Principles of
Comparative Politics

Principles of Comparative Politics

WILLIAM ROBERTS CLARK
University of Michigan

MATT GOLDER
Florida State University

SONA NADENICHEK GOLDER
Florida State University

CQ PRESS

A Division of SAGE
Washington, D.C.

CQ Press
2300 N Street, NW, Suite 800
Washington, DC 20037

Phone: 202-729-1900; toll-free, 1-866-4CQ-PRESS (1-866-427-7737)

Web: www.cqpress.com

Cover design: Matthew Simmons
Maps: International Mapping Associates
Composition: Auburn Associates, Inc.

♾ The paper used in this publication exceeds the requirements of the American National Standard for Information Sciences—Permanence of Paper for Printed Library Materials, ANSI Z39.48-1992.

Printed and bound in the United States of America

12   11   10   09   08   1   2   3   4   5

Library of Congress Cataloging-in-Publication Data
Clark, William Roberts
  Principles of comparative politics / William Roberts Clark, Matt Golder, Sona Nadenichek Golder.
      p. cm.
  Includes bibliographical references and index.
  ISBN 978-0-87289-289-7 (alk. paper)
  1. Comparative government. 2. Democracy. 3. Political science—Research—Methodology. I. Golder, Matt. II. Golder, Sona Nadenichek. III. Title.

  JF51.C53 2009
  320.3—dc22

                                                        2008033442

~ To our most important students:
Meaghan, Brian, Liam, Cameron, and Sean. ~

About the Authors

William Roberts Clark is associate professor of political science at the University of Michigan. He is the author of *Capitalism, Not Globalism,* and his articles have appeared in *American Political Science Review, Comparative Political Studies, Political Analysis,* and *European Union Politics,* among other journals. He has been teaching at a wide variety of public and private schools (William Paterson College, Rutgers University, Georgia Tech, Princeton, New York University, and the University of Michigan) for over a decade.

Matt Golder is assistant professor of political science at Florida State University. His articles have appeared in the *American Journal of Political Science, British Journal of Political Science, Comparative Political Studies, Electoral Studies,* and *Political Analysis,* among other journals. He has taught classes on comparative politics, advanced industrialized democracies, quantitative methods, and European politics at the University of Iowa, Florida State University, and the University of Essex.

Sona Nadenichek Golder is assistant professor of political science at Florida State University. She is the author of *The Logic of Pre-Electoral Coalition Formation* and articles published in the *British Journal of Political Science, Electoral Studies,* and *European Union Politics.* She teaches courses on European politics, democracies and dictatorships, comparative institutions, game theory, and comparative politics at Florida State University and was a mentor-in-residence for the 2007 Empirical Implications of Theoretical Models Summer Program at UCLA.

Brief Contents

Contents   xi

Boxes, Figures, Tables, and Maps   xvii

Preface   xxvii

PART I: WHAT IS COMPARATIVE POLITICS?

Chapter 1: Introduction   1

Chapter 2: What Is Science?   17

Chapter 3: What Is Politics?   55

PART II: THE MODERN STATE AND DEMOCRATIZATION

Chapter 4: The Origins of the Modern State   91

Chapter 5: Conceptualizing and Measuring Democracy   147

Chapter 6: The Economic Determinants of Democracy   169

Chapter 7: Cultural Determinants of Democracy   207

Chapter 8: Democratic Transitions   255

Chapter 9: Does Democracy Make a Difference?   311

PART III: VARIETIES OF DEMOCRACY

Chapter 10: Democracy and Its Varieties   355

Chapter 11: Parliamentary, Presidential, and Mixed Democracies:
Making and Breaking Governments   395

Chapter 12: Elections and Electoral Systems   463

Chapter 13: Social Cleavages and Party Systems   533

Chapter 14: Institutional Veto Players   603

PART IV: VARIETIES OF DEMOCRACY AND POLITICAL OUTCOMES

Chapter 15: Consequences of Democratic Institutions   675

Appendix A: The 2007 Failed States Index   A-1

Appendix B: Three Different Measures of Regime Type in 2002   A-7

Appendix C: 188 Independent Countries and Their Electoral Systems in 2004   A-13

References   R-1

Photo Credits   P-1

Index   I-1

Contents

Boxes, Figures, Tables, and Maps   xvii

Preface   xxvii

PART I: WHAT IS COMPARATIVE POLITICS?

CHAPTER 1: INTRODUCTION   1

Overview of the Book   6

  State Failure   7

  Economic Determinants of Democracy   7

  Cultural Determinants of Democracy   8

  What's So Good about Democracy Anyway?   9

  Institutional Design   10

The Approach Taken in this Book   13

Key Concepts   15

CHAPTER 2: WHAT IS SCIENCE?   17

Introduction   18

The Comparative Method   19

  Necessary and Sufficient Conditions   19

  Mill's Method of Agreement   21

  Mill's Method of Difference   25

  A Critique of Mill's Methods   27

An Introduction to Logic   32

  Valid and Invalid Arguments   33

  Testing Theories   37

  The Comparative Method Revisited   39

Science and Falsificationism   40

  What Is Science?   40

  The Scientific Method   42

  Myths about Science   50

Conclusion   51

Key Concepts   51

Problems   51

CHAPTER 3: WHAT IS POLITICS?   **55**
The Exit, Voice, and Loyalty Game   56
Solving the Exit, Voice, and Loyalty Game   65
Evaluating the Exit, Voice, and Loyalty Game   74
Conclusion   79
Key Concepts   79
Preparation for the Problems   80
Problems   84

PART II: THE MODERN STATE AND DEMOCRATIZATION

CHAPTER 4: THE ORIGINS OF THE MODERN STATE   **91**
What Is a State?   92
A Brief History of a Failed State: Somalia   95
The Contractarian View of the State   105
  The State of Nature   105
  Civil Society and the Social Contract   113
The Predatory View of the State   119
Conclusion   122
Key Concepts   123
Preparation for the Problems   123
Problems   128

CHAPTER 5: CONCEPTUALIZING AND MEASURING DEMOCRACY   **147**
Democracy and Dictatorship in Historical Perspective   148
Classifying Democracies and Dictatorships   151
  Dahl's View of Democracy   152
  Three Measures of Democracy   154
  Evaluating Measures of Democracy160
Conclusion   166
Key Concepts   167
Problems   167

CHAPTER 6: THE ECONOMIC DETERMINANTS OF DEMOCRACY   **169**
Classic Modernization Theory   170
A Variant of Modernization Theory   182
  Economic Development, Natural Resources, and Democracy   182
  Foreign Aid, Inequality, and Economic Performance   195
Some More Empirical Evidence   198
Conclusion   201
Key Concepts   202
Problems   202

CHAPTER 7: CULTURAL DETERMINANTS OF DEMOCRACY   207

Classical Cultural Arguments: Mill and Montesquieu   208

Does Democracy Require a Civic Culture?   212

Religion and Democracy   221

Are Some Religions Incompatible with Democracy?   221

Some Empirical Evidence   227

Are Some Religions Incompatible with Democracy? A New Test   232

Experiments and Culture   239

Conclusion   249

Key Concepts   250

Problems   251

CHAPTER 8: DEMOCRATIC TRANSITIONS   255

Bottom-Up Transitions to Democracy   258

East Germany 1989   258

Collective Action Theory   266

Tipping Models   271

Top-Down Transitions to Democracy   276

A Game-Theoretic Model of Top-Down Transitions   277

Applying the Transition Game to Poland   288

Conclusion   291

Key Concepts   293

Problems   293

CHAPTER 9: DOES DEMOCRACY MAKE A DIFFERENCE?   311

The Effect of Regime Type on Government Performance   313

The Effect of Democracy on Economic Growth   313

Empirical Evidence of the Effect of Democracy on
Government Performance   328

Selectorate Theory   331

Institutions   332

Mapping W and S onto a Typology of Regimes   335

Government Performance   337

Conclusion   349

Key Concepts   350

Problems   350

PART III: VARIETIES OF DEMOCRACY

CHAPTER 10: DEMOCRACY AND ITS VARIETIES   355

Problems with Group Decision Making   357

Majority Rule and Condorcet's Paradox   357

The Borda Count and the Reversal Paradox 363
Majority Rule with an Agenda Setter 366
Restrictions on Preferences: The Median Voter Theorem 368
Arrow's Theorem **379**
Arrow's Fairness Conditions 381
Conclusion **384**
Key Concepts **386**
Problems **386**

**CHAPTER 11: PARLIAMENTARY, PRESIDENTIAL, AND MIXED
DEMOCRACIES: MAKING AND BREAKING
GOVERNMENTS** **395**
Classifying Parliamentary, Presidential, and Mixed Democracies **396**
Is the Government Responsible to the Elected Legislature? 397
Is There an Independently (Directly or Indirectly) Elected President? 398
Is the Government Responsible to the President? 399
An Overview of Parliamentary, Presidential, and Mixed Democracies 400
Making and Breaking Governments: Parliamentary Democracies **400**
The Government 402
The Government Formation Process 404
A Simple Model of Government Formation 413
Different Types of Government 418
Preelectoral Coalitions 428
Duration of Governments: Formation and Survival 434
Making and Breaking Governments: Presidential Democracies **443**
Government Formation Process 444
The Size of Presidential Cabinets 445
The Composition of Presidential Cabinets 447
Making and Breaking Governments: Mixed Democracies **449**
Conclusion **453**
Key Concepts **456**
Problems **456**

CHAPTER 12: ELECTIONS AND ELECTORAL SYSTEMS **463**
Elections: An Overview **464**
Majoritarian Electoral Systems **473**
Single-Member District Plurality System 474
Alternative Vote 477
Two-Round Systems 484
Majoritarian Electoral Systems in Multimember Districts 490
Proportional Electoral Systems **493**

List PR Systems   495
Single Transferable Vote   507
Mixed Electoral Systems   **511**
Independent Mixed Electoral Systems   511
Dependent Mixed Electoral Systems   513
An Overview of Electoral Systems around the World   **517**
Conclusion   **526**
Key Concepts   **527**
Problems   **528**

CHAPTER 13: SOCIAL CLEAVAGES AND PARTY SYSTEMS   **533**
Political Parties: What Are They and What Do They Do?   **534**
Political Parties Structure the Political World   535
Recruitment and Socialization of the Political Elite   536
Mobilization of the Masses   538
The Link between Rulers and the Ruled   539
Party Systems   **543**
Where Do Parties Come From?   **551**
Types of Parties: Social Cleavages and Political Identity Formation **551**
Origins of the British Party System   552
Social Cleavages   554
Theorizing about Politicized Cleavages   565
Number of Parties: Duverger's Theory   **572**
Social Cleavages   572
Electoral Institutions   574
The Mechanical Effect of Electoral Laws   575
The Strategic Effect of Electoral Laws   579
Summarizing Duverger's Theory   583
Evidence for Duverger's Theory   585
Conclusion   **597**
Key Concepts   **598**
Problems   **598**

CHAPTER 14: INSTITUTIONAL VETO PLAYERS   **603**
Federalism   **604**
Federalism: Federalism in Structure   605
Decentralization: Federalism in Practice   612
Why Federalism?   616
Bicameralism   **620**
Types of Bicameralism   622
Why Bicameralism?   630

Constitutionalism   **634**
   The Shift to a New Constitutionalism   635
   Different Systems of Constitutional Justice   642
Veto Players   **648**
Conclusion   **655**
Key Concepts   **657**
Problems   **657**

PART IV: VARIETIES OF DEMOCRACY AND POLITICAL OUTCOMES

CHAPTER 15: CONSEQUENCES OF DEMOCRATIC INSTITUTIONS   **675**
  Combining Institutions: Majoritarian or Consensus Democracy? **677**
   Majoritarian and Consensus Visions of Democracy   677
   Majoritarian and Consensus Institutions   681
   Evaluating Majoritarian and Consensus Visions of Democracy 688
  The Effect of Political Institutions on Fiscal Policy   **700**
   Economic and Cultural Determinants of Fiscal Policy   703
   How Electoral Laws Influence Fiscal Policy   713
   Summary   723
  Electoral Laws, Federalism, and Ethnic Conflict   **723**
   Ethnic Diversity and Conflict   724
   The Hypothesized Effect of Electoral Laws on Ethnic Conflict 733
   The Hypothesized Effect of Federalism   738
  Presidentialism and Democratic Survival   **742**
   The Perils of Presidentialism   743
   The Difficult Combination: Presidentialism and Multipartism 752
   Summary   760
  Conclusion   **762**
  Key Concepts   **763**
  Problems   **763**

Appendix A: The 2007 Failed States Index   **A-1**
Appendix B: Three Different Measures of Regime Type in 2002   **A-7**
Appendix C: 188 Independent Countries and Their Electoral
  Systems in 2004   **A-13**
References   **R-1**
Photo Credits   **P-1**
Index   **I-1**

Boxes, Figures, Tables, and Maps

BOXES

1.1	What Is Comparative Politics?	3
2.1	John Stuart Mill	23
2.2	An Example of the Scientific Process	47
3.1	Origins of Game Theory	60
4.1	Can Cooperation Occur without the State?	142
5.1	Dictatorships	151
5.2	Alternation in Power	155
6.1	Comparing Wealth across Countries	173
6.2	Credible Commitment Problems	185
7.1	Does Good Democratic Performance Require a Civic Culture?	213
7.2	What Makes a Civic Culture?	215
7.3	The Clash of Civilizations	223
7.4	The Constitution of Medina—622 A.D.	229
7.5	Experiments in Political Science	244
8.1	Three Waves of Democracy	257
8.2	Externally Imposed Democracy	259
8.3	Tiananmen Square, Beijing (June 4, 1989)	261
8.4	A Brief History of East Germany, 1945–1990	263
8.5	Prague Spring 1968	280
8.6	Transition Game with Incomplete Information	307
9.1	Aesop's Fable	325
9.2	Consumption versus Investment	326
9.3	An Example of a Small Winning Coalition	334
9.4	The Tale of Two Leopolds	345
10.1	The Median Voter Theorem and Party Competition	371
10.2	Stability in Two-Dimensional Majority-Rule Voting	392
11.1	Investiture Votes	405
11.2	Principal-Agent, or Delegation, Problems	411
11.3	Portfolio Allocation and Gamson's Law	415
11.4	Endogenous Election Timing	441
12.1	Who Can Vote in Democracies?	469

12.2	The Borda Count in the South Pacific	478
12.3	The Supplementary Vote and Sri Lanka	488
12.4	Hungary: The World's Most Complicated Electoral System?	515
12.5	Strategic Miscalculation: Electoral System Choice in Poland in 1989	523
13.1	Party Whips in the United Kingdom	540
13.2	One-Party Dominant Systems in Japan: The Case of the LDP	545
13.3	Allies or Adversaries? Chewas and Tumbukas in Zambia and Malawi	570
13.4	Nationalizing Party Systems	586
14.1	Devolution versus Federalism	609
14.2	Hereditary Peers in the British House of Lords	623
14.3	Conflict Resolution in Bicameral Systems	629
14.4	Judicial Power and the Judicialization of Politics	639
14.5	Systems of Constitutional Justice	644
14.6	Checks and Balances in 191 Independent Countries	668
15.1	Ethnic Conflict in Sudan	726

FIGURES

1.1	One View of Political Science	4
2.1	A Visual Representation of a Necessary Cause	20
2.2	A Visual Representation of a Sufficient Cause	20
2.3	A Visual Representation of a Necessary and Sufficient Cause	21
2.4	Major Premise: If P, then Q	34
3.1	Exit, Voice, and Loyalty Game without Payoffs	62
3.2	Exit, Voice, and Loyalty Game with Payoffs	65
3.3	Solving the Exit, Voice, and Loyalty Game When the Citizen Has a Credible Exit Threat ($E > 0$): Step One	67
3.4	Solving the Exit, Voice, and Loyalty Game When the Citizen Has a Credible Exit Threat ($E > 0$) and the State Is Dependent ($L > 1$): Step Two	68
3.5	Solving the Exit, Voice, and Loyalty Game When the Citizen Has a Credible Exit Threat ($E > 0$) and the State Is Dependent ($L > 1$): Third and Final Step	69
3.6	Solving the Exit, Voice, and Loyalty Game When the Citizen Does Not Have a Credible Exit Threat ($E < 0$) and the State Is Dependent ($L > 1$)	71
3.7	Solving the Exit, Voice, and Loyalty Game When the Citizen Has a Credible Exit Threat ($E > 0$) and the State Is Autonomous ($L < 1$)	72
3.8	Solving the Exit, Voice, and Loyalty Game When the Citizen Does Not Have a Credible Exit Threat ($E < 0$) and the State Is Autonomous ($L < 1$)	73
3.9	Senate Race Game	81
3.10	Generic Game I	84
3.11	Generic Game II	85

3.12	Generic Game III	85
3.13	New Senate Race Game	86
3.14	Basic Terrorism Game Showing Outcomes but Not Payoffs	87
3.15	Legislative Pay Raise Game	89
4.1	State of Nature Game without Payoffs	107
4.2	State of Nature Game with Payoffs	109
4.3	Solving the State of Nature Game I	110
4.4	Solving the State of Nature Game II	110
4.5	Solving the State of Nature Game III	111
4.6	Solving the State of Nature Game IV	111
4.7	Civil Society Game	115
4.8	Civil Society Game when $p > 1$	116
4.9	Choosing between the State of Nature and Civil Society	117
4.10	Prisoner's Dilemma	125
4.11	Nuclear Arms Race Game as a Prisoner's Dilemma	128
4.12	A Game of Chicken: The Tractor Face-Off	129
4.13	The Stag Hunt Game	130
4.14	Pure Coordination Game	131
4.15	The Battle of the Sexes	132
4.16	Rock, Paper, Scissors Game	133
4.17	American Football Game	134
4.18	Mafia Game	135
4.19	Counterterrorism Preemption Game	137
4.20	Counterterrorism Deterrence Game I	138
4.21	Counterterrorism Deterrence Game II	139
4.22	Free Trade Game	140
4.23	State of Nature Game Revisited	144
5.1	Dahl's Two Dimensions of Democracy: Contestation and Inclusion	153
5.2A	PACL's Dichotomous Conceptualization of Regime Type	156
5.2B	Dahl's Continuous Conceptualization of Regime Type	156
5.3	Comparing the Reliability and Validity of Three Measures	165
6.1	Classic Modernization Theory	171
6.2	Proportion of Democracies at Various Levels of Wealth, 1950–1990	172
6.3	Expected Probability of Regime Transitions as Wealth Increases according to Modernization Theory and the Survival Story	176
6.4	Country Years under Democracy and Dictatorship, 1950–1990	177
6.5	Number of Regime Transitions as a Function of Wealth, 1950–1990	178
6.6	Probability of Regime Transitions as a Function of Wealth, 1950–1990	179
6.7	Probability of Transitions to Democracy and Dictatorship as a Function of Wealth, 1950–1990	180

6.8	Exit, Voice, and Loyalty Game without Payoffs between the Parliamentarians and the Crown	189
6.9	Solving the Exit, Voice, and Loyalty Game When the Parliamentarians Have a Credible Exit Threat ($E > 0$) and the Crown Is Dependent ($L > 1$)	190
6.10	Solving the Exit, Voice, and Loyalty Game When the Parliamentarians Do Not Have a Credible Exit Threat ($E < 0$) and the Crown Is Dependent ($L > 1$)	191
6.11	EVL Game with Payoffs	204
7.1	Culture, Economic Development, and Democracy: Some Potential Causal Relationships	211
7.2	Support for Democracy	219
7.3	Support for Gradual Change	220
7.4	Offers from an Ultimatum Game	243
7.5	Coordination and Democracy Game	253
7.6	Group Subgame	254
8.1	Independent Countries, Democracies, and Dictatorships, 1946–2000	256
8.2	Transition Game without Payoffs	282
8.3	Transition Game with Payoffs	284
8.4	Democratic Consolidation Game	294
8.5	Complete Information Terrorism Game	298
8.6	Incomplete Information Terrorism Game	299
8.7	Dictatorship Party Game	302
8.8	Religious Party Game	304
8.9	Incomplete Information Transition Game	308
9.1	Hypothesized Causal Path between Democracy and Economic Growth	314
9.2	Individual Productivity and Desired Tax Rate according to the Meltzer-Richard Model	318
9.3	The Potential Trade-off between Growth and Equality	321
9.4	The Effect of Democracy on Various Indicators of Material Well-Being	329
9.5	The Institutional Environment in the Selectorate Theory	333
9.6	Selectorate Theory and Regime-Type Locations	336
9.7	The Selectorate Model and Government Performance	343
9.8	Winning Coalition Size, Selectorate Size, and Government Type	351
10.1	An Example of Cyclical Majorities	361
10.2	Right-Wing Councillor's Utility Function	369
10.3	Centrist Councillor's Utility Function	370
10.4	When All Three Councillors Have Single-Peaked Preference Orderings	372
10.5	Illustrating the Power of the Median Voter	373
10.6	Two-Dimensional Voting	375
10.7	Two-Dimensional Voting with Winsets	376
10.8	Two-Dimensional Voting with a New Status Quo (P_1)	377

10.9	Two-Dimensional Voting with Cyclical Majorities	378
10.10	Arrow's Institutional Trilemma	383
10.11	Illustrating the Median Voter Theorem	388
10.12	Illustrating the Median Voter Theorem—A Centrist Electorate	388
10.13	Illustrating the Median Voter Theorem—A Polarized Electorate	389
10.14	Choosing a Level of Public Goods Provision: Scenario 1	390
10.15	Choosing a Level of Public Goods Provision: Scenario 2	391
10.16	Choosing a Level of Public Goods Provision: Scenario 3	391
10.17	Stability in Two-Dimensional Voting	393
10.18	Instability in Two-Dimensional Voting	394
11.1	Classifying Parliamentary, Presidential, and Mixed Democracies	397
11.2	Parliamentary, Presidential, and Mixed Democracies, 1946–2002	401
11.3	Government Formation Process in Parliamentary Democracies	408
11.4	German Party Positions on the Left-Right Economic Division, 1987	417
11.5	Government Types in Thirteen West European Parliamentary Democracies, 1945–1998	419
11.6	Average Government Duration by Cabinet Type, 1945–1998	438
11.7	Minimum and Average Duration of Governments, 1945–1998	439
11.8	Average Cabinet Duration, Political Experience, and Portfolio Experience, 1945–1999	443
12.1	Electoral System Families	473
12.2	Australian "How-to-Vote" Card from the 2004 Legislative Elections	481
12.3	Fijian AV Ballot Paper for the Tailevu Constituency in the 2001 Legislative Elections	482
12.4	Nicaraguan Closed List PR Ballot Paper	503
12.5	South African Closed List PR Ballot Paper	504
12.6	Danish Open List PR Ballot Paper	505
12.7	Electoral Systems in 177 Countries in 2004	518
12.8	Freedom House and Electoral Systems, 2004	521
13.1	Politicized Cleavages and the Role of Electoral Institutions	572
13.2	Duvergerland: A Hypothetical Polity Using an SMDP Electoral System	576
13.3	Distribution of Seats in Duvergerland under SMDP and PR Electoral Rules	576
13.4	Distribution of Votes and Seats in Legislative Elections in the United Kingdom, 1992	578
13.5	Strategic Entry Game: Coordination between Competing Left-Wing Parties	582
13.6	Party Systems: Social Cleavages and the Modifying Effect of Electoral Institutions	584
13.7	Number of Parties at the National and District Levels in the United States, 1790–1990	587
13.8	The Effective Number of Electoral and Legislative Parties in Fifty-two Democracies in the 1980s	591

13.9   The Effective Number of Electoral and Legislative Parties in
         Nonpermissive and Permissive Electoral Systems   592

13.10   The Effective Number of Ethnic Groups and Electoral Parties in
         Nonpermissive and Permissive Electoral Systems   594

13.11   The Effective Number of Ethnic Groups and Legislative Parties in
         Nonpermissive and Permissive Electoral Systems   595

13.12   Number of Parties at the National and District Level in India, 1957–1995   601

14.1   Revenue Centralization: Central Government's Share of Tax Revenue   615

14.2   Two Dimensions of Federalism   616

14.3   Two Dimensions of Bicameralism   628

14.4   An Application of Veto Player Theory   651

14.5   The Number of Veto Players and the Size of the Winset   653

14.6   The Ideological Distance between Veto Players and the Size of the Winset   654

14.7   Illustrating a Unicameral Legislature   658

14.8   Illustrating a Bicameral Legislature   658

14.9   Agency Policymaking Model   659

14.10   Statutory Review Model, Scenario 1   660

14.11   Statutory Review Model, Scenario 2   661

14.12   Statutory Review Model, Scenario 3   661

14.13   Two Veto Players   663

14.14   Three Veto Players   664

14.15   Illustrating the Unanimity Core   665

14.16   Activist Judges with Agenda-Setting Power   666

15.1   How Majoritarian Is Your Democracy?   686

15.2   Political Systems, Accountability, and Clarity of Responsibility   692

15.3   Two Ideals of Democratic Responsiveness   696

15.4   Total Public Fiscal Activity in Twenty-one OECD Countries, 1947–1997   702

15.5   Total Public Fiscal Activity by Year in Twenty-one OECD Countries,
         1947–1997   704

15.6   The Relationship between Income, Taxes, and Government Subsidies
         in a Hypothetical Tax and Transfer System   706

15.7   The Partisan Composition of Government and the Expansion of the
         Public Economy, 1960–1975   710

15.8   Relationship between Social Spending and the Belief that Luck
         Determines Income   712

15.9   Possible Causal Paths by which Ethnic Heterogeneity Encourages Civil War   730

15.10   Political Decentralization and Ethnic Conflict   740

15.11   Effect of Presidentialism on the Probability of Democratic Survival across
         Different Levels of Legislative Fractionalization   759

15.12   Veto Players, Policy Stability, and Different Types of Political Instability   761

TABLES

2.1	Mill's Method of Agreement I	22
2.2	Mill's Method of Agreement II	24
2.3	Mill's Method of Agreement III	24
2.4	Mill's Method of Difference	26
2.5	Combining Mill's Methods of Agreement and Difference	27
2.6	Mill's Method of Agreement Revisited	30
2.7	An Example of Mill's Method of Difference	31
2.8	Affirming the Antecedent: A Valid Argument	33
2.9	Denying the Antecedent: An Invalid Argument	35
2.10	Affirming the Consequent: An Invalid Argument I	35
2.11	Denying the Consequent: A Valid Argument I	36
2.12	What Types of Conditional Arguments Are Valid?	36
2.13	Affirming the Consequent: An Invalid Argument II	38
2.14	Denying the Consequent: A Valid Argument II	39
2.15	Three Critical Tests	49
3.1	Exit, Voice, and Loyalty	58
3.2	Turning Outcomes into Payoffs	63
3.3	Summary of Subgame Perfect Nash Equilibria and Outcomes	74
5.1	Aristotle's Classification of Regimes	149
5.2	Competitiveness of Political Participation	157
5.3	Regulation of Political Participation	158
5.4	Three Different Measures of Regime Type in 2002	159
6.1	Implications from Modernization Theory and the Survival Story	177
6.2	Modernization Theory and the Survival Story: A Summary of the Evidence	181
6.3	Summary of Outcomes in the Exit, Voice, and Loyalty Game	192
6.4	Economic Determinants of Transitions to Democracy	199
6.5	Economic Determinants of Democratic Survival	201
7.1	Countries with a Majority Muslim, Protestant, or Catholic Population	233
7.2	Effect of a Muslim, Catholic, or Protestant Majority on the Probability That a Country Will Become Democratic, 1950–2000	235
7.3	Effect of a Muslim, Catholic, or Protestant Majority on the Probability of Democratic Survival, 1950–2000	237
7.4	Fifteen Small-Scale Societies	242
8.1	Pro-Democracy Protest: Do I Participate or Not?	269
8.2	Turning Outcomes into Payoffs in the Transition Game	283
9.1	Countries with Large Gaps between Rule of Law and Electoral Rights Indexes	316
9.2	Effect of W and W/S on Six Indicators of Material Well-Being	347

10.1	City Council Preferences for the Level of Social Service Provision	358
10.2	Outcomes from the Round-Robin Tournament	358
10.3	Proportion of Possible Strict Preference Orderings without a Condorcet Winner	362
10.4	Determining the Level of Social Service Provision Using the Borda Count	364
10.5	City Council Preferences for the Level of Social Service Provision (Four Alternatives)	364
10.6	Determining the Level of Social Service Provision Using the Borda Count with a Fourth Alternative	365
10.7	Pair-Wise Contests and Different Voting Agendas	368
11.1	Parliamentary, Presidential, and Mixed Democracies, 2002	402
11.2	British Government, May 2005	403
11.3	German Legislative Elections, 1987	404
11.4	Potential West German Governments, 1987	406
11.5	Remaining Potential West German Governments, 1987	414
11.6	Allocation of Cabinet Seats in the Netherlands, 1998	416
11.7	Government Types in Thirteen West European Parliamentary Democracies, 1945–1998	420
11.8	Testing Theories of Minority Governments	425
11.9	Different Types of Preelectoral Coalition	429
11.10	Summary Information on National-Level Preelectoral Coalitions, 1946–2002	431
11.11	Duration of Government Formation Process after Elections, 1945–1998	435
11.12	Number of Governments That Fell for Technical and Discretionary Reasons in Thirteen West European Parliamentary Democracies, 1945–1998	440
11.13	Government Types in Presidential Systems, late 1970s–2000	446
11.14	Government Composition in Thirteen Presidential and Thirty Parliamentary Democracies, 1980–2000	448
11.15	Government Composition in Presidential Systems, late 1970s–2000	449
11.16	Legislative Election Results in Finland, 2007	459
11.17	Legislative Election Results in Ecuador, 1996	460
11.18	Legislative Election Results in Germany, 2002	461
12.1	Democratic Elections by Decade	468
12.2	Democratic Elections by Geographical Region, 1946–2000	469
12.3	Election Results from the Kettering Constituency, UK Legislative Elections, 2005	474
12.4	Buada District, Nauru Legislative Elections, 2004	479
12.5	Richmond Constituency, New South Wales, Australian Legislative Elections, 1990	480

12.6	Fourth District in the Puy-de-Dôme, French Legislative Elections, 2002	486
12.7	Translating Votes into Seats Using the Hare Quota	496
12.8	Hare Quota with Largest Remainders	497
12.9	Hare Quota with Highest Average Remainders	497
12.10	Translating Votes into Seats Using the d'Hondt System	498
12.11	The Proportionality of Proportional Electoral System Formulas	499
12.12	Results from Twenty Ballots in an STV Election	508
12.13	The STV in a Three-Seat District with Twenty Voters	508
12.14	Translating Votes into Seats in an Independent Mixed Electoral System	512
12.15	Translating Votes into Seats in a Dependent Mixed Electoral System	514
12.16	An Example of Overhang Seats	514
12.17	Electoral Systems by Geographic Region, 2004	519
12.18	Legislative Elections in Oslo, Norway, 2005	528
12.19	Legislative Elections in Oslo, Norway, 2005 (Using Quota Systems)	530
12.20	Legislative Elections in Oslo, Norway, 2005 (Using Divisor Systems)	531
13.1	Political Parties with Seats in the Israeli Knesset, 2006	547
13.2	Party Systems in Fifty-four Democracies in the mid-1980s	549
13.3	Some Dimensions of Whig-Tory Conflict	553
13.4	Individual Attributes and Possible Attribute Values	566
13.5	Attributes and Possible Combinations of Attributes in a Hypothetical Country	566
13.6	Potential Identity Categories in a Hypothetical Country	567
13.7	Cross-Cutting Attributes	567
13.8	Reinforcing Attributes	568
13.9	A Hypothetical Distribution of Attributes	568
13.10	An Alternative Hypothetical Distribution of Attributes	570
13.11	The Distribution of Identity Attributes in Hypothetical Country A	573
13.12	The Distribution of Identity Attributes in Hypothetical Country B	574
13.13	Legislative Elections Results, St. Ives Constituency, United Kingdom, 1992	577
13.14	Legislative Elections Results, National Totals, United Kingdom, 1992	578
13.15	The Interplay of Social Heterogeneity and Electoral System Permissiveness on Party System Size	589
13.16	The Observed Number of Parties under Alternative Conditions	590
13.17	The Effect of an Additional Ethnic Group on the Effective Number of Electoral and Legislative Parties as District Magnitude Changes	596
13.18	Parliamentary Election Results in the Republic of South Africa, 2004	599
13.19	Distribution of Attributes in a Hypothetical Los Angeles Community	601
14.1	Federal Countries, 1990–2000	606
14.2	Hereditary Peers in the United Kingdom, 1999	623
14.3	Life Peers in the United Kingdom, 1958–2007	624

14.4	Malapportionment in the Upper Chambers, 1996	627
14.5	Legislative Supremacy Constitution versus Higher Law Constitution	638
14.6	Different Systems of Constitutional Justice	643
14.7	American and European Models of Constitutional Justice	647
14.8	The Geographic Distribution of Different Models of Constitutional Justice, 2004	648
15.1	Institutions and the Majoritarian-Consensus Dimension	682
15.2	Government Identifiability and Expected Government Formation Scenario	694
15.3	European and American Attitudes toward the Poor	711
15.4	Electoral Systems and the Number of Years with Left and Right Governments, 1945–1998	714
15.5	Actual and Potential Communal Violence in Thirty-six Sub-Saharan African Countries, 1960–1979	725
15.6	Democratic Survival in Newly Independent States after World War II	748
15.7	Democratic Survival in Fifty-three Non-OECD Countries, 1973–1989	749
15.8	Military Coups in Fifty-three Non-OECD Countries, 1973–1989	749
15.9	Democracy Underachievers and Overachievers by Regime Type	750
15.10	Effect of Regime Type on Democratic Survival	751
15.11	Presidential Regimes that Sustained Democracy from 1967 to 1992 and Their Party System Size	756
15.12	Regime Type, Party System Size, and Democratic Consolidation, 1945–1992	757
15.13	Consolidated Democracies by Regime Type and Party System Size	758

MAPS

	World Map	ii
4.1	Somali Civil War, 2006	101
4.2	Failed States Index, 2007	104
8.1	Divided Germany	263
8.2	The Division of Berlin	264
12.1	Ethnoreligious Groups of Iraq	529
14.1	The Federal States of the United Arab Emirates	607
14.2	Brazil's States and Federal District	608
14.3	India's States and Union Territories	610

Preface

This book began as a syllabus for an introductory comparative politics class taught by a newly minted PhD—one of the book's authors, Bill Clark—at Georgia Tech in the early 1990s. The class had three goals: (1) to introduce students to the major questions in comparative politics, (2) to acquaint them with the field's best answers to those questions, and (3) to give them the tools to think critically about the answers. The decision to write this textbook was born out of the frustration caused by our inability, ten years later, to find a single text that accomplished these goals. The intervening period, however, allowed us to conduct what turned out to be a useful experiment, because along the way, our frustration led us to gradually develop an ambitious syllabus from research monographs and refereed journal articles. The benefit of this approach has been our ability to respond flexibly to the changes in the discipline of political science and the field of comparative politics that have, for the most part, not made their way into textbooks. As a result, we have had the satisfaction of introducing many students to exciting work being done at the cutting edge of this field. And we learned that students were by and large up to the task. Nonetheless, we have also recognized the frustration of students confronting material that was not written with them in mind. The goal of this text is to try to maximize these upside benefits while minimizing the downside risks of our previous approach. We want students to be challenged to confront work being done at the cutting edge of the field, and we believe we have packaged this work in a way that is comprehensible to ambitious undergraduates with no prior training in political science.

THE APPROACH OF THIS BOOK

With these goals in mind, we have organized the book around a set of questions that comparative scholars have asked repeatedly over the past several decades:

- What is the state and where did it come from?
- What is democracy?
- Why are some countries democracies whereas others are dictatorships?
- How might we explain transitions to democracy?
- Does the kind of regime a country has affect the material well-being of its citizens?
- Why are ethnic groups politicized in some countries but not in others?
- Why do some countries have many parties whereas some have only a few?

- How do governments form, and what determines the type of governments that take office?
- What are the material and normative implications associated with these different types of government?
- How does the type of democracy in a country affect the survival of that regime?

Using the latest research in the field of comparative politics, we examine competing answers to substantively important questions such as these and evaluate the proposed arguments for their logical consistency and empirical accuracy. At times our approach requires us to present substantial amounts of original research, although we believe that this research is closely tied to existing studies in the field.

The book itself is designed and organized to build upon the questions asked above, starting with a section that defines comparative politics. In Part I, after an overview of the book and its goals in Chapter 1, we define the parameters of our inquiry in Chapters 2 and 3 in a discussion of the fundamental questions of "What Is Science?" and "What Is Politics?" In Chapters 4 through 8 in Part II, "The Modern State and Democratization," we look at the origins of the modern state, measurements of democracy, the economic and cultural determinants of democracy, and the issue of democratic transitions. In Chapter 9 we ask whether and in precisely what ways democracy makes a material difference in people's lives. We explore the varieties of democracy in Part III, looking in Chapter 10 at the problems of democratic group decision making and the implications of Arrow's Theorem. In Chapter 11 we look at the major types of democracies and the forms of government that they have, in Chapter 12 at elections and electoral systems, in Chapter 13 at social cleavages and party systems, and in Chapter 14 at institutional veto players. In Part IV, Chapter 15, we investigate the relationships between types of democracy and economic and political outcomes.

As you can see, our approach to comparative politics is quite different from the standard approach taken by existing comparative politics textbooks. The traditional approach is to organize the text around a series of case studies. Roughly the same set of case studies appears in most of these texts because the Educational Testing Service (ETS) has, for the past few decades, appointed a committee of college and high school teachers to design an Advanced Placement test that allows students to get college credit for an introductory comparative politics course taught in high school. Until quite recently (Richards and Mitchell 2006), the ETS required teachers of courses aimed at preparing students for this test "to cover four core countries (China, France, Great Britain, and Russia), and one of three other countries (India, Mexico, or Nigeria)" as well as six major content areas (many of which we don't understand and one of which is called "Introduction to Comparative Politics"). Since there are many more high schools than colleges in the United States, many publishers have wanted to sell "college textbooks" that would also be assigned in high schools for classes connected to the Advanced Placement test. Thus, instead of advanced high school courses being modeled after college courses, it seems many college courses are being shaped by the desire to sell books to high school students. Space does not allow for a full discussion of everything we find troubling about this situation, but we will say this: we feel no compulsion to meet the goals of the ETS committee. Although it is true that ETS has made great strides in bringing its test up to date with the concerns of the field, and there is a fair amount of overlap between the current test and the material covered in this book, we have arrived at the content of this book by assessing where the field is and where it is going, rather than by attempting to meet ETS's guidelines.[1] Still, we do hope to effectively address one of its six major content areas—Introduction to Comparative Politics.

We explain in greater length in the first chapter why we have written a book that is quite different from other introductory comparative politics texts and hope you find our reasoning compelling. Here we will just say that we adopt a strategic approach to politics. We believe that the behavior of rulers and the ruled is most easily understood as the interaction between individuals seeking goals in an environment in which goal attainment is complicated by the choices of other actors. Game theory is a useful tool for understanding such interactions, and it will be used wherever we think it illuminating. We also believe that explanations should be confronted with as much potentially falsifying evidence as possible. Consequently, we make every effort to present students with information about rigorous empirical tests of the theoretical arguments we offer and try to give them tools to begin to critically engage such evidence themselves. We view comparative politics as a subfield of political science, which, like all of science, is about comparison. And the only bad comparison is one that shelters a hypothesis from disconfirming evidence. As the cover illustration demonstrates, one *can* compare apples and oranges. Indeed, the claim that "you cannot compare apples and oranges" seems contradictory. How would you support this claim without conducting such a comparison—an act that would contradict the very claim being asserted.

Of course, the usefulness of such a comparison depends on the question one is asking. In this book we make many comparisons across disparate contexts and attempt to use such comparisons to test claims made about the political world. In doing so, we highlight the similarities and differences among countries. We also aim to show the conditions under which some claims about the political world apply or do not apply. Exactly what should or should not be compared is a question of research design, not a matter of religion. In sum, there are no invalid comparisons, only invalid inferences.

METHODOLOGY

In addressing the substantive questions that form the backbone of this textbook, we introduce students to a variety of methods that have become central to the study of comparative politics. For example, students will be exposed to tools such as decision theory, social choice theory, game theory, experiments, and statistical analysis, although we have written this book

---

1. There is now a single list of six core countries (China, Great Britain, Iran, Mexico, Nigeria, and Russia), and the six content areas are now Introduction to Comparative Politics; Sovereignty, Authority, and Power; Political Institutions; Citizens, Society, and the State; Political and Economic Change; and Public Policy (see: http://www.collegeboard.com/prod_downloads/ap/students/govpol/ap-cd-govpol-0708.pdf).

under the assumption that students have no prior knowledge of any of these. Basic high school algebra is the only mathematical prerequisite. We show students how to calculate expected utilities, how to solve complete information games in strategic and extensive form, how to solve repeated games, how to solve simple games with incomplete information, how to evaluate one-dimensional and two-dimensional spatial models, and how to interpret simple statistical results. Although the tools that we employ may appear sophisticated, we believe (and our experience teaching this material tells us) that students beginning their college careers have the necessary skills to learn them and apply them to new questions of more direct interest to themselves personally. Given the relative youth of the scientific approach to politics, we believe that students can successfully contribute to the accumulation of knowledge in comparative politics if they are given some basic tools. In fact, on more than one occasion we have made contributions to the literature through collaborations with our own comparative politics undergraduate students (Clark and Reichert 1998; Brambor, Clark, and Golder 2006, 2007).

PEDAGOGY

Although this book differs in content and approach from other comparative politics textbooks, we do appreciate the usefulness of textbook features that genuinely assist the reader in digesting and applying the ideas presented. To that end, we have created chapter-opener overviews that help orient the reader toward each chapter's main goals. To establish a common understanding of the most important concepts we discuss, we've defined each new key term in a box near its first mention. Lists of those same terms appear at the end of each chapter along with page references to aid in review and study. We have schematized a great deal of our data and information in tables, charts, and maps, thereby allowing students to better visualize the issues and arguments at hand.

Two important features are unique to this book and in keeping with our focus on methods and current research. The first is extensive class-tested problem sets at the end of each chapter. Our emphasis on problem sets comes from the belief that there is a lot of art in science and one learns an art by doing, not by simply watching others do. Developing a command over analytical materials and building a capacity to engage in analysis require practice and repetition, and the problem sets are meant to provide such opportunities for students. We, together and separately, have been assigning these problem sets and others like them in large introductory classes for several years now and find they work particularly well in classes with discussion sections. Consistently, we have found that students who seriously engage the problem sets perform better on tests and appear grateful for the opportunity to apply what they have learned. We suspect they also perform better in upper-division classes and graduate school as well, although we admit that we have anecdotes, not data, to support this claim. Graduate students who lead discussion sections in such classes seem to welcome the direction provided by the problem sets while also being inspired to contribute to the ever-expanding bank of questions. We believe that the best way to learn is to teach, and we have the distinct impression that this approach to undergraduate education has contributed directly to the training of graduate students. (A solutions manual for the problems is available via download at college.cqpress.com. Adopters need only click on "Ancillaries for Download" to get what they need.)

The second important feature in the book is the rich appendix material containing important data for further research and also additional material on games. We've included, for instance, results of the most recent failed states index for all countries in the sample, three different democracy measures for countries in 2002, and information on the types of institutional checks and balances for 188 countries.

Finally, to help instructors "tool up," we offer a set of downloadable resources, materials we've developed for our own classes over the years. At the URL listed above, instructors will find a set of PowerPoint lecture slides, a test bank with multiple-choice and short-essay questions, a glossary of key terms that can be used as handouts or for quizzing, and all of the book's graphics.

ACKNOWLEDGMENTS

Given the long gestation of this text, we have accumulated many, many debts and would like to acknowledge just a few of them. Dong-Hun Kim, Oakland University; Amy Linch, Lehigh University; Will Moore, Florida State University; Laura Potter, University of Michigan; Joel Simmons, Stonybrook University; Jeff Staton, Emory University; and various graduate students at the University of Michigan and Florida State University were kind enough to assign trial versions of chapters in their classes and offer us feedback and constructive criticism. In addition, André Blais, Sabri Ciftci, Steffen Ganghof, Brad Gomez, Mark Hallerberg, Marek Kaminski, Özge Kemahlioglu, Masayuki Kudamatsu, Jerry Loewenberg, Monika Nalepa, Chris Reenock, Courtenay Ryals, David Siegel, Mark Souva, Mike Thies, Josh Tucker, Tom Walker, and Carol Weissert read portions of the manuscript and offered helpful comments. We would also like to thank the reviewers CQ Press commissioned to vet the book at both proposal and manuscript stages and who have helped shape this project over the past three years: Kathleen Bawn, University of California, Los Angeles; Charles Blake, James Madison University; Clifford Carrubba, Emory University; Karen Ferree, University of California, San Diego; Erik Herron, University of Kansas; Monika Nalepa, Rice University; Irfan Nooruddin, Ohio State University; Andrew Roberts, Northwestern University; Boyka Stefanova, University of Texas, San Antonio; Joshua Tucker, New York University; and Christopher Way, Cornell University. Finally, we should thank the many hundreds of undergraduate students at the Georgia Institute of Technology, the University of Iowa, New York University, the University of Michigan, and Florida State University who forced us to find better ways of explaining the material in this book by asking questions and challenging our presentation of this material.

We are hugely indebted to the entire team at CQ Press. Brenda Carter, director of the College Publishing Group, demonstrated early in the process that she was totally committed to supporting our vision for this text. Charisse Kiino and Elise Frasier were all one could hope for in editors: insightful, patient, critical, encouraging, and honest coaches. Joanne S. Ainsworth did a wonderful job of copyediting the manuscript, and production editor Allyson Rudolph helped us find photographs and maps and was, in general, a cheerful teammate during the tense final days of page proofs.

On a more personal note, we are grateful to the comparative politics scholars who inspired us and trained us at both the undergraduate and graduate levels (Neal Beck, André Blais, Maya Chadda, Mike Gilligan, Robert Kaufman, Anand Menon, Jonathan Nagler, Bing Powell, Adam Przeworski, Michael Shafer, Stephen Rosskam Shalom, Daniel Verdier, Richard W. Wilson, and Vincent Wright [and a couple of us would include Bill Clark in this list]). By declaring the truth clearly, while encouraging heresy, they have given us direction at the same time as giving us the freedom to grow. We are also grateful to New York University's Department of Politics, where much of this book was formed in us, and our current departments at Florida State University and the University of Michigan. They say that iron sharpens iron, and although we've been rubbed in uncomfortable ways at times, we are grateful for being shaped by such competent hands. Our thanks go out to our colleagues, teachers, and mentors of various stripes for their criticism, encouragement, inspiration, and companionship over the years, including Robert Bates, Jenna Bednar, Fred Boehmke, Ted Brader, Lawrence Broz, Bruce Bueno de Mesquita, George Downs, Rob Franzese, Jeff Frieden, Mary Gallagher, Jen Gandhi, Mike Gilligan, Brad Gomez, Anna Gryzmala-Busse, Anna Harvey, Allen Hicken, Ron Inglehart, Stathis Kalyvas, Orit Kedar, Ken Kollman, Jack Levy, Michael Lewis-Beck, Jerry Loewenberg, Skip Lupia, Fiona McGillivray, Rob Mickey, Sara McLaughlin Mitchell, Will Moore, Jim Morrow, Rebecca Morton, Scott Page, Chris Reenock, Sebastian Saiegh, Rob Salmond, Shanker Satyanath, Chuck Shipan, Dave Siegel, Alastair Smith, Jeff Staton, George Tsebelis, Ashu Varshney, John Vasquez, Leonard Wantchekon, Libby Wood, and Bill Zimmerman.

Principles of
Comparative Politics

1 Introduction

My purpose is to consider if, in political society, there can be any legitimate and sure principle of government, taking men as they are, and laws as they might be. I shall try always to bring together what right permits with what interest prescribes so that justice and utility are in no way divided.

Jean Jacques Rousseau, *The Social Contract*

OVERVIEW

- Political science is the study of politics in a scientific manner. Whereas international politics is the study of politics predominantly between countries, comparative politics is the study of politics predominantly within countries.

- In this chapter, we outline the central questions in comparative politics that we address in the remainder of this book. These questions are all related to the causes and consequences of democracy as well as to the tremendous variety of democratic institutions seen in the world.

- We argue that attempts to engineer democracy, should they occur, should rest on foundations provided by the study of comparative politics.

- We also discuss why we adopt an explicitly cross-national approach to introduce students to the study of comparative politics.

On February 26, 2003, just a few weeks prior to ordering the invasion of Iraq to remove Iraqi president Saddam Hussein, American president George W. Bush declared that the United States would ensure that "one brutal dictator is not replaced by another." He asserted that "[a]ll Iraqis must have a voice in the new government, and all citizens must have their rights protected." He then drew an analogy between his plans for "postwar" Iraq and what had happened in Japan and Germany after World War II. In particular, he highlighted how the United States left behind "constitutions and parliaments" rather than "occupying armies" in Japan and Germany. The result of this was that "in societies that once bred fascism and militarism, liberty found a permanent home" despite the presence of cultures in both countries that "many said . . . were incapable of sustaining democracy." He went on to state that the "nation of Iraq—with its proud heritage, abundant resources and skilled and educated people—is fully capable of moving toward democracy and living in freedom." Later in his speech, President Bush tempered this optimistic statement with a warning: "It will be difficult to help freedom take hold in a country that has known three decades of dictatorship, secret police, internal divisions, and war." [1]

This speech came twelve days after the chief United Nations weapons inspector Hans Blix challenged various elements of Secretary of State Colin Powell's presentation before the UN Security Council, which had claimed that Iraq possessed weapons of mass destruction. Blix accused the U.S. and British governments of dramatizing the threat of weapons of mass destruction in Iraq in order to strengthen the case for toppling Saddam Hussein. In his speech, President Bush was clearly making the case that the desirability and feasibility of encouraging democratization in Iraq (and the broader Middle East) should be taken into account when weighing the pros and cons of invading Iraq. In effect, he was suggesting that the goal of establishing a democracy in the Middle East could legitimately be used to justify overthrowing Saddam Hussein even in the absence of any weapons of mass destruction. Less than a month after this historic speech, the U.S.-led invasion of Iraq was under way; less than a month after that, U.S. forces were involved in toppling a statue of Saddam Hussein in Baghdad's Firdos Square—this event, captured by the invited media and press, symbolized, more than any other, the toppling of the Iraqi dictator.

Every generation seems to have its own motivation for studying comparative politics. The unfortunate truth is that each generation seems beset by a problem that is both devastatingly complex and extraordinarily

An American marine watches as a Saddam Hussein statue is toppled in Bagdad's Firdos Square, April 19, 2003.

1. White House, Office of the Press Secretary, February 26, 2003, http://www.whitehouse.gov/news/releases/2003/02/20030226-11.html.

WHAT IS COMPARATIVE POLITICS?

Traditionally, the field of comparative politics has been characterized by many related, but distinct, endeavors. An influential comparative politics textbook by Joseph LaPalombara (1974) was entitled *Politics **within** Nations*. LaPalombara's title distinguished **comparative politics** from **international politics,** which Hans Morgenthau (1948) famously called *Politics **among** Nations*. This definition of comparative politics, with its complementary definition of international politics, has one of the desirable features of all good scientific typologies in that it is logically exhaustive. By defining comparative and international politics in this way, these scholars have exhausted the logical possibilities involved in the study of politics—political phenomena occur either within countries or between countries.

Still, all good scientific typologies should also be mutually exclusive. Whereas logical exhaustion implies that we have a place to categorize every entity that is observed, mutual exclusivity requires that it not be possible to assign any single case into more than one category. Unfortunately, the typology just presented does not satisfy mutual exclusivity. A quick glance at today's newspapers clearly reveals that many contemporary political issues contain healthy doses of both "within country" and "between country" factors. As a consequence, the line between comparative and international politics is often blurred. This is particularly the case when it comes to studying how politics and economics interact. For example, ask yourself whether it is possible to fully understand American trade policy, say, toward China, without taking account of U.S. domestic politics or to fully understand European Union economic policies without taking into account the domestic policies of its member states. Similarly, many environmental issues involve factors both within and across a country's borders. In addition, because many violent antistate movements receive support from abroad, it is hard to categorize the study of revolutions, terrorism, and civil war as being solely in the domain of either comparative or international politics.

Nonetheless, it is possible to retain the basic insights of LaPalombara and Morgenthau by simply saying that comparative politics is the study of political phenomena that are predominantly "within country" relationships and that international politics is the study of political phenomena that are predominantly "between country" relationships. This view of comparative politics, and political science more generally, is illustrated in Figure 1.1. As you can see, international politics addresses things like conflict, foreign policy, and international organizations that shape the relationships between countries. In contrast, comparative politics focuses on issues such as party systems, elections, identity politics, and interest group relations within countries like Brazil, China, France, and Nigeria. Scholars interested in political economy issues such as trade, central bank independence, and exchange rate policy cross the divide between international and comparative politics.

Students in the United States may wonder where American politics fits into this description. In most political science departments in the United States, American politics is considered a separate subfield. Does the fact that American politics focuses predominantly on politics within the United States mean that it should be considered part of comparative politics? This is a question that, for some reason, generates quite heated debate among political scientists.

FIGURE 1.1   One View of Political Science

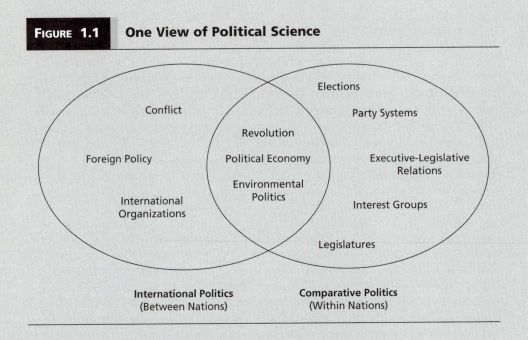

International Politics
(Between Nations)

Comparative Politics
(Within Nations)

Historically, a second traditional definition of comparative politics has been that it is the study of politics in every country except the one in which the student resides. Thus, according to this definition, comparative politics is the study of what economists often like to call "the rest of the world." This definition, however, seems rather silly to us because it means that the study of Nigerian politics is part of comparative politics unless one happens to be studying it in Nigeria, in which case it is simply "Nigerian politics." We leave it up to you to decide whether you think American politics should be considered part of comparative politics or not.

In addition to the two definitions just outlined, comparative politics has sometimes been defined as the study of politics using the method of comparison. In fact, as seen in Chapter 2, scholars of comparative politics who seek to define their subject in this way typically have a particular type of comparative method in mind. This tradition, which dates back at least as far as Aristotle's attempt to classify constitutional forms, seeks to answer questions about politics by comparing and contrasting attributes of different polities (predominantly city-states in Aristotle's day but nation-states today). Although this third definition is, to some extent, descriptively accurate, it is not particularly useful. As we show in Chapter 2, comparison is central to any and all scientific endeavor. As a result, defining comparative politics in terms of a "comparative" method would make it synonymous with political science itself. If this is the case, it makes one wonder why there are two phrases—comparative politics and political science—to describe the same thing.

We believe that comparative politics is best understood as the study of politics occurring predominantly within countries. As such, it is a rather vast field of research. For reasons that

Comparative politics is the study of political phenomena that occur predominantly within countries. **International politics** is the study of political phenomena that occur predominantly between countries.

we explain in this chapter, we choose not to focus on the politics of a single nation or a particular collection of nations in this book. Instead, we try to understand political behavior through the explicit comparison of important national-level attributes. In other words, we compare domestic political behavior from a cross-national perspective. As an example of our approach, we prefer to ask why some countries have two parties (like the United States) but others have many (like France) rather than examine the party systems in the United States and France separately. By taking this approach, we do not mean to suggest that the study of politics within individual countries should be excluded from the field of comparative politics. Nor do we mean to imply that cross-national comparison is a more worthy endeavor than studying a single country. Having said that, we believe that a comparison of national-level attributes is a reasonable introduction to comparative politics and one that will set a broad framework for the closer study of politics within individual polities at an advanced level.

urgent. For example, the Great Depression and the rise of fascism in Europe compelled comparative politics scholars in the middle of the last century to address two important topics. The first was what governments can and should do to encourage stable economic growth. In other words, what, if anything, can governments do to protect their citizens from the devastating consequences of market instability? The second was how to design electoral institutions in such a way as to reduce the likelihood that political extremists who oppose democracy, like the Nazi Party in Germany's Weimar Republic, might be elected. Both of these topics remain central to the field of comparative politics today.

In the aftermath of World War II, decolonization and the onset of the cold war combined to drive many comparative politics scholars to focus on the question of "political development." What, if anything, could be done to reduce political and economic instability in poor and underdeveloped countries? Research conducted at that time frequently focused on the proper relationship between the government and the market, with the central concerns of the day perhaps being best summarized in the title of Joseph Schumpeter's 1942 classic *Capitalism, Socialism, and Democracy*. The cold war between the United States and the Soviet Union only heightened the urgency with which scholars struggled to understand the causes and consequences of communist revolutions in China and Cuba, as well as the political turmoil in places like Vietnam and Chile.

By the 1970s, economic instability, brought on by the Middle East oil crisis, returned to wealthy industrial countries. As a result, many comparative politics scholars revisited questions raised during the interwar years on their home turf of Western Europe. By now, however, the discussion had been narrowed somewhat because many scholars had come to accept the "postwar settlement," or "class compromise," that had essentially seen workers accept a capitalist economy and free trade in return for the expansion of the welfare state and other benefits. With the widespread acceptance of capitalist economies across Western Europe, researchers now turned their attention to how the specific variety of capitalism that existed in a particular country might influence that country's capacity to weather economic storms created elsewhere.

In the waning days of the twentieth century, attention turned to the fallout created by the end of the cold war. Suddenly, dozens of countries in eastern and central Europe were negotiating the twin transitions from centrally planned economies to market-based ones and from one-party dictatorships to democracy. Now, in the twenty-first century, attention appears to be turning once again to questions of political and economic development.

President Bush's speech cited earlier is full of statements about the desirability and feasibility of democratization in Iraq. In effect, his speech sought to make the case that invading Iraq was an option that should be seriously considered because an Iraqi democracy was both desirable and achievable. To that end, much of what President Bush had to say was designed to convince people that democratization in Iraq was a realistic possibility, even if it was going to be difficult to achieve. It is worth noting that President Bush did not say that because democracy is a good thing, a democratic Iraq should be pursued no matter what the cost.[2] By raising the issue of whether it was actually feasible to establish a democracy, he was essentially stating that any decision about whether to invade Iraq would have to involve weighing the purported benefits of successful democratization against the expected costs in light of the probability of success.

President Bush made many claims about the benefits of democracy and the likelihood of successful democratization in Iraq in his speech. But what is the theoretical basis for these claims? What does the empirical evidence say? Exactly how would you begin to evaluate these and other, similar claims? In this book we introduce you to what comparative political scientists have to say about these types of questions. One of the central goals of this book is to provide you with the substantive knowledge and methodological tools to begin evaluating such claims for yourself.

OVERVIEW OF THE BOOK

Political science is the study of politics in a scientific manner. It is easy to see that, as it stands, this definition of political science is not particularly informative. For example, what is politics? What is science? We explicitly address these questions in Chapters 2 and 3 of Part I. With these preliminaries out of the way, we begin to examine the substantive questions relating to the causes and consequences of democracy that are the book's central focus. In Part II we contrast democracies and dictatorships. Specifically, we explore the origins of the modern state and ask two questions that have been central to the study of comparative politics. First, why are some countries democracies and others dictatorships? And second, does it matter?

---

2. President Bush could have made such an argument. Arguments to do the right thing, however, quickly encounter the problem of scarce resources. If there is an infinite number of ways that we can "do the right thing," how should we choose to deploy our limited resources?

In Part III we turn our attention to the different types of democracy that exist around the world. In particular, we examine the sometimes dizzying array of institutional forms that democracy can take on. Finally, in Part IV, we investigate how different types of democracy affect government performance and the survival of democracy itself.

Our goal in writing this book is to provide answers that are relevant to the problems motivating the study of comparative politics today and that are reliable—that is, built on the best practices of contemporary political scientists. In what follows, we highlight some of the questions and issues that we address in the upcoming chapters. These issues have been of long-standing interest to comparative political scientists and remain vitally important for understanding the contemporary world.

State Failure

Although state failure has long been recognized as one of the key sources of political and economic instability around the globe, the horrific events of September 11, 2001, have lent a new urgency to the need to understand the conditions under which states fail and the conditions under which such power vacuums might foster international terrorism. The reason for this is that the September 11 terrorist attacks were planned from Afghanistan—a failed state in which the Taliban provided sanctuary for al-Qaida to train terrorists and plan attacks against various targets around the world. In Chapter 4 we define what political scientists mean when they speak of the "state" and describe what life is like in a failed state by looking in detail at Somalia since 1991. To a large extent, the case of Somalia resembles that of Afghanistan in that an Islamic group, the Supreme Council of Islamic Courts, is attempting to establish an Islamic state and is vying for control of the country against the internationally backed Transitional Federal Government and various other militias and warlords. The fear that Somalia will become a safe haven for terrorist activity as Afghanistan did in the 1990s has led the United States to become increasingly involved in Somali affairs over the past few years. To understand how one might fill the power vacuum that exists in failed states like Somalia and Afghanistan, it is necessary to understand the historical development of the modern state. What distinguishes the modern state from other forms of political organization? What led to its development? The rest of Chapter 4 focuses on addressing these types of questions.

Economic Determinants of Democracy

In October 2001 the United States responded to the September 11 terrorist attacks by invading Afghanistan to overthrow the Taliban. In addition to trying to capture Osama bin Laden and destroy al-Qaida's terrorist infrastructure, one of the stated goals of this attack was to replace the Taliban with a more democratic form of government. In order to establish democracy intentionally and successfully in countries like Afghanistan and Iraq, however, it is important that we first understand the factors that encourage or discourage the emergence and survival of democracy. In other words, to critically evaluate President Bush's suggestions about the types of factors that make democracy feasible in places like Iraq, we need to turn both to the facts of the specific case at hand and the considerable body of theoretical and empirical evidence that comparative political scientists have compiled on the determinants of democracy.

Recall that President Bush pointed to Iraq's "abundant resources" and its "skilled and educated people" as two factors that make democracy feasible in Iraq. Iraq is an oil-rich country (only Saudi Arabia has larger oil reserves) that has, either in spite of or because of this fact, an ailing economy. In 2005 Iraq had a gross domestic product (GDP) per capita of $3,400 and it derived 95 percent of its foreign exchange earnings (assets denominated in foreign currencies that are needed to purchase imports) from oil. Between 1950 and 1980, the Iraqi economy underwent a rapid modernization process that transformed it from a traditional agricultural economy to the third largest economy in the Middle East. Over the next quarter of a century, however, war, international sanctions, and inefficiencies encouraged by a centrally planned economy undid many of these economic gains. The net effect of these recent developments has been an Iraqi economy that is poor by global standards. Since Iraq gained independence from British colonial rule in 1932, the country has been ruled by a monarchy and a series of dictatorships. It is reasonable to ask whether recent economic conditions such as the ones just described make it more or less likely for democracy to be established in a land in which it has not yet taken root.

In Chapter 6 we explore in great detail whether successful democracies can be created under such circumstances. Specifically, we examine how economic development and the structure of a country's economy influence the likelihood that a country will become and remain democratic. Some scholars have argued that countries are more likely to experience transitions from dictatorship to democracy as their economies become more modern—that is, less reliant on natural resource exports, more productive, more industrial, more highly educated, and so on. Other scholars have argued that such modernization may affect the survival of democracy but does not influence the emergence of democracy. In other words, they argue that modernization helps democracies stay democratic but does not help dictatorships become democratic. Although debate continues over the precise relation between economic modernization and democracy, the fact that Iraq does not fulfill many of the basic requirements of "modernization" means that comparative politics scholars on both sides of the debate would reach essentially the same conclusion regarding the prospects for democracy in Iraq—they are poor. On a related note, many political scientists have argued that democracy is unlikely to arise in countries whose economies are dependent on natural resource extraction, particularly if this extraction is capital intensive and has huge economies of scale, as is the case with oil. If you find such arguments persuasive after reading Chapter 6, then the "abundant resources" that President Bush pointed to in his speech may be a cause for concern, rather than hope, in regard to the attempt to build democracy in Iraq.

Cultural Determinants of Democracy

In the speech that we cited at the beginning of the chapter, President Bush also refers to cultural factors that might influence the process of democratization in Iraq. In doing so, he was responding to arguments that democratization in Iraq may be an uphill battle for cultural reasons. Over the years, many scholars have argued that democracy is incompatible with particular cultures. As President Bush correctly notes, though, precisely which culture is thought to be bad for democracy tends to change from one time period to the next, depending on which countries in the world are democratic at a particular point in time. For example, Catholicism was seen as inimical to democracy during the 1950s and 1960s, when few Catholic countries in the world were democratic. As Catholic countries in southern Europe and Latin America became democratic in the 1970s and 1980s, the earlier view began to wane. Today, of course, the culture that is deemed most antithetical to democracy is Islam. Again, the basic reason why people commonly view Islam as bad for democracy tends to be that they do not see many contemporary Islamic democracies.

In Chapter 7 we examine the theoretical and empirical evidence behind arguments that some cultures are bad for democracy. In doing so, we suggest that the type of after-the-fact (or post-hoc) theorizing that leads people to conclude, for example, that there must be something about Islam that discourages democracy because there aren't many predominantly Muslim democracies in the contemporary world should be treated with considerable skepticism. If you find the case for such skepticism convincing, then you might be inclined to agree with President Bush's suggestion that Iraq's status as a majority Muslim country does not rule out the possibility of democratization there. Although you might agree with President Bush on this point, we explain in our discussion of the scientific method in Chapter 2 why you should still be suspicious of his claim that because Japan and Germany overcame alleged cultural barriers to democracy, Iraq can too. Such an argument is similar in structure to the claim that because we have two elderly relatives who smoked cigarettes their whole lives and did not develop lung cancer, we can safely do so as well.

If, after reading Chapters 6 and 7, you believe that the economic and cultural factors in Iraq make democratization feasible, you might begin to wonder whether military force is the best way to bring it about. We do not examine the attempts of foreign countries to impose democracy by force in any great detail, but we do examine the process by which countries transition from dictatorship to democracy in Chapter 8. In particular, we look at bottom-up transitions to democracy, in which the people rise up as part of a popular revolution to overthrow the dictator, and top-down transitions, in which authoritarian elites introduce liberalization policies that ultimately lead to democracy. Our discussion in this chapter offers an explanation for why dictatorships frequently appear so stable, why popular revolutions are so rare, and why popular revolutions, when they do occur, nearly always come as a surprise even though they often appear so inevitable in hindsight. By focusing on the strategic interaction of elites and masses involved in top-down transitions, we also emphasize the important role that information, beliefs, and uncertainty can play in these types of democratic transitions. Given that the United States and its allies have already invaded and are actively trying to encourage a democratic transition and consolidation, an understanding of the actual dynamics of democratic transitions as outlined in Chapter 8 should prove useful.

What's So Good about Democracy Anyway?

President Bush suggests that we should support "freedom" and "democracy" in Iraq because the Iraqi people, like people everywhere, want good things for themselves and their children. For example, he says in his speech that "[i]n our desire to care for our children and give them a better life, we are the same." Although difficult to establish scientifically, a combination of introspection and human empathy would probably lead most of us to accept President Bush's claim that people all over the world want better lives for themselves and their children.[3] The claim that democracy actually produces these "good things" is, in contrast, well within the purview of social science. Consequently, in Chapter 9 we examine whether democracy really does make a material difference in people's lives or not. Is it an accident that years of dictatorship have produced war and economic ruin in Iraq, or is this an outcome to be expected from all dictatorships? And, perhaps more important, will changing the type of regime in Iraq reverse these outcomes?

Our time has been referred to as the "age of democracy." Even dictatorships spend a fair amount of time and energy paying lip service to the wonders of democracy. The benefits of democracy that many people speak of may be real, but political scientists like to reach conclusions on the basis of logic and evidence rather than conventional wisdom and ideology. As a result, we devote considerable effort in Chapters 9 and 10 to examining whether or not there is a sound basis for pursuing democracy in the first place. In Chapter 9 we examine what the comparative politics literature has to say about the relative policy performance of democracies and dictatorships. As we demonstrate, the picture that emerges from this literature is significantly more nuanced than the rhetoric that politicians around the world typically employ. Although democracies seldom perform poorly in regard to the level of material well-being that they provide their citizens, they frequently fail to outperform a substantial number of dictatorships. In Chapter 10 we examine whether the actual process of democracy has some inherently attractive properties that would make it morally or normatively attractive over and above any material benefits it might produce. The picture that emerges from the comparative politics literature on this matter may surprise you. The bottom line is that there is no support for the idea that there is an ideal form of political organization—this includes democracy.

Institutional Design

Presumably referring to Germany and Japan, President Bush, in his speech with which we started this chapter, suggests that the United States left behind "constitutions and parliaments, not occupying armies" after World War II. This is not entirely accurate. For example, the U.S. army continued to occupy Japan for seven years after the war; it finally left in 1952. The situation in Germany was slightly more complicated in that the occupying force was an alliance between France, the Soviet Union, the United Kingdom, and the United States. Although the Federal Republic of Germany (West Germany) was created in 1949, four years after the end of the war, the occupation by the Allied forces of France, the United Kingdom, and the United States did not officially end until 1955. East Germany was controlled by the Soviet Union, and many would date the end of that occupation as 1990, when East Germany was finally reunited with West Germany. Although the claim that the United States did not leave occupying forces behind in Japan and Germany at the end of World War II is somewhat inaccurate, there is considerable truth in President Bush's broader intimation that the

---

3. As we note in Chapter 2, this book is devoted to the social scientific route to knowledge, but we accept that this is just one way to know things.

United States played an important role in encouraging the growth of democracy in these two countries. First, the United States gave billions of dollars in economic aid to both countries in an effort to rebuild war-torn economies. Second, U.S. government officials and scholars had a considerable influence over the design of the new constitutions in these countries. Interestingly, the new constitutions in West Germany and Japan were quite different from one another, and both were very different from the U.S. Constitution.

The decision to adopt different constitutions in West Germany and Japan might be explained by the fact that the constitutional designers were aware that the effects and suitability of particular institutions are likely to depend on local conditions, such as a country's social structure, political environment, geography, economy, and history. Although the German, Japanese, and American constitutions exhibit a great deal of variety in regard to the democratic institutions that they establish, they come nowhere close to exhausting the extraordinary number of possible combinations of these institutions seen around the world—there are many, many different ways to structure a democracy. This suggests that if one were convinced that democracy was the best alternative for a country like Iraq (without implying that there is any reason to believe that this decision should be one person's to make), then the next logical question is how one should design such a democracy. Designing a democracy presumes that we know both how various democratic institutions work and what their consequences will be. In Parts III and IV of this book, we examine what the comparative politics literature has to say in these regards.

A comparison of the German, Japanese, and U.S. constitutions might give us some idea of the variety of democratic institutions in the world, but only a systematic examination of the way these institutions work and the broader historical experience with them can give us any sense of the consequences of particular institutional choices. Chapters 11 through 14 in Part III are devoted to explaining how various democratic institutions work. Unlike the United States, which is a presidential democracy, Germany and Japan are parliamentary democracies. In Chapter 11 we explore differences between these types of democracy in detail. In particular, we focus on how governments form and survive in parliamentary and presidential democracies. Germany, Japan, and the United States exhibit even more variety in the electoral systems that they employ. The United States uses a single-member district plurality (SMDP) system for its national-level legislative elections. From 1948 to 1993, Japan used the single non-transferable vote (SNTV) to elect its legislators in multimember districts. The Federal Republic of Germany uses a mixed electoral system that basically combines a proportional representation electoral system with an SMDP one. In Chapter 12 we explore the dizzying variety of electoral systems that have been employed around the world and attempt to understand each of their strengths and weaknesses as regards things like proportionality, ethnic accommodation, accountability, minority representation, and the revelation of sincere preferences.

In Chapter 13 we discuss one of the primary effects of electoral laws: that they help shape a country's political party system. Some countries have many political parties, whereas others have few. Some party systems are divided mainly along ethnic lines, whereas others are divided primarily along class, religious, linguistic, or regional ones. Although the type of government and electoral system in a country is nearly always enshrined in a constitution or some other legal document, this is not the case for the type of party system. Instead, party systems take their shape from the evolving nature of political competition in a country. In Chapter 13 we examine how the choice of electoral system combines with attributes of a country's social structure to determine both the number and types of parties that are likely to exist. In Iraq, there are substantial divisions between the two largest ethnic identity groups—Arabs (about 75 percent) and Kurds (about 25 percent)—and the two largest religious groups—Shia Muslims (about 60 percent) and Sunni Muslims (about 40 percent). We show in Chapter 13 that under these conditions, the choice of electoral laws is likely to play an important role in determining what types of political parties a democratic Iraq (should it survive its birth) will have and whether there will be many parties or few.

In Chapter 14 we briefly examine other institutional ways in which democracies vary. In particular, we focus on whether democracies are federal or unitary, whether they have a bicameral or unicameral legislature, and the extent to which they exhibit judicial independence. Continuing our comparison from before, Germany—as its name, the Federal Republic of Germany, would suggest—and the United States both employ a federal system, in which the activities of government are constitutionally divided between regional governments and the central government. In contrast, Japan employs a unitary system, in which all political power is constitutionally given to the central government. Germany, Japan, and the United States all have a bicameral legislature, in which legislative power is divided between two houses, but roughly 60% of the world's democracies have a unicameral legislature, in which legislative power is concentrated in a single house. Democracies also differ in the extent to which judges are independent from the influence of other branches of government. It turns out, however, that this is one area in which the written constitution is typically of little help to scholars seeking to understand the actual degree of judicial independence that exists in a country. For example, consider the United States and Japan. Although the U.S. Constitution makes no mention of judicial review—the idea that courts can decide whether a law is unconstitutional or not—judicial review has, nonetheless, developed in the United States. In contrast, the Japanese constitution explicitly states that judges shall be "independent in the exercise of their conscience and bound only by this Constitution and its laws," but a recent study of Japanese judges suggests that they are, in practice, quite responsive to political pressures. In other words, simply looking at a constitution can be quite misleading if one wishes to determine the actual degree of judicial independence in a country. All three of these institutional choices—federal versus unitary, unicameral versus bicameral, and judicial independence—can be thought of as forms of checks and balances that create institutional veto players in a political system. As such, their causes and consequences are closely related, and therefore we consider these different institutions in a single chapter.

As indicated in Chapters 11 through 14, democracies around the world exhibit many different institutional forms. Although President Bush appears to see the consequences of such institutional choices as straightforward, we do not. As a result, we believe that it is important to examine what comparative politics has to say about the expected outcomes associated with these different institutional forms. This is precisely what we do at some length in Chapter 15 (Part IV). In Chapter 15 we begin by examining the normative and material consequences associated with different combinations of democratic institutions. For example, we ask whether all democracies produce equally satisfactory forms of representation. Are governments in some types of democracy more accountable, representative, and responsive than governments in other types of democracy? What are the expected economic consequences associated with different types of democracy?

We then review what the comparative politics literature has to say about how the institutions adopted by a country affect the survival of democracy. Many scholars have argued that the kind of ethnic and religious diversity observed in Iraq is a destabilizing force in democracies. Indeed, the divisions noted in Iraq have produced a history of violence and brutality, including the use of chemical weapons by the Arab-dominated government against the Kurds and sectarian violence between Sunnis and Shias. The decade-long war conducted by Saddam Hussein's Sunni-dominated government against the Shia-dominated government in Iran exacerbated all of this hostility and violence. But do these types of divisions make democratic stability impossible, or are there institutional mechanisms that can be put in place that might mitigate the effects of ethnic and religious differences? In addition to examining how institutions might mitigate the effects of ethnic and religious diversity, we also look at whether a country's choice of government—parliamentary or presidential—influences the prospects for democratic survival. There is considerable evidence that parliamentary democracies survive significantly longer than presidential democracies. But if this is true, one might wonder what explains the persistence of democracy in the United States? Comparative politics scholars have an answer to this question, but to appreciate it, we must be willing to travel through both time and space.

THE APPROACH TAKEN IN THIS BOOK

Many introductory comparative politics texts are organized around a sequence of individual country studies. Typically, one starts with Britain, before moving on to France and Germany. Next it's on to Russia, Japan, India, Brazil, and, nearly always, Nigeria. Occasionally, China and Mexico might make an appearance somewhere along the line. We believe that this approach has some limitations if the goal of an introductory class is to teach something other than descriptive information about a tiny fraction of the world's countries. The eight countries that make up the domain of a typical comparative politics textbook constitute little more than 4 percent of the world's 193 widely recognized independent states. Why should we focus on these countries and not others? The response from the authors of these textbooks might be that these countries are, in some sense, either the most important or the most representative countries in the world. We find the first of these claims—that they are the most important countries—to be displeasing and the second—that they are the most representative countries—to be questionable.

An introductory class in comparative politics has many goals. We believe that it should stimulate students' interest in the particular subject matter and introduce them to the principal concerns and findings of the field. It should also give students an insight into the extent to which there is consensus or ongoing debate concerning those findings. Consequently, we have endeavored to focus our attention on the questions that comparative politics scholars have historically considered vitally important and those on which there is some growing consensus. It is undeniable that the causes and consequences of democracy are a central issue in comparative politics. It is for this reason that they are a central concern of our book. Less obvious perhaps is a growing consensus regarding the causes and consequences of particular sets of democratic institutions. We endeavor both to make this emerging consensus clearer and to provide the analytical tools required to critically engage it.

In light of the types of research questions that we want to address here, the traditional series of country studies found in most textbooks would not provide the most useful approach. First, very few countries exhibit sufficient variance across time with their experience of democracy to allow questions about democracy's causes and consequences to be answered by a single country study. Similarly, very few countries experience sufficient variation in their institutions across time to give us much leverage in gaining an understanding of their causes and consequences. For example, countries that adopt presidentialism or a particular set of electoral laws tend to retain these choices for long periods of time. In fact, when forced to choose those institutions again (for example, at the end of an authoritarian interruption), countries frequently make the same choice. It is for these reasons that comparisons across countries are important for understanding the research questions that are at the heart of this book—they provide the much-needed variation not often found in any one country.

Second, we—personally—do not possess the required memory and attentiveness to remember the relevant details of particular countries' institutions and cultures across many weeks and we, perhaps incorrectly, do not expect our students to either. Overall, we are not hopeful that we, or our students, can be expected in week ten of the semester when studying the intricacies of the Russian Duma to make comparisons with the Japanese Diet or the British House of Commons studied weeks earlier. Even if we could retain the relevant information across the course of a semester, it is not obvious that eight or ten countries would produce a sufficiently large variety of socioeconomic and institutional experiences to allow us to adequately evaluate the hypotheses that are central to the comparative politics subfield and this book. Given that our primary concern in this textbook surrounds institutional, social, economic, and cultural factors that remain fairly constant across time within countries, the most a comparison of a relatively small number of observations could accomplish is a collection of confirming cases. In Chapter 2 we discuss why such a practice is problematic from the standpoint of the scientific method.

We also believe that the traditional approach adopted by most textbooks has the unfortunate consequence of creating a significant disjuncture between what comparative political scientists teach students and what these scholars actually do for a living. Comparative politics scholars do sometimes engage in descriptive exercises such as detailing how laws are made, how institutions function, or who has power in various countries. This is the traditional subject matter of most textbooks. However, it is much more common for comparative scholars to spend their time constructing and testing theories about political phenomena in the world. In reality, they are primarily interested in explaining, rather than describing, why politics is organized along ethnic lines in some countries but class lines in others, or why some countries are democracies but others dictatorships. Some textbook authors seem reluctant to present this sort of material to students because they believe it to be too complicated. However, we strongly believe that comparative political science is not rocket science. The fact that it is only relatively recently that the scientific method has begun to be applied to the study of political phenomena suggests to us that students should be able to engage the political science literature with relative ease. Indeed, we believe that, compared with other disciplines such as physics or mathematics, there is unusual room for students actually to make significant contributions to the accumulation of knowledge in comparative political science. As a result, one of the goals of our book is to introduce you to what comparative political scientists spend most of their time doing and to begin to give you the tools to contribute to the debates in our discipline.[4]

KEY CONCEPTS

comparative politics, *5*
international politics, *5*

---

4. Clark and Reichert (1998) and Brambor, Clark, and Golder (2006, 2007) are examples of original research published in scientific journals in which our own undergraduate students have played significant roles.

2 | What Is Science?

OVERVIEW

- Comparative politics is the subfield of political science that focuses primarily on politics within countries. In Chapter 3 we define and examine the nature of politics. In this chapter we define and examine the nature of science.

- Science is a strategy for understanding and explaining the social and natural world that emphasizes the use of statements that can be examined to see whether they are wrong.

- Scientific explanations should explain previously puzzling facts, be logically consistent, and produce (many) potentially falsifiable predictions.

- All scientific statements are tentative. We accept some statements as provisionally true when they have withstood vigorous attempts at refutation more successfully than competing statements.

INTRODUCTION

Consider the following five statements. What do they all have in common?

1. Science is a collection of facts that tell us what we know about the world.
2. A scientific theory is one that has been proven.
3. "The sun revolves around the earth" is not a scientific statement.
4. If my theory is correct, then I should observe that rich countries are more likely to be democracies. I do observe that rich countries are more likely to be democracies. Therefore, my theory is correct.
5. Politics cannot be studied in a scientific manner.

The common element in these statements is that they are all, in some sense, wrong. Science is not a collection of facts that tell us what we know about the world. Scientific theories cannot be proven; thus, a scientific theory is not one that has been proven. The statement that the sun revolves around the earth is a scientific statement (even though it is false). The argument outlined in statement 4 is invalid and, therefore, I cannot conclude that my theory is correct. And finally, politics can be studied in a scientific manner. We suspect that many of you will have thought that at least some of these statements were correct. To know why all of these statements about science are wrong, you will need to continue reading this chapter.

Science certainly has its detractors, largely because of what was experienced in the twentieth century. Some horrendous things were either done in the name of science or "justified" on scientific grounds or, at a minimum, made possible by science. Although we should never close our eyes to the harm that is sometimes done with science, we believe that it is as much a mistake to blame science for what some scientists have done in its name as it is to blame religion for what some believers have done in its name.

But what is science? First and foremost, science is a method; however, it is also a culture. The epigraphs at the start of this chapter are meant to capture what we might call the "culture" of science. Some of the negative views of science come from what people perceive the culture of science to be—cold, calculating, self-assured, and arrogant. We believe, however, that at its best, the culture of science displays the characteristics encouraged by the otherwise very different thinkers who are quoted. The scientific method is, at its very core, a critical method, and those reflective individuals who use it are much more likely to be humbled than emboldened. Sir Karl Popper ([1959] 2003) reminds us that science is not a static set of beliefs to be conserved and that all knowledge is tentative. Socrates reminds us that an acute awareness of our own ignorance is always the first step toward knowledge. Saint Paul offers hope that our willingness to test all of our ideas will leave us something good to hang on to. As we'll demonstrate in this chapter, science isn't about certainty, it isn't merely about the orderly collection of facts, and it isn't about invoking authority to protect our ideas from uncomfortable evidence. Instead, science is about asking tough questions and providing answers that invite criticism. Science is about recognizing the limits of our knowledge without lapsing into irresponsible cynicism. And science is about using the best logic, methods, and evidence available to provide answers today, even though we recognize that they may be overturned tomorrow.

Comparative politics is a subfield of political science. But what exactly is political science? Well, it is the study of politics in a scientific way. How's that for a tautology? It is easy to see that, as it stands, this definition is not particularly informative. For example, what is politics? And what is science? In the next chapter we answer the first of these questions and seek to demarcate politics from other forms of social phenomena. In this chapter, though, we focus on the second question—what is science? Our goal is to provide an answer that resembles the way most practicing scientists would answer this question.

THE COMPARATIVE METHOD

A common method employed today by comparative political scientists to learn about the world is known as the **comparative method.** It is also known as Mill's methods because it is based on a formal set of rules outlined by John Stuart Mill in his 1843 book, *A System of Logic*. Mill actually outlined two different methods.

> The **comparative method,** also known as Mill's methods, involves the systematic search for the necessary and sufficient causes of political phenomena. The comparative method comprises the Method of Agreement and the Method of Difference.

One is called the *Method of Agreement;* the other is called the *Method of Difference*. Political scientists who employ these methods collect observations of the world and then use these observations to develop general laws and theories about why certain political phenomena occur.[1] In employing these methods, the goal is to identify the causes of political events. Before we evaluate Mill's Method of Agreement and his Method of Difference in detail, we should first define what we mean by the word *cause*. For the moment, let us restrict ourselves to two relatively straightforward conceptions of causation: necessary and sufficient conditions.

Necessary and Sufficient Conditions

A *necessary condition* is a circumstance in whose absence the event in question cannot occur. In other words, the effect (E) never happens unless the purported necessary condition or cause (C_N) is present: "If E, then C_N" or "If no C_N, then no E." Barrington Moore's ([1966] 1993) magisterial 559-page *Social Origins of Dictatorship and Democracy* can be summarized, somewhat simplistically, with the following necessary condition: "no bourgeoisie, no democracy." This necessary condition captures Moore's claim that without a strong urban class, there will be no stable democracy, and if there is a stable democracy, there must be a strong urban class. Because some of you, like us, think better visually, we provide a visual representation of a necessary condition in Figure 2.1. As you can see, the claim that C_N is a necessary condition for effect E to occur is logically equivalent to the claim that occurrences of E form a subset of the instances where C_N is present. Note that C_N can occur without the effect E occurring—this is because C_N is only a necessary, but not a sufficient, condition for E. As another example, oxygen is a necessary, but not a sufficient, condition for fire. Take oxygen

---

1. For example, Weber ([1930] 1992) employs Mill's methods to explain the rise of capitalism; Moore ([1966] 1993), to determine why some countries are democracies but others are dictatorships; Skocpol (1979), to examine social revolutions; Katznelson (1985), to analyze the variation in the organizational patterns of the working class in the United States and the United Kingdom; and Kalyvas (1996), to explain the rise of Christian democracy in Western Europe.

A Visual Representation of a Necessary Cause

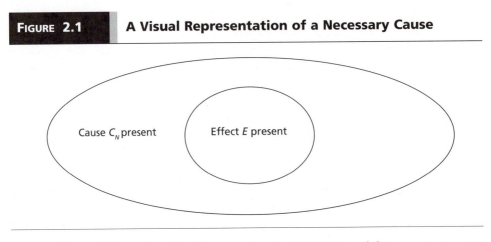

away and there will be no fire, but add oxygen to a given situation and there may or may not be fire, depending on other circumstances.

A *sufficient condition* is a circumstance in whose presence the event in question must occur. In other words, the sufficient condition or cause (C_S) never occurs without the effect (E) also happening; that is, "If C_S, then E" or "If no E, then no C_S." As an example, fire is a sufficient condition for smoke. If there is a fire, there will be smoke. And if there is no smoke, there can be no fire. Figure 2.2 provides a visual representation of a sufficient condition. It is easy to see that the claim that C_S is a sufficient condition for E to occur is logically equivalent to the claim that occurrences of the sufficient condition C_S form a subset of the instances where effect E occurs. Note that effect E can occur even when condition C_S is not present—this is because C_S is a sufficient, but not a necessary, condition for E. Put differently, there may be causes of E other than C_S. A second example might illustrate the point. Jumping is a sufficient, but not a necessary, condition for leaving the ground. Jumping will always cause us to leave the ground; however, the fact that we are not on the ground does not automatically mean that we jumped—there are many other ways of leaving the ground.

FIGURE 2.2   **A Visual Representation of a Sufficient Cause**

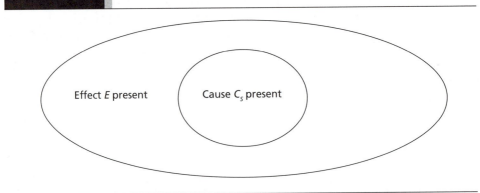

| FIGURE 2.3 | **A Visual Representation of a Necessary and Sufficient Cause** |

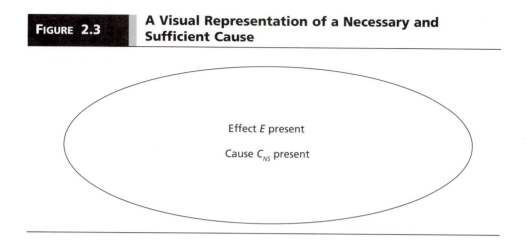

A **necessary and sufficient condition** is a circumstance in whose absence the event in question will not occur and in whose presence the event in question must occur. A statement about necessary and sufficient conditions is equivalent to an "if and only if" statement. In other words, the effect (E) occurs *if and only if*

> A **necessary condition** is a circumstance in whose absence the event in question cannot occur. A **sufficient condition** is a circumstance in whose presence the event in question must occur. A **necessary and sufficient condition** is a circumstance in whose absence the event in question will not occur and in whose presence the event in question must occur.

the necessary and sufficient condition (C_{NS}) is present: "If C_{NS}, then E" and "If no C_{NS}, then no E" or "If E, then C_{NS}" and "If no E, then no C_{NS}." Figure 2.3 provides a visual representation of a necessary and sufficient condition. The claim that C_{NS} is a necessary and sufficient condition for E to occur is logically equivalent to the claim that occurrences of C_{NS} are a subset of E and that occurrences of E are a subset of C_{NS}. In other words, you cannot get one without the other. Visually, this means that there are no subsets where effect E occurs without cause C_{NS} or vice versa.

The systematic search for "necessary," "sufficient," and "necessary and sufficient" conditions has come to be known as Mill's methods or simply the comparative method. Having defined what we mean by a cause, we can now turn our attention to Mill's methods of agreement and difference.

Mill's Method of Agreement

As an illustration of Mill's **Method of Agreement,** suppose we want to explain the occurrence of democracy. Common sense might suggest that if we want to know what causes democracy, we should study democracies.[2] We could observe two contemporary democracies and take note of their features. For example, we might compare the United Kingdom and Belgium, as we do in Table 2.1. Both the United Kingdom and Belgium "agree" in regard to

---

2. As we will see, the kind of sense needed to do good science often turns out to be very "uncommon."

TABLE 2.1	**Mill's Method of Agreement I**			
Country	Democracy	Ethnically homogeneous	Multiparty system	Parliamentary system
United Kingdom	Yes	Yes	No	Yes
Belgium	Yes	No	Yes	Yes

the outcome to be explained—they are both democracies. This is why Mill calls the method being employed here the Method of Agreement.

What, if anything, can we infer from this comparison? Well, we observe that the United Kingdom has a relatively homogeneous population and a two-party parliamentary system. We also observe that Belgium has a relatively heterogeneous population and a multiparty parliamentary system.[3] Assuming that the classification of our observations is correct, we can conclude that ethnic homogeneity is not a necessary condition for democracy. This is because Belgium is a democracy despite being ethnically diverse. We can also conclude that having a multiparty system is not a necessary condition for democracy, because the United Kingdom is a democracy even though it has only two parties. Thus, we have used Mill's Method of Agreement to eliminate two of the three potential causes. Does this mean that we can now conclude that having a parliamentary system is the cause of democracy? It certainly looks that way from Table 2.1. After all, Belgium and the United Kingdom are both democracies and they both have parliamentary systems.

Before we can declare success and put a lot of comparative politics scholars out of work, however, we should look more carefully at Mill's Method of Agreement. Mill ([1874] 1986, 280) wrote:

> If two or more instances of the phenomenon under investigation have only one circumstance in common, the circumstance in which alone all the instances agree, is the cause (or effect) of the given phenomenon.

Mill's logic is unassailable given the way he has defined a "cause." The key phrase to note from a practical standpoint, however, is that our observations of the world should have "only one circumstance in common." In other words, we must be entirely sure that the two observations have nothing else in common that might cause democracy other than the hypothesized cause (a parliamentary system in this case).

Therefore, before we can place much confidence in the statement "[i]f a country adopts a parliamentary system, then it will be a democracy," we must eliminate all other factors that

---

3. Belgium's population is fairly evenly split between Dutch-speaking Flemish and French-speaking Walloons. There is also a sizable German-speaking population in the east of the country and a nontrivial number of non-European immigrants.

Box 2.1

JOHN STUART MILL
(May 20, 1806–May 8, 1873)

John Stuart Mill was born in London, England, the oldest son of a Scottish philosopher. He was educated by his father with the assistance of one of the most famous philosophers of the day, Jeremy Bentham. Mill's education was quite rigorous and he was deliberately shielded from contact with children other than his siblings. By the age of eight he was fluent in Latin and Greek. By the time he was thirteen, Mill had been introduced to Euclidean geometry, algebra, and political economy. The rigor of his academic studies eventually took its toll and he suffered a nervous breakdown when he was twenty-one.

At various points in his life, Mill worked for the British East India Company and was elected to the British House of Commons, where he became the first member of Parliament to advocate for a woman's right to vote. Mill produced many influential works of political philos-

An undated portrait of John Stuart Mill

ophy. In *On Liberty* (1859), Mill set out the nature and limits of the power that can be exercised by society over the individual. It was here that he famously argued that people should be free to do whatever they liked so long as it did not harm others. It was in his most famous book, *A System of Logic* (1843), that he laid out his rules for the scientific method. Among his other famous works are *Utilitarianism* (1861), in which he argued for the philosophy of utilitarianism proposed by Bentham, and *The Subjection of Women* (1869), in which he claimed that the continuing oppression of women was an impediment to the progress of humanity.

might be considered relevant to the establishment of democracy. Until such a time, all we can do is continue to try to eliminate possible necessary conditions. Note that those factors that cannot be eliminated must be retained as potential necessary conditions. Thus, all we can really conclude on the basis of our two observations is that parliamentary rule may be a necessary condition for democracy—in other words, it's still in the running as a potential cause.

But let's dig a little deeper. Can you think of another possible cause of democracy? For some time now, scholars have suspected a causal connection between the wealth of a country and whether that country will be a democracy. We address this potential relationship in some detail in Chapter 6 of this book. But ask yourself right now, how might you test this claim? Scholars using Mill's Method of Agreement would suggest going back out into the "real world" to observe whether Belgium and the United Kingdom are wealthy or not. It turns out that both countries are wealthy. This new information is shown in Table 2.2.

Since Belgium and the United Kingdom are both wealthy democracies, it now seems that wealth might be a necessary condition for democracy. But note that this violates Mill's stipulation that a cause must be unique—recall that there must be "only one circumstance in common." This means that either wealth or a parliamentary form of government cannot be

TABLE 2.2	Mill's Method of Agreement II				
Country	Democracy	Wealth	Ethnically homogeneous	Multiparty system	Parliamentary system
United Kingdom	Yes	Yes	Yes	No	Yes
Belgium	Yes	Yes	No	Yes	Yes

the cause of democracy.[4] How can we determine which is the "real" cause? The answer is that we can't with just these two observations. So, it's back out into the real world for us to do some more observing.

What type of observation would allow us to determine whether wealth or a parliamentary form of government is a necessary condition for democracy? Clearly, we would need to observe either a wealthy democracy that is not parliamentary or a parliamentary democracy that is not wealthy. Suppose that the next country we observe happens to be the United States. Like the United Kingdom, the United States is a wealthy democracy. In contrast to the United Kingdom, though, the United States has a presidential system of government. We can now add our new observation to the two observations that we already have. We do this in Table 2.3.

What can we now infer from these three observations? Remember that a necessary condition is one in whose absence the event in question cannot occur. This means that we can eliminate any factor that is absent when the outcome being explained is present. In other words, we can eliminate any of the potential necessary causes of democracy in Table 2.3 that are absent when the country is a democracy. Thus, the conditions present in the United Kingdom demonstrate that a multiparty system is not necessary for democracy. Those in Belgium demonstrate that ethnic homogeneity is not necessary for democracy. Finally, con-

TABLE 2.3	Mill's Method of Agreement III				
Country	Democracy	Wealth	Ethnically homogeneous	Multiparty system	Parliamentary system
United Kingdom	Yes	Yes	Yes	No	Yes
Belgium	Yes	Yes	No	Yes	Yes
United States	Yes	Yes	Yes	No	No

---

4. It might be the case that neither wealth nor a parliamentary form of government causes democracy. We cannot be sure because we may not have eliminated all of the other possible causes of democracy. But let's ignore this for now.

ditions in the United States demonstrate that a parliamentary system is not necessary for democracy. Wealth alone survives as a potential necessary condition for democracy in our three cases.

It may be that wealth is the cause we are looking for. Still, we cannot emphasize enough that we can be confident in this only to the extent that we have identified all of the potential causes. In addition, we can say only that wealth may be necessary for democracy; Mill's Method of Agreement does not allow us to determine whether wealth is sufficient for democracy. Ask yourself what type of observation would allow you to determine whether wealth was a sufficient condition for democracy? Well, you would need to look for wealthy countries that are not democracies. If you found such a country, you would know that wealth is not sufficient for democracy. Thus, to evaluate whether wealth is sufficient for democracy, we need to examine non-democracies as well as democracies. This obviously cannot be done with Mill's Method of Agreement, however, because the outcome to be explained would not "agree" for all of the cases. It turns out that we can evaluate claims about sufficient (and necessary) causes using Mill's Method of Difference.

Mill's Method of Difference

Mill's **Method of Difference** compares cases that "differ" in regard to the outcome to be explained. Mill ([1874] 1986, 280) wrote:

> If an instance in which the phenomenon under investigation occurs, and an instance in which it does not occur, have every circumstance in common save one, that one occurring only in the former; the circumstance in which alone the two instances differ, is the effect, or the cause, or an indispensable part of the cause, of the phenomenon.

In other words, the analyst employing this method takes cases that differ in their outcome. She then tries to reject potential conditions for the difference in outcomes by eliminating those conditions that do not vary in exactly the same way as the outcome. If there is one and only one condition that cannot be eliminated by this process, then, Mill's Method of Difference states, this condition must be the cause of the outcome.

> The **Method of Agreement** compares cases that "agree" in regard to the outcome to be explained. The **Method of Difference** compares cases that "differ" in regard to the outcome to be explained.

Now that we know how the Method of Difference works, let's return to our question about whether wealth is a sufficient cause for democracy. To evaluate this claim we must go back out into the real world to observe some non-democracies.[5] Imagine that the first non-democracy that we observe is Mexico prior to 1990. Mexico in this period had a presidential system dominated by a single party. It was also relatively wealthy and ethnically homogeneous. Suppose that we compare Mexico prior to 1990 with the United States. We do this in Table 2.4.

---

5. Here's an example of science depending on uncommon sense. Note the somewhat surprising implication that if you want to know what is sufficient to produce democracy, you must study non-democracies.

TABLE 2.4	Mill's Method of Difference				
Country	Democracy	Wealth	Ethnically homogeneous	Multiparty system	Parliamentary system
United States	Yes	Yes	Yes	No	No
Mexico	No	Yes	Yes	No	No

What can we learn from this comparison? Remember that a sufficient condition requires that if the condition is present, then the outcome or effect should also be present. This means that we can eliminate from consideration any condition that is present when democracy is absent. The case of Mexico prior to 1990 tells us that wealth is not a sufficient condition for democracy, because it is wealthy but not a democracy. It also indicates that ethnic homogeneity is not a sufficient condition for democracy, because it is homogeneous and yet it is not a democracy. The Mexican case can shed no light on whether having multiple parties or a parliamentary system is a sufficient condition for democracy.

Not only does Mill's Method of Difference allow us to determine sufficient conditions, but it also allows us to find out if the conditions are necessary for democracy. In this sense, it is "stronger" than the Method of Agreement. For example, the United States case indicates that having multiple parties or a parliamentary system is not necessary for democracy. This is because the United States is a democracy even though it has only two parties and a presidential system. The information shown in Table 2.4 indicates that ethnic homogeneity, like wealth, may be necessary for democracy. Note, though, that the conclusion from the comparison of the United States and Mexico that ethnic homogeneity may be a necessary condition for democracy contradicts the conclusion drawn from our earlier comparison of the United Kingdom and Belgium that ethnic homogeneity was not a necessary condition for democracy. This point highlights an important limitation when one draws inferences from Mill's methods based on a small number of observations—the conclusions drawn may be extremely sensitive to the set of cases observed. As our examples illustrate, comparing the United Kingdom and Belgium would lead to a very different conclusion about the effect of ethnic homogeneity on whether a country will be a democracy than comparing the United States and Mexico prior to 1990. This is just one of the problems associated with drawing inferences using Mill's methods. Before we explore other problems in more detail, let's imagine that we had observed all four cases described above. The four cases are shown in Table 2.5.

From this set of four observations, we can make the following conclusions. Be sure you understand where each conclusion comes from.

- Wealth is not a sufficient condition for democracy in light of the Mexican case. It may, however, be a necessary condition.
- Ethnic homogeneity is not necessary for democracy in light of the Belgian case. Nor is it sufficient for democracy because of the Mexican case.

TABLE 2.5	Combining Mill's Methods of Agreement and Difference				
Country	Democracy	Wealth	Ethnically homogeneous	Multiparty system	Parliamentary system
United Kingdom	Yes	Yes	Yes	No	Yes
Belgium	Yes	Yes	No	Yes	Yes
United States	Yes	Yes	Yes	No	No
Mexico	No	Yes	Yes	No	No

Note: Mill refers to the combination of the Method of Agreement and the Method of Difference as the Indirect Method of Difference or the Joint Method of Agreement and Difference.

- Multipartism is not a necessary condition for democracy in light of the United Kingdom and United States cases. Multipartism may, however, be sufficient for democracy according to the Belgian case.
- A parliamentary system is not necessary for democracy in light of the United States case. It may, however, be a sufficient condition based on the Belgium and United Kingdom cases.

Note that our four observations allow us to rule out only ethnic homogeneity as a cause for democracy; that is, ethnic homogeneity is neither necessary nor sufficient for democracy. Mill's methods cannot determine whether multipartism or a parliamentary system is a sufficient condition for democracy or not based on these four observations. Note also that it is difficult to know if wealth as an apparent necessity for democracy is meaningful, because we have not observed any cases in which wealth is absent. This reveals an interesting aspect of Mill's methods. Although they are often presented as a useful tool when the phenomenon under study is relatively rare, once the number of potential causes expands, the number of cases logically required to isolate their individual effects can get very large rather quickly.[6]

A Critique of Mill's Methods

As we noted earlier, Mill's methods are widely employed in comparative political science. Indeed, they form the basis of the popular "most similar systems" and "most different systems" research designs (Przeworski and Teune 1970; Lijphart 1971, 1975; Collier 1993).[7] We suspect that you will have come across numerous studies using Mill-like methods in many

---

6. Skocpol (1979) argues that she must rely on Mill's methods because the subject she wishes to study (social revolutions) is historically rare. Ragin (1987) actually defines the comparative method as a technique to be used when the number of instances under study is sufficiently small that a scholar can study the full universe of observations rather than a sample.

7. Somewhat confusingly, the most similar systems design is the equivalent of Mill's Method of Difference. It requires that the analyst find cases that are identical to each other except in regard to the outcome to be explained and one key condition. The most different systems design is equivalent to Mill's Method of Agreement. It requires the analyst to choose cases that are as different as possible except in regard to the outcome to be explained and one key condition.

of your classes in political science, economics, sociology, anthropology, or history. Despite their prevalence, though, we now turn to what we consider a compelling critique of these methods (Lieberson 1991, 1994; Sekhon 2004). In order to draw valid inferences from Mill's methods of agreement and difference, several very special assumptions must be met.

- The causal process must be deterministic.
- There can be no interaction effects.
- There can be only one cause of the outcome.
- All of the possible causes must be identified.
- All the instances of the phenomena that could ever occur have been observed by us *or* all the unobserved instances (including future instances) must be just like the instances we have observed.

We believe that these assumptions are almost impossible to satisfy in the social sciences. Nonetheless, some "researchers seem to be unaware or unconvinced of these methodological difficulties, even though Mill himself clearly described many of their limitations" (Sekhon 2004, 281).[8] Moreover, most introductory books on comparative politics seem to ignore these methodological issues and continue to advocate the use of Mill's methods. Given that we seem to be challenging a certain view of how the study of comparative politics should be conducted, let us briefly examine whether these assumptions really are necessary for drawing valid inferences and what consequences they have for research in the social sciences.

> A **deterministic cause** is one that always produces a specific outcome. A **probabilistic cause** is one that influences the probability of a specific outcome.

A **deterministic** cause is one in which a cause always leads to a specific outcome. The assumption that causes must be deterministic logically follows from the fact that both the Method of Agreement and the Method of Difference employ a process of elimination. The Method of Agreement is based on the argument that whatever can be eliminated is not a cause of the outcome being explained, whereas the Method of Difference is based on the argument that what cannot be eliminated is the cause of the outcome being explained. Scholars employing Mill's methods recognize (and often appear to laud) their deterministic nature.[9] For example, Theda Skocpol (1984, 378) states: "Comparative historical analyses proceed through logical juxtapositions of aspects of small numbers of cases. They attempt to identify invariant causal configurations that necessarily (rather than probably) combine to account for outcomes of interest." The problem with deterministic causal processes, though, is that a single "disconfirming" observation can force the analyst to eliminate X as a cause of Y no matter how many other "confirming" observations she has found.

We believe that it is much more appropriate to view the social world in **probabilistic** terms than in deterministic ones. Up to this point, we have defined *cause* in terms of sufficiency and

---

8. Mill ([1874] 1986, 275) states that "in the sciences which deal with phenomena in which artificial experiments are impossible (as in the case of astronomy), or in which they have a very limited range (as in mental philosophy, *social science*, and even physiology), induction from direct experience is practiced at a disadvantage *in most cases equivalent to impracticability*" (italics added).

9. Mill also recognized that his methods are deterministic ([1874] 1986, 271, 373).

necessity; that is, "If C_S, then E" (C is sufficient for E) or "If no C_N, then no E" (C is necessary for E). In practice, though, it is often advisable to restrict ourselves to simply saying that the presence of C increases the probability or likelihood of E rather than that C always produces E. As we'll see, this is the case even if we truly believe that the causal process is deterministic. So why is thinking about causal processes in a probabilistic way better?

First, thinking in probabilistic terms helps us take account of the fact that we may have measured some or all of our cases incorrectly. Measurement error is common in the social sciences and may cause us to incorrectly eliminate (or fail to eliminate) a potential cause for the outcome we seek to explain.[10] This suggests that we should not claim that wealth always causes (or does not cause) democracy based on empirical evidence—our instruments for measuring wealth and democracy are imperfect, and the indicators that we choose to capture wealth may not perfectly fit the concept of wealth that we hope to capture with them. Given the likelihood of some measurement error, we believe that all we can really claim is that wealth increases (decreases, or has no effect on) the probability that a country will be democratic.

Second, thinking in probabilistic terms may be necessary because the phenomenon under study is inherently probabilistic. For example, what if you are trying to predict the behavior of someone who uses the roll of a die to determine his behavior? What if you are trying to predict the movement of subatomic particles? What if an outcome depends on the smooth operation of voting machines in Florida? Given that outcomes in the social sciences are nearly always the result of decisions made by human beings, we believe that it is preferable to think of their causes as being probabilistic rather than deterministic.[11] In sum, the first reason for thinking probabilistically has to do with the limits of our knowledge, whereas the second has to do with the nature of our subject matter.[12]

The second assumption required for drawing valid inferences from Mill's methods is that there can be no interaction effects—all of the causal factors must be independent of each other. An **interaction effect** is when two (or more) conditions jointly cause the outcome. Recall that we used Mill's methods to infer that ethnic homogeneity is neither a necessary nor a sufficient condition for democracy based on the cases in Table 2.5. Can Mill's methods, however, rule out the possibility that ethnic homogeneity and a two-party system are both necessary for democracy? The answer is that they cannot.[13] Mill himself recognized that interactions of this sort are widespread in the social world and admitted that his methods were inappropriate for identifying them. He

> An **interaction effect** occurs when the effect of one variable on an outcome depends on the value of another variable.

10. We address measurement issues in more detail in Chapter 5. As that discussion suggests, we rarely measure our observations perfectly. Moreover, there is often great controversy about which particular measurement process is most appropriate.

11. It is probably wise to think probabilistically even if one's research is in the natural sciences. The discoveries in the field of quantum physics, such as Heisenberg's uncertainty principle, make this particularly clear.

12. Several techniques have been proposed to extend Mill's methods to take account of probabilistic causes (Hildebrand, Laing, and Rosenthal 1977; Braumoeller and Goertz 2000). These techniques, however, all require that there be only one cause (Clark, Gilligan, and Golder 2006).

13. The information in Table 2-5 cannot rule out the possibility that ethnic homogeneity in combination with a two-party parliamentary system causes democracy based on the United Kingdom case or that ethnic heterogeneity in combination with a multiparty system causes democracy based on the Belgian case.

believed that "if so little can be done by the experimental method to determine the conditions of an effect of many combined causes, in the case of medical science; still less is this method applicable . . . to the phenomena of politics and history" (Mill [1874] 1986, 324). It turns out that there are techniques for extending Mill's methods to include complex combinations of individual causal factors (Ragin 1987). Several important difficulties arise with these techniques, however. First, the number of cases required to evaluate the many combinations of causal factors (which increase geometrically) becomes large very quickly. Second, all of the combinations of causal factors required to test one's claims may not actually exist as real world observations. As a result, these extensions are often impractical.

The third assumption underlying Mill's methods is that there can be only one cause. Mill himself indicates this when he says that the Method of Agreement requires cases to "have only one circumstance in common" and that the Method of Difference requires cases to "have every circumstance in common save one." The inability of Mill's methods to deal with multiple causes is illustrated with an example adapted from Lieberson (1994). Consider first the information shown in Table 2.6. Scholars employing the Method of Agreement would conclude that wealth, ethnic homogeneity, and a multiparty system are not necessary for democracy. They cannot, however, rule out the possibility that one or more of these variables are sufficient to cause democracy. As a result, the Method of Agreement cannot handle the possibility of multiple causes.

Is the Method of Difference any better? Imagine that we now add two new observations of non-democracies to our previous four observations. This new set of observations is shown in Table 2.7. As you can see, the Method of Difference cannot determine whether one or more of the conditions—wealth, multipartism, parliamentary system—are sufficient conditions for democracy either. In sum, Mill's methods require that there be only one possible cause of the outcome of interest if scholars are to draw valid inferences.

The fourth assumption is that we have identified all of the possible causes. Recall how our conclusions changed when we added wealth as a potential cause in Table 2.2. Although we were studying the exact same two observations (Belgium and the United Kingdom), our conclusions changed dramatically just because we turned our attention to a new causal fac-

TABLE 2.6	Mill's Method of Agreement Revisited			
Country	Democracy	Wealth	Ethnically homogeneous	Multiparty system
A	Yes	Yes	No	No
B	Yes	No	Yes	No
C	Yes	No	Yes	Yes
D	Yes	No	No	Yes

TABLE 2.7	An Example of Mill's Method of Difference			
Country	Democracy	Wealth	Ethnically homogeneous	Multiparty system
A	Yes	Yes	No	No
B	Yes	No	Yes	No
C	Yes	No	Yes	Yes
D	Yes	No	No	Yes
E	No	No	No	No
F	No	No	No	No

tor. When wealth was omitted, we thought that parliamentary systems caused democracy. Once we added wealth as a potential cause, however, we could not determine whether it was wealth or parliamentary systems that led to democracy. The point here is that we can reach conclusions that have logical force using Mill's methods only if we assume that we have identified all the relevant factors. To convince ourselves that we have done so we must examine a great number of alternative causal factors. To do this, we must examine many cases in order to isolate the independent effect of these alternative causal factors.

Finally, even if we are convinced that the causal process is deterministic, that there are no interaction effects, that there is only one cause, and that we have identified all the possible causes, we are still justified in inferring that a factor is a necessary or sufficient cause only if we accept either (a) that the cases we have observed are all the instances of the phenomena or (b) that all unobserved instances (including future instances) of the phenomena are just like the instances we have already observed. The problem is that we might well draw an inference after N observations that must be discarded after $N + 1$ observations. We saw this earlier when our conclusions about the causal role of wealth changed with the addition of Mexico to our set of observations. Before we added Mexico, we concluded that wealth was a sufficient condition for democracy; afterward, we concluded that wealth was not a sufficient condition. Who's to say that any of our remaining conclusions would not need to be altered in light of as yet unobserved cases? Drawing inferences from observed cases to unobserved cases is problematic.

What are the strengths and weaknesses of the comparative method? A key strength is that it allows us to test whether something is a necessary, sufficient, or necessary and sufficient condition. But it can do so only when many fairly restrictive assumptions are met. If one or more of these assumptions are not met, then we cannot draw valid inferences from the application of Mill's methods. This problem is exacerbated by the fact that the comparative method does not provide us with any help in determining when these assumptions will be met. In our view, at least one of these assumptions is likely to be violated in almost any social science application. This is perhaps why Mill ([1874] 1986, 324) so clearly warned scholars not to employ his methods for examining the political world. As he put it,

> Nothing can be more ludicrous than the sort of parodies on experimental reasoning which one is accustomed to meet with, not in popular discussion only, but in grave treatises, when the affairs of nations are the theme. "How," it is asked, "can an institution be bad, when the country has prospered under it?" "How can such or such causes have contributed to the prosperity of one country, when another has prospered without them?" Whoever makes use of an argument of this kind, not intending to deceive, should be sent back to learn the elements of some one of the more easy physical sciences.

These reservations are sufficiently worrisome on their own that analysts should be reluctant to accept uncritically claims based on the application of Mill's methods. A more fundamental problem is at issue here, however. Even if the analyst could get around the problems listed above, she would have established only that certain phenomena occur together; she would not have provided an explanation of the outcome in question. That is, Mill's methods are empirical methods—they tell us what happens, not why the phenomena occur together. Put differently, all they say is that Y happened when X was present; this is roughly equivalent to saying that the sun came up because the rooster crowed. An essential missing ingredient is a sense of process, a story about why Y appears to happen when X happens. The story about the process that produces the outcomes we see is what scientists call a *theory,* and these stories cannot necessarily be reduced to a set of circumstances that covary with the outcome we wish to explain.

Later in this chapter we discuss the role of theory in the scientific process. First, however, we show that scholars employing Mill's methods would confront a problem even if the cause of a phenomenon was no deeper or more complicated than the factors that covary with it. This problem applies to the analyst who runs millions of regressions on large data sets looking for patterns that might explain her outcome of interest as well as it does to scholars who apply the comparative method to a few cases. Next we address this problem head on by examining when an argument is valid and when it is invalid.

AN INTRODUCTION TO LOGIC

Throughout our lives we are confronted by people trying to convince us of certain things through arguments. Politicians make arguments as to why we should vote for their party rather than the party of their opponents. National leaders provide arguments for why certain policies should be implemented or abandoned. Lawyers make arguments as to why certain individuals should be found guilty or innocent. Professors make arguments as to why students should spend more time in the library and in class rather than at parties. It is important for you to know when these arguments are logically valid and when they are not. If you cannot distinguish between a valid and an invalid argument, other people will be able to manipulate and exploit you. You will be one of life's suckers. In this section, we give you some tools to determine whether an argument is valid or not.

Valid and Invalid Arguments

What is an argument? An **argument** is a set of logically connected statements, typically in the form of a set of **premises** and a **conclusion**. An argument is **valid** when accepting its premises compels us to accept its conclusions. An argument is **invalid** if, when we accept the premises of an argument, we are free to accept or reject its conclusions. One way to represent an argument is in the form of a **categorical syllogism** that consists of a major premise, a minor premise, and a conclusion. The major premise is typically presented as a

> An **argument** is a set of logically connected statements, typically in the form of a set of premises and a conclusion. A **premise** is a statement that is presumed to be true within the context of an argument leading to a conclusion. A **conclusion** in an argument is a claim that is thought to be supported by the premises. A **valid argument** is one in which, if you accept the premises, then you are compelled to accept the conclusion. An **invalid argument** is one in which, if you accept the premises, then you are free to accept or reject the conclusion. A **categorical syllogism** is a specific type of argument that consists of a major premise, a minor premise, and a conclusion.

conditional statement such as, "If P, then Q." The "if" part of the conditional statement (in this case "If P") is called the "antecedent," whereas the "then" part of it (in this case "then Q") is called the "consequent." An example of a conditional statement is: "If a country is wealthy [antecedent], then it will be a democracy [consequent]." The minor premise consists of a claim about either the antecedent or the consequent in the conditional statement (major premise). The conclusion is a claim that is thought to be supported by the premises.

Four types of conditional argument can be represented with a syllogism—arguments that affirm or deny the antecedent and those that affirm or deny the consequent. Which of these four types of argument are valid and which are invalid? Recall that a valid argument is one such that if you accept that the premises are true, then you are compelled to accept the conclusion as true. Let's start by considering what happens when we affirm the antecedent. An example is shown in Table 2.8.

TABLE 2.8	**Affirming the Antecedent: A Valid Argument**	
	General form	**Specific example**
Major premise	If P, then Q	If a country is wealthy, then it will be a democracy
Minor premise	P	The country is wealthy.
Conclusion	Therefore, Q.	Therefore, the country will be a democracy.

The major premise states, "If *P* is true, then *Q* must be true." The minor premise says that "*P* is true." Together, these premises compel us to accept that the conclusion is true. As a result, the argument is valid. In other words, the major premise states, "If a country is wealthy (antecedent), then it will be a democracy (consequent)." The minor premise says, "The observed country is wealthy." It logically follows from this that the observed country must be a democracy. To see why this type of argument is valid, consider the general form of this argument in set-theoretic form. This is shown in Figure 2.4. The major premise indicates that the set of cases where *P* occurs is a subset of the cases where *Q* occurs.[14] The minor premise maintains that *P* does occur. Figure 2.4 clearly shows that if the case in question is in *P*, as the minor premise affirms, then the case must also be in *Q*. Thus, the argument is valid—we are compelled to conclude *Q*.

Now let's consider what happens when we deny the antecedent. An example is shown in Table 2.9. Once again, the major premise can be represented in set-theoretic terms by Figure 2.4. The difference from the previous example is that the minor premise now asserts that *P* is not the case; that is, it denies the antecedent. If we accept this, does it necessarily follow that *Q* is not the case, as the conclusion maintains? Figure 2.4 clearly illustrates that even if our case is not in *P*, it could still be in *Q*. As a result, it does not logically follow from observing "not *P*" that *Q* is not the case. Therefore, this is an invalid argument. This is because we can contradict the conclusion (not *Q*) without running into a contradiction with either the major premise or the minor premise. Since a valid argument compels us to accept its conclusion given that its premises are true, this is sufficient to demonstrate that arguments that deny the antecedent are invalid.

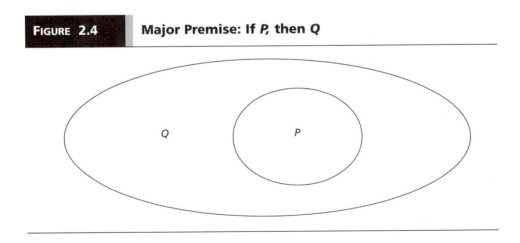

FIGURE 2.4   Major Premise: If *P*, then *Q*

Q   *P*

---

14. Earlier in the chapter we would have said that the major premise indicates that *P* is sufficient for *Q*.

TABLE 2.9	**Denying the Antecedent: An Invalid Argument**	
	General form	Specific example
Major premise	If *P*, then *Q*	If a country is wealthy, then it will be a democracy
Minor premise	Not *P*	The country is not wealthy.
Conclusion	Therefore, not *Q*.	Therefore, the country will not be a democracy.

In the context of our running example, does it follow from the fact that the observed country is not wealthy that it will not be a democracy? Intuitively, we can imagine that there may be other reasons why a country is a democracy even though it is not wealthy. Indeed, one example of a nonwealthy democracy is India. An important point here, though, is that the argument is invalid, not because we can come up with an example of a real democracy that is not wealthy, but rather because we are not compelled to accept the conclusion based on the truthfulness of the major and minor premises. It may be confusing for readers that there is no direct connection between the factual accuracy of an argument's conclusion and the validity of the argument itself—a valid argument can have a conclusion that is factually false and an invalid argument can have a conclusion that is factually true. If we restrict our attention only to whether the argument is valid as it applies to our democracy example, we must ask, "Does the major premise claim that wealth is the only reason why a country will be a democracy?" The answer is clearly no. The major premise states only what will happen if a country is wealthy. It makes no claim as to what might happen if a country is not wealthy. It is for this reason, and this reason alone, that the argument is invalid.

Now let's consider what happens when we affirm the consequent. An example is shown in Table 2.10. As before, the major premise can be represented in set-theoretic terms by Figure 2.4. The difference this time is that the minor premise now asserts that *Q* is the case; that is, it affirms the consequent. If we accept that the premises are true, are we compelled to accept the conclusion that *P* is the case? Figure 2.4 clearly illustrates that the fact that our case is in *Q* does not necessarily mean that it is also in *P*. As a result, the argument is invalid—we are not compelled to accept the conclusion based on the premises.

In the context of our running example, an argument that affirms the consequent confuses necessity and sufficiency. The major premise does not maintain that wealth is the only cause

TABLE 2.10	**Affirming the Consequent: An Invalid Argument I**	
	General form	Specific example
Major premise	If *P*, then *Q*	If a country is wealthy, then it will be a democracy
Minor premise	*Q*	The country is a democracy.
Conclusion	Therefore, *P*.	Therefore, the country is wealthy.

TABLE 2.11	**Denying the Consequent: A Valid Argument I**	
	General form	**Specific example**
Major premise	If *P*, then *Q*	If a country is wealthy, then it will be a democracy
Minor premise	Not *Q*	The country is not a democracy.
Conclusion	Therefore, not *P*.	Therefore, the country is not wealthy.

of a country's democracy. Consequently, we cannot make a valid inference from the fact that a country is a democracy to the claim that the country must be wealthy—it may be wealthy or it may not be. Recall that to show that an argument is invalid, it is not necessary to show that its conclusion is false, we have to show only that it doesn't have to be true.

Finally, let's consider what happens when we deny the consequent. An example is shown in Table 2.11. As always, the major premise can be represented in set-theoretic terms by Figure 2.4. The difference this time is that the minor premise now denies that *Q* is the case; that is, it denies the consequent. If we accept that the premises are true, are we compelled to accept the conclusion that "not *P*" is the case? Figure 2.4 clearly shows that the fact that our case is not in *Q* necessarily means that it is not in *P*. As a result, the argument is valid—we are compelled to accept the conclusion based on the premises. In the context of our running example, the major premise indicates that all wealthy countries are democracies and the minor premise states that the country is not a democratic one. If these premises are both true, then it logically follows that our country cannot be wealthy.

Our brief foray into the study of logic indicates that if complex arguments can be broken down into categorical syllogisms, then it is possible to classify all arguments into one of four types according to whether they affirm or deny the consequent or antecedent. Two of these arguments are valid but the other two are invalid. Specifically, affirming the antecedent and denying the consequent are valid arguments—if you accept the major and minor premises, you are compelled to accept the conclusion. In contrast, denying the antecedent and affirming the consequent are invalid arguments—if you accept the major and minor premises, you are not compelled to accept the conclusion. These results are summarized in Table 2.12.

TABLE 2.12	**What Types of Conditional Arguments Are Valid?**	
	Antecedent	**Consequent**
Affirm	Valid	Invalid
Deny	Invalid	Valid

Testing Theories

We believe that it is important for you to be able to distinguish between valid and invalid arguments so that you are not manipulated or exploited by others. This brief introduction to logic, however, is also important because it tells us something about the way scientists test their theories and explanations. Suppose we want to explain why wealthy countries are much more likely to be democracies than poor countries. One possible explanation for why this might be the case is given in the following statements:[15]

1. Living in an autocracy is risky—if you are one of the autocrat's friends you will do extremely well; but if you are not, you will do extremely poorly.
2. Living in a democracy is less risky—democratic leaders have to spread the goodies (and the pain) around more evenly. This means that you are less likely to do extremely well or extremely poorly in a democracy.
3. Wealthy people are less likely to take risks than poor people because they have more to lose. This means that countries with lots of wealthy people are more likely to be democracies than autocracies.

This short explanation provides reasons why rich countries might be more likely to be democracies than poor countries. How good is this explanation, though? Does this argument have any testable implications? One implication is that rich democracies should live longer than poor democracies. This is because people in rich democracies should be less likely to take the "risk" of becoming a dictatorship; in contrast, people in poor democracies might wonder what they have to lose.

How can we use observations of the real world to evaluate our proposed explanation? It is often the case that the implications of an explanation are more readily observable than the elements of the explanation itself. Consider the example we are using. Although it may be possible to compare the distribution of good and bad outcomes in autocracies and democracies, the claims that people differ in their propensity to take risks and that this propensity is related to their level of income are difficult to observe. This is because the propensity to take risks is an internal and psychological attribute of individuals.[16] For similar reasons, scholars typically evaluate their explanations by observing the real world to see if the implications of their explanations appear to be true based on the assumption, "If my theory is true, then its implications will be true." If we take this to be our major premise and the truth or falsity of the theory's implications as the minor premise, then we might be able to use observations to draw inferences about our theory or explanation.

---

15. This is a simplified version of an argument presented by Przeworski (2005). It is discussed more fully in Chapter 6.

16. Although an individual's propensity to take risks is difficult to observe, experimental social scientists are doing clever work to make progress on this front. For a summary of this work, see the relevant chapters in Davis and Holt (1993), Kagel and Roth (1995), and Camerer (2003).

Suppose our theory's implications were borne out by our observation that wealthy democracies do live longer than poor democracies. Can we conclude that our theory is true? If we were to do so, we would be engaging in reasoning that affirmed the consequent. This fact is shown more clearly in Table 2.13. However, as you know by now, affirming the consequent is an invalid form of argument. The major premise only says that if the theory is correct, then the implications should be observed. It never says that the only way for these implications to be produced is if the theory is correct. In other words, processes other than those described in our theory may produce the observation that wealthy countries live longer than poor countries. Put differently, the mere fact of observing the predicted implication does not allow us to categorically accept or reject our theory.

Suppose now that our observations did not bear out our theory's implications, that we did not observe that wealthy democracies live longer than poor democracies. Can we conclude that our theory is incorrect? If we were to do so, we would be engaging in reasoning that denies the consequent. This fact is shown more clearly in Table 2.14. As you know by now, denying the consequent is a valid form of argument. In other words, by accepting the premises, we are compelled to accept the conclusion that our theory is not correct.

If we compare the two previous examples, we can see an important asymmetry as regards the logical claims that can be made on the basis of "confirming" and "disconfirming" observations. When an implication of our theory is confirmed, the most we can say is that the theory may be correct. This is because neither of the two possible conclusions—our theory is correct or our theory is not correct—contradicts our major and minor premises. In other words, we cannot say that our theory is correct or verified. In contrast, if we find that an implication of a theory is inconsistent with observation, then we are compelled by logic to accept that the theory is false—this is the only conclusion that is consistent with our observation. Thus, although we can know that a theory must be incorrect in light of a disconfirming case, all that we can say in light of a confirming case is that a theory may be correct (it may also be wrong). What does this mean? It means that we are logically justified in having more confidence when we reject a theory than when we do not.

TABLE 2.13	**Affirming the Consequent: An Invalid Argument II**	
General form	**Example**	**Specific example**
If *P,* then *Q*	If our theory is correct (*T*), then we should observe some implication *I*.	If our theory is correct, then we should observe that wealthy democracies live longer than poor democracies
Q	We observe implication *I*.	Wealthy democracies live longer than poor democracies.
Therefore, *P.*	Therefore, our theory *T* is correct.	Therefore, our theory is correct.

TABLE 2.14	Denying the Consequent: A Valid Argument II	
General form	**Example**	**Specific example**
If *P,* then *Q*	If our theory is correct, then we should observe some implication *I.*	If our theory is correct, then we should observe that wealthy democracies live longer than poor democracies
Not *Q*	We do not observe implication *I.*	Wealthy democracies do not live longer than poor democracies.
Therefore, not *P.*	Therefore, our theory *T* is incorrect.	Therefore, our theory is incorrect.

This, in turn, implies that the knowledge encapsulated in theories that have not been rejected remains tentative and can never be proven for sure—scientific theories can never be proven. Even if we are utterly convinced that our major and minor premises are true, all that we can logically conclude from a confirming instance is that the theory has not yet been falsified.

This asymmetry between confirming and disconfirming cases led the philosopher of science Sir Karl Popper ([1959] 2003, 280–281) to conclude:

> The old scientific ideal of *episteme*—of absolutely certain, demonstrable knowledge—has proved to be an idol. The demand for scientific objectivity makes it inevitable that every scientific statement must remain *tentative for ever.* . . . With the idol of certainty . . . there falls one of the defenses of obscurantism which bar the way to scientific advance. For the worship of this idol hampers not only the boldness of our questions, but also the rigor and integrity of our tests. The wrong view of science betrays itself in the craving to be right; for it is not his *possession* of knowledge, of irrefutable truth, that makes the man of science, but his persistent and recklessly critical *quest* for truth.

The Comparative Method Revisited

It is important to recognize that the asymmetry between confirmation and falsification has important implications for the method we use to build knowledge. When scholars use Mill's methods, they go out into the real world to collect observations and look for patterns in the data. Those factors that cannot be eliminated as potential causes by Mill's methods become our explanation. Each new case that exhibits the same pattern in the data confirms or verifies our conclusion. We have already seen that one problem with Mill's methods is that many assumptions have to be satisfied before valid inferences can be drawn. This problem is complicated by that fact that the approach itself does not provide us with much guidance in determining if those assumptions are satisfied in any particular case.

It should be clear by now that Mill's methods pose yet another problem. Because they start with observations, they rely entirely on the process of affirming the consequent. If we identify causes only after we have observed the data, as Mill's methods require, we have no chance of ever coming across disconfirming observations. This is because our "theory" is essentially just a restatement of the patterns in our observations.[17] This is a real problem, whether the researcher is employing Mill's methods on a small number of cases or analyzing large data sets looking for patterns. No matter how many cases these researchers observe that appear to exhibit the predicted pattern, they are never logically justified in claiming that their conclusions have been confirmed or verified.

You might wonder whether there is any way to avoid these problems. The answer is yes. Imagine that we start with a set of implications derived from a theory and then observe some facts. In other words, let's start with the theory and then observe the world rather than the other way around. It is now at least possible for our observations to contradict our theory. If it turns out that our observations are consistent with our theory, then we can have a greater measure of confidence in our theory because it withstood the very real chance of being falsified. Even now, though, it is important to recognize that we still can never say that our theory is verified or confirmed. If our observations are inconsistent with our theory, then we can draw valid inferences about the truthfulness of our theory—we can conclude that it is wrong. This approach to doing science is called **falsificationism.** Falsificationism forms the basis for the view of science employed in this book. It is to this view of science that we now turn.

Falsificationism is an approach to science in which scientists generate testable hypotheses from theories designed to explain phenomena of interest. It emphasizes that scientific theories are constantly called into question and that their merit lies only in how well they stand up to rigorous testing.

SCIENCE AND FALSIFICATIONISM

In the previous section, we argued that the comparative method is deeply flawed. We hope that this is not taken as evidence that we believe that the whole scientific endeavor is inherently flawed and that we should look elsewhere for an understanding of the world. We truly believe that science is the best way to learn about the world and that it can fruitfully be applied to the study of politics. But let us be clear about what our view of science is.

What Is Science?

Is science simply a body of knowledge or a collection of facts, as many of us learn in high school? There was a time when scientists may have given this as the most common answer, but this response is fundamentally unsatisfactory. If this answer were correct, then many of the claims about how the universe worked, such as those developed through Newtonian physics, would now have to be called unscientific, because they have been replaced by claims based on

---

17. This suggests that the comparative method is, at most, suitable only for developing theories and not testing them.

more recent theories, such as Einstein's theory of relativity. Moreover, if science were simply a collection of statements about how the world works, then we would not be able to appeal to science to justify our knowledge of the world without falling into the following circular reasoning:

> "Science is a collection of statements about how the world works."
> *"How do we know if these statements are accurate?"*
> "Well, of course they're accurate! They're scientific!"

The body of knowledge that we call "scientific" may well be a product of science, but it is not science itself. Rather, science is a method for provisionally understanding the world. The reason for saying "provisionally" will become clear in a moment. Science is one answer to the central question in epistemology (the study of knowledge): "How do we know what we know?" The scientist's answer to that question is, "Because we have subjected our ideas to the scientific method." Science, as Karl Popper indicates in one of the epigraphs at the start of this chapter, is the quest for knowledge. At this point, you might say that there are many ways to seek knowledge. Does this mean that meditation, reading scripture, and gazing at sunsets are all scientific activities? Although we agree that these are all ways of seeking knowledge, none of them is scientific. Science is a particular quest for knowledge. To use Popper's phrase, it is the "recklessly critical" pursuit of knowledge, in which the scientist continually subjects her ideas to the cold light of logic and evidence.

Although science is not the only route to knowledge, it may be unique in its emphasis on self-criticism. Scientists, like other scholars, can derive their propositions from an infinite number of sources. For example, Gregory Derry (1999) tells the story of how August Kekulé made an extremely important scientific breakthrough while hallucinating—half asleep—in front of the fireplace in his laboratory one night. He had spent days struggling to understand the spatial arrangement of atoms in a benzene molecule. In a state of mental and physical exhaustion, his answer appeared to him as he "saw" swirls of atoms joined in a particular formation dancing among the embers of his fireplace. In a flash of inspiration, he saw how the pieces of the puzzle he had been struggling with fit together. This inspired understanding of the physical properties of organic compounds did not become a part of science that night. It did so only after the implications of his vision had withstood the critical and sober onslaught that came with the light of day. Thus, although flashes of insight can come from a variety of sources, science begins only when one asks, "If that is true, what else ought to be true?" And it ends—if ever—when researchers are satisfied that they have taken every reasonable pain to show that the implications of the insight are false and have failed to do so.

So, science is the quest for knowledge that relies on criticism. The thing that allows for criticism is the possibility that our claims, theories, hypotheses, and the like could be wrong. Thus, what distinguishes science from nonscience is that scientific statements are **falsifiable**—there must be some imaginable observation or set of observations that could falsify or refute it. This

> Scientific statements are **falsifiable.** This means that they are potentially testable—there must be some imaginable observation that could falsify or refute it.

does not mean that the scientific statement will ever be falsified, just that there must be a possibility that it could be falsified. Only if a statement is potentially testable is it scientific. We deliberately say "potentially testable" because a statement does not have to have been tested to be scientific; all that is required is that we can conceive of a way to test it.[18]

What sorts of statements are not falsifiable? **Tautologies** are not falsifiable because they are true by definition. For example, the statement "Strong states are able to overcome special interests in order to implement policies that are best for the nation" is a tautology. This statement may be true, but unless we

A **tautology** is a statement that is true by definition.

can think of a way to identify a strong state without referring to its ability to overcome special interests, then it is just a definition and is, therefore, unscientific. Other hypotheses are not falsifiable, not because they are tautological, but because they refer to inherently unobservable phenomena. For example, the claims "God exists" or "God created the world" are not falsifiable because they cannot be tested; as a result, they are unscientific. Note that these claims may well be true, but it is important to recognize that science has nothing to do with the truth or falsity of statements. All that is required for a statement to be scientific is that it is falsifiable. It should be clear from this that we are not claiming that nonscience is nonsense or lacks meaning—this would clearly be a mistake. Non-falsifiable statements like "God exists" may very well be true and have important and meaningful consequences—our claim is simply that they do not form a part of science. Having defined science as a critical method for learning about the world, we can now evaluate the basic elements of the scientific method in more detail.

The Scientific Method

The **scientific method** describes the process by which scientists learn about the world.

Although there is no **scientific method** clearly written down that is followed by all scientists, it is possible to characterize its basic features in the following manner.

Step 1: Question

The first step in the scientific process is to observe the world and come up with a question or puzzle. The very need for a theory or explanation begins when we observe something that is so unexpected or surprising that we ask, "Why did that occur?" Note that the surprise that greets such an observation, and that makes the observation a puzzle worth exploring, implies that the observation does not match some prior expectation or theory that we held about how the world works. Thus, we always have a preexisting theory or expectation when we observe the world; if we did not have one, we could never be surprised and there would be no puzzles.

---

18. Indeed, a statement can be scientific even if we do not currently have the data or the technical equipment to test it. Our upcoming discussion of Einstein's special theory of relativity illustrates this point quite clearly.

Step 2: Theory or Model

Once we have observed something puzzling, the next step is to come up with a theory or model to explain it. In what follows, we will talk of theories, models, and explanations interchangeably. Scientists use the word **theory** to describe a set of logically consistent statements that tell us why the things that we observe occur. It is important that these statements be logically consistent, otherwise we have no way of determining what their empirical predictions will be and, hence, no way to test them. Put differently, theories that are logically inconsistent should not, indeed cannot, be tested, because we have no way of knowing what observations would truly falsify them.

> A **theory** is a set of logically consistent statements that tell us why the things that we observe occur. A theory is sometimes referred to as a model or an explanation.

Most philosophers of science assume that all phenomena occur as a result of some recurring process. The principle of the **uniformity of nature** asserts that nature's operating mechanisms are unchanging in the sense that if X causes Y today, then it will also cause Y tomorrow and the next day and so on.[19] If it does not, then we should not consider X a cause. Be careful to note that the principle of uniformity is not a statement that nature is unchanging, only that the laws of nature do not change (although our understanding of those laws will likely change over time). This is an important principle, because if this principle is rejected, we must accept the possibility that things "just happen." That is, we must accept that things happen for no reason. Casual observation of the sometimes-maddening world around us suggests that this may, indeed, be true, but it is the job of scientists to attempt to impose order on the apparent chaos around them.[20] In the social world, this process often begins by dividing the behavior we observe into systematic and unsystematic components. The social scientist then focuses her attention on explaining only the systematic components.[21]

> The principle of the **uniformity of nature** asserts that nature's operating mechanisms are unchanging in the sense that if X causes Y today, then it will also cause Y tomorrow and the next day and so on.

So, what should theories or models look like? It is useful to think of our starting puzzle or observation as the end result of some previously unknown process (Lave and March 1975).[22] We can then speculate about what (hidden) processes might have produced such a result. In effect, we try to imagine a prior world that, if it had existed, would have produced

---

19. For a layman's discussion of the uniformity of nature, see Stephen Jay Gould's book (1985) *The Flamingo's Smile: Reflections in Natural History.*

20. Indeed, at least one paradigm for understanding the world embraces *chaos* as its starting point. See James Gleick's book (1987) *Chaos: Making a New Science* for a compelling introduction to chaos theory aimed at the nonspecialist.

21. This suggests that you should be wary of anyone who tells you that you need to know everything before you can know anything.

22. Note that thinking in terms of a process takes us away from the strictly correlational models used by scholars trying to apply the comparative method and brings us closer to a more commonsensical notion of an explanation. It also encourages the development of interesting implications via counterfactuals like, "What would happen if we changed a part of the causal process?"

the otherwise puzzling observation before us. This prior world then becomes our model explaining the observation.

Notice that this process of imagining prior worlds is one place—but surely not the only one—where imagination and creativity enter the scientific process. What scientists do to stimulate this creative process is itself not part of the scientific method. Essentially, anything goes. Nobel Prize–winning physicist Richard Feynman, who himself spent a lot time hanging out in bars, drawing "exotic" dancers, and playing Brazilian hand drums, describes science as "imagination in a straightjacket"—it is imagination constrained by what we already know about the world (Feynman 1967). Consequently, he suggests that there is no point engaging in flights of fancy about things that we know cannot exist (like antigravity machines). Whatever means we use to stimulate speculation about a prior world, if we can show through logical deduction that if that prior world existed, it would have produced the puzzling observation we started with, then we have a theory, or model. Note that we only have "a" theory; we do not necessarily have "the" theory. This is why we continually subject our theories to tests.

The model that we end up with will be a simplified picture of the world. It will be something that helps us understand how some aspect of the world works and helps us explain it to others. Because a model is a simplified picture of the world, it is always going to leave lots of things out. Much of the art of modeling is in deciding what to leave out and what to keep in. A good model contains only what is needed to explain the phenomenon that puzzles us and nothing else. If we made our models too complex, we would have no way of knowing which elements were crucial for explaining our puzzling observation that we started with and which were superfluous. The purpose of a model is not to describe the world but to explain it, so descriptive accuracy is not a core value in model building.[23] Details are important only to the extent that they are relevant to what we are trying to explain. For example, if we are interested in explaining an aircraft's response to turbulence, it is not important whether our model of the aircraft includes LCD screens on the back of the passengers' seats.[24] In fact, such irrelevant details can easily distract our attention from the question at hand. Another benefit of simple models is that they invite falsification because they make it very clear what we should not observe. The more amendments and conditions placed on an explanation, the easier it is for scholars to dismiss apparently contradictory evidence. We now know from our earlier discussion that we learn more when a theory is falsified; this may be another reason for keeping our models simple.

Step 3: Implications (Hypotheses)

Once we have a model, the third step in the scientific process is to deduce implications from the model other than those that we set out to explain. Why do we say "other than those that

---

23. As the late Dutch economist Henri Theil (1971) once said, "models should be used, not believed." In other words, a model is a tool to be used to create knowledge; it is not a repository of descriptive knowledge.

24. Of course, if we were explaining our children's choice of airlines, this might well be a crucial detail.

we set out to explain"? Well, presumably the model will provide a logical explanation for the puzzling observation that we started with; after all, that is what it was designed to do. In other words, there is no way that a model can ever be falsified if only the observations that were employed to develop the model in the first place are used to test it. To actually test the model and allow for the possibility that it will be falsified, we will have to find other implications that can be deduced from it. We must ask ourselves "If the prior world that we created to explain the phenomena that we originally found puzzling really did exist, what else ought to exist? What else should we be able to observe?" As before, there is often room for incredible imagination here, because the complete list of logical implications of a model is seldom self-evident.

Good models are those that produce many different implications. This is so because each prediction represents another opportunity for the model to fail and, therefore, makes the model easier to falsify. This is good because if the model fails to be falsified, we gain more confidence in its usefulness. Fertile models—models with many implications—are also desirable because they encourage the synthesis of knowledge by encouraging us to see connections between ostensibly disparate events. Good models also produce surprising implications— they tell us something we would not know in the absence of the model. Models are not particularly useful if they tell us only what we already know. Surprise, however, is best appreciated in small doses. If every implication of a model is surprising, then either everything we thought about the world is wrong, or the model is.

Step 4: Observe the World (Test Hypotheses)

The fourth step is to examine whether the implications of the model are consistent with observation. Remember that the goal is not to dogmatically uphold the implications or defend them in order to prove how right they are. On the contrary, we should try our best to falsify them, because it is only after a theory has withstood these attempts to overthrow it that we can reasonably start to have confidence in it. Although as many of the model's implications as possible should be tested, testing those that are most likely to be falsified is particularly important. Always submit a model to the harshest test that you can devise.

It is standard practice to stop and ask if other models—models that describe altogether different processes—might also explain the phenomena of interest. When this is the case (and it almost always is), it is incumbent upon the scientist to compare the implications of those other models with the implications of her own model. Although it is always the case that competing models have some of the same implications (otherwise they could not explain the same observations to begin with), it is typically the case that they will differ in some of their implications (otherwise they are not different models). The trick for a researcher is to identify these points of conflict between the different models and identify the relevant observations in the real world that would help her decide between them. This is what scientists refer to as a **critical test**. Ultimately, if a critical test is possible, observation will prove decisive

A **critical test** is one that allows the analyst to use observation to distinguish between two or more competing explanations of the same phenomenon.

in choosing between the models. This is because we know that there is only one world and the creative scientist has managed to get competing theories to say contradictory things about it—only one of the models can be consistent with the real world.

Step 5: Evaluation

If we observe the implications deduced from our theory, we simply say that our theory has been corroborated. As we showed earlier, we cannot say that our theory has been verified or proven.[25] This is why we earlier called science a method for "provisionally" understanding the world. Our theory may or may not be true. All we know is that it has not been falsified so far; we cannot rule out that it will not be falsified the next time it is tested. As you can see, the scientific method is an inherently critical method when it is "successful" (when a theory's predictions seem to be borne out), because it is precisely under these circumstances that it is most cautious in the claims that it makes.

Although we cannot ever prove our theories, we can claim that some theories are better corroborated than others. As a result, we can have more confidence in their conclusions. One might think that a theory that has been subjected to multiple tests is better corroborated than one that has not been subjected to many tests at all. However, this is not always the case. If we keep testing the same implication over and over again, it is not clear how much an additional test actually adds to the degree to which the theory is corroborated. What really matters is not so much how many times a theory has been corroborated, but the severity of the tests to which it has been subjected. This, in turn, will depend on the degree to which the theory is falsifiable. Again, this is why we like our models to be simple and have multiple implications. In general, we will have more confidence in a theory that has survived a few harsh tests than a theory that has survived many easy ones. This is why scientists often talk about the world as if it were black and white rather than gray. Bold statements should not be interpreted as scientific hubris but rather as attempts to invite criticism—they are easier to falsify.

What happens if we do not observe the implications deduced from our theory? Can we conclude that our theory is incorrect based on one observation? The answer is probably not. It is entirely possible that we have not observed and measured the world without error. Moreover, if we believe that human behavior is inherently probabilistic, then we might not want to reject theories on the basis of a single observation. In a world in which our tests are potentially fallible, we should not relegate a theory to the dustbin of intellectual history the minute one of its implications is shown to be false. Instead, we must weigh the number, severity, and quality of the tests that the theory's implications are subjected to and make a judgment. And most important, this judgment should be made with an eye toward what would replace the theory should we decide to discard it. This is why some scientists say that it takes a theory to kill a theory.

---

25. Many scientists, however, slip into the language of verification when reporting their results. Instead of simply saying that their test has failed to falsify their hypotheses or is consistent with their theory, they will claim that the test has shown that their theory is correct. For example, they might claim that their test shows that wealth causes democracies to live longer when, in fact, all they can conclude is that they were unable to falsify the claim that wealth causes democracies to live longer.

Box 2.2

AN EXAMPLE OF THE SCIENTIFIC PROCESS

The Case of Smart Female Athletes

Because student athletes often miss classes to compete out of state, they frequently submit a letter from the athletic director asking for cooperation from their professors. Over the years a certain professor has noticed through casual observation that women engaged in athletic competition frequently perform better academically than the average student. It is puzzling why female athletes would perform better in spite of missing classes. Can you think of a model—a process—that might produce such a puzzling observation?

You might start with the following conjecture:

- Female athletes are smart.

This is an explanation, but it is not a particularly good one. For example, it comes very close to simply restating the observation to be explained. One thing that could improve the explanation is to make it more general. This might lead you to a new explanation:

- Athletes are smart.

This model is certainly more general (but not necessarily more correct). Still, there are at least two problems with this model as things stand. First, it has no sense of process; it basically says that athletes share some inherent quality of smartness that leads them to perform better academically. In effect, this only pushes the phenomenon to be explained back one step, that is, we now need to know why athletes are smart. Second, the model comes close to being a tautology. It essentially says that athletes perform better academically because they are defined as being smart. This is problematic, as we saw earlier, because tautologies are not falsifiable—they cannot be tested and, hence, they are not part of the scientific endeavor.

This might lead you to look for a new explanation or model that includes some sort of process that makes female athletes appear smart. You might come up with the following model:

- Being a good athlete requires a lot of hard work; performing well academically in college requires a lot of work. Students who develop a strong work ethic in athletics are able to translate this to their studies.

This is a much more satisfying model because it provides a process or mechanism explaining why female athletes might be more academically successful than other students. An appealing feature of the model is that the logic of the argument applies not only to female athletes but to any athlete. Indeed, it applies to any person involved in an activity that rewards hard work. Thus, we might generalize this model by removing the specific reference to athletes:

- **Work Ethic Theory:** Some activities provide a clear, immediate, and tangible reward to hard work—in fact, they may provide an external stimulus to work hard (coaches shouting through bullhorns, manipulating rewards and punishments based on effort, and so on). Individuals who engage in these activities develop a habit of working hard and so will be successful in other areas of life as well.

At this point, you should stop and ask yourself whether there are any alternative explanations for why female athletes are successful. Can you think of any? One alternative explanation is the following:

- **Excellence Theory:** Everyone wants to feel successful but some people go long periods without success and become discouraged. Those individuals that experience success in one area of their life (perhaps based on talent, rather than hard work) develop a "taste" for it and devise strategies to be successful in other parts of their life. Anyone who achieves success in nonacademic areas, such as athletics, will be more motivated to succeed in class.

Another alternative explanation is the following:

- **Gender Theory:** In many social and academic settings, women are treated differently from men. This differential treatment often leads women to draw inferences that certain activities are "not for them." Because many athletic endeavors are gender specific, they provide an environment for women to develop their potential free from the stultifying effects of gender bias. The resulting sense of efficacy and autonomy encourages success when these women return to gendered environments like the classroom.

We now have three different or competing models, all of which explain the puzzling observation that we started with. But how can one evaluate which model is best? One way is to test some of the implications that can be derived from these theories. In particular, we would like to find some new question(s) to which the three models give different answers. In other words, we would like to conduct a critical test that would allow us to choose among the alternative reasonable models.

We might start by wondering whether being an athlete helps the academic performance of women more than men. Whereas the Work Ethic Theory and the Excellence Theory both predict that being an athlete will help men and women equally, the Gender Theory predicts that female athletes will perform better than nonathletic women, but that male athletes will have no advantage over nonathletic men. Thus, collecting information on how well male and female athletes perform in class relative to male and female nonathletes, respectively, would allow us to distinguish between the Gender Theory and the other theories.

But how can we distinguish between the Excellence Theory and the Work Ethic Theory? One difficulty frequently encountered when trying to devise critical tests is that alternative theories do not always produce clearly differentiated predictions. For example, we just saw that the Excellence Theory and the Work Ethic Theory both predict that athletics will help men and women academically. It turns out that these two theories have other predictions in common as well. The Excellence Theory clearly suggests that success in any nonacademic area of life is likely to encourage academic success. In other words, the Excellence Theory predicts that academic success will be associated with success in other areas of life. The problem is that success in many of these nonacademic areas may require hard work.

As a result, if we observe, for instance, accomplished musicians performing well in our political science classes, it will be difficult to discern whether this is because they learned the value of hard work in music and transferred it to political science (Work Ethic Theory) or because they developed a "taste" for success as musicians that then inspired success in political science (Excellence Theory). In effect, the Excellence Theory and the Work Ethic Theory both predict that academic success will be associated with success in other areas of life.

If we want to distinguish between the Work Ethic Theory and the Excellence Theory, we need to imagine observations in which they produce different expectations. Sometimes, this requires further development of a theory. For example, we might expand the Excellence Theory to say that those people who develop a taste for excellence also develop a more competitive spirit. If this is true, then the Excellence Theory would predict that student athletes are likely to be more competitive and will perform better than other students even when playing relatively frivolous board games. Since even the most driven athletes are not likely to devote time to training for board games, the Work Ethic theory predicts that athletes will perform the same as nonathletes in such trivial pursuits. Thus, we could look at the performance of athletes and nonathletes at board games to distinguish between the Excellence Theory and the Work Ethic Theory.

The three critical tests that we have come up with and their predictions are listed in Table 2.15. All that is now required is to collect the appropriate data and decide which model, if any, is best.

It is worth noting that there is considerable overlap between the predictions of our three theories. This is often the case in political science settings as well. The crucial point is not that each theory should yield a complete set of unique predictions, but that our theories should have sufficiently many distinct predictions that we can use observation to help us make decisions about which theories to embrace, however tentatively. Table 2-15 lists just some of the predictions that might help us to distinguish between the three theories outlined above. Can you think of any more?

TABLE 2.15   Three Critical Tests

Question	Theory		
	Gender	Excellence	Work ethic
Will athletics help women more than men?	Yes	No	No
Is academic success associated with success in other areas of life?	No	Yes	Yes
Are female athletes more successful at board games than women who are not athletes?	Yes	Yes	No

Having described the scientific method, we would like to briefly dispel certain myths that have developed about science. Some of these myths have been promoted by opponents to the scientific project, but others, unfortunately, have been sustained by scientists themselves.

Myths about Science

The first myth is that science proves things and leads to certain and verifiable truth. This is not the best way to think about science. It should be clear by now from our discussion that the best science can hope to offer are tentative statements about what seems reasonable in light of the best available logic and evidence. It may be frustrating for students to realize this, but science can speak with more confidence about what we do not know than what we do know. In this sense, the process of scientific accumulation can be thought of as the evolution of our ignorance. We use the scientific method because it is the best tool available to interrogate our beliefs about the (political) world. If we hold onto any beliefs about the (political) world, it is because, after we have subjected them to the most stringent tests we can come up with, they remain the most plausible explanations for the phenomena that concern us.

The second myth is that science can be done only when experimental manipulation is possible. This is clearly false. For theories to be scientific, they need only be falsifiable. There is no claim that tests of these theories need to be carried out in the experimental setting. Many of the natural sciences engage in research that is not susceptible to manipulation. For example, all research on extinct animals such as dinosaurs must be conducted without the aid of experimental manipulation because the subjects are long dead. In fact, there is also no claim that a theory must be tested before it can be called scientific. Einstein presented a special theory of relativity in 1905 that stated, among other things, that space had to be curved, or warped. It took fourteen years before his theory was tested with the help of a solar eclipse. No scientist would claim that Einstein's theory was unscientific until it was tested. Put simply, scientific theories must be potentially testable, but this does not mean that they stop being scientific if they are yet to be actually tested.

The third myth is that science is value-neutral. It is important to remember that the pursuit of knowledge about the world is closely entangled with attempts by people to change the world. This poses difficulties for social scientists. For example, the people we study may read what we write and act upon it. For that reason, we have to be very clear about the limits of our knowledge and not encourage others to act upon knowledge that is not highly corroborated. And although we should not resist the conclusions of our research because we had hoped that the world worked differently, there is nothing wrong with raising the evidentiary bar before accepting results that could lead to policies we would deeply regret if we found out later that we were wrong.

The fourth myth, that politics cannot be studied in a scientific manner, can easily be dispelled by now. Our description of the scientific method clearly shows that this myth is false. The study of politics generates falsifiable hypotheses and hence generates scientific statements. These theories of politics can be tested just like any other scientific theory. We will further demonstrate that politics can be studied in a scientific manner in the remaining chapters of this book. The fact, though, that our subjects can read our work and change their behavior makes our job quite a bit harder than if we were working in one of the natural sciences.

CONCLUSION

In this chapter we have argued that it is useful to think about politics in a scientific manner. We have also tried to offer a clear view of what most practicing scientists have in mind when they use the word *science*. It is a fairly minimalist view. What unites all scientists is the idea that one ought to present one's ideas in a way that invites refutation (Popper 1962). It is incumbent upon the scientist to answer the question "What ought I to observe if what I claim to be true about the world is false?" This view of science recognizes that scientific knowledge is tentative and should be objective. Although it is certainly likely that our prejudices and biases motivate our work and will creep into our conclusions, the goal of science is to present our conclusions in a way that will make it easy for others to determine whether it is reasonable for people who do not share those prejudices and biases to view our conclusions as reasonable.

KEY CONCEPTS

argument, *33*
categorical syllogism, *33*
comparative method, *19*
conclusion (in an argument), *33*
critical test, *45*
deterministic cause, *28*
falsifiable, *41*
falsificationism, *40*
interaction effect, *29*
invalid argument, *33*
Method of Agreement, *25*

Method of Difference, *25*
necessary and sufficient condition, *21*
necessary condition, *21*
premise, *33*
probabilistic cause, *28*
scientific method, *42*
sufficient condition, *21*
tautology, *42*
theory, *43*
uniformity of nature, *43*
valid argument, *33*

PROBLEMS

The four categories of problems that follow address some of the more important concepts and methods introduced in this chapter.

Logic: Valid and Invalid Arguments

1. Consider the following argument.

Major Premise: If a country has a strong economy, the government will be popular.
Minor Premise: The government is not popular.
Conclusion: Therefore, the country does not have a strong economy.

   a. Is this a valid or invalid argument?

    b. What form of categorical syllogism is this (affirming the antecedent/consequent or deny-
      ing the antecedent/consequent)?

2. Consider the following argument.

Major Premise: If the president commits a criminal act, then he can be impeached.
Minor Premise: The president does not commit a criminal act.
Conclusion: Therefore, the president cannot be impeached.

    a. Is this a valid or invalid argument?
    b. What form of categorical syllogism is this?

3. Consider the following argument.

Major Premise: If a country employs proportional representation electoral rules, it will have
    many parties.
Minor Premise: The country does not employ proportional representation electoral rules.
Conclusion: Therefore, the country does not have many parties.

    a. Is this a valid or invalid argument?
    b. What form of categorical syllogism is this?

4. Consider the following argument.

Major Premise: If theory T is correct, all rich countries will be democracies.
Minor Premise: All rich countries are democracies.
Conclusion: Therefore, theory T is correct.

    a. Is this a valid or invalid argument?
    b. What form of categorical syllogism is this?
    c. If you wanted to demonstrate that theory T is wrong, what would you have to observe?

Scientific Statements

5. A statement is scientific if it is falsifiable. Which of the following statements are scientific
    and why?

- Smoking increases the probability of getting cancer.
- A square is a shape with four sides of equal length.
- The sun revolves around the earth.
- It always rains in England during the winter.
- Education spending increases under left-wing governments.
- Iceland is a country.
- Religious faith assures a person a place in the afterlife.
- Democracies are less likely to go to war than dictatorships.

6. Some statements are nonscientific because they are tautologies and some because they
    refer to inherently nonobservable phenomena. Come up with an example of both types of
    nonscientific statement.

7. Sometimes it is hard to know whether a statement is scientific or not. Much depends on how we define certain terms. Consider the following statement.

- If the USA PATRIOT Act is successfully implemented, then the United States will not be attacked.

Whether this statement is falsifiable depends on how we define "successfully implemented." On the one hand, if we define successful implementation as not being attacked, then this statement becomes tautological or true by definition—no observation could falsify it. On the other hand, if we define successful implementation as actually passing the Patriot Act in Congress, then this statement becomes scientific—it could be falsified by an attack on the United States.

Consider the following statement.

- All mainstream U.S. senators agree that the House bill is unacceptable.
  a. Is this statement scientific if "mainstream" is defined in terms of the acceptability of the House bill?
  b. Is this statement scientific if "mainstream" is defined in terms of the ideology of the senators?

Now consider the following statement.

- All good students get high grades.
  a. Is this statement scientific if "good" is defined in terms of a student's grade?
  b. Is this statement scientific if "good" is defined in terms of a student's enthusiasm?

Necessary and Sufficient Conditions

8. Consider the following statements. After looking at the structure of each statement, would you say that the conditions shown in boldface type are necessary or sufficient to produce the effects shown?

- If a person contracts measles, then she was **exposed to the measles virus.**
- If a **democracy is wealthy,** then it will stay a democracy.
- A country cannot maintain a democratic form of government unless **it has a culture that promotes civic participation.**
- Countries have many parties only **when they employ proportional electoral rules.**
- Countries always have few parties **when they employ majoritarian electoral rules.**

Model Building in the Scientific Method

9. It has frequently been observed that students coming into a lecture hall tend to fill up the rear of the hall first (Lave and March 1975; Schelling 1978). Here are two possible explanations, or models, that predict this kind of behavior.

Minimum Effort Theory: People try to minimize effort; having entered at the rear of the hall, they sit there rather than walk to the front.

"Coolness" Theory: General student norms say that it is not cool to be deeply involved in school work. Sitting in front would display interest in the class, whereas sitting in the rear displays detachment.

a. Make up two facts (that is, derive two specific predictions) that, if they were true, would tend to support the Minimum Effort Theory. Do the same thing for the "Coolness" Theory.

b. Make up a critical fact or experiment (specific prediction) that, if it were true, would tend to support one theory and contradict the other.

c. Propose a third theory to explain student seating results and explain how you might test it against the other two theories.

10. It has frequently been observed that democracies do not go to war with each other. This has come to be known as the Democratic Peace.

a. Make up two theories or models that would account for this observation.

b. Generate a total of three interesting predictions from the two models and identify from which model they were derived.

c. Find some critical fact/situation/observation/prediction that will distinguish between the two models. Be explicit about how it simultaneously confirms one model and contradicts the other.

11. A casual look around the world reveals that some governments treat their citizens better than other governments do.

a. Make up two theories or models that would account for this observation.

b. Generate a total of three interesting predictions from the two models and identify from which model they were derived.

c. Find some critical fact/situation/observation/prediction that will distinguish between the two models. Be explicit about how it simultaneously confirms one model and contradicts the other.

3 | What Is Politics?

OVERVIEW

- Political science is the study of politics in a scientific manner. Politics is the subset of human behavior that involves the use of power or influence. Power is involved whenever individuals cannot accomplish their goals without either trying to influence the behavior of others or trying to wrestle free from the influence exerted by others.

- We introduce an Exit, Voice, and Loyalty (EVL) game that captures key elements of many political situations. We use the game to analyze the balance of power between citizens and states.

- Among other things, the EVL game helps us think about when citizens will take direct action against the state, when states will respond positively to the demands of their citizenry, and how citizens can strengthen their position vis-à-vis the state. In other words, it helps us think about the role of power in politics: Who has it? Why do they have it? How and when is it used?

Political science is the study of politics in a scientific manner. In the previous chapter we described what we mean by science and examined the various components that constitute the scientific process. In this chapter we define what we mean by politics. What makes one situation political and another not? What is politics? Although many answers have been given to these questions over the years, most share the intuition that **politics** is the subset of human behavior that involves the use of power

> **Politics** is the subset of human behavior that involves the use of power or influence.

or influence. Broadly speaking, power is involved whenever individuals cannot accomplish their goals without either trying to influence the behavior of others or trying to wrestle free from the influence exerted by others. That all forms of social interaction, whether at home, at work, or at play, typically involve some person or group trying to influence, or avoid the influence of, others illustrates that politics is a key aspect of much of our everyday lives.

In this chapter, we introduce a simple model that captures what we think are the key elements of many political situations.[1] Our model represents a reformulation and extension of an argument put forth in a famous book by Albert Hirschman (1970) entitled *Exit, Voice, and Loyalty: Responses to Decline in Firms, Organizations, and States*.[2] Whereas Hirschman primarily addresses the relationship between consumers and firms, we focus here on the power relationship between citizens and states. The model helps us understand when citizens will take direct action against the state, when states will respond positively to the demands of their citizenry, and when states will ignore their citizens. More generally, the model throws light on who has power, when and why they have it, and how they use it. In other words, it helps us think about what politics is and how politics works.

THE EXIT, VOICE, AND LOYALTY GAME

Throughout our lives we will all experience changes to our environment that we do not like. Below are examples of what some people might consider deleterious changes to their environment:

- The state increases taxes.
- The state imposes a ban on handguns.
- The Supreme Court rules that prayer in public schools is unconstitutional.
- The national currency drops in value.
- Fuel-efficient cars are imported from a foreign country.
- The quality of peaches at your local fruit stand declines.

Note that although some people will not like these changes and will see them as deleterious, others will see them as improvements. For example, those people who have to pay higher taxes will be unhappy when the state raises the tax rate, but recipients of state benefits might be better off. Although consumers in the domestic market are likely to suffer when the

---

1. This chapter draws heavily on the ideas presented in Clark, Golder, and Golder (2008).

2. Hirschman's *Exit, Voice, and Loyalty* has generated a huge literature in political science, economics, psychology, management studies, public administration, and other fields. For a good introduction to this literature, see Dowding et al. (2000).

national currency drops in value because imports are now more expensive, exporters are likely to benefit because their goods are more competitive. The importation of fuel-efficient cars may well have negative consequences for domestic car manufacturers who can no longer compete, but it provides benefits for consumers who are struggling with high gas prices. Similarly, the decision by the Supreme Court that prayer in schools is unconstitutional would obviously upset some people, but it would just as likely make others happy. On the whole, political situations nearly always involve some individuals or groups benefiting at the expense of other individuals and groups. As we'll see, politics is frequently about winners and losers.

Let's say that there has been some change in your environment that you do not like. What can you do about it? Broadly speaking, there are three possible responses that you might have—you can **exit**, use **voice**, or demonstrate **loyalty**. Choosing to exit means that you accept the deleterious change in your environment and alter your behavior to achieve the best outcome possible given your new environment. For example, if you do not like the fact that your state has introduced a ban on hand-

> **Exit:** You accept that there has been a deleterious change in your environment and you alter your behavior to achieve the best outcome possible given your new environment.
>
> **Voice:** You use your "voice" (complain, protest, lobby, or take direct action) to try to change the environment back to its original condition.
>
> **Loyalty:** You accept the fact that your environment has changed and make no change to your behavior.

guns, you could accept the policy change as inevitable and simply move to another state where handguns are allowed. Similarly, if you do not like a decline in the quality of peaches at your local fruit stand, you could accept the decline in peach quality and either go to a different fruit stand to buy your peaches or start buying mangoes instead. Choosing to use voice means complaining, protesting, lobbying, or taking other forms of direct action to try to change the environment back to its original condition. For example, if the state increases your tax rate, you might join an anti-tax protest to pressure the state to reverse its tax hike. Similarly, if the importation of fuel-efficient cars is having negative effects on your automobile firm, you could consider lobbying the government to place import restrictions or tariffs on these cars. Choosing to demonstrate loyalty means that you accept the deleterious change in your environment and you make no change to your behavior. For example, if the state rules that prayer in public schools is unconstitutional, you could accept the situation and keep your children in the public school system. In Table 3.1, we illustrate what it means to use exit, voice, or loyalty in response to several potentially deleterious changes in your environment.

Consider the situation in which the state introduces a policy—say, a tax hike—that deleteriously affects the environment of one of its citizens. How should the citizen respond? When should the citizen choose to exit, use voice, or remain loyal? The citizen's choice will depend on what she expects to happen when she chooses one of these options. In order for the citizen to know what to do, she needs to know what the state would do if she used voice. On the one hand, the fact that the citizen complains or protests might cause the state to respond positively to the citizen. This would lead to a tax reduction and the restoration of the citizen's original environment. On the other hand, the state might simply ignore the citizen's use of voice. If the state did ignore her, then the citizen would have to decide what to do next.

TABLE 3.1	Exit, Voice, and Loyalty		
Stimulus	**Exit**	**Voice**	**Loyalty**
State increases taxes.	Reallocate portfolio to to avoid tax increase.	Organize tax revolt.	Pay taxes, keep your mouth shut.
Decline in the quality of peaches at the local fruit stand.	Buy mangoes, or buy peaches somewhere else.	Complain to the store owner.	Eat peaches, keep your mouth shut.
Supreme Court rules that prayer in public schools is unconstitutional.	Home school your children.	Lobby the government to change the constitution.	Keep your children in the public school system, keep your mouth shut.
Your state outlaws handguns.	Move to Idaho.	Join the NRA or a militia group to put pressure on the state to allow handguns.	Turn in your handguns, keep your mouth shut.

After all, even though the citizen's use of voice failed, she would still have the choice of exiting or remaining loyal. What should the citizen do? What should the state do?

The problem facing the citizen and state is complicated because the citizen's choice of what to do depends on what she thinks the state will do, and the state's choice of what to do depends on what it thinks the citizen will do. This strategic aspect of social interactions is the essence of politics. **Game theory** is a fundamental tool that political scientists use for analyzing these types of **strategic situations** in which the choices of one actor depend on the choices made by other

> **Game theory** is a fundamental tool for analyzing strategic situations.
>
> A **strategic situation** is one in which the choices of one actor depend on the choices made by other actors.

actors.[3] Throughout this book, we will use game theory as a conceptual tool to analyze, and better understand, a variety of strategic situations relating to the emergence of the state (Chapter 4), how the socioeconomic structure of a country affects the emergence and survival of democracy (Chapter 6), how culture affects bargaining behavior (Chapter 7), transitions to democracy (Chapter 8), and the electoral coordination of political parties (Chapter 13).

> A **game** is a situation in which an individual's ability to achieve her goals depends on the choices made by other actors.

We can think of the decisions to be made by the citizen and the state as a game. A **game** is a situation in which an individual's ability to achieve his or her goals depends on the choices made by other identifiable actors. It is important to recognize that there is nothing trivial about political games; as will be seen throughout this book, the way they are "played" may mean the difference

---

3. In addition to political science, game theory is also widely applied in biology, economics, anthropology, sociology, social psychology, computer science, philosophy, and many other fields. Those students interested in learning more about game theory might want to begin by consulting Morrow (1994), Dixit and Skeath (1999), Dutta (1999), or Osborne (2004).

between life and death. Games have a set of players, and each player has a set of possible choices to make. There are two players in the story that we are presenting in this chapter—a citizen and the state. The citizen has to choose whether to exit, use voice, or remain loyal. If the citizen uses voice, then the state has to choose whether to respond positively to it or ignore it. And if the state ignores the citizen's voice, then the citizen has to choose whether to exit or remain loyal. A **strategy** for playing the game is a complete plan of action that specifies what a player would do under every possible circumstance that might arise in the game.

> A **strategy** for playing a game is a complete plan of action that specifies what a player would do under every possible circumstance.

To solve a game we have to identify the strategies that a rational decision maker, who is trying to do as well as possible, would employ. By rational, all we mean is that the player does what she believes is in her best interest given what she knows at the time of choosing.[4] By solving a game, it becomes possible to say something about what we expect the players to do in the type of strategic situation being examined.

An important solution concept for games is called a **Nash equilibrium**. A Nash equilibrium is a set of strategies in a game (one for each player) such that no player has an incentive to unilaterally switch to another strategy. In other words, no player has an incentive to change his or her mind given what the other players are doing. Games have rules about how decisions are made. The basic rule is that players choose to do what they believe is in their best interest. The interests are reflected in the **payoffs** associated with each possible outcome of the game. Players prefer outcomes with higher payoffs to outcomes with lower payoffs. A game can be represented by a game tree (extensive form games) or by a matrix of payoffs (normal, or strategic, form games). **Extensive form games** help us examine strategic situations in which players take turns to make decisions; that is, players make choices sequentially. **Normal, or strategic, form games** help us examine strategic situations in which players make their decisions at the same time; that is, decisions are made simultaneously rather than sequentially. In this chapter, we are going to use an extensive form game to examine the balance of power between citizens and states. In the next chapter, we employ a strategic form game to think about the emergence of the state.

> A **Nash equilibrium** is a set of strategies in a game (one for each player) such that no player has an incentive to unilaterally change her mind given what the other players are doing.

> **Payoffs** in a game indicate how the players value each of the possible outcomes.

> In an **extensive form game,** players make their choices sequentially. In a **normal, or strategic, form game,** players make their choices simultaneously.

An extensive form game consists of **choice nodes** linked in a sequence. Choice nodes are points at which a player must choose an action. The choice nodes are linked to other choice

> A **choice node** is a point in an extensive form game at which a player must choose an action. A **terminal node** is a place where the game ends. The **initial node** is a place where the game begins. The **branches** represent the actions that can be taken at choice nodes. A **game tree** is the entire specification of choice nodes and branches that comprise an extensive form game.

---

4. We provide a more detailed definition of rationality in Chapter 10.

Box 3.1 ## ORIGINS OF GAME THEORY

John von Neumann with his wife Klari in Princeton, NJ, in 1954.

Some ideas relating to game theory can be traced back as far as the eighteenth century (Osborne 2004, 2). However, game theory really emerged as a field of study only in the 1920s with a series of papers written by a Hungarian mathematician called John von Neumann (1903–1957). Von Neumann was born in Budapest and was immediately recognized as a child prodigy. For example, he could divide two eight-digit numbers in his head by the age of six, and he had mastered calculus by the age of eight. Having obtained his doctorate in chemical engineering from the University of Zurich, he then went on to receive his Ph.D. in mathematics from the University of Budapest in 1926. With political unrest spreading in central Europe, von Neumann was invited to Princeton University in 1930. In 1933 he became the youngest of six professors (another being Albert Einstein) from the School of Mathematics to be appointed to the newly established Institute for Advanced Study at Princeton. Together with the German economist Oskar Morgenstern, von Neumann wrote a book in 1944 entitled *Theory of Games and Economic Behavior* that is widely recognized as establishing the foundations of modern game theory. As Morrow (1994, 2) writes, this "book became an instant classic and triggered an explosion of interest in game theory among mathematicians and economists." In addition to this theoretical research, Von Neumann was also involved in more applied work. For example, he became a consultant to the Manhattan Project, which was helping to develop an atomic bomb, in 1943. In 1944 he became involved in the development of the first electronic computer.

Much of the early work on game theory focused on what are called "cooperative games"—games that assume that agreements between players can be enforced. As you can imagine, this assumption placed a significant restriction on the application of game theory to real-world situations. However, an American mathematician named John Nash (1928–) then wrote a series of papers between 1948 and 1950 that were to revolutionize game theory. Nash was born in West

Noble laureate John Nash beside Fine Hall, current home of Princeton University's Mathematics Department.

Virginia, and after receiving his undergraduate degree in mathematics at the Carnegie Institute of Technology (now Carnegie Mellon University), he went on to study mathematics at the graduate level at Princeton in 1948. As Osborne (2004, 23) remarks, one of Nash's letters of recommendation from a professor at the Carnegie Institute of Technology was just a single sentence long: "This man is a genius" (Kuhn et al. 1996). A little over two years after he started at Princeton, Nash graduated in 1950 having written a twenty-eight-page dissertation. By developing the concept of a Nash equilibrium in his dissertation, Nash was able to extend game theory to analyze what are known as "non-cooperative games." This was an extremely important development that greatly increased the applicability of game theory to real-world concerns.

In 1958 John Nash was struck by paranoid schizophrenia and he was virtually incapacitated for the next two decades of his life. Recently, the disease has begun to wane and he has gradually been able to return to his research at Princeton University. In 1994 he was awarded the Nobel Prize in Economics for his work on game theory, along with two other game theorists, John C. Harsanyi and Reinhard Selten. The life of John Nash was famously portrayed in the 2001 Oscar-winning film, *A Beautiful Mind,* based on the best-selling book of the same name by Sylvia Nasar (2001).

Since Nash wrote his dissertation, game theory, and particularly non-cooperative game theory, has become a key methodological tool in numerous academic disciplines such as political science, economics, biology, computer science, social psychology, anthropology, and philosophy. Game theory has been used to study a whole host of things ranging from auctions and social network formation to evolutionary change and international conflict.

nodes or outcomes by **branches**. The branches represent the actions that can be taken at each choice node. The branches lead to either another choice node or a **terminal node**. A terminal node is a place where the game ends. The entire specification of choice nodes and branches is called a **game tree** because it resembles a tree.

Figure 3.1 illustrates a game in extensive form between two players—a citizen and the state—going from left to right. The choice nodes are identified by the name of the player making a choice at that point of the game. Branches are shown as lines linking choice nodes to other choice nodes or terminal nodes. The "prehistory," or background, to the game is that the state has caused a deleterious change in the environment of the citizen that resulted in a transfer of some benefit from the citizen to the state. For example, the state might have introduced a tax hike leading to an increase in revenue for the state and less income for the citizen. Now the game displayed in Figure 3.1 begins.

The game starts at the left-most choice node (the **initial node**) with the citizen deciding whether to exit, use voice, or remain loyal. If the citizen decides to exit, then the state gets to keep the benefit that it seized in the game's prehistory and the citizen opts for some substitute. This is outcome 1 (O1). If the citizen chooses to remain loyal, then the state gets to keep the benefit that it seized and the citizen just suffers the loss in silence. This is outcome 2 (O2). If the citizen chooses to use voice, then the state must decide whether to respond positively to the citizen or ignore her. If the state responds positively, then the state returns the bene-

---

| FIGURE 3.1 | **Exit, Voice, and Loyalty Game without Payoffs** |

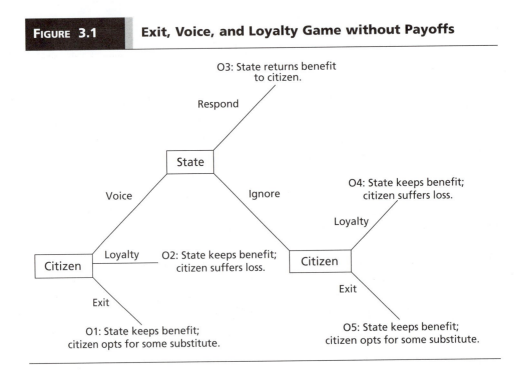

fit to the citizen. This is outcome 3 (O3). If the state ignores the citizen's use of voice, then the citizen must decide whether to remain loyal or exit.[5] If the citizen remains loyal, the state gets to keep the benefit that it took and the citizen suffers the loss. This is outcome 4 (O4). If the citizen chooses to exit, then the state gets to keep the benefit but the citizen opts for some substitute. This is outcome 5 (O5).

What do you expect the players to do in this game? This is actually an unfair question because you cannot really answer it without knowing how much each of the players values the different possible outcomes. In Table 3.2, we indicate the payoffs for the players that are associated with each of the five possible outcomes. If the citizen chooses to exit at any point in the game, then she gets what we call her "exit payoff." We arbitrarily set the value of the citizen's exit payoff at E. The precise value of E in any specific situation will depend on the attractiveness of the citizen's exit option. Some citizens will have attractive exit options (E will be high), whereas others will not (E will be low). If the citizen chooses to remain loyal at any point in the game, then she accepts the loss of her benefit and she gets nothing, 0. We assume that the use of voice is costly for the citizen, because protesting, complaining, lobbying, or taking direct action all require effort that could be put to alternative use. Depending on the state in which she lives, voice might be costly in other respects as well. For example, one's involvement in a protest might be met by imprisonment, loss of employment, or even death. In other words, the degree of state repression will likely affect the citizen's cost of using voice. For these reasons, the citizen must pay a cost (c), where $c > 0$, whenever she chooses to use voice.

TABLE 3.2	Turning Outcomes into Payoffs		
Outcome	Description	Citizen	State
O1	State keeps benefit of new situation; citizen opts for some substitute	E	1
O2	State keeps benefit of new situation; citizen suffers loss	0	$1 + L$
O3	State returns benefits to citizen	$1 - c$	L
O4	State keeps benefit; citizen suffers loss	$0 - c$	$1 + L$
O5	State keeps benefit but loses support of the citizen; citizen opts for some substitute	$E - c$	1

Note: E = citizen's exit payoff; 1 = value of benefit taken from the citizen by the state; L = state's value from having a loyal citizen who does not exit; c = cost of using voice.

---

5. You might be wondering why the citizen cannot choose to use her voice again at this point in the game. Well, obviously, she could. But ask yourself whether the state would behave any differently this time around if nothing else has changed. If the state ignored the citizen's voice before, it will do so again. Thus, allowing the citizen to use her voice at this point in the game does not add anything substantively new. This is why we allow the citizen to choose only between exiting and remaining loyal if the state decides to ignore her use of voice.

If the state gets to keep the benefit that it transferred from the citizen in the prehistory of the game, then the state gets a payoff of 1. We could have chosen any number other than 1, but 1 is the easiest for presentational purposes. If the citizen chooses to remain loyal, then the state gets, in addition, a loyalty payoff (L), where $L > 0$. This additional loyalty payoff captures the notion that states value having a loyal citizenry and can be thought of in at least a couple of ways. One is that loyal citizens can make life easier for state officials by providing them with support to help them stay in power or by providing them with what could be thought of as "legitimacy." The other is that loyal citizens continue to invest in the economy or other activities that provide meaningful resources and support to the state. Whatever the precise source of this additional loyalty payoff, its size will obviously vary across states and citizens. Some states desire or require more support from their citizenry than others, and some citizens are more important to state officials than others.

We can now put these payoffs together to see what the citizen and state get in each of the five possible outcomes. These are the payoffs shown in Table 3.2. In outcome 1 (O1), the citizen's payoff is E, because she exits, and the state's payoff is 1, because it gets to keep the benefit it took from the citizen. In outcome 2 (O2), the citizen's payoff is 0, because she remains loyal, and the state's payoff is $1 + L$, because it gets to keep the benefit it took from the citizen and it retains a loyal citizen. In outcome 3 (O3), the citizen's payoff is $1 - c$, because the state returns the benefit to the citizen but the citizen had to use her voice to get it, and the state's payoff is L, because the state retains a loyal citizen. In outcome 4 (O4), the citizen's payoff is $0 - c$, because the citizen chooses to remain loyal but only after using her voice, and the state's payoff is $1 + L$, because it gets to keep the benefit it took from the citizen as well as retaining a loyal citizen. In outcome 5 (O5), the citizen's payoff is $E - c$, because she exits but only after using her voice, and the state's payoff is 1, because it gets to keep the benefit that it took from the citizen. We can now add these payoffs to the game tree shown in Figure 3.1. The new game tree is shown in Figure 3.2. The citizen's payoffs are shown first because she is the first player to make a choice; the state's payoffs are shown second. A semicolon separates the payoffs for the players associated with each outcome.

We are almost ready to try to determine what the citizen and state will do in this game. Before we do this, however, we make one final assumption. Specifically, we assume that $E < 1 - c$. Think about what this assumption means for a moment. This assumption states that the value the citizen gets from exiting is less than the value that the citizen gets from successfully using her voice and regaining the benefit taken by the state. This assumption simply says that we are considering only the set of political situations in which exit is sufficiently unattractive that the value of the state's responding positively minus the cost of using voice is greater than the value offered by exit. If this assumption were not the case, then the citizen would always exit irrespective of how the state would respond to the use of voice. We believe that this assumption makes the situation we are examining between the citizen and state more interesting from a political point of view because there is now at least the possibility that the citizen might choose to use voice.

| FIGURE 3.2 | **Exit, Voice, and Loyalty Game with Payoffs** |

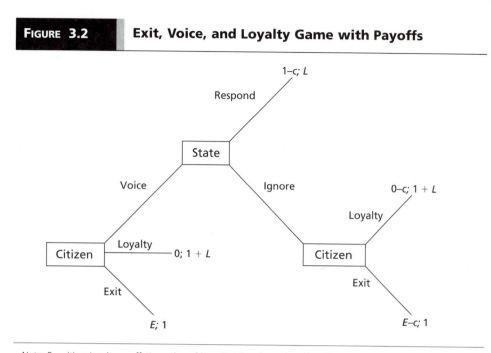

Note: E = citizen's exit payoff; 1 = value of benefit taken from the citizen by the state; L = state's value from having a loyal citizen who does not exit; c = cost of using voice. It is assumed that c, $L > 0$, and that $E < 1 - c$. The citizen's payoffs are shown first because she is the first player to make a choice; the state's payoffs are shown second. A semicolon separates the payoffs for the players associated with each outcome.

SOLVING THE EXIT, VOICE, AND LOYALTY GAME

Earlier, we noted that an important solution concept for games is a Nash equilibrium. It turns out, however, that there are several different types of Nash equilibrium. Typically, political scientists solve extensive form games like the Exit, Voice, and Loyalty game shown in Figure 3.2 for a particular type of Nash equilibrium called a **subgame perfect Nash equilibrium** (SPNE). A subgame is the part of a game beginning at one choice node and including all subsequent nodes. Thus, our EVL game has three subgames (one of which is the whole game), because there are three choice nodes. An SPNE is a set of strategies such that each player plays a Nash equilibrium in every subgame. Put differently, no player can have an incentive to unilaterally change his mind *in each subgame* given what the other players are doing. We can find the SPNE by using something called the method of **backward induction**. This probably

> A **subgame perfect Nash equilibrium** is a set of strategies such that each player is playing a Nash equilibrium in every subgame.

> A **subgame** is the part of an extensive form game beginning at one choice node and including all succeeding nodes.
>
> **Backward induction** is the process of reasoning backward, from the end of a game or situation to the beginning, in order to determine an optimal course of action.

all sounds quite complicated, but it really isn't. We will go through it with you step-by-step with our EVL game. In the problem section at the end of this chapter, we will also go through the whole process of constructing and solving extensive form games again.

Players in a game care about the consequences of their choices and, therefore, think ahead. They try to think about, and anticipate, how the other players will respond to their choices. For example, a player might ask himself how some other player would respond if he chooses action A and how that same player would respond if he chooses action B. The player then chooses the action (A or B) that is expected to give him the highest payoff. This process is quite familiar to chess players. Before making a move in a chess game, a player takes into consideration what she thinks the other player will do if she takes each of the possible moves open to her. Based on how she thinks the other player will respond to each of these possible moves, she then chooses the move that she thinks will be the best. The logical extension of this thought process leads players to begin at the end of the game and reason backward. This process is called backward induction and is probably something that most of us do when making decisions in our everyday lives without even thinking about it.

In the context of a game tree, backward induction requires starting at the end of the game tree (at a terminal node) and working our way back to the beginning of the game tree (the initial choice node). By doing this, each player can decide which choices are optimal in regard to obtaining the best possible payoff, given how she expects the other player to respond. The players must exhaust the choices at all of the terminal nodes first, then at all of the choice nodes that come before the terminal nodes, then at all of the choice nodes that come before these nodes, and so on until they reach the initial choice node. At each choice node, the players will choose the action that provides them with the highest payoff, given how they expect the other players to respond farther down the game tree. At the terminal node, the players simply choose the action that provides them with the highest payoff.

So, how does this work in practice? We now solve the EVL game shown in Figure 3.2 by backward induction. The terminal node of the game has the citizen deciding whether to exit or remain loyal. If the citizen chooses to exit, she will receive a payoff of $E - c$. If the citizen chooses to remain loyal, she will receive a payoff of $0 - c$. It is easy to see that the decision as to whether to exit or remain loyal will depend on whether $0 - c$ is larger or smaller than $E - c$. For now, let us assume that $E > 0$; that is, the citizen's exit payoff is greater than her loyalty payoff. One way to interpret this is to say that the citizen has a credible exit threat, because she might realistically choose to exit under this assumption. Had the citizen's exit payoff been smaller than her loyalty payoff ($E < 0$), the citizen would never choose to exit. Once we make the assumption that $E > 0$, it becomes clear that $E - c > 0 - c$. As a result, the citizen will choose to exit rather than remain loyal. We indicate this choice by making the exit branch at this terminal node bold. This is shown in Figure 3.3.

Now we move backward to the choice node prior to the terminal node. At this choice node, the state has to decide whether to respond positively to the citizen or ignore her. If the state responds positively, then it receives a payoff of L. If the state ignores the citizen, then it

FIGURE 3.3	**Solving the Exit, Voice, and Loyalty Game When the Citizen Has a Credible Exit Threat ($E > 0$): Step One**

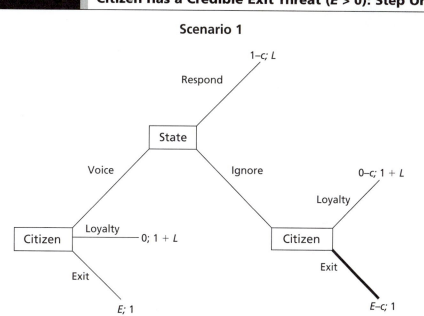

Scenario 1

Note: E = citizen's exit payoff; 1 = value of benefit taken from the citizen by the state; L = state's value from having a loyal citizen who does not exit; c = cost of using voice. It is assumed that c, $L > 0$; $E < 1 - c$; $E > 0$.

can look down the game tree (follow the bold line) and see that the citizen will choose to exit at the terminal node and that its payoff will be 1. The decision whether to respond positively to the citizen or ignore her will obviously depend on whether L is larger or smaller than 1. For now, let us assume that $L > 1$. One way to interpret this is to say that the state is *dependent* on the citizen—the state values having the loyalty of the citizen more than the benefit that it took from her. Once we make this assumption, it becomes clear that the state will choose to back down. We indicate this choice by making the respond branch at this choice node bold. This is shown in Figure 3.4.

Now we move backward to the choice node prior to this one. In this particular game, this is the initial choice node. At this node, the citizen has to choose whether to exit, remain loyal, or use her voice. If the citizen chooses to exit, then she receives a payoff of E. If the citizen chooses to remain loyal, then she receives a payoff of 0. And if the citizen chooses to use her voice, then she can look down the game tree (follow the bold lines) and see that the state will respond positively and that her payoff will be $1 - c$. As always, the citizen will choose the action that provides her with the highest payoff. Remember that we have assumed in this particular example that the citizen has a credible exit threat ($E > 0$) and that $E < 1 - c$. Given

| FIGURE 3.4 | Solving the Exit, Voice, and Loyalty Game When the Citizen Has a Credible Exit Threat ($E > 0$) and the State Is Dependent ($L > 1$): Step Two |

Scenario 1

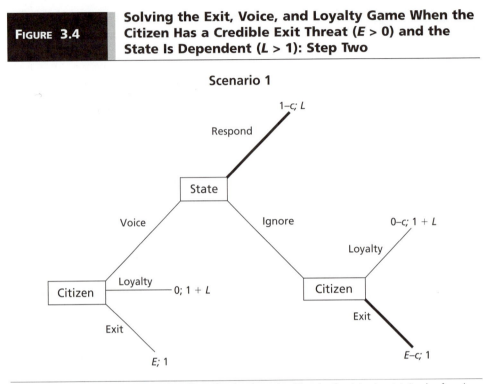

Note: E = citizen's exit payoff; 1 = value of benefit taken from the citizen by the state; L = state's value from having a loyal citizen who does not exit; c = cost of using voice. It is assumed that $c, L > 0$; $E < 1 - c$; $E > 0$; $L > 1$.

these assumptions, it is easy to see that the citizen will choose to use voice to get a payoff of $1 - c$ instead of E or 0. Again, we indicate this choice by making the voice branch at this choice node bold. This is shown in Figure 3.5.

We have now solved the game using backward induction. Once we have solved a game, we are often interested in identifying three things: the expected outcome of the game, the payoffs that each player receives, and the equilibrium of the game. Let's start by identifying the expected outcome of the game. We do this by starting at the beginning of the game and following the bold lines until we reach a terminal node. The expected outcome of the game in Figure 3.5 is that the citizen uses her voice and the state responds positively (Voice, Respond). The payoffs next to the terminal node that is identified as the expected outcome indicate the payoffs that each player will receive. In this case, the citizen obtains $1 - c$ and the state obtains L ($1 - c$; L).

To find the subgame perfect Nash equilibrium for the EVL game in Figure 3.5, we must list the actions chosen by both the citizen and the state at all of the choice nodes in the game. By convention, the SPNE first lists all the choices that the first player (citizen) makes at each of the choice nodes where she gets to make a choice, and then lists all of the choices that the

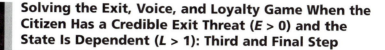

FIGURE 3.5	**Solving the Exit, Voice, and Loyalty Game When the Citizen Has a Credible Exit Threat ($E > 0$) and the State Is Dependent ($L > 1$): Third and Final Step**

Scenario 1

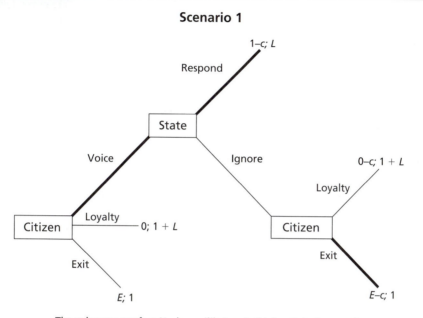

The subgame perfect Nash equilibrium is (Voice, Exit; Respond).

Note: E = citizen's exit payoff; 1 = value of benefit taken from the citizen by the state; L = state's value from having a loyal citizen who does not exit; c = cost of using voice. It is assumed that c, $L > 0$; $E < 1 - c$; $E > 0$; $L > 1$.

second player (state) makes at each of the choice nodes where it gets to make a choice. We distinguish between the choices (strategy) of the first player and the choices (strategy) of the second player by using a semicolon. In our EVL game, the citizen could make a choice at two choice nodes and the state could make a choice at only one. As a result, the SPNE first lists two actions for the citizen (Voice, Exit) and then lists one action for the state (Respond). As a result, we would write the SPNE for the EVL game shown in Figure 3.5 as (Voice, Exit; Respond). This equilibrium indicates that the citizen chooses to use voice at her first choice node and would choose exit at the terminal node if the game ever arrived at this choice node; the state chooses to respond positively at its one and only choice node.

You are probably wondering why we bother to list what the citizen does at the terminal node in the SPNE given that the citizen never actually gets to make a choice at this node because the state chooses to respond positively earlier in the game. Ask yourself, however, exactly why the game never reaches this node. In other words, why did the state choose to respond positively to the citizen's use of voice rather than ignore it? The answer to this question is that the state chooses to respond positively because it anticipates that the citizen will exit at the terminal node if it chooses to ignore her. In other words, knowledge about what the citizen will choose at the terminal node if this node were to be reached is crucial in determining the outcome of the game. It is for this reason that the SPNE always includes the choices of each actor at all of their choice nodes even if these choice nodes are never actually reached when the game is played.[6] An important point to take away from this, more generally, is that choices that are not taken are often as important to understanding the outcomes of strategic interactions as choices that we actually observe. As seen later in the chapter, power is often most effective when it is least observable. One of the benefits of game theory is that it forces the analyst to consider the influence of anticipated events. These anticipated events can have a tremendous impact on people's behavior even though they might never actually occur; they never occur precisely because people anticipate them and change their behavior to avoid them.

The SPNE that we just found indicates that the citizen's use of voice will be successful. This particular equilibrium, however, rests on the assumptions that the citizen has a credible exit threat ($E > 0$) and that the state is dependent ($L > 1$). What happens if we change these assumptions? What happens, for example, if we retain the assumption that the state is dependent ($L > 1$) but now assume that the citizen does not have a credible exit threat ($E < 0$)? In other words, let's assume that, as unhappy as the citizen may be with the state's pregame behavior, remaining loyal is preferred to exiting. The solution to this game is shown in Figure 3.6.

At the terminal node, the citizen has to choose whether to remain loyal with a payoff of $0 - c$ or exit with a payoff of $E - c$. Because $E < 0$, the citizen will receive a higher payoff if she remains loyal. As a result, the loyalty branch from the terminal node is bold. At the choice node prior to the terminal node, the state must choose whether to respond positively to the citizen's use of voice or ignore it. If the state responds positively, then it receives a payoff of L. If the state ignores the citizen, then it can look down the game tree (follow the bold line) and see that the citizen will choose to remain loyal at the terminal node and that its payoff will be $1 + L$. No matter what the value of L, the state will always choose to ignore the citizen because $1 + L > L$. As a result, the ignore branch from this choice node is bold. At the initial choice node, the citizen must choose whether to exit, remain loyal, or use voice. If she exits, her payoff will be E. If she remains loyal, her payoff will be 0. And if she uses voice, she can look down the game tree (follow the bold lines) and see that her payoff will be $0 - c$. Because the citizen does not have a credible exit threat ($E < 0$) in this scenario, she will get her highest payoff (0) by remaining loyal. As a result, the loyalty branch from the initial

---

6. You can think about this in a different way. Imagine that, for some reason, the citizen and state cannot turn up on game day to play the EVL game. Instead, they have to send some agent to take their places. The citizen and the state have to give their respective agents a complete set of instructions as to what to do at every place in the game at which they might have to make a choice. If you think about it, an SPNE is essentially just a combination of two complete sets of instructions on how to play the game, one from the citizen and one from the state. But why tell their agents what to do at choice nodes that the citizen and state do not expect to be reached? The simple answer is that one of the agents might make a mistake. Unless the other agent has been given a complete set of instructions, he will not know what to do if this happens.

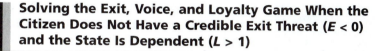

FIGURE 3.6 **Solving the Exit, Voice, and Loyalty Game When the Citizen Does Not Have a Credible Exit Threat ($E < 0$) and the State Is Dependent ($L > 1$)**

Scenario 2

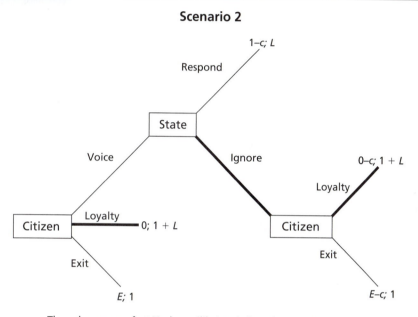

The subgame perfect Nash equilibrium is (Loyalty, Loyalty; Ignore).

Note: E = citizen's exit payoff; 1 = value of benefit taken from the citizen by the state; L = state's value from having a loyal citizen who does not exit; c = cost of using voice. It is assumed that c, $L > 0$; $E < 1 - c$; $E < 0$; $L > 1$.

choice node is bold. We have now solved this new scenario of the EVL game using backward induction. The SPNE is (Loyalty, Loyalty; Ignore). This indicates that the citizen will choose to be loyal from the beginning of the game. If the citizen had used her voice, the state would have ignored her, at which point the citizen would have remained loyal. The expected outcome of this game is that the citizen remains loyal and the state gets to keep the benefit it took from her. The payoffs associated with this outcome are 0 for the citizen and $1 + L$ for the state $(0; 1 + L)$.

What happens if we change the assumptions again? What happens, for example, if we assume that the citizen has a credible exit threat ($E > 0$) but that the state is autonomous and does not depend on the citizen ($L < 1$)? The solution to this game is shown in Figure 3.7. At the terminal node, the citizen has to choose whether to remain loyal with a payoff of $0 - c$ or exit with a payoff of $E - c$. Since the citizen has a credible exit threat once again ($E > 0$), she will receive a higher payoff if she exits because $E - c > 0 - C$. As a result, the exit branch from the terminal node is bold. At the choice node prior to the terminal node, the state must choose whether to respond positively to the citizen's use of voice or ignore it. If the state

FIGURE 3.7

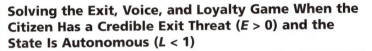

Solving the Exit, Voice, and Loyalty Game When the Citizen Has a Credible Exit Threat (*E* > 0) and the State Is Autonomous (*L* < 1)

Scenario 3

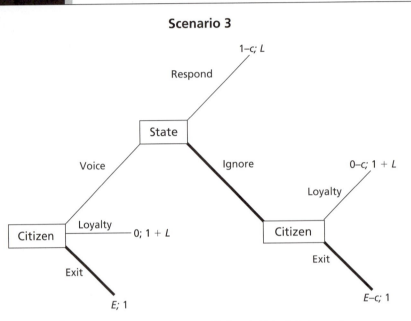

The subgame perfect Nash equilibrium is (Exit, Exit; Ignore).

Note: E = citizen's exit payoff; 1 = value of benefit taken from the citizen by the state; *L* = state's value from having a loyal citizen who does not exit; *c* = cost of using voice. It is assumed that *c, L* > 0; *E* < 1 − *c; E* > 0; *L* < 1.

responds positively, its payoff will be *L*. If the state ignores the citizen, it can look down the game tree (follow the bold line) and see that the citizen will exit and that its payoff will be 1. Because the state is now autonomous (*L* < 1), it will choose to ignore the citizen. As a result, the ignore branch from this choice node is bold. At the initial choice node, the citizen must choose whether to exit, remain loyal, or use voice. If she exits, her payoff will be *E*. If she remains loyal, her payoff will be 0. And if she uses voice, she can look down the game tree (follow the bold lines) and see that her payoff will be *E* − *c*. Because the citizen has a credible exit threat (*E* > 0), she will receive her highest payoff by choosing to exit. As a result, the exit branch from the first choice node is bold. The SPNE is, therefore, (Exit, Exit; Ignore). This indicates that the citizen will choose to exit at the beginning of the game. If the citizen had used her voice, the state would have ignored her, at which point the citizen would have exited. The observed outcome of this version of the game is that the citizen simply exits and the state gets to keep the benefit. The payoffs associated with this outcome are *E* for the citizen and 1 for the state (*E*; 1).

What happens if we change the assumptions one last time? For example, what happens if we assume that the citizen does not have a credible exit threat ($E < 0$) and that the state is autonomous ($L < 1$)? The solution to this game is shown in Figure 3.8. At the terminal node, the citizen has to choose once again whether to remain loyal with a payoff of $0 - c$ or exit with a payoff of $E - c$. Because the citizen does not have a credible exit threat ($E < 0$), she will receive a higher payoff if she remains loyal. As a result, the loyalty branch from the terminal node is bold. At the choice node prior to the terminal node, the state must choose whether to respond positively to the citizen's use of voice or ignore it. If the state responds positively, its payoff will be L. If the state ignores the citizen, it can look down the game tree (follow the bold line) and see that its payoff will be $1 + L$. It is easy to see that no matter what the value of L, the state will always choose to ignore the citizen. As a result, the ignore branch from this choice node is bold. At the initial choice node, the citizen must choose whether to exit, remain loyal, or use voice. If the citizen exits, her payoff will be E. If she remains loyal, her payoff will be 0. And if she uses voice, she can look down the game tree

FIGURE 3.8	**Solving the Exit, Voice, and Loyalty Game When the Citizen Does Not Have a Credible Exit Threat ($E < 0$) and the State Is Autonomous ($L < 1$)**

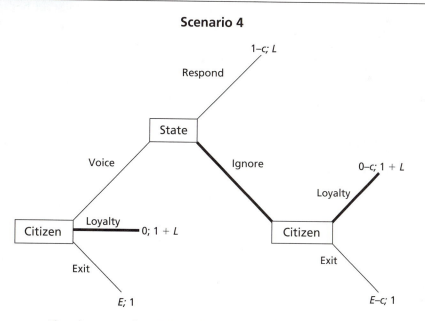

Scenario 4

The subgame perfect Nash equilibrium is (Loyalty, Loyalty; Ignore).

Note: E = citizen's exit payoff; 1 = value of benefit taken from the citizen by the state; L = state's value from having a loyal citizen who does not exit; c = cost of using voice. It is assumed that c, $L > 0$; $E < 1 - c$; $E < 0$; $L < 1$.

(follow the bold lines) and see that her payoff will be $0 - C$. Because the citizen has no credible exit threat ($E < 0$), she will receive her highest payoff if she remains loyal. As a result, the loyalty branch from the first choice node is bold. Thus, the SPNE is (Loyalty, Loyalty; Ignore). This indicates that the citizen will choose to remain loyal at the beginning of the game. If the citizen had used her voice, the state would have ignored her, at which point the citizen would have decided to remain loyal. The observed outcome of this game is that the citizen remains loyal from the beginning and the state gets to keep the benefit. The payoffs associated with this outcome are 0 for the citizen and $1 + L$ for the state $(0; 1 + L)$.

EVALUATING THE EXIT, VOICE, AND LOYALTY GAME

What can we learn from these various scenarios in the EVL game about the balance of power between citizens and the state? A summary of the subgame perfect Nash equilibria with their expected outcomes is shown in Table 3.3. Several important conclusions about the power relationship between citizens and states can be learned from this game. The first is that the state will be willing to respond positively to the citizen only when two conditions are met: the citizen must have a credible exit threat ($E > 0$), and the state must be dependent on the citizen ($L > 1$). You might have thought that a citizen would have a significant advantage over the state whenever she has a credible exit threat. This is clearly not the case, however. The state must also be dependent for the citizen with a credible exit threat to be able to influence it.[7] Put differently, an autonomous state will never respond positively even if the citizen has a credible exit threat.

Think about what this means for your life more generally. If you want to be able to influence others (say, for example, you want your employer to give you a pay raise), then you should try to make sure that you have a credible exit threat (there are other jobs you could

TABLE 3.3	**Summary of Subgame Perfect Nash Equilibria and Outcomes**	
	The State	
The Citizen	**Is autonomous** ($L < 1$)	**Is dependent** ($L > 1$)
Has a credible exit threat ($E > 0$)	(Exit, Exit; Ignore) Outcome 1	(Voice, Exit; Respond) Outcome 3
Has no credible exit threat ($E < 0$)	(Loyalty, Loyalty; Ignore) Outcome 2	(Loyalty, Loyalty; Ignore) Outcome 2

---

7. A citizen with a credible exit threat has an advantage in relation to one without such a threat, because the citizen with a credible exit threat has the realistic option of exiting, whereas the other citizen does not. Our point here, though, is that having a credible exit option itself is not sufficient for the citizen to be able to influence the state.

do or other firms that would hire you) and that the person you are interacting with depends on you in some way (perhaps you are the only one who knows how the firm's accounts work). If other firms are willing to hire you but your employer does not depend on you, then your employer will feel free to ignore you. Similarly, if your employer depends on you but other firms are not willing to hire you, then your employer will again feel free to ignore you. The only way to have power and be able to influence others is if you have a credible exit threat and the person or group that you want to influence depends on you. Think about how this applies to other relationships in your life. What about the relationship between you and your parents, your professors, or your friends?

The second important conclusion is that, in the absence of a credible exit option ($E < 0$), the citizen is, in some sense, a sitting duck. Under these conditions, the state can take away the citizen's benefits and there is nothing that the citizen can do about it but accept the new state of affairs. How can we see this conclusion at work in the real world? Well, some have argued that the Democratic Party in the United States has not done enough to take account of the concerns of African American voters. If this is true—and we do not wish to enter that particular debate—then our EVL game throws some light on why this might be the case. Clearly, Democrats depend on African American voters. Without their vote, Democrats have little chance of winning national office as things stand. But ask yourself whether African American voters have a credible exit option. In other words, is there another party that African Americans could credibly threaten to vote for instead of the Democrats? Some might argue that the fact that African Americans rarely vote for the Republican Party sends a signal to the Democratic Party that African Americans do not have a credible exit threat. Think about it this way. If the Republican Party were a credible option for African Americans, wouldn't more of them vote for it? Observing this signal, the Democratic Party can, to some extent, ignore (and exploit) African Americans even though it depends heavily on this particular constituency for its electoral success. The bottom line is that we should always strive to make sure that we have credible exit options in our life because they are a necessary, though not sufficient, condition to make sure we are not exploited. Going back to our example, this suggests, perhaps somewhat counterintuitively, that African Americans who want the Democratic Party to pay more attention to their concerns and to treat them better should start voting for the Republican Party as a way of signaling that they have a credible exit option. Only then will the Democratic Party feel that it has to take African Americans seriously.

We have argued that the state is free to take away the citizen's benefits whenever the citizen does not have a credible exit threat. Note, though, that we can think of the "benefits" that the state takes away in the game's prehistory in many ways. It could be that the state has denied the citizen some of her civil rights or civil liberties. Alternatively, it could be that the state has taken property away from the citizen—either through taxation or appropriation. In our discussion to this point, it has implicitly been assumed that the state has taken something away from the citizen that in some sense rightfully belonged to her. That need not be the case for this model to be useful in understanding the role of power in the relationship between the citizen and the state. For example, it could be the case that the state has taken away the citizen's ability to seize an unfair advantage over other citizens—say, through a licensing agreement that grants the holder of the license a market advantage. Thus, there is nothing inherently good about the state's being responsive to the citizen's use of voice; nor is it necessarily loathsome for the state to turn a deaf ear to citizen demands. In fact, we often refer to the demands that some people make on the state as "special interests," and state officials are as likely to be applauded, as lambasted, for ignoring them.

A third point made by our model is that it is often difficult to learn very much from observing real-world political situations. Consider the following. It is always possible to infer whether a citizen has a credible exit threat from observing her action. This is because the decision to exit or use voice requires a credible exit threat, whereas the decision to demonstrate loyalty implies the lack of such a threat. It is not so easy to learn whether a state is dependent or autonomous when the citizen has no credible exit threat, however, because both types of state will respond to the use of voice by this type of citizen in exactly the same way—they will simply ignore her. It is precisely because she expects to be ignored in these circumstances that the citizen without a credible exit threat always chooses to remain loyal in the first place. This is an important point, because it means that we should not make the mistake of inferring that states in which the use of voice and public opposition are rare, such as contemporary Burma, China, Iran, and North Korea, are autonomous or that they do not rely on the support of their citizenry. These regimes may be very dependent yet feel entirely free to ignore their citizens because their citizens lack credible exit threats.

The history of the collapse of the Communist regime in East Germany bears this logic out. For example, one can argue that, with the exception of the Berlin Uprising in 1953, the East German population was very loyal prior to 1989 because it lacked a credible exit threat. To many outsiders (and insiders), it appeared that the Communist regime was very stable and relatively autonomous from its citizens (Kuran 1991). The opening of the Hungarian border to Austria in May 1989, however, provided East Germans with a credible exit option for the first time since the construction of the Berlin Wall in 1961.[8] It was this change that transformed the seemingly "loyal" and rather docile East German population into enthusiastic protesters who used voice in large numbers on the streets of Leipzig and East Berlin (Garton Ash 1999). One can argue that it was precisely because the East German Communist Party did depend on its citizens, despite all evidence to the contrary for almost three decades, that the Communist regime eventually responded by opening the Berlin Wall. This particular historical example should make us wary of inferring that a state is autonomous when its citizens have no credible exit threat—it might be, but it also might not be.

Similarly, our model suggests that it is also inappropriate to use political mobilization (voting, lobbying, campaign contributions, and so on), or the lack thereof, as a straightforward revelation of citizen preferences. Citizens may remain silent on particular issues either

8. By 1961 the East German state had come to recognize that it relied on its citizens to keep the economy afloat and itself in power. By building the Berlin Wall and removing the one credible exit option available to its citizens, the Communist regime was able to deprive its citizens of any influence that they might have over it.

because they are satisfied with the status quo or because they do not expect their use of voice to be effective.

The EVL game raises a fourth important point. If the state is responsive to those citizens on whom it depends for loyalty whenever those citizens possess credible exit threats, why would the state ever take a benefit away from these citizens in the first place? This question cannot be answered with the game as it stands. It is relatively easy, however, to think about how we might answer this question if we were to incorporate the prehistory of the game into the game itself. For example, imagine that we added a move at the beginning of the game in which the state decides whether or not to take the benefit away from the citizen. We can think of this as a decision by the state about whether to exploit the citizen by taking away some of her resources or not. If the state chooses to seize the citizen's resource, then the version of the EVL game that we have just examined begins. If the state chooses not to exploit the citizen, however, the citizen simply has to choose whether to exit or remain loyal. Although we do not show this extended game here, you should think about what it would look like and how you could solve it. As the question above suggests, it turns out that the state will choose not to exploit the citzen whenever it depends on a citizen who has a credible exit threat. This in turn means that the citizen will never have to use her voice. Why is this the case? Well, put yourself in the shoes of the dependent state. You can see that if you attempt to exploit the citizen, the citizen will use her voice and, because you depend on her, you will respond positively. Because you know that you will eventually have to respond positively, you will choose not to seize the citizen's resources in the first place. As a result, the citizen will never have to use her voice (Clark, Golder, and Golder 2008).

An important point to note here is that those citizens who have credible exit options wield considerable influence without ever needing to open their mouths (use voice) whenever the state depends on them. Consider the politically incorrect epigraph attributed to the former British prime minister Margaret Thatcher at the beginning of this chapter: "Being powerful is like being a lady. If you have to tell people you are, you aren't." Thatcher's major insight was that sufficiently powerful people never need to use their voice because they are already getting other people to do what they want. This insight corresponds exactly to the results that we have just discussed from a version of the EVL model that incorporates the game's prehistory.

There are striking similarities between the argument just presented here and the so-called structural Marxist view of the state (Althusser 1969; Poulantzas 1975, 1980). According to this view, capitalists exercise tremendous power over the state despite speaking in a soft voice because they possess credible exit threats and the state is dependent on them for the deployment of investment that fosters job creation, economic growth, and tax revenues (Block 1977; Lindbloom 1982; Przeworski and Wallerstein 1988). It is precisely because capital is generally more mobile than labor (has more credible exit options) that capitalists typically have significantly more influence over the state than workers. This is the case even if the state depends on both labor and capital. We examine the structural Marxist view of the state in more detail in Chapter 9.

This central insight—that powerful people never need to use their voice—poses a particularly troubling problem for political scientists and other scholars who wish to empirically evaluate who has power in a given society. In many cases, the most powerful actors are precisely those citizens who are least likely to take action or use their voice—in other words, the political scientist will never be able to observe them using their power. Our EVL game suggests that it might be misleading to infer that citizens who do not engage in protests, strikes, lobbying, advertising, and so forth have no significant influence over state policy. To provide a specific example, our game indicates that it would be wrong to infer that presidents lack power because they rarely use their right to veto legislation. The possibility that presidents will veto legislation is enough to ensure that legislatures send presidents only the bills that the president wants. In effect, the president gets what he wants without having to use his veto power (Cameron 2000). The basic point here is that it is difficult to determine who has power and who does not simply by observing the world. This is one reason game-theoretic analysis, which allows us to analyze the way strategic dynamics may encourage nonaction, has become central to the scientific study of politics.

Finally, the EVL game is as noteworthy for what it does not explain as for what it does. Notice that in the game as it stands, citizens use voice only when they expect it to be effective. This means that the model cannot explain why we sometimes see states being unresponsive to the demands of their citizens. One reason states might ignore their citizens is that the citizens may not view the use of voice as costly. It is not altogether hard to imagine, at least in university towns, that some citizens might derive intrinsic benefits from the use of voice. For example, some citizens might welcome the opportunity simply to express themselves. Alternatively, they might use protest rallies as an opportunity to network with other like-minded individuals. Or they might feel a certain pride in the fact that they are living up to their civic responsibilities. If citizens do indeed derive such "consumption" benefits from the use of voice, we could capture this in our model by relaxing the assumption that $c > 0$. In effect, we could assume that $c < 0$ and treat these "negative costs" as benefits. If we do this, it is relatively easy to see that the citizen will always get a higher payoff from using voice than from either choosing to exit or remain loyal regardless of what the state does. In other words, the citizen will always use her voice even when she knows that it will not be successful.[9]

Another reason for sometimes seeing a state ignore its citizens has to do with information. The EVL game that we present in this chapter is currently one of complete information—each player knows everything about the game and about the preferences of all the other players. More advanced game-theoretic models, some of which are presented later in this book (Chapter 8), relax the assumption that the actors know enough about each other's preferences to be able to predict each other's responses perfectly. These more advanced games contain incomplete information. Perhaps the state does not know whether the citizen has a

---

9. Of course, this only leaves us with a different puzzle, namely, why citizens sometimes choose not to use voice when the state deleteriously affects their environment.

credible exit threat or not. Or perhaps the citizen does not know whether the state is dependent or not. A citizen with a credible exit option might overestimate the value of her loyalty to the state and might find out the hard way that the state is perfectly happy to let her exit. Conversely, a state may believe that a citizen who uses voice is bluffing—that the citizen does not intend to make good on her threat to exit.

CONCLUSION

We spend a fair amount of time in later chapters critically evaluating some of the claims that we have just made. Our goal in this chapter, though, was to demonstrate that the EVL game can be used to reveal something about what politics is and how politics works. Human interactions are considered political whenever actors cannot accomplish their goals without considering the behavior of other actors. Under such circumstances, the attempt to influence—or to avoid the influence of—others becomes relevant. It is here that power can, and will, be exercised. Attempts to influence, or break free of the influence of, others involve three basic strategies. Political actors can, as in the primordial response of "fight or flight," attempt to change their environment by using voice or change their location by using exit. "Voice" and "exit" are to be understood metaphorically here. A citizen's use of exit in response to a government policy need not involve emigration. Instead, a citizen might change industries, production processes, or political parties. Similarly, a citizen's use of voice might come as one of a host of behaviors, ranging from a ballot to a bullet. Finally, a citizen's best response to government policy might be to "keep on keepin' on." That is, throughout most of human history, the vast majority of humanity has often found itself between a rock and a hard place. Under such circumstances it is possible that neither voice nor exit is a feasible option. It should be clear that here too, the term *loyalty* is being used metaphorically—indeed, euphemistically.

In this chapter, we have used the words *state* and *citizen* without much explanation. In the next chapter, we devote our attention to the subject of where these entities come from and what they might be expected to do.

KEY CONCEPTS

backward induction, *65*
branches, *59*
choice node, *59*
exit, *57*
extensive form game, *59*
game, *58*
game theory, *58*
game tree, *59*
initial node, *59*
loyalty, *57*

Nash equilibrium, *59*
normal or strategic form game, *59*
payoffs, *59*
politics, *56*
strategic situation, *58*
strategy, *59*
subgame, *65*
subgame perfect Nash equilibrium, *65*
terminal node, *59*
voice, *57*

PREPARATION FOR THE PROBLEMS

As we have noted, game theory is a useful tool for examining strategic situations in which decision makers interact with one another. But how do we use it? We start by identifying a strategic situation of interest. Let's suppose that this strategic situation involves actors making sequential choices as in this chapter. The next step is to write an extensive form game that captures our strategic situation.

1. Writing the game
   a. Identify the players involved in the strategic situation.
   b. Draw the game tree to indicate what choices each of the players have and the order in which they make them. Label the choice nodes where players must make a choice with the names of the players making them.
   c. Determine the payoffs that the players receive for each of the possible outcomes that could occur in the game.
   d. Write the payoffs for each player in the game tree next to the relevant terminal node. By convention, start by writing the payoffs belonging to the player who moves first in the game, then the payoffs belonging to the player who moves second, then the payoffs belonging to the player (if there is one) who moves third, and so on. Use a semicolon to distinguish between the players' payoffs.

Once written, the game must be solved by backward induction.

2. Solving the game by backward induction
   a. Start at the end of the game tree. At each terminal node, determine which of the available actions provide the highest payoff to the player making the choice. Highlight the branch of the game tree associated with this "most-preferred" action by making it bold.
   b. Now go to the previous choice node. Again, determine which of the available actions provide the highest payoff to the player now making the choice. Highlight this branch of the game tree by making it bold.
   c. Continue this process of backward induction all the way back to the beginning of the game.

After the game has been solved by backward induction, it is often interesting to identify three things: the expected outcome of the game, the payoffs that each player receives, and the equilibrium of the game.

3. Identifying the outcome, payoffs, and equilibrium
   a. Start at the beginning of the game and follow the bold lines until you reach a terminal node. The path that you have just followed is called the equilibrium path. The terminal node that you reach is the expected outcome.
   b. The payoffs next to the terminal node that you have identified as the expected outcome indicate the payoffs that each player will receive.

c. To find the subgame perfect Nash equilibrium, list the actions chosen by each of the players at all of the choice nodes in the game. By convention, we first write down all the choices made by the first player, then all the choices made by the second player, then all the choices made by the third player (if there is one), and so on. We use a semicolon to distinguish between each player's choices.

Example: Potential Entry in a Senate Race

Suppose the strategic situation that we are interested in is a U.S. Senate race between an incumbent senator called Staton and a potential challenger called Reenock.[10] Imagine that Staton (incumbent) must decide whether to start a preemptive advertising campaign for the Senate seat and that Reenock (potential challenger) must decide whether to enter the race or not. We will assume that Staton chooses whether to launch a preemptive advertising campaign first and that Reenock then decides whether or not to enter the race. Now that we have identified our strategic situation, we can go through the steps outlined earlier.

The game tree for the Senate Race Game going from left to right is shown in Figure 3.9. At the beginning of the game, Staton must decide whether to advertise or not. Whatever

FIGURE 3.9	Senate Race Game

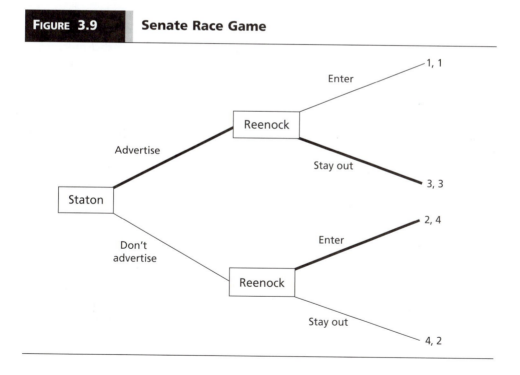

10. The following example is based on a strategic situation described in Dixit and Skeath (1999, 44–47).

Staton decides, Reenock must then choose whether to enter the race or stay out. The choice nodes in the game tree indicate who is making the choice at each point in the game and the branches coming from each choice node indicate what actions are available to the named player. As you can see, there are four possible outcomes: (a) Staton advertises and Reenock enters (advertise; enter); (b) Staton advertises and Reenock stays out (advertise; stay out); (c) Staton does not advertise and Reenock enters (don't advertise; enter); and (d) Staton does not advertise and Reenock stays out (don't advertise; stay out).

How do we determine the payoffs that the players associate with each outcome? One way to do this is to think about how each of the players would rank the four possible outcomes. Let's start by thinking about how Staton might rank the possible outcomes. If you know anything about U.S. senatorial races, you will know that there is a large incumbency advantage—incumbents typically enjoy a reelection rate of over 90 percent (Jacobson 2001). As a result, Staton can probably expect to be reelected no matter whether he advertises or not. Given that advertising is costly, this means that the best outcome for Staton is for him not to advertise and for Reenock to stay out of the race; the worst outcome for him would probably be to advertise and for Reenock to enter the race anyway. Of the remaining two outcomes, we might think that Staton prefers the situation in which he advertises and Reenock stays out to the situation in which he does not advertise and Reenock enters, because running unopposed (even with the cost of advertising) increases his reputation more than winning a tightly contested race in which he does not advertise. Thus, Staton's preference ordering, or ranking, of the four possible outcomes might be:

- (don't advertise; stay out) $\succ$ (advertise; stay out) $\succ$ (don't advertise; enter) $\succ$ (advertise; enter), where "$\succ$" means "is strictly preferred to."

How might Reenock rank the four possible outcomes? Reenock knows that he is probably going to lose if he enters. Let's assume, however, that he would like to do as well as possible so as to build name recognition in his party for the future. This suggests that the best outcome for Reenock is for Staton not to advertise and for him to enter; his worst outcome would probably be for Staton to advertise and for him to enter, because he is likely to be trounced and see his reputation severely damaged. Of the remaining two outcomes, we might think that Reenock prefers the situation in which Staton advertises and he stays out to the one in which Staton does not advertise and he stays out. Why? Well, Reenock can plausibly tell his party leaders that he did not enter because he had no chance of winning because of Staton's advertising, whereas he comes across as a bit of a wimp if he does not enter and Staton did not advertise. Thus, Reenock's preference ordering, or ranking, of the four possible outcomes might be:

- (don't advertise; enter) $\succ$ (advertise; stay out) $\succ$ (don't advertise; stay out) $\succ$ (advertise; enter).

Because there are four possible outcomes, we can assign the value "4" to each player's most preferred outcome, "3" to their second preferred outcome, "2" to their third preferred outcome, and "1" to their least preferred outcome. These are called "ordinal payoffs" because they tell us how the players rank the possible outcomes.

Now that we have written the game, we must solve it by backward induction. We start by looking for terminal nodes. As you can see in Figure 3.9, the Senate Race Game has two terminal nodes. At the top terminal node, Reenock must choose whether to enter or stay out after Staton has decided to advertise. If Reenock enters, his payoff is 1. If Reenock stays out, his payoff is 3. Because 3 is bigger than 1, Reenock will choose to stay out. We indicate this choice by making the "stay out" branch bold. At the bottom terminal node, Reenock must choose whether to enter or stay out after Staton has decided not to advertise. If Reenock enters, his payoff is 4. If Reenock stays out, his payoff is 2. Because 4 is bigger than 2, Reenock will choose to enter. We indicate this choice by making the "enter" branch bold. Now we move backward to the previous choice node, which in this game is the initial choice node. At this choice node, Staton must choose whether to advertise or not. If he advertises, he can see that Reenock will stay out and his payoff will be 3. If he does not advertise, he can see that Reenock will enter and his payoff will be 2. Because 3 is bigger than 2, Staton will choose to advertise. We indicate this choice by making the "advertise" branch bold. We have now solved the Senate Race Game by backward induction.

We now need to identify the expected outcome of the game, the payoffs that each player receives, and the equilibrium of the game. In order to find the expected outcome, we start at the beginning of the game and follow the highlighted branches until we reach a terminal node. As you can see, the expected outcome of the Senate Race Game is that the incumbent, Staton, advertises and the potential challenger, Reenock, stays out (advertise, stay out). In order to find the payoffs that each player receives in this game, we simply look at the payoffs associated with the terminal node that we have identified as the expected outcome. In this case, we can see that Staton receives 3 and Reenock receives 3 (3, 3). This indicates that both players obtained their second-best outcome. In order to find the subgame perfect Nash equilibrium, we must list the actions chosen by each of the players at all the choice nodes in the game. Staton chooses "advertise" at the one choice node where he gets to make a decision, whereas Reenock chooses "stay out" at his top choice node and "enter" in his bottom choice node. As a result, the subgame perfect Nash equilibrium for this game is (advertise; stay out, enter).

As you will notice, the Senate Race Game offers a potential explanation for why incumbents might choose to run an advertising campaign even when they do not face any challengers. In effect, the incumbent launches a preemptive advertising game in order to deter the entry of a potential challenger. As a result, the Senate Race Game is a generic type of Entry Deterrence Game. Epstein and Zemsky (1995) offer a slightly different version of our Senate Race Game to explain entry deterrence in electoral contests. In their model, a potential challenger would like to enter an electoral contest but only if the incumbent is politically weak. If the incumbent is strong, the potential challenger would prefer to stay out. As you can imagine, incumbents may want to signal to potential challengers that they are strong by raising large amounts of campaign money. If this "war chest" convinces the potential challenger that the incumbent is strong, then he is deterred from entering. As you can see, the Epstein and Zemsky game is, in its basic form, very similar to the Senate Race Game examined here.

PROBLEMS

1. Backward induction: some generic games to solve

We now present some generic extensive form games. As always, higher-valued payoffs are preferred to lower-valued payoffs. Solve each of the games by backward induction. For each game, write down the expected outcome, the payoffs that each player receives, and the subgame perfect Nash equilibrium.

    a. Generic Game I: Figure 3.10

    b. Generic Game II: Figure 3.11

    c. Generic Game III: Figure 3.12

FIGURE 3.10   **Generic Game I**

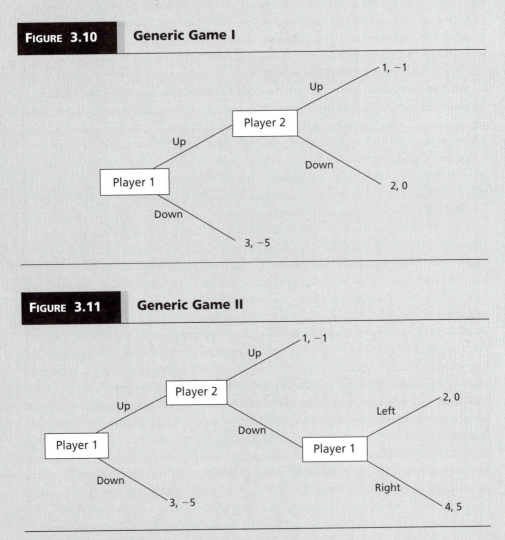

FIGURE 3.11   **Generic Game II**

FIGURE 3.12   **Generic Game III**

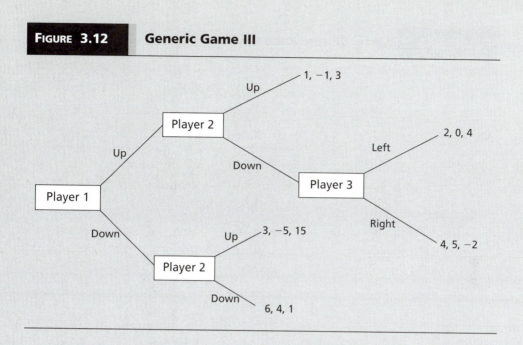

2. Senate Race Game revisited

Earlier we solved the Senate Race Game assuming that the incumbent, Staton, first decided whether or not to advertise and that the potential challenger, Reenock, then decided whether to enter or stay out. What happens, though, if we reverse the order in which the choices are made? In other words, what happens if Reenock has to decide whether to enter or stay out before Staton decides whether to advertise or not? The game tree for this scenario is shown in Figure 3.13. Assume that the two players have the same preference orderings as before, that is, Reenock's preference ordering is:

- (enter; don't advertise) ≻ (stay out; advertise) ≻ (stay out; don't advertise) ≻ (enter; advertise).

Staton's preference ordering is:

- (stay out; don't advertise) ≻ (stay out; advertise) ≻ (enter; don't advertise) ≻ (enter; advertise).
  a. Put the payoffs for each player associated with the four possible outcomes into the game tree. Use the numbers 4, 3, 2, and 1 to indicate the preference ordering for each player as we did with the original Senate Race Game.
  b. Solve the game by backward induction. Write down the expected outcome of the game, the payoffs that each player receives, and the subgame perfect Nash equilibrium.
  c. Based on what you have found, does it matter in regard to the outcome which player gets to move first? If it does matter, explain why it matters. If it does not matter, explain why it does not matter.

| FIGURE 3.13 | **New Senate Race Game** |

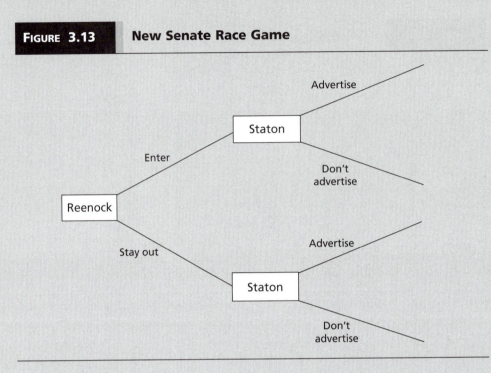

3. Terrorism Game

Terrorism is a problem that afflicts countries around the world, from Northern Ireland to Spain to Chechnya to Bali to Iraq. We can use game theory to think about the circumstances in which groups in society might engage in terrorist activities.[11] Imagine that there are two types of groups in society who might become terrorists and who can be distinguished by their preference for negotiations or violence. One type might be called "True Believers." These are fanatics who wish to engage in violent acts even if governments are willing to negotiate with them. We might think of al-Qaida members when we think of this type of social group. The second type might be called "Reluctant Terrorists" or "Freedom Fighters." These are people who would prefer to solve problems through negotiation but who will engage in terrorist acts if they are repressed by the government. One could argue that members of the Palestine Liberation Organization (PLO) or the Irish Republican Army (IRA) fall into this category. Imagine also that there are two types of governments that can be distinguished by their preference for negotiations and repression. One type of government might be called "Repressive Governments" because they wish to repress all social groups that oppose them. The second type of government might be called "Responsive Governments" because they are willing to listen to the demands of opposition groups and enter good faith negotiations with them.

---

11. The following terrorism game is based on a game found in Bueno de Mesquita (2006, 395–401).

We can think of a strategic situation in which a group in society must decide whether to request some policy concession from the government that will satisfy them politically or engage in a violent terrorist act. If the social group chooses violence, then the game ends with a terrorist act that leads to no cooperative negotiations and no change in the government position. If the social group requests some policy concession, the government must decide whether to repress the social group now that it has identified itself or enter good faith negotiations with it. As you can see, this Terrorism Game has three possible outcomes: Terrorist act, Repression, or Good faith negotiations. The basic game tree for the Terrorism Game is shown in Figure 3.14.

Based on the story that we have just told, the preference ordering for the True Believers over the three possible outcomes might be:

- Terrorist act ≻ Good faith negotiations ≻ Being repressed.

The preference ordering for the Reluctant Terrorists might be:

- Good faith negotiations ≻ Terrorist act ≻ Being repressed.

The preference ordering for the Repressive Government might be:

- Repression ≻ Good faith negotiations ≻ Terrorist act.

The preference ordering for the Responsive Government might be:

- Good faith negotiations ≻ Repression ≻ Terrorist act.
  a. Draw the game tree for the Terrorism Game with the social group True Believers and a repressive government. Using the preference orderings shown above, write in the appro-

| FIGURE 3.14 | **Basic Terrorism Game Showing Outcomes but Not Payoffs** |

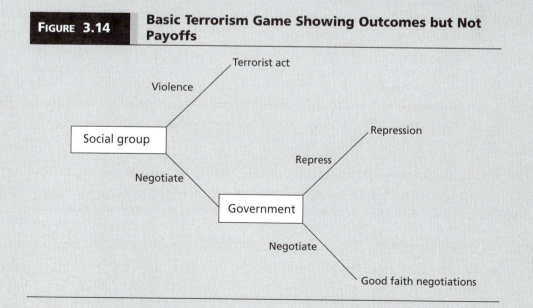

priate payoffs for each possible outcome. Use the numbers 3, 2, 1 to indicate the preference ordering for the players as we did with the Senate Race Game. Solve the game using backward induction. What is the expected outcome of the game? What are the payoffs that each player receives? What is the subgame perfect Nash equilibrium?

b. Draw the game tree for the Terrorism Game with the social group True Believers and a responsive government. Using the preference orderings shown above, write in the appropriate payoffs for each possible outcome. As before, use the numbers 3, 2, 1 to indicate the preference ordering for the players. Solve the game using backward induction. What is the expected outcome of the game? What are the payoffs that each player receives? What is the subgame perfect Nash equilibrium?

c. Does the type of government matter for the expected outcome of the Terrorism Game if the social group is True Believers?

d. Draw the game tree for the Terrorism Game with the social group Reluctant Terrorists and a repressive government. Using the preference orderings shown above, write in the appropriate payoffs for each possible outcome. As before, use the numbers 3, 2, 1 to indicate the preference ordering for the players. Solve the game using backward induction. What is the expected outcome of the game? What are the payoffs that each player receives? What is the subgame perfect Nash equilibrium?

e. Draw the game tree for the Terrorism Game with the social group Reluctant Terrorists and a responsive government. Using the preference orderings shown above, write in the appropriate payoffs for each possible outcome. As before, use the numbers 3, 2, 1 to indicate the preference ordering for the players. Solve the game using backward induction. What is the expected outcome of the game? What are the payoffs that each player receives? What is the subgame perfect Nash equilibrium?

f. Does the type of government matter for the expected outcome of the Terrorism Game if the social group is Reluctant Terrorists?

g. It is commonly assumed that terrorist acts are always committed by crazy, irrational fanatics. According to the various versions of the Terrorism Game that you have examined, is it necessarily the case that terrorist acts are committed by fanatics?

h. The common assumption that terrorist acts are committed by crazy, irrational fanatics helps to explain why so many Western countries, such as the United States and the United Kingdom, make public declarations that they will never negotiate with terrorists under any circumstances. Given that governments do not want terrorist acts, think about whether making such declarations matter for whether terrorist acts actually occur. What if the social group is made up of True Believers? What if the social group is made up of Reluctant Terrorists? *Hint:* Think about how these declarations influence the perception of the social group about whether the government they are interacting with is responsive or repressive.

4. Legislative Pay Raise Game

Imagine a strategic situation in which three legislators vote sequentially on whether they should receive a pay raise. Let's assume that decisions are made by majority rule. This means that if at least two legislators vote yes, then each legislator will receive a pay raise. Although all the legis-lators would like to receive a pay raise, each knows that they will pay a cost with their constituents if they are seen to vote for the raise. From the perspective of each legislator, four possible out-comes can occur. The most preferred outcome for each legislator is that they get the pay raise even though they personally vote no. The worst possible outcome is that they do not get the pay raise and they voted yes. Of the remaining two outcomes, let us assume that the legislators pre-fer the outcome in which they get the pay raise when they voted yes to the outcome in which they do not get the pay raise when they voted no. As a result, the preference ordering for each legislator is:

- Get raise, vote no ≻ Get raise, vote yes ≻ No raise, vote no ≻ No raise, vote yes.

   a. Imagine that you are one of the legislators. Would you prefer to vote first, second, or third? Explain your answer.

   b. The game tree for the Legislative Pay Raise Game is shown in Figure 3.15. Using the pref-erence orderings shown above, we have written in appropriate payoffs for some, but not

FIGURE 3.15   **Legislative Pay Raise Game**

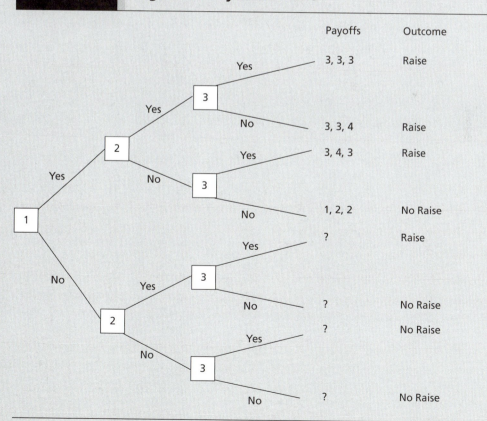

	Payoffs	Outcome
Yes	3, 3, 3	Raise
No	3, 3, 4	Raise
Yes	3, 4, 3	Raise
No	1, 2, 2	No Raise
Yes	?	Raise
No	?	No Raise
Yes	?	No Raise
No	?	No Raise

all, of the outcomes. As before, we have used the numbers 4, 3, 2, and 1 to indicate the preference ordering of the players. Legislator 1's payoff is shown first, Legislator 2's payoff is shown second, and Legislator 3's payoff is shown third. Fill in the missing payoffs to complete the game.

c. Solve the game by backward induction. Be careful to make sure that you are comparing the payoffs of the correct legislator. What is the expected outcome of the game? What are the payoffs that each player receives? What is the subgame perfect Nash equilibrium?

d. Imagine that you are one of the legislators again. Now that you have solved the game, would you prefer to vote first, second, or third? Explain your answer. Did your answer change from before?

e. Does the Legislative Pay Raise Game have any implications for whether you would want to be in a position to set the rules or the agenda in business meetings or other official settings? Explain your answer.

5. Writing and solving your own games

a. Think of a strategic situation in which two players make choices sequentially. Write down the game tree, establish preferences, and solve by backward induction. What is the expected outcome? What are the payoffs that each player receives? What is the subgame perfect Nash equilibrium?

b. Think of a strategic situation in which three players make choices sequentially. Write down the game tree, establish preferences, and solve by backward induction. What is the expected outcome? What are the payoffs that each player receives? What is the subgame perfect Nash equilibrium?

4 The Origins of the Modern State

In framing a government which is to be administered by men over men, the great difficulty lies in this: you must first enable the government to control the governed; and in the next place oblige it to control itself.

James Madison, *The Federalist Papers* No. 51

- A state is an entity that relies on coercion and the threat of force to rule in a given territory. A failed state is a statelike entity that cannot coerce and is unable to successfully control the inhabitants of a given territory.

- We present two views of the state: a contractarian view and a predatory view. According to the contractarian view, the creation of the state helps to solve political disputes that citizens might have with one another. Although the emergence of the state helps to solve these sorts of problems, it creates a potential new problem between the citizens and the state itself: if the state has sufficient power to prevent conflict between its citizens, what is to stop the state from using this power against the citizens?

- The predatory view of the state focuses on the potential conflicts of interest that exist between citizens and the state. According to the predatory view, states emerge as an unintended consequence of the strategies employed by actors like lords and kings to seize and maintain their hold on power. In many respects, a state can be viewed as an "extortion racket" that threatens the well-being of its citizens and then sells them protection from itself.

OVERVIEW

In the previous chapter, we defined the domain of politics as the subset of human behavior that involves the use of power or influence. This includes any situation in which individuals cannot accomplish their goals without either trying to influence the behavior of others or trying to wrestle free from the influence exerted by others. As anyone who has tried to get his roommate to wash the dishes or his professor to change a grade knows, political behavior is ubiquitous. Politics affects virtually every aspect of our lives, but the study of comparative politics tends to focus on political behavior that occurs at the level of the state. In this chapter, we focus on the state; we explain what it is, where it comes from, and what its function is. To do this, we concentrate on two common views of the state—the contractarian view of the state and the predatory view of the state. According to the contractarian view, the state emerges to help individuals in situations in which decentralized cooperation is likely to be difficult. Although those who subscribe to this view see the creation of the state as a solution to conflicts of interest between citizens, it leads to a new problem—a conflict of interest between citizens and the state itself. The predatory view of the state looks squarely at this new conflict of interest. We will use the predatory view of the state as a lens through which to study the historical origins of the state in early modern Europe. We begin, though, by examining standard definitions of the state.

WHAT IS A STATE?

The most famous definition of the **state** comes from the German sociologist Max Weber ([1918] 1958, 78): The state, he said, "is a human community that (successfully) claims the *monopoly of the legitimate use of physical force* within a given territory [Weber's italics]." Weber's definition has several different components. One is that a state requires a "given territory." In some sense, this component of Weber's definition distinguishes "states" from "nations." At a basic level, a **nation** is a group of people who share some sort of common identity like a language, a religion, or an ethnicity—there is no obvious requirement that the nation be geographically located in a particular place, as a state must. For example, many Jews believed that they belonged to a nation long before Israel was established; indeed, many Jews in the interwar period in Europe advocated an extraterritorial view of the Jewish nation (Mendelsohn 1983).[1] Of course, the gradual emergence of the "**nation-state**" since the nineteenth century has led many to associate nations with states and, hence, with a given territory.[2] It is important to recognize,

> A **nation** is a group of people who share some sort of common identity like a language, religion, ethnicity, or shared history. A **nation-state** is a state in which a single nation predominates and the legal, social, demographic, and geographic boundaries of the state are connected in important ways to that nation.

---

1. Mendelsohn (1983) describes a struggle in interwar Europe between Zionists and those that preferred a religious or cultural definition of the Jewish nation. He notes that some Zionists even preferred an extraterritorial view of Jewish nationality.

2. The literature on the emergence of the nation-state is vast. Spruyt (1994) examines how the nation-state in Europe won out in a competition with other forms of political organization such as city-states and trade blocs like the Hanseatic League. Numerous other scholars have focused on whether states were created around nations or whether states created nations (Gellner 1983; Anderson 1991; Hobsbawm 1997; Hobsbawm and Ranger 1997). Whereas France is often portrayed as the stereotypical case of a state that built a nation (Weber 1976; Sahlins 1991; Ford 1993), Germany, under Bismarck, is depicted as the stereotypical case of a nation that built a state (Blackbourn and Eley 1984; Brubaker 1996).

however, that although the nation-state has become by far the most predominant political entity in the world, there are still "stateless nations," like the Kurds in Iraq, and "diasporic nations" without a clearly identified homeland, such as the Roma. As a result, nations and states remain distinct concepts even if they increasingly seem to occur together. On the whole, all definitions of a state since Weber's have retained his assertion that some kind of "given territory" is a required characteristic for a state.

A second component of Weber's definition is that the state must have a "monopoly on the *legitimate* use of physical force." This focus on "legitimacy" has troubled many scholars over the years because it is not always easy to determine what is, and is not, a legitimate use of force. In fact, we can all probably think of situations in which the use of force by the state lacks legitimacy. For example, many of you will think that the violence perpetrated by state officials on the civil rights protesters of the 1960s in the United States was illegitimate. Martin Luther King Jr. clearly considered certain actions by the U.S. state to be illegitimate when he criticized it for being "the greatest purveyor of violence in the world" during an anti–Vietnam War speech in New York City in 1967. These examples suggest that a state's use of force need not always be legitimate, at least in the minds of some of its citizens. It is because of this that subsequent scholars have largely dropped any reference to legitimacy in their definitions of the state.

Members of the Cambridge Nonviolent Action Committee watched by members of the National Guard at a protest on July 21, 1963, in Cambridge, Maryland.

A third component of Weber's definition is that the state must have a "*monopoly* on the legitimate use of physical force [italics added]." This focus on "monopoly" has also troubled many scholars. The primary reason for this is that it is relatively easy to think of examples in which nonstate actors have the ability to use physical force and in which this use of force might be considered legitimate. For instance, many people believe that the use of force by groups such as the Irish Republican Army in Northern Ireland, Hamas and Islamic Jihad in the Palestinian territories, or al-Qaida in Iraq and Afghanistan is a legitimate response to foreign occupation and repression. Similarly, many people believe that the violent resistance by the Islamic mujahideen to Soviet control in Afghanistan during the 1980s was legitimate. Of course, one man's freedom fighter is another man's terrorist and whether you agree that the violent actions of these nonstate groups are legitimate or not will probably depend on which side of the conflict you are on. Thus, it is not obvious that a state always has a "monopoly" on the legitimate use of force. It is for this reason that subsequent scholars have tended to shy away from using the term *monopoly* when defining the state's use of physical force.

Below are two more recent definitions of a state. The first is by a sociologist named Charles Tilly and the second is by the Nobel-laureate economist Douglass North.

> [States are] relatively centralized, differentiated organizations, the officials of which, more or less, successfully claim control over the chief concentrated means of violence within a population inhabiting a large contiguous territory. (Tilly 1985, 170)

> A state is an organization with a comparative advantage in violence, extending over a geographic area whose boundaries are determined by its power to tax constituents. (North 1981, 21)

Although these definitions differ from that provided by Weber in that they no longer refer to legitimacy or a monopoly over the use of force, they share his belief that all states must have a given territory and that they inherently rely on the threat of force to rule. That states rely on the threat of forceful coercion cannot be overemphasized. The economic historian Frederick Lane (1958) even refers to a state as a violence-producing enterprise. All states use at least the threat of force to organize public life. This is true whether we are referring to the harshest of dictatorships or the most laudable of democracies. The more obvious use of force by dictatorships should not hide the fact that state rule in democracies is also based on the threat of force (and often the use of force). To see this, think about how many of us would actually pay our taxes in full if the threat of imprisonment from the state for tax avoidance was not implicit. Even if the state uses force in the best interests of society and is authorized to use force by its citizens, we should never forget that it still rules by coercion.

That states rule through the use of force does not mean that they are all-powerful. As we noted earlier, states never perfectly monopolize force in any country. This explains why North claims only that states must have a "comparative advantage in violence" and Tilly that they have control "over the chief concentrated means of violence." Nor does the state's ability to use force necessarily mean that it can always enforce its will. All states tolerate some noncompliance. For example, the state does not punish every driver who runs a red light or every underage student who drinks alcohol. At some point, the marginal cost of enforcing laws becomes so great for any state that it prefers to allow some degree of noncompliance rather than spend more resources on improving law enforcement. The bottom line is that although various states justify coercion in different ways (through elections, through birthright, through religion, and so on), although they may use coercion for different purposes (to improve social welfare or to enrich themselves, and so on), and although their use of coercion may have different effects (higher levels of investment and economic growth or increased poverty and conflict, and so on), all states rely on, and use, coercion to rule.

A **state** is an entity that uses coercion and the threat of force to rule in a given territory. A **failed state** is a statelike entity that cannot coerce and is unable to successfully control the inhabitants of a given territory.

States that cannot coerce and are unable to use force to successfully control the inhabitants of a given territory are often described as **failed states** (King and Zeng 2001; Rotberg 2002; Millikin 2003). For example, observers frequently referred to countries like Afghanistan, Bosnia, the Democratic Republic of Congo, Haiti, Liberia, Sierra Leone, Somalia, and Yemen as failed states during the 1990s. Note that these states did not "fail" because they were unable to meet some policy objective; they "failed" because they were unable to provide the functions that define them as states—they were unable to coerce or successfully control the inhabitants in their territory. In effect, states in these countries failed to exist. But what does a failed state look like exactly?

A BRIEF HISTORY OF A FAILED STATE: SOMALIA

In a 2006 U.S. congressional hearing, it was pointed out that the African country of Somalia had become synonymous with "chaos" and, for the past sixteen years, had been considered to be a "classic failed state." [3] One scholar of failed states writes the following about his experience in Somalia:

> In 1993 I did emergency relief work in Baidoa, Somalia. This was a time when the Somali state had truly collapsed: there was no army, no state bureaucracy, no police force or courts, and no state to provide electricity, water, road maintenance, schools, or health services. I have a passport full of immigration exit and entry stamps from Wilson Airport in Nairobi [Kenya], the departure point for Baidoa, but there is no evidence that I was ever in Somalia because there was no immigration service to stamp my passport. I would get off the plane, and simply walk though the airport gates and go to town. As journalists often remarked, Somalia during this era had similarities with the *Mad Max/Road Warrior* movies: water wells guarded by armed gangs, diesel fuel was society's most precious commodity, and ubiquitous "technicals"—4WD vehicles with heavy machine guns mounted onto their rear trays—cruised the streets hoping for trouble. (Nest 2002, vi)

Since 1991 there have been at least fourteen attempts to establish a national government in Somalia, but none has been successful. At the time of writing this chapter, the Transitional Federal Government (TFG) is generally recognized by foreign countries as the legitimate Somali government. However, the TFG controls only a part of the central region of the country. Indeed, prior to an Ethiopian invasion in December 2006 on behalf of the transitional government, the TFG barely controlled the area immediately surrounding Baidoa. The TFG is officially recognized by international organizations like the United Nations, but its authority is not widely accepted throughout Somalia itself. Outside of the central region controlled by the TFG—with the aid of Ethiopian and African Union troops—rival militias continue to fight each other and the TFG has no national military with which to reestablish order.

How did this situation develop? Somalia represents one of the clearest recent examples of state failure, so it is worth briefly probing the history of its collapse in a little more detail. As is often the case with failed states, the failure of the Somali state was precipitated by a civil war in 1991 (Mukhtar 2003, 46). The origins of this civil war can be traced back to an interstate

---

3. For the full report of the hearing, see U.S. Congress (2006).

war with Ethiopia that was waged on and off from the late 1970s into the 1980s. One might even argue that the origins of state failure in Somalia can be traced even further back to the colonial period inasmuch as the arbitrary borders drawn by European powers at the time have generated ongoing interstate disputes in the region. It is worth noting that there is still no internationally recognized border between Somalia and Ethiopia; there is only a "provisional administrative line" between these countries.

The Somalia that we know today was formed through the coordinated merger of a former British protectorate called Somaliland and a former Italian trust territory called Somalia in 1960. Somaliland became independent from Britain on June 26, 1960, and Somalia became independent from Italy on June 30, 1960.[4] On July 1 of that year, the two legislatures from these countries met in a joint session to form what we now recognize as Somalia and elect a Somali president.

Democratic legislative elections were held in Somalia in 1964 and 1969 (Nohlen, Krennerich, and Thibaut 1999). Charges of electoral fraud accompanied the March 1969 elections, and many, including the army and the police, perceived the government that ultimately formed as nepotistic and corrupt. In October 1969 a military coup took place. The coup was precipitated by the assassination on October 15 of the Somali president, Shermaarke, by his own bodyguard, a member of a clan that was said to be badly treated by the president. When it became obvious that the Somali prime minister, Igaal, was about to appoint a new president from the same clan as the former president, the army stepped in. On October 21, 1969, the army took up strategic positions in Mogadishu, the capital, and established a new governing body called the Supreme Revolutionary Council (SRC) with General Mohamed Siad Barre as its president. The SRC banned political parties, abolished the National Assembly, suspended the constitution, and established a socialist dictatorship under the name of the Somali Democratic Republic.

Throughout the first few decades of independence, an important political issue for all Somali leaders was the presence of ethnic Somalis living outside the borders of Somalia in neighboring states. Indeed, one of the stated goals of the Siad Barre dictatorship was to support Somali national liberation movements in other countries and their eventual reunification with the rest of Somalia. The Somali leadership had designs on creating a "Greater Somalia," but neighboring countries were understandably less than enthusiastic about this plan. In 1977, after several border incidents and an attempt to gain control of Ethiopia's Ogaden region, a region with a large population of ethnic Somalis, Somalia went to war with Ethiopia.

This conflict between Ethiopia and Somalia is often brought up as an example of a "proxy war" fought between the United States and the Soviet Union during the cold war. Being a client state of one of the two superpowers during the cold war meant receiving money and weapons, something that was not always conducive to peaceful government policies, either

---

4. French Somaliland did not merge into Somalia but eventually won independence as Djibouti in 1977. The Somalis living in Djibouti have shown little interest in merging with their fellow Somalis to create a greater Somalia.

internally or externally. Traditionally, Ethiopia was thought to have a military advantage over Somalia. This changed, however, when the Soviet Union responded to Siad Barre's new ideological policy of "Scientific Socialism" by giving Somalia a significant amount of military aid in the early 1970s. For the most part, this aid was simply funneled to Siad Barre's supporters. At the same time, Ethiopia (then backed by the United States) was in the midst of domestic political turmoil. When a new Ethiopian government was established that seemed to be developing along Marxist-Leninist lines, the Soviet Union took notice, and in early 1977 the two countries began secret negotiations. In response to these Soviet overtures (and to U.S. pressure on Ethiopia to negotiate a settlement for its war with neighboring Eritrea), Ethiopia cut off its relationship with the United States. Thus, when Somalia decided to go to war with Ethiopia in the summer of 1977 over its territorial claims to the Ogaden region, the Soviet Union found itself in the awkward position of supplying military aid to both sides of the conflict. After attempts to broker a ceasefire failed, the Soviets turned their back on Somalia and began funneling additional aid to Ethiopia. Other Communist regimes offered assistance to Ethiopia as well. This led Somalia, in turn, to sever its links with the Soviet Union. Ethiopian and Cuban troops eventually pushed the Somali army back to its original position, and the war ended in 1978 with a Somali defeat and thousands of refugees fleeing from Ethiopia to Somalia.

The 1977–1978 Ogaden War had many important consequences. One was the significant weakening of the Somali military. Another was the increased dissatisfaction felt by many toward Siad Barre's leadership. Significantly, various dissident groups around the country now had ready access to weapons that had been provided by a variety of international sources. A third consequence was that Somalia switched cold war loyalties to the American side, becoming a client state of the United States in exchange for the Americans' being able to set up military bases on Somali territory (Lewis 2002).

Various disputes and conflicts with Ethiopia continued to arise in the 1980s. For example, Somali dissidents and Ethiopian army units made repeated forays across the border in the early 1980s. In 1982, Somali dissidents, backed by Ethiopian air support, briefly invaded central Somalia, an act that threatened to divide the country in two. Siad Barre declared a state of emergency in the war zone and called on Western nations to provide aid to repel the invasion. The United States helped by speeding up shipments of already promised weapons to prop up the regime.

Protests and dissident movements unhappy with Siad Barre's rule, many of which were encouraged by Ethiopian interests, continued to grow during the 1980s. Siad Barre responded to this opposition by unleashing a brutal wave of repression against Somali clans such as the Hawiye, Majeerteen, and the Isaaq (Mukhtar 2003). This wave of repression was carried out by an elite unit called the Red Berets (Duub Cas), made up of members of the president's Mareehaan clan. One consequence of this increased repression was a surge in refugee flows (often into Ethiopia). Given the cause of the refugee flows, foreign aid donors became unwilling to provide money to alleviate the refugee crisis that was growing in Somalia. In many parts of the country, murder and torture had become the normal state of affairs by the end of the 1980s. In July 1989 Somalia's Italian-born Roman Catholic bishop was assassinated; it is generally believed that the order for this assassination came from the presidential palace. In the same month, 450 Muslims demonstrating against the arrest of their spiritual leaders were killed; 2,000 were seriously injured. These "July Massacres" finally prompted the United States to start distancing itself from the Siad Barre regime. With the loss of U.S. support, the dictatorship became more desperate, with Siad Barre ordering ever more massacres of civilians in an attempt to hold on to power.

By 1990 Siad Barre's control over the entire territory of Somalia was waning, with some opposition figures referring to him mockingly as the "mayor of Mogadishu" because he dared not travel to other parts of the country (Lewis 2002). In January 1991 Siad Barre was finally driven out of Mogadishu by troops led by Mohamed Farah Aideed, a career army officer who at one point had been imprisoned by Barre. This turned out to be a significant turning point for Somalia, because it marked the collapse of the Somali state. Despite repeated attempts, Somalis have failed to reestablish an effective central government since the overthrow of the Siad Barre regime in 1991.

Aideed's forces quickly became embroiled in a battle for Mogadishu with the forces of the prominent politician Ali Mahdi Mohamed after the two were unable to agree on how to share power in the post–Siad Barre era. Mogadishu was split into two armed camps, north and south, and the battle "quickly engulfed what was left of the capital in a protracted bloodbath, killing an estimated 14,000 and wounding three times that number. . . . Ferocious fighting extended outside Mogadishu, spreading devastation and starvation through most of southern Somalia" (Lewis 2002, 264). Militia groups terrorized the population of the countryside, destroying crops and creating conditions for widespread famine—the United Nations estimated that as many as 300,000 people died as a result (Prendergast 1997). Nearly a million others sought refuge outside Somalia.

Various military factions, all armed to the teeth, were drawn into the conflict. The international media began referring to the militia leaders as "warlords." The civil war in the southern part of Somalia, with its devastating famine, attracted international attention.[5] In March 1992 a United Nations humanitarian mission to Somalia was organized following a tentative ceasefire. The appropriate international response to the situation was not clear, though, because of the continued violence. Although aid agencies were publicizing the Somali crisis, the "international response was slow, not least because of the novelty of the situation: a country without a government whose people desperately lacked food and medical supplies, which could only be delivered to the most needy by running the gauntlet of hostile, predatory militias abundantly equipped with modern weapons" (Lewis 2002, 267). By the

---

5. In the northwestern part of the country, the independent Republic of Somaliland was proclaimed in 1991 and has been relatively peaceful compared with the rest of Somalia. In the northeastern part of the country, Puntland was declared an autonomous state; it has been self-governing since 1998 but does not seek full independence. The Republic of Somaliland and Puntland do not agree on the exact placement of their common border. As of this writing, neither entity has been recognized by any foreign government.

summer of 1992, a million children were estimated to be at risk of malnutrition and 4.5 million to be in urgent need of food assistance.

Later that year, a military coalition backed by the United Nations and largely staffed by American troops went into Somalia under the code name "Operation Restore Hope." The initial success of the international coalition provoked a violent response from Somali factions who viewed the UN force as a threat to their own power. UN forces were regularly ambushed by Somali militiamen. In reaction to the ambushes, the American forces launched a series of attacks on Aideed's bases in Mogadishu. In the ensuing combat, two American helicopters were shot down. Eighteen American soldiers were killed and another seventy-nine were injured in the 1993 "Battle of Mogadishu." [6] Readers may be familiar with this incident from the book *Black Hawk Down* (later made into a movie) by the war correspondent Mark Bowden. At the time, the media broadcast images of an American soldier being dragged through the streets of Mogadishu. The American public called for an immediate withdrawal of U.S. forces from Somalia.[7] The withdrawal of the U.S. contingent forced the rest of the UN forces to leave as well.

By January 1995, all the international peacekeeping troops in Somalia had been evacuated. Fighting between various Somali militias continued, with new factions continually emerging to claim power. The most important of these new factions is the Supreme Council of Islamic Courts (SCIC).[8] Initially these were local Islamic courts set up by businessmen who needed a minimum level of law and order to deal with thieves and to enforce contracts. These courts (and their affiliated gunmen) then joined together and the SCIC began to be a major player in the southern section of the country.

In the years that followed the withdrawal of the UN mission, a series of unsuccessful peace talks was held. Talks held in Arta, Djibouti, in August 2000 saw Abdikassim Salad Hassan elected as a transitional president of Somalia by various clan leaders. Other clan leaders, unhappy with the results of the Arta talks, continued to fight in Somalia. In 2002 the transitional government signed a new ceasefire agreement at the fourteenth round of peace talks. It was two more years before the 275 members of parliament for the new Transitional Federal Government were sworn in, in August 2004. Because Somalia was deemed unsafe, the swearing-in ceremony was held in Nairobi, Kenya.

The SCIC stood as one of the main opponents to the TFG and by 2006 controlled much of the south, including the capital city of Mogadishu. One of its goals was the establishment of an Islamic state in Somalia. It is clear that the U.S. government considers the SCIC to be

---

6. Estimates of the number of Somalis that were killed range from 500 to more than 2,000. These casualties were a mixture of militiamen and local civilians caught in the crossfire.

7. The Battle of Mogadishu led to a profound change in U.S. foreign policy at the time, with the Clinton administration increasingly reluctant to intervene militarily in developing-country conflicts, such as the genocide of 800,000 Tutsis by Hutu militia groups in Rwanda in 1994 (Gourevitch 1998). It also led to a preference for using "air power alone," rather than ground troops, in the Balkan conflicts later in the 1990s. These policy changes, in turn, were reversed when the Bush administration decided to topple the Taliban regime in Afghanistan in 2001 and invade Iraq in 2003.

8. The Supreme Council of Islamic Courts is sometimes referred to as the Islamic Courts Union (ICU).

a serious potential terrorist threat and has actively supported opposition to it. Some intelligence analysts suspect that the individuals behind the bombings of U.S. embassies in Tanzania and Kenya in 1998 later went into hiding in the area of Somalia controlled by the SCIC.[9] It has been widely reported that the United States began backing several "secular" warlords in Mogadishu who were opposed to the expansion of SCIC rule. Many of these warlords styled themselves as a counterterrorism coalition, called the Alliance for the Restoration of Peace and Counter-Terrorism, in an attempt to obtain U.S. support. U.S. support for these warlords was opposed by the TFG at the time, with Prime Minister Mohamed Gedi stating, "We would prefer that the U.S. work with the transitional government and not with the criminals. . . . This is a dangerous game. Somalia is not a stable place and we want the U.S. in Somalia. But in a more constructive way. Clearly we have a common objective to stabilize Somalia, but the U.S. is using the wrong channels" (*Washington Post,* May 17, 2006). Despite reported U.S. backing, the warlords were defeated and driven out of Mogadishu in June 2006 by the SCIC.

The potential rise of an Islamic state led by the SCIC in Somalia and the example that it would provide to radical Islamic groups within its own borders caused great concern in neighboring Ethiopia. On October 25, 2006, Ethiopia's prime minister, Meles Zenawi, declared that Ethiopia was "technically at war" with the SCIC (see Map 4.1). Initially, Ethiopia intervened in Somalia by assisting and training the forces of the TFG. In late December, however, Ethiopian forces actually went into Somalia to back the TFG and rid the capital of the Supreme Council of Islamic Courts. Not only did the U.S. government publicly support this Ethiopian incursion into Somalia, but the U.S. Air Force attacked various SCIC targets with air strikes in January 2007. Although most of the SCIC has been removed from the capital, law and order has not been firmly established. In fact, Mogadishu has seen a peak in violence since the Ethiopian-led invasion. Groups of SCIC fighters have dispersed and are now fighting a guerrilla war against the Ethiopian and Somali government forces. In addition, existing conflicts between different Somali clans have reemerged, and the militias of various warlords have been seen setting up roadblocks to extort money from hapless motorists as they try to escape the capital. An April 2007 report from the British Broadcasting Corporation notes that since the beginning of 2007, at least 2,000 Somalis have died, mostly civilians caught in the crossfire.[10] Hundreds of thousands of Somalis have fled Mogadishu, creating a humanitarian disaster. Seventy-one percent of the Somali population is classified as undernourished, and the UN Office for the Coordination of Humanitarian Affairs reports that the number of Somalis in need of help is 1.8 million.

Where now? As many commentators have recently noted, Ethiopia is trapped. It wants to get out of Somalia, but it cannot do so until the "Islamist threat" is finally defeated. Unfortunately, the very presence of Ethiopian troops on Somali soil, as the brief history that we

---

9. See the reports on Somalia on the Council on Foreign Relations Web site, http://www.cfr.org/publication/13389. For a more detailed discussion of terrorist activities in this region, see Rotberg 2005.

10. Adam Mynott, "Somalia's 'Total Nightmare,' " *BBC News,* April 28, 2007. http://news.bbc.co.uk/1/hi/programmes/from_our_own_correspondent/6600027.stm.

MAP 4.1	**Somali Civil War, 2006**

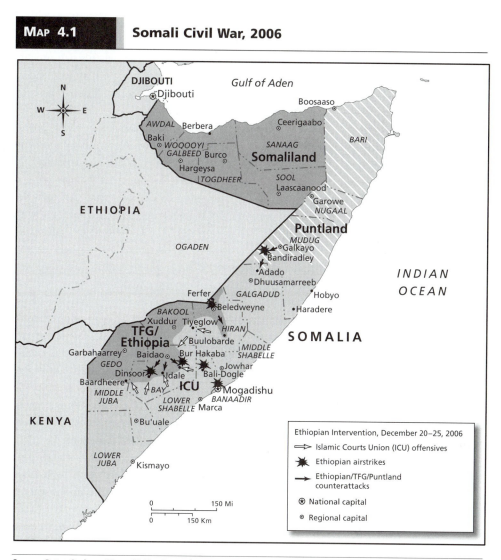

Source: Peter Corless, "Somali War, December 25, 2006 (rev. 1952)," available at http://fr.wikipedia.org/wiki/Image:Somali-war-12252006-1952.svg.

have provided should make clear, creates resentment among ordinary Somalis and acts as a useful recruiting tool for insurgents who say that they will die trying to rid their country of the Ethiopian invaders. As you can see, the establishment of a functioning Somali state still remains a long way off.

Why has the United States become involved in Somali affairs again? A major concern on the part of the American administration is that a Somalia controlled by the SCIC would be a safe haven for terrorists. At its most anarchic, of course, Somalia would not be a particularly safe place for anyone to hide, regroup, or set up training camps. The lack of a state does not, on its own, "make Somalia a potential bastion of terror. In a number of ways, the implanting of terrorist cells and the free movement of terrorists is always easier when a nation-state emerges from the chaos of collapse and forms a weak central government. It and its leaders become more, rather than less, susceptible to the blandishments and intimidations, and even to the arguments and ideologies, of terror and terrorists" (Rotberg 2005, 8–9). One can see a parallel here with Afghanistan, which became a particularly attractive safe haven for al-Qaida groups once the Taliban had taken control following the civil war in that country in 1995. It is worth noting at this point that the existence of failed states like Somalia and Afghanistan poses particular problems for countries like the United States that are worried about terrorism. If these failed states had well-functioning central governments, then the United States might be able to punish them for supporting terrorists or provide them with incentives to control terrorist activities. But what tools does the United States realistically have for disciplining failed states that harbor terrorists? The absence of a strong central government in failed states means that imposing sanctions or other punitive measures are unlikely to be effective. As a result, the United States and other countries frequently have little leverage over terrorist activities that occur in failed states other than to intervene directly.

To complicate matters in Somalia, the African country of Eritrea, which is embroiled in a difficult territorial dispute with Ethiopia, has been supporting various Islamic groups, including the SCIC. Eritrea has presumably been following the old adage that the "the enemy of my enemy is my friend." These interventions by Eritrea in Somali politics raise additional concerns within the international community that the political instability in Somalia could lead to a regional conflagration. They raise particular concerns for Washington because American relations with Eritrea are extremely poor and some in the intelligence community recommend that Eritrea be placed on the list of countries that sponsor terrorism.

Although international interest in Somalia often centers on concerns with terrorism, one should not forget or underestimate the humanitarian cost of state failure there. It has been estimated that since 1991 a million Somalis have died from fighting, famine, and disease.[11] The combination of violence and piracy has made it extremely difficult for international groups to provide humanitarian aid, such as emergency drugs and food, to the more than two million people in southern Somalia who need it. Drought is a common threat, and the absence of any actors who can maintain law and order prevents the distribution of water as well. More than a decade and a half of living without a state has meant a generation of Somali children growing up without proper schools, health care, or recreational activities. Somalia has one of the highest child mortality rates in the world. Roughly a tenth of all children die at birth, and a quarter of those who survive die before the age of five; many are subject to violence and extreme poverty. Indeed, according to the United Nations Development Fund, Somalia consistently ranks among the poorest countries in the world. Fully 43 percent

---

11. See "Country Profile: Somalia," *BBC News.* http://news.bbc.co.uk/2/hi/africa/country_profiles/1072592.stm (accessed September 4, 2007).

of Somalis are estimated to live under extreme poverty with the average per capita income in Somalia being less than $1 a day. Although many groups in the international community are concerned about Somalia for the humanitarian crisis it presents, it appears as though action is more likely to be taken because of fears that it could facilitate terrorist activities. Unfortunately, neither the international actors nor the citizens of Somalia have yet figured out how to successfully establish a national government that would be able to maintain law and order domestically, provide its population with basic services, and, ideally, not provide a safe haven for terrorists.

We have described the history of Somalia's failed state in some detail. But how typical is the Somali situation? Although it tends to stand out as a particularly disturbing case of state failure, it is, unfortunately, not unique. According to the 2007 Failed States Index, calculated by the think tank the Fund for Peace, Somalia ranks third in overall instability out of 177 countries; Sudan ranks first, whereas Norway ranks 177th.[12] The Failed States Index classifies countries of the world into four categories—Alert, Warning, Moderate, and Sustainable—based on their scores from twelve social, economic, and political indicators of state vulnerability. These indicators include things like (a) the massive movement of refugees creating complex humanitarian emergencies, (b) the legacy of vengeance-seeking group grievances, (c) uneven economic development along group lines, (d) the criminalization or delegitimization of the state, (e) progressive deterioration of public services, (f) the suspension or arbitrary application of the rule of law and the widespread violation of human rights, (g) the security apparatus operating as a state within a state, and (h) the intervention of other states or external political actors. Each indicator is scaled from 0 to 10, with 0 being the most stable and 10 being the least stable. A country's overall "vulnerability" or "instability" score, which runs from 0 to 120, is determined by simply adding up its scores on the twelve indicators.

In Map 4.2 we provide a graphic look at the distribution of failed or unstable states around the world. Appendix A, at the end of the book, contains the complete ranking of all 177 countries along with their individual scores on the twelve different indicators. Precisely where the lines can be drawn between a "failed state," a "collapsing state," a "state in danger," and a "stable state" is not entirely obvious, and presumably different country experts will not agree on how to classify all the countries in the world. What should be clear, though, is that there is a continuum of "stateness" or state effectiveness around the world. At one end of this continuum are countries like Iraq, Somalia, and Sudan, which are almost completely stateless and whose weak or nonexistent central governments are ineffective at controlling inhabitants throughout their territory. At the other end of the continuum are countries like Finland, Norway, and Sweden, which have strong and effective central governments that rule in an effectively unchallenged manner. In between are countries like Colombia, Russia, and Turkey, which have somewhat effective central governments that nonetheless fail to fully

---

12. For information and data on state failure, see the Web site of the State Failure Task Force at http://globalpolicy.gmu .edu/pitf/pitfpset.htm and the Failed States Index from the Fund for Peace at http://www.fundforpeace.org/programs/fsi/ fsindex.php.

MAP 4.2

Failed States Index, 2007

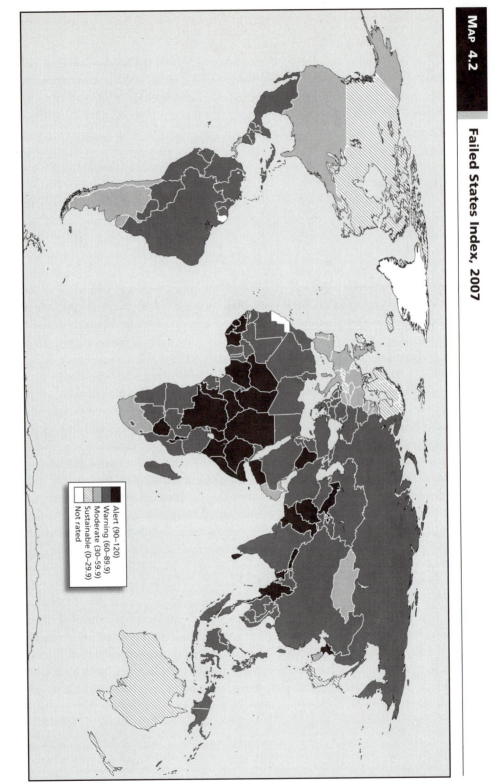

Alert (90–120)
Warning (60–89.9)
Moderate (30–59.9)
Sustainable (0–29.9)
Not rated

Source: Reproduced with permission from The Fund for Peace.

control all parts of their territory and that frequently leave specific areas ungoverned. In Colombia, the challenge to the state comes from drug cartels that control safe areas from which they engage in drug trafficking, kidnapping, and extortion; in Russia, it comes primarily from separatist movements like the one in the mountainous region of Chechnya; and in Turkey, it comes from Kurdish separatist groups in the southeastern part of the country. When comparing countries around the world, a famous political scientist, Samuel P. Huntington (1968, 1), once wrote that "[t]he most important political distinction among countries concerns not their form of government but their *degree of government*" (italics added). In many ways, it is hard to disagree with this claim.

The brief history of Somalia that we have just presented should clearly illustrate what life is like without a state. It should also underline the importance of understanding where the "state" actually comes from. This is a question that has drawn the attention of political theorists and political scientists for centuries. In what follows, we take a look at the **contractarian view of the state** and the quite different predatory view of the state.

> The **contractarian view of the state** sees the creation of the state as resulting from a social contract between individuals in the state of nature in which the state provides security in exchange for obedience from the citizen.

THE CONTRACTARIAN VIEW OF THE STATE

Early modern political thinkers like Hobbes ([1651] 1994), Locke ([1690] 1980), and Rousseau (1762) engaged in thought experiments in order to help them think more clearly about the role of the state in contemporary life. What, they asked, would social relationships among men (and, we would add, women) be like in a world without states or governments? How would people behave if they did not have to fear being punished by authorities if they stole things or engaged in opportunistic behavior at the expense of their neighbors? In effect, they asked what life would be like in a "state of nature," in which there was no government?[13]

The State of Nature

Thomas Hobbes famously described life in the **state of nature** as a "war of every man against every man" in which life was "solitary,

> The **state of nature** is a term used to describe situations in which there is no state.

poor, nasty, brutish, and short" (Hobbes [1651] 1994, chap. 13).[14] He believed that individuals in the state of nature faced a dilemma. Given a certain degree of equality between individuals,

---

13. We have described these theorists as engaging in thought experiments, but some have claimed that these theorists really believed that government was not a natural condition and that people had at one time actually lived in a state of nature (Baradat 2006, 65).

14. Hobbes's notion of the "state of nature" is remarkably similar to the notion of "anarchy" used by realist international relations scholars today. Just as Hobbes referred to the condition in which individuals lived in the absence of government as the state of nature, realist international relations scholars refer to the international environment in which individual states live in the absence of a world government as anarchy (Waltz 1979). Like Hobbes, realist international relations scholars believe that anarchy is characterized by a security dilemma in which states are constantly engaged in conflict as they seek to increase their power.

each citizen recognized that he could gain by attacking his neighbor in a moment of vulnerability (say, while his neighbor slept). Each citizen knew, however, that his neighbors were probably thinking exactly the same thing about him. Hobbes believed that even the weakest individual in the state of nature had enough power to overcome the strongest, either by trickery or by joining forces with others threatened by the power of the strongest, if he chose (chap. 13). In this type of situation, it is clear that the individuals in the state of nature would all be better off if they abstained from taking advantage of their neighbors than they would be in a "war of all against all." Still, if an act of violence or theft were to take place, it would obviously be far better to be the attacker or thief than the victim. Without a "common power to keep them all in awe," this was the dilemma that faced individuals in the state of nature (chap. 13).

You might think that this discussion is really about barbarous individuals and that it is, therefore, quite remote from the concerns of elevated individuals such as ourselves. It is important to recognize, however, that social contract theorists like Hobbes, Locke, and Rousseau did not claim that life in the state of nature was problematic because of any particular moral failing on the part of the individuals involved. In fact, Jean Jacques Rousseau worried about "modern" man and had quite romantic notions about the "noble savages" that we might expect to find in the state of nature. Social contract theorists argued that there was something fundamental about the very structure of the situation characterizing the state of nature that made it difficult for citizens to behave themselves.

Game theory can be used to shed light on the structural aspects of the state of nature that might lead to problems. We begin by describing a stylized interaction between two individuals in the state of nature using Hobbes's ([1651] 1994, chap. 13) own language. Imagine that there are two individuals who both desire "the same thing [say, a plot of land], which nevertheless they cannot both enjoy." In the absence of protection from a third-party enforcer, an "invader hath no more to fear than another man's single power." Consequently, "if one plants, sows, builds, or possesses a convenient seat, others may probably be expected to come prepared with forces united, to dispossess and deprive him, not only of the fruit of his labour, but also of his life or liberty. And the invader again is in the like danger of another." Under these conditions, "there is no place for industry" because the industrious have no confidence that they will be able to control the fruit of their labor.

What is Hobbes really saying here? In this stylized interaction, both men have essentially two actions that they can take: they can choose to "steal" or they can choose to "forbear." [15] If a man forbears, then he is essentially choosing to earn a living by doing something productive rather than by stealing. What should the men do? The choice facing each man is complicated because one man's choice of what to do depends on what he thinks the other man will do. As we saw in the last chapter, game theory is an extremely useful tool for analyzing these types of strategic situations. We can think of this interaction between two men in the state of nature as a game. In the previous chapter, we used an extensive form game to

---

15. To the extent that "steal" presupposes the concept of property, this choice in the state of nature is slightly inaccurate. This is because Hobbes explicitly denies that the concept of property can exist in the state of nature. A more accurate term, then, might be "dispossess."

examine how individuals respond to deleterious changes in their environment. In this chapter, we are going to use a normal, or strategic, form game to examine how individuals might behave in the state of nature. Recall that an extensive form game employs a game tree that allows us to see what happens when the players take turns to make decisions; that is, there is a specific sequence of play as illustrated by the branches and decision nodes in the game tree.

In contrast, a normal or strategic form game employs a **payoff matrix** that allows us to see what happens when the players make decisions at the same time; that is, decisions are made simultaneously in normal form games rather than sequentially.[16]

> A **payoff matrix** is a table that represents the strategies and payoffs available to players in strategic or normal form games.

Figure 4.1 illustrates the "empty" payoff matrix of the normal form game that captures our stylized interaction between two men, whom we'll call A and B, in the Hobbesian state of nature. Each player must decide whether to steal or forbear. There are four possible outcomes: both players forbear (top left cell), both players steal (bottom right cell), player A steals but player B forbears (bottom left cell), and player A forbears but player B steals (top right cell).

What do you expect the players to do in this game? As before, you cannot really answer this question without knowing how much each of the players values the possible outcomes. In other words, you need to know the payoffs that the players associate with each outcome. Based on what Hobbes says, how do you think that the players might rank each outcome? One interpretation is that each player's best outcome is to steal the other actor's belongings and to keep his own. In other words, a player's best outcome occurs when he steals and the other player forbears. The worst outcome is the exact opposite of this; that is, he forbears and the other player steals his belongings. Between these two fates are the outcomes in which

FIGURE 4.1   **State of Nature Game without Payoffs**

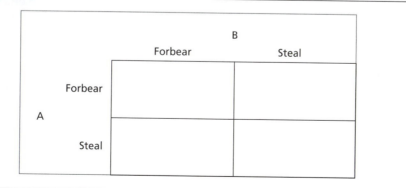

---

16. Extensive form and normal form games are connected in that all normal form games can be represented as extensive form games.

both players forbear and both steal. It seems clear from Hobbes's description of the state of nature that individuals would prefer the former (both forbear) to the latter (both steal). They would prefer this outcome because when both actors choose to "steal" they live in a state of war, which prevents them from engaging in productive activities and makes them reluctant to invest in things that would make their lives better.

> A **preference ordering** indicates how a player ranks the possible outcomes of a game.

Based on Hobbes's view of the state of nature, we can provide a **preference ordering** for each player over the four possible outcomes; that is, we can determine how both players would rank the outcomes. Player A's preference ordering over the four outcomes is:

- (Steal; Forbear) ≻ (Forbear; Forbear) ≻ (Steal; Steal) ≻ (Forbear; Steal),

and player B's preference ordering is:

- (Forbear; Steal) ≻ (Forbear; Forbear) ≻ (Steal; Steal) ≻ (Steal; Forbear),

where player A's action is given first, player B's action is given second, and "≻" means "is strictly preferred to." Given that there are four possible outcomes, we can assign the number 4 to each player's most preferred outcome, 3 to the second preferred outcome, 2 to the third preferred outcome, and 1 to the least preferred outcome. These payoffs are called **ordinal payoffs** because they tell us about the order in which the players rank each of the outcomes.

> **Ordinal payoffs** allow us to know how a player ranks the possible outcomes; they do not tell us how much more a player prefers one outcome to another.

Note that ordinal payoffs can tell us only whether one outcome is preferred by a player to another (the one with the higher number); they cannot tell us how much more the player prefers one outcome to the other.[17] In other words, we can say that an outcome worth 4 is preferred to an outcome worth 1; however, we cannot say that the outcome worth 4 is preferred four times as much as the outcome worth 1.

We can now add these payoffs to the normal form game shown in Figure 4.1. The new game is shown in Figure 4.2. Player A's (the row player's) payoffs are shown first in each cell; player B's (the column player's) payoffs are shown second. A comma separates the payoffs for the players in each cell. Thus, player A receives a payoff of 1 if he forbears and player B steals; player B receives a payoff of 4 in this situation. Player A receives a payoff of 4 if he steals and player B forbears; player B receives a payoff of 1 in this situation. Now that we have the payoffs, we can try to figure out what the players will do.

We solve this State of Nature Game for Nash equilibria.[18] Recall from Chapter 3 that a Nash equilibrium is a set of strategies such that no player has an incentive to unilaterally change his

---

17. As a result, we could use any sequence of numbers that retains the theorized ranking of the outcomes. For example, we could have chosen the numbers 50, 12, 1, −10 to indicate how the players rank the four possible outcomes in the game, because these numbers retain the correct preference ordering. Using the numbers 4, 3, 2, and 1 is just simpler.

18. We refer to this game as a State of Nature Game because of the topic under discussion. As we note later in the chapter (pp. 125–128), however, games with this same payoff structure are more familiarly known as Prisoner's Dilemma games. Prisoner's Dilemma games are used widely in political science to examine a whole host of phenomena, ranging from arms races and democratic transitions to resource exploitation and international cooperation. They are also commonly used in other disciplines such as biology, economics, and sociology.

		B	
		Forbear	Steal
	Forbear	3, 3	1, 4
A			
	Steal	4, 1	2, 2

Note: Player A's (the row player's) payoffs are shown first in each cell; player B's (the column player's) payoffs are shown second. A comma separates the payoffs for the players in each cell.

mind in light of what the other player is doing. We often say that both players are playing **best replies** in a Nash equilibrium—each player is doing the best that he can given what the other player is doing. If we think in terms of "best replies," it is quite easy to find Nash equilibria in

> A **best reply** is the action that yields the highest payoff given what the other player is doing.

normal form games like the one in Figure 4.2. We show you how to do this step-by-step. Just before the problem section at the end of this chapter, we review the whole process of constructing and solving normal form games again.

Step one is to put yourself in the shoes of one of the players (say, player A). Ask yourself, "What is my best reply (forbear or steal) if player B chooses to forbear?" We are now just looking at the left-hand column where player B chooses to forbear. If you choose to forbear, you will get a payoff of 3, and if you choose to steal, you will get a payoff of 4. Thus, your best reply to player B's forbearing is for you to steal. We indicate this by placing a line under the number 4. This is shown in Figure 4.3.

Now ask yourself, "What is my best reply if player B chooses to steal?" We are now just looking at the right-hand column where player B chooses to steal. If you choose to forbear, you will get a payoff of 1, and if you choose to steal, you will get a payoff of 2. Thus, your best reply to player B's stealing is for you to steal as well. We indicate this by placing a line under the 2. This is shown in Figure 4.4. You have now identified the best replies for player A to any choice made by player B.

Step two is to put yourself in the shoes of the other player, in this case player B. Ask yourself, "What is my best reply (forbear or steal) if player A chooses to forbear?" We are now just looking at the top row where player A chooses to forbear. If you choose to forbear, you will get a payoff of 3, and if you choose to steal, you will get a payoff of 4 (recall that you are look-

 **Solving the State of Nature Game I**

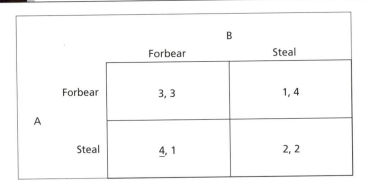

		B	
		Forbear	Steal
A	Forbear	3, 3	1, 4
	Steal	<u>4</u>, 1	2, 2

Note: Player A's (the row player's) payoffs are shown first in each cell; player B's (the column player's) payoffs are shown second. A comma separates the payoffs for the players in each cell. Payoffs associated with best replies are underlined.

ing at the second number in each cell, because you are now player B). Thus, your best reply to player A's forbearing is for you to steal. We indicate this by placing a line under the 4. We show this in Figure 4.5.

Now ask yourself, "What is my best reply if player A chooses to steal?" We are now just looking at the bottom row where player A chooses to steal. If you choose to forbear, you will get a payoff of 1, and if you choose to steal, you will get a payoff of 2. Thus, your best reply

FIGURE 4.4   **Solving the State of Nature Game II**

		B	
		Forbear	Steal
A	Forbear	3, 3	1, 4
	Steal	<u>4</u>, 1	2, <u>2</u>

Note: Player A's (the row player's) payoffs are shown first in each cell; player B's (the column player's) payoffs are shown second. A comma separates the payoffs for the players in each cell. Payoffs associated with best replies are underlined.

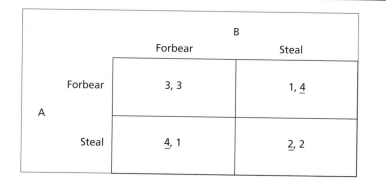

FIGURE 4.5	**Solving the State of Nature Game III**

Note: Player A's (the row player's) payoffs are shown first in each cell; player B's (the column player's) payoffs are shown second. A comma separates the payoffs for the players in each cell. Payoffs associated with best replies are underlined.

to player A's stealing is for you to steal as well. We indicate this by placing a line under the 2. This is shown in Figure 4.6. You have now identified the best replies for player B to any choice made by player A.

Recall that a Nash equilibrium is a set of strategies in which each player is making a best reply. Thus, to locate any Nash equilibrium, you need only look at the payoff matrix in Figure 4.6 for cells in which both numbers are underlined, that is, those in which both players are playing best replies. As you can see, the one cell in which both numbers are underlined is the

FIGURE 4.6	**Solving the State of Nature Game IV**

The matrix shows:

	B: Forbear	B: Steal
A: Forbear	3,3	1, <u>4</u>
A: Steal	<u>4</u>, 1	<u>2</u>, <u>2</u>

Note: Player A's (the row player's) payoffs are shown first in each cell; player B's (the column player's) payoffs are shown second. A comma separates the payoffs for the players in each cell. Payoffs associated with best replies are underlined.

one in which both players choose to steal. Thus, the unique Nash equilibrium in our State of Nature Game is (Steal; Steal).[19] The outcome of the game is that both players steal and the payoff to each player is 2.

An interesting feature of this particular game is that both players choose to steal (because they are better off doing so) no matter what the other player chooses. When this occurs, we say that both players have a **dominant strategy**—in this case their dominant strategy is to steal. Because both players have dominant strategies, we have what is known as a **dominant-strategy Nash equilibrium.** Thus, the expected outcome from our State of Nature Game is that forbearance will be unlikely and that theft will be endemic.[20] This is precisely why Hobbes described life in the state of nature as a "war of every man against every man" in which life was "solitary, poor, nasty, brutish, and short."

> A player has a **dominant strategy** if that strategy is a best reply to all of the other player's strategies. A **dominant-strategy Nash equilibrium** occurs when both players have a dominant strategy.

Keep in mind that we have simplified the state of nature quite considerably here in order to isolate only the most important aspects of the environment in which player A and player B find themselves. For example, it is hard to imagine a world in which theft and mutual predation are constantly occurring. In the real world, even the weak are able to fend off attack some of the time. When both actors are equal in strength, attacks will be successful only in moments of temporary vulnerability. Nevertheless, in the absence of someone to keep the actors in a permanent state of "awe," attacks will come when the opportunity arises. As a result, individuals will live in a persistent state of fear that can be debilitating, even in moments of relative calm.

Although this "abstract" state of nature probably seems remote from many of our own experiences, recall the troubled recent history of Somalia. Many commentators have described the environment in Somalia as a modern-day version of Hobbes's state of nature. Similar descriptions might be given of other situations in which no single actor is able to "awe" everyone in society, such as Iraq during the U.S. occupation, the Darfur region in Sudan, south central Los Angeles and New York City in the 1980s, New Orleans directly after Hurricane Katrina in 2005, or suburban New Jersey in the world of the Sopranos. In fact, according to the economic historian and Nobel laureate Robert Fogel, the world described by Hobbes as the absence of invention, trade, arts, and letters fairly accurately describes most of human history (Fogel 2004). Consider that prior to the first agricultural revolution in roughly 10,000 B.C., the life expectancy for our hunter-gatherer ancestors was estimated at

---

19. In this particular game, there is only one Nash equilibrium. Other games with different payoff structures, however, may have no equilibria in pure strategies or multiple equilibria—there is no rule that there will always be a unique equilibrium.

20. This is the expected outcome when the State of Nature Game is played once. But what do you think happens if player A and player B get to play the game over and over again? Do you think things change? To find out, you'll have to look at Box 4.1 "Can Cooperation Occur Without the State" at the end of the chapter (p. 141).

no more than twenty-five years. Even by 1700, life expectancy in England, the second richest country in the world at the time after the Netherlands, was still only thirty-seven years.

When we solved the State of Nature Game for the Nash equilibrium, you may have noticed something that seemed odd. The Nash equilibrium outcome from this game happens to be the second worst outcome for both players. Indeed, both players could be made better off if they chose to forbear—they would both get 3 instead of the 2 they get from both stealing in the Nash equilibrium. For this reason, the absence of cooperation represents a dilemma—individual rationality leads actors to an outcome that they both agree is inferior to an alternative outcome. The class of problems in which individual rationality produces outcomes that everyone in society sees as inferior has fascinated political thinkers since at least the time of Hobbes. One of the many ways in which they are interesting is that it doesn't seem to be enough for the players to recognize their mutually destructive behavior for cooperation to occur. Ask yourself what would happen if player A and player B met with each other one sunny afternoon and promised not to steal from each other because this would make them both better off. Do you think that they would feel comforted by such promises as they lay down to sleep that night?

Part of the problem is that each actor may come to feel that they are being taken advantage of. What if you are the only one that is sticking to your promise of good behavior? If your opponent breaks his promise and starts to steal, your best response is to stop forbearing and start stealing as well. As the State of Nature Game illustrates, you will increase your payoff from 1 to 2 by doing this. But part of the problem is that you also have an incentive to steal even if you think that your opponent is going to keep his promise. Say you knew for sure that your opponent was going to forbear and that, under these circumstances, you could benefit. What would you do? As the State of Nature Game illustrates, you will choose to break your promise to forbear and start stealing, because this will increase your payoff from 3 to 4. Thus, promising to stop stealing because it is mutually destructive is not sufficient to actually stop the players from stealing. As Garrett Hardin (1968) points out, relying on promises of good behavior or moral suasion may actually have perverse evolutionary consequences in any case. If the world is truly set up as in the State of Nature Game, then individuals who are swayed by entreaties to "behave" and to "do unto others as you would have them do unto you" are not likely to survive long enough to pass such ideas on to their progeny (whether one thinks that the mechanism of transmission is genetics or socialization). In effect, Hardin suggests that to rely on moral suasion is to run the risk that moral people will be eliminated from society.

Civil Society and the Social Contract

Hobbes's solution to the problems that individuals experience in the state of nature was to create someone or something—the "Sovereign"—that had sufficient force that people would stand in awe of it. Like us, Hobbes realized that simply promising not to steal would be insufficient to prevent people from stealing. Instead, he believed that "there must be

A **natural right** is a universal right that is inherent in the nature of living beings; as such, a natural right can exist even in the state of nature. A **civil right** does not arise naturally but is instead created by the state through laws; as such, a civil right cannot exist in the state of nature.

A **social contract** is an implicit agreement among individuals in the state of nature to create and empower the state. In doing so, it outlines the rights and responsibilities of the state and the citizens in regard to each other.

some coercive power to compel men equally to the performance of their covenants, by the terror of some punishment greater than the benefit they expect by breach of their covenant" (Hobbes [1651] 1994, chap. 15). In other words, Hobbes wanted a sovereign that could "force" people to forbear—for their own good, of course. The sovereign was to be created by an implicit **social contract** between individuals in the state of nature. Individuals would "contract" with each other to give up their **natural rights** (rights given to them by nature) in exchange for **civil rights** (rights given to them by laws) that would be protected by the sovereign.[21] In effect, individuals would give up what they had to the sovereign in return for protection.

Hobbes believed that life in the state of nature was sufficiently bad that individuals would, and should, be willing to transfer everything they had to the sovereign in exchange for protection. In many ways, Hobbes's pessimistic view of the state of nature helps to explain why so many Afghans and Somalis were quick to welcome the "law and order" brought by the Taliban and the Supreme Council of Islamic Courts in their respective countries even though they may have strongly disagreed with the ideologies of these particular movements. Other social contract theorists, like Jean Jacques Rousseau and John Locke, were more hopeful that individuals in the state of nature could find ways to achieve limited degrees of cooperation. As a result, these latter theorists believed that the extent to which individuals in the state of nature should delegate authority to a "third-party enforcer" such as the sovereign should always be evaluated in light of the particular conditions in which they found themselves. Although there are important differences between them, social contract theorists all view the state as a third-party enforcer who can dole out punishments to individuals who engage in socially destructive behavior that violates the social contract. These punishments were to be structured in such a way that "steal" would no longer be a dominant strategy for individuals in society. How does this happen?

Figure 4.7 illustrates the exact same stylized interaction between two people, A and B, as we saw in the state of nature, except that now there is a "passive player"—the state—lurking in the background who has sufficient physical force to punish those people if they choose to steal rather than forbear. We refer to this as the Civil Society Game because social contract theorists use the term *civil society* to describe the situation in which individuals live with a state. Again, each player must decide whether to steal or forbear. The state will dole out a

---

21. Although social contract theorists use the language of "contracts," it should be noted that the social contract does not necessarily share some of the defining characteristics of contracts—universal agreement, voluntary agreement, and third-party enforcement. For example, the state may be created in the face of opposition by some individuals—universal agreement may be violated. Individuals who disagree with the state are also pressured under the threat of physical force to enter into it and obey it—voluntary agreement may be violated. There is also no third-party enforcer to the social contract, because the sovereign does not exist until the contract is accepted—third-party enforcement may be violated.

| FIGURE 4.7 | **Civil Society Game** |

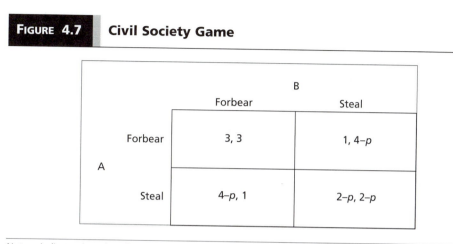

Note: p indicates the value of the punishment doled out by the state to anyone who steals.

punishment of value p to anyone who steals. We assume, for simplicity, that the state can see every infraction by the players and always doles out this punishment in response. The four possible outcomes are the same as before: both players forbear, both players steal, player A steals but player B forbears, and player A forbears but player B steals. To keep the discussion that follows as simple as possible, we will now treat the payoffs in the Civil Society Game as though they were **cardinal payoffs.** Unlike ordinal payoffs, cardinal payoffs tell us exactly

> **Cardinal payoffs** allow us to know how much more the players prefer one outcome to another.

how much more a player values one outcome compared with another. In other words, a player values an outcome with a payoff of 4 four times as much as an outcome with a payoff of 1. Now that we have determined the payoff matrix for the Civil Society Game, we can examine whether the creation of a state that can dole out punishments is sufficient to induce good behavior on the part of the individuals in question? As is often the case in this book, the answer is "it depends."

We can see exactly what it depends on by solving the Civil Society Game for Nash equilibria in the same way that we solved the State of Nature Game earlier. Recall that you start by putting yourself in the shoes of one of the players (say, player A). Ask yourself, "What is my best reply (forbear or steal) if player B chooses to forbear?" If you choose to forbear, you will get a payoff of 3, and if you choose to steal, you will get a payoff of $4 - p$ (remember that player A's payoffs in each cell are shown first and player B's payoffs second). It is relatively easy to see that you will choose to forbear if $3 > 4 - p$. This means that player A can be encouraged to give up his criminal ways if the state sets the punishment for stealing sufficiently high. How high is sufficiently high? A tiny bit of high school algebra should convince you that as long as the punishment is greater than 1 (that is, bigger than the difference between 4 and 3), then player A will choose to forbear.

Presumably, the state has a relatively easy job in getting player A to forbear if player B is going to forbear. But what if player B steals? Put yourself in the shoes of player A again and ask yourself, "What is my best reply if player B chooses to steal?" If you choose to forbear, you will get a payoff of 1 and if you choose to steal, you will get a payoff of $2 - p$. It is relatively easy to see that you will choose to forbear if $1 > 2 - p$. This means that as long as the state chooses a punishment greater than 1 (that is, bigger than the difference between 2 and 1), player A will "do the right thing" and forbear.

Because player B's payoffs are symmetrical to player A's—they are the same in the equivalent situation—we know that player B will also choose to forbear under the same conditions that player A chooses to forbear; namely, when $p > 1$. Figure 4.8 indicates the best replies for players A and B when $p > 1$. As you can see, when the punishment doled out by the state is sufficiently high ($p > 1$), the unique Nash equilibrium is (Forbear; Forbear). The outcome is that both players forbear and the payoff to each player is 3. Note that both players now have a dominant strategy to forbear. In other words, as long as the punishment level imposed by the state is sufficiently high, players will choose to forbear no matter what the other player decides to do.

It seems that by creating a third-party enforcer (the state) that dutifully doles out punishments for bad behavior, we can get individuals to give up the sorts of behavior that made life in the state of nature "solitary, poor, nasty, brutish, and short." Problem solved, right? Well, as you might suspect, the fact that we're still studying politics some three hundred and fifty years after Hobbes wrote suggests that there are some problems with his solution. Start by asking yourself why anyone would want to be the sovereign and why he or she would be willing to do us all a favor by acting as our policeman.

One common answer to this question portrays the members of civil society as being engaged in an exchange relationship with the sovereign. In effect, the sovereign agrees to police us in

---

FIGURE 4.8   **Civil Society Game when *p* > 1**

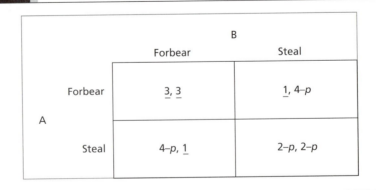

Note: p = the value of the punishment doled out by the state to anyone who steals. Payoffs associated with best replies are underlined.

exchange for taxes that citizens pay.[22] One of the uses of this taxation will be to build up the state's "comparative advantage in violence" and its "control over the chief concentrated means of violence" so that it can keep the citizens in awe and carry out its duties as a state. Given that a sovereign will demand tax revenue to carry out his job, it is not immediately obvious that the citizens will choose to leave the state of nature for civil society; much will depend on the level of taxation imposed by the state. In other words, citizens will not always choose to create a state.

To illustrate this point, compare our State of Nature and our Civil Society Games in Figure 4.9. The Civil Society Game now illustrates that the state will impose a tax of size *t* on the citizens for allowing them to live in civil society. We indicate this by subtracting *t* from the payoffs of each player in each cell. Note, though, that because the citizen must pay the tax in every cell of the game, the expected outcome of the Civil Society Game does not

FIGURE 4.9 **Choosing between the State of Nature and Civil Society**

State of Nature

A \ B	Forbear	Steal
Forbear	3, 3	1, 4
Steal	4, 1	2, 2

Civil Society

A \ B	Forbear	Steal
Forbear	$3-t$, $3-t$	$1-t$, $4-t$
Steal	$4-p-t$, $1-t$	$2-p-t$, $2-p-t$

Note: p = the value of the punishment doled out by the state to anyone who steals; t = the value of the tax imposed by the state. It is assumed that $p > 1$. Payoffs associated with best replies are underlined.

22. Most obviously, we can think of these "taxes" as money that citizens give to the state in return for security. It is possible, however, to conceptualize these taxes much more broadly. For example, we might think of required behavioral patterns—for example, regularly attending religious institutions or following dress codes such as wearing a burqa—as a kind of taxation that citizens give in exchange for state-provided security.

change—both players will still choose to forbear (check this for yourself). The expected outcomes of the two games are shown in the shaded cells.

Now ask yourself, "Under what conditions will citizens prefer to leave the state of nature and enter civil society?" The citizen can decide whether to leave the state of nature by comparing the payoffs she expects to receive from playing each game. As you can see, the citizen will get a payoff of 2 if she chooses to remain in the state of nature and a payoff of $3 - t$ if she chooses to live in civil society. It is easy to see that the citizen will prefer to leave the state of nature and live in civil society if $3 - t > 2$. This means that as long as the state does not charge a tax rate larger than 1 (that is, bigger than the difference between 3 and 2), the citizen will prefer to create a state and live in civil society.

Thus, for the state to be a solution to the state of nature as social contract theorists claim, it must be the case that (a) the punishment imposed by the state for stealing is sufficiently large that individuals prefer to forbear rather than steal and (b) that the taxation rate charged by the state for acting as the policeman is not so large that individuals prefer the state of nature to civil society.[23] With the particular payoffs that we have used in our State of Nature Game and Civil Society Game (Figure 4.9), this requires that $p > 1$ and $t < 1$.

This comparison between the responsibilities that the state imposes on its citizens (here thought of in terms of a level of taxation) and the benefits that the citizen can obtain from living in civil society is central to the very nature of politics. Thinkers who see the state of nature as dire are going to expect citizens to accept a draconian set of responsibilities in exchange for the "protection" that the state provides. In contrast, those who see civil society as a mere convenience over a workable, if inefficient, state of nature, are going to place much greater restrictions on what the state can ask of its citizens. It is, perhaps, not an accident that Hobbes was writing at the end of a long period of religious war in Europe and civil war in his home country. It was because he had had a firsthand glimpse of what the "war of every man against every man" looked like that he believed that the difference between civil society and the state of nature was effectively infinite. For Hobbes, almost any level of taxation that the state might choose to levy on its citizens in exchange for protection looked like a good deal. You might think that many of the people living in Somalia right now share a similar view of the world. In contrast, Thomas Jefferson—borrowing from social contract theorists like John Locke—believed, from the relative calm of Monticello, that we had a natural right (that is, the possibility of obtaining in the state of nature) to "life, liberty, and the pursuit of happiness," and that our commitment to the state was so

---

23. This point may throw light on the continued absence of a Somali state. For example, Leesom (2006) has recently argued that state taxation in all its forms under the Siad Barre regime was so great that many people's social welfare was actually lower when the Somali state existed than it is right now. In effect, he claims that the Somali state did more harm than good. To support his case, Leesom presents evidence suggesting that things like life expectancy, immunization rates, child mortality rates, and access to health-care facilities are all better now than they were under the Siad Barre dictatorship. To the extent that Leesom is providing an accurate assessment of the state of affairs in Somalia—and we should note that many scholars of African politics disagree with his data—individual Somalis may not be in a rush to reestablish civil society and strengthen the power of the Transitional Federal Government.

conditional that we should probably engage in revolution, or at least the rewriting of the Constitution, every couple of decades.

The reader is likely to have noticed that contemporary disputes in the United States and elsewhere over whether we should reduce civil liberties by giving more power to the state in an attempt to better protect ourselves against terrorist threats directly echo this historical debate between such scholars as Hobbes and Jefferson. Those politicians who argue that the threat of terrorism warrants a reduction in our civil liberties on the grounds that freedom means little without security are taking a distinctly Hobbesian view of the world. Whether you ultimately agree more with Hobbes or Jefferson, it seems clear that although the creation of the state may solve the political problem we have with each other, it may also create a potential new problem between us and the state. Put simply, if we surrender control over the means of violence to the state, what is to prevent the state from using this power against us? As some have put it, "Who will guard the guardian?" [24] At the very least, once the state has developed a "comparative advantage" in the use of violence, we would expect a renegotiation of the social contract that, at a minimum, would set the tax rate so high as to leave the citizen indifferent between living in the state of nature and living in civil society. It is the fear that this might occur that drives civil libertarians around the world to challenge ongoing attempts to locate ever-increasing amounts of power in the hands of the state. As you can see, one of the grim, but true, implications of many game-theoretic models is that solutions to political problems frequently lead to changes in behavior that erase the benefits of those solutions. The sovereign: can't live with him, can't live without him.

THE PREDATORY VIEW OF THE STATE

Whereas the contractarian view of the state focuses on the conflicts of interest that exist between individuals, the **predatory view of the state** focuses more on the potential conflicts of interest that exist between citizens and the state. Scholars who employ a predatory view of the state seek to understand the conditions under which the state can be expected to enforce rules

> The **predatory view of the state** holds that states that exercise an effective control over the use of violence are in a position to threaten the security of citizens. This makes it possible for them to exploit the citizens that, according to the social contract view of the state, they have a duty to protect.

and foster cooperation rather than use its "comparative advantage in violence" to prey upon the citizenry. According to the predatory view of the state, rulers can be viewed as similar to individuals in the state of nature. They are so because they face their own sort of security dilemma in that they have potential rivals constantly vying to take their place. The concern for security on the part of rulers leads them to use their power to extract resources from others, both because these resources can be used to help ensure their continued existence and because leaving these resources in the hands of rivals is potentially dangerous.

---

24. The original quotation, "Quis custodiet ipsos custodies?" is from Juvenal, *Satire* IV ("On Women").

The sociologist Charles Tilly (1985) went as far as to say that states resemble a form of organized crime and should be viewed as extortion rackets. Why? As with the contract theory of the state, the predatory approach to the state sees the state as an organization that trades security for revenue. The difference, though, is that the seller of the security in the predatory view of the state happens to represent a key threat to the buyer's continued security. In other words, the state resembles an extortion racket in that it demands tribute (taxes and obedience) from citizens within its jurisdiction in return for protection from, among other things, itself. The British comedy troupe Monty Python's Flying Circus once performed a skit in which members of an organized crime group walked into the office of a British army colonel and said, "Nice operation you have here, colonel. It would be a shame if something should happen to it." The implication here was a thinly veiled threat that if the army didn't pay for "protection," then the criminal organization would take actions that would result in damage to the army's resources. According to the predatory view of the state, the role of the crime group in this sketch is precisely the role that the state is thought to play in relation to its own citizens. Proponents of the predatory theory of the state are essentially pointing out that if we don't think that individuals are trustworthy and public-spirited (if they were, there would be no need for a state in the first place) then why would we imagine that representatives of the state, who wield a near monopoly on the use of force, would be? In this regard, those who take a predatory view of the state are arguing that Rousseau's (1762) admonition to "take men as they are and laws as they might be" applies at least as much to rulers as to the ruled.

Tilly argues that the level of predation inflicted by rulers in early modern Europe on their subjects varied from place to place because rulers faced a complex set of cross-pressures. To some extent, these rulers emerged out of what would look to us like a period of lawlessness during the Middle Ages. After the decline of the Roman Empire, Europe comprised a hodgepodge of local lords who offered protection to peasants in exchange for rents paid either in kind or in service on the lord's land. Like the heads of organized crime syndicates, feudal lords were constantly trying to put rivals down. These rivals included external competitors, such as other lords seeking to expand their territory, as well as internal challengers from within their own ranks. In part because of changes in military technology, lords who could seize control over larger numbers of peasants and more extensive areas of land were able to gain competitive advantages over their rivals. In time, feudal lands were consolidated into larger holdings under the control of feudal kings. For some time, feudal kings coexisted somewhat uneasily with local lords; although the kings controlled some lands themselves, they often relied on local lords to control other territories on their behalf. As time went on, however, the balance of power tended to tilt toward feudal kings, and local lords eventually became their subjects. The lands controlled by these kings gradually began to look like the territories that we would recognize as the political geography of contemporary Europe. To a large extent, the fighting between different militias and clans for supremacy in present-day Somalia closely resembles this process of state formation in early modern Europe.

According to Tilly, the political geography of modern Europe is essentially an unintended consequence of the strategies employed by lords and kings to keep a grasp on power. To remain in power, lords and kings engaged in four primary activities:

1. War making: Eliminating or neutralizing their own rivals outside the territories in which they had clear and continuous priority as wielders of force.
2. State making: Eliminating or neutralizing their rivals inside those territories.
3. Protection: Eliminating or neutralizing the enemies of their clients.
4. Extraction: Acquiring the means of carrying out the first three activities.

As Tilly (1985, 172) notes,

> Power holders' pursuit of war involved them [the state] willy-nilly in the extraction of resources for war making from the populations over which they had control and in the promotion of capital accumulation by those who could help them borrow and buy. Warmaking, extraction, and capital accumulation interacted to shape European State making. Power holders did not undertake those three momentous tasks with the intention of creating national states—centralized, differentiated, autonomous, extensive political organizations. Nor did they ordinarily foresee that national states would emerge from war making, extraction, and capital accumulation. Instead, the people who controlled European states and states in the making warred in order to check or overcome their competitors and thus to enjoy the advantages of power within a secure or expanding territory. To make more effective war, they attempted to locate more capital. In the short run, they might acquire that capital by conquest, by selling off their assets, or by coercing or dispossessing accumulators of capital. In the long run, the quest inevitably involved them in establishing regular access to capitalists who could supply and arrange credit and in imposing one form of regular taxation or another on the people and activities within their spheres of control.

In this sense, the modern state arose as a by-product of the attempts of leaders to survive. External geopolitical pressures and changes in military technology meant that lords needed to increase their war-making capacity to protect themselves and their subjects from the attack of external rivals. At the same time, this greater war-making capacity could be turned against their own subjects in order to increase their capacity to extract more resources—which, in turn, were needed to put their rivals down. The act of extraction,

> entailed the elimination, neutralization, or cooptation of the great lord's [internal] rivals; thus it led to state making. As a by-product, it created organization in the form of tax-collection agencies, police forces, courts, exchequers, account keepers; thus it again led to state making. To a lesser extent, war making likewise led to state making through the expansion of military organization itself, as a standing army, war industries, supporting bureaucracies, and (rather later) schools grew up within the state apparatus. All of these structures checked potential rivals and opponents. (Tilly 1985, 183)

In effect, "[w]ar makes states" (Tilly 1985, 170). The "kill or be killed" dynamic that, to a large extent, underpins the predatory view of the state makes it abundantly clear that those states that exist today do so only because they managed to out-compete their rivals who are now gone.

The need to extract resources from their subjects placed constraints on the predation of some early modern leaders (North 1981; Levi 1989). Rulers could extract the resources they needed to respond to geopolitical pressures in one of two ways. On the one hand, they could simply seize the assets of their subjects outright. We can think of this as the strategy that a predatory state would adopt. On the other hand, rulers could try to extract the resources they needed through what Levi (1989) terms "quasi-voluntary compliance." Quasi-voluntary compliance refers to a situation in which the subject feels that he is getting something— maybe policy concessions or limits on future state behavior—in return for the tax dollars that the state is extracting. We can think of this as the strategy that a limited state would adopt. As you might expect, quasi-voluntary compliance has several positive advantages over outright predation. For example, rulers would need to use fewer resources to coerce their subjects if their subjects voluntarily complied with their demands. Moreover, subjects might feel freer to invest and innovate in ways that expanded the tax base if the state limited its level of predation. In this way, leaders who managed to build "quasi-voluntary compliance" could succeed in extracting the resources they needed to meet external challenges without "killing the goose that laid the golden egg." By regulating their predatory instincts, rulers could opt, in effect, to increase their net extractive capacity by reducing the costs of conducting business and by taking a smaller portion of a larger pie. As it turned out, not all states were successful in limiting their predation in this way and, as a result, the character and consequences of rule exhibited quite a variety across early modern Europe. We return to the question of why some leaders chose to limit their predation more than others in Chapter 6.

CONCLUSION

In this chapter, we have examined different definitions of the state, as well as two conceptions of where the state comes from. The contract theory of the state explains how the state solves conflict between members of society. Although the literature on the evolution of cooperation points out that a state isn't strictly necessary for solving conflicts between members of society (see Box 4.1, "Can Cooperation Occur Without the State," at the end of this chapter), it does not conclusively show that decentralized cooperation is sufficient to ensure optimal outcomes. Although the contract theory of the state does identify key functions played by the state, it has little to say about the conflicts of interest that are likely to arise between rulers and the ruled. The predatory theory of the state assumes that such conflicts exist and attempts to explain why states do not always exploit their monopoly on the use of force to run roughshod over the citizens it came into being to protect.

Because the predatory view of the state both recognizes the possibility of exchange between rulers and the ruled and explains the nature and character of that exchange relationship, philosophers of science would call it a "progressive problem shift." That is, it seems to explain all of what the contract theory of the state explains while also answering at least some of the questions that the contract theory of the state raises. It should be noted, however, that the predatory theory of the state is almost exclusively "positive" in its orientation—that is, it seeks to explain the way that states and citizens behave without necessarily answering questions about what rulers or their citizens ought to do. In contrast, the contract theory of the state arose largely as a way of exploring the moral responsibilities of citizens to the state.

The predatory approach to the state has several other advantages over the contract theory of the state. First, it views rulers as egoistic, maximizing, rational actors. Consequently, we can imagine integrating explanations of leaders' behavior with other models of human behavior. Political leaders are not qualitatively different from the rest of us—they are concerned about their survival, their livelihood, and so on. Second, it shows how goal-oriented behavior leads to changes in the institutional environment in which political actors operate and, in addition, how changes in the institutional environment change leader behavior. For example, it can explain why political units grew large over time: so that they might benefit from economies of scale in the production of violence. Finally, it has the potential to explain why some rulers share power or limit their extractive activity whereas others do not. This is an issue that we return to in Chapter 6 when we examine economic explanations for why some states are democracies and others are not. In Chapter 5 we investigate how it is that we know a democracy when we see one—that is, how we conceptualize and measure democracy.

KEY CONCEPTS

best reply, *109*
cardinal payoffs, *115*
civil right, *114*
contractarian view of the state, *105*
discount factor, *142*
dominant strategy, *112*
dominant-strategy Nash equilibrium, *112*
failed state, *94*
nation, *92*
nation-state, *92*

natural right, *114*
ordinal payoffs, *108*
payoff matrix, *107*
predatory view of the state, *119*
preference ordering, *108*
present value, *142*
social contract, *114*
state, *92*
state of nature, *105*

PREPARATION FOR THE PROBLEMS

As we have sought to demonstrate throughout this book, game theory is a useful tool for examining strategic situations in which decision makers interact with one another. In the previous chapter, we employed extensive form games to examine strategic situations where actors make sequential choices. In this chapter, we introduced normal form, or strategic form, games to examine strategic situations in which actors make simultaneous choices. We now review how to construct and solve normal form games. The first thing to do is identify a strategic situation of interest. The next step is to draw a payoff matrix that captures our strategic situation.

1. Drawing the payoff matrix
   a. Identify the players involved in the strategic situation.
   b. Draw the payoff matrix to indicate the choices available to each player.
   c. Determine the payoffs that the players receive for each of the possible outcomes that could occur in the game.
   d. Write the payoffs for each player in the appropriate cell of the payoff matrix. By convention, the payoffs belonging to the row player come first and the payoffs belonging to the column player second. Use a comma to distinguish between each player's payoffs.

Once you have drawn the payoff matrix, you must solve the game.

2. Solving the game
   a. Choose to be one of the players, say, the row player. Determine which of the choices available to you is best for each of the possible choices that the other (column) player might make. In other words, identify your best replies. Indicate these choices by underlining or circling the payoffs that you will receive.
   b. Now choose to be the other player, say, the column player. Again, determine which of the choices available to you is best for each of the possible choices that the other (row) player might make. In other words, identify your best replies. Indicate these choices by underlining or circling the payoffs that you will receive.

Once you have solved the game, you will be able to identify any Nash equilibria that exist.

3. Identifying Nash equilibria:
   a. To find any Nash equilibria, identify those cells in the payoff matrix in which both players are playing their best replies. In other words, identify the cells of the payoff matrix in which both players' payoffs are underlined or circled. Then, in parentheses, list the actions chosen by each player that together lead to those cells. By convention, the action taken by the row player comes first and then the action taken by the column player. Use a semicolon to distinguish between each player's actions.
   b. Note that there may be multiple Nash equilibria. In other words, there may be more than one cell in which both players' payoffs are circled or underlined. List each of these equilibria separately in their own set of parentheses.
   c. If there are no cells in the payoff matrix in which both players' payoffs are circled or underlined, then there are no Nash equilibria in pure strategies.

Sometimes, we are interested in determining whether any of the players in the strategic situation have a dominant strategy.

4. Identifying a player who has a dominant strategy
   a. A player has a dominant strategy if she makes the same choice no matter what the other player chooses to do.
   b. If both players have a dominant strategy, then there is a dominant-strategy Nash equilibrium.

Example: Prisoner's Dilemma Game

One of the most well-known strategic form games employed by political scientists is called the Prisoner's Dilemma. The name "Prisoner's Dilemma" comes from the fact that it was originally used to describe a strategic interaction between two criminals. Here's the basic story. Two suspects in a major crime are arrested and placed in separate cells. Although there is enough evidence to convict each of them of some minor offense, there is not enough evidence to convict either of them of the major crime unless one of them rats the other one out (Talk). If they both stay quiet (Quiet), each will be convicted of the minor offense. If one and only one of them talks, then the one who talks will be freed and used as a witness against the other, who will be convicted of the major crime. If they both talk, then each will be convicted of the major crime but some leniency will be shown for their cooperation. The situation that the prisoners find themselves in is clearly strategic because the outcome of any action taken by suspect 1 depends on the choices made by suspect 2 and vice versa. Now that we have identified the strategic situation, we can go through the steps outlined earlier.

The payoff matrix for the Prisoner's Dilemma is shown in Figure 4.10. There are two players, suspect 1 and suspect 2. Both players must decide whether to keep quiet or talk. As

FIGURE 4.10 **Prisoner's Dilemma**

		Suspect 2	
		Quiet	Talk
Suspect 1	Quiet	3, 3	1, <u>4</u>
	Talk	<u>4</u>, 1	<u>2</u>, <u>2</u>

Note: Suspect 1's (the row player's) payoffs are shown first in each cell; suspect 2's (the column player's) payoffs are shown second. A comma separates the payoffs for the players in each cell. Payoffs associated with best replies are underlined.

you can see, there are four possible outcomes: both suspects keep quiet, both suspects talk, suspect 1 talks but suspect 2 keeps quiet, and suspect 1 keeps quiet but suspect 2 talks. How are the payoffs that the players associate with each outcome determined? One way to do this is to think about how each of the players would rank the four possible outcomes in the game. Based on the strategic situation that the prisoners find themselves in and the story that we have just told, the best outcome for each player would be for them to talk and for their partner to keep quiet, because this means that they would be set free. The worst outcome for each player would be for them to keep quiet and for their partner to rat them out, because they would be convicted of the major crime. Of the remaining two outcomes, both players prefer the outcome in which they both keep quiet and get convicted of the minor crime to the one in which they both talk and get convicted of the major crime with some leniency for talking. Based on this, we can write suspect 1's preference ordering as:

- (Talk; Quiet) ≻ (Quiet; Quiet) ≻ (Talk; Talk) ≻ (Quiet; Talk)

and suspect 2's preference ordering as:

- (Quiet; Talk) ≻ (Quiet; Quiet) ≻ (Talk; Talk) ≻ (Talk; Quiet),

where suspect 1's action is given first, suspect 2's action is given second, and "≻" means "is strictly preferred to." Because there are four possible outcomes, the value 4 can be assigned to each player's most preferred outcome, 3 to their second preferred outcome, 2 to their third preferred outcome, and 1 to their least preferred outcome. These numbers are the ordinal payoffs shown in the payoff matrix in Figure 4.10.

Now that you have drawn the payoff matrix, you must solve the game. You can start by putting yourselves in the shoes of suspect 1. What is suspect 1's best choice (Quiet or Talk) if suspect 2 chooses to keep quiet? The left-hand side of the payoff matrix indicates that suspect 1's payoff will be 3 if he keeps quiet and 4 if he talks in the scenario in which suspect 2 keeps quiet. As a result, suspect 1 will prefer to talk. To indicate this, underline the number 4. What is suspect 1's best choice if suspect 2 talks? The right-hand side of the payoff matrix indicates that suspect 1's payoff will be 1 if he keeps quiet and 2 if he talks in the scenario in which suspect 2 talks. As a result, suspect 1 will prefer to talk. To indicate this, underline the number 2.

Now, put yourselves in the shoes of suspect 2. What is suspect 2's best choice (Quiet or Talk) if suspect 1 chooses to keep quiet? The top part of the payoff matrix indicates that suspect 2's payoff will be 3 if he keeps quiet and 4 if he talks in the scenario in which suspect 1 keeps quiet. As a result, suspect 2 will talk. To indicate this, underline the number 4. What is suspect 2's best choice if suspect 1 talks? The bottom part of the payoff matrix indicates that suspect 2's payoff will be 1 if he keeps quiet and 2 if he talks in the scenario in which suspect 1 talks. As a result, suspect 2 will prefer to talk. To indicate this, underline the number 2. Now you have found the best replies for both suspect 1 and suspect 2.

To identify any Nash equilibria, look for cells in the payoff matrix in which both suspects are playing their best replies. In other words, look for cells in which the payoffs of both players are underlined. The only cell in which this is the case in the Prisoner's Dilemma is the one in which suspect 1 talks and suspect 2 talks. Thus, the unique Nash equilibrium for the Prisoner's Dilemma is (Talk; Talk). The expected outcome is that both players talk. The payoff to both players is 2. To find out if any player has a dominant strategy, look to see if any of the players always makes the same choice (Quiet or Talk) no matter what the other player does. As you can see, suspect 1 always talks irrespective of whether suspect 2 talks or keeps quiet. As a result, suspect 1 has a dominant strategy to talk. It turns out that suspect 2 also has a dominant strategy to talk, because he always chooses to talk irrespective of what the other suspect does as well. Because both players have a dominant strategy, the Nash equilibrium (Talk; Talk) in the Prisoner's Dilemma is a dominant-strategy Nash equilibrium.

Interestingly, both players in the Prisoner's Dilemma would be better off if they kept quiet (their payoffs would be 3) than if they played their Nash equilibrium strategies (their payoffs are 2). Given this, you might wonder why it is not an equilibrium for both players to keep quiet. Think about this for a moment. If you were suspect 1 and you knew that suspect 2 was going to keep quiet, would you talk (payoff of 4) or keep quiet (payoff of 3)? You would talk. And if you were suspect 2 and you knew that suspect 1 was going to keep quiet, would you talk (payoff of 4) or keep quiet (payoff of 3)? You would talk as well. In other words, no player will want to keep quiet if he thinks that the other player is going to keep quiet. Note that the criminals may well have promised each other prior to committing the crime that if they were both caught they would keep quiet. The problem is that these promises are not credible. Once they are caught, the criminals have a dominant strategy to talk. It is in their interests to talk if they think their partner will keep quiet, and it is in their interests to talk if their partner talks. The end result is that both criminals talk even though this means that they get a lower payoff than if they keep quiet. This is one of the central characteristics of the Prisoner's Dilemma—the Nash equilibrium is suboptimal from the perspective of the players; both players prefer another outcome.

The importance of the Prisoner's Dilemma Game and the reason why it is so frequently used by political scientists has to do with the huge variety of strategic situations in which people face similar incentives to those faced by the suspects in the crime story we have just described. As we noted earlier, the State of Nature Game has the same basic structure as a Prisoner's Dilemma Game. In addition to helping to explain the origins of the state, the Prisoner's Dilemma Game has also been used to explain a whole host of things, including arms races (Powell 1999). To see how it might throw light on arms races, think about the cold war strategic situation in which the United States and the Soviet Union had to decide whether to reduce or increase their nuclear arsenals. Arguably, the best outcome for the United States and the Soviet Union was the one in which they built up their nuclear weapons but the other country did not; this would give them a military advantage. The worst outcome for both countries, of course, was one in which they reduced their weapons while their opponents built up their arsenal. Of the other two possible outcomes, each country preferred the outcome in which they both reduced their nuclear weapons (lower cost and maintained security) to the one in which they both increased their nuclear weapons (higher cost and no increased security). If you write out the preference orderings for the United States and the Soviet Union in this Nuclear Arms Race Game, you will see that they have the same basic structure as the preference orderings in the Prisoner's Dilemma Game. We illustrate the payoff matrix for the Nuclear Arms Race Game in Figure 4.11. The Nash equilibrium is (Continue Buildup; Continue Buildup) and the expected outcome is a nuclear arms race.

FIGURE 4.11   **Nuclear Arms Race Game as a Prisoner's Dilemma**

		Soviet Union	
		Reduce arms	Continue buildup
United States	Reduce Arms	3, 3	1, <u>4</u>
	Continue buildup	<u>4</u>, 1	<u>2</u>, <u>2</u>

Note: The United States' (the row player's) payoffs are shown first in each cell; the Soviet Union's (the column player's) payoffs are shown second. A comma separates the payoffs for the players in each cell. Payoffs associated with best replies are underlined.

PROBLEMS

The Prisoner's Dilemma is just one type of strategic form game. Below, we present other strategic form games and ask various questions.

1. The Game of Chicken

Footloose is a 1984 rock musical film about a Chicago teenager called Ren McCormack (played by Kevin Bacon) who moves to a small conservative town in Iowa. Ren's love of dancing and partying to rock music causes friction with the straitlaced townspeople, who have passed a law prohibiting dancing within the town limits. Much of the film centers on the competition between Ren and a local tough guy named Chuck for the affections of the local reverend's daughter, Ariel. At one stage, Chuck challenges Ren to a "tractor face-off." In this face-off, Ren and Chuck have to drive tractors directly at each other as Ariel and others watch. Whoever swerves out of the way first is considered a "chicken."

As you can see, this part of the film captures a strategic situation in which Ren and Chuck both have to decide whether to "swerve" or "drive straight." Political scientists generally call the strategic situation described here the Game of Chicken. The best outcome for both characters is one in which they continue to drive straight but their competitor swerves; their status among their peers rises and the other character is seen as a wimp. The worst possible outcome is the one in which neither of them swerves, because they will end up dead or badly injured. Of the other two possible outcomes, both Ren and Chuck prefer the outcome in which they both swerve to the one in which he swerves but the other does not. If they both swerve, neither of them gains or loses anything; they may both even gain some credit simply for participating in the face-off in the first place. If one swerves and the other does not, then the one who swerved loses face. The payoff matrix for this Game of Chicken is shown in Figure 4.12.

a. Use the numbers in each cell of the payoff matrix in Figure 4.12 to write out the preference ordering for Ren and Chuck over the four possible outcomes.

b. Solve the Game of Chicken for Nash equilibria. *Hint:* There are actually two possible pure-strategy Nash equilibria.

c. Does either Ren or Chuck have a dominant strategy? If so, what is it?

d. What strategic situations in comparative politics might fit the basic structure of the Game of Chicken? In other words, provide a specific example in which actors might have preferences and interactions like those in the Game of Chicken.

FIGURE 4.12   A Game of Chicken: The Tractor Face-Off

		Chuck	
		Swerve	Drive straight
Ren	Swerve	3, 3	2, 4
	Drive straight	4, 2	1, 1

Note: Ren's (the row player's) payoffs are shown first in each cell; Chuck's (the column player's) payoffs are shown second. A comma separates the payoffs for the players in each cell.

2. The Stag Hunt Game

In a *Discourse on the Origin and Foundations of Inequality among Men,* the French philosopher Jean Jacques Rousseau (1988, 36) describes a strategic situation in which a group of hunters are trying to catch a stag. To keep things simple, imagine that there are just two hunters. The hunters have two options: they can work together and pursue the stag or they can hunt independently and catch a hare. If both hunters pursue the stag, they catch it and share it equally. If either of the hunters chooses to go after the hare, they catch it but the stag escapes. Each hunter prefers a share of the stag to a hare. The strategic situation that Rousseau describes has come to be known by political scientists as the Stag Hunt Game. The payoff matrix for the Stag Hunt Game is shown in Figure 4.13.

a. Use the numbers in each cell of the payoff matrix in Figure 4.13 to write out the preference ordering for the two hunters over the four possible outcomes.

b. Solve the game in Figure 4.13 for all Nash equilibria.

c. Do any of the hunters have a dominant strategy? If so, what is it?

d. What strategic situations in comparative politics might fit the basic structure of the Stag Hunt Game? In other words, provide a specific example in which actors might have preferences and interactions like those in the Stag Hung Game.

FIGURE 4.13   **The Stag Hunt Game**

		Hunter 2	
		Stag	Hare
Hunter 1	Stag	4, 4	1, 3
	Hare	3, 1	2, 2

Note: Hunter 1's (the row player's) payoffs are shown first in each cell; hunter 2's (the column player's) payoffs are shown second. A comma separates the payoffs for the players in each cell.

3. Pure Coordination Game

People often find themselves in strategic situations in which they must agree on adopting just one of several potential solutions to their problems. For example, it does not really matter whether cars drive on the left of the road, as they do in the United Kingdom, or on the right of the road, as they do in France. All that really matters is that all the drivers in a given country choose to drive on the same side of the road. Strategic situations like this have come to be known by political scientists as Pure Coordination Games. The payoff matrix for a situation in which two drivers are deciding to drive on the left or right of the road is shown in Figure 4.14.

a. Use the numbers in each cell of the payoff matrix in Figure 4.14 to write out the preference ordering for the two drivers over the four possible outcomes.
b. Solve the game in Figure 4.14 for all Nash equilibria.
c. Do any of the drivers have a dominant strategy? If so, what is it?
d. What strategic situations in comparative politics might fit the basic structure of the Pure Coordination Game? In other words, provide a specific example in which actors might have preferences and interactions like those in the Pure Coordination Game.

FIGURE 4.14   **Pure Coordination Game**

		Driver 2	
		Left	Right
Driver 1	Left	1, 1	0, 0
	Right	0, 0	1, 1

Note: Driver 1's (the row player's) payoffs are shown first in each cell; driver 2's (the column player's) payoffs are shown second. A comma separates the payoffs for the players in each cell.

4. Asymmetric Coordination Game: The Battle of the Sexes

Consider the following strategic situation. Archie and Edith are two people who would like to go on a date with each other. Archie likes going to boxing matches and Edith likes going to flower shows. Unfortunately, Archie and Edith work on different sides of town and, for some reason, they have no way of contacting each other to decide whether the date will be at the boxing match or the flower show. The main goal for both Archie and Edith is that they be together in the evening. In other words, they prefer to go to the same venue, whether it is the boxing match or the flower show, rather than miss each other. Of course, if they could guarantee being together, Archie would prefer to be together at the boxing match and Edith would prefer to be together at the flower show. Political scientists call strategic situations like this Asymmetric Coordination Games because both actors want to coordinate on some outcome, but their preferences conflict over what that outcome should be. These games are also sometimes referred to as Battle of the Sexes Games. The payoff matrix for the Battle of the Sexes Game is shown in Figure 4.15.

a. Use the numbers in each cell of the payoff matrix in Figure 4.15 to write out the preference ordering for Archie and Edith over the four possible outcomes.

b. Solve the game in Figure 4.15 for all Nash equilibria.

c. Does either Edith or Archie have a dominant strategy? If so, what is it?

d. What strategic situations in comparative politics might fit the basic structure of the Battle of the Sexes Game? In other words, provide a specific example, in which actors might have preferences and interactions like those in the Battle of the Sexes Game.

e. If you solved the Pure Coordination Game from the previous question and the Asymmetric Coordination Game from this question correctly, you should have found that each game has two possible Nash equilibria. In the real world, actors must try to "coordinate" on one of these equilibria. Use your intuition to say whether you think actors will generally find it easier to coordinate when they are in a strategic situation characterized by a Pure Coordination Game or one characterized by an Asymmetric Coordination Game. Explain your answer.

FIGURE 4.15   The Battle of the Sexes

| | | Edith | |
		Flower show	Boxing
Archie	Flower show	3, 4	1, 1
	Boxing	2, 2	4, 3

Note: Archie's (the row player's) payoffs are shown first in each cell; Edith's (the column player's) payoffs are shown second. A comma separates the payoffs for the players in each cell.

5. Rock, Paper, Scissors Game

All of the strategic form games that we have looked at so far involve actors deciding between two choices. There is no reason, however, why actors in strategic form games cannot have more than two potential choices. Consider the famous children's game of Rock, Paper, Scissors. In this game, two children simultaneously choose to play "rock," "paper," or "scissors." "Rock" beats "scissors," "paper" beats "rock," and "scissors" beats "paper." If the two children ever choose the same thing, then there is a draw. Let's assume that you get one point for a win, you lose one point for a loss, and you get 0 for a draw. The payoff matrix for this version of the Rock, Paper, Scissors Game is shown in Figure 4.16.

  a. Solve the game in Figure 4.16. Are there any pure-strategy Nash equilibria in this game?
  b. Imagine that you were going to play this game over and over again. Would you choose to play rock, paper, or scissors, or would you randomize over all three choices? Explain your answer.

FIGURE 4.16   Rock, Paper, Scissors Game

		Player 2		
		Scissors	Paper	Rock
	Scissors	0, 0	1, −1	−1, 1
Player 1	Paper	−1, 1	0, 0	1, −1
	Rock	1, −1	−1, 1	0, 0

Note: Player 1's (the row player's) payoffs are shown first in each cell; player 2's (the column player's) payoffs are shown second. A comma separates the payoffs for the players in each cell.

6. American Football Game

Another example of a strategic situation in which actors have more than two choices might be called the American Football Game. In an American football game, we can think that the offense has four possible strategies to progress down the field: run the ball, make a short throw, make a medium throw, and make a long throw. The defense has three strategies to try to stop this: counter the run, counter the pass, or blitz the quarterback. Let's say that after studying many games, statisticians have come up with the payoff matrix shown in Figure 4.17, in which the numbers in each cell indicate the expected number of yards either gained by the offense or lost by the defense. As you can see, every yard gained by the offense is a yard lost by the defense. As always, the players prefer higher numbers to lower numbers.

    a. Solve the game in Figure 4.17 for all Nash equilibria.

    b. Does the offense or defense have a dominant strategy? If so, what is it?

FIGURE 4.17   **American Football Game**

		Defense		
		Counter run	Counter pass	Blitz
Offense	Run	2, –2	5, –5	13, –13
	Short pass	6, –6	5.6, –5.6	10.5, –10.5
	Medium pass	6, –6	4.5, –4.5	1, –1
	Long pass	10, –10	3, –3	–2, 2

Note: The offense's (the row player's) payoffs are shown first in each cell; the defense's (the column player's) payoffs are shown second. A comma separates the payoffs for the players in each cell.

7. Mafia Game

Earlier we described the Prisoner's Dilemma Game, in which two prisoners had to choose between ratting out their partner or keeping quiet. The Nash equilibrium in this game involved both prisoners' deciding to talk even though they would both have been better off keeping quiet. This scenario will probably be familiar to anyone who watches *Law and Order*, TV's longest running crime series. As many of you are probably aware, however, certain types of criminals in the real world rarely talk or rat out their accomplices. In particular, it is well known that members of the Mafia or Cosa Nostra rarely provide incriminating evidence against their accomplices. Why is this? The answer is that the Mafia organization imposes a cost (c), often physical and deadly, on anyone who talks to the police. This additional cost changes the structure of the strategic situation in which the two prisoners find themselves. Rather than playing the traditional Prisoner's Dilemma, we can think that the prisoners are playing a Mafia Game with a payoff matrix like the one shown in Figure 4.18.

a. Solve the game in Figure 4.18 for any Nash equilibria assuming that $c = 0$. What type of game is this?

b. Given the payoffs shown in the payoff matrix in the Mafia Game, what is the minimum cost that the Mafia needs to impose on members who talk in order for the Nash equilibrium to be one in which both suspects keep quiet? Explain your answer.

c. The role of the Mafia in the Mafia Game can be thought of as that of a third-party enforcer. What do we mean by that? How is this role that the Mafia plays in this game related to the role that the state plays in the Civil Society Game examined earlier?

FIGURE 4.18   Mafia Game

		Mafia suspect 2	
		Quiet	Talk
Mafia suspect 1	Quiet	30, 30	10, 40–c
	Talk	40–c, 10	20–c, 20–c

Note: c = the cost imposed by the Mafia on a suspect who talks. Suspect 1's (the row player's) payoffs are shown first in each cell; suspect 2's (the column player's) payoffs are shown second. A comma separates the payoffs for the players in each cell.

8. Counterterrorism Games

On September 11, 2001, nineteen terrorists affiliated with al-Qaida hijacked four commercial passenger jets and flew them into two American landmarks (the World Trade Center in New York City and the Pentagon in Washington, D.C.) in coordinated terrorist attacks. Since 9/11, governments around the world have spent tens of billions of dollars on a variety of counterterrorism policies. Counterterrorism policies generally fall into two types: preemption and deterrence. Preemption involves proactive policies such as destroying terrorist training camps, retaliating against state sponsors of terrorism, infiltrating terrorist groups, freezing terrorist assets, and the like. The goal of preemption is to curb future terrorist attacks. One thing to note about preemption policies is that they not only make the country that carries out the preemptive strike safer, they also make all countries that are potential targets safer. Deterrence involves defensive policies such as placing bomb detectors in airports, fortifying potential targets, and securing borders. The goal is to deter an attack either by making success more difficult or by increasing the likely negative consequences for the terrorists. One thing to note about deterrence policies is that they often end up displacing terrorist attacks away from the country introducing the defensive measures to other countries or regions where targets are now relatively more vulnerable (Enders and Sandler 1993; Sandler and Enders 2004).

In an article entitled "Counterterrorism: A Game-Theoretic Analysis," Arce and Sandler (2005) use strategic form games to examine these two types of counterterrorism policies. They argue that governments around the world overinvest in deterrence policies at the expense of preemption policies and that this results in a socially suboptimal outcome from the perspective of world security. The following questions deal with some of the strategic form games examined by Arce and Sandler.

Let's start with preemption policies. Imagine that the United States and the European Union must decide whether to preempt a terrorist attack or do nothing. A terrorist group is a "passive player" in this game and will attack the weaker of the two targets. For illustrative purposes, let's suppose that each preemptive action provides a public benefit worth 4 to the United States and the European Union. Recall that preemptive action increases the safety of all countries. Preemptive action comes at a private cost of 6 to the preemptor, though. Consider an outcome in which only the United States preempts. In this situation, the United States will get –2 (i.e., 4 – 6) and the European Union will get 4. If the United States and the European Union both preempt, they each get a payoff of 2 (i.e., 8 – 6). If both the United States and the European Union do nothing, they each get 0. The payoff matrix for this Counterterrorism Preemption Game is shown in Figure 4.19.

a. Use the numbers in each cell of the payoff matrix in Figure 4.19 to write out the preference ordering for the United States and the European Union over the four possible outcomes.

b. Solve the game in Figure 4.19 for all Nash equilibria.

c. Does either the United States or the European Union have a dominant strategy? If so, what is it?

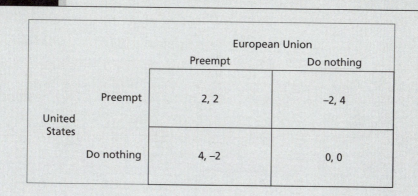

FIGURE 4.19   Counterterrorism Preemption Game

		European Union	
		Preempt	Do nothing
United States	Preempt	2, 2	–2, 4
	Do nothing	4, –2	0, 0

Note: The United States' (the row player's) payoffs are shown first in each cell; the European Union's (the column player's) payoffs are shown second. A comma separates the payoffs for the players in each cell.

Now let's look at deterrence policies. Imagine that the United States and the European Union must decide whether to deter a terrorist attack or do nothing. Terrorists will attack the weaker of the two targets. For illustrative purposes, let's suppose that deterrence is associated with a cost of 4 for both the deterring country and the other country. The deterrer's costs arise from the actual deterrence action that it takes, whereas the non-deterrer's costs arise from now being the terrorists' target of choice. Each deterrence action provides a private benefit worth 6 (prior to costs being deducted) to the deterring country because it is now safer. Recall that deterrence increases the safety only of the deterring country. Consider an outcome in which only the United States deters. In this situation, the United States will get 2, that is, 6 − 4, and the European Union will get −4. Net benefits are 0 if the United States and European Union do nothing, whereas each receives a net payoff of −2, that is, 6 − (2 × 4), from mutual deterrence, because costs of 8 are deducted from private gains of 6. The payoff matrix for this Counterterrorism Deterrence Game is shown in Figure 4.20.

    d. Use the numbers in each cell of the payoff matrix in Figure 4.20 to write out the preference ordering for the United States and the European Union over the four possible outcomes.

    e. Solve the game in Figure 4.20 for all Nash equilibria.

    f. Does either the United States or the European Union have a dominant strategy? If so, what is it?

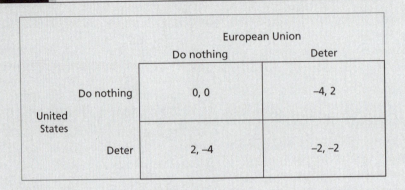

Counterterrorism Deterrence Game I

Note: The United States' (the row player's) payoffs are shown first in each cell; the European Union's (the column player's) payoffs are shown second. A comma separates the payoffs for the players in each cell.

Instead of assuming that governments can implement only preemption or deterrence policies, let's now look at a situation in which they can implement both types of counterterrorism policy. We can do this by combining the last two games. The only thing we need to do is determine the payoffs that the countries receive when one preempts and the other deters. In this situation, the deterrer gets a payoff of 6, that is, $6 + 4 - 4$. In other words, the deterrer gets 6 from the private benefit associated with the deterrence policy, -4 from the cost of the deterrence policy, and 4 from the public benefit associated with the other country's taking a preemptive action. The preemptor receives a payoff of -6, that is, $4 - 6 - 4$. In other words, they get 4 from the public benefit associated with their provision of preemption, -6 from the cost of the preemption policy, and -4 from the deflected costs associated with becoming the target country. The payoff matrix for this more general Counterterrorism Game is shown in Figure 4.21.

g. Solve the game in Figure 4.21 for all Nash equilibria.

h. Does either the United States or the European Union have a dominant strategy? If so, what is it?

i. Is the Nash equilibrium in this game suboptimal? In other words, are there other outcomes that both countries would prefer? If so, what are they?

j. If you have solved these games correctly, you will see that states overinvest in counterterrorism deterrence policies and underinvest in counterterrorism preemption policies. This is not only a theoretical prediction but something that terrorist experts have observed in the real world. Looking at the structure of these three games, can you explain why states do this? *Hint:* The answer to this question has something to do with what political scientists call the "free-rider problem" and is something that we examine in more detail in Chapter 8.

			European Union	
		Preempt	Do nothing	Deter
	Preempt	2, 2	–2, 4	–6, 6
United States	Do nothing	4, –2	0, 0	–4, 2
	Deter	6, –6	2, –4	–2, –2

FIGURE 4.21   Counterterrorism Deterrence Game II

Note: The United States' (the row player's) payoffs are shown first in each cell; the European Union's (the column player's) payoffs are shown second. A comma separates the payoffs for the players in each cell.

9. Free Trade Game

Free trade occurs when goods and services between countries flow unhindered by government-imposed restrictions such as tariffs, quotas, and antidumping laws that are often designed to protect domestic industries. Although it is well known that free trade creates winners and losers, a broad consensus exists among most economists that free trade has a large and unambiguous net gain for society as a whole. For example, Robert Whaples (2006) finds in a survey of economists that "87.5% agree that the U.S. should eliminate remaining tariffs and other barriers to trade" and that "90.1% disagree with the suggestion that the U.S. should restrict employers from outsourcing work to foreign countries." Despite this consensus, it is not at all clear that countries will actually adopt policies promoting free trade.

Consider the following strategic situation in which the United States and the European Union are engaged in trade negotiations. Both countries must decide whether to reduce their tariffs or impose new tariffs. The best outcome for both countries is for them to impose new tariffs and for the other side to reduce tariffs; they can export more easily to the other country and they obtain increased revenue from the new tariffs. The worst outcome for both countries is for them to reduce tariffs and for the other country to increase tariffs; they will lose jobs due to reduced exports and the other country will benefit from their lower tariffs. Of the remaining two outcomes, both countries would prefer the reduction of tariffs than the imposition of new tariffs. If both countries reduce their tariffs, then each country can benefit from increased free trade. If both countries impose new tariffs, a trade war begins in which each country sees a decline in trade and a loss of jobs. Based on this story, the preference ordering for the European Union over the four possible outcomes is:

- Impose; Reduce ≻ Reduce; Reduce ≻ Impose; Impose ≻ Reduce; Impose,

and the preference ordering for the United States is

- Reduce; Impose ≻ Reduce; Reduce ≻ Impose; Impose ≻ Impose; Reduce,

where the European Union's action is given first, the United States' action is given second, and "≻" means "is strictly preferred to." An empty payoff matrix for this Free Trade Game is shown in Figure 4.22.

a. Use the preference orderings shown above to fill in the payoff matrix shown in Figure 4.22 with the payoffs for each player. Use the numbers 4, 3, 2, 1 to indicate the preference ordering for the players.
b. Based on the preference orderings in the Free Trade Game, what is this sort of game more generally called?
c. Solve the game in Figure 4.22 for all Nash equilibria. What is the expected outcome of the game?
d. Does either the European Union or the United States have a dominant strategy? If so, what is it?

So far, you have solved the Free Trade Game assuming that it is played only once. In reality, though, countries often trade with each other many times and engage in multiple rounds of trade negotiations. We now examine the Free Trade Game assuming that it is played over and over again. In order to answer the following questions, you should first read Box 4.1 (pages 141–145) at the end of the chapter. The European Union and the United States must now decide how to

FIGURE 4.22 Free Trade Game

		United States	
		Reduce tariffs	Impose tariffs
European Union	Reduce tariffs		
	Impose new tariffs		

play the Free Trade Game in each round. Let's assume that both countries play grim trigger strategies. In the present context, recall that a grim trigger strategy means that a country will continue to reduce tariffs as long as the other country reduces its tariffs; but if the other country ever imposes new tariffs, it will impose new tariffs in the next round and in all future rounds.

e. Using the payoffs from the Free Trade Game, what is the present value of reducing tariffs?

f. Using the payoffs from the Free Trade Game, what is the present value of imposing new tariffs?

g. Is there a discount factor (δ) at which it is possible to sustain (Reduce Tariffs; Reduce Tariffs) as a Nash equilibrium in this repeated Free Trade Game if the European Union and the United States use grim trigger strategies? What is this discount rate?

h. Interpret the results from the "one-shot" Free Trade Game and the infinitely repeated Free Trade Game. In other words, what do they mean for free trade in substantive terms?

10. Writing and Solving Your Own Games

a. Think of a strategic situation in which two players must simultaneously choose between two possible actions. Establish preference orderings over the four possible outcomes and use them to write down a payoff matrix. Solve the game for any Nash equilibria.

b. Think of a strategic situation in which two players make choices simultaneously. At least one player should have to choose between more than two possible actions. Write down a payoff matrix for this strategic situation. Solve the game for any Nash equilibria.

Box 4.1   **CAN COOPERATION OCCUR WITHOUT THE STATE?**

According to Hobbes ([1651] 1994), life in the state of nature is "solitary, poor, nasty, brutish, and short." This seemed to be confirmed when we found that both players in our State of Nature Game had a dominant strategy to steal rather than forbear—both players were better off stealing no matter what the other player was doing. Hobbes believed that the only way to get individuals in the state of nature to cooperate and forbear was to create a state with sufficient power to "awe" them. As we saw in our Civil Society Game, the threat of a large enough punishment by the state was sufficient to get the players to forbear. In fact, both players now had a dominant strategy to cooperate and forbear. In effect, this is Hobbes's justification for the existence of the state. Some scholars, however, have challenged this justification by arguing that cooperation can emerge through a decentralized process in the state of nature; you do not always need to create a sovereign or a state (Taylor 1976; Axelrod 1981, 1984). These scholars claim that cooperation can occur without a sovereign as long as the individuals in the state of nature repeatedly interact with each other and care sufficiently about the future benefits of cooperation. Earlier in the chapter, we saw that cooperation or forbearance was not possible when the State of Nature Game was played once. But let's now examine what happens if the individuals in the state of nature play the game over and over again.

Before we do this, we need to introduce two new concepts that will come in handy. The first is called the **discount factor.** A discount factor essentially tells us how much people care about

A **discount factor** tells us the rate at which future benefits are discounted compared with today's benefits; in effect, it tells us how much people value the future.

the future. Specifically, the discount factor tells us how much future benefits are discounted compared with today's benefits. Low discount factors mean that people do not value the future very much—they value the benefits they receive today much more than the benefits they will get tomorrow. High discount factors mean that people value the future a lot—they value the benefits they will receive tomorrow almost as much as the benefits they receive today. This probably all sounds a little abstract. To make the idea of a discount factor more concrete, consider the following numerical example. Imagine that you had a choice of receiving $1,000 today or $1,000 in a month's time. If it didn't matter to you whether you received the money today or in a month's time, your discount rate (δ) would be 1; that is, future payoffs are worth as much to you as today's payoffs. In contrast, if receiving the money in a month's time was worthless to you, perhaps because you will be dead in a month's time, then your discount factor would be 0; that is, future payoffs are worth nothing to you. And if the $1,000 in a month's time was worth something to you, but not as much as getting it today, then your discount factor would be $0 < \delta < 1$. As you can see, the discount factor is always bounded by 0 and 1; that is, $0 \leq \delta \leq 1$. The important point to remember is that the higher the discount factor, the more you care about the future; the lower the discount factor, the less you care about the future.

The second concept is called the **present value** of some stream of payoffs. This concept is easiest explained with an example. Imagine

> The **present value** of a stream of benefits tells us how much this stream of future benefits is worth to us today.

that your parents promise to give you $1 every day from now into the future. How much is this promise of a stream of payments into the future worth to you today? In other words, what is the "present value" of this stream of future payments? The $1 you receive today is obviously worth $1 to you today. But what about all the dollars that you expect to receive in the future? How much are they worth to you today? The $1 you expect to receive tomorrow is not going to be worth quite as much to you as if you had received it today—it will be discounted by your discount factor. Thus, the $1 you expect to get tomorrow is only worth 1\delta$ today. The $1 you expect to receive in two days time is worth even less to you today because it will be discounted by your discount factor a second time. Thus, the $1 you receive in two days time is worth only 1\delta^2$ today. Similarly, the $1 you expect to get in three days time is worth only 1\delta^3$ today. Continuing with this logic, it is easy to see that the present value of the stream of payments promised to you by your parents is:

$$\text{Present Value (Promise)} = 1 + 1\delta + 1\delta^2 + 1\delta^3 + 1\delta^4 + 1\delta^5 + \ldots + 1\delta^\infty, \tag{4-1}$$

or

$$\text{Present Value (Promise)} = 1 + \delta + \delta^2 + \delta^3 + \delta^4 + \delta^5 + \ldots + \delta^\infty. \tag{4-2}$$

Can we simplify this in any way? Although we don't show it here, it turns out that this sum of numbers is equal to $1 / (1 - \delta)$:

$$\text{Present Value (Promise)} = 1 + \delta + \delta^2 + \delta^3 + \delta^4 + \delta^5 + \ldots + \delta^\infty = 1 / (1 - \delta). \tag{4-3}$$

What if your parents had promised you $5 every day indefinitely into the future instead of $1? In this case the present value of their promise would be $5 / (1 - \delta)$. If they had promised you $3, the present value would be $3 / (1 - \delta)$, and so on.

Now that we know what a discount factor is and how to calculate the present value of a future stream of payments, we can examine what happens when the State of Nature Game is played over and over again. The State of Nature Game is shown in Figure 4.23.

Now that Players A and B have to play the State of Nature Game over and over again, they have to decide how to play the game in each round (or period). One strategy that the players might employ is called a grim trigger strategy. A grim trigger strategy says that a player will forbear (cooperate) as long as the other player forbears; but if the other player ever steals instead, the first player will steal from him in the next round and in all future rounds. Imagine that both players decide to use a grim trigger strategy when playing the State of Nature game. How much will the players get if they both choose to forbear? The present value of forbearing is:

$$\text{Present Value (Forbear)} = 3 + 3\delta + 3\delta^2 + 3\delta^3 + 3\delta^4 + 3\delta^5 + \ldots + \delta^\infty$$
$$= 3 / (1 - \delta). \tag{4-4}$$

Where do these numbers come from? If both players forbear, we can see from the payoff matrix in Figure 4.23 that they will get a payoff of 3 in every period; this payoff will be discounted by the discount rate (δ) every time the game is played. This leads to equation 4-4.

What we want to know is whether it is ever a Nash equilibrium for both players to forbear now that the State of Nature Game is infinitely repeated. Recall that a Nash equilibrium requires that no player has an incentive to unilaterally deviate, given what the other player is doing. Well, we know that the players will get a payoff of $3 / (1 - \delta)$ if they always forbear. But how much would they get if they deviated from this? In other words, how much would players get if they stole instead? Let's imagine that Player A deviated and started to steal. As the payoff matrix in Figure 4.23 illustrates, Player A would get 4 in the first period—this is the payoff from stealing while Player B forbears. The fact that Player B is using a grim trigger strategy, however, means that he will respond to Player A's stealing by stealing himself in all the future rounds of the game. Given that Player B is always going to steal, the best that Player A can do now is to continue stealing. As a result, Player A will get a payoff of 4 in the first period but a payoff of only 2 discounted by the discount factor in every period thereafter. Thus, the present value of deviating—stealing—is given by equation 4-5.

$$\text{Present Value (Steal)} = 4 + 2\delta + 2\delta^2 + 2\delta^3 + 2\delta^4 + 2\delta^5 + \ldots + 2\delta^\infty. \tag{4-5}$$

Notice that equation (4-5) can be rewritten as:

$$\text{Present Value (Steal)} = 4 + 2\delta(1 + \delta + \delta^2 + \delta^3 + \delta^4 + \delta^5 + \ldots + \delta^\infty). \tag{4-6}$$

We saw earlier in equation (4–3) that $1 + \delta + \delta^2 + \delta^3 + \delta^4 + \delta^5 + \ldots + \delta^\infty = 1 / (1 - \delta)$. Thus, we can rewrite and simplify equation (4-6) as:

$$\text{Present Value (Steal)} = 4 + 2\delta / (1 - \delta). \tag{4-7}$$

FIGURE 4.23   State of Nature Game Revisited

		B	
		Forbear	Steal
A	Forbear	3, 3	1, 4
	Steal	4, 1	2, 2

Player A will choose not to deviate—that is, not to steal—if the present value of forbearance is greater than the present value of stealing. This will occur when $3 / (1 - \delta) > 4 + 2\delta / (1 - \delta)$. A little algebra (equations 4-8 through 4-13) indicates that Player A will prefer to forbear rather than steal when $\delta > 1/2$. Given that Player B has the same payoffs as Player A, he will also prefer to forbear rather than steal when $\delta > 1/2$.

Present Value (Forbear) > Present Value (Steal)

$$\Rightarrow 3 / (1 - \delta) > 4 + 2\delta / (1 - \delta) \tag{4-8}$$

$$\Rightarrow 3 / (1 - \delta) > (4 - 4\delta + 2\delta) / (1 - \delta) \tag{4-9}$$

$$\Rightarrow 3 / (1 - \delta) > (4 - 2\delta) / (1 - \delta) \tag{4-10}$$

$$\Rightarrow 3 > 4 - 2\delta \tag{4-11}$$

$$\Rightarrow 2\delta > 1 \tag{4-12}$$

$$\Rightarrow \delta > 1/2 \tag{4-13}$$

What we have just shown is that (Forbear; Forbear) can be sustained as a Nash equilibrium in the infinitely repeated State of Nature Game when both players use a grim trigger strategy and the discount factor is greater than a half. The condition that the discount rate must be greater than a half is specific to the payoffs that we have chosen for our particular State of Nature Game. The result, however, is quite general. Players using a grim trigger strategy in an infinitely repeated State of Nature Game can sustain cooperation as part of a Nash equilibrium as long as the discount factor is sufficiently high.[1] It turns out that other strategies can also sustain cooperation. One of the most famous strategies is called the tit-for-tat strategy, or TFT. According to TFT, players will start by cooperating and will then choose whatever action the other player did in the last period to determine how they will behave in subsequent rounds. Thus, if one player chose to cooperate the last time the game was played, the other player will cooperate in the next round. In contrast, if the first player chose to steal the last time the game was played, the other player will steal in the next round. And so on. If the players care enough about the future (if the discount factor is sufficiently high), then cooperation can be sustained in an infinitely repeated State of Nature Game using TFT. The important point here is that cooperation can occur in the state of nature without needing to create a state. In effect, cooperation can evolve in the state of nature as long as the players are sufficiently concerned about the potential benefits of future cooperation. This conclusion runs directly counter to the claims of social contract theorists like Hobbes and provides support for groups like anarchists who believe that society can survive, and thrive, without a state.

---

1. That the game is infinitely repeated (or alternatively, that the players do not know when the game will end) is very important. If the players know that the game will be played for a finite or fixed number of periods, it is no longer possible to sustain cooperation. We do not actually show this, but here is the basic logic. In whatever is the last period, the best reply for both players will be to steal. Because both players know that they will both steal in the last period, however, the best they can do in the penultimate period is also to steal. Knowing that they will both steal in the penultimate period leads them to steal in the period before that and so on. This logic continues to the point that both players steal from the very first period.

That cooperation can be sustained in equilibrium without a state does not necessarily mean that we should all become anarchists, though. It turns out that cooperation is only one of a whole host of possible equilibria in the infinitely repeated State of Nature Game. For example, it is also a Nash equilibrium for both players to steal. This is relatively easy to see. If your opponent is always going to steal, then you never have an incentive to unilaterally deviate—you will always steal as well. Thus, (Steal; Steal) is another Nash equilibrium. Game theory cannot tell us which equilibrium is most likely to occur in these circumstances. As a result, there is no reason to believe that the cooperative outcome will be any more likely to occur than any of the other equilibrium outcomes. That cooperation can be sustained in equilibrium without a state does not guarantee that cooperation will, in fact, occur. Moreover, it actually takes a lot of effort for the players to sustain cooperation in the state of nature because everyone has to monitor everyone else to see who is stealing and who is not. It also requires that the individuals get together to punish those people who have been caught stealing. In sum, although it is possible for cooperation to occur in the state of nature without a state, relying on it to emerge through some decentralized process may not be the best thing to do—the creation of a state may be a more preferable and reliable route to cooperative outcomes.

5 Conceptualizing and Measuring Democracy

> If you can think about something, you can conceptualize it; if you can conceptualize it, you can operationalize it; and if you can operationalize it, you can measure it.
>
> J. David Singer

> If you can not measure it, you can not improve it.
>
> Lord Kelvin

> Not everything that counts can be counted, and not everything that can be counted counts.
>
> From a sign in Einstein's office at Princeton

OVERVIEW

- Although a strong consensus exists that democracy is the most desirable form of government, this has not always been the case. In fact, historically, democracy was commonly viewed as an obsolete political system that was both dangerous and unstable.

- Given the current widespread agreement concerning the importance and desirability of democracy, one might wonder how a country becomes a democracy and about the sorts of things that influence democratic survival. Answering these types of questions presupposes that we can measure democracy and classify countries as democracies or dictatorships.

- In this chapter, we examine how political scientists conceptualize and measure democracy. What makes a democracy a democracy? Should democracy be conceptualized in substantive or minimalist terms? Should democracies and dictatorships be conceptualized as two separate categories or two ends of a single democratic–dictatorial continuum? We also discuss different criteria—validity, reliability, replicability—for evaluating the different measures of democracy commonly employed by political scientists.

We live in a world in which there is now strong agreement concerning the importance and desirability of democracy. It is important to recognize, however, that this has historically not always been the case. "For two millennia politicians and philosophers regarded democracy as an inferior form of politics" dominated by mob rule and class warfare (Hanson 1989, 70). As C. B. Macpherson (1966, 1) puts it, "Democracy used to be a bad word. Everybody who was anybody knew that democracy, in its original sense of rule by the people or government in accordance with the will of the bulk of the people, would be a bad thing—fatal to individual freedom and to all graces of civilized living. That was the position taken by pretty nearly all men of intelligence from the earliest historical times down to about a hundred years ago. Then, within fifty years, democracy became a good thing." It is only relatively recently, then, that democracy has come to be considered a political system to be championed and exported around the world. It is for this reason that we begin this chapter by briefly examining how the meaning and appeal of democracy has changed over time.

Given the consensus that now exists in favor of democracy, we might ask ourselves what causes democracy to emerge and survive. In the last chapter, we examined contractarian and predatory views of the state. We argued that the predatory view of the state had the potential to explain why some rulers share power or limit their extractive activity, or both, whereas others do not. Put differently, the predatory view of the state has the potential to explain why some states are democratic but others are dictatorial. In the next two chapters, we take a closer look at this issue by analyzing economic and cultural explanations for the emergence and survival of democracy. Empirical tests of these arguments, however, presuppose that we know a democracy when we see one. Is it obvious which countries are democracies and which are not? How do we know which ones are democracies? What makes a democracy a democracy? In the second half of this chapter, we investigate how comparative politics scholars have tried to conceptualize and measure democracy.

DEMOCRACY AND DICTATORSHIP IN HISTORICAL PERSPECTIVE

Democracy acquired a highly positive connotation during the second half of the twentieth century. Even countries widely considered dictatorships have professed their support for democracy and simply adjusted their definition of democracy so that the word could be applied to their form of government. Indeed, many acknowledged dictatorships make reference to "people" or "democracy" in their very name—the Democratic People's Republic of North Korea, the Democratic Republic of the Congo, the People's Republic of China—as if this would somehow make them democratic. As we will see in later chapters, these countries often go so far as to adopt seemingly democratic institutions such as elections, legislatures, and political parties. Still, until the middle of the nineteenth century, democracy was commonly viewed as an obsolete and ancient political system that was both dangerous and unstable. Of course, one reason for this view of democracy is that debate concerning the appropriate form that governments should take typically occurred among elites rather than the common people.

The earliest debates surrounding the merits of different forms of government, including democracy, can be dated to around 520 B.C. in Persia (Herodotus 2005, bk. 3, pp. 80–83).[1] It was perhaps Plato and Aristotle, however, who first began to think systematically about the different forms that regimes could take. In *The Republic,* Plato makes the case that political decision-making should be based on expertise and that "ochlocracy," or "mob rule," would result from allowing all people to rule in a democracy (1991: 427e–429a). In effect, just as only trained pilots should fly airplanes, Plato believed that only trained statesmen should guide the ship of state. The Greek word *demokratia* often gets translated as "rule by the people" with no mention about who these people are. In Plato and Aristotle's time, *demos* referred primarily to the "common people"— those people with little or no economic inde-

> ***Demokratia*** is a Greek word meaning "rule by the demos." Although the Greek word ***demos*** often gets translated as "the people," it refers more specifically to the "common people"— those people with little or no economic independence who were politically uneducated.

pendence who were politically uneducated (Hanson 1989, 71). Ultimately, Plato thought that democracy would not be government of the people but government of the poor and uneducated against the rich and educated. In addition, he believed that the uneducated mass would be open to demagoguery, leading to short-lived democracies in which the people quickly surrender power to a tyrant (Baradat 2006, 63).

Aristotle disagreed with Plato to the extent that he believed that there were some conditions under which the will of the many could be equal to or wiser than the will of the few (1996, 1281b). This is not to say, however, that he thought highly of democracy. In his *Politics,* Aristotle classified regimes in regard to the number of rulers that they had, stating that government "must be in the hands of one, or of a few, or of the many" (1996, 1279a.27–28). His classification is shown in Table 5.1. He believed that governments come in good and bad forms. In good forms of government the rulers govern for the good of all, whereas in bad forms they govern only for the good of themselves (1996, 1279a.17–21). The

TABLE 5.1	**Aristotle's Classification of Regimes**	
Number of rulers	Good form "For the Good of All"	Bad form "For the Good of the Rulers"
One	Monarchy	Tyranny
Few	Aristocracy	Oligarchy
Many	*Politeia*	Democracy

---

1. The earliest use of the word *demokratia* is in the *Histories* written by Herodotus sometime in the 440s to 420s B.C. (Rhodes 2003, 19). In this work, Herodotus mentions a debate among the Persians as to the relative merits of democracy, oligarchy, and monarchy. Athens is often considered the first recorded democracy (sixth century B.C.). Some scholars, however, argue that democracy existed in a recognizable form even earlier in the republics of ancient India (Muhlberger and Paine 1993).

good forms of government were monarchy, aristocracy, and *politeia;* the bad forms were tyranny, oligarchy, and democracy (1996, 1279b.4–10).

The concern for Aristotle was that each of the good forms of government could be corrupted in that the common good could be replaced by the good of the rulers. For example, a corrupted monarchy would become a tyranny, a corrupted aristocracy would become an oligarchy, and a corrupted *politeia* would become a democracy. Aristotle argues that we should choose the type of government that had the least dangerous corrupt form. For Aristotle, this was aristocracy. Like Plato, Aristotle believed that democracy would be the most dangerous form of government because it is characterized by class rule, in which poor and uneducated citizens govern for themselves rather than the commonweal. Some of the same fears about democracy—that it would result in class warfare, attempts by the poor to expropriate the rich, and so forth—were just as strong in the eighteenth and nineteenth centuries, when people were debating whether to extend the suffrage (Offe 1983; Roemer 1998). For example, Marx ([1850] 1952, 62) stated that universal suffrage and democracy inevitably "unchain the class struggle." These fears have also motivated efforts to restrict voting by certain categories of individuals during the twentieth century in the United States (Piven and Cloward 1988, 2000).

It should be noted that democracy at the time of Plato and Aristotle looked very different from what we understand democracy to be today. The most obvious difference is that democracy had nothing to do with elections when they wrote. In fact, leaders were chosen by elections in aristocratic forms of government, whereas they were decided by lot (that is, by drawing names from a hat) in democracies. As Montesquieu writes in his *Spirit of the Laws* ([1752] 1914, 2:2), "suffrage by lot is natural to democracy; as that by choice is to aristocracy." The notion that democracy was a system in which political offices were determined by lot continued all the way into the eighteenth century, and it is partly for this reason that many political theorists, such as Bodin, Hegel, Hobbes, Kant, Locke, Montesquieu, and Vico, all argued for the benefits of monarchy over democracy. Those people who were arguing for representative government in the eighteenth century did not see themselves as proponents of democracy. For them, democracy was associated with direct legislation by the people and, hence, was possible only in the city-states of the ancient world. In effect, democracy was seen as obsolete (Rosanvallon 1995, 141).

Only with the establishment of a major fault line between democracy and aristocracy in the age of revolution—French and American—did representative government and democracy come to be synonymous with each other (Hanson 1989; Rosanvallon 1995). Until this time, moves away from absolutism were motivated by attempts to get rid of unjust rulers rather than a desire to shift power to the people (Rhodes 2003, 28). In fact, lords and other members of the nobility would often side with commoners to get rid of unjust rulers. In this sense, corrupt monarchs, rather than the monarchy per se, were the target of opposition groups. This situation began to change during the French Revolution (1789) as the two opposing forces in the conflict solidified around the distinction between the aristocracy and the people. From this point on in time, the contemporary notion of democracy took on many of the characteristics that would be familiar to us today. It was also at this point that Aristotle's three-way distinction of government by one, a few, and many was replaced by a simple dichotomy between democracy (many) and autocracy/dictatorship (one or a few).

Box 5.1 | **DICTATORSHIPS**

It was really only after World War I that people began commonly to refer to autocracies as dictatorships. Historically, dictatorships have not always been seen as bad things. Although tyranny, despotism, and autocracy have always had negative connotations, this is not the case with dictatorships. A "dictator" was an extraordinary Roman magistrate nominated under exceptional emergency circumstances from about 500 B.C. to the third century A.D. This magistrate or dictator was nominated only for the duration of the extraordinary task entrusted to him. In his *Discourses,* Machiavelli argued that "dictatorial authority did good, not harm, to the republic of Rome" (1998, 34). Likewise, Rousseau, in *The Social Contract,* also suggested that dictators might be required in emergencies. He writes that "if the danger is such that the apparatus of law is itself an obstacle to safety, then a supreme head must be nominated with power to silence all laws and temporarily suspend the sovereign authority" (Rousseau 1987, bk. 4, chap. 6). Clearly, this positive connotation of a dictatorship has disappeared. Today, dictatorships are seen as largely synonymous with autocracy, tyranny, and despotism.

CLASSIFYING DEMOCRACIES AND DICTATORSHIPS

As political scientists, we often want to address questions such as why some countries are democracies but others are dictatorships, what factors influence democratic survival, and whether democracies or dictatorships produce better economic performance. To answer these questions we need to be able to measure democracy and classify countries as either democratic or dictatorial. This involves coming up with concrete observable phenomena or indicators that capture the abstract concept of democracy. Although our theories typically relate to abstract concepts, it is important to note that we do not actually observe these concepts when we look at the real world. Instead, we only get to evaluate indicators or measures of our concepts when we conduct empirical tests of our theories. We can think of a **measure** or **indicator** as a quantification of the thing in which we are interested.[2] As a result, we should

> A **measure** or **indicator** is a quantification of the concept or thing in which we are interested.

recognize that our empirical tests are good only to the extent that our selected indicators mirror the concept that we intend them to measure. In this section, we examine some of the various ways in which scholars have operationalized the abstract concept of democracy and discuss their strengths and weaknesses.

---

2. Although we use the terms *measure* and *indicator* interchangeably here, they are slightly different. A measure is a direct quantification of the concept or thing in which we are interested. For example, years are a measure of age. An indicator is a quantification of something that is known or believed to be correlated with the concept or thing in which we are interested. For instance, levels of corruption or transparency are indicators of characteristics of political systems, not measures of them.

Dahl's View of Democracy

Although our understanding of democracy has changed over time, the central notion underlying our contemporary concept of democracy is that "the people" rather than some subset of the people should rule. Exactly how this abstract concept is translated into a practical set of criteria for classifying political regimes varies enormously in political science (Collier and Levitsky 1997). In a highly influential book, Robert Dahl (1971) cautioned scholars against employing a substantive view of democracy. A **substantive view of democracy** classifies political regimes in regard to the outcomes they produce. To a large extent, Aristotle's view of democracy that we described earlier can be seen as substantive, because he distinguishes between good and bad versions of regimes based on the degree to which they serve the public good. Dahl argued that if scholars used normatively derived or substantive definitions of "ideal democracy"—that "true" democracies should rule in certain ways and should produce certain outcomes such as economic justice—then they may find it difficult to find real world examples of such regimes. For example, ask yourself how many regimes in the world actually produce economic justice? Dahl believed that researchers should employ a **minimalist,** or **procedural, view of democracy,** which classifies political regimes only in regard to their institutions and procedures.

> A **substantive view of democracy** classifies political regimes in regard to the outcomes that they produce. A **minimalist,** or **procedural, view of democracy** classifies political regimes in regard to their institutions and procedures.

Dahl identified two dimensions as being particularly important for classifying political regimes—levels of **contestation** and levels of **inclusion.** Contestation captures the extent to which citizens are free to organize themselves into competing blocs in order to press for the policies and outcomes they desire. Aspects of contestation include the freedom to form political parties, freedom of speech and assembly, and the extent to which leaders are chosen in free and fair elections. Contestation is, therefore, largely concerned with the procedures of democratic competition. Inclusion has to do with who gets to participate in the democratic process. Political regimes in which barriers to the naturalization of immigrants are low and all adult citizens are permitted to vote will rank high in regard to inclusion. In contrast, countries that have property requirements or that deny the effective right to vote based on place of birth, ethnicity, or gender would be considered less inclusive. We illustrate the two dimensions of contestation and inclusion in Figure 5.1.

> Dahl conceptualizes democracy along two dimensions: contestation and inclusion. **Contestation** captures the extent to which citizens are free to organize themselves into competing blocs in order to press for the policies and outcomes they desire. **Inclusion** has to do with who gets to participate in the democratic process.

The former Soviet Union is an example of a country that had high levels of inclusion because everyone was allowed to vote and participate, but it had low levels of contestation because there was only one political party. China has low levels of both inclusion and contestation, because there is only one party and there are no elections above the municipal level. In South Africa under apartheid and the United States prior to 1830 contestation was high, because there were multiparty elections, but inclusion was low, because vast segments of the population were not allowed to vote or participate. The expansion of the franchise in the United States during the 1830s represented an increase in inclusion, but substantial bar-

FIGURE 5.1	**Dahl's Two Dimensions of Democracy: Contestation and Inclusion**

Contestation

Polyarchies
(Ideal type)

Apartheid   Liechtenstein pre-1984,   U.S. today
South Africa,   Switzerland pre-1971,
U.S. before 1830   France pre-1945

China   Soviet Union

Inclusion

riers to full inclusion remained in place until at least 1964, when the Voting Rights Act gave many African Americans de facto access to the vote for the first time. As countries located in the top left of Figure 5.1 expand the right to vote, they begin to move rightward along the inclusion dimension. For example, Liechtenstein pre-1984, Switzerland pre-1971, and France pre-1945 had high levels of contestation due to multiparty elections, but because universal suffrage applied only to men, they had only moderate levels of inclusion. Most of the countries that we immediately recognize as being democracies today would be in the top right-hand corner of Figure 5.1 with high levels of both contestation and inclusion.

Dahl conceded that contestation and inclusion were only two aspects of what people take into account when they think of the concept of democracy. As a result, he was willing to drop the use of the term democracy altogether. Instead, he used the word **polyarchy** to describe a political regime with high levels of both contestation and inclusion. Another reason for preferring the term *polyarchy* was that he did not believe that any large country exhibited, or could exhibit, sufficient levels of contestation or inclusion to rightfully be considered a true democracy—countries could be closer or farther away from the ideal type of democracy, but they could never actually get there. Although the emphasis on contestation and inclusion has stuck and been incorporated into many of the subsequent measures of democracy, the term *polyarchy* has not. Comparative politics scholars continue to talk about democracy even when their operational definitions are no more ambitious (and frequently less ambitious) than Dahl's. We follow the practice of the comparative politics literature in using the word *democracy* even when discussing the procedural or minimalist definitions inspired by Dahl.

> A **polyarchy** is a political regime with high levels of both contestation and inclusion.

Three Measures of Democracy

How have comparative scholars operationalized the concept of democracy? What are the strengths and weaknesses of these operationalizations? Although there are several different measures of democracy (Munck and Verkuilen 2002), we focus here on three that are commonly used in the comparative politics literature—PACL, Polity IV, and Freedom House. As you will see, all three measures build, to differing extents, on Dahl's insights.

The PACL Measure

Przeworski, Alvarez, Cheibub, and Limongi (PACL) provide an annual measure of democracy for 199 countries from 1946 (or independence) to 2000. According to PACL, democracies are countries "in which those who govern are selected through contested elections" (2000, 15). The authors who constructed the PACL measure provide four rules for operationalizing their concept of democracy. A country is classified as a democracy if the following rules apply:

1. The chief executive is elected.
2. The legislature is elected.
3. There is more than one party competing in the elections.
4. An alternation in power under identical electoral rules has taken place.

A country is classified as a dictatorship if any of these four conditions do not hold. As you can see, the rules clearly recognize the centrality of elections to democracy. The authors rightly recognize, however, that elections are not sufficient to distinguish democracies from dictatorships. This is because virtually every country in the world has held legislative or presidential elections, or both, at one time or another (Golder 2005). Elections cannot fully distinguish between political regimes because almost all countries in the contemporary political world would be considered democratic by this standard.

The rules also recognize the importance of contestation to democracy (Schumpeter 1947; Dahl 1971). At a basic level, contestation requires that there be more than one party (rule 3). The authors who constructed the PACL measure, however, believe that contestation requires much more than just this. For them, contestation requires (a) *ex ante* uncertainty: the outcome of the election is unknown before it happens, (b) *ex post* irreversibility: the winner of the election actually takes office, and (c) repeatability: elections occur at regular and known intervals. *Ex ante* uncertainty rules out those countries, such as Iraq under Saddam Hussein, in which there was absolutely no uncertainty as to which candidate or party was going to win before the voters went to the polls. *Ex post* irreversibility rules out countries like Algeria in 1991, when the army intervened to prevent the Islamic Salvation Army from taking office following its success in the first round of legislative elections. Repeatability would rule out countries like Weimar Germany in the 1930s when the Nazi Party came to power through democratic elections but then canceled further electoral contests.

Together, these three characteristics of contestation provide the justification for the authors' fourth rule that an alternation in power under identical electoral rules must take place before a country can finally be considered a democracy. An alternation in power means that the individual who is the chief executive is replaced through the electoral process by someone else. Thus, an alternation occurred in the United States when Bill Clinton took over the presidency from George Bush in 1992. The authors who constructed the PACL measure believe that unless the incumbent ruler has demonstrated that he is willing to give up power after losing an election, then we have no way of truly knowing whether the country is a dictatorship or a democracy. For example, it is impossible without an alternation in power to distinguish between regimes in which the incumbents are always in power because they are popular (but would give up power if they lost) and those in which incumbents hold elections only because they know they will not lose—these two scenarios are observationally equivalent, that is, they look the same. Examples of this type of situation have occurred in several countries in which one party has been in power for long periods of time—Botswana, Japan, Malaysia, and Mexico (see Box 5.2).

The PACL measure builds on Dahl's insights in two respects. First, it is a purely procedural or minimalist view of democracy, because the classification rules make no mention of the outcomes produced by different political regimes. Second, it focuses strongly on Dahl's

ox 5.2

ALTERNATION IN POWER
Botswana, Japan, Malaysia, and Mexico

Multiparty elections have been held in Botswana, Japan, Malaysia, and Mexico. In each of these countries, however, a single party has been in power for long periods of time. Until the incumbents lost in Japan (LDP) and Mexico (PRI) and willingly gave up power, it was unclear whether these countries should be considered democracies or dictatorships. The difficulty in deciding whether these countries were democracies is illustrated by Malaysia, in which three multiparty elections were held between 1957 and 1969. The incumbent government won the first two multiparty elections. When it lost the third election, however, it declared a state of emergency, closed parliament, and rewrote the constitution such that it never lost another election (Ahmad 1988). Clearly, the holding of contested multiparty elections did not mean that Malaysia was a democracy. That the incumbent government was unwilling to give up power when it lost the third election suggests that it would have been unwilling to give up power if it had lost either of the two previous ones. Now consider Botswana. The incumbent government in Botswana has never lost an election since the country became independent in 1966. Should we consider Botswana to be a democracy? Many scholars do. According to the PACL measure of democracy, though, Botswana is coded as a dictatorship precisely because it is impossible to know for certain whether the incumbent government would willingly give up power if it lost—we have never seen it lose, so how would we know? In effect, the authors who constructed the PACL measure prefer to potentially mistake a democracy for a dictatorship rather than mistake a dictatorship for a democracy. This is a choice that all scholars obviously have to make.

notion of contestation. One obvious difference with Dahl is that the PACL measure completely ignores Dahl's dimension of inclusion. The authors justify this by saying that countries exhibit almost no variation in their level of inclusion for the time frame (1946–2000) of their measure (Przeworski et al. 2000, 16; Cheibub and Gandhi 2004). By 1946 all but a handful of countries around the world had adopted universal suffrage for their elections.[3] The biggest difference, though, between the PACL measure and Dahl's classification scheme is that the former treats regime type as a dichotomy—countries are either a democracy or a dictatorship—whereas Dahl treats regime type as a continuum with strong dictatorships at one end and strong democracies at the other. Although PACL accept that some regimes are more democratic than others, they believe that those countries with uncontested political offices should not be considered even partly democratic (Przeworski et al. 2000, 57). Put differently, the authors believe that there is a qualitative difference between democracies and dictatorships and that it does not make sense to think that there is a point at which a regime is equally democratic and dictatorial as implied by **continuous measures** of democracy. The abstract concepts of democracy proposed by PACL and Dahl are compared in Figure 5.2a and 5.2b. It is

A **dichotomous measure** is one that only has two discrete categories or values. (For example, "tall" or "short"). A **continuous measure** is one that can take on any intermediate value within a given range; for example, "height in centimeters."

because their conceptual view of regime type is dichotomous that the authors who constructed the PACL measure use a **dichotomous measure** to capture it, not because they think it is impossible to determine or measure whether some regimes are more democratic than others as some have implied (Elkins 2000).

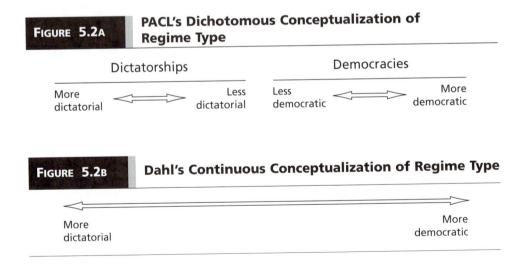

FIGURE 5.2A — **PACL's Dichotomous Conceptualization of Regime Type**

Dictatorships | Democracies

More dictatorial ⟵⟶ Less dictatorial | Less democratic ⟵⟶ More democratic

FIGURE 5.2B — **Dahl's Continuous Conceptualization of Regime Type**

⟵⟶

More dictatorial | More democratic

3. Given this justification, PACL would presumably have incorporated a country's level of inclusion into their measure of democracy had they gone further back in time to historical periods in which women and other groups were denied the right to vote.

Polity IV

An alternative measure of democracy comes from Polity IV. Polity IV provides an annual measure of democracy and autocracy for 184 countries from 1800 to the present (Marshall and Jaggers 2003). The Democracy and Autocracy scores for each country both range from zero to ten. From these two measures, a Polity Score is constructed for each country. The Polity Score is calculated as the Democracy Score minus the Autocracy Score. As a result, the Polity Score for each country ranges from a minimum of –10 (as autocratic or dictatorial as possible) to a maximum of 10 (as democratic as possible). Polity IV follows Dahl in conceptualizing and measuring democracy along a continuum like the one illustrated in Figure 5.2b. In practice, though, many scholars choose to code countries as democracies if their Polity Score is greater than 6, autocracies if their Polity Score is below –6, and mixed if the Polity Score is between –6 and 6.[4] Polity IV also follows Dahl in providing a largely minimalist or procedural measure of democracy, because it does not address substantive outcomes.

What are the precise rules that generate the Polity Score? A country's Polity Score is based on five different attributes or dimensions: (a) the competitiveness of executive recruitment, (b) the openness of executive recruitment, (c) the constraints that exist on the executive, (d) the regulation of political participation, and (e) the competitiveness of political participation. Together, these dimensions capture Dahl's notion of both contestation and inclusion. By including "constraints that exist on the executive," Polity IV actually adds an additional dimension to Dahl's concept of democracy—that democratic government must be limited government. Each of Polity IV's five attributes contributes a different number of points to a country's Democracy and Autocracy scores. As an illustration, consider the competitiveness of political participation dimension (an indicator of the degree of contestation) and the regulation of political participation dimension (an indicator of the degree of inclusion) in the political system. The possible scores for these dimensions are shown in Tables 5.2 and 5.3.

TABLE 5.2	**Competitiveness of Political Participation**		
	Contribution to democracy score	Contribution to autocracy score	Contribution to polity score
Competitive	3	0	3
Transitional	2	0	2
Factional	1	0	1
Restricted	0	1	–1
Suppressed	0	2	–2

---

4. Other scholars pick different cut-points for deciding whether a country should be considered a democracy or an autocracy. The decision of where to place the cut-points is rarely, if ever, justified in a theoretical manner. Unfortunately, there is reason to believe that the choice of where to place the cut-points matters in empirical tests (Coppedge 1997; Elkins 2000).

TABLE 5.3	Regulation of Political Participation		
	Contribution to democracy score	Contribution to autocracy score	Contribution to polity score
Regulated	0	0	0
Multiple identity	0	0	0
Sectarian	0	1	−1
Restricted	0	2	−2
Unregulated	0	0	0

If political participation is considered competitive in a country by those scholars coding it, then that country will have three added to its Democracy Score and nothing to its Autocracy Score.[5] In contrast, if political participation is considered suppressed by the coders, then two will be added to its autocracy score and nothing to its democracy score. If a country's political participation is considered restricted by the coder, then two will be added to that country's Autocracy Score and nothing to its Democracy Score. Note that the numbers or "weights" vary across these two dimensions. The scores from each of these dimensions are added together to come up with a country's overall Democracy, Autocracy, and Polity scores.

Freedom House

Freedom House (2005) has provided an annual measure of "global freedom" for 192 countries and eighteen territories since 1972. Although the measure provided by Freedom House is not technically a measure of democracy, many scholars use it as if it were, presumably under the assumption that democracy and freedom are synonymous. We leave it up to you to decide whether it is reasonable to assume that the more freedom exhibited by a country, the more democratic it is.

A country's Freedom House score is based on two dimensions capturing a country's level of political rights and civil rights. The amount of freedom on the political rights dimension is measured by a series of ten questions, each worth between zero and four points. The following are examples of the questions asked on the political dimension: Is the head of state elected in free and fair elections? Is there pervasive corruption? Is the government open, accountable, and transparent between elections? Do people have the right to organize? Is there a competitive opposition? Do minorities have reasonable autonomy? Whatever score a country gets out of the possible forty points is then converted to a seven-point scale. Thus, each country ultimately receives a score of 1 to 7 on the political rights dimension. The amount of freedom on the civil rights dimension is measured by a series of fifteen questions, each worth between zero and four points. The following are examples of questions asked on

---

5. To know precisely what is meant by competitive, transitional, factional, and so on, see the Polity IV Web site, http://www.cidcm.umd.edu/inscr/polity/index.htm.

the civil rights dimension: Is the media free and independent? Are there free religious organizations? Is there an independent judiciary? Is there equal treatment under the law? Are there free trade unions? Is there equality of opportunity? Do citizens have the right to own property? Whatever civil rights score a country gets out of the possible sixty points is also converted to a seven-point scale. Thus, each country ultimately receives a score of 1 to 7 on the civil rights dimension as well. The overall Freedom House score for each country is simply the average score on each of the two dimensions.

The questions relating to the political rights and civil rights dimensions take into account Dahl's concern with the levels of both contestation and inclusion in a country. Freedom House also follows Dahl in conceptualizing democracy along a continuum like the one illustrated in Figure 5.2b. In practice, though, many scholars choose to code countries as Free (Democratic), Partly Free (Mixed), and Not Free (Dictatorship) based on their Freedom House score: if a country scores 1 to 2.5, it is considered Free; if it scores 3 to 5.5, it is considered Partly Free; and if it scores 5.5 to 7, it is considered Not Free. In stark contrast to Polity IV, the PACL measure, and Dahl, Freedom House employs a substantive, rather than a procedural, view of democracy. Freedom House believes that although particular institutions are necessary for democracy, they are not sufficient. As a result, it takes into account the substantive outcomes produced by different political regimes, such as whether there is academic freedom, freedom from war, and freedom from socioeconomic inequalities.

In Appendix B at the end of the book, we illustrate how the three different measures classify political regimes in 188 independent countries for 2002. In Table 5.4, we show how the different measures classify political regimes in a handful of these countries. As you can see,

TABLE 5.4	Three Different Measures of Regime Type in 2002		
Country	PACL	Polity IV (–10 to 10)	Freedom House (1 to 7)
Egypt	Dictatorship	Dictatorship (–6)	Dictatorship (6)
Pakistan	Dictatorship	Dictatorship (–5)	Dictatorship (5.5)
China	Dictatorship	Dictatorship (–7)	Dictatorship (6.5)
Iraq	Dictatorship	Dictatorship (–9)	Dictatorship (7)
Rwanda	Dictatorship	Mixed (–4)	Dictatorship (6)
Iran	Dictatorship	Mixed (3)	Dictatorship (6)
Zimbabwe	Dictatorship	Mixed (–7)	Dictatorship (6)
Nigeria	Democracy	Mixed (4)	Mixed (4.5)
Turkey	Democracy	Democracy (7)	Mixed (3.5)
Argentina	Democracy	Democracy (8)	Mixed (3)
United States	Democracy	Democracy (10)	Democracy (1)
Israel	Democracy	Democracy (10)	Democracy (2)
France	Democracy	Democracy (9)	Democracy (1.5)

there are clearly some differences. For example, PACL and Polity IV both code Turkey as a democracy in 2002, but Freedom House codes it as a mixed regime (Partly Free). Similarly, Polity IV and Freedom House both code Nigeria as a mixed regime in 2002, but the PACL measure codes it as a democracy. On the whole though, these occasional differences are relatively few compared with the large degree of overlap between the measures. Overall, the measures from PACL, Polity IV, and Freedom House have been found to be highly correlated.[6]

Evaluating Measures of Democracy

In order to test our theories about abstract concepts such as democracy, we need to find measures of those concepts. The process by which scholars operationalize their measures will always involve some simplification or loss of meaning. It is important to recognize, however, that simplification is an essential part of the scientific process, for without it, empirical tests of our theories would be impossible. Still, this does not mean that all measures are created equal. Some measures are better than others. It is incumbent upon researchers to justify both the construction and use of whatever measure they employ in their research. Whether a particular measure is appropriate or not will depend heavily on the specific objective or research question of the scholar (Collier and Adcock 1999). With this in mind, we also often evaluate measures in terms of their conceptualization, validity, reliability, and replicability.

Conceptualization

Our three measures of democracy differ in their **conceptualization** of democracy. In particular, they differ in regard to whether they employ (a) a minimalist or substantive and (b) a dichotomous or continuous view of democracy. Let's begin by considering the distinction between minimalist and substantive views of democracy. Recall that the PACL measure and Polity IV provide a minimalist view of democracy, whereas Freedom House employs a more substantive view. To some extent, the appropriateness of these two views will depend on the particular research question the scholar asks.

> **Conceptualization** is the process of creating mental categories that capture the meaning of objects, events, or ideas.

For example, a substantive view of democracy runs into considerable problems if the researcher wants to know how regime type influences particular outcomes. Why? If we define democracy substantively in regard to, say, accountability, socioeconomic equality, and freedom from war, as Freedom House does, then using a country's Freedom House score to empirically examine whether democracy affects these very same things involves circular reasoning. Empirical tests will always suggest that a country's level of democracy increases accountability and the like in this situation because of the way the measure of democracy is constructed. Substantive measures of democracy, however, are arguably at least as appropriate as minimalist measures if the research question addressed

---

6. Despite high correlations, though, empirical results do seem to depend in some specific cases on which measure is used (Elkins 2000).

by the scholar is unrelated to any of the attributes that go into the construction of the democracy measure. For example, we might legitimately use the Freedom House score to examine whether regime type affects a country's proclivity to join international organizations or sign international treaties.

Irrespective of the research question, the very fact that minimalist views of democracy are *minimal* means that they have potential advantages when it comes to isolating causal processes. For example, if a study using Freedom House scores finds that democracy increases levels of economic development, how can the scholar determine which of the twenty-five underlying attributes (ten political rights questions and fifteen civil rights questions) is driving this observed relationship? In effect, many substantive measures of democracy conflate institutional and procedural factors with the outcomes they are thought to produce.

Finally, it should be noted that minimalist views of democracy do not place importance on things such as how the judiciary is organized or how the state intervenes in the economy. In effect, minimalist views recognize that democracies can be organized in many different ways. In contrast, Freedom House considers a country more free (democratic) if there is equality of opportunity, an independent judiciary, a right to own property, free trade unions, and so on. These are certainly important factors, but are they a part of what makes something a democracy or characteristics that vary from democracy to democracy that we might want to explain? In many ways, a free and democratic country according to Freedom House looks remarkably similar to an idealized version of the United States. Is this simply an accident or an example of analysts allowing what they view to be normatively appealing characteristics to color an ostensibly objective measure?

Now let's consider the distinction between dichotomous and continuous views of democracy. Recall that the PACL measure provides a dichotomous measure of democracy, whereas both Polity IV and Freedom House employ a continuous measure. There has been much debate about the relative merits of these two approaches (Collier and Adcock 1999; Elkins 2000). On the one hand, Bollen and Jackman (1989, 618, 612) argue for continuous measures of democracy, claiming that "democracy is always a matter of degree" and that treating it as dichotomous is a "flawed" practice. On the other hand, Alvarez and his colleagues (1996, 21) claim that Bollen and Jackman are "confused," because political regimes "cannot be half-democratic: there is a natural zero point." In effect, they suggest that democracy is like pregnancy in that women can't be half pregnant—they're either pregnant (democracy) or they're not (dictatorship). The debate essentially hinges on whether you think Figure 5.2a or 5.2b is the more appropriate conceptualization of regime type. In our opinion, scholars may reasonably disagree about this.

As with the distinction between minimalist and substantive views of democracy, though, the appropriateness of a dichotomous or continuous measure of democracy will depend to some extent on the researcher's question. On the one hand, the study of democratic transitions would suggest that a dichotomous measure is more appropriate, because a transition seems to imply movement from one distinct regime to another. This is, in fact, why we employ PACL's dichotomous measure of democracy when we examine the economic and cultural determinants of democratic transitions in Chapters 6 and 7. Similarly, research that examines whether parliamentary or presidential regimes affect democratic stability also seems to implicitly assume a dichotomy because parliamentary and presidential regimes are typically thought to exist only in democracies. On the other hand, studies that examine, say, the effect of foreign intervention on a country's level of democracy (see Box 8.2 on externally imposed democracy in Chapter 8) or the effect of the number of veto players on a country's level of democratic stability (see Chapter 15) don't seem to necessarily imply a dichotomous concept of democracy in the same way.

Validity

When we conduct empirical tests of our theories, we do not actually evaluate our abstract concepts. Instead, we only compare indicators or measures of those concepts. Consequently, our ability to use observations to understand the world is constrained by our ability to identify useful indicators or measures. This raises the question of what makes some indicators or measures more desirable than others. One thing that scholars would like their measures to be is valid. **Validity** refers to the extent to which our measures correspond to the concepts that they are intended to reflect (Adcock and

> **Validity** refers to the extent to which our measures correspond to the concepts that they are intended to reflect.

Collier 2001). Does our indicator actually measure the thing that it is supposed to measure? Several issues arise when we think about validity. Here, we briefly consider three: attributes, aggregation issues, and measurement level.

One of the initial tasks when constructing a measure is to determine the attributes that make up the abstract concept under consideration. You might ask whether a particular measure includes the "correct" attributes, whether it includes enough attributes to fully capture the concept, or whether it includes too many attributes. Unfortunately, there are no hard-and-fast rules for determining which attributes must be included when measuring a particular concept. Nonetheless, there are certain issues that scholars can take into account when constructing their measures. One issue has to do with having too many attributes. This is a particular concern with substantive measures of democracy such as the Freedom House measure. For example, Dahl was worried that there would be no actual countries in the world that could be classified as true democracies if too many attributes were included. Even if some countries can be classified as democracies, measures that employ many attributes may be of little analytical use. As we mentioned earlier, the inclusion of attributes such as accountability and socioeconomic equality in Freedom House's measure of democracy limits the scope of research questions that the measure can be used to answer. Of course, having too few attributes may also be problematic. Minimalist or procedural measures of democracy, such as those constructed by PACL and Polity IV, are open to the criticism that they do not really capture all of what we think of when we think of democracy. For example, some scholars criticize the PACL measure of democracy for not taking into account Dahl's notion of inclusion.

Even when the researcher has decided upon the attributes that constitute the abstract concept under consideration, he still has to decide how to aggregate or combine these attributes into a single measure of the concept. The measure of democracy from PACL does not require aggregation rules—a country is either a democracy or a dictatorship based on whether it passes a set of necessary and sufficient conditions. In contrast, the democracy measures from both Freedom House and Polity IV require aggregation rules to combine scores on multiple attributes into a single overall democracy score. None of the individual attributes used by Polity IV or Freedom House is explicitly necessary for a country to be considered democratic; instead, recall that a country is classified as democratic whenever it scores a high enough number of points across the range of included dimensions. As a good political scientist, you should ask yourself whether the aggregation rules employed by Freedom House and Polity IV are appropriate and justified.

Consider the aggregation rules used by Freedom House. Is it appropriate for Freedom House to weight each of the attributes (twenty-five questions) that make up a country's level of civil rights and political rights equally? Is academic freedom as important to democracy as an independent judiciary? Is it appropriate for Freedom House to weight the civil rights and political rights dimensions equally when coming up with a country's overall score? Now consider the aggregation rules employed by Polity IV. Is it appropriate for Polity IV to assume that moving from a one to a two on one of their five attributes will have the same effect on a country's level of democracy as, say, moving from a three to a four? Is Polity IV right to assume that all of their attributes measure democracy equally well? In other words, should Polity IV assume that moving from a one to a two on one attribute (competitiveness of political participation) will have the same impact on a country's level of democracy as moving from a one to a two on a different attribute (competitiveness of executive recruitment)? Is it appropriate for both Freedom House and Polity IV to assume that the different attributes of democracy can be aggregated along a single dimension? This last assumption would seem to run counter to Dahl's claim that democracy is inherently multidimensional. Although it is extremely rare to see scholars explicitly address these types of questions, Treier and Jackman (2008) recently examined aggregation issues as they relate to the Polity IV measure of democracy. They conclude that "skepticism as to the precision of the Polity democracy scale is well-founded, and that many researchers have been overly sanguine about the properties of the Polity democracy scale in applied statistical work."

Once a scholar has determined the best way to aggregate the attributes of a particular concept, he or she has to decide upon the most appropriate measurement level. There are three different measurement levels: nominal, ordinal, and interval. A **nominal measure** classifies observations into discrete categories that must be mutually exclusive and collectively exhaustive. This means that it must not be possible to assign any single case into more than one category (mutually exclusive) and that the categories must be set up so that all cases can be assigned to some category (collectively exhaustive). Essentially, a nominal measure is just a different way of naming cases. The PACL measure of regime type is a nominal measure in that it classifies, or "names," countries as either democracies or dictatorships. This is a valid way to measure democracy given the way the authors of the measure conceptualize democracy as a dichotomy.

A **nominal measure** classifies observations into discrete categories that must be mutually exclusive and collectively exhaustive. An **ordinal measure** rank-orders observations. An **interval measure** places observations on a scale so that we can tell how much more or less of the thing being measured each observation exhibits.

An ordinal measure allows us to rank order cases. As a result, an **ordinal measure** allows us to know whether a case has more or less of the thing that we are measuring. Thus, an ordinal measure of democracy would allow us to say whether country A was more or less democratic than country B. Note that we cannot say how much more or less democratic a country is using an ordinal measure. In contrast, an **interval measure** can allow us to determine exactly how much more or less of the thing that we are measuring a case exhibits. As a result, the claim that country A has two more units of democracy than country B is a meaningful statement only if we have an interval measure of democracy. Obviously, an interval measure requires that there be a standard unit of measurement. Both Polity IV and Freedom House employ an interval measure of democracy. This is a valid way of measuring democracy given the way that they conceptualize democracy as a continuum.

Reliability

When conducting empirical tests, not only do we want our measures to be valid, but we also want them to be reliable. A reliable measure is one that repeatedly and consistently produces the same score for a given case when we apply the same measurement process (Shively 1990, 48). A reliable measure of democracy would be one in which several people, when given the same rules for measuring democracy, all produce the same democracy score for a given country. What is the relationship between validity and **reliability?** A reliable measure does not necessarily imply a valid measure. Although a measurement process might produce results that do not change when repeated (reliability), this does not necessarily mean that the measure is an accurate reflection of the concept under consideration (validity). For example, an invalid measure might be reliable because it repeatedly and consistently produces the same "poor" score for a given case (Figure 5.3 left panel). Similarly, a measure may be valid in the sense that on "average" it captures the underlying concept, but unreliable in the sense that there might be a big difference in any two attempts to measure the phenomenon (Figure 5.3 center panel). Obviously, we would like our measures to be both valid and reliable (Figure 5.3 right panel).

Reliability refers to the extent to which the measurement process repeatedly and consistently produces the same score for a given case.

The reliability of a measure is likely to depend on the extent to which the measure depends on observable facts or subjective judgments. The PACL measure of democracy is likely to be highly reliable because it is based entirely on observables. For example, one only has to know whether the chief executive and legislature are elected, whether there is more than one party, and whether there has been an alternation in power under identical electoral

FIGURE 5.3	**Comparing the Reliability and Validity of Three Measures**

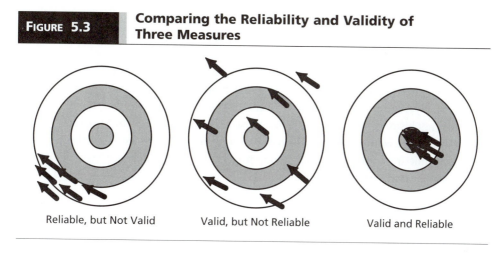

Reliable, but Not Valid	Valid, but Not Reliable	Valid and Reliable

rules to be able to code a country as a democracy or dictatorship. Given the ease with which we can observe elections, political parties, and so on, it is highly unlikely that two individuals would code the same country differently using PACL's rules. In contrast, the measures provided by Freedom House and Polity IV are likely to be less reliable because of their reliance on the subjective judgments of the individuals coding each country. For example, Freedom House asks country experts to code countries based on things such as *fair* electoral rules, *equal* campaigning opportunities, *free* and *independent* media, and *reasonable* self-determination. The fact that two individuals could reasonably disagree as to the meanings of the italicized words suggests that they might code the same country differently and, hence, that the resultant measure would be unreliable. A useful way to determine whether a measure suffers from reliability problems is to empirically assess inter-observer reliability by examining the degree to which different observers give consistent estimates of the same phenomenon. We do not know if Polity IV or Freedom House has ever conducted such tests.

Replicability

Another way to evaluate different measures is in regard to their replicability. **Replicability** refers to the ability of scholars to reproduce the

> **Replicability** refers to the ability of third-party scholars to reproduce the process through which a measure is created.

process through which a measure is created. King (1995, 2003) has been one of the strongest proponents of replication. He argues that for "any empirical work enough information should be made available that a third party can comprehend, analyze, replicate, and evaluate the results without further information from the original author" (2003, 72). Replicability is important because it allows researchers that were not party to the construction of a particular measure to independently evaluate the reliability and validity of that measure.

At a minimum, replicability requires that scholars provide clear coding rules and make their disaggregated data available. The three measures of democracy that we have examined vary in the extent to which they are replicable. For example, PACL and Polity IV provide much more detailed and clear coding rules for constructing their democracy measures than Freedom House does. In fact, Freedom House provides no coding rules for why a country might be given, say, a three on one of its twenty-five questions instead of any other score. Disaggregated data refer to the scores given to each observation on the different attributes that are combined to produce a country's overall democracy score. Although Polity IV makes all of the disaggregated data on each of its five attributes available to the public, Freedom House has not historically provided the disaggregated data from its twenty-five questions. In other words, there is no way to know what score a country was given on, say, the questions about academic freedom or personal autonomy. This has led Munck and Verkuilen (2002, 21) to conclude that "the aggregate data offered by Freedom House has to be accepted largely on faith." [7]

CONCLUSION

In this chapter, we have illustrated some of the difficulties that face political scientists when they try to transform abstract concepts such as democracy into measures or indicators that can be used to empirically test theories. Democracy has many meanings in our everyday language and it is just not possible to capture them all in a single measure; nor would we necessarily want to do this even if we could. Measurement implies simplification, and simplification implies choices and tradeoffs on the part of the scholar. Scholars should ask themselves what their research question is before creating or using a particular measure. Some measures will be appropriate for some research projects but not for others. You might think that it is always better to have the most multifaceted measure possible, but this is not always the case. As we have suggested, "minimalist" measures may be able to answer more questions, and more interesting questions at that, even though they do not perhaps capture the full complexity of the abstract concept under consideration. The validity and reliability of our measures will often be constrained by the practicalities of the measurement process. Unlike in most areas of the natural sciences, many of the measures in political science require subjective evaluations. This brings with it the danger of nonvalidity and poor reliability. Without these measures, however, we would be unable to test many of our most interesting and important theoretical claims.

Ultimately, we believe that political scientists should be aware of measurement issues and do the best that they can. This involves being aware of the limitations of their measures and not overstating the generality of theoretical claims made on the basis of these measures. The exact details of the process by which various measures are constructed should be made publicly available so that other scholars can replicate them and better evaluate their validity and reliability. At the same time, it is important for readers like you not to immediately reject measures because they appear to be poor reflections of the concept that they are trying to

---

7. Freedom House has recently responded to criticisms like this. Since 2006, it has begun to provide some information about its disaggregated data; however, it still does not provide scores for all twenty-five of its questions.

capture. Instead, ask yourself whether you can come up with a better measure. How can the measure be improved? Does the perceived quality of the measure affect the conclusions reached by the author, and in what way? Just as we do not reject an existing theory until a better one comes along, we should not immediately reject a particular measure until a better measure comes along. We hope that political scientists and students like you will construct better measures. Political scientists often spend their time developing better theories, but it may be better to spend a little more time developing better measures first.

KEY CONCEPTS

conceptualization, *160*

contestation, *152*

continuous measure, *156*

demokratia, 149

demos, 149

dichotomous measure, *156*

inclusion, *152*

interval measure, *164*

measure/indicator, *151*

minimalist, or procedural, view of democracy, *152*

nominal measure, *164*

ordinal measure, *164*

polyarchy, *153*

reliability, *164*

replicability, *165*

substantive view of democracy, *152*

validity, *162*

PROBLEMS

The problems that follow address some of the more important concepts and methods introduced in this chapter.

Conceptualizing and Measuring Democracy

1. Name some of the things that you associate with democracies. Would these things form part of a minimalist or a substantive view of democracy? Are these things observable or are they based on subjective evaluations? Do you think that the things you name enable you to classify countries as democracies or dictatorships in an unambiguous manner?

2. Do you think that a dichotomous or a continuous view of democracy is most appropriate? Does it depend? If so, what does it depend on?

3. Discuss the advantages and disadvantages of the three measures of democracy addressed in this chapter.

4. Say we wanted to test the following hypothesis:

   • Citizens in democracy have more equality of opportunity than citizens in dictatorships.

   If we want our hypothesis to be falsifiable, would it matter whether we used Freedom House or PACL to measure democracy? If so, why? If not, why not?

5. Say we wanted to test the following hypothesis:
   - Democracies are more likely to sign international treaties with other democracies than they are with dictatorships.

   If we want our hypothesis to be falsifiable, would it matter whether we used Freedom House or PACL to measure democracy? If so, why? If not, why not?

6. Can you think of other abstract concepts like democracy that might be of interest to political scientists and difficult to measure? How do you think that political scientists measure these concepts in practice?

Measures

7. In this chapter, we introduced different levels of measurement—nominal, ordinal, and interval.

   a. The economic growth rate in Bangladesh in 2000 was 3.7 percent. Is this an example of a nominal, ordinal, or interval measure of economic growth?
   b. If we classified national economies as "open" or "closed," then would we be creating a nominal, ordinal, or interval measure?
   c. Surveys such as the American National Elections Study often ask respondents to say how much they like a particular party or candidate. If the possible responses are "Very much," "Sort of," "Not really," and "Not at all," then is the measure nominal, ordinal, or interval?
   d. We often measure an individual's level of education in terms of the number of years that he or she has spent in school. As a result, is our measure of education nominal, ordinal, or interval?
   e. If we were to measure someone's eye color, would we typically use a nominal, ordinal, or interval measure? Could we measure eye color at more than one level of measurement? If so, explain how.
   f. Say we wanted to measure temperature. What might a nominal measure of temperature be? What might an ordinal measure be? What might an interval measure be?

8. Describe the difference between validity and reliability in your own words.

9. Imagine that the true value of democracy in country X is 5 on a scale of 0 to 10. Say there are four people who code the level of democracy in country X using two different measures of democracy, A and B. Measure A yields values of 4, 3, 6, and 4. Measure B yields values 6, 6, 7, and 6. Is Measure A or Measure B a more reliable measure of democracy in country X? Why?

10. Imagine that the true level of human rights violations in country X is 5 on a scale of 0 to 10. Say there are four people who code the level of human rights violations in country X using two different measures, A and B. Measure A yields values of 3, 4, 6 and 7. Measure B yields values 6, 5, 7, and 6. Is Measure A or Measure B a more valid measure of human rights violations? Why?

6 The Economic Determinants of Democracy

> Democracy endures only if it is self-enforcing. It is not a contract because there are no third parties to enforce it. To survive, democracy must be an equilibrium at least for those political forces which can over throw it.
>
> Przeworski 2006, 312–328

> The capacity for strategic calculations by maximizing monarch results in the owners of mobile factors, which the monarch seeks to tax, being . . . . given great voice over the policy choices of governments.
>
> Bates and Lien 1985, 53–70

OVERVIEW

- Classic modernization theory argues that countries are more likely both to become democratic and to stay democratic as they develop economically. We present empirical evidence to support these claims. Specifically, we show that democracy is more likely to emerge and survive in wealthy countries.

- One criticism of classic modernization theory is that it lacks a strong causal mechanism linking wealth with democracy. A more recent variant of modernization theory offers a potential solution to this criticism. The theory posits that changes in the socioeconomic structure of a country that accompany economic development in the modernization process (not wealth per se) promote the emergence and survival of democracy.

- This variant of modernization theory explains why democracies are more likely to emerge and survive in wealthy countries. It also helps to explain why countries that are abundant in natural resources such as oil, diamonds, or minerals tend to be dictatorships. The theory also has important insights for the role that foreign aid, economic inequality, and economic performance play in the democratization process.

In the post–cold war era, in which the world's only superpower has suggested that it is interested in spreading democracy, it is worth asking where democracy comes from and why it survives. In the previous chapter, we examined the criteria that political scientists use to classify a country as democratic or dictatorial. With this knowledge in hand, we can now ask the following two questions: Why do some states become democratic but not others? Why does democracy survive in some states but fail in others? In this chapter, we focus on so-called economic arguments for democracy. In particular, we investigate how economic development and the structure of the economy influence the likelihood that a country will become and remain democratic. In doing so, we illustrate how the predatory view of the state discussed in Chapter 4 can help to explain why some states are democratic and others dictatorial. In the next chapter, we turn to so-called cultural arguments for democracy.

CLASSIC MODERNIZATION THEORY

Most economic explanations for democracy can be linked to a paradigm—a family of explanations—called "modernization theory." Modernization theory argues that all societies pass through the same historical stages of economic development. The claim in the aftermath of post–World War II decolonization was that contemporary underdeveloped countries were merely at an earlier stage in this linear historical process of development than more developed countries. For example, economic historians, such as Rostow (1960) and Gerschenkron (1962), believed that countries in Africa, Asia, and Latin America in the 1950s and 1960s were just "primitive" versions of European nations and that they would eventually "develop" and come to look like Western Europe and the United States.[1] These primitive or immature societies were characterized by large agricultural sectors and small industrial and service sectors. Eventually these countries would "grow up" and become mature societies characterized by small agricultural sectors, large industrial and service sectors, rising urbanization, higher educational attainment, and increasing societal "complexity."

Although modernization theory was originally developed by economists and economic historians, it was later taken up by political scientists, most famously by Seymour Martin Lipset (1959, 1960). Modernization theorists in political science claim that as a society moves from being immature or "traditional" to being mature or "modern," it needs to change to a more appropriate type of government. Dictatorships might be sustainable in immature societies, but this is no longer the case in mature societies once they develop economically. Przeworski et al. (2000, 88) summarize modernization theory in the following way:

> As a country develops, its social structure becomes complex, new groups emerge and organize, labor processes require the active cooperation of employees, and, as a result, the system can no longer be effectively run by command: The society is too complex,

---

1. Modernization scholars eventually came to believe that countries could jump stages by copying and learning from countries further ahead of them. This was important because it helped to explain how the Soviet Union could advance so quickly during the middle of the twentieth century.

technological change endows the direct producers with autonomy and private information, civil society emerges, and dictatorial forms of control lose their effectiveness. Various groups, whether the bourgeoisie, workers, or just the amorphous "civil society," rise against the dictatorial regime, and it falls.

In effect, democracy is "secreted" out of dictatorship by economic development. Although Przeworski et al. (2000) highlight modernization theory's claim that countries will become democratic as they develop economically, Lipset (1959, 75) argues that modernization theory also implies that democracy will be more likely to survive in economically developed countries—as he puts it, "the more well-to-do a nation, the greater the chances that it will sustain democracy." In sum, classic modernization theory predicts that economic development will help both (a) the emergence of democracy and (b) the survival of democracy. The basic outline of classic modernization theory is shown in Figure 6.1.

For many people, the terminology used by modernization theory and its implications are unsettling and troubling. After all, the theory suggests that all countries, once they mature, will eventually come to look like the United States and Western Europe. In effect, countries just need to grow up—rather like a baby growing up into a responsible adult. Attempts have since been made to change the terminology used to describe these "primitive" countries. These countries used to be called primitive, but scholars started to refer to them as "backward." As this new terminology took on negative connotations of its own, "backward" countries soon became "third world" countries. With the collapse of the Berlin Wall, this new term began to seem outmoded because the "second world" countries—the command economies behind the "iron curtain"—were no longer set apart from the rest of the world in the way they once were. In addition, "third world" began to take on negative connotations because the term *third* implied that these countries were somehow behind the "first" and "second" worlds. As a result, scholars started referring to these countries as "underdeveloped." This too has recently changed to "developing" countries. Although scholars have

FIGURE 6.1   Classic Modernization Theory

"Traditional" society		"Modern" society
Large agriculture	⟶	Small agriculture
Small industry	⟶	Large industry
Small service	⟶	Large service
Dictatorship	⟶	Democracy

changed the terminology of classic modernization theory and felt disturbed by the implication that all countries will eventually come to look like the United States and Western Europe, we should not let political correctness stop us from asking whether this theory is actually falsified or not in the real world. Just because we do not like some of the implications of our theory is not a good reason to reject it—we have to ask what the empirical evidence says. Is classic modernization theory falsified or not?

One of the central implications of modernization theory is that there should be a strong relationship between how economically developed a country is and whether it is a democracy. Scholars often measure economic development in terms of a country's wealth because, as countries develop, they tend to become wealthier. So is there a relationship between wealth and democracy? Let's look at some data. Figure 6.2 graphs the proportion of countries that are democratic at different levels of wealth. In this case, wealth is measured by **GDP per capita** calculated in 1985 PPP United States dollars (see Box 6.1). Figure 6.2 clearly indicates that a country is much more likely to be a

GDP per capita stands for gross domestic product per capita. Gross domestic product measures the value of all goods and services produced in a country during a specified period, usually one year. GDP per capita is a country's gross domestic product divided by the size of the population. It is a common measure of the amount of wealth per person in an economy.

democracy if it is wealthy than if it is poor. Although virtually all countries with a GDP per capita above $8,000 are democratic (the proportion is close to 1), only 12 percent of the countries with a GDP per capita of less than $1,500 are democracies; that is, 88 percent of these countries are dictatorships.

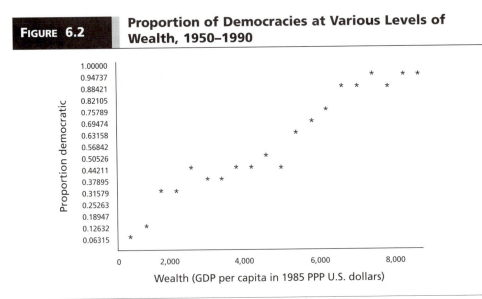

| FIGURE 6.2 | **Proportion of Democracies at Various Levels of Wealth, 1950–1990** |

Source: Data are from Przeworski et al. (2000, 80).

COMPARING WEALTH ACROSS COUNTRIES

In this chapter, we measure wealth as GDP per capita calculated in 1985 PPP U.S. dollars. What does this mean exactly? GDP stands for gross domestic product and measures the value of all goods and services produced in a country during a specified period. In effect, it is a measure of a country's wealth. GDP per capita is just a measure of a country's wealth per person; that is, GDP divided by the size of the population. GDP per capita is normally measured in each country's own currency. So, GDP per capita would be measured in pounds in the United Kingdom, pesos in Mexico, dinars in Iraq, rupees in India, euros in France, and so on.

If we want to compare one country's wealth with that of another, we have to express their GDP per capita in the same currency. One way to do this is to use one country's actual exchange rate to transform it into the currency of the other country. This method is considered problematic by most scholars, however, because a country's exchange rate does not appropriately reflect price differences on goods and services between countries. As a result, the standard method employed by economists and political scientists to transform each country's GDP per capita into the same currency is to use what is known as purchasing power parity (PPP) exchange rates. How does this work?

PPP calculates the price of a particular bundle of goods in each country using each country's local currency. To calculate the exchange rate between two countries, one simply takes the ratio of the two prices. A simple example of a measure of PPP is the Big Mac index popularized by the *Economist* magazine. The Big Mac index looks at the prices of a Big Mac burger in McDonald's restaurants in different countries. If a Big Mac costs US$4 in the United States and GB£3 in Britain, then the PPP exchange rate would be £3 for $4. The *Economist* magazine uses this Big Mac PPP exchange rate to see how much a country's actual exchange rate is under- or overvalued. Obviously, economists and political scientists use a much more representative bundle of goods than just a Big Mac, but the idea is the same.

The most common PPP exchange rate comes from comparing goods in each country with equivalent goods in the United States. As a result, we get what is known as a PPP U.S. dollar exchange rate. These PPP exchange rates are calculated at specific points in time; in our case, 1985. This is important because, over time, inflation can change the value of a currency even within countries. We hope that you are now able to understand what we mean when we say that a country's wealth is measured as the gross domestic product (GDP) per capita calculated in 1985 purchasing power parity (PPP) U.S. dollars.

Clearly, there seems to be a strong relationship between wealth and democracy. But does this necessarily mean that classic modernization theory is correct? Recall that modernization theory predicts that increases in wealth promote both the emergence and the survival of democracy. The data in Figure 6.2 are certainly consistent with modernization theory, but it turns out that they are also consistent with a slightly different story, which we will call the "survival story." According to the survival story, increasing wealth promotes the survival of democracy but does not affect whether a country becomes a democracy in the first place. But which story is more accurate? Does increased wealth only help the survival of democracy or does it also help the emergence of democracy? In recent years, scholars have conducted a great deal of research in an attempt to answer this question (Przeworski et al. 1996; Przeworski and Limongi 1997; Przeworski et al. 2000; Boix and Stokes 2003; Inglehart and Welzen 2005; Przeworski 2005; Epstein et al. 2006).

This new round of research began when a well-known comparative political scientist, Adam Przeworski, argued that increased wealth helps democracies survive but does not help countries become democratic in the first place. Why does Przeworski think that wealth helps democracy to survive? Well, he argues that the decision to choose democracy or dictatorship depends on the types of outcomes that you expect them to produce for you. Whereas Przeworski describes democracy as a system in which you can expect at least a moderate level of consumption, he describes dictatorship as a system in which you might win or lose everything. In democracies, citizens are normally guaranteed at least some minimal standard of living because resources are distributed relatively broadly. In a dictatorship, though, citizens are likely to do extremely well if they are part of the dictator's circle but extremely poorly if they are not. Not only is a dictatorship a world of extremes but it is also a world in which the probability of being part of the dictator's circle is very small.

Imagine that you are a wealthy person living in a democracy. Consider what life would be like for you in a dictatorship. There is a small probability that you would be in the dictator's circle, and you might become richer. Still, there is a very large possibility that you would not be in the dictator's circle and that you would lose everything and become much, much poorer. Thus, switching to a dictatorship is very much of a gamble if you are wealthy. According to Przeworski, this is why most wealthy people prefer to stay in democracies and, hence, why wealthy countries tend to remain democratic. Now imagine that you are a poor person living in a democracy. Consider what life would be like for you in a dictatorship. There is a large possibility that you would remain poor. There is, however, a small possibility that you could become very rich if you were in the dictator's group. Given that you are already poor and really have nothing to lose, you might want to take a gamble and switch to a dictatorship. According to Przeworski, this is why poor people may be more willing to take a chance with dictatorship and, hence, why democracy tends to be unstable in poor countries. As you can see, this line of reasoning implies that democracy is more likely to survive in a wealthy country than in a poor country.

Notice that Przeworski's "survival story" looks at the situation from the standpoint of decision makers who already find themselves in a democracy. He argues that the process by which countries become democratic may be unknowable, but if actors find themselves in a democracy at any given point in time, then the level of wealth will, for the reasons just indicated, influence whether they stay in a democracy. This has led Przeworski and various coauthors (1996, 1997, 2000, 2005) to argue that the emergence of democracy may be entirely unrelated to the level of wealth in a country but that we will still observe a long-run relationship between increased wealth and democracy because rich democracies survive longer than poor ones. Why? Well, imagine that a country flips between dictatorship and democracy at random. Sometimes a country will flip to democracy when it is wealthy. Although wealth did not cause this country to become democratic, it will help it stay democratic. Sometimes a country will flip to democracy when it is poor. Because the country is poor, it will likely collapse back into dictatorship. If this story is correct, then we will end up with a world in which nearly all the rich countries are democratic but in which the poor countries continue to alternate between democratic and dictatorial episodes. Unless countries for some unknown reason flip more frequently to democracy than they flip to dictatorship, democracies will—on average—be richer than dictatorships.

As you can now see, the evidence presented in Figure 6.2 showing a positive relationship between wealth and democracy is consistent with (a) **modernization theory** and its prediction that wealth promotes both the emergence and survival of democracy and (b) the **survival story**, in which wealth has no effect on the emergence of democracy but does help democracy to survive once it is established. The reason is that both of these stories predict that democracy is more likely in wealthy countries than in poor ones. As a result, we cannot simply look to see if democracy and wealth go together as we did in Figure 6.2 to determine whether modernization theory is consistent with the observed world. You may remember from our discussion of the scientific method back in Chapter 2 that political scientists often have competing theories to explain the same empirical observation. This is exactly what we have here, because modernization theory and the survival story both explain the observed positive association between wealth and democracy. When political scientists find themselves in this type of situation, they must try to deduce additional hypotheses from their theories in the hope that these additional hypotheses will help them decide which of the competing theories is most consistent with the observed world. As we saw in Chapter 2, competing stories will always share some implications in common (otherwise they would not be explanations for the same phenomena), but they must always differ in others (otherwise they would not be different explanations). It is up to the political scientist to identify these divergent implications and come up with a critical test to identify which story is most consistent with the observed world.

> **Modernization theory** predicts that democracy is more likely to emerge and survive as countries develop and become wealthier. Przeworski's **survival story** predicts that democracy is more likely to survive as countries develop and become wealthier but it is not more likely to emerge.

Boix and Stokes (2003) summarize the implications of modernization theory and the survival story by plotting how each story expects the probabilities of a transition to democracy and of a transition to dictatorship to change with increasing wealth. We reproduce their basic graph in Figure 6.3. Note that both modernization theory and the survival story predict that the probability of a transition to dictatorship decreases as wealth increases (the solid lines in both panels slope down). In other words, both stories predict that increased wealth helps democratic survival. What about transitions to democracy? Although modernization theory predicts that a transition to democracy increases with wealth (the dotted line in the

Expected Probability of Regime Transitions as Wealth Increases according to Modernization Theory and the Survival Story

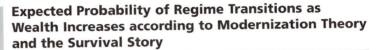

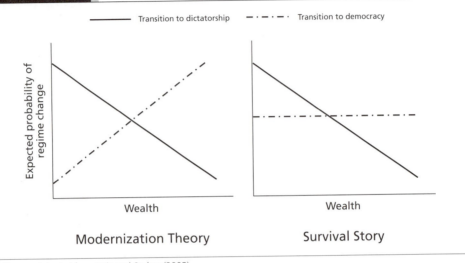

Modernization Theory   Survival Story

Source: Adapted from Boix and Stokes (2003).

left panel slopes up), the survival story predicts that the probability of a transition to democracy is unaffected by increasing wealth (the dotted line in the right panel is flat).

Note that the probability of any type of transition is simply the sum of the probability of a transition to dictatorship and the probability of a transition to democracy weighted by the frequency of each type of transition. According to the survival story, the probability that a country will experience any kind of regime transition declines with increased wealth. This is because the survival story predicts that increased wealth increases democratic stability (fewer transitions to dictatorship) but has no effect on the stability of dictatorships (no effect on transitions to democracy).[2] In contrast, the effect of increased wealth on the probability of any kind of regime transition is ambiguous in modernization theory. This is because increased wealth increases the stability of democracy but reduces the stability of dictatorships—modernization theory does not tell us which effect is stronger. In sum, then, modernization theory and the survival story share two implications in common but differ on two as well. All four implications are summarized in Table 6.1.

We now evaluate the implications of both modernization theory and the survival story using data from Przeworski et al. (2000). As predicted by both stories, democracies are more common in rich countries than poor countries (Implication 1). We saw this earlier in Figure 6.2,

---

2. Przeworski et al. (2000, 88–92) are very clear on this point—as wealth increases, the probability of transitioning to democracy remains constant but the probability of transitioning to dictatorship goes down.

TABLE 6.1	Implications from Modernization Theory and the Survival Story

Modernization theory and survival story

1. Democracy is more common in rich countries than poor countries.

2. Transitions to dictatorship become less likely as wealth increases.

Modernization theory	**Survival story**
3a. Transitions to democracy become more likely as wealth increases.	3b. Transitions to democracy are unaffected by increases in wealth.
4a. Regime transitions may or may not become less likely as countries become wealthier.	4b. Regime transitions become less likely as countries become wealthier.

which showed that the proportion of countries that were democratic at different levels of wealth was larger when wealth was high than when wealth was low. This result is further confirmed by Figure 6.4, which plots the number of years that all countries (country years) have lived under democracy or dictatorship at different levels of wealth between 1950 and 1990. As you can see, when countries are very poor (say, when GDP per capita is below $2,000), almost nine out of every ten country years in the data set are lived under dictatorship; that is, there are roughly 900 country years under dictatorship and 100 country years under democracy when GDP per capita is lower than $2,000. When countries are relatively rich, however (say, when GDP per capita is above $8,000), virtually all the country years in the data set are lived under democracy. For a broad swath of countries in between (say, when

FIGURE 6.4	Country Years under Democracy and Dictatorship, 1950–1990

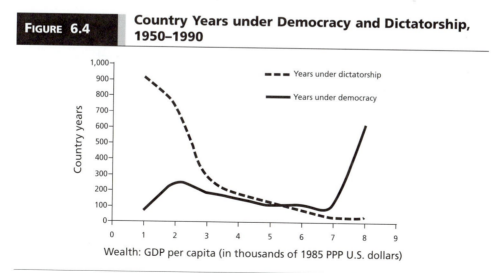

Source: Data are from Przeworski et al. (2000).
Note: The figure plots the number of years that all countries (country years) have lived under democracy or dictatorship at different levels of wealth.

GDP per capita is between $4,000 and $6,000), there are about as many country years under democracy as there are under dictatorship.

The two critical implications that allow us to distinguish between modernization theory and the survival story concern (a) the frequency of regime transitions in general and (b) the effect of increased wealth on transitions to democracy in particular. In Figure 6.5, we plot the number of transitions to democracy, the number of transitions to dictatorship, and the total number of regime transitions at different levels of wealth. Recall from Table 6.1 that the survival story predicts that regime transitions become less likely with increases in wealth. At first glance, there appears to be evidence in support of the survival story, because poor countries seem to experience more transitions than rich ones in Figure 6.5. Can you think why this evidence might be problematic? Comparing the raw number of transitions in this way can be quite misleading, because the number of transitions that might take place is limited by the number of countries that are democracies or dictatorships at each level of wealth. The problem is that both modernization theory and the survival story predict, and our observations have already shown, that the number of dictatorships and democracies are not constant across different levels of wealth. Moreover, we have also seen that the world has had more experience with poverty than with wealth. Thus, even if the probability of a regime transition were the same for poor countries and rich ones, the fact that there are more poor countries in the world will mean that the raw number of transitions in poor countries will be larger than that in rich countries. Thus, the evidence shown in Figure 6.5 is not sufficient to show that regime transitions become less likely with increases in wealth as the survival story predicts.

| FIGURE 6.5 | **Number of Regime Transitions as a Function of Wealth, 1950–1990** |

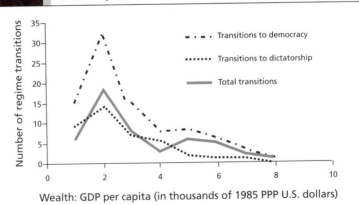

Source: Data are from Przeworski et al. (2000).

Instead, what we need to do is look at how wealth affects the probability of regime transition and not just at how it affects the raw number of regime transitions. The probability of a regime transition, given a particular level of wealth, is calculated as follows:

$$\text{Pr (Regime Transition} \mid \text{Wealth Level)} = \left. \frac{\text{Number of Transitions to Democracy or Dictatorship}}{\text{Number of Country Years}} \right| \text{Wealth Level}$$

This equation tells us that the probability of a regime transition given a particular level of wealth is equal to the total number of transitions at that wealth level divided by the number of cases (or country years) at that wealth level.

In Figure 6.6, we plot the probability of a regime transition at different levels of wealth. As you can see, there is no strong relationship between wealth and the probability of a regime transition. Specifically, it does not appear that the probability of regime transition decreases linearly with wealth as the survival story predicts. Thus, the evidence presented in Figure 6.6 would seem to falsify one of the implications of the survival story (Implication 4b, Table 6.1). In contrast, an increase in the probability of a regime transition when levels of wealth are low, as shown in Figure 6.6, is consistent with modernization theory; a certain amount of resources may be necessary for any change to take place. A decrease in the probability of a regime transition at high levels of wealth, as shown in Figure 6.6, is also consistent with modernization theory; by this point democracy should have emerged in nearly all countries, and there is no reason according to modernization theory for it not to survive.

| **FIGURE 6.6** | **Probability of Regime Transitions as a Function of Wealth, 1950–1990** |

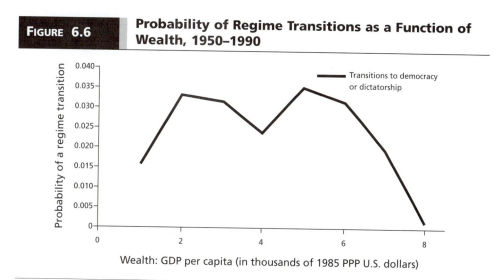

Source: Data are from Przeworski et al. (2000).

Although the evidence suggests that the survival story is incorrect when it predicts that the frequency of regime transitions declines linearly with wealth, the key implication that allows us to distinguish between the survival story and modernization theory has to do with whether increases in wealth actually make transitions to democracy become more likely. In Figure 6.6, we looked only at the effect of increases in wealth on regime transitions in general. We now need to examine the effect of increased wealth on transitions to democracy and transitions to dictatorship specifically. The probability of transitioning to democracy is calculated as:

$$\text{Pr (Transition to Democracy | Wealth Level)} = \left. \frac{\text{Number of Transitions to Democracy}}{\text{Number of Autocratic Country Years}} \right| \text{Wealth Level}$$

The probability of transitioning to dictatorship is calculated as:

$$\text{Pr (Transition to Dictatorship | Wealth Level)} = \left. \frac{\text{Number of Transitions to Dictatorship}}{\text{Number of Democratic Country Years}} \right| \text{Wealth Level}$$

In Figure 6.7, we plot the probability that a country will transition to democracy and that it will transition to dictatorship at different levels of wealth. The numbers in the figure indicate how many times more likely it is for a country to transition one way rather than the other. The numbers are gray whenever a country is more likely to transition to dictatorship than democracy and black whenever a country is more likely to transition to democracy than dictatorship. Although there was little evidence in Figure 6.6 that wealth affects the proba-

| **FIGURE 6.7** | **Probability of Transitions to Democracy and Dictatorship as a Function of Wealth, 1950–1990** |

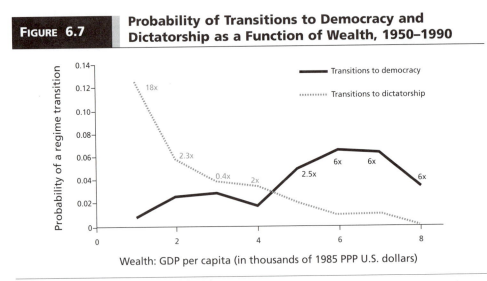

Source: Data are from Przeworski et al. (2000).

Note: The numbers in the figure indicate how many times more likely it is for a country to transition one way or another. For example, the gray "2x" indicates that a country is twice as likely to transition to dictatorship as transition to democracy when its GDP per capita is $4,000.

bility of regime transitions in a consistent way, Figure 6.7 clearly shows that the kind of transition that countries experience is a function of wealth. As predicted by both the survival story and modernization theory, the probability of transitioning to dictatorship (the gray dotted line) declines as wealth increases. In other words, the downward-sloping dotted line indicates that wealth encourages democratic survival (Implication 2, Table 6.1).

In direct contradiction to the survival story but entirely consistent with modernization theory, however, the probability of a democratic transition increases with wealth (the solid black line slopes upward). In other words, countries do seem more likely to become democratic as wealth increases (Implication 3a, Table 6.1). Note that the likelihood that a country transitions to democracy rather than dictatorship clearly increases with wealth. For example, transitions to dictatorship are eighteen times more likely than transitions to democracy when GDP per capita is less than $2,000. The reverse is true in rich countries, however—transitions from dictatorship to democracy are much more likely to occur than transitions from democracy to dictatorship. For instance, the probability of becoming democratic is six times larger than the probability of becoming dictatorial when GDP per capita is greater than $6,000.

In sum, the evidence that we have just presented suggests that the observed world looks more like the one envisioned by modernization theory than the one envisioned by the survival story. The bottom line is that wealth appears to increase both the likelihood that democracy will emerge and the likelihood that it will survive. This is entirely consistent with the predictions of classic modernization theory.[3] Later in the chapter, we show that these results continue to hold even when we take account of other factors that might affect the emergence and survival of democracy. We summarize our findings for now in Table 6.2. Those implications supported by the data are shown in the shaded cells.

TABLE 6.2	**Modernization Theory and the Survival Story: A Summary of the Evidence**

Modernization theory and survival story	
1. Democracy is more common in rich countries than poor countries: YES	
2. Transitions to dictatorship become less likely as wealth increases: YES	

Modernization theory	Survival story
3a. Transitions to democracy become more likely as wealth increases: YES	3b. Transitions to democracy are unaffected by increases in wealth: NO
4a. Regime transitions may or may not become less likely as countries become wealthier: YES	4b. Regime transitions become less likely as countries become wealthier: NO

Note: The hypotheses in the shaded cells are supported by the data, whereas those in the nonshaded cells are not.

---

3. Evidence in support of the theoretical predictions of classic modernization theory has been provided by a whole host of empirical analyses in recent years (Londregan and Poole 1996; Barro 1999; Ross 2001; Boix 2003; Boix and Stokes 2003; Inglehart and Welzen 2005; Epstein et al. 2006). While evidence to the contrary would seem to come from Przeworski et al. (2000), their famous claim that wealth does not increase the probability of democratic transitions is contradicted by results from their own fully specified model (124).

A VARIANT OF MODERNIZATION THEORY

In the previous section, we examined the claim made by classic modernization theorists that countries are more likely to become democratic and stay democratic as they become wealthier. One common criticism of classic modernization theory is that it lacks a strong causal mechanism and that it simply relies on an empirical correlation between wealth and democracy (Rueschemeyer, Stephens, and Stephens 1992; Acemoglu and Robinson 2006). We now examine a variant of classic modernization theory that explicitly provides a causal mechanism linking economic development and democracy.

This variant of modernization theory says that it is not wealth per se that encourages democracy but rather changes in the socioeconomic structure of a country that accompany economic development. This variant of modernization theory incorporates a predatory view of the state and helps to show why some rulers share power or limit their extractive activity (democracy) whereas others do not (dictatorship). As such it helps to answer one of the puzzles that we were confronted with at the end of Chapter 4 when we examined the origins of the modern state. Not only does this variant of modernization theory explain why democracies are more likely to emerge and survive in wealthy countries, but it also helps to explain why countries that are abundant in natural resources, such as oil, diamonds, or minerals, tend to be dictatorships rather than democracies. The theory also has important insights for the role that foreign aid, economic inequality, and economic performance play in the democratization process. Specifically, it offers a potential explanation for why foreign aid might be detrimental to democratization efforts (Easterly 2002; Bueno de Mesquita and Smith 2004), why economic inequality might not necessarily be harmful to the emergence and survival of democracy (Boix 2003; Reenock, Bernhard, and Sobek 2007), and why economic performance in dictatorships tends to be much more heterogeneous than in democracies (Przeworski et al. 2000; Bueno de Mesquita et al. 2003).

Economic Development, Natural Resources, and Democracy

As we mentioned earlier, one of the central features of modernization theory is the idea that all societies proceed through a similar series of economic and political stages (Rostow 1960). As a society proceeds through these stages, it undergoes structural changes. A key structural change has to do with the relative size of the "sectors" in the economy. According to this view, and illustrated in Figure 6.1, all economies can be divided into the same set of sectors—agricultural (sometimes referred to as the "traditional" sector) and manufacturing and services (sometimes referred to as the "modern" sector). Just as the relative sizes of a human's body parts change as they mature, so too—according to some modernization theorists—do the relative sizes of a society's economic sectors.[4] Specifically, countries tend to have large agricultural sectors but relatively small manufacturing and service sectors in the early stages of development. As the modernization process brings about efficiencies in the agricultural sector, resources are freed

---

4. Because maturity in humans is typically considered a good thing, the idea—put forth by scholars in "developed societies"— that "developing societies" are at an earlier stage of a maturation process (which, if all goes well, will culminate in those countries looking like "mature" societies) was, understandably, considered to be offensive to many in the developing world.

up for use in manufacturing and service sectors. Over time, and as countries continue to develop and mature, the manufacturing and service sectors become larger and larger relative to the agricultural sector.

Many scholars have argued that this is precisely what started to happen in early modern Europe. As agriculture became more efficient, fewer peasants were needed to work the land and traditional feudal bonds that tied peasants to the land were torn asunder. This, eventually, led to a population shift from rural areas to urban ones. This shift occurred both at the top and bottom of the social spectrum. Peasants found themselves dispossessed of lands that they had traditional claims to, and members of the gentry found themselves drawn into the commercial activities of the towns. A key feature of the commercialization of the agricultural gentry in England at this time was the shift from grain production to the grazing of sheep to feed the growing demand of wool producers (Moore 1966). As Bates and Lien (1985) have argued, this change in the composition of the British economy played a crucial role in the creation of representative government in England.

By the seventeenth century, the modernization process in England had brought about a shift in economic power from a relatively small number of traditional agricultural elites, who controlled large domains producing easily quantifiable agricultural products, to a rising class of wool producers, merchants, and financial intermediaries, who controlled assets that were much more difficult for the state to count—and, hence, more difficult for the state to tax. In contrast to the traditional agricultural elites, who were unable to hide their fields from the Crown's tax collectors, wool producers and the new commercialized gentry could better hide their sheep (by moving them around) and their business profits. According to Bates and Lien (1985), the ability of the gentry to hide their assets from state predation changed the balance of power between modernizing social groups and the traditional seats of power—specifically, the Crown. Suddenly, the kings and queens of England, who needed money to keep hold of power at home and to wage their wars abroad, found themselves in a position in which predation no longer worked; instead, they had to negotiate with economic elites in order to extract revenues. Because the growth of towns and the rise of the wool trade had also led to an increase in the number of economic decision makers whose actions determined the share of revenues available to the Crown, it was, perhaps, natural for these actors to use their newfound bargaining power to increase the strength of institutions, such as the Parliament, that helped aggregate their interests. The result was the supremacy of Parliament and the withering away of old avenues of representation, such as the Star Chamber, which had formerly served the traditional elites. Note that the increased mobility of assets—the ability to move and hide sheep or the ability to invest money in the Netherlands rather than in England, for example—can be thought of as equivalent to an increase in the value of the "exit option" possessed by economic elites. We return to this later in the chapter.

North and Weingast (1989) present a similar argument, in which they claim that the development of economic actors who could hide their assets led the Crown to look for ways to credibly commit to honoring its financial obligations to the emerging financial class from whom it wished to borrow money to fund its external wars. One way to do this was by strengthening the power of Parliament in relation to the king. To see how this argument works, imagine a king who has a temporary need to raise resources above and beyond what existing tax revenues can cover. Perhaps the king is conducting an expensive foreign war against a rival power. Although the king might like to simply exploit his citizens and take the money he needs by force as he did in the past, this option is less realistic now that the new gentry can hide their assets. Instead, it is likely that the king must borrow the money he needs from the gentry and promise to pay it back with interest at a later date. The problem is that the king controls the use of violence within his territory. As a result, private capital holders always have to worry that the king will default on his debts after the war is over and that they will not get their money back. In contrast to a student who takes on large amounts of debt while in college, there is no authority over the king who can threaten to forcefully collect the debt once the smoke has cleared and the battles have been fought. In other words, **sovereign debt**—debt accrued by the sovereign, or Crown—creates what is known as a **credible commitment problem** (see Box 6.2). Although the king would like to credibly commit, or promise, to pay back the money he borrows from the gentry, he cannot do this because there is nothing that the gentry can do to force the king to pay the debt back once the money has been borrowed. Knowing that they cannot force the king to pay the debt back, the lenders are unwilling to lend the king any money in the first place. As North and Weingast (1989) suggest, one solution to this problem is to make the Crown's potential financial backers more powerful by strengthening the role and importance of the Parliament vis-à-vis the king. If the king reneges on his debts now, he will suffer punishment at the hands of the Parliament. This is precisely the explanation proposed by many scholars to explain the institutional reforms that led to the establishment of modern parliamentary democracy in Britain during the Glorious Revolution of 1688 (Acemoglu and Robinson 2000, 2006; Stasavage 2002).

Sovereign debt refers to debt that is accrued by the sovereign, that is, the government.

A **credible commitment problem** or a time-inconsistency problem occurs when (a) an actor who makes a promise today may have an incentive to renege on that promise in the future and (b) power is in the hands of the actor who makes the promise and not in the hands of those expected to benefit from the promise.

Bates and Lien (1985) argue that the introduction of this more limited state occurred earlier and more definitively in England than it did in France because of the unique structure of the economy that early modernization had produced in England. To see why this is the case, it is useful to return to the Exit, Voice, and Loyalty game that we first analyzed in Chapter 3. In the prehistory of the game, the Crown, under the exigencies of war, has confiscated the assets of a segment of the elite represented by Parliament. We shall refer to this segment of the elite as the Parliamentarians. At this point, the Crown is still behaving in its usual predatory fashion as though the economic development sweeping through English society did not concern it directly. However, the Parliamentarians are operating from a newfound position of strength vis-à-vis the Crown. The Parliamentarians have three options. The first option is to take what assets remain and do everything they can to shield them from further confiscation—in part by taking their assets out of production or consuming them (exit). If the Parliamentarians no longer invest their assets, the economy is likely to stagnate and there will be less for the Crown to tax or confiscate in the future. The second option is

ox 6.2

CREDIBLE COMMITMENT PROBLEMS

North and Weingast (1989) suggest that kings who wish to borrow money from economic elites may have difficulty credibly committing or promising to repay any loans that they obtain. The basic reason is that although the king may promise today to repay the loans in the future, the king might use his power to renege on his promise when the loans actually come due. Credible commitment problems like the one outlined here have (at least) two basic characteristics. One is that they always involve a temporal dimension: what is in your interest to promise today may not be in your interest to do in the future. Some people refer to credible commitment problems as "time-inconsistency problems" for this very reason. The second is that they always involve situations in which power is in the hands of those who make the promise and not in the hands of those who expect to benefit from the promise. For instance, it is the king who has the power and not the economic elites in North and Weingast's example.

Credible commitment problems are not confined to politics; in fact, they occur in many areas of our lives. For example, consider an employer who promises to pay a worker at the end of the month for the work that she does. The worker must do her work before she actually gets paid. A commitment problem arises if the employer promises to pay the worker at the end of the month, but when payday comes, it is no longer in the interests of the employer to make the payment. You should immediately be able to see why the employer might have an incentive to not pay the worker once the work is done.

Society has developed at least three ways to deal with credible commitment problems like this: (a) contracts, (b) repeated interactions, and (c) institutions that alter the distribution of power (Acemoglu and Robinson 2006, 134).

1. *Enforceable contracts:* One of the most common ways to deal with a credible commitment problem like the one in our employer–worker example is with an enforceable contract. In effect, the worker and the employer could sign a contract in which the employer promises to pay the worker for her work. If the employer reneges and the contract is enforceable, the worker can file a complaint with an outside agency, such as a court of law, which can force the employer to pay up. As you might expect, this solution is not without its problems. For example, the court must presumably determine whether the quality of the work done by the worker is up to the standards promised in the contract. Although contracts may sometimes prove ineffective at solving credible commitment problems in economic settings for reasons such as this, they are likely to be even less useful in more political settings. This is primarily because the outside agency that typically enforces the contract (the state or the king perhaps) may well be one of the actors involved. For instance, it should be obvious that the economic elites and the king in North and Weingast's example cannot write a contract to solve their credible commitment problem for the simple reason that it would have been the king—who has an incentive to renege—who would have had to enforce it.

2. *Repeated interactions:* Another solution to potential credible commitment problems occurs when the two sets of actors are involved in repeated interactions. For example, employers may be deterred from reneging on their promise to pay workers at the end of the month if they need those workers (or others) to work the next month. In effect, employers do not want to develop a bad reputation because they need people to be willing to work for them in the future. Note that this solution to the credible commitment problem assumes that the actors making the promise care enough about the future that they are willing to forgo the benefits that they could get today from reneging on their promise. This assumption helps to explain why the repeated interactions solution to potential credible commitment problems is often not very useful in political settings. For example, the king's promise to repay his loans in the North and Weingast story is not particularly credible even though the king and the economic elites are likely to be involved in repeated interactions. The reason has to do with the fact that the king is often under financial stress, and hence in need of loans, precisely when foreign wars threaten his continued survival. In these circumstances, the king may not be particularly forward looking. In other words, he may come to discount the future so steeply that he is relatively unconcerned with the implications of his behavior on his future reputation. After all, we are only really concerned with our future reputation when we are reasonably confident that we will have a future.

3. *Institutions that alter the distribution of power:* Recall that one of the reasons for why certain promises suffer from a credibility problem is that the actor making the promise has power and the beneficiary of the promise does not. It is this asymmetric distribution of power that allows the promiser to renege. Given this, one solution to potential credible commitment problems is to create institutions that transfer power from the actor making the promise to the beneficiary of the promise. In our employer–worker example, one could create a trade union that would give workers the power to punish employers who renege on their promises through things like strikes. It is this ability to punish the employer that (a) encourages the employer to stick to his promise to pay the worker at the end of the month and that (b) makes the worker believe that the employer will follow through with his promise and thus provide the labor in the first place. This solution to potential credible commitment problems is quite common in political settings and is precisely the solution that the king of England employed in North and Weingast's example to make his promise to repay the loans from the economic elites credible. By transferring power to Parliament, which represented the interests of the economic elites and which could realistically punish the king if he reneged, the king was able to solve his credible commitment problem.

Despite these potential solutions, the difficulty in solving credible commitment problems should not be underestimated in politics. Consider the following three examples.

1. *Iraq:* Imagine that you are a member of an armed Sunni group in Iraq following the U.S. invasion in 2003. Both the United States and the Shia-dominated government want all armed militias to hand in their weapons to reduce the killing and violence. The problem is that if you hand in your weapons, you have no guarantee that the Shia-dominated government will not take advantage of this to repress you. Any promise by the Shia-dominated government not to repress Sunnis, to include Sunnis in the government, and to share funds from oil production with Sunnis is not credible, because the Shias have an obvious incentive to renege once you and your fellow Sunnis have handed in your weapons. As of writing this chapter, there appears to be no good solution to this problem.

2. *Northern Ireland:* Imagine that you are a member of the Irish Republican Army (IRA) which has been involved in violent activities designed to force the British government to give up control of Northern Ireland. Suppose that the British government and forces in Northern Ireland loyal to London promise to sit down and negotiate a political settlement as long as you first give up your weapons. The problem is that this promise is not necessarily credible. If you give up your weapons, then you are likely to lose any leverage that you would have in the upcoming negotiations. What's to stop the British government from ignoring or repressing you as soon as you give up your weapons? It is this credible commitment problem that has played a large role in hampering recent attempts to end the decades-long civil war in Northern Ireland. Attempts to solve the problem have typically involved both sides making small, incremental steps toward peace in an attempt to develop a reputation for following through on their word. For example, the IRA has periodically allowed an Independent Monitoring Commission to verify that it has put increasing numbers of its weapons beyond use. At the same time, the British government has periodically responded by removing army posts from Northern Ireland or making reforms to the Protestant-dominated Royal Ulster Constabulary (the Northern Irish police force) that has traditionally been closely linked to the British government in the minds of many Catholics. These incremental steps that have been necessary to develop reputations for not reneging on promises help to explain why moves toward a peaceful resolution of the civil war in Northern Ireland have been rather slow.

3. *South Africa:* Imagine that you are a member of the white minority that controlled South Africa during the apartheid era. Apartheid was a system of racial segregation that was enforced from 1948 to 1994 to ensure the economic and political dominance of whites over the indigenous African population. Suppose that you have come to believe that apartheid is unsustainable and that you think full democracy should be introduced in South

Africa. The problem is that in a democratic South Africa, the indigenous African population would represent a clear majority of the electorate and could pass policies to redistribute wealth and assets from the rich white minority to the poor black majority. This is likely to make you reluctant to introduce democracy. Imagine that the indigenous Africans, led by the African National Congress (ANC), promise that they will not redistribute too much if you allow democracy. Is this promise credible? Not really. Once democracy is established, what's to stop the ANC from reneging on its promise and using its large majority to redistribute wealth away from the white minority? This credible commitment problem may well help to explain why the apartheid system lasted so long. Note that the inability of the ANC to credibly promise not to redistribute too much may have prolonged the life of the apartheid system even if both the white minority and the black majority preferred to live in a low-redistribution democracy. You may be wondering why the apartheid regime finally came to an end in 1994. One answer is that the credible commitment problem faced by the ANC was solved by structural changes in the South African economy (Wood 2000). These changes included the increased mobility of the economic assets of the white minority that resulted from the globalization of the South African economy during the 1980s and early 1990s. In effect, this change in the mobility of the assets controlled by the white minority altered the power relationship between the white minority and the ANC. Now, if the ANC reneged on any promise not to redistribute too much, members of the white minority had the ability to simply remove their assets from South Africa and take them somewhere else. Because the economic performance of the South African economy depended heavily on these assets, the ANC's promise not to redistribute them became credible. This helps to explain why the transition to democracy in South Africa occurred when it did.

to petition the Crown for protections against future confiscations in exchange for a promise to continue investing their assets in the economy (voice). We will assume that the petition calls for the Crown to accept limits on future predatory behavior, say, by granting Parliament the right to veto all future increases in taxation or by constructing an independent judiciary capable of policing the Crown's behavior. The third option is for the Parliamentarians to continue investing their assets as they had before the confiscation (loyalty).

If the Parliamentarians decide to use voice and petition the Crown, the Crown can respond in one of two ways. First, it can accept the new limits on its power to tax (accept). In this case, we assume that the Parliamentarians will happily continue to invest their assets and the economy will grow. Second, it can reject the new limits (reject). If the Crown rejects the limits, then the Parliamentarians must choose whether to continue investing as before (loyalty) or to withdraw substantial portions of their assets from the market (exit). Depending on whether the Parliamentarians choose to continue investing their assets, the economy will either stagnate or grow. This strategic interaction between the Parliamentarians and the Crown is shown in Figure 6.8, going from left to right.

FIGURE 6.8	**Exit, Voice, and Loyalty Game without Payoffs between the Parliamentarians and the Crown**

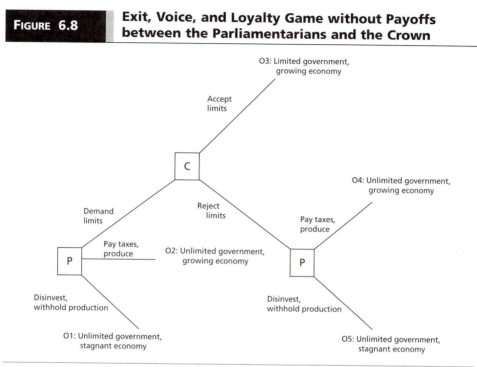

Note: C = Crown; P = Parliamentarians.

As you may recall from our analysis of game-theoretic models in Chapters 3 and 4, we cannot say what we expect the actors to do unless we can make statements about how they evaluate the potential outcomes. In what follows, we use the same payoffs as we did when evaluating the Exit, Voice, and Loyalty game in Chapter 3.[5]

According to the story that we have been telling, the Crown is dependent on the Parliamentarians—the Crown needs their money. In regard to the payoffs in our model, this means that $L > 1$. For now, let us assume that the Parliamentarians (P) have credible exit threats ($E > 0$). In other words, the Parliamentarians have mobile assets—the value they get from their assets when they hide them from the Crown is higher than it is when they obediently pay their taxes in a confiscatory environment. In Figure 6.9, we solve the Exit, Voice, and Loyalty game for the situation in which the Crown is dependent and the Parliamentarians have a credible exit option. The subgame perfect Nash equilibrium is (Demand limits, Disinvest; Accept limits), and the observed outcome is a limited government with a growing economy. In effect, the Crown decides to accept limits on its predatory behavior because it knows that it is dependent on the Parliamentarians for its money and because it knows that the Parliamentarians will disinvest and exit if it rejects the limits. Knowing that its petition

---

5. To see where these payoffs come from, we encourage the reader to refer back to Table 3.2 in Chapter 3.

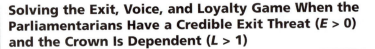

FIGURE 6.9

Solving the Exit, Voice, and Loyalty Game When the Parliamentarians Have a Credible Exit Threat ($E > 0$) and the Crown Is Dependent ($L > 1$)

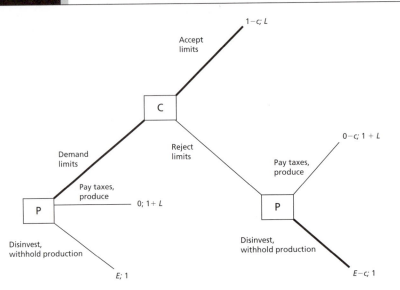

The subgame perfect Nash Equilibrium is (Demand limits, Disinvest; Accept limits).

Note: C = Crown; P = Parliamentarians; E = Parliamentarians' exit payoff; 1 = value of benefit taken from the Parliamentarians by the Crown; L = Crown's value from having loyal Parliamentarians who do not exit; c = cost of using voice for the Parliamentarians. It is assumed that $c, L > 0$; $E < 1 - c$; $E > 0$; and $L > 1$.

will be effective, the Parliamentarians use voice and demand limits from the Crown. This particular scenario helps to explain why the Crown in England, which was dependent on a social group with a credible exit threat (mobile assets), agreed to accept limits on state power.

In contrast to England, Bates and Lien (1985) argue that the agricultural sector in France had undergone considerably less modernization and, as a result, the engine of the economy—such as it was—continued to be a traditional oligarchy that derived its wealth from agricultural production based on quasi-feudal processes that were easy to observe and, therefore, easy to tax. In the terminology of our Exit, Voice, and Loyalty game, the relevant elites in France did not possess credible exit threats ($E < 0$). The French Crown, though, was as dependent on its economic elites as was the case in England. In Figure 6.10, we solve the EVL game for the situation in which the Crown is dependent and the Parliamentarians do not have a credible exit option. The subgame perfect Nash equilibrium is (Pay taxes, Pay taxes; Reject limits), and the observed outcome is unlimited government and a growing economy. In effect, the Crown will reject any demands to limit its predatory behavior in this situation because it knows that, although it is dependent on the Parliamentarians for money, the Parliamentarians will continue to invest and pay their taxes even in a predatory environment

FIGURE 6.10	**Solving the Exit, Voice, and Loyalty Game When the Parliamentarians Do Not Have a Credible Exit Threat (*E* < 0) and the Crown Is Dependent (*L* > 1)**

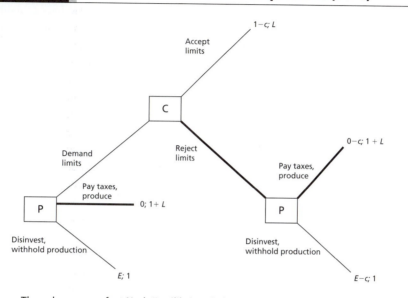

The subgame perfect Nash Equilibrium is (Pay taxes, Pay taxes; Reject limits).

Note: C = Crown; P = Parliamentarians; *E* = Parliamentarians' exit payoff; 1 = value of benefit taken from the Parliamentarians by the Crown; *L* = Crown's value from having loyal Parliamentarians who do not exit; *c* = cost of using voice for the Parliamentarians. It is assumed that *c*, *L* > 0; *E* < 1 − *c*; *E* < 0; and *L* > 1.

because they do not have a credible exit option. Knowing that the Crown will ignore their petitions, the Parliamentarians simply continue to invest and pay their taxes at the beginning of the game. This scenario helps to explain why the French Crown remained absolutist at a time when the English monarchy was accepting limits on its predatory behavior. For example, the Estates General, the chief French representative body at the time, did not meet between 1614 and May 1789, by which point financial crises had reached such proportions that the French Revolution may have been unavoidable. For nearly two centuries, then, French elites had little choice but to try to influence the Crown's behavior through the intricacies of court politics rather than through a parliament.

Up to this point, we have assumed that the Crown depends on the Parliamentarians for money and other resources. What happens, though, if the Crown is autonomous—it has other sources of money—and does not depend on the Parliamentarians? There are two scenarios to consider—one in which the Parliamentarians do not have a credible exit option and one in which they do. Instead of explicitly solving the EVL game for these two scenarios—we leave that for you to do—we simply describe the expected outcomes of the game. If the Parliamentarians do not have a credible exit option (mobile assets), then they will respond to state predation by continuing to invest and pay their taxes. They will do this because they know that the Crown does not depend on them in any way and so will ignore any of their petitions. In this scenario, the fact that the Parliamentarians continue to invest their assets means that the economy will grow. If the Parliamentarians do have a credible exit option, though, then they will choose to exit and disinvest in the economy—they realize that there is no point in petitioning the Crown to limit its predatory behavior because the Crown does not depend on them. In this scenario, the Parliamentarians' disinvesting means that the economy stagnates.

The outcomes of the four different scenarios are shown in Table 6.3. Note that we expect democracy (limited government) to emerge and survive only when the state (Crown) depends on economic elites (Parliamentarians) who have credible exit options (mobile assets). This was the case during the Glorious Revolution in England. The English Crown found itself dependent on a set of societal elites with whom it was forced to bargain. It had to bargain with them because a sufficient number of these elites possessed assets that were mobile and, hence, difficult to tax. It was as a result of this that the Crown ultimately accepted serious limitations on its power, thereby bringing limited and representative government into being in England. This central argument can be stated more broadly: representative government (of which democracy is an example) is more likely to emerge and survive when the rulers of a country depend on a segment of society consisting of a relatively large number of people holding liquid, or mobile, assets. Barrington Moore Jr. (1966, 418) essentially stated the same argument quite succinctly in his book about the social origins of democracy and dictatorship—"No bourgeois, no democracy."

The argument that we have just made helps alleviate some of the concern that political theorists such as Locke had with Hobbes's solution to the state of nature. Recall from our discussion in Chapter 4 that Hobbes saw the creation of a powerful state that would hold its cit-

TABLE 6.3	**Summary of Outcomes in the Exit, Voice, and Loyalty Game**	
	Crown	
	Is autonomous $L < 1$	Is dependent $L > 1$
Parliamentarians		
Have a credible exit threat (mobile assets) $E > 0$	*Poor dictatorship* (unlimited government, stagnant economy)	*Rich democracy* (limited government, growing economy)
Have no credible exit threat (fixed assets) $E < 0$	*Rich dictatorship* (unlimited government, growing economy)	*Rich dictatorship* (unlimited government, growing economy)

izens in "awe" as the solution to the "war of all against all" and the "solitary, poor, nasty, brutish, and short" life that characterizes the state of nature. Although theorists such as Locke recognized that the creation of the state might solve the political problem that citizens have with each other, they thought that it created a potential new problem between the citizens and the state. By surrendering control over the means of violence to the state, what was to prevent the state from using its power against its citizens? As some put it, "Who will guard the guardian?" [6] The argument that we have just presented here illustrates that there are some conditions under which the state will *voluntarily* agree to limit its predatory behavior: when the state depends on segments of society with mobile assets. At least under these conditions, no one needs to guard the guardian because the guardian will guard itself.

Our discussion of the Glorious Revolution in England makes it clear that it is not just a large group of actors with an interest in restricting the Crown's arbitrary behavior that produces parliamentary supremacy; the key is that this group has plausible exit options. A concept central to the viability of exit options is what economists call **quasi-rents.** A quasi-rent is the difference between an asset's value and its short-run opportunity cost. In other words, how much value does an asset return in its best case scenario usage compared with its second best case scenario usage? When this difference is large, the asset is said to generate large quasi-rents. For example, the first best use of a copper mine is to produce copper. If it is not producing copper, there is not a lot you can do with a copper mine. In fact, the second best use of a copper mine may be to fill it with water and use it as a not-so-attractive swimming pool. Similarly, if an off-shore oil platform is not used to produce oil, its second best usage might be for sunbathing, fishing, or, perhaps, bungee-jumping. As attractive as these activities might be, the return they are likely to bring the oil company is certain to be considerably less than that provided by oil. This is why things like copper mines and off-shore oil platforms are said to generate large quasi-rents.

> A **quasi-rent** is the difference between an asset's value and its short-run opportunity cost.

The concept of quasi-rents can be used to generalize the argument that we have made about the Glorious Revolution in England still further. All societies contain some actors who derive their wealth from the control of assets that produce huge quasi-rents. These actors, the owners of oil wells, copper mines, and other hard-to-redeploy assets, suffer great losses when the price of their commodity produced in the first best use of their asset plunges. Still, all societies also contain some actors who derive their wealth from the control of assets that can be relatively easily redeployed in response to price changes. These actors derive their wealth from their assets' flexibility, not from quasi-rents. Members of the first group (fixed asset holders), who control assets producing large quasi-rents, are not likely to possess credible exit options—it is hard for the owners of a copper mine or an oil company to profitably redeploy their assets (the mine, the oil rig, and so on) if the state decides to prey upon these assets. Members of the second group, however, who control relatively liquid assets, do possess

---

6. The original quotation, "Quis custodiet ipsos custodies?" is from Juvenal, Satire IV ("On Women").

credible exit options; if the state decides to prey upon them, they simply redeploy their assets elsewhere, out of the state's reach. According to the analysis of the Exit, Voice, and Loyalty game that we have just presented, the state will tend to be attentive to the needs of **liquid asset** holders and relatively unresponsive to **fixed asset** holders even if the state depends equally on both groups of actors. This suggests that when states depend on liquid asset holders for investment and resources, they are more likely to accept limits on their predatory behavior.

> A **fixed asset** is one that cannot easily be converted into cash. A **liquid asset** is one, such as cash, bank deposits, and the like, that can easily be turned into other types of assets.

This inference is supported by numerous empirical studies showing that democracy is unlikely to emerge and survive in countries in which fixed asset holders are prevalent. For example, many scholars have shown that democracy is less likely to emerge and survive in countries where oil production (perhaps the quintessential quasi-rent–generating fixed asset) is central to the economy (Barro 1999; Ross 2001). In fact, scholars have come to refer to the **rentier state** to describe the pervasive and negative effects of oil (Mahdavy 1970; Beblawi 1987). Other studies have also shown that democracy is less common and less stable in countries that rely on other primary resources, such as minerals, diamonds, and copper (Jensen and Wantchekon 2004), or whose economy is dominated by large landowners (Rueschemeyer, Stephens, and Stephens 1992). These empirical results have led some to speak of a **resource curse.**[7] Note that the existence of dictatorships that are rich due to their abundance in **natural resources** contradicts the claim of classic modernization theory that increased wealth produces democracy (Przeworski and Limongi 1997; Bueno de Mesquita and Downs 2005).[8] Although the existence of a few wealthy dictatorships, such as Saudi Arabia or Oman, might appear anomalous in the context of classic modernization theory, it is entirely compatible with the present variant of modernization theory, because these countries tend to rely for their wealth on fixed assets such as oil, gas, minerals, and so on.

> A **rentier state** is a state that derives all or a substantial portion of its revenue from the rent of indigenous natural resources to external clients.
>
> **Natural resources** are naturally occurring substances that are usually considered valuable, such as oil, diamonds, and minerals.
>
> The **resource curse** refers to the paradox that countries with an abundance of natural resources tend to experience things like poor governance, low levels of economic development, civil war, and dictatorship.

Whereas natural resources such as oil are seen as detrimental for democracy, Bates (1991) and Rogowski (1998) have both argued that when human capital (the quintessential liquid asset) becomes the engine of economic growth in an economy, states are forced to bargain with the holders of such assets in such a way that democracy is almost unavoidable.[9] To the extent

---

7. A large literature also shows that states that rely primarily on fixed assets such as oil are also prone to poor governance, low levels of economic development, and civil war (Shafer 1994; Karl 1997; Ross 1999; Collier and Hoeffler 2002, 2005; Dunning 2005; Fearon 2005; Humphreys 2005).

8. If you reexamine Figure 6.7, you will see that the probability that a country transitions to democracy actually declines slightly for wealthy countries with a GDP per capita over $7,000. The ability of rich dictatorships to sustain themselves can be explained by our variant of modernization theory in terms of their abundant natural resources.

9. Haber, Razo, and Maurer (2003) have recently argued that states are likely to be less predatory and more limited when the technology of production is sophisticated. In the terminology of our argument, one reason for this is that sophisticated technologies of production make states dependent on actors with high levels of human capital and credible exit threats.

that globalization leads to increased capital mobility and an increased reliance on human capital, the EVL framework would suggest that it should aid democratization efforts around the world. Suggestive evidence that this might be the case comes from the fact that both Huntington's (1991) first and third waves of democracy, which we describe later in Chapter 8, coincide with periods of increased economic globalization and financial integration.

In sum, the variant of modernization theory that we have just examined helps to explain both the relationship seen between (a) economic development and democracy and (b) the abundance of natural resources and dictatorship.

Foreign Aid, Inequality, and Economic Performance

This variant of modernization theory also has insights for the role of foreign aid, inequality, and economic performance in the democratization process.

Foreign Aid

As the outcomes in Table 6.3 illustrate, democracy is unlikely to emerge when the state is autonomous, that is, when it does not depend in any way on economic elites or its citizens more generally. This suggests that anything that reduces the dependence of a state on its citizens will harm the prospects for democracy, and it raises an interesting issue regarding the use of **foreign aid**. By giving foreign aid to a state, one is arguably reducing the dependence of that state on its citizens. In many cases, one is also reducing the incentive for the state to produce good economic performance, thereby making

> **Foreign aid** is aid—in the form of money, food, technical assistance, military weapons, and the like—that people in one country give to another. This aid can come from national governments, intergovernmental organizations, or private donations.

the life of the average citizen more miserable and making future donations of foreign aid more necessary. One implication of our argument, then, is that providing foreign aid to dictatorships—at least when aid reduces their dependence on citizens—may actually inhibit the emergence of democracy. Although it may be hard to see citizens living in destitution under harsh dictatorial rule, attempting to ease their pain by providing foreign aid to their governments may, under some circumstances, simply result in the prolonging of their suffering. This implication is consistent with many studies showing that foreign aid to dictatorships harms the welfare of the average citizen in these countries and helps dictators stay in office through corruption and exploitation rather than through the production of effective public policy (Morgenthau 1962; Burnside and Dollar 2000; Van de Walle 2001; Easterly 2002; Bueno de Mesquita et al. 2003; Bueno de Mesquita and Smith 2004; Clark, Doces, and Woodberry 2006).

Foreign aid is just one example of a policy that potentially undermines democracy by reducing the dependence of the state on its citizens. A similar story can be told about the policy of decolonization in Africa (Herbst 2000). By directly handing over power to particular elites and supporting their rule, European colonial powers essentially reduced the dependence of these new elites on their own citizens. A result was that these elites never felt particularly obliged to offer democratic concessions in return for the ability and right to rule. This helps to explain why almost all of the fledgling democracies that were established by the colonial powers in Africa before they left in the 1950s and 1960s soon collapsed into dictatorships.

Inequality

A number of recent studies have argued that economic inequality undermines democracy (Huntington 1991; Acemoglu and Robinson 2000, 2001, 2006; Rosendorf 2001; Boix 2003; Dunning 2006; Reenock, Bernhard, and Sobek 2007). The claim that inequality is bad for democracy actually goes back at least as far as De Tocqueville ([1835] 1988, 49–55, 128–136), who argued that economic equality was important for the introduction and persistence of democratic institutions. The basic argument in virtually all of these studies is that the emergence of democracy in unequal societies is likely to produce political cleavages based on divisions of wealth and income (class) and to significant pressures for economic redistribution from the rich to the poor. The possibility that the poor would attempt to expropriate the rich through the ballot box is thought to make democracy appear quite costly to elites. As a result, economic elites are expected to step in to block attempts at democratization or to conduct coups to reverse democratization in highly unequal societies. Empirical evidence in support of this type of theory comes from several Latin American countries (Argentina, 1976; Chile, 1973; Guatemala, 1954), where right-wing elites launched coups in order to block redistribution under democracy (O'Donnell 1973; Stepan 1985; Drake 1996). This type of argument also helps to explain why the framers of the U.S. Constitution extended suffrage only to (male) property holders—the framers believed that, were the poor to be given the vote, they would soon expropriate the rich (Roemer 1998).

Despite the strong intuitive nature of these arguments, the existing empirical evidence in support of them is not particularly consistent or compelling (Acemoglu and Robinson 2006; Reenock, Bernhard, and Sobek 2007). For example, Boix (2003) finds that economic inequality actually promotes democratic survival when a country's wealth is taken into account. Other scholars have found that inequality has no clear effect on the stability of democracy (Bollen and Jackman 1985, 1995; Barro 1997, Przeworski et al. 2000). That the spread of universal suffrage in the twentieth century has not historically led to the expropriation of the rich by the poor would also seem to call these arguments into question (Roemer 1998).

One potential explanation for these mixed or inconsistent findings has to do with the paucity or poor quality of the available inequality data (Barro 1997; Przeworski et al. 2000). The logic inherent in our variant of modernization theory offers an alternative explanation for the inconsistent results, however, because it offers a reason for why the poor do not always expropriate the rich and, hence, why economic inequality need not necessarily be bad for democracy. We saw earlier that economic elites who had credible exit options could force a dependent state to accept limits on its predatory behavior. That these economic elites have credible exit options and can realistically withdraw their much-needed investment in the economy also helps to explain why the poor will not vote to expropriate them (Przeworski and Sprague 1988). In effect, the poor "depend" on the economic elites for the economy to grow. If this is true, then existing empirical studies examining the link between economic inequality and democracy need to be modified. Economic inequality should be bad for democracy only in countries where the economic elites do not have credible exit options; where they have credible exit options, the elites should be willing to accept democracy know-

People queuing outside the polling station in the black township of Soweto, in the southwest suburbs of Johannesburg, South Africa, on Wednesday, April 27, 1994, during South Africa's first all-race elections.

ing that the poor will have incentives to curb their demands for redistribution. This may help to explain why the white minority in South Africa, who had increasingly mobile assets, were finally willing to introduce democracy to end the apartheid regime in 1994 despite the high level of economic inequality that characterized the country (see the earlier box on credible commitment problems for more detail). The failure of existing studies to take account of the way in which credible exit threats alter the impact of economic inequality on democracy may explain the inconsistent findings regarding inequality and democracy in the literature.

Economic Performance

In addition to providing predictions about whether we expect to see democracy or dictatorship, our EVL game also offers predictions about the conditions under which we expect to see growing or stagnant economies. In particular, the outcomes in Table 6.2 illustrate that although good economic performance should characterize democracies on the whole, the economic performance of dictatorships should vary considerably. Specifically, dictatorships in which citizens have no credible exit threat should perform relatively well, because citizens have little option other than to continue investing, making the best of what they have and hoping that the state does not exploit them too much. In contrast, dictatorships in which citizens have credible exit threats will perform poorly, because the citizens will redeploy their assets elsewhere to avoid state predation. The prediction that dictatorships should exhibit more variation in economic performance than democracies is consistent with several theoretical and empirical studies (Bueno de Mesquita et al. 2001, 2003). It is also supported by evidence from Przeworski et al. (2000, 176), who find that the standard deviation (a measure of how much something varies) in economic growth rates between 1950 and 1990 was 7.04 for dictatorships and just 4.85 for democracies. Further supportive evidence comes when they write that the "list of [economic] miracles and disasters are . . . populated almost exclusively by dictatorships."

That some dictatorships are expected to have growing economies may help to explain why so many economists and political scientists have failed to find compelling evidence that democracies routinely produce better economic performance than dictatorships (Sirowy and Inkeles 1991; Przeworski and Limongi 1993). The variant of modernization theory that we have examined here would suggest that it is inappropriate simply to compare the economic performance of democracies and dictatorships, because economic performance across these regimes should depend on the presence or absence of credible exit options. We look in more detail at the theoretical reasons as to why some dictatorships have incentives to produce good economic performance but others do not in Chapter 9.

SOME MORE EMPIRICAL EVIDENCE

Before turning to cultural explanations for the emergence and survival of democracy in the next chapter, we first evaluate some of the arguments that have been presented in this chapter using statistical analyses. We begin by examining how a country's status as an oil producer, its wealth, and its economic growth affect the probability that it will become a democracy using data provided by Przeworski et al. (2000) on all countries from 1946 to 1990. The results of our analyses are shown in Table 6.4. To estimate the effects of our economic variables, we use a dynamic probit model—this sounds somewhat complicated, but it really isn't. Let us briefly describe how to interpret the information shown in Table 6.4.

A **dependent variable** is an outcome or thing we want to explain. An **independent,** or **explanatory, variable** is what we think will explain, or determine the value of, the dependent variable.

The **dependent variable** listed at the top of the table is the thing we want to explain. In this case, the dependent variable is the probability that a country becomes a democracy given that it was a dictatorship in the previous year. The **independent,** or **explanatory, variables,** listed in the first column of Table 6.4 are the things we hypothesize might affect the emergence of democracy. In this case, our independent variables are wealth, growth, and oil production. Next to each independent variable (in the other columns) is a coefficient and beneath this is a standard error. The sign of the coefficient indicates the direction in which the explanatory variable affects the probability that a country will become a democracy. Thus, a positive coefficient indicates that an increase in the explanatory variable in question is associated with an increase in the probability that a country will become a democracy, whereas a negative coefficient indicates that an increase in the variable is associated with a reduction in the probability that a country will become a democracy. The standard error beneath the coefficient essentially tells us how confident we are in our results. We tend to be more confident in our results the smaller the standard error is relative to the size of the coefficient. Typically, as a rule of thumb, we claim that we can be 95 percent confident that the coefficient is correctly identified as being either positive or negative if the coefficient is bigger than twice the size of the standard error. If the coefficient is much larger than twice the size of the standard error, we become even more confident in our results. To save readers doing this calculation in their heads, authors often use stars next to the coefficient to indicate their confidence in the results. In Table 6.4, one star indicates that we are over 90 percent confident in our results, two stars indicate that we are over 95 percent confident in our results, and three stars indicate that we are over 99 percent confident in our results. No stars next to a coefficient indicates that we cannot be confident that this variable has any effect on the probability that a country becomes a democracy.

So, what do the results in Table 6.4 tell us? First, we can see that the coefficient on GDP per capita is positive and that it is highly significant. This indicates that the probability that

TABLE 6.4	Economic Determinants of Transitions to Democracy

Dependent variable: Probability that a country will be a democracy this year if it was a dictatorship last year.

Independent variables	1946–1990	1946–1990	
GDP per capita	0.00010***	0.00010***	◄——Coefficient
	(0.00003)	(0.00003)	◄——Standard error
Growth in GDP per capita		–0.02***	
		(0.01)	
Oil production		–0.48**	
		(0.24)	
Constant	–2.30***	–2.27***	
	(0.09)	(0.09)	
Number of observations	2,407	2,383	
Log-likelihood	–233.01	–227.27	

Source: Data are from Przeworski et al. (2000).

Note: Robust standard errors are in parentheses.

  * = greater than 90% significant.
 ** = greater than 95% significant.
*** = greater than 99% significant.

a dictatorship becomes a democracy increases with wealth as measured by GDP per capita. This result is entirely consistent with classic modernization theory. It is also consistent with a large body of empirical research that reaches the same conclusion (Londgregan and Poole 1996; Barro 1999; Ross 2001; Boix 2003; Boix and Stokes 2003; Inglehart and Welzen 2005; Epstein et al. 2006). Second, we can see that the coefficient on growth is negative and statistically significant. This indicates that a dictatorship that produces economic growth is less likely to become a democracy. In other words, dictatorships that do well with the economy are rewarded, as it were, by being allowed to continue to control the economy. This implies that dictatorships have an incentive to produce good economic performance. As we'll see in Chapter 9, some dictatorships have more of an incentive to produce good economic performance than others. Third, we can see that the coefficient on being an oil producer is negative and significant. This indicates that a dictatorship is less likely to become a democracy if it is an oil producer. This result is consistent with our earlier claim that countries with fixed or immobile assets producing quasi-rents are less likely to become democracies. It is also consistent with a large empirical literature that has tested the effect of oil on democratization (Barro 1999; Ross 2001; Jensen and Wantchekon 2004).

At this point you might be wondering exactly how much wealth, economic growth, and oil production really matter for the emergence of democracy? For example, how much more likely would it be for a dictatorship to transition to democracy if its GDP per capita rose by a certain amount? Take a country in Africa like Burkina Faso. In 1987 Burkina Faso was a dictatorship with a GDP per capita of $500; it was not an oil producer and it had a negative growth rate of –2.15 percent. The average GDP per capita in the world in 1987 was $4,022. How much more likely would a country like Burkina Faso have been to become a democracy in 1988 if its GDP per capita had been $4,022 instead of $500? Although we do not show exactly how to do this here, it is possible to answer this question using the results in Table 6.4. The answer is that it would have been 3.07 times more likely to become a democracy if its GDP per capita had increased from $500 to $4,022. In other words, its probability of becoming a democracy would have risen by fully 307 percent. As this example illustrates, wealth is quite an important determinant for the emergence of democracy.

Let's continue with the example of Burkina Faso. How much less likely would it be for a country like Burkina Faso in 1987 to have become a democracy in 1988 if its growth rate had been the same as that of the United States (2.55 percent) instead of –2.15 percent? Again using the results in Table 6.4, the answer is 23 percent less likely. In other words, increasing the growth rate of a dictatorial country like Burkina Faso from –2.15 percent to 2.55 percent could be expected to reduce the probability of a democratic transition by 23 percent. Finally, how much less likely would it be for a country like Burkina Faso in 1987 to have become a democracy in 1988 if it was an oil producer? The answer is 66 percent less likely. In other words, a dictatorship with a GDP per capita of $500 and a growth rate of –2.15 percent is 66 percent less likely to become a democracy if it is an oil producer than if it were not an oil producer.

Throughout the chapter we have claimed in line with classic modernization theory that economic factors affect not only the emergence of democracy but also the survival of democracy. Therefore, using the same data as before, we now examine how a country's status as an oil producer, its wealth, and its economic growth affects the probability that a democratic country will remain a democracy. The results of our analysis using a dynamic probit model are shown in Table 6.5.

Whether a coefficient is positive or negative now tells us whether an increase in our independent variables increases or decreases the probability of democratic survival. So what do the results tell us? First, we can see that the coefficient on GDP per capita is positive and that it is highly significant. This indicates that increased wealth, as measured by GDP per capita, increases the probability of democratic survival. As you will remember, this result is entirely consistent with the claims made by classic modernization theory that wealth should help democracies survive. Second, the coefficient on growth is positive and significant. This indicates that economic growth helps democracies survive. In other words, good economic performance appears to help both dictatorial and democratic regimes survive. Finally, the coefficient on oil production is negative but insignificant. This indicates that, although being an oil producer helps dictatorships to survive (see the result in Table 6.4), being an oil producer does not make democracies more stable.[10]

---

10. This result contradicts the finding by Smith (2004) that oil wealth helps the survival of all regimes, whether they are democratic or dictatorial.

TABLE 6.5	**Economic Determinants of Democratic Survival**

Dependent variable: Probability that a country will be a democracy this year if it was a democracy last year.

Independent variables	1946–1990	1946–1990
GDP per capita	0.00020***	0.00020***
	(0.00004)	(0.00004)
Growth in GDP per capita		0.04***
		(0.01)
Oil production		–0.21
		(0.269)
Constant	1.13***	1.12***
	(0.13)	(0.13)
Number of observations	1,584	1,576
Log-likelihood	–149.71	–144.11

Source: Data are from Przeworski et al. (2000).

Note: Robust standard errors are in parentheses.

   * = greater than 90% significant.
  ** = greater than 95% significant.
*** = greater than 99% significant.

But how much do wealth and economic growth really matter for democratic survival? To address this issue, let's return to the example of Burkina Faso. Let's imagine that Burkina Faso was a democracy in 1987. How would making it more wealthy or improving its economic growth affect the chances that a country like this would still be a democracy in 1988? What if we increased GDP per capita from $500 to the world average in 1987 of $4,022? The results in Table 6.5 indicate that an increase like this would increase the probability of democratic survival by 12 percent. What if we increased the economic growth rate from –2.15 percent to that of the United States in 1987 (2.55 percent)? The answer is that the probability of democratic survival would increase by 4 percent.

CONCLUSION

There is considerable evidence to support the claim made by classic modernization theory that countries are more likely to become democratic and remain democratic as their economies become more "modern." Higher levels of wealth encourage both the emergence and survival of democracy. Changes in economic structure that accompany wealth also matter. We have shown that limited government in early modern Europe was more likely to arise in polities in which the Crown was dependent on elites with mobile assets. As we stated earlier, this argument can be generalized to account for the emergence and survival of democracy in more contemporary periods. States that are more reliant on fixed assets that generate quasi-rents are less likely to sustain democracy. In support of this claim, we cited considerable evidence that democracy is less likely to arise in countries that are heavily dependent on oil production. In our own statistical analyses, wealth and economic growth continue to be important contributors to the emergence and survival of democracy even after taking account of oil production. In a more detailed study than the one presented here, Ross (2001) shows that wealth affects democratization by bringing about additional changes such as increased occupational differentiation, improved education, and the growth of the service economy. All of these changes can be thought of as parts of a broader process of modernization. Moreover, all of these changes can be expected to increase the "exit options" available to citizens. In the next chapter, we move away from economic arguments about democracy to consider whether cultural traits influence the emergence and survival of democracy.

KEY CONCEPTS

credible commitment problem, *184*

dependent variable, *198*

fixed asset, *194*

foreign aid, *195*

GDP per capita, *172*

independent, or explanatory variable, *198*

liquid asset, *194*

modernization theory, *175*

natural resource, *194*

quasi-rent, *193*

rentier state, *194*

resource curse, *194*

sovereign debt, *184*

survival story, *175*

PROBLEMS

The problems that follow address some of the more important concepts and methods introduced in this chapter.

Classic Modernization Theory

1. In this chapter we discussed classic modernization theory, which suggests that economic development is related to democracy. Answer the following questions.

   a. The basic idea with classic modernization theory is that as countries develop from traditional societies into modern societies, they shift from dictatorial forms of government to democratic ones. What are the general characteristics of "traditional societies" and "modern societies"?

   b. One implication of classic modernization theory is that rich countries tend to be democracies and poor countries tend to be dictatorships. In the chapter text, we argue that this association between wealth and democracy can be explained by both classic modernization theory and the survival story. Outline how these two stories explain the observed relationship between wealth and democracy.

c. Why does Przeworski say that wealth should help democratic survival?

d. Does the evidence presented in this chapter suggest that increased wealth makes the emergence of democracy more likely or less likely?

e. Does the evidence presented in this chapter suggest that increased wealth makes democratic survival more likely or less likely?

A Variant of Modernization Theory

2. In this chapter we discussed a variant of modernization theory. Answer the following questions.

   a. According to the variant of modernization theory that we examined, why does democracy emerge as economies develop?

   b. In early modern Europe, why did England develop a limited form of government and France develop an absolutist and autocratic form of government?

   c. Country A is characterized by the following features: it is wealthy, it has an abundance of natural resources, and its population is poorly educated. Country B is characterized by the following features: it is wealthy, its economy is dominated by the financial service sector, and its population is well-educated. Based on the variant of modernization theory that we examined, which country is most likely to be democratic and why?

   d. Why might increased globalization lead to democratization around the world?

   e. Many people have recently argued that countries with high levels of economic inequality are unlikely to become democratic. What is their basic argument? Based on the variant of modernization theory that we examined, do you expect economic inequality to always harm the prospects for democracy? Explain your answer.

Exit, Voice, and Loyalty Game

3. Earlier in the chapter we solved the Exit, Voice, and Loyalty game for (a) the scenario in which the Crown was dependent and the Parliamentarians had a credible exit threat and (b) the scenario in which the Crown was dependent and the Parliamentarians had no credible exit threat. We did not explicitly solve the EVL game for scenarios when the Crown was autonomous. The game tree for the Exit, Voice, and Loyalty game is shown in Figure 6.11. Answer the following questions.

   a. Use backward induction to solve the game for the scenario in which the Crown is autonomous ($L < 1$) and the Parliamentarians have a credible exit threat ($E > 0$). What is the subgame perfect Nash equilibrium? Do we get democracy or dictatorship? Do we get good economic performance or bad economic performance?

   b. Use backward induction to solve the game for the scenario in which the Crown is autonomous ($L < 1$) and the Parliamentarians do not have a credible exit threat ($E < 0$).

FIGURE 6.11	**EVL Game with Payoffs**

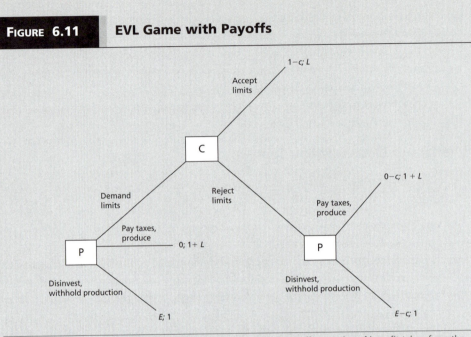

Note: C = Crown; P = Parliamentarians; *E* = Parliamentarians' exit payoff; 1 = value of benefit taken from the Parliamentarians by the Crown; *L* = Crown's value from having loyal Parliamentarians who do not exit. *c* = cost of using voice for the Parliamentarians. It is assumed that *c, L* > 0 and that *E* < 1 − *c*.

What is the subgame perfect Nash equilibrium? Do we get good economic performance or bad economic performance?

c. In the chapter we suggest that providing foreign aid to dictators may hinder the chances that democracy will emerge. Based on the outcomes from the two scenarios in the EVL game that you have just examined, explain why we reach this conclusion.

Credible Commitment Problems

4. In the chapter we introduce the concept of credible commitment problems. Answer the following questions about them.

a. What two factors characterize credible commitment problems?

b. Can you think of a nonpolitical situation in which actors face a credible commitment problem? Can you think of a way to solve this problem?

c. Can you think of a political situation in which actors face a credible commitment problem? Can you think of a way to solve this problem?

Dependent and Independent Variables

5. In this chapter we introduce the concept of dependent and independent variables. Dependent variables are the outcomes or things that we want to explain. They are the

"effects" in cause-and-effect relationships. Independent variables are the factors that we think might explain or determine the value of the dependent variable. They are the "causes" in cause-and-effect relationships. Look at the following statements and identify the independent variable and the dependent variable.

a. Smoking causes cancer.
b. Incumbents lose elections when economic performance is bad.
c. When a country develops economically, it will become a democracy.
d. Obesity is caused by eating too much food.
e. Democracy is stable in wealthy countries.
f. If citizens have mobile assets, then the government will not exploit them.
g. Crime is caused by poverty.
h. Economic inequality is bad for democracy.
i. Countries with high levels of natural resources are less likely to be democratic.
j. A good grade in class is the result of hard work.

Oil and Democracy: The Resource Curse

6. Obtain a copy of Michael L. Ross's article, "Does Oil Hinder Democracy?" from the journal *World Politics* 53 (April 2001): 325–361 using your institution's library resources. Read the article and then answer the following questions.[11]

    a. What is Ross's dependent variable? How is it measured? What is the main independent variable? How is it measured?
    b. What is the main hypothesis of this article? What evidence would falsify this hypothesis?
    c. Why does Ross believe that having oil might be detrimental to the development of democracy? Summarize the argument's three proposed causal mechanisms in a couple of sentences.
    d. Ross tests his theory using statistical analyses. Given his dependent variable, what sign (positive or negative) does Ross predict for the coefficient on his primary explanatory variable? (*Hint:* See your answers to parts a and b.) What sign does he find? Is the coefficient on this variable statistically significant? How do you know? (*Hint:* The answer is in Table 3, column 1, page 341.)
    e. Does Ross find that being an oil producer hinders the development of democracy only in the Middle East?
    f. Does Ross find any evidence that nonfuel (not oil or gas) minerals help or hinder the development of democracy?

---

11. The following series of questions is based on several similar questions posed by Powner and Bennett (2006, 118–120).

7 Cultural Determinants of Democracy

There was a time when many said that the cultures of Japan and Germany were incapable of sustaining democratic values. Well, they were wrong.

George W. Bush, in a speech to the American Enterprise Institute, Washington Hilton Hotel, February 26, 2003

I am a democrat only on principle, not by instinct—nobody is that. Doubtless some people say they are, but this world is grievously given to lying.

Mark Twain, *Notebook,* entry for February–March 1898

OVERVIEW

- Does democracy require a "democratic culture"? Are certain cultures incompatible with democracy? Does culture affect the emergence and survival of democracy?

- According to cultural modernization theory economic development produces certain cultural changes, and it is these cultural changes that lead to democracy. A key cultural change is the emergence of a "civic culture." For many, the existence of a civic culture is seen as a prerequisite for the successful emergence and survival of democracy. As we demonstrate, the empirical evidence in support of cultural modernization theory is somewhat mixed.

- We investigate recent claims that particular religions such as Islam are incompatible with democracy. As we indicate, all religions have some doctrinal elements that can be seen as compatible with democracy and others that can be seen as not compatible; Islam is no exception. Our empirical evidence suggests that there is little reason to believe that majority Muslim countries cannot sustain democracy once we take account of their wealth.

- We examine evidence from a series of experiments conducted around the world that throws light on why culture may be important for the emergence and survival of democracy.

In the previous chapter, we examined the vast literature linking economic factors to the emergence and survival of democracy. The literature addressing the relationship between culture and democracy is equally large and is the subject of this chapter. The notion that cultural differences drive significant elements of political and economic life is commonplace and has a long history. But does democracy really require a "democratic culture"? Are certain cultures incompatible with democracy? How does culture affect the emergence and survival of democracy? The claim that culture plays any role with respect to democracy obviously has important implications for those wishing to spread democracy to regions of the world such as the Middle East, Africa, and Asia.

Cultural arguments regarding democracy typically fall into two categories: primordialist and constructivist (Laitin 1983, 1986; Przeworski, Cheibub, and Limongi 1998). **Primordialist arguments** treat culture as something that is objective and inherited; something that has been fixed since "primordial" times. For example, Geertz (1973, 259–260) describes primordial cultural attachments, which for him includes things like blood lines, language, race, religion, and customs, as stemming "from the givens ... of social existence. ... For virtually every person, in every society, at almost all times, some attachments seem to flow more from a sense of natural—some would say spiritual—affinity than from social interaction." According to primordialists, culture exists prior to, and remains unchanged by, political interaction. Put differently, it is culture that affects political behavior by providing ideological guidelines for collective action rather than political behavior that shapes culture. As a result, political institutions such as democracy may not be compatible with all cultures. In effect, primordialist arguments imply that democracy is not for everyone.

> **Primordialist arguments** treat culture as something that is objective and inherited; something that has been fixed since "primordial" times. **Constructivist arguments** treat culture as something that is constructed or invented rather than inherited.

Constructivist arguments treat culture as something that is "constructed" or "invented" rather than "inherited." Like primordialist arguments, "constructivist" arguments claim that culture has a causal effect and that a democratic culture is required for democracy to emerge and prosper. Constructivists recognize, however, that cultures are malleable and are not given once and for all—cultures can change in response to social, economic, and political actors. As a result, cultures do not necessarily represent impenetrable barriers to democratization. Although cultures may not act as impenetrable barriers to democratization as they do in primordialist arguments, constructivists recognize that the speed with which cultures can change is likely to vary from culture to culture. In this sense, some cultures will find it easier to adopt democracy than others.

CLASSICAL CULTURAL ARGUMENTS: MILL AND MONTESQUIEU

The notion that political institutions such as democracy or dictatorship are more suited to some cultures than others is not new. As long ago as 472 B.C., Aeschylus contrasted the authoritarianism associated with the people of Asia with the democracy found in Athenian

Greece in his play *The Persians* (Emmerson 1995, 96). The views of Aeschylus would later be echoed in what would become known as the Asian Values debate in the 1990s. Although vague references to the compatibility of certain cultures with democracy have been around for some time, the first person to write in any great detail about the importance of culture to political institutions was Montesquieu in the eighteenth century. He claimed that monarchy was most suited to European states, that despotism was most suited to the Orient, and that democracy was most suited to the ancient world. He believed that the best government for a given country was that which "leads men by following their propensities and inclinations" (Montesquieu [1721] 1899, Persian Letter 81) and which "best agrees with the humor and disposition of the people in whose favor it is established" ([1752] 1914, 1:3). What did this entail exactly? He stated that political institutions "should be in relation to the climate of each country, to the quality of its soil, to its situation and extent, to the principal occupation of the natives, whether husbandmen, huntsmen, or shepherds: they should have relation to the degree of liberty which the constitution will bear; to the religion of the inhabitants, to their inclinations, riches, numbers, commerce, manners, and customs" (1:3). It is for this reason that he goes on to claim that it can be only by chance that the political institutions of one country can successfully be exported to another.

In his discussion entitled, "To What Extent Forms of Government Are a Matter of Choice," John Stuart Mill also argued that different cultures were suited to different political institutions. He stated, "No one believes that every people is capable of working every sort of institutions" ([1861] 2001, 7). To illustrate this, he claimed, "Nothing but foreign force would induce a tribe of North American Indians to submit to the restraints of a regular and civilized government" (8). Mill believed that even those people who recognized the benefits of a civilized government might still have to live under despotism if they did not have the requisite characteristics to support a better system of government. These necessary characteristics included "moral" or "mental habits," such as the willingness to "co-operate actively with the law and the public authorities in the repression of evil-doers" (9). They also included a certain degree of development characterized, for example, by a press capable of propagating public opinion and a tax system "sufficient for keeping up the force necessary to compel obedience throughout a large territory" (11). Mill was clearly a strong believer that legislators should take account of "pre-existing habits and feelings" when creating political institutions in a country (11).

It is important, however, not to interpret Mill's statements as if they are arguments that certain cultures are incompatible with political institutions such as democracy. In fact, Mill is highly critical of those who believe that culture prevents political actors from "choosing" the institutions that they desire. Although he thinks that "people are more easily induced to do, and do more easily, what they are already used to," he also believes that "people . . . learn to do things new to them. Familiarity is a great help; but much dwelling on an idea will make it familiar, even when strange at first" (11). Ultimately, Mill does not see particular cultural traits as "necessary conditions" for democracy, because he thinks that culture is inherently malleable and that, as a result, people can learn to be good democrats. Of course, Mill recognized that the speed with which culture can be transformed and molded varies significantly from country to country. He does not, however, speculate about what factors might systematically affect this speed of adjustment. As you can see, Mill asserts a constructivist cultural argument regarding the prospects for democracy.

Cultural modernization theory argues that socioeconomic development does not directly cause democracy; instead, economic development produces certain cultural changes, such as the emergence of a civic culture, and it is these cultural changes that ultimately produce democratic reform.

The cultural arguments put forth by both Montesquieu and Mill were later incorporated into strands of **cultural modernization theory.** As you will remember from the previous chapter, modernization theory predicts that "immature" societies (those with large agricultural sectors and authoritarian institutions) will eventually become "mature" societies (those with large industrial and service sectors and democratic institutions) as they develop economically. Cultural modernization theory states that socioeconomic development transforms societies with primitive cultures into societies with civilized cultures—only when this happens are societies ready for democracy. In other words, cultural modernization theory argues that socioeconomic development does not directly cause democracy; instead economic development produces certain cultural changes, and it is these cultural changes that produce democratic reform. As Inglehart and Welzen (2005, 15) put it, "Socioeconomic development brings roughly predictable cultural changes ... [and] these changes make democracy increasingly likely to emerge where it does not yet exist, and to become stronger and more direct where it already exists."

The claims made by Montesquieu and Mill regarding culture and democracy illustrate several potential problems that characterize some cultural arguments to this day. How would you test the claims made by Mill and Montesquieu? What exactly would the hypotheses be? Try to state one of them in a way that can be tested. One obvious problem is that neither scholar specifically says exactly what it is about culture that matters for democracy. Both men provide a whole host of cultural things that might affect the emergence and survival of democracy—religion, customs, morals, manners, marital institutions, and so on. Indeed, most of these things are left quite vague. For example, what particular morals are incompatible with democracy? Which customs are problematic? Moreover, both scholars point to numerous noncultural things that also affect democracy, such as the climate of a country, the quality of the soil, and the economy. The key point here is that cultural arguments must specify exactly what it is about culture that matters, otherwise it will never be possible to conclude that culture does not matter. Put simply, one of the problems with cultural arguments such as those made by Montesquieu and Mill is that they are so vague or nonspecific that they become non-falsifiable (Przeworski, Cheibub, and Limongi 1998). In effect, they become "nonscientific" in the terms we outlined in Chapter 2.

The second problem relates to the purported causal relationship between cultural, economic, and political factors. Does culture cause political institutions such as democracy to emerge and survive? Does it also cause economic development? Or do political institutions and economic development cause culture? In other words, which way does the causal arrow go? If culture does cause democracy, is it a necessary or a sufficient condition? If culture is a cause, does it cause the emergence of democracy or does it affect only the survival of democracy? In Figure 7.1, we illustrate some of the causal arguments that scholars have made con-

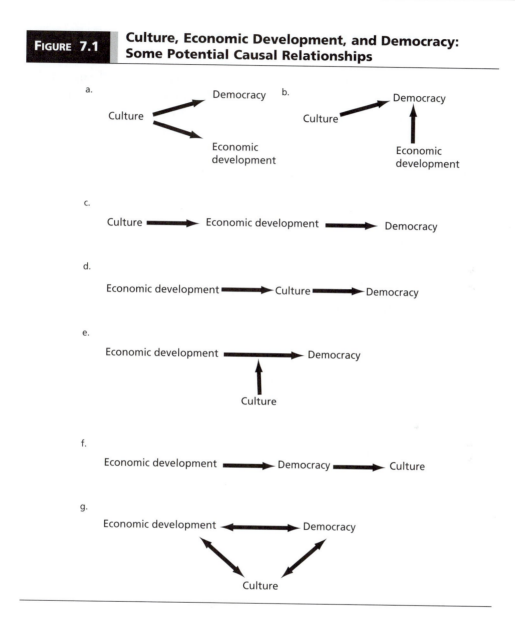

FIGURE 7.1   **Culture, Economic Development, and Democracy: Some Potential Causal Relationships**

cerning the interaction between culture, economic development, and democracy. Mill and Montesquieu clearly believed that economic development and culture both matter for democracy. From what they wrote, however, it is hard to discern what they thought the exact causal relationship was between these factors. As we will demonstrate, this problem of discerning the direction of causality continues to be an issue in many contemporary cultural arguments regarding democracy.

DOES DEMOCRACY REQUIRE A CIVIC CULTURE?

Gabriel Almond and Sidney Verba reopened the debate about culture and democracy in the 1960s with their book *The Civic Culture*. Although they recognized the importance of economic development for democracy, they believed that only culture could provide the "psychological basis of democratization" ([1963] 1989: 9) and that without this, the prospects for democratic survival were slim.[1] Almond and Verba claimed that there were three basic types of political culture in the world—parochial, subject, and participant. According to them, only "participant cultures" or "civic cultures" were compatible with democracy. In contrast, parochial cultures were compatible with the traditional political systems of African tribes, and subject cultures were congruent with centralized authoritarian institutions like those seen in Soviet-dominated Eastern Europe (20, 33).

For Almond and Verba, political culture is determined by how individuals think and feel about the political system. They believed that it was possible to study culture by conducting surveys and asking individuals about their feelings toward political institutions, actors, and processes; a nation's political culture is simply the distribution of the responses to these survey questions (13). Thus, a political culture reflects a relatively coherent cluster of attitudes in society in this conceptualization. According to Almond and Verba, a "participant" or "civic" culture reflects a particular cluster of attitudes that includes (a) the belief on the part of individuals that they can influence political decisions, (b) positive feelings toward the political system, (c) high levels of interpersonal trust, and (d) preferences for gradual societal change. In contrast, "parochial" and "subject" political cultures reflect different clusters of attitudes on these same issues. Applying their methodology to the study of Germany, Italy, Mexico, the United States, and the United Kingdom, Almond and Verba found that the United States and the United Kingdom were not only the most stable democracies in their sample but that they were also the countries that most closely resembled their ideal **civic culture.** As a result, they concluded that a civic culture was necessary for democratic stability.

On the whole, a **civic culture** is conceptualized as a shared cluster of attitudes that includes things like a high level of interpersonal trust, a preference for gradual societal change, a high level of support for the existing political system, and high levels of life satisfaction.

Inglehart (1990) reached a similar conclusion after studying survey responses from twenty-five industrial nations in the 1980s. Like Almond and Verba ([1963] 1989), he believed that "different societies are characterized to very different degrees by a specific syndrome of political cultural attitudes; that these cultural differences are relatively enduring, but not immutable; and that they can have major political consequences, one being that they are closely linked to the viability of democratic institutions" (15). According to Inglehart, political culture is determined by, among other things, the levels of overall life satisfaction, the

---

1. It is worth noting that Seymour Martin Lipset (1994a, 3), the father of classical modernization theory in political science, also claims that "[d]emocracy requires a supportive culture, the acceptance by the citizenry and political elites of principles underlying freedom of speech, media, assembly, religion, of the rights of opposition parties, of the rule of law, of human rights and the like."

DOES GOOD DEMOCRATIC PERFORMANCE REQUIRE A CIVIC CULTURE?

In this chapter, we are primarily interested in how political culture affects the emergence and survival of democracy. Several scholars have argued that political culture is also important for the overall performance of democracy (Inglehart and Welzen 2005). In *Making Democracy Work,* Robert Putnam (1993) argues that cultural norms affect the variation in economic and political performance exhibited by regional governments in Italy. In accordance with a long line of scholarship on Italy, Putnam found that regional governments in the north of Italy functioned far more effectively than those in the south. Putnam's research goal was to explain this variation across Italian regional governments and to determine the causes behind variation in governmental performance in democracies more generally.

In his study, Putnam measured government performance with twelve different indicators, including cabinet stability, the number of day-care centers and family clinics, spending on urban development, responsiveness of local bureaucracies to informational requests, and the like. Because the regional governments all across Italy shared a similar institutional structure, Putnam argued that institutions could not possibly be the explanation for the observed variation in government performance between the north and the south of Italy. Instead, he looked at cultural explanations and focused on the presence or absence of what he called "social capital" or "civic culture." At a basic level, social capital captures "norms of reciprocity and networks of civic engagement" (167). Putnam measured his concept of social capital with various indicators: the number of voluntary associations, levels of newspaper readership, turnout in referenda, and (a lack of) personalized preference voting. He found that regions with a civic culture had better governmental performance than regions that did not.

In his work, Putnam showed that northern regions in Italy were characterized by the "good" civic culture. In contrast, southern regions exhibited a "bad" culture of "amoral familism," in which norms of reciprocity and engagement were limited primarily to family relations and in which self-interest was the primary motivating force behind individual actions. According to Putnam, the civic culture in the north had a long history, which could be traced back to communal republican towns in Italy's medieval past; in contrast, the culture of amoral familism could be traced back to the south's monarchical past. Putnam claims that these two divergent historical traditions can be seen as "vicious and virtuous circles that have led to contrasting, path-dependent social equilibria" (180). He concludes by saying that *"social context and history profoundly condition the effectiveness of institutions"* (182; Putnam's italics).

Putnam's work on Italy energized many in the policymaking community. "From the World Bank to city hall, the creation of social capital [and civic culture] has been embraced as a solution for social problems as diverse as promoting economic development in Africa and stemming urban decay in Los Angeles" (Boix and Posner 1996). Putnam's study of Italy has also been a catalyst for research on political culture in the United States. In *Bowling Alone,* Putnam (2000) argues that the number of people participating in voluntary associations has been falling in the United States and that people have become disconnected from family, friends, and neighbors. Putnam's book created quite a stir, because the decline in social capital that it described was seen to have potentially negative consequences for the state of democracy in the United States.

levels of interpersonal trust, and the support for gradual societal change among the individuals of a nation.[2] Clearly, these determinants of political culture are very similar to those proposed by Almond and Verba. In his analysis, Inglehart found that countries in which levels of life satisfaction, interpersonal trust, and support for gradual societal change were high were more likely to be stable democracies than countries without these characteristics (43). In other words, he too found that some kind of civic culture is required for stable democracy.[3]

The studies conducted by Inglehart as well as Almond and Verba are obviously significant improvements from a scientific point of view over the rather vague cultural arguments made by Mill and Montesquieu in the eighteenth and nineteenth centuries. For example, both studies try to specify and test exactly what it is about culture that they think matters for democracy; in both cases, this includes attitudes toward revolutionary societal change and levels of interpersonal trust. These studies still suffer, however, from some of the same problems that we noted in Mill's and Montesquieu's arguments. For example, some confusion still remains about the exact causal relationship between culture, economic development, and democracy.[4] In line with cultural modernization theory, Inglehart (1990) argues that economic development leads to cultural changes and that it is these cultural changes that ultimately lead to democracy—this is the potential causal relationship shown in Figure 7-1d. For example, he writes that "political culture is a crucial intervening variable" (16) between economic development and democracy, and that the relationship between economic development and "the emergence and viability of mass-based democracy . . . is contingent on specific cultural changes" (65).

Other work, though, has raised concerns about this purported causal relationship. For example, Barry (1970, 88) has argued that scholars such as Almond and Verba have the direction of causality backward and that it is at least as plausible to think that experience with democracy causes the emergence of a democratic culture as it is to claim that a civic culture causes democracy. Indeed, Muller and Seligson (1994) provide empirical evidence for exactly this in a study of twenty-seven countries. Specifically, they find that levels of interpersonal trust in a country—a component of the civic culture—are determined by that country's level of democracy rather than the other way around. They also find that another element of Inglehart's civic culture—life satisfaction—has no noticeable effect on democracy. The only element of civic culture that they find to increase democracy is the level of support for revolutionary change—those countries in which few people support revolutionary change are

---

2. It is also determined by the support for the current social order, levels of political discussion, levels of postmaterialist values, and the proportion of the population that is Protestant (Jackman and Miller 1996, 645).

3. More recently, Inglehart and Welzen (2005, 245–271) have argued that it is primarily cultures characterized by self-expression (postmaterialist values) that are important for democracy, rather than cultures characterized by high levels of support for democracy or high levels of citizen participation. Using survey responses from eighty-one countries in the World Values Survey from 1981 to 2001, they found that countries with cultures characterized by self-expression were more likely to become and remain democratic than countries with other cultures.

4. There also seems to be some confusion as to whether a civic culture is necessary for the emergence of democracy or just for democratic stability.

ox **7.2**

WHAT MAKES A CIVIC CULTURE?

What comprises the civic culture? Below, we illustrate the main elements of the civic culture as proposed by Almond and Verba ([1963] 1989) and Inglehart (1990).

Almond and Verba's ([1963] 1989) civic culture included the following elements:

- Belief that individuals can influence political decisions.
- High support for the existing political system.
- High levels of interpersonal trust.
- Preference for gradual societal change.

Inglehart's (1990) civic culture included the following elements:

- High levels of life satisfaction.
- High levels of interpersonal trust.
- Preference for gradual societal change.
- High support for the current social order.
- High levels of post-materialist values.
- High levels of political discussion.
- High percentage of population comprised by Protestants.

Countries that have these characteristics, as measured by survey responses, are deemed to have a civic culture.

likely to be more democratic. It turns out that this last finding actually provides little support for the claim that a "civic culture" is required for democracy, because Muller and Seligson also find that attitudes toward revolutionary change are unrelated to other aspects of civic culture, such as life satisfaction and interpersonal trust.[5] In other words, they find that civic culture does not appear to be the coherent cluster of attitudes that some scholars have claimed (Seligson 2002). In sum, the empirical evidence that some kind of civic culture is necessary for democracy is not entirely overwhelming at present.

Despite this, Almond and Verba's (1963) *Civic Culture* and Inglehart's (1990) *Culture Shift* have encouraged the widespread use of surveys among political scientists to examine the relationship between culture and democracy. One of the most well known of these surveys is the World Values Survey at the University of Michigan. This survey is conducted by a network of social scientists at leading universities all around the world. Interviews have been conducted with nationally representative samples of more than eighty societies on all six

---

5. Jackman and Miller (1996) find a similar result when reanalyzing data from Inglehart (1990).

inhabited continents. Although the World Values Survey is often used to examine the relationship between culture and democratic institutions, it is designed to examine sociocultural and political change more broadly. For example, scholars can compare the basic values and beliefs of people cross-nationally to address such questions as how these values and beliefs affect things like economic growth and levels of environmental pollution.[6]

Scholars who are particularly interested in the relationship between culture and democracy are frequently drawn to the following question from the World Values Survey:

> Democracy may have problems, but it's better than any other form of government.
> Could you please tell me if you strongly agree, agree, disagree, or strongly disagree?

Many people believe that mass support for a particular system of government, and mass confidence in specific institutions, provides political systems with the legitimacy that they need to operate effectively (Newton and Norris 2000). In effect, mass support for democracy is seen by some as essential in delegitimizing dictatorial rule and legitimizing democratic rule (Inglehart and Welzen 2005). Thus, a low level of public support reported in questions like this one from the World Values Survey is often seen as a harbinger of democratic instability or collapse. Indeed, many scholars often anxiously examine the responses to this type of question for precisely this reason. One question that you might want to ask yourself at this point, though, is whether or not the answers to survey questions such as this really do predict democratic stability. This is a good question and, in our opinion, one that has been insufficiently examined.

Although we believe that surveys of this kind are extremely useful for addressing many important questions concerning the relationship between culture and democratic institutions, it is important to recognize their limitations. For example, one limitation is that surveys can really only get at how culture affects democratic stability; they are not well suited to addressing the question of whether a certain culture produces democracy. The reason for this is that to examine the emergence of democracy, we would have to conduct surveys in dictatorships. The obvious problem with this is that even if we were allowed to conduct a survey in an authoritarian regime, it is unclear whether the citizens in that country would be able to answer the questions freely. As we demonstrate more clearly in Chapter 8, citizens in dictatorships often engage in what political scientists call "preference falsification"—citizens do not reveal their true preferences in public for fear of being punished. As a result, any inferences drawn from a survey conducted in a dictatorship would have to be interpreted very carefully.

A second limitation, which relates to virtually all surveys, is that "[i]ndividuals [can] understand the 'same' question in vastly different ways" (Brady 1985).[7] To illustrate the

---

6. More detailed information concerning the World Values Survey can be found at http://www.worldvaluessurvey.org/.

7. For a good overview of this problem and a potential solution, see King et al. (2004) as well as King and Wand (2007).

problems that can arise if this is the case, consider the following example about self-reported health in India and the United States. Sen (2002, 860–861, quoted in King et al. 2004) writes:

> [T]he state of Kerala has the highest rates of literacy . . . and longevity . . . in India. But it also has, by a very wide margin, the highest rate of reported morbidity among all Indian states. . . . At the other extreme, states with low longevity, with woeful medical and educational facilities, such as Bihar, have the lowest rates of reported morbidity in India. Indeed, the lowness of reported morbidity runs almost fully in the opposite direction to life expectancy, in interstate comparisons. . . . In disease by disease comparisons, while Kerala has much higher reported morbidity rates than the rest of India, the United States has even higher rates for the same illnesses. If we insist on relying on self-reported morbidity as the measure, we would have to conclude that the United States is the least healthy in this comparison, followed by Kerala, with ill provided Bihar enjoying the highest level of health. In other words, the most common measure of the health of populations is negatively correlated with actual health.

Clearly, the respondents in the different regions of India and in the United States either understood the survey questions differently or evaluated their levels of health on very different scales. A key point here is that measuring or inferring reality by comparing people's attitudes or perceptions across different regions or countries can often be "extremely misleading" (Sen 2002). At the end of the day, one always has to wonder whether one is attempting to compare the incomparable (King and Wand 2007).

One reason that measuring the reality of democratic stability on the basis of people's attitudes or perceptions about democracy might be problematic is that people tend to conceive of democracy in different ways in different countries. For example, democracy may conjure up images of economic and political equality for some, but may simply mean holding competitive elections for others. These different views of democracy should not come as a surprise, given that we have already seen in Chapter 5 that political scientists disagree about whether to employ a minimalist or substantive view of democracy in their own work. If experts cannot agree on what they mean by democracy, why would we expect individuals in different countries to have the same concept in mind when answering survey questions about it? In addition, national history is likely to influence how individuals evaluate democracy. Democracy in newly democratic countries is likely to be judged on different criteria, depending on the nature of the previous regime and the transition process itself. For instance, individuals who have endured a civil war, such as those in Sri Lanka, may evaluate democracy in regard to whether it produces peace. In contrast, individuals who have lived and worked in a highly segregated economy like South Africa might judge democracy in regard to whether it produces social freedom and economic equality. The concern, then, is that it may not be possible to compare responses to survey questions concerning democracy across countries with any degree of validity because individuals may conceptualize democracy in very different ways.

We obviously cannot address the issue of validity here in any detail. Still, let us briefly examine responses to two questions from the World Values Survey that have often been taken as indicators of democratic stability and ask whether they have any face validity. By face validity, we mean, do the responses to these questions match our everyday or common-sensical understanding of which countries are stable democracies and which ones are not? Let's start with the question that we already introduced above.

> Democracy may have problems, but it's better than any other form of government.
> Could you please tell me if you strongly agree, agree, disagree, or strongly disagree?

In Figure 7.2, we illustrate the mean responses to this question among individuals from thirty-seven countries in the 1995 World Values Survey. Remember, the claim is that democratic rule in countries with a low score on this question should be more stable than democratic rule in countries with a high score on this question. We have rank ordered the countries in Figure 7.2 so that countries whose citizens tended to agree with the statement that democracy is the best form of government and that are, therefore, expected to have stable democratic rule are at the top and those whose citizens disagreed and are, therefore, expected to have unstable democratic rule are at the bottom. As you can see, Bangladesh should be the most stable democracy in this sample. In fact, democratic rule in Bangladesh, Croatia, the Dominican Republic, Nigeria, Argentina, and Montenegro should be more stable than democratic rule in the United States. In terms of face validity, we suspect that few individuals in the world would truly claim that the United States is less stable as a democracy than any of these countries.

The second question also comes from the 1995 World Values Survey and concerns the preference among individuals for gradual, as opposed to revolutionary, societal change.

> Do you believe that the entire way our society is organized should be radically changed
> by revolutionary action, that our society should be gradually improved by reforms, or
> that our society must be valiantly defended against all subversive forces?

Recall that Inglehart (1990), as well as Almond and Verba ([1963] 1989), believed that preferences for gradual societal change were important elements of civic culture. As a result, it should follow that societies with preferences for gradual change should be more democratically stable than societies with preferences for revolutionary change. In Figure 7.3, we illustrate the mean responses to this question for the same thirty-seven countries as before. We have again rank ordered the countries in Figure 7.3 so that countries that are expected to have stable democratic rule are at the top and those that are expected to have unstable democratic rule are at the bottom. As you can see, Peru, Venezuela, South Korea, Taiwan, Bangladesh, and Mexico should all be more stable democracies than the United States, because more people in these countries prefer gradual societal change than those in America. Again, in terms of face validity, we suspect that few individuals in the world would truly claim that the United States is less stable as a democracy than these other countries.

FIGURE 7.2 Support for Democracy

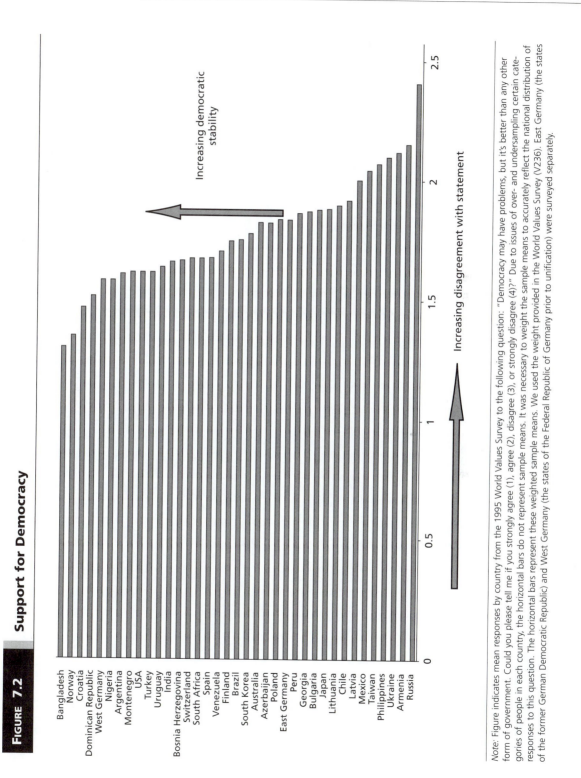

Note: Figure indicates mean responses by country from the 1995 World Values Survey to the following question: "Democracy may have problems, but it's better than any other form of government. Could you please tell me if you strongly agree (1), agree (2), disagree (3), or strongly disagree (4)?" Due to issues of over- and undersampling certain categories of people in each country, the horizontal bars do not represent sample means. It was necessary to weight the sample means to accurately reflect the national distribution of responses to this question. The horizontal bars represent these weighted sample means. We used the weight provided in the World Values Survey (V236). East Germany (the states of the former German Democratic Republic) and West Germany (the states of the Federal Republic of Germany prior to unification) were surveyed separately.

FIGURE 7.3   Support for Gradual Change

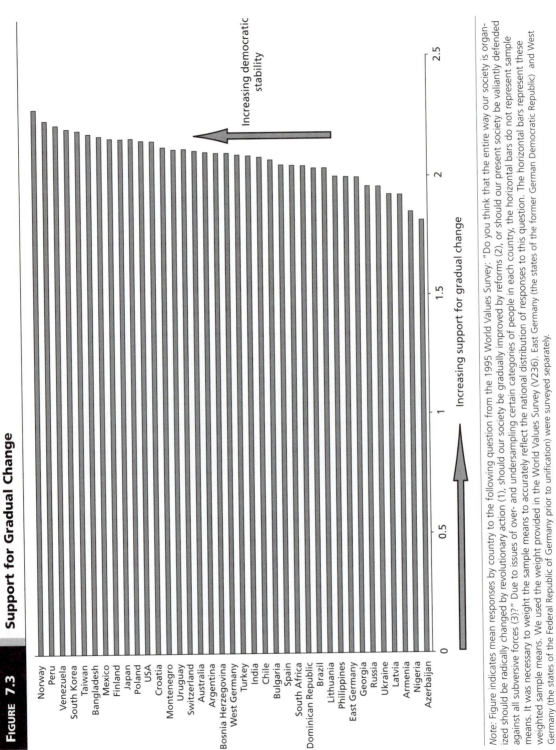

Note: Figure indicates mean responses by country to the following question from the 1995 World Values Survey: "Do you think that the entire way our society is organized should be radically changed by revolutionary action (1), should our society be gradually improved by reforms (2), or should our present society be valiantly defended against all subversive forces (3)?" Due to issues of over- and undersampling certain categories of people in each country, the horizontal bars do not represent sample means. It was necessary to weight the sample means to accurately reflect the national distribution of responses to this question. The horizontal bars represent these weighted sample means. We used the weight provided in the World Values Survey (V236). East Germany (the states of the former German Democratic Republic) and West Germany (the states of the Federal Republic of Germany prior to unification) were surveyed separately.

It is interesting to note that the countries with a strong belief that democracy is the best form of government (Figure 7.2) are not necessarily the same countries that have a high level of support for gradual societal change (Figure 7.3). For example, Nigeria is one of the highest ranked countries in regard to believing that democracy is the best form of government but is one of the lowest ranked countries in regard to believing that societal change should be conducted through gradual reform. Indeed, the correlation—a measure of association running from 0 to 1—between the responses to the two questions is only 0.38. This suggests that at least some of the attitudes that scholars think make up the civic culture required for democratic stability do not, in fact, represent a coherent cluster of beliefs. This result is supported by several previous empirical studies (Muller and Seligson 1994; Jackman and Miller 1996).

We do not mean to suggest from our brief analysis here that surveys are not an appropriate methodology for studying the relationship between culture and democracy. Much can be learned from surveys. Indeed, in many cases, the questions that interest political scientists can *only* be answered through the use of surveys. It seems clear to us, however, that we should be very careful about drawing strong inferences about the relationship between culture and democracy from the analysis of these surveys.

RELIGION AND DEMOCRACY

Instead of focusing primarily on the purported relationship between civic culture and democracy, recent cultural arguments have increasingly addressed the issue of whether religion affects the emergence or the stability of democracy, or both. Unlike many of their predecessors, these cultural arguments have not been confined to the halls of academia; instead, they have strongly influenced public discourse and shaped the direction of public policy. For example, Samuel Huntington's (1996) book *The Clash of Civilizations and the Remaking of World Order,* in which he argues that Islamic and Confucian cultures are incompatible with democracy, was reportedly recommended reading for many of the soldiers heading to Iraq during the second Gulf War in 2003. It is worth noting, however, that these contemporary debates concerning the causal relationship between religion and democracy actually have a long and storied history—a history that should perhaps make us wary of unthinkingly accepting claims that certain religions are incompatible with democracy.

Are Some Religions Incompatible with Democracy?

Historically, scholars have assumed that "there have been negative relationships between democracy and Catholicism, Orthodox Christianity, Islam, and Confucianism; conversely Protestantism and democracy have been positively interlinked" (Lipset 1994a, 5). Max Weber ([1930] 1992) is commonly thought to have provided the first argument linking Protestantism with democracy in his book *The Protestant Ethic and the Spirit of Capitalism.* For example, Lipset ([1959] 1994b, 57) writes, "It has been suggested, by Weber among others, that a historically unique concatenation of elements produced both democracy and capitalism in this area [northwest Europe, America, and Australasia]. . . . Protestantism's emphasis on individual responsibility furthered the emergence of democratic values in these countries."[8] The causal story connecting Protestantism to democracy here is the following: Protestantism encouraged economic development, which in turn created a bourgeoisie, whose existence was both a catalyst and a necessary condition for democracy (Moore [1966] 1999). In effect, the causal relationship mirrors the one shown earlier in Figure 7-1c. The notion that Protestantism promotes democracy was later taken up by other scholars, such as Inglehart (1990), for whom the percentage of Protestants in a country is one element of his civic culture (Jackman and Miller 1996, 645).

Recently, Rodney Stark (2004a, 2004b) has criticized the Weberian emphasis on Protestantism by pointing out that many of the attributes of modern capitalism were present in the Italian city-states before the Protestant Reformation. Stark's controversial new study suggests that it is Christianity in general, not Protestantism per se, that encouraged the growth of capitalism and democracy. He argues that because Christianity focuses on orthodoxy (correct belief) rather than orthopraxy (correct practice, which is the focus of Islam and Judaism) and posits a rational and personal God, a brand of science and philosophy arose in predominantly Christian countries that supported the development of democratic self-rule.

Other scholars have suggested that Protestantism really is a key determinant for contemporary levels of democracy but for reasons different from those linked to Weber. For example, Robert Woodberry (2004; Woodberry and Shah 2004) has argued that it is the depth and breadth of Protestant missionary activity during colonial periods that helps to explain why certain countries are democracies today and others are not. The reason has to do with the emphasis that Protestants placed on teaching people to read the scripture in their own language. These missionary efforts spearheaded mass education and the introduction of modern printing to colonial regions, which in turn unleashed many modernizing forces that encouraged democracy, such as increased literacy, greater equality, a more independent workforce, and a larger middle class. Whatever the causal process, Protestantism has historically been seen by many as a religion that encourages the emergence and survival of democracy.

In contrast to Protestantism, Catholicism has traditionally been seen as antithetical to democracy. For example, Lipset ([1959] 1994b, 72) has argued that Catholicism's emphasis on there being only one church and one truth is incompatible with democracy's need to accept various different and competing ideologies as legitimate.[9] The hierarchy in the Catholic Church and the clear distinction between the clergy and laity are also thought to

---

8. Lipset does not point to any specific part of Weber's writing to support his claim that Weber saw a causal relationship between Protestantism and democracy. In fact, Weber appears to have said very little at all about political institutions (Przeworski, Cheibub, and Limongi 1998). Nonetheless, political scientists frequently point to Weber as the source for arguments linking Protestantism to democracy.

9. Lipset (1994a, 5) claims that it was Tocqueville who first noted the negative effect of Catholicism on democracy but he does not provide a citation for this. In fact, Tocqueville said that Catholics were the most republican and democratic class in the United States and that it would be wrong to think that Catholicism was a natural enemy of democracy (cited in Przeworski, Cheibub, and Limongi 1998, 138).

THE CLASH OF CIVILIZATIONS

In 1992 Francis Fukuyama famously declared the "end of history." With the end of the cold war, Fukuyama believed that liberal democracy had finally won the battle with other rival ideologies such as monarchism, fascism, and communism. Liberal democracy was the "end point of mankind's ideological evolution," and hence the "end of history." Although Samuel Huntington (1993a, 1996) took issue with the claim that we were witnessing the end of history, he agreed with the claim that conflict in the world would no longer be based on ideological divisions. He wrote: "It is my hypothesis that the fundamental source of conflict in this new world will not be primarily ideological or primarily economic. The great divisions among humankind and the dominating source of conflict will be cultural. Nation states will remain the most powerful actors in world affairs, but the principal conflicts of global politics will occur between nations and groups of different civilizations. The clash of civilizations will dominate global politics. The fault lines between civilizations will be the battle lines of the future" (1993a, 22).

For Huntington, a civilization is the "highest cultural grouping of people and the broadest level of cultural identity people have short of that which distinguishes humans from other species" (1993a, 24). Huntington identifies many different civilizations in the world today—Western Christian, Confucian, Japanese, Islamic, Hindu, Slavic-Orthodox, Latin American, African, and others. The exact number is ambiguous because he refers to different civilizations in different studies. It is not always obvious how Huntington moves from his definition of a civilization to an indicator of them. On the whole, civilizations seem to be coded primarily in regard to religion, although linguistic differences and geographic proximity seem to play a role in some cases.

Huntington argues that the widespread Western belief in the universality of the West's values and its insistence on imposing these values through democratization efforts will only antagonize other civilizations and lead to conflict. Moreover, these conflicts will be less amenable to diplomacy and peaceful resolution than previous economic and ideological conflicts because cultural differences are less mutable and less easy to compromise. He writes: "Western ideas of individualism, liberalism, constitutionalism, human rights, equality, liberty, the rule of law, democracy, free markets, the separation of church and state, often have little resonance in Islamic, Confucian, Japanese, Hindu, Buddhist, or Orthodox cultures. Western efforts to propagate such ideas produce instead a reaction against 'human rights imperialism' and a reaffirmation of indigenous values, as can be seen in the support for religious fundamentalism by the younger generation in non-Western cultures" (1993a, 40–41). In effect, Huntington argues that certain cultures are incompatible with democracy. In particular, Islamic and Confucianist countries cannot sustain democracy; even Catholic countries will find it hard to sustain democratic regimes. He also notes that violent conflict will be "particularly prevalent between Muslims and non-Muslims" because Muslims are prone to violence (1996, 256–258). We should note that Huntington does not systematically test any of his assertions and simply relies on anecdotal evidence.

pose particular problems for the acceptance of more socially and politically egalitarian institutions such as democracy. Those who believe that democracy is difficult to establish in Catholic countries often point to the support that the Catholic Church has given to dictatorships around the world in the past. For example, the Catholic Church was an open supporter of fascist Italy under Mussolini and authoritarian Spain under Franco. The Catholic Church has historically also supported several dictatorships in South America and Asia.

Confucianism and Islam have come to be seen as posing even bigger problems for the successful establishment of democracy than Catholicism. Huntington (1993a) is perhaps the most vocal proponent of this belief. He argues that we are currently observing a clash of civilizations and that "Western concepts differ fundamentally from those prevalent in other civilizations. Western ideas of individualism, liberalism, constitutionalism, human rights, equality, liberty, the rule of law, democracy, free markets, the separation of church and state, often have little resonance in Islamic, Confucian, Japanese, Hindu, Buddhist or Orthodox cultures" (1993a, 40). He goes so far as to say that Confucian democracy is a contradiction in terms and that "[a]lmost no scholarly disagreement exists regarding the proposition that traditional Confucianism was either undemocratic or anti-democratic" (1993a, 24). Huntington is not alone in claiming that Confucianism is incompatible with democracy. In what became known as the Asian Values Debate in the 1990s, scholars argued that Confucianism's respect for authority and its emphasis on communalism and consensus rather than individual rights and competition made it incompatible with democracy (Pye 1985; Scalapino 1989; Kim 1997). To a large extent, the catalyst for this debate was the Bangkok Declaration that was signed in April 1993 by the political leaders of China, Indonesia, Malaysia, and Singapore. This declaration essentially stated that Asian values justify a different way of understanding human rights and democracy. Along these lines, Lee Kuan Yew (1994), Singapore's prime minister from 1959 to 1990, has suggested that Confucianism's respect for authority and its emphasis on the community are antithetical to Western images of liberalism.[10] This line of reasoning was used by various authoritarian leaders in Asia to justify the ongoing existence of their non-democratic forms of government (Dalton and Ong 2004, 3).

Like Confucianism, numerous reasons have been proposed for why Islam might be incompatible with democracy. One of the earliest arguments dates to Montesquieu, who claimed that Islam had a violent streak that predisposed Muslim societies to authoritarianism. While comparing Christianity and Islam, Montesquieu ([1752] 1914, 24:3–4) writes that "[t]he Christian religion is a stranger to mere despotic power. The mildness so frequently recommended in the Gospel is incompatible with the despotic rage with which a prince punishes his subjects, and exercises himself in cruelty. . . . The Mahometan [Islam]

---

10. Lee Kuan Yew (1994) claimed that the "expansion of the right of the individual to behave or misbehave as he pleases comes at the expense of orderly society. In the East the main object is to have a well-ordered society so that everybody can have maximum enjoyment of his freedoms. This freedom can only exist in an ordered state and not in a natural state of contention and anarchy [democracy]."

religion, which speaks only by the sword, acts still upon men with that destructive spirit with which it was founded." Huntington (1996, 256–258) is a modern-day proponent of the same idea, because he argues that one of the reasons democracy is so difficult to establish in Islamic countries is that Muslims are prone to political violence. A second proposed reason for the incompatibility of Islam and democracy concerns the purported inability of Islam to disassociate religious and political spheres. The recognition in Islam that God is sovereign and the primary lawgiver has led some to argue that the Islamic state is in principle a theocracy (Lewis 1993) or, as Huntington (1996, 70) succinctly puts it, that "[i]n Islam God is Caesar." A third proposed argument for the incompatibility of Islam and democracy concerns Islam's unequal treatment of women (Fish 2002; Norris and Inglehart 2004). Some believe that the repressiveness and dominance of the father in the family and of men in relation to women more generally in Islamic culture replicate themselves in the larger society, thereby creating a culture suitable for authoritarianism. Others claim that the social marginalization of women in the political sphere leaves society susceptible to authoritarianism because men hold attitudes that are more conducive to domination.

Although arguments that particular religions are incompatible with democracy have strong supporters around the world (notably among the authoritarian leaders of certain countries), there is good reason to doubt their veracity. Why might these arguments be flawed? Note that many of the arguments presented so far rest on claims that there is something about the doctrine of each religion that makes them particularly compatible or incompatible with democracy. One problem with this is that virtually all religions have some doctrinal elements that can be seen as compatible with democracy and others that are not (Stepan 2000, 44).[11] This is true even of "pro-democratic" Protestantism. For example, Przeworski, Cheibub, and Limongi (1998, 132) argue that Protestantism's legitimization of economic inequality and the ethic of individual self-interest associated with it provide "a poor moral basis for living together and resolving conflicts in a peaceful way."

What about Confucianism and Islam? Many would argue that these religions have elements that might make them compatible with democracy. For example, some claim that Confucianism's meritocratic system and its emphasis on the importance of education and religious tolerance suggest that it can sustain democracy (Fukuyama 1995a). Indeed, Taiwan's president from 1988 to 2000, Lee Teng Hui, even claims that traditional Confucianism calls for limited government. Other scholars have noted that Confucianism recognizes the right of rebellion against rulers who deviate from the prescribed "Way" (Leys 1997). In addition, the existence of a public sphere in Korea during the Joseon (Chosun or Choson) dynasty from 1392 to 1910 would seem to contradict those who assert that Confucianism cannot sustain democracy because it has no concept of civil society (Im 1997). Thus, despite claims to the contrary by some authoritarian leaders in Asian countries, there seems to be

---

11. In response to the Asian Values debate, Sen (1999) points out that authoritarian themes can be found in much of Western political philosophy. This did not stop the emergence of democracy in the West, and thus he sees no reason why it would necessarily stop the emergence of democracy in Asia.

nothing explicit in Confucianism itself that would necessitate an authoritarian government; in fact, many of the elements of Confucianism mentioned above seem quite well suited to a democratic form of government. Indeed, Friedman (2002) goes so far as to suggest that "Buddhist and Confucian cultures may actually have more democratic elements than Greco-Christian culture."

Many scholars have also taken issue with the claim that Islam is incompatible on doctrinal grounds with democracy (Rahman 1979; Esposito and Voll 1996; Abootalebi 1999; Filali-Ansary 1999; Price 1999; Hefner 2000; Sachedina 2000). For example, several scholars find a basis for democracy in the Koran's emphasis on "shura" (consultation). Shura requires that even the messenger of Allah should consult his people in worldly matters and that Muslims should consult each other in their secular affairs. This process of consultation is in many respects similar to the process of consultation that underpins elections and legislatures in democracies. Indeed, many Islamic scholars "have come to the conclusion that general elections and a parliament properly serve that concept of consultation" (Yazdi 1995, 18). Other scholars have interpreted Islamic concepts such as "ijma" (consensus of the community) and "ijtihad" (reinterpretation), as well as legal principles such as "maslaha" (public welfare), as providing a basis for Islamic forms of parliamentary governance, representative elections, and religious reform (Esposito 2003).

Still others have suggested that those who portray the rule of law in a democratic state ("law of man") as being inherently in conflict with sharia, or Islamic law ("law of god"), are creating a false dichotomy. It is true that the sovereign and primary lawgiver in Islam is God and that God's agents such as the Islamic state (Khilafa) enjoy only marginal autonomy to implement and enforce God's laws.[12] In other words, it is true that sovereignty lies in different places in democracy (with the people) and Islam (with God). Still, the reason this distinction should not be overemphasized is that, in practice, it is the state, and not God, that actually exercises sovereignty in Islam. Worth noting here is that one of the underlying concerns in both Islam and democracy is clearly the need to limit the power of the state and the people who rule. That this is achieved in Islam by arguing that God is the primary lawgiver and that the state should simply implement God's laws, whereas it is achieved in democracy by holding elections and implementing checks and balances, should not be allowed to hide the fact that both Islam and democracy share the same goal of limited government.

We should also point out that there is nothing inherent in democratic theory that requires a democratic state to be secular anyway (Stepan 2000, 40). It may be true that most contemporary democracies tend to separate church and state (although there is considerable variation even in this), but it is important to recognize that this is a choice and not necessarily part and parcel of democratic theory. Indeed, it is illuminating to remember that until the eighteenth century, the Christian church vehemently opposed both democracy and secularism, just like many proponents of Islam today. For decades, there was a great struggle between the church

---

12. A Khalifa is the successor to Prophet Muhammad's position as the political, military, and administrative leader of the Muslims. Khilafa is a related Arabic word which, in the context of Islam, is used to denote the government of the Muslim state, of which the Khalifa is the head.

and princely rulers on the one hand and between Christians and secularists on the other. It was only during the nineteenth century that democracy and secularism became acceptable within western Christian society. Even today, some Christians believe that the strict separation of church and state should be relaxed. In sum, Islamic doctrine, like the doctrines of other religions, contains elements that make it compatible with many traditional aspects of democracy.

Some Empirical Evidence

Given that almost all religions seem to contain doctrinal elements that can be seen as detrimental to democracy and others that can be seen as conducive to it, it becomes an empirical question as to whether certain religions pose particular difficulties for the establishment and survival of democracy. So what does the empirical evidence say?

The growing empirical evidence that cultures are invented, constructed, and malleable rather than primordial, inherited, and unchanging suggests that it is inappropriate to view particular religions or civilizations as being permanently incompatible with democracy. For example, Eickelman and Piscatori (1996) illustrate that Islamic doctrine has historically been interpreted in various ways to justify many different types of government. As to Confucianism, the fact that the comments of Singapore's former prime minister, Lee Kuan Yew, concerning the relationship between Confucianism and democracy run directly counter to the comments of Taiwan's former president, Lee Teng Hui, suggests that Confucianism can be interpreted differently by different people and that it can be adapted to suit different purposes.[13] As Przeworski, Cheibub, and Limongi (1998, 132) put it, "Cultures are made of cloth but the fabric of culture drapes differently in the hands of different tailors."

Considerable evidence supports the claim that the stance of different religions toward political institutions often depends less on the content of religious doctrine and more on the interests of religious leaders. For example, Kalyvas (1996) shows in his study of the rise of European Christian Democracy that the relationship between Catholicism and democracy had less to do with the actual content of Catholic faith and more to do with the strategic considerations of elites in the Catholic Church. Balmer (2006) makes a similar point with respect to Protestants in his account of the rise of the "religious right" in the United States. Elsewhere, Kalyvas (1998, 2000) examines why Catholic fundamentalism proved compatible with the successful establishment of democracy in nineteenth-century Belgium but Islamic fundamentalism did not in Algeria during the 1990s. He argues that the reasons for the different outcomes in the two countries had little to do with actual doctrinal issues and more to do with the different organizational structures of the two religions (see the Religious Party Game in the problem section at the end of Chapter 8 for more details). Numerous other scholars have similarly highlighted the role played by "cultural entrepreneurs" in producing

---

13. There is growing empirical evidence that it is misleading to talk of a single Confucian culture in Asia (Sen 1999). Indeed, some Asian countries are not predominantly Confucian at all. For example, Indonesians are overwhelmingly Muslim and Filipinos are primarily Catholic. Taoism and Buddhism have also had an important impact in some Asian countries. Using survey evidence, Dalton and Ong (2004) show that Asians do not share a single coherent set of values or attitudes. They also show that Asian values as a whole do not differ significantly from Western attitudes in the Pacific Rim. Given this, it is hard to argue that Asian values somehow prevent the successful establishment of democracy in Asia.

cultural change, thereby suggesting that conflicts over culture tend to be matters of interest and strategy rather than any primordially given cultural content (Laitin 1983, 1986, 1992; Posner 2004, 2005). In other words, a vast amount of empirical evidence undermines the implication made by scholars such as Huntington that the anti-democratic tendencies of certain religions and civilizations are given once and for all.

The empirical reality is that all religions have historically been compatible with a broad range of political institutions. For example, Fukuyama (1995b, 12) claims that the kinds of political structures that are compatible with Confucianism are indeterminate. The fact that it is possible to distinguish between "political" and "everyday" Confucianism helps to explain why the imperial system mandated by traditional political Confucianism could be abolished relatively easily in China with the overthrow of the Qing dynasty in 1911 and replaced with a variety of political-institutional forms without the loss of Chinese society's essential coherence. In this sense, the important legacy of traditional Confucianism is not its political teaching but, rather, the personal ethic that regulates attitudes toward family, work, education, and other elements of everyday life. This helps to explain why Confucian society can exist happily in democracies like Japan, South Korea, and Taiwan, in semi-authoritarian regimes like Singapore, or in more authoritarian regimes like Burma, China, and North Korea.

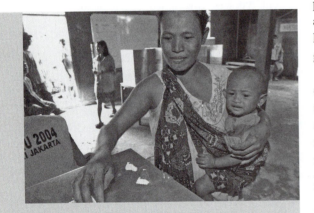

A Jakarta mother carries her child as she votes Monday, July 5, 2004, in the first direct presidential election in the vast archipelago of Indonesia, the world's most populous Muslim-majority country.

Islamic countries also have considerable experience with different forms of political systems. Despite the claim that Islam requires an Islamic state or Khilafa, it should be noted that, with the exception of Iran since the 1979 revolution and of Afghanistan during the period of Taliban rule in the 1990s, there have been few historical precedents for mullahs', or religious leaders', controlling political power in Islamic countries. On the whole, secular political elites have controlled political power in Islamic countries for the roughly 1,400 years since the Prophet Muhammad died in 632 A.D. Despite claims that Islam is incompatible with democracy, it is important to remember that hundreds of millions of Muslims live today in such democratic countries as Canada, France, India, the Netherlands, the United Kingdom, and the United States (Stepan 2000, 49). Indeed, several countries with majority Muslim populations are considered democracies—Albania, Bangladesh, Indonesia, Mali, Niger, Senegal, and Turkey.[14] Clearly, being Muslim does not preclude anyone from living a peaceful and constructive life in a democratic society.

---

14. We use the classification of democracies proposed by PACL to identify these countries (see Chapter 5).

Not only can we find evidence for the compatibility of Islam and democracy by looking at the world today, but we can also find evidence of at least quasi-democratic institutions and practices in the history of some Islamic states. One example is the Loya Jirga (Grand Assembly) in Afghanistan, which has functioned since at least 1709, when the country moved toward independence by breaking with the rule of the Persian Safavid dynasty. The Loya Jirga is a consultative council at which the country's elite, tribal chiefs, religious leaders, and political groupings decide issues, settle tribal disputes, enforce interim rule, and approve constitutions. Although the Loya Jirga itself stems from both pre-Islamic local practices and the Islamic concept of "shura," it is clear that it shares much in common with what we would consider a democratic legislature.

Another example is the Compact of Medina in 622 A.D. After the Prophet Muhammad migrated from Mecca to Medina in 622 A.D, he established the first Islamic state. He was not only the leader of the emerging Muslim population in Arabia but also the political head of Medina, where he ruled over both Muslims and non-Muslims. Important to note here is that he did not decide to rule purely through the revelations he received as the messenger of Allah. Instead, he felt compelled to write down a compact, or constitution. In other words, the Prophet Muhammad explicitly sought the consent of all who would be affected by his rule. As one Islamic scholar puts it, "the first Islamic state established in Medina was based on a social contract, was constitutional in character, and the ruler ruled with the explicit written consent of all the citizens of the state. It establishes the importance of consent and cooperation for governance. . . . The principles of equality, consensual governance and pluralism are beautifully enmeshed in the compact of Medina" (Khan 2003). The historical examples of the Loya Jirga in Afghanistan and the Compact of Medina would suggest that Islam is compatible with many aspects of democracy.

Despite the fact that cultures tend to be malleable and that all religions have been compatible with a variety of political institutions throughout history, one might still wonder

7.4

THE CONSTITUTION OF MEDINA—622 A.D.

In the year 622 the Prophet Muhammad established the first Islamic state when he migrated from Mecca to Medina (known as Yathrib at the time). In establishing the Islamic state, Muhammad wrote a constitution, or compact, that was signed by the Muslim, Jewish, Arabic, and other tribal communities then living in Medina. In many respects, the Constitution of Medina was a document of religious tolerance. Jews and Muslims were free to practice their own religions, and Jews were not to be attacked for being Jews. The constitution granted Jews social, legal, and economic equality as long as they remained loyal to the constitution. Jews and Muslims were supposed to come to the defense of each other if either was attacked.

whether certain religions are *more* or *less* compatible with democracy than others. In this vein, several empirical studies have recently suggested that Islam is particularly bad for democracy—Islamic countries seem to have lower Freedom House scores than non-Islamic countries (Barro 1999; Karatnycky 2002; Fish 2002). For example, Karatnycky (2002) finds that there was only one Islamic country in 2001 that was coded as Free, eighteen were coded as Partly Free, and twenty-eight were coded as Not Free. In contrast, eighty-five non-Islamic countries were coded as Free, thirty-nine as Partly Free, and twenty-one as Not Free. Fish (2002) concludes that the reason that Islam is so bad for democracy is its treatment of women and girls. Why? First, he finds that Islamic countries tend to be characterized by a wider literacy gap between men and women, fewer women in government, and lower measures of overall gender empowerment (UNDP 2000). Second, he finds that all these measures of the status of women reduce a country's Freedom House score. As a result, he infers that it is the treatment of women that is at least partially responsible for the poor democratic performance of Islamic countries.

Despite the evidence presented in these recent studies, we believe we should be cautious in concluding that Islam truly is bad for democracy. One reason for such caution is that several of the studies mentioned above examine the effect of Islam on democracy at a fixed point in time. For example, Karatnycky examines the effect of Islam on a country's Freedom House score in 2001 and Fish examines the effect of Islam on a country's average Freedom House score in the 1990s. Why might this be problematic? Ask yourself what a researcher would find if she examined the effect of Catholicism on a country's level of democracy in 1976? It turns out that she would find that of the forty-seven countries with a Catholic majority, fourteen were coded as Free and sixteen were coded as Not Free; in contrast, eleven of the sixteen countries with a Protestant majority were coded as Free and only one was coded as Not Free. This evidence would suggest that Catholicism is particularly bad for democracy, at least in comparison with Protestantism. If the same researcher examined the effect of Catholicism on a country's level of democracy in 2004, however, her conclusion would be very different. Of the fifty-seven countries with a Catholic majority in 2004, forty were coded as Free and only three were coded as Not Free; of the twenty-three countries with a Protestant majority, seventeen were coded as Free and one was coded as Not Free. As you can see, whereas Catholicism seemed to pose some difficulties for democracy from the perspective of 1976, this was no longer the case from the perspective of 2004. Thus, it can be dangerous to draw strong inferences about the incompatibility of a religion with democracy from a single point in time.

Note that it would be equally dangerous to draw inferences about the compatibility of a civilization with democracy from a single point in time as well. For example, consider Huntington's assertion that Western civilization is obviously compatible with democracy. Such a claim might seem eminently reasonable from our perspective today. It would hardly seem this way to someone living in Europe during the 1930s, however. As Mazower (1998, 5) notes, "it is hard to see the inter-war experiment with democracy for the novelty that it was: yet we should certainly not *assume* that democracy is suited to Europe. . . . Triumphant in

1918, it was virtually extinct twenty years on. . . . Europe found other, authoritarian, forms of political order no more foreign to its traditions" (Mazower's italics).

It turns out that most of the arguments claiming that particular religions or civilizations are incompatible with democracy are implicitly based on observations of the world at a particular point in time. For example, arguments linking Protestantism to democracy and Catholicism to authoritarianism tended to be made most frequently when Protestant countries around the world were predominantly democratic and when Catholic countries were largely authoritarian. This observed variation encouraged some scholars to look for reasons why Protestantism might promote democracy and why Catholicism might impede it. In other words, theory construction came after observing the world. Because explanation always begins with a puzzling observation, there is nothing inherently wrong with this. But if the explanation does not suggest testable implications other than those that led to it, we call this an *ex post,* or ad hoc, explanation. Such explanations violate the norms of science because they do not invite falsification.[15] Of course, the argument that Catholic countries are inherently anti-democratic has now lost most of its force because Catholic countries are predominantly democratic today. In fact, one might now even argue that Catholicism helps democratization, given the important role that the Catholic Church played in aiding democratic transitions in countries like Chile, Paraguay, the Philippines, and Poland in the 1980s. Despite this, the exact same type of argument that used to be made about Catholicism is now frequently made about Islam: we observe that there are few democratic Islamic countries at this point in time and we therefore conclude that there must be something about Islam that is anti-democratic. The history of arguments concerning Catholicism (and Confucianism) should make us wary of accepting this type of reasoning.

What about the evidence that Islam is particularly bad for democracy because of its treatment of women (Fish 2002)? Unfortunately, because of the author's decision to use Freedom House as his measure of democracy, it is hard to know if this evidence is truly compelling. If you remember our discussion in Chapter 5 of the Freedom House measure of democracy, you might recall that it is based on a series of questions regarding the level of political rights and civil liberties in a country. Countries that have more political rights and civil liberties are considered more free and, hence, more democratic. The problem is that some of these questions take into account, at least implicitly, the treatment and status of women. In other words, the overall Freedom House score for each country automatically varies with that country's treatment of women simply because of the way it is constructed. As a result, it is arguably inappropriate to test to see whether the measure of the treatment of women affects

---

15. Some of you may have noticed that this type of analysis is similar to employing Mill's Method of Difference. The analyst begins by observing democracies and dictatorships in the world. He then looks for things that only democracies have in common (such as Protestantism) and for things that only dictatorships have in common (Catholicism). From this pattern of observations, the analyst then generates a general theory claiming that Protestantism causes democracy and Catholicism impedes democracy. The fact that Catholic countries are largely democratic today clearly illustrates the central problem with the traditional mode of scientific analysis; that is, no matter how many times you observe a Catholic dictatorship, it does not logically follow that Catholicism causes dictatorship.

a country's Freedom House score—we already know that it will by construction. Thus, the question as to whether Islam is bad for democracy because of its treatment of women remains an open question.

Are Some Religions Incompatible with Democracy? A New Test

Given that questions remain about the compatibility or incompatibility of certain religions with democracy, it might be useful to reexamine the issue here. Let's start with what we know. We know that Protestant and Catholic countries are likely to be democratic and that Muslim countries are likely to be dictatorships today. This has already been demonstrated by some of the studies we have just mentioned (Barro 1999; Fish 2002; Karatnycky 2002). In and of itself, however, this does not establish a causal link between these religions and democracy. We also know that democracy originated in Protestant countries. But our question is not about where democracy originated. What we really want to know is whether democracy can be transplanted to countries dominated by different religions. The evidence to answer this question is not whether more Protestant countries are democratic than Catholic or Muslim countries at some specific moment in time. Instead, what we need to know is whether democracy is more or less likely to emerge and survive in countries that are dominated by Protestants, Muslims, or Catholics. In other words, we need to examine the effect of these religions on democracy across time. To do this, we need to know what effect being a Protestant, Catholic, or Muslim country has on (a) the probability of becoming democratic and (b) the probability of staying democratic. In other words, we would like to test the following hypotheses:

> *Catholic hypothesis:* Countries with a majority Catholic population are less likely to become and stay democratic.
> *Protestant hypothesis:* Countries with a majority Protestant population are more likely to become and stay democratic.
> *Islamic hypothesis:* Countries with a majority Muslim population are less likely to become and stay democratic.

In Table 7.1, we list the countries with majority Catholic, Protestant, and Muslim populations.[16]

Although we have not addressed cultural diversity in this chapter, there is reason to think that high levels of cultural diversity may make countries less compatible with democracy.[17] For example, Weingast (1997) argues that democracy can be sustained only if citizens can

---

16. Some scholars have tested the following type of hypothesis: Countries with more Muslims will be more anti-democratic than countries with fewer Muslims (Przeworski, Cheibub, and Limongi 1998; Barro 1999). There seems little theoretical justification in this literature, however, to suggest that a country with 10 percent Muslims is likely to be more anti-democratic than a country with 5 percent Muslims. Rather, the central claim is really that countries that are predominantly Muslim will be more anti-democratic than countries that are not predominantly Muslim. This is the reason we compare countries with a majority Muslim population to those without a majority Muslim population, and so on.

17. This idea goes back at least as far as John Stuart Mill in the nineteenth century, who writes that for democracy to endure, there must be shared values—a "consensus" (cited in Przeworski et al. 2000, 125).

| TABLE 7.1 | Countries with a Majority Muslim, Protestant, or Catholic Population |

Religion of majority	Countries
Muslim	Afghanistan, Albania, Algeria, Azerbaijan, Bahrain, Bangladesh, Brunei, Comoros, Djibouti, Egypt, Eritrea, Gambia, Guinea, Indonesia, Iran, Iraq, Jordan, Kuwait, Kyrgyzstan, Lebanon, Libya, Malaysia, Maldive Islands, Mali, Mauritania, Morocco, Niger, Oman, Pakistan, Qatar, Saudi Arabia, Senegal, Somalia, Sudan, Syria, Tajikistan, Tunisia, Turkey, Turkmenistan, United Arab Emirates, Uzbekistan, (Republic of) Yemen.
Protestant	Angola, Antigua, Bahamas, Barbados, Denmark, Fiji, Finland, Iceland, Liberia, Marshall Islands, Namibia, Norway, Papua New Guinea, St. Kitts and Nevis, St. Vincent, Solomon Islands, South Africa, Sweden, Tonga, United Kingdom, United States, Vanuatu, Western Samoa.
Catholic	Andorra, Argentina, Armenia, Austria, Belgium, Belize, Bolivia, Brazil, Burundi, Cape Verde, Chile, Colombia, Congo, Costa Rica, Croatia, Cyprus, Dominica, Dominican Republic, Ecuador, El Salvador, Equatorial Guinea, France, Gabon, Greece, Grenada, Guatemala, Haiti, Honduras, Hungary, Ireland, Italy, Kiribati, Liechtenstein, Lithuania, Luxembourg, Macedonia, Malta, Mexico, Micronesia, Nicaragua, Panama, Paraguay, Peru, Philippines, Poland, Portugal, Romania, Rwanda, St. Lucia, San Marino, Sao Tomé and Principe, Seychelles, Slovakia, Slovenia, Spain, Uruguay, Venezuela, Yugoslavia.

Source: Data are from Przeworski et al. (2000). Their data are based on Atlas Narodov Mira (1964).
Note: "Catholic" includes both Roman Catholic and Orthodox religions.

coordinate their beliefs about when the government has transgressed and when they should do something about it. In many ways, this coordination of beliefs might be considered a "democratic culture"—something that is necessary for democracy to emerge and survive. It seems reasonable to think that this type of coordination is likely to be more difficult when there are many cultural groups in society. Other scholars have argued that ethnic diversity is particularly bad for democracy because it makes reaching compromises difficult and because it raises the risk of intercommunal violence (Dahl 1971; Rabushka and Shepsle 1972; Lijphart 1977; Horowitz 1993). We might suspect that countries with a large number of religious groups or a large number of cultural groups might also be problematic for democracy on similar grounds. As a result, we also evaluate the following hypotheses in our upcoming empirical analyses:

Ethnic group hypothesis: Countries with a large number of ethnic groups are less likely to become and stay democratic.

Religious group hypothesis: Countries with a large number of religious groups are less likely to become and stay democratic.

Cultural group hypothesis: Countries with a large number of cultural groups are less likely to become and stay democratic.

Let's start by looking at the emergence of democracy. In order to test the hypotheses outlined above, we use the same dynamic probit model as the one we employed in Chapter 6 on data from 199 countries between 1950 and 2000. The results of our analyses are shown in Table 7-2. The dependent variable listed at the top of the table is what we want to explain. In this case, the dependent variable is the probability that a country will become a democracy given that it was a dictatorship in the previous year. In other words, our dependent variable is the emergence of democracy. Our independent, or explanatory, variables—the things we hypothesize might affect the emergence of democracy—are listed in the first column of Table 7-2. Next to each independent variable (in the other columns) is a "coefficient" and beneath this is a "standard error." Recall that the coefficient indicates the direction in which the independent variable affects the probability of becoming a democracy. Thus, a positive coefficient indicates that an increase in the independent variable in question increases the probability of becoming a democracy, whereas a negative coefficient indicates that an increase in the variable reduces the probability of becoming a democracy.

Recall also that the standard error beneath the coefficient essentially tells us how confident we are in our results. We tend to be more confident in our results the smaller the standard error is relative to the coefficient. Typically, as a rule of thumb, we claim that we can be 95 percent confident that the coefficient is correctly identified as being either positive or negative if the coefficient is bigger than twice the size of the standard error. If the coefficient is much larger than twice the size of the standard error, we become even more confident. To save readers from doing this calculation in their heads, authors often use stars next to the coefficient to indicate their confidence in the results. In Table 7-2, one star indicates that we are over 90 percent confident in our results; two stars indicate that we are over 95 percent confident; and three stars indicate that we are over 99 percent confident in our results. No stars next to a coefficient indicates that we cannot be confident that this variable has any effect on the probability that a country will become a democracy.

So what do the results in Table 7.2 tell us? Model 1 in the first column tells us how having a Muslim, Catholic, or Protestant majority affects the probability that a country will become democratic without taking anything else into account. Remember that our hypotheses are that Protestant majority countries will be more likely to become democracies, whereas Catholic and Muslim majority countries will be less likely to become democracies. What does the evidence say? As predicted, the coefficient on "Muslim majority" is negative and significant. This means that countries with a Muslim majority are significantly less likely to become democracies than other countries. There is no evidence, though, that Protestant majority countries are any more likely to become democracies than other countries. Indeed, the fact that the coefficient on "Protestant majority" is negative and almost significant at the 90 percent level might suggest that countries with a Protestant majority are, if anything, less

TABLE 7.2 Effect of a Muslim, Catholic, or Protestant Majority on the Probability That a Country Will Become Democratic, 1950–2000

Dependent variable: Probability of being a democracy this year if country was a dictatorship the previous year.

Independent variables	Model 1	Model 2	Model 3	Model 4	Model 5
Muslim majority	-0.28**	-0.18	-0.23	-0.25	-0.18
	(0.12)	(0.16)	(0.17)	(0.19)	(0.16)
Protestant majority	-0.56	-0.42	-0.40	-0.45	-0.43
	(0.35)	(0.38)	(0.38)	(0.39)	(0.38)
Catholic majority	0.33***	0.31***	0.26**	0.26**	0.31**
	(0.10)	(0.12)	(0.12)	(0.13)	(0.13)
GDP per capita		0.00004*	0.00003*	0.00003*	0.00004*
		(0.00002)	(0.00002)	(0.00002)	(0.00002)
Growth in GDP per capita		-0.02**	-0.02**	-0.02**	-0.02**
		(0.01)	(0.01)	(0.01)	(0.01)
Oil production		-0.15	-0.12	-0.13	-0.15
		(0.18)	(0.19)	(0.19)	(0.18)
Effective number of ethnic groups			-0.02		
			(0.02)		
Effective number of religious groups				-0.06	
				(0.09)	
Effective number of cultural groups					0.02
					(0.08)
Constant	-2.06***	-2.05***	-1.94***	-1.91***	-2.06***
	(0.07)	(0.10)	(0.13)	(0.23)	(0.19)
Number of observations	4,379	2,578	2,563	2,578	2,563
Log-likelihood	-418.75	-318.64	-317.85	-318.46	-318.35

(In Model 5 column) -0.18 ← Coefficient / (0.16) ← Standard error

Source: Data on religious groups and whether a country is a democracy are from Przeworski et al. (2000), updated through 2000; data on GDP per capita and growth in GDP per capita are from the Penn World Tables 6.1 (2004); and data on ethnic and cultural groups are from Fearon (2003).

Notes: Robust standard errors are in parentheses. A country is listed as an oil producer in those years in which fuel exports exceed one-third of a country's export revenue according to the World Bank (Fearon and Laitin 2003).

* = greater than 90% significant.
** = greater than 95% significant.
*** = greater than 99% significant.

likely to become democracies than others. The coefficient on "Catholic majority" is positive and significant. This means that countries with a Catholic majority are actually significantly more likely to become democratic than other countries. Thus, there is little evidence that Catholicism represents a barrier to the emergence of democracy—quite the opposite in fact.

If we looked only at the results from Model 1, we would conclude that majority Muslim countries are bad for the emergence of democracy. We know, however, that these countries tend to be poorer than most other countries. We also know that poor countries are less likely to become democracies than rich countries (see Chapter 6). Thus, it might be the case that Muslim countries are less likely to become democracies not because they are Muslim but because they are poor. To test this possibility, we included in Model 2 the three economic variables that were used in the previous chapter to examine the economic determinants of democracy: GDP per capita in 1996 international dollars, growth in GDP per capita, and whether a country is an oil producer. Once we take account of these economic determinants, there is no longer any evidence that majority Muslim countries are bad for the emergence of democracy. The coefficient on "Muslim majority" in Model 2 is still negative but it is no longer statistically significant. Thus, the evidence strongly suggests that Muslim countries are less likely to become democracies not because they are Muslim but because they are poor. If these countries can become wealthier, then there is no reason to think, based on the evidence presented here, that being majority Muslim will pose any more of a barrier to a country's becoming democratic than being majority Protestant. Despite adding the economic data, it still appears that countries with a Catholic majority are significantly more likely to become democratic than other countries.

What about our other hypotheses? Does having more ethnic, religious, or cultural groups decrease the likelihood that a country will become democratic? The results in Models 3–5 clearly indicate that we have no reason to suspect that ethnic, religious, or cultural diversity inhibits (or promotes) the emergence of democracy. This is because none of the coefficients on these variables is anywhere close to being statistically significant.

So what conclusions can we draw from our analysis of the emergence of democracy? As in the previous chapter, we find that increased wealth makes transitions to democracy more likely and that high economic growth tends to make transitions to democracy less likely. Countries that are predominantly Catholic are significantly more likely to become democracies than other countries. In contrast, having a Protestant or Muslim majority in a country has no significant effect on whether that country will become a democracy. Ethnic, religious, and cultural diversity do not appear to destabilize dictatorships or aid the emergence of democracy.

Having examined how these factors affect the emergence of democracy, we can now investigate how they influence the survival of democracies. The results of our analysis are shown in Table 7.3. The dependent variable listed at the top of the table is now the probability that a country remains a democracy given that it was a democracy in the previous year. The independent or explanatory variables are again listed in the first column. Whether a coefficient is positive or negative now tells us whether an increase in our independent variables increases or decreases the probability of democratic survival. Again, statistical significance is indicated

TABLE 7.3 **Effect of a Muslim, Catholic, or Protestant Majority on the Probability of Democratic Survival, 1950–2000**

Dependent variable: Probability of being a democracy this year if country was a democracy last year.

Independent variables	Model 1	Model 2	Model 3	Model 4	Model 5
Muslim majority	-0.61***	-0.30	-0.46	-0.48	-0.39
	(0.18)	(0.26)	(0.28)	(0.30)	(0.27)
Protestant majority[†]					
Catholic majority	0.02	-0.27*	-0.41**	-0.43*	-0.39**
	(0.13)	(0.16)	(0.20)	(0.22)	(0.18)
GDP per capita		0.0001***	0.0001***	0.0001***	0.0001***
		(0.00003)	(0.00003)	(0.00003)	(0.00003)
Growth in GDP per capita		0.02*	0.02*	0.02*	0.02*
		(0.01)	(0.01)	(0.01)	(0.01)
Oil production		0.29	0.43	0.35	0.40
		(0.31)	(0.31)	(0.29)	(0.31)
Effective number of ethnic groups			-0.09*		
			(0.05)		
Effective number of religious groups				-0.19	
				(0.15)	
Effective number of cultural groups					-0.23
					(0.12)
Constant	2.06***	1.50***	1.88***	1.92***	1.99***
	(0.10)	(0.16)	(0.28)	(0.37)	(0.30)
Number of observations	2,408	1,784	1,784	1,784	1,784
Log-likelihood	-252.28	-163.19	-161.41	-162.33	-161.74

Source: Data on religious groups and whether a country is a democracy are from Przeworski et al. (2000), updated through 2000; data on GDP per capita and growth in GDP per capita are from the Penn World Tables 6.1 (2004); and data on ethnic and cultural groups are from Fearon (2003).

Note: Robust standard errors are in parentheses. A country is listed as an oil producer in those years in which fuel exports exceed one-third of a country's export revenue according to the World Bank (Fearon and Laitin 2003).

[†] No democracy with a Protestant majority ever failed to survive in this time period. As a result, it is not possible to include this variable.
  * = greater than 90% significant.
 ** = greater than 95% significant.
*** = greater than 99% significant.

by the stars next to the coefficients. If the coefficient has no stars, then we have no evidence to suggest that the variable has an effect on democratic survival.

What do the results tell us? Model 1 in the first column tells us how having a Muslim, Protestant, or Catholic majority affects the probability that a democratic country remains democratic. It turns out that there were no democracies with a Protestant majority that ever collapsed into dictatorship in our sample of countries and time period. As a result, it was not possible to include this variable in the analysis. What this indicates, though, is that having a Protestant majority is strongly associated with democratic survival. What about having a Muslim or Catholic majority? Well, it appears that having a majority Muslim population is bad for democratic survival. This is because the coefficient on "Muslim majority" is both negative and highly significant. There seems to be no evidence in Model 1 that Catholicism is bad for democratic survival.

If we looked only at Model 1, we would conclude that having a Muslim majority is bad for democratic survival. But again, it is important to remember that majority Muslim countries tend to be poorer than most other countries. We know that poor countries are less likely to survive as democracies than rich countries (see Chapter 6). Thus, it might be the case that Muslim countries are less likely to survive as democracies not because they are Muslim but because they are poor. To test this possibility, we again included in Model 2 the three economic variables that were used in Chapter 6 to examine the economic determinants of democracy—GDP per capita in 1996 international dollars, growth in GDP per capita, and whether a country is an oil producer. Once we take account of these economic determinants, there is no longer any evidence that having a Muslim majority is bad for democratic survival. The coefficient on "Muslim majority" in Model 2 remains negative, but it is no longer statistically significant. Thus, the evidence strongly suggests that Muslim countries are less likely to stay democratic not because they are Muslim but because they are poor. If these countries can become wealthier, then the results presented here indicate that there is no reason to think that having a Muslim majority will pose a barrier to democratic survival.

What about the other hypotheses? Does having more ethnic, religious, or cultural groups decrease the likelihood that a country will remain democratic? The results in Models 3–5 indicate that countries with a large number of ethnic or cultural groups are less likely to stay democratic. This is because the coefficients on these variables are both negative and significant. In contrast, there is no evidence that having multiple religious groups affects democratic survival.

So what conclusions can we draw from our "cultural" analysis of the emergence and survival of democracy? First, there is no evidence that predominantly Muslim countries are less likely to become democratic or less likely to stay democratic. It is true that Muslim countries typically have authoritarian forms of government at present. There is reason to believe, however, that this has more to do with the fact that they tend to be poor than because they are Muslim. Thus, Huntington appears to be wrong in his famous claim that Islam has antidemocratic proclivities. Second, majority Protestant countries do not seem more likely to become democratic than other countries. Still, if a majority Protestant country does become democratic for some reason, then it is likely to stay democratic. This is illustrated by the fact that there are no examples in our data set (1950–2000) of a majority Protestant democracy ever collapsing into dictatorship, but it is difficult to determine whether this is the result of religion or wealth. Third, predominantly Catholic countries are significantly more likely to become democratic than other countries. This runs counter to the traditional argument that Catholic countries provide difficult terrain from which democracy can emerge. It is unclear why a majority Catholic country might increase the likelihood of transitioning to democracy. Still, even though Catholic countries are more likely to become democratic, they have a hard job staying democratic. The results in Table 7.3 when we take account of economic factors indicate that majority Catholic countries are significantly less likely to remain democratic than other countries.

Fourth, ethnically, religiously, or culturally diverse countries do not seem to be any less likely to undergo a transition to democracy than homogeneous countries. In other words, diversity of these kinds does not seem to destabilize dictatorships. In contrast, ethnic and cultural diversity does seem to destabilize democracies. Democracy is significantly less likely to survive in countries that have many ethnic or cultural groups; the number of religious groups does not seem to matter. One interpretation of these results is that some sort of shared values or beliefs is required for democracy, but not for authoritarianism, to persist (Weingast 1997).

Finally, economic factors continue to have an important impact on democracy even when we take account of various cultural features. As modernization theory would predict, and as we found in Chapter 6, wealthy countries are more likely to become democratic and they are more likely to remain democratic. Economic growth is good for both dictatorships and democracies; economic growth reduces the likelihood of a democratic transition and it reduces the likelihood of democratic collapse. One result that differs somewhat from those in the previous chapter is that there is now no evidence that being an oil producer has any significant effect on becoming democratic once we take account of various cultural features. This is a result that requires more study.

EXPERIMENTS AND CULTURE

So far we have examined how culture might affect democracy using survey evidence and statistical analyses. We now turn to some experimental results that also suggest that culture might be important for the establishment and survival of democracy. The experiments that we are going to examine involve individuals playing what are known as Ultimatum and Dictator Games. In an Ultimatum Game, individuals (known as subjects or players) are paired together. The first player, often called the "proposer," is provisionally allotted a divisible "pie" (usually money). The proposer then offers a portion of the total pie to the second player, called the "responder." The responder, knowing both the offer and the total amount of the pie, can then either accept or reject the proposer's offer. If the responder accepts, then he receives the amount offered and the proposer gets the remainder (the pie minus the offer). If the responder rejects the offer, then neither receives any money. In either case, the game ends and the two subjects receive their winnings and leave. In the experiments, the players are anonymous to each other and the games use substantial sums of money. An example might help. Imagine that the proposer is given $100 and offers $40 to the responder. If the responder accepts the offer, then the responder gets to keep the $40 and the proposer keeps the remaining $60. If the responder rejects the offer, then both the responder and proposer get nothing. The Dictator Game is essentially the same as the Ultimatum Game except that responders are not given an opportunity to reject the offer; they simply get whatever the proposer dictates. You should think about how much of the pie you would offer if you were the proposer. What types of offers would you accept or reject if you were the responder? Would the offer you make depend on whether you were playing the Ultimatum Game or the Dictator Game?

Why might an experimenter compare the behavior of individuals in the Ultimatum Game with their behavior in a Dictator Game? To answer this question, think about why someone might make a positive offer in the Ultimatum Game. There are two potential reasons. First, the proposer might make a positive offer out of a sense of fairness. In other words, the proposer realizes that he was randomly chosen to receive the pie and thinks it only fair that he should offer some of it to the responder. Second, the proposer might make a positive offer because of fear of rejection. In other words, the proposer only makes a positive offer in order to reduce the risk that he would get nothing if the responder rejects it. In the Dictator Game, there is no fear of rejection, because the responder cannot reject the proposer's offer. As a result, any positive offer in the Dictator Game must be from a sense of fairness. Thus, the Dictator Game allows the experimenter to distinguish between proposers who make positive offers out of a sense of fairness and those who make positive offers out of a fear of rejection.

What would you expect purely self-interested individuals to do if they acted as the proposer in an Ultimatum Game? What would they do if they acted as the responder? We sometimes refer to a purely self-interested actor as *homo economicus*. It turns out that we would expect a purely self-interested proposer to offer ϵ to the responder, where ϵ is only slightly larger than 0. We would then expect the responder to accept this offer because receiving ϵ is clearly better than getting nothing, which is what both players get if the responder refuses. Thus, if we continue our example from above and assume that we are in the world of homo economicus, we would expect the proposer to get $100 − \epsilon$ and the responder to get ϵ. Things look only slightly different in the Dictator Game. Now we would expect a purely self-interested proposer not to offer anything to the responder and to simply keep all of the $100 for himself. Remember, these are the theoretical predictions if we were in the world of homo economicus. But what do we actually observe when we ask individuals to play this game in an experimental setting?

Both the Ultimatum and Dictator Games have been played in numerous experimental settings in virtually all of the industrialized democracies in the world.[18] Typically, the experiment

---

18. For an overview of these experiments, see Davis and Holt (1993); and Kagel and Roth (1995).

involves a group of students who are paired up anonymously in a computer lab. One student is randomly chosen to be the proposer, and the other becomes the responder. The game then begins. What do you think happens in these games? Somewhat remarkably, there is a great deal of similarity in the results produced by these experiments despite the fact that they are conducted in different countries around the world. It turns out that the modal offer—the most common offer—in student populations playing the Ultimatum Game is almost always 50 percent, with the mean, or average, offer varying somewhere between 40 percent and 45 percent. Offers less than 20 percent of the pie are rejected by responders about half the time. In contrast, the modal offer in student populations playing the Dictator Game is normally 0 percent. The large difference in the modal offers between the two games would suggest that many of the positive offers in the Ultimatum Game come about because of a fear of rejection, rather than a sense of fairness, on the part of the proposer. Although this is certainly true, the mean offer in the Dictator Game is still in the 20 percent to 30 percent range. In other words, some individuals still make quite large positive offers even when they know that their offers cannot be rejected. These proposers are clearly acting out of a sense of fairness; they exhibit what some call a pro-social behavior. Overall, the results from these experiments clearly indicate that the students playing these games do not approximate the theoretical homo economicus.

Several scholars began to wonder whether these deviations from the theoretical predictions for homo economicus were evidence of a universal pattern of human behavior or whether the deviations varied with an individual's economic and cultural setting. Do some cultures exhibit behavior that more closely resembles that of homo economicus than other cultures? Of course, these questions cannot be answered with any satisfaction simply by looking at experimental results from student populations around the world. Although there are cultural differences among students in different countries, these differences are quite small compared with the range of cultural environments that exist in the world. As a result, a group composed primarily of anthropologists and economists decided to conduct experiments using Ultimatum and Dictator Games in fifteen small-scale societies in twelve countries on five continents (Henrich et al. 2001, 2004; Gintis 2003). These societies exhibited a wide range of cultural and economic environments: foraging societies; slash-and-burn horticulture groups; nomadic herding groups; and sedentary, small-scale agriculturalist societies. Information on these societies is shown in Table 7.4.

How did the individuals in these societies act in the Ultimatum and Dictator Games? The offers made in the Ultimatum Game are shown in a bubble plot in Figure 7.4. Data from an experiment using students at the University of Pittsburgh are included as a benchmark against which to compare the results from the fifteen small-scale societies. The size of the bubble at each location along each row represents the proportion of the sample that made a particular offer. The right edge of the lightly shaded horizontal gray bar gives the mean offer for that group. For example, if one looks at the row associated with the Machiguenga from Peru, then you can see that the mode (the most common offer) is 0.15, the secondary mode is 0.25, and the mean is 0.26.

TABLE 7.4	Fifteen Small-Scale Societies		
Group	**Country**	**Environment**	**Economic base**
Machiguenga	Peru	Tropical forest	Horticulture
Quichua	Ecuador	Tropical forest	Horticulture
Achuar	Ecuador	Tropical forest	Horticulture
Hadza	Tanzania	Savanna-woodlands	Foraging
Aché	Paraguay	Semi-tropical woodlands	Horticulture and foraging
Tsimané	Bolivia	Tropical forest	Horticulture
Au	Papua New Guinea	Mountainous tropical forest	Foraging and horticulture
Gnau	Papua New Guinea	Mountainous tropical forest	Foraging and horticulture
Mapuche	Chile	Temperate plains	Small-scale farming
Torguud	Mongolia	High altitude desert, seasonally flooded grassland	Pastoralism
Khazax	Mongolia	High-altitude desert, seasonally flooded grassland	Pastoralism
Sangu (farm/herd)	Tanzania	Savanna-woodlands, seasonally flooded grassland	Agro-pastoralists
Orma	Kenya	Savanna-woodlands	Pastoralism
Lamelara	Indonesia	Tropical island coast	Foraging-trade
Shona	Zimbabwe	Savanna-woodlands	Farming

The information in Figure 7.4 illustrates that no society matches the predictions for homo economicus. The second thing to note, though, is that there is much more variation in the offers made in the fifteen small-scale societies than in the student populations of the advanced industrial countries. Remember that the mean offer among students varies from about 40 to 45 percent in Ultimatum Games. In contrast, the range for the mean offers in the fifteen small-scale societies is much larger, varying from 26 percent for the Machiguenga in Peru to 58 percent for the Lamelara in Indonesia. Whereas the modal offer among students is 50 percent, the modal offer among the fifteen small-scale societies ranges from 15 percent to 50 percent.

Although we do not show any evidence here, it turns out that the rejection rates in these fifteen societies also vary quite considerably between the groups. Whereas offers below 20 percent

FIGURE 7.4   **Offers from an Ultimatum Game**

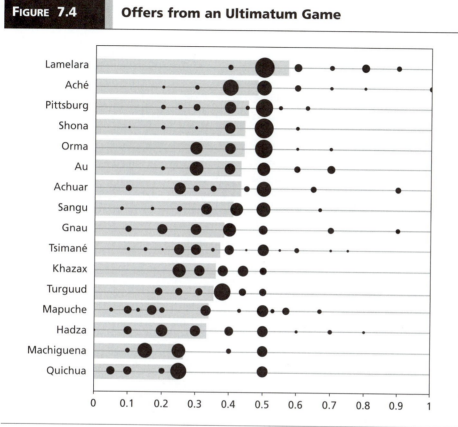

Source: Henrich et al. 2004.

Note: The size of the bubble at each location along each row represents the proportion of the sample that made a particular offer. The right edge of the lightly shaded horizontal gray bar gives the mean offer for that group.

in industrial democracies are rejected with a probability of 0.4 to 0.6, the experimenters found that rejections of very low offers such as this are quite rare in some groups. For example, the Machiguenga rejected only one offer even though 75 percent of the offers made were below 30 percent. In some groups, though, the experimenters found that rejection rates were quite high even when offers were over 50 percent of the pie. For example, the Au and the Gnau in Papua New Guinea were equally likely to reject offers that were below or above 50 percent. The results from the Dictator Game also showed considerable variation. Among student populations, the distribution of offers has a mode at zero and a secondary mode at 50 percent. In contrast, the Orma had a mode at 50 percent and the Hadza dictators had a mode at 10 percent. There were no zero offers among the Tsimané; the mean was 32 percent and the mode was 25 percent.

What explains this large variation in behavior between the different cultural groups? The experimenters claim that this variation can be explained by how group-specific conditions,

Box 7.5   **EXPERIMENTS IN POLITICAL SCIENCE**

Political scientists are increasingly turning to experiments as a way to learn about the world. In recent years, experiments have been employed to answer a wide range of interesting questions. For example, they have been used to examine whether mobilization efforts and increased information affect voter turnout (Gerber and Green 2000; Grosser and Schram 2006), whether preelectoral coalition agreements between political parties affect how people vote (Gschwend and Hooghe 2008), whether ethnic diversity affects the provision of public goods (Habyarimana et al. 2007), whether particular campaign messages influence voter behavior (Wantchekon 2003), and how legislative bargaining affects the distribution of resources (Frechette, Kagel, and Morelli 2005). In many respects, political science has reached a stage at which it can rightfully be considered an experimental discipline.

The **data-generating process** is the process by which data or observations are generated. The defining characteristic of **experimental research** is that the analyst deliberately introduces variation into the data-generating process. **Experimental data** are data from experimental research. **Non-experimental research** is when the researcher observes the data but does not have anything to do with how it is generated. **Observational data** are data from non-experimental research.

But what makes research "experimental"? The defining characteristic of **experimental research** is that the analyst deliberately introduces variation into what is called the **data-generating process** (Morton and Williams 2006). The data-generating process, as the name suggests, is just the process by which data or observations are generated—it is the process that produces the data we use in our research.

An example might help to clarify things. A medical researcher engages in experimental research to test the effects of a new drug when she deliberately introduces variation into the data-generating process by giving one group the new drug and a different group a placebo. The data that the medical researcher generates in this way is called **experimental data.** In contrast to this, research is non-experimental when the researcher observes the data but does not have anything to do with how it is generated. Data from **non-experimental research** is called **observational data.**

A **natural experiment** is one in which nature, rather than the analyst, exogenously intervenes in the data-generating process. The analyst acts *as if* she intervened in it when analyzing the data.

You may have heard of the term natural experiment. A **natural experiment** is one in which nature, rather than the analyst, exogenously intervenes in the data-generating process. For example, a researcher might use Hurricane Katrina as a natural experiment to examine how congressional representatives adapt to changing constituencies. Although a researcher does not intervene in the data-generating process in a natural experiment, she acts *as if* she did when analyzing the data. A natural experiment uses observational data, but observations of key causal variables are argued to be randomly distributed. For this reason natural experiments are often considered to be part of experimental research.

Experiments differ as to where they are conducted—they can be conducted in a laboratory, in the field, or on the Internet (Morton and Williams 2006). A **laboratory experiment** is an experiment that is conducted in a common location, such as a computer lab; the researcher controls all aspects of the environment except for the behavior of the participants, who are known as subjects. **Field experiments** and **Internet experiments,** by contrast, are those in which interactions between the analyst and subjects take place in the context of their everyday lives. Internet experiments differ from field experiments by taking place over the Internet, as their name would suggest. "For example, a field experiment would be a randomized mailing of campaign material and subsequent surveys about voter preferences, while an internet experiment would be a situation where the subjects were randomly assigned to view the campaign material on their computer and then surveyed afterwards about their preferences on the computer. . . . [I]n internet experiments the researcher has less control than in a physical laboratory but to some extent more control than in a traditional field experiment" (Morton and Williams 2006).

A **laboratory experiment** is an experiment that is conducted in a common location, such as a computer lab; the researcher controls all aspects of the environment except for the behavior of the participants, who are known as subjects. A **field experiment** is an experiment in which the interactions between the analyst and subjects take place in the context of the subjects' everyday lives. An **Internet experiment** is an experiment that occurs over the Internet.

One of the main advantages of experiments is that they give the researcher a great deal of control over how the data are generated and collected. As a result, it is easier for the researcher to identify causal processes at work and rule out spurious relationships. Experiments are particularly good for exploring causal relationships in situations in which observational data can tell us if two variables are correlated, but not if they are causally related. In fact, one of the reasons behind the recent increase in the number of experiments in political science has to do with a growing recognition of the limitations that exist when political scientists attempt to draw causal inferences from observational (non-experimental) data (Achen 1987).

To see how experiments might help us capture causality better than observational studies, consider the following example about whether television news coverage affects a person's opinion on various political issues. One approach to addressing this issue would be to examine people's survey responses to questions about their television viewing habits along with a variety of public opinion questions. Say you found evidence that certain television habits were associated (correlated) with particular beliefs. Is this enough to say that television coverage caused viewers to have these beliefs? The answer is, unfortunately, no. As Kinder and Palfrey (1992, 14) note, a survey of television habits and public opinion "cannot establish causal relationships. Observing that television news coverage and viewers' beliefs are correlated is not the same as establishing that television coverage influences viewers' beliefs. Citizens who rely primarily on television may differ in many ways from those who obtain their information elsewhere, and it may be these differences that are responsible for generating different outlooks on national problems." So what can you do? Well, you could run an experiment in which you control the television newscasts that citizens watch by randomly assigning them to different groups or treatments. By randomly assigning citizens to one treatment or another, the researcher tries to eliminate any systematic differences between the two groups other than the newscasts that the researcher makes them watch. As a result, any differences in the opinions between members of these two groups following the newscasts can be attributed to differences in the television programs each had been shown.

Although many experiments are designed to identify causal processes, others are designed to explore the accuracy of the assumptions underpinning our theories. In both political science and economics, many experimentalists are interested in finding the conditions under which people do (or do not) behave in accordance with some of the assumptions about human behavior that are often made in game-theoretic models. For example, imagine that we had a model about voting behavior when there is a majority rule requirement. The game theorist solves the game and generates some equilibrium predictions. An experimenter can then create a situation that closely matches the game theorist's assumptions about payoffs, voting rules, and types of voters, and run an experiment to see if subjects actually behave in the way the theory predicts. The results of such an experiment tell us something about how reasonable the game theorist's assumptions are about human behavior. These experimental results can be used by game theorists, in turn, to build new models with a different set of assumptions that are arguably more "reasonable." In the neighboring field of economics, "experiments that show violations of behavioral assumptions of formal theory" have been so influential "that it has resulted in the creation of a new field within the discipline, behavioral game theory, with a whole new set of perspectives on understanding economic behavior, something that was unthinkable twenty years ago" (Morton and Williams 2006).

You will notice that the experiments described in this chapter, in which participants in various places around the world were asked to play Ultimatum and Dictatorship Games, are experiments that are designed to see if people behave as game theorists predict. As we indicate, the results from these experiments differ from the equilibrium predictions of the games themselves. This forces the experimenters and game theorists to come up with an explanation for why the results differ. These experiments, as we note, have some extremely interesting implications for how we think about culture and democracy.

Let's briefly look at another interesting example of how experiments can be used to evaluate the assumptions of our theoretical models. Theories that highlight or rely on cultural or ethnic distinctions among different groups typically assume that individual actors can accurately determine who is a member of their own group and who is not. Thus, whether the theories assume that identity is primordial or constructed, they tend to assume that these identities are evident to everyone involved. But is this assumption realistic? Given that this assumption is often critical to our theories dealing with race, ethnicity, and politics, we might want to test it. One way to do this is with an experiment.

Such an experiment was conducted by Habyarimana et al. (2005). They test the assumption as to whether individual actors can determine who is a member of their own group and who is not by having subjects guess the ethnicity of various individuals after being shown a picture or watching a video clip of the individual. In the video clips, the individual provides varying amounts of either true or false information about his or her ethnic background. The researchers conducting the experiment used undergraduate students from the University of California, Los Angeles, and from the University of Southern California; each student self-identified as a member of one of seven ethnic groups that are well-represented on both campuses—African American, Arab, Asian, Caucasian, Indian, Latino, and Persian. Their results suggest that, contrary to the typical assumption that ethnic identities are obvious to political actors, there is significant variability within groups and among groups in how identifiable their members are. The level of distinctiveness between any two groups varies across individuals and across the groups in general. These results have interesting implications for many current theories. For example, consider the following:

> If ethnic identifiability varies across groups, then theorists of ethnic coalition building can use identifiability as a determinant of coalition choice. Theorists of in-group policing can use it to distinguish among communities with greater or lesser abilities to sanction their members, and thus greater or lesser abilities to execute business transactions, organize collectively, or prevent inter-group conflicts from degenerating into spirals of violence (Fearon and Laitin 1996). Theorists of ethnic mobilization can use it to account for variation in the ease with which political entrepreneurs may be able to organize—or organize against—particular communities. Theorists of ethnic violence can use it to explain the form that conflict takes. (Habyarimana et al. 2005, 5)

The authors of this study provide some anecdotal evidence to support their main claims with a brief comparison of wars in the north of Mali (1990–1995) and the south of Senegal (1982–present). Both conflicts involve separatist movements led by members of minority groups: the Tuaregs and Maures in Mali, and the Diola in the Casamance region of Senegal. In Mali, the Tuaregs and Maures are considered to be easily identifiable in comparison with the dominant ethnic group members. Thus, it is easier for the separatists to pressure members of their ethnic group to join the movement, and easier for the dominant group members and the Malian army to arbitrarily target Tuareg and Maure civilians for reprisals. As a result, the positions between the two camps were swiftly polarized and this led to communal violence. In Senegal, however, the members of the minority and majority groups are more difficult to identify. In this situation, both the mobilization of separatist partisans and the targeting of reprisals against members of the minority group have been more difficult, and the overall level of violence has been much lower. The authors suggest that this "contrasting degree of ethnic identifiability corresponds to a sharp difference in the form of group mobilization and the scope of violence in each case—a difference that would be hard to account for if we assumed erroneously that all ethnic groups were equally identifiable" (Habyarimana et al. 2005, 6).

As we have sought to demonstrate, experiments have been conducted in a wide range of areas in political science. Recently, political scientists have even been looking at images of the brain using Functional Magnetic Resonance Imaging (fMRI) scans to determine how the brain processes different political and economic situations (Tingley 2006). fMRI experiments focus on the fact that oxygen is required for the brain to function. Because oxygen is supplied to the brain by blood, experimenters have devised ways to measure the level of oxygenization in the blood. A growing body of evidence suggests that local changes in brain activity cause local changes in oxygen. These changes in oxygen can be measured by fMRI machines, the result being a relatively precise spatial and temporal picture of oxygen use in the brain. Rather than asking subjects why they react to certain stimuli the way that they do using some kind of survey or interview, experimenters using fMRI can try to determine this themselves by looking at which parts of the brain are illuminated, and in which order, when the stimuli are given. Among other things, political scientists have used fMRI experiments to examine how the brain processes different types of moral dilemmas (Greene et al. 2001), how it makes decisions (Camerer 2003; Bhatt and Camerer 2005), and how race and political sophistication affect judgment formation (Ochsner and Lieberman 2001; Lieberman, Schreiber, and Ochsner 2003; Phelps and Thomas 2003).

such as social institutions or cultural fairness norms, affect preferences or expectations.[19] They rank ordered the fifteen societies along two dimensions: payoffs to cooperation (how important and how large is a group's payoff from cooperation in economic production with non-immediate kin?) and market integration (how much do people rely on market exchange in their everyday lives?).

At the low end of the "payoffs to cooperation" dimension are the Machiguenga and Tsimané. Members of both of these groups are almost totally economically independent at the family level and rarely engage in cooperative production that involves individuals outside of the family. At the high end of the "payoffs to cooperation" dimension is the Lamelara, who hunt whales in large canoes manned by twelve or more people at a time. The expectation is that groups in which payoffs to cooperation are high, like the Lamelara, will make high offers in situations like the Ultimatum Game. At the low end of the "Market integration" dimension are the Hadza, because their lives would change little if markets suddenly disappeared. At the high end are the Orma, who often work for wages and engage in selling livestock. The expectation is that societies with greater market integration will make high offers in situations like the Ultimatum Game. This is because the more frequently people experience market transactions, the more they should also experience abstract sharing principles concerning behavior toward strangers. As predicted, a statistical analysis revealed that higher values on both dimensions were, indeed, associated with higher mean offers in the Ultimatum Game. In fact, fully 68 percent of the variance in offers could be explained by these two variables alone.

How should we interpret these results? One interpretation is that the individuals in these societies looked for analogues (similar situations) in their everyday lives when they were faced with the novel situation presented by the experiment. In effect, they asked themselves the following question, "What familiar situation is this game like?" and then acted in a way appropriate for this analogous situation. Consider the hyper-fair offers and the frequent rejections of these offers among the Au and Gnau in Papua New Guinea. This behavior can be explained by the culture of gift-giving in these societies. It is recognized that accepting gifts in these societies commits you to reciprocate at some future time determined by the gift giver. Moreover, particularly generous gifts put you in a clearly subordinate position. The culture of gift giving not only explains the generous offers made by the Au and Gnau, but it also explains why large offers were so readily rejected; these "excessively" large gifts tended to produce anxiety about the unspoken strings that were attached to them.

Consider now the low offers and high rejection rates of the Hadza. This behavior is entirely compatible with the fact that Hadza hunters often try to avoid sharing their meat. One ethnographer goes so far as to call this reluctance to share "tolerated theft." What about the Lamelara's tendency to divide the pie equally or to offer the respondent slightly more than a fair share? In real life, when a Lamelara whaling crew returns with a large catch, a designated person carefully divides the whale into predesignated parts allocated to the harpooner,

---

19. The experimenters examined whether individual level characteristics such as the proposer's (or responder's) sex, age, level of formal education, and their wealth relative to others in their group could explain the variation. Statistical analyses indicated that they could not.

crewmembers, and others participating in the hunt, as well as the sail maker, members of the hunters' corporate group, and other community members. The Lamelara may well have seen dividing the large pie in the Ultimatum Game as similar to dividing up a whale. Similar stories to these could be told to explain the behavior of individuals from the other societies.

By now, you are probably wondering what these experiments have to do with culture and democracy. The results from these experiments suggest that culture might be considered a shared way of playing everyday games that has evolved over many years (Bednar and Page 2007). It seems clear that individual choices are shaped by the economic and social interactions of everyday life. It appears that people search for analogous situations when trying to figure out how to act in new situations. If this is true, then it seems reasonable to think that the shared way of playing games in some societies might be less compatible with the game of democracy than that in other societies. For example, the game of democracy often requires cooperation, competition, and compromise. Societies that already require this type of behavior in their everyday "games" should find it easier to adopt and support democratic institutions. In contrast, societies in which individuals are engaged in games that do not encourage this type of behavior will find it much harder to consolidate democracy.

CONCLUSION

As we noted at the very beginning of this chapter, the notion that political institutions such as democracy or dictatorship are more suited to some cultures is not new. The rather vague claims made by scholars such as Montesquieu and Mill in the eighteenth and nineteenth centuries regarding the compatibility and incompatibility of democracy with particular cultures were later taken up in a more systematic fashion by cultural modernization theory. Cultural modernization theory argues that economic development produces certain cultural changes and that it is these cultural changes that lead to democracy (Inglehart and Welzen 2005). A key cultural change according to this line of reasoning is the emergence of what political scientists call a "civic culture."

For many, the existence of a civic culture is seen as a prerequisite for the successful emergence and survival of democracy (Almond and Verba [1963] 1989; Inglehart 1990; Inglehart and Welzen 2005). In addition to its importance for democracy, a civic culture is also seen by some as crucial for the good performance of government (Putnam 1993, 2000). But what is "civic culture"? On the whole, political scientists have conceptualized civic culture as a shared cluster of attitudes that includes things like a high level of interpersonal trust, a preference for gradual societal change, a high level of support for the existing political system, and high levels of life satisfaction. Although there are strong proponents of the idea that democracy requires a civic culture, the empirical evidence for this claim is somewhat mixed. Some studies have found that cultural modernization theory has the causal story backward (Barry 1970; Muller and Seligson 1994). In other words, some studies have found that it is experience with democracy that leads to the emergence of a civic culture and not experience with a civic culture that leads to the emergence of democracy. Other studies have shown that the elements of the shared cluster of attitudes that are thought to comprise the civic culture are not necessarily strongly related to each other or, in fact, with the stability of democracy (Muller and Selgison 1994; Jackman and Miller 1996; Seligson 2002).

More recently, the focus of cultural arguments regarding democracy has shifted to questions of whether certain religions are incompatible with democratic institutions. Given the current state of world affairs, it is not surprising that particular attention has been paid to whether Islam is incompatible with democracy. As we indicate in this chapter, though, a quick glance at the history of these types of arguments should make one very cautious of unthinkingly accepting that certain religions are incompatible with democracy. For example, some political scientists used to claim as recently as the 1970s that Catholicism was antithetical to democracy, but few do now, given how firmly established democracy has become in many Catholic countries around the world.

Many scholars point to particular doctrines to explain why such and such a religion is inimical to democracy. As we have sought to demonstrate, however, virtually all religions, including Islam, have some doctrinal elements that seem incompatible with democracy and others that do not (Przeworski, Cheibub, and Limongi 1998). This hardly seems a firm basis on which to draw such strong conclusions about the incompatibility of certain religions with democracy. Moreover, there is growing empirical evidence that the stance of different religions toward various political institutions often depends less on the content of their doctrine and more on the interests and strategic concerns of religious leaders (Kalyvas 1996, 1998, 2000). When combined with a vast literature indicating how culture is constructed and malleable rather than primordial and inherited, this helps to explain why all religions have historically been compatible with a broad range of political institutions, including democracy.

Despite the widely held belief by many that Islam is incompatible with democracy, the empirical analyses that we conducted in this chapter suggest that there is little reason to believe that majority Muslim countries cannot become and remain democratic once we take account of their wealth. To a large extent, our analyses indicate that the hurdle these majority Muslim countries need to overcome to be able to sustain democracy has less to do with the fact that they are Muslim and more to do with the fact that they are poor.

In the last two chapters, we have examined the economic and cultural determinants of the emergence and survival of democracy. Although these chapters are useful in giving us an aggregate view of democratization, you might be wondering how the democratic transition process actually plays out in practice. We focus on precisely that in the next chapter.

KEY CONCEPTS

civic culture, *212*
constructivist arguments, *208*
cultural modernization theory, *210*
data-generating process, *244*
experimental data, *244*
experimental research, *244*
field experiment, *245*

Internet experiment, *245*
laboratory experiment, *245*
natural experiment, *244*
non-experimental research, *244*
observational data, *244*
primordialist arguments, *208*

PROBLEMS

1. Consider the following argument.

Major premise: If Catholicism is antithetical to democracy, then Catholic countries are more likely to be dictatorships than democracies.

Minor premise: Catholic countries today are more likely to be democracies than dictatorships.

Conclusion: Therefore, Catholicism is compatible with democracy.

   a. Is this a valid or invalid argument?
   b. What form of categorical syllogism is this (affirming the antecedent/consequent or denying the antecedent/consequent)?

2. Consider the following argument.

Major premise: If Islam is antithetical to democracy, then Islamic countries are more likely to be dictatorships than democracies.

Minor Premise: Most Islamic countries around the world today are dictatorships.

Conclusion: Therefore, Islam is incompatible with democracy.

   a. Is this a valid or invalid argument?
   b. What form of categorical syllogism is this?

3. Obtain a copy of M. Steven Fish's article "Islam and Authoritarianism" from the journal *World Politics* 55 (2002): 4–37, using your institution's library resources. Read the article and then answer the following questions.

   a. What is Fish's dependent variable? How is it measured? What is the primary source for the dependent variable? What is the main independent variable? How is it measured?
   b. What is the main hypothesis of this article? What evidence would falsify this hypothesis?
   c. Why does Fish believe that countries with a predominantly Islamic religious tradition might be detrimental to the level of democracy in a country? Fish examines four proposed causal mechanisms for why this might be the case. Describe each of these four causal mechanisms in a sentence or two.
   d. Fish tests his theory using statistical analyses. Given his dependent variable, what sign (positive or negative) does Fish predict for the coefficient on his primary explanatory variable? *Hint:* See your answers to parts a and b. What sign does he find? Is the coefficient on this variable statistically significant? How do you know? *Hint:* The answer is in Table 3, column 1 on page 13. Interpret these results in substantive terms. In other words, what does Fish find about the relationship between Islam and a country's level of democracy?
   e. Which of the four potential causal mechanisms does Fish find the most evidence for? How do you know?
   f. One of the conclusions that Fish reaches is that Islam is antithetical to democracy because women are not treated equally in Islamic countries. He reaches this conclusion using Freedom House as his measure of democracy. Why might it be problematic to use

Freedom House to examine the impact that the unequal treatment of women in Islamic countries has on democracy? Find the complete list of questions that are used to create a country's Freedom House score by going to http://www.freedomhouse.org/. Identify which questions make it problematic to use Freedom House scores to test Fish's statement that Islam is bad for democracy because of its unequal treatment of women. Explain why these questions make Fish's statement more of a tautology than a scientific statement.

g. Fish (6) recognizes that one of the limitations to his analysis is that it looks at the relationship between Islam and a country's level of democracy only at a fixed point in time. Based on our discussion in the chapter, why might this be problematic for drawing inferences about whether Islam is incompatible with the emergence and the survival of democracy?

4. In this chapter, we discussed a couple of questions from the World Values Survey that are sometimes used as indicators of a country's level of democratic stability.

a. Re-read the possible responses to the two survey questions. Are these examples of nominal, ordinal, or interval measures of democratic stability?

b. Briefly describe some of the arguments for and against using such survey questions as a way of measuring democratic stability.

c. Write down two questions that you think should be put on a survey to elicit useful information about a country's level of democratic stability. Include the possible responses that you would provide as well.

d. Do you think that citizens of different countries might be likely to interpret your questions differently? Why or why not?

5. Coordination and Democracy Game

Some political scientists argue that democracy can be sustained only if citizens can coordinate their beliefs about (a) what types of government actions are unacceptable and (b) when they ought to take action against the government in response. Countries in which citizens have coordinated their beliefs on these matters might be said to be characterized by a "democratic culture." We now analyze a Coordination and Democracy Game inspired by Weingast (1997) to explore this argument further.

Our Coordination and Democracy Game has three actors—a state S, and two groups of citizens, A and B. The state must decide whether to transgress or not. If the state decides to transgress, then the two groups of citizens, A and B, must simultaneously decide whether to acquiesce to the state's transgression or challenge it. Only if both citizen groups "coordinate" on challenging the state will their challenge be successful. The most preferred outcome for the state is the one in which it transgresses and the two groups of citizens fail to coordinate on challenging it. The state prefers not to transgress if a transgression produces a successful challenge from the two citizen groups. The most preferred outcome for both citizen groups is obviously the one in which the state does not transgress in the first place. If the state does transgress, though, then both citizen groups prefer the outcome in which they successfully challenge the state to outcomes in which they either do not challenge it or they challenge unsuccessfully. Both citizen groups would rather not challenge the state than participate in an unsuccessful challenge. Figure 7.5 illustrates the game tree for our Coordination and Democracy Game along with cardinal payoffs capturing how the three actors evaluate the different outcomes. The payoffs to the state are listed first, those to group A are listed second, and those to group B are listed third.

The dashed line in Figure 7.5 indicates that when group A has to choose whether to acquiesce or challenge, it does not know whether group B will acquiesce or challenge. In other words, Group A and group B do not make their choices sequentially; they must make them simultaneously without knowing what the other is going to do. You are more familiar with seeing this sort of thing being captured by a strategic form game. As a result, let's rewrite this particular subgame (the part of the game tree in Figure 7.5 shown in gray) in its equivalent strategic form. This strategic form game is shown in Figure 7.6. The only thing that is unusual about this game is that the first payoff in each cell of the payoff matrix belongs to the state (even though it is not a player in this particular subgame).

 a. Solve the strategic form game in Figure 7.6 for any Nash equilibria. *Hint:* Ignore the payoffs belonging to the state, because the state is not a player in this game. If you solve the game correctly, you will find two Nash equilibria.

 b. What are the expected outcomes associated with the two Nash equilibria? What are the payoffs that each of the three players receive in the two Nash equilibria?

FIGURE 7.5	**Coordination and Democracy Game**

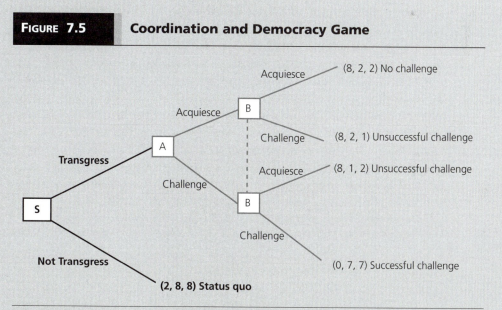

Note: A and B = citizen groups; S = state.

FIGURE 7.6	**Group Subgame**

		Group A	
		Acquiesce	Challenge
Group A	Acquiesce	8, 2, 2	8, 2, 1
	Challenge	8, 1, 2	0, 7, 7

c. By solving the game in Figure 7.6, you have found out that the state can expect to receive one of two possible payoffs if it transgresses. Compare each of the state's potential payoffs from transgressing with the state's payoff from not transgressing. What can you say about the circumstances under which the state will or will not transgress against its citizens?

d. How does the Coordination and Democracy Game help illustrate the notion that the coordination of beliefs between different groups in society might be considered a "democratic culture"—something that is necessary for democracy to emerge and survive?

e. In the chapter, we note that some political scientists believe that democracy is hard to sustain in countries that are characterized by a large number of ethnic or cultural groups. How does the Coordination and Democracy Game that you have just examined help to explain why this might be the case?

f. Weingast (1997) extends the game in Figure 7.5 to allow the state to transgress against only one group while keeping the other one satisfied. Without constructing and solving such a game, what difference do you think this would make to the conclusions from our original Coordination and Democracy Game? Do you think that groups will find it easier or harder to coordinate their beliefs in this new setting? What difference do you think this new setting makes to the likelihood that democracy can survive?

8 Democratic Transitions

The most radical revolutionary will become a conservative the day after the revolution.

Hannah Arendt, quoted in the *New Yorker,* 1970

Those who make peaceful revolution impossible will make violent revolution inevitable.

John F. Kennedy, in a speech at the White House, 1962

- In this chapter, we examine bottom-up and top-down processes by which democratic transitions might occur. A bottom-up process is one in which the people rise up to overthrow an authoritarian regime in a popular revolution. A top-down process is one in which the dictatorial ruling elite introduce liberalizing reforms that ultimately lead to a democratic transition.

- Collective action theory throws light on why popular revolutions are so rare and why authoritarian regimes frequently appear incredibly stable. The prevalence of preference falsification under dictatorships helps to explain the puzzle as to why revolutions nearly always come as a surprise yet appear so inevitable in hindsight. Tipping models provide further insight into why revolutions are so unpredictable and why even small changes in people's preferences can sometimes rapidly transform previously subservient individuals into revolutionary protesters.

- Authoritarian elites occasionally introduce liberalization policies. The goal of these policies is frequently the stabilization of dictatorial rule in the form of a broadened dictatorship, however, rather than a full democratic transition. We present a game-theoretic model of this liberalization process suggesting that top-down transitions cannot occur unless someone makes a mistake. Our analysis highlights the important role that information, beliefs, and uncertainty play in democratic transitions—and politics more generally.

OVERVIEW

The number of independent countries in the world grew from 67 in 1946 to 190 in 2000 (Przeworski et al. 2000). This large increase in the number of independent countries was largely the result of the accelerated decolonization process forced upon European powers in the 1950s and 1960s and the breakup of the Soviet Union in the early 1990s. Figure 8.1 illustrates how the number of independent countries, dictatorships, and democracies in the world has changed since 1946. Despite the consensus that now exists in favor of democracy, it is only since 1992 that the number of democracies worldwide has actually been greater than the number of dictatorships. Of those countries that gained independence in the 1950s and 1960s, the vast majority soon became dictatorships. By 1977 there were 2.6 times as many dictatorships as there were democracies—only 28 percent of the countries in the world were democratic.

The mid-1970s, though, ushered in an era of democratization that Samuel Huntington (1991) has called the "**third wave of democratization.**" On April 25, 1974, Portuguese military officers, unhappy with the ongoing colonial conflicts in Mozambique and Angola, con-

The **third wave of democratization** refers to the surge in democratic transitions that have occurred around the world since 1974.

ducted a coup, triggering events that eventually led to the first democratic multiparty elections in Portugal since 1926. Although it was not foreseen at the time, the movement toward

FIGURE 8.1 **Independent Countries, Democracies, and Dictatorships, 1946–2000**

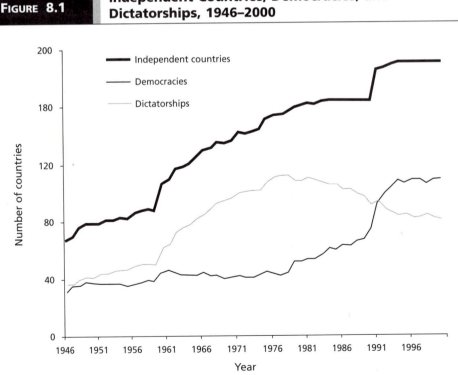

Source: Data are from Przeworski et al. (2000), updated through 2000.

democracy in Portugal was soon to be followed by democratic stirrings elsewhere. For example, Greece returned to the democratic fold in 1974 following conflict with Turkey over the island of Cyprus, and Spain finally threw off four decades of dictatorial rule under General Francisco Franco in 1977. This reemergence of democracy in much of southern Europe in the 1970s was followed by a global wave of democratization over the next twenty or so years in Africa, Asia, Eastern Europe, and Latin America.

In the previous two chapters, we examined the economic and cultural determinants of the emergence and survival of democracy. Although those chapters were useful in giving us an aggregate view of democratization, you may be wondering how the democratic transition process actually plays out in practice. In this chapter, we flesh out two types of democratic transition processes—bottom-up and top-down processes—drawing on historical evidence primarily from Eastern Europe. A **bottom-up democratic transition** process is one in which the people rise up to overthrow an authoritarian regime in a popular revolution. In contrast, a **top-down democratic transition** process is one in which the dictatorial ruling elite introduces liberalizing reforms that ultimately lead to a democratic transition. Although most real-world cases are probably characterized by aspects of both types of transition process, it can be illuminating to examine these two transition processes separately.

> A **bottom-up democratic transition** is one in which the people rise up to overthrow an authoritarian regime in a popular revolution. A **top-down democratic transition** is one in which the dictatorial ruling elite introduces liberalizing reforms that ultimately lead to a democratic transition.

BOX 8.1   THREE WAVES OF DEMOCRACY

Samuel Huntington (1991, 15) has argued that the spread of democracy around the world has come in waves, where a wave "is a group of transitions from non-democratic to democratic regimes that occur within a specified period of time and that significantly outnumber transitions in the opposite direction during that period of time." Specifically, Huntington argues that there have been three waves of democracy in the modern world. The first "long" wave between 1828 and 1926 had its roots in the American and French Revolutions. Countries that transitioned to democracy during the first wave include Argentina, France, Great Britain, Iceland, Ireland, Italy, Switzerland, and the United States. The second "short" wave between 1943 and 1962 had its origins in World War II. Countries that became democratic during the second wave include Austria, Brazil, Costa Rica, India, Israel, Italy, Japan, Malaysia, Nigeria, Sri Lanka, Turkey, Uruguay, and West Germany. The third wave started with the end of the Portuguese dictatorship in 1974 and, arguably, continues to this day. Numerous authoritarian regimes have been replaced by democratic forms of government in Africa, Asia, Latin America, and southern and eastern Europe since the mid-1970s.

- First wave of democratization   1828–1926
- First reverse wave   1922–1942
- Second wave of democratization   1943–1962

- Second reverse wave   1958–1975
- Third wave of democratization   1974–

As with real waves, the three waves of democracy have experienced weaker undercurrents flowing in the opposite direction. Thus, between the three waves of democracy have been periods in which some, but not all, of the countries that had previously made the transition to democracy slipped back into dictatorship. For example, the 1920s and 1930s saw the collapse of democracy in much of Europe and a return to traditional forms of authoritarian rule. Transitions to dictatorship also predominated in the 1960s and early 1970s, with military intervention in much of Latin American—Peru (1962), Bolivia (1964), Brazil (1964), Argentina (1966), Ecuador (1972), Chile (1973), and Uruguay (1973). Numerous authoritarian regimes also emerged during the 1960s in Asia and Africa. Thus, Huntington's analysis suggests that the global spread of democracy over the last two centuries has been marked by an ebb and flow, largely characterized by a two-step-forward and one-step-back pattern.

BOTTOM-UP TRANSITIONS TO DEMOCRACY

We begin by examining bottom-up transitions to democracy.

East Germany 1989

One of the most dramatic examples of a bottom-up transition to democracy occurred in East Germany in November 1989 when protests on the streets of Leipzig and Berlin forced the Communist East German government to open up the Berlin Wall and allow free multiparty elections. The end result was the emergence of a democratic East Germany and the eventual reunification of Germany in 1990. Few alive at the time will forget the scenes of East and West German citizens happily dancing together on top of the Berlin Wall under the watchful eyes of the East German border guards—guards who until recently had been under strict orders to shoot anyone who attempted to cross the border.

Although the collapse of communism in East Germany, and Eastern Europe more generally, seems inevitable from our vantage point, it came as a complete surprise to most observers at the time. Until 1989, Communist regimes had proved to be remarkably stable. Indeed, there had been extremely few major uprisings or revolts in Eastern Europe during the entire postwar period. With the exception of revolts in East Germany in 1953, in Poland and Hungary in 1956, in Czechoslovakia in 1968, and in Poland in 1981, the Communist regimes of Eastern Europe had been relatively unchallenged for forty years or more.[1] The

---

1. Of course, there were other small-scale uprisings in various East European countries (Ekiert 1996). For example, Poland experienced a student revolt in 1968, shipyard strikes in 1970, and workers' strikes in 1976. However, the Communist system always managed to quickly stabilize itself after these protests. On the whole, these smaller-scale revolts were not anti-system in character and were often self-limiting in nature.

EXTERNALLY IMPOSED DEMOCRACY

The 2003 U.S. invasion of Iraq has rekindled the debate as to whether democracy can be imposed on a country by military force or not. In particular, debate has centered on whether the success of democratic nation building depends on the identity of the external force. For example, some political leaders, such as French president Jacques Chirac (1995–2007), have argued that military intervention and democracy building is best achieved by a broad multilateral coalition of (European) democratic states. This is in contrast to leaders like U.S. president George W. Bush (2001–2009), who, at least implicitly, believe that a single democratic state acting alone or as part of a small coalition is best suited to democratic nation building. Still other political leaders, particularly those from the developing world and those closely associated with international institutions, argue that the United Nations should take the lead in building democratic states on the grounds that it possesses greater legitimacy than other actors.

Despite the obvious importance of the topic, it is perhaps surprising to note that there has been relatively little systematic research examining the factors that determine the success or failure of externally imposed democracy. What studies exist suggest that although intervention may promote democratic reform in the short run, it ultimately produces political instability in the long run (Kegley and Hermann 1997; Gleditsch, Christiansen, and Hegre 2004; Gilligan and Stedman 2003). Analyses that focus primarily on U.S. intervention have generally concluded that intervention does not lead to democracy (Lowenthal 1991; Forsythe 1992); some studies have been slightly more optimistic (Meernik 1996; Wantchekon and Neeman 2002).

A recent study by Bueno de Mesquita and Downs (2006, 1) suggests that although leaders of intervening states frequently assert that one of their main goals is to establish democracy, third-party intervention leads "to little if any improvement, and all too often erosion, in the trajectory of democratic development." Ultimately, the authors argue that it is cheaper for the intervening state to keep a compliant dictator in power than to guarantee that a sympathetic candidate will win a democratic election. As a result, we should not be terribly surprised that intervention frequently fails to produce democracy. The theory that underlies this argument is known as the "Selectorate Theory" of politics and is something that we examine in more detail in Chapter 9 (Bueno de Mesquita et al. 2003).

Bueno de Mesquita and Downs test their theory by examining the impact that military interventions have on the level of democratization in the "target state." They focus on military interventions that have occurred in the wake of civil wars and intrastate disputes, militarized interstate disputes, and interstate wars between 1946 and 2001. They find that military interventions by the United Nations or by dictatorships lead to a statistically significant reduction in democracy relative to what could have been expected if there had been no intervention. Although it is more likely to produce the trappings of democracy, such as elections and legislatures, intervention by democratic states, and the United States in particular, fails to increase the level of democracy in target countries to the point at which scholars would normally consider them democratic. In sum, there is little systematic evidence at present to suggest that externally imposed democracy will be successful. This is the case irrespective of the identity of the intervening actor.

revolts that did occur were put down by considerable force and direct Soviet military intervention, which only further discouraged East Europeans from publicly opposing their Communist governments. Of all the governments in the Eastern bloc in 1989, the one in East Germany was arguably the most stable, prosperous, and hard-line. The East German secret police—the *Staatssicherheitsdienst*, or *Stasi* for short—were infamous for their ability to monitor and control the lives of ordinary citizens (Rosenberg 1996). In 1989 there were 85,000 full-time Stasi officers and more than 100,000 informers (Lohmann 1994, 59). With a population of slightly less than 17 million, these figures reveal the shocking fact that there was one Stasi officer or informer for every ninety East German citizens. To most observers, East Germany looked far from the brink of collapse in 1989.

The eventual collapse of communism in East Germany had much to do with the election of Mikhail Gorbachev to the position of general secretary of the Communist Party in the Soviet Union on March 11, 1985. To a large extent, Gorbachev inherited a Soviet Union in crisis. The economy that had seemed to perform so well during much of the postwar period had begun to stagnate by the mid-1980s, and the Soviet invasion of Afghanistan in 1979 to prop up a Communist government against Islamic rebels was increasingly taking up valuable resources. The 1986 Chernobyl disaster, in which a nuclear reactor exploded and spread radioactive fallout across much of Europe, starkly revealed the dysfunctional nature of a deeply sclerotic and secretive Soviet state. As William I. Hitchcock (2004, 353) notes, the director of the Chernobyl nuclear plant "responded to the explosion in typical Soviet fashion: he reassured Moscow that despite the accident, radiation levels were normal; then he ordered all telephone lines to be cut"—it took the government more than two weeks to actually begin an evacuation of the area.

> **Perestroika,** or "economic restructuring," was a reform policy aimed at liberalizing and regenerating the Soviet economy. **Glasnost,** or "openness," was a reform policy aimed at increasing political openness.

Gorbachev responded to these crises with two reform policies, called perestroika and glasnost. **Perestroika** was a policy aimed at liberalizing and regenerating the Soviet economy; **glasnost** was a policy designed to increase political openness and encourage freedom of expression. We all know what happened to the Soviet Union and Eastern Europe, but it is important to recognize that Gorbachev was an ardent Communist who deeply believed in socialism. It was his hope that the policies of perestroika and glasnost would save the Soviet Union; he certainly did not intend for them to facilitate its breakup, as they arguably did.

The liberalizing reform policies introduced by Gorbachev in the Soviet Union had the effect of encouraging reformists and opposition groups in other countries in Eastern Europe. Following a big wave of strikes, the Polish government convened a conference in August 1988, known as the Roundtable Talks, with the main opposition group, Solidarity, to help reach a compromise on how to deal with the growing economic and political problems. The result of these talks was the legalization of the independent trade union—Solidarity—and nationwide elections in 1989, which produced the first non-Communist prime minister in Eastern Europe in forty years. These changes in Poland served to encourage liberalizers in other Communist countries. For example, talks in Hungary, known as the Triangular Table Talks, which began about three months after those in Poland, resulted in cautious moves toward easing censorship and legalizing an independent trade union. When this brought little response from the Soviet Union, further reforms were introduced—the Communist Party renamed itself the Socialist Party, the country's name was changed from the Hungarian People's Republic to the Republic of Hungary, and multiparty elections were planned for 1990.

Although these changes in Eastern Europe were clearly significant, it should be noted that people at the time did not see them as signs of the imminent collapse of Communist control. The Chinese Communist Party's use of tanks and soldiers to violently disperse thousands of protesters in Tiananmen Square in June 1989 clearly illustrated that some Communist regimes were willing to use overwhelming force to retain power; indeed, the East German government led by its hard-line leader, Eric Honecker, was one of the most vocal supporters of the Chinese government's forceful response.

The situation in East Germany began to change when Hungary decided to open its border with Austria in August 1989, thereby breaching the Iron Curtain for the first time. Although East Germans had always been relatively free to travel to other Communist countries in Eastern Europe, it had been all but impossible to get permission to travel to the West. In September 1989, 13,000 East Germans fled to the West across Hungary's open border.[2]

x 8.3

TIANANMEN SQUARE, BEIJING (JUNE 4, 1989)

Between April 15 and June 4, 1989, students, intellectuals, and labor activists held mass demonstrations against the Chinese Communist government in Tiananmen Square, Beijing. After the demonstrators refused to disperse, a hard-line faction in the Communist Party decided to use force against them. On May 20 the government declared martial law and on June 4 army tanks and infantry troops were sent in to crush the protest. Estimates of civilian deaths vary from a low of 23 according to the Chinese Communist Party to a high of 2,600 according to the Chinese Red Cross; several thousand people were injured. The Chinese government then conducted widespread arrests to suppress remaining opposition groups.

A Chinese man stands alone to block a line of tanks heading east on Beijing's Chang'an Boulevard in Tiananmen Square on June 4, 1989.

---

2. Some East Germans actually went to Warsaw, because Poland, by this time, had an open border with West Berlin. Thus, you had the rather odd sight of East Germans hopping on a train in East Berlin, going to Warsaw, changing trains, and going back to West Berlin. All this just to move a few hundred yards to the other side of the Berlin Wall.

Thousands of other East Germans tried to reach the West by staging sit-ins at West German embassies in other East European capitals such as Prague. In response to these "refugees," the East German government eventually provided special trains to carry them to the West. Before doing so, East German officials took away their East German passports and claimed that they were expelling "irresponsible antisocial traitors and criminals." In a matter of weeks, thousands of East Germans had left their possessions and relatives behind to make a dash for freedom. The willingness of East Germans to leave so much behind is further evidence that few at the time foresaw the imminent collapse of the Communist system in East Germany.

Although tens of thousands of East Germans fled the country, a fledgling opposition group called Neues Forum (New Forum) surfaced in East Germany demanding reform. Opposition protests began to take place on the streets of Leipzig and East Berlin. Initially, the crowds chanted, "Wir wollen 'raus!" (We want to leave!). Soon, however, they began to defiantly chant, "Wir bleiben hier!" (We are staying here!). It was the emergence of protesters demanding reform and refusing to simply leave that proved to be the real threat to the East German government's hold on power. The early protests were small, but they soon began to grow as the failure of the East German government to successfully intimidate and crack down on the initial demonstrators encouraged more and more people to participate. By October 1989 more than 250,000 people were regularly taking part in pro-democracy demonstrations. In a clear challenge to the Communist Party's claim to represent the East German people, the protesters famously chanted, "Wir sind das Volk!" (We are the People!).

Despite the protests, the East German government went ahead with celebrations on October 7 to mark the fortieth anniversary of the founding of the East German state. These celebrations included extravagant military parades, orchestrated pro-regime demonstrations, and a visit by Mikhail Gorbachev. To the embarrassment of the East German leadership, or politburo, the crowd at the parades, many of them handpicked by Communist Party officials, began chanting for Gorbachev to help them. In defiance of Gorbachev's advice that "Life will punish latecomers"—a clear reference to the necessity for reform—the hard-line East German leader, Eric Honecker, reacted within days of Gorbachev's departure by signing the *Schiessbefehl* (order to shoot) for a Chinese solution to the protests (Lohmann 1994, 69). East Germany was on the brink of civil war. As troops were being assembled and armed, the rest of the East German politburo rebelled, countermanded the order, and replaced Honecker with the more moderate Egon Krenz.

Despite the introduction of minor reforms, the mass protests continued and were only emboldened when, on a trip to Finland, Gorbachev announced that the Soviets would no longer intervene militarily in Eastern Europe to prop up Communist governments. On November 4, more than one million East Germans took to the streets of East Berlin. In a final attempt to ward off ever larger protests, the East German government agreed on November 9 to remove all restrictions on travel to the West. The announcement of this decision on television led to tens of thousands of East Berliners rushing to the Berlin Wall, where surprised

A BRIEF HISTORY OF EAST GERMANY, 1945–1990

At the Potsdam Conference in August 1945, the Allied powers divided Germany into four zones, to be occupied by France in the southwest, Britain in the northwest, the United States in the south, and the Soviet Union in the east. Berlin, which was more than 100 miles inside the eastern zone controlled by the Soviet Union, was also divided into four similar occupation zones. As the postwar rivalry between the Western powers and the Soviet Union increased, the Americans, French, and British signed the London Agreements in June 1948, joining their sectors together

MAP 8.1   Divided Germany

and introducing a new currency—the Deutschmark. In response to this perceived act of aggression, the Soviets responded by blocking all ground transportation between the western sectors and West Berlin on June 24, 1948. The next day, the Western powers began a massive airlift to supply West Berlin with essentials such as food and fuel. The Berlin Airlift, or the Berlin Blockade as it became known, finally ended ten months later when the Soviets realized that the West would not simply give up West Berlin. By now the division of Germany was almost inevitable. The Federal Republic of Germany (West Germany) was formally established on May 23, 1949, and the German Democratic Republic was established on October 7, 1949.

The first real challenge to the East German government came with the Berlin Uprising in June and July 1953. The uprising began when Berlin construction workers protested against increasingly repressive working conditions. As the protests began to spread, the East German government introduced martial law and finally managed to suppress the uprising with the help of hundreds of Soviet tanks; more than 100 people died.

Between 1949 and 1961, 2.7 million people reacted to the increasingly dismal economic and political conditions in East Germany by emigrating to the West. It was in response to this that the East German government closed the borders to the West and began construction of the ninety-six-mile-long Berlin Wall during the night of August 12–13, 1961. The Berlin Wall split numerous families and separated many Berliners from their places of employment.

MAP 8.2   The Division of Berlin

Although the whole length of the border between East and West Germany was closed with chain-link fences, walls, minefields, and other installations, it was the Berlin Wall that arguably became the most iconic symbol of the cold war. Over the years, thousands of attempts were made to breach the wall and reach the West. In all, about 200 people were killed trying to escape, with Chris Gueffroy being the last to be shot dead in February 1989.

In what became known as the Hallstein Doctrine, Konrad Adenauer, the first postwar West German chancellor, had tied West Germany firmly into a Western orbit and steadfastly refused to recognize the official existence of East Germany. The election of Willy Brandt in 1969, however, brought a change of direction in the policy of West Germany. Brandt's Ostpolitik, or "Eastern Policy," was designed to improve the lives of Germans caught up in the day-to-day reality of the cold war. As such, he sought to normalize and improve relations with East Germany. In a series of treaties in the 1970s, the leaders of East and West Germany agreed to recognize the political status quo; one treaty allowed for West Berliners to visit East Berlin. This normalization of relations essentially recognized the formal division of Germany for the first time; both Germanys joined the United Nations in 1973.

During the summer and autumn of 1989, massive changes occurred in East Germany that eventually led to the reunification of Germany. Tens of thousands of East Germans fled to the West, taking advantage of the Hungarian government's decision to open its border to Austria. Increasingly, growing numbers of East Germans began protesting on the streets of Leipzig and Berlin, demanding reform within East Germany itself. More than a million protesters took part in a demonstration in East Berlin on November 4, 1989. Under pressure from these protests, the East German government finally announced that it would allow unrestricted travel to the West. On hearing this announcement, tens of thousands of East Berliners rushed to the Berlin Wall, where astonished border guards had little choice but to allow them through. That night, East Berliners danced on top of the Berlin Wall with West Berliners; some took the opportunity to start dismantling the wall with whatever tools they had available. Ongoing protests forced the East German government to allow free, multiparty elections in March 1990. These elections produced a victory for the pro-unification forces headed by West German chancellor Helmut Kohl. East Germany entered into an economic and monetary union with West Germany in July 1990. On September 12, 1990, East Germany, West Germany, and the four powers that occupied Germany at the end of World War II signed the Treaty on the Final Settlement with Respect to Germany. This treaty paved the way for German reunification on October 3, 1990.

border guards eventually allowed them to pour through. In the following weeks, the whole socialist system in East Germany unraveled. Despite brief attempts to create a non-socialist East Germany, elections on March 18, 1990, demonstrated that an overwhelming majority of East Germans wanted reunification with West Germany. By now, instead of shouting, "Wir sind das Volk!" (We are the People!), the protesters were shouting, "Wir sind ein Volk!" (We are one people!). Reunification finally took place on October 3, 1990, when the areas of the former German Democratic Republic were incorporated into the Federal Republic of Germany.

East and West Germans stand on the Berlin Wall in front of the Brandenburg Gate the day after the wall opened on Nov. 9, 1989.

The transition to democracy that occurred in East Germany in 1989 represents but one case of a bottom-up transition, in which popular mobilization led to the overthrow of an authoritarian regime. There are numerous other examples. For instance, a few weeks after the fall of the Berlin Wall, mass protests forced the overthrow of the Communist government in Czechoslovakia in what became known as the Velvet Revolution because of its lack of violence (Garton Ash 1999). A few weeks after this, in December 1989, crowds played an integral role in removing the Communist dictator Nicolae Ceaușescu from power in Romania. Other examples include the EDSA Revolution, or the People Power Revolution, which saw massive demonstrations of up to three million people remove Ferdinand Marcos from power in the Philippines in 1986, or the June Resistance, which saw mass protests force South Korea's General Roh Tae Woo to allow direct presidential elections in mid-1987. The list could go on and on.

As political scientists, we need to ask ourselves how we can explain these types of bottom-up transitions. How can we capture the surprise with which actual participants greeted the events that were unfolding around them? Why did the collapse of communism in Eastern Europe occur in 1989 and not any earlier or any later? Why did Eastern Europe, which in retrospect seems to have been filled with extremely fragile Communist regimes, seem so stable before 1989? Why are revolutions like those in Eastern Europe and elsewhere so rare? Why are they so hard to predict? We believe that collective action theory and tipping models provide answers to some of these questions. We begin by examining collective action theory.

Collective Action Theory

Collective action theory focuses on forms of mass action, or "collective action," such as the protests in East Germany in 1989. Other examples of **collective action** are revolutions, interest group activities, strikes, elections, public television fund-raising drives, fraternities and sororities, and the like. Typically, collective action concerns the pursuit of public goods by

Collective action refers to the pursuit of some objective by groups of individuals. Typically, the objective is some form of public good.

groups of individuals. A **public good** has two characteristics: (a) **non-excludability** (a good is non-excludable if you cannot prevent those in the group who did not contribute to its supply from consuming it); and (b) (**non-rivalry**— a good is non-rivalrous if its consumption by one individual does not reduce the amount available for consumption by other individuals in the group).

> A **public good** is non-excludable and non-rivalrous. **Non-excludability** means that you cannot exclude people from enjoying the public good, and **non-rivalry** means that there is just as much public good for people to enjoy no matter how many people consume it.

Some examples should clarify the idea of a public good. One example of a public good is clean air. Clean air is non-excludable in the sense that you cannot stop people from breathing it if it is around, and it is non-rivalrous in the sense that one person's consumption of it does not diminish the amount of clean air that others can consume. Another example of a public good is a lighthouse. A lighthouse is non-excludable in that you cannot stop ships in the sea from seeing the light irrespective of whether they contribute to the building and upkeep of the lighthouse, and it is non-rivalrous in that there is just as much light for everyone to see no matter how many ships are taking advantage of it. Other examples of public goods include public parks, fire stations, public radio, and national defense. For the purposes of this chapter, we can also think of democracy as a public good—it is non-excludable in that anyone living in a democracy gets to enjoy living under democratic rule irrespective of whether they helped bring democracy about or whether they help to sustain it, and it is non-rivalrous because one person's enjoyment or consumption of democracy does not reduce the amount of democracy that others can consume.

Most people will recognize that the nature of public goods make them quite desirable. This might lead you to think that individuals who expect to benefit from a public good would be enthusiastic contributors to the provision of that good—at least as long as the benefit from the public good outweighed the cost of providing it. Put more starkly, you might expect that groups of individuals with common interests would act collectively to achieve those interests. Although this might seem reasonable to you, a famous economist, Mancur Olson ([1965] 1971), has shown that there are quite compelling reasons to doubt whether individuals will actually contribute to the provision of public goods or take collective action to achieve their common interests. The difficulty that groups of individuals have in providing public goods that all members of the group desire is commonly known as the **collective action, or free-rider, problem.** As we will see, the free-rider problem provides one explanation for why protests were so rare in Eastern

> The **collective action, or free-rider, problem** refers to the fact that individual members of a group often have little incentive to contribute to the provision of a public good that will benefit all members of the group.

Europe prior to 1989 and why the Communist regimes in that part of the world seemed stable for so long; in fact, it provides an explanation for why revolutions and public displays of opposition in dictatorships are so rare in general.

Start by asking yourself whether you would contribute to the provision of a public good that you value. Would you join a pro-democracy protest like those in East Germany in 1989 or would you stay at home? It is important to recognize that your *individual* decision to contribute to the public good or to participate in the pro-democracy protest is unlikely to be the decisive factor in determining whether the public good is provided or whether the protest is successful. What possible difference could one person make to the success of a mass protest? Given that you are individually unlikely to influence the outcome of the protest, why pay the costs that come with participation? The costs of participation include time, possibly expense, and perhaps even loss of life. It should be obvious that the potentially high costs associated with joining pro-democracy rallies in Communist Eastern Europe would have been only too clear to would-be participants at the time. All in all, the decision not to participate in a pro-democracy protest (or not to contribute to a public good more generally) is very appealing: if the pro-democracy rally fails, you will not have paid any costs or run the risk of incurring the dictatorship's wrath; and if the pro-democracy rally succeeds, you can "free ride" on the participation of others because everyone gets to benefit from the establishment of democracy irrespective of whether they participated in the rally or not. This is the basic logic underlying the collective action problem.

To better understand this logic, let's try to be a little more analytical. Imagine a group made up of N individuals. For example, we could think of the group as being the entire East German population. Now imagine that K individuals (where $K \leq N$) in the group must contribute or participate for the public good to be provided. We could think of the public good as being democracy and K as being the number of pro-democracy protesters that are necessary to make the Communist government in East Germany (or any other dictatorship) back down and allow democracy to emerge. If democracy is achieved, then everyone receives a benefit, B (where $B > 0$), irrespective of whether everyone participated in the pro-democracy rally or not. If you participate in the pro-democracy rally, you must pay a cost C (where $C > 0$). To capture the notion that the provision of the public good provides more benefits to you than the individual cost of participating in the protest, let's assume that $B > C$. If we did not make this assumption, then no one would ever have an incentive to contribute to the public good. Now ask yourself whether you would ever contribute to the public good under these circumstances. Would you participate in a pro-democracy protest? As Table 8.1 illustrates, your decision will depend on your conjecture or expectation about what other members of the group will do.

As you can see, if these payoffs capture your assessment of the situation, it makes no sense for you to participate in the pro-democracy protest if you expect that fewer than $K-1$ others will participate (Scenario 1).[3] This is because your individual participation will not make the

---

3. Some readers might say that participating in the provision of this and other public goods is the "right thing to do" and that a person should, therefore, participate despite the expected consequences. This is certainly a defensible moral position from the standpoint of several world religions and secular philosophies. For example, Immanuel Kant ([1785] 1993, 30) argued that it is a "categorical imperative" (that is, an unconditional requirement) that moral agents "act only according to that maxim whereby you can at the same time will that it should become a universal law." In other words, the "right thing to do" is to ask yourself, "What if everyone failed to contribute to public goods?" If you conclude that the outcome would be lamentable, you should contribute to the public good. Under such conditions doing the right thing is a desired end in itself. We are not endorsing the rejection of such moral concerns but merely suggesting that much of the political world can be understood by assuming that most actors are unencumbered by them. Put differently, if most people acted according to a moral rule along the lines of Kant's categorical imperative, the study of politics could well be unnecessary.

TABLE 8.1	**Pro-Democracy Protest: Do I Participate or Not?**

	Scenario 1 (Fewer than $K - 1$ participate)	Scenario 2 (Exactly $K - 1$ participate)	Scenario 3 (K or more participate)
Participate	$-C$	$\underline{B - C}$	$B - C$
Don't participate	$\underline{0}$	0	$\underline{B}$

K = the number of individuals that must participate for the pro-democracy protest to be successful; C = cost associated with participating; B = benefit associated with a successful pro-democracy protest; underlined letters indicate the payoffs associated with the actor's best response—participate or don't participate—in each scenario. It is assumed that $B > C > 0$.

protest successful and you will only end up incurring the cost of participation; you'd be better off staying at home. It also makes no sense for you to participate if you conjecture that at least K others will participate (Scenario 3). This is because your participation is not necessary for a successful protest; you might as well stay at home and free ride on the successful participation of others without paying any costs. It makes sense for you to participate only if you expect that exactly $K-1$ others will participate (Scenario 2). In this scenario, your participation is decisive because it turns an otherwise unsuccessful protest into a successful one; you get a payoff of $B–C$. By not participating, you condemn the protest to failure and your payoff is 0. Given that $B–C > 0$, it is rational for you to participate. The rational choices in each of the three possible scenarios are underlined in Table 8.1.

The fact that the logic behind these choices applies to every individual in the group suggests that there are only two possible types of equilibria here—either no one participates in the pro-democracy rally or exactly K individuals do. Think about it this way. If no one is participating in the rally, then no one will want to individually deviate by participating because he or she will pay the cost of participating but the one-person rally will be a failure. As a result, "no participation" is an equilibrium. If K individuals are participating, none of the K participants will want to individually deviate by staying home because the rally will fail without his or her participation, and none of the other group members will want to protest because his or her participation is costly and not crucial to the rally's success. As a result, exactly K participants is also an equilibrium. Thus, for the pro-democracy rally (or any form of collective action) to succeed, exactly K individuals must believe that they, and only they, are likely to participate. As we argue below, this insight suggests that two factors in particular are crucial for determining the likely success of collective action: (a) the difference between K and N, and (b) the size of N.[4]

---

4. It seems reasonable to think that the likelihood of successful collective action also depends on (a) the costs of participation (C) and (b) the size of the benefit (B) at issue. As participation becomes more costly (holding N, K, and B fixed), it is likely that group members will be less willing to participate. Similarly, as the benefit to be obtained from successful collective action increases (holding N, K, and C fixed), it seems likely that the group member will be more willing to participate.

Why would the difference between K and N matter? Suppose that the number of people required for a successful pro-democracy protest (K) was equal to the size of the group (N). In this situation, all in the group know that their participation is crucial for the success of the protest and that they each prefer a successful protest to a failed one. As a result, there is no incentive for any member of the group to free ride by staying at home.[5] Suppose now that only some of the group members are required for a successful pro-democracy protest, that is, $K < N$. In this situation, group members know that a successful rally can take place without everyone's participation. It is this realization that creates the incentive to free ride. It does not take much of a leap to realize that the incentive to free ride becomes greater the larger the difference between K and N. For example, if K is only slightly smaller than N, then most group members are still going to think that their participation will be crucial to the success of the protest. The result of this is that participation rates and, hence, the likelihood of a successful protest will remain relatively high. If K is much smaller than N, however, then most group members are going to think that they are not crucial to the success of the protest and that they can get away with free riding on the participation of others. Given the increased level of free riding, the likelihood of a successful protest is going to decline in this situation.

The bottom line here is that forms of collective action such as protests, strikes, revolutions, lobbying, and the like are less likely to be successful when the number of group members required for success (K) is significantly smaller than the number of people who will benefit from the success (N). Somewhat counterintuitively, this means that group leaders interested in some form of collective action such as a demonstration or a letter-writing campaign will be more successful if they tell their members that success depends on the participation of nearly all of their members rather than just a few of them. The logic of collective action that we have just presented helps to explain why political parties try to convince their supporters that all of their votes are crucial to their electoral success or why pledge drives for public television or National Public Radio in the United States continually state that the contribution of all listeners is crucial to the ongoing existence of these institutions even if this is not true—they are trying to persuade voters, listeners, and viewers to participate rather than to free ride.

Why would the size of the group matter? The size of N matters because it influences the likelihood that you will think of yourself as critical to the form of collective action under consideration. Should you run the risks associated with participating in a pro-democracy rally where N is large? Will it make a difference? If hardly anyone else participates, then the pro-democracy protest is unlikely to be successful. And if lots of people participate, it is unlikely that your individual participation will make much of a difference. Given this, why

---

5. It turns out that it is also an equilibrium for no one to participate if $K = N$. For example, if everyone else is choosing not to participate, it makes no sense for one person to deviate and participate, because the protest will obviously fail with only one protester. In this situation, the group is stuck in an equilibrium trap in which no one is participating, even though everyone would be better off if they all participated. Shepsle and Bonchek (1997, 228) have argued that this equilibrium is unlikely, because everyone "will realize that everyone else benefits from achieving the group goal, and that the only way for this to happen is if everyone" participates.

participate? The size of N also matters because it influences the ability of group members to monitor and punish free riders. The larger the group, the harder it is to monitor, identify, and punish those who do not participate in the protest. The result is that larger groups tend to be characterized by higher levels of free riding and a lower likelihood that collective action will be successful.

The relationship between group size and successful collective action has some important and counterintuitive implications. Most important, it suggests that small groups may be more effective than large groups because of the small group's increased ability to solve the free rider problem. In this sense, the relationship that we outline challenges the common concern in democratic theory that the majority will tyrannize and exploit the minority. In fact, the opposite may well occur in some circumstances. For example, the result about group size helps to explain why business groups (relatively small) seem to have greater lobbying power and influence over policy than, say, consumer groups or workers (relatively large). It also helps to explain why relatively small constituencies such as religious fundamentalists can have a significant influence on political outcomes compared with the much larger constituencies made up of religious moderates and secularists. In sum, the free-rider problem is likely to damage the ability of large groups to conduct forms of collective action much more than that of small groups.

Collective action theory provides a possible explanation for the apparent stability of communism in postwar East Germany and for why public demonstrations of regime opposition are so rare in dictatorships more generally. Collective action theory reminds us that the fact that many East Germans shared a common interest in the overthrow of the Communist regime and the establishment of democracy did not automatically translate into their taking collective action to bring this about. The public goods nature of democracy created an incentive for East Germans to avoid the potential costs of participating in pro-democracy rallies and to free ride on the participation of others. The incentives to free ride in East Germany were large because the number of people who would benefit from democracy (N)—virtually the entire 17 million population—was huge and because the number of protesters necessary to bring democracy about (K)—several hundred thousand in the end—was relatively small in comparison. The costs of participating in pro-democracy demonstrations were largely prohibitive as well. The violent and deadly outcome of the Berlin Uprising in 1953 was a stark reminder to potential protesters of the dangers that they faced if they publicly opposed the Communist government. It is important to recognize that the lack of public opposition in East Germany for most of the postwar period was not necessarily a sign that the Communist regime enjoyed widespread support; it may simply have been that the collective action problem made it difficult for the opposition to organize itself into a coherent force.

Tipping Models

Although collective action theory helps to explain why revolutions are so rare and why dictatorships often appear quite stable, it cannot really explain the mass protests that eventually brought communism to its knees in 1989–1990. Participation now becomes the puzzle that needs to be explained. One explanation for the mass protests that occurred in East Germany in 1989 can be found in what political scientists call "tipping," or "threshold," models (Granovetter 1978; DeNardo 1985; Kuran 1991; Lohmann 1994; Ginkel and Smith 1999).

As in the model of collective action that we have just examined, we start with an individual who must decide whether to publicly support or oppose a dictatorship. The individual has a private preference and a revealed public preference. His private preference is his true attitude toward the dictatorship, and his public preference is the attitude toward the dictatorship that he reveals to the outside world. The dangers that come from publicly revealing one's opposition to a dictatorship often mean that individuals who oppose the regime falsify their true preferences; instead of opposing the dictatorship in public, they support it. In East Germany, as elsewhere in Eastern Europe, "people routinely applauded speakers whose message they disliked, joined organizations whose mission they opposed, and signed defamatory letters against people they admired" (Kuran 1991, 26). One consequence of **preference falsification** is that individuals do not know the

> **Preference falsification** means not revealing one's true preferences in public.

true level of opposition in a dictatorship because they all seem to be publicly supporting it. The perception is that society is publicly behind the dictatorship and that there is no point opposing it. As the political dissident Aleksandr Solzhenitsyn (1975, 275) wrote about the Soviet Union, "The lie has been incorporated into the state system as the vital link holding everything together." Note that preference falsification provides an alternative, but complementary, explanation to that provided by collective action theory for the relative stability of Eastern Europe in the postwar period. It suggests that even if collective action could be effectively organized, individuals might still choose not to protest because they are not sure whether others really oppose the regime or not.

Although many people may be engaged in preference falsification, there is probably some protest size at which they would be willing to publicly reveal their true preferences. In other words, an opponent of the regime might not wish to participate in a pro-democracy rally that comprises a few hundred people but may be willing to participate in one that comprises tens of thousands or hundreds of thousands of people. We will refer to the protest size at which an individual is willing to participate as his **revolutionary threshold.** The intuition behind the notion of a revolutionary threshold

> A **revolutionary threshold** is the size of protest at which an individual is willing to participate.

is relatively straightforward. As the size of a protest grows, it becomes harder for the state to identify and punish individuals for participating. In other words, the costs of participation decline in rough proportion to the number of protesters.[6] That large numbers of people are willing to smoke marijuana in public each year at the National Organization for the Reform

---

6. Other tipping, or threshold, models do not focus purely on the number of people participating in protests. Instead, they point to the information that is revealed about the regime's support by having particular groups of individuals protest (Lohmann 1994). For example, Ginkel and Smith (1999) focus on the role that dissidents play in signaling whether the time is appropriate for the masses to rise up and overthrow the regime.

of Marijuana Laws' "smoke ins" is a prime example of the logic underlying the notion of revolutionary thresholds.

Individuals naturally have different revolutionary thresholds. Some people are really brave and are quite happy to oppose dictatorial rule irrespective of whether others do. These people are commonly referred to as political dissidents and often include academics, writers, or religious figures. For example, Aleksandr Solzhenitsyn and Andrei Sakharov were both political dissidents who, between them, challenged the police state and nuclear weapons policy of the Soviet Union. Other people may be scared and unwilling to publicly show their opposition to a dictatorship unless lots of others also do so. Still others may actually support the regime; these people are unlikely to join in a pro-democracy protest under any circumstances. As you might expect, people's thresholds are likely to depend on many different factors, such as whether they have benefited or suffered under the regime, whether they have much to lose from participating in protests, and whether they believe that the regime is fragile or stable. The point is that people's revolutionary thresholds vary.

An example might make this concept clearer.[7] Below is an example of a ten-person society labeled A.

$$A = \{0, 2, 2, 3, 4, 5, 6, 7, 8, 10\}.$$

The numbers in brackets indicate the revolutionary threshold of each of the ten people in society A. The first individual in this society has a revolutionary threshold of 0, meaning that he is willing to protest on his own. The second and third individuals in this society have a revolutionary threshold of 2, meaning that they need two other people to be protesting before they are willing to join in. In this example, the tenth individual has a revolutionary threshold of 10. Given that there are only ten people in this society, this means that the tenth individual will never participate in a protest, because there can never be ten people already protesting without his participation.

The distribution of revolutionary thresholds in a society is crucial for determining whether a revolution occurs or not. Consider the example of society A. In this society, only one person will protest. The individual with a revolutionary threshold of 0 will protest but no one else will. It is unlikely that a one-person protest will be successful. Now consider a slightly different society, A':

$$A' = \{0, 1, 2, 3, 4, 5, 6, 7, 8, 10\}.$$

The only difference between society A and society A' is that the second individual's revolutionary threshold has dropped from 2 to 1. We can think of these two examples as the same society at two different points in time. For example, we can think that the government took some action or introduced some policy that made the second individual more willing to publicly oppose the government. Although this small change in one person's revolutionary

---

7. Several of the examples that follow were provided by Marek Kaminski.

threshold might appear inconsequential, it actually has quite a dramatic effect on the size and likely success of a protest. The reason for this is that the second individual is now willing to join the first individual who is protesting. Now that there are two people protesting, the third individual with a revolutionary threshold of 2 is willing to join in as well. This, in turn, causes the fourth individual to join in. Before you know it, there is a nine-person protest going on. The fact that fully 90 percent of the people in this society are now protesting is likely to mean that this protest is successful. In this example, the slight shift in the revolutionary threshold of one individual has caused what we call a **revolutionary cascade.** This example should make it clear why these types of models are referred to as "tipping," or "threshold," models.

A **revolutionary cascade** is when one person's participation triggers the participation of another, which triggers the participation of another, and so on.

Note that a small shift in the revolutionary threshold like that in the previous example will not always produce a revolution or protest. Consider society *B*:

$$B = \{0, 2, 3, 3, 4, 5, 6, 7, 8, 10\}.$$

The only difference with society *A* is that the third individual now has a revolutionary threshold of 3 instead of 2. Notice, though, what happens when the government takes the same action or introduces the same policy as before, causing the second individual to reduce his threshold from 2 to 1.

$$B' = \{0, 1, 3, 3, 4, 5, 6, 7, 8, 10\}.$$

As you can see, the change of threshold only produces a two-person protest this time. In other words, there is a slight decline in the popularity of the regime but no revolution. Thus, a slightly different distribution of a society's revolutionary thresholds can mean the difference between a small, abortive, and ultimately unsuccessful protest (society *B'*) and a revolutionary cascade (society *A'*) that produces the overthrow of the dictatorship.

This result has implications for those who argue that revolutions and protests are caused by structural factors such as relative deprivation, grievances, or oppression (Gurr 1970). As the tipping model suggests, things like economic recession or the introduction of a repressive policy may cause private preferences and revolutionary thresholds to move against the regime without actually producing a revolution. For example, economic recession may cause the regime in some society *C* to become deeply unpopular (as exhibited by the relatively low revolutionary thresholds).

$$C = \{0, 2, 2, 2, 2, 2, 2, 2, 2, 10\}.$$

The low threshold of virtually every individual in this society indicates that it would not take much for a revolutionary cascade to occur. Despite this, though, the distribution of revolutionary thresholds indicates that the regime will not experience a revolution as things stand. Structural factors such as economic recession are not sufficient in and of themselves to produce revolutions. All we can say is that structural factors can make revolutions more likely by reducing individual thresholds; they do not make revolutions inevitable.

It is important to remember at this point that preference falsification means that a society's distribution of revolutionary thresholds is never known to the individuals of that society. Each individual knows his own revolutionary threshold, but not that of anyone else. This means that a society can come to the brink of revolution without anyone's ever knowing it. In effect, people may be ready to participate in a full-scale revolt as long as one more person goes out to protest. If that one extra person does not protest, however, then no revolution occurs and the dictatorship appears entirely stable. Note that even if people know for sure that preference falsification is occurring (as they surely must), they cannot know if they live in a society like *A* or one like *B*. This implies that it is often impossible for observers to distinguish between very stable and very fragile dictatorships. Moreover, our inability to observe both private preferences and thresholds conceals potential revolutionary cascades and makes it impossible to predict when a revolution will occur. In effect, revolutions will always come as a surprise. This is why we talk about the "predictability of unpredictability" of revolutions (Kuran 1989, 1991). Note, though, that our inability to predict revolutions such as the fall of communism in Eastern Europe in 1989 should not lead one to conclude that revolutions are somehow irrational. As the logic underlying the tipping model that we have just presented indicates, our failure to predict revolutions "is entirely consistent with calculated, purposeful human action" (Kuran 1991, 45).

Preference falsification helps explain why the Communist regimes in Eastern Europe were substantially more vulnerable than their subservient populations had made them seem prior to 1989. During the 1980s, a series of structural changes had the effect of lowering revolutionary thresholds in Eastern Europe to such an extent that they triggered a revolutionary cascade both within countries and between countries. For example, the appointment of Gorbachev to power in the Soviet Union and his introduction of reformist policies such as perestroika and glasnost reduced the perceived risk of challenging the political status quo, thereby reducing people's thresholds. Revolutionary thresholds were also lowered by the increasingly poor economic performance of many East European countries from the mid-1980s on and Gorbachev's statement in 1989 that the Soviet Union would not intervene militarily to help sustain Communist rule in Eastern Europe. Once pro-democracy reforms were successfully introduced in one East European country, they started to have demonstration effects in other countries, further reducing revolutionary thresholds. The end result was a democratic cascade with the diffusion of democracy from one country to another (O'Loughlin et al. 1998; Starr and Lindborg 2003; Brinks and Coppedge 2006). The democratic cascade that occurred in Eastern Europe is best summed up by a protest banner seen at a pro-democracy rally in Prague in 1989 stating simply, "Poland—10 years, Hungary—10 months, East Germany—10 weeks, Czechoslovakia—10 days" (Garton Ash 1999). The message of the banner was that a democratic transition had finally taken place roughly ten years since the rise of Solidarity in Poland, roughly ten months since the introduction of reforms in Hungary, roughly ten weeks since the start of mass protests in East Germany, and roughly ten days since pro-democracy rallies began in Czechoslovakia.

In hindsight, the collapse of communism in Eastern Europe has come to be seen by many as inevitable. Numerous historians, sociologists, and political scientists who interviewed individuals across Eastern Europe reported that there had been a huge pent-up pool of opposition to Communist rule and that this was bound to break out at some time. Almost all of the interviewees reported that they had opposed Communist rule and wanted it to end. These reports certainly make it seem that the collapse of communism was inevitable, but the notion of preference falsification should make us extremely wary of drawing this inference. For example, put yourself in the shoes of a Communist Party supporter. As the revolutionary cascade starts to snowball into an overwhelming majority, it becomes imprudent for you to remain a government supporter. You may even feel obliged to join the pro-democracy protests even though you would have preferred that they fail. We might call this a revolutionary bandwagon to distinguish it from a revolutionary cascade. Just as pro-democracy supporters falsify their preferences under dictatorship to avoid punishment, pro-dictatorship supporters will falsify their preferences under democracy for similar reasons. Supporters of the former Communist regime are likely to lie about their true preferences and indicate that they were long-standing opponents of the toppled government. In effect, the evidence from these people will make it seem as if the former dictatorship was much more unstable and unloved than it actually was. As Kuran (1991, 23) puts it, "Having misled everyone into seeing a revolution as highly unlikely, preference falsification now conceals the forces that were working against it. One of the consequences of post-revolutionary preference falsification is thus to make it even less comprehensible why the revolution was unforeseen." In other words, revolution will often seem inevitable in hindsight even though this is, in fact, far from the case at the time.

TOP-DOWN TRANSITIONS TO DEMOCRACY

Some transitions to democracy do not occur through a bottom-up process as occurred in East Germany. Instead, they result primarily from a policy of liberalization on the part of authoritarian elites themselves. This policy of liberalization is often designed to stabilize a dictatorship but sometimes inadvertently leads to democracy. Periods of liberalization have preceded numerous transitions to democracy throughout history. For example, Generals Ernesto Geisel and João Figueiredo introduced a period of liberalization (*distençao*) and opening (*abertura*) in Brazil between 1982 and 1985 as they tried to strengthen their position in relation to hard-liners like General Sylvio Frota. This period of liberalization ultimately led to an implicit pact between government soft-liners, the regime party, the military, and the opposition to name the opposition leader, Tancredo Neves, as president in 1985.

A similar period of liberalization preceded the democratic transition in Uruguay between 1983 and 1984. In this case, month-long discussions between soft-liners in the authoritarian regime and representatives of the opposition led to the Acuerdo del Club Naval (Naval Club Accord) and the reintroduction of presidential elections in 1984 (Colomer 1991, 1295). Chile, similarly, experienced a period of liberalization before its return to the democratic fold in 1988. Its transition to democracy began in 1980 with the introduction of a new constitution that contained provisions for the transfer of power from the military government of Augusto Pinochet to a civilian government within eight years. Chile's slow democratization process was tightly orchestrated, culminating in a defeat for Pinochet in a plebiscite on his leadership in October 1988 and the reintroduction of presidential elections later that year. As discussed in more detail a little later in this chapter, Poland's transition to democracy in 1989 was another case in which democracy was preceded by a period of liberalization introduced by authoritarian elites.

A Game-Theoretic Model of Top-Down Transitions

We now present a stylized story of top-down transitions.

The Story

Top-down transitions to democracy frequently result from a split between soft-liners and hard-liners in an authoritarian regime. Typically, the dictatorship has come under some sort of pressure, often having to do with declining economic conditions, and soft-liners have come to prominence. Whereas hard-liners tend to be satisfied with the political status quo, soft-liners may prefer to liberalize and broaden the social base of the dictatorship in an attempt to gain allies, strengthen their position in relation to the hard-liners, and manage opposition groups.[8] The soft-liners have a choice to make. Should they open up the political regime through a process of liberalization or should they stick with the status quo?

A **policy of liberalization** entails a controlled opening of the political space and might include the formation of political parties, holding elections, writing a constitution, establishing a judiciary, opening a legislature, and so on. It is important to recognize that the goal of any "opening" for the soft-liners is not to bring about democracy but to incorporate various opposition groups into authoritarian institutions. In effect, the liberalization process is typically an attempt by dictatorial elites to co-opt opposition groups or, at least, to divide and control them (Przeworski 1991; Lucas 2005; Lust-Okar 2005b; Gandhi and Przeworski 2006). The intended goal is not a democracy, but what we might call a "broadened dictatorship." [9] As an example, Lust-Okar (2005b) uses evidence from Egypt, Jordan, and Morocco, to illustrate how authoritarian elites have employed periods of liberalization and institutionalization to divide and control opposition groups. She shows how dictators in these countries have been able to influence the timing of

> A **policy of liberalization** entails a controlled opening of the political space and might include the formation of political parties, holding elections, writing a constitution, establishing a judiciary, opening a legislature, and so on.

---

8. The decision to liberalize is rarely taken in a vacuum. Instead, it often occurs after the authoritarian elites have come under some form of pressure from opposition groups in society. In this sense, it is hard to entirely disentangle bottom-up and top-down processes of democratization. As we noted at the beginning of the chapter, we believe that both processes typically interact with each other in the real world.

9. Different terms have been used by political scientists to capture the concept of a "broadened dictatorship." For example, scholars have sometimes referred to these regimes as "competitive authoritarianism," "electoral authoritarianism," "soft-authoritarianism," "semi-authoritarianism," "pseudo-democracy," "illiberal democracy," "hybrid regimes," and other terms. (Karl 1995; Zakaria 1997; Diamond 2002; Schedler 2002; Levitsky and Way 2002, 2003).

when political opponents unite and divide, as well as when they emerge and dissolve, by creating rules and institutions that allow some groups to participate in the formal political sphere but not others. In taking these steps, the authoritarian elites in these Middle Eastern states have been able to lower the opposition's willingness and ability to challenge them.

It is worth noting that broadened dictatorships characterized by seemingly democratic institutions such as elections and legislatures are increasingly common in the world today (Diamond 2002; Levitsky and Way 2002, 2003). Many people have championed the introduction of these types of institutions in several dictatorships as signs that these states are gradually moving toward democracy. The implication is that the liberalization process will eventually lead to a transition to full democracy. It is this belief that often encourages some scholars to label these regimes as "mixed," "hybrid," "partial democracies," or "partly free," as if they were some halfway house between dictatorship and democracy.[10] Strong, and growing, empirical evidence, however, shows that broadened dictatorships are not necessarily undergoing a prolonged democratic transition (Herbst 2001; Carothers 2002). Indeed, it appears that liberalization and institutionalization can, under some circumstances, significantly enhance the stability of dictatorial rule. This line of research strongly contradicts the common wisdom that institutions in dictatorships have no effect on anything of importance and are merely forms of window dressing.

Several scholars have recently demonstrated how particular institutions might be employed by authoritarian elites to co-opt or control opposition groups to enhance their hold on power. For example, Geddes (2005) argues that elections can be used to signal the overwhelming strength of the dictatorship to potential opposition groups thinking about challenging them. Similarly, Lust-Okar (2005a) suggests that elections can be a force for stability by providing an arena for patronage distribution and a means of recruiting and rewarding the political elite. Milton Obote, a former Ugandan president, trumpets the stabilizing potential of elections when he states that elections were a way for him to control the people rather than a means by which the people could control him (cited in Cohen 1983). Other institutions have also been shown to be useful tools in the hands of dictators. For instance, Gershenson and Grossman (2001) highlight how political parties can help dictatorships mobilize support, penetrate society, and control opposition elements down to the local level. Schwedler (2000) suggests that legislatures can be beneficial by allowing opposition groups to reveal their demands without having to oppose the dictatorship more publicly. She provides evidence for this when she notes that the offer of King Hussein of Jordan to give some influence over educational and religious policies to the Muslim Brotherhood led the Brotherhood to shift its strategy from denouncing the regime on the streets to articulating its demands in the legislature. Brown (2002) argues that written constitutions can make dictatorial rule more stable and effective. Although constitutions in dictatorships

---

10. These broadened dictatorships frequently score somewhere in the middle of the continuum used by the continuous measures of democracy (Freedom House and Polity IV) that we examined in Chapter 5, thereby giving the impression that they are moving toward democracy and away from dictatorship.

rarely place limits on the power of the ruler, as they typically do in democracies, they can serve to delineate the basic structures and chains of command. In effect, by organizing power without limiting it, dictatorial constitutions like the one introduced in Chile in 1980 by Augusto Pinochet help to make authoritarian rule more organized and efficient.

Given these potential benefits, you might wonder why authoritarian elites do not always push for liberalization. The problem is that the soft-liners cannot guarantee that liberalization will successfully produce a broadened dictatorship. As you might expect, the liberalization process is inherently unstable. If the soft-liners do liberalize, then the democratic opposition has two options. On the one hand, it can accept the concessions offered by the authoritarian elites and enter the institutions of a broadened dictatorship. In this case, the democratic opposition essentially agrees to maintain the dictatorial rules of the game in return for entrance into the formal political sphere. The soft-liners would obviously see this as a success. On the other hand, however, the democratic opposition can take advantage of its new freedoms to further organize and mobilize against the dictatorship. In many cases around the world, this is precisely what happened. For example, the Polish Communist Party agreed to allow the formation of the independent trade union Solidarity in September 1980. Within just two weeks, Solidarity had three million members and was rapidly becoming a direct threat to ongoing Communist rule (Garton Ash 1999, 34). It is easy to see that the soft-liners in the authoritarian regime are playing a dangerous game—they could unleash forces that might escape them.

Lech Walesa, head of the striking workers delegation, stands in the Lenin shipyard in Gdansk, Poland, as he addresses striking workers after negotiations on August 26, 1980, led to a preliminary contract between the striking workers and the Polish government.

If the democratic opposition does choose to continue organizing and mobilizing against the regime, then this is evidence that the controlled opening initiated by the soft-liners has failed. As a consequence, the position of the soft-liners in the dictatorship is likely to be undermined. At this point, two choices are available to the authoritarian elites. The first choice is to use force in an attempt to repress popular mobilization and to restore order. If the repression is successful, then the result will be a "narrow dictatorship" in which the soft-liners pay the consequence for having introduced a failed policy of liberalization and are replaced by hard-liners. This particular scenario has played out quite frequently throughout history. For example, the experiment with liberalization attempted by King Hussein of Jordan in the 1950s and by King Hassan II of Morocco in the 1960s failed to appease their opponents, who simply demanded more significant reductions in, and even the elimination of, the monarchs' power. The two kings both responded to ongoing mobilization by imposing martial law, removing the men they had assigned to implement liberalization, and excluding all opposition groups from the formal political system (Lust-Okar 2005b, 49–60). Periods of liberalization in Eastern Europe prior to 1989, such as the 1968 Prague Spring, also ended in repression and the establishment of narrow dictatorships led by hard-liners. Of course, state repression may prove to be unsuccessful, at which point the dictatorship is likely to have an insurgency on its hands. Clearly, authoritarian elites must weigh the likelihood that repression will be successful before deciding to take this route.

Box 8.5

PRAGUE SPRING 1968

By the mid-1960s, the Czechoslovak economy had stalled and moderate Communists were increasingly calling for economic, social, and political reform. In January 1968 the soft-liner Alexander Dubček replaced the hard-liner Antonín Novotný as leader of the Czechoslovak Communist Party. The period from March to August 1968 is known as the Prague Spring and was a period in which Dubček tried to open up the political regime and introduce a policy of liberalization that he called the "Action Program." The goal of these reforms was not the end of the socialist state but what Dubček called "socialism with a human face." Dubček wanted to overcome the disillusionment of the people with the previous two decades of Communist rule and breathe new life into socialism. He attempted to do this by increasing the freedom of the press, reducing censorship, and encouraging more participation in politics.

The introduction of these rather limited reforms encouraged further mobilization by the democratic opposition. Within weeks, the people were demanding still more reforms, and Communist control of the country was soon in doubt. Anti-Soviet statements appeared in the press, the Social Democrats began to form a separate party, and independent political clubs were created. At this point, the Soviet Union and its leader, Leonid Brezhnev, demanded that Dubček stop the reforms. Although Dubček had not originally intended for his policy of liberalization to go this far, he refused. The Soviets and their Warsaw Pact allies responded by invading Czechoslovakia in Operation Danube. The invaders included about 400,000 Soviet troops and 80,000 other troops from Bulgaria, East Germany, Hungary, and Poland. Although Dubček called on the people not to resist, there were numerous acts of nonviolent resistance. For example, one man, Jan Palach, set himself on fire in Prague's Wenceslas Square to protest the renewed suppression of free speech. Dubček was eventually replaced by the hard-liner Gustáv Husák, who introduced a period of "normalization." Husák reversed Dubček's reforms, purged the Communist Party of its soft-liners, and repressed remaining dissidents with the help of the secret police.

In 1987 Gorbachev acknowledged that his liberalizing policies of *glasnost* and *perestroika* owed a great deal to Dubček's vision of "socialism with a human face." When asked what the difference was between the Prague Spring and his own reforms, Gorbachev simply replied, "Nineteen years."

The second choice available to the soft-liners if the democratic opposition continues to mobilize is to accept its demands and allow the emergence of truly democratic institutions. This is essentially what happened in South Korea when pro-democracy rallies through the 1980s finally transformed the regime's soft-liners from liberalizers into democratizers; free elections were allowed in 1987. It is arguably what also happened in the Soviet Union under Gorbachev and, as we will see, it is what happened in Poland in 1989. The argument that we have presented basically suggests that failed "liberalizations are either reversed, leading to grim periods euphemistically termed normalization, or continue to democratization" (Przeworski 1991, 60).

The Model

Under what conditions do authoritarian elites introduce a period of liberalization? When does liberalization succeed in producing an institutionalized and broadened dictatorship? When does it fail? Put differently, when do opposition groups agree to enter authoritarian institutions and when do they choose to continue mobilizing independently of the regime? If liberalization fails, when do authoritarian elites respond with repression and when do they allow a transition to full democracy? Clearly, the choice by the authoritarian elite to stick with the political status quo or to open up the regime depends on how it thinks the democratic opposition will respond to liberalization. Similarly, the choice by the democratic opposition to enter a broadened dictatorship or to continue mobilizing depends on how it thinks the dictatorship will respond to ongoing mobilization. As we have argued in previous chapters, strategic situations like this, in which the decisions of one actor depend on the choices of other actors, are usefully analyzed with the help of game theory. In Figure 8.2, we present one way to model the strategic interaction between authoritarian soft-liners and democratic opposition groups using an extensive form game.[11]

The prehistory, or background, to the Transition Game is that a split has developed in the authoritarian elite between soft-liners and hard-liners. For some reason, the soft-liners have come to prominence and are in a position to open up the political space through a policy of liberalization if they so choose. The game illustrated in Figure 8.2 now begins. The soft-liners move first and must decide whether to do nothing or open up the regime. If the soft-liners do nothing, we are left with the political status quo (Outcome 1). If they decide to open up, then the democratic opposition groups must choose whether to enter the authoritarian institutions or to continue organizing. If they enter, the result is a broadened dictatorship (Outcome 2). If they organize, then the soft-liners must decide whether to repress or democratize. If they repress, there are two possible outcomes. If the repression is successful, there will be a narrow dictatorship in which the hard-liners return to prominence (Outcome 3). If the repression is unsuccessful, there will be an insurgency (Outcome 4). Whether state repression is successful

---

11. Our Transition Game is based on an outline of a similar game provided by Przeworski (1991).

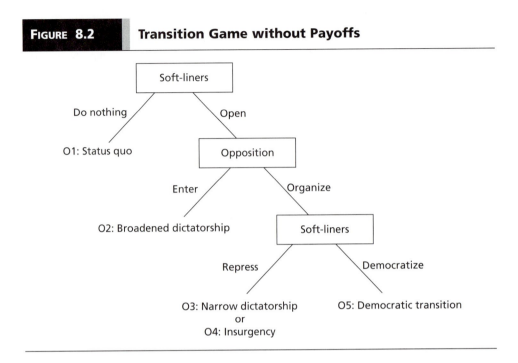

FIGURE 8.2 | **Transition Game without Payoffs**

or not is likely to depend, among other things, on the strength of the opposition groups. In what follows, we assume that state repression is successful and leads to a narrow dictatorship if the democratic opposition is weak but is unsuccessful and produces an insurgency if the democratic opposition is strong. Finally, if the soft-liners choose to democratize, the result is a democratic transition (Outcome 5).

Before we can determine what the players are likely to do in the Transition Game, we need to know how the players value the possible outcomes. Based on the argument that we have presented, we can provide a preference ordering for each player over the five possible outcomes; that is, we can determine how both players would rank the outcomes. The preference ordering for the soft-liners over the five outcomes is:

$$\text{Broadened dictatorship} \succ \text{Status quo} \succ \text{Narrow dictatorship} \succ$$
$$\text{Democratic transition} \succ \text{Insurgency,}$$

where "$\succ$" means "is strictly preferred to." As this preference ordering illustrates, the ideal outcome for the soft-liners is a broadened dictatorship in which opposition groups are co-opted and their position in the dictatorship is strengthened relative to that of the hard-liners. If they cannot obtain this outcome, then they would prefer the political status quo—the dictatorship is maintained and they are still in a position of power. If this outcome cannot be achieved, then they would prefer maintaining the dictatorship by handing power to the hard-liners in the form of a narrow dictatorship rather than having a democratic transition or an insurgency. If the dictatorship cannot be maintained in any form, we have assumed that the soft-liners would prefer a democratic transition to a potentially costly insurgency. We feel comfortable in making this assumption because it turns out that the results of the Transition Game do not depend on whether the soft-liners prefer a democratic transition or an insurgency.

The preference ordering for the democratic opposition groups is:

Democratic transition $\succ$ Broadened dictatorship $\succ$ Status quo $\succ$ Insurgency $\succ$ Narrow dictatorship.

The ideal outcome for the opposition is a full transition to democracy. If this outcome is not possible, however, then it prefers a broadened dictatorship in which it, at least, gets to enjoy some concessions from the soft-liners. The political status quo is better than both an insurgency in which many people are likely to die and a narrow dictatorship in which the democratic opposition is repressed by hard-liners. We have assumed that the opposition will prefer an insurgency to a narrow dictatorship. Again, we are comfortable making this assumption because the results of the game do not depend on whether the opposition prefers an insurgency or a narrow dictatorship.

Given that there are five possible outcomes, we can assign the number 5 to each player's most preferred outcome, 4 to their second preferred outcome, 3 to their third preferred outcome, and so on. The players' payoffs are illustrated in Table 8.2. Recall from the discussion in Chapter 4 that these "ordinal payoffs" tell us about the order in which the players rank each of the outcomes but do not tell us how much more each player prefers one outcome to another.

We can now add these payoffs into the game tree shown earlier. To distinguish between the situation in which the soft-liners face a strong democratic opposition and the one in which they face a weak democratic opposition, we present two separate game trees in Figure 8.3. The only difference between the game trees is that repression produces a narrow dictatorship when the democratic opposition is weak but an insurgency if the democratic opposition is strong. As in previous game-theoretic models that we have presented, the soft-liners' payoffs are shown first because they are the first mover in the game; the opposition's payoffs are shown second. A semicolon separates the payoffs for each player. Just as an illustration, this means that the soft-liners receive a payoff of 4 and the democratic opposition

Table 8.2	Turning Outcomes into Payoffs in the Transition Game		
Outcome	Description	Soft-liners	Opposition
O1	Status quo	4	3
O2	Broadened dictatorship	5	4
O3	Narrow dictatorship	3	1
O4	Insurgency	1	2
O5	Democratic transition	2	5

FIGURE 8.3 Transition Game with Payoffs

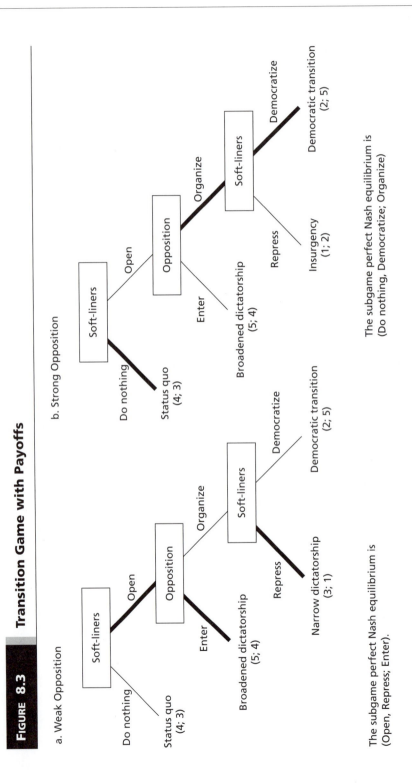

a. Weak Opposition

Soft-liners
- Do nothing → Status quo (4; 3)
- Open → Opposition
  - Enter → Broadened dictatorship (5; 4)
  - Organize → Soft-liners
    - Democratize → Democratic transition (2; 5)
    - Repress → Narrow dictatorship (3; 1)

The subgame perfect Nash equilibrium is (Open, Repress; Enter).

b. Strong Opposition

Soft-liners
- Do nothing → Status quo (4; 3)
- Open → Opposition
  - Enter → Broadened dictatorship (5; 4)
  - Organize → Soft-liners
    - Repress → Insurgency (1; 2)
    - Democratize → Democratic transition (2; 5)

The subgame perfect Nash equilibrium is (Do nothing, Democratize; Organize) receives a payoff of 3 if the outcome is the political status quo. Now that we have the payoffs, we can try to figure out what the players will do.

Let's start by looking at the situation in which the soft-liners are faced with a weak democratic opposition (Figure 8.3a). As usual, we solve the game for subgame perfect Nash equilibria using backward induction.[12] Recall that backward induction requires starting at the end of the game tree (at the terminal node) and working one's way back to the beginning of the game tree (initial node). The terminal node has the soft-liners' deciding whether to repress or democratize. The soft-liners get a payoff of 3 if they repress and a payoff of 2 if they democratize. As a result, the soft-liners will choose to repress. We indicate this choice by making the repress branch at this terminal node bold in Figure 8.3a. Now we move backward to the choice node prior to the terminal node. At this choice node, the democratic opposition must decide whether to enter a broadened dictatorship or continue to organize. If the democratic opposition enters, it will get a payoff of 4. If it organizes, it can look down the game tree (follow the bold lines) and see that the soft-liners will repress and that its payoff will be 1. As a result, the democratic opposition will choose to enter. We indicate this choice by making the enter branch at this choice node bold. We now move back to the choice node prior to this one, which happens to be the initial node in the Transition Game. At this node the soft-liners must decide whether to do nothing and stick with the status quo or to open up the political regime. If the soft-liners do nothing, they will get a payoff of 4. If they open up, they can look down the game tree (follow the bold lines) and see that the democratic opposition will enter and that their payoff will be 5. It is easy to see that the soft-liners will choose to liberalize and open up in these circumstances.

We have now solved the Transition Game when the democratic opposition is weak using backward induction. So, what is the subgame perfect Nash equilibrium? Recall that the SPNE lists the actions chosen by each player at all of the choice nodes in the game. Thus, the SPNE for this particular game is (Open, Repress; Enter). As before, we first list the choices made by the soft-liners (the first player) at each of the nodes at which they get to make a choice, and then we list the choices made by the democratic opposition (the second player) at each of the nodes at which it gets to make a choice. As a result, the SPNE indicates that the soft-liners choose to open up and would choose to repress at the terminal node if the game arrived at this node; the democratic opposition chooses to enter at its one and only choice node. The expected outcome of the game—what we actually observe when the soft-liners and the democratic opposition play the game—is a broadened dictatorship. The payoffs associated with a broadened dictatorship are 5 for the soft-liners and 4 for civil society.

Now let's examine the situation in which the soft-liners are faced with a strong democratic opposition (Figure 8.3b). The terminal node again has the soft-liners deciding whether to repress or democratize. This time, however, the soft-liners get a payoff of 1 if they repress

---

12. For a review of backward induction and subgame perfect Nash equilibria, return to our initial, and more detailed, discussion of these concepts in Chapter 3.

and a payoff of 2 if they democratize. As a result, the soft-liners will choose to democratize. We indicate this choice by making the repress branch at this terminal node bold in Figure 8.3b. At the choice node prior to this, the democratic opposition must decide whether to enter a broadened dictatorship or continue to organize. If the democratic opposition enters, it will get a payoff of 4. If it organizes, it can look down the game tree and see that the soft-liners will democratize and that its payoff will be 5. As a result, the democratic opposition will choose to continue organizing. We indicate this choice by making the organize branch at this choice node bold. At the first choice node, the soft-liners must decide whether to do nothing or open up the political regime. If the soft-liners do nothing, they will get a payoff of 4. If they open up, they can look down the game tree and see that the democratic opposition will organize. Given that the opposition organizes, the soft-liners will choose to democratize and their payoff will be 2. It is easy to see, then, that the soft-liners will choose to do nothing at the first choice node. We have now solved the Transition Game when the democratic opposition is strong using backward induction. The subgame perfect Nash equilibrium is (Do nothing, Democratize; Organize). The expected outcome of the game is the political status quo; the payoffs are 4 to the soft-liners and 3 to civil society.

What can be learned from the Transition Game? The most important insight is that a transition to democracy is *not* possible as things stand. The only two possible outcomes are a broadened dictatorship or the political status quo. It is worth reexamining why these were the only two outcomes. When the democratic opposition is weak, the soft-liners can obtain their most preferred outcome—a broadened dictatorship. Why? A weak opposition chooses to accept the concessions of the soft-liners and enter the authoritarian institutions because this is better than the status quo and because it knows that it is not strong enough to prevent the soft-liners from successfully repressing it if it chooses to continue organizing and mobilizing against the regime. Knowing that a weak opposition will prefer to enter a broadened dictatorship rather than organize, the soft-liners are willing to liberalize and the outcome is a broadened dictatorship.[13] When the democratic opposition is strong, though, the political status quo will prevail. Why? A strong opposition knows that if it organizes, then it is strong enough that the soft-liners will be unable to successfully repress it and they will, therefore, prefer to democratize at this point. The soft-liners in turn know that a strong opposition will respond to liberalization by organizing and that, as a result, they will eventually be forced to democratize. To avoid being forced into a democratization that they do not want, the soft-liners simply do nothing and stick with the political status quo.

But we know that top-down transitions to democracy do occur. So what is going on? Is there something wrong with the Transition Game? All of the game-theoretic models that we have examined in this book up to this point are what we call complete information games.

---

13. If we think of the democratic opposition's strength as being determined by how unified or divided it is, then this result is consistent with one of the insights in Lust-Okar's (2005b) study of authoritarian rule in Morocco, Egypt, and Jordan. She finds that political liberalization is more likely to be successful and stable in situations in which the opposition is divided (weak) rather than in those in which it is unified (strong).

A **complete information game** is essentially one in which each player knows all the information that there is to know about the game—the identity and type of the players, the choices

available to each player, the order of the choices, the possible outcomes, and the preferences of the players over the outcomes. The Transition Game shown in Figure 8.3 is also a complete information game. What we have shown to this point is that top-down transitions to democracy are not possible in situations in which the players know everything, or have complete information.

One of the key assumptions underlying our analysis is that the soft-liners know what type of opposition they are dealing with—they know whether they are dealing with a strong democratic opposition or a weak democratic opposition. In effect, we have assumed that the soft-liners know whether they are playing the game outlined in Figure 8.3a or the one shown in Figure 8.3b. What if this is not the case, though? What if we change our game into one of incomplete information, where the soft-liners are uncertain as to the type of opposition—weak or strong—that they are dealing with?[14] Given our earlier discussion of preference falsification, it seems almost certain that authoritarian soft-liners will not always have complete information and that they will often be uncertain or misinformed about the true strength of the democratic opposition. Although citizens are likely to support the regime in public, they may well oppose it quite vehemently in private. Opposition groups are likely to take great care to keep their activities hidden from the prying eyes of the dictatorship and its secret police. Despite their best efforts, it is almost impossible for dictatorships to successfully shut down all forms of autonomous organizations that escape their control; there will nearly always be underground resistance networks of some sort.

It turns out that top-down transitions to democracy can occur if authoritarian soft-liners are uncertain about the type of opposition (weak or strong) that they are facing. Suppose that the soft-liners think that the democratic opposition is weak, that is, that they are playing the Transition Game in Figure 8.3a. As we demonstrated earlier, the soft-liners will choose to liberalize and open up the political regime because they expect the opposition to enter into a broadened dictatorship. But what happens if the soft-liners are mistaken in their beliefs about the strength of the democratic opposition? What happens if the opposition is actually strong and the soft-liners are really playing the Transition Game in Figure 8.3b? If this is the case, then we have already seen that the strong democratic opposition will choose to continue organizing when the soft-liners open up. As soon as the soft-liners see the opposition organizing, they will immediately realize that they have made a dreadful mistake because they will know that only a strong opposition would take such an action; a weak opposition would enter

---

14. What follows is an informal discussion of the consequences of adding this type of incomplete information to our Transition Game. The interested and motivated student might wish to examine Box 8.6 "Transition Game with Incomplete Information" at the end of this chapter in which we present a slightly more formal elaboration of our argument.

a broadened dictatorship. Now that they know for sure that they are facing a strong democratic opposition, the soft-liners will realize that repression will be unsuccessful and that their best option is to democratize further. The end result is a top-down transition to democracy.

The central point to take away from this is that democratic transitions from above are not possible under complete information, that is, in situations in which everyone knows everything. They can occur only when there is some uncertainty or incomplete information. In effect, these types of transition occur only because someone makes a mistake. In regard to our particular version of the Transition Game, the mistake is that the soft-liners think they are dealing with a weak democratic opposition when, in fact, they are facing a strong one.

Our Transition Game has two further implications. The first has to do with when we are likely to see institutionalized dictatorships—those with legislatures, political parties, elections, and so on. If we conceive of a broadened dictatorship as an institutionalized one, then the results from our Transition Game indicate that dictatorial institutionalization is likely to occur only when the authoritarian soft-liners believe that the democratic opposition is weak; if the soft-liners think that the opposition is sufficiently strong, then they will choose not to open up or institutionalize. Although our Transition Game has something to say about the conditions under which we expect to see institutionalized dictatorships, it does not provide any firm predictions as to whether liberalization and institutionalization actually help the stability and survival of dictatorships. Dictators may well establish seemingly democratic institutions in the hope that they will improve their chances of staying in power. Our Transition Game illustrates that the effectiveness of the liberalization process in achieving this objective will depend heavily on whether the beliefs of the authoritarian elites about the strength or weakness of the democratic opposition are correct. If a dictatorship establishes institutions such as elections and legislatures under the mistaken belief that the democratic opposition is weak, then these institutions may, in fact, accelerate the dictatorship's collapse.

The second implication is that it is possible to have authoritarian soft-liners who would like to open up the political system by introducing liberalizing reforms but who choose nevertheless to do nothing because they know that they cannot control the liberalization process if they start it. This suggests that some people living in dictatorships are actually living under more repressive conditions than need be the case. If the democratic opposition could somehow commit to not taking advantage of the liberalization process by organizing and pushing for full democracy, then soft-liners might be willing to introduce some liberalizing reforms. The result would not be full democracy, but it may be a more palatable and less repressive form of broadened dictatorship.

Applying the Transition Game to Poland

We now illustrate the usefulness of our Transition Game for understanding top-down transitions by applying it to help explain the democratic transition that occurred in Poland in 1989. In the late 1970s, the Polish economy was in a state of crisis. The Communist government had borrowed money from the West that it then used to subsidize prices on things like food in an attempt to keep its citizens satisfied. From 1975 to 1981, Poland's foreign debt increased from $700 million to $23 billion (Hitchcock 2004). When the repayment of this huge debt began to come due, the leader of Poland's Communist Party, Edward Gierek, was forced to raise prices. This led to strikes that started in the Gdansk shipyards. The strikers presented twenty-one demands to the government. These demands included things like freedom of expression, a right to strike, access to the media, and better housing, but the most important one was for a trade union independent of Communist Party control. Unsure of whether the Polish army would actually fire on its own people, Gierek backed down and the independent trade union, Solidarity, was formed in September 1980. Within two weeks of its formation, three million Poles had joined Solidarity under the leadership of an electrician by the name of Lech Walesa. By 1981, Solidarity had ten million members and had come out in direct opposition to the Communist regime. At this point, Solidarity had become much more than just a trade union.

The Soviets were becoming increasingly worried about the situation in Poland and there were rumors that they were drawing up invasion plans involving tanks and infantrymen from Czechoslovakia, East Germany, and the Soviet Union. By now, Gierek had been replaced by the hard-liner General Wojciech Jaruzelski. In December 1981, Jaruzelski declared martial law. Overnight, thousands were arrested, the army occupied factories and smashed strikes, Solidarity was banned, and a military dictatorship was established under the name of the Military Council of National Salvation. Although Jaruzelski has always implied that he imposed martial law in order to prevent a Soviet invasion (he constantly spoke of the "lesser evil" when referring to martial law), most opposition groups at the time claimed that martial law was a desperate attempt by the Communist regime to retain power and put a stop to the newly born civil society that was developing. Recently released documents from the Soviet Union suggest that the Soviets had no intention of invading Poland and that, in fact, they had rejected Jaruzelski's request for military help in 1981 (Mazower 2000, 370). Martial law remained in place until 1983. This particular episode in Polish history illustrates just how a period of liberalization could get out of control and eventually produce a repressive backlash resulting in the coming to power of hard-liners like Jaruzelski.

Despite attempts to solve the economic problems that plagued Poland, the economy did not significantly improve over the next few years. As a new wave of strikes threatened to get out of control and turn violent in mid-1988, the Polish Communist Party (PUWP) attempted to introduce a new period of liberalization called the "big thaw." [15] In December 1988 the government agreed to convene a conference with the banned trade union Solidarity to see if they could hammer out a compromise. These talks, which took place between February and April 1989, became known as the Roundtable Talks. At these talks, it was agreed, among other things, that Solidarity would be legalized and that nationwide legislative elections would occur in June. The goal of this liberalization process was to defuse social

---

15. There had been a "little thaw" in 1986, when the Communists introduced an amnesty for some political prisoners and adopted certain initiatives from some opposition groups (not Solidarity).

unrest, co-opt the democratic opposition into authoritarian institutions without major changes in the political power structure, and get Solidarity to lend its moral authority to the electoral process. As Jaruzelski put it, "the game is about absorbing the opposition into our system" (Perzkowski 1994, 262).

Like most elections in dictatorships, the proposed legislative elections in Poland were not entirely open. All 100 seats in the Polish Senate were to be freely contested, but 65 percent of the seats in the lower house, or Sejm, were reserved for the Communists and their allies. With 65 percent of the seats in the Sejm, the Communists could expect to appoint the prime minister; they were already guaranteed the presidency because there were to be no presidential elections. The Polish Communist Party expected to do quite well in the legislative elections and did not believe that Solidarity was strong enough to realistically challenge its hold on power. Just after introducing martial law in 1981, General Jaruzelski had established a special Center for Public Opinion Research (CBOS; Kaminski 1999). CBOS was designed to provide information about the level of support enjoyed by the regime among the public and to reduce incentives for bureaucrats and administrators to paint an overly rosy picture of regime stability. Opinion polls since the mid-1980s had consistently shown that the Communist Party enjoyed more confidence than Solidarity. In fact, the support for Communist leaders like Jaruzelski was almost on a par with religious figures like the pope and considerably higher than that for the leader of Solidarity, Lech Walesa. In order to prevent Solidarity from having time to strengthen its position, the Communists set the election date for June 4, 1989, just two months after the last day of the Roundtable Talks.

Given the beliefs that the Communist Party had about the strength of Solidarity, the election results came as a complete surprise. Solidarity won all 35 percent of the Sejm seats that it was allowed to contest and 99 of the 100 seats in the Senate. Up until the time that the election results were announced, the process surrounding the Roundtable Talks had been understood as one designed to bring about a "big thaw" and not the end of Communist rule. The election results of June 4, 1989, and the overwhelming victory for Solidarity changed this understanding dramatically. That night, a popular Polish actress Joanna Szczepkowsa announced on official television: "Friends, this is the end of communism in our country!" What happened next, though, also came as a surprise. The 65 percent of the guaranteed seats had "symbolically" been divided between the Communist Party (37.6 percent) and the so-called "deaf and speechless" puppet parties that were allied to it (26.9 percent). After the election, two of these previously loyal parties joined forces with Solidarity to give it more than 50 percent of the Sejm seats. With this legislative majority, Solidarity was able to appoint the first non-Communist prime minister in Eastern Europe in forty years. In contrast to 1981, the Soviets now made it abundantly clear that they would not intervene in Polish affairs, which meant that the Communists could not feasibly break the agreement they had reached with Solidarity and reverse the liberalization process. As we saw earlier in the chapter, the events in Poland had the effect of encouraging the democratic opposition in other East European countries to challenge their own Communist rulers. Within months, Communist control in Eastern Europe had essentially come to an end.

As our Transition Game predicted, one of the key elements in Poland's democratic transition was the Communist Party's incorrect beliefs about the strength of Solidarity. The opinion surveys conducted by CBOS turned out to be poor indicators of the political support enjoyed by Solidarity. Although they were carefully conducted, they were deeply flawed in many ways. For example, roughly 30 percent of respondents refused to complete the surveys. To a large extent, this high refusal rate was the result of Solidarity supporters not wanting to interact with Communist institutions. As we saw earlier, many of those who opposed Communist rule but who actually agreed to complete the surveys would have falsified their preferences out of fear anyway. The effect of this "fear factor was . . . confirmed when the number of declared memberships in 1981 *Solidarity* was compared with the expected membership calculated on the basis of available statistics" (Kaminski 1999, 97). Much of the Solidarity organization remained underground, out of sight of the Communist Party. The considerable strength of this underground Solidarity network is described by a former colleague, Marek Kaminski, who also spent time in a Polish jail as a political prisoner:

> In 1985, I was running an underground publishing house, STOP, that employed about twenty full-time workers and up to 100 moonlighters. Between 1982 and 1989, we published about thirty-five titles of more than 100,000 books combined. We were a part of a decentralized network that included about 100 underground publishing houses, hundreds of periodicals, thousands of trade union organizations with a hierarchically organized leadership structure, a few Nobel prize winners, and even underground theaters, galleries, and video rentals. We called it an "independent society." (2004, 2)

It is worth noting that Kaminski was a twenty-two-year-old student at Warsaw University in 1985—probably not much older than most of the students reading this book. It is easy to see from what Kaminski writes why the Polish Communist Party might have seriously overestimated its own strength relative to that of Solidarity. Mistaken beliefs were crucial to the Polish transition to democracy in 1989, and they are, in fact, central to top-down transitions to democracy more generally.

CONCLUSION

Democratic transitions tend to result from bottom-up processes, in which the people rise up to overthrow an authoritarian regime in a popular revolution, or from top-down processes, in which dictatorial elites introduce liberalizing reforms that inadvertently lead to democracy. In this chapter, we have examined bottom-up and top-down democratic transitions drawing on historical evidence from Eastern Europe.

Collective action theory throws light on why bottom-up democratic transitions like those that took place in East Germany, Czechoslovakia, and Romania in 1989 are so rare and why authoritarian regimes frequently appear stable. Because democracy is a form of public good, attempts at collective action to bring it about suffer from a free-rider problem. This means that individuals have strong incentives not to participate in mass protests or demonstrations calling for democratic reforms and instead free ride on the actions of others. The end result is that public displays of opposition are extremely rare in dictatorships. A consequence of this is that authoritarian elites usually seem, at least on the surface, to have a strong hold on power.

Because there can be significant dangers associated with publicly opposing dictatorships, individuals who dislike authoritarian regimes tend not to reveal their true preferences—instead of opposing the dictatorship in public, they support it. The prevalence of this type of preference falsification helps to explain the puzzle of why popular revolutions nearly always come as a surprise yet appear so inevitable in hindsight. Revolutions come as a surprise because nobody can be exactly sure about the true level of opposition in a dictatorship—societies can come to the brink of revolution without anyone's realizing it. Revolutions frequently appear inevitable in hindsight because few people will openly claim to have supported the old dictatorial regime, even if they did, once it has been overthrown and replaced by a democracy; the danger now comes from publicly opposing the democracy. The tipping models that we examined in this chapter provide further insight into why revolutions are so unpredictable and why even small changes in people's preferences can sometimes rapidly transform previously subservient individuals into revolutionary protesters. Because each society has a different distribution of revolutionary thresholds, policies or actions that lead to a revolutionary cascade in one dictatorship may have little, or at least appear to have little, effect in some other dictatorship.

Our analysis of top-down democratic transitions like the one that occurred in Poland in 1989 suggests that they can happen only when someone makes a mistake. Although authoritarian elites sometimes introduce periods of liberalization, the goal of liberalization policies is typically to strengthen and stabilize the dictatorship rather than produce a democratic transition. In effect, the objective of the dictatorship is to broaden its social base in an attempt to maintain its hold on power. According to the Transition Game that we presented in this chapter, top-down transitions will not occur if the relevant actors—the authoritarian elite and democratic opposition groups—know everything there is to know about each other. They *can* occur, however, if incomplete information leads actors to have mistaken beliefs about the types of actors with whom they are interacting. For example, a democratic transition can occur in our Transition Game if the authoritarian elite mistakenly believes that the opposition is weak when, in fact, it is strong. Our game-theoretic analysis highlights the important role that information, beliefs, and uncertainty can play in democratic transitions—and politics more generally.

The last three chapters have examined the economic and cultural determinants of democracy as well as the dynamics of regime transition. An implicit assumption throughout has been that democracy is good and something that should be promoted. In the next chapter, we ask if it really matters whether someone lives in a democracy or a dictatorship. Specifically, we focus on whether democracy makes a material difference in people's lives.

KEY CONCEPTS

bottom-up democratic transition, *257*
collective action, *266*
collective action, or free-rider, problem, *267*
complete information game, *287*
expected payoff, *309*
glasnost, *260*
incomplete information game, *307*
information set, *307*
non-excludability, *267*

nonrivalry, *267*
perestroika, *260*
policy of liberalization, *277*
preference falsification, *272*
public good, *267*
revolutionary cascade, *274*
revolutionary threshold, *272*
third wave of democratization, *256*
top-down democratic transition, *257*

PROBLEMS

We start with two problems addressing issues to do with collective action and democratic consolidation. We then we go on to provide material to help prepare you for dealing with incomplete information games. You will find this material extremely helpful for answering problems 3 and 4.

Problems 1 and 2

1. Collective Action Problem

   a. Give three examples—not already provided in the chapter—of public goods.
   b. Suppose that you are a leader of an interest group trying to get the government to change one of its policies by holding a street protest. According to collective action theory, would you prefer to live in a world where you need 30 percent of your members to march in the streets in order to be successful or a world in which you need 60 percent of your members to march in the streets to be successful? Explain your answer.
   c. Suppose that there are two interest groups, A and B, trying to get the government to change its policies by holding street protests. Group A has 5,000 members and group B has 10,000 members. Assume that each group's protest will be successful if it gets 20 percent of their members marching in the streets. According to collective action theory, which interest group is most likely to get the government to change its policies? Explain your answer.

2. Democratic Consolidation Game

Political scientists sometimes distinguish between democratic transitions and democratic consolidation (Svolik 2007). "Transition and consolidation are conceptually distinct aspects of [democratic development], although in practice they may temporally overlap or sometimes even coincide. Transition begins with the breakdown of the former [dictatorial] regime and ends with the establishment of a relatively stable configuration of political institutions within a democratic regime. Consolidation . . . refers to the achievement of substantial attitudinal support for and behavioral compliance with the new democratic institutions and the rules of the game which they establish. . . . [T]ransition results in the creation of a new regime; consolidation results in the stability and persistence of that regime, even in the face of severe challenges" (Gunther, Puhle, and Diamandouros 1995, 3).

One of the stated goals behind the U.S. invasion of Iraq and the overthrow of Saddam Hussein in 2003 was to help establish a consolidated democracy in the Middle East. Although Iraq has undergone a transition that has seen the emergence of numerous political parties, elections, a new legislature, a new constitution, and so on, it is unclear that the end result will be a stable, consolidated democracy. As with other democratic transitions that have occurred around the world, much depends on the types of agreement that are possible between the supporters of the former authoritarian regime (primarily Sunnis) and the supporters of the new regime (primarily Shiites).

One way to think about this is whether or not the two sides are willing to take moderate approaches toward each other or not. The supporters of the new regime can take a moderate approach and offer amnesty and concessions to Saddam Hussein's former supporters (Sunnis) OR they can take a radical approach and refuse amnesty and any concessions. The authoritarian supporters (Sunnis) can take a moderate approach and agree to support the new regime OR they can take a radical approach that involves taking up arms and fighting. If the Sunnis decide to fight back, there will be a civil war no matter whether the Shiites offer an amnesty or not. If the Sunnis agree to support the new regime and the Shiites offer no amnesty or concessions, then there will be a full democracy. If the Sunnis agree to democratic reforms and the Shiites offer an amnesty, however, there will be a limited democracy—democracy will be limited because the Shiites had to make concessions to the Sunnis that probably include retaining some legacy of the Saddam Hussein dictatorship. This strategic situation is shown in the normal form Democratic Consolidation Game shown in Figure 8.4.

FIGURE 8.4   **Democratic Consolidation Game**

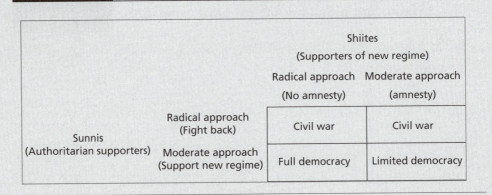

| | | Shiites (Supporters of new regime) | |
		Radical approach (No amnesty)	Moderate approach (amnesty)
Sunnis (Authoritarian supporters)	Radical approach (Fight back)	Civil war	Civil war
	Moderate approach (Support new regime)	Full democracy	Limited democracy

Let's suppose that the Sunnis have the following preference ordering:

Limited democracy ≻ Civil war (amnesty) ≻ Civil war (no amnesty) ≻ Full democracy.

and that the Shiites have the following preference ordering:

Full democracy ≻ Limited democracy ≻ Civil war (no amnesty) ≻ Civil war (amnesty).

a. Use the preference orderings shown above to fill in the matrix shown in Figure 8.4 with the payoffs for each player. Use the numbers 4, 3, 2, 1 to indicate the preference ordering for the players. What is the Nash equilibrium? What is the expected outcome? What are the payoffs that each player receives?

b. Is there another outcome that both the Sunnis and Shiites would prefer to the expected outcome? If so, what is it? Why isn't this outcome a Nash equilibrium?

Now let's suppose that the Shiites have a preference ordering slightly different from the one listed above. Specifically, let's assume that the Shiites have the following preference ordering, where "~" means "is indifferent between":

Full democracy ~ Limited democracy ≻ Civil war (no amnesty) ≻ Civil war (amnesty).

As you can see, the only difference is that the Shiites are now indifferent between having a full democracy and a limited democracy; before, they had strictly preferred a full democracy to a limited democracy.

c. Use the new preference ordering for the Shiites and the same preference ordering as before for the Sunnis to fill in the matrix shown in Figure 8.4 with the payoffs for each player. (Note that if any of the players are indifferent between two outcomes, then they receive the same payoff from both outcomes.) List any Nash equilibrium. List any expected outcomes. List the payoffs that each player receives from each expected outcome.

d. Is some form of consolidated democracy—limited or full—a possible equilibrium in this modified version of the Democratic Consolidation Game?

e. In May 2003 the U.S. administrator of Iraq, L. Paul Bremer, issued two orders. One order outlawed Saddam Hussein's Sunni-dominated Baath Party and dismissed all its senior members from their government posts. This order led to the firing of about 30,000 ex-Baathists from various government ministries. The second order dissolved Iraq's 500,000-member military and intelligence services. All military officers above the rank of colonel were barred from returning to work, as were all 100,000 members of the various Iraqi intelligence agencies. In November 2003 Bremer established a Supreme National Debaathification Commission to root out senior Baathists—primarily Sunnis—from Iraq's ministries. Imagine that you were an adviser to Bremer during this period and that your goal was to establish a consolidated democracy. Based on what you have learned from the two versions of the Democratic Consolidation Game that we examined, would you have advised Bremer to issue these two orders or not? Explain your answer.

f. Nouri al-Maliki became the first prime minister appointed under the provisions of Iraq's new constitution. If you were one of Maliki's advisers, would you tell him to offer an amnesty to Sunnis involved in terrorist activities? Explain your answer. Would it matter in your mind if the Sunnis were killing only fellow Iraqis or if they were killing coalition forces as well? If so, why?

g. One problem with promises of amnesty has to do with their credibility. Can you think of how credible commitment problems might affect the efficacy of amnesty promises? How might actors try to overcome these credible commitment problems?

h. Between 1936 and 1975, Spain was a dictatorship under the rule of General Franco. Spain finally underwent a transition to democracy in 1976 following a series of negotiations between elites who wanted to continue the dictatorship (Francoists) and elites who wanted to introduce democratic reforms (Reformists). In 1976 King Juan Carlos appointed a Reformist, Adolfo Suárez, as president. Upon coming to power Suárez presented a bill for political reform. Although a Reformist, Suárez's bill promised the Francoists the continuation of the monarchy in the person of King Juan Carlos, the maintenance of the unity of Spain, and the exclusion of the Communists. It also promised them an electoral system that rewarded representation in rural areas and a Senate in which a certain number of senators would be designated by the king (Colomer 1991). In effect, the newly democratic Spain was characterized by an institutional legacy from the dictatorial period under Franco. Based on what you have learned from the Democratic Consolidation Game, can you provide a potential reason why countries like Spain that are successfully able to consolidate democracy after a transition often have institutional legacies from the dictatorial period?

Preparation for Problems Dealing with Incomplete Information Games

Important: Before you attempt to solve the more advanced problems involving incomplete information games that follow this section, we strongly recommend that you first read Box 8.6 "Transition Game with Incomplete Information" at the end of this chapter (pp. 307–310). You should then read the following section, in which we provide a step-by-step overview of how to deal with incomplete information games.[16]

As we note in Box 8.6 "Transition Game with Incomplete Information," an incomplete information game is one in which a player does not know all of the relevant information about some other player's characteristics or type. For example, the soft-liners are unsure whether the democratic opposition is weak or strong in our incomplete information Transition Game. As a result, it becomes difficult for the soft-liners to know what to do at those nodes in the game tree where they have to make a choice. This is the essential problem facing actors in games of incomplete information.

As we can see with the incomplete information Transition Game in Figure 8.9 the key to dealing with incomplete information in game theory involves combining multiple games. In effect, we have to write alternative games to capture all of the possible ways that the world might look. This means that if some player has two possible types, say weak and strong, as in our Transition Game, then we

---

16. Our overview of incomplete information games draws on Powner and Bennett (2006, 87–89).

have to write two games, one in which the player is weak and one in which the player is strong. We then figure out what the players will do in each of the two games and find some way to combine the answers. Ultimately, we are going to engage in the following sort of reasoning: "If the world is like this, then I would choose to do X and the following thing would happen. But if the world is like that, then I would choose to do Y and the following would happen. I believe that the world is *probably* like *this,* and so I will do (X or Y)" (Powner and Bennett 2006, 87; italics in original).

The basic steps for writing and analyzing incomplete information games are:

1. Write out separate games for the different possible ways the world works.
2. Solve the separate games.
3. Put the games together with an information set that shows the uncertainty about the two games.
4. Compare the expected payoffs of the uncertain actor's choices in the combined game.

We will now walk you through an example of an incomplete information game by returning to the Terrorism Game that you first saw in the problems at the end of Chapter 3.

Example: Terrorism Game Revisited

If you recall, our Terrorism Game in Chapter 3 examines the interaction between a group of Reluctant Terrorists and a Government. Reluctant Terrorists are people who would prefer to solve problems through negotiation but who will engage in terrorist acts if they are repressed by the government. Let's assume that the government with which the Reluctant Terrorists interact comes in one of two types: "Responsive" or "Repressive." A Responsive Government is willing to listen to the demands of opposition groups and enter good faith negotiations with them. In contrast, a Repressive Government wishes to repress all social groups that oppose them.

The strategic situation that we are interested in is one in which the Reluctant Terrorists must decide whether to request some policy concession from the government that will satisfy them politically or to engage in a violent terrorist act. If the Reluctant Terrorists choose violence, then the game ends with a terrorist act that leads to no cooperative negotiations and no change in the government position. If the Reluctant Terrorists request some policy concession, the government must decide whether to repress them or enter good faith negotiations with them. The Terrorism Game that we have just described has three possible outcomes: Terrorist act, Repression, or Good faith negotiations. Based on the story that we have just told, the preference ordering for the Reluctant Terrorists and the Government are:

- Reluctant Terrorists: Good faith negotiations $\succ$ Terrorist act $\succ$ Being repressed
- Responsive Government: Good faith negotiations $\succ$ repression $\succ$ Terrorist act
- Repressive Government: Repression $\succ$ Good faith negotiations $\succ$ Terrorist act

Let's assume that the Reluctant Terrorists do not know whether they are interacting with a Responsive Government or a Repressive Government. How can we use game theory to examine this strategic situation?

1. Write out the separate games.

Figure 8.5 illustrates two versions of the Terrorism Game. Each game represents one of the two possible states of the world. The game at the top (Figure 8.5a) represents the situation in which the Reluctant Terrorists confront a Responsive Government, whereas the game at the bottom (Figure 8.5b) represents the situation in which they confront a Repressive Government. The payoffs shown in the two games are cardinal payoffs.

FIGURE 8.5   Complete Information Terrorism Game

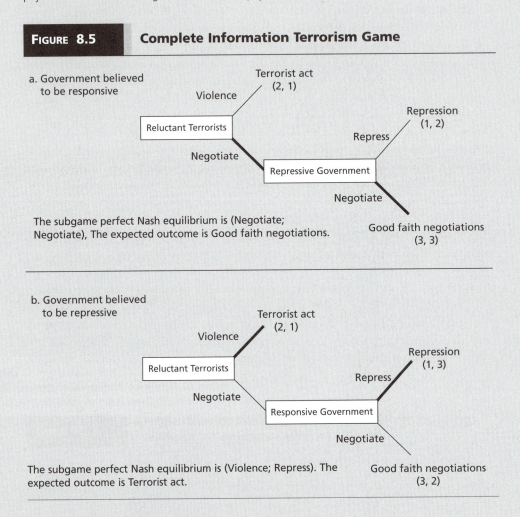

a. Government believed
   to be responsive

Terrorist act
(2, 1)

Violence

Reluctant Terrorists

Repress

Repression
(1, 2)

Negotiate

Repressive Government

Negotiate

Good faith negotiations
(3, 3)

The subgame perfect Nash equilibrium is (Negotiate; Negotiate), The expected outcome is Good faith negotiations.

b. Government believed
   to be repressive

Terrorist act
(2, 1)

Violence

Reluctant Terrorists

Repress

Repression
(1, 3)

Negotiate

Responsive Government

Negotiate

Good faith negotiations
(3, 2)

The subgame perfect Nash equilibrium is (Violence; Repress). The expected outcome is Terrorist act.

2. Solve the separate games.

If you solved these games correctly using backward induction in Chapter 3, you will know that the SPNE is (Negotiate; Negotiate) and that the expected outcome is Good faith negotiations when the Reluctant Terrorists are faced with a Responsive Government; the SPNE is (Violence; Repress) and the expected outcome is Terrorist act when they are faced with a Repressive Government. The problem is that the Reluctant Terrorists do not know which game they are actually playing.

3. Connect the games with an information set showing the uncertainty about the two games.

Figure 8.6 represents the Terrorism Game with uncertainty. Basically, Figure 8.6 combines the two games illustrated in Figure 8.5 and makes two changes. The first change is that we add a move by "Nature" at the initial choice node of the game. The move by Nature indicates that there are two possible states of the world, each of which exists with some probability. There is some probability p that the Reluctant Terrorists are in the top subgame, in which they are facing a Responsive Government. And there is some probability $1-p$ that they are in the bottom subgame, in which they are facing a Repressive Government. The second change is the dashed line connecting the choice nodes of the Reluctant Terrorists. As we noted in Box 8.6 "Transition Game with Incomplete Information," this dashed line indicates an information set, and tells us that the Reluctant Terrorists do not know which node they are at—they might be playing the top subgame or they might be playing the bottom subgame. The dashed line is how uncertainty is introduced into our model.

FIGURE 8.6   **Incomplete Information Terrorism Game**

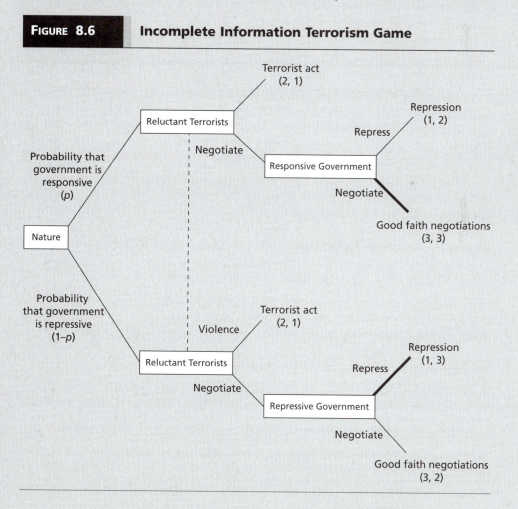

4. Compare the expected payoffs in the combined game.

In order to solve the combined game, we must do two things. The first thing we must do is calculate the payoffs that the Reluctant Terrorists can expect to get from each of their two possible choices—Violence and Negotiate. In other words, we need to calculate expected payoffs. The second thing we must do is calculate the critical probability that will make the Reluctant Terrorists choose Violence or Negotiate.

a. *Expected payoff of the choices.* What is the expected payoff from choosing Violence for the Reluctant Terrorists? With probability p, the Reluctant Terrorists are in the top subgame with the Responsive Government; the decision to use violence here will give them a payoff of 2. With probability $1-p$, they are in the bottom subgame with the Repressive Government; the decision to use violence here will also give them a payoff of 2. Thus, the Reluctant Terrorists' expected payoff from violence can be calculated as:

$$\text{Expected payoff (Violence)} = (p \times 2) + [(1-p) \times 2]$$
$$= 2p + 2 - 2p$$
$$= 2.$$

In other words, the Reluctant Terrorists can expect to get a payoff of 2 if they choose Violence at their choice node. As you can see, if the Reluctant Terrorists choose to use violence, it does not really matter which game is being played—the payoff is always 2. Now we must calculate the expected payoff from choosing Negotiate. With probability p, the Reluctant Terrorists are in the top subgame with the Responsive Government; the decision to negotiate will give them a payoff of 3. With probability $1-p$, they are in the bottom subgame with the Repressive Government; the decision to negotiate here will give them a payoff of 1. Thus, the Reluctant Terrorists' expected payoff from negotiating can be calculated as:

$$\text{Expected payoff (Negotiate)} = (p \times 3) + [(1-p) \times 1]$$
$$= 3p + 1 - 1p$$
$$= 2p + 1.$$

Now we must determine whether Violence or Negotiate gives the Reluctant Terrorists the larger expected payoff. If $2 > 2p + 1$, then the Reluctant Terrorists will use violence; if $2 < 2p + 1$, then they will negotiate. To see under which conditions one or the other situation will be true, we need to calculate the critical probability for p that will make the Reluctant Terrorists act one way or the other.

b. *Critical probability.* As we just noted, the Reluctant Terrorists will choose violence if $2 > 2p + 1$. We can calculate the critical probability at which the expected payoff from violence is larger than the expected payoff from negotiating in the following way:

$$\text{Expected payoff (Violence)} > \text{Expected payoff (Negotiate)}$$
$$2 > 2p + 1$$
$$1 > 2p$$
$$\tfrac{1}{2} > p.$$

This means that if $p < \frac{1}{2}$, then the Reluctant Terrorists will choose to use violence rather than negotiate. What does this mean in the real world? Essentially, it means that if the Reluctant Terrorists believe that the probability that the government is responsive is sufficiently small (less than 0.5, given our payoffs), then it will choose to engage in violence. It is important to note that what we have calculated is not the actual or perceived beliefs that the Reluctant Terrorists have about the type of government that they are facing; rather what we have calculated is the critical value of p that would make the Reluctant Terrorists prefer to use violence rather than negotiate. We have now solved the incomplete information version of the Terrorism Game introduced in Chapter 3.[17]

It should be obvious from the incomplete information version of the Terrorism Game that a terrorist act can occur even if reluctant terrorists are interacting with responsive governments. It can happen, for example, if the reluctant terrorists mistakenly believe that they are facing a repressive government when they are in fact facing a responsive one. Note that a terrorist act cannot occur between reluctant terrorists and responsive governments if there is complete information. This suggests that responsive governments who are dealing with reluctant terrorists should not take actions that might lead the reluctant terrorists to perceive them as repressive.

Problems 3 and 4

We now present two problems dealing with incomplete information games so that you may become more familiar with how these types of games work. Problem 3 involves an incomplete information game examining why dictatorships might choose to conduct elections and form political parties. Problem 4 involves an incomplete information game examining whether religious parties are compatible with secular and liberal democratic institutions.

3. Dictatorship Party Game

In a paper entitled "Why Parties and Elections in Authoritarian Regimes?" Barbara Geddes (2005) examines why dictators might choose to conduct elections and form political parties. Her basic argument is that dictators choose to establish these institutions because they help ward off potential coups from challengers within the authoritarian elite. Let's examine the logic of her "party" story a little more with the help of some game theory.

There are two different factions within the authoritarian elite—the "Regime" faction and the "Challenger" faction. The Regime is currently in charge. The Challenger is not in charge but would like to be. We can think that the Challenger comes in two types: "weak" and "strong." At the beginning of the game, the Regime has to decide whether or not to form a political party (and hold elections). We will assume that forming a political party is costly for both factions in the authoritarian elite. Once the Regime has made its choice, the Challenger must decide whether to launch a coup against the Regime or not. We will assume that launching a coup is costly and that

---

17. If you are particularly interested in games of incomplete information, we encourage you to consult a game theory textbook. Although we have shown you how to find the critical probability that determines what choice an uncertain actor should make, we have not shown you how to find and write down the equilibrium of this type of game.

launching an unsuccessful coup is particularly costly. Whether a coup is successful depends on the strength of the Challenger and whether the Regime has created a political party. Political parties provide a means by which the Regime can mobilize supporters to counter a coup and stay in power. To keep things simple, we will assume that coup attempts by both types of Challenger fail if the Regime has created a party. If there is no party, though, then the Regime is able to counter coups by weak Challengers, but not coups by strong Challengers. There are five possible outcomes in this game: Status quo, Party and no coup, Party and failed coup, No party and failed coup, No party and successful coup. Figure 8.7 illustrates an incomplete information game with cardinal payoffs in which the Regime does not know whether it is interacting with a weak Challenger or a strong Challenger.

FIGURE 8.7	Dictatorship Party Game

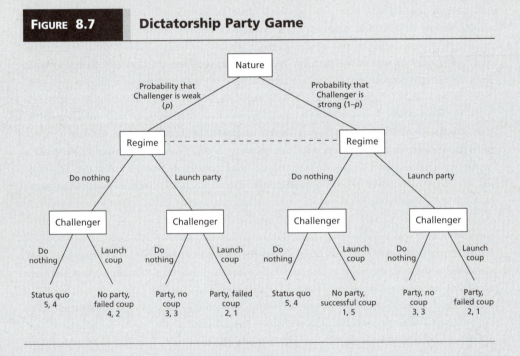

a. Based on the cardinal payoffs shown in Figure 8.7, write down the preference ordering for the Regime and for both types of Challenger over the possible outcomes.

b. Solve the subgame on the left, where the Challenger is weak, as if there were no uncertainty. What is the subgame perfect Nash equilibrium? What is the expected outcome? What are the payoffs that each player receives?

c. Solve the subgame on the right, where the Challenger is strong, as if there were no uncertainty. What is the subgame perfect Nash equilibrium? What is the expected outcome? What are the payoffs that each player receives?

d. What is the expected payoff for the Regime from "Do nothing"?

e. What is the expected payoff for the Regime from "Launch party"?

   f. Use the expected payoffs from the two previous questions to calculate the critical probability at which the Regime will choose to launch a party rather than do nothing.

   g. If the Regime believes that the Challenger is weak with a probability of 0.75, will it choose to do nothing, launch a party, or be indifferent between these two actions? Explain.

   h. If the Regime believes that the Challenger is weak with a probability of 0.25, will it choose to do nothing, launch a party, or be indifferent between these two actions? Explain.

   i. If the Regime believes that the Challenger is weak with a probability of 0.50, will it choose to do nothing, launch a party, or be indifferent between these two actions? Explain.

   j. If you were the Regime, would you prefer to be in a world in which you know the strength of the Challenger or one in which you don't? Would it make a difference? Explain your answer.

   k. If you were the Challenger and you were weak, would you prefer to be in a world in which the Regime knows your strength or one in which it doesn't? Would it make a difference? Explain your answer.

   l. If you were the Challenger and you were strong, would you prefer to be in a world in which the Regime knows your strength or one in which it doesn't? Would it make a difference? Explain your answer.

  4. Religious Party Game

In a paper entitled "Commitment Problems in Emerging Democracies: The Case of Religious Parties," Stathis Kalyvas (2000) examines whether religious parties are compatible with secular and liberal democratic institutions. He concludes that religious parties may be compatible with democracy as long as they can credibly commit not to impose a theocratic dictatorship if they come to power. He goes on to argue that some religions are better able to provide these credible commitments than others. We now provide a Religious Party Game that throws light on the credible commitment problem facing religious parties that Kalyvas describes.

    The two players in our game are a dictatorial regime (Regime) that has recently introduced a process of democratization and a religious party (Religious Party) that seeks to gain power through the newly proposed democratic elections. The Religious Party is expected to win the elections, and many fear that it will turn the country into a theocracy rather than continuing the process of democratic consolidation. The Regime has to decide whether to hold the elections as scheduled or to cancel them and retain power as a dictatorship. If elections are held and the Religious Party wins (which we are assuming will happen), then the Religious Party has to decide whether to pursue a moderate political agenda and support democratic consolidation or to subvert the democratization process and create a religious regime. The Religious Party comes in two types—moderate and radical. One way to think about these types is that religious parties have both moderate and radical factions; whichever faction is dominant determines the Religious Party's type. Moderate religious parties prefer democratic consolidation to establishing a theocracy, whereas radical religious parties prefer the opposite. There are three possible outcomes in this game: Continued dictatorship, Religious dictatorship, and Democratic consolidation. Figure 8.8 illustrates an incomplete information version of this game with cardinal payoffs in which the Regime does not know whether they are interacting with a moderate Religious Party or a radical Religious Party.

| FIGURE 8.8 | **Religious Party Game** |

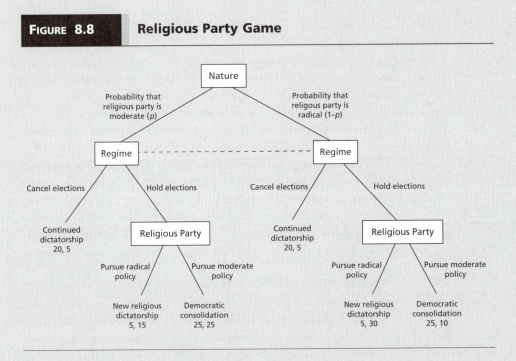

a. Based on the cardinal payoffs shown in Figure 8.8, write down the preference ordering for (a) the Regime, (b) the moderate Religious Party, and (c) the radical Religious Party over the three possible outcomes.

b. Solve the subgame on the left, where the Religious Party is moderate, as if there were no uncertainty. What is the subgame perfect Nash equilibrium? What is the expected outcome? What are the payoffs that each player receives?

c. Solve the subgame on the right, where the Religious Party is radical, as if there were no uncertainty. What is the subgame perfect Nash equilibrium? What is the expected outcome? What are the payoffs that each player receives?

d. What is the expected payoff for the Regime from "Cancel elections"?

e. What is the expected payoff for the Regime from "Hold elections"?

f. Use the expected payoffs from the two previous questions to calculate the critical probability at which the Regime will choose to hold elections rather than cancel them.

g. If the Regime believes that the Religious Party is moderate with a probability of 0.75, will it choose to hold elections, cancel elections, or will it be indifferent between these two actions? Explain.

h. If the Regime believes that the Religious Party is moderate with a probability of 0.8, will it choose to hold elections, cancel elections, or will it be indifferent between these two actions? Explain.

i. If the Regime believes that the Religious Party is moderate with a probability of 0.5, will it choose to hold elections, cancel elections, or will it be indifferent between these two actions? Explain.

j. If you represented a moderate religious party poised to win the elections, would you want the Regime to believe that the party was moderate or radical?

k. If you represented a radical religious party poised to win the elections, would you want the Regime to believe that the party was moderate or radical?

l. If you solved the game correctly, you will find that the Regime will hold elections as long as it believes that the Religious Party is moderate with a high enough probability. If there is some uncertainty on the part of the Regime and you are representing a moderate religious party that wants the elections to go ahead, why might it not be enough for you to simply announce to the Regime that the party is a moderate religious party and not a radical one?

In his article, Kalyvas (2000) claims that there have been only two cases in which religious parties won or were expected to win an electoral mandate—Belgium (1870–1884) and Algeria (1988–1992).[18] In January 1992 in Algeria, the Islamic Salvation Front (FIS) was deprived of a sweeping electoral victory when the military stepped in and aborted the country's electoral process. The result was a bloody civil war. In contrast, a Catholic party was able to come to power in Belgium in 1884 having won a large electoral victory on the basis of a religious program. The incumbent elite accepted the electoral outcome even though they had the power to abort it. In turn, the Catholic party did not apply its religious program in full, nor did it challenge Belgium's secular and liberal institutions.

Although the religious parties in both countries had moderate and radical factions, Kalyvas presents evidence that the moderate factions were dominant in each party. If our Religious Party Game is correct, then the reason why the Catholic party in Belgium was allowed to come to power but the Islamic party in Algeria was not must have been because only the promises from the Catholic party to pursue a moderate policy once in power were seen as credible. This raises the question as to why the promises to adopt a moderate policy once in power were credible coming from the Catholic party but not coming from the Islamic party. After examining several potential answers to this question, Kalyvas argues that it has to do with the different organizational structures of the two religions. In effect, he claims that commitments to pursue moderate policies when in power are more credible when they come from hierarchical religions like

18. The electoral success of religious parties in India, Jordan, Pakistan, and Turkey do not count as cases in which religious parties won an "electoral mandate" because, at the time of writing, these parties were either always in opposition or had been only in coalition governments--they never ruled on their own. Religious parties in Afghanistan, Iran, and Sudan have ruled on their own; however, they came to power through revolutions rather than an electoral process (Kalyvas 2000, 380).

Catholicism than when they come from more decentralized religions like Islam. The idea is that when someone at the top of a hierarchy orders its members to abide by liberal democratic rules, then this should be seen as a credible statement because that person actually has the ability to control the behavior of the members. This is exactly what Pope Leo XIII did in 1879 when he told Belgian Catholics to stop attacking the Belgian constitution and to purge prominent radical leaders (Kalyvas 2000, 389). In contrast, promises to pursue moderate policies are seen as less credible when there is no single religious leader who can speak for all believers. In Islam, different religious leaders compete with one another and each claims to speak for the masses.

Use the Internet and other sources to answer the following questions about democracy and Islamic religious parties in Turkey.

m. Is Turkey a democracy or a dictatorship? Is Turkey a secular or a religious state? What kind of party was the Refah (Welfare) Party? How did the Refah Party do in the 1995 legislative elections? What happened to the Refah Party and its leader Erbakan in 1997? What kind of party was the Fazilet (Virtue) Party? Where did it come from and what happened to it in 2001? What kind of party is the Saadet (Felicity) Party and where did it come from? What kind of party is the Adalet ve Kalkinma (Justice and Development) Party and where did it come from? Are there any religious differences between the Felicity Party and the Justice and Development Party? How did the Justice and Development Party do in the 2002 legislative elections? How did it do in the 2007 legislative elections? What were some of the main issues surrounding the 2007 legislative elections in Turkey?

n. In his article published in 2000, Kalyvas states that "No contemporary case of compliance with a religious party's mandate victory is available" (380). Based on what you have learned from Turkey, is this statement still true?

o. An implication from Kalyvas's analysis is that unlike Catholic parties, Islamic parties are unable, or at least find it more difficult, to be successfully incorporated into liberal democratic regimes because their decentralized organizational structures make it difficult for them to credibly promise to adopt moderate policies once in power. Does the history that you have examined from Turkey lend support for this implication or not? Explain.

p. Does the evidence from Turkey suggest that repeated interactions in the electoral arena can help religious parties to overcome the difficulty they face in credibly committing to pursue moderate policies once in power?

TRANSITION GAME WITH INCOMPLETE INFORMATION

In the main text of this chapter, we presented a game-theoretic analysis suggesting that top-down transitions to democracy cannot occur when there is complete information, that is, when the players know everything there is to know about the game. We then presented an informal discussion in which we claimed that top-down transitions are possible when there is incomplete information. Specifically, we claimed that they are possible when authoritarian soft-liners are uncertain as to whether they face a weak democratic opposition or a strong democratic opposition. We now examine this claim more formally with the help of an **incomplete information game.**

> An **incomplete information game** is one in which a player does not know all of the relevant information about some other player's characteristics.

Recall that we previously analyzed two complete information transition games. In one, the soft-liners know for sure that the democratic opposition is strong and in the other, they know for sure that it is weak (Figure 8.3). In our incomplete information Transition Game, we incorporate a new "actor" who determines whether we are playing the game with the strong opposition or the one with the weak opposition. We will refer to this new actor as "Nature." Unfortunately for the soft-liners, they do not know which game Nature is going to choose. All they know is that Nature chooses the game in which the opposition is weak with some probability p and that it chooses the game in which the opposition is strong with some probability $1 - p$.

We now incorporate this information into a new game tree shown in Figure 8.9. The dashed line indicates that when the soft-liners choose whether to do nothing or to open up at their first choice node, they do not know whether they are playing the game with the strong opposition or the weak opposition. This dashed line is called an **information set.** One other change should be pointed out. Unlike with games of complete information, we cannot use ordinal payoffs with games of incomplete infor-

> An **information set** is a dashed line connecting the choice nodes where the uncertain player has to make a choice; it indicates that the player does not know which of the connected choice nodes she is at when choosing.

mation. Instead, we have to use cardinal payoffs just as we did in Chapter 4 when we examined the emergence of the state. As you will remember, cardinal payoffs are different from ordinal payoffs in that they tell us exactly how much more a player values one outcome compared with another. In other words, a player values an outcome with a payoff of 4 four times as much as an outcome with a payoff of 1. To keep things as simple as possible, we have retained the same payoffs we used in our complete information Transition Game. Remember, however, these are now cardinal payoffs, not ordinal payoffs.

Now that we have specified the game, we can try to figure out what the players will do. We start with the usual method of backward induction. At the final two choice nodes, the soft-liners must choose whether to democratize or repress. As in our earlier analysis, the soft-liners will choose to repress in the left-hand side of the game tree (when they believe the democratic opposition is weak) and they will choose to democratize in the right-hand side of the game tree (when they believe the democratic opposition is strong). We indicate these choices by making the relevant branch at these final two choice nodes bold in Figure 8.9. We now move back to the two previous choice nodes where the democratic opposition must

| FIGURE 8.9 | **Incomplete Information Transition Game** |

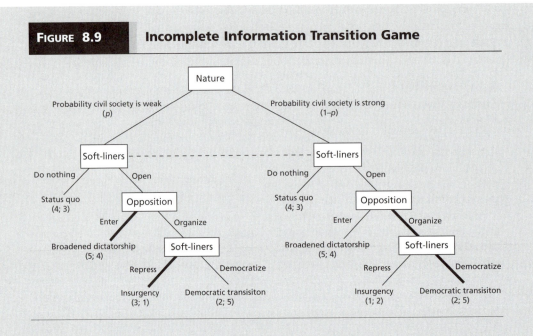

choose whether to continue organizing or enter a broadened dictatorship. From our earlier analysis, we have already seen that a weak opposition will enter and that a strong opposition will organize. As a result, we indicate these choices by making the relevant branch at these choice nodes bold in Figure 8.9 as well.

We must now determine whether the soft-liners will choose to do nothing or whether they will choose to open up at the initial choice nodes. Unfortunately, the method of backward induction can no longer help us here. The reason for this has to do with the dashed line between these two choice nodes in Figure 8.9 that indicates that the soft-liners do not know which side of the game tree they are on. Their uncertainty over the strength of the democratic opposition means that the soft-liners do not know for sure what their payoffs will be if they open up. On the one hand, if the soft-liners open up and the opposition is weak, they can look down the game tree (follow the bold lines on the left-hand side) and see that the outcome will be a broadened dictatorship with a payoff of 5. On the other hand, if they open up and the opposition is strong, they can again look down the game tree (follow the bold lines on the right-hand side) and see that the outcome will be a democratic transition with a payoff of 2. Whether the democratic opposition is weak or strong, the soft-liners will get a payoff of 4 if they do nothing; that is, the "do nothing" branch on either side of the game tree always gives the soft-liners a payoff of 4.

What should the soft-liners do? They know that they can get a payoff of 4 if they do nothing and they know that they will either get a payoff of 5 or a payoff of 2 if they open up. What would you do? The way political scientists approach this problem is to ask whether the payoff that the soft-liners can *expect* to get if they open up is greater than the payoff they *know* they will get if they do nothing. To answer this question, it is necessary to calculate the soft-liners' **expected payoff** from opening up. In general, the expected payoff of some choice (in this case to open up) is calculated by multiplying the payoff associated with each possible

An **expected payoff** is the sum of the payoffs associated with each outcome multiplied by the probability with which each outcome occurs.

outcome by the probability that that outcome occurs and then summing these values. Thus, if there are two possible outcomes associated with some choice, then the expected payoff is calculated as follows:

Expected payoff (Choice) = (Probability Outcome 1 occurs × Payoff from Outcome 1)

+

(Probability Outcome 2 occurs × Payoff from Outcome 2).

As some of you will no doubt have already realized, an expected payoff essentially tells the players what they could expect their average payoff to be if they were able to make their choice over and over again.

What is the expected payoff for the soft-liners if they open up? With probability p, the soft-liners are on the left-hand side of the game tree with a weak democratic opposition and we have already shown that the outcome is a broadened dictatorship with a payoff of 5. With probability $1 - p$, the soft-liners are on the right-hand side of the game tree with a strong democratic opposition and we have already shown that the outcome is a democratic transition with a payoff of 2. Thus, their expected payoff from opening up is:

$$\text{Expected payoff (Open)} = (p \times 5) + [(1 - p) \times 2]$$
$$= 5p + 2 - 2p$$
$$= 3p + 2$$

Now that we know this, will the soft-liners choose to do nothing and receive a payoff of 4 or will they choose to open up with an expected payoff of $3p + 2$? It should be immediately obvious that the soft-liners' choice will depend on the value of p; that is, their choice depends on the probability with which they believe that the democratic opposition is weak. The soft-liners will choose to open up and liberalize when the expected payoff from opening up is greater than the payoff from doing nothing. This occurs when:

$$\text{Expected payoff (Open)} > \text{Payoff (Do Nothing)}$$
$$\Rightarrow \quad 3p + 2 > 4$$
$$\Rightarrow \quad 3p > 2$$
$$\Rightarrow \quad p > \tfrac{2}{3}$$

As you can see, the soft-liners will choose to open up the political regime and liberalize if and only if they believe that the probability that the opposition is weak is greater than $\tfrac{2}{3}$. This is referred to as the "critical probability." If they believe that the opposition is weak with a probability less than this, then the soft-liners will choose to do nothing and the outcome will be the status quo.

Our analysis illustrates just how a top-down transition to democracy might occur. In effect, we have just demonstrated that authoritarian soft-liners will choose to open up and liberalize whenever they are sufficiently confident that the democratic opposition is weak.[1] The problem is that their beliefs about the strength of the opposition may be wrong; the democratic opposition may, in fact, be strong. As we saw earlier, the opposition will continue to organize and mobilize if it is strong. Because only a strong democratic opposition would organize, the soft-liners will realize that they have made a critical mistake and update their initial beliefs about the strength of the opposition. Their updated beliefs will now be that the democratic opposition is strong for sure, that is, $p = 0$. Having realized that the opposition is strong, the soft-liners will then choose to democratize because they know that repression will be unsuccessful and will lead to an unwanted insurgency. In effect, the authoritarian soft-liners inadvertently become democratizers in this situation because of their mistaken beliefs.

Games of incomplete information such as this highlight the important role that information and beliefs play in politics. One implication of this is that political actors will have incentives to take actions that influence the beliefs of other actors. For example, a strong democratic opposition in the prehistory of our incomplete information Transition Game will try to avoid taking actions that signal its strength to the authoritarian soft-liners if it thinks that they might liberalize. In effect, it will try to act just like a weak democratic opposition. By acting as if it were weak, a strong opposition makes it more likely that the soft-liners will choose to open up the regime. At this point, the democratic opposition can reveal that it is strong and push for a full transition to democracy. The incomplete information Transition Game that we have just presented here is one in which the soft-liners do not know what type (weak or strong) of democratic opposition they are dealing with. We could, however, easily adapt our game to examine situations in which the democratic opposition does not know what type of dictatorship (repressive or liberal) it is dealing with. Indeed, we could investigate the situation in which the opposition is unsure about the type of dictatorship it faces *and* the dictatorship is unsure about the type of opposition it faces. As you can see, incomplete information games have the potential to capture situations in the world in which there are quite complicated informational asymmetries and where actors have strong incentives to try to deceive each other.

To familiarize yourself even further with incomplete information games, we suggest that you answer problems 3 and 4 dealing with the Dictatorship Party Game and the Religious Party Game in the "Problems" section of this chapter.

---

1. Given the particular payoffs that we employed, the soft-liners had to believe that the democratic opposition was weak with a probability greater than 2/3.

9 Does Democracy Make a Difference?

A monarchy is the best kind of government because the King is the owner of the country. Like the owner of a house, when the wiring is wrong, he fixes it.

Italian peasant, quoted in Banfield and Banfield 1958, 26

In the terrible history of famines in the world, no substantial famine has ever occurred in any independent and democratic country with a relatively free press.

Amartya Sen, 1999

There can be no government without an army. No army without money. No money without prosperity. And no prosperity without justice and good administration.

Ibn Qutayba, ninth-century Muslim scholar

OVERVIEW

- We live in a world that tends to associate good outcomes with democracy and bad ones with dictatorships. In reality, the world is much more complex than this. Oftentimes, we have no compelling theoretical reason to expect that democracies will outperform dictatorships. Although the empirical evidence indicates that democracies tend to produce high levels of material well-being for their citizens, it also shows that they do not regularly outperform all dictatorships. In effect, some dictatorships perform quite well even though others perform extremely poorly. Classifying the world into democracies and dictatorships fails to explain the variation in the performance of dictatorships.

- Rather than categorize governments as either democratic or dictatorial, the Selectorate Theory characterizes all governments by their location in a two-dimensional institutional space. One dimension is the size of the selectorate—those with a say in choosing the leader—and the second is the size of the winning coalition—those in the selectorate whose support is essential for the leader to stay in office.

- Leaders in systems with large winning coalitions and large selectorates—democracies—have incentives to produce public goods. These leaders produce good government performance—high levels of wealth, efficient governance, and low rates of corruption and kleptocracy.

- Leaders in systems with small winning coalitions and large selectorates—rigged-election dictatorships—have incentives to provide private rewards to their winning coalition. These leaders produce poor government performance—low levels of wealth, inefficient governance, and high levels of corruption and kleptocracy.

- Leaders in systems with small winning coalitions and small selectorates—monarchies and military juntas—produce middling levels of government performance.

In previous chapters, we examined how political scientists distinguish between democracies and dictatorships, we explored economic and cultural explanations for the emergence and survival of democracy, and we investigated the dynamics of regime transition. Now we ask whether it really matters whether someone lives in a democracy or a dictatorship. We live in a world that tends to associate good outcomes with democracy and bad ones with dictatorships. But is this an accurate reflection of the real world? Although there may be many important normative arguments to justify democracy—that it protects certain freedoms, that it is fairer, or that it is more just—we focus our attention in this chapter on whether democracy makes a *material* difference in people's lives. Are government policies better for the average citizen in a democracy or in a dictatorship? For example, do economies grow faster in democracies or dictatorships? Do people live longer in democracies? Are they healthier? Are they more educated? Are they wealthier? It turns out that the answers to these types of questions are not as straightforward as you might imagine. It is not at all obvious, for example, that democracies experience lower levels of child mortality than dictatorships (Ross 2006), or that democracies produce better economic growth (Przeworski and Limongi 1993).

In the first part of this chapter, we examine the effect of regime type on various aspects of government performance. We begin by looking closely at the competing arguments concerning the effect of democracy on economic growth. Some of these arguments suggest that democracies should produce higher growth than dictatorships do, but others suggest the exact opposite. In other words, political scientists do not, as yet, have a clear theoretical prediction as to whether or when democracies will economically outperform dictatorships. We then report somewhat inconclusive results from tests in which we investigate the effect of regime type on a variety of indicators of material well-being, such as wealth, infant mortality, life expectancy, and health care spending. Overall, the empirical evidence suggests that although democracy is often sufficient for ensuring a high level of citizen material well-being, it is certainly not necessary; some dictatorships perform at relatively high levels as well.

In the second part of this chapter, we present a theory—the Selectorate Theory—that is able to explain our empirical results (Bueno de Mesquita et al. 2003). As we will demonstrate, this theory offers a potential explanation both for why democracies generally produce good government performance and for why some dictatorships perform better than others. According to the Selectorate Theory, though, the key to a country's material well-being has less to do with whether it is a democracy or dictatorship, and more to do with the size of what we refer to as a country's "winning coalition" and "selectorate." We will define these terms in more detail shortly. Once we start to think in terms of the size of the selectorate and winning coalition, rather than in terms of regime type per se, it becomes a lot easier to explain why some countries promote better economic policies and provide more public goods than others.

THE EFFECT OF REGIME TYPE ON GOVERNMENT PERFORMANCE

Before presenting the Selectorate Theory, we turn to a large body of research in comparative politics investigating the effects of regime type on government performance. This will give you a sense of what it is that we know about how democratic and authoritarian forms of government influence government performance. We begin by focusing on some of the theoretical arguments linking regime type and economic growth.

The Effect of Democracy on Economic Growth

Do democratic governments promote higher levels of economic growth than dictatorships? This question has generated an enormous literature in both political science and economics, but you'll perhaps be surprised to learn that there is, as yet, no strong consensus on what the answer is. Conflicting arguments abound. Some scholars suggest that democracy promotes economic growth (Barro 1989, 1990; North 1990; Olson 1991), some that it hinders it (de Schweinitz 1959; Galenson 1959; Huntington 1968; Huntington and Dominguez 1975), and some that it makes no difference (Sirowy and Inkeles 1991; Przeworski and Limongi 1993; Przeworski et al. 2000). Typically, theoretical arguments that attempt to link regime type to economic growth focus on three main factors: (a) the protection of property rights, (b) citizens' incentives to consume rather than invest, and (c) dictatorial autonomy. We look at all three in turn.

Property Rights

It is common today for scholars to argue that democracies will enjoy higher levels of economic growth than dictatorships because democracies are characterized by the rule of law and the protection of property rights (North and Thomas 1973; North 1990). According to these scholars, democracy places limits on the ability of governments to engage in the arbitrary seizure of private property. As a result, democracy encourages investment and, in turn, growth. In Chapter 6, one of the arguments for the emergence of democracy—or, at least, limited government—focused on the role that democratic institutions can play in providing a credible commitment mechanism to asset holders who wish to invest in the economy but who worry that the government will later seize their investments. As you'll recall, we illustrated this argument by examining the emergence of limited government in England during the seventeenth century. Although the emergence of a democratic form of government in England at this time was not originally brought about with the specific intention of promoting economic growth, it does appear to have had precisely this effect. Indeed, the fact that England had a limited government in early modern Europe but France did not offers a potential explanation for why the English economy grew so much faster during this period than the French one. In effect, the causal logic of this "property rights" argument in favor of democracy is that democracy helps ensure the rule of law, that the rule of law then helps secure stable property rights, and that stable property rights then encourage growth-boosting investment (see Figure 9.1).

This argument might seem extremely convincing at first, but Barro (2000) presents evidence that only parts of the causal chain outlined in Figure 9.1 actually work in the real world. As predicted, Barro finds that the rule of law does significantly encourage economic growth when he examines data from roughly 100 countries between 1960 and 1995. Indeed,

FIGURE 9.1	**Hypothesized Causal Path between Democracy and Economic Growth**

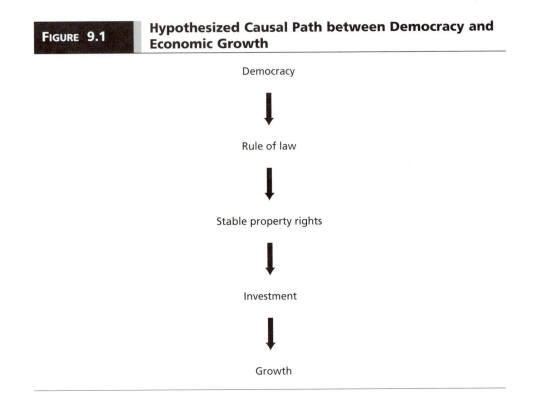

Democracy

Rule of law

Stable property rights

Investment

Growth

he claims that because a similar relationship exists between the rule of law and the ratio of investment to GDP, then "one route by which better rule of law promotes growth is by encouraging investment" (2000, 40). So far, everything seems good for the property rights argument linking democracy to economic growth. The problem, though, is that Barro does not find democracy to be strongly associated with the rule of law. In effect, the initial step in the causal chain linking democracy to economic growth appears to be missing.

As illustrated in Table 9.1, some countries score high on a rule of law index but poor on an electoral rights (democracy) index.[1] These countries are typically run by dictators who promote property rights and a reliable legal system. Examples of such dictators include Augusto Pinochet in Chile (1973–1990), Lee Kuan Yew in Singapore (1959–1990), and Shah Mohammed Reze Pahlavi in Iran (1941–1979). It is perhaps important to note that the legal systems in these countries are reliable—meaning rules tend to be applied in a consistent manner—but not necessarily fair or just. Investors (especially international investors who, by definition, live outside the country), though, are typically more concerned with reliability than fairness. This is because reliable laws, whether fair or not, allow investors to make accurate predictions about their ability to earn a return on their investments. In contrast to these countries, there are others, like Colombia, Israel, and Venezuela (1980s), and Bolivia, Honduras, and South Africa (1990s), that score high on the electoral rights index but poor on the rule of law index.[2] These countries are characterized by fairly advanced forms of electoral competition, but legal protection of property rights is largely absent.

Chee Soon Juan, leader of the Singapore Democratic Party, is arrested outside Singapore's presidential residence, May 1, 2002. Chee, an opposition politician and vocal government critic, was arrested shortly after addressing a small group of supporters and calling for free speech in Singapore.

---

1. Both indexes are compiled by a private firm (Political Risk Services) that monitors the investment climate in particular countries and sells their findings to international investors.

2. In some other countries, property rights are protected in some sectors of the economy but not in others. For example, Haber, Razo, and Maurer (2003) detail how the Mexican government between 1876 and 1929 failed to protect property rights in many sectors of the economy but did protect them in sectors in which the technology of production was sophisticated and in which the government relied on actors with high levels of human capital. In effect, the Mexican government protected property rights in those sectors of the economy in which it depended on actors who had credible exit threats. Haber, Razo, and Maurer go on to demonstrate that significant investment, industrial expansion, and economic growth occurred in precisely those sectors with protected property rights and that all of this occurred despite the tremendous social disorder and political instability that plagued Mexico during this period.

	Countries with Large Gaps between Rule of Law and Electoral Rights Indexes
TABLE 9.1	

a. High Rule of Law Relative to Electoral Rights in 1982

Country	Rule of law index	Electoral rights index
Burkina Faso	0.50	0.00
Chile	0.83	0.17
Ethiopia	0.50	0.00
Guinea	0.50	0.00
Hong Kong	1.00	0.50
Hungary[a]	0.83	0.33
Myanmar (Burma)	0.50	0.00
Niger	0.67	0.00
Poland[a]	0.67	0.17
Singapore	1.00	0.50
Somalia	0.50	0.00
Taiwan	1.00	0.33

b. High Rule of Law Relative to Electoral Rights in 1998

Country	Rule of law index	Electoral rights index
Bahrain	0.83	0.00
Cameroon	0.50	0.00
China	0.83	0.00
Egypt	0.67	0.17
Gambia	0.83	0.00
Hong Kong	0.83	0.33
Iran	0.83	0.17
Kuwait	0.83	0.33
Malaysia	0.83	0.33
Morocco	1.00	0.33
Myanmar (Burma)	0.50	0.00
Oman	0.83	0.17
Saudi Arabia	0.83	0.00
Singapore	1.00	0.33
Syria	0.83	0.00
Tanzania	0.83	0.33
Tunisia	0.83	0.17
United Arab Emirates	0.67	0.17
Yugoslavia	0.83	0.17

a. Data are unavailable for 1982 and are shown for 1985.

TABLE 9.1	Countries with Large Gaps between Rule of Law and Electoral Rights Indexes (continued)	

c. Low Rule of Law Relative to Electoral Rights in 1982

Country	Rule of law index	Electoral rights index
Bolivia	0.17	0.83
Colombia	0.33	0.83
Cyprus[a]	0.33	1.00
Dominican Republic	0.50	1.00
Greece	0.50	1.00
Honduras	0.17	0.83
South Africa	0.50	1.00
Uruguay	0.50	1.00

Source: Barro (2000), from Political Risk Services.

Note: The indexes run from 0 to 1 with higher numbers indicating greater rule of law or greater electoral rights. The table shows observations for which the magnitude of the gap between the rule of law and electoral rights indexes was at least 0.5.

a. Data are unavailable for 1982 and are shown for 1985.

Barro's evidence indicates that breakdowns in the rule of law and the protection of property rights occur under both dictatorships and democracies. As a consequence, he concludes that "the electoral rights index has no predictive content for the rule of law index" and, therefore, that encouraging democracy on the grounds that it will lead to economic growth "sounds pleasant, but is simply false" (Barro 2000, 46, 47). Other scholars, however, disagree. For example, some have found that more democratic countries *are* more likely to protect property rights (Leblang 1996; Rigobon and Rodrik 2004) and, as a consequence, experience higher growth rates (Leblang 1996, 1997). The precise relationship between democracy and economic growth clearly remains a hotly contested issue.

One reason why the relationship between democracy and economic growth is not clear cut has to do with the fact that democratic governments appear to be more than capable of abrogating or abolishing property rights when they want. One explanation for why democracy might fail to protect property rights can be derived from an influential model of the size of government that political scientists refer to as the "Meltzer-Richard" model (Meltzer and Richard 1981). The model starts with a situation in which everyone in society is asked to pay a portion of his or her income as a tax (t). The government then takes this tax revenue and divides it equally among all members of society. Because government spending is divided equally among all members of society in this imaginary world but the amount of tax paid is a function of each individual's income, anyone with above-average income ends up paying above-average taxes and gets back government benefits equal only to those received by the average taxpayer. As a result, any individual with below-average income in this society stands to be a net beneficiary of the tax system; in contrast, anyone with above-average income stands to be a net contributor to the tax system.[3] Because the Meltzer-Richard model assumes a balanced budget, the amount of redistribution a government can engage in is constrained by the amount of taxes it can raise. As a result, individuals who stand to be net recipients of the government's "tax and transfer system" will prefer high taxes (and the ensuing high transfers), whereas individuals who are net contributors to the system will prefer low taxes and few transfers.

In a market economy, income is likely to be tied to productivity. Highly productive individuals have high incomes and less productive individuals have low incomes. Consequently, people's preferred tax rate is related to their level of productivity in a manner similar to that shown in Figure 9.2. If their level of productivity is extremely low (say, below x_0), then they

FIGURE 9.2   **Individual Productivity and Desired Tax Rate according to the Meltzer-Richard Model**

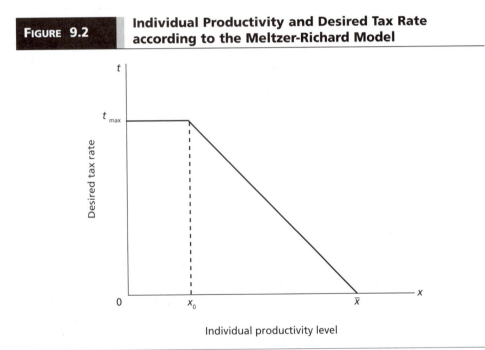

Individual productivity level

Note: x = an individual's level of productivity; $\bar{x}$ = the average level of individual productivity in society. Individuals with a productivity level below x_0 will choose not to work and to live entirely on government transfers. t = an individual's desired tax rate; t_{max} = the maximum desired tax rate.

3. Note that redistribution from the "rich" to the "poor" occurs in this society despite the fact that government spending is not targeted toward the poor and that both the poor and rich pay exactly the same tax rate. "Means tested" welfare programs that restrict access to government benefits to low-income families (such as food stamp programs in the United States) and "progressive" income tax systems that apply higher tax rates to rich people than poor people would make the system even *more* "redistributive." All that is necessary to make a system redistributive, though, is to have the total tax paid by each person be an increasing function of income while making benefits independent of income.

choose not to work at all and they survive purely on government transfers. As a result, individuals in this category have a preferred level of taxation that is uniformly high (t_{max}). In contrast, individuals whose level of productivity is above the societal average ($\bar{x}$) and, hence, have an above-average income, pay more taxes than the average citizen but receive only the societal average of government transfers. As a result, such individuals are net contributors to the tax and transfer system and prefer a tax rate of zero. Between these two groups are individuals with productivity levels that are somewhat high but below the societal average. Because these individuals are net beneficiaries of the tax and transfer system, they prefer a non-zero tax rate. The precise level of their desired tax rate (on the downward sloping line), however, depends on the distance between their productivity level and the societal average. Those with productivity rates very close to the societal average want tax rates close to zero, because they expect to benefit only slightly from the tax and transfer system, whereas those with low productivity rates want tax rates almost as high as do individuals that have left the labor market altogether, because they expect to benefit from the tax and transfer system a lot.

So far, we have used the Meltzer-Richard model to explain why some individuals might prefer a higher tax rate than others. In order to make predictions about what the tax rate will be, however, we need to say something about how policy is actually chosen. In general, democracies tend to represent the interests of a wider portion of society than dictatorships. This means that the interests of poor (low-productivity) people are given more effective representation in democracies than in dictatorships. If we assume that dictatorships make tax policy to reflect the preferences of individuals with above-average incomes but that democracies make tax policy to reflect the preferences of individuals with below-average incomes, then a change from autocracy to democracy can be expected to lead to an increase in the level of taxation and, therefore, an increase in the amount of redistribution from the rich to the poor. Indeed, this increase in the level of taxation and redistribution when countries transition to democracy is likely to be quite large if there is widespread inequality in society.

How might this affect economic growth? Well, consider that potential investors—in this story, the rich—are always deciding whether to consume (spend) their after-tax income or invest it. If they think that the tax rate is too high, then they will prefer to consume rather than invest. In the absence of investment, economic growth can be expected to grind to a halt. Although democracy might be expected to offer property owners protection against seizures by the state, the Meltzer-Richards model illustrates that democracy introduces the possibility that the poor will seize the property of the rich through a redistributive tax scheme. When left-wing parties come to power in democracies promising to "expropriate" the rich—take their wealth and redistribute it to the poor—wealthy citizens often feel threatened and sometimes call on the military to step in and protect their property rights. This is a story commonly told about right-wing military coups that toppled left-wing democratic regimes in Latin American countries, such as Argentina (1976), Chile (1973), and Guatemala (1954) (O'Donnell 1973; Stepan 1985; Drake 1996). The same theme can be found in the writings of the political elites setting up the American democracy in the late eighteenth century

(Roemer 1998). Why else did the founding fathers extend the suffrage only to male property holders and spend so long trying to write a constitution that protected property? [4]

There are, however, two criticisms of the Meltzer-Richard model. Both of these criticisms suggest that the model may overstate the extent to which democratic politics will lead to large-scale redistribution and, therefore, to growth-reducing disinvestment. First, it is well known that political participation in democracies is inversely related to income; poor people are much less likely to vote than rich people (Wolfinger and Rosenstone 1980; Leighley and Nagler 1992a, 1992b; Verba, Schlozman, and Brady 1995; Blais 2000). As a result, it is possible that, in reality, democracies implement tax and transfer policies that are not very different from the policies adopted in dictatorships. In fact, if the "decisive" voter in both systems has a level of productivity (and, therefore, income) higher than the societal average ($\bar{x}$), then there should be no difference in the tax and transfer system between the two regimes types.

The second criticism of the Meltzer-Richard model is related to a famous Marxist argument that highlights what political scientists call the "structural dependence of the state on capital" (Block 1977; Lindblom 1977; Przeworski and Wallerstein 1988). The important insight from this Marxist theory is clearly seen with the help of a model by Przeworski (1991, 9–10). The model starts with an economy comprising two groups: one group (P) derives its income from profits; the other group (W) derives it from wages. For any given level of technological development in society, there is a maximum level of output that the economy is capable of producing. We might think that the fruits of this output can be divided between profit takers and wage earners in any number of ways. The downward-sloping line in Figure 9.3 represents all of the feasible ways we could divide society's maximum output between profit takers and wage earners. At P^*, the profit takers receive all of the output and the wage earners receive nothing. At W^*, the wage earners receive all of the output and the profit takers receive nothing. In between these two points, there is a continuum of distributional possibilities that includes the perfectly egalitarian distribution (E), in which the profit takers and wage earners each receive half of society's maximum potential output. Political scientists sometimes refer to this downward-sloping line as the "technological possibility frontier" because it represents all the different divisions of what it is possible for society to technologically produce.

As just mentioned, there is a maximum level of output that an economy is capable of producing. It turns out that this level of output can be achieved only if profit takers and wage earners efficiently invest their resources—their capital and labor—in the economy. As we'll show, this will happen only if profit takers and wage earners receive a particular division of societal output whereby each group receives the entire return on the investments they make. In other words, only one of the points or divisions on the technological possibility frontier is actually consistent with the economy's producing the maximum that it is capable of pro-

---

4. Several political scientists have applied the basic argument of the Meltzer-Richard model to claim that economic inequality undermines the prospects for stable democracy (Huntington 1993; Acemoglu and Robinson 2000, 2001, 2006; Rosendorff 2001; Boix 2003; Dunning 2006). The logic of the claim is that as inequality rises, the poor become more likely to vote to expropriate the rich, and as a result the rich become more likely to try to undermine democracy to prevent this from happening.

FIGURE 9.3	The Potential Trade-off between Growth and Equality

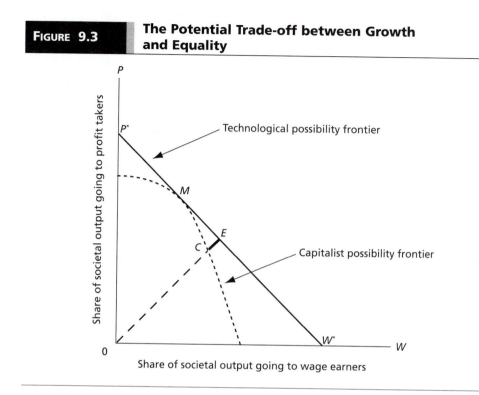

The answer to this question has to do with the fact that individuals in a capitalist economy always have a choice about how to allocate their resources. For example, profit takers are always comparing what they could get from investing their capital against the enjoyment they could get from simply consuming it. Similarly, wage earners are always comparing what they could get from an additional hour's work against the value they place on an

ducing. In Figure 9.3, this is point *M*. Because *M* is on the technological possibility frontier to the left of the egalitarian point (*E*) in this specific society, we are assuming that, in line with much of historical experience, profit takers will receive more of society's maximum output than wage earners.[5] But why, you might wonder, is there only one division of societal output between profit takers and wage earners that maximizes total economic output? Why wouldn't any of the other possible divisions on the technological possibility frontier also maximize output?

The answer to this question has to do with the fact that individuals in a capitalist economy always have a choice about how to allocate their resources. For example, profit takers are always comparing what they could get from investing their capital against the enjoyment they could get from simply consuming it. Similarly, wage earners are always comparing what they could get from an additional hour's work against the value they place on an

5. The precise position of point *M* on the technological possibility frontier depends on the relative rate of return on capital and labor. If the rate of return on capital is larger than the rate of return on labor, then the division of societal output will benefit capital and be on the technological possibility frontier to the left of the egalitarian point (*E*); if the rate of return on labor is greater, then the division of societal output will benefit labor and be to the right of the egalitarian point. What do we mean by "rate of return"? In everyday language, the rate of return on an investment is just the ratio of money gained on an investment relative to the amount of money invested. If capital and labor were measured in the same units, then the relative rate of return on capital would be higher than that on labor if one unit of capital produced more than one unit of labor.

additional hour of leisure. If profit takers or wage earners ever receive less than their entire return on their capital or labor investments—perhaps because the government taxes them—then profit takers will start consuming more of their capital rather than investing it and wage earners will start taking more leisure time rather than working. As a result, society's resources will be underutilized and there will be a decline in societal output away from what is technologically possible. The logic here leads to what we might call a "capitalism possibility frontier"—the curved line in Figure 9.3—that is entirely inside the technological possibility frontier except for the point at which capital and labor receive the entire return on their investments (*M*). In other words, a capitalist economy will always produce less than is technologically possible unless profit takers and wage earners divide societal output between them in a manner indicated by point *M*.

To help illustrate how the model works, imagine a society in which the tax and transfer system has historically been controlled by an autocratic government representing the interests of profit takers. Over time and through experience, the autocratic government has discovered that societal output is maximized by returning a larger share of society's product to the profit takers than to the wage earners. Recall that this is point *M* in Figure 9.3. Now, imagine that the autocratic government is replaced by a democratic one in which there are at least as many wage earners as profit takers. This change in regime would, presumably, put pressure on the government to use its tax and transfer system to redistribute wealth in a more egalitarian fashion—say, to a point like *E*. So far, the predicted effect of a shift to democracy is essentially the same as that generated by the Meltzer-Richard model that we examined earlier—there will be pressure for redistribution.

But note, now, what happens if the government actually uses its tax and transfer capability in this way. Because profit takers are no longer receiving the full value of their investments, they will begin to remove their capital assets from the economy, either by consuming them or by shifting them to a different economy—a process known as "capital flight." As a result, societal output will decline from point *E* on the technological possibility frontier to point *C* on the capitalist possibility frontier that is associated with the new egalitarian distribution of income. The distance between points *E* and *C* (the short boldface line in Figure 9.3) constitutes the cost in lost societal output that results from the redistributive policy. In effect, Przeworski's model illustrates that there is a potential trade-off between equality and growth—increased equality can be obtained only by accepting reduced economic growth.

Structural Marxists argue that governments will recognize this trade-off and choose to promote growth over equality. They argue that whether the government is controlled by capitalists or by workers, the fact that resource allocation decisions are in the hands of private individuals in a capitalist economy means that policies will be adopted that protect the interests of the capitalist class. As Fred Block (1977, 15) notes,

> Those who manage the state apparatus—regardless of their own political ideology—are dependent on the maintenance of some reasonable level of economic activity. This is true for two reasons. First, the capacity of the state to finance itself through taxation or borrowing depends on the state of the economy. If economic activity is in decline,

the state will have difficulty maintaining its revenues at an adequate level. Second, public support for a regime will decline sharply if the regime presides over a serious drop in the level of economic activity, with a parallel rise in unemployment and shortages of key goods. Such a drop in support increases the likelihood that the state managers will be removed from power one way or another.

In other words, even if the tax and transfer system comes under the control of actors who want to increase redistribution from profit takers to wage earners, either for ideological reasons or simply because they think it politically expedient, they probably will not introduce such a redistributive scheme in practice. This is because they recognize that they will pay a large price in the form of (a) reduced societal output and, therefore, a smaller tax base in the future and (b) increased unemployment and, hence, increased opposition, for doing so. Ironically, the very people redistribution is supposed to help—the poor—are most likely to suffer first from any economic downturn because the least productive members in society are likely to be the first to become unemployed (Hibbs 1987). As a result, structural Marxists argue that strongly redistributive tax and transfer systems are likely to be self-defeating—they hurt those they are intended to help—and that the political benefits of such policies will be fleeting—state managers are likely to be punished for causing an economic downturn. In this sense, capitalists "have a veto over state policies in that their failure to invest at adequate levels can create major political problems for the state managers" (Block 1977, 15). It is precisely for this reason that some political scientists talk of the "**structural dependence of the state on capital**" (Przeworski and Wallerstein 1988). If structural Marxists are correct, then a change in "who governs" is not likely to have

> The **structural dependence of the state on capital** is a theory suggesting that capitalists have a veto over state policies in that their failure to invest at adequate levels can create major problems for the state managers.

much of an effect on the tax and transfer system. Consequently, a change from dictatorship to democracy will *not* have the negative effect on economic growth suggested by the Meltzer-Richard model discussed earlier.

It is important to recognize that the predictions we have drawn from Przeworski's model depend on many implicit assumptions that may or may not be satisfied in any given situation. The first, and least problematic, assumption is that the distribution that maximizes societal output (*M*) returns a larger share of society's product to the profit takers than to the wage earners. Recall that it was this assumption that led us to place point *M* on the technological possibility frontier to the left of the egalitarian point in Figure 9.3. Historical experience tells us that this is probably a reasonable assumption. What happens, however, if the reverse is true and the distribution that maximizes societal output returns a larger share of society's product to the wage earners rather than the profit takers? In other words, what happens if point *M* is to the right of the egalitarian point? Well, it turns out that any attempt to reach a more egalitarian distribution from this point would still result in a decline in societal output. The difference is that the decline would now occur because workers choose to work less and not because capitalists decide to disinvest. In effect, we would be talking about the structural dependence of the state on labor in this scenario. The bottom line, though, is that there would be a drop in societal output and, as a result, there would be similar incentives not to implement a redistributive tax and transfer system; the potential trade-off between equality and growth remains.

The second assumption concerns the expected effect of capital flight on the amount of societal output going to wage earners. Although aggressive redistribution by wage earners in a democracy will reduce societal output, it is important to remember that wage earners will get a larger (more egalitarian) share of the "smaller" economic pie as a result of increased government transfers. Thus, there may be conditions under which wage earners are better off pushing for redistribution rather than opposing it. Ultimately, aggressive redistribution will be deterred only if the threat of capital flight by profit takers is sufficiently large to shrink societal output to such an extent that wage earners end up worse off than if there were no redistribution. Whether this is the case depends on the alternatives that capitalists have. For example, if it is relatively easy for capitalists to direct their resources away from investment into consumption or from domestic investment into foreign investment, then aggressive redistribution is likely to result in a sharp and immediate economic decline that hurts wage earners. Thus, democracy is less likely to lead to aggressive redistribution and, hence, lower economic growth when the capitalists that influence the economy have what we referred to in Chapters 3 and 6 as "credible exit threats." [6] In contrast, democracy is much more likely to lead to aggressive redistribution when there are constraints on international capital markets or when immobile asset holders dominate the economy. When capital markets are constrained or immobile asset holders dominate, the poor are relatively free to redistribute wealth from the rich to themselves, safe in the knowledge that it is hard for the rich to remove their assets from the economy. Evidence in support of this claim can be seen in the rapid expansion of redistributive tax and transfer systems that occurred when international capital markets collapsed between 1918 and 1939, and in the aggressive redistribution that occurs in a whole range of countries (the Persian Gulf states, Norway, Venezuela, and so on) whose economies are dominated by the "immobile" oil sector.

To this point, we have shown that any movement away from a distribution of resources that maximizes societal output (M) toward a more egalitarian division results in a reduction in output. We should note that *any* movement from point M, whether toward a more equal division of resources or a more unequal one, leads to a decline in output. For example, allocating a greater share of resources to profit takers—moving from M toward P^* in Figure 9.3—also leads to a decline in societal output. This is because workers no longer receive their full return on

---

6. As we noted earlier, many political scientists have argued that economic inequality undermines democratic stability. The idea is that as inequality rises, the poor become more likely to vote to expropriate the rich and, as a result, the rich become more likely to try to undermine democracy to prevent this from happening. It is worth noting that the argument that we have just presented indicates that inequality does not necessarily have a negative effect on democratic stability in all situations. Even in highly unequal societies, the poor may have few incentives to vote for the expropriation of the rich if they recognize that doing so will lead to capital flight, economic decline, and a worsening of their own situation. Given this, the rich may decide that there is no need to block or undermine democracy. In effect, our argument suggests that economic inequality should only harm the prospects for democracy in those countries where capitalist elites do not have sufficiently credible exit threats.

AESOP'S FABLE
The Goose with the Golden Eggs

"One day a countryman going to the nest of his Goose found there an egg all yellow and glittering. When he took it up it was as heavy as lead and he was going to throw it away, because he thought a trick had been played upon him. But he took it home on second thoughts, and soon found to his delight that it was an egg of pure gold. Every morning the same thing occurred, and he soon became rich by selling his eggs. As he grew rich he grew greedy; and thinking to get at once all the gold the Goose could give, he killed it and opened it only to find nothing." (www.aesopfables.com)

their labor and, therefore, decide to consume more leisure rather than work. At a certain point, this may even be involuntary—workers who receive less than subsistence will be too sick or malnourished to work. The Nobel Prize–winning economic historian Robert Fogel (2004) estimates that, throughout most of human history, the average person consumed enough food to work for only about two hours a day. As a result, even dictators are likely to try to move the distribution of societal output toward *M*, lest they "kill the goose that lays the golden eggs."

In conclusion, tracing a link between democracy and economic growth through the protection of property rights and the rule of law is extremely difficult. The basic problem is that although effective property rights and the rule of law appear to promote economic growth, it is not at all clear that democracies are better at protecting property rights or implementing the rule of law than dictatorships. As a result, it is extremely difficult to tell a compelling story about the effect of regime type on economic growth if the causal mechanism has to do with the protection of property rights. On the one hand, does the state itself or do the poor pose the more important threat to investment and production? If it is the state, then democracies (in which the predatory powers of the state are limited) should experience higher economic growth. If it is the ability of the poor to expropriate the rich through a redistributive tax scheme, then dictatorships should experience higher economic growth. On the other hand, if the structural Marxists are correct and state managers—whatever their ideological stripe—are able to figure out that tax and transfer systems that produce income distributions that fail to maximize societal output are self-defeating, then who rules—democrats or dictators, the bourgeoisie or the proletariat—will have little effect on the amount of redistribution in society, and, therefore, little effect (at least by the mechanism presently under consideration) on economic growth.

Consumption versus Investment

A second argument linking regime type and economic growth is based on the claim that democracy encourages workers to consume their assets immediately rather than invest them (de Schweinitz 1959; Galenson 1959). As a result of this consumption, democracies are expected to produce poor economic growth. Note that this story is different from the previ-

---

Box 9.2

CONSUMPTION VERSUS INVESTMENT
The Trade-off

For the sake of argument, let's say a potential investor has 100 units of after-tax income. Should she consume it immediately or invest it? If she consumes it, she can consume all of it. If she invests it, it may grow and she will have more to consume in the future. Let's assume that she is confident that the return on her investment will be 10 percent per year. Her choice between consumption and investment, therefore, comes down to a choice between consuming 100 units this year or 110 units next year. Clearly 110 units are better than 100 units, but most people "discount" the future. That is, 100 units of consumption today is typically better than waiting a year to consume the same 100 units. Whether 100 units today will be better than 110 units a year from now, however, will depend on a person's discount factor. Suppose, for example, that a person thinks that 105 units next year is as good as 100 units today. Given the choice between consuming today or investing with an expected return of 10 percent, the person will choose to invest. This is because if the person believes that 105 units next year is as good as 100 units today, then she must think that 110 units next year is *better* than 100 units today. Now, imagine that the government imposes a 55 percent tax on any profits that come from investments. This means that 5.5 units of the 10-unit profit that she expects to make from investing will have to be given to the government. As a result, investing 100 units today will allow her to walk away with only 104.5 units next year. Suddenly, consuming today is preferred to investing.

---

ous argument in that we are now talking about investment by workers rather than investment by economic elites. The claim is that poor people (workers) tend to consume rather than invest. The intuition is that the poor cannot afford to direct their assets away from immediate consumption—they need to eat and pay the rent today—toward investment for the future. When workers can organize by forming political parties or trade unions, as they can in democracies, they have the ability to drive wages up, thereby reducing profits for business owners and, hence, overall investment. Because workers can vote in democracies, the government also has incentives to direct money toward them and away from investment in the economy, thereby slowing economic growth even further. If democratic governments fail to do this and instead promote saving and investment too heavily, they will likely be voted out of office. In contrast, if dictators are future oriented—they care about the future—then they can use their power to force people to save, thereby launching economic growth. As Rao (1984, 75) puts it,

> Economic development is a process for which huge investments in personnel and material are required. Such investment programs imply cuts in current consumption that would be painful at the low levels of living that exist in almost all developing societies. Governments must resort to strong measures and they must enforce them with an iron hand in order to marshal the surpluses needed for investment. If such measures were put to a popular vote, they would surely be defeated. No political party can hope to win a democratic election on a platform of current sacrifices for a *bright future*. (Rao's italics)

As you may have noticed, a lot of implicit assumptions underpin this story. For example, it is assumed that the poor have a higher propensity to consume than the rich and that economic growth is primarily driven by capital investment. Even if we were to accept these assumptions, it still does not follow that dictatorships will produce better economic growth than democracies unless we happen to also assume that dictators care more about the future than democratic leaders. But why would this necessarily be the case? In effect, without a clear set of expectations about the incentives and constraints facing both democratic leaders and dictators, it is difficult to tell a compelling story about how each will behave. As a result, this second argument also fails to provide clear predictions about whether democracies or dictatorships will produce higher economic growth.

Autonomy from Special Interests

A third argument linking regime type and economic growth has to do with the claim that dictators are not subjected to as many pressures from special interests as democratic leaders. This claim is based on the intuition that democratic leaders are more heavily influenced by special interests because they can so easily be voted out of office if they fail to retain the political and financial support of powerful interest groups. Unfortunately, some political scientists use the claim that dictators enjoy more autonomy from special interests than democratic leaders do in order to argue that dictatorships are better for economic growth, and some use it to argue the exact opposite, that is, that dictatorships are worse for growth.

One story states that because dictators are insulated from the pressures of interest groups (both business and labor), they do not need to spend money in an inefficient manner to keep various electoral constituencies happy. In effect, dictators have the ability to make difficult short-term policy decisions that will have good long-term effects on the economy. As a result, dictatorships will produce better economic growth than democracies. We hope you have noticed the key assumption behind this story—the dictator *chooses* to promote economic growth. But why would the dictator necessarily choose to do this? As long as the dictator is satisfied with his own share of the annual revenue, why should the national level of economic growth matter? Do you think it is reasonable to assume that dictators are necessarily benevolent and that they behave in the national interest?

The second story basically states that dictators who are autonomous and insulated from pressure groups will be able to behave in a predatory way because there is no one to constrain their behavior. As a result, economic elites will be less likely to invest and continue to produce because they will be worried that a predatory dictator will confiscate all of their wealth and profits. Given the lack of investment, economic growth is expected to be low. Political scientists who make this type of argument go one step further and claim that economic growth will be lower in dictatorships than in democracies. As you'll quickly realize, the implicit assumption necessary to make this final leap is that democracies protect property rights (limit state predation) better than dictatorships. We have already seen from our earlier discussion of economic growth and property rights, however, that this assumption is extremely hard to defend from both a theoretical and empirical point of view.

We suspect that you have not found the various causal arguments that we have presented linking regime type and economic growth entirely convincing. You almost certainly have noticed that they reach quite different predictions. But what does the empirical evidence say? Do democracies or dictatorships produce higher economic growth in the real world? In an overview of eighteen different studies (with twenty-one different findings in total) examining the effect of regime type on economic growth, Przeworski and Limongi (1993) report that eight find that dictatorships grow faster, eight find that democracies grow faster, and five find that regime type has no effect on growth. They conclude that "we do not know whether democracy fosters or hinders economic growth. . . . Our own hunch is that politics does matter, but *'regimes' do not capture the relevant differences*" (65; italics added). Before looking further at how politics might matter for things like economic growth, we turn briefly to some data on other indicators of material well-being that should shed some light on how well different regimes perform.

Empirical Evidence of the Effect of Democracy on Government Performance

How does a country's level of democracy affect the material well-being of its citizens? In Figure 9.4, we show how the average level of democracy in eighty-eight countries between 1960 and 1990 is associated with six different indicators of material well-being: (a) wealth as measured by GDP per capita, (b) the percentage of births attended by a physician, (c) the percentage of pregnant women receiving prenatal care, (d) the percentage of infants and children receiving vaccinations, (e) infant and child (under five years of age) mortality rates per thousand, and (f) life expectancy as measured in years. Given that we are interested in how the *level* of democracy influences material well-being, we employ Polity IV's continuous measure of democracy in our plots (Marshall and Jaggers 2003). As you will recall from our discussion of democracy measures in Chapter 5, Polity IV codes a country's level of democracy on a scale that ranges from −10 (most dictatorial) to +10 (most democratic). Data on the various indicators of material well-being come from McGuire (2002).

Before examining the information in Figure 9.4, let's first stop to think about what relationship we would expect to find between a country's level of democracy and material well-being. Several theories of regime type suggest that democracies are better than dictatorships at improving the material well-being of their citizens, especially that of their poorest citizens—the people who, arguably, need government assistance the most. One idea is that the poor are able to vote leaders out of office in a democracy if their political leaders do not implement policies aimed at improving their situation. As a result, democratic leaders have an incentive to help the poor. A second idea has to do with the fact that democratic regimes are typically characterized by a greater freedom of the press than dictatorships (Sen 1981, 1999). This means that democratic governments—and their electorates—are more likely to be aware of the serious problems faced by the poor in the first place. Thus, democratic governments are in a position to act to alleviate the problems, and the electorate are in a position to evaluate these efforts. In contrast, dictatorships are more likely to be able to censor embarrassing new stories. For example, it seems reasonable to think that a dictatorship might well have tried to suppress the diffusion of the shocking images that were broadcast from New Orleans in the wake of hurricane Katrina in the

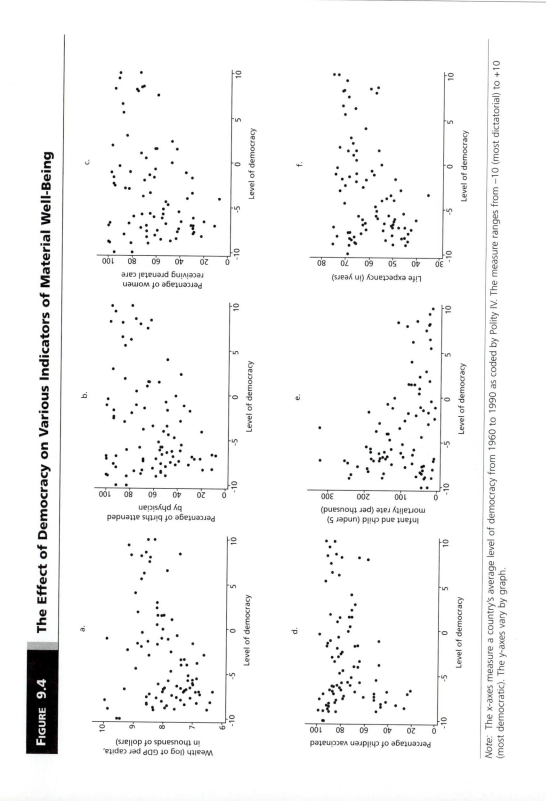

FIGURE 9.4 The Effect of Democracy on Various Indicators of Material Well-Being

Note: The x-axes measure a country's average level of democracy from 1960 to 1990 as coded by Polity IV. The measure ranges from −10 (most dictatorial) to +10 (most democratic). The y-axes vary by graph.

United States in 2005. The third idea is simply that democratic leaders provide more public goods and more redistribution from the rich to the poor than dictators. Some argue that democratic leaders do this because they expect it to help them win elections and stay in power (McGuire and Olson 1996; Lake and Baum 2001). Others argue that they do this because democratic governments have a broader range of supporters to appease, which creates incentives for democratic leaders to produce public, rather than private, goods (Ghorbarah, Huth, and Russett 2004).[7] If any of these arguments are correct, then we should see a clear trend in the data showing that government performance is better when countries are more democratic.

A first glance at the information in Figure 9.4 might lead one to think that there is very little relationship between democracy and the various indicators of material well-being. Notice, however, the "triangular" nature of the data in each of the plots. This feature of the data indicates an interesting asymmetry suggesting that although democracies seldom perform poorly in terms of these indicators of material well-being, they frequently fail to outperform a substantial number of dictatorships. Put differently, although it appears that dictatorships often produce outcomes that are substantially worse than most democracies, some seem to perform every bit as well as democracies. In other words, democracy appears to be *sufficient* for ensuring some degree of success in these various areas of material well-being, but it is obviously not *necessary* for success.

Triangular data like that seen in Figure 9.4 are often a sign that the variables being captured are related through a process of complex causation. In this case, they suggest that there is greater variability in the performance of dictatorships than in that of democracies. As a result, attempts to gauge the differences in performance between democracies and dictatorships that fail to take account of the variation *among* dictatorships are likely to be misleading at best and wrong at worst. Making sense of the variability in performance among dictatorships, therefore, is crucial if we are to get a clear picture of the effects of democracy on material well-being. That said, it will not do to just remove the high-performing dictatorships, declare them "different," and estimate the difference in performance between democracies and the remaining dictatorships in an attempt to confirm our prejudices about

Veiled students at computers in the library of the Zayed University in Abu Dhabi, United Arab Emirates, March 5, 2005.

---

7. Some have argued, however, that even if democracies do redistribute at higher levels than dictatorships, and even if democracies do provide more public goods than dictatorships, these policies are not necessarily directed *at the poor;* rather, they are directed at the middle class (Ross 2006).

bad dictatorial performance. Instead, it is important to understand *why* some dictatorships perform poorly and some do not.[8]

Thus far, we have seen contradictory theoretical and empirical evidence suggesting that we don't really know if, how, or why regime type matters for economic growth or a host of other political outcomes that we generally think are important for ensuring a good quality of life. Does this mean that political institutions such as regime type have no effect on policy and outcomes? We believe that this is too quick and too pessimistic a conclusion to draw. As we are about to demonstrate, political institutions do, in fact, matter a great deal for determining the type of performance that governments have incentives to provide. Institutions do matter for government performance, but you will see that thinking about the world in terms of democracies and dictatorships is not always the most useful approach to explaining how or why. In the next section, we lay out a theory—the Selectorate Theory—that clearly links institutions with governmental performance.

SELECTORATE THEORY

The basic assumption underpinning Selectorate Theory is that all political leaders, whether of democracies or dictatorships, are motivated by the desire to gain and maintain office. Of course, political leaders may have other goals as well, such as implementing particular policies or helping certain groups in society. Although the Selectorate Theory does not deny this, it argues that the competitive nature of politics forces leaders in all regimes to at least behave "as if" they desire to gain and maintain office. Political actors who fail to exert effort on gaining and retaining power are likely to be replaced by competitors who do exert such effort. Knowing that they can achieve whatever goals that motivate them only if they win, all political leaders are, therefore, forced to act as if they care about gaining and maintaining office even if this is not their primary motivation. It turns out that a large proportion of a leader's systematic behavior can be understood from this perspective. A key part of this perspective is that there is a competitor willing, at any moment, to replace the incumbent leader. It is important to recognize that leaders, whether democratic or dictatorial, always face political competition; someone else always wants to be the leader, and current leaders must continually guard against losing power to these competitors.[9]

The puzzle posed by the authors of the Selectorate Theory, Bueno de Mesquita, Smith, Siverson, and Morrow (2003; hereafter referred to as BDM^2S^2), is the following: if all political leaders have the same (induced) goals, why do we get variance in political outcomes? In other words, why do some leaders produce good economic outcomes and some leaders produce bad ones? Why do some leaders provide public goods but others don't? Why do some

---

8. The presence of oil wealth in mainly dictatorial countries leaps to mind as one possible explanation for the dictatorial "over-achievers" shown in Figure 9.4. A closer examination of the data, however, reveals that only some, and by no means most, of the dictatorial over-achievers are oil exporters. As you are no doubt aware, many OPEC members have less-than-distinguished performance records.

9. It is often much easier to identify political challengers in democracies than in dictatorships. Competitors who seek to replace a dictator are likely to face significant threats to their lives, and as a result they tend to keep a low profile until they deem the moment right to challenge the dictator. The fact that we are not always able to identify who the competitors are in a dictatorship should not lead us to think that there is no political competition or that the dictator is unchallenged.

leaders engage in kleptocracy or corruption but others don't? Why do some leaders adopt policies that lead to peace and prosperity but others adopt policies that lead to war and ruin?

Given that all political leaders wish to gain power and keep it, you might think that they would all want to produce good economic performance. It turns out, however, that good economic performance does not necessarily result in longevity in power. For example, BDM^{2}S^2 (2003, 273–276) provides both a list of the twenty-five "best" leaders in regard to their provision of peace and prosperity from 1955 to 2002 and a list of the top twenty-five longest-ruling leaders in the same time period.[10] There is *no overlap* between the leaders on the two lists. The twenty-five highest-performing leaders average an annual economic growth rate of 7 percent; fourteen of the twenty-five longest-ruling leaders average an annual growth rate of 4.4 percent (the others do not report their economic data). The high-performing leaders last just six years in office on average, whereas the longest-ruling leaders last 35.1 years. These data would seem to suggest that producing good performance leads to short terms in office, whereas poor performance produces long stretches of time in office. Why, then, do some political leaders ever produce good performance? What explains the variation in the performance of political leaders?

Institutions

Selectorate Theory characterizes all governments by their location in a two-dimensional institutional space. One dimension is the size of the selectorate, and the second dimension is the size of the winning coalition.

Selectorate Theory argues that the variation in the performance of political leaders can be explained in regard to the institutional environment in which they operate. Some institutional environments encourage political leaders to behave in ways that benefit society, whereas other environments encourage them to behave in ways that benefit only themselves and a few others. Each country has a fundamental set of institutions or rules that govern interactions between residents within its borders. These include rules that define who is **disenfranchised,** who is part of the **selectorate,** and who is part of the **winning coalition.** The relationship between the disenfranchised, the selectorate, and the winning coalition in a country is shown graphically in Figure 9.5.

The **disenfranchised** are those residents who do not have the legal right to participate in choosing the government. The **selectorate** is the set of people who can play a role in selecting the leader. The **winning coalition** includes those people whose support is necessary for the leader to stay in power.

The disenfranchised are all those residents who do not have the legal right to participate in choosing the government. As Bueno de Mesquita (2006, 416) notes, "Most people throughout history have been part of this group. In monarchies, everyone except a handful of aristocrats was in the disenfranchised group. When John Lackland became King John of England in 1199,

---

10. Membership on the first list is based on producing a long-term growth rate in the top quartile for all governments in the period, avoiding involvement in wars, and scoring in the top portion of the Freedom House rankings in regard to political rights and civil liberties.

FIGURE 9.5	The Institutional Environment in the Selectorate Theory

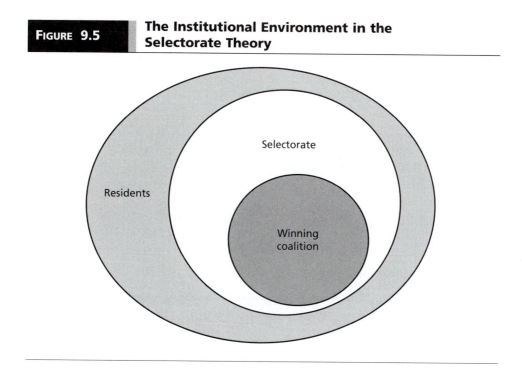

only 197 lay barons, and 39 ecclesiastical barons, had a say in his selection. Everyone else in England was essentially disenfranchised."

The selectorate (S) is the set of people who have a legitimate say, if they so choose, in the selection of the leader. The term *selectorate* is chosen deliberately so as to indicate that the people "selecting" a leader do not necessarily have to do so by voting. In other words, the selectorate is not always the same as an electorate. In some forms of dictatorship, the selectorate is quite small. For example, the selectorate in a monarchy, like that in Saudi Arabia or Oman, typically comprises only members of the royal family, or, perhaps, the wider nobility and certain religious leaders. For example, as we just saw, the selectorate in King John's England consisted of just 236 barons. Similarly, the selectorate in a military junta, like that in Chile under General Augusto Pinochet (1973–1990), usually consists only of members from the armed forces or, perhaps, the heads of each of the military branches. In other forms of dictatorship, though, the selectorate can be quite large. For example, the selectorate arguably consists of all adult citizens with the right to vote in dictatorships that hold rigged elections like Indonesia under President Suharto (1967–1998), Iraq under Saddam Hussein (1979–2003), the Philippines under Ferdinand Marcos (1965–1986), the Soviet Union (1922–1991), and many other states in the Middle East and Africa. Although the selectorate can be small or large in dictatorships, it is nearly always large in democracies. In a democracy, the selectorate comprises all those who are eligible to vote. In the past, certain groups, such as women, nonwhites, and those without property, were ineligible to vote in particular democracies. For example, nonwhites were banned from voting in apartheid South Africa between 1948 and 1994, and women did not get the right to vote until 1945 in France and until as late as 1971 in Switzerland. In most contemporary democracies, however, the selectorate means all adult citizens.

The winning coalition (W) consists of those members of the selectorate whose support is necessary for the leader to remain in power.[11] If the leader is ever unable to keep his win-

---

Box 9.3

AN EXAMPLE OF A SMALL WINNING COALITION
Kenya 1989

Bueno de Mesquita, Smith, Siverson, and Morrow (BDM^{2}S^2) (2003, 55–56) provides the following example from Kenya of how an extremely small winning coalition can determine a country's political leadership with the help of a rigged electoral system.

> The Kenyan government introduced what it called a queue voting system in 1986. Under these rules, instead of using a secret ballot, voters lined up publicly behind a representative of the candidate they supported. If a candidate was deemed to have received 70 percent or more of the vote, the candidate was elected. Otherwise a runoff was held by secret ballot. Many of these queuing elections were rigged by a simple mechanism of lying about how many people lined up in favor of this or that candidate. The ruling party ensured victory by cheating in about one-third of the elections. The case that is of particular interest is striking because of its egregious nature. In it the winning coalition—all the votes it took to elect an official—appears to have been just *one* man.
>
> In a by-election on February 1, 1989, in Kiharu, one candidate—Dr. Julius Kiano—was a former government minister who was highly regarded by the citizens of Kiharu. He was, however, distrusted by the ruling party because of his independence. Indeed, that was why he had been dropped from the government. He was opposed in the by-election by a relatively unknown and inexperienced man named Mweru. A local reporter happened to photograph a chalkboard with the tally of votes: 9,566 (92.46 percent) for Kiano and 780 (7.53 percent) for Mweru. The Returning Officer, charged with responsibility for determining and reporting who won the election, returned voter totals of 2,000 for Kiano and 9,000 for Mweru. Mweru won based on the support of a winning coalition of one man, the Returning Officer (Throup and Hornsby 1998, 42–45). Of course, the winning-coalition size for the whole country—where the same electoral procedure was used—was larger. It surely included at least one individual from each constituency and probably considerably more people whose loyalty to the ruling government was not in doubt. As surely, the winning coalitions in any district did not need to meet the test of majority rule, let alone the 70 percent stipulated for queuing elections.

---

11. To make meaningful cross-national comparisons, the winning coalition and the selectorate are not conceptualized in terms of the absolute numbers of residents who belong to them; rather, they are conceptualized in terms of the *proportion* of residents that they represent.

ning coalition loyal, he will lose his position to a challenger. In democracies, the winning coalition is always quite large and comprises those voters who are required to elect the winning candidate or government. If there are only two candidates or parties at election time, then the winning coalition is as large as a majority of the electorate. In contrast, the winning coalition in a dictatorship is always quite small. For example, the winning coalition in a military junta might be a majority of the officers or a small group of colonels and generals who together control the armed forces. In Communist countries like China or North Korea, the winning coalition is often just a small subset of the Communist Party. In fact, the winning coalition in North Korea was estimated several years ago at between 250 and 2,500 people out of a population of 20 million (Bueno de Mesquita 2006, 417); more recent estimates now put it as low as 73 people.[12] In a monarchy, the winning coalition might consist of a majority of the nobility. As Box 9.3 on a 1989 by-election in Kenya indicates, the winning coalition can, in some circumstances, be as small as one person—the person counting the votes—in dictatorships with rigged electoral systems.

Mapping *W* and *S* onto a Typology of Regimes

As we have noted, the Selectorate Theory is able to differentiate various forms of government—monarchies, military juntas, one-party rigged electoral systems, democracies, and so on—by the size of their selectorate and winning coalition. In Figure 9.6a, we plot the *theoretical* location of these various forms of government in a two-dimensional institutional space, where one dimension is the size of the selectorate and the other dimension is the size of the winning coalition. As you can see, the Selectorate Theory differentiates between different types of dictatorships as well as between dictatorships and democracies. The key factor that distinguishes democracies from dictatorships is the size of the winning coalition. Whereas all dictatorships have small winning coalitions, all democracies have large ones. And the key factor that distinguishes between the different varieties of dictatorships is the size of the selectorate. Dictatorships with rigged electoral systems have large selectorates, whereas military juntas and monarchies tend to have small ones.

As you can imagine, measuring the size of a country's winning coalition and selectorate in the real world is extremely difficult. Nonetheless, BDM^{2}S^2 have attempted to do precisely this. Although BDM^{2}S^2 (2003, 133) are quick to admit that the "measurement of selectorate size and winning-coalition size, especially in nondemocratic states, is in its infancy" and that their "approximations . . . are crude and primitive," their measures appear to have some face validity.[13] In Figure 9.6b we plot the *actual* location of different forms of government by their average selectorate and winning coalition scores from 1946

---

12. This number comes from correspondence with Alastair Smith and Bruce Bueno de Mesquita. These political scientists have recently begun to estimate the size of a country's selectorate and winning coalition through the use of expert surveys.

13. For precise details on how the size of a country's selectorate and winning coalition are measured, see BDM^{2}S^2 (2003, 133–140).

FIGURE 9.6 | Selectorate Theory and Regime-Type Locations

a. Theoretical Regime-Type Locations

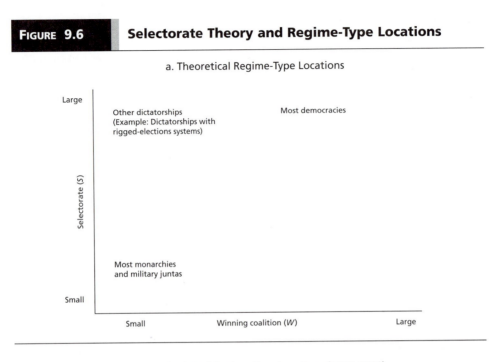

b. Actual Regime-Type Locations (1946–2000)

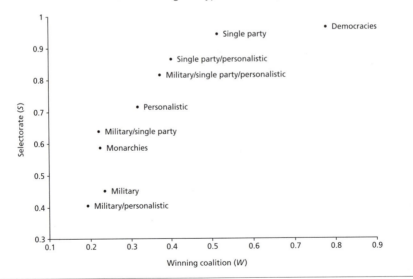

Source: Data on the size of *W* and *S* are from BDM²S² (2003); data on the different forms of dictatorships are from Geddes (2003).

Note: *W* and *S* both range from a minimum of 0 to a maximum of 1. Geddes classifies dictatorships into four types: (a) personalist, (b) military, (c) single-party, or (d) hybrid mixtures of these pure types. Countries that are not classified as one of these four types of dictatorships are either monarchies or democracies; we employ data from Polity IV to determine which were monarchies and which were democracies. For more detailed information about Geddes's classification of dictatorships, see footnote 14.

to 2000.[14] Even though BDM^{2}S^2 do not use information about the form of government to measure the size of a country's selectorate and winning coalition, Figure 9.6b reveals that the scores for each country situate the different forms of government in the two-dimensional institutional space in a manner that is entirely consistent with the theoretical locations shown in Figure 9.6a. As expected, the average size of the winning coalition in a democracy is much larger than that in any of the various forms of dictatorship. Also as predicted, there is considerable variation in the average size of the selectorate among dictatorships, with monarchies and military dictatorships having small selectorates and single-party dictatorships having large ones.

Government Performance

We now look at how the institutional environment in which a leader operates influences government performance. According to the Selectorate Theory, political leaders must keep members of their winning coalition happy in order to stay in power. They can do this by distributing public goods or private goods or both. As you will recall from Chapter 8, public goods benefit everyone in society regardless of whether they are in the winning coalition or not. This is because public goods are non-excludable (once it is provided, anyone can enjoy it) and non-rivalrous (the amount of the good available to be consumed is not diminished by the number of people who consume the good). Examples of public goods might be increased spending on education, health care, and infrastructure. In contrast, private goods benefit only some members of society and not others. In effect, private goods, such as business or export licenses, private jets, villas in the south of France, can be given directly to members of the winning coalition; those who are not members of the winning coalition cannot enjoy the benefits of these private goods. It is the job of an incumbent leader to figure out how many public and private goods to distribute in order to keep his winning coalition loyal.

---

14. The different forms of government are identified with the help of a data set on dictatorships from Geddes (2003, 50–53, 225–232). Geddes classifies all countries (with the exception of monarchies) that endured three or more years of dictatorial rule as (a) personalist, (b) military, (c) single-party, or (d) a hybrid mixture of these pure types. For Geddes, a *military dictatorship* is one in which a group of officers decides who will rule, and these officers exercise influence over policy, for example, Brazil (1964–1985), El Salvador (1948–1984), and South Korea (1960–1987). A *single-party dictatorship* has one party, which dominates both access to political office and control over policy. Poland under the Polish United Workers' Party (PUWP) prior to 1989 and Mexico under the Institutional Revolutionary Party (PRI) prior to 2000 represent examples of single-party dictatorships. A *personalist dictatorship* differs from a military or single-party dictatorship in that access to office and the benefits of office depend on the whims of an individual leader, such as Rafael Trujillo in the Dominican Republic (1930–1961), Ferdinand Marcos in the Philippines (1972–1986), and Idi Amin in Uganda (1971–1979). Dictatorships that exhibit a mixture of characteristics from these three pure types of dictatorship are classified as hybrid dictatorships. For example, Geddes classifies dictatorships like that of Sani Abacha in Nigeria (1993–1999) and Valentine Strasser in Sierra Leone (1992–1996) as military-personalist hybrids because they had personalist leaders with militaries that exerted considerable autonomy and influence. Countries that are not classified as one of these four types of dictatorships by Geddes are either monarchies or democracies. We employed data from Polity IV to determine which were monarchies and which were democracies; fortunately, distinguishing monarchies from democracies is relatively easy.

In addition to deciding what mix of public and private goods to hand out to his winning coalition, the leader must also pick a tax rate. This tax rate ultimately determines how much money the leader has at his disposal to pay for the provision of public and private goods. Depending on the tax rate chosen, residents decide how to allocate their time between economically productive activities and leisure. At the same time that the incumbent is deciding his tax rate and announcing his offer of public and private goods, a challenger also makes an offer to the selectorate (a combination of public goods, private goods, and a tax rate) in an attempt to put together an alternative winning coalition. The bottom line is that the political entrepreneur—the incumbent leader or challenger—who is best able to meet the needs of the relevant actors wins.

Loyalty Norm

It turns out that the manner in which leaders distribute public and private goods depends on the size of the winning coalition and the size of the selectorate. Recall that the goal of the incumbent leader is to stay in power and that to do this he must keep the winning coalition happy. The key for the leader, then, is to stop members of the current winning coalition from defecting. Given this, let's start by thinking about the conditions under which a member of the current winning coalition might decide to defect and shift his loyalty to a challenger. Clearly, any disgruntled member of the winning coalition must weigh the potential risks and rewards from defecting. Oftentimes, there will be more than one potential defector in a winning coalition or multiple challengers to whom they can defect, or both. Moreover, it is almost always the case that there will be members of the selectorate who are not in the winning coalition but who would like to be. As a result, individuals who defect from the current winning coalition have no guarantee that they will end up as part of the next leader's coalition. Indeed, any promise by a challenger to make them part of their future winning coalition if they defect and bring down the incumbent leader is not credible for obvious reasons. Thus, individuals who choose to defect risk losing access to the private goods that they presently enjoy as members of the current winning coalition.

The risk that members of the winning coalition face when they think about defecting is embodied in the ratio of the size of the winning coalition to the size of the selectorate (W/S). The ratio W/S essentially represents the probability that a member of the selectorate will be in any winning coalition. As a result, it indicates the probability that someone who defects from the current winning coalition will be in the next winning coalition. Members of the selectorate have only a small chance of being in the winning coalition when W/S is small (when few people in the selectorate are needed to form a winning coalition), but they have a large chance when W/S is large (when many people in the selectorate are needed to form a winning coalition). As you can imagine, the size of W/S has important implications for the loyalty of members in the current winning coalition. If W/S is small, then members of the winning coalition are likely to be intensely loyal to the incumbent leader because they realize that they are lucky to be part of the winning coalition and that they have a low probability of being in anyone else's winning coalition. As W/S gets larger and the probability of being in the next leader's winning coalition increases, this loyalty to the incumbent leader naturally declines.[15] In effect, W/S represents a sort of **loyalty norm**: there is a strong loyalty norm in small W/S systems and a weak loyalty norm in large W/S systems.

> The strength of the **loyalty norm** is determined by W/S—the probability that a member of the selectorate will be in the winning coalition. Members of the winning coalition are most loyal when W/S is small and least loyal when W/S is large.

The existence or absence of a strong loyalty norm has important implications for the performance of leaders in power. For example, political leaders in small W/S systems with strong loyalty norms have greater opportunities to engage in **kleptocracy** and **corruption** than leaders in large W/S systems with weak loyalty norms. Why? Consider the following example of two societies, A and B. In both societies, the

> **Corruption** is when public officials take illegal payments (bribes) in exchange for providing benefits for particular individuals. **Kleptocracy** is when corruption is organized by political leaders with the goal of personal enrichment.

political leader has $1 billion in tax revenue to distribute among the 1,000 members of his winning coalition and himself. The only difference between the two societies is that the selectorate is made up of 100,000 people in society A and just 10,000 people in society B. In effect, society A has a stronger loyalty norm (smaller W/S) than society B. It is easy to see that both of the leaders in societies A and B could pay each member of their winning coalitions up to $1 million in private goods to win over their support; that is, $1 billion divided equally among the 1,000 people in the winning coalition. As we'll see, though, neither leader has to actually pay out this much to ensure the loyalty of their winning coalition. In fact, it also turns out that the leader of society A, by taking advantage of the strong loyalty norm in his country, does not have to pay out as much as the leader of society B to keep his winning coalition happy. Ultimately, this means that the leader in society A can keep more of his tax revenue for his own discretionary use (kleptocracy)—perhaps to buy palaces, private jets, or whatever else he might desire. How does all this work exactly?

Let's start with society A. The probability that a member of the current winning coalition will be a member of the next leader's coalition if he defects is just 1 percent; that is, $W/S = 1,000/100,000 = 0.01$. It is this low probability of being in the next leader's coalition that generates the strong loyalty norm we mentioned earlier. Anyone who defects from the current winning coalition in society A has a 1 percent chance of obtaining (at most) $1 million in private goods and a 99 percent chance of obtaining nothing.[16] As a result, the expected value of defecting in terms of private goods is just $10,000, or $1 million $\times$ 0.01 + $0 $\times$ 0.99. All the incumbent leader, therefore, has to do to stay in power is to offer each member of his winning coalition slightly more than $10,000 in private

---

15. In the language of the Exit, Voice, and Loyalty model examined in Chapters 3 and 6, a large W/S indicates that members of the winning coalition have credible exit threats; that is, they can defect and still have a high probability of being in the next leader's winning coalition.

16. A million dollars is the most that a defector can receive because that is the most that a challenger can offer to each member of the winning coalition if all tax revenue is spent on private goods.

goods and come close to matching the provision of public goods promised by any challenger. In effect, the incumbent can skim off for himself the difference between the $1 million per supporter that he could have distributed and the something over $10,000 per supporter that he needs to distribute to stay in power. If the incumbent's challenger offers a particularly attractive set of public goods, then the incumbent can give some of this "slush fund" to his supporters to purchase their continued loyalty (Bueno de Mesquita 2006, 421).

What about society B? Well, the probability that someone in the current winning coalition will be a member of the next leader's coalition if he defects is now 10 percent; that is, $W/S = 1,000/10,000 = 0.1$. This is somewhat higher than in society A and, as a result, the loyalty norm in this society is weaker. The expected value of defecting from the current winning coalition in terms of private goods is $100,000, that is, $1,000,000 \times 0.1 + \$0 \times 0.9$. This means that the incumbent leader in society B has to pay a little more than $100,000 in private goods to each member of his winning coalition and come close to matching whatever provision of public goods a challenger has promised in order to stay in power. In society B, the incumbent gets to skim off for himself the difference between the $1 million per supporter that he could have distributed and the something over $100,000 per supporter that he needs to distribute to stay in power. This is still a lot of money, but it is considerably less than the leader in society A can skim off for himself.

Although we might think that all leaders want to engage in kleptocracy and corruption, the example that we have just provided illustrates that the institutional arrangements in a country influence their ability to do so without jeopardizing their hold on power. Specifically, leaders in small W/S systems (society A) have greater opportunities to "steal" from their citizens by skimming off tax revenue into their own pockets than leaders of large W/S systems (society B). As an example of widespread kleptocracy and corruption, consider the small W/S system of Zaire under Mobutu Sese Seko (1965–1997). Mobutu was reportedly able to put as much as a third of the national budget under his personal control and skim off a quarter of all the profits from the country's vast copper mines. As Rose-Ackerman (1999, 116) notes, "Corruption and predation undermined the formal private sector, and grandiose infrastructure projects were used as sources of payoffs" for Mobutu and his supporters. Indeed, in the thirty-two years that Mobutu was in power, he is estimated to have stolen a staggering $4 billion. As another example, consider the small W/S system of the Philippines under Ferdinand Marcos (1965–1986). Marcos is thought to have stolen somewhere between $5 billion and $10 billion during the thirty-one years that he was in office (BDM^{2}S^2 2003, 167).

The strong loyalty norm that encourages leaders in small W/S systems, such as dictatorships with rigged electoral systems, to engage in kleptocracy also generates incentives for poor public policy more generally. Note that members of the winning coalition in these systems are loyal because (a) the leader provides them with more private goods than any challenger can and (b) they have to worry about being cut out of the next leader's coalition if they decide to defect. It follows from this that as long as members of the winning coalition are being sufficiently "bribed," they do not really care about the material well-being of the citizenry more generally (Bueno de Mesquita 2006, 423). As a result, leaders in small W/S

systems have no incentive to produce good public policy—it does not help them stay in power. Leaders in small *W/S* systems recognize that they stay in power by keeping their supporters happy with private goods. "Just think of Saddam Hussein's success in holding on to power even after a worldwide trade embargo against Iraqi goods left his nation's economy in shambles. . . . As long as Saddam Hussein continued to pay the military well and keep his clansmen happy, he was unlikely to suffer an internal coup" (Bueno de Mesquita 2006, 424). We should note that not only does good public policy fail to help leaders in small *W/S* systems stay in power, it may actually get the leader ousted. This is because allocating resources to things like public goods that benefit the citizenry more widely opens up an opportunity for a challenger to credibly promise to provide more private goods to members of the winning coalition than are currently being provided by the incumbent.

In contrast to these types of systems, large *W/S* systems such as democracies do not have strong loyalty norms. For example, voters in a democracy are unlikely to lose access to private goods, such as particular tax policies or redistributive schemes, that benefit them if they switch their support from the incumbent leader to the leader of an opposition party. As a result, leaders in large *W/S* systems have to work harder to keep their supporters happy and cannot afford to skim off too many resources if they want to stay in power. Moreover, because leaders in large *W/S* systems need more resources to keep their winning coalition loyal, they have a strong incentive to produce good overall economic performance. As a result, they are unlikely to tax or steal from their citizens too much lest this cause the citizens to spend more time relaxing and less time working. Remember that if the citizens do not work, then there will be a smaller economic pie with which the leader can win over the winning coalition. All in all, government performance should be better in large *W/S* systems than in small *W/S* systems—kleptocracy should be lower, taxation and state predation should be lower, economic growth should be higher, and so on.[17]

The Size of the Winning Coalition

In addition to the strength of the loyalty norm (*W/S*), the Selectorate Theory indicates that the manner in which leaders distribute public and private goods also depends on the size of the winning coalition (*W*). Leaders always prefer to use private goods rather than public goods to satisfy their winning coalition. As our example of leaders in societies A and B illustrate, an incumbent leader is always able to defeat a challenger if competition is restricted to the distribution of private goods. This inherent advantage comes from the simple fact that challengers cannot credibly guarantee to put would-be defectors in their own winning coalition. Recognizing the uneven playing field, challengers, therefore, attempt to defeat incumbents by emphasizing the provision of public goods. Not only does this help to explain why challengers

---

17. Although large *W/S* systems encourage leaders to perform well in office, there is no guarantee that good performance will translate into longevity in office. Due to a weak loyalty norm, leaders in large *W/S* systems are likely to survive in office for shorter periods of time than leaders in small *W/S* systems even if they produce better government performance. This helps to explain why democratic leaders rarely last as long in office as even the poorest performing dictators in rigged electoral systems.

spend considerable time criticizing incumbents for their poor performance in tackling corruption and providing food, health care, education, and the like, but it also helps to explain why these same challengers frequently maintain the preexisting system of corruption and do little to increase the provision of public goods when they finally come to power. In this regard, we can think of people like Jomo Kenyatta, who railed against corruption in Kenya before coming to power in 1963, but who then did little to stamp it out while in office (BDM^{2}S^2 2003, 374–375). Kenya has consistently ranked at the bottom of Transparency International's list of corrupt countries.[18] The Selectorate Theory suggests that foreign countries that today promote and support seemingly public-minded opposition leaders, such as Morgan Tsvangirai of the Movement for Democratic Change in Zimbabwe, should not necessarily expect government performance to significantly improve if these opposition leaders ever come to power.

Although incumbent leaders always prefer to use private goods to keep their winning coalition loyal, it turns out that this is not always a viable strategy. Much depends on the size of the winning coalition. As the size of the winning coalition increases, the share of private goods that can go to each member of the winning coalition shrinks. In our earlier example, the leaders in societies A and B had $1 billion in tax revenues to distribute to the winning coalition. Because the winning coalition comprised 1,000 members, the maximum amount of private goods that any one member could receive was $1 million. If the winning coalition in these societies had comprised 1 million members, then the maximum amount of private goods that any one member could have received is just $1,000. Clearly, the private goods deal looks a lot better when the winning coalition is small than when it is large. It follows that the advantage the incumbent has over the challenger in regard to the provision of private goods shrinks as the winning coalition gets larger. At some point, the winning coalition is so large that it is no longer efficient or viable for the leader to buy the support of the winning coalition with just the help of private goods. In effect, the value of the private goods going to each member of the winning coalition becomes so small that the members would obtain more value if the leader provided public goods. An implication of this is that leaders in small W systems (dictatorships) will tend to use private goods to stay in power, whereas leaders in large W systems (democracies) will primarily use public goods. The fact that democratic leaders simply do not have sufficient resources to "bribe" all the people they need to win an election with private goods helps to explain why political competition in contemporary democracies is nearly always a contest over public goods—who has the best education policy, who has the best health care plan, and so on.

In Figure 9.7, we summarize how a leader's institutional environment (W and S) affects government performance and the material well-being of citizens. The dotted line indicates those positions where W/S is large; that is, the loyalty norm is low. Note that W/S can be large when both W and S are large, as in democracies, or when both W and S are small, as in military juntas and monarchies. As Figure 9.7 illustrates, we can think of three different levels of government performance—good, middling, poor—depending on the institutional environ-

---

18. Transparency International is a nongovernmental organization that produces an annual Corruptions Perceptions Index for countries around the world. Highly corrupt countries have low scores. This index is based on surveys that ask businessmen and analysts about their perceptions of the level of corruption in each country.

ment in place. Government performance is likely to be good when *W* and *W/S* are both large (democracies). This is because leaders are likely to provide public goods rather than private goods (*W* is large) and because the weak loyalty norm (*W/S* is large) forces leaders to work hard to stay in office.

In contrast, government performance is likely to be poor when *W* and *W/S* are both small (dictatorships with rigged electoral systems). In countries with this type of institutional environment, leaders have little incentive to care about the state of the national economy or the material well-being of the citizenry in general. Instead, they provide small amounts of private goods to members of their winning coalition and engage in highly kleptocratic and corrupt activities. The only thing keeping these types of leaders from excessive predation is the refusal of residents to work and therefore the lack of anything to prey on. This constraint is obviously much weaker if the country is rich in natural resources, such as oil and minerals, or if the leaders receive significant amounts of foreign aid (Smith 2007).

Government performance is likely to be middling when *W* is small and *W/S* is large (monarchies and military juntas). Although leaders in these types of system provide few public goods to the general citizenry, they are forced to care about their own overall performance in office because of the weak loyalty norm at work. For example, leaders have an incentive to produce reasonably good economic performance, because this is the only way

FIGURE 9.7   The Selectorate Model and Government Performance

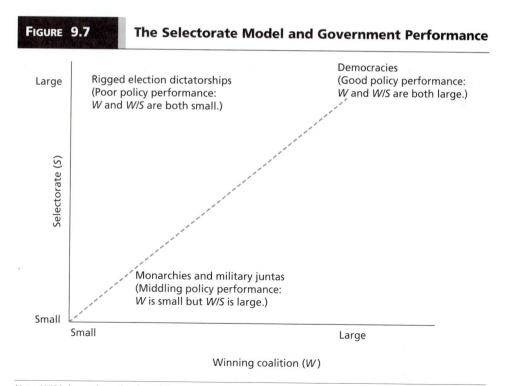

Note: W/S is large along the dotted line.

of generating the necessary resources to pay off their not-so-loyal winning coalition. That these leaders are interested in good economic performance necessarily means that they also care, to some extent, about the material well-being of the residents who make up the workforce, and thus have an incentive to provide some basic public goods.

As you'll no doubt have realized, the theoretical predictions about government performance shown in Figure 9.7 are entirely consistent with our earlier empirical results in Figure 9.4. Recall that those empirical results suggest that whereas democracies tend to produce relatively good government performance, the performance of dictatorships varies considerably. Some dictatorships appear to perform quite well, and others seem to perform extremely poorly. As we can now see, the Selectorate Theory offers a potential explanation for this variation in the performance of dictatorships. On the one hand, dictatorships with rigged electoral systems are likely to produce poor government performance because they are characterized by small winning coalitions and strong loyalty norms. On the other hand, monarchies and military juntas are likely to produce reasonably good government performance because they are characterized by weak loyalty norms.

Before examining whether there is any empirical evidence to support the Selectorate Theory, we should stop and ask ourselves what this all means for the *type* of leader necessary to generate good public policy. By now you should realize that implementing good public policy is not as simple as identifying decent human beings who genuinely want to improve their fellow citizens' lives and then ensuring that these people rise to political power. It turns out that having a civic-minded leader is neither necessary nor sufficient for successful public policies. Simply put, what is needed for good public policy is a set of institutions that creates a large *W*, large *W/S* system. If the political institutions in a country are such that a large proportion of the residents can participate in choosing their leader and the leader depends on a large proportion of that selectorate to remain in power, then only leaders who provide a sufficiently high level of government performance will be *able* to stay in power. It doesn't matter whether the leader cares about providing good government performance for its own sake or whether he cares about it only because it helps him stay in power; both goals dictate the same course of action. This results in competition to provide more, and better, public goods, as well as good economic policies designed to generate higher overall revenue. Under such conditions, residents have incentives to invest and the economy is expected to grow.

The bottom line is that even if there are two types of leaders in the world—those that are civic minded and those that are not—all leaders are forced to govern well in large *W*, large *W/S* systems and poorly in small *W*, small *W/S* systems if they want to stay in power. This point is well illustrated by leaders who had the opportunity to rule over very different systems of government. Consider Leopold II (1835–1909), who was king of Belgium (large *W*, large *W/S*) and ruler of the Congo Free State (small *W*, small *W/S*). Consider also Chiang Kai-shek (1887–1975) who ruled China (small *W*, small *W/S*) for twenty years and then Taiwan (large *W*, large *W/S*) for another twenty-five. In both of these cases, the two leaders provided more public goods and better government performance in the large *W*, large *W/S* systems that they governed (BDSM^{2}S^2 2003, 208–213). For more details, see Box 9.4 on Leopold II.

THE TALE OF TWO LEOPOLDS

Leopold II is remembered as an excellent king of Belgium (1865–1909) who provided his subjects with significant amounts of public goods, instituted progressive reforms, and promoted high levels of economic growth and industrial development. For example, he gave workers the right to strike, expanded the suffrage, set limits on child labor, introduced educational improvements, and supported massive public works projects designed to lower unemployment and enhance the economy.

While Leopold was presiding over this set of progressive policies in Belgium, he was taking a decidedly different approach in the Congo Free State (1885–1908), over which he also ruled. Leopold created a low-paid military force in the Congo, the Force Publique, and offered the soldiers additional wages based on commissions for goods such as rubber and ivory. Without laws to protect Congolese workers, the members of the Force Publique used slave labor, torture, and murder to meet its quotas. The soldiers were also given rewards for killing "anti-government rebels," although more often than not these were villagers who simply did not want to be forced into slave labor. The soldiers would bring hands (or heads) to the Belgium commissioner as proof of the number of "rebels" that had been killed; eyewitness accounts report that some of these hands obviously belonged to women and children, and suggested that ordinary Congolese were being killed because doing so meant that soldiers could get higher wages. Leopold and the Force Publique gained incredible riches from the sale of ivory and rubber on the world market. This revenue was not returned to the Congo Free State in the form of public goods to benefit its residents. The only goods exported to the Congo, in fact, were weapons for the Force Publique to keep the flow of goods (the result of slave labor) headed toward Belgium. Thus Leopold was allowing—even promoting—slave labor in the Congo at the same time as he was promoting laws protecting workers in Belgium.

What was different about the institutions in the two countries? Belgium was a constitutional monarchy, which means that Leopold's rule relied on the support of a popularly elected government. The winning coalition size was reasonably large. By contrast, the Congo Free State was considered to be Leopold's personal property. Leopold's winning coalition in the Congo consisted of just himself and the members of the Force Publique. As the Selectorate Theory predicts, Leopold worked hard to promote economic growth and provide significant amounts of public goods when his winning coalition was large (Belgium) but provided small amounts of private goods for his supporters and stole the rest of the revenue for himself when the winning coalition was small (Congo).

Which was the real Leopold? BDM^{2}S^2 (2003, 208–213), who provide the account of the two Leopolds that we have drawn on here, conclude that it must have been the "murderous ruler of the Congo" rather than the "civic-minded king of Belgium." Why? Well, Leopold simply inherited his institutions in Belgium and acted accordingly. In contrast, he had free reign to set up any type of government arrangement he wanted in the Congo. Leopold's actions in both countries were entirely consistent with the institutional incentives he faced.

It follows from this discussion that one's preference for the type of institutions in a country depends on one's position in the society: as the leader, a member of the selectorate, a member of the winning coalition, or just a member of the disenfranchised class. Leaders clearly prefer to set up institutions that encourage a small winning coalition and a large selectorate, because these institutions help them not only to stay in power but also to enrich themselves at the expense of their citizenry. Members of the winning coalition like institutions in which W is small but W/S is large: a small W means that the leader will provide its members with private goods, whereas a large W/S guarantees that the leader will have to provide large quantities of these goods to counteract the weak loyalty norm. Members of the selectorate and the disenfranchised classes like institutions in which both W and W/S are large; a large W forces the leader to provide its members with public goods, and the large W/S provides strong incentives for the leader to perform well in office to counteract the weak loyalty norm. In other words, leaders prefer to rule over rigged-electoral systems, members of the winning coalition prefer to live in monarchies or military juntas, and everyone else prefers to live in democracies.

Some Empirical Evidence

We now put some of the implications derived from the Selectorate Theory to the test. Specifically, we ask how the size of a country's W and the size of its W/S affect the material well-being of the citizenry. Recall that we expect better government performance as both W and W/S get larger. In Table 9.2, we show the effect of W and W/S on six different indicators of material well-being: economic growth, wealth as measured by GDP per capita, health care expenditures as a percentage of GDP, education expenditures as a percentage of GDP, infant mortality rates per thousand, and life expectancy in years. We control for the size of the selectorate (S) in each country.

Recall that it is the dependent variable that we want to explain—economic growth, life expectancy, and so on. Our independent or explanatory variables are what we hypothesize might affect the various dependent variables. In each table of results, our explanatory variables are W (and S) in Model 1 and W/S in Model 2. Next to each independent variable is a

TABLE 9.2	**Effect of *W* and *W/S* on Six Indicators of Material Well-Being**

a. Economic Growth

Dependent variable: Economic growth rate.

Independent variables	Model 1	Model 2
W	0.02***	
	(0.005)	
S	−0.004	
	(0.005)	
W/S		0.02***
		(0.004)
Constant	0.01***	0.009***
	(0.004)	(0.003)
N	3,772	3,772
R^2	0.0071	0.0067

b. Wealth

Dependent variable: Log of GDP per capita.

Independent variables	Model 1	Model 2
W	2.30***	
	(0.22)	
S	−0.67***	
	(0.17)	
W/S		1.83***
		(0.19)
Constant	6.97***	6.66***
	(0.15)	(0.13)
N	3,813	3,813
R^2	0.35	0.32

c. Education

Dependent variable: Government spending on education as share of GDP.

Independent variables	Model 1	Model 2
W	2.07***	
	(0.37)	
S	−0.44	
	(0.27)	
W/S		1.8***
		(0.30)
Constant	2.86***	2.63***
	(0.23)	(0.21)
N	3,313	3,313
R^2	0.12	0.12

d. Health Care

Dependent variable: Government spending on health care as share of GDP.

Independent variables	Model 1	Model 2
W	4.09***	
	(0.61)	
S	−0.35	
	(0.51)	
W/S		3.95***
		(0.49)
Constant	3.04***	2.80***
	(0.32)	(0.33)
N	1,204	1,204
R^2	0.22	0.22

continues

TABLE 9.2	Effect of *W* and *W/S* on Six Indicators of Material Well-being (continued)

e. Infant Mortality

Dependent variable: Infant mortality (deaths per 1,000 live births).

Independent variables	Model 1	Model 2
W	−101.5***	
	(8.3)	
S	10.1	
	(6.3)	
W/S		−96.4***
		(7.2)
Constant	113.1***	119.4***
	(6.7)	(6.4)
N	3,365	3,365
R^2	0.33	0.33

f. Life Expectancy

Dependent variable: Life expectancy at birth (in years).

Independent variables	Model 1	Model 2
W	24.6***	
	(1.9)	
S	−2.6*	
	(1.4)	
W/S		23.1***
		(1.5)
Constant	49.0***	47.5***
	(1.3)	(1.3)
N	2,692	2,692
R^2	.34	.33

Source: Data are from BDM²S² (2003) and McGuire (2002).

Note: *W* = winning coalition; *S* = selectorate; *W/S* = loyalty norm; data on *W*, *S*, and *W/S* cover all countries in the world averaged over the time period 1960–1999. Robust standard errors clustered by country are in parentheses.

  * = greater than 90% significant.
  ** = greater than 95% significant.
  *** = greater than 99% significant.

coefficient indicating how an increase in the independent variable affects the dependent variable. For instance, a positive coefficient on *W* would indicate that an increase in the size of the winning coalition increases whatever dependent variable we are considering. Beneath each coefficient is a standard error, which basically tells us how confident we are in our results. As we have done in previous chapters, we use stars, next to the coefficients to indicate our confidence in the results. A coefficient with no stars would suggest that there is no evidence that the independent variable in question has any impact on the dependent variable under consideration.

Let's start by looking at the effect of *W* and *W/S* on economic growth in Table 9.2a. First, we can see that the coefficient on *W* in Model 1 is positive and highly significant. As predicted, this indicates that larger winning coalitions are associated with higher levels of economic growth. Second, we can see that the coefficient on *W/S* in Model 2 is positive and highly significant as well. As predicted, this indicates that countries with weaker loyalty norms (that is, higher *W/S*) are associated with higher levels of economic growth. This same pattern of results is repeated for all of the different indicators of material well-being. Wealth, education, health care expenditures, and life expectancy are all higher and infant mortality is lower when *W* and *W/S* are large. These results offer a great deal of support for two of the key implications derived from the Selectorate Theory. Increasing the size of the winning coalition does lead to better outcomes from the point of view of the average citizen. Likewise, increasing the ratio of *W/S*, thereby making the loyalty norm weaker, also leads to better outcomes. In other words, political institutions do clearly have an effect on the kinds of government policies that are generally thought to be important for the material well-being of citizens around the world.

CONCLUSION

As we noted at the very beginning of this chapter, we live in a world that tends to clearly associate good outcomes with democracy and bad ones with dictatorships. As we have shown, the world, in reality, is much more complex than this. Oftentimes, we have no compelling theoretical reason to believe that democracies outperform dictatorships. For example, we presented several different stories linking regime type to economic growth. They all reached different conclusions. Some suggested that democracy is good for economic growth, whereas others suggested that dictatorship was better. When it comes to the empirical evidence, it does appear that democracies produce a relatively high level of material well-being for their citizens. It is not the case, however, that democracies regularly outperform all dictatorships. Although some dictatorships perform extremely poorly on many different indicators of material well-being, others perform relatively well. As a whole, the empirical evidence suggests that thinking of the world purely in terms of a democracy-dictatorship dichotomy may not be the best way to explain the variation in the performance levels of different countries.

In the second half of this chapter, we presented a new theory—the Selectorate Theory—that provides a potential story both for why democracies produce a relatively high level of material well-being for their citizens and for why some dictatorships perform better than others. Starting from the simple assumption that all political leaders care about winning and retaining power, the Selectorate Theory offers an explanation for the observed variation in the performance of different forms of government that focuses on the institutional structure surrounding political leaders. This "institutional structure" refers primarily to the size of a country's winning coalition and selectorate. As we saw, leaders in systems with large winning coalitions and weak loyalty norms like democracies have to provide public goods and a high level of overall government performance if they want to remain in office. In contrast, leaders in systems with small winning coalitions and strong loyalty norms, like dictatorships with rigged electoral systems, are "forced" to provide private goods and produce a poor level of overall government performance because this is the best way to stay in power in these countries. In between these two ends of the performance spectrum are leaders in systems with small winning coalitions and weak loyalty norms, such as monarchies and military juntas. Although these leaders are more likely to provide private than public goods, they do have to care about their overall government performance because of the weak loyalty norm at work.

KEY CONCEPTS

corruption, *339*
disenfranchised, *332*
kleptocracy, *339*
loyalty norm, *339*
selectorate, *332*

Selectorate Theory, *332*
structural dependence of the
  state on capital, *323*
winning coalition, *332*

PROBLEMS

The following problems address some of the more important concepts and theories introduced in this chapter.

Classifying Political Regimes

1. Rather than classify governments as either democratic or dictatorial, the Selectorate Theory characterizes all governments in regard to their location in a two-dimensional institutional space. One dimension is the size of the selectorate (S) and the second dimension is the size of the winning coalition (W). These two dimensions are graphically shown in Figure 9.8 along with the types of governments that fall into each cell. Use Internet and other resources to determine into which cell of the two-dimensional space in Figure 9.8 each of the following governments should be placed. Explain your answers.

   a. Cuba
   b. Iraq under Saddam Hussein (pre-2003)
   c. United States in 1776
   d. United Arab Emirates
   e. Chile under Augusto Pinochet
   f. Argentina
   g. South Africa under apartheid (pre-1991)
   h. Taiwan
   i. Jordan

FIGURE 9.8	Winning Coalition Size, Selectorate Size, and Government Type

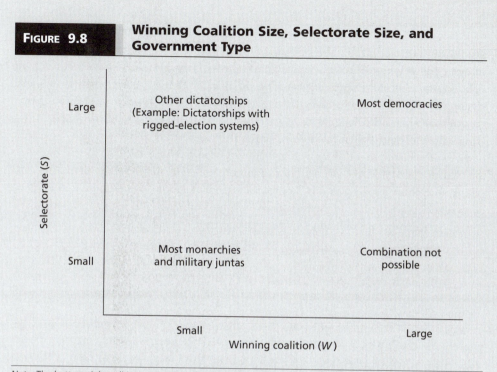

Note: The bottom right cell is empty because, by definition, the winning coalition cannot be larger than the selectorate.

Public and Private Goods

2. In Chapter 8 we introduced the notion of public and private goods.

   a. Name at least three examples of private goods that leaders might use to stay in power. Explain why they are private goods.

   b. Name at least three examples of public goods that leaders might use to stay in power. Explain why they are public goods.

The Distribution of Public and Private Goods: The Size of the Winning Coalition

3. Suppose that a political leader raises $1 billion in tax revenue. Assume that the leader can supply public goods worth $2,000 to each individual in society if he spends all of this tax revenue on providing public goods. Assume also that the size of the winning coalition is 250,000. With all of this in mind, answer the following questions.

a. If the leader were to spend all of the tax revenue on providing private goods, what would the maximum value of the private goods be for each member of the winning coalition if we assume that they all receive the same amount?

b. Would the leader prefer to provide only public goods or only private goods in this situation? Why?

Now suppose that the size of the winning coalition is 750,000. Keeping everything else the same, answer the following questions.

c. If the leader were now to spend all of the tax revenue on providing private goods, what would the maximum value of the private goods be for each member of the winning coalition if we assume that they all receive the same amount?

d. Would the leader prefer to provide only public goods or only private goods in this new situation? Why?

e. Based on the answers you have given and the description of the Selectorate Theory in this chapter, why is providing public goods a more efficient way for leaders in democracies to stay in power?

f. Based on the answers you have given and the description of the Selectorate Theory in this chapter, why is providing private goods a more efficient way for leaders in dictatorships to stay in power?

The Distribution of Public and Private Goods: The Loyalty Norm

4. Suppose that a political leader raises $1 billion in tax revenue. Assume that the size of the winning coalition is 250,000 and that the size of the selectorate is 50 million.

a. If the leader were to spend all of the tax revenue on providing private goods, what would the *maximum* value of the private goods be for each member of the winning coalition if we assume that they all receive the same amount?

b. How much are private goods worth to someone who is not a member of the winning coalition?

c. What is the probability that a member of the selectorate will be a member of the winning coalition?

d. What is the probability that a member of the selectorate will *not* be a member of the winning coalition?

e. Suppose that you, as a member of the winning coalition, are thinking of defecting to the challenger. What is the (maximum) expected value of defecting to the challenger in terms of private goods?

f. Based on your answer to the previous question, how much does the political leader have to give each member of the winning coalition in terms of private goods in order to ensure that the members remain loyal?

g. What is the difference between how much the political leader *could* give each member of the winning coalition and how much the political leader *needs* to give each member of the winning coalition to ensure the members' loyalty?

Now suppose that the size of the selectorate is just 1 million. Keeping everything else the same, answer the following questions.

h. What is the probability that a member of the selectorate will be a member of the winning coalition?

i. What is the probability that a member of the selectorate will *not* be a member of the winning coalition?

j. Suppose that you, as a member of the winning coalition, are thinking of defecting to the challenger. What is the (maximum) expected value of defecting to the challenger in terms of private goods?

k. Based on your answer to the previous question, how much does the political leader have to give each member of the winning coalition in terms of private goods in order to ensure that the members remain loyal?

l. What is the difference between how much the political leader *could* give each member of the winning coalition and how much the political leader *needs* to give each member of the winning coalition to ensure the members' loyalty?

m. Based on the answers you have given and the description of the Selectorate Theory in this chapter, why are leaders in rigged-election dictatorships particularly well placed to steal the state's wealth for themselves?

International Organizations and Economic Development

5. Many international organizations, such as the International Monetary Fund (IMF) and the World Bank (WB), have economic development and the alleviation of poverty as two of their central goals. Although international organizations frequently provide expertise and resources for economic development and poverty relief, these resources are often misappropriated. Consider the recent description of events in Kenya.

> In December 2002 Mwai Kibaki was elected president following the retirement of the long-term incumbent Daniel Arap Moi. Billions of dollars were stolen under Moi's regime. Given worsening economic conditions, aid agencies such as the IMF agreed to the resumption of aid to Kenya. The Kenyan government promised to reduce corruption. Unfortunately, rather than being used to root out corruption, these funds have been largely stolen. The BBC reports that graft has cost Kenya $1 billion under Kibaki's increasingly autocratic regime. A majority of Kenyans believe they are worse off under Kibaki than Moi. (Smith 2005, 566)

a. Would the ongoing corruption in Kenya come as a surprise to someone familiar with the Selectorate Theory? Explain your answer.

b. What does the Selectorate Theory have to say about the potential of international organizations such as the IMF and WB to achieve their goals of economic development and poverty reduction in countries with small winning coalitions? Explain your answer.

10 Democracy and Its Varieties

Democracy is the recurrent suspicion that more than half of the people are right more than half of the time.

E. B. White, *New Yorker,* July 3, 1944

- In this chapter, we look at whether the actual process by which democracies make decisions has appealing features that make it morally or normatively attractive above and beyond any material benefits that it might produce.

- At its very heart, democracy is a system in which the majority is supposed to rule. Still, making decisions that reflect the preferences of a majority can be a lot more complicated and less fair than one might think. Even if all the members of a group have rational preferences, Condorcet's Paradox shows that it might be impossible to reach a stable group decision using majority rule.

- The Median Voter Theorem indicates that stable group decisions can be achieved if we are willing to rule certain preferences out of bounds and reduce the policy space to a single-issue dimension. Unfortunately, neither of these restrictions is uncontroversial.

- Arrow's Theorem proves that no method of group decision making can guarantee a stable group decision while simultaneously satisfying minimal conditions of fairness. In effect, it proves that there is no perfect set of decision-making institutions; either fairness is compromised or there will be a potential for unstable group choices.

- The absence of an ideal decision-making mechanism means that institutional choice is an exercise in the choice of "second bests" and that trade-offs will need to be made. This helps to explain why we observe so many different types of democracy in the world.

OVERVIEW

What kinds of political institutions should we adopt when we have an opportunity to set up new institutions or change existing ones? One obvious way to begin answering this question is to see which sets of institutions produce good outcomes. For example, do democratic regimes produce better material outcomes, say, than dictatorial ones? If they do, then we should recommend adopting some set of democratic institutions. Although it is commonly believed that democracies outperform dictatorships in regard to providing material well-being, our analysis in Chapter 9 suggests that things are not this simple. As we demonstrated in that chapter, citizens living in certain types of dictatorship tend, on average, to enjoy a very high quality of life that easily rivals that of citizens in democracies, at least according to various measures of economic development and growth or the provision of government services, such as health care and education.[1] Indeed, several dictatorships regularly outperform many democracies when it comes to the measures of material outcomes that we examined.

At this point, the philosophy students among you might point out that we are overlooking some important criteria with which to evaluate sets of political institutions. Political philosophers usually use one of two broad approaches for evaluating the moral or ethical value of adopting a given set of institutions. On the one hand, those interested in **consequentialist ethics** ask whether the institutions in question produce good outcomes. This is the approach that we adopted in the previous chapter. On the other hand, those interested in **deontological ethics** attempt to evaluate institutions in a way that is independent of the outcomes that those institutions produce—they ask whether the institutions are good, fair, or just, in and of themselves. In this chapter, we consider democracy from a deontological perspective. In particular, we examine whether the actual process by which democratic governments make decisions for the entire country has appealing properties that make it morally or normatively attractive above and beyond any material benefits that it might produce. In other words, is the process by which decisions are made in democracies inherently good, fair, or just?

> **Consequentialist ethics** evaluate actions, policies, or institutions in regard to the outcomes they produce. **Deontological ethics** evaluate the intrinsic value of actions, policies, or institutions in light of the rights, duties, or obligations of the individuals involved.

People typically assume that a dictatorial decision-making process is inherently unfair, whereas a democratic decision-making process is inherently fair. In what follows, we explore this assumption in some detail and lay out several criteria for evaluating how groups of individuals make decisions.[2] Overall, we think that the results of our analysis will surprise many

---

1. In Chapter 9, we focused on the average level of well-being in a society. An alternative approach would have been to see if democracies are characterized by a more equitable distribution of well-being than dictatorships. We could also have examined a whole host of other measures of government performance in addition to the ones that we focused on.

2. The material in this chapter comes from a part of the political science literature called social choice theory. Social choice theory addresses the voting rules that govern and describe how individual preferences are aggregated to form a collective group preference. Much of this literature is highly mathematical. In this chapter, we focus on providing you with the intuition behind some of the more important ideas in social choice theory. For those of you interested in examining social choice theory in more depth, we suggest starting with Sen (1970), Riker (1982), and Hinich and Munger (1997).

of you. As we demonstrate, there are no perfect decision-making processes—all institutional choices, including the decision to adopt democratic institutions, entail a set of significant trade-offs. It is the existence of these trade-offs that helps to explain, as we will see throughout Part III of this book, why there are so many different types of democracies in the world. In effect, different countries choose to make different trade-offs when they decide to adopt democratic institutions.

PROBLEMS WITH GROUP DECISION MAKING

Many people say that they like democracy because they believe it to be a fair way to make group decisions. One commonsense notion of fairness is that group decisions should reflect the preferences of the majority of group members. We believe that most people would probably agree, for example, that a fair way to decide between two options is to choose the option that is preferred by the most people. When selecting among just two options, the option preferred by the most members of a group is necessarily the option preferred by a majority of the group.[3] At its very heart, democracy is a system in which the majority rules. In this section of the chapter, we show that there are many situations in which "majority rule" is a lot more complicated and less fair than our commonsense intuition about it would suggest. In effect, we demonstrate that allowing the majority to decide can be deeply problematic on many different dimensions.

Majority Rule and Condorcet's Paradox

If a group of people needs to choose between just two options, then majority rule can be quite straightforward, as we just saw. But what if a group needs to choose between more than two options? For example, imagine a city council deciding on the level of social services it should provide.[4] The proposed options are to increase (I), decrease (D), or maintain current (C) levels of social service provision. Assume that the council is made up of three members—a left-wing councillor, a right-wing councillor, and a centrist councillor—who all rank the proposed options differently. Specifically, the left-wing councillor prefers an increase in spending to current levels of spending, and prefers current levels of spending to a decrease. The centrist councillor most prefers current levels of spending, but would prefer a decrease in spending over any increase if it came to it. The right-wing councillor most prefers a decrease in spending. Because he views current levels of spending as unsustainable, however, the right-wing councillor would prefer to "break the bank" with an increase in spending in order to spur much-needed reforms than maintain the status quo. The preference ordering for each of the council members is summarized in Table 10.1.

---

3. A majority of a group is defined here as more than half. If we have a group of size N, and we assume that none of the members of the group are indifferent between the two options on offer, then a majority M of the group would be any subgroup, such that $M \geq \frac{N+1}{2}$. If indifference were allowed, then it is possible for the alternative receiving the most votes to win a plurality without winning a majority of the votes.
4. This example comes from Dixit and Skeath (2004).

TABLE 10.1	City Council Preferences for the Level of Social Service Provision	
Left-wing Councillors	**Centrist Councillors**	**Right-wing Councillors**
$I \succ C \succ D$	$C \succ D \succ I$	$D \succ I \succ C$

Note: I = increased social service provision; D = decreased social service provision; C = maintenance of current levels of social service provision; $\succ$ = "is strictly preferred to."

Let's assume that the council employs majority rule to make its group decisions. In this particular example, this means that any policy alternative that enjoys the support of two or more councillors will be adopted. How should the councillors vote, though? It's not obvious how they should vote given that there are more than two alternatives. One way they might proceed is to hold a **round-robin tournament** that pits each alternative against every other alternative in a set of "pair-wise votes"—I versus D, I versus C, and C versus D—and designates as the winner whichever alternative wins the most contests.[5] If we assume that the councillors all vote for their most preferred alternative in each pair-wise contest (or round), then we see that D defeats I, I defeats C, and C defeats D. The outcomes of these pair-wise contests and the majorities that produce them are summarized in Table 10.2. Notice that there is no alternative that wins most often—each alternative wins exactly one pair-wise contest. This multiplicity of "winners" does not provide the council with a clear policy direction. In other words, the council fails to reach a decision on whether to increase, decrease, or maintain current levels of social service provision.

> A **round-robin tournament** pits each competing alternative against every other alternative an equal number of times in a series of pair-wise votes.

This simple example produces several interesting results that we now examine in more detail. The first is that a group of three *rational* actors (the councillors) make up a group (the council) that appears to be incapable of making a rational decision for the group as a whole.

TABLE 10.2	Outcomes from the Round-Robin Tournament		
Round	**Contest**	**Winner**	**Majority that produced victory**
1	Increase vs. decrease	D	Centrist and right
2	Current vs. increase	I	Left and right
3	Current vs. decrease	C	Left and centrist

---

5. This voting method is also known as Copeland's rule (Riker 1982, 76).

What do we mean by "rational"? When political scientists use the word *rational*, they have a very specific meaning in mind. An actor is said to be **rational** if she possesses a complete and transitive preference ordering over a set of outcomes.[6] An actor has a **complete preference ordering** if she can compare each pair of elements (call them *x* and *y*) in a set of feasible outcomes in one of the following ways—either the actor prefers *x* to *y*, she prefers *y* to *x*, or she is indifferent between *x* and *y*. The assumption of completeness essentially states that an individual can always make up his mind as to whether he prefers one option or is indifferent when presented with a pair of options. What about the assumption of transitivity? Before we

> An actor is **rational** if she possesses a complete and transitive preference ordering over a set of outcomes. An actor has a **complete preference ordering** if she can compare each pair of elements (call them *x* and *y*) in a set of outcomes in one of the following ways—either the actor prefers *x* to *y*, *y* to *x*, or she is indifferent between them. An actor has a **transitive preference ordering** if for any *x*, *y*, and *z* in the set of outcomes it is the case that if *x* is weakly preferred to *y*, and *y* is weakly preferred to *z*, then it must be the case that *x* is weakly preferred to *z*.

get to this, we need to first make a distinction between strict and weak preferences. An actor is said to "strictly prefer" *x* to *y* if *x* is always better than *y*. And he is said to "weakly prefer" *x* to *y* if *x* is at least as good as *y*. An actor has a **transitive preference ordering** if for any *x*, *y*, and *z* in the set of outcomes it is the case that if *x* is weakly preferred to *y*, and *y* is weakly preferred to *z*, then it must be the case that *x* is weakly preferred to *z*. Actors whose preference orderings do *not* meet these conditions—completeness and transitivity—are said to be irrational.

In the example we have been examining, each of the councillors is rational because each has a complete and transitive preference ordering over the three policy alternatives. For example, the left-wing councillor prefers *I* to *C* and *C* to *D*, and also prefers *I* to *D*. The outcome of the round-robin tournament, however, reveals that this set of rational individuals becomes a group that acts like an individual with intransitive preferences. Recall that the group prefers *D* to *I* and *I* to *C*. Transitivity would require, therefore, that the group prefer *D* to *C*. Round three of the round-robin tournament reveals, however, that the group prefers *C* to *D*. This juxtaposition—of rational individuals forming a group that behaves irrationally—was first described in a paper in 1785 by Marie Jean Antoine Nicolas de Caritat, the Marquis de Condorcet, and is usually referred to as **Condorcet's Paradox.**

> **Condorcet's Paradox** illustrates that a group composed of individuals with rational preferences does not necessarily have rational preferences as a collectivity; individual rationality is not sufficient to ensure group rationality.

A second interesting aspect of our example is that a different majority supports the winning alternative or outcome in each round. In round one, the majority that votes in favor of a decrease in social service provision is made up of the centrist and right-wing councillors. In round two, the majority that votes in favor

---

6. Technically, a rational individual must also have a "reflexive" preference ordering. This means that any alternative in the set of outcomes can be thought of as at least as good as itself. As the Nobel Prize-winning economist Amartya Sen (1970, 2–3) has noted, the reflexivity "requirement is so mild that it is best looked at as a condition . . . of sanity rather than of rationality." Most political scientists focus on the conditions of completeness and transitivity as we do here.

of an increase in social service provision is a coalition of "odd bedfellows" comprising the left- and right-wing councillors. Finally, in round three, the majority that votes in favor of the status quo comprises the left-wing and centrist councillors. Although "letting the majority decide" may sound fair and straightforward, our example here makes it very clear that "a majority" does not necessarily exist until the policy debate is framed in a certain way.

As we just noted, Condorcet's Paradox points out that individual rationality is not sufficient to ensure group rationality. A set of actors, each with complete and transitive preference orderings, may behave in a way that reveals group intransitivity. When this occurs, there is no "majority" to speak of; instead, there is a cycle of different majorities. For example, suppose that we start with the current level of social service provision as the status quo. A council member who is unhappy with this status quo (say, the left-wing councillor) might propose a vote like that in round two of the round-robin tournament (*C* vs. *I*). In this vote, a majority would support an increase in social service provision over the maintenance of the status quo (see Table 10.2). But as soon as this vote ends, a disgruntled council member (say, the centrist) can propose a vote like that in round one of the round-robin tournament (*I* vs. *D*). In this vote, a majority would support a decrease in social service provision over an increase. But as soon as this vote ends, a different disgruntled council member—in this case, the left-wing councillor—can propose a vote like that in round three of the round-robin tournament (*C* vs. *D*). In this vote, a majority would support maintaining the current level of social service provision rather than decreasing it. Interestingly, the centrist who just one vote ago proposed decreasing the provision of social services now votes to maintain current levels of social service provision. Having arrived back where they began (*C*), and absent any institutional mechanism to end the succession of proposals and counter-proposals, the scene is set for the cycle to begin anew—with no end in sight. This cycle through the different majorities is illustrated in Figure 10.1.

Some of you may feel that our example of cyclical majorities is unlikely ever to occur in practice. After all, we see deliberative bodies make decisions all the time and, although we may sometimes think they are far from efficient, they do not seem to be caught in the type of endless cycle suggested by our example. On the whole, there are two broad reasons for this. One has to do with preference orderings and the other has to do with decision-making rules. Let's start with preference orderings. To some extent, our current example is special in the sense that it depends on the councillors having a particular set of preference orderings. For example, if the right-wing councillor's preferences were the mirror image of those of the left-wing councillor—that is, if the right-wing council member preferred a decrease to the current level but preferred the current level to an increase—then maintaining current levels of social service provision would win both rounds of the round-robin tournament in which it competes. In political science, we call an option like this—that is, one that beats all other options in a series of pair-wise contests—a **Condorcet winner.** Given the decision-making process adopted by the council, and assuming that all councillors vote for their most preferred option, this would mean that maintaining current levels of social service provision is a stable outcome.

An option is a **Condorcet winner** if it beats all other options in a series of pair-wise contests.

FIGURE 10.1	An Example of Cyclical Majorities

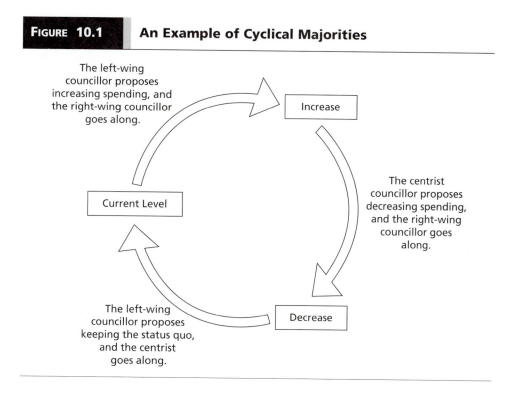

The left-wing councillor proposes increasing spending, and the right-wing councillor goes along.

Increase

The centrist councillor proposes decreasing spending, and the right-wing councillor goes along.

Current Level

Decrease

The left-wing councillor proposes keeping the status quo, and the centrist goes along.

To see why, imagine that maintaining current spending on social services is the status quo and ask yourself who would benefit from a change? The answer is that both the left- and right-wing councillors would like to propose a change. The right-wing council member prefers a decrease in social service provision to the status quo. If he proposed a decrease, however, both the centrist and left-wing councillors would vote against the proposal. Similarly, the left-wing council member prefers an increase in social service provision to the status quo. But if he proposed an increase, both the centrist and right-wing councillors would vote against the proposal. In other words, with this new profile of preferences in the group, there is no cycle of majorities, and, as a result, current levels of spending constitute a stable outcome. In effect, the group now behaves as if it were an individual with transitive (and complete) preferences—it prefers current levels of social service provision to a decrease, and a decrease to an increase.

The point here is that majority rule is not necessarily incompatible with rational group preferences. All that Condorcet showed was that it is *possible* for a group of individuals with transitive preferences to produce a group that behaves as if it has intransitive preferences. As a result, Condorcet's Paradox erodes our confidence in the ability of majority rule to produce stable outcomes only to the extent that we expect actors to hold the preferences that cause group intransitivity. So how likely is it that transitive individual preferences will lead to group intransitivity? Modern scholars have analyzed this problem in detail and found that the likelihood of group intransitivity increases with the number of alternatives under consideration or the number of voters, or both. In Table 10.3, we show estimates of the share of all possible strict preference orderings that fail to produce a Condorcet winner (that is, that produce group intransitivity) as the numbers of voters and alternatives increase (Riker 1982, 122).

As Table 10.3 illustrates, the example of the city council that we started with, in which a Condorcet winner fails to emerge from a contest among three alternatives and three voters, is indeed a rarity. Nearly all (94.4 percent) of the logically possible strict preference orderings produce a Condorcet winner and, hence, a stable outcome. As the number of voters increases, however, the probability of group intransitivity rises to some limit. When the number of alternatives is relatively small, this limit is still small enough that most of the logically possible preference orderings will not lead to group intransitivity. In contrast, although an increase in the number of alternatives also increases the probability of group intransitivity, this process continues until the point at which group intransitivity is certain to occur. In other words, as the number of alternatives goes to infinity, the probability of group intransitivity converges to one—even when the number of voters is small. This is an extremely important result because many political decisions involve a choice from, essentially, an infinite number of alternatives.

Imagine, for example, what would happen if we introduced a bit more realism into our example about a city council deciding on social welfare spending. Previously, we simplified the situation to one in which the councillors were deciding between three alternatives—increase, decrease, or maintain current spending. In reality, though, the councillors would normally be choosing an exact amount of money to spend on social services. In effect, they would be choosing a share of the budget to allocate to social service provision from 0 percent to 100 percent. Thus, there are an infinite number of choices that could be made in this

TABLE 10.3	**Proportion of Possible Strict Preference Orderings without a Condorcet Winner**					
	Number of voters					
Number of alternatives	**3**	**5**	**7**	**9**	**11**	➤ **. . . Limit**
3	0.056	0.069	0.075	0.078	0.080	0.088
4	0.111	0.139	0.150	0.156	0.160	0.176
5	0.160	0.200	0.215			0.251
6	0.202					0.315
↓ Limit	1.000	1.000	1.000	1.000	1.000	↓ 1.000

Source: Riker (1982, 122)

interval (0–100).[7] As a consequence, if no restrictions are placed on the councillors' preferences, then group intransitivity is all but guaranteed. Significantly, all policy decisions that involve bargaining—questions relating to things like the distribution of government resources, the allocation of the tax burden, the allocation of ministerial portfolios in the government, and the location of toxic waste—can be seen in a similar light.

To summarize, Condorcet's Paradox makes it clear that restricting group decision making to sets of rational individuals is no guarantee that the group as a whole will exhibit rational tendencies. Group intransitivity is unlikely when the set of feasible options is small, but it is almost certain that majority rule applied to a pair-wise competition among alternatives will fail to produce a stable outcome when the set of feasible options gets large. As a result, it is impossible to say that the majority "decides" except in very restricted circumstances.

The analytical insight from Condorcet's Paradox suggests that group intransitivity should be common, but, as we have already noted, we observe a surprising amount of stability in group decision making in the real world. Our discussion so far suggests that this must be the result of either of two factors. Either the number of decision makers or issues is kept small *and* the kinds of preferences that produce group intransitivity are rare, or a decision-making mechanism other than a simple pair-wise comparison of alternatives is being used. We have already seen that some of the most common types of political decisions involve a great number of alternatives, so it is likely that any stability we observe in the real world results from the use of alternative decision rules. It is to these alternative decision-making rules that we now turn.

The Borda Count and the Reversal Paradox

One alternative decision-making rule—the Borda Count—was suggested by Jean-Charles de Borda, a compatriot of Condorcet, in 1770 (published in 1781).[8] The Borda Count asks individuals to rank potential alternatives from their most to least preferred and then assigns numbers to reflect this ranking.[9] For instance, if there are three alternatives as in our city council example, then the Borda Count might assign a three to each councillor's most preferred option, a two to their second-best option, and a one to their least preferred option. The weighted votes for each alternative are then summed and the alternative with the largest score wins. Using the same preferences as shown earlier in Table 10.1, the Borda Count would again be indecisive in determining whether to increase, decrease, or maintain current levels of social service provision. This is because each alternative would garner a score of 6. This is shown in Table 10.4.

---

7. This is true in abstract games in which players bargain over the share of a "pie." In real life, budgets are denominated in currency and so the smallest accounting increment (like a penny) can place a limit on the divisibility of the pie. What is important here, though, is that there are many, many possible outcomes, and group intransitivity is therefore nearly certain to occur. Political scientists and economists both use formal bargaining models to examine these types of situation. Interestingly, political scientists tend to bargain over a "pie," whereas economists tend to bargain over a "cake" (Morrow 1994, 346).

8. Two men other than Charles de Borda are thought to have independently come up with this decision-making mechanism. Recent evidence suggests that Ramon Llull (1232–1315) first discovered the Borda Count in the thirteenth century. The Borda Count was "reinvented" by Nicholas of Cusa (1401–1464) when he suggested (unsuccessfully) that it should be used to elect the Holy Roman Emperor in 1433.

9. We discuss the Borda Count again in Chapter 12 when we investigate electoral systems in more detail.

TABLE 10.4	Determining the Level of Social Service Provision Using the Borda Count			
	Points awarded			
Alternative	Left-wing	Centrist	Right-wing	Borda Count total
Increase spending	3	1	2	6
Decrease spending	1	2	3	6
Current spending	2	3	1	6

Although the indecisiveness of the Borda Count is once again an artifact of the particular preference ordering we are examining,[10] a more troubling aspect of this decision rule can be seen if we consider the introduction of a possible fourth alternative. Let's assume, for example, that the councillors consider a new alternative: maintain current spending levels for another year (perhaps it's an election year) but commit future governments to a decrease in spending of, say, 10 percent in each successive year.[11] Suppose that the left-wing councillor likes this new option the least, the right-wing councillor prefers it to all alternatives except an immediate decrease, and the centrist councillor prefers all options except an increase to this new alternative. The preference ordering for each of the council members over the four alternatives is summarized in Table 10.5.

If we apply the Borda Count in this new situation by assigning a three to each councillor's most preferred alternative, a two to his second-best alternative, a one to his third-best alternative, and a zero to his least preferred alternative, then we find that the vote tally looks

TABLE 10.5	City Council Preferences for the Level of Social Service Provision (Four Alternatives)	
Left-wing	Centrist	Right-wing
$I \succ C \succ D \succ FC$	$C \succ D \succ FC \succ I$	$D \succ FC \succ I \succ C$

Note: I = an increase in social service provision; D = a decrease in social service provision; C = a maintenance of current levels of social service provision; FC = future cuts in social service provision; $\succ$ = "is strictly preferred to."

10. We could, of course, conclude that the group actually is indifferent between these alternatives, given this aggregation of citizen preferences. Doing so, however, requires us to make what political scientists call "interpersonal comparisons of utility." For example, we would have to believe that the welfare improvement that a left-wing councillor feels when a decrease in social service provision is replaced by an increase is exactly equal to the sum of the decline in welfare experienced by the centrist and left-wing councillors when this happens. Most modern scholars are reluctant to make these types of interpersonal comparisons of utility and so would be reluctant to make normative statements about the appropriateness of this outcome.

11. This example is not as fanciful as it might sound. In fact, it shares many qualities with the "balanced budget" proposals of politicians who are all too eager to be "fiscally conservative" tomorrow (when an election is no longer looming).

like the one shown in Table 10.6. As you can see, the council now has a strict preference ordering over the alternatives. Based on their votes, the council would decrease the level of social service provision.

You will immediately notice that something very strange has happened. Despite the fact that the new alternative receives a lower score than all of the original options and that it is not the first choice of any of the councillors, its addition as an active alternative for consideration changes how the councillors, as a collectivity, rank the three original options. In doing so, it changes the outcome of the vote. Whereas the group had previously been "indifferent" between the three original options, it now possesses a strict and transitive preference ordering over them, with "decreased spending" as the group's "most preferred" outcome. Note that this is the case despite the fact that none of the councillors has changed the way that he rank orders *I, D,* and *C.* In effect, the choice that the council now makes has been influenced by the introduction of what might be called an "irrelevant alternative." As this example illustrates, the Borda Count does not demonstrate the property that political scientists refer to as the "independence from irrelevant alternatives." [12]

Many analysts find the susceptibility of the Borda Count to the introduction of what they consider "irrelevant alternatives" disconcerting. Note that in our city council example, there was no change in the individual preference ordering of any of the actors over the original three alternatives, and yet, the introduction of an "irrelevant alternative" had a marked effect on the outcome of the decision-making process. One reason why we might like a decision rule to be "independent from irrelevant alternatives" is that if it is not, wily politicians can more easily manipulate the outcome of a decision process in order to produce their most

TABLE 10.6	**Determining the Level of Social Service Provision Using the Borda Count with a Fourth Alternative**			
	Points awarded			
Alternative	Left-wing	Centrist	Right-wing	Borda Count total
Increase spending	3	0	1	4
Decrease spending	1	2	3	6
Current spending	2	3	0	5
Future cuts in spending	0	1	2	3

---

12. Technically, the "independence from irrelevant alternatives" (IIA) property in the social choice literature refers to the independence from the "ranking" (and not the "presence") of an irrelevant alternative. This is the requirement that the ranking of an irrelevant alternative in a *fixed* set of alternatives should not affect the alternative that is chosen (Arrow 1963; Sen 1970). Our city council example can be understood in these terms too. For example, we can imagine that the city councillors all originally ranked the alternative of future spending cuts last but through some kind of deliberation process came to rank it in the way shown in Table 10-5. When the future spending cuts are ranked last, the council is indifferent between *D, I,* and *C.* But when the future spending cuts are ranked according to the preference orderings in Table 10-5, then the council has a strict preference ordering $D \succ C \succ I$.

preferred outcome. For example, instead of making persuasive arguments about the desirability of her preferred outcome or seeking compromise solutions that leave all parties better off, a politician might get her way by the imaginative introduction of an alternative that has no chance of winning, but that—by its sheer presence—changes the weights attached to other alternatives and, therefore, changes the alternative that is ultimately chosen.

Majority Rule with an Agenda Setter

An alternative decision-making mechanism that overcomes the potential instability of majority rule in round-robin tournaments requires actors to begin by considering only a subset of the available pair-wise alternatives. For instance, in our original city council example, we might require that both departures from the status quo (that is, increases and decreases in social service spending) first face each other in a pair-wise contest and that the winner then go on to compete in a vote against the status quo. Imposing a voting agenda such as this turns the voting process into a sequential game with three players—each player simultaneously chooses between increasing and decreasing social service provision, and then each player simultaneously chooses between the winning alternative from the first round and the maintenance of current spending levels in the second round.

Let's assume for a moment that each council member votes for her preferred option when confronted with any two choices. In other words, let's assume that each councillor casts what is known as a **sincere vote.** In the first round, the councillors choose between increasing social service spending and decreasing it. Given the preferences of the councillors in our example, we know that both the centrist and the right-wing council members prefer a decrease in spending over an increase. As a result, the vote in the first round would be 2-1 in favor of a decrease. This means that the second (and final) round of voting is a choice between decreasing social service spending and maintaining current levels of spending. Because the left-wing and centrist councillors both prefer the current level of social service spending to a decrease, the outcome of this game is the status quo; that is, current spending levels are maintained. (Stop for a moment and ask yourself which of the councillors is likely to have set this voting agenda.)

But should we expect all of the councillors to vote sincerely in our example? Consider that the councillors know that there are only two possible contests in the second round—either D vs. C or I vs. C. Given the preference orderings in our example, the councillors know that these potential second-round contests will either end up with C defeating D or I defeating C. It follows from this that the councillors know that if D wins in the first round against I, then the final outcome will be the status quo, C. In other words, voting for D in the first round is essentially equivalent to voting for the status quo in the end. As a result, the first round of voting should, in reality, be seen as a contest between I and C (even if the councillors are actually voting between I and D).

Think about how the right-wing councillor might reason through the logic of this voting procedure. Recall that her favorite outcome is a decrease in social service spending, her second-best outcome is an increase in social service spending, and her least preferred outcome is maintaining the current level of social service spending. If she casts her vote in the first round for her most preferred outcome without thinking about the consequences for the rest of the game, then we have already seen that option D will be victorious in the first round but will go on to lose to C in the second and final round. This is, of course, the right-wing councillor's worst possible outcome. As a result, she has a strong incentive to change her vote in the first round from D to I even though this new vote does not conform to her sincere preferences. If she does this and votes for an increase in social service spending in the first round, then I will win and be pitted against C in the final round. In this final round, I will defeat C. In other words, the final outcome will be an increase in social service provision. Note that by deviating from her sincere preferences in the first round, the right-wing councillor is able to alter the final outcome from her least preferred outcome to her second-best one. In this example, the right-wing councillor casts what political scientists call a **strategic, or sophisticated, vote**—a vote in which an individual votes in favor of a less preferred option because she believes doing so will ultimately produce a more preferred outcome than would otherwise be the case. Some

> A **strategic, or sophisticated, vote** is a vote in which an individual votes in favor of a less preferred option because she believes doing so will ultimately produce a more preferred outcome. A **sincere vote** is a vote for an individual's most preferred option.

analysts find strategic voting lamentable and would prefer decision rules that induce **sincere voting**—voting that constitutes a sincere revelation of an individual's preferences.[13]

The incentives to vote strategically are not the only thing that scholars find lamentable with voting agendas like the one that we just examined. Another thing that many scholars find disconcerting is that alternative agendas can produce very different outcomes even if we hold all of the actors' preferences constant. In fact, the three alternatives in our city council example can face each other in three different two-round tournaments, all of which produce a different outcome. The three different two-round tournaments and the outcomes that they produce are shown in Table 10.7. As you can see, choosing the agenda is essentially equivalent to choosing which outcome will win. For example, if you decide to have a first-round contest between I and D, you know that the eventual outcome will be a victory for C. If you decide to have a first-round contest between C and I, you know that the eventual outcome will be D. And if you decide to have a first-round contest between C and D, you know that the eventual outcome will be I. Consequently, if one of the councillors is given the power to choose the agenda, she is, effectively, given the power to dictate the outcome of the decision-making process. This phenomenon, in which choosing the agenda is tantamount to choosing which alternative will win, is referred to as the "power of the agenda setter" and it exists in many institutional settings. In our example, the agenda setter can obtain her most preferred outcome simply by deciding what the order of pair-wise contests should be. For example, the centrist councillor would choose agenda 1 in Table 10.7 if she were the agenda setter; the right-wing councillor would choose agenda 2; and the left-wing councillor would choose agenda 3.

---

13. We return to a more detailed discussion of sincere and strategic voting in Chapters 12 and 13.

TABLE 10.7		Pair-Wise Contests and Different Voting Agendas			
Agenda	1st round	1st-round winner	2nd round	2nd-round winner	Councillor obtaining her most preferred outcome
1	*I* vs. *D*	*D*	*D* vs. *C*	*C*	Centrist councillor
2	*C* vs. *I*	*I*	*I* vs. *D*	*D*	Right-wing councillor
3	*C* vs. *D*	*C*	*C* vs. *I*	*I*	Left-wing councillor

Note: I = an increase in social service provision; *D* = a decrease in social service provision; *C* = a maintenance of current levels of social service provision.

In sum, it is possible to avoid the potential for group intransitivity that arises in majority rule round-robin tournaments by imposing an agenda—by designating which outcomes will be voted on first and which outcome will, in effect, be granted entry into a second round, in which it will compete against the winner of the first round. Unfortunately, the outcome of such a process is extremely sensitive to the agenda chosen and, consequently, either of two things is likely to happen. Either the instability of group decision making shifts from votes on outcomes to votes on the agendas expected to produce those outcomes, or some subset of actors is given power to control the agenda and, therefore, given considerable influence over the outcome likely to be produced.

Restrictions on Preferences: The Median Voter Theorem

As was the case with the Borda Count, it appears that institutional factors restricting the agenda may produce stable outcomes, but only at the expense of creating incentives for actors to attempt to manipulate the decision-making process. This obviously raises questions about our ability to design our way around the instability of majority rule in such a way that the cure is not worse than the disease. In the next section of this chapter, we discuss important work that suggests that it may be impossible to design a decision-making mechanism that ensures group transitivity while simultaneously meeting minimal criteria for fairness. But before we get there, let's pause briefly to consider the behavior of majority rule in one more special case.

Recall that group intransitivity in our original city council example seemed to stem from the fact that the right-wing councillor has a particular type of preference ordering. Specifically, the right-wing council member prefers both lower and higher levels of social service provision to the maintenance of current levels of social service provision. The right-wing councillor's most preferred option is to decrease social service spending. But if it came to it, she would rather increase spending in the hope that this would "break the bank" and force the city to adjust to lower levels of spending in the future than maintain current levels of spending (which she thinks are too high) that would slowly bleed the city dry.

A **utility function** is essentially a numerical scaling in which higher numbers stand for higher positions in an individual's preference ordering.

It is possible to represent the right-wing councillor's preferences with what political scientists call a **utility function.** A utility function can be thought of as a numerical scale in which higher numbers stand for higher positions in an individual's preference ordering. It essentially indicates how satisfied an individual is with the available alternatives. In Figure 10.2 we display a utility function that is consistent with the preference ordering of the right-wing councillor over the level of social service provision in our example. The utility function is highest over the proposal to decrease social service provision (D), it is lowest over the proposal to maintain current levels of social service provision (C), and it is between these two extremes over the proposal to increase social service provision (I).

Let's now examine the utility function of the centrist councillor. This is shown in Figure 10.3. You will immediately notice that the centrist councillor's utility function looks very different from that of the right-wing councillor in Figure 10.2. In particular, the centrist councillor's utility function captures what political scientists call a **single-peaked preference ordering.** In other words, the utility function reaches a "peak" above the centrist councillor's most preferred point. In this particular example, her most preferred point, sometimes called her "ideal point," is C. As proposals move away from this "ideal point" in either direction, the centrist councillor experiences a decline in her utility function.[14] The basic intuition behind single peakedness is that individuals prefer outcomes that are closer to their ideal point than those that are farther away. A quick glance at Figure 10.2 again shows that the right-wing

> A **single-peaked preference ordering** is characterized by a utility function that reaches a maximum at some point and slopes away from this maximum on either side.

| FIGURE 10.2 | **Right-Wing Councillor's Utility Function** |

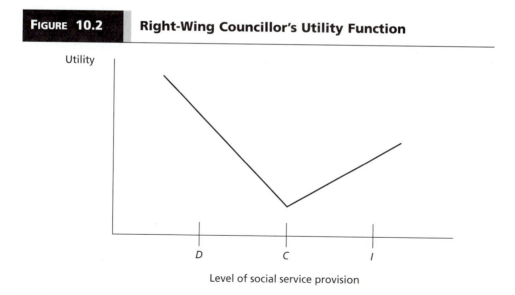

Note: D = decreased social service provision; C = maintenance of current levels of social service provision; I = increased social service provision.

---

14. Note that the decline in utility may occur more rapidly when moving in one direction away from an individual's ideal point than the other.

| FIGURE 10.3 | **Centrist Councillor's Utility Function** |

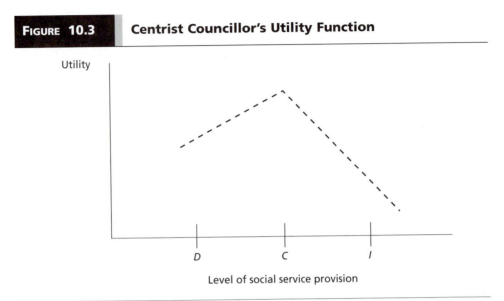

Note: D = decreased social service provision; C = maintenance of current levels of social service provision; I = increased social service provision.

councillor's utility function is not single peaked. Although there is a point at which the right-wing councillor's utility function reaches a maximum (around *D*), the utility function does not continuously decline as it moves farther away from this point—it starts to go back up to the right of *C*. In other words, the right-wing councillor prefers some outcomes that are farther from her ideal point (say, *I*) than outcomes that are closer (say, *C*).

The **Median Voter Theorem** (MVT) states that the ideal point of the median voter will win against any alternative in a pair-wise majority-rule election if the number of voters is odd, voter preferences are single-peaked over a single-policy dimension, and voters vote sincerely. When arrayed along a single-policy dimension in terms of their ideal points, the **median voter** is the individual who has at least half of all the voters at his position or to his right and at least half of all voters at his position or to his left.

One of the most important results in all of political science is called the **Median Voter Theorem** (Black 1948). The Median Voter Theorem (MVT) states that no alternative can beat the one preferred by the median voter in pair-wise majority-rule elections if the number of voters is odd, voter preferences are single-peaked over a single-policy dimension, and voters vote sincerely. When arrayed along a single-issue dimension in terms of their ideal points, the **median voter** is the individual who has at least half of all the voters at his position or to his right and at least half of all voters at his position or to his left.

Suppose that we placed a restriction on the preferences of the councillors in our city council example such that they all had single-peaked preference orderings. For example, we could restrict the preferences of the right-wing councillor such that her most preferred proposal is *D*, her second-best proposal is *C*, and her least preferred proposal is *I*. If we did this,

ox 10.1

THE MEDIAN VOTER THEOREM AND PARTY COMPETITION

The Median Voter Theorem (MVT) was originally constructed in the context of committee voting (Black 1948). In his classic book, *An Economic Theory of Democracy,* Anthony Downs (1957) then extended the MVT to elections more generally. Building on an earlier model of economic competition presented by Harold Hotelling (1929), Downs shows that if we assume that there is a single-issue dimension, an odd number of voters with single-peaked preferences who vote sincerely, and that there are only two parties, then both parties will converge to the ideal point of the median voter. Any other point in the policy space will lose in a pair-wise contest against the policy position preferred by the median voter. Thus, if one party is located at the median voter's ideal point and the competing party is not, then the first party will win a majority of the votes. The losing party, therefore, has an incentive to move to the median voter's ideal point as well. The consequence is that both parties will be located at the position of the median voter, resulting in a tied election in which each party wins with equal probability.

The logic of the MVT indicates that political parties have an incentive to converge to the position of the median voter and adopt similar policy positions in two-party systems. The fact that observers of two-party systems frequently criticize the dominant parties in these countries for being ideologically indistinguishable on the major issues provides some evidence that policy convergence does, indeed, occur. These observers complain that the parties are giving voters an "echo" rather than a "choice" (Page 1978; Monroe 1983). A common expression for the convergence of party platforms in these countries is "Tweedledee-Tweedledum politics" (Goodin and Pettit 1993, 6). For example, while campaigning in the midwestern states in 1968, third-party presidential candidate George Wallace famously referred to the Democratic and Republican Parties in a speech as "Tweedledum and Tweedledee." He argued that both were serving the interests of the "Eastern establishment" and that since around the time of the Civil War, "both parties have looked down their noses and called us rednecks down here in this part of the country. I'm sick and tired of it, and on November 5, they're goin' to find out there are a lot of rednecks in this country" ("Neither Tweedledum Nor Tweedledee," *Time Magazine,* September 20, 1968). Similar criticisms are made by smaller parties or outsider candidates in nearly every country that has two large parties that dominate elections. Indeed, political discourse in Britain often refers explicitly to the Tweedledum-Tweedledee phrase. Non-English-speaking countries, of course, have their own expressions for this phenomenon.

then the preference orderings of all the councillors would be single peaked.[15] In Figure 10.4, we illustrate utility functions that are consistent with the single-peaked preferences of all three councillors. As we saw earlier in the chapter, maintaining current levels of social service provision (C) would win a round-robin tournament in which the councillors have preferences consistent with the utility functions shown in Figure 10.4.

---

15. We already showed in Figure 10-3 that the centrist councillor has a single-peaked preference ordering over the level of social service provision. You can check for yourself that the left-wing councillor also has a single-peaked preference ordering.

FIGURE 10.4	When All Three Councillors Have Single-Peaked Preference Orderings

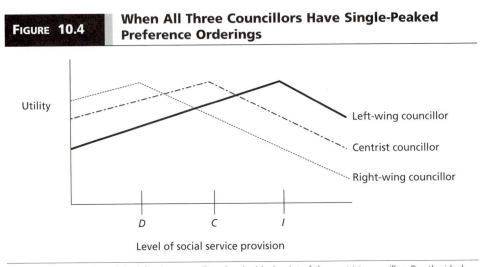

Note: I = the ideal point of the left-wing councillor; C = the ideal point of the centrist councillor; D = the ideal point of the right-wing councillor.

Up to this point, we have allowed the city councillors to choose between only three alternatives—increase, decrease, and maintain current levels of social service provision. We are now in a position to consider what might happen if the councillors are free to propose any level of social service spending. In other words, we can now look at the situation in which the councillors can pick any point on the x-axis of Figure 10.4 as their proposed level of social service spending.

Let's look at what happens if we assume that all the councillors vote sincerely for whichever proposal is closest to their ideal point. We will look at two kinds of scenarios. First, suppose that the status quo level of social service spending is given by point C—the ideal point of the centrist councillor. Clearly, the left-wing councillor would like to move social service spending to the right, toward her own ideal point I. Any proposal to do this, however, would be opposed by the centrist and right-wing councillors because any such proposal would be farther from their ideal points than the existing status quo. The right-wing councillor would like to move social spending to the left, toward her own ideal point D. Any proposal to do this would now be opposed by the centrist and the left-wing councillors because any such proposal would be farther from their ideal points than the existing status quo. As a result, if the status quo is at the centrist councillor's ideal point, then it is an equilibrium.

Second, suppose that the status quo level of social service spending is anywhere other than C—let's say somewhere to the left of C. This type of scenario is shown in Figure 10.5, with the status quo policy arbitrarily placed at SQ (status quo). In this type of situation, both the centrist and left-wing councillors are likely to propose moving social service spending closer to C. Let's suppose they propose A. Proposal A beats the SQ because the left-wing and

| FIGURE 10.5 | **Illustrating the Power of the Median Voter** |

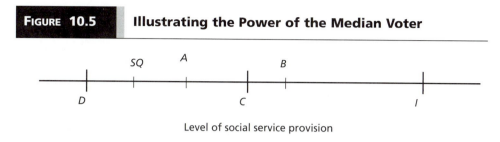

Level of social service provision

Note: D = the ideal point of the right-wing councillor ; *C* = the ideal point of the centrist councillor; *I* = the ideal point of the left-wing councillor; *SQ* = status quo level of social service provision; *A* and *B* = proposals for a new level of social service provision.

centrist councillors vote for it and only the right-wing councillor votes against. But is policy A an equilibrium? The answer is no. The left-wing and centrist councillors would like to move social service provision farther to the right, closer to their ideal points. Let's suppose that they now propose B. Proposal B will be adopted because it is closer to the ideal points of both the left-wing and centrist councillors than proposal A; the right-wing councillor will vote against the new proposal but will lose. Is proposal B an equilibrium? Again, the answer is no. The right-wing and centrist councillors will now want to move social service provision to the left, closer to their ideal points. Any proposal that is closer to *C* than B is will win with the support of the right-wing and centrist councillors. This process will continue until policy fully converges to the ideal point of the centrist councillor at *C*. Only then will the policy outcome be stable. A similar process of convergence to the position of the centrist councillor would occur if the status quo started off to the right of *C* instead of to the left.

Even if the centrist councillor is never given the opportunity to propose a policy change, we would still expect to see alternative offers by the left- and right-wing council members that slowly converge to the most preferred policy of the centrist candidate. In fact, if making different policy proposals was sufficiently costly, far-sighted councillors of the left and right might look to the end of this convergence process and simply propose a policy that matched the policy preferences of the centrist candidate from the very beginning. Whatever the process that produces the convergence to the centrist councillor's ideal point, once policy arrives there, there is no longer any impetus for change in the system. In other words, the policy that is most preferred by the centrist councillor is the only point on the policy continuum for which there is no policy alternative that is preferred by a majority of the councilors—it is the only equilibrium. This is so not because we have labeled the policymaker in the center a "centrist" but because the centrist happens to be the median voter.[16]

---

16. The Median Voter Theorem does not assert that the equilibrium policy outcome will be centrist in terms of the underlying issue dimension. All it states is that the equilibrium policy will be the ideal point of the median voter. Whether it is centrist or not will, therefore, depend on the location of the median voter in the issue space.

The Median Voter Theorem essentially shows that the difficulties we encountered earlier with Condorcet's Paradox, such as group intransitivity and cyclical majorities, can be avoided if we are willing to both rule certain preference orderings "out of bounds" and reduce the policy space to a single-issue dimension. Unfortunately, neither of these restrictions is uncontroversial. For example, there is nothing intrinsically troubling about individual preferences that are not single peaked. In fact, there are a whole host of issues for which voters might, like the right-wing councillor in our example, legitimately prefer a lot or a little of something to a moderate amount.[17] As a result, we might have moral objections to a decision-making procedure that prohibits individuals from holding preferences that are not single-peaked.

The restriction of politics to a single-issue dimension can also be controversial. This is because many political questions are inherently multidimensional. As an example, consider a situation in which the representatives of three constituencies—labor, capital, and agriculture—are deciding how to divide a pot of subsidies from the government's budget. This decision-making situation can be represented by a two-dimensional policy space in which the percentage of subsidies going to labor is one dimension and the percentage of subsidies going to capital owners is the other; anything left over goes to agriculture. This decision-making situation is depicted in Figure 10.6. The downward-sloping dashed line sets an upper bound on all the possible distributions of subsidies. This limit is necessary because there is a finite amount of resources that can be spent on subsidies. In what follows, we assume that the entire pot of subsidies will be distributed between the three constituencies. At point L, all of the subsidies go to labor. At point C, all of the subsidies go to capital. And at point A, all of the subsidies go to agriculture. Any point along the sloping dashed line between L and C is some distribution of the subsidies between labor and capital; agriculture gets nothing. Any point along the solid vertical line between L and A is some distribution of the subsidies between labor and agriculture; capital gets nothing. And any point along the solid horizontal line between A and C is some distribution of the subsidies between agriculture and capital; labor gets nothing. Finally, any point within the triangle LAC is some distribution of the subsidies between all three constituencies. For example, at point E, the subsidies are divided equally between labor, capital, and agriculture.

Imagine that each constituency wants to maximize its share of the government subsidies but has no opinion about how the portion it does not receive is divided among the other constituencies. If each constituency votes to allocate the subsidies by majority rule and can propose a change in the division at any time, then the problem of cyclical majorities that we encountered with Condorcet's Paradox will rear its ugly head again. To see why, imagine that someone, perhaps the national government, proposes to divide the subsidies equally between all three constituencies. This point can be thought of as the status quo proposal, and

---

17. We suspect that many of you probably have the following non-single-peaked preference ordering over coffee when the single dimension under consideration is the temperature of the coffee—you prefer both hot coffee and iced coffee to lukewarm coffee. We see nothing inherently wrong with a preference ordering like this.

FIGURE 10.6	**Two-Dimensional Voting**

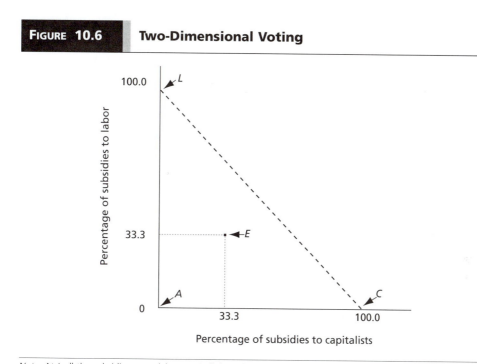

Note: At *L* all the subsidies go to labor; at *C* all the subsidies go to capital; at *A* all the subsidies go to agriculture; and at *E* the subsidies are divided equally between labor, capital, and agriculture.

it is marked as *SQ* in Figure 10.7. Given the assumptions that we have made, the most preferred outcome for each constituency will be to get 100 percent of the subsidies for itself. Recall that these ideal points are given by points *L* (labor), *A* (agriculture), and *C* (capital) in Figure 10.6.

The gray sloping line through the status quo proposal in Figure 10.7 indicates all of the ways that the pot of subsidies can be divided between labor and capital such that agriculture receives one-third of the pot. Because agriculture cares only about how much it is getting, agriculture is essentially indifferent between any of the points on this line and the status quo proposal made by the national government. For this reason, the gray sloping line is called agriculture's **indifference curve** (with respect to the status quo).[18] Any point to the southwest of this indifference curve involves a division of subsidies in which agriculture receives more than one-third of the pot. As a result, agriculture strictly prefers any point to the

> An **indifference curve** is a set of points such that an individual is indifferent between any two points in the set.

southwest of its indifference curve to any point on its indifference curve. The vertical gray line through the status quo proposal is capital's indifference curve because it indicates all of

18. This is despite the fact that, in this case, it is not actually a curve but a straight line.

the ways that the pot of subsidies can be divided between labor and agriculture so that capital receives one-third of the pot. Any point to the right of this indifference curve involves a division of subsidies in which capital receives more than one-third of the pot. As a result, capital strictly prefers any point to the right of its indifference curve to any point on its indifference curve. Finally, the horizontal gray line through the status quo proposal is labor's indifference curve because it indicates all of the ways that the pot of subsidies can be divided between capital and agriculture so that labor receives one-third of the pot. Although labor is indifferent among any of the points along this line, it strictly prefers any point above this line because it will receive more than one-third of the pot.

Because labor prefers any point above the horizontal gray line to the status quo, capital prefers any point to the right of the vertical gray line, and agriculture prefers any point below the sloping gray line, each of the triangle-shaped petals radiating from the status quo represents a set of alternative divisions of the subsidies that a majority of the constituency representatives prefer to the status quo. Such sets of alternatives that would win a majority vote if

> The **winset** of some alternative z is the set of alternatives that will defeat z in a pair-wise contest if everyone votes sincerely according to whatever voting rules are being used.

pitted against the status quo in a pair-wise contest are sometimes referred to as **winsets** of the status quo. The triangle to the northwest of the status quo, labeled $A + L$, represents outcomes

| **FIGURE 10.7** | **Two-Dimensional Voting with Winsets** |

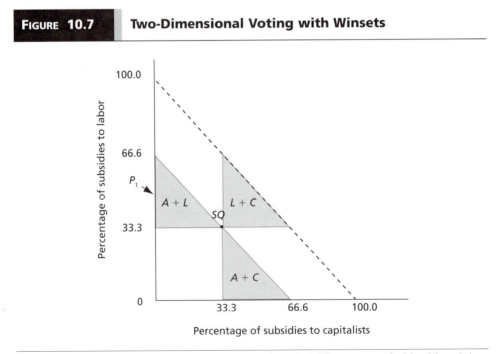

Note: The three solid gray lines going through *SQ* (status quo) are the indifference curves for labor (*L*), capital (*C*), and agriculture (*A*); P_1 = proposal 1. The shaded triangles are winsets that represent alternative divisions of the subsidies that are preferred by a majority to the status quo; the majority in question is shown in each winset.

that are preferred by labor and agriculture to the status quo. The triangle to the northeast of the status quo, labeled $L + C$, represents outcomes that are preferred by labor and capital to the status quo. Finally, the triangle to the southeast of the status quo, labeled $A + C$, represents outcomes that are preferred by capital and agriculture to the status quo.

The existence of these non-empty winsets indicates that if any of the three constituencies has an opportunity to propose a change in the division of subsidies, they will. For example, the labor representative might propose a 50-50 split of the subsidies with agriculture. This proposal is denoted by P_1 in Figure 10.7. Because this proposal leaves both agriculture and labor better off vis-à-vis the status quo, the agriculture and labor representatives will vote to accept this proposal; the capital representative will vote against the proposal because capital would be worse off. Hence, proposal P_1 will defeat the original status quo 2 to 1 and become the new status quo proposal. Are there any alternative divisions of the subsidies that a majority of representatives prefer to the new status quo proposal P_1? To answer this question, we must draw the indifference curves of the three constituencies with respect to P_1 and see if there are any non-empty winsets. We do this in Figure 10.8.

As before, the indifference curves for each constituency are shown by the gray lines going through the new status quo proposal P_1. As Figure 10.8 illustrates, there are two winsets. The

| **FIGURE 10.8** | **Two-Dimensional Voting with a New Status Quo (P_1)** |

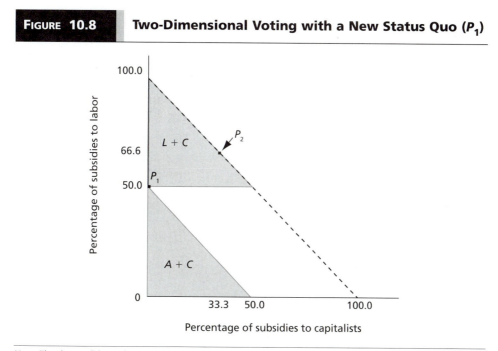

Note: The three solid gray lines going through P_1 are the indifference curves for labor (L), capital (C), and agriculture (A). The shaded triangles are winsets that represent alternative divisions of the subsidies that are preferred by a majority to the status quo; the majority in question is shown in each winset.

winset labeled $L + C$ contains alternatives that are preferred to P_1 by both labor and capital. The winset labeled $A + C$ contains alternatives that are preferred to P_1 by both agriculture and capital. In other words, there are several alternative divisions of the subsidies that are preferred by a majority to the new status quo proposal P_1. For example, the capital representative might propose to give two-thirds of the subsidies to labor and one-third of the subsidies to capital. This proposal is denoted by P_2 in Figure 10.8. Because this proposal leaves labor better off (labor receives 66.6 percent instead of 50 percent) and capital better off (capital gets 33.3 percent instead of 0 percent), the labor and capital representatives will vote to accept proposal P_2; the agriculture representative will vote against the proposal because agriculture will be worse off (agriculture receives 0 percent instead of 50 percent). Hence, proposal P_2 will defeat proposal P_1 2 to 1 and become the new status quo proposal.

Is P_2 a stable division of subsidies? The answer is no. Agriculture, which is not getting any share of the subsidies under proposal P_2, could propose a 50-50 division of the subsidies between itself and capital. This is proposal P_3 in Figure 10.9. This proposal would defeat P_2 because agriculture would vote for it (agriculture receives 50 percent instead of 0 percent), and capital would also vote for it (capital receives 50 percent instead of 33 percent). Thus, proposal P_3 would dislodge proposal P_2 as the new status quo proposal. Because there is always some division of the subsidies that gives the excluded constituency a share of the pot while giving one of the other constituencies a bigger share of the pot than they are receiving

| FIGURE 10.9 | **Two-Dimensional Voting with Cyclical Majorities** |

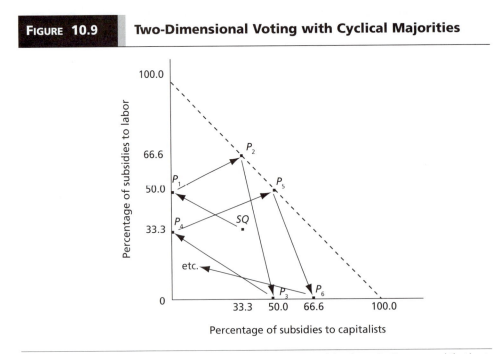

Note: SQ = original status quo; P_1 = proposal that beats SQ; P_2 = proposal that beats P_1; P_3 = proposal that beats P_2; P_4 = proposal that beats P_3, and so on.

with the status quo proposal, this process of ever-shifting divisions of the subsidy pot can be expected to go on forever. This is illustrated in Figure 10.9.

The process of cyclical majorities highlighted in Figure 10.9 exemplifies a famously unsettling theorem about politics relating to majority rule in multidimensional settings (Plott 1967; McKelvey 1976; Schofield 1978). According to the **Chaos Theorem,** if there are two or more issue dimensions and three or more voters with preferences in the issue space who all vote sincerely, then except in the case of a rare distribution of ideal points, there will be no Condorcet winner. As a result, whoever controls the order of voting can determine the final outcome.

> The **Chaos Theorem** states that if there are two or more issue dimensions and three or more voters with preferences in the issue space who all vote sincerely, then except in the case of a rare distribution of ideal points, there will be no Condorcet winner.

Like Condorcet's Paradox, the Chaos Theorem suggests that unless we are lucky enough to have a set of actors who hold preferences that do not lead to cyclical majorities, either of two things will happen: (a) the decision-making process will be indeterminate and policy outcomes hopelessly unstable; or (b) there will exist an actor —the agenda setter—with the power to determine the order of votes in such a way that she can produce her most favored outcome.

In the absence of institutions that provide an actor with agenda-setting powers, stable outcomes are even less likely to occur in the circumstances covered by the Chaos Theorem than those covered by Condorcet's Paradox. This is because the set of preferences that prevent majority cycling in two or more dimensions are extremely rare and special. Students who are interested in learning more about the conditions for stable outcomes in multi-dimensional policy spaces are referred to Box 1.2 titled "Stability in Two-Dimensional Majority-Rule Voting" at the end of this chapter (p. 392).

The important lesson to draw from the Chaos Theorem is that if politics cannot be reduced to a single-issue dimension, then there is a wide set of circumstances under which either (a) stable outcomes will not occur, or (b) stable outcomes will be imposed by whichever actor controls the agenda. The results of the Chaos Theorem highlight "the importance of investigating the effects of the political institutions within which collective choices are made" (McCarty and Meirowitz 2007, 80), because it is likely that it is these institutions that play a significant role in alleviating the "chaos" that might otherwise reign.

ARROW'S THEOREM

Up to this point, we have seen that thinking about democracy as simply a matter of allowing the majority to make decisions runs into difficulties on several fronts. First, Condorcet's Paradox shows that a set of rational individuals can form a group that is incapable of choosing rationally in round-robin tournaments. Specifically, situations might arise in which majorities cycle indefinitely, rendering the group incapable of reaching a decision. We learned that although voting schemes, like the Borda Count, that allow voters to rank order all possible alternatives might allow clear winners to emerge under some conditions, the outcomes that are produced by such decision-making processes are not robust. In particular, altering rankings over irrelevant alternatives could change the way votes are counted and, therefore, change the outcome. Next, we learned that if round-robin tournaments are replaced by "single elimination" tournaments that form a voting agenda, then cyclical majorities may be avoided and a stable outcome achieved. Unfortunately, we also saw that whoever controls the agenda—the order by which alternatives are pitted against each other and submitted to a vote—could dictate the outcome of such procedures.

We saw, though, that the problem of instability could be overcome if the political question to be decided can be thought of as a single-issue dimension *and* if each voter has single-peaked preferences over that dimension. When these and other conditions are met, the alternative that is most preferred by the median voter is a stable outcome in the sense that no other alternative exists that can defeat it in a majority-rule pair-wise contest. Unfortunately, the Median Voter Theorem is, at best, cold comfort for a couple of reasons. First, it requires restrictions on the types of preferences that individuals can have. If some voters have non-single-peaked preferences, it is possible for a cycle of majorities to arise—just as in round-robin tournaments. Consequently, the Median Voter Theorem tells us only that we can avoid the potential for decision-making instability if certain preference orderings do not occur, either because we are lucky or because we are willing to rule them out of bounds. This is problematic because it seems reasonable that an individual's preferences should be treated as sacrosanct. It seems to us that a "democratic" decision-making process that works reliably only when we restrict participation to those with the "right kind" of preferences loses much of its ethical appeal. Second, it is likely that many crucial political questions involve more than one dimension. We presented an example of distributional bargaining between three groups as an illustration of a two-dimensional political question that is, in many ways, the very essence of politics. In this example, the decision-making process was unstable and "chaotic." As we noted at the time, the stability implied by the Median Voter Theorem occurs in situations in which there are two or more dimensions to a political problem only in exceedingly rare circumstances.

Each of these complications with majority rule raises fundamental questions about the ethical appeal of democracy—understood as majority rule—as a mechanism for making group decisions. Specifically, we have seen that it is difficult to guarantee that majority rule will produce a stable group choice without either granting someone agenda-setting power or restricting the kinds of preferences that individuals may hold. In a famous book, Kenneth Arrow (1963) put forth a theorem that shows that these problems with majority rule are, in some ways, special cases of a more fundamental problem. **Arrow's Theorem** demonstrates that it is impossible to design any decision-making system—not just majority rule—for aggregating the preferences of a set of individuals that can guarantee producing a rational outcome while simultaneously meeting what he argued was a minimal standard of fairness.[19] When deciding which set of conditions a fair decision-making procedure should

---

19. It is common to see Arrow's Theorem referred to as Arrow's "Impossibility" Theorem. In fact, Arrow himself labeled it the "Possibility Theorem."

meet, Arrow sought a minimal set in the sense that violations of these fairness conditions would lead to a procedure that is unfair in a way that would be evident to all.

Arrow's Fairness Conditions

Arrow presented four fairness conditions that he believed all decision-making processes should meet. Each of these four conditions is related to issues that have already arisen during our examination of majority rule and can reasonably be argued to be a part of any conception of democracy. We will discuss each of the four conditions in turn.

Non-Dictatorship

The **non-dictatorship condition** states that there must be no individual who fully determines the outcome of the group decision-making process in disregard of the preferences of the other group members. In fact, this condition is an extremely minimal fairness condition because it only says that there can be no individual who, if she prefers x to y, forces the group choice to be x instead of y, irrespective of the preferences of everyone else. A group decision-making process that pays attention to only one member of the group and disregards the preferences of all the other members is clearly not democratic. Although it is possible that a dictator would be benevolent and choose an outcome that benefits the group, it is clear that a *mechanism* that allows a single individual to determine group outcomes for everyone else is inherently unfair.

> The **non-dictatorship condition** states that there must be no individual who fully determines the outcome of the group decision-making process in disregard of the preferences of the other group members.

Universal Admissibility

The **universal admissibility condition** states that any fair group decision-making rule must work with any logically possible set of individual preference orderings. This allows actors to adopt any rational preference ordering they want. This condition is closely related to the philosophical doctrine of individualism. According to this perspective, individuals should be free to formulate their own desires. Although it may be appropriate under some conditions to prohibit individuals from acting on those desires, it is inappropriate to comment on the intrinsic social desirability of another's desires per se. It is on this basis that Arrow believed it inappropriate to exclude individuals from group decision-making processes simply on the basis of the types of preferences that they happen to hold. Riker (1982, 117) defends the universal admissibility condition by stating that "if social outcomes are to be based exclusively on individual judgments—as seems implicit in any interpretation of democratic methods—then to restrict individual persons' judgments in any way means that the social outcome is based as much on the restriction as it is on individual judgments." In the context of voting, this condition states that every voter may vote as she pleases.

> The **universal admissibility condition** states that individuals can adopt any rational preference ordering over the available alternatives.

Unanimity, or Pareto Optimality

The **unanimity, or pareto optimality, condition** states that if all individuals in a group prefer x to y, then the group preference must reflect a preference for x to y as well.

The **unanimity, or pareto optimality, condition** states that if all individuals in a group prefer x to y, then the group preference must reflect a preference for x to y as well. A decision-making process that fails to meet this condition is not only unfair, it is perverse. Imagine pressing the Coke button on a vending machine and having a Sprite come out. The unanimity condition is extremely minimal in that it merely states that if everybody in the group is unanimous in sharing a preference for x to y, then the group must not choose y when x is available.

Independence from Irrelevant Alternatives

The **independence from irrelevant alternatives condition** states that group choice should be unperturbed by changes in the rankings of irrelevant alternatives.

The **independence from irrelevant alternatives condition** states that when groups are choosing between alternatives in a subset, the group choice should be influenced only by the rankings of these alternatives and not by the rankings of any (irrelevant) alternatives that are not in the subset. Suppose that, when confronted with a choice between x, y, and z, a group prefers x to y. The independence from irrelevant alternatives condition states that if one or more individuals alter their ranking of z, the group must still prefer x to y. Or as Varian (1993, 535) puts it, the group's preference "between x and y should depend only on how people rank x versus y, and not on how they rank other alternatives." We saw earlier that the Borda Count can violate this condition. A decision rule respects the independence from irrelevant alternatives condition whenever the group's ranking of any two alternatives x and y depends only on the relative ranking of these alternatives by every individual in the group (Geanakoplos 2005). Some scholars have, therefore, interpreted this condition to mean that the decision rule should be reliable in the sense that it always returns the same decision if the way individuals rank relevant alternatives remains unchanged (Riker 1982). In this respect, the independence from irrelevant alternatives condition is as much a condition about the reliability of the preference aggregation technology as it is a condition about the fairness of the decision-making mechanism.

In sum, Arrow's four conditions suggest that any fair group decision-making mechanism must prevent dictatorship (non-dictatorship), must not restrict the type of preferences that individuals can hold (universal admissibility), and must link group choice, in at least some rudimentary sense, to individual preferences (unanimity and independence from irrelevant alternatives). We have already seen examples of how particular majority-rule decision-making mechanisms must violate at least one of these requirements if we wish to guarantee that the group's preference ordering will be transitive. As we have seen, group transitivity is necessary in order for the group decision-making process to produce a stable outcome. The real power of Arrow's Theorem, though, comes from demonstrating that *every* decision-making process that we could possibly design, including any majority-rule one, must sacrifice at least one of Arrow's fairness conditions if it is to guarantee group transitivity and, hence, stable outcomes. Put differently, if we insist that Arrow's four fairness conditions be met, we must accept the possibility of group intransitivity—there is no way around it.

The implications of Arrow's Theorem are far reaching. Suppose that we take Arrow's conditions of unanimity and independence from irrelevant alternatives as uncontroversial and given. If we do this, Arrow's Theorem tells us that we face an institutional "trilemma" between stable outcomes, universal admissibility, and non-dictatorship. In other words, we can design decision-making institutions that have at most two of these three desirable attributes. In Figure 10.10, we illustrate Arrow's institutional trilemma with the help of a triangle.

> **Arrow's Theorem** states that every decision-making process that we could possibly design must sacrifice at least one of Arrow's fairness conditions—non-dictatorship, universal admissibility, unanimity, or independence from irrelevant alternatives—if it is to guarantee group transitivity and, hence, stable outcomes.

Basically, Arrow's Theorem states that when we design decision-making institutions, we can choose one and only one side of the triangle shown in Figure 10.10. If we want decision-making institutions that guarantee group transitivity and stable outcomes (A), then we must give up either non-dictatorship (B) or universal admissibility (C). If, on the other hand, we want to avoid dictatorship (B), then we must give up either transitivity (A) or universal admissibility (C). Finally, if we hold individual preferences as inviolable (C), then we must give up either transitivity (A) or non-dictatorship (B). To summarize, Arrow's Theorem proves that if the independence from irrelevant alternatives and the unanimity conditions

FIGURE 10.10   Arrow's Institutional Trilemma

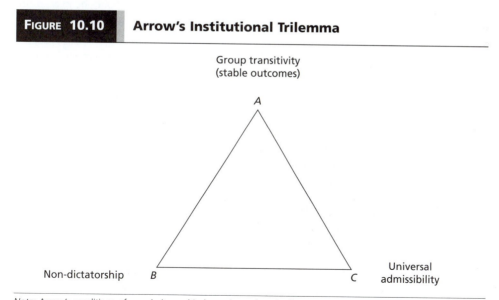

Note: Arrow's conditions of unanimity and independence from irrelevant alternatives are assumed as given here.

are assumed, then designers of group decision-making institutions will be forced to choose their poison from the following set: restrictions on individual preferences, dictatorship, or the possibility of group intransitivity.

In addition, Arrow's Theorem shows that it is, at the very least, difficult to interpret the outcome of any group decision-making process as *necessarily* reflecting the will of the group (Shepsle 1992). When a group comes to a clear decision it *may* mean that individual preferences lined up in a way that allowed for a clear outcome that represented, in some meaningful way, the desires of a large portion of the group. But it may also mean that individuals with inconvenient preferences were excluded from the process, or that some actor exercised agenda control. In such cases, outcomes may reflect the interest of some powerful subset of the group rather than the preferences of the group as a whole, or even some majority of the individuals in the group.

CONCLUSION

Most people associate democracy with majority rule. In this chapter we have examined various problems with majority-rule decision-making procedures. We have shown, for example, that there is a fundamental tension between the desire to guarantee that a group of individuals will be able to make coherent and stable choices on the one hand and the ability to guarantee the freedom of these individuals to form their own preferences and have those preferences influence group decisions on the other. Arrow's Theorem shows that these tensions extend far beyond majority rule to encompass a wide set of minimally fair group decision-making methods. Because most conceptions of democracy would probably be even more ambitious than Arrow's fairness criteria, these results have important and profound implications for democracy.

It is important to note at this point that the most direct implications of Arrow's Theorem concern particular mechanisms for group decision making. Arrow's Theorem is not in any direct sense about *collections* of decision-making procedures. Consider constitutions. A constitution does not typically stipulate *a* decision-making procedure to be used in a country but rather an entire set of decision-making procedures. For example, a constitution may stipulate how the head of the executive branch will be chosen, how legislators are chosen, how legislators choose laws, how the executive and legislative branches interact, how and if courts decide whether legislation is constitutional, which laws are under the jurisdiction of the national government and which are under local control, and the like. Arrow's Theorem applies to each and every one of these decision-making mechanisms, and the way the trilemma that Arrow's Theorem poses is resolved may vary from mechanism to mechanism within a particular constitution.[20] Some mechanisms, or institutions, may privilege group

---

20. Arrow's Theorem also applies to decision-making bodies we are involved with on a day-to-day basis—student organizations, faculties, labor unions, religious congregations, corporate boards, families, and groups of friends deciding which movie to see.

transitivity by reducing the number of alternatives from which people can choose—the two-party system used for electing presidents in the United States can be seen as an example of this. Other mechanisms or institutions may avoid group intransitivity by granting agenda-setting powers to an individual. A large literature on the U.S. Congress argues that committee chairs play this role in the legislative process. Cabinet ministers play a similar role in many parliamentary systems.

The key point is that *every* decision-making mechanism must grapple with the trade-offs posed by Arrow's Theorem and *every* system of government represents a collection of such decision-making mechanisms. Consequently, we can think of a system of government in terms of how its decision-making mechanisms tend to resolve the trade-offs between group transitivity and Arrow's fairness criteria. And to the extent that a set of decision-making mechanisms privileges group transitivity, it is useful to think about *which* of Arrow's fairness criteria tends to be sacrificed. For example, is stability produced because strong agenda setters are produced or because restrictions are placed on the preferences that actors hold? If it is the latter, we might ask whether this is achieved because some actors are excluded from deliberations or because strong mechanisms are in place to socialize participants so that they adopt the "right" preferences.

It should be clear by now that the most basic implication of Arrow's Theorem is this: there is no perfect set of decision-making institutions. Every set of institutions either runs the risk of group intransitivity or compromises a fairness condition. As such, democracy must in some sense be imperfect—either fairness is compromised or there will be a potential for instability. Perhaps this is what inspired former British prime minister Winston Churchill to say, "Democracy is the worst form of government, except for all those other forms that have been tried from time to time." [21] In Part II of this book, we compared democracy with dictatorship. In the following chapters, we examine the immense variety of democratic forms of government, focusing specifically on different configurations and their consequences.

In the next chapter, we examine the different ways we can choose the head of government and structure the relationship between the head of government and the legislative branch. In Chapter 12 we look at the myriad ways in which legislators are elected around the world. In Chapter 13 we investigate the ways in which group preferences interact with electoral laws to shape party systems. From the perspective of Arrow's Theorem, party systems can be thought of as a way of encouraging stability by reducing the number of alternatives to be considered in an election. In Chapter 14 we examine a whole host of other institutional mechanisms, such as the division of powers between national and subnational governments (federalism), the division of powers between different houses of the legislature (bicameralism), and the division of powers between the legislative and judicial branches (constitutional review). From the standpoint of Arrow's Theorem, these institutional mechanisms can be thought of as attempts to limit the control of powerful agenda setters by pitting them against each other.

---

21. House of Commons speech, November 11, 1947.

The immense variety of democratic institutions observed in the world is itself implied by Arrow's Theorem. Because there is no ideal decision-making mechanism, institutional choice is an exercise in the choice of "second bests," and which institution (or set of institutions) is adopted in any given time or place is going to be dictated by context—some situations make instability sufficiently threatening to make the sacrifice of fairness conditions reasonable, whereas others may permit individuals to accept a certain degree of instability in exchange for protecting the fairness of the decision-making process. Of course, the suggestion that we, as a society, may "choose" optimal institutions is itself in tension with Arrow's Theorem. Perhaps the institutions we confront today are the product of choices by agenda setters in the past, or inherited from times when actors with certain preferences were restricted from participating in the constitutional deliberations.

KEY CONCEPTS

Arrow's Theorem, *383*
Chaos Theorem, *379*
complete preference ordering, *359*
Condorcet's Paradox, *359*
Condorcet winner, *360*
consequentialist ethics, *356*
deontological ethics, *356*
independence from irrelevant
   alternatives condition, *382*
indifference curve, *375*
median voter, *370*
Median Voter Theorem, *370*

non-dictatorship condition, *381*
rational, *359*
round-robin tournament, *358*
sincere vote, *367*
single-peaked utility function, *369*
strategic, or sophisticated, vote, *367*
transitive preference ordering, *359*
unanimity, or pareto optimality, condition, *382*
universal admissibility condition, *381*
utility function, *368*
winset, *376*

PROBLEMS

The following problems address some of the more important concepts, theories, and methods introduced in this chapter.

Individual Preferences

1. What does it mean for an individual to be "rational"? Give a brief definition of the concept in your own words. If you use terms like *complete* and *transitive* to define the concept, be sure to define those terms as well.

2. In the problems at the end of Chapter 4, you were asked to consider the children's game of Rock, Paper, Scissors. In this game, two children simultaneously choose "rock," "paper," or "scissors." Rock beats scissors, paper beats rock, and scissors beat paper. Let's say that you prefer the winner in each of these pair-wise comparisons. That is, you prefer rock to scissors, scissors to paper, and paper to rock. Is your preference ordering complete? Explain

your answer. Is your preference ordering transitive? Explain your answer. Are you rational? Explain your answer.

3. Construct a complete and transitive preference ordering between three or more alternatives that you think some people might hold (or that you yourself hold). Now construct another (reasonable) preference ordering that does *not* satisfy completeness or transitivity.

4. Choose some issue dimension. With the help of a diagram, construct one preference ordering over the issue dimension that is single peaked and one that is not. Explain what single-peaked preferences are in your own words.

Agenda Setting

5. Imagine that you are one of three judges for a singing competition. You need to decide which of three finalists should win. You have no qualifications to evaluate actual singing ability, so you plan to make your choice based entirely on your preferences for the style of music that each performer chose: a sappy ballad, a traditional Irish folk song, and a heavy metal song. Luckily for you, you happened to see the notes written by the other judges, and so you know how your fellow judges ranked the finalists. One judge had the following preference ordering: ballad ≻ Irish folk song ≻ heavy metal. The other judge had the following preference ordering: heavy metal ≻ ballad ≻ Irish folk song. Your preference ordering, however, is the following: Irish folk song ≻ heavy metal ≻ ballad. The rules of the competition do not specify how the judges are to reach their decision.

   a. Let's suppose that you suggest a round-robin tournament in which everyone votes on the finalists in a series of pair-wise contests. How many pair-wise contests does each of the finalists win? Is there a Condorcet winner? Explain. Does this decision-making process identify a clear winner? Explain.

   b. Now let's suppose that you propose a decision-making procedure by which all of the judges begin by considering only a subset of the available pair-wise contests. The specific decision-making procedure that you propose is that two finalists should compete in a pair-wise contest with the winner competing in a second and final round against the remaining finalist. Given your preference ordering, which finalist do you want to win? If you were in charge of setting the voting agenda and could determine the order in which the pair-wise contests took place, what order would you pick and why?

Median Voter Theorem and Party Competition

6. In Figure 10.11, we illustrate an election in which there are seven voters (A, B, C, D, E, F, G) arrayed along a single left-right issue dimension that runs from 0 (most left) to 10 (most right). Each voter is assumed to have single-peaked utility functions and to vote for the party that is located closest to her ideal point. The voters are participating in a majority-rule election in which there are two parties, P_1 and P_2, competing for office. These parties can be thought of as "office-seeking" parties because they care only about winning the election and getting into office.

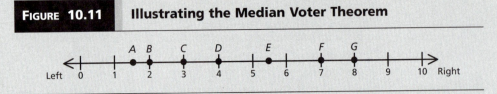

FIGURE 10.11   **Illustrating the Median Voter Theorem**

a. Which voter is the median voter? What is her ideological position?

b. Let's suppose that P_1 locates at position 2 on the left-right issue dimension and that P_2 locates at position 7. How many votes does P_1 win? How many votes does P_2 win? Who wins the election? Where does the winner implement policy on the left-right issue dimension? Will P_1 and P_2 want to stay at these policy positions for the next election? If not, what policy positions do you think they will adopt and why?

c. Now let's suppose that P_1 locates at position 4 and P_2 locates at position 4. What is the outcome of this election? Does P_1 or P_2 want to change policy positions given where the other party is located? If so, why? If not, why not?

Instead of office-seeking parties in our example, let's now assume that we have two "policy-seeking" parties, L and R. L is a left-wing party whose ideal point is 2, and R is a right-wing party whose ideal point is 7. Policy-seeking parties care about where policy is implemented.

d. Let's suppose that L locates at its ideal point (2) on the left-right issue dimension and that R locates at its ideal point (7). How many votes does L win? How many votes does R win? Who wins the election? Where does the winner implement policy on the left-right issue dimension? Will L and R want to stay at their ideal points for the next election? If not, what policy positions do you think they will adopt and why?

e. Now let's suppose that L locates at position 4 and R locates at position 4. What is the outcome of this election? Where will policy be implemented on the left-right issue dimension? Does L or R want to change policy positions given where the other party is located? If so, why? If not, why not?

f. Based on your answers so far, does the result from the Median Voter Theorem stating that parties will converge to the position of the median voter depend on whether political parties are office seeking or policy seeking? Explain.

g. Suppose that some event occurs that causes several voters to adopt more centrist positions on the left-right issue dimension. The new distribution of voters is shown in Figure 10.12. Where will parties P_1 and P_2 locate in the left-right space, given the centrist nature of the electorate? Why?

FIGURE 10.12   **Illustrating the Median Voter Theorem—A Centrist Electorate**

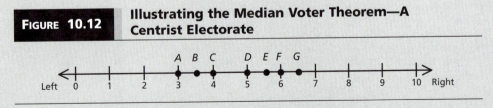

h. Suppose now that some polarizing event occurs that causes several voters to adopt more extreme positions on the left-right issue dimension. The new distribution of voters is shown in Figure 10.13. Where will parties P_1 and P_2 locate in the left-right space, given the polarized nature of the electorate? Why?

FIGURE 10.13	**Illustrating the Median Voter Theorem—A Polarized Electorate**

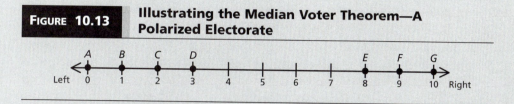

i. Based on your answers to the two previous questions, does the result from the Median Voter Theorem stating that parties will converge to the position of the median voter depend on the distribution of voter ideal points? Explain.

j. Suppose now that three parties instead of just two are competing in the election. Imagine that all three of the parties locate at the position of the median voter. Would any of the parties want to change their position? If so, why? If not, why not? If it helps, you can think of all three parties locating at the position of the median voter in any of the three figures (10.11, 10.12, or 10.13).

k. Based on your answer to the previous question, does the result from the Median Voter Theorem stating that parties will converge to the position of the median voter depend on there being only two parties? Explain.

Spatial Models

7. The Median Voter Theorem is an example of a larger class of models known as spatial models. The primary characteristic of spatial models is that the preferences of actors can usefully be conceived as points in some kind of policy "space" (Hinich and Munger 1997, 5). Political scientists have employed spatial models to examine a diverse array of political situations, from leaders of countries negotiating territorial conflicts, to the relations between Congress, the president, and the Supreme Court in the United States, to party factions choosing a policy platform, to a policy adviser making recommendations to an elected official, and so on.

We now employ a simple spatial model to examine a situation in which a president (P) and a legislature (L) are considering whether to change the current level of public goods provision in a country. We can think of the level of public goods provision in a country as a single-issue dimension ranging from low public goods provision (0) to high public goods provision (10). The current level of public goods provision is referred to as the status quo (SQ). Both the president and the legislature have preferences over what the level of public goods provision should be. We will assume that the legislature gets to make proposals on what the level of public goods provision should be and that the president can either accept or veto these proposals. If the president vetoes the legislature's proposal, then the status quo policy is maintained. If the president approves the legislature's proposal, then the proposal is implemented and becomes the new status quo.

In Figure 10.14, we illustrate one possible scenario in which a president and a legislature could find themselves. The status quo level of public goods provision is 2. The president's most preferred level of public goods provision is 7, and the legislature's most preferred level is 4. Recall that in spatial models, actors are assumed to prefer policy outcomes that are closer to their ideal points than ones that are farther away. In other words, if an actor has to vote over two alternatives, then she will choose the one that is closer to her ideal point. If an actor has to choose between two policy outcomes that are equidistant from her ideal point, then she is indifferent between them and could choose either as a best response. For example, the president would be indifferent between having public goods provision at 6 or 8 because both of these outcomes are one unit away from her ideal point, 7.

| FIGURE 10.14 | **Choosing a Level of Public Goods Provision: Scenario 1** |

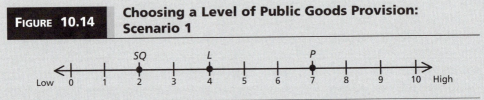

Note: SQ = the current level of public goods provision; L = the ideal point of the legislature; P = the ideal point of the president.

a. Given that the status quo is at 2, what is the range of policy outcomes that the president prefers to the status quo? Recall that the president prefers any policy that is closer to her ideal point than the status quo.

b. Given that the status quo is at 2, what is the range of policy outcomes that the legislature prefers to the status quo? Recall that the legislature prefers any policy that is closer to its ideal point than the status quo.

c. Do the ranges of policy outcomes that the president and legislature prefer to the status quo overlap? If they do overlap, how would you interpret the set of points where they overlap?

d. If the legislature proposes a new policy, and if it needs the president's approval for the new policy to be implemented, what level of public goods provision do you think the legislature will propose? Why? *Hint:* If the legislature proposes a new policy, it will want to choose the level of public goods provision that is closest to its ideal point and that is acceptable to the president.

Now imagine that the ideal points of the president and the legislature are reversed. In other words, the president's ideal point is now 4 and the legislature's ideal point is now 7. This scenario is illustrated in Figure 10.15.

FIGURE 10.15   **Choosing a Level of Public Goods Provision:**
Scenario 2

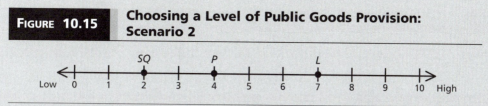

Note: SQ = the current level of public goods provision; L = the ideal point of the legislature; P = the ideal point of the president.

e. Given that the status quo is at 2, what is the range of policy outcomes that the president prefers to the status quo?

f. Given that the status quo is at 2, what is the range of policy outcomes that the legislature prefers to the status quo?

g. Do the ranges of policy outcomes that the president and legislature prefer to the status quo overlap? If they do overlap, how would you interpret the set of points where they overlap?

h. If the legislature proposes a new policy, and its implementation needs the president's approval, what level of public goods provision do you think the legislature will propose? Why?

Now imagine that the ideal points of the president and the legislature are on opposite sides of the status quo. Let's assume that the president's ideal point is now 1 and the legislature's ideal point is now 4. This scenario is illustrated in Figure 10.16.

FIGURE 10.16   **Choosing a Level of Public Goods Provision:**
Scenario 3

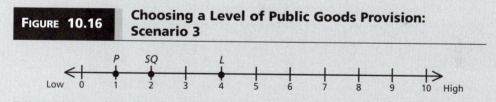

Note: SQ = the current level of public goods provision; L = the ideal point of the legislature; P = the ideal point of the president.

i. Given that the status quo is at 2, what is the range of policy outcomes that the president prefers to the status quo?

j. Given that the status quo is at 2, what is the range of policy outcomes that the legislature prefers to the status quo?

k. Do the ranges of policy outcomes that the president and legislature prefer to the status quo overlap? If they do overlap, how would you interpret the set of points where they overlap? If they do not overlap, what does this mean?

l. Can the legislature make a successful proposal to change the status quo? If so, why? If not, why not?

m. Given your analysis of the three scenarios above, what can you say about the conditions under which policy will change versus when it will be stable?

Box 10.2

STABILITY IN TWO-DIMENSIONAL MAJORITY-RULE VOTING

Earlier in this chapter, we argued that multidimensional voting was almost always going to be characterized by instability and cyclical majorities. Recall that this was the central insight gleaned from the Chaos Theorem. Only in extremely rare circumstances can stability be achieved. At the time, we did not present any evidence for why the conditions necessary to achieve stability in multidimensional voting were likely to be so rare. Although a full treatment of this subject exceeds the space and technical limits of this book, we now present some informal evidence to support this assertion. To keep things simple, we focus on two-dimensional voting. The logic of our argument, though, applies equally well to multidimensional scenarios in general.

One way instability is avoided in two-dimensional voting is if the individuals in a group have radially symmetric preferences (Plott 1967). This involves having a single individual be the median voter in both dimensions and all of the other voters be aligned symmetrically around this person. In Figure 10-17, we present a situation in which three individuals (voters A, B, and C) must make decisions on two issue dimensions simultaneously. For example, perhaps Issue 1 is the amount of money spent on education and Issue 2 is the amount of money spent on health care. As you can see, the voters in Figure 10-17 have radially symmetric preferences. Voter B is the median voter on both Issue 1 and Issue 2. For example, voter B has one voter to her left and one to her right on Issue 2, and one voter above her and one below her on Issue 1. As the dashed line indicates, the two other voters, A and C, are aligned symmetrically around voter B; that is, they are exactly opposite each other with voter B in between. Given this arrangement of voter preferences, if voter B's ideal point were ever to become the status quo, there would be no majority that could displace it. In effect, voter B's ideal point is an equilibrium in this two-dimensional majority-rule voting scenario.

To see why, we must examine the indifference curves of voters A and C with respect to voter B's ideal point (the status quo)—these are the circles that surround the ideal points of voters A and C. These circles show all of the policy outcomes for which voters A and C would be indifferent between that policy and the status quo. Note that each indifference curve goes through B. Consequently, any point inside a circle is closer (and, therefore, preferred) to the relevant voter's ideal point than the status quo (represented by voter B's ideal point. There is no circle with B as its center because there are no alternatives that voter B prefers to his own ideal point.[1] The two circles in Figure 10-17, therefore, represent the set of policy proposals that A and C prefer to the status quo. Majority rule means that two out of the three voters would have to prefer an alternative to B's position for a policy proposal to dislodge B. The fact that the two circles never overlap, though, means that A and C cannot agree on an alternative to replace the status quo. If C proposed an alternative closer to his ideal point, A and B would vote against it. Similarly, if A proposed an alternative closer to his ideal point, B and C would vote against it. In other words, any alternative to B's position

---

1. That is the definition of an ideal point, after all.

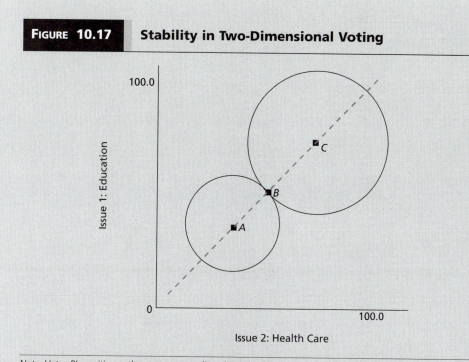

FIGURE 10.17   **Stability in Two-Dimensional Voting**

Note: Voter *B*'s position = the status quo policy; the two circles = the indifference curves for voters *A* and *C* with respect to the status quo policy *B*.

would never get more than one vote and would, therefore, lose. As this example illustrates, it is possible to obtain a stable outcome—in this case *B*'s position—in two-dimensional majority-rule voting.

Although stability is *possible* in two-dimensional majority-rule voting games, is it *likely*? Many scholars think not. To see why, imagine what happens if one of the voter's ideal points moves just a little. In Figure 10-18, we shift voter *C*'s ideal point by an arbitrary amount off of the dashed line to the southeast. You will immediately notice that there is now a lens-shaped area south of *B* in which the indifference curves of voters *A* and *C* overlap. This lens-shaped area is the winset of *B* and contains all of the alternative policy outcomes that both voters *A* and *C* prefer to *B*. This means that if either voter *A* or *C* has an opportunity to propose a change in policy to a point in the winset, say P_1, he will do so and the new policy proposal will win a majority vote. Once this happens, all the indifference curves will need to be redrawn so that they go through this new status quo point. If we were to do this, we would find another lens-shaped area, thereby demonstrating that at least two voters will prefer yet another policy combination to this new status quo. At this point we will be off to the races, and the instability of the Chaos Theorem will ensue because the condition that had previously made *B* a stable outcome no longer pertains.

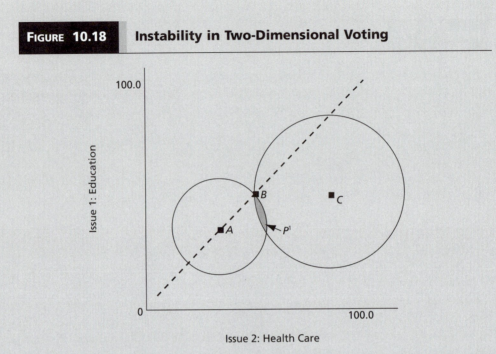

| FIGURE 10.18 | **Instability in Two-Dimensional Voting** |

Note: Voter *B*'s position = the status quo policy; the two circles = the indifference curves for voters *A* and *C* with respect to the status quo policy; the shaded oval area = the winset of *B* and represents the alternative policy outcomes that voters *A* and *C* prefer to voter *B*'s position. P^1 = a policy proposal that would defeat the status quo policy (*B*) in a majority rule vote.

Recall what made *B* stable in the first place. First, there was a voter whose ideal point made her a median voter in both issue dimensions. Second, all of the other voters' ideal points radiated from *B* in just the right way. Specifically, *A* and *C* were aligned on a straight line with *B* (the dashed line in Figure 10-17). Charles Plott (1967) proved that such "radial symmetry" is sufficient to guarantee the existence of a stable outcome in a two-dimensional majority-rule voting scenario. Radial symmetry, however, is not strictly necessary, and subsequent scholars have identified other conditions that are sufficient to produce stability.[2] These further conditions, like Plott's condition, though, are quite restrictive. As a result, it is reasonable to conclude that majority rule is unstable in multidimensional situations except under very unusual circumstances in which voter preferences line up in just the right way.

2. Hinich and Munger's *Analytical Politics* (1997) is a good resource for ambitious students who would like to pursue this topic further.

11 Parliamentary, Presidential, and Mixed Democracies

Making and Breaking Governments

The essence of pure parliamentarism is mutual dependence. . . . The essence of pure presidentialism is mutual independence.

Alfred Stepan and Cindy Skach, "Constitutional Frameworks and Democratic Consolidation"

A cabinet is a combining committee—a *hyphen* which joins, a *buckle* which fastens, the legislative part of the state to the executive part of the state. In its origin it belongs to the one, in its functions it belongs to the other.

Walter Bagehot, *The English Constitution*

- Political scientists often classify democracies as parliamentary, presidential, or mixed. Whether a democracy is parliamentary, presidential, or mixed depends on the relationship between the government, the legislature, and (if there is one) the president.

- The government formation process in parliamentary democracies can be quite complicated and take a long time. Several different types of government can form: single-party majority governments, minimal winning coalitions, minority governments, surplus majority governments, and so on. The type of government that forms depends on many factors, including whether the political actors in a country are office seeking or policy seeking. Although some governments in parliamentary democracies last several years, others last just a few days.

- The government formation process in presidential democracies is different in many ways from that in parliamentary democracies. Presidential democracies have more minority governments but fewer coalition governments on average than parliamentary ones. They also have more nonpartisan ministers and a lower proportionality in the allocation of ministerial posts. Governments in presidential democracies look more like those in parliamentary democracies if the president is weak.

- The government formation process in mixed democracies is relatively understudied. There is evidence, however, that governments in mixed democracies share characteristics from governments in both parliamentary and presidential democracies.

In Chapter 5 we looked at how political scientists distinguish between democracies and dictatorships. For example, one set of scholars classifies countries as democratic if (a) the chief executive is elected, (b) the legislature is elected, (c) there is more than one party competing in elections, and (d) there has been an alternation of power under identical electoral rules (Przeworski et al. 2000). Our focus now turns to examining the different types of democracy that exist around the world. As you can imagine, we could distinguish between democracies in many, many different ways. Most political scientists, however, tend to classify democracies according to the form of government they have, that is, according to the rules that define who the government is, how the government comes to power, and how the government remains in power (Cheibub 2007). This classification scheme includes three basic types of democracy: parliamentary, presidential, and mixed.[1] In this chapter, we examine how scholars distinguish between these three types. We then take a close look at how governments form and survive in these democratic systems.

CLASSIFYING PARLIAMENTARY, PRESIDENTIAL, AND MIXED DEMOCRACIES

Whether a democracy is parliamentary, presidential, or mixed depends on the relationship between (a) the government, which comprises the political chief executive and the ministers that head the various government departments, (b) the legislature, and (c) the president (if there is one; Cheibub 2007).[2] Ultimately, distinguishing between the three types of democracy requires identifying which actors can remove the government from office. Democracies in which the legislature cannot remove the government are presidential; democracies in which only the legislature can remove the government are parliamentary; and democracies in which both the legislature and the president can remove the government are mixed. In effect, three basic questions are necessary to be able to unambiguously classify democracies as parliamentary, presidential, or mixed.[3] These questions are shown in Figure 11-1.

---

1. Mixed regimes are sometimes called semi-presidential or premier-presidential (Duverger 1980; Shugart and Carey 1992; Sartori 1997; Elgie 1999).

2. Our upcoming discussion about how to classify parliamentary, presidential, and mixed democracies draws heavily on Cheibub (2007). Interested scholars should also see Cheibub and Gandhi (2004).

3. Some political scientists employ slightly different criteria to those we are about to present for classifying democracies as parliamentary, presidential, or mixed (Verney 1959; Lijphart 1984, 1999; Shugart and Carey 1992; Stepan and Skach 1993; Sartori 1997; Shugart and Mainwaring 1997). These alternative criteria are, however, among other things, operationally ambiguous because they do not allow one to unambiguously code all democracies as either parliamentary, presidential, or mixed (Elgie 1998; Müller, Bergman, and Strøm 2003; Cheibub 2007).

FIGURE 11.1	**Classifying Parliamentary, Presidential, and Mixed Democracies**

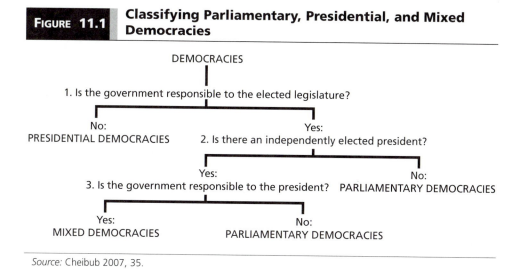

Source: Cheibub 2007, 35.

Is the Government Responsible to the Elected Legislature?

The first question is whether the government is responsible to the elected legislature. Recall that the government is made up of the political chief executive and the ministers that head the various government departments. **Legislative responsibility** means that a legislative majority has the constitutional power to remove the government from office without cause.[4] In those democracies that are characterized by legislative responsibility, the mechanism that the legislature can initiate to remove a government is called the **vote of no confidence.** Basically, a vote of no confidence involves a vote in the legislature on whether the government should remain in office. If a majority of legislators vote against the government, then the government must resign. Some countries, such as Belgium, Germany, Israel, and Spain, adopt a slightly different version of this procedure called a **constructive vote of no confidence.** A constructive vote of no confidence requires that those who oppose the government also indicate who should replace the government if the incumbent loses. In effect, a successful constructive vote of no confidence removes one government from office and replaces it with another in a single step. One of the reasons for adopting a constructive vote of no confidence is that it tends to reduce government instability. As you can imagine, it is often easier to get people to

> **Legislative responsibility** refers to a situation in which a legislative majority has the constitutional power to remove a government from office without cause.

> A **vote of no confidence** is initiated by the legislature; if the government does not obtain a legislative majority in this vote, it must resign. A **constructive vote of no confidence** must indicate who will replace the government if the incumbent loses a vote of no confidence. A **vote of confidence** is initiated by the government; if the government does not obtain a legislative majority in this vote, it must resign.

---

4. Legislatures may be able to remove members of the government from office in presidential systems, but only "for cause" —typically incapacitation or criminal behavior.

vote against a government than it is to get them to agree on who should replace it. During the interwar period in Weimar Germany, it was relatively easy to build legislative majorities who opposed the incumbent government. It was extremely difficult, however, to construct and maintain majorities in favor of a particular alternative. As a result, governments tended to be extremely short-lived. It was in response to this that the postwar German constitution adopted the *constructive* vote of no confidence. With this new provision, an incumbent German government can be brought down only if a legislative majority can also agree on an alternative government to replace it.

In addition to votes of no confidence, some countries have what is known as a **vote of confidence** (Huber 1996). A vote of confidence is similar to a vote of no confidence in that governments who do not obtain a legislative majority must resign.[5] The difference is that votes of confidence are initiated by governments, whereas votes of no confidence are initiated by the legislature. You might be wondering why a government would ever call a vote of confidence in itself. There are a number of reasons. For example, one has to do with the fact that votes of confidence can be attached to pieces of legislation in many countries. If a government is unsure about its ability to gain sufficient legislative support to pass some piece of legislation, then it can choose to make the vote on this legislation a vote on the continued existence of the government. Oftentimes, legislators who do not like the particular piece of legislation that the government is trying to pass may nonetheless decide to vote for it under these circumstances because they do not actually wish to bring the government down over it. This is particularly the case if bringing the government down means new elections and the possibility of losing their seats. Similarly, governments can employ votes of confidence in an attempt to unite a divided party or to humiliate critics who publicly criticize the government but who are unwilling to actually vote the government out of office. Of course, these tactical uses of the vote of confidence can backfire against those who use them if the government misjudges the willingness of its opponents to call its bluff and vote against the motion.

In sum, legislatures in democracies that exhibit legislative responsibility can remove governments by successfully passing a vote of no confidence or defeating a government-initiated vote of confidence. As Figure 11.1 illustrates, democracies in which there is no legislative responsibility are presidential; democracies that have legislative responsibility may be either parliamentary or mixed. To help determine whether these latter democracies are parliamentary or mixed, we must start by asking a second question.

Is There an Independently (Directly or Indirectly) Elected President?

The second question is whether there is an independently elected president. "Independently elected" refers to the independence of the president from the legislature—the president is

---

5. Germany represents a slight exception. Article 81 of the German constitution allows a government that has lost a vote of confidence in the lower house (Bundestag) to retain power for six months if it continues to enjoy the support of a majority in the upper house (Bundesrat).

elected to serve a fixed term in office and cannot be removed by the legislature.[6] Presidents can be either directly elected if the voters cast ballots for the candidate they wish to elect (such as Benin, Mexico, and South Korea) or indirectly elected if voters cast ballots to elect an assembly whose role it is to elect a president (such as the Czech Republic, Italy, and the United States). The mere presence or absence of an independently elected political actor with the title of president, though, is neither a necessary nor sufficient condition in and of itself to classify a democracy as parliamentary, presidential, or mixed. As Figure 11.1 indicates, the defining characteristic of a presidential regime is not that there is an independently elected president; rather, it is that there is no legislative responsibility. In fact, independently elected presidents can exist in all three types of democracy.[7] For example, directly elected presidents exist in presidential democracies (such as Guatemala, Malawi, and Russia), parliamentary democracies (such as Cape Verde, Ireland, and Slovakia), and mixed democracies (such as France, Mali, and Poland). Similarly, indirectly elected presidents exist in presidential democracies (such as the United States), parliamentary democracies (such as Germany, Greece, and Italy), and mixed democracies (such as Finland prior to 1999).[8]

Although the presence of an independently elected president is neither a necessary nor sufficient condition for distinguishing between the three types of democracy, we can conclude that any democracy that has legislative responsibility but no independently-elected president must be parliamentary. Most parliamentary democracies fall into this category (Cheibub 2007, 37). Still, as we have already indicated, some parliamentary democracies do have independently elected presidents. To distinguish between these parliamentary democracies and mixed democracies, we must ask a third and final question.

Is the Government Responsible to the President?

The third question is whether the government is responsible to an independently elected president. Governments are responsible to a president in a direct way if the president can unilaterally dismiss the government in its entirety or one minister at a time (such as in Iceland and Portugal). They are responsible to the president in an indirect way if the president can dismiss the government by dissolving the legislature (such as in France and Portugal). Democracies in which the government is responsible to both the legislature and an independently elected president are mixed. Democracies in which the government is responsible only to the legislature

---

6. Some democracies, like the United States, allow for the possibility of removing the president only through the extraordinary and costly procedure of impeachment.

7. It is worth noting that simply bestowing the title of president on a political actor does not necessarily make that actor an independently elected president. For example, Kiribati, the Marshall Islands, and South Africa all have political actors that are called "presidents." The fact that these actors can all be removed from office through a vote of no confidence by the legislature, though, means that they are not *independently* elected. In effect, these actors are the same as prime ministers in parliamentary democracies even though they go by the title of president. It is for this reason, in combination with the existence of legislative responsibility in these countries, that these democracies are considered parliamentary (Cheibub 2007, 39–40).

8. In 2000, Finland adopted a new constitution that removed the president's power to dissolve the legislature and appoint or remove the government. As a result, Finland is today a parliamentary, rather than a mixed, democracy.

(irrespective of whether they have an independently elected president) are parliamentary. In those parliamentary democracies with independently elected presidents, the president may be the "head of state," but he is not the "head of government." Instead, the prime minister is the "head of government" and the president's duties are restricted to the largely ceremonial tasks of the "head of state." When the head of state in a parliamentary democracy is not a president, it is typically a monarch—again, with largely ceremonial duties.

> A **presidential democracy** is one in which the government does not depend on a legislative majority to exist. A **parliamentary democracy** is one in which the government depends only on a legislative majority to exist. A **mixed democracy** is one in which the government depends on a legislative majority and on an independently elected president to exist.

As our discussion indicates, we can classify our three types of democracy in the following way:

- **Presidential democracy:** Democracies in which the government does not depend on a legislative majority to exist are presidential.
- **Parliamentary democracy:** Democracies in which the government depends only on a legislative majority to exist are parliamentary.
- **Mixed democracy:** Democracies in which the government depends on a legislative majority and on an independently elected president to exist are mixed.

An Overview of Parliamentary, Presidential, and Mixed Democracies

Figure 11.2 shows the number and percentage of parliamentary, presidential, and mixed democracies that there were in the world each year from 1946 to 2002. As the figure indicates, the parliamentary form of democracy is the most common in the world. Almost half (56 out of 114) of the world's democracies in 2002 were parliamentary. The percentage of parliamentary democracies in the world has been much higher than this in the past, though, with fully 74 percent of democracies being parliamentary in 1978. About a third (37 out of 114) of the world's democracies were presidential in 2002 and about a fifth (21 out of 114) were mixed. A striking feature of Figure 11.2 is the rapid increase in the number and percentage of mixed democracies in the world from 1946 to 2002. For example, out of the world's 31 democracies in 1946, only those of Finland and Iceland (6 percent) were mixed. In contrast, by 2002 fully 21 (18 percent) of the world's 114 democracies were mixed. In Table 11.1 we list those democracies that were parliamentary, presidential, and mixed in 2002.

MAKING AND BREAKING GOVERNMENTS: PARLIAMENTARY DEMOCRACIES

Having addressed the criteria for classifying democracies as parliamentary, presidential, or mixed, we now try to give a more in-depth insight into how these different democratic systems operate in the real world. We do so by carefully examining how governments form and survive. We start with parliamentary democracies.

FIGURE 11.2 **Parliamentary, Presidential, and Mixed Democracies, 1946–2002**

a: Number of Democracies by Democracy Type

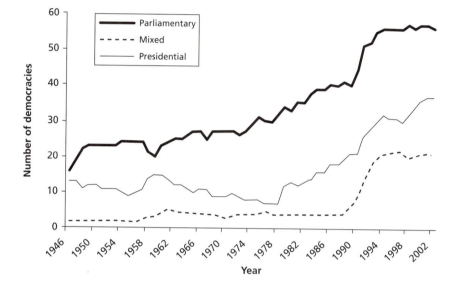

b: Percentage of Democracies by Democracy Type

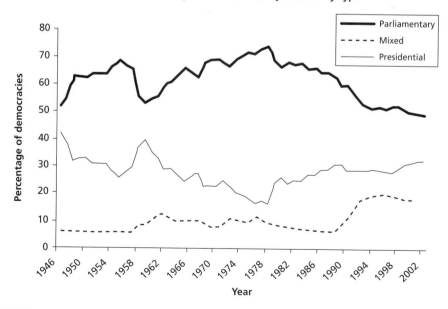

Source: Data were generously provided by José Antonio Cheibub. Przeworski and colleagues' criteria were employed to determine whether a country was a democracy or a dictatorship.

TABLE 11.1	**Parliamentary, Presidential, and Mixed Democracies, 2002**

Parliamentary	Presidential	Mixed
Albania, Andorra, Antigua, Australia, Austria, Bahamas, Bangladesh, Barbados, Belgium, Belize, Bulgaria, Canada, Cape Verde, Czech Republic, Denmark, Dominica, Estonia, Finland, Germany, Greece, Grenada, Hungary, India, Ireland, Israel, Italy, Jamaica, Japan, Kiribati, Latvia, Lesotho, Liechtenstein, Luxembourg, Macedonia, Malta, Marshall Islands, Mauritius, Nauru, Netherlands, New Zealand, Norway, Papua New Guinea, Slovakia, Slovenia, Solomon Islands, South Africa, Spain, St. Kitts and Nevis, St. Vincent, Sweden, Thailand, Trinidad and Tobago, Turkey, United Kingdom, Vanuatu	Argentina, Benin, Bolivia, Brazil, Chile, Colombia, Costa Rica, Ivory Coast, Dominican Republic, El Salvador, Ghana, Greek Cyprus, Guatemala, Guinea-Bissau, Guyana, Honduras, Indonesia, Kenya, South Korea, Malawi, Mexico, Micronesia, Namibia, Nicaragua, Nigeria, Palau, Panama, Peru, Philippines, San Marino, Sierra Leone, Suriname, Switzerland, United States, Uruguay, Venezuela, Zambia	Armenia, Central African Republic, Croatia, France, Haiti, Iceland, Lithuania, Madagascar, Mali, Moldova, Mongolia, Niger, Poland, Portugal, Romania, Russia, Sao Tomé and Principe, Senegal, Sri Lanka, Taiwan, Ukraine

The Government

The **government in a parliamentary democracy** comprises a prime minister and the cabinet. The **prime minister** is the political chief executive and head of the government in a parliamentary democracy. The **cabinet** is composed of ministers whose job it is to be in the cabinet and head the various government departments. In a parliamentary democracy, the executive branch and the government are the same thing.

The **government in a parliamentary democracy** is essentially made up of a prime minister and a cabinet. As an example, the British government is shown in Table 11.2. The **prime minister** (PM) in a parliamentary democracy is the political chief executive and head of the government. The position of prime minister goes under a number of different titles in various countries—"prime minister" in the United Kingdom, "chancellor" in Austria and Germany, "taoiseach" in Ireland, "premier" in Italy and Poland, and even "president" in the Marshall Islands and South Africa. Here, and throughout, we will follow convention and refer to the political chief executive in a parliamentary system as prime minister. The **cabinet** is equivalent in many ways to a "country's board of directors" (Gallagher, Laver, and Mair 2006, 40). The cabinet comprises ministers whose job it is to be in the cabinet and to head one of the government's various departments, such as Education, Finance, Foreign Affairs, and Social Policy. The department of which the minister is head is often referred to as the

TABLE 11.2	British Government, May 2005		
Minister	**Department**	**Minister**	**Department**
Tony Blair	Prime Minister	Jacqui Smith	Chief Whip
John Prescott	Deputy Prime Minister	Alan Johnson	Education
Gordon Brown	Chancellor of the Exchequer	Stephen Timms	Treasury
Margaret Beckett	Foreign Affairs	Hazel Blears	Without Portfolio
John Reid	Home Department	Baroness Amos	House of Lords
David Miliband	Environment	Lord Falconer	Constitution
Douglas Alexander	Transport/Scotland	Hilary Benn	Development
Patricia Hewitt	Health	Des Brown	Defence
Peter Hain	Northern Ireland/Wales	Tessa Jowell	Culture/Sport
John Hutton	Work and Pensions	Ruth Kelly	Local Government
Alistair Darling	Trade & Industry	Jack Straw	House of Commons leader/
Hilary Armstrong	Social Exclusion/ Duchy of Lancaster		Lords Reform

minister's portfolio. Each minister is directly responsible to the cabinet for what happens in her department. If a problem arises in a particular department, then the minister is supposed to be held responsible for it. This practice is known as the constitutional doctrine of **ministerial responsibility.** Although this practice is part of the constitutional theory of almost all parliamentary democracies, it is now relatively rare to see ministers actually resign when things go wrong under their supervision.

> **Ministerial responsibility** refers to the constitutional doctrine by which cabinet ministers must bear ultimate responsibility for what happens in their ministry.

As a member of the cabinet, as well as the head of a government department, a minister is part of a collective entity that is responsible for making the most important decisions about the direction of governmental policy. Cabinet ministers are typically bound by the doctrine of **collective cabinet responsibility.** This doctrine means that, although ministers may air their disagreements about policy freely in cabinet meetings, once a cabinet decision has been made, each minister must defend the government policy in public. Cabinet ministers who feel that they cannot do this must resign, as Robin Cook did as foreign minister in the United Kingdom in 2003 when he disagreed with the British government's decision to go to war over Iraq. This notion of collective cabinet responsibility stands in stark contrast to the behavior and expectations about cabinet ministers in presidential democracies. This is because cabinet members in presidential democracies are in charge of particular policy areas and are not responsible for, or expected to influence, the overall direction of government policy; that is the domain of the president and his staff.

> **Collective cabinet responsibility** refers to the doctrine by which ministers must publicly support collective cabinet decisions or resign.

The Government Formation Process

In parliamentary democracies, citizens do not elect the prime minister or cabinet members; they elect only members of the legislature. So, how, you might wonder, do governments actually form and take office? Consider the results from the 1987 West German legislative elections shown in Table 11.3. Can you figure out what German government formed after these elections just by looking at the table? It's not obvious, right?

When thinking about the government formation process, it is important to remember that any proposed government must enjoy the "confidence" of the legislature, both to come to power and to stay in power. As we saw earlier, this is the defining characteristic of a parliamentary democracy—the government must always enjoy the support of a legislative majority. In some countries, a potential government may have to demonstrate that it has such support before it can take office by holding what's known as an **investiture vote** (see Box 11.1). If the proposed government does not win a majority in this vote, it cannot take office. Even if there is no formal investiture vote, though, a potential government in a parliamentary democracy must still have the *implicit* support of a legislative majority at all times. This is because of the ability of the legislature to call a vote of no confidence in the government at any time. If the government ever loses such a vote because it cannot garner the support of a legislative majority, then it must resign. Ultimately, a parliamentary government can be removed from office any time a majority of legislators decides that this is what should happen. As a result, governments that come to power in parliamentary systems must always enjoy the implicit support of a legislative majority even if they never have to explicitly demonstrate this in an investiture vote or a vote of no confidence.

If a single party controlled a majority of the seats in the legislature, then one might expect that party to form a **single-party majority government.** In fact, this expectation is strongly supported by data from the Constitutional

A **single-party majority government** is a government in which a single party controls a legislative majority.

Change and Parliamentary Democracy (CCPD) Project. These data show that a party controlling a majority (50 percent plus 1 or more) of legislative seats nearly always forms a gov-

TABLE 11.3	German Legislative Elections, 1987	
Party	**Seats**	**Percentage**
Christian Democrats (CDU/CSU)	223	44.9
Social Democrats (SPD)	186	37.4
Free Democrats (FDP)	46	9.3
Greens	42	8.5
Other parties	0	0.0
Total	497	100

Source: Data are from Adam Carr at http://psephos.adam-carr.net.

An **investiture vote** is a formal vote in the legislature to determine whether a proposed government can take office.

ox 11.1   ## INVESTITURE VOTES

An **investiture vote** is a formal vote in the legislature to determine whether a proposed government can take office. The precise rules governing investiture votes vary from country to country (Bergman 1993). Some constitutions require an absolute majority—more than half of all legislative members must vote for the proposed government. Other constitutions require only a plurality—more people should vote for the proposed government than vote against it. In Germany and Spain, a proposed government must win an absolute majority in a first vote of investiture but only a plurality if a second vote is needed. In Belgium, Ireland, and Italy, a new government requires only a plurality in the first vote. If abstentions are allowed, they may count for or against the government, depending on the country. For example, abstentions count in favor of the government in Italy. As Strøm (1995, 75) reports, "Giulio Andreotti's famous [1976] government of *non sfiducia* ('non-no confidence') was supported by no more than 258 deputies out of 630. Yet Andreotti comfortably gained office, since all but 44 of the remaining members abstained."

ernment on its own. For example, a single party controlling a majority of seats formed a government on its own fifty (85 percent) out of a possible fifty-nine times that such a party existed in thirteen West European parliamentary democracies from 1945 to 1998.[9]

But what happens when no single party commands a legislative majority, as in Germany in 1987? This is, in fact, the normal situation in most parliamentary democracies. As the CCPD data reveal, fully 251 of the 310 governments (81 percent) that formed in the thirteen West European parliamentary democracies in their sample emerged from political situations in which no single party controlled a majority of legislative seats. As we shall see in more detail when we examine electoral rules in the next two chapters, the frequent use of proportional representation electoral systems helps to explain why so few parties ever win a majority of votes or seats. Only countries like the United Kingdom that employ disproportional electoral rules, such as single-member district plurality systems, regularly produce single parties that control a legislative majority. Even in these countries, it is rare for a single party to actually win a majority of the votes; instead, the mechanical effect of the disproportional electoral rules awards legislative majorities to parties with less than 50 percent of the vote.

9. The countries included here are Austria, Belgium, Denmark, Germany, Greece, Ireland, Italy, Luxembourg, Netherlands, Norway, Spain, Sweden, and the United Kingdom. The Comparative Parliamentary Democracy Project can be found at http://www.pol.umu.se/ccpd/CCPD/index.asp (Müller and Strøm 2000; Strøm, Müller, and Bergman 2003). Data are from the March 2006 release.

We know that any potential government must implicitly control a legislative majority before coming to office. There are no rules about who should be in this legislative majority. As a result, any legislator could conceivably be a part of the government's majority support and, hence, play a role in appointing the government. In practice, though, the tight discipline of political parties in many countries means that the actual business of forming a government tends to be done by a small group of senior politicians in each party (Gallagher, Laver, and Mair 2006, 49). These politicians typically include party leaders and potential cabinet members. After an election or the fall of a previous government, these party leaders bargain with one another and a government forms as soon as enough party leaders have committed their support (and that of their party) for it to command a legislative majority. But can we say anything more about the government formation process and the type of government that these actors are likely to choose?

Table 11.4 illustrates all of the potential governments that could have formed in West Germany in 1987. It also indicates the number of surplus seats controlled by each potential government that were not required for obtaining a legislative majority. For example, a coalition between the SPD, FDP, and the Greens would have twenty-five "surplus" seats more than they actually needed to guarantee a legislative majority. In contrast, a coalition between just

TABLE 11.4	Potential West German Governments, 1987		
Party	**Seats**	**Percentage**	**Surplus seats**
CDU/CSU + SPD + Greens + FDP	497	100.0	248
CDU/CSU + SPD + Greens	451	90.7	202
CDU/CSU + SPD + FDP	455	91.5	206
CDU/CSU + FDP + Greens	311	62.6	62
SPD + FDP + Greens	274	55.1	25
CDU/CSU + SPD	409	82.2	160
CDU/CSU + FDP	269	54.1	20
CDU/CSU + Greens	265	53.3	16
SPD + FDP	232	46.7	−17
SPD + Greens	228	45.9	−21
FDP + Greens	88	17.7	−161
SPD	186	37.4	−63
CDU/CSU	223	44.9	−26
Greens	42	8.5	−207
FDP	46	9.3	−203

Note: The numbers in the "Surplus seats" column are the number of seats controlled by each potential government that were not required for obtaining a legislative majority.

the SPD and Greens would be twenty-one seats shy of a majority. One question you should ask yourself is whether all of these potential governments are equally plausible. To answer this question, you really need to know more about the exact process by which governments form in parliamentary democracies.

A graphical depiction of the government formation process in parliamentary regimes is shown in Figure 11.3. The head of state, typically a monarch or president, presides over the government formation process and it is he who ultimately invests a government with the constitutional authority to take office.[10] The extent to which the head of state actively becomes involved in the actual bargaining varies from country to country. In some countries, the head of state is limited to simply swearing in the government proposed by the party elites. If there is an investiture vote, then the proposed government must demonstrate that it has a legislative majority. Once this is done, the head of state simply appoints the government. This government stays in power until the next election, until it loses in a vote of no confidence, or until it resigns. In other countries, the head of state plays a more active role by choosing a particular politician to initiate the government formation process. This politician is known as a **formateur.** It is her job to construct a government.

> A **formateur** is the person designated to form the government in a parliamentary regime. The formateur is often the PM designate.

In some countries, the constitution explicitly states who the formateur will be. For example, the Greek constitution states that the head of state must appoint the leader of the largest party as the formateur. If this person fails to form a government, then the head of state allows the leader of the second largest party to try to build a government by making him the new formateur. This process continues until a formateur successfully forms a government. Obviously, the head of state has little discretion in these countries because the election results determine the order in which parties get to try to form the government.

In other countries, the formateur is determined by tradition. For instance, there is an implicit convention in the United Kingdom that the outgoing prime minister gets the first chance to form the government. Only if the old prime minister cannot form a government does one of his rivals get the chance. Thus, even if the outgoing prime minister loses support in the polls, he still gets to be the first formateur. Of course, if the outgoing prime minister loses significant electoral support, he will be unable to form a government and, thus, his right to get first crack at forming a government is little more than a formality; in practice, a beaten prime minister usually admits defeat on election night. There have been a few notable exceptions to this, though. For example, the outgoing prime minister Edward Heath remained in office for a few days after losing the February 1974 legislative elections in the United Kingdom before conceding that he could not form a government. Again, the head of state enjoys little discretion in appointing the formateur in countries like the United Kingdom.

---

10. Our description of the government formation process in parliamentary democracies builds on Gallagher, Laver and Mair (2006, 47–54).

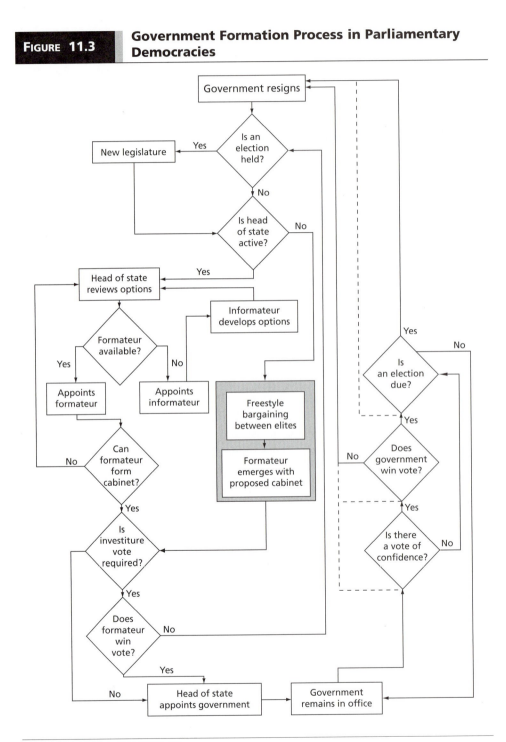

FIGURE 11.3 — **Government Formation Process in Parliamentary Democracies**

Source: Laver and Schofield (1998, 63).

In contrast to these countries, there are others in which the head of state is less constrained and can actually "choose" the formateur in a more meaningful sense. For example, choosing the formateur has been one of the more important duties belonging to the head of state in countries like Iceland and the Czech Republic. The Icelandic president's prerogative of choosing the formateur was critical in the formation of a coalition between the Social Democratic Party and the Independence Party, which governed from 1959 to 1971. The president's ability to choose the formateur also played a crucial role in the formation of subsequent nonpartisan governments in Iceland (Kristinsson 1999, 93–94). Following legislative elections in June 2006, the Czech president, Vaclav Klaus, was able to influence the government formation process in a starkly partisan way because of his power to appoint the formateur. The Czech elections resulted in a dead heat in the 200-seat legislature: a coalition of left-wing parties won 100 seats, and a coalition of right-wing parties won 100 seats. The Czech president, who belonged to a right-wing party called the Civic Democratic Party (ODS), appointed a member of his own party—Mirek Topolanek—to be the first formateur. When his nominated formateur failed to get his proposed government passed in an investiture vote that saw all 100 legislators from the right vote for it and all 100 legislators from the left vote against it, the Czech president simply renominated the same person to be the next formateur. In somewhat dubious circumstances, Topolanek managed to win a second investiture vote even though he proposed the same government as before—he won the vote 100 to 98 when two left-wing legislators surprisingly decided to abstain rather than vote against the proposed government.

In other countries, the ability of the head of state to engage in partisan politics is seen as inappropriate. As a result, such countries have limited the power of the head of state to appointing an **informateur.** An informateur is someone who is supposed to lack personal political ambition and whose job it is to look at

> An **informateur** examines politically feasible coalitions and nominates the formateur.

politically feasible coalitions and recommend people who would make good formateurs. In the Netherlands, the monarch chooses an informateur, who then chooses a formateur. The existence of an informateur means that the head of state is, at least theoretically, one step removed from the partisan nature of the government formation process.

Despite the discretion enjoyed by some heads of state, it turns out that the formateur is nearly always the leader of the largest party in the legislature. In most cases, the formateur is also the prime minister designate. All of this is to be expected, given that the leader of the largest party can often credibly threaten to veto any proposal by other possible formateurs. Once the formateur has been chosen, she has to put a cabinet together that is acceptable to a legislative majority.

The ability to nominate cabinet members is one of the most important powers held by the prime minister (formateur). In single-party majority cabinets, the prime minister has enormous discretion in regard to whom to appoint to the cabinet and is constrained only by the internal politics of her party. Politicians might be rewarded with cabinet appointments because they have demonstrated loyalty to the party or the prime minister, because they represent a particular ideological faction within a party, or because they have useful administrative skills. In some cases, a PM might feel that internal party politics require her to appoint internal party opponents to the cabinet. In fact, the British PM Margaret Thatcher, later to be called the "iron lady," felt compelled to appoint a cabinet in which her own party supporters were in a distinct minority on first being elected in 1979 (Young 1990, 138). Still, even at this initial moment of relative weakness, Thatcher (1993, 26) later recalled, "I made sure that the key economic ministers would be true believers in our economic strategy."

In coalition cabinets, the discretion that the PM has in nominating cabinet members is obviously more constrained. Typically, party leaders in the proposed cabinet will nominate particular ministers to the subset of portfolios that have been allocated to their party during the initial stages of the government formation process. Although possible, it is rare to see the PM or party leaders veto a nomination by another party leader. On the face of it, this would seem to suggest that the leaders of each government party are generally free to pick the people they want for "their" portfolios. The fact that we do not see nominations vetoed, though, does not necessarily mean that party leaders have full discretion in whom they nominate. It might simply be the case that objectionable ministerial choices are not proposed in the first place (Indriðason and Kam 2005). Given the considerable influence that cabinet members have over policy in their respective portfolios, party leaders will bargain hard, first over how many ministers they get, and second over who should be appointed to these posts, before deciding whether to support the proposed cabinet.

Once a cabinet has been formed, the support of a legislative majority may or may not have to be demonstrated by a formal investiture vote. If the investiture vote is unsuccessful, then the government formation process starts all over again; there may or may not be a new election before this happens. If the investiture vote is successful (or there is no required vote), however, then the head of state simply appoints the cabinet nominated by the formateur to office. At this point, the government is free to rule until it is defeated in a vote of no confidence or until a new election is necessary. If the government is defeated in a vote of no confidence or a new election is called, then the incumbent government remains in office to run the country as a **caretaker government**.[11] This caretaker government remains in office until the next round of the government formation process is complete and a new government is ready to take its place. In most countries, there is a strong constitutional convention that caretaker governments will not make any important policy changes to those in place when the outgoing government loses its parliamentary basis (Herman and Pope 1973; Golder 2007). Ireland represents somewhat of an exception to this in that Irish caretaker governments can, and do, use the full range of powers available to any "normal" government (Laver and Shepsle 1994, 292). As you can

> A **caretaker government** occurs when an election is called or when an incumbent government either resigns or is defeated in a vote of no confidence. It rules the country for an interim period until a new government is formed.

---

11. In Germany, the "constructive" vote of no confidence means that an alternative government must be proposed as part of a no confidence motion. As a result, there is no caretaker government in Germany if the legislature ever passes such a motion, because there is no interim period between governments.

ox 11.2 | **PRINCIPAL-AGENT, OR DELEGATION, PROBLEMS**

Forming a coalition cabinet raises an interesting problem. Each party in government (principal) delegates the discretion and resources to make policy in a particular ministry to a cabinet minister (agent). In a single-party government, the cabinet ministers all come from the same party. As a result, we expect that each cabinet minister is likely to implement his party's preferred policy. In coalition governments, though, the leaders of each government party delegate power to make policy to cabinet ministers from *different* parties. It is often the case that party leaders will agree to a coalition policy that is some mix of each party's preferred policy during the government formation process. But what's to stop cabinet ministers from implementing their own party's preferred policy in the ministries that they control rather than the policy that they had agreed to before coming to power? This is

A **principal-agent, or delegation, problem** refers to the difficulties that arise when a principal delegates authority to an agent that (a) has different goals than the principal, and (b) cannot be perfectly monitored.

known generally as a **principal-agent, or delegation, problem.** The problem is that the cabinet minister has more information about the available policy options in her ministry than the rest of the cabinet and can take advantage of this informational asymmetry if she wants.

Müller and Strøm (2000) suggest that problems of delegation that arise in the context of coalition governments can be resolved simply by writing very detailed coalition agreements in an attempt to bind the relevant parties to an agreed government policy. In effect, parties promise, in writing, to implement the coalition policy. But what makes these promises credible? Why would parties keep these promises just because they have written them down in detail? Political parties have recognized that there is a delegation problem when forming a cabinet and have come up with a couple of institutional solutions to help monitor and keep tabs on what their coalition partners are doing.

One solution is to use what are known as "junior ministers." These individuals are also sometimes known as ministers of state or undersecretaries. Although it is rare for government parties to veto cabinet nominations by another party, Michael Thies (2001) has argued that they often appoint their own junior ministers to cabinet portfolios controlled by their coalition partners in order to ensure that their coalition partners do not stray too far from the agreed government policy. The appointment of junior ministers is part and parcel of the deal that sets up the cabinet, but these junior ministers are not actually full members of the cabinet—they generally do not share power with ministers, they do not vote in cabinet, and they only occasionally participate in cabinet meetings. Nonetheless, the cabinet minister to whom they have been appointed cannot unilaterally dismiss them. Thies finds that parties purposely assign their own junior ministers to ministries headed by their partners in Italy, Japan, and the Netherlands but not in Germany.

A second solution that helps to resolve Thies's "German anomaly" focuses on legislative committees. Martin and Vanberg (2004) show that the legislative committees in the Dutch and German parliaments scrutinize government bills more extensively when the ideological divergence between coalition partners on the issues addressed in the bill is large. Kim and Loewenberg (2005) examine the importance of legislative committees further and show that government parties in the German Bundestag from 1961 to 1998 have appointed members of their own party to chair legislative committees that oversee ministries controlled by their coalition partners. In effect, German parties use legislative committees, and not junior ministers, to monitor the actions of their coalition partners.

The appointment of junior ministers and legislative committee chairs are both mechanisms

Lawmakers in the German parliament in Berlin cast their ballots for a confidence vote on July 1, 2005. German chancellor Gerhard Schroeder called the confidence vote, which he intentionally lost, in order to enable early elections to be held that fall.

that can be used to help cope with the delegation problems that arise in the relationship between government parties, as principals, and members of the cabinet, as their agents. Why some countries choose to use both mechanisms, whereas others prefer to employ one rather than the other, is an open question that requires more research.

As you can imagine, the types of principal-agent, or delegation, problems that we have mentioned in the context of forming coalition governments are ubiquitous in political (and other) settings. For example, think about elections and the government formation process in parliamentary democracies more broadly for a moment. At election time, voters (principals) are delegating policymaking power to legislators (agents). Following elections, these legislators (principals) then delegate policymaking power to the prime minister and her cabinet (agents). When the cabinet is being constructed, each party in government (principals) delegates policymaking power in a particular ministry to a cabinet minister (agent), who may or may not be from the same party. This process of delegation continues, with cabinet ministers (principals) delegating policymaking and policy-implementing power to civil servants or bureaucrats (agents) within their government departments. In effect, parliamentary democracy is, by its very nature, a long chain of delegation and accountability, from the voters to the ultimate policymakers in the cabinet (and civil service), in which, at each link, a principal (in whom authority is placed) delegates to an agent, whom the principal has conditionally authorized to act on her behalf (Strøm, Müller, and Bergman 2003). This chain of delegation is indirect in that voters (the original principal) get to directly elect only the legislators; all other agents are only indirectly elected and indirectly accountable to the voters.

Some form of delegation is required in any large political system. After all, citizens simply do not have the time or expertise to make all the necessary policy decisions in a country. Still, although delegation allows principals to benefit from the expertise and abilities of others, it can also be perilous. This is because delegation involves a transfer of power, and there is always a danger that the people to whom power is transferred will abuse that power and not do as the principal wants (Lupia 2003, 34). One of the Founding Fathers in the United States, James Madison, famously recognized this problem in the *Federalist,* number 51, when he noted, "In framing a government to be administered by men over men, the great difficulty lies in this: you must first enable the government to control the governed; and in the next place oblige it to control itself."

imagine, the fact that caretaker governments generally have no authority to take major policy initiatives can be problematic if the government formation process takes a long time. This is particularly the case if the government has collapsed as the result of some sort of political, economic, or military crisis. We will return to the issue of how long it takes to form a government a little later in the chapter.

A Simple Model of Government Formation

Now that we know more details about the government formation process in parliamentary democracies, we can return to our West German example from 1987. Remember that all of the potential governments are listed in Table 11.4. Given what you now know about the government formation process, ask yourself whether all of these governments are equally plausible. Who is likely to be the formateur? The leader of the CDU/CSU was appointed formateur because he controlled the largest party in the Bundestag at the time. As the leader of the largest party, Helmut Kohl (CDU/CSU) was given the first chance to form the government. If you were Helmut Kohl, would you form a government that did not include your own party? The obvious answer is no. As a result, you can immediately eliminate those potential governments in Table 11.4 that do not include the CDU/CSU.

Are any of the remaining potential governments more plausible than others? The fact that a government must control a legislative majority in order to come to power suggests that the government formation process may be easier if the proposed government actually controls a majority of legislative seats. As a result, you might think to eliminate those potential governments that do not have a positive number of surplus seats, that is, those governments that do not control a legislative majority.[12] Table 11.5 lists the remaining potential governments in boldface type. Which of the seven remaining possibilities do you think is most likely to become the government? To answer this question, you should start to think about the goals of the political actors engaged in the government formation process. What do they want?

---

12. As we'll see a little later, governments that do not explicitly control a legislative majority do sometimes come to power. You should start to think about how and why this might happen.

TABLE 11.5	Remaining Potential West German Governments, 1987		
Party	Seats	Percentage	Surplus seats
CDU/CSU + SPD + Greens + FDP	497	100.0	248
CDU/CSU + SPD + Greens	451	90.7	202
CDU/CSU + SPD + FDP	455	91.5	206
CDU/CSU + FDP + Greens	311	62.6	62
SPD + FDP + Greens	274	55.1	25
CDU/CSU + SPD	409	82.2	160
CDU/CSU + FDP	269	54.1	20
CDU/CSU + Greens	265	53.3	16
SPD + FDP	232	46.7	−17
SPD + Greens	228	45.9	−21
FDP + Greens	88	17.7	−161
SPD	186	37.4	−63
CDU/CSU	223	44.9	−26
Greens	42	8.5	−207
FDP	46	9.3	−203

Note: Entries that are not shown in boldface type either do not contain the CDU/CSU or do not control a majority of legislative seats.

Political scientists often divide politicians into those who are office seeking and those who are policy seeking. When forming a government, an office-seeking politician will want to secure as many ministerial portfolios as he can. After the position of prime minister, cabinet positions represent the highest political posts in a parliamentary regime. In effect, landing a cabinet portfolio is often a signal of a successful political career and is a prize that many politicians seek. Being in the cabinet brings power and fame. An **office-seeking politician** is interested in the "intrinsic" benefits of office. In contrast, a **policy-seeking politician** will, when forming a government, want to secure ministerial portfolios in order to be able to influence public policy. This type of politician is not interested in the "intrinsic" benefits of office; he does not want to be a minister simply for the sake of being a minister. Instead, a policy-seeking politician wants ministerial portfolios so that he can make a difference in how the country is run.

An **office-seeking politician** is interested in the intrinsic benefits of office; he wants as much office as possible. A **policy-seeking politician** only wants to shape policy.

A Purely Office-Seeking World

Imagine again that you are Helmut Kohl, the CDU/CSU leader, in Germany in 1987. If you lived in a purely office-seeking world, what government would you propose? In order to control a legislative majority, you know that you must get the support of other party leaders because your party controls only a minority of legislative seats. Because you live in a purely office-seeking world, you can win their support only by giving them office. In effect, you say to them, "I will give you X ministerial posts in the government in exchange for your legislative support." You will obviously want to give them as few portfolios as possible, however, so that you can keep the rest for yourself. In order to win their support you will probably have to give up more cabinet positions to a party leader who controls a large number of legislative seats than to a party leader who controls a small number of seats. In fact, there is quite strong empirical evidence that a prime minister must give portfolios to other parties in proportion to the number of seats that each party contributes to the government's legislative majority. This apparent empirical regularity is known as **Gamson's Law** (see Box 11.3).

> **Gamson's Law** states that cabinet portfolios will be distributed among government parties in strict proportion to the number of seats that each party contributes to the government's legislative majority.

---

x 11.3   **PORTFOLIO ALLOCATION AND GAMSON'S LAW**

Gamson's Law: Cabinet portfolios will be distributed among government parties in strict proportion to the number of seats that each party contributes to the government's legislative majority (Gamson 1961).

The allocation of cabinet seats in the Netherlands following the 1998 legislative elections is shown in Table 11.6. On the whole, the last two columns indicate that the distribution of cabinet portfolios is quite proportional to the relative size of each party in the government. Often, there is some evidence that the degree of proportionality declines as the parties become smaller. One reason for this is the "lumpy" nature of cabinet positions. Once a party is invited and agrees to join the government, it must get at least one cabinet seat irrespective of the number of legislative seats that it contributes to the government's majority—it cannot receive half a cabinet portfolio or a third of one. The lumpy nature of cabinet portfolios means that small parties tend to be slightly overrepresented and large parties slightly underrepresented in the portfolio allocation process. There is some evidence for this in the 1998 Dutch government.

Several recent studies have questioned the extent to which Gamson's Law holds in practice. For example, Druckman and Warwick (2001) point out that some ministerial portfolios are more important or more powerful than others. As a result, a party may agree to receive fewer cabinet positions than its size would indicate under Gamson's Law in exchange for more powerful portfolios. The 1998 Dutch government provides some evidence for this. Both the PvdA and the VVD received a smaller percentage of cabinet portfolios than they could have

| TABLE 11.6 | Allocation of Cabinet Seats in the Netherlands, 1998 |

Party	No. of legislative seats	No. of cabinet ministers	Proportion of government seats	Proportion of cabinet ministers
Social Democrats (PvdA)	45	6	46.4	42.9
Liberal Democrats (D66)	14	3	14.4	21.4
Liberals (VVD)	38	5	39.2	35.7

Note: 150 seats in legislature.

expected given their size. These parties did, however, get the more important portfolios, such as the prime minister and interior minister (PvdA) or the foreign minister, finance minister, and defense minister (VVD). Although the D66 appears to be overcompensated, one of its three cabinet appointments is a "minister without portfolio," that is, a minister who has no specific responsibility. For further studies examining the applicability of Gamson's Law, see Frechette, Kagel, and Morelli (2005); Druckman and Warwick (2006); Carroll and Cox (2007); and Laver, de Marchi, and Mutlu (2007).

One of the implications of the office-seeking logic that we have just outlined is that you will not want more parties in government than are strictly necessary for you to obtain a legislative majority. Thus, you will want to form a particular type of coalition government called a **minimal winning coalition** (MWC). A minimal winning coalition is one in which there are just enough parties (and no more) to control a legislative majority. Of the seven remaining potential governments in Table 11.5, there are three MWCs: (CDU/CSU + SPD), (CDU/CSU + FDP), and (CDU/CSU + Greens). In none of these coalitions is it possible to remove a party without, at the same time, giving up your legislative majority. A second implication of the purely office-seeking logic is that you will choose the smallest MWC, or the **least minimal winning coalition.** The least MWC is the one with the lowest number of surplus seats. You want the least MWC because you do not want to "buy" more legislative seats with office than you strictly have to. This leads to the hypothesis that if the world is purely office seeking, then we should observe least minimal winning coalitions. In terms of our example of the 1987 German election, this means that we should expect the leader of the CDU/CSU to form a minimal winning coalition with the Greens because this MWC has the fewest surplus seats.

> A **minimal winning coalition** (MWC) is one in which there are no parties that are not required to control a legislative majority. A **least minimal winning coalition** is the MWC with the lowest number of surplus seats.

A Purely Policy-Seeking World

Imagine that you are Helmut Kohl again but that you now live in a purely policy-seeking world. Which of the remaining potential governments in Table 11.5 would you propose? To answer that question, you will need to know something about the policy positions of the parties along the salient issue dimensions in Germany in 1987. Figure 11.4 illustrates the policy positions or "ideal points" of the four German parties with legislative seats on the left-right dimension of economic policy. As the leader of the CDU/CSU, you know that you must get the support of other party leaders in order to control a legislative majority. Because you now live in a purely policy-seeking world, you can win their support only by giving them policy concessions. This means that instead of being able to implement policy at your own ideal point, you will have to implement a coalition policy that lies somewhere between the ideal points of all your coalition partners. It is likely that you will have to make more policy concessions to win the support of a party leader who controls a large number of legislative seats than you will to win the support of a party leader who controls a small number of legislative seats. In other words, large parties will tend to be able to pull policy more toward their ideal point than small parties.

One of the implications of this logic is that you will want to form governments with parties that are located close to you in the policy space. Political scientists often refer to this type of coalition as a "compact coalition," or **connected coalition.** A connected coalition is one in which all members of the coalition are located next to each other in the policy space. For example, a coalition between the CDU/CSU and the FDP is a connected coalition. A coalition between the CDU/CSU and the Greens, however, is not a connected coalition because there is a noncoalition party (the SPD) that lies between them in the policy space. Of the seven remaining potential governments in Table 11.5, there are five connected coalitions: (CDU/CSU + SPD + Greens + FDP), (CDU/CSU + SPD + Greens), (CDU/CSU + SPD + FDP), (CDU/CSU + SPD), and (CDU/CSU + FDP). The parties in all of these coalitions are located directly next to each other in the policy space. A second implication of the purely policy-seeking logic is that you will choose the connected least minimal winning coalition. You want the connected least MWC because you do not want to "buy" more legislative seats with policy than you strictly have to. This leads to the hypothesis that if the world is purely policy seeking, then we should observe connected least minimal winning coalitions. In terms of our German example, this means that we should expect the leader of the CDU/CSU to form a coalition government with the FDP.

> A **connected coalition** is one in which the member parties are located directly next to each other in the policy space.

| **FIGURE 11.4** | **German Party Positions on the Left-Right Economic Dimension, 1987** |

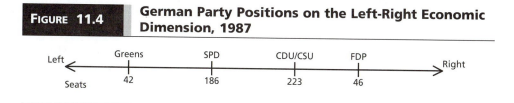

The Trade-off between Office and Policy

The actual government formed by Helmut Kohl in 1987 was a coalition between the CDU/CSU and the FDP. This was the prediction from the purely policy-seeking logic. Does this mean that policy seeking dominates office seeking in Germany? There is a vast literature in political science that seeks to answer questions like this, but we believe that this sort of question is hard, if not impossible, to answer empirically. Consider our example again. It is difficult to know if policy seeking really dominated office seeking in Germany, because the CDU/CSU did not have to give up too much extra office in order to get a coalition policy closer to its ideal point. In effect, the CDU/CSU preferred to give up slightly more office by forming a government coalition with the FDP (four extra surplus seats) in exchange for a coalition policy that was likely to be much closer to its ideal point than if it had formed a coalition with the Greens. In practice, we believe that politicians probably care about both office and policy and are, therefore, always making trade-offs. They are always asking how much extra office they should give up to get policy closer to their ideal point or how much policy they should give up to get more office. If this is the case, then it probably makes little sense to categorize real-world politicians into purely policy-seeking or purely office-seeking types.

Even if politicians were purely office seekers or purely policy seekers, we believe that the reality of political competition would force them to act *as if they cared about both policy and office*. For example, a politician who wishes to affect policy must win office in order to be in a position to change policy. As a result, a purely policy-seeking politician will have to care about office, if only as a means to affect policy. Similarly, an office-seeking politician will realize that voters are unlikely to elect or reelect him if he cares only about office and being famous. A consequence is that an office-seeking politician will have to care about policy, if only to make sure that he wins election. Ultimately, we see no way to distinguish between office-seeking and policy-seeking politicians simply by observing the world, because all politicians will act as if they care about both office and policy. If we are right, then it probably makes slightly more sense to think that government coalitions are likely to be connected least MWCs rather than just least MWCs.

Different Types of Government

We know that a government must control an implicit legislative majority in order to come to power and remain in office in a parliamentary democracy. Up to this point, we have assumed that governments must contain enough parties that they *explicitly* control a majority of legislative seats. In fact, the logic presented in the previous section suggests that governments should contain just enough parties to obtain this legislative majority and no more. It is for this reason that we have focused up to this point on single-party majority governments and various forms of minimal winning coalitions. When we look around the world, however, we sometimes observe other types of parliamentary government—minority governments and surplus majority governments. Table 11.7 provides information on 310 cabinets by country that formed in thirteen West European parliamentary democracies from 1945 to 1998. Figure 11.5 illustrates the percentage of cabinets of each government type and the percentage of time spent under each government type.

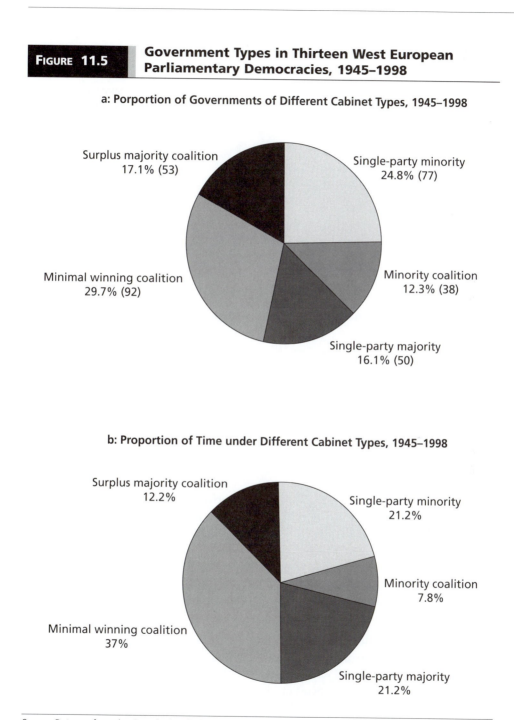

FIGURE 11.5 Government Types in Thirteen West European Parliamentary Democracies, 1945–1998

a: Porportion of Governments of Different Cabinet Types, 1945–1998

Surplus majority coalition
17.1% (53)

Single-party minority
24.8% (77)

Minority coalition
12.3% (38)

Single-party majority
16.1% (50)

Minimal winning coalition
29.7% (92)

b: Proportion of Time under Different Cabinet Types, 1945–1998

Surplus majority coalition
12.2%

Single-party minority
21.2%

Minority coalition
7.8%

Single-party majority
21.2%

Minimal winning coalition
37%

Source: Data are from the Constitutional Change and Parliamentary Democracies project. (Müller and Strøm 2000; Strøm, Müller, and Bergman 2003).

Note: Data do not include caretaker or nonpartisan governments. The numbers in parentheses indicate the number of governments of different cabinet types.

	Single-party majority	Minimal winning coalition	Single-party minority	Minority coalition	Surplus majority	Total
Country						
Austria	4	14	1	0	3	22
Belgium	3	16	2	1	11	33
Denmark	0	4	14	13	0	31
Germany	1	17	3	0	5	26
Greece	7	1	1	0	1	10
Ireland	6	5	6	5	0	22
Italy	0	3	14	9	22	48
Luxembourg	0	15	0	0	1	16
Netherlands	0	9	0	3	10	22
Norway	6	3	12	5	0	26
Spain	2	0	6	0	0	8
Sweden	2	5	17	2	0	26
United Kingdom	19	0	1	0	0	20
Total	50	92	77	38	53	310

TABLE 11.7 Government Types in Thirteen West European Parliamentary Democracies, 1945–1998

Source: Data are from the Constitutional Change and Parliamentary Democracies project. (Müller and Strøm 2000; Strøm, Müller, and Bergman 2003).
Note: Data do not include caretaker or nonpartisan governments.

Minority Governments

A **minority government** is one in which the governmental parties do not together command a majority of legislative seats.

A **minority government** is one in which the party or parties in power do not explicitly command a majority of legislative seats. Minority governments may be single-party minority governments or minority coalition governments. You are probably wondering how a minority government could come to power and why it would stay in power in a parliamentary democracy. After all, the opposition in parliament controls enough seats that it could remove the government through a vote of no confidence whenever it agrees to do so. A minority government can exist only as long as the opposition chooses not to bring it down. This means that whenever we observe a minority government, we know that there must be an implicit majority in the legislature that supports it. Every day that a government is not defeated in a vote of no confidence, it implicitly enjoys the support of a legislative majority.

In some countries, we know precisely who makes up this implicit majority because some nongovernmental party or parties publicly state that they will sustain the government against votes to overthrow it but do not want to be in the cabinet (Powell 2000, 102). In exchange, the government usually agrees to consult these "support parties" on various policy matters. This occurred in Britain in 1977 when the Liberals agreed to support the Labour Party when it lost its majority. This also occurred more recently after the 2005 legislative elections in New Zealand when two minor parties—the Progressive Party and United Future—publicly agreed to support a minority coalition government made up of the Labour Party and New Zealand First. In other countries, the government does not rely on specific support parties but builds legislative majorities on an ad hoc basis. In effect, the government builds different majorities for each piece of legislation that it wants to pass. For example, the minority Socialist government in France in 1988 formed legislative majorities with the Communists on their left to pass some policies and with the UDF on their right to pass other policies (Powell 2000, 105). In these countries, it is not always easy to figure out exactly who in the legislature is keeping the minority government in power; all we know is that at least one of the nongovernmental parties must be helping it at any given point in time. One consequence of this is that it becomes difficult for voters to know who is responsible for policy and to hold them accountable for it.

For a long time, minority governments were seen as undemocratic and an unfortunate anomaly. They were seen as something that should occur only infrequently and something that, if they did occur, should be short-lived. Strøm (1984, 1990) was one of the first political scientists to challenge this accepted wisdom. He argued that minority governments should be seen as a normal and "democratic" outcome of party competition in parliamentary regimes. One thing that he illustrated was the frequency with which minority governments formed in West European democracies and the relative stability that characterized these cabinets. As Figure 11.5a indicates, over a third (37.1 percent) of all governments that formed in West European parliamentary democracies from 1945 to 1998 were minority governments. In countries like Denmark (82 percent), Sweden (81 percent), and Norway (65 percent), minority governments were the norm in this period. In addition to their numerical frequency, minority governments have also been in power for long stretches of time. For example, minority cabinets have ruled in West European parliamentary democracies for well over a quarter (29 percent) of the postwar period (Figure 11.5b). Each minority government that formed remained in power for well over a year (513 days) on average.

Several theories have been proposed to explain the apparent puzzle of why minority governments exist. All of these theories point to the importance of policy in the government formation process. If politicians cared only about office, then it is hard to understand why any nongovernmental party would ever choose not to be in the cabinet when it has the power to force its way into it. In other words, why would nongovernmental parties ever allow a minority government to enjoy all the benefits of office without controlling a legislative majority? The simple answer is that they wouldn't. If politicians care about policy, however, then we can think of situations in which a party might decide that it can better achieve its policy objectives by remaining outside the cabinet.

Strøm (1984, 1990) claims that minority governments are more likely in countries in which nongovernmental (opposition) parties have a strong say over policy. The strength of the opposition typically depends on the structure of the legislative committee system in each country. All legislatures have committee systems to help them carry out their work. In some countries, the opposition has little influence over policy because the committee system largely accepts whatever the government proposes. The opposition is in a much stronger position in those countries in which the committee system is specifically designed to facilitate the dispersal of policymaking influence to many groups, including nongovernmental parties. The extent to which policy is made in parliamentary committees and the degree to which opposition parties can exert influence in these committees obviously varies from country to country.[13] Strøm hypothesizes that the more powerful a country's committee system and the greater the influence of the opposition in it, the lower the incentive for opposition parties to enter government, because they can shape policy without actually being in the cabinet. As a result, we should expect to see more minority governments in these countries. This leads to the following hypothesis:

> *Opposition strength hypothesis:* Minority governments will be more likely when opposition influence is strong.

Of course, you might be wondering why a party would ever choose to influence policy from outside the government rather than from inside it. Although all countries typically allow some degree of opposition influence over policy, this influence is never stronger than that of the government itself. So, why not influence policy from within the cabinet? In fact, why not enjoy the benefits of office while shaping policy? There are several reasons, most having to do with future electoral prospects, why a party might choose not to be in the cabinet despite the loss of office benefits and the decreased ability to shape policy. First, parties may be reluctant to take responsibility for the policy that will be implemented. Governing parties are much more likely to be held responsible for failed policies than opposition parties. Indeed, there is strong evidence that incumbent parties tend to lose votes in subsequent elections. In a study of twenty democracies over twenty-five years, Powell (2000, 47–48) finds that incumbent governments lose about 2 percent of their vote on average. By remaining in the opposition, parties can often achieve some of their policy objectives while being held less accountable if things go wrong. Second, a party may have made a preelection pledge not to go into government with certain parties. Breaking this promise might be electoral suicide at the next election. Third, opposition parties have much more flexibility in choosing their campaign strategies in future elections because they do not have a past record in office to constrain them. These are all possible reasons why parties might choose not to be in government in countries that allow them to influence policy from the opposition benches.

Luebbert (1984) provides a related, but slightly different, explanation for the existence of minority governments. Like Strøm, he claims that minority governments are more likely in

---

13. The committees in Belgium, Denmark, Germany, the Netherlands, Norway, and Sweden are very influential in the policymaking process. Moreover, committee chairs are allocated in strict proportion to the size of each party in the legislature (subject to some minimal size requirement) irrespective of whether these parties are in the government or in opposition. In contrast, the legislative committees in France, Greece, Ireland, and the United Kingdom are quite weak and opposition parties are almost never allowed to chair them (Powell 2000; Döring 1995).

countries in which nongovernmental parties have a strong say over policy. Rather than focusing on a country's legislative committee system, though, Luebbert argues that the abil-ity of opposition groups to influence policy depends heavily on whether a country has **corporatist** or **pluralist interest group relations.** A pluralist country is one in which interest groups compete in the political marketplace outside of the formal policymaking process. In contrast, a corporatist country is one in which

> **Corporatist interest group relations** occur when key social and economic actors, such as labor, business, and agriculture groups, are integrated into the formal policy-making process. **Pluralist interest group relations** occur when interest groups compete in the political marketplace outside of the formal policy-making process.

key social and economic actors have a formal institutional role in making policy. In these countries, interest groups are organized into national, specialized, hierarchical, and monop-olistic peak organizations that sit down with each other and the government to hammer out public policy. As Luebbert (1984, 235) notes, corporatism "allows, indeed guarantees, access to policymaking by a variety of groups." For example, ministries in Norway and Sweden that contemplate legislative or administrative action that might affect a particular interest group are obliged to consult that interest group before proceeding. In Austria the formal represen-tation of labor, business, and agricultural interests is guaranteed by the existence of "cham-bers," which have a formal right to be consulted on a wide range of policy matters and to which all working citizens are obliged by law to belong. Thus, the cabinet is only one of the sites in which fundamental social and economic decisions are made in corporatist countries. Interest groups, and political parties that represent these groups, have a range of alternatives for the expression of their concerns beyond the cabinet. As a result, we should expect to see more minority governments in corporatist countries because of the lower incentive for opposition parties to enter government. This leads to the following hypothesis:

Corporatist hypothesis: Minority governments will be more likely in corporatist countries.

Strøm has also argued that minority governments are less likely in countries that require a formal investiture vote because potential minority governments face a higher hurdle to tak-ing office than in countries in which no investiture vote is required. If a formal investiture vote is required, then opposition parties must choose to openly support a minority govern-ment. Some parties who would not necessarily support a particular minority government in a public vote, however, may find it acceptable to tacitly lend their support to a government if no investiture vote is required. Bergman (1993) distinguishes between "positive" and "neg-ative" government formation rules. He notes that when rules are positive (investiture votes are required), then the onus is on the government to demonstrate that it is supported by a legislative majority. In contrast, when rules are negative (no investiture votes are required), the onus is on the parliament to show that the government is not tolerated. This distinction between being *supported* and *tolerated* suggests that investiture votes might pose particular difficulties for minority governments.

Investiture hypothesis: Minority governments will be less likely when there is a formal investiture vote.

Another explanation for the existence of minority governments focuses on policy divisions within the opposition. In effect, a minority government can survive and be relatively stable if opposition parties cannot reach an agreement on whom to replace it with. For example, the Congress Party was able to dominate Indian politics as a minority government for many years because the opposition parties on each side of it could not agree on a suitable replacement.[14] A similar situation occurred with the Social Democrats in Sweden and the Christian Democrats in Italy. These parties were consistently able to form minority governments by being relatively large parties located in the middle of the ideological spectrum with opposition parties on either side. These parties, often referred to as "strong" parties, could credibly demand to govern alone because their ideological opponents could not agree on an alternative government to replace them with. This has led Laver and Shepsle (1996) to hypothesize that minority governments should be more likely when there is a strong party.

Strong party hypothesis: Minority governments are more likely when there is a "strong" party.

As good political scientists, you should be wondering if these hypotheses are supported by the empirical evidence. In Table 11.8, we present the results from a statistical analysis in which we examine the effect of opposition strength, corporatism, investiture votes, and strong parties on the probability that a government will be a minority (single party or coalition) government. Our sample includes all governments that formed in thirteen West European parliamentary democracies from 1945 to 1998. We omit nonpartisan governments and those that formed in the presence of a majority party (Strøm 1990, 75). Majority situations are excluded because minority governments are not a feasible option, and nonpartisan governments are omitted because they cannot be assigned a majority or minority status by their very nature. If the theories that we have presented are correct, then we should observe that higher levels of opposition strength, corporatism, and the existence of strong parties make minority governments more likely and that investiture vote requirements make them less likely.

Opposition strength ranges from 1 (low) to 9 (high) and comes from a survey of country experts who were asked to rate their country in regard to the potential impact the opposition has on policy (Laver and Hunt 1992). *Corporatism* ranges from 0 (low) to 5 (high) and captures both the proportion of unionized workers in the workforce and the overall number of unions—a country is more corporatist when it has only a few unions but a high proportion of unionized workers (Garrett 1998). *Investiture* captures whether there is a formal investiture vote or not. *Strong party* indicates whether a "merely strong" or a "very strong" party exists.[15] According to theory, the existence of a strong party should make the formation of a minority government more likely. This is particularly the case if the party is "very strong" rather than just "merely strong" (Laver and Shepsle 1996). Our upcoming results do not depend on whether we treat these two types of strong party separately or together as we do here.

---

14. It was only when the opposition parties decided to fight the Congress Party on an anticorruption platform rather than an ideological platform that they were able to unite to defeat it (Andersen 1990, 528–530).

15. This measure comes from Martin and Stevenson (2001). It was originally created by Paul Warwick using Laver and Shepsle's WINSET program.

TABLE 11.8	**Testing Theories of Minority Governments**				

Dependent Variable: Did a Minority Government Form? 1 = Yes, 0 = No

Variables	Model 1	Model 2	Model 3	Model 4	Model 5
Opposition strength	0.31***				0.39***
	(0.05)				(0.11)
Corporatism		0.57**			0.60*
		(0.22)			(0.31)
Investiture vote			−0.54***		−0.84**
			(0.16)		(0.34)
Strong party				−0.52**	−0.08
				(0.21)	(0.33)
Constant	−1.63***	−2.06***	0.20	0.29*	−3.86***
	(0.28)	(0.79)	(0.12)	(0.17)	(1.42)
N	251	106	251	155	85
Log likelihood	−152.46	−69.53	−167.55	−104.28	−39.66

Source: Data are from the Constitutional Change and Parliamentary Democracies project. (Müller and Strøm 2000; Strøm, Müller, and Bergman 2003).

Note: Cells show coefficients from a probit model with robust standard errors in parentheses.

* = greater than 90% significant.
** = greater than 95% significant.
*** = greater than 99% significant.

So what do the results in Table 11.8 reveal? Remember that next to each variable is a "co-efficient," and beneath this is a "standard error." The coefficient indicates the direction in which the variable affects the probability of forming a minority government. Thus, a positive coefficient indicates that an increase in the variable makes it more likely that a minority government will form and a negative coefficient indicates that an increase in the variable makes it less likely. The standard error beneath the coefficient essentially tells us how confident we are in our results; we tend to be more confident the smaller the standard error relative to the coefficient. To help indicate how confident we are in our results, we use stars, next to the coefficient. In Table 11.8, one star indicates that we are over 90 percent confident in our results; two stars that we are over 95 percent confident; and three stars that we are over 99 percent confident in our results. A coefficient with no stars indicates that we cannot be very confident that this variable has any effect on the probability that a minority government will form.

As you can see, there is very strong evidence to support the claims made by Luebbert and Strøm that countries with high levels of corporatism and opposition strength are more likely to have minority governments. This is because the coefficients associated with *Opposition strength* and *Corporatism* are always positive and significant. To see the substantive effect of these variables, imagine a country with no strong parties, no investiture votes, and a mean level of corporatism (3.5). If we increased the strength of opposition parties in this country from 2.2 (Greece) to 5.2 (Sweden), then the results from Model 5 indicate that we would increase the probability of a minority government by 438 percent.[16] Now imagine a country with no strong parties, no investiture votes, and a mean level of opposition strength (4.9). If we increased the degree of corporatism in this country from 1.7 (United Kingdom in 1990) to 3.0 (Italy in 1990), then the results from Model 5 indicate that we would increase the probability of a minority government by 446 percent. There is also very strong evidence to support Strøm's conjecture that countries with formal investiture votes are much less likely to have minority governments. This is because the coefficient associated with *Investiture* is always negative and significant. If a country without a strong party and with mean levels of opposition strength and corporatism decided to adopt formal investiture requirements, then the results from Model 5 indicate that it could expect to cut the probability of minority governments in half (53 percent). These are all very large substantive effects.

In stark contrast to these results, there is no compelling evidence for Laver and Shepsle's (1996) claim that the existence of strong parties makes minority governments more likely. In fact, the coefficient on *Strong party* is always negative. This is the exact opposite of what their theory predicts and suggests that, if anything, the presence of strong parties reduces the likelihood of minority governments. These results are consistent with the findings of a more detailed and complicated analysis conducted by Golder (2006). Thus, although it seems entirely plausible that the existence of parties located in the middle of the ideological spectrum with opposition parties on either side might increase the likelihood of minority governments, there is no systematic evidence, as yet, to support this hypothesis.[17] In sum, we have presented evidence that minority governments are more likely in countries where (a) opposition parties are able to strongly influence policy, (b) interest group relations are organized along corporatist lines, and (c) there are no formal investiture vote requirements.

Surplus Majority Governments

Although governments that appear "too small" (minority) often form, cabinets that appear "too large" (surplus majority or oversized) also emerge from time to time. A **surplus majority government** is one in which the cabinet contains more parties than are strictly necessary to control a legislative majority. In effect, the government could lose or remove a party and still control a majority of the seats in the legislature. Like minority governments, surplus majority cabinets have often been considered peculiar and uncommon forms of government in parliamentary democracies. The data do not support this view, however. As Figure 11.5a

> A **surplus majority government** is one in which the cabinet includes more parties than are strictly necessary to control a majority of legislative seats.

---

16. We do not show exactly how to make these calculations here because they are beyond the methodological scope of this book. Students who are interested in how to make these types of calculations are encouraged to take classes in statistics.

17. Martin and Stevenson (2001, 46) present results consistent with the claim that minority governments are more likely when there are strong parties. Specifically, they find that strong parties "tend to get into government and, even more, to rule alone." Golder (2006), however, shows that Martin and Stevenson's results come from a slightly misspecified model. Once corrected, their model provides no evidence that minority governments are more common in the presence of strong parties.

indicates, a little under a fifth (17.1 percent) of all governments that formed in West European parliamentary democracies from 1945 to 1998 were surplus majority governments. In fact, surplus majority governments have made up almost half the governments in Italy (46 percent) and the Netherlands (45 percent). In addition to their numerical frequency, surplus majority governments have also been in power for reasonably long stretches of time. For example, surplus majority cabinets have ruled in Western Europe for about 12.2 percent of the postwar period (Figure 11.5b). Moreover, each surplus majority government remained in power for well over a year (536 days) on average.

Several arguments have been proposed to explain the apparent puzzle as to why surplus majority governments form. Just as with minority governments, these arguments emphasize the importance of policy in the government formation process. If politicians were purely office seekers, then it is hard to see why surplus majority governments would ever form, because they require political actors to give up office when they do not have to. This implies that the very existence of surplus majority governments must be a signal that policy matters.

Surplus majority governments have often formed in times of political, economic, or military crisis. These crisis governments are sometimes referred to as "national unity" governments. For example, national unity governments formed in Austria, Belgium, Finland, France, Germany, Italy, Luxembourg, and the Netherlands immediately after World War II. They also formed in several East European countries following the collapse of communism in 1989. A national unity government formed in Iraq following the 2006 legislative elections. The belief is that only by bringing together parties from across the ideological spectrum and giving them a reason to be invested in the existing political system is it possible to resolve whatever crisis is afflicting the country. The goal is to put the everyday partisan, ethnic, or religious nature of politics on hold for the sake of the country's immediate future. Although governments of national unity often have strong popular support, this particular type of surplus majority government tends to be short-lived in practice. Political parties that are not required to sustain a legislative majority are often quickly pushed into opposition. The reason is that the desire on the part of politicians to enjoy as much office and policy influence as possible often overrides the wishes of the electorate that parties work together to rescue a country from whatever ails it.

In some circumstances, the formation of a surplus majority government may actually be necessary to pass particular pieces of legislation. For example, constitutional amendments often require "supermajorities," which are made up of more than a legislative majority. If a government wants to pass a constitutional amendment that requires a supermajority, then it might choose to have more parties in the cabinet than are strictly necessary just to remain in power. Of course, the surplus majority government in this case does not actually contain more parties than are strictly necessary to pass the constitutional amendment. In fact, you might say that this type of government is "oversized" in name only and that in practice it is no different from a minimal winning coalition, given its policy objectives. A country that produces this type of surplus majority government is Belgium (Gallagher, Laver, and Mair 2006, 392). The Belgian constitution requires that laws affecting the relationship between different language groups in the country require the support of two-thirds of the legislators and a majority of each language group. This has led to several surplus majority governments in Belgium.

Another explanation for the formation of surplus majority governments focuses on the strategic interaction between coalition partners or between actors within parties. If a minimal winning coalition takes office, any party in the cabinet, no matter how small, can bring the government down simply by resigning. This situation allows for the possibility of blackmail by a single dissatisfied party (Luebbert 1984, 254). In particular, it allows a small party to extract significant policy concessions from its coalition partners in vast disproportion to its size simply because its votes are critical to the government's continuing existence. To prevent this scenario, larger parties in the coalition may decide to form surplus majority coalitions so that the government is not automatically brought down if a single party decides to resign. Parties that lack party discipline and suffer from high levels of internal dissent may also choose to form surplus majority governments for similar reasons. In effect, parties that cannot guarantee that their own legislators will always vote the party line might agree to share office and policy influence with other parties in return for the legislative support necessary to remain in power. Finally, the fact that parties typically agree on a set of coalition policies prior to forming the government but ultimately have to implement these policies in some order also creates incentives for surplus majority governments (Carruba and Volden 2000). Consider two parties that agree on a set of coalition policies prior to coming to power. As soon as one of the parties has managed to implement the policies that it wants, it will have an incentive to defect from the government and bring it down if it does not like any of the policies still to be introduced. This incentive is reduced with a surplus majority coalition, because the defection of one party will not prevent the government from implementing the remaining policies.

Preelectoral Coalitions

So far we have assumed that parties in parliamentary democracies wait until after elections before thinking about what government to form. This is certainly how most political scientists have thought about the government formation process. This, however, is not always the case. The fact that single parties are unable to command a majority of support in the legislature in most democracies typically means that parties who wish to be in the government have to form some sort of coalition. In effect, parties can either form a **preelectoral coalition** with another party (or parties) prior to election in the hope of governing together afterward if successful at the polls, or they can compete independently and hope to form a **government coalition** after the election. Most scholars have focused almost exclusively on the government coalitions that form after elections and ignored preelectoral coalitions. An exception is Golder (2006). In an analysis of twenty-three advanced industrial democracies, she shows that preelectoral coalitions are not only common but also that they affect election

> A **preelectoral coalition** is a collection of parties that do not compete independently at election time. A **government coalition** is one that forms after the election.

outcomes, have a strong impact on the government formation process, and have significant policy and normative implications.[18]

A preelectoral coalition is a collection of parties that do not compete independently at election time either because they publicly agree to coordinate their campaigns, run joint candidates or joint lists, or enter government together following the election. Preelectoral coalitions come in various types that differ in the extent to which parties coordinate their electoral strategies. These types are shown in Table 11.9.

Nomination agreements between parties represent a relatively high level of electoral coordination because the parties agree to present a coalition candidate in each district rather than each party putting up their own candidate. Nomination agreements are a typical form of electoral coordination in countries with single-member districts. For example, parties in France often choose to nominate a single coalition candidate in each district before the first round of elections or they agree to withdraw their respective candidates in favor of a coalition candidate prior to the second round of voting. The Liberal Party and the newly formed Social Democratic Party also reached nomination agreements in the United Kingdom during the 1980s. The two parties "recognized that competition between them would be mutually destructive . . . [and] they quickly worked out an electoral pact in which constituencies were allocated between the two parties, so that nowhere would they oppose each other" (Rasmussen 1991, 168). Joint lists also represent a relatively high level of electoral coordination because they involve parties agreeing to a single list of coalition candidates. Joint party lists are quite common in Israel, where parties run under a new coalition name. They also occur in Greece, the Netherlands, and Portugal.

A slightly lower level of electoral coordination often occurs in countries where individuals get to cast two votes in different electoral tiers. In these countries, electoral coalitions often take the form of party leaders' telling their supporters to cast one vote for their party and the second vote for their coalition partner (dual ballot instructions). This type of elec-

---

TABLE 11.9   **Different Types of Preelectoral Coalition**

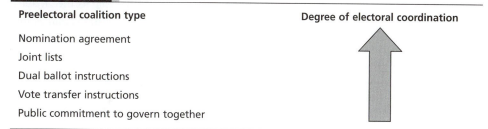

Preelectoral coalition type	Degree of electoral coordination
Nomination agreement	
Joint lists	
Dual ballot instructions	
Vote transfer instructions	
Public commitment to govern together	

---

18. Other recent studies examining preelectoral coalitions include Ferrara and Herron (2005); Blais and Indriðason (2007); and Carroll and Cox (2007).

toral coalition occurs quite frequently in Germany, where individuals cast one vote for a constituency candidate elected by plurality rule and a second vote for a party list in a multi-member (regional) district. In Germany it is usually understood that the constituency vote will go to the candidate from the larger coalition member, whereas the list vote will go to the smaller partner to ensure that the small party passes the 5 percent electoral threshold. In countries in which voters get to rank their preferences over candidates and preferences are transferable, electoral coalitions often take the form of party leaders' telling their supporters to rank their own party first and a coalition partner second. For example, parties in Australia often give individuals "how-to-vote" cards outside polling stations with clear instructions on how to rank candidates so that the flow of preferences will benefit the party if it is running separately or the coalition if a preelectoral agreement is in place. Similar instructions are provided by party leaders to their supporters in Ireland.

Publicly stating an intention to govern together if successful at the polls represents the lowest level of electoral coordination.[19] This type of electoral coalition occurs in many countries, such as Germany, the Netherlands, and New Zealand. For example, the Alliance and Labour Party in New Zealand formed a loose electoral coalition in 1999 stating that they would govern together if they won the elections. Some parties actually make public commitments to *not* govern with certain other parties in Austria, Germany, the Netherlands, and Norway, thereby effectively ruling out certain cabinet configurations (Strøm, Budge and Laver 1994; Müller and Strøm 2000). For example, all parties in Germany publicly rejected the possibility of forming a government with the Party of Democratic Socialism (the former Communist Party in East Germany) prior to the 1990, 1994, and 1998 elections.

Preelectoral coalitions are quite common. Table 11.10 provides information on 240 preelectoral coalitions at the national level in twenty-three advanced industrialized democracies from 1946 to 2002. Only Canada and Malta have no experience with preelectoral coalitions at the national level. Although some countries, such as Japan, Luxembourg, New Zealand, and the United Kingdom have had few electoral coalitions, others, such as Australia, France, Germany, Greece, Israel, and Portugal have had many. Preelectoral coalitions have competed in all Australian elections, 93.3 percent of Germany's elections, and 90 percent of Portugal's elections. About a third (29.2 percent) of the 240 preelectoral coalitions that formed made it into government. Indeed, about two-thirds of all the governments in Australia and France

---

19. Publicly stating that you will form a government if successful at the polls is another explanation for the formation of surplus majority governments. When coalition partners make a public statement such as this, they do not know if all of them will be needed to control a majority of the legislative seats. For example, it may turn out that one of the coalition partners can be jettisoned after the elections without losing the government's legislative majority. This situation occurred when the Socialists and Communists agreed to enter government together if they won the French legislative elections in 1981. Although the elections resulted in a majority for the Socialists, both parties honored their agreement and entered office as a surplus majority government. Why didn't the Socialists renege on their preelectoral pact and form a government on their own? It turns out that there is quite strong empirical evidence that public commitments to form governments are nearly always honored (Laver and Schofield 1998; Martin and Stevenson 2001). One explanation for this has to do with reputational effects—other parties may not agree to form preelectoral coalitions with parties that have reneged on such pacts in the past.

TABLE 11.10	**Summary Information on National-Level Preelectoral Coalitions, 1946–2002**

Country	Election years	Elections (no.)	PECs (no.)	Elections with PECs (%)	Governments based on PECs	
					(no.)	(%)
Australia	1946–2001	23	25	100.0	15	65.2
Austria	1949–2002	17	12	58.8	9	52.9
Belgium	1946–1999	18	14	61.1	1	5.6
Canada	1949–2000	17	0	0.0	0	0.0
Denmark	1947–2001	22	8	36.4	1	4.5
Finland	1948–1999	15	3	20.0	1	6.7
France	1946–2002	15	23	73.3	10	66.7
Germany	1949–2002	15	19	93.3	8	53.3
Greece[a]	1946–2000	19	25	73.7	4	21.1
Iceland	1946–1999	17	8	47.1	0	0.0
Ireland	1948–2002	17	9	47.1	5	29.4
Israel	1949–1999	15	26	86.7	0	0.0
Italy	1948–2001	14	9	35.7	2	14.3
Japan	1947–2000	20	2	5.0	0	0.0
Luxembourg	1954–1999	10	3	30.0	0	0.0
Malta	1966–1998	8	0	0.0	0	0.0
Netherlands	1946–2002	17	8	35.3	3	17.6
New Zealand	1946–2002	20	2	10.0	1	5.0
Norway	1949–2001	14	9	64.3	5	35.7
Portugal	1976–2002	10	14	90.0	2	20.0
Spain	1977–2000	8	11	87.5	1	12.5
Sweden	1948–2002	18	8	38.9	2	11.1
United Kingdom	1950–2001	15	2	13.3	0	0.0
Total		364	240		70	

Source: Data are from Golder (2006).

[a] The years 1968–1973 are not included.

during this time period, and one-half of German governments, have been based on preelectoral alliances. These data serve to demonstrate that coalition bargaining often occurs prior to elections in a wide range of countries and that a large proportion of government coalitions that ultimately form are based on preelectoral agreements. Golder (2006) finds that potential government coalitions are 123 times more likely to become the actual government if they are based on a preelectoral pact than if they are not.

As with the governments that form after elections, the emergence of preelectoral coalitions is the result of a bargaining process among party leaders. For example, party leaders who wish to form a preelectoral coalition must reach agreement over a joint electoral strategy and the distribution of office benefits that might accrue to them. This may involve outlining a common coalition platform, deciding which party gets to run the more powerful ministerial posts, choosing which party's candidates should step down in favor of candidates from their coalition partners in particular districts, or determining which leader is to become prime minister. Clearly, the preelectoral coalition bargaining process involves a similar set of thorny distributional and ideological issues as the postelection government coalition bargaining process. One difference, though, between the preelectoral coalition formation process and the government coalition formation process is that there are electoral advantages from competing as a coalition at election time that are no longer relevant in the postelection context. This is particularly the case in countries with disproportional electoral systems that punish small parties. Ultimately, electoral coalitions can influence the probability of electoral victory, whereas government coalitions can't. It is largely for this reason that political parties sometimes choose to form a coalition prior to an election rather than wait until afterward.

In the simple model of government formation that we presented earlier, we suggested that government coalitions are more likely to form between ideologically similar parties. This led to the prediction that we should observe "connected" coalitions. There is good reason to believe that governments based on preelectoral coalitions will be even more ideologically compatible than government coalitions that are not based on electoral pacts. The reason for this is that the "ideological compatibility constraint" facing potential coalitions is likely to be stronger prior to elections than afterward, because voters might be unwilling to vote for electoral coalitions made up of parties with incompatible or incoherent policy preferences; after the election, parties have more leeway to enter into these types of government coalitions because voters are no longer such an immediate constraint on politicians' actions.[20] Of course, parties do feel constrained to some extent in their coalition choices even after an election because voters could potentially punish ideologically incompatible governments at subsequent elections. If party leaders think that a particular incompatible coalition is likely to be successful in office, however, then they may gamble that voters will not punish them at the next election. Party leaders may also prefer to get the benefits of office and the ability to make policy today even though they know that they will be punished in the future.

---

20. The fact that party leaders often invest considerable resources to explicitly measure the expected electoral consequences of a coalition indicates that they are fully aware of the dangers of forming an ideologically incompatible coalition (Kaminski 2002). Some parties employ private polling companies to carry out surveys asking voters whether they would support particular coalition arrangements (Kaminski 2001). Others engage in coalition experiments at the regional level to evaluate the performance of particular combinations of parties. Based on these local experiences, party leaders then decide whether these coalitions should be implemented at the national level (Downs 1998).

The Manifesto Research Group provides estimates of the ideological position of parties on the traditional left-right policy dimension by examining the manifestos of political parties in numerous countries around the world (Budge et al. 2001). From these data it is possible to create a measure of a government's ideological spread—the distance between the left-most and right-most government party. Using such a measure, Golder (2006) finds that governments based on preelectoral coalitions are, indeed, more ideologically compatible than government coalitions that are not based on electoral pacts. She also finds that these governments are significantly more likely to be connected coalitions as well. One of the implications of her analysis is that the policy position of a government based on an electoral pact is likely to be more congruent with the preferences of its electorate than the policy position of governments that are not constrained by a preelectoral agreement.

Preelectoral coalitions can have quite significant effects on election outcomes and government policies. Consider the following simple example. Imagine a legislative election with single-member districts in which there are two blocs of parties, one on the left and one on the right. The left-wing bloc has more electoral support than the right. Suppose that the parties on the right form an electoral coalition and field a common candidate in each district but the parties on the left compete independently. The left would most likely lose in this situation. In this example, the possibility arises that a majority of voters could vote for a group of politicians who support similar policies and that these politicians might still lose the election by failing to coordinate sufficiently. The result is that a right-wing party is elected to implement policies that a majority of the voters do not want. In other words, the absence of a preelectoral coalition on the left can have a significant impact on the election outcome, the government that forms, and the policies that are likely to be implemented. If you believe that the candidate with the most support among the electorate should be elected to implement policy, it matters whether political elites choose electoral strategies and coalitions that make them more or less likely to win elections.

The simple example that we just outlined might be considered a good description of what happened in the French presidential elections in 2002. It had widely been expected that Jacques Chirac, the president and leader of the mainstream right, would make it through to the second round of voting along with Lionel Jospin, the Socialist prime minister and leader of the mainstream left. The real question for months had been which of the two men would win the second round. Then, unexpectedly, the left vote was split among so many candidates in the first round that the Socialist leader came in third, behind the extreme-right politician Jean-Marie Le Pen. The French press described the event as an earthquake, and the French elections were for a couple of weeks the subject of world-wide speculation. In reality, there was little chance that Le Pen would be elected president, and Chirac easily won the runoff election two weeks later. Most analyses of this particular election focus on the disturbing success of the extreme right. This political "earthquake," however, had as much to do with the inability of the French left to form a coherent preelectoral coalition as it did with an increase in the strength of the extreme right. The result of the left's failure to form a preelectoral coalition was that the French electorate got a right-wing government implementing right-wing policies even though there was good reason to think that a relative majority of the voters wanted a left-wing cabinet—opinion polls at the time suggested that Jospin may well have won a head-to-head contest with Chirac if he could have just made it to the second round. Ironically, the popularity of left-wing parties among the voters may have emboldened their leaders to run alone rather than in coalition—a decision that, in the end, led to their electoral failure.

A voter compares the campaign manifestos of Jacques Chirac and Jean-Marie Le Pen ahead of the second round of voting in the French presidential elections, held on May 5, 2002.

Preelectoral coalitions also have important normative implications. One would like to think that voters choose their governments through the electoral process. A government, however, forms beyond the scrutiny of the electorate whenever the election does not produce a single-party majority government or whenever parties begin the government formation process after the election. In countries that employ proportional electoral rules, elections often serve "primarily as devices for electing representative agents in postelection bargaining processes, rather than as devices for choosing a specific executive" (Huber 1996, 185). Voters often end up voting for a single, unaligned party, not knowing what, if any, government it would join. This disconnect between the voters and the government formation process in these countries is a problem, because it is not always clear whether the final coalition that takes office has the support of the electorate in a meaningful sense. Preelectoral coalitions can help to alleviate this problem by helping voters to identify government alternatives and register their support for one of them (Powell 2000). In fact, party leaders in Germany, Ireland, and the Netherlands have made this type of argument publicly to appeal to voters. Arguably, electoral coalitions also increase democratic transparency and provide coalitions with as much of a mandate as single parties. By providing a direct link between the voters and the cabinet that proposes and implements policy, preelectoral coalitions help to undermine the criticism of parliamentary democracies that employ proportional representation electoral rules, namely, that governments lack a convincing mandate from the voters and that the quality of representative democracy is thereby diminished. We return to some of these normative issues in Chapter 15.

Duration of Governments: Formation and Survival

As we have illustrated, the government formation process in parliamentary democracies can be very complicated and quite complex. Even if parties agree to go into government together, they still have to haggle over who gets which portfolio and what the government policy should be. This bargaining process can sometimes last a long time. Table 11.11 presents

TABLE 11.11	**Duration of Government Formation Process after Elections, 1945–1998 (days)**			
Country	Minimum	Maximum	Average	N
Austria	23	129	52.1	15
Belgium	2	148	59.7	17
Denmark	0	35	9.5	21
Finland	25	80	54.7	14
France (5th Republic)	1	11	3.5	11
Germany	23	73	36.4	14
Iceland	1	76	30.6	16
Ireland	7	48	18.7	16
Italy	11	126	47.3	14
Luxembourg	19	52	32.0	9
Netherlands	31	208	85.7	16
Norway	0	16	2.50	13
Portugal	1	45	24.0	7
Spain	2	58	28.6	7
Sweden	0	25	5.7	17
United Kingdom	1	18	7.8	14
All	0	208	31.8	221

Source: Data are from the Constitutional Change and Parliamentary Democracies project. (Müller and Strøm 2000; Strøm, Müller, and Bergman 2003).

Note: Bargaining duration measures the number of days between the election and the day on which the new government is officially inaugurated.

information about the length of time in days that it typically takes governments to form after an election in sixteen West European countries from 1945 to 1998.[21]

As Table 11.11 illustrates, there is considerable cross-national variation in the length of time that it takes to form a government following an election. If a single party obtains a majority of the legislative seats, then it is normally understood that this party will form a cabinet on its own and the only question is who from this party will get which portfolio. This explains why it takes only about a week (7.8 days) on average for a cabinet to form in the United Kingdom. In countries in which many parties gain legislative representation, it can

---

21. The data in Table 11.11 refer only to governments that form after elections. However, governments also form in interelection periods after an incumbent cabinet falls. The average length of time that it takes to form a government in an interelection period is only 13.5 days. This is a statistically significantly shorter period of time than the government formation process that follows an election. Only in Norway and Spain do interelection cabinets take longer to form on average.

take much longer to form a cabinet, because it is not always obvious which combination of parties will be able to form the government, how these parties will allocate portfolios among themselves, and what the coalition policy will be.[22] For example, the average length of the government formation process in the Netherlands is about three months (85.7 days). In fact, the longest delay in government formation in this sample of countries occurred in the Netherlands at almost seven months, or 208 days. It is not uncommon for a formateur to fail to form a coalition on the first or even the second attempt in some countries without single-party majorities. For instance, it took seven different government coalition proposals more than 106 days for a government to finally form after the 1979 Belgian legislative elections. Overall, the average length of time that it takes to form a government after an election in Western Europe is about a month (31.8 days).

The first democratic elections in Iraq occurred on January 30, 2005. It was not until April 28, however, fully 88 days later, that an Iraqi government actually took office. This delay in the Iraqi government formation process was a cause of some concern around the world. Much of the world's media, along with the American government, blamed the delay on the lack of democratic experience among Iraqi politicians—they simply did not have any experience with democracy or putting a government coalition together. Although the Iraqis were certainly faced with some additional difficulties not present in most other parliamentary systems, it should be noted that the length of time that it took them to form a government was about the same as the average length of time it takes the Dutch to form a government after elections. In fact, there are at least sixteen instances in which cabinet negotiations in Western Europe lasted longer than 88 days—in some cases much longer. The Iraqis did not come close to matching the 208 days that it took to form the Dutch government in 1977. The point here is that we do not argue that such delays in Austria, Belgium, Iceland, Italy, or the Netherlands were caused by unfamiliarity with democratic politics. It is simply part and parcel of most parliamentary systems that election results do not regularly determine the identity of the government. Instead, elections usher in what can be quite a long period of negotiations in which party leaders bargain over the composition of the government cabinet. Delays of several months are not infrequent, even in highly established democracies with considerable experience in building coalition governments.

Delays in the government formation process can have important implications for governance. You may recall that caretaker governments, which administer the affairs of state while negotiations are proceeding, do not generally have the authority to make major policy initiatives. This means that delays in the government formation process can be quite problematic, particularly if the previous cabinet has fallen because of some sort of crisis. Until a cabinet is finally formed, the identity of government parties, the allocation of portfolios to

---

22. In addition, nonpolitical factors such as holidays affect the length of time between the election and the date the new government takes office. For instance, forming the German government at the end of the year in 1990 took extra time because of the Christmas holidays.

particular politicians, and the content of policy compromises among coalition partners have yet to be determined. The uncertainty that surrounds the future direction of government policy can have serious consequences on the behavior of economic and political actors, both domestic and international (Martin and Vanberg 2003, 323–324). For example, consider the seven-month delay in forming a government that followed the June 2006 elections in the Czech Republic. By August, the Czech media were already reporting on the deleterious consequences of the prolonged period under a caretaker government. The *Prague Post Online* (August 24, 2006) wrote, "Lawmakers are getting nothing done, while legislation and important reforms rest in a state of limbo, including long awaited pension reform, the privatization of many state-owned companies, an overhaul of the country's Criminal Code, and the fate of the controversial flat tax. A nonfunctioning parliament costs taxpayers as much as 3 million Kč ($136,500) a day." A number of recent empirical studies paint a similar picture, finding that uncertainty over the government formation process affects exchange rate markets (Leblang 2002), stock market volatility (Leblang and Mukherjee 2006), and the types of assets that market actors choose to invest in (Bernhard and Leblang 2006). Delays in government formation have real consequences for many people.

Only limited research has been conducted on the factors that affect the length of bargaining delays in forming governments. Diermeier and van Roozendaal (1998) argue that delays are caused by uncertainty regarding the preferences of the parties involved in the formation process. For example, it may take time to figure out the best offer of policy and portfolio allocation that would be acceptable to the party leaders involved in the coalition negotiations— the greater the uncertainty regarding the relevant bargaining parameters, the longer the formation time. Martin and Vanberg (2003) argue that delays are caused by complexity in the bargaining environment. The more complex the bargaining situation, the longer the bargaining delays.

More recently, Golder (2007) has argued that uncertainty and bargaining complexity both matter. Using data on sixteen countries from 1946 to 1998, she finds that governments take longer to form after elections (increased uncertainty) than during interelection periods and when there are many ideologically diverse parties in the legislature (increased complexity). Following an election, the party composition in the legislature is different, parties may have new platforms, and there may be membership turnover within the parties. Party leaders are likely to learn about what policies are feasible for potential government cabinets and which would likely lead to their breakup through their day-to-day negotiations over legislative proposals. As a result, policy leaders will be less certain about which potential cabinets are acceptable to a legislative majority right after an election than after an extended period of legislative interaction. This increased uncertainty after elections leads to delays in the government formation process. Having many ideologically diverse parties increases the complexity of the bargaining environment facing formateurs. For example, the formateur will likely have to negotiate with many potential coalition partners and make many offers and counteroffers if there are many parties. If the parties in the legislature are also ideologically diverse, then it is likely that the formateur will have to bargain with at least one party that does not hold similar positions on several different types of policy as well. In effect, bargaining complexity leads to delays in the formation of governments because it makes it difficult for the formateur to gather the information that the formateur is uncertain about, that is, the parameters of the best offer that would be acceptable to potential government partners.

Not only is there considerable variation in the length of time that it takes to form governments, but there are also large differences in the amount of time that various governments survive in power. Of the governments that formed in thirteen West European parliamentary democracies from 1945 to 1998, only 20 percent actually stayed in office for their maximum permitted term. On average, governments lasted only 60 percent of their permitted time in office; this average ranged from 84 percent in the Netherlands to 33 percent in Italy. In Figure 11.6, we illustrate the average duration of governments in days by cabinet type in thirteen parliamentary democracies in Western Europe from 1945 to 1998. Single-party majority governments last the longest at 967 days on average. Minimal winning coalitions last only slightly less time at 864 days. Both of these types of government last considerably longer (about a year in all) than minority or surplus majority governments.

| FIGURE 11.6 | Average Government Duration by Cabinet Type, 1945–1998 (days) |

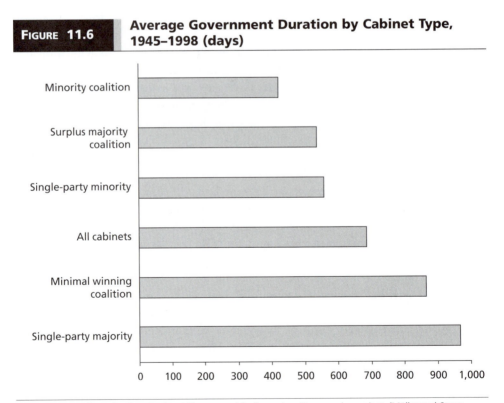

Source: Data are from the Constitutional Change and Parliamentary Democracies project. (Müller and Strøm 2000; Strøm, Müller, and Bergman 2003).

Note: Data cover thirteen West European parliamentary democracies.

In Figure 11.7, we illustrate the minimum and average duration of governments by country in days. As you can see, there is considerable cross-national variation in the length of time a government stays in office. Governments last longest on average in Luxembourg (1,170 days), the United Kingdom (981 days), and Spain (957 days). They last much less time in Italy (354 days) and Belgium (520 days).

You might think that all political scientists measure government duration in the same way. How hard can it be to measure how long a government lasts? Unfortunately, scholars measure government duration in many different ways. All agree that a government ends if the party composition of the cabinet changes either because an incumbent party leaves or a new party joins. But that's about it. What's the problem? Ask yourself whether we should classify a government as new if the same parties are in power after an election as before the election. Would you consider it a new government if the same parties are in power but completely different individuals fill the ministerial portfolios (cabinet reshuffle)? What if the prime minister changes? What if the party composition of the cabinet changes slightly but virtually all the incumbent ministers get to keep their old positions? Measuring government duration is a surprisingly difficult issue (Golder and Ryals 2008). The data that we present on government duration in this chapter define the end of a government as occurring if (a) there is any change in the set of parties holding cabinet membership, (b) there is any change in the identity of the prime minister, or (c) there has been a general election.

| FIGURE 11.7 | **Minimum and Average Duration of Governments, 1945–1998 (days)** |

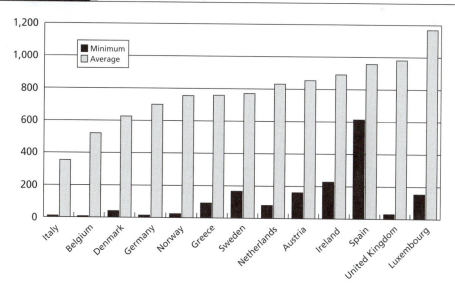

Source: Data are from the Constitutional Change and Parliamentary Democracies project. (Müller and Strøm 2000; Strøm, Müller, and Bergman 2003).

Governments end for both "technical" and "discretionary" reasons (Müller and Strøm 2000, 25–27). Technical reasons are things that are beyond the control of the government. For example, a government might end because the prime minister dies or resigns due to ill health, or because there is a constitutionally mandated election. In our sample of thirteen West European parliamentary democracies from 1945 to 1998, 37 percent of governments ended for technical reasons. Discretionary reasons are political acts on the part of the government or opposition. For instance, a government might end because the government dissolves the parliament and calls early elections, because the opposition defeats the government in a vote of no confidence, or because conflicts between or within the coalition parties force the government to resign. These discretionary reasons are obviously not mutually exclusive. Of the governments in our sample, 63 percent ended for discretionary reasons. We indicate how many governments fell for particular technical and discretionary reasons in Table 11.12. Over a quarter of the cabinets ended because the government called early elections. The ability of governments to choose when to have an election is known as endogenous election timing (see Box 11.4). Only thirty-four governments ended as a result of a parliamentary defeat. Still, not too much should be read into this relatively low number, because governments often resign in order to avoid being defeated in a vote of no confidence.

TABLE 11.12	**Number of Governments That Fell for Technical and Discretionary Reasons in Thirteen West European Parliamentary Democracies, 1945–1998**	
	Specific reason	No.
Technical		
	Constitutionally mandated election	81
	Other constitutional reason	25
	Death of PM	6
Discretionary		
	Early election	91
	Enlargement of government	13
	Parliamentary defeat	34
	Intercoalition conflict over policy	62
	Intercoalition conflict not related to policy	20
	Intraparty conflict	51
Technical		111
Discretionary		191
Total		302

Source: Data are from the Constitutional Change and Parliamentary Democracies project. (Müller and Strøm 2000; Strøm, Müller, and Bergman 2003).

Note: The different technical and discretionary reasons for why governments fall are not mutually exclusive. In other words, governments can fall, within the technical or discretionary categories, for more than one reason. This explains why the numbers shown above do not sum exactly to the total number of governments that end because of technical (111) or discretionary (191) reasons.

ENDOGENOUS ELECTION TIMING

In some countries, the government gets to choose when it wants to hold elections. For example, the government in the United Kingdom is constrained to hold an election at least once every five years but can choose exactly when to hold the election in this five-year window. We refer to this possibility as endogenous election timing. Three different stories have been proposed to explain the timing of elections. All three stories assume that politicians want to win elections and that voters hold governments accountable for their past economic performance.

1. *Political surfing:* The government waits until the economic conditions are right before calling an election. The government does not actively manipulate the economy but waits until the economy, for whatever reason, is at a high point before announcing the election (Kayser 2005).

2. *Political business cycle:* The government actively manipulates the economy to engineer a short-term economic high and then calls an election. The election is then followed by an economic decline. Thus, the economy goes through cycles of boom and bust that are politically driven (Clark 2003).

3. *Signaling:* The government is better informed about future economic performance than the voters and so can time elections to occur prior to any expected economic decline. In other words, the government calls early elections in order to cash in on its past successes by censoring the public's ability to observe the future decline. The very act of calling an early election, however, effectively sends a signal to voters that the future performance of the economy looks bad. If voters are naive or have short-term memories, or if the opposition is unprepared, the government may prefer to call an early election. Otherwise, governments might be reluctant to take advantage of good economic times by calling an early election because they want to avoid sending voters a signal that they don't expect the good times to last (Smith 2003).

Several different predictions can be derived from these stories. First, let's consider predictions about economic performance. Both the political surfing and political business cycle stories predict that elections are called when the economy is doing well, whereas the signaling story says that current economic conditions should not matter. Both the political business cycle and signaling stories predict that calls for early elections should be followed by economic declines (if for different reasons), but the political surfing story makes no prediction about future economic performance. The signaling story predicts that the support of the government in the opinion polls will fall if it calls early elections because voters learn that the government is about to produce bad economic outcomes; the other stories have nothing to say about the electoral support of the government. The signaling story predicts that the earlier an election is called, the greater the economic decline to come—why else risk losing office? The other stories make no such prediction.

continues

Smith (2004) has tested these predictions on data from the United Kingdom and finds strongest support for the signaling story. He finds that when elections are called early relative to expectations, then the support for the government declines, postelection outcomes decline, electoral campaigns are short, and stock market indexes decline. When elections are called especially early, he finds that the economy later performs particularly badly. There was little evidence that the current performance of the economy affected the likelihood that a government would call an early election. All of these findings are consistent with the signaling story but not the other stories.

Over the past few decades, there have been numerous studies of government duration (King et al. 1990; Warwick 1994; Lupia and Strøm 1995; Diermeier and Stevenson 1999). They have examined how various attributes of the government, the legislature, and the country affect the survival of governments. In regard to government attributes, it has been found that cabinets last longer if they are majority governments (rather than minority governments), if they are single-party governments (rather than coalition governments), and if the government exhibits low ideological diversity in its party membership. In regard to legislative attributes, it has been found that more legislative parties lead to a reduction in government duration. In regard to country attributes, some have found that investiture vote requirements diminish average government duration (King et al. 1990; Warwick 1994).

How and why does it matter whether or not a government survives for a long time? It is perhaps a natural reaction to think that cabinet instability is a bad thing, but why exactly might this be the case? You might think that governments that do not survive long result in policy instability and cabinet ministers who lack portfolio experience and political experience more generally. It has long been known, however, that cabinet instability does not automatically imply ministerial instability. For example, Allum (1973, 119) found that a set of politicians had been "in office almost continuously for over twenty years" during the heyday of cabinet instability in Italy. In a recent study, Huber and Martinez-Gallardo (2004) also show that cabinet instability does not necessarily lead to high levels of turnover in cabinet membership. Huber and Martinez-Gallardo measured cabinet duration, portfolio experience, and political experience in nineteen democracies from 1945 to 1999. Portfolio experience is measured as the average amount of experience in days that ministers have in the specific cabinet portfolio that they hold. Political experience is measured as the average amount of experience in days that ministers have in *any* significant cabinet portfolio. The results of their analysis are shown in Figure 11.8.[23]

---

23. The average cabinet duration shown in Figure 11.8 may differ slightly from that in Figure 11.7 because Huber and Martinez-Gallardo use a different source and measure: Woldendorp, Keman, and Budge 1998.

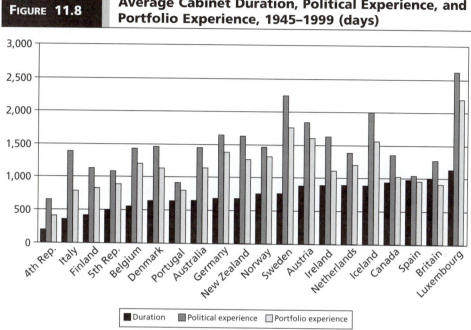

FIGURE 11.8 **Average Cabinet Duration, Political Experience, and Portfolio Experience, 1945–1999 (days)**

Source: Huber and Martinez-Gallardo (2004, 38).

Note: "4th Rep[ublic]" refers to France in 1946–1958; "5th Rep[ublic]" refers to France in 1958.

As Figure 11.8 clearly illustrates, cabinet duration is not necessarily the same thing as political or portfolio experience. For example, cabinets in Britain, Canada, and the Netherlands last quite a long time but have low levels of portfolio and political experience because of the frequent cabinet reshuffles in these countries (Allum 1973; Indriðason and Kam 2005). In contrast, cabinets in Germany, Sweden, and Belgium do not last a long time but they have relatively high levels of portfolio and political experience because the same individuals are often returned to the cabinet and their former ministries. Huber and Martinez-Gallardo's analysis suggests that we should, perhaps, be less concerned about what affects cabinet duration and more interested in discovering what influences the degree of portfolio and political experience in a country. As yet, little research has been done in this area.

MAKING AND BREAKING GOVERNMENTS: PRESIDENTIAL DEMOCRACIES

As you can see, the literature on the government formation process in parliamentary democracies is vast and much has been learned. In contrast, relatively little is known about government formation in presidential regimes. One reason for this has been a lack of data. This situation has recently begun to change. With the emergence of new data has come a promising and ambitious research agenda examining various aspects of governments in presidential democracies (Cheibub and Limongi 2002; Cheibub, Przeworski, and Saiegh 2004; Amorim Neto 2006; Amorim Neto and Samuels 2006; Amorim Neto and Strøm 2006; Cheibub 2007). In this section we summarize some of the principal lines of research that have been followed so far.

Government Formation Process

The **government in a presidential democracy** comprises the president and the cabinet. The **president** is the political chief executive in a presidential democracy; he is also the head of state. In a presidential democracy, the executive branch and the government are the same thing.

The **government in a presidential democracy** is essentially made up of the president and his cabinet. The **president** is the political chief executive and head of the government in a presidential system; he is also the head of state. The government formation process in presidential democracies is different in many important ways from that in parliamentary ones. First, and most fundamentally, legislative responsibility does not exist in presidential democracies. As a result, governments in presidential systems do not have to maintain majority legislative support as cabinets do in order to remain in office in parliamentary systems. Second, there is no uncertainty about the identity of the formateur in presidential democracies unlike in most parliamentary systems. This is because the president is always the formateur, irrespective of whether his party does well or poorly in legislative elections. Coupled with the absence of legislative responsibility, this means that the president appoints whomever he wants to the cabinet (and dismisses them as he wishes).[24] Third, the fact that the president is always the formateur means that the president's party must be included in each cabinet regardless of its legislative size. Note that this does not necessarily mean that the cabinet will exclude all other parties, just that it must include the president's party.

Finally, the "reversion point" of the government formation process is different in presidential democracies from that in parliamentary ones. A "reversion point" here refers to what happens when a minority formateur fails to form a coalition. In a parliamentary system, the failure of a minority prime minister to obtain an implicit legislative majority results in—or causes the actors to "revert" to—an early election, a new round of bargaining, or a caretaker government. In a presidential system, though, the failure of a minority president to win the support of opposition parties simply results in the president's party ruling alone. As a consequence, members of the legislative delegation of a government party can often vote against cabinet-sponsored bills

A **portfolio coalition** is composed of those legislators belonging to parties in the cabinet. A **legislative coalition** is a voting bloc composed of legislators who support a piece of legislation.

without the fear of forcing new elections (which they may lose). Consequently, a **portfolio coalition** does not imply a **legislative coalition** in presidential democracies to the extent that it does in parliamentary democracies.

---

24. Although it is true that presidents in the United States require senatorial consent to appoint each of their cabinet secretaries, this rarely prevents them from obtaining a cabinet of their own choosing.

These differences create particular incentives and opportunities that help to distinguish presidential governments from parliamentary ones. We will focus here on differences in the size and composition of governments.

The Size of Presidential Cabinets

In a parliamentary system, the prime minister must appoint a cabinet that enjoys an implicit legislative majority. We have seen that this does not necessarily imply that she must appoint a cabinet that controls a majority of legislative seats—opposition parties in the legislature may be willing to support minority cabinets on policy grounds. Clearly, presidents will form majority cabinets whenever their party controls a majority of the legislative seats. But what happens when the president's party is not a majority party? Presidents have no constitutional imperative to form majority cabinets—they are free to form minority cabinets whenever they want. Some of these minority presidential governments will rule with the support of an implicit legislative majority, just like minority governments in parliamentary systems; that is, some opposition party or parties in the legislature will support the government without receiving posts in the cabinet. Other minority presidential governments, however, will rule without this kind of support. This second type of minority government is not possible in a parliamentary system because of the existence of legislative responsibility. This difference suggests that, all things being equal, minority governments will be more frequent in presidential systems than in parliamentary systems.

The empirical evidence supports this claim. It is widely recognized that about a third of all parliamentary governments are minority governments (Strøm 1990). In contrast, Amorim Neto (2006) finds that 46 percent (49) of the governments in presidential regimes in Latin America from the late 1970s to 2000 were minority governments. This information is shown in Table 11.13. This difference in the frequency of minority governments in presidential and parliamentary systems is even more marked if we focus explicitly on minority situations, that is, situations in which the party of the president or prime minister does not control a majority of legislative seats. Data from Cheibub, Przeworski, and Saiegh (2004, 574) on minority situations in the world from 1946 to 1999 indicate that 65 percent of these situations resulted in minority governments in presidential democracies compared with just 35 percent in parliamentary ones.

The fact that presidents can appoint whomever they like to the cabinet might lead you to think that they would rarely form coalition governments. Indeed, Linz (1994, 19) claims that coalition governments in presidential democracies are "exceptional." Coalition governments would certainly be unexpected if political actors lived in a purely office-seeking world—why would they form a coalition and give up cabinet seats if they didn't have to? As we noted earlier, however, political actors are likely to care to some extent about policy or, at least, to act as if they care about policy. If this is the case, then it is easy to see why presidents might have an incentive to form coalition governments. The extent to which this incentive is felt will depend to a large extent on the legislative powers of the president.

TABLE 11.13	Government Types in Presidential Systems, late 1970s–2000				
Country	Single-party majority	Majority coalition	Single-party minority	Minority coalition	Total
Argentina	1	0	3	2	6
Bolivia	0	4	1	3	8
Brazil	0	11	0	4	15
Chile	0	5	0	0	5
Colombia	0	10	1	0	11
Costa Rica	3	0	3	0	6
Ecuador	0	1	4	15	20
Mexico	2	0	0	0	2
Panama	0	3	0	4	7
Peru	2	4	1	2	9
United States	2	1	2	0	5
Uruguay	0	6	0	0	6
Venezuela	1	1	3	1	6
Total	11	46	18	31	106

Source: Data are from Amorim Neto (2006).

A presidential **decree** is an order by the president that has the force of law. The scope and extent of these decrees vary from country to country.

All presidents have the ability to issue a **decree**—a presidential order that has the force of law. The scope and strength of these decrees, however, vary from country to country (Shugart and Carey 1992). For example, decrees in the United States, known as executive orders, allow the president only to regulate and interpret statutes already enacted by the legislature and give orders to the public administration; the president cannot enact *new* laws. In other countries, though, presidents can issue "decree-laws"—decrees that immediately become law—even when faced with a hostile legislature. Presidents who have relatively weak decree power and whose party does not control a majority of legislative seats need support from other parties if they are to achieve any of their policy goals. As a result, these presidents will have an incentive to try to form coalitions. The bottom line is that coalition governments should not be exceptional in presidential systems for this reason. In fact, the empirical evidence suggests that coalition governments occur quite frequently in presidential democracies. As Table 11.13 indicates, fully 73 percent (77) of the governments studied by Amorim Neto (2006) were coalition governments.

The frequency with which coalition governments form in presidential systems has led some scholars to conclude that "it is not true that incentives for coalition formation are any different in presidential than in parliamentary democracies" (Cheibub and Limongi 2002, 18). This conclusion is probably premature, however. Why? Much has to do with the "reversion point" that we mentioned earlier. If negotiations over the formation of a coalition government break down in a presidential regime, the result is that the president's party gets to rule on its own. This implies that the president ultimately has the last word over policy in a way that is not true of a prime minister (Samuels 2007). In a parliamentary system, we have seen that the prime minister may have to concede control over particular ministries to her cabinet partners in order to be able to form a government (Laver and Shepsle 1996). In a presidential system, the president does not face the same need to make such policy concessions. This is particularly the case if he can use presidential decrees or vetoes to achieve his policy goals. Even if the president does make policy concessions in order to get opposition parties to join his cabinet, these policy promises lack a certain amount of credibility, because the president has the right to dismiss these parties without losing office whenever he wants. The ability of some presidents to use decrees and the inability of opposition parties to bring the government down, therefore, reduces the expected benefits (in regard to both office and policy) of opposition parties that are thinking about joining the government. The fact that legislators belonging to coalition parties can vote against government-sponsored bills without running the risk of causing the government to fall, however, implies that the costs (in regard to committing support to the government's legislative agenda) of belonging to a coalition may also be lower. Thus, although presidents may want to form coalition governments in some circumstances, it is not clear that they will always find willing coalition partners; if they do find coalition partners, they are likely to be less reliable.

Two implications follow from this logic. First, although coalition governments should not be exceptional in presidential democracies, they should definitely be less common than in parliamentary ones. Again, there is some empirical evidence to support this. When examining minority situations in the world between 1946 and 1999, Cheibub, Przeworski, and Saiegh (2004) found that coalitions formed 78 percent of the time in parliamentary democracies but only 54 percent of the time in presidential ones. The second implication is that coalition governments in presidential systems may be more unstable and survive a shorter amount of time, all things being equal, than coalition governments in parliamentary countries. Alternatively, coalitions in presidential regimes may survive as long as coalitions in parliamentary regimes, but they may not govern as effectively because it is possible for a portfolio coalition to outlive the legislative coalition implied by its membership. To our knowledge, these last two hypotheses are yet to be tested. Can you think of how someone might test them?

The Composition of Presidential Cabinets

We have just illustrated that presidential democracies tend to be characterized by more minority governments and fewer coalition governments than parliamentary ones. It turns out that the composition of presidential cabinets also differs systematically from parliamentary cabinets. On average, presidents appoint cabinets that contain a higher proportion of nonpartisan ministers. A nonpartisan minister is someone who does not come from the legislature; he might be someone like a technocrat, a crony, or a representative of an interest group. On average, presidents also allocate cabinet portfolios in a less proportional way than prime ministers (Amorim Neto and Samuels 2006). Table 11.14 provides empirical evidence in support of these claims from thirty parliamentary and thirteen presidential democracies from 1980 to 2000.

To a large extent, the composition of cabinets in any type of democracy will reflect the extent to which formateurs must negotiate with political parties. Although political parties exert a relatively strong impact over the allocation of cabinet seats in parliamentary systems, this is not necessarily the case in presidential democracies. Prime ministers almost always appoint partisan ministers—individuals from political parties in the legislature—to the cabinet as a way of building the legislative majority that they need to stay in power. As we saw earlier, it is for precisely the same reason that prime ministers tend to allocate cabinet seats in proportion to the seats each party provides to the government coalition. Recall that this was the basis for Gamson's Law. Because presidents do not depend on having a legislative majority to stay in office, they do not have to negotiate with political parties to the same extent as prime ministers. As a result, they are much freer to vary both the partisan nature and proportionality of their cabinets.

On the whole, presidential democracies will have fewer partisan ministers and lower cabinet proportionality than parliamentary ones. Some presidential cabinets, however, will look more like parliamentary ones than others. This is because of the variation in the legislative powers of presidents that we mentioned earlier. Presidents can choose to achieve their policy goals either through the legislature or through decrees. Those presidents who have relatively weak decree power, whose parties in the legislature are quite small, and whose parties exhibit low levels of party discipline are likely to appoint cabinets that look more like those from parliamentary democracies—more partisan ministers and a more proportional allocation of cabinet portfolios—because they rely on winning the support of opposition parties to pass their policies. As Table 11.15 illustrates, there is considerable variation in the extent to which presidents appoint partisan and proportional cabinets. Cabinets tend to be very partisan and highly proportional in countries like Costa Rica, Mexico, and the United States but much less so in countries like Brazil, Peru, and Venezuela. Amorim Neto (2006) has shown that this variation is systematically related to the need of presidents to negotiate with opposition parties to achieve their policy objectives.

TABLE 11.14	Government Composition in Thirteen Presidential and Thirty Parliamentary Democracies, 1980–2000	
Democratic system	Average percentage of nonpartisan ministers	Average proportionality of cabinet portfolio allocation
Parliamentary	2.12	0.90
Presidential	29.17	0.65

Source: Numbers are based on data from Amorim Neto and Samuels (2006).
Note: Proportionality is measured from 0 to 1, with 1 being perfect proportionality.

TABLE 11.15	Government Composition in Presidential Systems, late 1970s–2000	
Country	Average percentage of nonpartisan ministers	Average proportionality of cabinet portfolio allocation
Argentina	7.2	0.89
Bolivia	20.5	0.73
Brazil	46.9	0.50
Chile	6.7	0.85
Colombia	5.6	0.87
Costa Rica	1.8	0.98
Ecuador	65.3	0.27
Mexico	3.6	0.96
Panama	17.8	0.71
Peru	40.8	0.54
United States	0.0	0.91
Uruguay	1.5	0.77
Venezuela	43.7	0.56
Total	29.2	0.64

Source: Data are from Amorim Neto (2006).

Note: The proportionality of cabinet portfolio allocation refers to the extent to which government parties receive the same percentage of cabinet posts as the percentage of seats they provide to the government majority.

MAKING AND BREAKING GOVERNMENTS: MIXED DEMOCRACIES

A mixed democracy is one in which the government depends on both the legislature and president to stay in power. Relatively little research has been conducted on government formation in presidential democracies, but even less has been done on mixed democracies. This is likely to change with the growing number of countries that have become mixed democracies in recent years. In Eastern Europe, Armenia, Croatia, Lithuania, Moldova, Poland, Romania, Russia, and the Ukraine all adopted mixed forms of democracy following their democratic transitions in the late 1980s and early 1990s.

The **government in a mixed democracy** comprises a prime minister and a cabinet, as in a parliamentary democracy. Whereas the executive branch and the government are the same thing in a parliamentary democracy, however, this is not the case in a mixed democracy. In a mixed democracy, the executive branch comprises the government *and* a president—the

> The **government in a mixed democracy** comprises a prime minister and a cabinet. In a mixed democracy, the executive branch comprises the government and a president—the president is part of the executive branch but not part of the government.

president is part of the executive branch but not part of the government. Both the president and prime minister are involved in the day-to-day administration of the state. The precise way in which executive power is divided between the president and the prime minister varies from one mixed democracy to another. It is often the case, however, that the president has more influence in matters of foreign policy, whereas the prime minister is more powerful in domestic politics. For example, a political convention has evolved to some extent in France that the president is responsible for foreign policy and the prime minister for domestic policy. In other countries, this type of division of power is more clearly stated in the constitution.

In mixed democracies, there is nothing to guarantee that the president and the prime minister will come from the same political party. Periods in which politicians from different political parties or blocs hold the positions of the president and prime minister are often referred to as **cohabitation.** Because the president nearly always gets to appoint the prime minister in mixed democracies, why would the president ever appoint a prime minister from an opposing political party? The answer has to do with the fact that the government (prime minister and cabinet) must enjoy the support of a legislative majority to remain in office. Thus, a president may need to appoint a prime minister from an opposition party when the president's party or political bloc does not control a majority of legislative seats. In effect, the potential for cohabitation results from the duality of the executive—an independently elected president, and a prime minister who must enjoy a legislative majority.

Cohabitation—a president from one political bloc and a prime minister from another—occurs when the party of the president does not control a majority in the legislature.

At first glance, cohabitation sounds very similar to divided government in the context of presidential democracies. Still, even though presidential democracies such as the United States have seen power shared between a president and a legislature of different political blocs, cohabitation is not a characteristic of such democracies. The main reason for this is that unlike in a mixed democracy, a president in a presidential system is free to appoint whomever he likes to the cabinet (and the legislature is able to appoint whomever it wants as its presiding officers). To make things a littler clearer, consider the United States in 2006 after the Democrats had regained control of the House of Representatives from the Republicans. If the United States had allowed for cohabitation, then the new Democratic speaker of the House, Nancy Pelosi, would have been able to remove the cabinet appointed by the Republican president, George W. Bush, and replace it with a cabinet of her own choosing. This was not possible, though. The United States of 2006 had divided government, not cohabitation.

France has experienced three periods of cohabitation since 1986. Cohabitation could have occurred even earlier, in 1981, when a Socialist president, François Mitterrand, was voted into office (for a seven-year term) by the French electorate; at that time the legislature was controlled by a right-wing coalition. On coming to office, though, Mitterrand used his constitutional power to dissolve the legislature and call new legislative elections. In these elections, Mitterrand's Socialist Party won an absolute majority of seats, thereby preempting a period of cohabitation. France's first experience with cohabitation came just five years later when a right-wing coalition won a two-seat majority in the constitutionally mandated legislative elections in 1986. Despite the small size of the legislative majority, Mitterrand was forced to appoint Jacques Chirac, the leader of the right-wing Gaullist RPR party, as prime minister because a left-wing prime minister would have been unacceptable to the right-wing majority in the legislature. An uneasy two-year period of cohabitation ensued in which each leader felt constrained by the powers of the other. This initial period of cohabitation came to an end in 1988 when Mitterrand defeated Chirac in presidential elections. Mitterrand immediately dissolved the legislature, and the Socialist Party won a sufficient number of legislative seats for him to be able, with the help of some centrist legislators, to appoint a left-wing prime minister.

In 1993 President Mitterrand found himself in a similar position to that in 1986, when a right-wing coalition won an 80 percent majority in the legislative elections. Mitterrand was again forced to appoint a right-wing politician, Edouard Balladur, to be prime minister. This second period of cohabitation ended when the right-wing candidate Jacques Chirac was elected president in 1995. Because the right already controlled a legislative majority, Chirac was able to appoint the right-wing's Alain Juppé as prime minister. This alignment of a right-wing president and a right-wing legislature should have lasted until the normally scheduled legislative elections in 1998. President Chirac made the ill-fated decision, however, to dissolve the legislature and call early elections in a strategic attempt to build more support for his reform policies. Chirac's plan backfired and the left won the 1997 legislative elections. As a result, Chirac was forced to appoint the leader of the Socialist Party, Lionel Jospin, as prime minister. Jospin remained prime minister until 2002, when Chirac was reelected president. On winning the presidential elections, Chirac immediately dissolved the legislature. Chirac's right-wing party, the UMP, won an overwhelming majority in the legislative elections that followed, allowing Chirac to appoint a right-wing prime minister, Jean-Pierre Raffarin, and to end France's third period of cohabitation after five years.

For much of the history of the French Fifth Republic, it was thought that the president was the dominant political figure in French politics. The constitution provides the president with significant powers, such as the power to appoint the prime minister, the authority to dissolve the legislature (not more than once a year), and the ability to take on emergency powers if the integrity of France's territory is under threat. From 1958 to 1986, the president seemed to dominate both domestic and foreign policy in France. To all intents and purposes, France appeared to function like a presidential democracy during this period. The first period of cohabitation, though, quickly revealed that the dominance of the French president prior to 1986 was not automatic but was, in fact, contingent on the president's controlling a majority in the legislature. Without a legislative majority, the president is forced to defer on domestic politics and, to some extent, on foreign policy, to the prime minister.[25] In periods

---

25. The French constitution is somewhat ambiguous about the relative roles of the president and prime minister in regard to foreign policy. For example, although the president is the commander in chief of the armed forces and is authorized to negotiate and ratify international treaties (articles 14 and 15), the prime minister is responsible for national defense (article 21) and only the legislature is able to declare war (article 35). Over time a convention has emerged that foreign policy is a "reserved domain" of the president. However, this is occasionally challenged during periods of cohabitation. For example, both President Mitterrand and Prime Minister Chirac turned up at the 1986 G7 meeting in Tokyo. Unfortunately for Chirac, G7 protocol allowed only heads of state (Mitterrand) to attend the most important meetings and Chirac was able to attend only the plenary sessions (Giesbert 1996, 498).

of cohabitation, France functions very much like a parliamentary democracy with executive power lying in the hands of the prime minister and the cabinet. This has led some to claim that mixed democracy, at least in the case of France, is really just an alternation between presidential and parliamentary forms of government, depending on whether the president controls a legislative majority or not (Duverger 1980).

Other mixed democracies, such as Sri Lanka and the Ukraine, have also experienced cohabitation. In 2001 Sri Lanka experienced a bitter episode of cohabitation when President Chandrika Kumaratunga of the People's Alliance (PA) was forced to appoint her political opponent, Ranil Wickremasinghe of the United National Party (UNP), as prime minister following the success of the UNP in legislative elections. These two politicians held starkly different positions regarding the need to negotiate with the Liberation Tigers of Tamil Eelam (LTTE), or Tamil Tigers, to end the decades-long civil war. President Kumaratunga had taken a staunchly militaristic approach to dealing with the LTTE prior to 2001, but Wickremasinghe immediately opened negotiations and eventually signed a permanent ceasefire with the LTTE in 2002. After indicating that she was willing to sack the prime minister if too many concessions were made, President Kumaratunga suspended the parliament and deployed troops to take control of the country when Wickremasinghe was away visiting the United States in 2003. The period of cohabitation that had started in 2001, therefore, ended with the president's putting Sri Lanka under a state of emergency.

Ukraine has also experienced cohabitation; in 2006 President Viktor Yuschenko was forced to appoint his political rival, Viktor Yanukovych, as prime minister. The rivalry between these two men dates back at least as far as the 2004 presidential elections, when the pro-Western Yuschenko eventually defeated the pro-Russian Yanukovych in rather controversial circumstances. During the bitter and often violent presidential electoral campaign, Yuschenko became extremely ill, and it was later alleged that he had been poisoned with dioxin, possibly by elements associated with the Security Service of the Ukraine (SBU) or the Russian Federal Security Service (FSB). Neither candidate won the required majority in the first round of voting to be elected president: Yuschenko obtained 39.87 percent of the vote just ahead of Yanukovych with 39.32 percent. The second round of voting, which was marred by significant electoral fraud, saw Yanukovych declared president. Due to the electoral irregularities, Yuschenko and his supporters refused to recognize the results. Following thirteen days of protest that became known as the Orange Revolution, the Ukrainian Supreme Court overturned the election results and ordered a rerun of the second round runoff, which Yuschenko eventually won with 51.99 percent of the vote. A year and a half later, the Party of Regions, led by Yanukovych, won the most seats in the 2006 legislative elections. Despite the obvious personal hostility between the two men, the legislative election results forced Yuschenko and Yanukovych to reach a compromise. Yuschenko eventually appointed Yanukovych to be prime minister in a coalition government that included both men's parties. Relations between the president and prime minister have not been smooth since this government formed, with both actors involved in an apparent power struggle. In April 2007, President Yuschenko dissolved parliament and called for new elections that he hoped would reduce the power of Yanukovych. This decision plunged Ukraine into a political crisis, with legislators calling it a coup d'état and refusing to recognize it until the constitutional court ruled it legal. Eventually, both the president and prime minister agreed to hold new elections in an attempt to end weeks of political deadlock. For many, periods of cohabitation in mixed democracies can be characterized as an effective system of checks and balances. As these examples from Sri Lanka and the Ukraine illustrate, however, cohabitation can also be characterized by bitter and violent conflict when the political actors involved share starkly different ideologies and goals.

Viktor Yushchenko, a Western-leaning reformer (on the right), and Prime Minister Viktor Yanukovych, seen as an ally of Russia (on the left), appear in a television debate in Ukraine's capital, Kiev, on Monday, November 15, 2004, between the first and second rounds of the presidential elections. Due to allegations of voter fraud following the second round, an unprecedented third round was held, and Yushchenko eventually took office in January 2005.

Very few studies have examined the composition of governments in mixed democracies. The most recent study, though, comes from Amorim Neto and Strøm (2006). They argue that, although the government formation process varies across mixed democracies, it is perhaps appropriate to think that both the president and the prime minister have de facto vetoes over cabinet appointments. Thus, the president is not as strong as he would be in a presidential regime and the prime minister is not as strong as she would be in a parliamentary regime. This suggests that we might expect mixed democracies to possess both parliamentary and presidential characteristics when it comes to the composition of cabinets. An implication of this is that cabinets in mixed democracies should be characterized by fewer partisan ministers and a lower proportionality in the allocation of portfolios than in parliamentary regimes but more partisan ministers and a higher proportionality in the allocation of portfolios than in presidential regimes. In fact, this is precisely what Amorim Neto and Strøm find in their study of twelve parliamentary and twelve mixed democracies in Europe during the 1990s. As with presidential democracies, we would expect there to be variation in cabinet partisanship and proportionality across different mixed democracies. For example, when the president's party controls a legislative majority, we should expect cabinets in a mixed democracy to look more like those commonly found in a presidential democracy. In contrast, when the president is faced by a legislature dominated by an opposition party, we should expect cabinets in a mixed democracy to look more like those commonly found in a parliamentary democracy. The historical experience of the government formation process in France seems to bear this out (Duverger 1980).

CONCLUSION

One way to classify democracies is in terms of whether they are parliamentary, presidential, or mixed. As we have seen, whether a democracy is parliamentary, presidential, or mixed basically depends on the relationship between three "actors"—the president, the government, and the legislature. In effect, the different institutional forms of democracy examined in this chapter represent three alternative ways to structure the relationship between the executive and legislative branches of government.

The defining feature of presidentialism is the absence of legislative responsibility—the government serves at the pleasure of the president, not the legislature. Consequently, even when members of the president's own party call for the resignation of one of his cabinet appointees, the most the legislature can do when faced with a president who fails to heed its council by asking for the resignation of the cabinet member is to hold a *symbolic* "no confidence vote" to register its disapproval. These forms of symbolic no confidence votes are rare in presidential systems, in part because they are not binding. At the time of writing this chapter, a Democrat-led Senate in the United States had scheduled a no confidence vote to register its disapproval of the activities of the Attorney General Alberto Gonzales (*New York Times*, May 17, 2007).[26] Although such a measure might convey the "sense of the Senate," any successful vote would have no legal status to compel Gonzales's removal from the government. For example, the Senate passed a similar vote in 1950 when it determined that Secretary of State Dean Acheson was not doing enough to combat the spread of communism; despite the vote, Acheson retained his post for the remainder of the Truman administration.[27] The ability of a cabinet member to stay in office despite the explicit disapproval of a legislative majority demonstrates a key feature of presidential systems—a separation of powers between the executive and legislative branches.

In stark contrast, the defining feature of parliamentary systems is that the composition of the government is directly controlled by the legislature. In this chapter we have outlined the negotiations among party elites that result in the appointment of prime ministers and cabinets in parliamentary systems in some detail. The prime minister—typically the head of the largest legislative party—will, de facto, play a central role in the appointment of the heads of the ministries. Nevertheless, the members of the cabinet—including the prime minister herself—ultimately serve at the pleasure of the legislature in parliamentary systems. Consequently, in 1990 when the United Kingdom's Margaret Thatcher—who had been elected prime minister three times, most recently in 1987 with a 102-seat majority for the Conservative Party—lost the support of party members in the cabinet and in the House of Commons, she stepped down, thereby avoiding a vote of no confidence that had been proposed by Neil Kinnock, the leader of the opposition Labour Party. Before a vote of no confidence occurred, Thatcher was subjected to a leadership challenge from within her own party. After Thatcher's long-time supporter Deputy Prime Minister Sir Geoffrey Howe

---

26. The Democrat-led Senate eventually failed in its attempt to hold a vote of no confidence in Attorney General Alberto Gonzales. Although the vote on June 11, 2007, in the U.S. Senate was 53 to 38 in favor of holding such a vote, the Democrats did not obtain the sixty votes necessary to prevent a Republican filibuster. As a result, there was no vote of no confidence.

27. "Vote of No Consequence," *Slate*, May 21, 2007.

resigned in frustration with her opposition to agreeing to a single European currency, Michael Heseltine (who had resigned from the cabinet four years earlier to return to the "backbench") challenged her in a Conservative Party leadership vote. Although Thatcher managed to win more votes than Heseltine, she fell short of the supermajority needed under Conservative Party rules to prevent a second-round election. She agreed to step down before the second ballot, which was eventually won by John Major.

Although the intricacies of party leadership elections vary from country to country and from party to party, this dramatic episode highlights important characteristics of parliamentary systems. Ministers serve at the pleasure of the legislature. Shifts in opinion or circumstances in the legislature can remove the head of government—oftentimes without recourse to the voting public. Margaret Thatcher was elected to the House of Commons as a representative of a London suburb and was elevated to the head of the government by a vote of her fellow Conservative members of Parliament. Eleven years later a similar vote, in which she garnered support from 204 of the 362 valid votes cast by Conservative members of Parliament, led to her removal from the position of prime minister. For students familiar with the working of the United States government, a simple (but fairly accurate) way to think about parliamentary government is to imagine a U.S. government in which the Speaker of the House, rather than the president, is the head of government.

Mixed systems are as they sound. Cabinets can be formed and reformed by either presidential or legislative initiative. Earlier in the chapter, we described how France's Socialist president François Mitterrand decided to dismiss the right-wing-dominated cabinet in 1981 by dissolving the legislature to which it was responsible. The ensuing election returned a Socialist majority in the National Assembly and, as a result, Mitterrand was free to appoint a Socialist, Pierre Mauroy, as prime minister. The 1986 legislative elections, however, produced a slight majority for a coalition of right-wing parties and as a consequence, the cabinet was changed to reflect the new parliamentary reality—most visibly in the form of a new right-wing prime minister—Jacques Chirac. In mixed systems, therefore, governments can be said to have two masters—the president and the legislature. Which one dictates at any given time, though, depends on the electoral fortunes of the political parties involved.

Thus, the relationship between the country's chief executive officer (whatever his title), the cabinet, and the legislature is fundamentally different in presidential and parliamentary democracies. Some political scientists have used these differences to conclude that presidentialism is a system of governance based on the division of executive and legislative powers, whereas parliamentarism is a system based on the fusion of these powers. There is, indeed, a good deal of truth in Stepan and Skach's (1993) assertion that the essence of parliamentarism is "mutual dependence" and that the essence of presidentialism is "mutual independence." In Chapter 15, we will examine the strategic dynamic between the executive and legislative branches in more detail when we explore how the decision to adopt parliamentary or presidential systems of government affects the survival of democracy.

KEY CONCEPTS

cabinet, *402*
caretaker government, *410*
cohabitation, *450*
collective cabinet responsibility, *403*
connected coalition, *417*
constructive vote of no confidence, *397*
corporatist interest group relations, *423*
decree, *446*
formateur, *407*
Gamson's Law, *415*
government coalition, *428*
government in a mixed democracy, *449*
government in a parliamentary democracy, *402*
government in a presidential democracy, *444*
informateur, *409*
investiture vote, *405*
least minimal winning coalition, *416*
legislative coalition, *444*
legislative responsibility, *397*

minimal winning coalition, *416*
ministerial responsibility, *403*
minority government, *420*
mixed democracy, *400*
office-seeking politician, *414*
parliamentary democracy, *400*
pluralist interest group relations, *423*
policy-seeking politician, *414*
portfolio coalition, *444*
preelectoral coalition, *428*
president, *444*
presidential democracy, *400*
prime minister, *402*
principal-agent, or delegation, problem, *411*
single-party majority government, *404*
surplus majority government, *426*
vote of confidence, *397*
vote of no confidence, *397*

PROBLEMS

The problems that follow address some of the more important concepts and ideas introduced in this chapter.

Classifying Democracies

1. In this chapter, we discussed the rules for classifying democracies as parliamentary, presidential, or mixed. Look at the information from the following constitutions and decide whether these democracies are parliamentary, presidential, or mixed. Explain your decision.

   a. 1919 Weimar Constitution in Germany

   - Article 25: The Reich president has the right to dissolve the Reichstag, but only once for the same reason. New elections are held no later than sixty days after the dissolution.
   - Article 53: The Reich chancellor, and, at his request, the Reich ministers, are appointed and dismissed by the Reich President.
   - Article 54: The Reich chancellor and the Reich ministers, in order to exercise their mandates, require the confidence of the Reichstag. Any one of them must resign if the Reichstag votes by explicit decision to withdraw its confidence.
   - Article 55: The Reich chancellor presides over the Reich government and conducts its affairs according to the rules of procedure, to be decided upon by the Reich government and to be approved by the Reich president.

- Article 56: The Reich chancellor determines the political guidelines and is responsible for them to the Reichstag. Within these guidelines every Reich minister leads his portfolio independently and is responsible to the Reichstag.

b. 1937 Irish Constitution

- Article 12: There shall be a President of Ireland (Uachtarán na hÉireann), hereinafter called the President, who shall take precedence over all other persons in the State and who shall exercise and perform the powers and functions conferred on the President by this Constitution and by law. The President shall be elected by direct vote of the people.
- Article 13: The President shall, on the nomination of the Dáil Éireann, appoint the Taoiseach, that is, the head of the Government or Prime Minister. The president shall, on the nomination of the Taoiseach with the previous approval of Dáil Éireann, appoint the other members of the Government. The President shall, on the advice of the Taoiseach, accept the resignation or terminate the appointment of any member of the Government. Dáil Éireann shall be summoned and dissolved by the President on the advice of the Taoiseach. The President may in his absolute discretion refuse to dissolve Dáil Éireann on the advice of a Taoiseach who has ceased to retain the support of a majority in Dáil Éireann. . . . The President shall not be answerable to either House of the Oireachtas or to any court for the exercise and performance of the powers and functions of his office or for any act done or purporting to be done by him in the exercise and performance of these powers and functions.
- Article 15: The National Parliament shall be called and known, and is in this Constitution generally referred to, as the Oireachtas. The Oireachtas shall consist of the President and two Houses, viz.: a House of Representatives to be called Dáil Éireann and a Senate to be called Seanad Éireann.
- Article 28: The Government shall consist of not less than seven and not more than fifteen members who shall be appointed by the President in accordance with the provisions of this Constitution. . . . The Government shall be responsible to the Dáil Éireann. The head of the government, or Prime Minister, shall be called, and is in this Constitution referred to as, the Taoiseach.

c. 1980 Chilean Constitution

- Article 4: Chile is a democratic republic.
- Article 24: The government and administration of the State are vested in the President of the Republic, who is the Chief of the State.
- Article 25: The President of the Republic shall hold office for a term of eight years and may not be reelected for the consecutive period.
- Article 26: The President shall be elected by direct ballot, with an absolute majority of the votes validly cast.
- Article 32: The special powers vested in the President of the Republic are the following: . . . To appoint, and remove at will Ministers of State, Undersecretaries, Intendants, Governors and Mayors appointed by him.

- Article 33: The Ministers of State are the direct and immediate collaborators of the President of the Republic in governing and administering the State.

d. 1947 Japanese Constitution

- Article 1: The Emperor shall be the symbol of the State and of the unit of the People, deriving his position from the will of the people with whom resides sovereign power.
- Article 4: The Emperor shall perform only such acts in matters of state as are provided in the Constitution and he shall not have powers related to government.
- Article 6: The Emperor shall appoint the Prime Minister as designated by the Diet.
- Article 41: The Diet shall be the highest organ of state power, and shall be the sole law-making organ of the State.
- Article 42: The Diet shall consist of two Houses, namely the House of Representatives and the House of Councillors.
- Article 65: Executive power shall be vested in the Cabinet.
- Article 66: The Cabinet shall consist of the Prime Minister, who shall be its head, and other Ministers of State, as provided for by law. The Prime Minister and other Ministers of State must be civilians. The Cabinet, in the exercise of executive power, shall be collectively responsible to the Diet.
- Article 69: If the House of Representatives passes a non-confidence resolution, or rejects a confidence resolution, the Cabinet shall resign en masse, unless the House of Representatives is dissolved within ten (10) days.

2. Canada held an early general election on January 23, 2006, after the Liberal Party's minority government was toppled in a no-confidence vote on November 28, 2005. Canada does not have an independently elected president. Based on these two pieces of information, is Canada a presidential, parliamentary, or mixed democracy? Explain your answer.
3. If a democracy has an independently (directly or indirectly) elected president, then we automatically consider it to be a presidential democracy. True or false?

Institutions

4. A constructive vote of no confidence is essentially a vote of no confidence and an investiture vote rolled into one. What does this mean?
5. Which of the following statements best describe a vote of confidence?

a. A new government must pass a vote (on the cabinet's composition and proposed policies) in the legislature before it can take office.
b. A government declares that a vote on a particular piece of legislation is also a vote on support for the government itself; if the legislators do not support the legislation, then the government will resign (and new elections might result).
c. A group of legislators propose a vote on support for the incumbent government. If the government passes the vote, then it stays in office. If it fails the vote, then it must resign (and new elections might result).

6. The March 2007 "unity" or "grand coalition" cabinet of the Palestinian Territories has twelve Hamas members and six Fatah members (The other seven members are nonpartisan or from much smaller parties). Of the legislative seats controlled by the government parties, Hamas controls about 59 percent. Hamas received 48 percent of the government positions. Is this a good example of Gamson's Law? Explain.

Government Formation

7. A story in the *International Herald Tribune* from 2006 stated the following: "Dutch political parties began the complicated task of forming a new government on Thursday, one day after national elections thrust the Netherlands into the same kind of inconclusive terrain that Austria and Germany experienced in their votes. Austria has yet to form a government after its election two months ago, and in Germany last year, it took six weeks of grueling negotiations to form a coalition government under Angela Merkel." How would you explain what this means to a roommate or family member who has no idea what a parliamentary government is? Your explanation should include what the government is, how it forms, what factors affect how long this formation process takes, and who gets into government, and so on.

8. Legislative elections were held in Finland on March 18, 2007. Eight parties won seats in parliament. Based on what you have learned in this chapter and the information in Table 11.16, the leader of which party is likely to be appointed formateur? Explain.

TABLE 11.16	Legislative Election Results in Finland, 2007	
	Seats	
Party	**(no.)**	**(%)**
Centre Party	51	25.5
National Coalition Party	50	25.0
Social Democratic Party	45	22.5
Left Alliance	17	8.5
Green League	15	7.5
Christian Democrats	7	3.5
Swedish People's Party	9	4.5
True Finns	5	2.5
Other	1[a]	0.5
Total	200	100

[a]Province of Åland representative.

9. Legislative elections were held in Sweden on September 17, 2006, and seven parties won seats. Although the left-wing Social Democratic Party won more seats than any other party, the leader of the largest right-wing party was appointed to be the first formateur. Which of the following statements might explain this choice?

a. The choice of formateur is random. As a result, the leader of the largest right-wing party had the same chance of being chosen as did each of the other party leaders.

b. In this particular election, four right-wing parties ran as a preelectoral coalition and together won a majority of the seats. Because they had pledged to govern together if successful, it made sense to give the leader of the largest coalition party the position of formateur.

c. The position of formateur is always offered first to a party on the right; if the first attempt to form a government fails, the second formateur will be chosen from a left-wing party, and so on.

10. In Table 11.17, we show the results from the 1996 legislative elections in Ecuador.

TABLE 11.17   **Legislative Election Results in Ecuador, 1996**

Party	Seats (no.)	Seats (%)
Social Christian Party (PSC)	28	34.1
Ecuadorian Roldosista Party (PRE)	19	23.2
Popular Democracy (DP)	12	14.6
New Country Movement	8	9.6
Democratic Left (ID)	4	4.9
Alfarist Radical Front (FRA)	3	3.7
Ecuadorian Popular Revolutionary Action (APRE)	2	2.4
Democratic Popular Movement (MPD)	2	2.4
Ecuadorian Conservative Party (PCE)	2	2.4
Concentration of Popular Forces (CFP)	1	1.2
Independents	1	1.2
Total	82	100

a. Based on the results in Table 11.17, from which party would you expect the formateur to come if Ecuador were a parliamentary democracy?

b. Ecuador is in fact a presidential democracy. In the 1996 presidential elections, Abdalá Bucaram Ortz of the Ecuadorian Roldosista Party (PRE) was elected president ahead of Jaime Nebot Saadi of the Social Christian Party (PSC). Based on this new information, from which party would you now expect the formateur to come? Why is this?

11. A new government took office on October 6, 2006, in Sweden. A couple of weeks later, two ministers in the government (in charge of commerce and culture, respectively) had to resign as a result of revelations in the press regarding personal financial improprieties. Because two cabinet ministers had changed, would most political scientists consider that the government had ended?

Government Types

12. Look back at the information about the 2006 Finnish elections in Table 11.16. Based on the information in this table, indicate at least five of the possible minimal winning coalitions that could form. What is the least minimal winning coalition out of this set of five MWC?

13. In Table 11.18, we show the results from the 2002 legislative elections in Germany. Answer the following questions.

TABLE 11.18	**Legislative Election Results in Germany, 2002**	
Party	**Seats**	**Ideology**
Party of Democratic Socialism	2	Most left
Greens	55	
Social Democratic Party	251	
Christian Democratic Party	248	
Free Democratic Party	47	Most right
Total	603	

a. If a government formed between the Christian Democratic Party and the Free Democratic Party, what type of government would it be?

b. If a government formed between the Social Democratic Party and the Greens, what type of government would it be?

c. If a government formed between the Social Democratic Party, the Greens, and the Party of Democratic Socialism, what type of government would it be?

14. Minority governments are more likely to form in parliamentary democracies when opposition parties have a significant role in the policymaking process. True or false? Explain your answer.

15. Explain why minority governments should be more frequent on average in presidential democracies than parliamentary ones.

12 Elections and Electoral Systems

> **It's not the voting that's democracy; it's the counting.**
>
> Tom Stoppard, *Jumpers*

> **The most important choice facing constitution writers is that of a legislative electoral system.**
>
> Arend Lijphart, "Constitutional Design for Divided Societies"

OVERVIEW

- Almost every country in the world, whether democratic or authoritarian, has had some experience with holding elections. Although elections play a minimal role in choosing who rules in dictatorships, evidence suggests that authoritarian elections are not merely forms of institutional window dressing; they can be useful tools for stabilizing dictatorial rule. In contrast, elections are one of the defining characteristics of democracies and provide the primary mechanism by which democratic governments obtain the authority to rule.

- Although there is a great deal of variety in the types of electoral systems that are employed around the world, most political scientists categorize them into three main families based on the electoral formula that is used to translate votes into seats: majoritarian, proportional, and mixed.

- We illustrate how each of the different electoral systems used for national-level legislative and presidential elections works in practice. We also discuss their effect on things like proportionality, ethnic accommodation, accountability, minority representation, and the revelation of sincere preferences. Finally, we provide an overview of electoral systems by geographic region and regime type.

In the previous chapter, we described how political scientists often classify democracies in terms of the form of government that they have: parliamentary, presidential, or mixed. We also noted, however, that there are many other ways that one can distinguish between different types of democracy. As you will no doubt remember from our discussion of the different ways of defining democracy in Chapter 5, one of the key elements of any democracy is the use of elections. It is perhaps no surprise then that political scientists sometimes distinguish between democracies by the type of electoral system employed in these elections. An **electoral system** is a set of laws and regulations that govern the electoral competition between candidates or parties or both (Cox 1997, 38). As we will see, these laws and regulations include a whole host of things, such as the **electoral formula** (how votes are translated into seats), the **ballot structure** (whether individuals vote for candidates or parties or both and whether they cast a single vote or express a series of preferences), and the **district magnitude** (the number of representatives elected in a district). They also include various administrative rules dealing with things like the nomination of candidates, the registration of voters, and the distribution of polling places (Reynolds, Reilly, and Ellis 2005). Despite the different dimensions along which electoral systems can vary, most political scientists categorize electoral systems into three main families based on the electoral formula that they use to translate votes into seats: majoritarian, proportional, and mixed. It is partly on this basis that some political scientists talk of majoritarian and proportional democracies (Lijphart 1999; Powell 2000; Golder and Stramski 2007).

> An **electoral system** is a set of laws that regulate electoral competition between candidates or parties or both. An **electoral formula** determines how votes are translated into seats. The **ballot structure** is how electoral choices are presented on the ballot paper. **District magnitude** is the number of representatives elected in a district.

In this chapter, we explore how various forms of majoritarian, proportional, and mixed electoral systems work in some detail. We also discuss some of the advantages and disadvantages associated with each of these systems. Before we address these issues, though, we briefly provide an overview of elections around the world. Elections are frequently used to select people for a wide range of offices. For example, they are used in various countries to fill offices in the legislature, the executive, and the judiciary, as well as in a whole variety of private and business organizations, ranging from clubs and voluntary associations to corporations and school boards. In what follows, we focus on national-level legislative and presidential elections.

ELECTIONS: AN OVERVIEW

All modern democracies, by their very nature, hold regular elections.[1] This does not mean, however, that all elections are held in democracies; as we noted in Chapter 8, elections are

---

1. If you recall from Chapter 5, citizens in older "democracies," such as that in ancient Athens, selected their representatives by lot (for instance, by drawing names out of a hat) rather than by election.

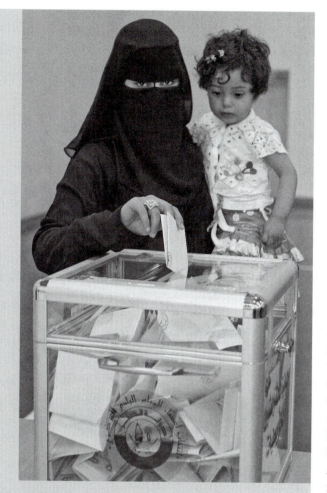

A Qatari woman places her vote in the ballot box in Doha, Qatar, Sunday, April 1, 2007. About 28,000 Qataris had a chance to vote in these municipal elections, which were seen as the last democratic test, a practice run, before parliamentary elections scheduled for 2008. Vying for seats on Qatar's Central Municipal Council—a 29-member chamber with limited, advisory powers—were 3 women and 122 men. Although some Qataris complained that the municipal vote was meaningless because of the council's limited powers, government officials said it was watched closely to see how the women candidates fared. One of the three female candidates, Shaikha Al Jufairi, was elected with the highest amount of votes of all 125 candidates.

quite common in dictatorships as well. In fact, about half of the legislative and presidential elections that occurred in the world between 1946 and 2000 took place in dictatorships (Golder 2005, 106). Indeed, virtually every independent country in the world, whether democratic or dictatorial, has held national-level elections at one time or another. As of early 2007, only six countries—Bhutan, Brunei, China, Eritrea, Qatar, and Saudi Arabia—have failed to hold national-level elections in the postwar period. Arguably, there has been considerable experience with, or interest in, electoral politics even among these six countries. For example, Bhutan regularly experiences something akin to legislative elections when village heads and family representatives gather to nominate members of the legislature in village-level meetings (Nohlen, Grotz, and Hartmann 2001). Although elections do not occur at regional, provincial, or national levels in China, Chinese voters have the opportunity to cast their ballots in township and county elections. Saudi Arabia held its first elections at the municipal level in 2005. Local and regional elections have taken place in Eritrea, most recently in 2004. In April 2003, Qataris overwhelmingly voted in favor of a referendum on a new constitution that would allow them to vote for a partially elected legislature.[2] The new Qatar constitution went into effect in June 2005. An electoral law was finally passed in May 2008 and legislative elections are planned for later

---

2. The legislature would have forty-five seats, of which thirty would be filled by direct elections and the remaining fifteen would be appointed by the emir.

in the year, although no precise date has yet been set. In sum, it is only in Brunei that electoral politics has failed to put down any roots at all.[3]

Elections in dictatorships vary quite a lot, both in their level of competitiveness and their inclusiveness (Blaydes 2006b). Some elections, like those in Iraq under Saddam Hussein, are little more than referenda in which voters are able to vote only yes or no on the incumbent. In contrast, some dictatorships allow elections in which voters are able to choose between multiple candidates from a single party. In the 1960s, for example, two ruling-party candidates were allowed to compete for the voters' mandate in each single-member district in Tanzania; similar elections were held in Kenya and Zambia during periods of one-party rule. Other dictatorships, like Burkina Faso, Ghana, Nigeria, Senegal, and Uganda in the 1970s, actually allowed voters to choose between competing candidates from multiple parties (Nohlen, Krennerich, and Thibaut 1999, 6). In contrast to most contemporary democracies, in which all adult citizens are generally eligible to vote, the rules on who can vote in dictatorships vary quite a lot. Some dictatorships, like the former Soviet Union, basically allow all adult citizens to vote, but others place strong restrictions on who can vote. For example, in December 2006, in the first legislative elections held in the United Arab Emirates, only 6,689 people, or just 1 percent of the population, were allowed to vote; indeed, all of the eligible voters were handpicked by the rulers of the seven emirates (*Gulf Times,* December 21, 2006).

In most dictatorships, elections have a predetermined outcome, whether this is victory for the incumbent or some other candidate(s) supported by the ruling elite. Ultimately, voters in dictatorships have little or no say in who rules them. The predetermined outcome of elections is often the result of voter coercion, vote rigging, or simply some official making up arbitrary vote totals.[4] In Chapter 9 we presented an example from the 1989 legislative elections in Kenya, where the Returning Officer simply reported false election results to ensure the victory of the incumbent party's preferred candidate. Many election results reported in dictatorships are ridiculously one-sided. For example, Saddam Hussein was declared the winner of the 2002 elections in Iraq just before the second Gulf War after polling 100 percent of the votes with a 100 percent turnout; he had won only 99.96 percent of the votes in the previous elections in 1995 (CNN.com, October 16, 2002). The predetermined nature of dictatorial elections has led some to refer to them as "show" or "sham" elections. These terms can be somewhat misleading, however, because they suggest that these elections are merely forms of institutional window dressing with few political consequences. Ask yourself, though, why so many dictatorships bother to hold elections if this is the case.

Although elections rarely offer citizens the opportunity to change the existing leadership in dictatorships, as they do in democracies, it is becoming increasingly clear to many politi-

---

3. Brunei is a small country on the island of Borneo in Southeast Asia that obtained its independence from the United Kingdom in 1984. Brunei did hold one legislative election in January 1962, when all ten of the elected seats in the twenty-one-seat legislature were won by the Brunei People's Party (BPP). Before the BPP could take power, though, the sultan annulled the results and banned the BPP, leading to a five-month-long insurrection. No legislative elections have been held since.

4. Some elections in dictatorships are manipulated in less obvious ways. For example, thousands of candidates, including virtually all reformist ones, hoping to run in the 2004 legislative elections in Iran were deemed "unfit" by the religiously conservative Council of Guardians, primarily on the grounds that they were enemies of the Islamic Revolution.

cal scientists that authoritarian elections do have substantively meaningful consequences. To a large extent, dictatorships hold elections because they think that it is somehow in their interest to do this. For example, some dictatorships hold elections because they have come under pressure from the United States and international financial institutions, such as the International Monetary Fund, to democratize. In effect, the holding of elections is an attempt to maintain the *appearance* of democratic competition in these countries and keep international goodwill and monetary funds flowing.

Elections can be a force for stability in dictatorial regimes in several ways. For instance, they can provide a mechanism for resolving intra-elite conflicts, an arena for patronage distribution, a means of recruiting and rewarding local political elites, and a way for leaders to obtain information about the performance of local officials (Geddes 2005; Blaydes 2006a; Lust-Okar 2006). Elections can also help to institutionalize the dominance of a single party in one-party dictatorships and provide a relatively stable mechanism for dictatorial succession (Blaydes 2006b). Elections may also provide information to the regime about the relative strengths of supporters and opponents (Magaloni 2006). Indeed, one-sided elections—even when the outcome is known to be fixed—can undermine the willingness of opposition groups to challenge the dictatorship, because these groups have no way of knowing the true level of opposition in society; all public evidence points to an overwhelming level of support for the dictatorship (Geddes 2005). There is also evidence that elections provide a way for dictatorships to co-opt opposition groups, or at least to divide and control them (Przeworski 1991; Gandhi and Przeworski 2006). By allowing some opposition groups but not others to legitimately compete in elections, dictators can sow the seeds of division within the opposition, thereby making it harder for opposition groups to overthrow them (Lust-Okar 2005).

Finally, dictatorial elections offer citizens an opportunity to register their dissatisfaction with the ruling regime. As Blaydes (2006b) notes, acts of voter abstention or ballot nullification can provide meaningful signals of discontent and voter preference. For example, studies of voting in the former Soviet Union suggest that nonvoting can be seen and, indeed, was interpreted at the time, as an act of protest whereby relatively well-educated individuals consciously decided to ignore mandatory voting laws or spoil their ballots (Karklins 1986; Roeder 1989). Blank and spoiled ballots were similarly interpreted as a form of protest against military rule in Brazil from 1964 to 1985 (Powers and Roberts 1995). By offering this controlled opening for citizens to register their discontent, dictatorships may be attempting to channel citizen dissatisfaction with the regime into the electoral process instead of other more destabilizing activities. In sum, elections appear to be an important strategy for survival in authoritarian regimes. Empirical evidence in support of this comes from Gandhi (2003). Using data on 512 dictators between 1946 and 1996 in 138 countries, she finds that dictators who hold elections stay in power longer than those who do not hold elections.

Although elections play a meaningful role in dictatorships, they are not a defining characteristic of authoritarian regimes. In contrast, elections are seen as central to the very nature of contemporary democratic rule. In democracies, elections serve both a practical and a symbolic role. In a practical sense, elections provide the primary means by which citizens select their representatives. As such, they provide citizens with an opportunity to influence the government formation process, to reward or punish politicians for their time in power, and to shape the direction of future policy. In a symbolic sense, the legitimacy of a democratic government comes from the fact that it was chosen through an electoral process—citizens have an equal and relatively low-cost opportunity to participate in selecting the people who rule over them and, hence, the types of policy that should be implemented. The bottom line is that it is recognized in democracies that the authority of governments to rule comes solely from the consent of the governed; elections provide the primary mechanism by which this consent is translated into the authority to rule.

We now provide some summary statistics on the legislative and presidential elections that have taken place in democracies around the world from 1946 to 2000. In this time period, 125 countries experienced at least one democratic election. Table 12.1 illustrates that roughly one-third of the democratic legislative and presidential elections that took place between 1950 and 2000 occurred in the 1990s. The number of legislative and presidential elections remained fairly constant until the end of the 1980s. The collapse of the Soviet Union and the return of multiparty elections in Africa in the 1990s, however, led to a large increase in the number of democratic countries and, hence, democratic elections. As Table 12.2 illustrates, almost half of the world's democratic presidential elections between 1946 and 2000 occurred in Latin America; a third of the world's legislative elections took place in Western Europe.

Elections always involve citizens casting votes for candidates or political parties or both, but there is a great deal of variation in the precise set of rules employed by the world's electoral systems. Consider the rules on who is eligible to vote. Although all contemporary democracies allow for **universal suffrage**—the right to vote is not restricted by race, gender, belief, or social status—they still place differing restrictions of one kind or another on who can vote. For example, democracies vary in regard to whether they restrict felons, noncitizens, the mentally ill, nonresidents, and so on from voting (see Box 12.1, titled "Who Can Vote in Democracies?").

> Suffrage is the civil right to vote and is sometimes referred to as the franchise. **Universal suffrage** is when the right to vote is not restricted by race, gender, belief, or social status.

		Number of elections	
Decade	Average number of democracies	Legislative	Presidential
1950s	36.5	111	33
1960s	42.3	121	37
1970s	42.7	127	35
1980s	58.6	162	48
1990s	100.7	281	114

TABLE 12.1   Democratic Elections by Decade

Source: Data are from Golder 2005.

TABLE 12.2	**Democratic Elections by Geographical Region, 1946–2000**		
Region	Number of countries	Number of legislative elections	Number of presidential elections
Sub-Saharan Africa	52	49	26
Eastern Europe	31	50	31
Middle East/North Africa	21	33	0
Latin America	19	164	133
Asia	23	86	18
Western Europe	25	285	60
Pacific Islands/Oceana	13	83	8
Caribbean/Non-Iberic America	16	117	18
Total	199	867	294

Source: Data are from Golder 2005.

Electoral systems vary in many other ways as well. Some allow citizens to vote for candidates, whereas others allow them to vote only for political parties; some allow citizens to cast only one vote, whereas others allow them to cast multiple votes; some allow for only one round of voting, whereas others allow for two or more; some involve electing only one representative in each district, whereas others involve electing many. The list of differences could go on and on. Despite the many different ways in which one might think to distinguish among the world's electoral systems, most political scientists categorize electoral systems into the three main families mentioned earlier—majoritarian, proportional, and mixed; they base these categories on the electoral formula they use to translate votes into seats.

ox 12.1   ## WHO CAN VOTE IN DEMOCRACIES?

If you recall from our discussion in Chapter 5, Dahl (1971) argues that two dimensions are important for classifying democracies: contestation and inclusion. Contestation is largely concerned with the procedures of democratic competition. In contrast, inclusion has to do with who gets to participate in the democratic process; that is, who can vote. To classify a country as democratic, it should be characterized by high levels of both contestation and inclusion. As Dahl (1989, 233) notes, it is a requirement that "practically all adults have the right to vote" for a country to be considered democratic. In the real world, though, "no country allows all adults to vote. . . . Although the basic trend over the last 200 years has been to remove one barrier after another, many restrictions remain" (Katz 1997, 216).

Historically, many groups of people have been excluded from the right to vote. For example, many countries did not allow women to vote. The first country to give unrestricted voting rights to women was New Zealand in 1893. In contrast, it was not until 1984 that Liechtenstein finally gave women the right to vote. Some countries excluded people from the right to vote based on religion. For instance, Roman Catholics were not allowed to vote in the United Kingdom until 1788. A more common basis on which to exclude various groups was social class. Indeed, most countries employed some sort of property qualification for people to vote until the nineteenth century. Other countries have prevented people from voting based on race. For example, indigenous Australians were barred from voting in Australia until 1967, African Americans were effectively barred from voting in the southern United States until 1964, and blacks were unable to vote in apartheid South Africa from 1948 to 1993. Much of electoral history is about the efforts to extend the suffrage, or franchise, to these various excluded groups.

Today, virtually all democracies allow for universal suffrage, under which the right to vote is not restricted by race, gender, religious belief, or social status. The United States does not quite enjoy universal suffrage because there are limitations on the voting rights of citizens in the District of Columbia (DC); citizens in DC are subject to federal laws and taxation, but their only congressional representative is a nonvoting delegate. Although all democracies generally enjoy universal suffrage, this does not mean that everyone in contemporary democracies can vote; many restrictions remain. For example, various countries restrict the right to vote based on issues having to do with age, mental health, citizenship, residency (district, country, citizens abroad), and prison sentences (Blais, Massicotte, and Yoshinaka 2001).

Age

Most countries exclude nonadults on the ground that only mature people can make reasoned choices. These countries typically use age as a proxy for maturity. Almost all democracies use eighteen years of age as the point at which individuals obtain the right to vote. For example, Blais, Massicotte, and Yoshinaka (2001) find that fifty-nine out of sixty-one democracies in their sample do not allow individuals under eighteen to vote. If we look at all countries (democracies and dictatorships), the minimum age requirement ranges from a low of sixteen in Brazil to a high of twenty-one in Malaysia, the Maldives, Pakistan, and Singapore. Historically, there have been circumstances in which the minimum age requirement depended on the married status of the individuals (Katz 1997, 218–229). For example, until 1995, Bolivia allowed people to vote at eighteen if they were married and twenty-one if they were not.

Mental Health

Most countries have voting restrictions for individuals who suffer from mental health problems. Indeed, some countries, like Bulgaria, Chile, and the Netherlands, have these restrictions explicitly written into their constitutions. Of course, the criteria for determining mental health vary across both time and space. Many countries require judicial courts to rule whether individuals are incompetent before their right to vote is removed. Only four countries—Canada, Ireland, Italy, and Sweden—have no mental health requirements for voting.

Citizenship

Some people argue that the right to vote should be given only to citizens of a country because only citizens have the interests of the national community at heart. Others counter that immigrants should be able to vote if they pay taxes and obey the laws of the country. Blais, Massicotte, and Yoshinaka (2001) find that forty-eight out of sixty-one democracies in their sample restrict the right to vote to citizens. A few countries allow noncitizens to vote but impose certain residency requirements. For example, Chile allows noncitizens to vote as long as they have been residents for five years. Several other countries allow noncitizens to vote but only if these noncitizens come from specific countries. For instance, several former British colonies, such as Barbados, Belize, and Trinidad and Tobago allow members of various British Commonwealth countries to vote. In Ireland, British citizens can vote in legislative elections but not presidential ones. Any member of a European Union country residing in Portugal can vote there.

District Residency

A small number of democracies have district residency requirements. The justification for these requirements is that individuals should be informed about local issues if they are to vote. Of course, this raises the issue of what happens when people have recently moved to an area. The length of district residency requirements varies from a low of one month in Australia and New Zealand to a high of six months in France, Mali, and the Philippines.

Country Residency

A few countries allow only those individuals who have resided within their borders for a certain amount of time to vote. In these countries, the minimum amount of residency time before an individual can vote ranges from a low of three months in Germany to a high of seven years in Malawi and St. Lucia.

Citizens Abroad

Historically, citizens who reside in foreign countries have been unable to vote in their home countries. This restriction was initially removed for soldiers fighting abroad; it was later removed for civil servants and diplomats working abroad. Blais, Massicotte, and Yoshinaka (2001) find that forty of the sixty-one democracies in their sample allow citizens who reside abroad to vote. Thirty of these countries, including France, Mali, and Venezuela, allow these citizens to vote indefinitely; others allow these citizens to vote only for a certain period of time, ranging from three years in New Zealand to twenty years in the United Kingdom. Several democracies, however, such as Barbados, the Czech Republic, Italy, Malta, and Slovakia, require individuals to return to their home country to cast their vote, so the right to vote for these citizens is more symbolic than practical.

Prison Sentences

Some people argue that citizens who are convicted of breaking laws have broken some kind of "social contract" with the rest of society and should, therefore, be barred from voting. At one end of the spectrum are democracies such as Brazil, India, Portugal, the United Kingdom, and Venezuela, which do not allow individuals convicted of any crime to vote while in prison. At the other end of the spectrum are countries like Germany, Namibia, and Sweden, which allow all prisoners to vote. In between are countries that allow some prisoners to vote, depending on the length of their prison sentence and the type of crime that they committed. In some countries, individuals lose the right to vote for periods beyond the length of their prison sentence. For example, prisoners in Belgium lose the right to vote for five years beyond the end of their prison sentence. In Iowa, Kentucky, and Virginia in the United States, individuals convicted of a felony lose the right to vote for life (unless the governor or state legislature intervenes).

Registration

In all democracies, only those who are registered are able to vote. In many countries, voter registration is done by the local or national government. Until 1992, for example, Elections Canada hired temporary employees from the public to go to each residence in order to determine all the eligible voters. This system was ultimately abandoned as being too costly. In some countries, all eligible voters must legally register themselves. For instance, voter registration is compulsory in the United Kingdom and Australia. In other democracies, like the United States, it is up to the eligible voters whether they choose to register to vote.

You may be wondering why political scientists focus on the electoral formula when there are so many other ways to distinguish between electoral systems. To be honest, there is no really good answer—it has just become an established convention. The closest thing to an answer that we can come up with is that political scientists have found that the electoral formula strongly influences the proportionality of the electoral system and the type of government that forms (Rae 1967; Powell 1982; Blais and Carty 1987; Lijphart 1994). For example, majoritarian electoral systems tend to produce a more disproportional translation of votes into seats and to increase the probability of single-party majority governments. In contrast, proportional electoral systems tend to produce more proportional results—as the name "proportional representation" would suggest—and to lower the probability of single-party majority governments. Given that most political scientists think that the proportionality of an electoral system

| FIGURE 12.1 | **Electoral System Families** |

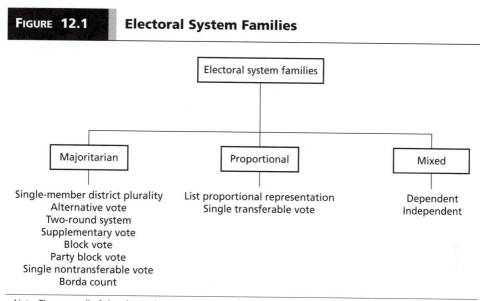

Note: These are all of the electoral systems used in contemporary national-level legislative and presidential elections in independent countries.

and the type of government that forms are important, it is perhaps not surprising that they typically distinguish electoral system families on the basis of their electoral formulas. We illustrate these electoral system families in Figure 12.1 along with the names of the various electoral systems they include. The electoral systems shown are all those that are employed in contemporary national-level legislative and presidential elections around the world.[5]

MAJORITARIAN ELECTORAL SYSTEMS

A **majoritarian electoral system** is one in which the candidates or parties that receive the most votes win. We should note that the word "majoritarian" is somewhat misleading. Although some majoritarian electoral systems require the winning candidate or party to obtain an absolute majority of the votes (absolute majority systems), others require only that they win more votes than anyone else (relative majority or plurality systems). In other words, not all majoritarian electoral systems actually require the winning candidates or parties to obtain an absolute majority of the votes. Probably the main reason why majoritarian electoral systems are referred to as "majoritarian" is, as we will see, that they frequently produce outcomes in which the largest party wins an absolute majority of the legislative seats even if the party does not win an absolute majority of the votes. In effect, majoritarian electoral systems tend to help the largest party obtain a leg-

> A **majoritarian electoral system** is one in which the candidates or parties that receive the most votes win.

---

5. There are, of course, numerous other electoral systems, such as approval voting (Brams and Fishburn 1978), that are used for different types of elections.

islative majority. Eight different varieties of majoritarian electoral systems are used for national-level elections around the world: single-member-district plurality (SMDP), alternative vote (AV), Borda Count (BC), two-round systems (TRS), single nontransferable vote (SNTV), block vote (BV), party block vote (PBV), and supplementary vote (SV).

Single-Member District Plurality System

A **single-member district plurality system** is one in which individuals cast a single vote for a candidate in a single-member district. The candidate with the most votes is elected.

A **single-member district plurality system** is the simplest and most commonly used majoritarian electoral system in the world. It is employed primarily in the United Kingdom and in former British colonies, such as Belize, Canada, India, Nepal, Nigeria, Trinidad and Tobago, and the United States. An SMDP system involves individuals voting for candidates in single-member districts. On being presented with a list of the nominated candidates in the district, each individual votes for one, and only one, candidate; they typically do this by placing an X next to their chosen candidate. The candidate with the most votes, even if this is not a majority of the votes, is elected from the district. SMDP systems are sometimes referred to as "first-past-the-post" systems in an analogy to horse racing. This analogy is misleading, however, because there is no particular "post" that a candidate must move beyond before he or she can win; all a candidate needs to win is to get more votes than anyone else. In theory, a candidate can win in an SMDP system with as few as two votes if all the other candidates win only one vote each. An example of the operation of an SMDP system in the Kettering constituency in the United Kingdom in the 2005 legislative elections is shown in Table 12.3. Philip Hollobone of the Conservative Party won the most votes and was, therefore, elected as the member of Parliament for this district.

SMDP electoral systems have both advantages and disadvantages. Perhaps the greatest strength of SMDP systems is their relative simplicity. This means that they are easy to explain to voters and easy for them to understand. It also suggests that they are easy to administer and, hence, relatively low in cost. A second advantage of SMDP systems has to do with the fact that only one representative is elected in each district. Having only one representative per constituency means that responsibility for what happens in the district lies squarely with

TABLE 12.3	**Election Results from the Kettering Constituency, UK Legislative Elections, 2005**		
Candidate	Party	Votes	Percentage
Philip Hollobone	Conservatives	25,401	45.6
Phil Sawford	Labour	22,100	39.7
Roger Aron	Liberal Democrats	6,882	12.4
Rosemarie Clarke	United Kingdom Independence Party	1,263	2.3

that person. In other words, SMDP systems make it easy for voters to identify who is responsible for policies in their district and, therefore, to hold them accountable in the next election. By making it easier for voters to hold representatives accountable, SMDP systems create incentives for representatives to perform well in office. This helps to explain why political scientists often link SMDP electoral systems with high levels of constituency service and close bonds between constituents and representatives. For some scholars, a third advantage of SMDP systems is that these electoral systems are associated with single-party majority governments (Blais and Carty 1987). As we'll see in more detail in Chapter 15, single-party majority governments increase the ability of voters to identify who is responsible for national policy and hold them accountable; we already saw in the previous chapter that single-party majority governments are more stable than other forms of government.

Despite these advantages, SMDP electoral systems have many critics. Some critics point to the fact that SMDP systems have the potential to produce extremely unrepresentative outcomes. As our example in Table 12.3 illustrates, it is possible for a candidate to win without obtaining a majority of the votes; in fact, 54.4 percent of the Kettering constituents who voted did not vote for the winning candidate. Although it is true that the winning candidate did not obtain a majority of the votes in the Kettering constituency, one could argue that he came quite close (45.6 percent). Still, it is important to note that candidates can win in SMDP systems with a much lower vote share than that obtained by the winning candidate in Kettering. As an example, the winning candidate in the Kerowagi constituency in Papua New Guinea won with just 7.9 percent of the vote in the 1987 legislative elections; fully 92.1 percent of the constituents voted for someone else (Cox 1997, 85). That this can happen helps to explain why SMDP systems are often criticized for leading to the election of legislators who are not representative of the voters' wishes.

Not only are SMDP systems criticized for being able to produce unrepresentative outcomes at the district level, they are also frequently criticized for their potential to produce unrepresentative outcomes at the national level as well. Under an SMDP system, it is entirely possible for a party that wins a significant percentage of the overall national vote to obtain very few legislative seats because it fails to come first in many constituencies. For instance, consider the 1983 legislative elections in the United Kingdom. In these elections, the coalition between the Social Democratic Party and the Liberal Party, which was known as the Alliance, won 25.4 percent of the national vote but received just 3.5 percent of the seats. In fact, the Alliance won only 675,985 votes (out of 30,661,309 votes) fewer than the Labour Party but received 186 fewer legislative seats. In stark contrast to the Alliance, the Conservative Party won 61.1 percent of the seats and formed a single-party government in the 1983 elections even though it had only won 42.4 percent of the votes. As this example demonstrates, SMDP systems can produce a highly disproportionate translation of votes into seats that tends to favor larger parties at the expense of smaller ones. We should note, though, that the level of disproportionality seen in SMDP systems is sometimes not as high as was the case in the 1983 elections in the United Kingdom. One reason for this is that some parties may finish second and fail to win seats in some districts but come in first and win seats in others. This situation can translate into a fairly proportional outcome at the national level even if the outcomes at the local level are not proportional (Barkan 1995). For example, the 1994 legislative elections in Malawi saw the United Democratic Front win 48 percent of the seats with 46 percent of the votes, the Malawian Congress Party win 32 percent of the seats with 34 percent of the votes, and the Alliance for Democracy win 20 percent of the seats with 19 percent of the votes.

SMDP systems are also criticized by some for encouraging individuals to vote strategically rather than in accordance with their true preferences. Sincere voting means voting for your most preferred candidate or party. In contrast, strategic voting means voting for your most preferred candidate *who has a realistic chance of winning*.[6] To see how the SMDP system creates an incentive to vote strategically, consider the Kettering example again. Imagine an individual who prefers the Liberal Democrat candidate to the Labour Candidate and the Labour Candidate to the Conservative candidate, that is, LD ≻ L ≻ C. If this individual votes for the Liberal Democrat candidate, she will be voting sincerely. However, this individual has an incentive to vote strategically because opinion polls are likely to show that the Liberal Democrat candidate is going to finish in third place and has little to no chance of coming in first. Thus, a vote for the Liberal Democrat candidate is likely to be "wasted"; that is, it will not affect the outcome of the election. As a result, the individual may decide to vote strategically for the Labour candidate (who has a more realistic chance of winning) in an attempt to stop the Conservative candidate (the least-preferred candidate) from winning. Clearly, we prefer democratic electoral systems that encourage voters to express their sincere preferences. Unfortunately, though, scholars have shown that *all* reasonable electoral systems create incentives for individuals to act strategically; there are no "strategy-proof" systems (Gibbard 1973; Satterthwaite 1975). Nonetheless, some electoral systems, such as SMDP, create stronger incentives to act strategically than others. We address these incentives to vote strategically and their effects in more detail in the next chapter.

Another criticism of SMDP systems is that they can encourage the creation of ethnic or clan-based parties in countries in which ethnic groups and clans are regionally concentrated. This can result in regional fiefdoms or party strongholds in which there is little electoral competition, the party of the majority ethnic group is dominant, and minorities have little sway over public policy or the allocation of private goods. This type of situation frequently occurs in African countries like Malawi and Kenya, where ethnic groups are geographically concentrated in particular regions (Barkan 1995; Posner 2005). In effect, the use of SMDP electoral systems in Africa has helped produce countries that are "divided into geographically separate party strongholds, with little incentive for parties to make appeals outside their home region and cultural-political base" (Reynolds, Reilly, and Ellis 2005, 43). Similarly, the use of SMDP probably helped segregationist Democrats maintain single-party dominance in the southern United States for almost a century (Mickey, forthcoming).

---

6. For more detailed definitions of sincere and strategic voting, see Chapter 10.

Alternative Vote

One of the criticisms of SMDP systems is that they allow candidates to win without obtaining a majority of the votes. One simple way to avoid this possibility involves having individuals rank order the candidates on the ballot rather than simply vote for one of them. When voters rank order candidates in this way, they are engaging in what is called **preference,** or **preferential, voting.** A majoritarian electoral system that involves preferential voting is called the **alternative vote** (AV).

> **Preference,** or **preferential, voting** involves voters ranking one or more candidates or parties in order of preference on the ballots.
>
> The **alternative vote,** used in single-member districts, is an electoral system in which voters mark their preferences by rank ordering the candidates. A candidate who receives an absolute majority is elected. If no candidate wins an absolute majority, then the candidate with the fewest votes is eliminated and her votes are reallocated until one candidate has an absolute majority of the valid votes remaining.

In the alternative vote system, a candidate-centered system used in single-member districts, voters are required to rank at least one candidate in order of preference. Voters typically do this by placing numbers next to the names of the candidates to indicate whether each is the voter's first choice, second choice, third choice, and so on. AV systems in which voters have to rank order all of the candidates are called "full preferential" systems, whereas AV systems in which voters have to rank order only some candidates are called "optional preferential" systems. If a candidate wins an absolute majority of first-preference votes, he is immediately elected. If no candidate wins an absolute majority, then the candidate with the lowest number of first-preference votes is eliminated and his ballots are examined for their second-preference votes. Each ballot from the eliminated candidate is then reallocated among the remaining candidates according to these second preferences. This process is repeated until one candidate has obtained an absolute majority of the votes cast (full preferential system) or an absolute majority of the valid votes remaining (optional preferential system). The alternative vote is sometimes referred to as an instant-runoff vote (IRV) because it is much like holding a series of runoff elections in which the candidate with the fewest votes is eliminated in each round until someone receives an absolute majority of the vote.

Australia is perhaps the most famous country to use the AV system.[7] The alternative vote was first introduced in Queensland, Australia, in 1893 and soon spread to the other Australian colonies after 1901. The AV system has been used to elect the Australian House of Representatives since 1919. Australian voters must rank order all of the candidates on the ballot because they employ a full preferential AV system. An example of the operation of an AV system in the Richmond constituency of New South Wales in the 1990 Australian legislative elections is shown in Table 12.5. When the first-preference votes from all the voters were initially tallied up, Charles Blunt came first with 40.9 percent of the vote. Because no candidate won an absolute majority, the candidate with the lowest number of votes (Gavin Baillie) was eliminated. As Table 12.5 illustrates, Baillie was ranked first on 187 ballots. These

---

7. Australians refer to the AV system as "preferential voting." This term, however, is slightly ambiguous, because there are several different types of preferential voting, as we will see.

Box 12.2 **THE BORDA COUNT IN THE SOUTH PACIFIC**

The **Borda Count** is a candidate-centered electoral system used in either single- or multimember districts in which voters must use numbers to mark their preferences for all of the nominated candidates. These preferences are then assigned a value using equal steps to reflect the voter's preference ordering. These values are then summed and the candidate(s) with the most "valuable" votes is (are) elected.

Another majoritarian electoral system that involves preferential voting is the **Borda Count** (BC).[1] The BC is a candidate-centered electoral system used in either single- or multimember districts in which voters must use numbers to mark their preferences for all of the nominated candidates. These preferences are then assigned a value using equal steps to reflect the voter's preference ordering. For example, if there are ten candidates, a voter's first preference might be worth one, his second preference 0.9, his third preference 0.8, and so on until his tenth preference, which would be worth 0.1. These values are then summed and the candidate(s) with the most "valuable" votes is (are) elected. Although the Borda Count was officially designed by a French scientist, Charles de Borda, in the eighteenth century, the history of this particular voting method goes back even further, because a variant of it was used after 105 AD to make decisions in the Roman Senate. The BC is the forerunner of more recent and more common preferential-voting systems, such as the alternative vote that we are discussing in the main text. The BC is currently used to select presidential candidates from among the members of parliament on the Pacific island of Kiribati (Reilly 2002a). It is also used to elect two ethnic minority members to the legislature in Slovenia and by major league baseball to choose its Most Valuable Player.

Although it is otherwise rarely employed, the BC is "often advocated as an 'ideal' electoral system by voting theorists" (Reilly 2002a, 357). The BC tends to favor candidates with broadly based support rather than candidates who are supported by the majority. In some sense, it favors what you might think of as the least-unpopular candidates. Although this might seem anti-democratic to some, others like this feature because it encourages consensus-based politics. It can be particularly attractive in a highly divided society in which the majority candidate is strongly opposed by a large minority of the electorate. It is on these grounds that scholars have advocated the use of the BC for divided countries in the Balkans, Northern Ireland, and elsewhere (Emerson 1998). The BC also tends to elect candidates that are close to the center of the distribution of citizen preferences (Cox 1987). As Dummett (1997, 161–162) puts it, the BC "will be far more favourable to candidates occupying moderate positions than will the plurality system [SMDP] or AV, and will likewise be unfavourable to those representing extreme positions."

As with all electoral systems, though, the BC creates incentives for voters to act strategically. In particular, it encourages voters to engage in what is termed "compromising" and "burying." Imagine that there are five candidates in a single-member district and your sincere preference ordering between them is A ≻ B ≻ C ≻ D ≻ E. Suppose that opinion polls prior to the elec-

---

1. Recall that we briefly mentioned the Borda Count in Chapter 10.

tion indicate that only candidates B and C have a realistic chance of winning. Because you have a clear preference for whether B or C wins, you may want to vote strategically by ranking B first. This is called "compromising," because you are ranking candidate B higher than your sincere preferences would imply in an attempt to stop C from winning. You may also want to vote strategically by ranking C last. This is called "burying," because you are placing candidate C lower than your sincere preferences would imply in an attempt to help B get elected.

A slightly different electoral system, called the **modified Borda Count,** has been employed to elect members of parliament on the Pacific island of Nauru since 1971 (Reilly 2002a). The modified BC is different in that

> The **modified Borda Count** is essentially the same as the Borda Count except that the value of each preference no longer declines in equal steps; it assumes that voters care more about higher-ranked candidates than lower-ranked ones.

each of the voter's preferences are assigned a value calculated by using a series of divisors— 1, 2, 3, 4, and so on. For example, if there were ten candidates, then a voter's first preference would be worth 1, his second preference 0.5, his third preference 0.33, his fourth preference 0.25, and so on until his tenth preference, which would be worth 0.1. These values are then summed and the candidate(s) with the most valuable votes is (are) elected. Note that the value of each preference no longer declines in equal steps as with the normal BC. As a result, the modified BC assumes that voters care more about their higher-ranked candidates than their lower ones. This makes the electoral system more majoritarian, because candidates need to attract more lower-order preferences to overtake a leading candidate.

Table 12.4 illustrates how votes are translated into seats using the modified BC by presenting the results in the two-seat Buada district from the 2004 legislative elections in Nauru. As you can see, Table 12.4 does not list the "number" of votes won by each candidate; instead, it lists the "value" of the votes won by each candidate. Roland Kun and Lyn Terangi Adam were elected as the representatives for this district because the values of their votes were the two highest.

TABLE 12.4	**Buada District, Nauru Legislative Elections, 2004**	
Candidate	Value of votes cast	
Lyn Terangi Adam	131.967	Elected second
Palik Agir	109.110	
Manfred Depaune	84.890	
Vinson Detenamo	122.610	
Roland Kun	145.324	Elected first
Thomas Star	123.243	
Nelson Tamakin	104.793	

Source: Adam Carr's Election Archive, http://psephos.adam-carr.net.

TABLE 12.5   Richmond Constituency, New South Wales, Australian Legislative Elections, 1990

Candidate	First count (no.)	(%)	Second count (no.)	(%)	Third count (no.)	(%)	Fourth count (no.)	(%)	Fifth count (no.)	(%)	Sixth count (no.)	(%)	Seventh count (no.)	(%)
Stan Gibbs	4,346	6.3	4,380	6.3	4,420	6.4	4,504	6.5	4,683	6.8				
Neville Newell	18,423	26.7	18,467	26.7	18,484	26.8	18,544	26.9	18,683	27.1	20,238	29.4	34,664	50.5
Gavin Baillie	187	0.3												
Alan Sims	1,032	1.5	1,053	1.5	1,059	1.5	1,116	1.6						
Ian Paterson	445	0.6	480	0.7	530	0.8								
Dudley Leggett	279	0.4	294	0.4										
Charles Blunt	28,257	40.9	28,274	41.0	28,303	41.0	28,416	41.2	28,978	42	29,778	43.2	33,980	49.5
Helen Caldicott	16,072	23.3	16,091	23.3	16,237	23.5	16,438	23.8	16,658	24.1	18,903	27.4		

Note: Blank cells indicate that a candidate was eliminated.

FIGURE 12.2	**Australian "How-to-Vote" Card from the 2004 Legislative Elections**

Source: http://en.wikipedia.org/wiki/Image:Liberalhtv.jpg

187 ballots were then reallocated to whichever of the remaining candidates the voters ranked second after Gavin Baillie. For example, the fact that Ian Paterson received 445 votes in the first count but 480 votes in the second count indicates that 35 of the people who had listed Gavin Baillie as their most preferred candidate listed Ian Paterson as their second-choice candidate. Because there was still no candidate with an absolute majority after this second count, the new candidate with the lowest number of votes (Dudley Leggett) was eliminated and his ballots were reallocated among the remaining candidates in the same manner as before. This process continued until the seventh round of counting, when Neville Newell became the first candidate to finally obtain an absolute majority of the votes. The overall result, then, was that Neville Newell became the representative elected from the Richmond constituency of New South Wales.

It is worth noting that Charles Blunt had won by far the most votes in the first round and had been leading on all of the counts up until the very last one. It was only when the last votes were reallocated according to the preferences of the voters that it became clear that an absolute majority of those who voted in Richmond preferred Neville Newell to Charles Blunt. As this example illustrates, the reallocation of votes from eliminated candidates to remaining candidates can play an important role in determining the outcome of elections in AV systems. It is for this reason that political parties in Australia often give voters "how-to-vote" cards outside polling stations with clear instructions on how to rank candidates so that the flow of preferences will benefit them either directly or, by helping any allied parties, indirectly. An example of a how-to-vote card for the Liberal Party is illustrated in Figure 12.2.

Fiji also employs a full-preferential AV system to elect its House of Representatives. The Fijian system is somewhat unusual, though, in that it allows for "default preferences" specified by the political parties and "custom preferences" specified by the voter. In effect, each political party or candidate ranks all of the competing candidates according to their own preferences. Voters who are happy with this ranking simply vote for their preferred party, and voter preferences are automatically reallocated according to the ranking chosen by their preferred party. Voters who do not like the ranking provided by their preferred party can opt to rank the candidates themselves. To see how this works, examine the ballot paper for the Tailevu constituency in the 2001 Fijian legislative elections shown in Figure 12.3. As you can see, the Fijian ballot paper is divided by a thick black line. If the voter checks one of the boxes above the black line (default preferences), then he is opting for the rank ordering of the candidates chosen by one of the eleven political parties shown. In many ways, the upper portion of the Fijian ballot paper is the equivalent of a how-to-vote card handed out to voters by political parties in Australia. If the voter does not like these default preferences, then he must

| **FIGURE 12.3** | **Fijian AV Ballot Paper for the Tailevu Constituency in the 2001 Legislative Elections** |

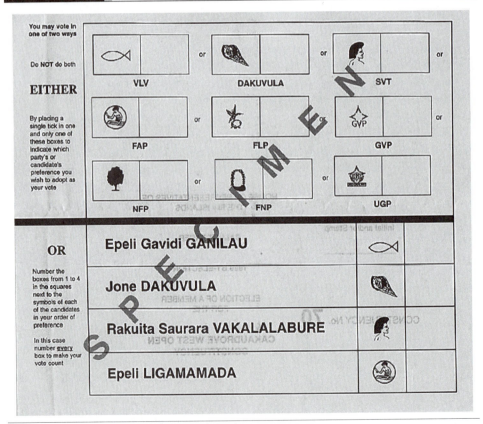

Source: www.unc.edu/~asreynol/ballot_pages/fiji.html

rank order all of the candidates that are listed below the line (custom preferences) by putting numbers next to each candidate's name. In the 2001 elections, less than 10 percent of Fijian voters chose to fill out the custom preferences; the vast majority preferred to simply go along with the rank ordering of their preferred political party. It is worth noting in this particular district that there are more party options above the line than there are actual candidates. For example, several parties—FAP, FLP, NVTLP, DNT, PANU, and VLV—do not have any candidates competing in the Tailevu district. What this illustrates is that political parties often have an incentive to tell their supporters how to rank order the competing candidates even if they do not necessarily have their own candidate in the race. By doing this, they can try to influence the outcome of elections in specific districts and, hence, the outcome of the national election.

Several other countries also employ AV systems. For example, Ireland uses a full-preferential AV system to elect its president.[8] In 2003 the legislature in Papua New Guinea voted to reintroduce an AV system for its legislative elections. Papua New Guinea had used an AV system between 1964 and 1975, when it was an Australian territory. In June 2007, Papua New Guinea elected its first legislature using an optional-preferential AV system in which voters have to rank only their top three preferences.

To a large extent, AV systems retain many of the advantages associated with SMDP electoral systems. For example, the fact that there is only one representative elected per constituency means that it is easy for voters to identify who is responsible for district policy and hold them accountable. As a result, we can expect high levels of constituency service and strong bonds between citizens and their representatives. AV systems have several additional advantages, though. One is that voters have a greater opportunity to convey information about their preferences than they have under an SMDP system. This is because they get to rank order the candidates rather than simply vote yes and no for one (or more) of them. Another advantage is that there is less of an incentive for voters to engage in strategic voting because they know that their vote will not be wasted if the candidate they most prefer is unpopular and unlikely to win; their vote is simply transferred to the candidate they prefer next. We should note, though, that strategic incentives do not disappear entirely. For example, voters may decide not to rank the candidates according to their sincere preferences in an attempt to influence the order in which candidates are eliminated and, hence, who ultimately wins in a district. That this type of strategic concern matters is one explanation for why Australian parties hand out how-to-vote cards at the polling stations.

A third advantage is that AV systems encourage candidates and parties to win not only the votes from their base supporters but also the "second preferences" of others. This is because these second preferences may end up being crucial to their election. To attract these votes,

---

8. The Irish Constitution states that the president is elected by means of the single transferable vote (Article 12-2.3). This is technically incorrect, because the single transferable vote is used only in multimember districts, whereas the alternative vote is only used in single-member districts. Nonetheless, the Irish still refer to their presidential electoral system as the single transferable vote.

candidates are likely to have to make broadly based centrist appeals to all interests rather than focus on narrow sectarian or extremist issues. Some evidence for this comes from Australia, where the major parties frequently attempt to negotiate deals with smaller parties for their second preferences prior to an election in a process known as "preference swapping" (Reilly 2001, 45). The incentive to build broadly based support helps to explain why the AV system is often advocated for elections in deeply divided societies, such as the ethnically fragmented Bosnia-Herzegovina, Fiji, Papua New Guinea, and South Africa (Horowitz 1991; Reilly 2001).

Recall that one of the most common criticisms with SMDP electoral systems was that they allow candidates to win who do not obtain majority support. This problem is addressed by AV systems because candidates are eliminated one at a time until one has an overall majority. Although this would appear to be one of the main advantages of AV systems, some critics claim that the winning candidate does not necessarily obtain a "genuine" majority. By this, they mean that it is possible for a majority of the voters in a district to prefer some other candidate to the one who actually wins. The reason why this possibility exists is that a candidate who is preferred to all the other candidates in a series of head-to-head races can be eliminated early on in an AV system because they receive an insufficient number of first-place votes. A clear disadvantage of the AV system is that it is rather complicated. From the point of view of the voters, it requires a reasonable degree of literacy and numeracy; from the point of view of the authorities, the counting process can be costly and drawn out.

Two-Round Systems

A **two-round system** (TRS) is a majoritarian electoral system that, as its name would suggest, has the potential for two rounds of elections.[9] In TRSs, candidates or parties are automatically elected in the first round if they obtain a specified level of votes, nearly always an absolute majority. If no candidate or party wins this level of votes, then a second round of elections takes place, normally one or two weeks later. Although the precise details of how this second round of elections is conducted vary from country to country, the candidates or parties with the most votes in the second round are elected. TRSs are sometimes referred to as "runoff" or "double-ballot" electoral systems in recognition of their potential for two rounds of elections. Although TRSs are quite diverse, they can be divided into two main types: the majority-runoff TRS and the majority-plurality TRS.

> A **two-round system** has the potential for two rounds of elections. Candidates or parties are automatically elected in the first round if they obtain a specified level of votes, typically an absolute majority. Those candidates or parties that win the most votes in the second round are elected.

Majority-Runoff Two-Round Systems

Most majority-runoff TRSs are candidate-centered electoral systems in single-member districts in which voters have a single vote. Each voter chooses his most preferred candidate.

---

9. Although highly unusual, some TRSs can require more than two rounds of voting to determine the winner. Thus, it might be more descriptively accurate to call this electoral system a multiple-round system (MRS).

Any candidate who obtains an absolute majority of the votes in the first round is automatically elected. If no candidate obtains an absolute majority, then the top two vote winners go on to compete in a runoff election one or two weeks later. Whoever wins the most votes in this runoff election is elected. Given that there are only two candidates in this second election, the winner necessarily has the support of an absolute majority of the voters (as long as there is not an exact tie). This type of majority-runoff TRS is used to elect the president in many countries, such as France, Mali, and most Latin American countries. In fact, the majority-runoff TRS is the most common method for electing presidents around the world today (Golder 2005). The majority-runoff TRS is also used for legislative elections in several countries, such as the Central African Republic, Comoros, Haiti, Kyrgyzstan, and Ukraine.

Although extremely unusual, majority-runoff TRSs are sometimes employed in multi-member districts. For example, Mali employs a party-centered majority-runoff system in its multimember districts. Malian voters cast a single vote for their preferred party. Any party that obtains an absolute majority of the votes wins all of the seats in the district. If no party wins an absolute majority, however, then the top two parties are placed on a second ballot and compete in a runoff election. Whichever party obtains the most votes wins all of the district seats.

Majority-Plurality Two-Round Systems

Almost all majority-plurality TRSs are candidate-centered electoral systems in single-member districts in which voters have a single vote. As in the majority-runoff TRSs, a candidate who receives an absolute majority of the vote in the first round is automatically elected. The difference is that now if no candidate obtains an absolute majority, then *all* candidates who overcome some preordained threshold of votes can contest the second round. Whichever candidate obtains the most votes in this second round, whether it is an absolute majority or not, is duly elected.

Perhaps the most famous country to employ a majority-plurality TRS for its legislative elections is France. All candidates who obtain more than 12.5 percent of the registered electorate in the first round of French legislative elections are eligible to compete in any second round that might be necessary.[10] Table 12.6 illustrates how the French majority-plurality TRS operated in the fourth district in the Puy-de-Dôme during the 2002 French legislative elections. No candidate won an absolute majority in the first round. Of the two candidates who received more than the 12.5 percent of the registered electorate required to compete in the second round, J. Paul Bacquet of the Socialist Party won the most votes and was elected. In France it is often the case that only two candidates will compete in the second round of elections even if more candidates are eligible to do so. The reason for this is that parties on the left or right often agree to withdraw the least popular of their eligible candidates and support the best-placed candidate from their side of the political spectrum. By doing this, they

---

10. A candidate who wishes to compete in the second round of French legislative elections must win 12.5 percent of the registered electorate, not 12.5 percent of the actual vote. In effect, this often means that a candidate must win about 17 percent of the actual vote to be eligible to run in the second round.

TABLE 12.6	Fourth District in the Puy-de-Dôme, French Legislative Elections, 2002	

First Round		
Candidate	**Party**	**Vote share (%)**
J. Paul Bacquet	Socialist Party	42.8
Pierre Pascallon	Union for a Presidential Majority	38.1
Christophe Picard	National Republican Movement	0.9
M. Germaine Wilwertz	National Front	6.3
Marie Savre	Workers' Struggle	1.3
Laura Artusi	Communist Party	2.8
Rémi Aufrere	Republican Pole	1.3
J. Paul Russier	Green Party	2.8
Nicolas Bagel	Rally for Independence from Europe	0.0
Bernard Bouzon	Hunting, Fishing, Nature, and Tradition Party	1.4
Patrick Goyeau	Communist Revolutionary League (100% Left)	2.4
Second Round		
J. Paul Bacquet	Socialist Party	56.1
Pierre Pascallon	Union for a Presidential Majority	43.9

are hoping to increase the chance that their side of the political spectrum will win the second round by preventing their electorate from splitting its support among multiple candidates. In fact, no more than two candidates competed in all of the second-round elections in the 2007 legislative elections in France.

In one country—the Pacific island of Kiribati—a majority-plurality TRS is used in multimember districts. Kiribati's voters have as many votes as there are seats available. Although they can use as many or as few of their votes as they wish, they can give at most only one vote to any particular candidate. Any candidate that receives a vote on an absolute majority of the ballots is automatically elected. If a sufficient number of candidates do not receive a vote on more than 50 percent of the ballots, then a second round of elections takes place. In three-member districts with no first-round victors, the top five candidates contest the second round; in two-member districts, the top four candidates contest it. Those candidates with the most votes in this second round are elected (Brechtenfeld 1993, 44).

In both types of TRS systems that we have examined so far, a candidate who obtains an absolute majority of votes in the first round is automatically elected. There are, however, some TRSs in which a candidate can be elected in the first round without an absolute majority. We might want to call these qualified-majority TRSs. The precise threshold of votes that needs to be overcome to win in the first round varies quite considerably in these systems. For example, a candidate had to come first and win more than 33 percent of the votes to be elected in the first round of the 1956 and 1963 presidential elections in Peru. In contrast, a candidate currently has to win more than 55 percent of the vote to be elected in the first round of presidential elections in Sierra Leone. The threshold employed in the first round can be quite complicated in some countries. For instance, a candidate can be declared president in Argentina today without the need for a second round if he either (a) comes first and wins more than 40 percent of the votes or (b) if he wins 35 percent of the votes and 5 percent more than the nearest competitor. Qualified-majority TRSs are not restricted to presidential elections. For example, the first-placed candidate in Mongolian legislative elections has to win 25 percent of the district vote in order to avoid a second round. Although the voting procedure employed in the second round of these TRSs varies from country to country, most employ a runoff between the top two vote winners. This is the procedure used for presidential elections in Argentina, Costa Rica, Nicaragua, and Sierra Leone.

TRSs have many attractive features, particularly when compared with SMDP electoral systems. One is that TRSs give voters more choice than they enjoy in SMDP systems. For example, individuals who vote for a candidate who "loses" in the first round get a second opportunity to influence who gets elected in the second round. TRSs also allow voters to change their mind and switch their votes even if the candidate they supported in the first round actually makes it into the second round. Voters might want to change their mind as a result of new information that emerges between the first and second rounds. It is worth noting that changing one's ranking of candidates in this way is not possible in preferential voting systems such as the alternative vote that we examined earlier.

A second attractive feature of TRSs is that voters have less incentive to behave strategically than they do in SMDP systems because they have a second opportunity to affect the election outcome. Individuals can vote for their most preferred candidate in the first round even if this candidate has little chance of winning in the end and then switch their support to a more well-placed candidate in the second round. Of course, strategic incentives do not disappear entirely and things can go wrong if individuals vote sincerely in this way. Voters need to think about whether their decision to vote sincerely in the first round positively affects the likelihood that a candidate whom they do not like will win either the first or second round. For example, consider the 2002 presidential elections in France that we described in Chapter 11. The second round of these elections involved a candidate from the mainstream right, Jacques Chirac, and a candidate from the extreme right, Jean-Marie Le Pen. One reason why there was no left-wing candidate was that the left-wing electorate split its vote among so many left-wing candidates in the first round that none made it into the second round. As a result, the only choice that left-wing voters had in this second round was between a candidate whom they disliked and a candidate whom they really disliked. It is arguable that France's left-wing voters would have been better off had they voted more strategically in the first round.

Another attractive feature of TRSs is that they create incentives for candidates who make it into the second round to look beyond their own electoral base and reach compromises with the leaders of parties who are already eliminated in an attempt to win over their supporters. In addition, because voters are not required to rank order candidates with numbers to express their second choice, some have argued that TRSs are more suitable to countries

| Box 12.3 | **THE SUPPLEMENTARY VOTE AND SRI LANKA** |

One of the disadvantages of two-round systems is that they are costly. An electoral system that acts like a majority-runoff TRS but with lower costs is the **supplementary vote** (SV). In the SV, a candidate-centered electoral system used in single-member districts, voters are required to rank at least one and at most two candidates in order of preference. Typically, voters are presented with a ballot with two columns alongside a list of names. Voters place an X in the first column to indicate their most preferred candidate and, if they wish, an X in the second column to indicate their second choice. A candidate who wins an absolute majority of the first-preference votes is automatically elected. If no candidate wins such an absolute majority, however, all but the two leading candidates are eliminated. The second-preference votes of those who voted for eliminated candidates are then reallocated to determine the winner. The SV is, in many ways, like a majority-runoff TRS except that there is only one round of voting. It is this characteristic that makes the SV less costly than the TRS. As you will have noticed, the SV is also a special variant of the preferential AV system in which voters are restricted to expressing only a first and second choice and in which there can be at most two counts of the votes. This means that, unlike in an AV system, voters affect the outcome of the election only if they indicate a preference for at least one of the top two candidates; if individuals vote for candidates who finish outside the top two, then their votes are wasted. The Australian state of Queensland first used a variant of the SV, then known as the contingent vote, between 1892 and 1942. A form of SV was also used in Alabama from 1915 to 1931. The SV system is currently used to elect various mayors, including the mayor of London (Kolk, Rallings, and Thrasher 2006).

The **supplementary vote** is a candidate-centered electoral system used in single-member districts, in which voters are required to rank at least one and at most two candidates in order of preference. A candidate who wins an absolute majority of the first-preference votes is automatically elected. If no candidate wins an absolute majority, then all but the two leading candidates are eliminated. The second-preference votes of those who voted for eliminated candidates are then reallocated to determine the winner.

A slight variant of the SV is used in contemporary Sri Lanka to elect its president (Reilly 2002b). The only difference with the SV system described above is that voters can mark their preferences for the top three, instead of the top two, candidates. If no candidate wins an absolute majority of the first-preference votes, then all but the top two candidates are eliminated and the second- and third-preference votes of the eliminated candidates are reallocated to determine the winner. As a former British colony, Sri Lanka originally employed an SMDP electoral system with a parliamentary form of government. Over time, though, concern grew that this institutional structure was unable to adequately represent minority interests. In 1978, political actors decided to transform the parliamentary democracy into a mixed democracy along French lines (Reilly 2001, 112–115). The need to elect a president raised particular concerns, given that Sri Lanka had a long history of bitter ethnic conflict between the majority Sinhalese and the minority Tamil communities. The goal was to have a president who would

Kumaratunga greets her cabinet colleagues on April 10, 2004, after a swearing-in ceremony at the president's house in Colombo, Sri Lanka.

be a national figure capable of representing all the groups in society and who could encourage different factions in the parliament and beyond to compromise and reach a consensus. But what was the best way to elect such a president?

Two objectives were seen as being particularly important. One was that the minority Tamil community should have a meaningful role in electing the president. The other was that the president should have the explicit support of an absolute majority of the voters. Given the origins of the 1978 Sri Lankan constitution in the French model, political actors were initially interested in adopting a majority-runoff TRS. "However, the extreme costs and security issues associated with holding two separate elections within a two-week period was seen as being a major defect, particularly since Sri Lanka was in the midst of a violent civil war at the time" (Reilly 2002b, 115). These concerns ultimately led to the adoption of the supplementary vote system that combines the two rounds of voting into one election.

In addition to ensuring that the president is elected with majority support, the SV creates incentives for candidates to look beyond their own political party or ethnic constituency to win over the second- and third-preference votes from other groups. Sri Lanka has conducted five presidential elections—1982, 1988, 1994, 1999, 2005—since adopting the SV. So far, the winning presidential candidate has won an absolute majority (if only just) in the first round and has had no need to rely on the transfer of preference votes to be elected. Despite this, some scholars have argued that the possibility that winning candidates might have to rely on these preference votes has led presidential candidates to pay more attention to minority groups during their campaigning than political actors typically did under the old SMDP electoral system (Reilly 2001, 119–120). For example, Chandrika Kumaratunga, the winning candidate in the 1994 presidential elections, made formal coalition arrangements with the major Muslim party in Sri Lanka. In addition, her moderate approach to ethnic matters led parties representing Sri Lankan and Indian Tamils to support her as well (Schaffer 1995, 423).

with widespread illiteracy and low levels of education than preferential voting systems such as the alternative vote (Reynolds, Reilly, and Ellis 2005, 53).

Despite these attractive features, TRSs also have many disadvantages. One is that they impose significant costs on the electoral administration. After all, the electoral administration has to conduct two sets of elections instead of one. Indeed, these additional costs have led some countries, such as Sri Lanka, that were initially interested in the TRS, to adopt a different electoral system (see Box 12.3, on the supplementary vote and Sri Lanka). TRSs also impose additional costs on individuals, who potentially have to vote twice; empirical evidence suggests that there is a considerable drop-off in the level of turnout between the two rounds of elections. A second disadvantage is that, like SMDP electoral systems, TRSs also produce a disproportional translation of votes into seats. Indeed, there is some evidence that the TRS produces the most disproportional results of any electoral system used in Western democracies (Reynolds, Reilly, and Ellis 2005, 53). According to some, a third disadvantage is that the TRS hurts minority representation. For example, Guinier (1994) has argued that, on extending the right to vote to African Americans, several southern states in the United States adopted the majority-runoff TRS in an attempt to reduce the ability of African American candidates to win. Evidence that the majority-runoff TRS does, indeed, hurt minority candidates comes from a series of elections conducted in the laboratory by Morton and Rietz (forthcoming).

Majoritarian Electoral Systems in Multimember Districts

Most, though not all, of the majoritarian electoral systems that we have examined so far can be employed only in single-member districts. We now briefly turn to some majoritarian electoral systems that are employed in multimember districts.

Single Nontransferable Vote

> The **single nontransferable vote** is a system in which voters cast a single candidate-centered vote in a multimember district. The candidates with the highest number of votes are elected.

The **single nontransferable vote** is essentially the equivalent of an SMDP electoral system applied in multimember districts. Both systems involve individuals casting a single vote for some candidate. The only difference is that voters in an SNTV system are now electing more than one candidate in each district. Basically, each party competing in a district puts up a list of candidates, and individuals vote for one of them. The candidates that win the most votes are elected. Candidates in an SNTV system know how many votes they need to win in order to guarantee their election. For example, if there are n seats to be filled, then any candidate A can guarantee being elected by receiving one more than $1 / (n + 1)$ of the votes. This is because n other candidates cannot all receive more than candidate A. Thus, in a four-seat district, a candidate can guarantee winning one of the seats by winning more than 20 percent of the vote. An SNTV system was employed for legislative elections in Japan from 1948 to 1993. It is currently employed for filling some seats in the Taiwanese parliament and for legislative elections in Jordan and the pacific island of Vanuatu.

One advantage of SNTV systems over SMDP ones is that they tend to produce more proportional outcomes and improve the representation of smaller parties and minority ethnic groups. This is because candidates from smaller parties and minority ethnic groups can now get elected even though they do not win the most votes in a district. Indeed, the fact that some countries have adopted the SNTV system to explicitly improve minority representation and that it tends to produce more proportional outcomes than other majoritarian electoral systems has led some scholars to classify SNTV as a "semi-proportional," rather than a majoritarian, electoral system (Lijphart 1994). This line of reasoning, however, confuses the outcome of an electoral system—proportionality or minority representation—with its actual mechanics (Massicotte and Blais 1999; Golder 2005). As we noted earlier, the defining feature of majoritarian electoral systems is that the candidates or parties that ultimately win must obtain the most votes. Because this is precisely what happens with the SNTV system, it should rightfully be classified as a majoritarian electoral system.[11]

Several disadvantages are associated with SNTV systems. One is that they tend to create incentives for intraparty fighting and factionalization. This is because the candidates from one party are not only competing against candidates from other parties in their district but also against candidates from their own party. The fact that candidates can guarantee their own election with a specific percentage of votes also encourages clientelistic behavior, in which candidates target subtle "electoral bribes to groups of defined voters" (Reynolds, Reilly, and Ellis 2005, 117). Another disadvantage is that candidates have few incentives to build broadly based coalitions because their election does not depend on the transfer of any preference votes from other parties or candidates.

Finally, it should be noted that SNTV systems raise certain strategic quandaries for political parties and voters. Although every party in an SNTV system wants to win as many seats as they can in each multimember district, they do not want to put up too many candidates in case their party supporters split their vote between these candidates to such an extent that none, or only a few, of the candidates actually finish among the top vote winners. If we go to an extreme, it is possible in an SNTV system for a party whose candidates together obtain a substantial percentage of the votes, even an absolute majority, to win no seats. This suggests that political parties have to be very careful in choosing how many candidates to run in each district. Similarly, supporters of each party must think hard about which candidate from their party most needs their vote to be elected; if they give their vote to a candidate that is already likely to obtain a sufficient number of votes, then their vote will be wasted.

---

11. The Institute for Democracy and Electoral Assistance (IDEA), which provides the most widely cited classification of electoral systems, classifies electoral systems into four major families—majoritarian, proportional, mixed, and other. The SNTV is among several electoral systems that fall into the "other" category. In effect, the "other" category is a residual category for all of the cases that cannot unambiguously be assigned according to IDEA's classification rules. The existence of such a residual category suggests that the IDEA's classification rules are flawed.

Block Vote and Party Block Vote

> The **block vote** (BV) is a candidate-centered system used in multimember districts in which voters have as many votes as there are candidates to be elected. The candidates with the most votes are elected.

The **block vote** (BV) is essentially the same as the SNTV electoral system except that individuals now have as many votes as there are seats to be filled.[12] When presented with a list of candidates from various parties, voters can use as many or as few of their votes as they wish; however, they can give only one vote to any one candidate. The candidates with the most votes are elected.[13] This system was used in the two-member districts in United Kingdom legislative elections until their complete abolition in the 1950s and is still used for some local elections in England and Wales. It is currently used in such countries as Kuwait, Laos, Lebanon, Mauritius, Syria, and Tonga. One disadvantage of the BV worth noting is that it has the potential to produce extremely disproportional outcomes if voters allocate their votes to candidates from the same party. In Mauritius in 1982 and 1995, for example, the opposition party won all of the legislative seats with just 64 percent and 65 percent of the votes, respectively (Reynolds, Reilly, and Ellis 2005, 44).

> The **party block vote** is used in multimember districts in which voters cast a single party-centered vote for their party of choice. The party with the most votes wins all of the district seats.

Like the block vote, the **party block vote** (PBV) is employed in multimember districts. The difference is that individuals in the PBV have only a single vote and they allocate this to a list of party candidates rather than an individual candidate. In effect, voters are choosing the party or list of people that they want to win all of the district seats. The party that obtains the most votes in a PBV system wins all of the seats; all of the candidates on the party list are elected. The PBV is a potentially useful electoral system for those political actors who wish to encourage minority representation. Consider the use of the PBV in the East African country of Djibouti. Each party list in Djibouti must, by law, include a mix of candidates from different ethnic groups. By making this a requirement, voters in Djibouti are essentially forced to elect candidates from minority ethnic groups that they might never have chosen to elect if they had been able to vote for individual candidates rather than party lists. It is important to note, though, that the increased representation of minority groups is not inherent to the PBV; instead, it arises because the PBV is combined with a law requiring parties to have minority candidates on the party lists. Without such a law, the PBV is likely to produce highly disproportional results that are harmful to minority groups. Other countries that employ the PBV to elect all or significant portions of their legislatures include Cameroon, Chad, and Singapore.

---

12. If individuals have multiple votes but not as many as there are seats available, then the electoral system is referred to as the limited vote. This is the electoral system used to elect the legislature in Gibraltar.

13. This helps to explain why the block vote is sometimes referred to as plurality-at-large voting.

PROPORTIONAL ELECTORAL SYSTEMS

The rationale behind most **proportional,** or **proportional representation, electoral systems** is to consciously reduce the disparity between a party's share of the vote and its share

> A **proportional,** or **proportional representation, electoral system** is a quota- or divisor-based electoral system employed in multimember districts.

of the seats. In other words, the goal of proportional representation (PR) systems is to produce proportional outcomes—if a party wins 10 percent of the vote, it should win 10 percent of the seats; if it wins 20 percent of the vote, it should win 20 percent of the seats, and so on. This proportionality should exist both within districts and in the nation as a whole. This has led some scholars to define PR systems as those that produce proportional outcomes (Cox 1997). As we noted earlier, however, defining electoral systems in terms of the outcome that they produce rather than in terms of how they work—their mechanics—is problematic. One reason for this is that PR systems differ in the extent to which they produce proportional outcomes; some are more proportional than others. Indeed, it is even possible, under some circumstances, for a majoritarian electoral system to regularly produce more proportional outcomes than a PR system (Barkan 1995). A second reason is that we often want to explain the proportionality of an electoral outcome in terms of the type of electoral system that is being used. If we have already defined electoral systems in terms of the proportionality that they produce, we would be engaging in circular reasoning. For these reasons, we might want to define PR systems without reference to their relative ability or inability to produce proportional outcomes. So how should we define a PR system? Well, all PR systems share two things in common. One is that they employ multimember districts. This is basically because it is impossible to divide a single seat proportionally. The second is that they use either a quota or a divisor to determine who is elected in each district. As we will see, a quota or a divisor essentially determines the number of votes that a candidate or party needs in order to win a seat. In sum, then, we can define a proportional electoral system as a quota- or divisor-based system that is employed in multimember districts.[14] Although there are important variations among proportional systems, they are typically divided into the two main types illustrated in Figure 12.1: list proportional representation (list PR) systems and the single transferable vote (STV).

Many scholars have argued that proportional electoral systems have a number of advantages over majoritarian ones (Lijphart 1999). Perhaps the main advantage of PR systems is that they tend to produce a more accurate translation of votes into seats. In other words, they tend to produce more proportional outcomes. This means that PR systems avoid the possi-

---

14. Some majoritarian systems can be considered quota-based systems. For example, the majority-runoff TRS and the AV all require the winning candidate to obtain the quota of an absolute majority in order to win a seat. However, all but one of these quota-based majoritarian systems are employed in single-member districts. The one exception is the electoral system employed in Mali, where the party block vote with an absolute majority requirement is used in a two-round format in multimember districts. To avoid any ambiguity that might arise from the one case of Mali, we could define PR systems as "non-majoritarian" electoral systems that employ quotas or divisors to allocate seats in multimember districts.

bility that a party wins a large percentage of the vote but few legislative seats. Recall that this was one of the possible anomalies with majoritarian systems. It also means that small parties are able to win representation in proportion to their size. As a result, minorities are likely to be better represented in a PR system than in a majoritarian one. The fact that small parties have a greater chance of winning seats means that individuals face weaker incentives to vote strategically. As a result, electoral outcomes in PR systems should be a more accurate reflection of voters' sincere preferences. Arguably, it is also the case that individuals are more likely to turn out and vote in PR systems because they know that their votes are less likely to be wasted (Blais and Carty 1990; Blais and Dobrzynska 1998).

Some have argued that PR systems are all but essential for ethnically and religiously divided societies (Lijphart 1990, 1991). PR makes it easy for social groups to organize into ethnic and religious parties that can obtain legislative representation in proportion to their size. This, in turn, produces legislatures that reflect all the significant segments of society and leads to coalition governments based on power-sharing arrangements. The implicit assumption here, of course, is that the different ethnic groups will ultimately choose to work together in the legislature and the government. The notion that PR systems are essential for stability and democratic rule in divided societies is challenged by a set of scholars that advocates the use of preferential voting systems such as the alternative vote and the supplementary vote (Horowitz 1985, 1991; Reilly 1997, 2001). These scholars note that PR systems essentially replicate societal divisions in the legislature without creating incentives for cooperation and accommodation across the different ethnic parties. In contrast, they argue that preferential voting systems encourage political parties to make broadly based centrist appeals beyond their core set of supporters because they know that their electoral success is likely to depend on the transfer of preference votes from other ethnic groups. In effect, one can think of the choice as being between replicating ethnic divisions in the legislature and hoping that political leaders will cooperate after the election, and creating institutional incentives that seek to weaken or even transcend the political salience of ethnicity altogether. One complaint made of preferential voting systems like the AV and SV is that they are majoritarian and produce disproportional outcomes (Lijphart 1997). As we will see, however, an alternative preferential voting system that works in multimember districts and produces relatively proportional outcomes is the single transferable vote.

Other scholars have offered more general criticisms of proportional electoral systems. One of the most common is that they tend to produce coalition governments. As we noted earlier, it is often difficult to hold political parties accountable in coalition governments because it is hard to identify who is responsible for policy and, hence, who to hold accountable at election time. Even if those responsible for policy could be identified, it is still difficult to hold them accountable because parties that lose significant numbers of votes frequently make it back into coalition governments anyway. As the empirical evidence we presented in Chapter 11 indicates, coalition governments are also more unstable than the single-party majority governments that are typically produced by majoritarian electoral systems. Another criticism of PR systems is that they allow small, extremist parties to win representation. This is frequently seen as problematic. For example, some have argued that the existence of extremist parties, such as the Nazi Party in the Weimar Republic, undermines democracy. A third criticism is that small parties in PR systems frequently have a strong role in the government formation process and receive concessions that are disproportionate to their actual level of support in the electorate. It is rare for parties to obtain a majority of the legislative seats in PR systems, so large parties often rely on the support of some smaller party to get into government. These smaller parties can often use their leverage to wring concessions from the larger party. Some of these concessions may be quite radical and lack the support of an electoral majority. In Israel, for example, ultra-religious parties have won support for many of their policies by threatening to pull out of the government. A fourth criticism is that PR systems create a weak link between constituents and their representatives, because no single representative is responsible for policy in a given district. Voters might also wonder which of the elected representatives from their districts actually represent them.

List PR Systems

How do proportional electoral systems actually work? We start by looking at list PR systems. In a **list PR system** each party presents a list of candidates in each multimember district. Parties then receive seats in proportion to their overall share of the votes. Despite obvious similarities, list systems differ in important ways. These differences include (a) the precise formula for allocating seats to parties, (b) the district magnitude and the use of higher electoral tiers, (c) the use of electoral thresholds, and (d) the type of party list that is employed (Gallagher, Laver, and Mair 2005, 354). We discuss each of these in turn.

> In a **list PR system,** each party presents a list of candidates for a multimember district. Parties receive seats in proportion to their overall share of the votes.

Electoral Formulas: Quotas and Divisors

All proportional electoral systems either employ quotas or divisors to determine how many seats each party wins. In the quota system the **quota** indicates the number of votes that guarantees a party a seat in a particular district.

> A **quota** is the number of votes that guarantees a party a seat in a particular electoral district.

Four different quotas are in common use around the world: Hare, Droop, Imperiali, and Reinforced Imperiali.[15] A quota, $Q(n)$, is defined as:

$$Q(n) = \frac{V_d}{M_d + n},$$

where V_d is the total number of valid votes in district d, M_d is the number of seats available in district d, and n is the modifier of the quota. When $n = 0$, the system employs the Hare

---

15. The Hare quota is sometimes referred to as the Hare-Niemeyer quota or the simple quota. It was first invented in the United States to apportion seats among the states; it was originally called the Hamilton quota. The Droop quota is sometimes referred to as the Hagenbach-Bischoff quota.

quota; when $n = 1$, the system employs the Droop quota; when $n = 2$, the system employs the Imperiali quota; and when $n = 3$, the system employs the Reinforced Imperiali quota. For example, the Hare quota in an electoral district with 10 seats and 100,000 valid votes would be 10,000. This means that a political party obtains a seat for every 10,000 votes that it wins. The Droop quota in the same electoral district would be 9,091 votes, the Imperiali quota would be 8,333 votes, and the Reinforced Imperiali quota would be 7,692.

We now provide an example of how votes are translated into seats in a list PR system that employs the Hare quota system. Table 12.7 illustrates the election results for a ten-seat district in which 100,000 valid votes are split among parties A through F. How many seats does each party win? As we already illustrated, the Hare quota in this case is 10,000. Because Party A has 47,000 votes, it has 4.7 full quotas. This means that it automatically receives four seats. Following the same logic, Parties B, C, and D all automatically win one seat. You'll have noticed that we have allocated only seven of the ten seats available in this district so far. What happens to the three "remainder" seats? How are these seats allocated?

The issue of remainder seats arises with all list PR systems that use quotas to allocate seats. Three different methods are employed to allocate these seats: largest remainder (LR), highest average (HA), and modified highest average (mHA). By far the most common is the largest remainder method. Table 12.8 illustrates how the largest remainder method works in our sample district. After all of the automatic seats are allocated, we calculate the fraction of a Hare quota that was left unused (remainder) by each party. The first remainder seat is then allocated to the party with the largest remainder. Thus, Party A wins the first remainder seat because its remainder (0.7) is the largest. The second remainder seat is then allocated to the party with the next largest remainder. The remainder seats are allocated in this way until all of the district seats have been allocated. Thus, the total number of seats won by each party in a district is the sum of their automatic and remainder seats. As Table 12.8 illustrates, Party A wins five seats, Party B wins two seats, and Parties C, D, and E each win one seat. Countries that use the Hare quota with largest remainders include Colombia, Honduras, Namibia, and Sierra Leone.

TABLE 12.7	Translating Votes into Seats Using the Hare Quota						
	Party A	Party B	Party C	Party D	Party E	Party F	Total
Votes	47,000	16,000	15,800	12,000	6,100	3,100	100,000
Seats							10
Quota							10,000
Votes/quota	4.7	1.6	1.58	1.2	0.61	0.31	
Automatic seats	4	1	1	1	0	0	7
Remainder seats							3

| TABLE 12.8 | **Hare Quota with Largest Remainders** | | | | | | |

	Party A	Party B	Party C	Party D	Party E	Party F	Total
Votes	47,000	16,000	15,800	12,000	6,100	3,100	100,000
Seats							10
Quota							10,000
Votes/quota	4.7	1.6	1.58	1.2	0.61	0.31	
Automatic seats	4	1	1	1	0	0	7
Remainder	0.7	0.6	0.58	0.2	0.61	0.31	
Remainder seats	1	1	0	0	1	0	3
Total seats	5	2	1	1	1	0	10

In Table 12.9, we illustrate what would have happened in our sample district if we had employed the highest average method to allocate the remainder seats. The highest average method requires that the number of votes won by each party be divided by the number of automatic seats that they obtain.[16] This gives the average number of votes "paid" by each party for the automatic seats that they won. The highest average method then allocates the remainder seats to the parties that paid the most votes (highest average) for their seats. As Table 12.9 illustrates, Party B gets the first remainder seat because it paid 16,000 votes for its one seat; Party C gets the second remainder seat, and Party D gets the third. Countries that use the Hare quota with the highest average method include Benin and Brazil.

| TABLE 12.9 | **Hare Quota with Highest Average Remainders** | | | | | | |

	Party A	Party B	Party C	Party D	Party E	Party F	Total
Votes	47,000	16,000	15,800	12,000	6,100	3,100	100,000
Seats							10
Quota							10,000
Votes/quota	4.7	1.6	1.58	1.2	0.61	0.31	
Automatic seats	4	1	1	1			7
Votes/Automatic seats	11,750	16,000	15,800	12,000	0	0	
Remainder seats	0	1	1	1	0	0	3
Total seats	4	2	2	2	0	0	10

16. The modified highest average method for allocating remainder seats is basically the same except that it requires the number of votes won by each party to be divided by the number of automatic seats plus one. Although no countries use the modified highest average method with the Hare quota, Luxembourg uses it in combination with the Droop quota.

A **divisor,** or **highest average, system** divides the total number of votes won by each party in a district by a series of numbers (divisors) to obtain quotients. District seats are then allocated according to which parties have the highest quotients.

A list PR system that does not employ quotas to translate votes into seats is known as a **divisor,** or **highest average, system.** Three divisor systems are commonly employed around the world: d'Hondt, Sainte-Laguë, and Modified Sainte-Laguë.[17] In divisor systems, the total number of votes won by each party in a district is divided by a series of numbers called divisors to give quotients. District seats are then allocated according to which parties have the highest quotients.

To illustrate how these systems work, we apply the d'Hondt method to the same ten-seat district that we used to examine quota systems. The results are shown in Table 12.10. Under the d'Hondt system, we divide the total number of votes won by each party by 1, 2, 3, 4, 5, and so on to obtain a series of quotients.[18] The ten largest quotients are shown in boldface type. The exact order in which the ten district seats are allocated among these ten quotients is shown by the numbers in parentheses next to them. For example, Party A receives the first and second seat, Party B wins the third seat, Party C wins the fourth seat, Party A the fifth seat, and so on. Unlike quota systems, it is easy to see that divisor systems do not leave any remainder seats. The final allocation of the ten district seats is five to Party A, two each to Party B and Party C, and one to Party D. The d'Hondt system is the most common divisor system and is used by Argentina, Bulgaria, the Dominican Republic, Portugal, Turkey, and others.

TABLE 12.10	**Translating Votes into Seats Using the d'Hondt System**						
	Party A	**Party B**	**Party C**	**Party D**	**Party E**	**Party F**	**Total**
Votes	47,000	16,000	15,800	12,000	6,100	3,100	100,000
Seats							10
Votes/1	**47,000 (1)**	**16,000 (3)**	**15,800 (4)**	**12,000 (6)**	6,100	3,100	
Votes/2	**23,500 (2)**	**8,000 (9)**	**7,900 (10)**	6,000	3,050	1,550	
Votes/3	**15,666 (5)**	5,333	5,266	4,000	2,033	1,033	
Votes/4	**11,750 (7)**	4,000	3,950	3,000	1,525	775	
Votes/5	**9,400 (8)**	3,200	3,160	2,400	1,220	620	
Total seats	5	2	2	1	0	0	10

Note: The numbers in parentheses indicate the order in which the ten seats in the district are allocated among the parties.

---

17. Like the Hare quota, these divisor systems were first invented in the United States to apportion seats among the states and districts. D'Hondt was known as the Jefferson Method and Sainte-Laguë was known as the Webster Method (Young 1994).

18. The general formula for the d'Hondt quotient is $V / (S + 1)$, where V is the total number of valid votes won by a party list and S is the total number of seats allocated to the party so far (S is initially 0 for all parties). Whichever party has the highest quotient gets the next seat to be allocated and then its quotient is recalculated given its new seat total.

The Sainte-Laguë system works in a similar way except that the divisors are different. Under the Sainte-Laguë system, the votes of each party are divided by 1, 3, 5, 7, and so on to obtain the quotients.[19] The Sainte-Laguë system is currently employed for legislative elections in Latvia. The divisors in the Modified Sainte-Laguë system, currently used for legislative elections in Sweden, are 1.4, 3, 5, 7, 9, and so on.

The electoral formulas used to allocate seats to parties in list PR systems differ in their proportionality; some produce a more proportional translation of votes into seats than others (Lijphart 1986; Gallagher 1991, 1992; Benoit 2000). Another way to think about this is that some proportional formulas help small parties more than others. Although the proportionality of an electoral outcome depends to some extent on the distribution of votes given to the parties in a district, a widely accepted overall ranking of the different proportional formulas is shown in Table 12.11. As you can see, the Hare and Droop quotas with largest remainders are the most proportional; the d'Hondt divisor and Imperiali quota systems are the least proportional. All of these systems are more proportional than SMDP systems.

District Magnitude and Higher Electoral Tiers

The different formulas used to translate votes into seats clearly affect the proportionality of an electoral system. The factor that political scientists generally recognize as the most important factor influencing the proportionality of an electoral system, however, is the district magnitude (Rae 1967; Taagepera and Shugart 1989; Lijphart 1994; Cox 1997). Recall that the district magnitude is the number of representatives that are elected in a district. Electoral systems are more proportional when the district magnitude is large. This is because smaller parties are much more likely to win seats when the district magnitude is large. For example, a party would need to win more than 25 percent of the vote to guarantee winning a seat in a three-seat district, but it would need to win only a little more than 10 percent of the vote

TABLE 12.11	**The Proportionality of Proportional Electoral System Formulas**
Formula	**Proportionality**
Hare LR	
Droop LR	
Sainte-Laguë	
Imperiali LR	
Modified Sainte-Laguë	
d'Hondt	
Imperiali HA	

19. The general formula for the quotient is $V / (2S + 1)$, where V and S are the same as before. Whichever party has the highest quotient gets the next seat to be allocated and then its quotient is recalculated given its new seat total.

to guarantee winning a seat in a nine-seat district. One thing to note is that the electoral outcome is likely to be disproportional whenever the district magnitude is small, irrespective of the particular formula used to translate votes into seats. It is for this reason that political scientists argue that the district magnitude is the most important factor for the proportionality of the electoral system.

Although all PR systems use multimember districts, the average size of these districts—the average district magnitude—can vary quite a lot from one country to another. At one extreme are the Netherlands and Slovakia, who elect all 150 of their legislators in a single national district. At the other extreme is Chile, which elects all its legislators in sixty two-seat districts. Other countries have district magnitudes of varying size between these two extremes. Countries with low average district magnitudes include Chile (2.00), Benin (3.50), Cape Verde (3.79), and the Dominican Republic (5.00). Countries with high average district magnitudes include the Netherlands (150.00), Slovakia (150.00), Israel (120.00), Brazil (19.00), and Indonesia (17.11).

In addition to the proportionality of the electoral system, the district magnitude also affects the strength of the linkage between elected representatives and their constituency. As district magnitude increases and with it the geographical size of the district, the linkage between representatives and their voters is likely to weaken. Some countries have attempted to provide a relatively strong link between representatives and voters as well as high levels of proportionality by allocating seats in two **electoral tiers.** How does this work? Typically, some seats are allocated at the constituency level in small districts in an attempt to create a clear connection between the representatives and the voters. In addition, some supplemental seats are kept aside to be allocated

An **electoral tier** is a level at which votes are translated into seats. The lowest tier is the district or constituency level. Higher tiers are constituted by grouping together different lower tier constituencies; they are typically at the regional or national level.

in some higher electoral tier above the constituency level, normally at the regional or national level. These "higher tier" seats are distributed among those parties that do not receive their fair or proportional share of the seats at the constituency level. In other words, they go to parties that earn fewer seats than their share of the votes would suggest is appropriate. The way this works is that each party's votes that are not used to obtain seats at the constituency level are gathered up and pooled in the higher tier; the supplemental seats are then allocated among the parties on the basis of these "unused votes." As an example, about 11 percent of the legislative seats in Sweden are allocated in a national tier to parties and cartels whose share of the seats at the constituency level is less than their share of the votes. Likewise, parties in Venezuela that are underrepresented in the allocation of constituency-level seats relative to their national vote share are eligible to receive a limited number of compensatory seats (Golder 2005, 111).[20]

---

20. In our examples, the two electoral tiers are "linked" in the sense that the allocation of seats in the higher tier depends on the seats received in the lower tier (Shvetsova 1999). This is by far the most common situation for proportional electoral systems that employ multiple tiers (Golder 2005). Still, a few countries like Poland and Guatemala employ multiple electoral tiers that are unlinked. The level of proportionality produced by these unlinked systems is not usually as high as that produced by the linked systems. The reason is that unlinked systems are constrained in their ability to increase proportionality because they do not take account of the unused votes in the lower tier.

Electoral Thresholds

All proportional electoral systems have an **electoral threshold** that stipulates the minimum percentage of votes that a party must win, either nationally or in a particular district, to gain representation. This threshold is either legally imposed (**formal threshold**) or it exists as a mathematical property of the electoral system (**natural threshold**). The size of the electoral threshold has a strong effect on the proportionality of the electoral system.[21]

> An **electoral threshold** is the minimum level of support a party needs to obtain representation. A **natural threshold** is a mathematical by-product of the electoral system. A **formal threshold** is explicitly written into the electoral law.

Natural thresholds are not written into electoral laws; instead, they are a mathematical by-product of certain features of the electoral system, such as the district magnitude. For example, any candidate in the Netherlands must win more than 0.67 percent of the national vote, not because this is legally stipulated somewhere, but simply because there are 150 legislative seats allocated in a single national district, that is, 100 percent $\div$ 150 = 0.67 percent. All electoral systems have a natural threshold. In contrast to natural thresholds, formal thresholds are explicitly written into the electoral law. For example, political parties in Israel have had to win 2 percent of the national vote before they can win seats in the Knesset since 2003 (the natural threshold in Israel is only 0.83 percent). In Turkey, political parties must win more than 10 percent of the national vote before they can gain representation in parliament. In Poland, parties and coalitions must win 5 percent and 8 percent of the national vote, respectively, before they can win seats in the Sejm. Some countries have more complicated formal thresholds. For instance, political parties in Germany must win either 5 percent of the national vote *or* three constituency seats before they are eligible to win legislative seats. Formal thresholds always increase the disproportionality of an electoral system because the votes for parties that might otherwise have won representation are wasted.

Formal thresholds are often introduced in an attempt to reduce party system fragmentation by preventing very small parties from gaining representation. For example, the imposition of the 5 percent threshold in Germany was largely a response to the fractious and unstable party system of Weimar Germany in the interwar period. Similarly, many East European countries have imposed high formal thresholds in an attempt to reduce the number of parties and encourage the consolidation of a stable party system (Gallagher, Laver, and Mair 2006, 357). Although some countries would like to prevent all small parties from winning seats, others want to prevent only small *extremist* parties from gaining representation. One potential way to do this is to combine a formal threshold with a provision known as **apparentement.** Apparentement allows small parties to group together and form a cartel to contest

> **Apparentement** is the provision in a list PR system for two or more separate parties to reach an agreement that their votes will be combined for the purposes of seat allocation.

---

21. Majoritarian systems also have thresholds. For example, the requirement that the winning candidate obtain an absolute majority in AV systems can be considered an electoral threshold. Despite this, electoral thresholds are considered more of an issue in proportional systems because the underlying goal of these systems is to produce proportional outcomes.

elections. The parties in the cartel remain as separate entities on the ballot and campaign independently; however, the votes gained by each party are counted as if they belonged to the single cartel for the purposes of surpassing the threshold. To the extent that getting other parties to join a cartel will be more difficult for extremist parties, apparentement helps nonextremist small parties win a share of seats proportional to their support while making it difficult for extremist parties to win any representation. Apparentement is a provision employed in Israel and some countries in Latin America and Europe.

It should be noted that formal thresholds can have a significant effect on election outcomes. For example, there were so many parties that did not surpass the 10 percent threshold in the Turkish legislative elections of 2002 that fully 46 percent of all votes cast in these elections were wasted. Similarly, 34 percent of the votes cast in the Polish legislative elections of 1993 were wasted because of the 5 percent threshold for parties and 8 percent threshold for coalitions. In the Polish case, these wasted votes were crucial in allowing the former Communists to return to power only a few years after the collapse of communism in that country (Kaminski, Lissowski, and Swistak 1998). These examples from Turkey and Poland force us to think about whether the problems arising from formal thresholds (wasted votes and increased disproportionality) are more or less acceptable than the problems they are designed to solve (fragmented party systems).

Types of Party List

To this point we have discussed how seats are allocated between parties competing in multi-member districts. However, we know that parties present lists of candidates in each district. You may be wondering which candidates on the lists actually get the seats that their party wins. This depends on which of the three types of party list is being used: the **closed party list,** the **open party list,** or the **free party list.**

> In a **closed party list,** the order of candidates elected is determined by the party itself, and voters are not able to express a preference for a particular candidate. In an **open party list,** voters can indicate not just their preferred party but also their favored candidate within that party. In a **free party list,** voters have multiple votes that they can allocate either within a single party list or across different party lists.

In a closed party list, which is sometimes known as a nonpreferential or blocked list, the order of candidates elected is determined by the party itself, and voters are not able to express a preference for a particular candidate.

In a closed list system, political parties receive seats in proportion to the number of votes that they obtain using one of the formulas described earlier. The first seat won by the party goes to the candidate listed first on the party's list; the second seat goes to the second candidate, and so on. Thus, if a party wins four seats in a district, then the top four candidates on the list gain seats and the remaining candidates do not win any. In some cases, the ballot paper in a closed list system will contain the names of the individual candidates and their positions on the list, as with the Nicaraguan ballot paper illustrated in Figure 12.4. More frequently, though, ballot papers in closed list systems do not contain the names of individual candidates. Instead, the only information on the list is the party names and symbols, and perhaps a photograph of the party leader. As Figure 12.5 illustrates, this type of ballot paper was used in South Africa's 1994 legislative elections.

| FIGURE 12.4 | **Nicaraguan Closed List PR Ballot Paper** |

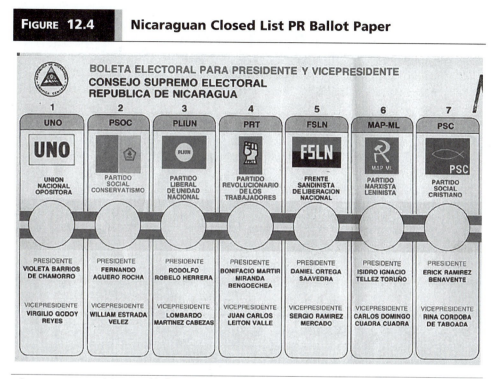

Source: www.unc.edu/~asreynol/ballot_pages/nicaragua.html

One of the potential advantages of closed party lists is that parties can more easily include some candidates, such as minority ethnic and linguistic candidates, or female candidates, who might otherwise have had difficulty getting elected. Of course, some voters may consider this potential advantage a disadvantage in that they are unable to choose the candidates that they most desire and may have to elect unpopular and undesirable candidates if they wish to vote for their preferred party.

Closed party lists are often preferred by the leaders of political parties because they provide a useful way of disciplining and rewarding candidates. Candidates that are important in the party hierarchy can be guaranteed relatively safe seats by being placed toward the top of the party list, whereas candidates who fail to toe the party line can be placed toward the bottom of the party list. Political parties tend to be more important than individual candidates in closed list systems for this reason.

In an open party list, which is sometimes known as a preferential or unblocked list, voters can indicate not just their preferred party but their favored candidate within that party. In most open list systems, it is up to the voter to choose whether to indicate her preferred candidate as well as her preferred party. If individuals simply vote for a party and do not indicate a preferred candidate, then the candidate-choice option of the ballot paper will obviously have little effect. If we look at Sweden and its open list system, we find that over 25 percent of Swedish voters regularly choose an individual candidate within a party list;

FIGURE 12.5 **South African Closed List PR Ballot Paper**

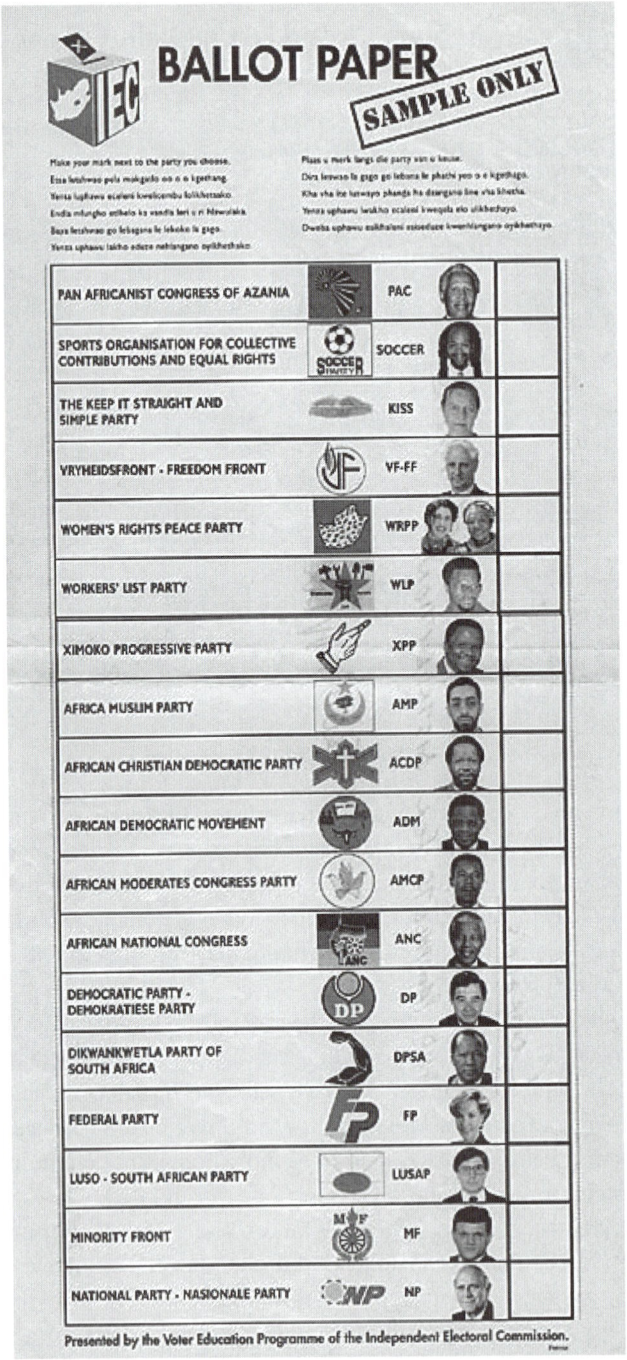

Source: www.unc.edu/~asreynol/ballot_pages/south_africa.html

many of these candidates would not have been elected had the party list been closed (Reynolds, Reilly, and Ellis 2005, 84).

Figure 12.6 illustrates an open list ballot from the 1994 legislative elections in Denmark. In Danish elections, voters cast a single vote either for their preferred party (party vote) or for their preferred candidate from among that party's list of candidates (preferential or personal vote). The total number of seats won by each party is determined equally by both types of votes. Each individual candidate is credited with all of the personal votes given to him plus a share of the votes cast for his party. The order in which the party's seats are allocated among the individual candidates is determined by the number of total votes (personal and party) that are credited to them.

| **FIGURE 12.6** | **Danish Open List PR Ballot Paper** |

Nordjyllands amts 2. kreds
Folketingsvalget 1990

A. Socialdemokratiet
Ole Stavad
Martin Glerup
Holger Graversen
Ilse Hansen
Arne Jensen
Frank Jensen
J. Risgaard Knudsen
Bjarne Laustsen
Kaj Poulsen

B. Det Radikale Venstre
Lars Schönberg-Hemme
Bent Bundgaard
Marianne Jelved
Bent Jørgensen
Hans Larsen-Ledet
Axel E. Mortensen
Lars Lammert Nielsen
Ove Nielsen
Preben Pedersen

C. Det Konservative Folkeparti
Karsten Frederiksen
Niels Ahlmann-Ohlsen
H. P. Clausen
Suzanne Kogsbøll
Jørgen Lund
Allan Nygaard
Gerda Thymann Pedersen
Per Seeberg
Søren Pflug

D. Centrum-Demokraterne
Peter Duetoft
Gregers Folke Gregersen
Bodil Melgaard Haakonsen
Anton Jepsen
Tove Kattrup
Hartvig Kjeldgaard
Bent V. Villadsen

E. Danmarks Retsforbund
Knud Christensen
Aase Bak-Nielsen
Jane Dyrdal
Karen Hansen
Ejnar Pedersen
Ole Thielemann
Egon Thomsen

Source: www.unc.edu/~asreynol/ballot_pages/denmark.html

Although voters normally have a choice in open list systems as to whether to vote for a candidate, this is not the case in all open list PR systems. For example, individuals have to vote for a party candidate in countries like Brazil, Finland, and the Netherlands. The total number of seats won by each party in these countries is determined by the total number of votes given to its candidates, and the order in which each party's candidates receive these seats is determined by the number of individual votes that they receive.

Open list systems clearly give voters greater freedom over their choice of candidates and weaken the control of party leaders over their party's candidates compared with closed list systems. A frequent consequence of open lists, though, is that they generate internal party fighting, because candidates from the same party are effectively competing with each other for the same votes. A result of this is that political candidates in open list systems have incentives to cultivate a personal vote rather than a party vote (Carey and Shugart 1995). A personal vote occurs when an individual votes based on the characteristics of a particular candidate rather than the characteristics of the party to which the candidate belongs. Building a personal vote is frequently associated in the United States with legislators bringing back pork-barrel projects to their single-member districts. As you can see, though, incentives to build personal votes also exist in multimember districts, where the election of candidates can depend on personal reputations in open list systems. In addition to internal party fighting, some scholars worry that open lists make it less likely that minority candidates will be elected. In Sri Lanka, for instance, majority Sinhalese parties tried to place minority Tamil candidates in winnable positions on their open party lists. These efforts at improving minority representation were rendered ineffective, however, when many voters deliberately voted for lower-placed Sinhalese candidates instead (Reynolds, Reilly, and Ellis 2005, 90).

Voters have even more flexibility in free list systems than in open list systems. This is because voters in free list systems have multiple votes that they can allocate to candidates either within a single party list or across different party lists as they see fit. The capacity to vote for candidates from different party lists—split voting—is known as **panachage** (Cox 1997, 43). In Luxembourg, voters can either cast their ballot for a party and accept the party's rank ordering of the candidates, or they can vote for as many individual candidates as there are seats available, irrespective of whether they come from the same party. Switzerland has a similar system with the added freedom that voters can give up to two of their votes to the same candidate. The capacity to give more than one vote for a single highly favored candidate is known as **cumulation.** Swiss parties simply present a list of names in no particular rank order (often alphabetically) and voters have a choice of (a) choosing a candidate from the list, (b) choosing a candidate twice from the list, (c) dropping a candidate from the list, (d) writing in one or more candidates from a different party list (up to two times each), or (e) voting for the party without revealing any preference for a particular individual candidate. The sole condition is that Swiss voters have only as many votes as there are seats available in their district. The seats allocated to each party are determined by the total number of votes won by

> **Panachage** is the ability to vote for candidates from different party lists. **Cumulation** is the capacity to give more than one vote to a single candidate.

the party. Seats are then given to individual party candidates based on the number of times their names appear on the party lists, including write-ins on other parties' lists.

Single Transferable Vote

The only proportional electoral system that does not employ a party list is the **single transferable vote.** This electoral system was invented by the English lawyer, Thomas Hare, in 1857 and is currently used to elect the Australian Senate and the Irish and Maltese legislatures. The STV is used in multimember districts, and voters must rank at least one candidate in order of preference. Voters usually do this by placing a number next to the name of the candidates, indicating whether they are the voter's first choice, second choice, third choice, and so on. Because voters indicate their preference ordering of competing candidates, the STV is another form of preferential voting like the alternative vote, supplementary vote, and Borda Count that we discussed earlier.

The **single transferable vote** is a preferential candidate-centered PR electoral system used in multimember districts. Candidates that surpass a specified quota of first-preference votes are immediately elected. In successive counts, votes from eliminated candidates and surplus votes from elected candidates are reallocated to the remaining candidates until all the seats are filled.

In order to win a seat, candidates must obtain a particular quota or threshold of votes. Votes initially go to each voter's most preferred candidate. If an insufficient number of candidates obtain the necessary quota to fill all of the district seats, then the candidate with the lowest number of first-choice votes is eliminated. The votes from the eliminated candidate, as well as any surplus votes from candidates that are already elected, are then reallocated to the remaining candidates. This process continues until enough candidates meet the quota to fill all of the district seats. The exact process by which the STV system transfers votes and the exact size of the quota used to determine the winning candidates vary from country to country. Although the Hare quota is sometimes employed, it turns out that the most common quota is the Droop quota. If you think that the STV system sounds familiar, you would be right: it is essentially the same as the alternative vote but applied in multimember districts.

The STV is quite a complicated electoral system and so an example of how it works might help. Our specific example illustrates how the STV works when a Droop quota is used with the Clarke method for reallocating surplus votes.[22] This is the STV system employed to elect the Australian Senate. Imagine that there are five candidates—Bruce, Shane, Sheila, Glen, and Ella—competing in a three-seat district containing twenty voters. Table 12.12 illustrates how the twenty voters marked their preferences on their ballots; each icon represents a ballot and each type of icon reflects a particular preference ordering. Thus, four people (👤) placed Bruce first and Shane second; two people (👤) placed Shane first and Bruce second, and so on. One thing to note is that not everybody provided a complete preference ordering of all the candidates. For example, two people (👤 and 👤)marked only their first preferences.[23]

---

22. There are a variety of different ways of reallocating surplus votes—Hare's method, Cincinnati method, Clarke method, senatorial rules, and Meek's method (Tideman and Richardson 2000, 248–258).

23. In the actual elections to the Australian Senate, individuals must rank order all of the candidates if they want their vote to count.

TABLE 12.12	**Results from Twenty Ballots in an STV Election**

Voting round					
1st	Bruce	Shane	Sheila	Sheila	Glen	Ella
2nd	Shane	Bruce	Glen	Ella		
3rd			Ella	Glen		

Note: Each icon represents a ballot and each type of icon reflects a particular rank ordering of the candidates.

As we noted earlier, a Droop quota is normally calculated by dividing the total number of valid votes in a district by the number of seats plus one. If the Droop quota turns out to be a whole number, however, as is the case here, then a one is added to it. Thus, in our example of a three-seat district and twenty voters, the Droop quota is 20 / (3 + 1)+1 = 6. In other words, each candidate must win six votes in order to be elected. We can now begin examining how votes are translated into seats in an STV system. The whole process is outlined in Table 12.13.

TABLE 12.13	**The STV in a Three-Seat District with Twenty Voters**

	Candidates					
Voting round	Bruce	Shane	Sheila	Glen	Ella	Result
1st						Sheila is elected and Sheila's surplus votes are reallocated
2nd						Shane is eliminated
3rd						Bruce is elected
4th						Ella is eliminated and Glen is elected

Note: Each icon represents a ballot and each type of icon reflects a particular rank ordering of the candidates. See Table 12.12 to see the particular rank ordering of the candidates associated with each icon.

The first thing to do is to see if any candidates obtained a Droop quota in the first-choice votes. If they did, they are automatically elected. Because Sheila has twelve first-choice votes, she is elected in the first round. Next, it is necessary to reallocate any surplus votes from already elected candidates to the remaining candidates. In the example, Sheila has six surplus votes, that is, she received six votes more than she needed to be elected. As we noted at the beginning, we are going to use the Clarke method for reallocating these six surplus votes to the remaining candidates. To do this, it is necessary to separate Sheila's ballots into bundles based on who the second-choice candidates are. Because those who voted for Sheila list either Glen 👤 or Ella 👤 as their second choice, there would be two bundles. Because the eight 👤 votes make up two-thirds of Sheila's twelve total votes, two-thirds of Sheila's surplus votes (four) go to Glen. Because the four 👤 votes make up one-third of Sheila's total votes, one-third of Sheila's surplus votes (two) go to Ella. After reallocating these surplus votes to Glen and Ella, votes are recounted a second time to see if any new candidate has now obtained the Droop quota. In our example, no candidate meets the Droop quota in the second count. As a result, the next step is to eliminate the candidate with the lowest number of votes (Shane) and reallocate his votes to the remaining candidates. Because the second choice of Shane's voters is Bruce, Shane's two votes are reallocated to Bruce. Votes are now recounted a third time to see if any candidate now meets the Droop quota. As you can see, Bruce meets the Droop quota on the third count because he has six votes and he is, therefore, elected. If there were any surplus votes for Bruce, then we would reallocate them among the remaining candidates. In this case, though, Bruce has no surplus votes. To this point, we have filled two of the three district seats. No one else meets the Droop quota, so the candidate with the next lowest number of votes (Ella) is eliminated. Because there is only one candidate left, there is no need for a fourth recount; Glen is the third and last candidate to be elected. Thus, the STV with the Droop quota and the Clarke method for reallocating surplus votes results in the election of Sheila, Bruce, and Glen in this three-seat district.

How does the STV system compare with other electoral systems? One of the advantages of STV systems is that they provide voters with an opportunity to convey a lot of information about their preferences (Bowler and Grofman 2000, 1). Like other preferential voting systems, individuals in STV systems have the opportunity to rank order all of the candidates rather than simply voting yes or no to one (or more) of the candidates as in most majoritarian and list PR systems. Because an individual's preferences end up being reallocated whenever a candidate is elected or eliminated, the STV minimizes wasted votes. STV systems also allow individuals to vote for candidates from different parties. This means that individuals can vote for candidates who share a similar policy stance even though the candidates may come from different parties. This might be useful in cases in which an issue cuts across traditional party lines, such as abortion. With the exception of those that allow for panachage, the vast majority of list PR systems do not allow this type of cross-party voting. Another advantage is that the STV is a proportional electoral system that does not require the existence of political parties—individuals vote for candidates, not parties. This could be important in countries in which political parties are yet to organize or political elites do not wish to allow the formation of political parties (see Box 12.5 on electoral system choice in Poland on pages 523–524). STV systems are also advantageous in that they give voters total control over how their votes will be used; a candidate cannot receive support from a voter unless that voter expresses a preference for her. As Gallagher, Laver, and Mair (2006, 360–361) note, "This sets STV apart from all list systems, where a preference given to one candidate of a party might end up helping another candidate of the same party—a candidate whom, perhaps, the voter does not like. Under STV, voters can continue to give preferences after their first, knowing that a preference given to a candidate can never help that person against a candidate to whom the voter gave a higher preference."

Like other preferential voting systems, an additional advantage of STV systems is that they create incentives for candidates to appeal to groups outside their core set of supporters and campaign on broadly based centrist platforms. This is because a candidate's election may well depend on the transfer of votes from different social groups. Recall that it is for this reason that some scholars advocate the use of preferential voting systems in divided societies (Horowitz 1985, 1991; Reilly 1997, 2001). One criticism of the preferential voting systems that we have examined to this point, such as the alternative and supplementary votes, is that they are majoritarian and can produce highly disproportional outcomes (Lijphart 1997). A benefit of the STV, though, is that it works in multimember districts and typically produces more proportional outcomes than majoritarian systems. Thus, the STV holds out the possibility of combining relatively proportional outcomes with incentives for candidates to make cross-cleavage appeals and build electorates that bridge religious and ethnic lines.

Another advantage of the STV highlighted by its supporters is that it tends to create a strong link between representatives and their constituents. Since the STV is a candidate-rather than a party-centered system, candidates have an incentive to build personal votes and engage in constituency service. For example, there is evidence that the STV in Ireland leads to an emphasis on local campaigning, a focus on district work and local concerns, and a low importance attached to ideology and national issues (Katz 1980). In this respect, the STV "involves a notion of the connection between the individual representative and his or her constituency that is much closer to the notion of representation implicit in the first past the post [SMDP] system than to the notion of representation of parties underlying list systems" (Sinnott 1992, 68). Another benefit of STV systems is that they reduce the incentive for voters to behave strategically, because their votes are less likely to be wasted. As with any electoral system, though, strategic concerns are never entirely absent. In an attempt to strategically channel the transfer of votes in an STV system so as to benefit their candidates as much as possible, parties in Ireland hand out "candidate cards" in a similar way to how parties hand out how-to-vote cards in the AV system used in Australia.

Despite these advantages, the STV system has its critics. One criticism is that it tends to weaken the internal unity of parties and make them less cohesive. Because voters are allowed to rank order candidates from the same party, these candidates have incentives to criticize and campaign against one another. As Farrell and McAllister (2000, 18) note, "[T]he problems of intraparty factionalism and excessive attention to localist, particularistic concerns [in Ireland] are attributed to politicians who must compete with each other for votes on ordinally ranked STV ballots." You will perhaps recall that the single nontransferable vote also created incentives for intraparty factionalism. It is worth noting, though, that the incentives for factionalism are weaker under the STV because candidates can expect to receive votes from fellow party members who are eliminated. This means that candidates from the same party in an STV system do not want to harm each other too much.

A second criticism of the STV is that it is hard to operate in large districts. As a result, the system tends to produce outcomes that are not as proportional as those produced by list PR systems. For practical reasons, the STV is hard to operate in districts whose magnitude is greater than ten; the ballot paper could contain fifty or more names. In fact, the ballot for the Australian Senate in New South Wales in 1995 contained the names of ninety-nine candidates and was several feet long (Farrell and McAllister 2000, 29). It is difficult to believe that voters would have sufficient information to rank candidates beyond the first ten or so names on a ballot. For this reason, constituencies in STV systems tend to be relatively small. For example, the largest district magnitude in Ireland and Malta is five.

MIXED ELECTORAL SYSTEMS

A way to think about a **mixed electoral system** is that there are two electoral systems using different formulas running alongside each other. One electoral system uses a majoritarian formula to allocate seats, and the other uses a proportional formula. Thus, a mixed electoral system is one in which voters elect representatives through two different systems, one majoritarian and one proportional. Many mixed systems have more than one electoral tier, with majoritarian formulas employed in one tier and proportional formulas used in another. Multiple electoral tiers, however, are not a necessary characteristic of mixed electoral systems, as some have claimed (Shugart and Wattenberg 2001). Mixed systems can, and do, function in countries that have only one electoral tier. The defining characteristic of mixed systems is simply that they combine majoritarian and proportional electoral formulas in the same election. Although there are important variations among mixed systems, we can divide them into two main types: independent and dependent (see Figure 12.1).

> A **mixed electoral system** is one in which voters elect representatives through two different systems, one majoritarian and one proportional.

Independent Mixed Electoral Systems

An **independent mixed electoral system** is one in which the majoritarian and proportional components of the electoral system are implemented independently of one another. This type of mixed system is often referred to as a parallel system. The most common form of

> An **independent mixed electoral system** is one in which the application of one electoral formula does not depend on the outcome produced by the other.

independent mixed electoral system involves the use of majoritarian and proportional formulas in two separate electoral tiers. For example, Russia elects 225 of its legislators using an SMDP system at the constituency level and another 225 using list PR in a single district at the national level. The precise balance between "proportional" and "majoritarian" seats varies from country to country. Only Andorra, Russia, and the Ukraine have a 50-50 split (Reynolds, Reilly, and Ellis 2005, 104). Although in some countries, such as South Korea, individuals have only one vote, which is used for both parts of the electoral system, in other countries, such as Japan and Lithuania, they have two votes—one for the majoritarian component and one for the proportional component.

Table 12.14 illustrates how votes are translated into seats in an independent mixed electoral system with two electoral tiers. Two parties, A and B, are competing over ten seats. Five seats are allocated at the constituency level using an SMDP system, and five seats are allocated in a single district at the national level using some type of list PR system. Given the distribution of votes shown in Table 12.14, Party A wins eight seats. Why? First, it wins all five constituency seats because it came first in each constituency. Second, because Party A wins 60 percent of the party list vote, it wins 60 percent of the five seats allocated in the national tier, that is, three seats. As a result, Party A wins eight seats altogether. Party B wins 2 seats—it gets no constituency seats but it gets 40 percent of the five party list seats in the national tier, or two seats.

Although rare, some independent mixed systems involve the use of different electoral formulas in a single electoral tier. For example, Madagascar elects eighty-two legislators using an SMDP system in some constituencies and another seventy-eight legislators using list PR in other districts. Even rarer are independent mixed systems that use different electoral formulas in a single constituency. The Turkish electoral system did precisely that between 1987 and 1994. During this period, Turkey employed a "contingency mandate," in which the first seat in a constituency was allocated to the largest party, as in an SMDP system. The remaining seats were then allocated using a list PR system. In effect, the Turkish system gave a bonus seat to the largest party.

TABLE 12.14 **Translating Votes into Seats in an Independent Mixed Electoral System**

| | Votes won in each electoral district | | | | | | | Seats won | | |
	1	2	3	4	5	National district votes won	% of votes won	SMDP	List PR	Total
Party A	3,000	3,000	3,000	3,000	3,000	15,000	60	5	3	8
Party B	2,000	2,000	2,000	2,000	2,000	10,000	40	0	2	2
Total	5,000	5,000	5,000	5,000	5,000	25,000	100	5	5	10

Dependent Mixed Electoral Systems

A **dependent mixed electoral system** is one in which the application of the proportional formula is dependent on the distribution of seats or votes produced by the majoritarian formula.

> A **dependent mixed electoral system** is one in which the application of the proportional formula is dependent on the distribution of seats or votes produced by the majoritarian formula.

This is because the proportional component of the electoral system is used to compensate for any disproportionality produced by the majoritarian formula at the constituency level. This type of mixed system is sometimes referred to as a mixed member proportional (MMP) system. Dependent mixed electoral systems involve the use of majoritarian and proportional formulas in two separate electoral tiers. For example, Mexico elects 300 of its legislators using an SMDP system at the constituency level and another 200 using list PR in five 40-member districts at the regional level. Other countries that employ dependent mixed systems include Albania, Germany, and New Zealand.

In most dependent mixed electoral systems, such as those used in Germany and New Zealand, individuals have two votes. They cast their first vote for a representative at the constituency level (candidate vote) and their second vote for a party list in a higher electoral tier (party vote). These types of mixed dependent systems allow individuals to give their first vote to a constituency candidate from one party and to give their second vote to a different party if they wish. This is called split-ticket voting. In systems in which voters have only one vote, the vote for the constituency candidate also counts as a vote for that candidate's party.

In order to illustrate how votes are translated into seats in a dependent mixed electoral system, consider the example shown in Table 12.15. This is identical to the example shown in Table 12.14 except that our mixed system is now dependent rather than independent. The first thing that happens is that each party receives legislative seats in proportion to the total number of votes that they obtained nationally. This means that because Party A won 60 percent of the vote overall, it receives 60 percent of the party list seats, or six seats. And since Party B won 40 percent of the vote overall, it receives 40 percent of the party list seats, or four seats. We then look to see how many constituency seats each party won. In our example, Party A won all five constituency seats because it came first in each constituency. Party A already has five constituency seats, so it gets to keep only one of its six party list seats. Party B has no constituency seats, so it gets to keep all four of its party list seats. In effect, the party list seats "correct" or "compensate" for the fact that Party B won no seats at the district level even though it won 40 percent of the vote. Overall, then, Party A receives six seats (five constituency seats and one party list seat), and Party B gets four seats (no constituency seats and four party list seats). As you can see, the party list vote determines how many seats a party gets, whereas the candidate vote determines whether these seats will be constituency or party list seats. This particular version of the dependent mixed system is used in Germany and New Zealand.

If you compare the results in Tables 12.14 and 12.15, you'll notice that the election outcome is much more proportional in the dependent mixed electoral system than in the independent one even though the starting distribution of votes is exactly the same. This is to be expected, because the list PR component of dependent mixed systems is specifically designed

| TABLE 12.15 | Translating Votes into Seats in a Dependent Mixed Electoral System | | | | | | | | | |

	Votes won in each electoral district					National district votes won	% of votes won	Seats won		
	1	2	3	4	5			SMDP	List PR	Total
Party A	3,000	3,000	3,000	3,000	3,000	15,000	60	5	1	6
Party B	2,000	2,000	2,000	2,000	2,000	10,000	40	0	4	4
Total	5,000	5,000	5,000	5,000	5,000	25,000	100	5	5	10

to reduce the disproportionality created by the majoritarian component of the electoral system; this is not the case in independent mixed systems.

Two issues crop up in dependent mixed systems. First, some candidates compete for a constituency seat but are also placed on the party list. You may wonder what happens if a candidate wins a constituency seat but is also placed high enough on a party list that she could win a party list seat as well. In this circumstance, the candidate would keep the constituency seat, and her name would be crossed off the party list. Second, some parties win more constituency seats than is justified by their party list vote. An example is shown in Table 12.16. Three parties competed for ten legislative seats. Party B and Party C each won 30 percent of the vote and so get three party list seats. They did not win any constituency seats, so they get to keep all three of their party list seats. Party A won 40 percent of the vote and so gets four party list seats. Party A, however, won all five of the constituency seats. What happens now? Well, Party A loses all of its party lists seats but gets to keep all five of its constituency seats. Overall, then, Party A gets five constituency seats, and Party B and Party C each get three party list seats. You'll notice that the total number of allocated seats is eleven even though the original district magnitude was just ten. Because Party A won more constituency seats than its party list vote justified, the legislature in this example ends up being one seat larger than expected. This extra seat is known as an "overhang seat." This means that

| TABLE 12.16 | An Example of Overhang Seats | | | | | | | | | |

	Votes won in each electoral district					National district	%	Seats won		
	1	2	3	4	5			SMDP	List PR	Total
Party A	3,000	3,000	3,000	3,000	3,000	15,000	40	5	0	5
Party B	2,250	2,250	2,250	2,250	2,250	11,250	30	0	3	3
Party C	2,250	2,250	2,250	2,250	2,250	11,250	30	0	3	3
Total	7,500	7,500	7,500	7,500	7,500	37,500	100	5	6	11

the size of a legislature in a dependent mixed electoral system is not fixed and ultimately depends on the outcome of the election. In New Zealand's 2005 legislative elections, the fact that the Maori Party won 2.1 percent of the party vote entitled it to three legislative seats. Because it won four constituencies, however, it ended up with four seats. As a result, the New Zealand legislature had 121 seats instead of the normal 120.

In many respects, mixed electoral systems are an attempt to combine the positive attributes of both majoritarian and proportional systems. In particular, mixed electoral systems help produce proportional outcomes at the same time as ensuring that some elected representatives are linked to particular geographic districts. The extent to which mixed systems produce proportional outcomes is likely to depend on the institutional features that characterize them. As we have already seen, dependent mixed systems are likely to be more proportional than independent systems because the allocation of seats in the proportional component of the electoral system is specifically designed to counteract the distortions created by the majoritarian component. It is perhaps interesting to note that the vast majority of the new democracies in Eastern Europe did not adopt the dependent mixed electoral system of Germany, as is often assumed, but actually chose an independent mixed electoral system. Institutional features, such as the percentage of seats distributed by list PR, the size of the district magnitude used in the proportional component of the electoral system, and the proportional formula itself are likely to affect the degree of proportionality in independent mixed systems (Golder 2005).

Dependent mixed electoral systems produce outcomes as proportional as those found in pure list PR systems. As a result, they share many of the advantages and disadvantages of list PR systems that we have already discussed. Some issues arise that are specific to dependent mixed systems, though. One is that dependent mixed systems can create two classes of legislators—one that is responsible and accountable to a geographic constituency and one that is more beholden to the party. This can influence the cohesiveness of political parties (Reynolds, Reilly, and Ellis 2005, 95). In addition, there is some concern that individuals who have two votes in dependent mixed systems are unaware that it is their party vote rather than their candidate vote that ultimately determines the number of seats that each party wins in the legislature.

x 12.4

HUNGARY: THE WORLD'S MOST COMPLICATED ELECTORAL SYSTEM?

The electoral system used for Hungary's legislative elections has been described as the world's most complicated electoral system (Benoit 1996, 2005; Benoit and Schiemann 2001). Let us explain exactly how it works. There are three electoral tiers—a constituency tier, a regional tier, and a national tier—and candidates can compete simultaneously in all of them. Voters cast two ballots, one for an individual candidate in a single-member district at the constituency level and one for a closed party list in the regional tier. The 176 seats that are available at the constituency level are allocated using a majority-plurality TRS. If a candidate obtains an

Watched by her daughters, Anna, left, and Eva, right, local teacher Eva Toth, center, leaves the booth after casting her ballot during the first round of the third free democratic parliamentary elections polling station in Boldog, Hungary, some 50 kilometers west of Budapest, Sunday, May 10, 1998. There are about 8.1 million people with suffrage in Hungary.

absolute majority in the first round, then he is automatically elected. If no candidate obtains this number of votes, however, the top three candidates, as well as any candidate gaining more than 15 percent of the vote, are eligible to compete in a second round if they want. The candidate with the most votes in the second round is elected. This part of the electoral system is further complicated by the fact that if fewer than 50 percent of the eligible voters cast a ballot in the first round, then the whole constituency election is repeated in the second round. This occurred in thirty-one of the districts in the 1998 elections.

The regional tier has 152 seats allocated in twenty regions. These seats are allocated according to a regional closed party list vote using the Droop quota with largest remainders. There is a slight twist, however. No party in the Hungarian system can receive a seat in the remainder process if their remainder is less than two-thirds of a Droop quota. The application of the two-thirds limit typically means that some of the 152 seats in the regional tier are left unallocated. These unallocated seats are added to the 58 seats reserved for the single district national tier. Thus, the regional tier has a *maximum* of 152 seats and the national tier has a *minimum* of 58 seats. In practice, about 85 to 90 seats end up being allocated in the national tier. Remainder votes from the regional tier are all transferred to the national vote pool in the following manner. If the remainder votes for a party were not used to obtain an additional seat in the regional tier, then these remainder votes are *added* to that party's national vote pool. However, if the remainder votes for a party were used to obtain an additional seat, then the difference between the Droop quota and the remainder used to obtain the additional seat is *subtracted* from that party's national vote pool. Therefore, each vote is used only once and no seat will be allocated at a "discount." For example, suppose that the regional district has a Droop quota of 10,000 votes and that after the quota allocation of automatic seats has been done, Party A has 7,500 remainder votes and Party B has 6,500 remainder votes. Party A has the highest number of remainder votes, and so gets the next seat. Because Party B's remainder votes are less than the two-thirds (6,666) requirement, it does not receive an additional seat at the regional level. For Party B, 6,500 votes are *added* to the national vote pool. For Party A, 2,500 votes (10,000–7,500) are *subtracted* from its national vote total.

How are seats allocated in the national tier? In order to be eligible to receive any national closed party list seats, a party list must have won at least 5 percent of the national vote in the regional party lists. As we indicated earlier, there is no ballot for these national tier seats. Instead, the national tier seats are awarded on the basis of compensation votes—votes that are unused to allocate seats in a lower electoral tier. Compensation votes come from two sources. First, there are the votes from the first round of the majority-plurality TRS elections at the constituency level that went to candidates who did not end up winning seats. Second, there are the remainder votes from the party list vote at the regional level that we just described. Having obtained the total number of votes for each party in the national tier, the remaining seats are allocated using the d'Hondt proportional electoral system. Because only the first-round single-member-district votes of losing candidates transfer to the national list, and because most single-member districts are decided in the second round, the national list seats cannot be allocated until these second-round elections have taken place. And that's how votes are translated into seats in Hungary.

As you can see, the Hungarian electoral system is extremely complicated and has characteristics of both a dependent and independent mixed system. The majoritarian system at the district level and the list PR system at the regional level occur completely independently of each other. This is similar to an independent mixed system. The list PR system at the national level, however, does depend on the results of the majoritarian system at the district level and the list PR system at the regional level. This is similar to a dependent mixed system. Because the Hungarian system combines dependent and independent mixed systems, we might want to classify it as a "super" mixed system.

AN OVERVIEW OF ELECTORAL SYSTEMS AROUND THE WORLD

The electoral systems used in 188 independent countries in the world in 2004 are shown in Appendix B at the end of this book. Eleven of these countries were either holding no elections in 2004 or were in transition and an electoral system still had to be adopted. We now examine some summary statistics on the 177 electoral systems employed for legislative elections as of 2004. In Figure 12.7, we show the number of countries that use each of the different electoral systems examined in this chapter. We also show the number of people in the world that live under these systems. As you can see, the most popular electoral system in terms of the number of countries that use it is the list PR system (65). The second most popular system is the SMDP electoral system (41). Very few countries use the BV, PBV, AV, SNTV, BC, or STV systems (17). Although more countries use the list PR system than any other electoral system, more people actually live under the SMDP system than any other. Fully two-thirds of the world's population live in countries that use either SMDP systems (2.2 billion) or list PR (1.2 billion) to elect their representatives.

In Table 12.17, we illustrate how electoral systems are distributed across geographic regions in 2004. Some regions are relatively homogeneous in the type of electoral systems that they use. For example, 81 percent of the countries in the Caribbean and North America use an SMDP electoral system; only three different electoral systems (SMDP, TRS, list PR) were

FIGURE 12.7 **Electoral Systems in 177 Countries in 2004**

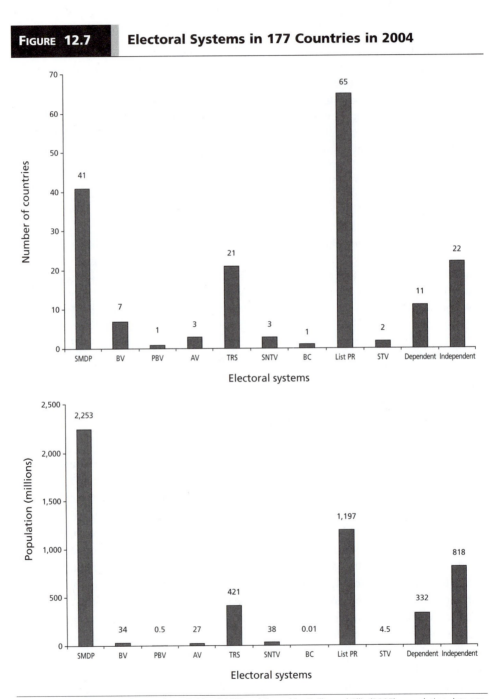

Source: Electoral system data are from Golder (2005) and Reynolds, Reilly, and Ellis (2005); population data are from the *CIA World Factbook* (2007).

Note: Electoral system data are for 2004; population data are for 2007. The numbers above the bars indicate either the precise number of countries (top figure) or the precise population in millions (bottom figure).

TABLE 12.17 Electoral Systems by Geographic Region, 2004

	Sub-Saharan Africa	North Africa and Middle East	Asia	Oceana	Latin America	Caribbean and North America	Eastern Europe	Western Europe	Total
	No. of countries using electoral system								
SMDP	14	2	6	5	0	13	0	1	41
BV	1	3	2	1	0	0	0	0	7
PBV	1	0	0	0	0	0	0	0	1
AV	0	0	0	3	0	0	0	0	3
TRS	7	3	3	1	1	1	4	1	21
SNTV	0	1	0	1	0	0	1	0	3
BC	0	0	0	1	0	0	0	0	1
List PR	13	5	3	0	14	2	12	16	65
STV	0	0	0	0	0	0	0	2	2
Dependent	3	0	0	1	3	0	2	2	11
Independent	5	1	6	0	1	0	8	1	22
Total	44	15	20	13	19	16	27	23	177
	No. of countries using electoral system family								
Majoritarian	26	11	12	9	1	14	5	2	80
Proportional	12	3	0	5	14	2	12	18	66
Mixed	6	6	1	1	4	0	10	3	31
Total	44	20	13	15	19	16	27	23	177

used by the sixteen different countries in this region. Similarly, 74 percent of the countries in Latin America and 70 percent of the countries in Western Europe use list PR. In contrast, there are other regions where countries employ a highly diverse set of electoral systems. This is the case in Oceana, North Africa and the Middle East, and Sub-Saharan Africa. In fact, the thirteen countries in Oceana use seven different electoral systems; many of these systems are rarely used elsewhere around the world (BC, BV, PBV, AV, SNTV, and so on). The information in Table 12.17 also indicates that majoritarian electoral systems of all kinds are largely absent in regions such as Latin America and both Western Europe and Eastern Europe; they are much more common in other regions of the world, such as Africa, Asia, and the Caribbean and North America.

Do dictatorships and democracies use different types of electoral systems? In Figure 12.8, we use Freedom House to classify countries into three categories: Not Free, Partially Free, and Free. If you remember from Chapter 5, these categories are frequently used to classify countries as democracies or dictatorships. Not Free countries are dictatorships, Free countries are democracies, and Partially Free countries are somewhere in between. Figure 12.8 illustrates that the percentage of countries employing majoritarian electoral systems declines as we move from the dictatorial end of the spectrum to the democratic end. In other words, dictatorships are much more likely to use majoritarian electoral systems than democracies. Why might this be the case? Unfortunately, relatively little work has been done examining the choice of electoral systems under dictatorships. We might come up with a few conjectures, however. One explanation for why dictatorships tend to adopt majoritarian systems might be that they are easier to manipulate. Some evidence for this comes from a study of twenty-four former Communist countries showing that elections conducted using a majoritarian SMDP system were much more likely to be the object of manipulation than those run under list PR systems (Birch 2007).

In one of the few studies on electoral system choice under dictatorship, Lust-Okar and Jamal (2002) argue that different types of dictatorships choose different types of electoral systems. Specifically, they claim that majoritarian electoral systems are more likely to be adopted by one-party-dominated dictatorships, and proportional systems are more likely to be employed by monarchies. The idea is that leaders in these two types of dictatorship have divergent preferences. Monarchs are political arbitrators; their legitimacy typically comes from things like the royal family, religious authority, or historical tradition rather than popular support. "For the monarch, then, political division and competition in popular politics, not unity, is the basis of stability. Kings have no interest in creating a single contender who could vie with them for power" (Lust-Okar and Jamal 2002, 353). As a result, monarchs prefer proportional systems that allow for the representation of competing political parties while they maintain their role as chief arbiter. In contrast, leaders in states dominated by a single party are forced to enter politics to maintain their rule. As a result, they want majoritarian systems that disproportionately favor their (large) political party. This line of reasoning is supported with empirical evidence from the Middle East. Clearly, more research needs to be done on why particular dictatorships adopt the electoral systems that they do and how these decisions affect the stability and other aspects of authoritarian rule.

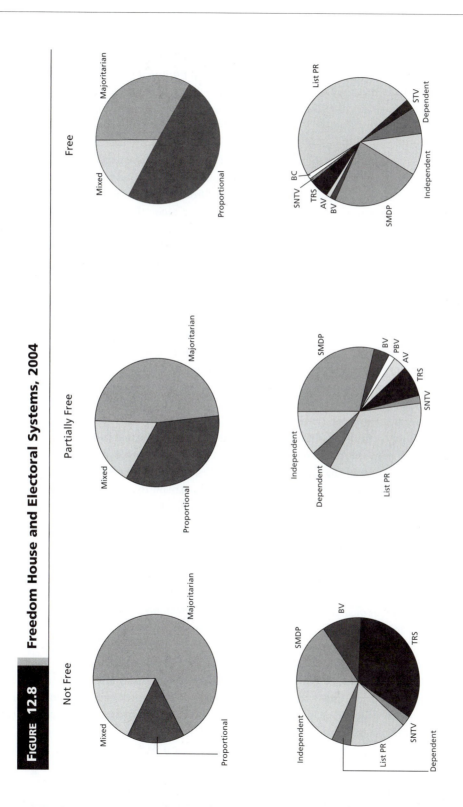

FIGURE 12.8 Freedom House and Electoral Systems, 2004

The literature addressing electoral system choice in democracies is relatively new but growing quite rapidly. Various explanations have been proposed for why countries have the electoral systems that they do. These explanations point to things like the self-interest of political parties, general interest concerns, historical precedent, external pressures, and idiosyncratic occurrences (Benoit 2004, 2007). Self-interest explanations tend to focus on the preferences that political parties have for various electoral systems. Because electoral systems are basically distribution mechanisms that reward one party at the expense of another, parties are likely to have conflicting preferences for alternative electoral rules. The adoption of an electoral system is, then, an outcome that arises from a struggle between political parties with competing interests. In this struggle, political parties are thought to care about either policy or office. In policy-seeking stories, leaders care about how different electoral alternatives affect the types of policy that are likely to be adopted in the legislature. Bawn (1993) adopts such an approach to explain why Germany first used a proportional electoral system in 1949 and then switched to a mixed system four years later in 1953. In office-seeking stories, leaders care about how different electoral rules influence their seat share and the likelihood that they will be in government. As an example, Boix (1999) uses an office-seeking story to explain the spread of proportional electoral systems around the world at the beginning of the twentieth century. He argues that ruling elites who were historically elected using some kind of majoritarian electoral system chose to adopt proportional systems at a time when suffrage was being extended to the poor and the support of socialist parties was growing. The incentive to adopt a proportional system was particularly strong in those countries in which conservative parties on the right were fragmented and the presence of strong socialist parties posed a threat to their continued rule. In effect, Boix claims that conservative parties at the beginning of the twentieth century chose to adopt proportional systems as a preemptive strategy to guarantee strong representation in the legislature even if they remained divided. Office-seeking stories like this have also been used to explain the choice of electoral system in Hungary, Poland, Russia, and Taiwan (Brady and Mo 1992; Remington and Smith 1996; Kaminski 1999; Benoit and Schiemann 2001; Benoit and Hayden 2004).

Rather than argue that electoral systems are adopted because they are in the interest of particular parties, others claim that they are chosen because they serve some kind of general interest like promoting legitimacy, fairness, ethnic accommodation, participation, accountability, and the revelation of sincere preferences. For example, we discussed earlier how the adoption of the supplementary vote to elect the Sri Lankan president was driven by a desire to allow the minority Tamil community to have a meaningful role in the election, to ensure that any president enjoyed majority support, and to keep the administrative costs of running the election low (Reilly 2001). Some have argued that the leaders charged with choosing electoral institutions in Eastern Europe after the collapse of communism were motivated by a desire to maximize legitimacy and fairness by promoting proportionality and the development of political parties (Birch et al. 2002). It is worth noting that there can be high levels of uncertainty in newly democratic countries about how people will vote (Andrews and Jackman 2005). As a result, it becomes harder for political parties to know which electoral

STRATEGIC MISCALCULATION: ELECTORAL SYSTEM CHOICE IN POLAND IN 1989

As we note in the text, one explanation for why countries adopt the electoral systems that they do focuses on the strategic calculations of political parties. In effect, parties in power choose to adopt electoral rules that benefit them at the expense of their rivals. Although the stakes involved in choosing an electoral system can often be extremely high, history has shown us that political parties frequently make strategic miscalculations.

In an article entitled, "How Communism Could Have Been Saved," Marek Kaminski describes the bargaining that took place between the opposition movement, Solidarity, and the Communist Party over the electoral law to be used for the 1989 legislative elections in Poland. At the time, these elections were to be the first semifree elections held in the Soviet bloc. During these negotiations, the Communist Polish United Workers' Party (PUWP) made two strategic miscalculations.

Mistake 1: The first mistake was that the PUWP overestimated its support in the electorate. Following the imposition of martial law in 1981, the PUWP under General Jaruzelski set up a Center for Public Opinion Research (CBOS) to keep better track of public opinion and support for the Communist regime. If you recall from our discussion of democratic transitions in Chapter 8, preference falsification is likely to be rampant in dictatorships because members of opposition groups are unlikely to publicly reveal their opposition for fear of punishment. This was certainly the case in Poland, where roughly 30 percent of respondents simply refused to complete surveys conducted by CBOS. Much of the opposition in Poland essentially remained underground and out of the sight of the PUWP. The result was that the PUWP went into the negotiations over the electoral law with Solidarity in 1989 with an overly optimistic belief about their electoral strength.

Mistake 2: The second mistake was that the PUWP did not adopt a proportional electoral system. As you may recall, the 1989 legislative elections turned into an electoral disaster for the PUWP with Solidarity winning all 35 percent of the legislative seats that they were able to compete for. The size of Solidarity's victory and the subsequent divisions that appeared between the PUWP and its supporters eventually led to the appointment of the first non-Communist prime minister in Eastern Europe. The reason that Solidarity won all the seats in these elections had a lot to do with the electoral system that was chosen—a majority-runoff TRS. Because Solidarity turned out to have the largest support in each district, this electoral system translated the 70 percent of the vote won by Solidarity into 100 percent of the seats and the roughly 25 percent of the vote won by the PUWP into zero seats. Had the PUWP adopted a proportional electoral system, though, the outcome of the elections would have been very different.

So why did the PUWP not adopt a proportional system? One reason has to do with the PUWP's belief that it had sufficient support to win seats in a majoritarian system. A second reason, however, has to do with the fact that the PUWP did not want to legalize any additional political parties. The maximum concession the PUWP was willing to make during the negotiations was to legalize Solidarity as a trade union; Poland was to remain a one-party state. As a result, the PUWP refused to consider adopting any electoral system that required individuals to vote for parties rather than candidates. At the time, the PUWP believed that all proportional systems required the presence of political parties. As you now know from reading this chapter, this is not true. The STV is a proportional electoral system in which individuals vote for candidates. It appears that the PUWP was simply unaware that the STV system existed. In his article, Kaminski indicates that had the option of the STV come up, it would have been acceptable to both Solidarity and the PUWP. STV would have guaranteed a significant representation for Solidarity in the legislature and provided a greater margin of safety for the PUWP. It seems likely that with a more proportional allocation of seats, as would have occurred under an STV system, the PUWP may have been able to hold on to power and not had to appoint a prime minister from Solidarity.

This leads to an interesting counterfactual question that one might ask. What would have happened to communism in Eastern Europe had the PUWP adopted a proportional STV system in 1989 rather than the majoritarian TRS? What we know is that the collapse of communism in Poland had a snowball effect, to a large extent, on the rest of the Eastern bloc; a different course of events in Poland could perhaps have restrained the breakdown of the Communist regime. This leads one to wonder whether communism in Eastern Europe could have been saved if the political leaders in Poland had only been more aware of the information on electoral systems presented in this chapter.

After the Polish version of Kaminski's article was published, he received several letters from Premier Tadeusz Mazowiecki and other Solidarity leaders. Below, we list some of the more emotional responses that he received from former Communist dignitaries.

Jerzy Urban (former Communist spokesman, number 4 in Poland in the 1980s):

> You are absolutely right that we did not read the surveys properly . . . we were ignorant about various electoral laws . . . probably nobody knew STV. . . . I distributed copies of your paper among General Jaruzelski, Premier Rakowski, and [the present] President Kwasniewski.

Hieronim Kubiak (former Politburo member, top political adviser):

> The negative heroes of Kaminski's article are the "ignoramus"—we, communist experts. . . . [He thinks that the communist regime could have survived] if General Jaruzelski had known the STV electoral law and if he had chosen differently!

Janusz Reykowski (former Politburo member, the designer of the 1989 electoral law):

> [The value of Kaminski's work] is in showing that technical political decisions [that is, the choice of the electoral law] may have fundamental importance for a historical process.

Maria Terese Kiszczak (the wife of General Czeslaw Kiszczak, number 2 in Poland in the 1980s):

> You based your story on the bourgeois literature. . . . [C]ommunists did not really want to keep power. . . . [My husband] resisted a temptation to cancel the 1989 elections and to seize power.

system will be in their self-interest. It is partially for this reason that Birch (2003) claims that East European leaders often chose electoral systems less to maximize seat share than to promote general interest concerns and minimize risk.

External pressures and historical precedent help to explain why other countries have the electoral system that they do. For example, the particular electoral system adopted by many countries is heavily influenced by their former colonial ruler (Blais and Massicotte 1997). Nearly every African country that employs an SMDP system is a former British colony, and the former French colonies of the Central African Republic, Comoros, and Mali all use the TRS adopted by the French Fifth Republic; the former colonies of Portugal (Cape Verde, Sao Tomé and Principe) and Italy (Somalia) use proportional electoral systems (Golder and Wantchekon 2004, 408). Similar to African countries, Iraq and Afghanistan adopted their current electoral rules as the result of pressure from a victorious invading power. Other countries appear to have adopted a particular electoral system for the simple reason that they have had some previous historical experience with it. For example, there is some evidence that the newly democratic Czechoslovakia chose a proportional electoral system in 1990 because it had used a similar system in the interwar period. Similarly, France's adoption of a TRS in 1958 can perhaps be traced back to its use in the Second Empire (1852–1870) and much of the Third Republic (1870–1940; Benoit 2004, 370).

It appears that some electoral systems are even chosen by accident. As an example, consider the following description from Benoit (2007, 376–377) of how New Zealand came to adopt a mixed electoral system in 1993.

> In a now famous incident of electoral reform through accident, ruling parties in New Zealand found themselves bound to implement a sweeping electoral reform that traced back in essence to a chance remark, later described as a gaffe, by Prime Minister David Lange during a televised debate. In New Zealand, the use of first-past-the-post [SMDP] had virtually guaranteed a two-party duopoly of the Labor Party and the National Party, producing continuous single-party majority governments since 1914—often cited as the textbook example of the "majoritarian" or Westminster type of democracy (Nagel 2004). Grassroots dissatisfaction with the electoral system began in the 1970s among Maori and minor-party supporters who consistently found it difficult to obtain any representation, and increased with the 1978 and 1981 elections, in which Labor received a plurality of the vote yet National won a majority of the seats. This led Labor to pledge in the 1980s to establish a Royal Commission to reappraise the electoral law. The commission compared many options and finally recommended the "mixed-member plurality" (MMP) system combining single-member districts with lists, although the majority of Labor's Members of Parliament opposed this system. Because the commission was politically independent and had very broad terms of reference, its considerations were disconnected from the strategic considerations of any particular party. After the commission's report, "horrified politicians of both parties attempted to put the genie of reform back in the bottle" (Nagel 2004, 534). This succeeded for six years, until the televised leaders' debate in which Labor Prime Minister David Lange inadvertently promised to hold a binding referendum on electoral reform in response to a question from the leader of the Electoral Reform Coalition. Labor initially refused to honor this pledge when elected in 1987, but after the

National Party politically exploited the incident as a broken promise, both parties promised a referendum in their 1990s manifestos. The National Party elected in 1990 finally held a referendum on electoral system reform in 1992, in which voters rejected the existing first-past-the-post system by 84.7 percent in favor of an MMP alternative (70.5 percent) (Roberts 1997). New Zealand's long-standing first-past-the-post system owes its changeover to the mixed-member system not so much to "a revolution from below [as to] an accident from above" (Rudd and Taichi 1994, p. 11, quoted in Nagel 2004).

CONCLUSION

As we saw at the beginning of this chapter, almost every country in the world has had some experience with holding national-level elections in the postwar period. This is true of both democracies and dictatorships. As Appendix B indicates, only seven out of 188 independent countries were not holding national-level legislative elections as of 2004. Although elections obviously play a minimal role in choosing who rules in dictatorships, growing evidence suggests that authoritarian elections are not merely forms of institutional window dressing. Dictatorial elections appear to matter, although probably not in the way that most democratic reformers around the world would like. Rather than encourage ongoing reforms and an eventual transition to democracy, the weight of existing evidence suggests that authoritarian elections are designed to stabilize dictatorial rule. In dictatorships, as the former president of Uganda, Milton Obote (1966–1971, 1980–1985), said many years ago, elections are a way of controlling the people rather than being a means through which they can control the leader (Cohen 1983). In contrast, elections are one of the defining characteristics of democracies and they provide the primary mechanism by which democratic governments obtain the authority to rule from the people.

Although there is a great deal of variety in the types of electoral systems that are employed around the world, most political scientists tend to classify electoral systems into three main families, depending on the electoral formula that is used to translate votes into seats: majoritarian, proportional, and mixed. In this chapter, we illustrated how these electoral systems work in some detail. We are often asked whether there is a single electoral system that is better than all of the others. As our discussion indicates, though, each electoral system has its advantages and disadvantages. For example, some electoral systems promote proportionality but lower the ability of voters to hold representatives accountable. Others allow voters to more accurately convey their sincere preferences but are complicated for individuals to understand and costly for electoral agencies to administer. In an echo of our comments from Chapter 10, there is no perfect electoral system—there are always trade-offs to be made.

Of course, you may be more willing to make certain trade-offs than others. Perhaps you think proportionality is the key criteria for evaluating different electoral systems and are less concerned with having a close link between the representative and his constituents. When we think about the actual adoption of an electoral system, though, we need to stop and ask what is in the interests of the actors involved in choosing the electoral system. Rather than thinking about which electoral system is best at meeting some objective criteria that we might care about, such as proportionality, we now need to think of which electoral systems are politically feasible, given the preferences of the actors involved. We can then try to choose the "best" electoral system from within the set of politically feasible electoral systems.

As we noted earlier, electoral systems are distributive mechanisms that reward one set of actors at the expense of another. This means that no electoral system is a winning situation for everyone involved. This has important consequences for any budding electoral reformers among you. It is nearly always the case that the political actors who won under the existing electoral system are the ones who are in a position to determine whether electoral reform should take place. Given that these actors won under the existing system, they are unlikely to be willing to reform the electoral system except in ways that solidify their ability to win in the future. Only when there is some impending threat to their continued electoral success, as was the case with conservative parties at the beginning of the twentieth century when the right to vote was extended to the working class, are they likely to consider major electoral reform. Although many people in the United States complain about the existing SMDP electoral system and advocate for the adoption of a more proportional one, we suggest that they not hold their breath. Why would either the Democratic or Republican parties choose to adopt a more proportional electoral system that would hurt their chances to be reelected and help smaller political parties? Of course, as the New Zealand case that we just described illustrates, electoral reform can happen "by accident."

In the next chapter, we discuss how electoral systems affect the size of the party system. Why do some countries have few parties but others have many? As we will demonstrate, whether a country has few or many parties depends to a great extent on the proportionality of the electoral system that is employed. It also depends on the social and ethnic makeup of a country. This last point forces us to think about which social and ethnic differences in a country become politicized.

KEY CONCEPTS

alternative vote (AV), *477*
apparentement, *501*
ballot structure, *464*
block vote (BV), *492*
Borda count (BC), *478*
closed party list, *502*
cumulation, *506*
dependent mixed electoral system, *513*
district magnitude, *464*
divisor, or highest average, system, *498*
electoral formula, *464*
electoral system, *464*
electoral threshold, *501*
electoral tier, *500*
formal threshold, *501*
free party list, *502*
independent mixed electoral system, *511*
list PR system, *495*

majoritarian electoral system, *473*
mixed electoral system, *511*
modified Borda count, *479*
natural threshold, *501*
open party list, *502*
panachage, *506*
party block vote, *492*
preference, or preferential, voting, *477*
proportional, or proportional repesentation, electoral system, *493*
quota, *495*
single-member district plurality system, *474*
single nontransferable vote, *490*
single transferable vote, *507*
supplementary vote, *488*
two-round system (TRS), *484*
universal suffrage, *468*

PROBLEMS

The following problems address various issues relating to electoral systems that were raised in this chapter.

Electoral System Design

1. What criteria do you think are important for evaluating electoral systems? Explain and justify your answer.
2. Electoral formulas are rules that allow us to translate votes into seats. As we note in the chapter, the rationale behind proportional representation (PR) electoral systems is that they should produce highly proportional outcomes. In other words, the percentage of seats that a party wins should accurately reflect the percentage of votes that it receives. Proportionality is often taken as a criterion of an electoral system's "fairness." However, it is not always clear how to design a system that produces "fair" results even when we employ multimember districts. We now provide an example in which you can try for yourself. In Table 12.18, we present actual results from the 2005 Norwegian legislative elections for the Oslo district. Seventeen seats were allocated to Oslo. Answer the following questions (based on a modified series of questions asked by Professor Kaare Strøm, University of California, San Diego).

TABLE 12.18	**Legislative Elections in Oslo, Norway, 2005**		
Party	Votes (no.)	Votes (%)	Seats (no.)
Center Party (SP)	3,270	1.1	
Christian People's Party (KrF)	11,168	3.6	
Coast Party (Kyst)	551	0.2	
Conservative Party (H)	61,130	19.8	
Labour Party (Ap)	97,246	31.5	
Left Party (V)	28,639	9.3	
Socialist Left Party (SV)	41,434	13.4	
Progress Party (FrP)	53,280	17.3	
Other	12,116	3.9	
Total	308,834	100	17

a. Copy Table 12.18. Now decide how you would allocate the seventeen seats between the parties. Put the number of seats you give to each party in your table.
b. Explain your method and attempt to justify how you arrived at your distribution of seats among the parties. Are there any problems with fairness that would arise from the seat allocation that you suggest?

c. How would your choice be affected if there were only three seats in Oslo instead of seventeen? What if there were thirty seats instead of fifteen? Under what conditions would it be easier to produce a "fairer" outcome?

3. Iraq is an ethnically and religiously diverse country. See Map 12.1, which illustrates the geographic location and size of Iraq's different ethnic groups. In December 2005, Iraqis elected 275 legislators to the Iraq Council of Representatives. Answer the following questions.

a. The electoral system used for the 2005 legislative elections in Iraq was a list PR system. Use Internet resources to find out more detailed information about the electoral system. For example, how many districts and electoral tiers were there? How many legislators

MAP 12.1   **Ethnoreligious Groups of Iraq**

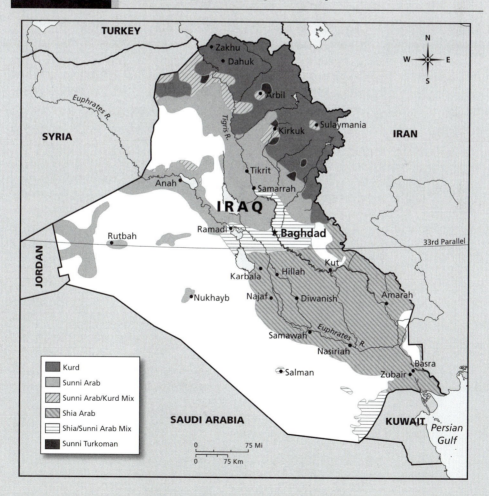

were elected in each district? What type of party list was employed? Did the Iraqis use a quota or divisor system? What type of quota and remainder system or what type of divisor method was employed? Were there any other special features of the Iraqi electoral system?

b. Given the ethnically diverse character of Iraq, what are the advantages and disadvantages of the electoral system that was adopted?

c. If you were in charge of designing an electoral system for Iraq, what would it be and why?

How Do Electoral Systems Work?

4. In Table 12.19 we again show the results from the Oslo district in the 2005 Norwegian elections. Answer the following questions.

TABLE 12.19   **Legislative Elections in Oslo, Norway, 2005 (Using Quota Systems)**

	SP	KrF	Kyst	H	Ap	V	SV	FrP	Others	Total
					Party					
Votes	3,270	11,168	551	61,130	97,246	28,639	41,434	53,280	12,116	308,834
Seats										17
Quota										
Votes/quota										
Automatic seats										
Remainder										
Remainder seats										
Total seats										

a. Copy Table 12.19. Imagine that the seventeen seats in Oslo are to be allocated according to the Hare quota with largest remainders. Fill in your table and indicate how Oslo's seventeen seats are allocated among the parties. How many automatic, remainder, and total seats does each party obtain?

b. Now make another table like Table 12.19 and repeat the process using the Droop quota with largest remainders. Does the allocation of seats change?

5. In Table 12.20, we again show the same results from the Oslo district in the 2005 Norwegian elections. Answer the following questions.

TABLE 12.20			Legislative Elections in Oslo, Norway, 2005 (Using Divisor Systems)							
				Party						
	SP	KrF	Kyst	H	Ap	V	SV	FrP	Others	Total
					Votes					
	3,270	11,168	551	61,130	97,246	28,639	41,434	53,280	12,116	308,834
Divisors					Quotients					
1										
2										
3										
4										
5										
6										
Total seats										

a. Copy Table 12.20. Imagine that the seventeen seats in Oslo are to be allocated according to the d'Hondt divisor method. Show the different quotients that are calculated when you divide each party's vote total by the d'Hondt divisors in your table. How many seats does each party obtain?

b. Now repeat the process using the St. Lagüe divisor method and then the Modified St. Lagüe divisor method. Note that you will need to change the integers used to estimate the quotients. How many seats does each party obtain under these divisor systems?

c. Are there any differences if you examine the seat allocations from the two quota systems and the three divisor systems? Does one method produce a more proportional or fairer outcome in your opinion than another?

13 Social Cleavages and Party Systems

Party is organized opinion.

Benjamin Disraeli

- Political scientists sometimes categorize democracies in terms of the type of party system that they exhibit. When they do this, they typically distinguish between party systems based on the number and size of the parties that they contain.

- A political party is an organization that includes officials who hold office and people who help get and keep them there. Parties help to structure the political world, recruit and socialize the political elite, mobilize the masses, and provide a link between rulers and the ruled.

- In this chapter, we examine why some party systems are divided primarily along ethnic lines, whereas others are divided mainly along class, religious, linguistic, or regional ones. We also investigate why some countries have few parties and others have many. As we will see, the general structure of a country's party system results from the complex interplay of both social and institutional forces.

OVERVIEW

In addition to classifying democracies according to the type of government that they have or the type of electoral system that they employ, political scientists sometimes categorize democracies by the type of party system that they exhibit. Although there are obviously many facets to a party system that one might examine, political scientists often focus on the number and size of the parties in a country. As a result, you will frequently see scholars distinguish between democracies that have a two-party system, like the United States, and democracies that have a multiparty system, like the Netherlands. Although the type of government and electoral system in a country is nearly always enshrined in a constitution or some other legal document, this is not the case for the type of party system (Stokes 1999, 245). Instead, party systems take the form that they do as a result of the evolving nature of political competition in each country. Like the structure of an economic market or the grammar of a language, the structure of a country's party system is not intentionally designed by particular individuals; rather, it arises from the complex interplay of decisions made by such actors as party leaders and voters. We will suggest in this chapter that socioeconomic forces largely drive the structure of a country's party system, but we will also demonstrate that these forces are channeled in powerful and important ways by the kinds of political institutions that we have examined in the last two chapters. In effect, the structure of a country's party system results from the complex interplay of both social and institutional forces.

We begin this chapter by asking what a party is and what a party does. After briefly describing the different types of party system that exist around the world, we then explore the social and institutional factors that interact to influence both the number and types of parties that exist in a country. As such, our goal is to help explain why some countries have few parties but others have many, and why some party systems are divided primarily along ethnic lines and others are divided mainly along class, religious, linguistic, or regional ones.

POLITICAL PARTIES: WHAT ARE THEY AND WHAT DO THEY DO?

> A **political party** can be thought of as a group of people that includes those who hold office and those who help get and keep them there.

A **political party** "is a group of officials or would-be officials who are linked with a sizeable group of citizens into an organization; a chief object of this organization is to ensure that its officials attain power or are maintained in power" (Shively 2001, 234). As this definition suggests, a political party comprises a broad collection of actors that can range from officials who actually attain power to individuals who regularly vote for the party and people who contribute money or time to campaign for a party member. In other words, a party can be thought of as a group of people that includes those who hold office and those who help get and keep them there. One of the primary goals of political parties is to attain power; it is this goal that differentiates them from interest groups. In contrast to political parties, interest groups, such as the National Rifle Association, the American Medical Association, and Greenpeace, are organizations that attempt to influence policy without actually taking power.

One thing to note about the definition that we have just given is that political parties are not restricted to democracies or electoral activity. As we saw in Chapter 12, political parties exist in many dictatorships around the world. Some of these parties, such as Communist parties in China and Cuba, control the levers of power without holding national-level elections. That some dictatorships have chosen to have political parties even in the absence of elections should immediately alert you to the fact that political parties can serve important purposes beyond simply helping officials get elected to power.

Political parties perform many important functions that are crucial to the operation of modern political systems in both democracies and dictatorships. In what follows, we focus on (a) how political parties structure the political world, (b) how they recruit and socialize the political elite, (c) how they mobilize the masses, and (d) how they provide a link between rulers and the ruled (Shively 2001).

Political Parties Structure the Political World

Political parties help to structure the political world for both political elites and the masses. For the elites, political parties provide some kind of order to the policymaking process. Imagine, for a moment, a world in which there are no political parties. In other words, imagine a world in which every legislator is an independent with no institutionalized link to other legislators. Given that legislators must make policy decisions in numerous issue areas and that there is likely to be disagreement over which policies are most appropriate, the outcome of the policymaking process in this type of environment is probably going to be highly chaotic and unstable. You will no doubt recall that this is precisely the prediction that we saw in Chapter 10 when we examined the Chaos Theorem and Arrow's (1963) Impossibility Theorem. Political parties help to overcome some of these problems by coordinating the actions of individual legislators and simplifying the issue space. In effect, parties help to provide structure to an otherwise unstable policymaking process. Aldrich (1995) argues that the need to coordinate votes on many issues among congressional representatives with similar, but not identical, preferences is precisely the explanation for why political parties were formed in the United States in the eighteenth century.

Just as for elites, political parties also structure the political world for voters. One way in which they do this is by providing "information shortcuts" to voters (Downs 1957; Fiorina 1981). Voters seldom have the opportunity, time, energy, or even the inclination to gather information about particular political issues. For these uninformed voters, party labels and party attachments can be an information shortcut in the sense that these things tell voters how to feel about certain issues. In effect, voters might decide that they are against a particular piece of legislation not because they have read up on it and realized that it is not in their interests but simply because the party to which they feel attached dislikes it. In many ways, one's political identity is frequently tied up with one's **party identification** (Campbell et al. 1960). Campbell et al. (1986, 100) note this when they describe "party identification [as] an attachment to a party that helps the citizen

> **Party identification** is an attachment to a party that helps citizens locate themselves on the political landscape.

locate him/herself and others on the political landscape." For example, simply admitting to being a Democrat or a Republican in the United States or a Labour or Conservative supporter in the United Kingdom can convey a lot of information about a person's likely stance on a whole host of different issues. All of this helps to explain why so many people seem to view politics in terms of the fortunes of political parties rather than the fate of political issues.

Recruitment and Socialization of the Political Elite

In addition to structuring the political world, parties play an important role in recruiting and socializing the political elite. In many countries, it is extremely difficult to get elected as an independent. In other words, being selected as a party's candidate is often a necessary condition for a successful run for office. Similarly, cabinet positions are frequently restricted to senior members of a political party. In effect, "gaining access to political power requires being accepted by a party, and usually being a leading figure in it. Parties also socialize the political elite; most government ministers have spent a number of years as party members, working with other party members and learning to see the political world from the party's perspective" (Gallagher, Laver, and Mair 2006, 308). To see a more concrete example of this, consider the description Shively (2001, 238) gives of how an ambitious young woman interested in entering politics in Britain might behave.

> [She] might work for a while at lesser tasks for one of the major parties, such as the Conservative Party. Before too long, if she were interested in standing for Parliament, she might be nominated from a district. To get the nomination, she would have to convince the local selection committee of the Conservative Party in that district that she was their best nominee. As a beginner, she would probably be selected in a hopeless district, where no Conservative had much of a chance; but once she had proved she could campaign well in one or two lost causes, she might get the nomination from a decent district, win, and enter the House. In the House, she would continue to be molded and guided by the party. If she were the sort that party leaders like—witty in debate, hard working, and above all a faithful party voter—she might advance into positions of real responsibility, such as party spokesperson on defense or on health. Eventually, she might aim so high as to be prime minister. To be selected for this position, she would have to win an internal election at which all the Conservative members of Parliament vote to choose their leader. Throughout this career, her advancement would have been primarily due to her support from her party organization, and she would have risen to the top only because she was the sort of person her party wanted and because, in each position she held, she had learned from the rest of the party how to behave in ways they preferred. This is essentially the only way to make a political career in Great Britain.

To some extent, the role played by parties in recruiting and socializing the political elite is more important in parliamentary democracies than in presidential ones. Although it is true that much of the political elite in presidential democracies will have worked their way into place through the apparatus of one political party or another, parties are not the monopolistic gatekeepers to power that they frequently are in parliamentary systems. For example, our discussion of the government formation process in presidential democracies in Chapter 11 indicated that presidents are much more likely to appoint nonpartisan ministers to their cabinets than prime ministers are in parliamentary systems. If you recall, the reason for this is that the president has less need to negotiate with political parties in the legislature over the composition of the cabinet because the vote of no confidence is absent in presidential systems. Presidential regimes that allow for primaries, like the United States, and, increasingly, many Latin American countries (Carey and Polga-Hecimovich 2006, 2007), further weaken the role that political parties play in recruiting and socializing the political elite. By allowing candidates to appeal directly to the voters rather than rely on party leaders, primaries can allow candidates with little political or party experience to win elections. The existence of primary elections is often posited as the key reason for the organizational weakness of political parties and the dominance of candidate-centered, rather than party-centered, electoral campaigns in the United States (Aldrich 1995). In presidential democracies, it is even possible for complete political outsiders to win the presidency. This is precisely what happened when the academic and TV presenter Alberto Fujimori surprisingly won the 1990 presidential elections in Peru. The election of such a candidate to a position equivalent to that of prime minister in a parliamentary democracy is almost unthinkable. That political parties do not exert the same degree of control over the recruitment and socialization of the political elite across different types of democracy suggests that the political direction of leaders in presidential democracies is inclined to be inherently less stable and more unpredictable than that of political leaders in parliamentary democracies (Gallagher, Laver, and Mair 2006, 308).

Just as political parties play an important role in recruiting and socializing the political elite in democracies, they can perform a similar function in dictatorships. Consider the role that the Communist Party (CPSU) played in the former Soviet Union. For all intents and purposes, membership in the CPSU was a necessary condition for becoming part of the political, economic, and academic ruling class—the *nomenklatura* (Gershenson and Grossman 2001). Describing the Soviet nomenklatura in the 1980s, Voslensky (1984, 98) writes, "While a party card is of course no guarantee of success, lack of it is a guarantee that you will not have a career of any kind." Power and authority increased the higher one rose in the party, as did the monetary and nonmonetary benefits. For example, members of the nomenklatura got to enjoy many of the things that were denied to the average citizen—they got to shop in well-stocked stores, they had access to foreign goods, and, more important, they were allowed to travel abroad. As George Orwell ([1949] 1977, 192) describes in his book *1984,*

> By the standards of the early twentieth century, even a member of the Inner Party lives an austere, laborious kind of life. Nevertheless, the few luxuries that he does enjoy—his large well-appointed flat, the better texture of his clothes, the better quality of his food and drink and tobacco, his two or three servants, his private motorcar or helicopter— set him in a different world from a member of the Outer Party, and the members of the Outer Party have a similar advantage in comparison with the submerged masses.

As citizens gained membership into the CPSU and advanced up its ranks, they would be increasingly socialized into following the party line; demonstrating loyalty to the party was crucial to gaining and retaining the benefits of power associated with membership in the nomenklatura.

Mobilization of the Masses

Political parties are also key tools for mobilizing the masses. This is particularly important at election time, when ordinary citizens need to be encouraged to turn out to vote. A large literature in political science suggests that people will not necessarily choose to vote given that turning out to vote is costly—it takes time, they could be doing something else, it might be raining, and so on—and the likelihood that anyone's individual vote will determine the outcome of the election is incredibly small (Aldrich 1993; Gomez, Hansford, and Krause 2007). This suggests that organizations such as political parties have a significant role to play in getting people to the polls (Morton 1991; Uhlaner 1989). Political parties are well-placed to carry out this role because they are likely to have membership and organizational structures that extend deeply into each constituency. Moreover, they have a strong incentive to get people (at least particular people) to the polls—they want to win elections. In a one-party dictatorship like the Soviet Union, there was obviously no need for the Communist Party (CPSU) to mobilize the electorate in order to win elections—it was guaranteed to win. The CPSU did many of the same things that political parties do in democracies to encourage voter turnout, however, because it wanted to generate a good show and enhance the legitimacy of the regime (Shively 2001, 237). It is worth noting that political parties in democracies also frequently play this role as well—they encourage general voter turnout in an attempt to build support for the democratic regime as a whole.

The ability of political parties to mobilize the masses can be important even when elections are not being held. For example, French president Charles de Gaulle used his Gaullist Party to help mobilize party supporters against student and worker protests in 1968 (Lacouture 1986, 719–720). What was originally a relatively small, student-led protest soon got out of hand as police used tear gas, water cannons, mass arrests, and beatings to disperse the protesting students. In an attempt to take advantage of the situation, the French trade unions went out on the streets and formed an alliance with the students. Over a two-week period, as many as ten million workers went on strike. The student protest quickly became a social crisis that seemed to threaten the very existence of the French Fifth Republic. De Gaulle, who had initially kept a low profile as events developed, finally delivered a radio address that preyed on the French people's fears of a Communist revolution. He said that he would dissolve the National Assembly, that he would hold new elections, and that the country was "threatened with dictatorship, that of totalitarian communism." He also called on the people to come to the defense of the republic against the "Communist" students and workers. As Hitchcock (2003, 251) notes, "Within an hour of de Gaulle's address, crowds began to form on the place de la Concorde. . . . Perhaps as many as half a million people poured out of their homes into the streets, and marched up the Champs-Elysées behind the major political leaders of the Gaullist and right-wing parties." In the new elections that took place about a month later, the electorate gave a huge majority to the Gaullist candidates.

The previous example illustrates how political parties might be used to mobilize the masses in support of a regime, but there are numerous other instances in which parties are used to mobilize people *against* the ruling order. For example, the main opposition movement against the rule of Robert Mugabe in Zimbabwe comes from the Movement for Democratic Change (MDC), which is an opposition party established in 1999 by the trade unionist Morgan Tsvangirai. The MDC has frequently organized street protests against the government's failure to address the crumbling economy and mounting food shortages.

Morgan Tsvangirai, the leader of the Movement for Democratic Change opposition party, addressing about 3,000 supporters at an election rally in the border town of Mutare, Zimbabwe, about 300 kilometers (186 miles) east of Harare, Sunday June 4, 2000. The MDC said the then-recent farm takeovers and plans for immediate land redistribution were aimed at bolstering President Robert Mugabe's flagging popularity and to punish white farmers for supporting the opposition.

Political parties and their leaders were also the central mobilizing forces behind the protests against Ukrainian authorities from November 2004 to January 2005 that became known as the Orange Revolution. These protests started after presidential elections in which the authorities were deemed by many to have engaged in widespread corruption, voter intimidation, and electoral fraud to help Viktor Yanukovych come to power. Viktor Yuschenko, the leader of Our Ukraine, and his party supporters refused to recognize the results of these elections and helped to organize demonstrations. Kiev, the Ukrainian capital, became the focal point for the opposition movement with thousands of protesters demonstrating daily in the city. On some days, the number of protesters in the center of Kiev reached into the hundreds of thousands; one million by some estimates.

Across the country, the opposition movement led by Yuschenko and his party organized sit-ins and general strikes. Following thirteen days of protests, the Ukrainian Supreme Court overturned the election results and ordered a rerun of the presidential elections, which Viktor Yuschenko eventually won with 51.99 percent of the vote. Other examples of political parties mobilizing the masses against the ruling regime include the Congress Party in India and the National Front for Liberation in Algeria. Both of these parties were originally established as a means to mobilize the masses against British and French colonial rule (Shively 2001, 237).

The Link between Rulers and the Ruled

Political parties provide a link between rulers and the ruled. According to most democratic theorists, democratic governments are supposed to reflect the preferences of their citizens (Mill [1861] 1991; Dahl 1956; Pitkin 1967). As discussed in Chapter 11 in our examination of the government formation process, the political party is the primary vehicle ensuring that citizen preferences are reflected in government policy. In fact, it is probably the central function of a political party in a democracy to represent, articulate, and champion the interests and political causes of its membership. Political parties are also the main means by which democracies can be induced to be responsive. Some people claim that "political parties created democracy . . . modern democracy is unthinkable save in terms of parties" (Schattschneider 1942, 3). In democracies, it should be possible for the people to hold elected leaders accountable for their actions in office. The problem is that government policy is frequently determined by the collective actions of many officeholders. As a collective group, the political party provides the main means by which voters can hold elected officials responsible for what they do collectively. Fiorina (1980, 26) goes so far as to write, "[T]he only way collective responsibility has ever existed, and can exist . . . is through the agency of the political party."

It is important to recognize that the link that parties create between officials and citizens runs both ways. We have just described the political party as an organization that citizens can use to control the actions of officials and hold them responsible for what they do in office, but we should recognize that political parties can also help officials exert control over other political actors and citizens as well. For example, party leaders have many carrots and sticks at their disposal that they can use to deliberately force the obedience of legislators when it comes to voting in the legislature. Party leaders can use promotion within the party, promises of campaign resources, threats of expulsion, and the like to induce legislators to vote the "right" way on pieces of legislation. Most political parties have an individual called a **whip,** whose job it is to ensure that members of the party attend legislative sessions and vote as the

A **whip** is an individual whose job it is to ensure that members of the party attend legislative sessions and vote as the party leadership desires.

Box 13.1 **PARTY WHIPS IN THE UNITED KINGDOM**

The term *whip* to describe someone who ensures that party members attend legislative sessions and vote as the party leadership desires originated in the English Parliament in the 1880s. The term derives from the "whipper-in" at a fox hunt, whose job it is to keep the pack together and prevent the hounds from running riot. As you can imagine, the role of the whips is particularly important when the voting strengths of the government and the opposition are close as they were in the Parliament between 1992 and 1997. The duties of whips include (a) keeping legislators informed of forthcoming parliamentary business, (b) maintaining the party's voting strength by ensuring that members attend important debates and vote as the party leadership desires, and (c) passing on the opinions of legislators to the party leadership. Each of the three major parties in the United Kingdom—the Conservatives, the Labour Party, and the Liberals—have a chief whip, a deputy chief whip, and a varying number of junior whips. The government chief whip has the formal title of parliamentary secretary to the treasury; he is directly answerable to the prime minister, attends cabinet meetings, and makes the day-to-day arrangements for the government's program of business.

The term *whip* also applies to a weekly circular sent out by each party's whips to all their Members of Parliament notifying them of parliamentary business and the schedule for the days ahead. This circular includes the sentence "Your attendance is absolutely essential" next to each debate in which there will be a vote. The degree of importance of each debate is indicated by the number of times this sentence is underlined. Sentences that are underlined once are considered routine and attendance is optional. Those that are underlined twice are more important and attendance is required unless a "pair"—a member of the Opposition who also intends to be absent from the debate—has been arranged. Those that are underlined three times are highly important and pairing is not normally allowed. The number of underlines determines whether there is a one-line, two-line, or three-line whip on a vote. Three-line whips are imposed on important occasions, such as for votes of no confidence and the second reading of significant bills.

The consequences of defying the party leadership depend on the circumstances surrounding a vote and are usually negotiated with the party whips in advance. Cabinet ministers who defy the whips are immediately dismissed, assuming that they have not already resigned. The consequences for defying the party whip for a backbencher—someone who is not in the cabinet or the "shadow" cabinet of the Opposition—can include being overlooked for future promotions to a cabinet post, being given little support by the party organization when seeking reelection, being de-selected by local party activists or moved to a different, and less safe, constituency seat, or being expelled from the party altogether. Failure by MPs to attend a vote with a three-line whip is usually treated as a rebellion against the party and, theoretically, leads to suspension from the party. As an example, nine Conservative MPs were suspended from the party in 1994 when they voted against the position of John Major's government regarding the European Union.

Party whips can be extremely forceful in obtaining the votes of their backbenchers, even engaging in "blackmail, verbal intimidation, sexual harassment and physical aggression" from time to time to force some unpopular votes (Dixon 1996, 160). Occasionally, whips bring in very sick MPs for what are sometimes referred to as "death" or "stretcher" votes. For example, Labour Party whips brought in heart attack victims and an MP who had just had brain surgery to vote in an attempt to bring down the government of John Major in the 1990s. A former MP, Joe Ashton, refers to a similar case from the final days of James Callaghan's government (1976–1979).

> I remember the famous case of Leslie Spriggs, the then Member for St. Helens. We had a tied vote and he was brought to the House in an ambulance having suffered a severe heart attack. The two Whips [from the Government and the Opposition] went out to look in the ambulance and there was Leslie Spriggs laid there as though he was dead. I believe that John Stradling Thomas said to Joe Harper, "How do we know that he is alive?" So he leaned forward, turned the knob on the heart machine, the green light went around, and he said, "There, you've lost—it's 311." [The vote had been tied 310–310.] That is an absolutely true story. It is the sort of nonsense that used to happen. No one believes it, but it is true.

party leadership desires. Although the power of whips varies from country to country, whips are frequently some of the most important political actors in a country. The importance of whips often goes unrecognized by the public because these actors rarely appear in the media, at least in their capacity as whips.

Political parties can also be used to control the behavior of actual citizens. As you might suspect, this is much more common in dictatorships than in democracies. As Friedrich and Brzezinski (1961, 29) put it in their book on dictatorships, "the role of the party [is] to provide a following for the dictator." Single-party dictatorships frequently use the party organization as a means to control the citizenry. In exchange for perks, privileges, and prospects for career advancement, party members agree to mobilize popular support and supervise the behavior of people who are unwilling to identify themselves with the dictator. As an example, Gershenson and Grossman (2001) describe how the Communist Party in the Soviet Union used party membership to co-opt and repress various segments of society. In particular, they detail how the CPSU systematically eased and tightened the restrictions on who could become a member of the party to undermine potential opposition at different points in time. Hough (1980, 33) makes a similar point, claiming that "[t]he Soviet government has thus far been skillful in the way it has tied the fate of many individuals in the country to the fate of the regime. By admitting such a broad range of the educated public into the party, it has provided full opportunities for upward social mobility for those who avoid dissidence, while giving everyone in the managerial class reason to wonder what the impact of an anti-Communist revolution would be on him or her personally."

A further illustration of how political parties can be used to control the masses comes from Przeworski and Gandhi (2006, 25).

> Consider communist Poland. Even though in 1948 communists forced their major rival, the Polish Socialist Party, into a "merger," thus creating the Polish United Workers Party (PUWP), they tolerated a pre-war left-wing United Peasant Party (ZSL), a small private business party (SD), and a Catholic group with direct ties to Moscow. After 1956, two other Catholic groups were allowed to organize. Even though these parties functioned under separate labels in the legislature, they were presented to the voters as a single list, with all candidates approved by the communists. Hence, elections only ratified the distribution of parliamentary seats and the specific appointees of the Communist Party. One way to think of this "multipartism" is that it represented a menu of contracts, allowing people characterized by different political attitudes (and differing degrees of opportunism) to sort themselves out. Membership in each party entailed a different degree of identification with the regime: highest for members of the PUWP, lower for those joining the Peasant Party, the lowest for the Catholic groups. In exchange, these memberships offered varying amounts of perks and privileges, in the same order. Someone not willing to join the Communist Party, with the social opprobrium this membership evoked among Catholic peasants, may have joined the Peasant Party. This choice entailed a less direct commitment and fewer perks, but it did signify identification with the regime, and it did furnish perks and privileges. This separating equilibrium maximized support for the regime and visibly isolated those who were not willing to make any gesture of support.

Having examined what it is that political parties do, we now briefly describe the different types of party systems that are observed around the world.

PARTY SYSTEMS

As we noted at the beginning, political scientists sometimes categorize democracies in terms of the type of party system that they exhibit. When they do this, they typically distinguish between party systems by the number and size of the parties that they contain. In what follows, we identify five different types of party system: **nonpartisan democracy, single-party system, one-party dominant system, two-party system,** and **multiparty system.** Single-party systems exist only in dictatorships, and nonpartisan and one-party dominant systems are relatively rare in democracies. It is for this reason that political scientists usually distinguish between democracies on the basis of whether they have a two-party system, like the United States, or a multiparty system, like the Netherlands.

A **nonpartisan democracy** is a democracy with no official political parties.

A **single-party system** is one in which only one political party is legally allowed to hold power.

A **one-party dominant system** is one in which multiple parties may legally operate but in which only one particular party has a realistic chance of gaining power.

A **two-party system** is one in which only two major political parties have a realistic chance of holding power.

A **multiparty system** is one in which more than two parties have a realistic chance of holding power.

The existence of political parties is often seen as a necessary condition for the existence of modern democracy. For example, scholars have claimed that "parties are the core institution of democratic politics" (Lipset 1996), that "democracy is unthinkable save in terms of parties" (Schattschneider 1942), and that "modern democracy is party democracy" (Katz 1980). Despite these claims, though, it turns out that a small handful of democracies in the world can be considered nonpartisan, that is, ones in which there are no official political parties. The absence of political parties may be because a law prohibits their existence or simply because they have yet to form. Historically, the administration of George Washington and the first few sessions of the U.S. Congress were nonpartisan. Today, the only democracies that can be considered nonpartisan are the small Pacific islands of Kiribati, the Marshall Islands, Micronesia, Nauru, Palau, and Tuvalu (Anckar and Anckar 2000).[1] These islands have extremely small populations; Nauru, Palau, and Tuvalu all have fewer than 15,000 residents. Although nonpartisan democracies at the national level are extremely rare, a few countries have some nonpartisan governments at the subnational level. For example, the unicameral legislature of Nebraska is nonpartisan, as are some Swiss cantons and some Canadian territories.

In single-party systems, only one political party is legally allowed to hold power. Liberia is generally considered the first single-party state in the world. The True Whig Party ruled

---

1. Of these six countries, it is widely accepted that Micronesia, Palau, and Tuvalu are nonpartisan democracies. There is some disagreement, however, as to whether political parties have existed in certain periods in the other countries, particularly in Kiribati. Much depends on how one exactly defines a political party.

Liberia from 1878 to 1980, when it was ousted by a military coup. Current single-party states include such countries as China, Cuba, Eritrea, Laos, North Korea, Syria, Turkmenistan, and Vietnam. Although these party systems are called single-party systems, minor parties are sometimes allowed to exist. These minor parties, however, are always legally required to accept the leadership of the dominant party. As an example, consider our earlier discussion of single-party rule in Communist Poland. Although minor parties were allowed to coexist under separate labels in the legislature alongside the Polish Communist Party (PUWP), the candidates of these parties were always presented to the voters on a single PUWP party list; in other words, the candidates of the minor parties had to be approved by the PUWP ahead of time. All single-party systems occur in dictatorships.

In some countries, multiple parties are legally allowed to exist but only one party has a realistic chance of gaining power. States in which this is the case are said to have one-party dominant systems. Many of these one-party dominant systems occur in dictatorships. In these countries, the dictatorship might allow certain opposition parties to legally operate but they then use various means to prevent them from actually coming to power (Lust-Okar 2005). Examples of one-party dominant systems in dictatorships include the National Democratic Party (NDP) of Hosni Mubarak in Egypt and the Zimbabwe African National Union-Patriotic Front (ZANU-PF) of Robert Mugabe in Zimbabwe.

Not all one-party dominant systems are necessarily undemocratic, though. For example, there are several cases of democracies in which a single party is dominant for long periods of time. This dominance is normally attributed to things like long-running popularity, a divided opposition, the efficient use of patronage systems, and, occasionally, electoral fraud. Examples of one-party dominant systems in states that many consider, or considered, democratic include the African National Congress in South Africa since 1994, the Botswana Democratic Party in Botswana since 1966, the Democratic Party in the southern United States from the 1880s to the 1960s, the Liberal Democratic Party in Japan from 1955 to 1993, and the Congress Party in India from 1947 to 1977. Although a one-party dominant system is similar in many ways to a single-party system, "the availability of other active parties does guarantee that there will be fairly open discussion and debate, and it also provides for possible long-term flexibility and adjustment in the system" (Shively 2001, 249).

Japanese Prime Minister Ryutaro Hashimoto (1996–1998) raises his hand to fellow Liberal Democratic Party members, who wore victory headbands, while campaigning ahead of upper house elections in 1998. Hashimoto was the leader of one of the largest factions within the ruling LDP through most of the 1990s and remained a powerful actor in Japanese politics until a scandal forced him to resign his leadership position in 2004.

x 13.2   **ONE-PARTY DOMINANT SYSTEMS IN JAPAN: THE CASE OF THE LDP**

The Liberal Democratic Party (LDP) was the dominant political force in Japan from 1955 to 1993, regularly winning more than 50 percent of the vote and managing to form single-party majority governments throughout this period. Although the LDP can trace its roots back to the 1880s, it officially came into existence in 1955 when the Liberal Party and the Japan Democratic Party merged to form a united front against the popular Japan Socialist Party. Given the emerging cold war, the merger that led to the creation of the LDP was strongly supported by the United States. Indeed, the CIA spent millions of dollars over the following two decades to help the LDP win elections against the Communists and Socialists (*New York Times*, March 31, 1997).

Since its formation, the LDP has been a large party representing a broad spectrum of interests. The party has failed to espouse a well-defined ideology, however, which has led many to claim that the LDP might more accurately be considered a coalition of factions rather than a party. Throughout its history, there have been between six and thirteen different factions in the LDP. Every LDP member of parliament is typically associated with one of these factions and each faction is headed by a senior party figure. Faction leaders offer their followers such services as financial support during election campaigns and contact with influential bureaucrats and business people. Without these funds and contacts, it is extremely difficult for LDP legislators to survive politically. To a large extent, the sole thing that kept all of these factions together within the LDP tent was the desire to win elections and share in the spoils of office. Given the electoral dominance of the LDP from 1955 to 1993, much of the real struggle for political power in Japan during this period occurred between factions within the LDP rather than among the different Japanese parties. The central role of these factions has led some to joke that the LDP is neither liberal, nor democratic, nor even a party.

If you recall from our discussion of electoral systems in Chapter 12, Japan employed the single nontransferable vote (SNTV) to elect its legislators during the period of LDP dominance. As we noted at the time, SNTV creates incentives for intraparty fighting and factionalization because candidates from one party are competing not only against candidates from other parties in their district but also against candidates from their own party. One consequence of this was that LDP legislators went to enormous lengths to cultivate personal reputations in their districts to differentiate themselves from competing LDP candidates (Cox and Niou 1994). This led scholars to conclude that Japan was characterized by the most candidate-centered politics of any democracy in the world during this period of time (Reed and Thies 2000).

As Hirano (2005, 8) notes, LDP legislators were notorious for engaging in constituency service and targeting subsidy (pork) allocations to their districts. "The constituency services, which are organized through the candidates' personal support networks (*koenkai*), provide a wide range of events for the constituents, such as local fund raisers, study groups, cultural events (such as sumo matches), tours of the Diet [parliament], and in some cases trips to hot springs. LDP candidates were also expected to perform personal favors for their constituents, such as providing monetary gifts at weddings and funerals, helping with job or school placement, and mediating disputes between constituents." Hirano (2005, 9) goes on to describe Tanaka

Kakuei as the most extreme example of a candidate's using services and pork provision to cater to his electorate. For example, he writes that "one of Tanaka's final activities while in office was to take 11,000 people to Nukumi hot springs in Yamagata prefecture at a cost of $1.4 million (Richardson 1997, 28). He is also known for bringing Japan's high speed rail line to his home prefecture, a project that took 11 years to build at a cost of millions of dollars per kilometer. Four of the eight bullet train stops are in Tanaka's home prefecture, and two of the stops are less than 14 miles apart (Schlesinger 1997, 104)."

The importance and pervasiveness of personal ties between LDP legislators and their faction leaders, as well as between LDP legislators and their constituents, created a strong, multitiered patronage structure in which large numbers of people had incentives to preserve the LDP's political dominance. The success of the LDP's system "depended less on generalized mass appeals than on the three 'bans': *jiban* (a strong, well-organized constituency), *kaban* (a brief-case full of money), and *kanban* (prestigious appointments, particularly on the cabinet level)" (Dolan and Worden 1994). The LDP's modus operandi led to numerous corruption and bribery scandals over the years. For example, several members of Japan's political, business, and underworld classes were involved in the 1976 Lockheed bribery scandal, when Japanese prime minister Tanaka Kakuei was arrested for taking $3 million in bribes from the U.S. aerospace company Lockheed during negotiations over the sale of aircraft.

In the wake of further corruption scandals and a strong downturn in the Japanese economy, the LDP's hold on power finally ended in the 1993 elections when a coalition of opposition parties entered office. Prior to these elections, more than fifty LDP members had left the party to form the Shinseito and Sakigake parties. This was enough to prevent the LDP from obtaining the legislative majority it needed to form the government. In 1994 a package of reform laws was introduced that was specifically designed to reduce corruption. Not only did these laws create a new electoral system, but they also introduced a public subsidy program to fund political parties and stricter regulations for political donations. Despite these changes, it was not long before the LDP was back in power. In that same year, 1994, the Japan Socialist Party formed a coalition with the LDP, its former archrival, when several opposition parties left the government. In the 1996 elections, the LDP was triumphantly returned to power as the majority party. Although the LDP has lost some of its popularity since then, as of June 2008 it was still in power alongside the much smaller Buddhist New Komeito Party. The LDP remains by far the largest party in the lower house; however, during the July 2007 elections, it lost its majority status in the upper house.

A two-party system is one in which only two major political parties have a realistic chance of holding power. In democracies with this type of party system, nearly all elected offices are held by candidates endorsed by one of the two major parties; electoral success under the label of some third party, although not impossible, is extremely difficult. Examples of two-party systems include the systems in Jamaica, the United Kingdom, and the United States. As of 2006, 434 of the 435 seats in the U.S. House of Representatives and 98 of the 100 seats in the U.S. Senate were controlled by either the Democratic Party or the Republican Party.

The 2007 elections in Jamaica resulted in all sixty legislative seats going to either the Jamaica Labour Party or the People's National Party. Although the United Kingdom has recently seen some electoral success for third parties, the two major parties—the Conservatives and Labour—still managed to win 86 percent of the legislatives seats in the 2005 elections. Despite their name, virtually all two-party systems have many more than two parties competing for office. As of 2007, for instance, there were 185 registered political parties in England and 50 national-level parties in the United States with endorsed candidates. Both the United Kingdom and the United States, however, are traditionally seen as two-party systems because only the two major parties usually have any expectation of winning.

A multiparty system is one in which more than two political parties have a realistic chance of holding power, either separately or as part of a coalition. Most democracies have multiparty systems. Examples include France, Israel, and the Netherlands. In Table 13.1, we list those parties holding legislative seats in the 2006 Israeli Knesset. As you can see, the seats in the legislature are split among numerous political parties, with no single party coming close to obtaining a legislative majority. The coalition government formed by Israeli prime minister Olmert after the 2006 elections included his own Kadima Party, Labour, Shas, and Gil.

We have just described how political scientists frequently distinguish between democracies based on the number and size of the parties that exist. In general, they tend to distinguish between two-party and multiparty democracies. Rather than lump democracies into just these two categories, however, we might want to know how many parties there are in each country. This requires us to think about how we count political parties. It turns out that the most appropriate way of doing this is not as obvious as you might think.

TABLE 13.1	**Political Parties with Seats in the Israeli Knesset, 2006**
Political party	**No. of seats**
Kadima	29
Labour	19
Shas	12
Likud	12
Yisrael Beiteinu	11
National Union-National Religious Party	9
Gil	7
United Torah Judaism	6
Meretz-Yachad	5
United Arab List-Ta'al	4
Hadash	3
Balad	3
Total	120

You might think to count every party that contests national elections. If you did this, though, the number of parties in many countries would be extremely large and include "joke" parties, such as the "Mongolian Barbecue Great Place to Party" Party and the "Monster Raving Loony" Party in the United Kingdom, the "Church of the Militant Elvis" Party and the "Guns and Dope" Party—which advocates replacing one-third of Congress with ostriches—in the United States, the "Sun Ripened Warm Tomato" Party in Australia, and the "Beer Drinkers" Party in Russia (and many other countries). The problem is that a party system in which votes are divided evenly among ten parties is quite different from a system in which two parties get 90 percent of the votes with eight parties splitting the rest; this difference would be lost if we simply described both systems as "ten-party" systems.

The **effective number of parties** is a measure that captures both the number and size of parties in a country. The **effective number of electoral parties** is a measure of the number of parties that win votes. The **effective number of legislative parties** is a measure of the number of parties that win seats.

To take account of this, political scientists have frequently used a measure called the **effective number of parties** to count political parties (Laakso and Taagepera 1979). This measure counts each party that wins votes or seats, but it attaches to each party a weight that is related to the share of votes or seats that it wins. The precise formula for the effective number of parties in a system in which four parties receive votes would be:

$$\text{effective number of parties} = \frac{1}{v_1^2 + v_2^2 + v_3^2 + v_4^2},$$

where v_1 is the vote share of party 1, v_2 is the vote share of party 2, and so on. If all four parties received the same percentage of votes (0.25), then the effective number of parties would be 4, that is,

$$\text{effective number of parties} = \frac{1}{0.25^2 + 0.25^2 + 0.25^2 + 0.25^2} = \frac{1}{0.25} = 4.$$

Contrast this with the situation in which two parties split 90 percent of the vote equally and the two other parties split the remaining 10 percent equally. In this situation, the effective number of parties would be 2.44, that is,

$$\text{effective number of parties} = \frac{1}{0.45^2 + 0.45^2 + 0.05^2 + 0.05^2} = \frac{1}{0.41} = 2.44.$$

The "effective number of parties" is a desirable measure if we think that this latter situation is more like a two-party system than a four-party one.

If we use the "vote share" of political parties to weight each party as we did in the example above, then we are measuring what political scientists call the **effective number of electoral parties**. This gives us a sense of how many parties earned votes and how the electorate's votes were distributed across the parties. If we use the "seat share" of political parties to weight each party, then we are measuring what political scientists call the **effective number of legislative parties.** This gives us a sense of how many parties won seats in the legislature and how those seats were distributed across the parties. In effect, both measures of the effective number of parties not only take account of the number, but also the size, of the parties in a country. Note that we can use the effective number of parties in a country to classify democracies as having two-party or multiparty systems. One common way to do this is to classify democracies as having a two-party system if the effective number of parties is less than three and a multiparty system if the effective number of parties is three or more.

In Table 13.2, we list the effective number of electoral and legislative parties in fifty-four democracies around the world in the mid-1980s (Amorim Neto and Cox 1997). The country with the lowest effective number of electoral (1.84) and legislative (1.18) parties is Trinidad and Tobago. The reason why the effective number of parties is so low in Trinidad and Tobago is that the National Alliance for Reconstruction won 65.8 percent of the vote and

| TABLE 13.2 | Party Systems in Fifty-four Democracies in the mid-1980s | | |

Country	Year	Effective number of electoral parties	Effective number of legislative parties	Effective number of ethnic groups
Argentina	1985	3.37	2.37	1.34
Australia	1984	2.79	2.38	1.11
Austria	1986	2.72	2.63	1.01
Bahamas	1987	2.11	1.96	1.34
Barbados	1986	1.93	1.25	1.50
Belgium	1985	8.13	7.01	2.35
Belize	1984	2.06	1.60	3.46
Bolivia	1985	4.58	4.32	3.77
Botswana	1984	1.96	1.35	1.11
Brazil	1990	9.68	8.69	2.22
Canada	1984	2.75	1.69	3.49
Colombia	1986	2.68	2.45	2.51
Costa Rica	1986	2.49	2.21	1.08
Cyprus	1985	3.62	3.57	1.56
Czech Republic	1990	3.10	2.04	1.12
Denmark	1984	5.25	5.04	1.02
Dominica	1985	2.10	1.76	1.68
Dominican Republic	1986	3.19	2.53	1.75
Ecuador	1984	10.32	5.78	2.60
El Salvador	1985	2.68	2.10	1.25
Finland	1983	5.45	5.14	1.13

continues

TABLE 13.2	Party Systems in Fifty-four Democracies in the mid-1980s (continued)			
Country	Year	Effective number of electoral parties	Effective number of legislative parties	Effective number of ethnic groups
France	1981	4.13	2.68	1.17
Germany	1983	3.21	3.16	1.15
Greece	1985	2.59	2.14	1.04
Grenada	1990	3.84	3.08	1.06
Honduras	1985	3.49	2.80	1.23
Iceland	1983	4.26	4.07	1.06
India	1984	3.98	1.69	1.72
Ireland	1987	3.46	2.89	1.08
Israel	1984	4.28	3.86	1.39
Italy	1983	4.51	4.11	1.04
Jamaica	1989	1.97	1.60	1.65
Japan	1986	3.35	2.57	1.01
Korea, South	1988	4.22	3.56	1.01
Liechtenstein	1986	2.28	1.99	1.11
Luxembourg	1984	3.56	3.22	1.63
Malta	1987	2.01	2.00	1.13
Mauritius	1983	1.96	2.16	1.86
Netherlands	1986	3.77	3.49	1.08
New Zealand	1984	2.99	1.98	1.28
Norway	1985	3.63	3.09	1.04
Peru	1985	3.00	2.32	2.76
Portugal	1983	3.73	3.41	1.02
Spain	1986	3.59	2.81	1.65
St. Kitts & Nevis	1984	2.45	2.46	1.22
St. Lucia	1987	2.32	1.99	1.22
St. Vincent	1984	2.28	1.74	1.66
Sweden	1985	3.52	3.39	1.26
Switzerland	1983	5.99	5.26	2.13
Trinidad & Tobago	1986	1.84	1.18	2.74
United Kingdom	1983	3.12	2.09	1.48
United States	1984	2.03	1.95	1.36
Uruguay	1989	3.38	3.35	1.28
Venezuela	1983	2.97	2.42	1.99

Source: Amorim Neto and Cox (1997).

Note: The effective number of parties is a measure that captures both the number and size of parties in a country. The effective number of *electoral* parties is a measure of the number of parties that wins votes and the effective number of *legislative* parties is a measure of the number of parties that wins seats. The effective number of ethnic groups is a measure that captures both the number and size of ethnic groups in a country.

92 percent of the legislative seats in the 1986 elections. In effect, one party dominated the elections, and this is reflected in the two measures of the effective number of parties. The country with the highest effective number of electoral parties (10.32) is Ecuador, and the one with the highest effective number of legislative parties (8.69) is Brazil. In both of these countries, votes and seats were shared fairly evenly among a very large number of parties.

WHERE DO PARTIES COME FROM?

You might be wondering at this stage why democracies have the types of party systems that they do. To answer this question, we need to understand where parties come from. Political scientists have two basic views—primordial and instrumental—on this. The primordial view treats parties as the natural representatives of people who share common interests. In effect, this view takes it as given that there are "natural" divisions, or cleavages, in society. As groups of individuals form around these cleavages, political parties emerge and evolve to represent these interests. This is sometimes referred to as the "bottom up" approach to party formation. The instrumental view of party formation treats parties as teams of office seekers and focuses on the role played by political elites and entrepreneurs. According to this "top down" approach, political parties are created by individuals who, perhaps because of certain informational advantages and additional resources, are able to discern an opportunity to represent a previously unrepresented interest. Indeed, the instrumental approach recognizes that political entrepreneurs may even help citizens become aware that such an interest exists; in other words, they can even "create" divisions, or cleavages, in society.

These two views of party formation are similar to what economists would call supply and demand factors. The primordial view takes the social demand for the representation of particular interests as given and explains the existence of political parties as a response to those demands. In contrast, the instrumental view, along the lines of "Say's Law" in economics, holds that "supply creates its own demand." Just as advertising and marketing firms can shape the tastes of consumers, savvy political entrepreneurs might help create the demand for particular policies and ideologies. As in the case with supply and demand, it turns out that understanding the origins of political parties involves recognizing the interaction of both primordial and instrumental forces. To a large extent, social demands for representation drive the formation of political parties. These demands, however, are channeled in powerful and important ways by political institutions that structure the environment of would-be political entrepreneurs and voters. In what follows, we examine how social (primordial) and institutional (instrumental) forces interact to determine both the *type* and *number* of political parties that form in a democracy. We begin by looking at the types of parties that form. This requires us to examine societal cleavages and the process of political identity formation.

TYPES OF PARTIES: SOCIAL CLEAVAGES AND POLITICAL IDENTITY FORMATION

As we noted earlier, perhaps the central function of a political party in a democracy is to represent, articulate, and champion the interests and causes of its membership. These interests and causes are, by their very nature, shared by only a part of the overall population. The *Oxford English Dictionary* recognizes this when it defines a party as "a division of a whole; a part, portion, or share." By this definition, political parties arise when officials or would-be officials seek office to pursue goals that are shared by a *part*, but not all, of society. The origins of the British party system can be understood from this perspective.

Origins of the British Party System

The British party system first emerged in the seventeenth century out of a conflict in Parliament over the appropriate relationship between the church and state. In 1679 the first Earl of Shaftesbury introduced an Exclusion Bill to Parliament with the goal of preventing King Charles II's Catholic brother, James, the Duke of York, from succeeding him. Supporters of the Exclusion Bill were known as Whigs, whereas opponents of the bill were known as Tories. Although these names were originally meant to be insults (one meaning of Whigs being "Scottish horse thieves" and one meaning of Tories being "Irish outlaws"), parliamentary leaders embraced the terms—probably because the insults gave them a sense of shared offense that could be mobilized to create a sense of group loyalty. These group identities survived even after the resolution of the Exclusion Crisis in 1681—King Charles II dissolved Parliament twice over the Exclusion Bill, and the Duke of York did eventually become King James II after Charles's death in 1685—in part because they helped parliamentarians who shared similar views on several issue dimensions to organize their work. Compared with most modern political parties, "Tories" and "Whigs" stood for loose groupings of men. Nonetheless, they did capture important dispositional, confessional, and professional distinctions.

According to Ivor Bulmer-Thomas (1965), Tories and Whigs were divided most fundamentally in regard to their attitudes toward change. Forged in a time of revolution, with epic struggles between the Crown and Parliament, town and country, commerce and agriculture, capitalism and the remnants of feudalism, religious tradition and religious toleration—in short, tradition and modernity—Tories were associated with the status quo and Whigs with change or, as they would say, "progress." Although not fully determined by material relations, people's attitudes toward change were not entirely unrelated to their position in society. For example, Tories tended to come from the landed agricultural elite that had been long dominant in England, whereas the Whigs were more likely to come from the rising commercial elite. Tories and Whigs also differed in their attitudes toward the relationship between church and state. The Tories tended to support the Church of England's attempt to monopolize religious and political life by barring people who did not belong to the Church of England from holding public office, whereas the Whigs tended to support religious toleration.[2] These differences in social and economic background also influenced foreign policy

---

2. The tolerance of the Whigs went only so far, though. For instance, although the 1689 Act of Toleration, which was supported by the Whigs, granted freedom to worship to Nonconformist Protestants (such as Baptists, Congregationalists, and Quakers), it did not extend the same right to Catholics or Unitarians.

preferences. Because Whigs were more associated with commerce, they tended to be more "internationalist" in their outlook. For instance, they were willing to finance Queen Anne's military efforts because they saw such actions as important for protecting their commercial interests. Tories, by contrast, tended toward isolationism—they supported only those claimants to the Crown who came from the British line of succession and sought to avoid continental royalty that might bring foreign entanglements.

As you can see, the embryonic parties at the end of the seventeenth and beginning of the eighteenth centuries tended to sort members of Parliament into two distinct camps that were cleaved along several dimensions. The correlation or mapping across these dimensions was not entirely perfect. For example, there were nonconformist Tories and Whigs representing rural districts. Similarly, some Tories joined with the Whigs in inviting William of Orange and, later, George of Hanover to pursue the British Crown. As is the case with modern political parties, some members toed the "party line" more comfortably on some issues than on others. On the whole, though, the Whigs and Tories comprised parliamentarians who shared views across different policy dimensions. It is (only) at this point that these "like-minded" parliamentarians began to resemble what we would call a political party. Some of the policy dimensions along which Tories and Whigs competed at the beginning of the eighteenth century are shown in Table 13.3. As we will see, some of these same issue dimensions have been central to party systems in other times and places as well.

The Tories and Whigs went from groups of like-minded parliamentarians to competing teams of office seekers during the early eighteenth century. By excluding Tories from his ministry, George I was the first king (1714–1727) to compose his inner circle of advisers from a single party. One consequence of this "party ministry" was that gaining office now meant a party had greater control over policy and a greater control over public resources for the purpose of furthering the party's interests than before. Not only did this shift power from the Crown to the parliamentary elite, but it also raised the utility and benefit of holding office. Thus, what appeared to be differences of opinion within a bipartisan administration

TABLE 13.3   **Some Dimensions of Whig-Tory Conflict**

Whigs	Tories
"Progress"	"Tradition"
Limited government	Monarchy
Gentry	Nobility
Nonconformity and toleration	High Church orthodoxy
Commerce	Agriculture
Urban	Rural
Internationalism	Isolationism

now became congealed into competing teams that had incentives to help get their fellow party members elected and an increased capacity to use patronage to further a party's electoral goals.

Social Cleavages

As we noted earlier, some of the dimensions of political conflict between Tories and Whigs have been salient in other political systems as well. These cleavages have been used by political scientists to analyze the structure of party systems around the world. Before we begin to discuss why certain cleavages have become salient in some countries but not others, it is worthwhile to list a few of the more common cleavages that occur and talk about the evolution of their salience over time.

The Urban-Rural Cleavage

The conflict between rural and urban interests is one of the oldest political conflicts in the world. Moreover, it remains salient in many countries to this day. The conflict in early modern Europe between feudal lords on the one hand and town dwellers—freemen, burghers, or the bourgeoisie—on the other had both an economic and a cultural dimension. Economically, rural dwellers were typically associated with agricultural production and city dwellers with trade, crafts, and commerce. The most basic point of conflict between rural and urban interests, therefore, involved the price of food. Town dwellers were *consumers*, not producers, of food and, as a result, they typically experienced an increase in their living standards when food prices dropped. Rural dwellers were more likely to be *producers* of food and, so, benefited from increased food prices. In addition, much of rural life took place through a barter system that involved the trading of goods and services. Reputation was an important element in making the complex set of commitments surrounding such trades "credible," and reputation typically rested upon ties of kinship. In contrast, economic exchange in towns tended to be monetized and to take place between relatively anonymous actors. Consequently, urban commitment problems often surrounded the credibility of the money used to buy goods or the weights and measures employed to apportion them. It was because of this that the development of contract law, clearly defined property rights, and financial innovation became more of a priority in towns than in rural areas. Culturally, rural actors tended to value tradition, whereas town dwellers favored change.

The Confessional Cleavage

Another important conflict in many countries centers on confessional, or religious, differences. Conflict over religious differences emerged in European countries during the Protestant Reformation in the early sixteenth century. At this time, the authority of the Roman Catholic Church was challenged by the rise of Protestantism and men like Martin Luther in Germany and John Calvin in Geneva. For several decades, Europe was thrown into tumult as struggles between Protestants and Catholics, which would later become known as the Wars of Religion, tore apart countries, principalities, and the Holy Roman Empire. Religious conflict also fueled war between various political entities that lasted well into the seventeenth century. When the Peace of Westphalia (1648) ended both the Thirty Years' War and the Eighty Years' War (or Dutch Revolt), it also re-invigorated the norm of *cuius regio, eius religio*. This Latin phrase means "Whose region, his religion" and is used to describe the notion that the leader of a country, city-state, or principality is entitled to choose the religion for those who live under his or her rule. The idea dates back to the days of Emperor Constantine in the fourth century. Although the Peace of Westphalia may have led to a reduction in religious conflict between jurisdictions and helped create the modern state by rendering the Holy Roman Empire irrelevant, it did little to resolve religious conflicts within states. In fact, by empowering leaders to declare a state religion, it all but dictated religious intolerance.

The result was that individuals who confessed a commitment to a particular brand of Christianity often found themselves in conflict with devotees of other denominations. The exact way that this played out varied across different contexts. Britain, for example, was cleaved along confessional lines on at least two fronts. On the one hand, religious conflicts arose between supporters of the Church of England and the Nonconformists, such as Congregationalists (also known as Puritans), Presbyterians, and Quakers. This conflict was most acute during the English Civil War of 1642. On the other hand, religious conflicts also arose between supporters of the Church of England and Catholic Jacobites. The Jacobites supported the exiled King James II, his son James Edward ("the Old Pretender"), and his grandson Charles Edward ("the Young Pretender") in various conflicts. In addition, there was a long and brutal conflict between Protestants and Catholics in Ireland (and later, Northern Ireland).

The Protestant-Catholic cleavage has been important in many other European countries as well. Its continued salience, however, depends largely on whether or not one or the other side has been able to establish its dominance. In some places, the division has led to two different countries. For example, the Eighty Years' War split the Low Countries into the Protestant- (mostly Calvinist) dominated Dutch Republic (now the Netherlands) and the Catholic-dominated southern Netherlands (today's Belgium). In some places, such as Germany, Catholics and Protestants eventually formed an uneasy truce, and in other countries, such as Sweden (Lutheran) or France (Catholic), one or the other church became dominant. Finally, it is worth mentioning that in some countries, such as Italy and Spain, the Protestant Reformation never made any significant inroads. Whatever the settlement, many European party systems bear the imprint of the now centuries-old conflict between Protestants and Catholics.

Confessional cleavages continue to be salient in many non-European countries as well. For example, conflict between Hindus and Muslims led to the partition of India into a predominantly Hindu India and a Muslim-dominated Pakistan in 1947. Following the creation of Pakistan, millions of Muslims moved from India to Pakistan and millions of Hindus and

Sikhs moved from Pakistan to India. The conflict between Hindus and Muslims continues to be salient in this region today, particularly in the disputed region of Kashmir. Deep divisions between Sunni and Shia Muslims have been central to the politics of many Middle Eastern countries for centuries. The removal of Saddam Hussein by U.S. forces in 2003 exacerbated these divisions in Iraq and beyond. Nigeria is another country with deep confessional divisions, this time between a predominantly Muslim north and a predominantly Christian south. Finally, nowhere is the confessional cleavage more institutionalized than in Lebanon, where high political offices are explicitly reserved for representatives of different religious groups. For example, the president, prime minister, deputy prime minister, and the speaker of the parliament are constitutionally mandated to be held by a Maronite Christian, Sunni Muslim, Orthodox Christian, and Shia Muslim, respectively.

The Secular-Clerical Cleavage

In the last two centuries, political competition around religious issues in European democracies has taken place primarily along a church-state axis (Lipset and Rokkan 1967). The conflict "between the growing state, which sought to dominate, and the church, which tried to maintain its historic corporate rights" had been growing for some time (Lipset 2001, 6). This conflict was particularly pronounced in France, where close cooperation between the nobility and the Catholic clergy had helped maintain the Bourbon monarchy in power since the sixteenth century. The Roman Catholic Church was the largest landowner in the country and had, since 585 AD, the right to exact a tax of 10 percent (or *la dîme*) on all agricultural products. These church taxes fueled resentment among many French people, in part because these resources, which were originally meant to provide for local parishes, were often siphoned off by the church hierarchy to support remote monasteries and bishops. Consequently, when the French Revolution was launched in 1789 against Louis XVI, the popular uprising was, to a large extent, aimed at the church as much as the monarchy. Legislation that was passed in 1790 abolished the church's authority to levy *la dîme*, confiscated church property, and canceled special privileges for the clergy. The 1790 Civil Constitution of the Clergy turned clergy into employees of the state, thereby subordinating the Roman Catholic Church to the French government and removing it from the authority of the pope.

In order to solidify his hold on power after a coup d'état in 1799, though, Napoleon Bonaparte reached an agreement with the Roman Catholic Church—the Concordat of 1801—to restore some of the church's power. With the brief restoration of the monarchy in 1814, the Catholic Church regained even more of its former status, and the clergy continued to enjoy privileges into the late nineteenth century. French **anti-clericalism**—opposition to religious institutional power and influence in public and political life—once again grew stronger as the nineteenth century drew to a close. In the 1880s, religious figures began to be expelled from public schools, and the Jules Ferry laws mandated that the French state provide

Anti-clericalism is opposition to religious institutional power and influence in public and political life. **Laïcité** is the notion that there is a division between private life, where religion belongs, and public life, where it does not; it does not necessarily imply any hostility to religion.

a free and *lay* education for its citizens. Numerous conflicts broke out at this time between supporters of the Catholic Church and supporters of a secular state. One such conflict was the Dreyfus Affair, which divided French society from the 1890s to the early 1900s (Bredin 1986). The Dreyfus Affair was a political scandal centering on the wrongful conviction of Captain Alfred Dreyfus, a Jew, for treason. This scandal was about many things, including pervasive anti-Semitism in French society, but it divided the country into supporters of Dreyfus (republicans, socialists, and anti-clericalists) and opponents of Dreyfus (royalists, conservatives, and the Catholic Church). In effect, the Dreyfus Affair divided France into those groups that supported the ideas behind the French Revolution and those that opposed them.

In 1905 France passed a law requiring the complete separation of church and state. The law states, "The Republic neither recognizes, nor salaries, nor subsidizes any religion." In effect, this law established state secularism in France and is the backbone of the current French principle of **laïcité.** *Laïcité* refers to the division between private life, where religion belongs, and public life, where religion does not. To a large extent, this principle rests on the belief that citizens should be treated equally in the public sphere and that things like religion (and ethnicity), which might distinguish between individuals and lead to unequal treatment by the state, should be ignored. Laïcité is distinct from anti-clericalism in that it does not necessarily imply any hostility on the part of the state toward religion; it is simply the idea that the state and political issues should be kept separate from religious organizations and religious issues.

Although the secular state is now well-established and laïcité is overwhelmingly supported by the French people, religion remains a source of political conflict in contemporary France. Since the 1990s, for example, it has led to a political conflict that has come to be known as the Headscarf Debate. This debate has primarily been about whether Muslim girls wearing headscarves in public schools are violating the principle of laïcité by wearing a religious symbol (the headscarf) in a state-funded institution (public school). After several years without a clear policy, the French National Assembly overwhelmingly passed a law against pupils wearing "conspicuous" or "ostentatious" symbols of belonging to a religion in 2005. Although the law does not mention any particular religious symbol, the prohibited items are generally recognized to include headscarves for Muslim girls, yarmulkes for Jewish boys, turbans for Sikhs, and large Christian crosses. Although the law initially led to several demonstrations and protests from affected groups, the law has been implemented fairly smoothly. Nonetheless, there is ongoing debate as to whether this specific law, and the strict implementation of laïcité more generally, is actually encouraging the integration of religious groups, mainly Muslims, into mainstream French society or alienating them. The current French president, Nicolas Sarkozy, has recently proposed weakening the strict separation of church and state, for example, by allowing the state to subsidize Muslim prayer rooms in schools.

The specifics of the French case should not distract us from a broader trend toward secularism in Europe from the dawn of the Enlightenment in the eighteenth century into the twenty-first century. Although the degree of secularization in terms of individual piety is the subject of considerable debate among sociologists, there is no debate that this period saw a

Lila Levy, 18, left, and her sister Alma, 16, stand outside the headquarters of the Movement Against Racism and for Friendship Between People, or MRAP, after giving a news conference in the premises, Monday, Oct. 13, 2003 in Paris. The two sisters were expelled the previous Friday from their high school in Aubervilliers, outside Paris, after administrators said their headscarves were ostentatious symbols of religion. The girls' father, Laurent Levy, blamed the decision on what he claimed was a phobia of Islam "eating away at French society."

persistent retreat by religious institutions from the public square. Modernizing elites around the world argued persuasively that the state and church should be separated. Much of the popular appeal of this argument stemmed from the frequent association of the church with the unpopular ancien régime—conservative, monarchist forces seeking to protect aristocratic privilege.

Church officials and some believers resisted the separation of church and state, arguing that Christian values of charity for the poor, protection of the family, and the like needed to be protected against what they saw as the corrosive effects of secularism. As a consequence, religious parties formed in many countries. For example, the Tories in Britain originally rallied around the slogan "For Church and King." Separate Protestant and Catholic parties competed in the Netherlands, although by the late nineteenth century they were typically making common cause against "secular" parties. Indeed, political conflicts between Catholics and Protestants subsided in many countries as the cleavage between confessional and secular groups became increasingly salient. For example, the Christian Democratic Appeal (CDA) in the Netherlands is explicitly nondenominational and seeks to unite Catholics and Protestants. In many countries in Europe and Latin America, Christian Democratic parties combine a conservative position on social issues like abortion and same-sex marriage with an activist position on economic policy. Although staunchly anti-Communist, many Christian Democratic parties take an organic or corporatist view of the economy that emphasizes individuals' obligation to serve their community. This stands in stark contrast to the economic position of Liberal parties in Europe, which derive their identity from the defense of individual, rather than group, rights. European liberals are staunchly secular in their social orientation and champion free-market capitalism in the economic world.

The Class Cleavage

Lipset and Rokkan (1967) refer to the preceding cleavages as "pre-industrial cleavages." This is in marked contrast to the class cleavage, which is said to have become salient during the Industrial Revolution at the end of the eighteenth century. Like the urban-rural cleavage, the class cleavage pits actors against each other over conflicting economic interests. Whereas the urban-rural cleavage involves horizontal conflicts *between* different sectors in society, however, the class cleavage involves vertical conflicts *within* sectors between actors who derive their livelihood from the use of their labor and those who derive their livelihood from the use of their property or capital. Class conflict takes place most fundamentally between workers and capitalists in industrial sectors of the economy, but it takes place primarily between peasants (or, later, agricultural workers) and large landowners in the agricultural sectors. Class conflict typically involves attempts to use the state to redistribute wealth from the rich to the poor. Capitalists tend to favor the free market, a small state, and a restricted franchise; in contrast, workers support greater state intervention in the economy and an expansion of the franchise.

The class cleavage became increasingly salient in most European countries during the nineteenth century as demands for franchise expansion, particularly from the working class, grew. At the beginning of the nineteenth century, the right to vote was typically restricted to adult male citizens who owned large amounts of property. Although the Great Reform Act of 1832 expanded the franchise in Great Britain, it still allowed only about one in five male adults to vote. The 1867 Reform Act expanded the suffrage further to include all working-class males. Through this process, and analogous processes in other European states, workers became relevant at the ballot box, and the state was set for full-scale competition between parties claiming to represent the industrial working class and parties that represented economic elites.

For the next hundred years, politics in Europe revolved around the "left-right" divide. The terms *left* and *right* were first used to describe the seating location of competing factions in the French National Assembly in 1791. From the viewpoint of the speaker's chair, monarchists sat to the right and bourgeois reformers sat to the left. This pattern was replicated in other continental parliaments: protectors of aristocratic and clerical interests sat on the right and middle-class reformers sat on the left. At the time, people sitting on the left—the "left-wingers"—were advocating laissez-fair capitalism and democratization. Through the nineteenth century, though, the political center of gravity shifted further leftward throughout Europe so that by the beginning of the twentieth century, protectors of free markets and democracy were considered "right-wing" and those in favor of workers' rights and socialist revolution were considered "left-wing." Eventually the "Left" came to be represented by Communist and Social Democratic parties and the "Right" by Christian Democratic and Liberal parties.

In the nineteenth century, many socialists were in favor of democracy and the socialist transformation of society. Marxist theory predicted the expansion of the industrial working class (proletariat) as capitalism expanded. Under such conditions it was thought that the expansion of the franchise and the natural course of economic development would in short order produce huge Socialist majorities that would then implement the transition to a socialist society by legislative means (Przeworski and Sprague 1986, 22–25). Several factors, however, conspired to inhibit the unfolding of this set of historical developments that many Marxists had once thought inevitable.

First, not all actors voted according to their class interests. In his book *The Poverty of Philosophy*, Karl Marx ([1847] 1995) makes the distinction between a class "in itself" and a class "for itself." Individuals are members of a class "in itself" simply by virtue of their objective "relation to the means of production." In other words, individuals who sell their labor for a wage are workers; those who earn a profit are capitalists. In contrast, individuals are members of a "class for itself" only if they are actually conscious of their status as a member of that class. Thus, the socialist project can be thought of as a process of class formation. In effect, the goal was to make workers realize that they were workers and to transform the proletariat from a "class in itself" to a "class for itself." Although Marxist orthodoxy held that this process of class formation was a historical inevitability, individual Marxists differed on the extent to which this process could be accelerated or delayed by the strategic organizational practices of the leaders of the proletariat and the bourgeoisie. What is clear is that the process by which workers were radicalized took longer than many Marxist theorists expected, leading scholars to label the continued commitment of some workers to bourgeois parties and institutions as "false consciousness" in which "the real motive forces impelling (an actor) remain unknown to him" (Engels [1893] 1968). Whether workers perceived their interests differently from the way that Marxist theorists suggested they should, or whether they were, in fact, suffering from "false consciousness," it is a historical fact that across a wide range of countries and time periods, a nontrivial portion of manual laborers voted *against* left-wing parties and a substantial share of managers and professionals voted *for* left-wing parties.

Second, workers "never were and never would become a numerical majority in their respective societies" (Przeworski and Sprague 1986, 31). As a consequence, Socialist parties found it necessary either to broaden their appeals to attract salaried workers and other members of the bourgeoisie or to govern in coalition with bourgeois parties. Przeworski and Sprague (1986) note how these strategies, which were designed to help win elections and gain office, ultimately ended up diluting the salience of class as a basis for individual behavior in some countries.

Finally, even where Socialist parties were electorally successful, there were structural factors at work to limit the extent to which they could bring about a socialist transformation. As we discussed in Chapters 6 and 9, part of the reason for why Socialist parties did not institute a socialist transformation had to do with the disciplining effects that investors can play in deterring radical policies. As you will recall, this disciplining effect is referred to as the "structural dependence of the state on capital." In addition to this pressure from external actors, scholars have identified organizational factors that helped to moderate the policy positions of Socialist parties. With some irony, German sociologist Robert Michels ([1911] 2001, 13) noted that "[i]n theory, the principal aim of social and democratic parties is the struggle against oligarchy in all its forms. The question therefore arises how we are to explain the development in such parties of the very tendencies against which they have declared war." Michels responded to this puzzle by arguing that in all sufficiently complex organizations, including political parties, a division of labor must arise between rank-and-file members and professional managers. Because the leaders of the organization develop lifestyles, skills, and interests different from those of the rank and file, the organization will, inevitably, begin to pursue goals that are different from those it was originally formed to pursue. In the case of labor unions and Socialist parties, although the leadership may exist to represent the "ruled," it is inevitably transformed into part of the ruling class by virtue of its position at the head of the organization. This notion that the leadership of an organization will develop goals that are distinct from those of the organization's rank and file, and that because they *are* leaders their goals will become dominant, is known as **Michels' iron law of oligarchy.** Michels' iron law of oligarchy has been used to explain organizational dynamics in many different social

> **Michels' iron law of oligarchy** states that the leadership of organizations such as political parties will never be faithful to the program and constituency that gave rise to the organization in the first place.

settings, from trade unions and political parties to religious denominations, corporations, and nonprofit organizations.

The Post-Material Cleavage

Lipset and Rokkan (1967) observed that European party systems were remarkably stable during most of the twentieth century. They observed that the preceding cleavages were all activated during a period when new groups were in the process of being politically mobilized. For example, the urban-rural cleavage and the various religious cleavages became salient at the same time that new elites (the landed gentry and commercial elites in urban areas) were being incorporated into national politics in competition with traditional elites (the nobility and the clergy). The class cleavage became salient during a period when the franchise was expanded to include male workers and eventually women. As these cleavages were activated, new parties could be formed to capture segments of the population that had not previously been active in electoral politics. Lipset and Rokkan argued that European party systems became "frozen" with the achievement of universal suffrage during the 1920s. Social structures might change, as they had in the past, but there was no longer any untapped electoral base to be mobilized into new parties. In effect, the barriers to successful entry for new parties seeking to represent emerging interests became too high after the 1920s. As a consequence, political positions associated with new cleavages would either go unrepresented or existing parties would alter their positions to capture "unrepresented" voters. Lipset and Rokkan's famous **"freezing hypothesis"** was used to explain why the ideological dimensions of most European party systems

> Lipset and Rokkan's **freezing hypothesis** states that West European party systems became frozen following the extension of universal suffrage in most countries during the 1920s.

were so similar. Although there was some interesting variety across cases, the modal European party system in the middle of the twentieth century had two parties on the left (Socialist and Communist, with Socialists being more hostile to Soviet influence than the Communists) and a Conservative Party (often Christian Democratic) and a Liberal Party on the right. The freezing hypothesis was also used to explain why the political parties dominating elections in the 1960s were the same parties that had dominated elections decades earlier in the 1920s and 1930s.

Two challenges to Lipset and Rokkan's freezing hypothesis have arisen in Europe since the 1960s. One is the emergence in the 1960s and 1970s of new political parties that Kitschelt (1988) terms "left-libertarian" parties.[3] These parties differ from the "Old Left" in that they are less closely tied to the industrial working class and are likely to privilege issues such as environmentalism and immigration that can be perceived to run against working-class interests. Inglehart (1977, 1997) argues that these new parties are a response to a fundamental value shift in advanced industrial democracies from "materialist" to "post-materialist" values. In effect, he claims that they are a response to the relative decline in the salience of more traditional cleavages and the emergence of a new post-materialist cleavage. Having been raised in an environment of plenty in which their existential security was taken for granted, new generations of voters prioritize the expansion of human freedom. This new generation of voters is more concerned with issues relating to multiculturalism, gender and racial equality, reproductive choice, and sexual freedom than the traditional bread-and-butter issues that concerned the left in previous decades.

According to Kitschelt (1988, 195):

> All left-libertarian parties are critical of the logic of societal development and the institutions that underlie the postwar compromise between capital and labor in industrial societies. They oppose the priority that economic growth has on the political agenda, the patterns of policy making that restrict democratic participation to elite bargaining among centralized interest groups and party leaders, and the bureaucratic welfare state. Their political alternatives conform neither to traditional conservative nor to socialist programs, but link libertarian commitments to individual autonomy and popular participation, with a leftist concern for equality.

Kitschelt goes on to show that there is a strong correlation between a country's level of development and the electoral success of left-libertarian parties such as the Greens. Using survey evidence, he suggests that these parties "overproportionally draw voters from the ranks of the younger, well-educated middle class; they are employed in human services (teaching, health care, social work), have left-of-center political convictions, subscribe to 'post-materialist' values, and sympathize with environmental, feminist, and peace movements" (1988, 198).

The second challenge to the freezing hypothesis comes from the successful emergence of populist extreme right parties in some European countries during the 1980s and 1990s (Kitschelt 1996; Golder 2003). Several scholars have linked the emergence of these parties to the same new post-materialist cleavage that supposedly led to left-libertarian parties (Flanagan 1987; Inglehart 1990; Ignazi 1992; Minkenberg 1992; Betz 1994). In fact, these

---

3. This is an unfortunate label because there are at least two other distinct intellectual movements that use this term. One is influenced by the Austrian-School economist Murray Rothbard and the other is associated with such philosophers as Hillel Steiner, Peter Vallentyne, and Michael Otsuka. Both of these intellectual movements are largely unrelated to Kitschelt's "left-libertarian" parties.

scholars see the successful emergence of populist extreme right parties as a direct reaction to the post-materialist agenda of the libertarian left. In contrast to the libertarian left, populist parties on the extreme right tend to emphasize traditional values and highlight how things like immigration are not only threatening national identity and culture but also the jobs and economic welfare of native workers (Golder 2003). For example, Jean-Marie Le Pen, the leader of the National Front in France used the slogan, "Two million immigrants are the cause of two million French people out of work" during the 1984 European elections (Mitra 1988), and the Republicans in Germany have campaigned under a similar slogan: "Eliminate Unemployment: Stop Immigration." Populist parties have also managed to exploit the shift from an industrial to a postindustrial economy, in which certain sections of the population, such as the uneducated, feel alienated and unable to compete and prosper (Betz 1994).

Despite the emergence of these new left-libertarian and populist parties in Europe since the 1960s, there is considerable debate about the extent to which European party systems have truly changed (Bartolini and Mair 1990; Mair 1997). Although the policies of left-libertarian parties have found some resonance in the wider citizenry, these parties managed to poll only about 5 percent of the vote on average during the 1990s in Western Europe. Populist parties on the extreme right were, on average, polling about the same during this period. Although these averages obviously hide some significant variation across different countries, it is hard to argue that they represent a large-scale change in aggregate voter alignments. If one looks at the left and right as a whole "the most remarkable feature of all is the extraordinary persistence across the postwar decades" (Gallagher, Laver, and Mair 2006, 286). On the whole, the parties that dominate West European elections and governments today tend to be the same parties that dominated elections and governments as far back as the 1920s (Golder 2002).

Ethnic and Linguistic Cleavages

In various countries around the world, ethnic or linguistic cleavages or both are another important source of conflict. Exactly what counts as an "ethnic" cleavage is not obvious because there are many different definitions of what makes a group an "ethnic" group. One common characteristic in definitions of an **ethnic group,** though, is an emphasis on the role of "descent" (Chandra 2006). In effect, members of ethnic groups share some characteristic more closely with fellow group members

> An **ethnic group** is one in which members possess some attributes, believed to be related to descent, which are shared more closely with fellow group members than with nongroup members.

than with nongroup members, and this characteristic is inherited in some way from their parents. What scholars tend to differ with one another about is what the particular characteristic or trait is that is shared by the ethnic group members. Thus, an individual's eligibility for membership in an ethnic group is based on the possession of certain attributes that are, at least believed to be, related to descent. We say "believed to be" because the claims of many ethnic groups to having a common ancestry or common place of origin are simply myths. Chandra (2006, 400) notes that "descent-based attributes" shared by ethnic group members can be "acquired genetically (e.g., skin color, gender, hair type, eye color, height, and physical features), through cultural and historical inheritance (e.g., the names, languages, places of birth and origin of one's parents and ancestors), or in the course of one's lifetime as markers of such an inheritance (e.g., last name or tribal markings)."

Eligibility in an ethnic group does not mean the same thing as "membership." As with class, there is a natural tension between ethnic groups "in themselves" and ethnic groups "for themselves." On the one hand, there are circumstances in which individuals can choose the extent to which they identify with an ethnic group. For example, one of the authors of this book (Clark) might embrace his Irish-American heritage at a Celtic music performance or poetry reading but shy away from that same heritage when confronted with particularly crass and distasteful "St. Paddy's Day" debauchery. On the other hand, there are circumstances in which individuals might be classified by others, such as in-group "gatekeepers" or government officials, as belonging or not belonging to a particular ethnic group. In addition, as the experiments on ethnic identity that we mentioned in Chapter 7 indicate, it is not always the case that the ethnic identity of an individual can be easily identified by other actors, even by other members of the individual's ethnic group (Habyarimana et al. 2005). Ethnic identity is not always self-evident.

As with class, social scientists have differed on the extent to which they see ethnic group membership as based on objective or subjective traits. Scholars who emphasize the objective nature of ethnic identification have been termed "primordialists," and those who emphasize the subjective nature of ethnic identification have been called "constructivists" or "instrumentalists." Briefly, primordialists believe that ethnic attachments are transmitted automatically and that group composition is naturally and externally determined. Constructivists, in contrast, believe that group attachments are socially constructed. In other words, they believe that group identities today are the result of choices made by social actors in the past; social groups do not fall from heaven, nor do they spring from some primordial ooze. "Instrumentalism" might be thought of as a subcategory of constructivism in that instrumentalists believe that group attachments result from the intentional acts of social actors who see group attachments as *serving some other purpose,* such as aiding their political survival or giving them access to state resources.

Given the salience of various ethnic cleavages around the world, it is little surprise that ethnic parties exist in many countries. An **ethnic party** is one that "appeals to voters as the champion of the interests of one ethnic category or set of categories to the exclusion of others, and makes such an appeal central to its mobilizing strategy. The key aspect of this definition is *exclusion*. An ethnic party may champion the interests of more than one ethnic category, but only by identifying the common ethnic enemy to be excluded" (Chandra 2005, 236). Although most people probably think of Africa when they think of ethnic parties, ethnic parties exist and do well in most regions of the world. In fact, probably the first ethnic parties were Jewish parties in the Russian and Austro-Hungarian empires and the Swedish

> An **ethnic party** is one that champions the interests of one ethnic category or set of categories to the exclusion of others, and does so as a central component of its mobilizing strategy.

Party in Finland, all founded in the nineteenth century or the first decade of the twentieth century. Relatively successful ethnic parties exist today in countries as far afield as Canada, Fiji, India, Ireland, Israel, Macedonia, New Zealand, Romania, Russia, Spain, Sri Lanka, and Turkey. One continent where there have historically been few ethnic parties is Latin America. This has recently begun to change, however, with the emergence of various ethnic parties in countries such as Bolivia, Colombia, Ecuador, and Venezuela to represent indigenous populations (Van Cott 2005).

Theorizing about Politicized Cleavages

So far we have identified a number of salient social cleavages that define political conflict in party systems around the world. But why are some party systems divided primarily along ethnic lines, whereas others are divided mainly along class, religious, linguistic, or regional ones? What determines which social cleavages become politicized and salient? In sum, what explains why we get the types of parties that we do? Unfortunately, comparative political scientists have only just begun to examine these sorts of questions in any great detail. As yet, they have not developed a fully worked out theory of politicized cleavages. Nonetheless, recent research suggests that the distribution of individual attributes in society and the electoral institutions in a country are likely to be key parts of any such theory (Chandra and Boulet 2003; Posner 2004, 2005; Chandra 2004, 2006).[4] In what follows, we present the general contours of this research, drawing heavily on insights from Chandra and Boulet (2003).

The basic premise in this new research is that individuals are multifaceted and have a repertoire of **attributes,** such as religion, language, class, gender, skin color, and so on, that makes them eligible for membership in some **identity category** or social group. The attributes of individuals can obviously take on different values. For example, consider the attribute of religion. An individual might be Catholic, Protestant, Jewish, Muslim, Hindu, atheist, or something else. In Table 13.4, we list some attributes that individuals might have and possible values that these attributes can take on. Chandra and Boulet (2003) take an individual's attributes as given, self-evident, and sticky (hard to change). In contrast, they assume that identity categories are socially constructed. In other words, whether identity categories or social groups form around all workers, just black workers, just male workers, or just black male workers who are tall and who happen to be political scientists, and so on is not something that is natural or objective but something that is determined by the choices of social actors over time (and the institutional context in which they make those choices). By taking attributes as given but identity categories as socially constructed, Chandra and Boulet (2003) provide a "thinly-constructivist" approach to political identity formation.

> An **attribute** is a characteristic that qualifies an individual for membership in an identity category. An **identity category** is a social group in which an individual can place herself.

---

4. The roots of this recent research can be traced to Laitin (1986, 1992, 1998).

TABLE 13.4	**Individual Attributes and Possible Attribute Values**
Attribute	**Possible attribute values**
Class	Worker, bourgeoisie
Skin color	Black, white
Nationality	English, American, Nigerian
Profession	Political scientist, plumber, doctor
Region	North, south, east, west
Origin	Foreign, native
Height	Tall, short

Assignment to an identity category or social group, either by oneself or by someone else, will involve a shared understanding about the ways in which possession of certain attributes corresponds to membership in particular groups. This shared understanding is likely to have been built up over many years, decades, centuries, or even longer. As an example, suppose that a country's population is divided according to the region (North or South) and language (French or Dutch) associated with one's parents and that a social understanding has developed over the years that "who you are" is related to your ancestral language and ancestral region. Potential identity categories in this country would, therefore, be drawn from the possible combinations of these two attributes. The attributes of individuals in this country will obviously be distributed in a particular way. In Table 13.5, we list the two attributes in our hypothetical country and the share of the population (a, b, c, d) embodying each possible combination of attributes.

In Table 13.6, we list all nine of the potential identity categories (social groups) that could be formed (socially constructed) in our hypothetical country. These "potential" identity categories are sometimes referred to as "latent" identity categories. But which of the potential identity categories shown in Table 13.6 will be "activated" or "politicized"? The answer to this question is not immediately obvious.

To some extent, how attributes map onto actual identity categories is likely to depend on the distribution and correlation of those attributes. For example, if the attributes are uncorrelated with each other and fairly evenly distributed across the population, then there may be a propensity for each combination of attributes to be thought of as a separate identity

TABLE 13.5	**Attributes and Possible Combinations of Attributes in a Hypothetical Country**	
	French speaker	**Dutch speaker**
Northerner	a	b
Southerner	c	d

Note: Letters indicate the share of the population embodying each possible combination of attributes.

TABLE 13.6	Potential Identity Categories in a Hypothetical Country
Potential identity category	**Size (%)**
Northerner	a + b
Southerner	c + d
French speaker	a + c
Dutch speaker	b + d
Northerner and French speaker	a
Northerner and Dutch speaker	b
Southerner and French speaker	c
Southerner and Dutch speaker	d
Everyone	a + b + c + d

Note: Letters indicate the share of the population embodying the potential identity category shown.

group and activated as such. For example, suppose that the attributes in our hypothetical country are uncorrelated and that the population is evenly distributed as in Table 13.7. In this scenario, our hypothetical country is said to have **cross-cutting attributes.** All other things being equal, the identity categories (Northerner, Southerner) and (French speaker, Dutch speaker)

> A country with uncorrelated attributes has **cross-cutting attributes** (cleavages), whereas a country with correlated attributes has **reinforcing attributes** (cleavages).

are equally distinctive and, presumably, equally likely to be activated. Indeed, either of these cleavages—North versus South or French speaking versus Dutch speaking—are as likely to be activated and politicized as the four-way cleavage (French-speaking northerner, Dutch-speaking northerner, French-speaking southerner, Dutch-speaking southerner).

Now suppose that the attributes in our hypothetical country are highly correlated as in Table 13.8. When attributes are highly correlated like this, then the effective number of attribute repertoires is likely to be smaller. A country with highly correlated attributes is said to have **reinforcing attributes.** In regard to our hypothetical country in Table 13.8, this is because knowing that a person's family is from the North allows one to predict with a fair amount of confidence that his or her ancestral language is Dutch; similarly, knowing that a person's family is from the South allows one to predict that his or her ancestral language is French. In such circumstances it seems plausible, all other things being equal, to predict that

TABLE 13.7	Cross-Cutting Attributes	
	French speaker	**Dutch speaker**
Northerner	0.25	0.25
Southerner	0.25	0.25

TABLE 13.8	Reinforcing Attributes	
	French speaker	Dutch speaker
Northerner	0.03	0.57
Southerner	0.36	0.04

the identity categories that will be activated or politicized will be "French-speaking southerners" and "Dutch-speaking northerners." In fact, a similar distribution of attributes to that shown in Table 13.8 is found in contemporary Belgium. Belgium is a country that is profoundly cleaved along ethno-linguistic and regional lines. Indeed, Belgians are constitutionally divided into three communities: a French-speaking community that lives primarily in the South (Wallonia), a Dutch-speaking community that lives primarily in the North (Flanders), and a German-speaking community that lives primarily in the East in a region that was part of Germany before World War I.

Clearly, the division of the people of Belgium into separate ethnic "communities" is the product of deep-seated historical processes. For example, the East-West line dividing French-speaking Wallonia from Dutch-speaking Flanders has been said to mark the northernmost reaches of the Roman province of Gaul in the fourth century. Thus, the line represents, in many ways, a historic dividing line between Frankish and Germanic cultures. If one drives through the region, one can immediately sense the change as one travels between towns such as Lille and Charleroi on the southern side of the line and Ghent and Leuven on the northern side. It is hard to overstate the cultural and political salience of such a boundary; a boundary, we should note, that is centuries older than the Mason-Dixon Line that is said to divide the North and South in the United States.

Although it is hard to overstate the salience of these types of boundaries, it is important to recognize that many such divisions exist around the world, and their salience rises and falls in different periods and different places. This variation in salience suggests that we should look for other factors that might influence which potential identity categories in a society get activated or politicized. The electoral rules that we examined in the previous chapter are one such factor. Different electoral rules can lead to the activation of different identity categories in countries that have identical distributions of attributes. For example, imagine that we have two countries, A and B, in which attributes are identically distributed as shown in Table 13.9. The only difference between the two countries is that the electoral institutions in country A

TABLE 13.9	A Hypothetical Distribution of Attributes	
	French speaker	Dutch speaker
Northerner	0.40	0.10
Southerner	0.40	0.10

are such that gaining national office requires 50 percent of the vote and the electoral institutions in country B are such that gaining national office requires 60 percent of the vote. How do you think this difference in electoral rules will influence which identity categories will get activated or politicized in the two countries? If you were a political entrepreneur, which identity categories would you try to politicize if you wanted to gain national office?

One way to think about this is to recall the logic of building government coalitions that we presented in Chapter 11. Let's start by thinking about country A. According to the logic of "least minimal winning coalitions," French-speaking northerners in country A have strong incentives to form a coalition with Dutch-speaking northerners; similarly, French-speaking southerners have strong incentives to form a coalition with Dutch-speaking southerners. Both coalitions could expect to win the required 50 percent of the vote to win national office.[5] In this scenario, each national election would effectively be decided by a flip of a coin. In fact, whoever was more effective out of the French-speaking northerners and French-speaking southerners at building ties with the Dutch speakers could expect to win every national election. This means that political parties in country A are likely to compete on the basis of how effective they are at generating interlinguistic cooperation. By doing this, though, the political parties would, in effect, be reinforcing regional divisions. As a result, the main politicized cleavage in country A is likely to be regional, and the party system is likely to be characterized by regional parties.[6]

What about country B? Recall that gaining national office in country B requires 60 percent of the vote. One possible scenario in country B is that a coalition will form between northern French speakers and southern French speakers. Such a coalition could expect to win 80 percent of the vote. In these circumstances, Dutch speakers would be a permanent minority.[7] In this case, the main politicized cleavage (and the party system) would be linguistic rather than regional. The only thing that has changed between country A, where interlinguistic cooperation is likely, and country B, where the exclusion of linguistic outgroups is likely, is the electoral threshold.

The importance of electoral institutions to the politicization of social cleavages can also be seen if we examine how identity categories might be activated in countries that share the same electoral rules but differ in their distribution of attributes. For example, imagine that two countries, C and D, have the same electoral institutions such that gaining national office requires 60 percent of the vote. The only difference between the two countries is that the attributes in country C are distributed as shown in Table 13.9 and the attributes in country D are distributed as shown in Table 13.10. Following the same logic as before, we might expect the identity categories that will be activated or politicized to be linguistic in country C and regional

---

5. You might think that French-speaking northerners and French-speaking southerners would form a coalition together. However, this coalition would require that government resources and offices be split among 80 percent of the population rather than among 50 percent of the population. The lower average "payoffs" associated with this coalition help to explain why political entrepreneurs have incentives to form *least* minimal winning coalitions rather than just minimal winning coalitions.

6. Readers who see the United States as being divided between the "Blue coasts" and the "Red heartland" might see something familiar in this example.

7. We explore the potentially disastrous consequences of such a situation in Chapter 15.

TABLE 13.10	An Alternative Hypothetical Distribution of Attributes	
	French speaker	Dutch speaker
Northerner	0.25	0.35
Southerner	0.15	0.15

in country D. Posner (2004) employs a similar argument to help explain why Chewas and Tumbukas are political allies in Zambia but rivals in Malawi (see Box 13.3 for more details).

What these examples illustrate is that politicized cleavages are likely to be the result of an interaction between latent social cleavages and electoral (and other) institutions. In other words, each country has a certain set of latent social cleavages that is determined by its distribution of individual attributes. Which of these latent social cleavages become politicized, though, is going to be influenced by the electoral institutions employed in that country. This causal story is illustrated in Figure 13.1. An implication of this story is that the cleavages that are politicized and, hence, the types of parties that exist in a country can change either because the underlying set of latent social cleavages changes or because the electoral rules change or both.

Box 13.3

ALLIES OR ADVERSARIES? CHEWAS AND TUMBUKAS IN ZAMBIA AND MALAWI

In an article published in 2004, Daniel Posner examines why cultural differences become politicized in some contexts but not others. Specifically, he tries to explain why two ethnic groups, Chewas and Tumbukas, are allies in Zambia but adversaries in Malawi. Zambia and Malawi are two neighboring countries in sub-Saharan Africa. The border between the two countries was arbitrarily drawn by the British South Africa company in 1891. No attention was paid to the distribution of ethnic groups when the border was drawn, so roughly two-thirds of all Chewas and Tumbukas found themselves living in Malawi, whereas the remaining third found themselves living in Zambia.

In his study of the Chewas and Tumbukas, Posner examined life in four villages along the Malawi-Zambia border. Two of the four villages were Chewa villages—one was just inside Malawi and the other was just a few miles away across the border in Zambia. The other two villages were Tumbuka villages—again, one was just inside Malawi and the other was just a few miles away in Zambia. Using survey questions, Posner first attempted to see if the Chewas and Tumbukas really were distinct cultural and ethnic groups. On numerous important dimensions, he found that they were. For example, he found that Chewas speak Chichewa and dance the *nyau*, whereas Tumbukas speak Chitumbuka and dance the *vinbuza*. In addition, he found that although Tumbuka parents must pay seven cows to have their daughters married, Chewa parents need pay only one chicken. These cultural and ethnic differences between

Chewas and Tumbukas were equally strong in Malawi and Zambia. In other words, Chewas and Tumbukas represented distinct identity categories in both countries.

To examine whether these identity categories were actually salient and politicized, Posner asked other survey questions. One question asked whether the respondent would vote for a presidential candidate from the other ethnic group. Sixty-one percent of Chewas and Tumbukas in Malawi said that they would *not* vote for a presidential candidate from the other ethnic group; in contrast, just 21 percent of Chewas and Tumbukas in Zambia made a similar statement. A second survey question asked whether the respondent would marry a member of the other ethnic group. Fifty-five percent of the Chewas and Tumbukas in Malawi said that they would *not* marry a member of the other ethnic group; in contrast, just 24 percent of them made a similar statement in Zambia. These (and other) survey results clearly indicate that the cultural and ethnic differences between Chewas and Tumbukas were salient in Malawi but not in Zambia.

But why would these cultural differences be salient in one country but not in the other? Perhaps it has something to do with the electoral system, the colonial history, or the party systems in the two countries. As Posner notes, though, both countries employ a single-member district plurality (SMDP) electoral system, both countries are former British colonies, and both countries have experienced one-party and multiparty rule. As a result, Posner argues that we must look elsewhere for an explanation for why Chewa-Tumbuka relations are so different in Malawi and Zambia.

Specifically, Posner argues that we must look to the different distribution of Chewas and Tumbukas in the two countries. Chewas and Tumbukas represent relatively large ethnic groups in Malawi. For example, Chewas comprise roughly 57 percent of the population, whereas Tumbukas account for about 12 percent. Because groups of this size have a realistic chance of winning Malawi's SMDP elections, it makes sense for political entrepreneurs to politicize the Chewa-Tumbuka cleavage and form political parties around the two different groups. In fact, this is precisely what has happened. The Malawi Congress Party (MCP) is widely recognized as the Chewa party and the Alliance for Democracy (AFORD) is seen as the Tumbuka party.

Contrast this situation to the one in Zambia, where Chewas and Tumbukas represent only very small segments of the overall population. For instance, Chewas comprise about 7 percent of the population, and the Tumbukas comprise just 4 percent. These relatively small ethnic groups in Zambia do not represent good political vehicles for winning office because such small groups have little realistic chance of winning SMDP elections. As a result, political entrepreneurs in Zambia have had to look for other cleavages to politicize rather than the Chewa-Tumbuka cleavage. The main politicized cleavage in Zambia is a regional one, pitting easterners (Chewas and Tumbukas together) against northerners, westerners, and southerners. In this political environment, Chewas and Tumbukas (easterners) have to work together, rather than against one another, if they are to have any hope of winning political power.

Posner's story illustrates how the logic of political competition focuses the attention of both voters and political entrepreneurs on some cleavages rather than others. His story also recognizes that political actors need to build winning coalitions to achieve their goals. If they are going to emphasize cultural or ethnic differences, they will choose divisions that define the most usefully sized building blocks. As a result, not all latent cultural and ethnic differences will become politicized. Which differences become politicized will ultimately depend on the interaction between institutions like electoral rules and the distribution of latent social cleavages.

FIGURE 13.1	**Politicized Cleavages and the Role of Electoral Institutions**

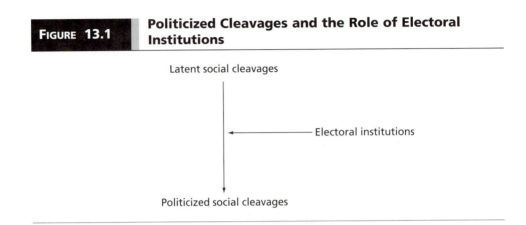

NUMBER OF PARTIES: DUVERGER'S THEORY

Although comparative political scientists currently lack a strong understanding of *which* parties will form in a country, we know a fair amount about *how many* parties will form.

Social Cleavages

Our current understanding of the factors influencing the size of party systems is due, in large part, to the seminal work of a French political scientist, Maurice Duverger ([1954] 1963). Duverger argued that the primary engine behind the formation of political parties can be found in social divisions—the more divisions there are, the greater the demand for political parties to form (Afonso Da Silva 2006; Clark and Golder 2006).[8] In effect, he believed that there is some natural tendency for cleavages within society, such as those discussed earlier, to be represented in the party system. We should recall from our earlier discussion, though, that it is not just the number of cleavages per se, but the way in which membership in society is distributed across those divisions that determines the pressures for distinctive representation.

For example, imagine that two societies, A and B, have the same number of identity attributes as each other. Let's suppose that the identity attributes are income, place of origin, and religion. Our two hypothetical countries might be from Latin America, where divisions between the rich and poor, European and indigenous populations, and Catholics and Protestants are common.[9] In both of our hypothetical countries, let's imagine that exactly half the citizens are rich and half are poor, half have European ancestry and half have indigenous ancestry, and half are Catholic and half are Protestant.

---

8. Duverger ([1954] 1963, 205) claimed that "the most decisive influences [leading to more political parties] are aspects of the life of the nation such as ideologies and particularly the socio-economic structure."

9. Actually, the Latin American "religious market" is much more complex than this. In addition to Catholics and Protestants, there are a substantial number of Mormons, as well as people who practice indigenous religions or religions that combine elements from various indigenous, European, and African faiths. For an interesting discussion of competition between Catholic and Protestant groups in Latin America, see Anthony Gill's (1998) book *Rendering unto Caesar.*

In country A, we will assume that exactly half of the rich people are European and half are indigenous; half of the rich European people and half of the poor indigenous people are Catholic. The full distribution of identity attributes in country A is shown in Table 13.11. As you can see, the attributes that might contribute to the formation of identity categories are evenly distributed. This means that country A is entirely characterized by cross-cutting cleavages—there is no correlation between one's income level, one's place of origin, or one's religion. As a result, this means that there is a whole host of identity categories—rich, rich Catholic, rich Protestant, rich European, rich indigenous, rich Catholic European, rich Protestant European, and so on—that are equally distinctive and, presumably, equally likely to be activated.[10] According to Duverger, and assuming that policy preferences are associated with wealth, place of origin, and religious confession, the "engine" of social forces in country A is propelling the party system toward a large multiparty system.

In contrast to country A, let's assume that some of the attributes that might map onto identity categories are perfectly correlated in country B. Specifically, we'll imagine that although exactly half of the rich and poor people are of European descent as in country A, all rich people are Catholic and all poor people are Protestant. The full distribution of identity attributes in country B is shown in Table 13.12. As you can see, the distribution of attributes reveals a mixture of both cross-cutting and reinforcing cleavages. As in country A, the income and place of origin cleavages are cross-cutting. In other words, knowing someone's place of origin is of no help in predicting that person's income. Unlike in country A, though, the income and religious cleavages are now reinforcing. In other words, knowing someone's religion allows one to predict which income group they are from. As the distribution of attributes in Table 13.12 indicates, there are now, in some sense, four latent identity categories to be represented by the party system: rich Catholic Europeans, rich Catholic indigenous people, poor Protestant Europeans, and poor Protestant indigenous people. In other words, the total number of latent identity categories is considerably lower in country B than in country A even though both countries have the same three cleavages—income, place of

TABLE 13.11	**The Distribution of Identity Attributes in Hypothetical Country A (percent)**				
	European		Indigenous		
	Catholic	Protestant	Catholic	Protestant	Total
Rich	12.5	12.5	12.5	12.5	50.0
Poor	12.5	12.5	12.5	12.5	50.0
Total	25.0	25.0	25.0	25.0	

10. We are deliberately ignoring the effect of the country's electoral system at this point.

TABLE 13.12	The Distribution of Identity Attributes in Hypothetical Country B (percent)				
	European		Indigenous		
	Catholic	Protestant	Catholic	Protestant	Total
Rich	(25.0)	0.0	(25.0)	0.0	50.0
Poor	0.0	(25.0)	0.0	(25.0)	50.0
Total	25.0	25.0	25.0	25.0	

origin, and religion. It should be clear that if one's place of origin was also perfectly corre-lated with income—for example, if all rich citizens had European ancestry and all poor cit-izens had indigenous ancestry—then there would be only two latent groups needing repre-sentation: rich Catholic Europeans and poor Protestant indigenous people.

The key aspect of a country's social structure influencing the demand for the number of parties, therefore, is not necessarily the total number of cleavages in a country but rather the total number of *cross-cutting* cleavages. As you might suspect, most cleavages in a country will not be perfectly cross-cutting or perfectly reinforcing as in our example. The same logic as that outlined above, however, suggests that the social pressure for distinctive representa-tion (and a large party system) depends on the number of cleavages in a country and increases with the degree to which these cleavages are cross-cutting rather than reinforcing.

Electoral Institutions

Although Duverger believed that social divisions create the demand for political parties, he argued that electoral institutions play an important role in determining whether this latent demand for representation actually leads to the existence of new political parties. Recall the earlier claim that European societies have seen the emergence of a new post-materialist cleavage since the 1960s (Inglehart 1977, 1997). If social cleavages were the only factor influ-encing the size of party systems, then all European countries should have experienced an increase in the number of parties competing for office. However, Kitschelt (1988) finds that there was a significant increase only in the share of votes going to "left-libertarian parties" in some countries. This should make one wonder why an increase in the number of cleavages would have a different effect on the size of party systems in different countries.

Although one explanation for this might be that the shift to post-materialist values was more pronounced in some countries than others, Duverger claims that it is likely to have something to do with the electoral institutions used in each country. In other words, he argues that the same value change can have a significant effect on the party structure of one country but not on that of another due to differences in electoral rules. The reason for this is that nonproportional electoral systems, such as the single-member district plurality sys-tem, act as a "brake" on the tendency for social cleavages to be translated into new parties. Put differently, Duverger's theory states that increasing the number of social cleavages in a country has less of an effect on party system size if the electoral system is nonproportional than if it is proportional. There are two reasons, commonly known as the "mechanical" and "strategic" effects of electoral laws, for why nonproportional electoral systems have this moderating effect. We now examine each of these effects in turn.

The Mechanical Effect of Electoral Laws

The **mechanical effect of electoral laws** refers to the way that votes are translated into seats. As we discussed in Chapter 12, the mechanical effect of all electoral systems systematically punishes small parties and rewards large parties. The extent to which small parties are punished and large parties are rewarded, however,

> The **mechanical effect of electoral laws** refers to the way votes are translated into seats. When electoral systems are disproportional, the mechanical effect punishes small parties and rewards large parties.

depends on the proportionality of the electoral system. Specifically, small parties will find it harder to win seats, and large parties are more likely to be rewarded, when the electoral system is highly disproportional, as in an SMDP system. To illustrate how the mechanical effect of electoral laws affects parties of different sizes, consider the following two examples. One is based on a hypothetical country called "Duvergerland," and the other is based on real-world electoral returns from the United Kingdom.

Duvergerland is a country that has historically been divided by a single class cleavage—the electorate has been divided fairly evenly between supporters of a workers' party and supporters of a party that represents the interests of the business class. The 100-person legislature in Duvergerland is elected using an SMDP electoral system. Recently, social transformation has led to an increase in the number of voters holding post-materialist values. In recent elections, 20 percent of voters cast ballots for the newly formed Green Party, with the rest split in different ways between the Business and Labor Parties in each district. In Figure 13.2, we illustrate the distribution of electoral results across twenty of the one hundred districts using a "doughnut" graph.[11] Although the Green Party wins 20 percent of the vote in each district, at least one of the other parties always wins more votes than this. As a result, the Green Party does not win a single legislative seat under the SMDP electoral system.

In Figure 13.3a, we illustrate the distribution of legislative seats if the pattern in the twenty districts shown in Figure 13.2 is reproduced throughout Duvergerland. The Labor and Business Parties each get close to 50 percent of the seats in the legislature and the Green Party goes completely unrepresented even though it won 20 percent of the vote. Simply as a result of the way in which votes are translated into seats—the mechanical effect of the SMDP system—a party in Duvergerland that receives 20 percent of the population's support receives 0 percent of the legislative seats being contested. Moreover, although there is clearly support for three parties in the electorate, there are only two parties in the legislature.

---

11. Interestingly, different disciplines have different habits when using such metaphors. Economists often refer to "dividing the dollar" or "dividing the pie," whereas mathematicians often refer to "dividing the cake." We suggest that "dividing the doughnut" is a fitting visual metaphor for political scientists to use when discussing distributional struggles, because political scientists should be reminded that it is not uncommon for powerless actors to be left holding nothing but the "hole" in the middle of the doughnut.

| FIGURE 13.2 | Duvergerland: A Hypothetical Polity Using an SMDP Electoral System |

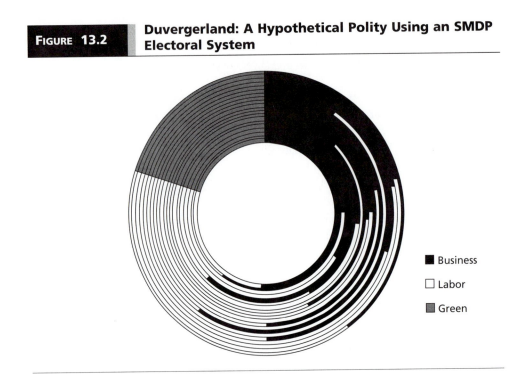

Now contrast the way this same distribution of votes would have been translated into seats if Duvergerland had used a proportional representation system in a single national district. Given that the Green Party won 20 percent of the vote, it now obtains twenty legislative seats. This distribution of seats in this new legislature is shown in Figure 13.3b. As you

| FIGURE 13.3 | Distribution of Seats in Duvergerland under SMDP and PR Electoral Rules |

a. SMDP   b. PR

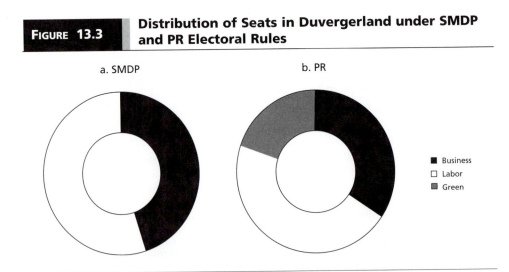

can see, the fate of the small party—the Green Party—is substantially different under the two different electoral systems. The Green Party goes from controlling 20 percent of the legislative seats under PR to being excluded entirely from the legislature under SMDP. This reductive effect in the representation of the small party, as well as the electoral bonus given to the two large parties, is a direct result of the mechanical effect of the SMDP electoral system employed in Duvergerland.

The mechanical effect of the SMDP electoral system that reduces the number of parties in the legislature by penalizing parties that win smaller shares of the vote is not just a matter of theoretical interest. In Table 13.13 we report the electoral returns for the St. Ives constituency during the 1992 legislative elections in the United Kingdom. In these elections, the Conservative Party candidate, David Harris, edges out the Liberal Democrat candidate, Andrew George, by fewer than 2,000 votes. Harris, who won just under 43 percent of the vote, becomes the sole representative of the St. Ives constituency. In contrast, Andrew George, who was supported by 40 percent of the voters in his constituency, is awarded nothing.

If the type of situation that occurred in the St. Ives constituency is repeated in a large number of constituencies, the "winner-take-all" logic of SMDP systems can lead to the introduction of a large gap between the share of votes that a party obtains and the share of seats that it ultimately wins. In Table 13.14 we show some fairly typical national election results from the United Kingdom. One thing to notice about these results is that both of the two larger parties—the Conservatives (Tories) and Labour—won about 20 percent more seats than their percentage of votes would suggest that they should have won. In the case of the Conservative Party, this "electoral bonus" resulting from the mechanical way in which the SMDP system translates votes into seats was enough to turn an electoral plurality into a legislative majority.[12] The other thing to notice is that the smaller party—the Liberal Democrats—won only 3.1 percent of the legislative seats even though they won 17.8 percent of the vote. In Figure 13.4 we illustrate graphically how the mechanical effect of the SMDP electoral system used in the 1992 UK legislative elections rewarded the larger parties and punished the smaller ones.

TABLE 13.13	**Legislative Elections Results, St. Ives Constituency, United Kingdom, 1992**	
	Votes	% of vote
David Harris (Conservative)	24,528	42.9
Andrew George (Liberal Democrat)	22,883	40.1
Stephen Warr (Labour)	9,144	16
Graham Stevens (Liberal)	577	1
Harris is elected		

---

12. The tendency for this to happen is the reason why some scholars refer to SMDP systems as "majoritarian" systems despite the fact that only a plurality of the votes in a district, not a majority, is needed to win a seat.

TABLE 13.14	Legislative Elections Results, National Totals, United Kingdom, 1992 (percent)	
	Votes	Seats
Conservative	41.9	51.6
Labour	34.9	41.6
Liberal Democrats	17.8	3.1
Others	5.4	3.7
Total	100	100

A quick comparison of the hypothetical case of Duvergerland and the real-world example from the 1992 UK legislative elections reveals that the extent to which nonproportional electoral systems such as SMDP punish small parties depends on the way that the votes for these parties are distributed across electoral districts. In Duvergerland, we assumed that the support for the Green Party was evenly distributed across all of the electoral districts. This particular distribution of support resulted in the Green Party's failing to win a single seat. Contrast this with the fact that the Liberal Democrats managed to win twenty seats (3.1 percent) in the 1992 UK elections even though they won a smaller share of the national vote than the Greens did in Duvergerland. The reason for this difference is that the size of the support for the Liberal Democrats varied across different districts. Although the support for the Liberal Democrats was not sufficient to produce victory in the St. Ives constituency, it was big enough to win seats in twenty other districts. This indicates that the extent to which the mechanical effect of the SMDP system punishes small parties is directly related to how dispersed their electoral support is. The Liberal Democratic Party (and its predecessor, the

FIGURE 13.4	Distribution of Votes and Seats in Legislative Elections in the United Kingdom, 1992

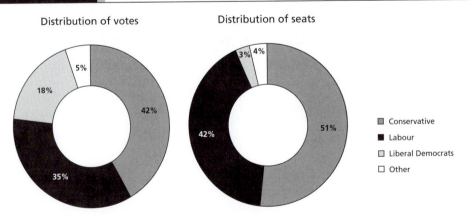

Distribution of votes

Distribution of seats

- Conservative
- Labour
- Liberal Democrats
- Other

Liberal Party) in the United Kingdom has generally been penalized quite heavily by the UK's SMDP electoral system because its support tends to be broadly distributed across many electoral districts. In contrast, small regional parties, such as Plaid Cymru in Wales, the Scottish National Party in Scotland, Sinn Fein and the Ulster Unionists in Northern Ireland, which garner a much smaller share of the national vote, have experienced very little disadvantage from the way in which the UK's SMDP system translates votes into seats. This is because the support for these parties is heavily concentrated in a small number of districts.

The Strategic Effect of Electoral Laws

As we have just seen, the mechanical way in which votes are translated into seats in nonproportional systems penalizes small parties and rewards large parties. The benefits that systems like SMDP bestow on large parties are further enhanced by a second institutional effect called the **strategic effect of electoral laws.** To this point we have isolated the mechanical effect of electoral laws by taking the way votes are distributed as given. Now we must ask how

> The **strategic effect of electoral laws** refers to how the way in which votes are translated into seats influences the "strategic" behavior of voters and political elites.

voters and party elites are likely to respond to the mechanical effect of electoral systems. The strategic effect of electoral laws refers to how the way in which votes are translated into seats influences the "strategic" behavior of voters and political elites. When electoral systems are disproportional, their mechanical effect can be expected to reward large parties and punish small parties. Recognizing that this is going to happen, voters in these systems have an incentive to engage in strategic voting, whereas political elites have an incentive to engage in what is called strategic entry. As we will see, both of these actions—strategic voting and strategic entry—bestow even more benefits on large parties and further penalize small parties.

Strategic Voting

As you will recall, we discussed strategic and sincere voting in Chapters 10 and 12. Strategic voting essentially means voting for your most preferred candidate *who has a realistic chance of winning.* In contrast, sincere voting means voting for your most preferred candidate or party. To help refresh your mind about the logic of strategic voting in nonproportional electoral systems, such as SMDP, take a look again at the election results from the St. Ives constituency in the 1992 UK elections (Table 13.12). Imagine that you preferred the Labour candidate to the Liberal Democrat candidate and the Liberal Democrat candidate to the Conservative candidate, that is, L ≻ LD ≻ C. Imagine also that you had reliable polling data indicating that the Labour candidate was trailing the Conservative and Liberal Democrat candidates by a wide margin. If you cast a sincere vote, then you would vote for the Labour candidate. However, a sincere vote is likely to be "wasted" in the sense that it has little chance of affecting the outcome of the election given how far the Labour candidate trails behind the other candidates. As a result, you have an incentive to vote strategically for the Liberal Democrat candidate (who has a more realistic chance of winning) in order to try to stop the Conservative candidate (your least-preferred candidate) from winning.

As this example illustrates, supporters of small parties that have little realistic chance of winning seats due to the way that votes are translated into seats have an incentive to vote strategically. In other words, they have an incentive not to vote for their most preferred party—a small party—and, instead, give their support to one of the larger parties that they like. This incentive to vote strategically increases as the electoral system becomes more disproportional. As a result, small parties are not only penalized in nonproportional systems because of the way that votes are translated into seats but also because voters in these systems have an incentive not to vote for them in the first place. Similarly, large parties not only benefit in nonproportional systems due to the electoral bonus that they receive from the way that votes are translated into seats but also because voters who prefer other parties often have an incentive to strategically vote for them.

Strategic Entry

Although nonproportional electoral systems create incentives for voters to engage in strategic voting, they also create similar incentives for political elites to engage in what is called **strategic entry.** Strategic entry refers to the decision by political elites about whether to enter the political scene under the label of their most preferred party or under the label of their most preferred party *that has a realistic chance of winning.* Imagine that you are an aspiring political entrepreneur in Duvergerland who has an interest in environmental politics. If this is the case, then you confront a dilemma. On the one hand, you could run as a candidate for the Green Party. The Green Party is your most preferred party because it will likely share your attitudes on environmental policy. The problem is that you will not get elected as a candidate for the Green Party given the use of an SMDP electoral system and the way that the party's support is distributed across Duvergerland. On the other hand, you could decide to run in the "lesser of two evils" from among those parties that you estimate to have a realistic chance of winning seats. Furthermore, even if the party that reflects your policy preference (Green Party) is able to gain a few seats in the legislature, you must consider whether you can better further your policy agenda by representing that party or by working within a different party that actually stands a chance of commanding a legislative majority.

In contrast to political elites who compete under an SMDP electoral system, political entrepreneurs in proportional systems do not face such a stark trade-off. This is because even a small amount of electoral success in garnering votes can often allow one to win legislative seats. Indeed, if there are many parties in the legislature, leaders of small parties might even find themselves in the enviable position of being a kingmaker in the government formation process and a highly sought-after junior coalition partner. The difference in opportunities for small party leaders between the SMDP and PR systems is evident if we compare the postwar experience of leaders of the Liberal Party in the United Kingdom (under the SMDP system) with that of leaders of the Free Democratic Party (FDP) in Germany (under the pro-

> **Strategic entry** refers to the decision by political elites about whether to enter the political scene under the label of their most preferred party or under the label of their most preferred party that has a realistic chance of winning.

portional mixed system). Although these two parties have historically shared similar ideological positions in their respective party systems, the FDP was a nearly constant fixture in German cabinets, whereas the Liberal Party in the United Kingdom was consigned to watch from the sidelines as the Conservative and Labour Parties rotated in and out of office. The different trajectories of these two parties would have to enter the calculations of ambitious young politicians. This suggests that small parties in SMDP systems will find it more difficult to attract and retain high-quality leaders than small parties in more proportional systems. For similar reasons, small parties in SMDP systems will also find it harder to attract private financial support. The lack of high-quality candidates and other resources in small parties that compete in SMDP systems will, in turn, make it harder for these parties to win votes.

Note that the example we have just presented assumed that the Green Party actually existed in Duvergerland. Now imagine that you are the same political entrepreneur as before with a strong interest in environmental politics. The social transformation that has seen an increase in the number of voters holding post-materialist values has just taken place. You must decide whether to form a Green Party to represent this new constituency or try to represent it within one of the established parties. Given that a Green Party is unlikely to win any seats in Duvergerland, you will have a strong incentive to work within one of the existing parties to achieve your political and policy goals. As this example illustrates, not only do disproportional electoral systems mean that small parties will receive a lower percentage of the vote because they are less likely to attract high-quality candidates and other resources, they also mean that these small parties are less likely to exist in the first place.

The dilemma confronting political elites in an SMDP system can be demonstrated in another way with the help of the following Strategic Entry Game. Suppose that there are two left-wing parties (L_1 and L_2) and one right-wing party (R). Let's assume that if both left-wing parties compete in the election, then the right-wing party will win for sure, because the vote of the left-wing electorate will be split between two parties. Let's also assume that the right-wing party will be defeated if only one left-wing party runs. Because each left-wing party prefers that the right-wing party be defeated for ideological reasons, its worst possible outcome occurs if both left-wing parties run. Note, though, that if only one of the left-wing parties is going to run, then each left-wing party would prefer that its own party be it. This is because an electoral victory would not only allow it to implement left-wing policies, but it also allows the party to consume the benefits that come with holding office. Without any loss of generality, we can assign to each party a value of 0 for its worst outcome (both left-wing parties run and the right-wing party wins) and a value of 1 to its most preferred outcome (the other left-wing party drops out and it, the remaining one, wins). We can use a parameter λ (lambda) to represent the value that each left-wing party places on seeing its fellow left-wing party run instead of it. Because having the other left-wing party win is better than having the right-wing party win but not as good as winning oneself, it follows that $0 \succ \lambda \succ 1$. Ultimately, the two left-wing parties must decide whether to run or not run. The normal form of this Strategic Entry Game is shown in Figure 13.5.

FIGURE 13.5	**Strategic Entry Game: Coordination between Competing Left-Wing Parties**

		Left Party L$_2$	
		Run	Don't Run
Left party L$_1$	Run	0, 0	1, λ
	Don't run	λ, 1	0, 0

Notice that the two left-wing parties face a coordination dilemma. They share a common goal—defeat the right-wing party. They differ, however, on how that goal should be met—each party wants to be the party that rules in the event of a right-wing defeat.[13] If you solve the Strategic Entry Game, you will find that there are two pure strategy Nash equilibria: (Run; Don't run) and (Don't run; Run). In other words, each party has an incentive to drop out of the race if the other player does not drop out. Such mixed-motive games present a dilemma that is often difficult for the actors involved to solve. In some countries, parties on the left (or right) realize that they have an incentive to withdraw from an electoral contest but cannot coordinate on which one should do it. As a result parties that do not "drop out" wind up contributing to the election of their most bitter rivals. A good example of this occurred in the 2002 French presidential elections (S. Golder 2006, 56–57). It had widely been expected that Jacques Chirac, the president and leader of the mainstream right, would make it through to the second round, along with Lionel Jospin, Socialist prime minister and leader of the mainstream left. The real question for months had been which of the two men would win the second round. Then, unexpectedly, the left vote was split among so many candidates that the Socialist leader came in third behind the extreme-right politician, Jean-Marie Le Pen. Although many people have naturally focused on the disturbing success of the extreme right, this political earthquake, as it became known, had as much to do with the inability of the French left to solve its coordination problems as it did with an increase in the strength of the extreme right. A similar example occurred in the 2000 U.S. presidential elections when the presence of Ralph Nader on the ballot split the left-wing vote, particularly in Florida, to such an extent that the right-wing Republican George W. Bush was able to defeat the left-wing Democrat, Al Gore, in the Electoral College.

---

13. As you will recall from the problems at the end of Chapter 4, this sort of game is commonly referred to as an asymmetric coordination game.

One way to prevent this type of worst case scenario is for the parties splitting the vote to merge into a single party.[14] This is exactly what the Liberal Party and the Social Democratic Party did to create the Liberal Democratic Party in the United Kingdom in 1988. As several scholars have noted, the more disproportional the electoral system, the greater the incentive that small parties have to merge or form coalitions rather than compete as independent entities at election time (Strøm, Budge, and Laver 1994; Cox 1997; S. Golder 2005, 2006).[15] It is worth noting that this incentive not only encourages mergers between small parties but can also even deter the entry of small parties in the first place. Even when disgruntled by the current direction of their party, forward-looking political entrepreneurs may decide that it is better to work within an existing party rather than break away to form a new party and risk contributing to the election of a party that they find less desirable than their current one. As all of these examples illustrate, small parties that represent relatively small segments of the population will be less likely to form or be successful in disproportional electoral systems because of the strategic incentives that these electoral rules create for both voters and political elites.

Summarizing Duverger's Theory

To sum up, **Duverger's theory** states that the size of a country's party system depends on the complex interplay of both social and institutional forces. The precise causal story underlying Duverger's theory is illustrated in Figure 13.6. Characteristics of a country's social structure provide the driving force behind the formation of parties. When there are many cross-cutting cleavages, there are many distinct positions that, in some sense, need to be represented. Whether these distinct positions are ultimately translated into distinct parties, however, will depend on the proportionality of the electoral system. Disproportional electoral systems translate votes into seats in such a way that small parties are penalized and large parties are rewarded. In other words, the "input-output" ratio by which votes are turned into seats in disproportional systems is smaller for small parties than it is for large parties. In contrast, proportional electoral systems translate

> **Duverger's theory** states that the size of a country's party system depends on the complex interplay of both social and institutional factors. Social divisions create the "demand" for political parties and electoral institutions then determine the extent to which this demand is translated into parties that win votes (electoral parties) and parties that win seats (legislative parties).

---

14. An alternative strategy for avoiding this type of "worst case scenario" is for the parties splitting the vote to form a preelectoral coalition at election time rather than compete as independent entities (S. Golder 2005, 2006; Blais and Indriðason 2007).

15. Determining when and why some small political parties retain their separate identities rather than merge or coalesce into a larger party is a complex question. As we have already seen, it will depend to a large extent on the disproportionality of the electoral system. However, a number of other institutions are known to influence how likely it is that parties retain their separate identities. One such institution is the use of fusion candidates, where multiple parties can nominate the same candidate (S. Golder 2005, 2006). Fusion candidates were employed in many U.S. states in the nineteenth century. Although this practice continues in New York State, it was stopped in most other states more than a century ago. The end of fusion candidates contributed quite markedly to the evolution of a party system in which the Democratic and Republican parties were the only viable parties outside of New York State (Argersinger 1980). Two-round electoral systems are also thought to encourage parties to retain their separate identities since small parties might think that they can at least make it into the second round (Duverger [1954] 1963).

| FIGURE 13.6 | Party Systems: Social Cleavages and the Modifying Effect of Electoral Institutions |

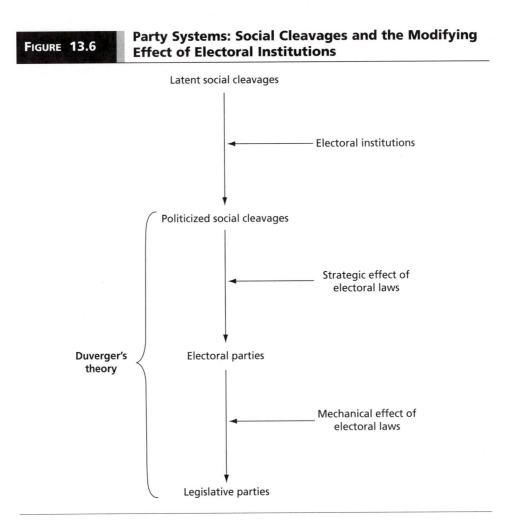

votes into seats at a relatively constant rate. The way in which the mechanical effect of disproportional systems helps large parties and hurts small parties creates incentives for voters and political elites in these systems to engage in strategic voting and strategic entry. Supporters of small parties are more likely to see a vote for their most preferred party as a "wasted vote" in disproportional systems than in more proportional ones. Consequently, these voters are more likely to transfer their support to a larger party that is lower ranked in their preference ordering but that has a realistic chance of winning. Similarly, political entrepreneurs connected to policy positions that are not represented by existing parties or are associated with small parties have strong incentives to work within existing large parties if the electoral system is disproportional. As a result, disproportional electoral systems discourage the formation and electoral success of new parties in two related ways. First, the mechanical effect of these systems leaves small parties with fewer seats in the legislature than the votes cast for them would have produced in a PR system. Second, the strategic effect of these systems leaves small parties with fewer votes than the latent support for their policies in the electorate would suggest they could attract.

Evidence for Duverger's Theory

Duverger succinctly summed up the observational implications of his theory in two statements that have become known as **Duverger's Law** and **Duverger's Hypothesis**:

> **Duverger's Law** states that single-member district plurality systems encourage two-party systems. **Duverger's Hypothesis** states that proportional representation electoral rules favor multiparty systems.

> *Duverger's Law:* Single-member district plurality systems encourage two-party systems.
> *Duverger's Hypothesis:* Proportional representation electoral rules favor multiparty systems.

Unfortunately, it turns out that the simple prediction that we should expect to find two-party systems if SMDP electoral laws are employed is a valid inference from Duverger's broader theory only when some auxiliary assumptions are satisfied. As Duverger himself noted, the logic by which the mechanical and strategic effects of SMDP electoral systems produce two-party systems works only at the district, and not the national, level. To see why, recall our example from the St. Ives constituency in the United Kingdom. If voters know that the Labour Party has no chance of winning *in this district,* then the benefits of strategic voting accrue to the Conservatives and the Liberal Democrats *in this district*. In other districts—indeed, in most districts in the UK—it is the Liberal Democrats who are the "also ran" party. As a result, it is the Conservative and Labour Parties that benefit in most districts from the strategic voting induced by the mechanical effect of the SMDP electoral system.

As you can see, the logic of Duverger's argument leads us to expect a national two-party system in SMDP countries only to the extent that the same two parties are favored by strategic voting across the lion's share of the electoral districts. It is possible, for example, for some parties to be favored by SMDP in some regions of the country and other parties to receive an electoral boost from SMDP in other parts of the country. The net effect of these off-setting distortions may leave the country with a multiparty system in which the national seat shares of several parties are very close to their national vote shares. In short, if the party system is not fully nationalized with the same parties advantaged in each district, SMDP electoral systems could very well have more than two parties. Among other things, the extent to which a party system is nationalized depends on a host of factors, including whether economic and political power is centralized in the national government, how this power is shared between the branches of government, and whether there are presidential elections (Chhibber and Kollman 1998, 2004; M. Golder 2006; Hicken, forthcoming).

These cautions, however, do little damage to Duverger's broader theory. This is because his theory is more concerned with how changes in social conditions or electoral laws result in changes in the number of parties, and there is considerable evidence consistent with his predictions in this area (Ordeshook and Shvetsova 1994; Amorim Neto and Cox 1997; Cox 1997; Clark, Gilligan, and Golder 2006; Clark and Golder 2006; Brambor, Clark, and Golder 2007).

Box 13.4

NATIONALIZING PARTY SYSTEMS

Duverger's Law states that countries with SMDP electoral systems will be characterized by two-party systems. However, the logic by which the mechanical and strategic effects of SMDP electoral rules produce two-party systems really works only at the district level (Duverger [1954] 1963; Cox 1997). Because the SMDP system is a winner-take-all system, it is often the case that only the two largest parties in a district have a realistic chance of winning the seat. That two parties are likely to predominate in each district, though, does not necessarily mean that there is a two-party system at the national level. Whether this is the case or not depends on whether the same two parties predominate across the lion's share of the districts. In other words, there can be a discrepancy between the size of local party systems and the size of the national party system. In effect, there can be more parties competing nationally than there are, on average, competing in each district. Political scientists say that a country's party system has been nationalized if the local and national party systems are of a similar size.

Several factors have been found to influence the extent to which party systems are nationalized. For example, party systems are more likely to be nationalized when political and economic power is centralized in the national government (Chhibber and Kollman 1998, 2004). The logic is that as power is centralized, it becomes increasingly important to gain control of the national government. As a result, parties that have little chance of gaining control of the national government, even if they are one of the two largest parties in their district, are likely to find themselves abandoned by both voters and political entrepreneurs at election time. Parties that are able to compete nationally, rather than in just one or two districts, are likely to benefit from this strategic behavior. To illustrate this point, Chhibber and Kollman (1998) examine the size of local and national party systems in the United States from 1790 to 1990. Their data are shown in Figure 13.7.

As you can see, the average number of parties at the district level has been about two, as Duverger's theory predicts, throughout U.S. history. The size of the national party system has varied quite considerably over this 200-year period, however. Prior to the New Deal in the 1930s, the number of parties at the national level was frequently much larger than two. This reflects the fact that several minor parties were able to enjoy regional success throughout this period. For example, a minor party, such as Labor, the Progressives, the Socialists, the Prohibitionists, or Farmers, was one of the two locally dominant political parties in certain regions and time periods. Ever since the 1930s, though, there has been little difference in how many parties compete at the local and national level in the United States. In effect, the U.S. party system became nationalized in the 1930s with the same two parties—Democrats and Republicans—dominating both the local and national party systems. Minor parties have enjoyed relatively little success since this time. Chhibber and Kollman explain this dramatic change by the increased centralization of political and economic power in the U.S. national government that occurred in the 1930s. As they note, national government spending as a percentage of total government spending (including state and local spending) more than doubled in this period; national government spending increased almost tenfold as a proportion of gross national product as well. In effect, holding national office became increasingly important in the 1930s. Minor parties that were unable to credibly compete for national office were, therefore, at a strategic disadvantage, and the party system became nationalized.

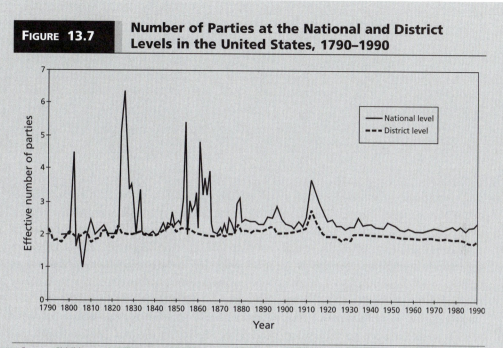

FIGURE 13.7   **Number of Parties at the National and District Levels in the United States, 1790–1990**

Source: Chhibber and Kollman (1998, 331).

Hicken (forthcoming) has recently built on this argument to suggest that the extent to which power is shared between different branches of the national government also matters. If political power is centralized in the national government and this power is not shared between different branches of government, the value of holding national office is particularly high. This creates even greater incentives for political parties to solve cross-district coordination problems, such as those highlighted in our Strategic Entry Game. The result is a party system in which Duvergerian dynamics are reflected at both the national and district level.

Another factor that influences the nationalization of party systems is the presence of presidential elections (M. Golder 2006). The presidency is nearly always the most important electoral prize in a presidential regime. There is typically, however, only a small number of viable presidential candidates because only one person can become the president. Given the importance of the presidency, parties that do not have a viable presidential candidate, even if they are electorally strong in their local regions, are likely to find themselves abandoned by both voters and political entrepreneurs at election time. Parties that have a national base and, hence, viable presidential candidates will naturally benefit from this strategic behavior. The end result is a nationalized party system where regionally based parties can struggle to compete. The extent to which presidential elections exert nationalizing pressures on a country's party system depends on how important it is to win the presidency and the temporal proximity between presidential and legislative elections. Specifically, party systems in presidential democracies are more likely to be nationalized if the president's power is large relative to that of other political actors and if presidential elections occur at the same time as legislative ones.

Another obvious factor influencing the extent to which party systems are nationalized has to do with the distribution of politicized cleavages in a country. If these cleavages are national in the sense that the same cleavages dominate political competition in each region, then the party system as a whole is likely to be national in character. If a country's politicized cleavages vary from region to region, however, the party system is likely to be less nationalized. As our discussion in this chapter makes clear, though, the extent to which regional cleavages are actually translated into distinct parties still depends on the permissiveness of the electoral system.

Duverger used the metaphor of a car to explain why some countries have many parties and other countries have few. Social structure is the "engine" that drives the multiplication of parties, whereas electoral laws serve as the brake pedal. Disproportional electoral systems, such as SMDP, depress the brake pedal and, therefore, prevent the engine of social division from producing multiparty systems. Another metaphor that describes this process focuses on how social divisions create a storm of policy demands and how the electoral system determines if those demands will be permitted to flow downstream and be translated into distinctive parties. Just as a dam in a river moderates the flow of water, electoral laws *moderate* the way social divisions get turned into parties (see Figure 13.6). When the dam is closed, it prevents some of the water from flowing downstream; when the dam is open, it permits more of the water to flow downstream. SMDP electoral systems are like a closed dam that, for the reasons described above, prevents some societal demands from being transformed into political parties. Proportional electoral systems are like an open dam in that they permit *more* of these demands to be translated into parties. It is for this reason that political scientists frequently say that proportional electoral systems are permissive and nonproportional ones are nonpermissive.

As we have seen, the effect of social structure on the size of a country's party system depends on the permissiveness of the electoral system. Similarly, the effect of the electoral system on party system size depends on a country's social structure. Consider the four different scenarios shown in Table 13.15. The case in which there are many social divisions—high social heterogeneity—and a permissive electoral system (top right) is like a river filled with storm water meeting an open dam. Because the dam is open, it has little effect on the current of the river, and most, if not all, of the water flows unimpeded downstream. In other words, social heterogeneity is expected to result in the formation of many parties when a PR electoral system *permits* it to. Contrast this with the case in which there are many social divisions and a nonpermissive electoral system (top left). This situation is like having a storm-filled river confront a closed dam—some of the water will not get to flow downriver and, instead, it will form a reservoir on the upstream side of the dam. In other words, some of the societal demands in a socially heterogeneous country that employs a nonpermissive electoral system will not be translated into political parties.

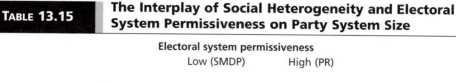

TABLE 13.15 — **The Interplay of Social Heterogeneity and Electoral System Permissiveness on Party System Size**

		Electoral system permissiveness	
		Low (SMDP)	High (PR)
Social heterogeneity	High	Few parties	Many parties
	Low	Few parties	Few parties

Now consider the two cases in which there are few social divisions—social heterogeneity is low (bottom left and bottom right). This situation is equivalent to having a dry season that results in an almost entirely dry river. We can imagine that the river is so low that water cannot reach the gates or valves in the dam. Clearly, little water will be getting downstream in this situation, irrespective of whether the dam is open or closed. In other words, when social heterogeneity is low, we do not expect much of a demand for political parties. As a result, few parties will be formed whether or not the electoral system is permissive.

A key implication of Duverger's theory, then, is that there are two reasons why a party system may have few parties. Some countries may have few parties, despite the fact that they are socially heterogeneous, because they have a nonpermissive electoral system that prevents this heterogeneity from being reflected in the party system. Alternatively, some countries may have few parties regardless of how permissive their electoral system is because they have few social divisions. In contrast, there is only one way, according to Duverger's theory, to end up with many parties—you need a heterogeneous society and a permissive electoral system.

Clark, Gilligan, and Golder (2006) present empirical evidence that is consistent with this interpretation of Duverger's theory. Their data, which are based on fifty-four democracies in the 1980s, are shown in Table 13.16. As is standard in the literature on party systems, party system size is measured by the effective number of legislative parties. As predicted by Duverger's theory, the average number of legislative parties is highest when high social heterogeneity is combined with a highly permissive electoral system.[16] Specifically, the number of legislative parties in socially heterogeneous societies with multimember electoral districts is 3.88. In contrast, the number of legislative parties in socially heterogeneous countries

---

16. Electoral system permissiveness depends on whether a country employs single-member electoral districts (low permissiveness) or multimember electoral districts (high permissiveness). Social heterogeneity is measured by the effective number of ethnic groups in a country. Countries that have more effective ethnic groups than the median in the sample are coded as having high social heterogeneity; those with fewer ethnic groups than the median are coded as having low social heterogeneity. For more details, see Clark, Gilligan, and Golder (2006).

	The Observed Number of Parties under Alternative Conditions	
TABLE 13.16		

		Electoral system permissiveness	
		Low	High
Social heterogeneity	High	1.68	3.88
	Low	2.52	3.06

Source: Clark, Gilligan, and Golder (2006, 15).

Note: Party system size is measured by the effective number of legislative parties. Electoral system permissiveness depends on whether a country employs single-member electoral districts (low permissiveness) or multimember electoral districts (high permissiveness). Social heterogeneity is measured by the effective number of ethnic groups in a country. Countries that have more effective ethnic groups than the median in the sample are coded as having high social heterogeneity; those with fewer ethnic groups than the median are coded as having low social heterogeneity. Data cover fifty-four democracies in the 1980s (Amorim Neto and Cox 1997).

using single-member electoral districts is just 1.68. The difference between these two numbers can be thought of as the reductive effect of nonpermissive electoral laws when social heterogeneity is high—this is the effect of closing the floodgates when the river is high. It turns out that the number of legislative parties is not significantly different between socially homogeneous countries that use single-member electoral districts (2.52) and socially homogeneous countries that use multimember districts (3.06). This suggests that closing the floodgates has a smaller effect on how much water gets downstream when the river is low than when the river is high. In other words, adopting a permissive electoral law will have little effect on party system size in socially homogeneous countries. This is exactly as predicted by Duverger's theory.

Another way to observe the important modifying effect that electoral laws play in influencing the size of party systems is to observe the way in which social cleavages are translated into votes for parties (electoral parties) and the way in which votes for parties are translated into seats (legislative parties). If an electoral system were perfectly proportional, political parties would receive the same share of seats in the legislature as the share of votes they receive in the electorate.

In Figure 13.8, we plot the relationship between the effective number of electoral and legislative parties in fifty-two democracies during the 1980s.[17] If a country's electoral system translates votes into seats without any distortion, it will have the same number of legislative

17. There are fifty-four observations in the original dataset (Amorim Neto and Cox 1997). Two of these observations, however, are recorded as having slightly more legislative parties than electoral parties. This is not actually possible, because there cannot be more parties that win seats than parties that win votes unless some seats are reserved for parties irrespective of how well they do at the polls. As a result, we drop these two observations here.

FIGURE 13.8	**The Effective Number of Electoral and Legislative Parties in Fifty-two Democracies in the 1980s**

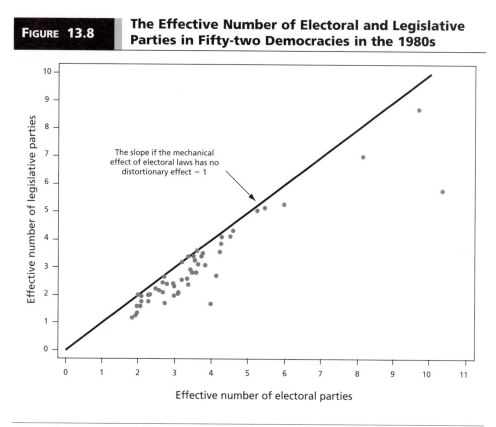

Source: Data are from Amorim Neto and Cox (1997).

parties as it does electoral parties. If this is the case, the country will fall somewhere on the 45-degree line in Figure 13.8. As you can see, some countries fall on or very close to this line. That most countries fall below this line, however, suggests that the mechanical process by which votes are turned into seats leads to a reduction in the number of parties as we go from parties with votes to parties with seats. The vertical distance between a country's position in Figure 13.8 and the 45-degree line can be thought of as a graphical representation of the "mechanical" effect of the particular country's electoral laws. In effect, this vertical distance is a measure of the distortion introduced by the process by which votes are turned into seats.

According to Duverger's theory, this distortion should be greater in countries that employ nonpermissive electoral systems than in countries that use permissive ones. In other words, the slope of the line that best fits observations from nonpermissive systems should be smaller (indicating more distortion) than the slope of the line that best fits observations from permissive systems. To see if this is the case, we split our sample into two groups—one with single-member districts (nonpermissive) and one with multimember districts (permissive). We then separately plotted the lines that best fits these two groups in Figure 13.9. As you can see, the slope of the line that best fits electoral systems with multimember districts is 0.92,

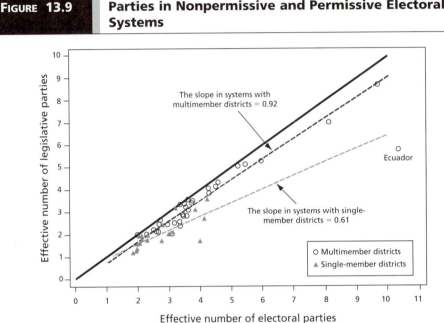

FIGURE 13.9

The Effective Number of Electoral and Legislative Parties in Nonpermissive and Permissive Electoral Systems

Source: Data are from Amorim Neto and Cox (1997).

Note: Because Ecuador is a huge outlier, we ignored it when plotting the line that best fits the observations from countries employing multimember districts. Had we included it, the slope of the line for multimember districts would have been smaller (0.73) but still significantly larger than the slope of the line for single-member districts.

whereas the slope of the line that best fits electoral systems with single-member districts is 0.61. In other words, an additional electoral party is expected to result in 0.92 legislative parties in a permissive electoral system but just 0.61 legislative parties in a nonpermissive one. Put differently, the distortionary effect induced by the mechanical way in which votes are translated into seats reduces the effective number of parties by 8 percent in permissive electoral systems and by 39 percent in nonpermissive systems. On average, then, nonpermissive systems are almost five times more distortionary when it comes to translating votes into seats than are permissive electoral systems.

Duverger's theory indicates that the strong distortionary effect exhibited by nonpermissive electoral systems induces voters and political elites to engage in strategic behavior. The end result is that some social divisions are not represented in the party system. As we saw earlier in the chapter, there are many different social divisions in a given country that might create pressure for new parties. Political scientists interested in party system size, however, have tended to focus primarily on ethnic divisions. The number of ethnic divisions in a country is commonly measured in regard to the effective number of ethnic groups that exist.

This measure is constructed in exactly the same way as our measures of the effective number of parties except that we use each ethnic group's share of the population in our calculations rather than each party's share of the vote or legislative seats. The effective numbers of ethnic groups for fifty-four democracies in the mid-1980s are shown in Table 13.2.

In a completely "permissive" electoral system, we might expect each ethnic group to have its own party. In contrast, Duverger's theory indicates that nonpermissive systems will discourage the formation of small political parties to represent ethnic minorities. Since SMDP systems are "winner-take-all" systems, members of ethnic groups are likely to engage in what Chandra (2004) calls an "ethnic head count." They will look to see if fellow group members are sufficiently numerous to win representation in their constituency. If they are, they are likely to form and vote for an ethnic party. If there are insufficient numbers of co-ethnics, however, they will either vote for a nonethnic party or redefine the boundaries of the ethnic group. As an example of this, Chandra (2004) describes how political entrepreneurs from the Kshatriya warrior caste in the state of Gujarat in India redefined the boundaries of their ethnic group to improve their electoral chances following India's independence in 1947. Kshatriyas constituted just 5 percent of the Gujarat population, which made it extremely unlikely that they would win SMDP elections. "Rather than bowing to the 'predetermined' fate of a minority group . . . [Kshatriya entrepreneurs] engaged in a large-scale attempt to swell the numbers of their 'own' ethnic group by relaxing the strict criteria for membership. As one such entrepreneur openly admitted: 'We have taken all the backward people who are martial by nature and called them Kshatriyas. Bhils, Ahirs, Bariyas and Dharalas are all Kshatriyas' " (Chandra 2004, 289).[18]

Nonpermissive electoral systems, such as SMDP, raise the bar on what constitutes a critical number of co-ethnics. Plurality rule means that an ethnic group has to be bigger than any other ethnic group in the district to win the seat. In contrast, ethnic parties looking to win seats in permissive systems just have to be big enough to surpass whatever natural or legal threshold exists. As a consequence, multimember district systems are permissive in that ethnic identity is likely to be translated into ethnic parties, whereas single-member district systems are nonpermissive in that they encourage ethnic voters and their leaders to cast their net more widely—by making cross-ethnic appeals or by defining their ethnic group more broadly. All of this implies that we should expect the existence of large numbers of ethnic groups to lead to a large number of parties in permissive electoral systems but not in nonpermissive ones.

The information in Figure 13.10 provides considerable support for this prediction. In this figure, we plot the relationship between the number of ethnic groups in a country and the number of electoral parties. To see if this relationship depends on the type of electoral system used in these countries, we split our sample into the same two groups as before. We then separately plotted the lines that best fit those observations coming from countries

---

18. Another example of where ethnic boundaries are redefined in order to increase political influence can be seen in the United States, where Dominicans, Mexicans, Puerto Ricans, and others are often mobilized as "Hispanics" or "Latinos."

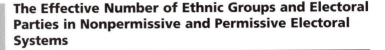

FIGURE 13.10 **The Effective Number of Ethnic Groups and Electoral Parties in Nonpermissive and Permissive Electoral Systems**

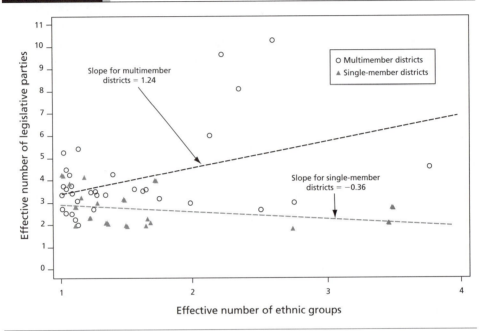

Source: Data are from Amorim Neto and Cox (1997).

using single-member districts and that best fit those observations coming from countries using multimember districts.

The first thing to note is that an additional ethnic group is associated with 1.24 additional electoral parties in permissive electoral systems. The upward sloping line in the figure indicates that more ethnic groups lead to more parties in countries with permissive electoral systems. In contrast, an additional ethnic group is associated with 0.36 fewer parties in nonpermissive electoral systems. This negative relationship in nonpermissive electoral systems is not statistically significant. As a result, the evidence in Figure 13.10 indicates that there is no relationship between the number of ethnic groups and the number of electoral parties in countries employing nonpermissive electoral systems. The difference in the slopes of the two lines can be seen as the differential impact of the strategic effect of permissive and nonpermissive electoral systems on how ethnic groups are translated into electoral parties. A second thing to note from Figure 13.10 is that the slope of the line best fitting those observations from countries employing permissive systems is greater than one (1.24). This indicates that each effective ethnic group is represented by more than one party. One way to interpret this, as our earlier discussion notes, is that ethnicity is just one source of conflict within society, and some parties are formed to represent different cleavages.

The best way to look at the *total* modifying effect of electoral laws—a combination of their mechanical and strategic effects—is to examine the relationship between the number of ethnic groups and the number of legislative parties. This relationship is plotted in Figure 13.11. As you can see, an additional ethnic group yields close to a full, effective party in the legislature in a permissive electoral system but essentially zero legislative parties in nonpermissive systems. In other words, ethnic heterogeneity increases the size of party systems in permissive systems but not in nonpermissive ones. This is exactly as Duverger's theory predicts.

So far, our analysis has been rather simple in that we have assumed that there are precisely two kinds of electoral laws—nonpermissive ones and permissive ones. Elsewhere in his classic work, Duverger says that the single most important dimension by which electoral systems differ is their district magnitude. Since single-member districts elect precisely one legislator, their district magnitude is obviously one. There is, however, a tremendous amount of variety in the district magnitude of multimember districts. Rather than simply distinguish

FIGURE 13.11 **The Effective Number of Ethnic Groups and Legislative Parties in Nonpermissive and Permissive Electoral Systems**

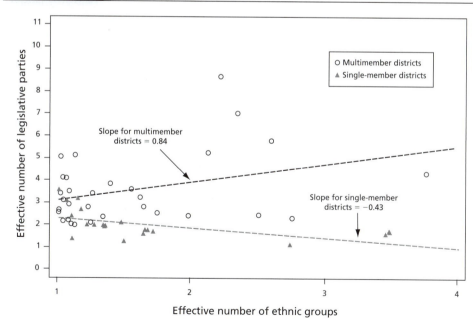

Source: Data are from Amorim Neto and Cox (1997).

between single-member and multimember districts, Clark and Golder (2006) use a country's average district magnitude to measure the permissiveness of the electoral system in a continuous, rather than a dichotomous, way. Results from their analyses, which are based on data from all democracies in the world from 1946 to 2000, are shown in Table 13.17. As you can see, increasing the number of ethnic groups by one when the average district magnitude is very large, such as in the Netherlands, yields about one and a half electoral parties and one and a quarter legislative parties. Increasing the number of ethnic groups by one when the average district magnitude is moderately large, such as in Greece, Spain, or Argentina, yields about 0.6 electoral parties and 0.5 legislative parties. Increasing the number of ethnic groups by one has no appreciable effect on party system size in countries that employ single-member districts; although there is an estimated increase of 0.11 electoral parties and 0.07 legislative parties in these countries, neither of these estimates is statistically distinguishable from zero. Overall, then, there is strong evidence that the size of a country's party system

TABLE 13.17	The Effect of an Additional Ethnic Group on the Effective Number of Electoral and Legislative Parties as District Magnitude Changes		
District magnitude	Sample countries	Strategic effect Electoral parties	Mechanical effect Legislative parties
1	Australia Canada United States United Kingdom	0.11	0.07
2 to 5	Chile Thailand Ireland	0.29 to 0.54	0.20 to 0.39
5 to 10	Greece Argentina Spain Honduras	0.54 to 0.72	0.39 to 0.55
10 to 20	Portugal Finland Brazil Luxembourg	0.72 to 0.90	0.55 to 0.72
120 to 150	Israel Netherlands	1.37 to 1.43	1.24 to 1.31

Source: Clark and Golder (2006, 705).

depends on the interaction between social and institutional forces in the manner predicted by Duverger's theory.

CONCLUSION

Political scientists sometimes categorize democracies in terms of the type of party system that they employ. When they do this, they tend to focus on the number and size of the parties in a country. But what explains why some countries have many parties and others have few? As we have seen, party system size is shaped by the interaction between social heterogeneity and the permissiveness of electoral institutions. Social divisions provide the demand for distinctive representation and, hence, the driving force behind the multiplication of political parties. However, electoral laws modify the way that these social divisions are translated into parties that win votes (electoral parties) and parties that win seats (legislative parties). According to Duverger's theory, countries will only have large multiparty systems if they are characterized both by high levels of social heterogeneity *and* permissive electoral systems.

When electoral systems are permissive (high district magnitude), social heterogeneity is translated into electoral and legislative parties with very little distortion. In contrast, nonpermissive (low district magnitude) electoral institutions are likely to produce party systems that are much smaller than the number of social cleavages in a country might lead us to imagine. In effect, nonpermissive electoral laws introduce a large amount of distortion in how social heterogeneity is translated into parties at the electoral and legislative levels. It is important to remember, though, that the precise amount of distortion that is introduced by nonpermissive electoral rules depends on the way that social heterogeneity is geographically distributed in a country. For example, if the supporters of small parties are distributed fairly evenly across electoral districts, then we should expect nonpermissive electoral laws to produce legislatures with many fewer parties than social cleavages. If the supporters of small parties are geographically concentrated, however, the reductive effect that nonpermissive electoral rules exercise on the number of parties will be greatly curtailed.

In this chapter, we also examined why it is that some party systems are divided primarily along ethnic lines, whereas others are divided mainly along class, religious, or linguistic ones. In other words, we looked at why countries have the types of parties that they do. As with party system size, we argued that the types of parties in a country are determined by the complex interplay of social and institutional forces. At some basic level, the patterns of social cleavages in a country provide the potential lines of conflict that could underpin the existence of distinct political parties. We also saw that institutions, such as electoral rules, are likely to determine which of these cleavages become activated or politicized. Overall, comparative politics scholars have made much greater progress in understanding the number of parties that exist in a country than in understanding the likely ideological or programmatic orientation of the parties. Given this, we hope that readers of this text will contribute to the construction and testing of theories relating to the types of parties found in different countries.

KEY CONCEPTS

anti-clericalism, 556
attribute, 565
cross-cutting attributes, 567
Duverger's Hypothesis, 585
Duverger's Law, 585
Duverger's theory, 583
effective number of electoral parties, 548
effective number of legislative parties, 548
effective number of parties, 548
ethnic group, 563
ethnic party, 564
freezing hypothesis, 561
identity category, 565
laïcité, 556

mechanical effect of electoral laws, 575
Michels' iron law of oligarchy, 561
multiparty system, 543
nonpartisan democracy, 543
one-party dominant system, 543
party identification, 535
political party, 534
reinforcing attributes, 567
single-party system, 543
strategic effect of electoral laws, 579
strategic entry, 580
two-party system, 543
whip, 540

PROBLEMS

The problems that follow address some of the more important concepts and ideas introduced in this chapter.

Party System Size

1. As we note in the chapter, the actual number of parties competing in an election or winning seats is not necessarily a good reflection of "how big" a country's party system is. As a result, political scientists often prefer to use a measure of the *effective* number of parties in a country to capture party system size. If you recall, the effective number of electoral parties when there are four actual parties is calculated as:

$$\text{effective number of electoral parties} = \frac{1}{v_1^2 + v_2^2 + v_3^2 + v_4^2},$$

where v_1 is the vote share of party 1, v_2 is the vote share of party 2, and so on. The effective number of legislative parties when there are four actual parties is calculated as:

$$\text{effective number of legislative parties} = \frac{1}{s_1^2 + s_2^2 + s_3^2 + s_4^2},$$

where s_1 is the seat share of party 1, s_2 is the seat share of party 2, and so on. These measures can easily be adapted to cases in which there are more parties or fewer parties. For example, the general formulas for the effective number of parties are:

$$\text{effective number of electoral parties} = \frac{1}{\sum_{i=1}^{P} v_i^2},$$

and

$$\text{effective number of legislative parties} = \frac{1}{\sum_{i=1}^{P} s_i^2},$$

where P is the total number of actual parties.

In Table 13.18, we show the results from the 2004 parliamentary elections in the Republic of South Africa. As you can see, nineteen parties won votes and twelve parties won seats. This would seem to suggest that South Africa has a large multiparty system. Answer the following questions.

TABLE 13.18	**Parliamentary Election Results in the Republic of South Africa, 2004**		
Party name	**Votes (%)**	**Seats (no.)**	**Seats (%)**
African National Congress (ANC)	69.70	279	69.80
Democratic Alliance/Demokratiese Alliansie (DA)	12.40	50	12.50
Inkatha Freedom Party (IFP)	7.00	28	7.00
United Democratic Movement (UDM)	2.30	9	2.30
Independent Democrats (ID)	1.70	7	1.80
Nuwe Nasionale Party/New National Party (NNP)	1.70	7	1.80
African Christian Democratic Party (ACDP)	1.60	7	1.80
Vryheidsfront Plus (VF Plus)	0.90	4	1.00
United Christian Democratic Party (UCDP)	0.80	3	0.80
Pan Africanist Congress of Azania (PAC)	0.70	3	0.80
Minority Front (MF)	0.40	2	0.50
Azanian People's Organisation (AZAPO)	0.30	1	0.25
Christian Democratic Party (CDP)	0.10	0	0.00
Nasionale Aksie (NA)	0.10	0	0.00
Peace and Justice Congress (PJC)	0.10	0	0.00
The Socialist Party of Azania (SOPA)	0.10	0	0.00
New Labour Party (NLP)	0.10	0	0.00
United Front (UF)	0.10	0	0.00
Employment Movement for South Africa (EMSA)	0.10	0	0.00
The Organisation Party (TOP)	0.00	0	0.00
Keep It Straight and Simple Party (KISS)	0.00	0	0.00

a. What is the effective number of electoral parties in the 2004 South African elections? What is the effective number of legislative parties? (You should probably use a calculator for this.)

b. Compare the effective numbers of electoral and legislative parties in these elections with the actual number of parties winning votes and seats. Which measure—the actual or effective number of parties—does a better job, in your opinion, of capturing the size of the South African party system? Why? Are there circumstances in which you would be more likely to use the actual number of parties as the measure of party system size? Are there circumstances in which you would be more likely to use the effective number of parties?

c. Based on your answers to the previous questions and the information in Table 13.18, what do you think is the most accurate classification of the South African party system: nonpartisan, single party, one-party dominant, two party, or multiparty?

d. Based on the effective numbers of electoral and legislative parties that you calculated, does the mechanical effect of South Africa's electoral system introduce much distortion in the way that votes are translated into seats? Based on your answer to this question, what type of electoral system do you think South Africa employs—a permissive or nonpermissive one? Use Internet resources to find out whether South Africa really does use a permissive or a nonpermissive electoral system.

Party System Nationalization

2. India uses an SMDP electoral system to elect its legislators to the Lok Sabha, the Indian lower house of parliament. In the 2004 elections, nearly forty different political parties won seats. The effective number of legislative parties was 6.52.[19]

a. Given that India employs the highly nonpermissive SMDP electoral system, can you think of reasons why we don't see a two-party system similar to the ones found in the United States or Jamaica?

b. In Figure 13.12, we illustrate the effective number of parties at the district and national level in India from 1957 to 1995. As you can see, the effective number of parties at the district level always hovers around two. Explain why this is the case with reference to the mechanical and strategic effects of electoral laws.

---

19. See the Electoral Systems Web site at http://www.tcd.ie/Political_Science/Staff/Michael.Gallagher/ElSystems/index.php.

FIGURE 13.12	**Number of Parties at the National and District Level in India, 1957–1995**

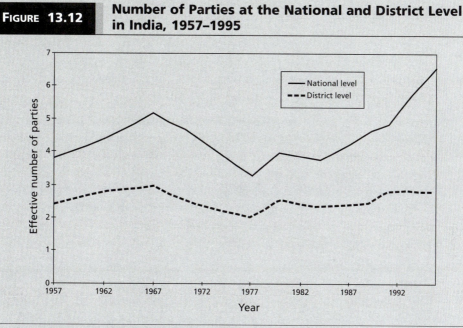

Source: Chhibber and Kollman (1998).

c. Although the effective number of parties at the district level in India always hovers around two, the number of parties at the national level exhibits a considerable amount of variation, ranging from a low of about three in the mid-1970s to a high of over six in the 1990s. One thing that is noticeable in Figure 13.12 is that the size of the national party system in India was lower in the 1970s than in the 1960s or in the 1980s and 1990s. In effect, there is evidence that the Indian party system was more nationalized in the 1970s than in other periods. Without knowing anything in particular about Indian politics, can you try to explain this variation over time?

Political Identity Formation

3. In Table 13.19, we illustrate the distribution of attributes in a hypothetical Los Angeles community that is divided along language and race lines.

TABLE 13.19	**Distribution of Attributes in a Hypothetical Los Angeles Community (percent)**		
	English speaker	**Spanish speaker**	**Korean speaker**
Latino	20	31	0
Asian	17	0	14
Black	10	0	0
White	8	0	0

a. If you know that someone is an English speaker, can you predict with much certainty what racial group he or she belongs to? If you know that someone is a Latino, can you predict with much certainty what language he or she speaks? If you know that someone is Asian, can you predict with much certainty what language he or she speaks? Based on your answers to these questions, would you say that the attributes in this hypothetical Los Angeles community are cross-cutting or reinforcing?

b. Let's assume that in order to win political office in this Los Angeles community, a candidate needs to win 50 percent of the vote. Let's also assume that political entrepreneurs will try to mobilize voters along either racial or linguistic lines. If this is the case, what identity categories could be activated or politicized to win the election? In other words, what identity categories (racial or linguistic) form minimal winning coalitions? If you have answered this question correctly, you will find that there are two identity categories that form minimal winning coalitions. Which of these two identity categories do you think is most likely to be politicized and why?

c. In the previous question, you found that there were two identity categories that could form minimal winning coalitions in this Los Angeles community. Are there any groups of individuals that are members of both minimal winning coalitions? If so, who are they? Do you think that being in both potential winning coalitions is politically advantageous? If so, why?

14 Institutional Veto Players

The accumulation of all powers, legislative, executive, and judiciary, in the same hands, whether of one, a few, or many, and whether hereditary, self appointed, or elective, may justly be pronounced the very definition of tyranny.

James Madison, *Federalist,* no. 47

It is very dangerous to allow the nation as a whole to decide on matters which concern only a small section, whether that section be geographical or industrial or defined in any other way. The best cure for this evil, so far as can be seen at present, lies in allowing self-government to every important group within a nation in all matters that affect that group much more than they affect the rest of the community.

Bertrand Russell, *Proposed Roads To Freedom,* 1919

[In government] the constant aim is to divide and arrange the several offices in such a manner as that each may be a check on the other; that the private interest of every individual may be a sentinel over the public rights.

James Madison, *Federalist,* no. 51

OVERVIEW

- In this chapter, we examine the origins and consequences of federalism, bicameralism, and constitutionalism.

- A federal state is one in which sovereignty is constitutionally split between at least two territorial levels so that independent governmental units at each level have final authority in at least one policy realm. It is important to distinguish between "federalism in structure" and "federalism in practice."

- A bicameral state is one in which legislative deliberations occur in two distinct assemblies. Although bicameral legislatures were originally designed to represent different social classes, they are now more closely associated with the representation of different territorial units.

- Constitutionalism refers to the commitment of governments to be governed by a set of authoritative rules and principles that are laid out in a constitution. Constitutionalism requires a codified constitution, a bill of rights, and constitutional review.

- Rather than view the world in terms of institutional dichotomies, comparative scholars are increasingly recognizing that institutions such as federalism, bicameralism, and constitutionalism are conceptually the same. In effect, all three of these institutions act as checks and balances, thereby influencing how easy it is to change the political status quo. This new approach to understanding political institutions is called veto player theory.

As we noted in Chapter 10, there are many, many different types of democracy in the world. In subsequent chapters, we looked at how political scientists sometimes distinguish between democracies in terms of the type of government that they have (Chapter 11), the type of electoral system that they employ (Chapter 12), and the type of party system that they have (Chapter 13). In this chapter, we focus on other institutional dimensions of democracy. Specifically, we examine federalism, bicameralism, and constitutionalism. All three of these institutions can be thought of as forms of checks and balances on the political system. In effect, they can all be conceptualized as "institutional veto players" that influence the ease with which the political status quo in a country can be changed. As such, their causes and consequences are closely related. It is for this reason that we consider these different institutions in a single chapter.

FEDERALISM

Political scientists sometimes distinguish between states according to whether they are federal or unitary. Unfortunately, there remains a great deal of uncertainty and confusion about exactly what it is that makes a state federal. At present, there are several rather vague definitions of federalism in the existing literature (Riker 1975; Elazar 1987; Wright 1988; Ostrom 1991; O'Toole 1993). This causes a problem in that scholars regularly come up with different lists of federal states. Although there is a widespread consensus that about a dozen countries, such as Argentina, Canada, Germany, and the United States, are federal, there is considerable disagreement over the federal-unitary status of many other countries. For example, countries like China, India, Italy, Russia, Spain, the United Kingdom, and Venezuela are considered federal by some political scientists but not others.

To a large extent, the source of this confusion can be traced to whether one thinks that a country needs to be both federal *in structure* (de jure) and federal *in practice* (de facto) in order to be considered truly federal. For our part, we believe that it is useful to retain a conceptual distinction between de jure federalism and de facto federalism (Bednar, forthcoming). Only by making this distinction can political scientists examine why it is that some states that are federal on paper actually *behave* federally but others do not. In what follows, we refer to de jure federalism (federalism in structure) as **federalism** and de facto federalism (federalism in practice) as **decentralization.**

Federalism: Federalism in Structure

To be classified as federal, a country must satisfy three structural criteria: (a) geopolitical division, (b) independence, and (c) direct governance (Bednar forthcoming). Typically we can determine whether a country satisfies these criteria simply by looking at its constitution.

1. *Geopolitical division:* The country must be divided into mutually exclusive regional governments that are constitutionally recognized and that cannot be unilaterally abolished by the national or central government.
2. *Independence:* The regional and national governments must have independent bases of authority. Typically, this independence is established constitutionally by having the regional and national governments elected independently of one another.
3. *Direct governance:* Authority must be shared between the regional governments and the national government; each governs its citizens directly, so that each citizen is governed by at least two authorities. In addition, each level of government must have the authority to act independently of the other in at least one policy realm; this policy sovereignty must be constitutionally declared.

The regional units in a federal polity go under different names, depending on the country concerned. For example, they are called states in Australia, the United States, and Venezuela; provinces in Canada; Länder in Germany and Austria; cantons in Switzerland; and regions in Belgium. Taken together, the three criteria outlined above indicate that a **federal state** is one in which sovereignty is constitutionally split between at least two territorial levels so that independent governmental units at each level have final authority in at least one policy realm.

> **Federalism** has three structural components: (a) geopolitical division, (b) independence, and (c) direct governance. A **federal state** is one in which sovereignty is constitutionally split between at least two territorial levels so that independent governmental units at each level have final authority in at least one policy realm. States that are not federal are known as **unitary states.**

In Table 14.1, we list all twenty-four countries that could be considered federal at some point between 1990 and 2000.[1] We also list whether these countries are democratic or authoritarian based on their Polity IV scores (Marshall and Jaggers 2003). By definition, all countries that do not appear in Table 14.1 are **unitary states.** As the information in Table 14.1 indicates, federalism is relatively rare in the world. As of 2000, only about 10 percent of the world's independent countries were federal; slightly less than 20 percent of the world's population lived in a federal country. On the whole, those countries that are federal tend to be either relatively large countries, such as Australia, Brazil, the former Soviet Union, and the United States, or relatively heterogeneous and diverse countries, such as Belgium, Ethiopia, Malaysia, Switzerland, and Yugoslavia.

---

1. The European Union also meets our criteria for a federal system. We do not include it in Table 14.1, however, because the European Union is not an independent state.

TABLE 14.1		Federal Countries, 1990–2000	
	Country	**Regime**	**Years**
1	Argentina	Democracy	1990–2000
2	Australia	Democracy	1990–2000
3	Austria	Democracy	1990–2000
4	Belgium	Democracy	1994–2000
5	Bosnia & Herzegovina	Dictatorship	1990–2000
6	Brazil	Democracy	1990–2000
7	Canada	Democracy	1990–2000
8	Czechoslovakia	Democracy	1990–1992
9	Ethiopia	Dictatorship	1995–2000
10	Germany	Democracy	1990–2000
11	Malaysia	Dictatorship	1990–2000
12	Mexico	Dictatorship	1990–1995
		Democracy	1996-2000
13	Micronesia	Democracy	1990–2000
14	Nigeria	Democracy	1999–2000
15	Pakistan	Democracy	1990–1999
16	Russia	Democracy	1992–2000
17	South Africa	Democracy	1993–2000
18	Switzerland	Democracy	1990–2000
19	USSR	Dictatorship	1990–1991
20	United Arab Emirates	Dictatorship	1990–2000
21	United States of America	Democracy	1990–2000
22	Venezuela	Democracy	1990–2000
23	Yugoslavia	Dictatorship	1990–1991
24	Yugoslavia (Serbia & Montenegro)	Dictatorship	1992–2000

Source: Data are from Bednar (forthcoming); the coding for regime type is from the Polity IV dataset.
Note: All of these countries satisfy the criteria of (a) geopolitical division, (b) independence, and (c) direct governance.

The United Arab Emirates (UAE) is an example of a federal dictatorship. The UAE currently comprises seven emirates in the Middle East—Abu Dhabi, Ajman, Dubai, Fujairah, Ra's al-Khaimah, Sharjah, and Umm al-Qawain. See Map 14.1, which shows the seven emirates. Originally, the seven emirates were known as the Trucial States and they formed part of a British protectorate along with Bahrain and Qatar. Following Britain's stated decision to withdraw from the Gulf in 1968, the seven Trucial States, along with Bahrain and Qatar, began negotiations to form a federation of Arab Emirates. Bahrain and Qatar ultimately decided to go their separate ways, but six Trucial States went on to form the United Arab Emirates in

December 1971; the seventh Trucial State—Ra's al-Khaimah—joined in February 1972 (Peterson 1988). The provisional constitution of the UAE, which only became permanent in 1996, established a federal form of government (Peck 2001). This essentially involved constructing federal authorities above the preexisting local governments in each of the seven emirates. The federal nature of the UAE is guaranteed in Articles 116 and 122 of the constitution. These articles state that all powers that are not explicitly given to the federal authorities in the constitution belong to the individual emirates.[2] Not only is the UAE the only current example of a federal state in the Middle East, but it also represents the only successful attempt to form a political union among Arabs. Egypt and Syria had formed a United Arab Republic in 1958. This experiment with Arab political union proved short-lived, however, collapsing in 1961 when Syria began to believe that it was being treated like an Egyptian province. The

| MAP 14.1 | The Federal States of the United Arab Emirates |

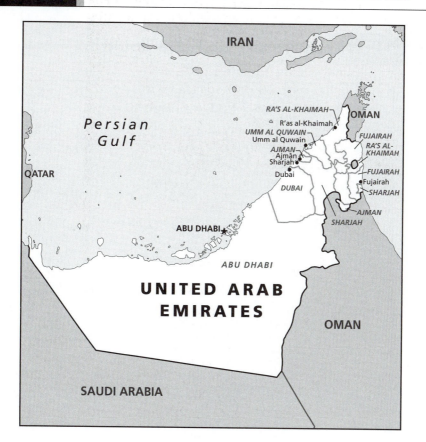

---

2. Very few powers are explicitly given to the federal authorities. Articles 120 and 121 state that the federal authorities are in charge of foreign affairs, security, defense, nationality and immigration issues, education, public health, currency, and a few other areas; everything else is determined by the local governments in the individual emirates.

merger of North and South Yemen in 1990 was another attempt at Arab political union. This attempt essentially ended in failure when the South tried to secede militarily in 1994.

Whereas the United Arab Emirates is an example of a federal dictatorship, Brazil is an example of a federal democracy. Brazil has a long history with federalism dating back to the 1891 constitution of the Old Republic (1889–1930). The existing federal arrangements date to the 1988 constitution, which was written following the re-emergence of democracy from military dictatorship in 1985. Unlike most federal countries, which have two different levels of territorial units, Brazil has three—federal, state, and municipal. At the federal level, executive power is in the hands of the president. At the state level, there are twenty-six states based on historical borders that have developed over centuries and a "federal district" that comprises Brazil's capital, Brasília. As Map 14.2 illustrates, the federal district is in the state of Goiás. Executive power at the state level is in the hands of governors. At the municipal level, there are 5,560 different municipalities with their own legislative council; executive power is in the hands of mayors. Each of the municipalities has its own "little constitution," called an "organic law."

MAP 14.2   **Brazil's States and Federal District**

The federal nature of Brazil's government is guaranteed in Article 1 of the constitution, which states that Brazil is formed by "the indissoluble union of the states and municipalities and of the federal district." Political authority is constitutionally shared among all three levels of government. In effect, state governments are allowed to pass legislation in any area that is not explicitly prohibited to them in the constitution (Article 25). Similarly, municipal governments are permitted to pass laws on any matter that does not contradict either the state or national constitutions (Article 30). Brazil is one of four federal states in Latin America, the others being Argentina, Mexico, and Venezuela.

DEVOLUTION VERSUS FEDERALISM

Although only twenty-four countries satisfied all three structural criteria for federalism at some point during the 1990s, several other countries, such as Comoros, India, Italy, Spain, Sudan, St. Kitts and Nevis, Tanzania, Ukraine, and the United Kingdom, satisfied two of them (Bednar, forthcoming). On the whole, the criterion that most of these unitary countries failed to meet was that of geopolitical division. Recall that this criterion requires that a country be divided into mutually exclusive regional governments that are constitutionally recognized and that cannot be unilaterally abolished by the national or central government. Many of the aforementioned countries, like India, Spain, and the United Kingdom, have transferred quite a considerable amount of power from the central government to regional governments. In all of these countries, however, the central government retains the right to unilaterally recall or reshape the powers given to the regional governments. Ultimately, political power resides in the central government of these countries and nowhere else; regional governments do not have a constitutional right to any of their powers. This type of situation is known as **devolution** and not federalism. To further illustrate this point, consider the United Kingdom and India.

Devolution occurs when a unitary state grants powers to subnational governments but retains the right to unilaterally recall or reshape those powers.

Although the United Kingdom has historically had a very powerful central government, things have recently begun to change. Following successful referenda on the establishment of regional parliaments in 1997, elections were held for a Scottish parliament and a Welsh Senate in 1999. In accordance with the 1998 Good Friday Agreement, a provincial assembly was also established in Northern Ireland in 1999. These regional governments have had the legal right to act independently of the central government in London in numerous policy areas. As a result of these developments, the United Kingdom has come to satisfy two of the criteria for a federal state: independence and direct governance. The United Kingdom is not a federal state, however, because it fails to satisfy the criterion of geopolitical division; the UK central government retains the unilateral right to recall or reshape the powers that it has delegated or devolved to the regional governments. Indeed, the history of the Northern Ireland Assembly clearly illustrates this point. On four separate occasions since the establishment of the Assembly in 1999, the central government in London has suspended it; the fourth suspension lasted for over four years, from October 14, 2002, to May 7, 2007.

India also has many characteristics of a federal state. For example, it has two different levels of government—national and state. At present, twenty-eight states have their own local governments. There are also seven union territories, which differ from states in that they do not have their own local governments and are, instead, governed directly by the national government. Map 14.3 shows the states and union territories of India. Article 246 of the Indian constitution divides political authority between policy areas that are the exclusive concern of the national government (Union List) and policy areas that are the exclusive concern of the state governments. India clearly satisfies two of the criteria for a federal state: independence and direct governance. Like the United Kingdom, however, India is not a federal state, because it fails to satisfy the criterion of geopolitical division.

MAP 14.3   **India's States and Union Territories**

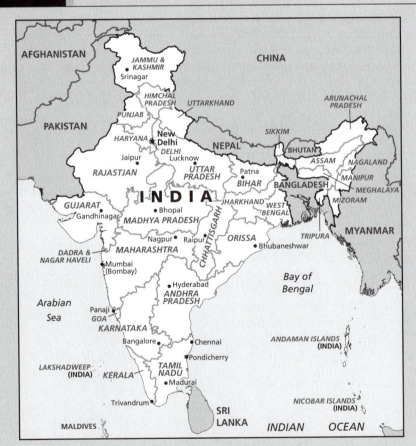

Two articles in the Indian constitution are of particular relevance here. The first is Article 3, which states that the national legislature has the power to change the boundaries of individual states and to create new states by separating territories from existing ones. The second is Article 356, which allows for the imposition of emergency presidential rule in a state that cannot be governed "in accordance with the provisions of the Constitution." In effect, this article, commonly known as "President's Rule," allows India's president to take over a state's executive and rule directly through his appointed state governor. The state's legislature may be dismissed or simply put in suspended animation during this period of emergency rule. President's Rule can last anywhere from six months to three years. It can last even longer than this if a constitutional amendment is passed, as has happened in the state of Punjab and the state of Jammu and Kashmir. Although Article 356 was originally designed to allow the central government to take over when a state was unable to end civil unrest, such as riots, it has taken on obvious political significance, with Indian presidents frequently using the power to dissolve state governments ruled by political opponents. Since the adoption of the Indian constitution in 1950, Article 356 has been invoked more than one hundred times to impose direct rule. President's Rule was first used in 1959 to dismiss the democratically elected Communist government in the state of Kerala. It was most recently used on November 20, 2007, in the south Indian state of Karnataka to help resolve difficulties in the state government formation process (Thaindian News online).

Despite sharing some of the features of a federal state, both the United Kingdom and India remain unitary states in structure even though they have devolved power to the regions.

Although all of the states shown in Table 14.1 can be considered federal, there is a great deal of variation in the precise form that federalism takes in these countries. When it comes to distinguishing between different forms of federalism, political scientists frequently focus on whether a federal system is (a) congruent or incongruent and (b) symmetric or asymmetric (Lijphart 1999).

Congruent federalism exists when the territorial units of a federal state share a similar demographic (ethnic, cultural, linguistic, religious, and so on) makeup. In a perfectly congruent federal state, each of the territorial units would be a precise miniature reflection of the

> **Congruent federalism** exists when the territorial units of a federal state share a similar demographic makeup with one another and the country as a whole. **Incongruent federalism** exists when the demographic makeup of territorial units differs among the units and the country as a whole.

country as a whole. Examples of a congruent federal state include the United States and Brazil. In both of these countries, the demographic composition of the territorial units does not vary significantly along ethnic, linguistic, cultural, or religious lines. In contrast, **incongruent federalism** exists when the demographic makeup of the territorial units differs among the units and the country as a whole. Examples of an incongruent federal state include Switzerland and Belgium. In both of these countries, the territorial units differ from one another along linguistic lines.

One way to think about congruent and incongruent federalism is in regard to whether the political boundaries of the territorial units line up with the geographic boundaries of ethnic, linguistic, cultural, or religious groups in a country. In an incongruent federal state, political boundaries tend to be aligned with the geographic boundaries of these social groups, whereas they tend to cut across them in congruent federal systems (Lijphart 1999, 196). One of the purported advantages of incongruent federalism is that it can transform highly diverse and heterogeneous countries that have geographically concentrated social groups into a federation of relatively homogeneous territorial units. As an example, consider Switzerland. Although Switzerland has four official language groups—German, French, Italian, and Romansch—the way that the territorial boundaries are drawn in the Swiss system of incongruent federalism means that twenty-two of the twenty-six cantons officially have only one language; three cantons—Bern, Fribourg, and Valais—are bilingual, and only one—Graubünden—is trilingual (McRae 1983, 172–179). In effect, Switzerland comprises a collection of homogeneous cantons within a relatively diverse country.

Symmetric federalism exists when the territorial units of a federal state possess equal powers relative to the central government. **Asymmetric federalism** exists when some territorial units enjoy more extensive powers than others relative to the central government.

Symmetric federalism exists when the territorial units of a federal state possess equal powers relative to the central government. This is the case in the United States: the Constitution gives each state equal standing and power vis-à-vis the central government. In contrast, **asymmetric federalism** exists when some territorial units of a federal state enjoy more extensive powers than others relative to the central government. On the whole, asymmetries in the division of power are designed to satisfy the different needs and demands that arise from ethnic, linguistic, demographic, or cultural differences between the separate subnational units. Examples of asymmetric federal states include Belgium, Canada, Malaysia, Russia, and Switzerland.[3] In Canada, the French-speaking province of Quebec enjoys significantly more autonomy in relation to the central government than the other nine English-speaking provinces. In addition to having special powers to promote and protect its French-Canadian culture, Quebec has considerable authority over employment and immigration issues within its borders; it is also the only Canadian province to have its own pension plan.

Decentralization: Federalism in Practice

Decentralization refers to the extent to which actual policy-making power lies with the central or regional governments in a country. Most political scientists see decentralization as a revenue issue: the greater the share of all tax revenues going to the central government, the less decentralized the state.

As we noted earlier, it is possible to make a conceptual distinction between federalism in structure (federalism) and federalism in practice (decentralization). As we have just seen, whether a state is federal or unitary is ultimately a consti-

---

3. In a similar manner to federal states, unitary states can also devolve power in an asymmetric manner. For example, the Navarra and Basque communities have significantly more extensive tax and expenditure powers than the other "autonomous communities" in Spain; Galicia and Catalonia enjoy special authority in the areas of education, language, and culture (Congleton 2006). In the United Kingdom the Scottish Parliament enjoys significantly more power, particularly in the area of taxation, than the Welsh senate.

tutional issue. It depends on whether a country has certain structural characteristics written into its constitution. Note, though, that whether a country is federal or unitary says very little about exactly *where* policy is made in practice. Recall that our definition of federalism simply states that each level of government has the authority to act independently of the other in *at least one policy realm*. Not only does this definition not specify a particular ratio of policy realms between the central and regional governments, it also does not specify whether the regional governments have the necessary resources to actually implement the policy decisions they might make.[4] In other words, simply knowing that a state is federal does not immediately imply that significant policymaking power is in the hands of regional governments at the subnational level. Similarly, knowing that a state is unitary does not necessarily mean that all policymaking power is in the hands of the central government. The degree to which actual policymaking power lies with the central or regional governments in both federal and unitary states determines the extent to which political scientists view these states as centralized or decentralized.

Determining the extent to which a state is centralized or decentralized can be quite difficult. You might think that we need only look at what a state's constitution has to say about the division of power between different levels of government. This, however, can be problematic for several reasons. Consider unitary states. In almost all unitary states, policymaking authority constitutionally resides with the central government. Still, as indicated in Box 14.1, significant amounts of policymaking power can be devolved to regional governments in unitary countries. In other words, subnational governments can play an important policymaking role even when they derive no explicit authority to do so from the constitution.

Now consider federal states. Oftentimes, the constitution of a federal country will delineate the specific policy realms in which the central or regional governments can act. Although this is somewhat informative, it is important to remember that having the *authority to act* in a policy realm can be very different from having the practical *ability to act* in that area. Consider, for example, a country in which the regional governments have the authority to make health or education policy. Unless these regional governments also have the ability to raise their own tax revenue, they may find themselves significantly constrained when it comes to actually making and implementing policy in these areas. Put another way, regional governments in a federal state may have a much weaker role in the policymaking process than a reading of the state's constitution might suggest, because they do not have the financial wherewithal to implement their policy choices. The bottom line is that looking at a constitution, whether in a federal or unitary country, can be misleading if one wants to know the extent to which that country is centralized or decentralized in practice.

In recognition of these difficulties, political scientists frequently use the percentage of all tax revenue that is collected by the central government as a measure of state centralization.[5]

---

4. We should note that this is not specific to our particular definition of federalism. For example, both Elazar and Riker allow for a wide range of actual power exercised by the different levels of government. As Lijphart (1999, 187) notes, "Riker (1975, 101) states that each level [of government] 'has some activities on which it makes final decisions.' . . . Likewise, Elazar (1997, 239) states that 'the powers assigned to each [of the] multiple centers' in federalism may be large or small."

5. For a good discussion of various measures of federalism and decentralization, see Rodden (2004).

This is often referred to as "fiscal (de)centralization." The basic assumption underlying this measure is that governments need tax revenue in order to implement policies. Thus, the scope of policymaking activities at any one level of government will ultimately depend on the share of tax revenues that it collects. The higher the share of all tax revenues collected by the central government, the more centralized the state. The lower the share of all tax revenues collected by the central government, the more decentralized the state. In sum, although political scientists tend to see federalism as a constitutional issue, they tend to see decentralization as a budgetary one.

In Figure 14.1, we illustrate the share of tax revenue collected by the central government out of the total tax revenue collected by all levels of government for fifty-three countries in 1997. Of these fifty-three countries, thirteen are federal and forty are unitary. In some countries, particularly federal ones, a proportion of the tax revenue collected by the central government is automatically transferred to regional governments through a legally mandated "revenue-sharing" scheme.[6] For example, roughly 28 percent of all the revenue collected by the central government in Argentina was automatically transferred to regional governments in 1997 (Diaz-Cayeros 2006, 184). Although this tax revenue was originally collected by the central government, the data in Figure 14.1 treat it as if it were collected by regional governments because they are its legal recipients.[7] With this in mind, what does the information in Figure 14.1 tell us about the relationship between federalism and decentralization?

On the whole, it is clear that the average degree of revenue centralization is lower in federal states (74.6 percent) than in unitary ones (87.95 percent). In other words, federalism and decentralization tend to go together, as one would expect. It should be noted, however, that there is a substantial amount of variation in revenue centralization in both unitary and federal countries (Arzaghi and Henderson 2005). For example, some unitary states (China, Denmark, Finland, India, Japan, Sweden) are more decentralized than the average federal state. Indeed, China, where the central government collects only 48.6 percent of the country's tax revenue, is the most decentralized state in the whole sample. Similarly, some federal states (Belgium, Malaysia, South Africa) are much more centralized than the average unitary state. Fully 97.6 percent of the tax revenue collected in federal Malaysia is collected by the central government.

---

6. Although mandated revenue-sharing schemes legally require central governments to transfer a certain percentage of their tax revenue to regional governments, central governments do not always fully comply with them. In a study of Latin America's four federal states—Mexico, Venezuela, Argentina, and Brazil—Diaz-Cayeros (2006) finds that central governments come much closer to transferring the mandated amount of tax revenue to regional governments when they are democratic rather than autocratic. To the extent that central governments do not abide by revenue-sharing schemes, the data in Figure 14.1 overstate the degree of decentralization in some, mainly federal, states.

7. In addition to these mandatory tax transfers, some countries also have nonmandatory transfers. On the whole, these nonmandatory transfers do not typically increase the power of regional governments vis-à-vis the central government (Lijphart 1999, 192). One reason for this is that many of them are conditional in the sense that they must be spent on things specified by the central government. As a result, these nonmandatory tax transfers are treated as belonging to the central government in Figure 14.1; only mandatory transfers are treated as belonging to regional governments.

| FIGURE 14.1 | **Revenue Centralization: Central Government's Share of Tax Revenue** |

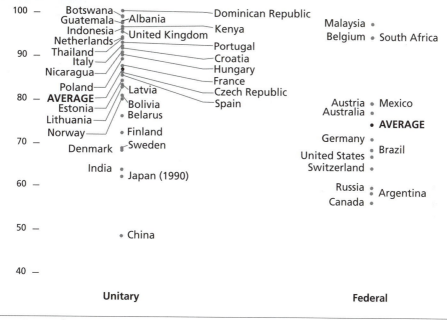

Source: Data are from World Bank (2000, 216–217).

Note: With the exception of Japan, all data points are for 1997; Japan's data point is for 1990. Tax revenue that is legally mandated to be transferred to regional governments through a revenue-sharing scheme is treated as belonging to the regional governments even if it is first collected by the central government. The names of some unitary countries have been omitted simply for visual clarity.

To summarize, federalism can be distinguished along two dimensions: federalism in structure (federal versus unitary) and federalism in practice (decentralized versus centralized). Whereas federalism in structure is a dichotomy—a country is either federal or unitary—decentralization is best thought of as a continuum, with some states being more decentralized than others. In Figure 14.2, we simplify the world somewhat and plot the names of various countries in a two-by-two matrix. Those countries in the top right quadrant, such as Brazil, Canada, and Germany, are federal, both in structure and in practice. Those countries in the bottom left quadrant, such as Botswana, the Dominican Republic, and Kenya, are unitary, both in structure and practice. Those countries in the top left quadrant, such as China, India, and Sweden, are unitary in structure but federal in practice. Finally, those countries in the bottom right quadrant, such as Belgium, Malaysia, and Venezuela, are federal in structure but unitary in practice.

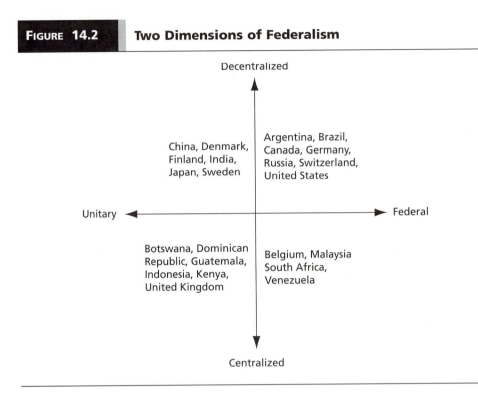

FIGURE 14.2   **Two Dimensions of Federalism**

Why Federalism?

Why do some states adopt federal arrangements? [8] To a large extent, political scientists distinguish between "coming-together" and "holding-together" federalism to explain the origins of federalism in various countries around the world (Stepan 1999, 21–22). **Coming-together federalism** results from a bottom-up bargaining process in which previously sovereign polities come together and voluntarily agree to give up part of their sovereignty in order to pool together their resources so as to improve their collective security and achieve

> **Coming-together federalism** is the result of a bargaining process in which previously sovereign polities voluntarily agree to give up part of their sovereignty in order to pool together their resources and improve their collective security or achieve other, economic goals. **Holding-together federalism** is the result of a process in which the central government of a polity chooses to decentralize its power to subnational governments in order to diffuse secessionist pressures.

other, typically economic, goals, such as a common currency and freer trade (Riker 1964). Australia, Switzerland, and the United States are examples of coming-together federal states. Although there is some variation, coming-together federations are typically characterized by a symmetric form of federalism.

---

8. In this section, we use the term *federalism* quite broadly to capture both dimensions of federalism—"federalism in structure" and "federalism in practice."

In contrast, **holding-together federalism** is the result of a top-down process in which the central government of a polity chooses to decentralize its power to subnational governments. This process typically occurs in multiethnic states in which the central government fears that the continued existence of the state is somehow threatened by one or more territorially based "ethnic" groups that wish to secede. In order to appease these secessionist groups and keep the country together, the central government decentralizes power to subnational units in which the aggrieved ethnic group dominates, thereby making the group more content to live within a unified state. For example, Belgium adopted federal arrangements in the 1990s to placate the demands of its different linguistic groups. Although they remain unitary states in their constitutional structure, India, Spain, and the United Kingdom are also examples of states that have engaged in "holding-together federalism"—they have all devolved significant policymaking power to regional governments in an attempt to diffuse secessionist pressures. In general, holding-together federations are characterized by both incongruent and asymmetric federalism. These federations are incongruent because their whole *raison d'être* is to decentralize power to territorially based ethnic groups; they tend to be asymmetric because they are trying to satisfy the different needs and preferences of the various ethnic groups in the country.

Over the years, supporters of federalism have sought to highlight its advantages over other forms of government. For example, some scholars have argued that decentralized forms of government are best for satisfying popular preferences in democratic countries in which individuals hold heterogeneous preferences (Tiebout 1956; Buchanan and Tullock 1962; Tullock 1969; Alesina and Spolaore 1997). On the whole, it seems reasonable to expect that fewer citizens will be dissatisfied with public policy in a federal state than in a unitary one. Consider the following example. Suppose that sixty citizens in a unitary state prefer policy A and forty citizens prefer policy B. In this situation, policy A will be adopted and forty citizens will be unhappy. Suppose now that we have a federal state with two regions. Imagine that fifty citizens prefer policy A and ten prefer policy B in the first region, whereas thirty citizens prefer policy B and ten prefer policy A in the second region. In this scenario, policy A will be adopted in one region and policy B will be adopted in another. Only twenty citizens will now be dissatisfied with government policy in our federal state. Obviously, if citizens are free to move from one region to another, then even greater citizen satisfaction can be achieved—citizens can simply "sort" themselves by moving to the region that best satisfies their policy preferences. As this example suggests, government policy is more likely to match citizen preferences in a federal state than in a unitary one. This is particularly the case in large countries in which individuals hold diverse policy preferences.

Another purported advantage of federalism is that it brings the "government" closer to the people. Some have claimed that this leads to an increase in the amount of information that is available to both citizens and governments (Hayek [1939] 1948; Oates 1972). By being closer to the people, subnational governments in federal systems should have better information about exactly what it is that their citizens want. This means that they will be able to tailor policies to the specific needs of their citizens. By being closer to the government, citizens in federal systems should have better information about exactly what it is that their government is doing. This means that they will be better placed to hold their government accountable. As a result, federalism is frequently linked to increased government accountability and responsiveness to citizen preferences (Lijphart 1999). By bringing the government closer to the people and, thereby, making it more relevant to their daily lives, federalism is also thought to encourage political participation and enhance perceived levels of legitimacy in the democratic process. As Alexander Hamilton put it in 1787 when discussing the United States, people will maintain stronger "affection, esteem, and reverence" toward their subnational government because of its public visibility in the day-to-day "administration of criminal and civil justice" (*Federalist,* no. 17).

If federal arrangements are combined with the ability of citizens and investors to move from one region to another, it has been argued, subnational governments will also have strong incentives to perform well in office, because poor performance will cause citizens and investors to move to better performing regions, taking their tax dollars and assets with them. This is sometimes referred to as "voting with one's feet" (Tiebout 1956), and it is a quite literal example of the benefits of having an exit option, discussed in Chapters 3 and 6. The competition between subnational governments for investment and citizens that is engendered by federalism is often expected to result in smaller, more efficient, and less corrupt government (Buchanan 1995). This competition is also at the heart of arguments suggesting that federalism enhances market economies and produces higher economic growth (Montinola, Qian, and Weingast 1994; Weingast 1995; Cao, Qian, and Weingast 1999).

Advocates of federalism also point to its ability to encourage policy experimentation and innovation. For example, subnational governments in federal systems have the opportunity to experiment with, and evaluate, different policies for tackling social, economic, and political problems. As U.S. Supreme Court Justice Louis D. Brandeis put it in 1932, subnational governments in federal systems are "laboratories" for democracy and innovative government action. The ability to experiment with different policies is important because it means that policymakers can learn more quickly about which policies work and which ones do not. In effect, federalism allows subnational governments to quickly learn from the experimentation of others without putting the whole country at risk of a single failed policy. In the United States, welfare reform during the 1990s is perhaps the most famous example of what some consider a successful policy that grew out of experimentation at the regional level.

Ever since Montesquieu, numerous individuals have also promoted federalism as a bulwark against tyranny. For instance, many of the founding fathers in the United States believed that the interlocking arrangements of federalism reduced the risk of tyranny because the subnational governments could, and would, check each other. As James Madison put it, "A rage for paper money, for an abolition of debts, for an equal division of property, or for any improper or wicked project, will be less likely to pervade the whole body of the Union than a particular member of it" (*Federalist,* no. 10). Alexander Hamilton also believed that the interlocking nature of federalism protected individual rights against abuse by authorities both at the national and subnational levels (*Federalist,* no. 9). Others have argued that federalism also has the ability to protect territorially based groups whose preferences diverge from those of the majority population from being subject to majority decisions that run counter to their preferences (Horowitz 1985). As such, federalism can be thought to minimize citizen coercion.

Although federalism has many supporters, several scholars have recently begun to question its purported benefits (Rose-Ackerman 2000). Rather than leading to a more efficient form of government as the proponents of federalism maintain, critics claim that the different layers of federalism can lead to the unnecessary duplication of government and the inefficient overlapping of potentially contradictory policies. Critics also argue that federalism exacerbates collective action problems in the formulation and implementation of economic and other politics, particularly in developing countries. For example, Rodden and Wibbels (2002, 500) argue that "[f]ederalism empowers regional politicians who face incentives to undermine macroeconomic management, market reforms, and other policies that have characteristics of national public goods. Self-interested regional elites do this either through autonomous policies made at the local level or through their [ability to block] the policy-making process at the center." Because provincial politicians ultimately care about their own political success, they face only weak incentives to make economic and other decisions in the interests of the federal system as a whole. For example, regional governments often block attempts at fiscal reform by the central government, particularly if these reforms are expected to be painful for their constituents. Regional governments also have incentives to spend beyond their means if there is an expectation that the central government will come to their rescue and bail them out. Evidence in support of this line of reasoning comes from several scholars who have found that federal systems are more prone to economic mismanagement and crises than unitary systems (Treisman 2000; Wibbels 2000; Rodden 2002).

Although supporters of federalism regularly point to the benefits that accrue from having competition between different subnational governments, critics point to the possible deleterious consequences that such competition can have. For example, in attempting to attract investment and retain their citizens, competition between subnational governments may lead to "downward harmonization" or a "race-to-the-bottom" in which levels of regulation, welfare, taxes, and trade barriers are continuously lowered (Hallerberg 1996). One consequence of downward harmonization is that it becomes difficult to implement local redistributive tax systems because the wealthy simply move to those regions with the lowest tax rates. Another potential consequence is increased poverty, with the poor migrating to those regions that still maintain some form of welfare protection; these regions will, in turn, be forced to lower their welfare protection as a result of the added fiscal strain of dealing with the arrival of poor immigrants from other regions.

Competition, particularly in asymmetric federations in which some regions enjoy more power and discretion than others, may also lead to the amplification of preexisting inequalities in population, wealth, and political power (Peterson 1995; Congleton 2006). If favored regional governments can take advantage of their additional authority to attract residents and enlarge their tax base, then they will likely prosper relative to other regional governments. The expectation of greater regional inequality is, in turn, likely to create conflict and political instability, with advantaged communities demanding increased autonomy and disadvantaged communities attempting to reverse asymmetries in the regional distribution of power.

Far from enhancing government accountability, as its supporters claim, critics argue that federalism is just as likely to undermine it. By adding layers of government and expanding areas of shared responsibility, federalism facilitates blame shifting and credit claiming (Rodden 2004, 494). This is because federalism can make it difficult for citizens to know which level of government is responsible for policy successes and which is to blame for policy failures. For example, if the regional economy performs poorly, is this the result of policies adopted by the subnational government or those implemented by the national government? In this type of situation, neither the subnational nor the national government will want to take responsibility for the poor economic performance and will likely try to blame the other. If federalism does lower government accountability, as critics maintain, it may actually increase, rather than reduce, levels of corruption (Rose-Ackerman 1978; Schleifer and Vishny 1993). Indeed, this is precisely what Treisman (2002) finds in a study examining the effect of decentralization on the quality of government. He concludes that countries with higher levels of decentralization have higher levels of corruption and lower levels of public goods provision.

BICAMERALISM

In addition to distinguishing states according to whether they are federal or unitary, political scientists sometimes distinguish between them by whether they have unicameral or bicameral legislatures.[9] A **unicameral legislature** is one in which legislative deliberations occur in a single assembly. In contrast, a **bicameral legislature** is one in which legislative deliberations occur in two distinct assemblies (Tsebelis and Money 1997, 15). Information from 2007 about whether a country has a unicameral or bicameral legislature is shown in Box 14.6 at the end of this chapter.[10] According to the Inter-Parliamentary Union, 76 (39.8 percent) of the 191 independent states listed in the box have a bicameral legislature (http://www.ipu.org/english/home.htm).

> A **unicameral legislature** is one in which legislative deliberation occurs in a single assembly. A **bicameral legislature** is one in which legislative deliberation occurs in two distinct assemblies.

We should note from the beginning that whether a country has a unicameral or bicameral legislature does not affect the relationship between the legislature and the executive. Recall

---

9. Surprisingly little has been written on the causes and consequences of unicameral versus bicameral legislatures. Much of the information in this section comes from Tsebelis and Money (1997) and Lijphart (1999).

10. On the whole, it is relatively easy to divide countries into unicameral or bicameral systems. However, one or two odd cases do not fit neatly into either category (Lijphart 1999, 201–202). For example, Norwegian legislators are elected as one body. After the election, though, they divide themselves into two chambers by selecting a quarter of their members to form a second chamber. Any disagreements that emerge between the two chambers are resolved in a joint session of both chambers. It is because of this that we code Norway as having a unicameral legislature in the appendix to this chapter.

from Chapter 11 that a presidential democracy is one in which the government does not depend on a legislative majority to exist, that a parliamentary democracy is one in which the government depends only on a legislative majority to exist, and that a mixed democracy is one in which the government depends on both a legislative majority and an independently elected president to exist. In almost every country, legislative responsibility refers exclusively to having a legislative majority in the popularly elected lower house.[11] As a result, there is no inherent conflict between bicameralism and the parliamentary form of government. The existence of a second legislative chamber does not influence the relationship between the legislature and the executive and, hence, whether a democracy is presidential, parliamentary, or mixed.

As we will see, though, having a second assembly can have a significant effect on a country's legislative process. This is fairly obvious in those countries in which the upper chamber is quite powerful, as in the United States. In the United States the House of Representatives and the Senate are equal partners in the legislative process—the agreement of both chambers is required for the passage of legislation. As a result, both chambers have the power to veto bills and amendments proposed by the other chamber. The equal power of the two chambers in the United States opens up all sorts of strategic possibilities that are not always available to legislators in unicameral systems. For example, U.S. legislators in one chamber can sometimes get away with voting for a politically popular, but ideologically unpalatable (for them), version of a bill if they know that the other chamber is going to reject it. This type of position-taking or credit-claiming behavior is frequently not possible in a unicameral legislature; whenever legislators vote in a unicameral legislature, they are more often than not legislating.[12]

The existence of a second chamber can still have a significant effect on the legislative process even in countries in which the upper house is relatively weak, such as the United Kingdom. Ever since the Parliament Acts of 1911 and 1949, the power to make legislative decisions in the United Kingdom has been firmly placed in the lower house, the House of Commons. The only real power that the upper house, the House of Lords, has in the legislative process is the ability to delay the passage of nonfinancial legislation for two parliamentary sessions or one calendar year.[13] Although this might not seem like much, this ability to delay legislation takes on a whole new light in the year before an election, when delaying a bill may, in effect, mean killing it. As Tsebelis and Money (1997, 2) point out, this ability to

---

11. The two most notable exceptions to this are Germany and Italy. Article 81 of the German constitution allows a government that has lost a vote of confidence in the lower house (Bundestag) to retain power for six months if it continues to enjoy the support of a majority in the upper house (Bundesrat). In Italy, two governments, one led by Andreotti in 1979 and the other led by Prodi in 2008, resigned after losing votes of confidence in the Italian upper house, the Senate.

12. Credit claiming or position taking is possible in unicameral democracies in which a president has the power to veto legislation. In effect, legislators in these systems can also vote for politically popular, but ideologically unpalatable, bills if they know that the president will veto them.

13. The House of Lords can delay "money bills"—those bills that, in the view of the Speaker of the House of Commons, are solely about national taxation or public funds—only for up to one month. The power of the House of Lords is further restricted by a constitutional convention, known as the Salisbury Convention, which rules out opposing legislation promised in the government's election manifesto.

delay legislation in the year prior to an election has enabled the House of Lords to abort significant pieces of legislation proposed by both Conservative and Labour governments. For example, Conservative prime minister Margaret Thatcher was forced to postpone her project to dissolve the Greater London Council in 1984 when the House of Lords rejected her legislation. This type of outcome—the reversal of a floor vote—is obviously impossible in unicameral legislatures. As this example illustrates, the existence of an upper chamber, even one widely considered to be weak, like the British House of Lords, can significantly influence the legislative process.

Types of Bicameralism

Although seventy-six states had a bicameral legislature in 2007, there is a great deal of variation in the precise form that bicameralism takes in these countries. When it comes to distinguishing between different forms of bicameralism, political scientists frequently focus on whether a bicameral system is (a) congruent or incongruent and (b) symmetric or asymmetric (Lijphart 1999). Congruence and incongruence refer to the membership of the two chambers and the categories of citizens represented, whereas symmetry and asymmetry refer to the relative power of the two chambers.

Congruent and Incongruent Bicameralism

Congruent bicameralism occurs when the two legislative chambers have a similar political composition. **Incongruent bicameralism** occurs when the two legislative chambers differ in their political composition. The level of congruence depends on how the membership of the two chambers is selected and whom that membership is supposed to represent.

Congruent bicameralism occurs when the two chambers have a similar political composition; **incongruent bicameralism** occurs when they differ in their political composition. Whether bicameralism is congruent or incongruent typically depends on *how* the membership of the two chambers is elected and *whom* that membership is supposed to represent. If the same methods are used to elect the members of each legislative chamber and both chambers represent the same set of citizens, then the political composition of each chamber is likely to be congruent. When this is the case, it is often assumed that the policy preferences of the two chambers will be identical or, at least, very similar.

When it comes to electing bicameral legislatures, it is almost always the case that the members of the lower chamber are directly elected through systems in which all eligible voters are given equal weight. This is not necessarily the case with members of the upper chamber, though. On the whole, four common methods are used to select members of upper chambers around the world: heredity, appointment, indirect elections, and direct elections (Tsebelis and Money 1997, 46). Historically, it was quite common for monarchs to grant seats in the upper chamber to members of the aristocracy, which would be passed down from generation to generation. Since the 1999 House of Lords Act in the United Kingdom (see Box 14.2), however, there are no longer any contemporary bicameral systems that use heredity as the predominant means for selecting members of the upper chamber.

HEREDITARY PEERS IN THE BRITISH HOUSE OF LORDS

The United Kingdom employs a bicameral system in which the lower chamber is called the House of Commons and the upper chamber is called the House of Lords. As of 2008, the House of Commons had 646 members and the House of Lords 738 members. Historically, members of the House of Lords have comprised a section of the nobility known as hereditary peers. The peerage is the system of titles of nobility granted by the monarch in the United Kingdom. Hereditary peers are individuals that have been given a title of nobility—duke, marquess, earl, viscount, baron—that can be passed on from one generation to the next. Peerages are passed on to the next holder on the death of the previous holder and disappear only when all the possible heirs have died out.

The House of Lords was originally quite small and rather exclusive. For example, there were only 29 hereditary peers during the fifteenth century under Henry VII (reigned 1457–1509). Although some subsequent monarchs were reluctant to create additional peerages, others did so quite freely. In many cases, peerages were specifically created to ensure that there was a majority in the House of Lords that supported the policies of the monarch. Indeed, Queen Anne (reigned 1702–1714) created twelve peerages in a single day with this particular goal in mind. The nineteenth century, starting with George III (reigned 1760–1820), probably witnessed the most prolific expansion in the number of hereditary peers. By 1999 there were 759 hereditary peers in the United Kingdom; a breakdown of these hereditary peers is shown in Table 14.2.

The predominantly hereditary nature of the House of Lords began to change in 1958 when the Life Peerages Act authorized the unlimited creation of life baronies. Life peers are members of the House of Lords who are appointed for life-long terms; their membership in the House of Lords cannot be passed on to their heirs when they die. Although life baronies are formally created by the monarch just like hereditary peers, in practice all are granted after being proposed by the prime minister. As a result, the 1958 Life Peerages Act greatly increased the ability of the prime minister to change the composition of the House of Lords and weaken the influence of hereditary peers. It also allowed for the creation of female peers. Information about the number of life peers created since 1958 is shown in Table 14.3.

TABLE 14.2	Hereditary Peers in the United Kingdom, 1999		
Type	**Male**	**Female**	**Total**
Prince	1	0	1
Duke	28	0	28
Marquess	34	0	34
Earl	170	5	175
Viscount	102	0	102
Baron/Lord	407	12	419
Total	742	17	759

TABLE 14.3	Life Peers in the United Kingdom, 1958–2007		
Prime minister	**Party**	**Tenure**	**Peers**
Harold Macmillan	Conservative	1957–1963	48
Alec Douglas-Home	Conservative	1963–1964	14
Harold Wilson	Labour	1964–1970	123
Edward Heath	Conservative	1970–1974	56
Harold Wilson	Labour	1974–1976	80
James Callaghan	Labour	1976–1979	57
Margaret Thatcher	Conservative	1979–1990	200
John Major	Conservative	1990–1997	141
Tony Blair	Labour	1997–2007	357
Total			1,076

As a working-class party, the British Labour Party has historically had a commitment either to abolish the House of Lords or, at least, to eliminate its hereditary element. After several failed attempts to reform the House of Lords in the 1960s and 1970s, the election of Tony Blair as prime minister in 1997 appeared to signal the end of the traditional House of Lords. In its 1997 election manifesto, the Labour Party committed itself to removing all hereditary peers from the House of Lords. Despite introducing legislation to do precisely this, the Labour Party ultimately agreed to a compromise—the 1999 House of Lords Act—in which ninety-two hereditary peers would remain in the House of Lords on an interim basis until all other reforms were completed. This means that, as of now, the British House of Lords is predominantly appointed; just ninety-two of its members are hereditary peers.

Attempts to further reform the House of Lords have stalled, with various proposals failing to win legislative support. The Wakeham Commission, which was set up to examine how best to reform the House of Lords, proposed in 2000 that roughly 20 percent of the House of Lords should be elected and the rest appointed by an independent Honours and Appointments Commission. This proposal was quickly rejected. Another committee, established in 2001 to look at reforms in the House of Lords, came up with several different proposals: fully appointed, 20 percent elected, 40 percent elected, 50 percent elected, 60 percent elected, 80 percent elected, or fully elected. All of these proposals were rejected in a series of legislative votes in 2003. Senior members of Parliament from all the leading parties then proposed that 70 percent of the House of Lords be elected and the remainder appointed by a commission with the goal of ensuring a mix of "skills, knowledge, and experience" in 2005. This proposal was also rejected. In a series of votes in early 2007, a majority of the House of Commons finally supported proposals in which 80 percent or 100 percent of the House of Lords would be elected. These proposals, however, were rejected by the House of Lords, whose members preferred a fully appointed second chamber. What ultimately will be decided about the composition of the House of Lords still remains up in the air. What is clear is that the membership of the British House of Lords will no longer be based predominantly on hereditary lines.

A second method of selecting members to the upper chamber is appointment. For example, a whole host of countries, such as Belize, Germany, Ireland, Jordan, Madagascar, Russia, and Thailand, have fully or partially appointed upper chambers. Although in a handful of countries appointments to the upper chamber are made by the monarch (Jordan, Malaysia, Thailand), it is much more common for these appointments to be made by an elected government of some kind. Germany is somewhat unusual in that the members of the upper chamber are appointed by regional governments. In almost every other case, it is the national government that appoints individuals to serve in the upper chamber. One of the rationales behind appointing, rather than electing, members of the upper chamber is that it facilitates the selection of individuals who have particular skills, knowledge, or experience that might come in useful when debating particular pieces of legislation.

Like hereditary methods, though, appointing individuals to an upper chamber is often perceived as undemocratic. As a result, many countries allow their citizens to *indirectly* or *directly* elect the members of the upper chamber. Austria, France, India, Madagascar, Mauritania, the Netherlands, and Swaziland, for example, all employ indirect elections. In most of these countries, citizens directly elect the members of local or regional governments, and it is these local or regional representatives who then elect the members of the upper chamber. Although indirect elections like this are somewhat common, it is much more often the case that citizens get to directly elect individuals to the upper chamber. This is the case in a wide range of countries, such as Argentina, Australia, Bolivia, Brazil, Chile, Colombia, Japan, Malaysia, Mexico, Norway, Poland, Romania, the United States, and Venezuela. Some countries, such as Spain, employ a mix of both indirect and direct elections. For example, the Spanish Senate comprises 264 members, of whom 208 are directly elected by popular vote and 56 are appointed by regional legislatures.

Whether a bicameral legislature is congruent or not depends not only on whether the members of the two chambers are selected in the same way but also on whether they represent the same set of citizens. In almost all countries, the members of the lower legislative chamber are supposed to represent all citizens equally under the general principle of "one person, one vote." In a few countries, such as Italy and Japan, this is also the case for members of the upper chamber. In these countries, the political composition of the upper house tends to mimic that of the lower house. On the whole, though, this type of situation is quite rare. In the vast majority of bicameral systems, the upper chamber is not designed to represent the entire population equally. For example, representation in the Irish Senate is based largely on certain professional occupations—most Irish senators are elected by five vocational panels representing culture and education, labor, industry and commerce, agriculture, and administration. In other countries, the upper chamber is supposed to ensure that minorities (Venezuela) or linguistic communities (Belgium) are represented.

By far the most common role for the upper chamber in a bicameral system is to represent the citizens of subnational geographic units. Although this is always the case in federal systems, such as Austria, Germany, Mexico, Switzerland, and the United States, it is also the case in some unitary countries, such as Bolivia, the Netherlands, and Spain. The frequently unequal distribution of citizens across the different subnational geographic units in a country—some

> **Malapportionment** occurs when the distribution of political representation between constituencies is not based on the size of each constituency's population. In a malapportioned system, the votes of some citizens weigh more than the votes of others.

regions have many people and others have few—often leads to **malapportionment** in the upper legislative chamber, with some citizens receiving greater representation than others (Monroe 1994; Samuels and Snyder 2001). In other words, the unequal geographic distribution of citizens frequently leads to the violation of the "one person, one vote" principle in territorially based upper chambers. This is clearly the case in such countries as Australia, Switzerland, Venezuela, and the United States, where the different geographic units all receive the same level of representation irrespective of how many residents they have. For example, each of the fifty U.S. states is represented by two senators. This means that California, with its approximately 36 million residents, receives the same level of representation in the U.S. Senate as Wyoming, with its half-million residents. Other countries, such as Canada and Germany, do not give equal representation to each of their subnational regions but still tend to overrepresent less populous regions and underrepresent more populous ones. Austria is unusual in that the allocation of upper chamber representatives to each subnational unit is roughly proportional to the size of each unit's population.

To get a better idea of the level of malapportionment found in upper chambers that are designed to represent subnational geographic units, consider Table 14.4. Here we illustrate the percentage of seats in the upper chamber going to the most favorably represented citizens in nine countries in 1996 (Lijphart 1999, 208). To see where these numbers come from, imagine that all of the subnational units in a country are lined up from left to right based on the size of their populations, with smaller units to the left and larger units to the right. Starting with the smallest unit and working our way to the right, we identify those units that together comprise 10 percent, 20 percent, 30 percent, and 50 percent of the country's overall population. We then determine the percentage of upper chamber seats that are allocated to these regions. These are the percentages shown in Table 14.4. As an example, consider the case of the United States. Table 14.4 indicates that the smallest states that together comprise 10 percent of the national population control 39.7 percent of the seats in the U.S. Senate. In other words, they receive almost four times the amount of representation in the Senate as their population would imply they should. The smallest states, which together comprise 20 percent of the overall U.S. population, control 55 percent of the Senate seats—an overall majority. The other percentages in Table 14.4 can be interpreted in a similar way. As you can see, there is a great deal of variation in the level of malapportionment seen in upper chambers around the world. Countries like the United States and Switzerland exhibit high levels of malapportionment, whereas countries like Austria and Belgium exhibit low levels.

In sum, the degree of congruence in a bicameral system depends on whether the two legislative chambers employ similar methods for selecting their members and on whether the two chambers represent the same set of citizens. On the whole, congruent bicameralism is relatively rare. Lijphart (1999, 212) identifies the following countries as being characterized by congruent bicameralism at the end of the 1990s: Austria, Bahamas, Barbados, Ireland, Italy, Jamaica, Japan, the Netherlands, Norway, the Philippines, and Trinidad.

TABLE 14.4	**Malapportionment in Upper Chambers, 1996**			
	Seats held by the percentages of the most favorably represented citizens (percent)			
	10	20	30	50
United States	39.7	55.0	67.7	83.8
Switzerland	38.4	53.2	64.7	80.6
Venezuela	31.6	47.2	60.0	77.5
Australia	28.7	47.8	58.7	74.0
Canada	33.4	46.3	55.6	71.3
Germany	24.0	41.7	54.3	72.6
India	15.4	26.9	37.4	56.8
Austria	11.9	22.5	32.8	52.9
Belgium	10.8	20.9	31.0	50.9

Source: Data are from Lijphart (1999, 208).

Symmetric and Asymmetric Bicameralism

Symmetric bicameralism occurs when the two legislative chambers have equal or near equal constitutional power (Lijphart 1999, 206). Total symmetry exists when the agreement of both chambers is necessary to enact a law. In practice, symmetric bicameralism is extremely rare. Countries in which the upper chamber has formally equal powers with the lower chamber include Colombia, Italy, Switzerland, and the United States.[14] Countries in which the two chambers enjoy similar, but not quite equal, power include Australia, Germany, Japan, and the Netherlands. **Asymmetric bicameralism** is much more common and occurs when the two legislative chambers have unequal constitu-

> **Symmetric bicameralism** occurs when the two legislative chambers have equal or near equal constitutional power.
> **Asymmetric bicameralism** occurs when the two legislative chambers have unequal constitutional powers.

tional power. Total asymmetry exists when one chamber is granted ultimate decision-making power. In all cases of asymmetric bicameralism, it is the lower house that has more power. To a large extent, the degree of symmetry in the powers of the two chambers is related to how the members of the upper chamber are selected. Upper chambers are much more likely to have co-equal power with the lower house when citizens play a direct role in electing upper chamber representatives (Mastias and Grangé 1987). This is likely due to the increased democratic legitimacy that these upper chambers are perceived to have from being

14. Belgium, Denmark, and Sweden are three other countries that used to have symmetric bicameral legislatures. Denmark and Sweden both abolished their second chambers in 1953 and 1970, respectively. The power of the Belgian senate was significantly reduced in 1994 following the introduction of a federal form of government.

directly (or indirectly) elected as opposed to appointed. Of the four countries we just mentioned in which the upper chamber enjoys formally equal power with the lower chamber, Colombia, Italy, and the United States all have directly elected upper chambers; most of the members of the Swiss upper chamber are also popularly elected.

To summarize, it is possible to distinguish bicameral systems based on their level of congruence and symmetry. In Figure 14.3, we simplify the world somewhat and plot the names of various countries along these two dimensions of bicameralism. Countries such as those in the upper right quadrant—Australia, Germany, Switzerland, and the United States—exhibit a strong form of bicameralism. In a strong bicameral system, the upper house is likely to be an important political actor because it enjoys similar constitutional powers to the lower house and because the different political composition of the upper chamber tends to mean that it has different policy preferences to the lower chamber. Countries such as those in the lower left quadrant—Austria, the Bahamas, and Jamaica—exhibit what might be thought of as an insignificant form of bicameralism. In an insignificant bicameral system, the upper chamber is unlikely to be an important political actor because its constitutional powers are extremely weak and because its political composition tends to mirror that of the lower chamber.

| **FIGURE 14.3** | **Two Dimensions of Bicameralism** |

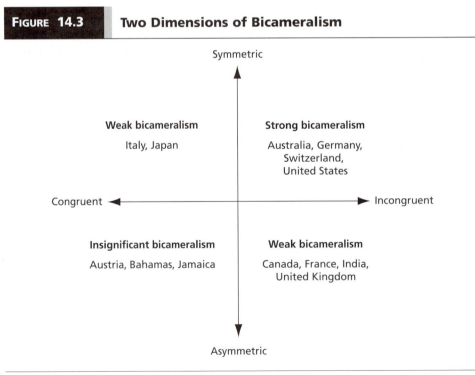

Source: Based on information in Lijphart (1999, 212).

Countries in the upper left and lower right quadrants exhibit a weak form of bicameralism. In weak bicameral systems, the upper chamber is likely to be a weak political actor. Although such countries as those in the upper left quadrant—Italy and Japan—have a powerful upper chamber (symmetry), the upper chamber is not expected to significantly affect the policymaking process given its political makeup, which is like that in the lower chamber (congruence). Similarly, although such countries as those in the lower right quadrant—Canada, France, India, and the United Kingdom—have an upper chamber that is likely to conflict with the lower chamber as a result of its differing political composition (incongruence), the upper chamber is not expected to play a significant role in the policymaking process because its constitutional powers are weak (asymmetry).

Box 14.3

CONFLICT RESOLUTION IN BICAMERAL SYSTEMS

What happens when there are disagreements between the upper and lower legislative chambers in a country? Bicameral systems have many different ways for resolving intercameral conflict: the *navette,* the conference committee, the joint session, the ultimate decision by one chamber, and new elections (Tsebelis and Money 1997, 54–69).

Almost all bicameral systems use the navette, or shuttle, system to help resolve policy differences between the two legislative chambers. Essentially, the chamber that first passes a bill sends it to the second chamber for consideration. If the second chamber accepts the bill, then the legislation is accepted and promulgated. If the second chamber disagrees with the bill, it can make amendments and send it back to the first chamber. In this way, legislation "shuttles" back and forth between the two chambers until an agreement is reached. But what happens if no agreement can be reached? In some countries, such as France, Madagascar, and Mauritania, the shuttling back and forth simply continues indefinitely unless the government steps in to end the process. In other countries, such as Italy, Liberia, and the Philippines, legislation that continuously fails to reach agreement in both chambers is simply aborted after a certain amount of time.

Most countries, though, have adopted additional institutional mechanisms to resolve intercameral conflict when the navette system breaks down. Typically, there are rules about how many times a bill needs to have shuttled back and forth without success before political actors can turn to these additional institutional mechanisms for resolving conflict. For example, a bill needs to shuttle between the two chambers in Belgium for two readings before an alternative conflict resolution mechanism is employed. South Africa and Pakistan represent the unusual case in which disagreement by the second chamber in the very first round automatically triggers a joint session of the lower and upper legislative chambers.

A variety of different mechanisms can be employed to resolve intercameral conflict when the navette system breaks down. One possibility is a conference committee. Typically, a conference committee involves the two chambers, each appointing an equal number of delegates to meet jointly and hammer out a compromise. In most cases, a conference committee can be thought of as a mini-legislature that reaches agreement by majority rule. Once an agreement is reached, the committee's compromise proposal is put to the parent legislative chambers for an up or down vote; this proposal cannot be amended at this point. Conference committees are employed in a wide range of countries, including Chile, Colombia, France, Germany, Ireland, Japan, Madagascar, Romania, South Africa, and the United States.

An alternative dispute resolution mechanism is for the two legislative chambers to meet in a joint session to vote on the legislation. Because the lower chamber (nearly) always has more members than the upper chamber, joint sessions tend to favor the position of the lower chamber. Joint legislative sessions are employed by many countries, including Australia, Bolivia, Brazil, India, Jordan, Norway, Pakistan, Romania, Swaziland, and Venezuela. In some countries, one chamber has the ultimate decision-making power when intercameral agreement cannot be reached. In France, the government can intervene following the breakdown of the navette system and ask the lower chamber to decide the outcome. In most cases, though, ultimate decision-making power automatically reverts to one of the chambers. For example, the lower chamber is decisive in such countries as Austria, Belize, Croatia, Ireland, Japan, Mauritania, Poland, Spain, Swaziland, and the United Kingdom. In a few countries, the chamber that initiated the piece of legislation or the one that is reviewing it is decisive. This is the case in, for example, Argentina, Brazil, Chile, the Dominican Republic, and Mexico. Although extremely rare, some countries, such as Australia, call legislative elections in the hope that they will resolve any intercameral dispute.

Why Bicameralism?

The ideas on which contemporary bicameralism are based have their origins in the political institutions of ancient Greece (Tsebelis and Money 1997, 17). Greek philosophers, like Aristotle and Plato, frequently evaluated the merits of political institutions in terms of whether they produced "mixed government." In contrast to "simple government," where the interests of only one social class—the one (monarchy), the few (aristocracy), or the many (people)—would be represented, the Greek notion of "mixed government" called for the representation of all social classes. Many governments in both ancient Greece and early Rome developed this type of mixed structure, with dual advisory-legislative councils that had overlapping functions and that represented different classes. For example, Sparta, Crete, and Carthage all had separate assemblies to represent various social classes. These assemblies deliberated on the same issues in a way similar to bicameral legislatures today.[15]

Many Greek philosophers admired aspects of aristocratic government, such as having the educated and wise rule, but they recognized, as we noted in Chapter 5, the danger that aristocracy might degenerate into oligarchy. For many, a mixed form of government was an anti-

---

15. It is because the executive, legislative, and judicial functions of these assemblies were not clearly delineated that they cannot be viewed as bicameral legislatures in the modern sense (Tsebelis and Money 1997, 17).

dote that could prevent this sort of degeneration from occurring. By representing the interests of different social classes, mixed government essentially created a system of checks and balances that would prevent the degeneration of the political system into oligarchy. In effect, mixed government was thought to combine the benefits of having the aristocracy play a role in government with the benefits of having a balance of power in which no single class could gain control of the state for itself. In this way, mixed government was thought to be both an efficient and stable form of government.

The first bicameral legislature in a modern sense appeared in fourteenth-century England. In many ways, it mirrored the notion of mixed government that had been advocated centuries earlier by Greek philosophers. For example, Tsebelis and Money (1997, 23) write that "the lower house represented the democratic element of society; the upper house, the aristocratic element; and the king's veto power, the monarchic element." Over the next few centuries, political philosophers continued to adapt the notion of mixed government in such a way that it essentially became synonymous with bicameralism. For example, consider the ideas of Montesquieu. Like the Greek philosophers before him, Montesquieu worried that the reins of government might be captured by a single social class and that it would then use its control against the rest of society. As he wrote in his *Spirit of the Laws* ([1752] 1914, 11:6), "There would be an end of everything, were the same man or the same body, whether of the nobles or of the people, to exercise those three powers, that of enacting laws, that of executing the public resolutions, and of trying the causes of individuals." Although Montesquieu believed that "executive power ought to be in the hands of a monarch, because this branch of government, having need of dispatch, is better administered by one than by many," he thought that legislative power should be in the hands of the aristocracy and the people because legislative power "is oftentimes better regulated by many than by a single person." Rather than placing the aristocracy and the people in a single legislative body, though, Montesquieu recommended separate and equal chambers for these two social groups. He wanted separate chambers because he believed that the aristocracy would always be outvoted by the common people in a single legislative body as a result of its smaller size. As Montesquieu ([1752] 1914, 11:6) put it,

> In . . . a state there are always persons distinguished by their birth, riches, or honors: but were they to be confounded with the common people, and to have only the weight of a single vote like the rest, the common liberty would be their slavery, and they would have not interest in supporting it, as most of the popular resolutions would be against them. The share they have, therefore, in the legislature ought to be proportioned to their other advantages in the state; which happens only when they form a body that has a right to check the licentiousness of the people, as the people have a right to oppose any encroachment of theirs.
>
> The legislative power is therefore committed to the body of the nobles, and to that which represents the people, each having their assemblies and deliberations apart, each their separate views and interests.

Greek principles of mixed government, particularly the emphasis on checks and balances, also influenced John Adams's support for bicameralism in the American colonies during the eighteenth century. For example, Adams wrote that in a bicameral system, "[t]he three natural orders in society, the monarchical, the aristocratical and the democratical are . . . constitutionally placed to watch and control each other. . . . Thereby, also, each will balance the other two" (quoted in Walsh 1915, 80–81). Given that Adams was writing at a time when the American colonies were trying to gain their independence from the British monarchy, we need to recognize that he was using terms like "monarchy" and "aristocracy" in an unusual way. For Adams, "monarchy" was equivalent to an elected executive, and "aristocracy" meant a natural (not hereditary) aristocracy that had achieved superiority in wealth and education over the common people.

As these examples from Montesquieu and Adams illustrate, most political theorists by the eighteenth century had come to interpret the Greek notion of mixed government as a bicameral legislature in which the aristocracy would deliberate in one chamber and the common people in another. These two legislative chambers, along with a monarch (either a hereditary or elected ruler) as executive, would create a system of checks and balances to ensure the stability of the political system. Moreover, the aristocracy, with its supposed characteristics of knowledge, age, wisdom, and training, would be able to use its position in the upper chamber to improve upon the legislation coming from the common people in the lower chamber. For roughly two thousand years, then, bicameralism essentially meant the separate representation of social classes in different legislative bodies.

This view of bicameralism was eventually challenged at the end of the eighteenth century by the rise of republicanism and its emphasis on the representation of the people as a whole rather than as a set of competing social classes. In this new environment, bicameralism came to be viewed and justified in a completely different way. Specifically, the existence of bicameral legislatures was increasingly justified not as an institutional means to represent different social classes but as one that federal states could use to represent their constituent territorial units. For example, the "Great Compromise" reached during the Philadelphia Convention of 1787 saw the establishment in the United States of the House of Representatives, elected on the basis of a state's population, and the Senate, which granted equal representation to each state. This compromise, particularly the creation of an upper chamber in which each state received equal representation, was specifically designed to protect the interests of the small states against the power of the large states and, thereby, encourage them to sign on to the new Constitution. Essentially, the lower house was to represent the popular dimension of the people's will and the upper house was to represent its territorial dimension.

This form of "incongruent bicameralism" established in the United States was justified on the grounds that different states were likely to have specific and distinct needs from the population as a whole (*Federalist*, no. 62). In effect, the U.S. Senate was to be a forum in which these different needs could be addressed and protected. To fully protect the specific needs of the constituent territorial units and, indeed, the federal system as a whole, the founding fathers realized that the upper house needed sufficient power to prevent the lower house from overriding it. As a result, they promoted a symmetric form of bicameralism in which the agreement of both legislative chambers was needed to change the status quo. This type of incongruent and symmetric bicameral system established in the United States was subsequently adopted by other federal countries, such as Australia, Germany, and Switzerland.

Class-based upper chambers increasingly came to be repudiated over time, but territorial-based upper chambers like the U.S. Senate were able to retain their legitimacy and power. In effect, territory came to provide a competing legitimacy for powerful upper chambers that social class now lacked (Tsebelis and Money 1997, 33). It is perhaps no surprise then that all of the examples of "strong"—symmetric and incongruent—bicameral systems illustrated in Figure 14.3 are in federal countries.

Strong bicameral systems like the ones that emerged in the United States and Switzerland were harder to justify in unitary states with no constituent territorial units to explicitly represent. Some unitary countries with bicameral systems responded to the growing adoption of democratic values and the spread of universal suffrage by significantly curtailing the power of the upper chamber to block or reverse the policies of the popularly elected lower house. For example, this occurred in the United Kingdom with the passage of the 1911 and 1949 Parliament Acts. The 1911 Parliament Act asserted the legislative supremacy of the House of Commons by limiting the ability of the House of Lords to block legislation. The 1949 Parliament Act further weakened the House of Lords by reducing the maximum amount of time that the upper chamber could delay legislation to one year.[16] Although co-equal in power with the National Assembly during the Third Republic (1870–1940), the French Senate has also seen its power drastically reduced over time. For instance, the constitution of the Fourth Republic (1946–1958) limited the role of the French Senate to delaying legislation. The constitution of the Fifth Republic (1958–) further weakened the French Senate by allowing the government to grant the National Assembly the right to make final decisions on pieces of legislation.

To a large extent, the argument for keeping these weak upper chambers rather than just getting rid of them rests on the belief, going back to ancient Greece, that the members of the upper chamber have characteristics of value—typically things like wisdom, age, knowledge, and training—that members of the popularly elected lower chamber do not have. It also rests on the belief that upper chambers can play an important role in delaying the legislative process, thereby reducing the likelihood that "bad" laws will be made in haste. In effect, the argument for keeping weak upper chambers in unitary countries ultimately rests on the belief that they improve the overall quality of legislation. This line of reasoning obviously requires that the political composition of the upper and lower chambers be different; that is, incongruent. In many countries, this incongruence is achieved by having appointed upper chambers in which members are selected on the basis of some special skill, expertise, or experience.

---

16. In practice, the Parliament Acts have been used to pass legislation against the wishes of the House of Lords on only seven occasions since 1911. This does not mean, however, that these acts were not important. For example, it is generally recognized that the mere threat of using the Parliament Acts has forced the House of Lords to accept legislation that it wanted to block on several other occasions.

Whereas many unitary countries historically responded to the spread of democratic values by establishing asymmetric, but still incongruent, forms of bicameralism, a few, like Denmark and Sweden, responded by trying to "democratize" the selection procedures used in the upper chamber. This typically involved adopting a similar selection procedure for the upper chamber to the one employed in the popularly elected lower chamber. The result, as one would expect, was that the political composition of the upper chamber in these countries came to increasingly match that of the lower chamber. In many places, this congruence between the upper and lower chambers raised questions as to the actual purpose of the upper chamber. As Tsebelis and Money (1997) point out, the general thrust of these questions is best summed up in the famous words of the seventeenth-century philosopher, Abbé Sieyès: "If the second chamber agrees with the first, it is useless, and if not, it is bad." Like several other countries that initially decided to establish congruent upper chambers, Denmark (in 1953) and Sweden (in 1959) essentially resolved the debate over the value of the upper chamber by abolishing it and establishing a unicameral legislature.

Contemporary debates over bicameralism largely mirror those that have driven the evolution and justification of bicameral systems in the past. In effect, there are two basic arguments in favor of bicameralism. In federal countries, bicameralism is primarily defended as an institutional means for protecting the federal system and promoting the distinct preferences of different territorial units. In unitary countries, bicameralism is primarily defended as an institutional means for improving the quality of legislation.

CONSTITUTIONALISM

Another way in which political scientists distinguish between states is by the extent to which they accept **constitutionalism.** Constitutionalism refers to the commitment of governments to accept the legitimacy of, and be governed by, a set of authoritative rules and principles that are laid out in a constitution (Stone Sweet 2000, 20). A central part of any commitment to constitutionalism is the establishment of a set of institutions and procedures to protect constitutional rules and principles. These institutions and procedures are known as **systems of constitutional justice.** The commitment to

> **Constitutionalism** refers to the commitment of governments to accept the legitimacy of, and be governed by, a set of authoritative rules and principles that are laid out in a constitution. A **system of constitutional justice** comprises the set of institutions and procedures that are established to protect constitutional rules and principles.

abide by a constitution varies across both space and time. Historically, few countries have had any system of constitutional justice. Indeed, there was no system of constitutional justice in the world when the first fully codified and written constitution was emerging in the United States in 1787 (Stone Sweet 2008, 218). The historical norm has, instead, been one of legislative supremacy. The norm of legislative supremacy essentially states that the laws created by the people's elected representatives in the legislature should not be constrained by other authorities, such as the constitution. Looking around the world today, though, we see that the norm of legislative supremacy has been replaced by what Shapiro and Stone (1994) call a "new constitutionalism." This new constitutionalism describes a situation in which virtually all new constitutions contain a charter of human rights that is protected by such institutions as constitutional courts. These institutions can use the power of constitutional review to invalidate legislation that is deemed to violate individual rights, thereby substantively constraining legislative authority.

Although there has been a general shift toward this new constitutionalism since 1945, there is considerable variation in the extent to which states have delegated constitutional control over their actions to judges. Although formal judicial power has expanded around the world, it has not been expanded in the same way in all countries (Tate and Vallinder 1995; Ginsburg 2003). In this section we briefly describe the historical shift from a norm of legislative supremacy to a situation in which most states now agree to live within the constraints imposed by a constitution. This shift toward a new constitutionalism has increasingly involved judges in the legislative process, leading some to worry about a possible "government of judges." [17] Following this, we outline some of the distinctive features of the different systems of constitutional justice that have been adopted around the world. As we will see, there are, to a large extent, two basic systems of constitutional justice. These systems of constitutional justice are commonly referred to as the American and European models.

The Shift to a New Constitutionalism

A **constitution,** in a very general sense, provides the formal source of state authority. For example, a constitution establishes governmental institutions, such as legislatures, executives, and courts, and then gives these institu-

> A **constitution** provides the formal source of state authority. In addition to establishing the structure, procedures, powers, and duties of governmental institutions, more recent constitutions also contain a list of guaranteed rights.

tions the power to make, enforce, and interpret laws. In addition to outlining how these institutions should be constituted and function, a constitution also indicates how these institutions should interact with one another. Recent constitutions, such as those adopted in the last sixty years or so, also tend to contain a list of rights that are protected by some kind of constitutional body and that act as substantive constraints on the actions of the government.

Almost all current constitutions are **codified constitutions** in that they are written in a single document. An **uncodified constitution** is one that has several sources, which may be

> A **codified constitution** is one that is written in a single document. An **uncodified constitution** is one that has several sources, which may be written or unwritten.

written or unwritten. As of 2007, only three countries—Israel, New Zealand, and the United Kingdom—had uncodified constitutions. Some of the United Kingdom's uncodified constitution is written and some of it is not. The written part includes constitutional statutes passed by the legislature, such as the 1998 Scotland Act and the 1998 Human Rights Act,

---

17. The first known reference to a "government of judges" came in a 1921 book by Edouard Lambert, a French law professor, which examined the control that the U.S. Supreme Court exerted over legislation.

whereas the unwritten part includes things like constitutional conventions, royal preroga-tives, customs and traditions, and observations of precedents.[18]

In addition to whether constitutions are codified or not, constitutions also differ in regard to whether they are entrenched or not. An **entrenched constitution** is one that can be modified only through a procedure of constitu-tional amendment. Constitutional amendments require more than the approval of a legislative majority. Exactly what is required to pass a con-stitutional amendment varies from country to country. In federal systems, for example, it is often the case that constitutional amendments require the support of a majority of the regional legislatures. Some countries require a popular referendum. Australia and Switzerland both require that a successful amendment win not only a majority of votes nationwide in a popular referendum but also a majority of the votes in every state or canton. Other countries require legislative supermajorities. Successful amendments in Japan must obtain a two-thirds super-majority in both legislative chambers and a majority in a popular referendum (Lijphart 1999, 222). Sometimes the precise constitutional amendment procedure depends on the particular constitutional provision that is to be modified. Entrenched constitutions, by requiring a spe-cial constitutional amendment procedure to be modified, implicitly (sometimes explicitly) rec-ognize that constitutional law has a higher legal status than ordinary statute law. **Unentrenched constitutions** have no special amendment procedures; they can be modified at any point in time by a simple legislative majority just like any other law. As a result, it makes no sense to talk of constitutional amendments in countries like the United Kingdom that have unentrenched constitutions. By their very nature, unentrenched constitutions do not recognize that constitutions have any legal status that is higher than or different from ordinary statutes. Almost all contemporary constitutions are entrenched.

> An **entrenched constitution** is one that can be modified only through a special procedure of constitutional amendment. An **unentrenched constitution** has no special amendment procedure and can be modified at any point in time with the support of a legislative majority.

Historically, we can identify two ideal types of constitutions: the **legislative supremacy constitution** and the **higher law constitution.**

Legislative Supremacy Constitution

The underlying principle behind the system of government established by legislative supremacy constitutions is that "elections legitimize legislative authority, and legislative majorities legitimize statutory authority" (Stone Sweet 2000, 20). In a legislative supremacy constitution, there is an explicit recognition that legislatures can do no legal wrong, because they derive their legitimacy from being elected by the people. Legislative supremacy consti-tutions have three basic features. One is that they are not entrenched and can be revised at

---

18. Constitutional conventions include things like the duty of the monarch to act on the advice of government ministers and the Salisbury Convention, which states that the upper house will not oppose legislation promised in the government's election manifesto. Customs and traditions include things like always holding general elections on Thursdays. And royal prerogatives include things like appointing and dismissing government ministers, declaring war, and the issue and revoca-tion of passports.

the discretion of the legislature. Legislative supremacy constitutions have no special legal status and are the same as ordinary laws in that they can be modified or replaced without recourse to special amendment procedures. In effect, these constitutions can be changed at any time through a simple majority vote in the legislature. The second distinctive feature is that there is no institution that can review the constitutional legality of statutes. Because legislative authority resides only with the legislature, no statute can be challenged once promulgated; a law can be replaced or modified only by a new statute. If there is a perceived conflict between a statute and some constitutional rule or principle, then judges are to ignore this or rule in favor of the statute. The third distinctive feature of legislative supremacy constitutions is that they do not contain a bill of rights that might act as a substantive constraint on legislative authority. This is not to say that all countries with this type of constitution do not protect rights; some do. Rather, the source of these rights should be the legislature itself and not the constitution. The constitutions of the United Kingdom and New Zealand, along with the historical constitutions of the French Third (1870–1940) and Fourth (1946–1958) Republics, are examples of legislative supremacy constitutions.

Higher Law Constitution

The second ideal type of constitution is the higher law constitution. In contrast to legislative supremacy constitutions, higher law constitutions start from the premise that the state *can* do legal wrong and that, in particular, individual and minority rights must be protected from the state. As a result, higher law constitutions reject the notion of legislative supremacy and include a layer of substantive constraints, in the form of a bill of rights, on the legislature. The inclusion of these constitutionally protected rights constrains states because they give nonstate actors a basis on which to make claims against the state. In effect, nonstate actors can claim that legislative statutes are invalid to the extent that they violate their protected rights.

Higher law constitutions also establish a mechanism—**constitutional review**—for defending the supremacy of the constitution and the rights that it contains. Constitutional review is the authority of an institution to invalidate acts of government, such as legislation, administrative decisions, and judicial rulings, that violate constitutional rules (Stone Sweet 2000, 21). As we will see, constitutional review can be exercised by judges sitting on special tribunals—constitutional courts—that are not part of the regular judicial system, as in most European countries, or by ordinary judges in the regular judicial system, as in the United States. When constitutional review is conducted by ordinary judges from the regular judicial system, it is commonly referred to as **judicial review.** The ability to engage in constitutional review gives constitutional judges the opportunity to directly intervene in the legislative process and even draft the precise terms of legislation. By allowing constitutional

> A **legislative supremacy constitution** has no constitutional review, has no bill of rights, and is not entrenched. A **higher law constitution** has constitutional review, has a bill of rights, and is entrenched.
>
> **Constitutional review** is the authority of an institution to invalidate legislation, administration decisions, judicial rulings, and other acts of government that violate constitutional rules, such as rights. When constitutional review is conducted by ordinary judges from the regular judicial system, it is commonly referred to as **judicial review**.

review, higher law constitutions signal that constitutional laws are superior to "ordinary" laws passed by the legislature. In recognition of the special status of constitutional law, higher law constitutions are entrenched and stipulate special amendment procedures for modifying constitutional provisions. The differences between legislative supremacy constitutions and higher law constitutions are summarized in Table 14.5.

Legislative supremacy constitutions were historically quite common, particularly in Europe, where there has traditionally been a deep political hostility toward judges, but they tend be relatively rare now. Virtually all new constitutions—both democratic and authoritarian—are higher law constitutions that establish constitutional review and include an extensive list of political and social rights.[19] For example, all 106 constitutions that have been adopted since 1985 and for which we have reliable data contain a catalogue of rights. And all but five of these constitutions—those of Iraq (1990), Laos, North Korea, Saudi Arabia, and Vietnam—have established provisions for constitutional review (Stone Sweet 2008, 233–234). As we noted earlier, this convergence around the idea that higher law constitutions are somehow better than legislative supremacy constitutions has been called the **new constitutionalism** (Shapiro and Stone 1994). But why did this shift to the new constitutionalism happen?

> The **new constitutionalism** describes a situation in which almost all countries now have an entrenched constitution, a bill of rights, and a procedure of constitutional review to protect rights.

The shift toward this new constitutionalism began in Europe after 1945 with constitutional courts being established in Austria (1945), Italy (1948), and West Germany (1949).[20]

TABLE 14.5	**Legislative Supremacy Constitution versus Higher Law Constitution**	
Characteristic	**Legislative supremacy**	**Higher law**
Entrenched	No	Yes
Constitutional review	No	Yes
Bill of rights	No	Yes

---

19. The rights that are included in these constitutions are fairly extensive (Stone Sweet 2000, 42–43). In addition to many of the rights that we commonly think of, such as equal rights for men and women, equality before the law, the right to religion, and the right of asylum, some constitutions contain additional rights, such as the right to adequate health care (France, Italy), the right to resist political oppression (France, Germany), the right to unemployment compensation (France, Italy, Spain), and the right to adequate housing (Italy, Spain). Higher law constitutions also tend to establish duties on the part of the citizens and the state. For example, some constitutions require citizens to work (Italy, Spain) and financially support and educate their children (Italy, Spain). States are sometimes required to provide public health care (France, Italy, Spain), pursue full employment (Spain), protect consumers (Spain), and protect the environment (Italy, Spain).

20. Higher law constitutions with constitutional review were adopted by many countries in the interwar period: Czechoslovakia (1920), Liechtenstein (1925), Greece (1927), Spain (1931), Ireland (1937), and Egypt (1941). With the exception of Ireland, however, constitutional review was largely ineffective and little utilized. Only the Irish constitutional court survived World War II. Many other countries in addition to Austria, Italy, and West Germany adopted higher law constitutions shortly after World War II: Brazil (1946), Burma (1947), Japan (1947), India (1949), and Thailand (1949).

The adoption of higher law constitutions in these countries was partly a response to the experience with fascism in the interwar period (Stone Sweet 2000, 37). The experience of fascist governments in Italy and Germany made it abundantly clear that states could, indeed, do wrong and that individuals would sometimes need protection from the state. In effect, Europe's experience with fascism undermined much of Europe's faith in a powerful and unconstrained state and highlighted the need to protect individual rights. The adoption of higher law constitutions in Germany and Italy can also be traced to the presence of U.S. troops on their soil after World War II and the pressure that the United States put on these countries to incorporate a bill of rights and constitutional review into their constitutions.

To a large extent, the subsequent adoption of higher law constitutions in other countries has coincided with democratic transitions. For example, both Portugal (1976) and Spain (1978) adopted constitutional courts following their democratic transitions in the 1970s. Central and East European countries, such as the Czech Republic, Hungary, Poland, Romania, Russia, Slovakia, the Baltic states, and the states of the former Yugoslavia, also adopted constitutional courts following the collapse of Communist rule in 1989 (Ludwikowski 1996; Schwartz 1999). The strengthening of constitutional courts in Latin America and Asia during the 1980s and 1990s has also been seen as part of a concerted effort to consolidate democracy in these regions of the world (Helmke 2002; Ginsburg 2003; Navia and Ríos-Figueroa 2005). In all of these cases, the adoption of higher law constitutions can, in part, be viewed as an attempt to prevent a repetition of the individual abuses inflicted by the state in the recent past.

14.4 JUDICIAL POWER AND THE JUDICIALIZATION OF POLITICS

The spread of constitutional review around the world has raised fears about the power of constitutional judges and the possible judicialization of politics. This raises the question of how powerful courts really are in practice. Here we outline what we mean by judicial power and examine the conditions under which courts can effectively influence policy outcomes.

Traditionally, there have been two main approaches to understanding judicial power. One approach looks at the formal, or de jure, powers given to courts. This approach essentially involves determining the jurisdiction of a particular court (Billikopf 1973; Lasser 1988; Gunther 1991; Barber 1993). Under this notion of judicial power, a court is powerful whenever it is granted significant legal authority. One obvious problem with this approach is that it does not take into account whether courts use their legal authority or whether their decisions are actually implemented. As several political scientists have pointed out, there is ample empirical evidence of courts that appear to be powerful on paper being ignored (Staton 2004). For example, local governments in the United States and Germany have refused to implement various constitutional decisions relating to equal protection and religious establishment (Rosenberg

1991; Vanberg 2005). There is also plenty of evidence to suggest that courts strategically try to avoid conflict by not making decisions that they know will be opposed by the other branches of government (Volcansek 1991; Clinton 1994; Epstein and Knight 1998a). To illustrate this point, Staton (2008) recounts the story of the president of the Venezuelan Supreme Court, Cecilia Sosa Gomez, who resigned her post in 1999 in protest at the Court's approval of a decision by allies of Hugo Chavez to declare a state of emergency in which judges could be fired without cause. On resigning, Sosa stated that the Court had "committed suicide to avoid being assassinated. But the result is the same. It is dead."

The problem with simply looking at judicial power in terms of the jurisdiction that courts are granted on paper has led most political scientists to focus on the de facto power of courts. In other words, they focus on whether courts have the power to change policy outcomes in practice, not in theory. In this sense, political scientists define judicial power as the ability of courts to bring about policy outcomes that they prefer (Cameron 2002). This definition, along with empirical evidence that courts act strategically, necessarily implies that courts are not always the impartial interpreters of laws that legal scholars and judges frequently claim them to be. Just like other political actors, judges have their own policy preferences that influence how they make legal decisions.

Of course, the extent to which judges can make legal decisions in line with their own preferences is likely to depend on the specific environment in which those decisions are made. This brings us to the following question: Under what conditions can courts effectively influence policy outcomes? The central difficulty faced by all courts is that they are inherently weak institutions in that they rely on others to implement and enforce their decisions. As Alexander Hamilton recognized in the *Federalist,* no. 78, a court "must ultimately depend upon the aid of the executive arm even for the efficacy of its judgements," because it has no financial or physical coercive powers of its own. As you might expect, this "implementation problem" can be particularly constraining in situations in which courts are required to make decisions against the very actors on whom they rely to implement their decisions (Vanberg 2001). It is the existence of this implementation problem that drives the strategic behavior of courts. Given their inability to independently enforce their decisions, it is little wonder that judges sometimes rule policies constitutional so as to avoid conflict with elected officials even when they know that these policies are constitutionally suspect (Epstein and Knight 1998b; Rogers 2001; Ramseyer and Rasmusen 2003; Carrubba 2005; Helmke 2005).

The fundamental insight from the "implementation problem" and strategic models of judicial politics would seem to be that judicial power is inherently bounded and constrained. Although there is plenty of evidence that judicial power is often constrained, we do sometimes see courts acting powerfully. For example, Staton (2008) notes that even in periods of serious national security threats the Israeli Supreme Court has placed limits on interrogation techniques that can be used against terrorist suspects by the General Security Service. What explains this? Why is it that courts can act powerfully in some situations but not others?

Two conditions need to be met for courts to exert judicial power (Vanberg 2001, 2005). The first is that courts must enjoy public support. If courts enjoy public support and, hence, high levels of legitimacy, then elected officials can expect to suffer a negative electoral backlash if they do not comply with court decisions (Gibson and Caldeira 1992; Caldeira and Gibson 1995; Gibson, Caldeira, and Baird 1998). The fear of such a backlash creates a powerful incentive for legislative majorities to respect judicial decisions (Vanberg 2000), thereby allowing courts to make decisions in a relatively unconstrained manner. Of course, this "electoral connection" mechanism works only if voters know about court decisions and can identify noncompliance by elected officials. Thus, the second necessary condition for a powerful court is that voters must be able to effectively and reliably monitor legislative responses to judicial rulings. At a minimum, this requires that court decisions be transparent and available to the public. Without this information, voters cannot hold elected representatives accountable for noncompliance. Only when these two conditions are met can courts be expected to influence policy decisions effectively.

The existence of these necessary conditions for judicial power creates strong incentives for courts to act strategically when publicizing their decisions (Staton 2006, 2008). Courts can expect to gain public support and legitimacy by publicizing their work if their decisions show them to be impartial interpreters of the constitution. We have already seen, however, that judges sometimes act politically and seek to impose their own personal preferences on the legislative process. It is likely that publicizing these types of decisions will not increase public support for the judicial system. As a result, courts will have a strong incentive to publicize only some of their decisions—the impartial-looking ones.

That constitutional judges regularly engage in public relations exercises suggests that they are well aware of the role that public support plays in their ability to assert judicial power. For example, virtually all constitutional courts throughout the world maintain a Web site on which they provide information on pending and completed cases, descriptions of their jurisdiction, and biographical summaries of their membership. Constitutional judges also give university lectures and media interviews and participate in other public forums to publicize their decisions and explain their legal reasoning (Staton 2008). Although this type of behavior is to be expected of legislative representatives, who can be held electorally accountable, it is sometimes seen as puzzling as to why unelected and unaccountable constitutional judges would engage in these types of public relations activities. Of course, this kind of behavior immediately becomes understandable once one recognizes that public support is necessary for courts to exert judicial power as we have argued. As noted earlier, constitutional judges have a strategic incentive to be selective in the types of cases, decisions, and legal reasoning that they publicize. Staton (2008) provides strong evidence to support this claim from an in-depth study of the Mexican Supreme Court and a cross-national analysis of constitutional courts around the world. That constitutional judges are strategic in publicizing their decisions only goes to underscore the very political nature of constitutional review.

Different Systems of Constitutional Justice

That higher law constitutions have increasingly been adopted around the world in the last sixty years does not mean that countries are adopting the exact same system of constitutional justice. Systems of constitutional justice vary along many different dimensions (Epstein, Knight, and Shvetsova 2001; Murphy, Pritchett, and Epstein 2001). In what follows we focus on three in particular: (a) the type of constitutional review, (b) the timing of constitutional review, and (c) the jurisdiction of constitutional review; we briefly examine other aspects of constitutional justice systems in Box 14.5.

Abstract constitutional review involves the constitutional review of legislation in the absence of a concrete legal case. **Concrete constitutional review** involves the constitutional review of legislation with respect to a specific legal case. **A priori constitutional review** occurs before a law is formally enacted, whereas **a posteriori constitutional review** occurs only after a law is formally enacted.

The two basic types of constitutional review are **abstract constitutional review** and **concrete constitutional review.** Abstract review is "abstract" in that it involves the constitutional review of legislation in the absence of a concrete legal case. In contrast, concrete review is "concrete" in that it involves the constitutional review of legislation with respect to a specific case before the court. These two types of constitutional review are not mutually exclusive in that countries can allow both types of review. Constitutional review can take place at two points in time during the legislative process. If constitutional review occurs before a law is formally enacted, then it is referred to as **a priori constitutional review.** If constitutional review occurs after a law is formally enacted, then we speak of **a posteriori constitutional review.** Again, a priori and a posteriori review are not mutually exclusive in that countries can allow constitutional review to take place both before and after a law is enacted.

The jurisdiction of constitutional review can be centralized or decentralized. **Centralized constitutional review** refers to a situation in which only one court is responsible for conducting constitutional review. This single court, called a constitutional court, exists entirely outside of the normal judicial system and settles only constitutional disputes; it does not get involved in normal litigation. As such, we might want to think of it more as a special tribunal than a court. **Decentralized constitutional review** refers to a situation in which more than one court can interpret the constitution and render laws, decrees, and administrative decisions unconstitutional. These courts and the judges that sit on them are part of the regular judicial system. The highest court in a decentralized jurisdiction system, typically called a Supreme Court, has general jurisdiction in that it can settle all legal disputes and not just constitutional ones.

Centralized constitutional review refers to a situation in which only one court can conduct constitutional review. **Decentralized constitutional review** refers to a situation in which more than one court can interpret the constitution.

TABLE 14.6	**Different Systems of Constitutional Justice**			
	Concrete		Abstract	
Jurisdiction/timing	*A priori*	*A posteriori*	*A priori*	*A posteriori*
Centralized (European)	Not possible	Yes	Yes	Yes
Decentralized (American)	Not possible	Yes	Not observed	Not observed

Source: Navia and Ríos-Figueroa (2005, 199).

If we focus on these three dimensions of constitutional review, we can distinguish between eight different systems of constitutional justice (Navia and Ríos-Figueroa 2005, 199). As Table 14.6 illustrates, only four of these systems actually exist in the real world. Two of the systems of constitutional justice are ruled out on the grounds that they are not logically possible—concrete review cannot take place a priori because it requires a legal case challenging the constitutionality of an existing statute. Two other systems of constitutional justice are not observed in the real world at the national level. Although logically possible, the combination of abstract review and a decentralized jurisdiction is theoretically unappealing. In effect, this combination would allow local judges to nullify laws in the abstract with the consequence being that such laws, or parts of such laws, would simply disappear in particular districts. Not only would this create legal insecurity, but it would also create a chaotic situation with legal holes around the country.[21] This helps to explain why the combination of abstract review and a decentralized jurisdiction is not observed at the national level in the real world.

Although it is possible to distinguish between four different systems of constitutional justice, as we do in Table 14.6, most political scientists focus on the distinction between centralized and decentralized systems. They refer to decentralized systems as the American model of constitutional justice and to centralized systems as the European model of constitutional justice.[22]

---

21. Somewhat similar concerns exist with any decentralized jurisdiction system. Indeed, the desire to have uniform legal decisions across the country was one reason why many countries have adopted centralized jurisdiction systems. Combining a decentralized jurisdiction system with concrete review (as opposed to abstract review) is somewhat less problematic because any local court decisions apply only to the specific case at hand.

22. The European model is sometimes referred to as the Kelsenian model after the Austrian legal theorist, Hans Kelsen, who helped establish the Austrian Constitutional Court in 1920.

Box 14.5 **SYSTEMS OF CONSTITUTIONAL JUSTICE**

As we noted earlier, systems of constitutional justice differ along many different dimensions. In the main text of this chapter, we focus on the type, timing, and jurisdiction of constitutional review. We now examine other aspects of constitutional justice systems. Specifically, we look at who can challenge the constitutionality of a law, how constitutional judges are selected, and the qualifications that are necessary to become a constitutional judge.

Who Can Challenge the Constitutionality of a Law?

In abstract review systems, constitutional challenges are typically initiated by a specifically designated group of elected politicians (Stone Sweet 2000, 45). These politicians might be members of the executive or legislature as in France, Germany, and Spain. For example, the president of the Republic, the president of the National Assembly, and the president of the Senate in France can all refer constitutional questions to the French Constitutional Council. Since 1974, constitutional referrals can also be made by sixty representatives in either the National Assembly or the Senate. In other countries, such as Germany, Italy, and Spain, regional governments get to challenge the constitutionality of laws. Whoever the designated politicians are, they must make referrals or petitions to the constitutional court within some prescribed period of time. For instance, laws must be referred to the French Constitutional Council within fifteen days of their adoption by the legislature. In practice, most attempts to challenge the constitutionality of legislative initiatives are made by opposition politicians. In many cases, constitutional review is the last chance that opposition groups have to delay or block a piece of government legislation. That abstract review allows opposition groups to challenge the constitutionality of laws encourages legislative majorities to consider opposition interests when drafting legislation, thereby fostering policy compromise (Stone 1992; Vanberg 1998).

In concrete review systems, constitutional challenges are usually initiated by the judiciary itself. For example, a constitutional question may become relevant during the course of litigation in the courts. In centralized jurisdiction systems, the judge dealing with the case would refer the constitutional question to the constitutional court. At this point, the proceedings in the case would be suspended until the constitutional court has ruled. In decentralized jurisdiction systems, the judge dealing with the case would rule on the constitutional question; any challenge to the court's ruling would be referred up the judicial hierarchy, potentially all the way to the Supreme Court.

Although somewhat rarer, some countries allow private individuals to bring complaints. For example, individuals in Germany and Spain have the right to go directly to the constitutional court once other judicial remedies have been exhausted. These individual constitutional complaint procedures can occur in both abstract and concrete review situations.

How Are Constitutional Judges Selected?

On the whole, judges in constitutional courts are selected either through a nomination process or by election. If a nomination procedure is used, then the nominating authority simply names a judge or set of judges to the constitutional court. In France, for example, the Constitutional Council comprises nine judges who serve nonrenewable nine-year terms. One-third of these judges are appointed every three years. The president of the Republic, the president of the National Assembly, and the president of the Senate each get to appoint one of the three judges. Former presidents of the Republic, who are no longer engaged in political activities, are also entitled to sit on the Constitutional Council. This helps to explain why, as of 2007, the French Constitutional Council actually had eleven members; two former presidents— Valéry Giscard d'Estaing and Jacques Chirac—had both taken up positions on the court.

If an election procedure is used, then a qualified or super-majority within the legislature is usually necessary for appointment. In Germany, for example, the Federal Constitutional Court consists of two "senates," each with eight judges who serve a twelve-year term. The lower legislative chamber (Bundestag) and the upper legislative chamber (Bundesrat) each get to elect four judges to each of the senates. The election of the judges requires a two-thirds majority in the relevant legislative chamber.

Some countries use nomination *and* election procedures to select their constitutional courts. For example, the Spanish Constitutional Court consists of twelve judges who serve for nine-year terms. The lower legislative chamber (congress) and the upper legislative chamber (senate) each elect four judges. These judges must obtain the support of 60 percent of the representatives in the relevant legislative chamber to be elected. Of the remaining four judges, two are nominated by the government and two are nominated by the General Council of the Judiciary.

What Qualifications Are Necessary to Become a Constitutional Judge?

Most countries, such as Germany, Italy, and Spain, require that judges on constitutional courts have advanced legal training as well as professional experience in some domain of law. In some countries a quota guarantees that a minimum number of constitutional judges be drawn from the ordinary court system (Stone Sweet 2000, 48). In Germany, for example, the sixteen-member Federal Constitutional Court must contain at least six federal judges. Similarly, one-third of the fifteen members on the Italian Constitutional Court are elected by representatives of the judiciary. Law professors comprise the largest group of constitutional court appointees in most countries. In direct contrast to the vast majority of countries, France does not require that the judges on the French Constitutional Council have any legal training at all. In fact, a majority of the French Constitutional Council has always been made up of former ministers and parliamentarians, although many of these individuals have had some legal training.

The American Model

In the United States, "any judge of any court, in any case, at any time, at the behest of any litigating party, has the power to declare a law unconstitutional" (Shapiro and Stone 1994, 400). As this quotation makes clear, constitutional review in the United States is decentralized and carried out by ordinary judges in the regular judicial system. Constitutional review in the United States is, as a result, judicial review. The American separation-of-powers system, in which the executive, legislature, and judiciary are separate but co-equal branches of government, attempts to mark a clear distinction between what we can think of as the "judicial function"—resolving legal cases—and the "political function"—legislating. American courts are supposed to avoid legislating because that is the function of the people's elected representatives in the legislature. Still, it is recognized that a constitutional issue that needs resolving might arise in the course of a legal case. It is for this reason that ordinary judges in the United States have the right to conduct concrete a posteriori constitutional review—they need it to do their prescribed job. Courts in the American model are prohibited, though, from engaging in abstract review or giving advisory opinions on the constitutionality of legislative bills because this is not part of their job and would be usurping the rightful role of the legislature.

The European Model

As mentioned earlier, the judiciary has traditionally been seen as subordinate to the legislature in Europe. In other words, the judiciary has never been seen as a co-equal branch of the government. Indeed, *judicial* review has been explicitly prohibited in French and German constitutions since the end of the eighteenth century. This view of the judiciary helps to explain why American-style judicial review has faced so much hostility in much of Europe. From a European perspective, "American-style judicial review, rather than corresponding to a separation of powers, actually establishes a permanent *confusion* of powers, because it enables the judiciary to participate in the legislative function" (Stone Sweet 2000, 33). To avoid judicial review and a "government of judges" that might ensue, Europeans invented a completely new institution, the constitutional court, to conduct *constitutional* review.

Constitutional courts have several defining characteristics. First, they have a monopoly on conducting constitutional review. Ordinary courts cannot engage in constitutional review and cannot appeal any of the decisions made by a constitutional court. Second, constitutional courts are formally detached from the regular judicial system. A constitutional court is, therefore, not a "judicial" institution. These two defining characteristics mean that judicial review remains prohibited in the European model. Third, constitutional courts have jurisdiction only over constitutional matters; they cannot preside over judicial disputes or litigation as, say, the U.S. Supreme Court can. Fourth, most constitutional courts can engage in abstract constitutional review. In other words, they can evaluate legislative initiatives to see if they are unconstitutional before they actually have the oppor-

TABLE 14.7	**American and European Models of Constitutional Justice**	
Characteristic	American model	European model
Jurisdiction: Who has the power to engage in constitutional review?	Decentralized; ordinary courts can engage in constitutional review	Centralized; only a single constitutional court can engage in constitutional review; other courts are barred from doing so, although they may refer to the constitutional court.
Timing: When can constitutional review occur?	A posteriori	A priori or a posteriori or both; some courts have a priori review over treaties or government acts; others have both, and some have either but not both.
Type: Can constitutional review occur in the absence of a real case or controversy?	Concrete	Abstract and concrete; most constitutional courts can exercise review in the absence of a real case, and many can also exercise concrete review.
Standing: Who can initiate disputes?	Litigants engaged in a case or controversy and who have a personal stake in the outcome can initiate a dispute.	The range can be broad, from governmental actors (including executives and members of the legislature) to individual citizens.

Source: Adapted from Navia and Ríos-Figueroa (2005, 192).

tunity to harm anyone. This is the only type of constitutional review that is allowed in France. Many constitutional courts can also exercise concrete constitutional review. The main characteristics of the American and European models of constitutional justice are shown in Table 14.7.

Information from 2004 on whether a country employs an American or European model of constitutional justice is shown in Box 14.6 on page 668. In Table 14.8, we illustrate the geographic distribution of the American and European models of constitutional justice around the world. As you can see, the European model of constitutional justice is more popular than the American one, although there are clear regional differences. For example, the American model is predominant in Asia, North America, and the Caribbean, whereas the European model is predominant everywhere else. Some countries, most notably in Central and South America, employ a mixture of the American and European models.

TABLE 14.8	The Geographic Distribution of Different Models of Constitutional Justice, 2004				
Region	**American model**	**European model**	**Mixed**	**Other**	**None**
Europe	5	31	3	1	2
Africa	12	30	1	6	3
Middle East	2	4	0	3	1
Asia and Southeast Asia	17	14	2	9	0
North America	2	0	0	0	0
Central America	3	3	3	0	0
South America	3	4	5	0	0
Caribbean	11	0	0	1	0
Total	55	86	14	20	6

Source: Data are from Dr. Arne Mavčič and are available at http://www.concourts.net.

Note: "Mixed" means some combination of the American and European models; "Other" means that the system of constitutional justice is unique or unclassifiable; "None" means that there are no mechanisms for constitutional review. Systems based on France are coded as European.

VETO PLAYERS

As we have noted in this chapter, political scientists sometimes distinguish between democracies by whether they are federal or unitary, bicameral or unicameral, and whether they accept constitutionalism or not. In effect, these political scientists see the world in terms of different institutional dichotomies. Recently, though, comparative scholars have begun to move away from this position and to recognize that these institutions are conceptually the same in that they all act as checks and balances on the political system. Put differently, they all affect the ease with which the political status quo in a country can be changed. This new approach to understanding political institutions is called **veto player theory** (Tsebelis 1995, 1999, 2002).

Veto player theory argues that important characteristics of any country's institutional structure are determined by its configuration of veto players. A **veto player** is an individual (such as a president) or collective actor (such as a legislative chamber) whose agreement is necessary for a change of the political status quo.[23] In any given country, there are two types of veto player. First, there is the **institutional**

> **Veto player theory** offers a way to think about political institutions in a consistent way across countries. In effect, veto player theory conceptualizes the institutional structure of a given country in terms of its configuration of veto players.
>
> A **veto player** is an individual or collective actor whose agreement is necessary for a change in the political status quo. There are two types of veto player. An **institutional veto player** is generated by a country's constitution. A **partisan veto player** is generated by the way the political game is played.

---

23. Note that veto player theory is not restricted to democracies. In dictatorships, veto players might include the military or particular religious leaders and so on. The key to applying veto player theory in any given setting involves identifying which actors are in a position to block changes to the political status quo. This will vary both across countries, across time, and potentially across policy areas.

veto player. Institutional veto players are those generated by a country's constitution. For example, the U.S. Constitution identifies actors like the president, the Congress, and the Senate as institutional veto players because it gives these actors the right to block legislative changes to the status quo. Second, there is the **partisan veto player.** Partisan veto players are those generated by the political game. In other words, partisan veto players are not specified in a constitution but are determined by the way political competition plays out in a given country. For example, particular parties in a legislature or a coalition government might be considered partisan veto players if they are in a position to block changes to the status quo. Such parties are veto players not because they have been identified as such in some document but, rather, because of the way that citizens vote, how votes are translated into seats, how governments form, and so on. Whereas the identity of institutional veto players is essentially fixed across time as long as the constitution remains the same, the identity of partisan veto players changes with the vagaries of political competition.

Rather than see federalism, bicameralism, and constitutional review as entirely different institutions that need to be studied separately, as most political scientists have traditionally done, veto player theory suggests that we might constructively view them as just different types of the same thing; that is, as different types of institutional veto player.[24] All three institutions place hurdles on the ability of political actors to change the status quo. For example, a legislative majority in the lower chamber may require the support of a powerful upper chamber to change some policy status quo. As we saw earlier, this is the case in the United States, where the agreement of both legislative chambers is required to pass legislation. Courts are not veto players when they interpret ordinary statutes, because their decisions can be overridden by subsequent legislation. They are veto players, however, when they engage in constitutional review (Tsebelis 2002, 226). Recall that the French Constitutional Council has the ability to invalidate laws on constitutional grounds before they are applied. This suggests that, in many ways, we can think of constitutional courts like the French Constitutional Council as a third legislative chamber (Stone 1992). Similarly, the support of a subnational government in a federal system may be necessary for political actors to change the status quo. This is particularly the case for those policy areas that are constitutionally delegated to subnational governments. In this framework, then, adopting federalism, bicameralism, or constitutional review can be thought of as equivalent to increasing the number of institutional veto players in a country.

As we will see, veto player theory shows that the number of veto players in a country, as well as the ideological distance between them, has important consequences for policy stability. Specifically, veto player theory indicates that countries in which there are many veto players with conflicting policy preferences are likely to be characterized by (a) greater policy sta-

---

24. In previous chapters, we have looked at whether countries have single party or coalition governments and whether they have two-party or multiparty systems. Just as federalism, bicameralism, and constitutional review can be reconceptualized in terms of institutional veto players, the type of government and the size of the party system in a country can be reconceptualized in terms of partisan veto players. If we do this, then we can think of countries with coalition governments as having more partisan veto players than countries with single-party majority governments.

bility, (b) smaller shifts in policy, (c) less variation in the size of policy shifts, and (d) weaker agenda-setter powers. This, in turn, has important consequences for things like judicial and bureaucratic activism, government stability, and regime stability.

To see where these results come from, let's start with the basic building blocks of veto player theory. Veto players can be represented by their preferred policy positions or ideal points in some issue space.[25] In Figure 14.4, we have three veto players, *A*, *B*, and *C*, who are located in a two-dimensional issue space on the basis of their most preferred position on two different policies. To give our example some substance, we can think of one issue dimension as being about the appropriate level of state intervention in the economy and the other issue dimension as being about the appropriate amount of money to be spent on education. The status quo policy in the two-dimensional policy space is given by the point *SQ*. In Figure 14.4, we illustrate the indifference curves for each veto player with respect to the status quo—these are the circles that surround the ideal points of the three veto players and go through the status quo point. These indifference curves, as you will remember, indicate all of the policy outcomes that are equally distant from each veto player's ideal point as the status quo. As a result, each veto player is indifferent between any point on his indifference curve and the status quo. More important, each veto player will prefer any policy outcome inside his indifference curve to the status quo because this policy outcome will necessarily be closer to his ideal point.

A central concept in veto player theory is the winset. Recall that a winset is the set of policy alternatives that would defeat the status quo in a pair-wise contest under whatever voting rules are being employed. Given the very definition of a veto player, unanimity is required to change the status quo. As a result, the winset in a veto player setting is the set of policy alternatives that falls within the indifference circle of *every* veto player. In Figure 14.4, this winset is represented by the shaded petal-shaped area coming from the status quo. Any policy alternative in this shaded area will win the support of all veto players in a pair-wise vote against the status quo.

According to veto player theory, the size of the winset has a significant impact on policy outcomes. First, the size of the winset affects policy stability. When the winset is large, policy is less stable, because there are many policy alternatives that can defeat the status quo. In contrast, when the winset is small, policy is more stable, because there are few policy alternatives that can defeat the status quo. Second, the size of the winset determines the likely size of policy shifts. When the winset is small, policy shifts must necessarily be small; it is impossible to move policy very far from the status quo. When the winset is large, though, the possibility arises for more radical policy shifts. If we think that every policy alternative in a winset is equally possible, then it follows that the average size of policy shifts will increase with the size of the winset. Third, the size of the winset influences how much variation we are

---

25. At this point, readers may well benefit from rereading the material on spatial models first presented in Chapter 10.

| FIGURE 14.4 | **An Application of Veto Player Theory** |

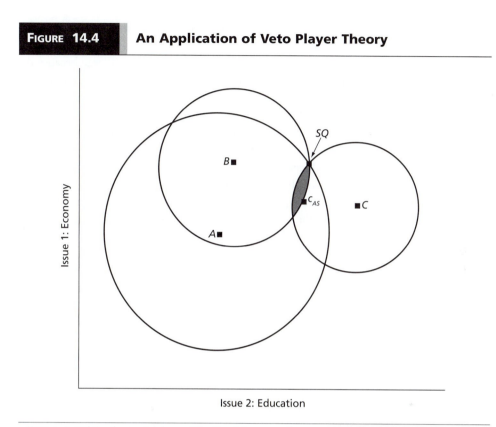

Note: *A, B,* and *C* = three veto players; *SQ* = the status quo policy; c_{AS} = the policy alternative that *C* would propose if he were the agenda setter; the three circles = the indifference curves of *A, B,* and *C* with respect to the status quo; the shaded area = the winset, assuming decisions are made by unanimity rule.

likely to see in the size of policy shifts. As we have already noted, policy shifts must be small when the winset is small. When the winset is large, however, policy shifts may be small or large. As a result, we are likely to observe more variation in the size of policy shifts the larger the size of the winset.

Fourth, the size of the winset affects the power of an agenda setter to influence the policy outcome. So far, we have assumed that all veto players are created equal. Although this assumption allows us to identify the feasible set of policy alternatives that can defeat the status quo (the winset), it does not permit us to identify a specific policy outcome. In reality, it is often the case that some veto players are also agenda setters in that they get to make take-it-or-leave-it policy proposals to the other veto players. Clearly, any veto player who is an agenda setter is at an advantage because he can view the winset as his constraint and select the outcome within it that is closest to his ideal point. For example, if veto player *C* were the agenda setter in Figure 14.4, then he would propose shifting policy to c_{AS} because this is the closest point in the winset to his ideal point. The size of the winset affects the importance of agenda setting. When the winset is small, the agenda setter cannot move policy far from where the other veto players would want to move it if they were the agenda setter. In contrast, agenda setting becomes much more important when the winset is large because the agenda setter now has the possibility to move policy far from where the other veto players would choose if they were the agenda setters.

We now know that the size of the winset has a significant impact on policy outcomes. But how do the number of veto players in a country and the ideological distance between them affect the size of the winset? Let's start by examining how the number of veto players influences the size of the winset with the help of Figure 14.5. In the first panel (a) there are two veto players and in the second panel (b) there are three veto players. In this particular comparison, increasing the number of veto players shrinks the size of the winset; that is, the winset in the second panel is smaller than the winset in the first one. But does this mean that increasing the number of veto players *always* shrinks the size of the winset? The answer to this question is no. To see why, let's now compare the second and third panels (b and c). In the third panel there are two veto players and in the second panel there are three veto players. As this comparison indicates, increasing the number of veto players does not shrink the size of the winset; the size of the winset in the second panel is exactly the same as the size of the winset in the third one. The reason for this is that the new veto player (*B*) is ideologically located in such a way that if we were to draw a line connecting the two existing veto players (*A* and *C*), she would be on it.[26] What this means, practically speaking, is that it is impossible for veto players *A* and *C* to jointly prefer alternatives to the status quo that veto player *B* will not also prefer. In the language of veto player theory, we say that veto player *B* is "absorbed" by the existing veto players. It is because of this that the winset remains the same size as we move from the third panel (c) to the second panel (b). The bottom line is that veto player theory shows that an increase in the number of veto players decreases the size of the winset or leaves it the same; it never increases the size of the winset.

Let's now examine how the ideological distance between veto players influences the size of the winset with the help of Figure 14.6. The two veto players in the first panel (a) have more similar ideal points than the two veto players in the second panel (b). As you can see, increasing the ideological distance between veto players—moving from the first panel (a) to the second panel (b)—shrinks the size of the winset. This is a general result from veto player theory that always holds.

As Figures 14.5 and 14.6 illustrate, the size of the winset in any particular situation is determined jointly by the number of veto players and the ideological distance between these veto players. In general, we can expect the size of the winset to shrink as we increase the number of veto players or the ideological distance between them or both. As we noted earlier, federalism, bicameralism, and constitutional review are all institutions that can be

---

26. In this particular example, the line connecting the two existing veto players (*A* and *C*) is known as the "unanimity core." Whenever an additional veto player is added to the unanimity core, the size of the winset remains unchanged. We discuss the unanimity core in more detail in problems 7 and 8 at the end of this chapter.

FIGURE 14.5

The Number of Veto Players and the Size of the Winset

a. Two Veto Players, *A* and *B*

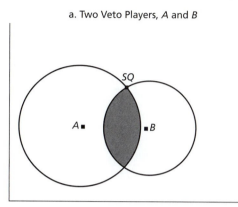

b. Three Veto Players, *A, B,* and *C*

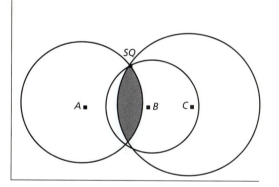

c. Two Veto Players, *A* and *C*

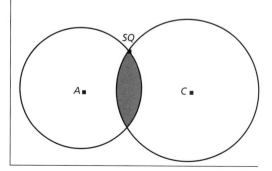

Note: A, B, C = veto players; *SQ* = the status quo policy; the shaded area = the winset, assuming decisions are made by unanimity rule.

| **FIGURE 14.6** | **The Ideological Distance between Veto Players and the Size of the Winset** |

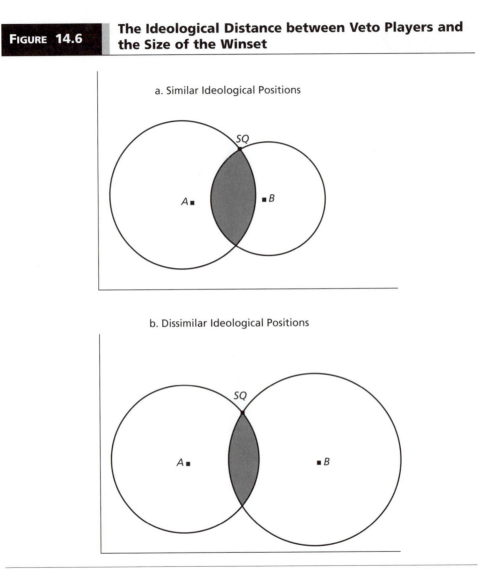

a. Similar Ideological Positions

b. Dissimilar Ideological Positions

Note: A, B = veto players; SQ = the status quo policy; the shaded area = the winset, assuming decisions are made by unanimity rule.

reconceptualized as institutional veto players. In regard to policy outcomes, this means that we can expect countries with these types of institutions to be characterized by (a) policy stability, (b) small policy shifts, (c) little variation in the size of policy shifts, and (d) weak agenda-setting powers. These characteristics are likely to be particularly prevalent if the institutional veto players have dissimilar policy preferences. For example, we would expect policy output to be lower and less radical during periods of divided government or cohabitation (Mayhew 1991; Binder 1999, 2003; Erikson, MacKuen, and Stimson 2002) and when coalition governments are ideologically diverse (Tsebelis 2002, 173). We would also expect greater policy stability when the two legislative chambers in a bicameral system or the central and subnational governments in a federal system are controlled by different political parties.

We should note at this point that there is nothing inherently good or bad about policy stability. After all, policy stability is typically viewed as a good thing by those who like the status quo, but a bad thing by those who do not. Policy stability, though, can have important consequences for various aspects of a political system, such as government stability, regime stability, and judicial or bureaucratic activism. Let's first briefly consider the effect of policy stability on government and regime stability. Imagine that a government comes to power in a country with the promise to shake up some policy area. Perhaps some crisis requires radical reform. If the configuration of veto players in the country is such that the status quo cannot be changed or can be altered only a little, the government will likely appear ineffective and immobilized. If we are in a parliamentary democracy, political and social actors who want to resolve the crisis will likely push for a vote of no confidence in the government. As a result, veto player theory predicts a connection between policy stability and the likelihood of *government* instability in parliamentary democracies. If we are in a presidential democracy, though, there is no institutional mechanism, such as a vote of no confidence, to remove the ineffective government from office. This may lead political and social actors who want to resolve the crisis to look to extra-constitutional means, such as a military coup, to replace the government. As a result, veto player theory predicts that policy stability will increase the likelihood of *regime* instability in presidential democracies. We return to the connection between policy stability and regime instability in the next chapter, where we examine the effect of institutions on the survival of democracy in more detail.

Let's now briefly consider the effect of policy stability on judicial and bureaucratic activism. Veto player theory suggests that policy stability leads to high levels of judicial and bureaucratic activism (Tsebelis 2002, 222–247). Why? In many situations, judges have the opportunity to make policy through their ability to interpret statutes. Similarly, bureaucrats get to make policy by virtue of actually implementing policy. Obviously, if the members of the legislature do not like policies made by the judges and bureaucrats, they can write new legislation that will effectively overrule the judiciary or bureaucracy. When policy is stable because there are many legislative veto players with dissimilar policy preferences, however, judges and bureaucrats get to interpret and implement laws close to their own ideal points, safe in the knowledge that the legislature will not be able to reach an agreement on overriding them. This suggests that we should expect to see higher levels of judicial and bureaucratic activism in federal and bicameral countries than in unitary and unicameral ones.

CONCLUSION

In Chapter 10, we examined some theoretical results suggesting that constitutional designers necessarily face trade-offs when designing democratic institutions. In particular, Arrow's Theorem demonstrates that stable outcomes (group transitivity) can be guaranteed only if the freedom of individuals to form their own preferences (universal admissibility) or the ability of individuals to have their preferences influence group decisions (non-dictatorship) are compromised.[27] If we accept universal admissibility as inalienable, then the basic tension that exists in democratic regimes is between instability and dictatorship. As we have noted before, increased stability of outcomes is likely to be the result of someone's having been given agenda power.

In this and the three preceding chapters, we have examined many of the dimensions along which democratic institutions vary. For example, in Chapter 11 we looked at the ways in which the relationship between the executive and legislative branches can be organized. In Chapter 12, we examined the tremendous variety of ways in which elections have been organized. And in Chapter 13, we investigated the structure of party systems. In this chapter, we looked at three more ways in which institutions might vary from democracy to democracy—federalism, bicameralism, and constitutionalism. We suggested that these three institutional forms have a common feature—they create political actors capable of blocking a change in the political status quo. Federalism, for instance, has the potential to create powerful regional actors capable of blocking the implementation of national law. Bicameralism creates a second legislative body capable of blocking legislation. And constitutionalism creates the possibility that judges might overturn laws that the legislature approves of. Each of these institutions, therefore, has the effect of creating an institutional veto player.[28]

Veto player theory can be thought of as a modern-day version of arguments about the effects of mixed government and checks and balances that can be traced back to such political theorists as Aristotle and Montesquieu. As we have demonstrated, countries with many veto players with conflicting preferences are expected to be characterized by great policy stability, smaller shifts in policy, less variation in the size of policy shifts, and weaker agenda-setter powers. As a result, systems with many veto players may, in some sense, overcome the instability of democratic institutions without creating a single powerful agenda setter. Unfortunately, the existence of multiple veto players doesn't fully overcome the dilemmas posed by Arrow's Theorem, because complex veto structures necessarily mean that current policy decisions are profoundly influenced by the status quo policy. In this sense, they grant something like dictatorial power to the policymakers who chose those policies in the past. As a consequence, circumstances or tastes may change in such a way that a large share of the populace might desire policy change but be unable to achieve it. As implied by Arrow's Theorem, then, there appears to be some trade-off between policy stability and the responsiveness of decisions to voters' preferences.

In the next chapter, we have more to say about the way democratic institutions influence the way voters' preferences are translated into policy decisions. We will also have more to say about the potentially explosive effects that can be produced by policy stability in presiden-

---

27. As we note in Chapter 10, this trade-off—something we called the "institutional trilemma"—assumes that the independence from irrelevant alternatives and unanimity conditions are met.

28. Presidentialism (see Chapter 11) also creates an institutional veto player—the president—who can check the power of the legislature.

tial democracies—policy stability, it seems, may come at the expense of regime instability. A comprehensive examination of the varieties of democracy observed in the world is well beyond the scope of our book, but in the next chapter we attempt to highlight some prominent findings in the comparative politics literature regarding the consequences of the varieties of democracy. Specifically, we look at how variations in democratic institutions influence four sets of important outcomes—the quality of representation, the size of the welfare state, the propensity for ethnic conflict, and the survival of democracy.

KEY CONCEPTS

a posteriori constitutional review, *642*
a priori constitutional review, *642*
abstract constitutional review, *642*
asymmetric bicameralism, *627*
asymmetric federalism, *612*
bicameral legislature, *620*
centralized constitutional review, *635*
codified constitution, *616*
coming-together federalism, *642*
concrete constitutional review, *622*
congruent bicameralism, *611*
congruent federalism, *635*
constitution, *634*
constitutionalism, *637*
constitutional review, *612*
decentralization, *642*
decentralized constitutional review, *609*
devolution, *609*
entrenched constitution, *636*
federalism, *605*
federal state, *605*

higher law constitution, *637*
holding-together federalism, *616*
incongruent bicameralism, *622*
incongruent federalism, *611*
institutional veto player, *648*
judicial review, *637*
legislative supremacy constitution, *637*
malapportionment, *626*
new constitutionalism, *638*
partisan veto player, *648*
symmetric bicameralism, *627*
symmetric federalism, *612*
system of constitutional justice, *634*
unanimity core, *664*
uncodified constitution, *635*
unentrenched constitution, *636*
unicameral legislature, *620*
unitary state, *605*
veto player, *648*
veto player theory, *648*

PROBLEMS

The problems that follow address some of the more important concepts and ideas introduced in this chapter.

Spatial Model of Bicameralism

1. In Figure 14.7, we illustrate a situation in which we have a unicameral legislature that includes a median voter (*MV*) and a status quo policy (*SQ*) arrayed along a single left-right issue dimension that runs from 0 (most left) to 10 (most right). The median voter is assumed to have a single-peaked utility function and to vote for the policy that is located closest to her ideal point.

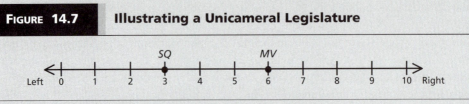

Figure 14.7   **Illustrating a Unicameral Legislature**

Note: *MV* = the median voter in the legislature; *SQ* = the policy status quo.

a. What is the range of policies that the median voter prefers to the status quo? If the median voter in the legislature gets to propose a new policy, what would she propose? What would the outcome be?

In Figure 14.8, we illustrate a situation in which we have a bicameral legislature. The location of the status quo policy is *SQ*, the location of the median voter in the lower chamber is *LC*, and the location of the median voter in the upper chamber is *UC*. Assume that both median voters have a single-peaked utility function and that the support of both chambers is needed to pass a new policy.

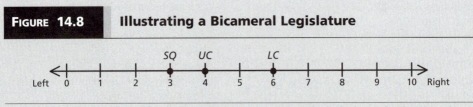

Figure 14.8   **Illustrating a Bicameral Legislature**

Note: *UC* = the median voter in the upper chamber; *LC* = the median voter in the lower chamber; *SQ* = the policy status quo.

b. What is the range of policies preferred to the status quo by the median voter in the lower chamber? What is the range of policies preferred to the status quo by the median voter in the upper chamber? What is the overlapping range of policies preferred by both chambers to the status quo?

c. If the lower chamber is the agenda setter and can make take-it-or-leave-it proposals, where on the left-right issue dimension will the lower chamber make its policy proposal? Would your answer change if the upper chamber is the agenda setter instead? If so, how and why?

Now imagine that the status quo policy is located at 5 instead of 3 on the left-right issue dimension and that the ideal points of the two median voters remain the same as in Figure 14.8.

d. Answer parts (b) and (c) again for this new situation. What changes? That is, how do the expected policy outcomes compare across these different scenarios?

Spatial Model of Judicial Review

2. We now use a spatial model to examine the effects of judicial review. In our model, a bureaucratic agency, such as the Environmental Protection Agency (EPA), sets the initial policy. If the agency's policy is not challenged by the legislature or the courts, then the policy prevails. Our model is loosely based on one by Ferejohn and Shipan (1990, 3), who argue that policymaking by bureaucratic agencies is

> the ordinary or routine decision-making practice throughout modern government. Relatively few governmental decisions are directly mandated by government acts. For the most part, statutes serve as constraints on what bureaucrats can do rather than as detailed directives. Thus, while not denying the importance of the classical statutory model of democratic government—in which a democratically elected legislature instructs its delegates in public action—it seems likely that a model of administrative action that puts agency actions at the front is more relevant for explaining government action most of the time.

To start with, imagine that we have three actors: a legislature, a legislative committee, and a regulatory agency (we will add a court shortly). We will call this the Agency Policymaking Model. Suppose that the legislature has delegated supervision of the regulatory agency to the legislative committee. In Figure 14.9, we show the ideal points of the median member of the legislature (L), the median member of the legislative committee (LC), and the regulatory agency (A). The agency makes the first move by choosing a policy position. If it wishes, the legislative committee can initiate legislation to alter the agency's policy. If it does so, legislation is sent to the floor of the legislature, where it can be amended freely. If the committee does not wish to initiate legislation, then the policy chosen by the agency stands. As always, you should assume that all actors have single-peaked preferences and that they will vote over alternatives sincerely.

FIGURE 14.9	Agency Policymaking Model

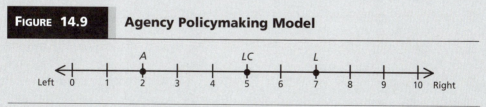

Note: A = the regulatory agency; LC = the median voter on the legislative committee; L = the median voter in the legislature.

a. If the legislature gets a chance to amend a proposal from the legislative committee, what will the outcome of the amendment process be? In other words, where will the legislature set policy if it gets the chance?

b. What is the range of policies that the legislative committee would prefer to the policy outcome that the legislature would choose in an amendment process?

c. Given your previous answer, when will the legislative committee initiate legislation to alter the agency's policy? When will the legislative committee not initiate legislation to alter the agency's policy? In your own words, explain your answers.

d. Given your previous answer, where do you think the agency should initiate policy so that it will not be overturned?

Now imagine that we add a fourth actor: a court. Assume that the court has the ability to review agency actions and can strike them down if it wants to. If this happens, policy reverts to some status quo policy that we will label *SQ*. Ferejohn and Shipan (1990) refer to this as the "Statutory Review Model." After the court has decided whether to strike down the agency's policy, the committee can choose to initiate new legislation if it wants to. If it does so, legislation is sent to the floor of the legislature, where it can be amended freely, as in the Agency Policymaking Model that we just examined. In Figure 14.10, we show the status quo reversion point (*SQ*) and the ideal points of the median member of the legislature (*L*), the median member of the legislative committee (*LC*), the regulatory agency (*A*), and the median judge on the court (*C*).

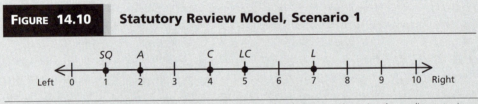

FIGURE 14.10   **Statutory Review Model, Scenario 1**

Note: A = the regulatory agency; *LC* = the median voter in the legislative committee; *L* = the median voter in the legislature; *C* = the median judge on the court; *SQ* = the reversion status quo.

e. Imagine for some reason that the court decides to strike down the agency's policy (wherever it might be). If this happens, policy will revert to the status quo point shown in Figure 14.10. How do you think the legislative committee will react? Will it initiate legislation to change the status quo policy? If the legislative committee does initiate legislation to change the status quo policy, what will the legislature do? What will the final policy position be in this situation if the court decides to strike down the agency's policy?

f. In the previous question, we did not specify where the agency would implement policy. Let's suppose that the agency chooses to implement its policy at 3.1 on the left-right issue dimension. Would the court prefer to have policy at 3.1 or at the final policy position you found in the previous question (e)? In other words, if the agency chooses to implement policy at 3.1, will the court want to strike it down? Explain your answer.

g. If the agency chooses to implement its policy at 3.1, the legislative committee will not bother to initiate legislation to change the agency's policy. Explain, in your own words, why this is the case.

h. Given your answers to the last three questions (e, f, g), what will the final policy outcome be if the agency initially sets policy at 3.1? Explain your answer.

Imagine now that we change the ideal point of the median judge on the court. The new scenario is shown in Figure 14.11.

FIGURE 14.11   Statutory Review Model, Scenario 2

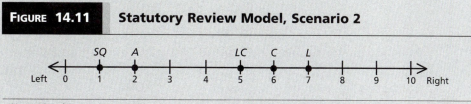

Note: SQ = the reversion status quo; A = the regulatory agency; LC = the median voter on the legislative committee; C = the median judge on the court; L = the median voter in the legislature.

i. What is the range of policies that the court prefers to the ideal point of the median voter in the legislature?
j. If the court strikes down the agency's policy (wherever it might be), it is easy to see that the legislative committee will initiate legislation to try to change the status quo policy (make sure that you understand why). We also know that policy will end up at the ideal point of the median voter in the legislature if the legislative committee initiates legislation to change the status quo. Given this, where should the agency implement policy in order to keep the court from striking down its policy in the first place? Will this be the final policy outcome? Explain your answers.

Imagine that we now change the ideal point of the median judge on the court one more time. The new scenario is shown in Figure 14.12.

FIGURE 14.12   Statutory Review Model, Scenario 3

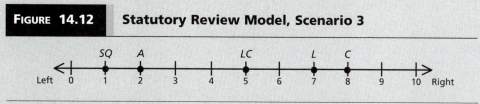

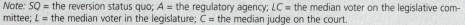

Note: SQ = the reversion status quo; A = the regulatory agency; LC = the median voter on the legislative committee; L = the median voter in the legislature; C = the median judge on the court.

k. What is the range of policies that the court prefers to the ideal point of the median voter in the legislature?

l. As before, if the court strikes down the agency's policy, it is easy to see that the legislative committee will initiate legislation to try to change the status quo policy. We also know that policy will end up at the ideal point of the median voter in the legislature if the legislative committee initiates legislation to change the status quo. Given this, where should the agency implement policy in order to keep the court from striking down its policy in the first place? Will this be the final policy outcome? Explain your answers.

m. Does the effect of having a court that can engage in judicial review affect policy outcomes? To answer this question, compare the final policy outcome from the Agency Policymaking Model and the final outcome(s) across the three Statutory Review Scenarios. Does the court actually have to do anything, such as make rulings, to affect policy outcomes?

n. In the particular scenarios that we have evaluated, does the presence of a court with the power of judicial review move policy toward or away from the ideal point of the median voter in the legislature? Again, compare the final policy outcome from the Agency Policymaking Model without a court and the final outcome(s) across the three Statutory Review Scenarios with a court.

o. Many people worry that judicial review is anti-democratic because judges are making policy instead of the people's elected representatives in the legislature. In this particular model of judicial review, should people be worried by the anti-democratic nature of judicial activism? Explain your answer.

Constitutions, the Provision of Rights, and Constitutional Courts

3. Use the "Constitution Finder" at the University of Richmond (http://confinder.richmond.edu) to find the constitutions from at least three countries. What rights are explicitly delineated in each constitution? What are the duties expected of citizens? What are the duties expected of the state?

4. Use the hyperlinks maintained by the Venice Commission of the Council of Europe to find out more information about three constitutional or supreme courts around the world. For example, what is the composition of the courts? how are judges appointed? what is the competency of the court? how are decisions made? what are some of the recent decisions? (http://www.venice.coe.int/site/dynamics/N_court_links_ef.asp?L=E).

Veto Player Theory

5. In Figure 14.13, we have two veto players, *A* and *B,* who are located in a two-dimensional issue space. The status quo policy is given by the point *SQ.*

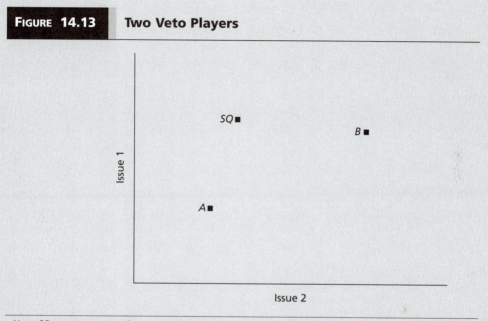

FIGURE **14.13**   **Two Veto Players**

Note: SQ = a status quo policy; *A, B* = veto players.

   a. Using Figure 14.13, draw indifference curves for each veto player with respect to the status quo. Shade in the winset if there is one.

   b. In your own words, describe what a winset is in the context of veto player theory.

6. In Figure 14.14, we have three veto players, *A, B,* and *C,* who are located in a two-dimensional issue space. The status quo policy is given by the point *SQ.*

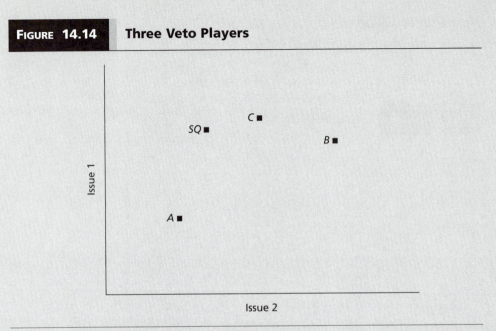

FIGURE 14.14   **Three Veto Players**

Notes: SQ = a status quo policy; A, B, C = veto players.

a. Using Figure 14.14, draw indifference curves for each veto player with respect to the status quo. Shade in the winset if there is one.

b. Is the winset in Figure 14.14 smaller than the winset in Figure 14.13? What does this mean for policy outcomes?

7. In the chapter, we argued that a central concept in veto player theory is the winset. Recall that in the context of veto player theory, the winset is the set of policy alternatives that would defeat the status quo in a pair-wise contest by unanimity rule. In fact, there is another important concept in veto player theory called the **unanimity core.** The unanimity core is the set of policy alternatives that cannot be defeated in a pair-wise contest by unanimity rule. In other words, the unanimity core can be thought of as a region of policy stability—if policy ever gets into the unanimity core, it cannot be moved. It turns out that the size of the unanimity core is directly related to the size of the winset. Specifically, whatever makes the winset smaller makes the unanimity core bigger. And whatever makes the winset bigger makes the unanimity core smaller. This means that all of the results from veto player theory that we presented in the chapter in the context of the winset can also be presented in the context of the unanimity core. For example, whereas policy stability is associated with having a small winset, it is associated with having a large unanimity core. The following questions examine veto player theory in the context of the unanimity core.

> The **unanimity core** is the set of policy alternatives that cannot be defeated in a pair-wise contest under unanimity rule.

Finding the unanimity core is relatively simple.[29] Imagine that the ideal points of the veto players are pins sticking up out of a board. If you were to wrap a piece of string around the outside of these pins, you would have located the unanimity core. For example, the unanimity core for the situation in Figure 14.15 is given by the triangle connecting the three veto players, A, B, and C.

FIGURE 14.15 | **Illustrating the Unanimity Core**

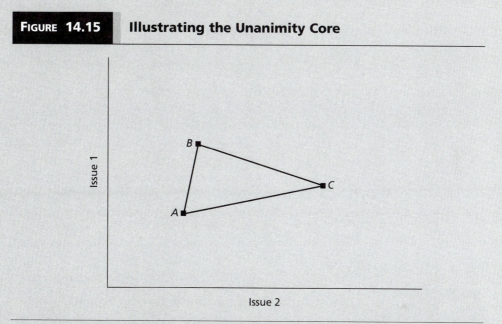

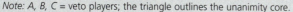

Note: A, B, C = veto players; the triangle outlines the unanimity core.

---

a. Demonstrate that a policy inside the unanimity core in Figure 14.15 *cannot* be defeated by an alternative policy in a pair-wise vote under unanimity rule. To do this, choose some point inside the triangle and label it the status quo. Now draw indifference curves for each veto player with respect to the status quo policy. Is there a winset? What does it mean if you find one? What does it mean if you do not find one?

b. Now demonstrate that a policy outside the unanimity core in Figure 14.15 *can* be defeated by an alternative policy in a pair-wise vote under unanimity rule. To do this, choose some point outside the triangle and label it the status quo. Now draw indifference curves for each veto player with respect to the status quo policy. Is there a winset? What does it mean if you find one? What does it mean if you do not find one?

---

29. Note that another word for the "unanimity core" is the "Pareto set" (Tsebelis 2002, 21). The unanimity core, or Pareto set, is the "smallest set of points that contains all ideal points, and the line segments connecting them. These line segments . . . represent the boundaries of the set of possible unanimous agreements. . . . For points inside the Pareto set, any change makes at least one [veto player] worse off" (Hinich and Munger 1997, 61).

c. What would happen to the size of the unanimity core if the ideal points of the veto players were further apart? What do you think the relationship is between the size of the unanimity core and policy stability? Why?

d. Suppose that we were to add an additional veto player within the area captured by the triangle in Figure 14.15. Would the size of the unanimity core change? Explain your answer.

e. Suppose that we were to add an additional veto player outside of the area captured by the triangle in Figure 14.15. Would the size of the unanimity core change?

f. Based on your answers to questions (d) and (e), does increasing the number of veto players *always* increase policy stability by increasing the size of the unanimity core?

8. Imagine a set of institutional arrangements in which judges have the opportunity to make policy through their ability to interpret statutes. If the members of the legislature don't like the policy made by the judges, they can write new legislation to change it, effectively overruling the judiciary. In this scenario, the judge moves first and sets policy by interpreting the law. The legislature then moves and decides whether to change the law by overruling the judge. Consider the situation outlined in Figure 14.16, where we have three legislative veto players, L_1, L_2, and L_3, located in a two-dimensional policy space. We are going to examine two scenarios with two different judges ruling on separate laws. The ideal points of the two judges are shown in Figure 14.16 as J_1 and J_2.

FIGURE 14.16   **Activist Judges with Agenda-Setting Power**

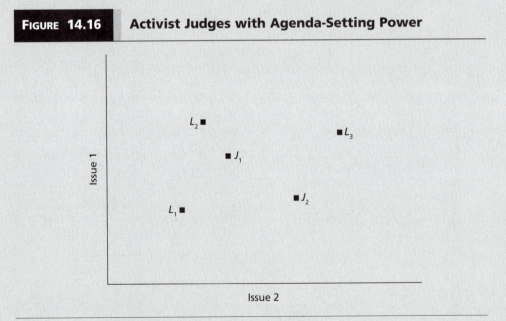

Note: L_1, L_2, L_3 = legislative veto players; J_1, J_2 = judicial agenda setters.

a. Draw the unanimity core for this situation.

b. First consider judge J_1. If she interprets statutes so that the new policy is exactly at her ideal point, will the legislative veto players be able to overturn it and move it anywhere else? If so, where could they move it? If not, why not? Where should judge J_1 set policy?

c. Now consider judge J_2. If she interprets statutes so that the new policy is exactly at her ideal point, will the legislative veto players be able to overturn it and move it anywhere else? If so, where could they move it? If not, why not? Where should judge J_2 set policy?

d. What do you think would happen to the agenda-setting power of judges if the ideal points of the legislative veto players were further apart? What do you think the relationship is between the size of the unanimity core and the amount of discretion judicial activists can exercise over policy outcomes? Why?

e. Based on your answers to question (d), do you think that we should expect to see more judicial activism in federal and bicameral countries or in unitary and unicameral ones? Why?

Box 14.6   CHECKS AND BALANCES IN 191 INDEPENDENT COUNTRIES

Country	Unitary/federal	Unicameral/bicameral	System of constitutional justice
Afghanistan	Unitary	Bicameral	American
Albania	Unitary	Unicameral	European
Algeria	Unitary	Bicameral	European
Andorra	Unitary	Unicameral	European
Angola	Unitary	Unicameral	European
Antigua	Unitary	Bicameral	American
Argentina	Federal	Bicameral	American
Armenia	Unitary	Unicameral	European
Australia	Federal	Bicameral	Other
Austria	Federal	Bicameral	European
Azerbaijan	Unitary	Unicameral	European
Bahamas	Unitary	Bicameral	American
Bahrain	Unitary	Bicameral	Other
Bangladesh	Unitary	Unicameral	American
Barbados	Unitary	Bicameral	American
Belarus	Unitary	Bicameral	European
Belgium	Federal	Bicameral	European
Belize	Unitary	Bicameral	American
Benin	Unitary	Unicameral	European
Bhutan	Unitary	Bicameral	?
Bolivia	Unitary	Bicameral	American
Bosnia-Herzegovina	Federal	Bicameral	European
Botswana	Unitary	Unicameral	American
Brazil	Federal	Bicameral	Mixed
Brunei	Unitary	No Legislature	Other
Bulgaria	Unitary	Unicameral	European
Burkina Faso	Unitary	Unicameral	European
Burma	Unitary	No Legislature	Other
Burundi	Unitary	Bicameral	European

Country	Unitary/federal	Unicameral/bicameral	System of constitutional justice
Cambodia	Unitary	Bicameral	European
Cameroon	Unitary	Unicameral	European
Canada	Federal	Bicameral	American
Cape Verde	Unitary	Unicameral	Mixed
Central African Republic	Unitary	Unicameral	European
Chad	Unitary	Unicameral	European
Chile	Unitary	Bicameral	European
China	Unitary	Unicameral	Other
Colombia	Unitary	Bicameral	Mixed
Comoros	Unitary	Unicameral	European
Congo (Brazzaville)	Unitary	Bicameral	Other
Congo (Kinshasa)	Unitary	Bicameral	European
Costa Rica	Unitary	Unicameral	European
Ivory Coast	Unitary	Unicameral	European
Croatia	Unitary	Unicameral	European
Cuba	Unitary	Unicameral	Other
Cyprus	Unitary	Unicameral	European
Czech Republic	Unitary	Bicameral	European
Denmark	Unitary	Unicameral	American
Djibouti	Unitary	Unicameral	European
Dominica	Unitary	Unicameral	American
Dominican Republic	Unitary	Bicameral	American
Ecuador	Unitary	Unicameral	Mixed
Egypt	Unitary	Bicameral	European
El Salvador	Unitary	Unicameral	Mixed
Equatorial Guinea	Unitary	Unicameral	European
Eritrea	Unitary	Unicameral	European
Estonia	Unitary	Unicameral	American
Ethiopia	Federal	Bicameral	Other
Fiji	Unitary	Unicameral	American
Finland	Unitary	Unicameral	Other

Box 14.6

CHECKS AND BALANCES IN 191 INDEPENDENT COUNTRIES (continued)

Country	Unitary/federal	Unicameral/bicameral	System of constitutional justice
France	Unitary	Bicameral	European
Gabon	Unitary	Bicameral	European
Gambia	Unitary	Unicameral	American
Georgia	Unitary	Unicameral	European
Germany	Federal	Bicameral	European
Ghana	Unitary	Unicameral	American
Greece	Unitary	Unicameral	Mixed
Grenada	Unitary	Bicameral	American
Guatemala	Unitary	Unicameral	Mixed
Guinea	Unitary	Unicameral	American
Guinea-Bissau	Unitary	Unicameral	Other
Guyana	Unitary	Unicameral	American
Haiti	Unitary	Bicameral	American
Honduras	Unitary	Bicameral	Mixed
Hungary	Unitary	Unicameral	European
Iceland	Unitary	Unicameral	European
India	Unitary	Bicameral	American
Indonesia	Unitary	Unicameral	Mixed
Iran	Unitary	Unicameral	American
Iraq	Unitary	Unicameral	?
Ireland	Unitary	Bicameral	American
Israel	Unitary	Unicameral	American
Italy	Unitary	Bicameral	European
Jamaica	Unitary	Bicameral	American
Japan	Unitary	Bicameral	American
Jordon	Unitary	Bicameral	Other
Kazakhstan	Unitary	Bicameral	European
Kenya	Unitary	Unicameral	American
Kiribati	Unitary	Unicameral	American

Country	Unitary/federal	Unicameral/bicameral	System of constitutional justice
Korea, North	Unitary	Unicameral	Other
Korea, South	Unitary	Unicameral	European
Kuwait	Unitary	Unicameral	Other
Kyrgyzstan	Unitary	Unicameral	European
Laos	Unitary	Unicameral	Other
Latvia	Unitary	Unicameral	European
Lebanon	Unitary	Unicameral	European
Lesotho	Unitary	Bicameral	None
Liberia	Unitary	Bicameral	None
Libya	Unitary	Unicameral	None
Liechtenstein	Unitary	Unicameral	European
Lithuania	Unitary	Unicameral	European
Luxembourg	Unitary	Unicameral	European
Macedonia	Unitary	Unicameral	European
Madagascar	Unitary	Bicameral	European
Malawi	Unitary	Unicameral	American
Malaysia	Federal	Bicameral	American
Maldives	Unitary	Unicameral	?
Mali	Unitary	Unicameral	European
Malta	Unitary	Unicameral	European
Marshall Islands	Unitary	Unicameral	?
Mauritania	Unitary	Unicameral	European
Mauritius	Unitary	Unicameral	European
Mexico	Federal	Bicameral	American
Micronesia	Federal	Unicameral	American
Moldova	Unitary	Unicameral	European
Mongolia	Unitary	Unicameral	European
Montenegro	Unitary	Unicameral	European
Morocco	Unitary	Bicameral	European
Mozambique	Unitary	Unicameral	European
Namibia	Unitary	Bicameral	American
Nauru	Unitary	Unicameral	American

CHECKS AND BALANCES IN 191 INDEPENDENT COUNTRIES (continued)

Country	Unitary/federal	Unicameral/bicameral	System of constitutional justice
Nepal	Unitary	Unicameral	American
Netherlands	Unitary	Bicameral	None
New Zealand	Unitary	Unicameral	American
Nicaragua	Unitary	Unicameral	European
Niger	Unitary	Unicameral	European
Nigeria	Federal	Bicameral	American
Norway	Unitary	Unicameral	American
Oman	Unitary	Bicameral	Other
Pakistan	Unitary	Bicameral	Other
Palau	Unitary	Bicameral	American
Panama	Unitary	Unicameral	European
Papua New Guinea	Unitary	Unicameral	American
Paraguay	Unitary	Bicameral	European
Peru	Unitary	Unicameral	Mixed
Philippines	Unitary	Bicameral	European
Poland	Unitary	Bicameral	European
Portugal	Unitary	Unicameral	Mixed
Qatar	Unitary	Unicameral	?
Romania	Unitary	Bicameral	European
Russia	Federal	Bicameral	European
Rwanda	Unitary	Bicameral	European
St. Kitts & Nevis	Unitary	Unicameral	American
St. Lucia	Unitary	Bicameral	American
St. Vincent	Unitary	Unicameral	American
Samoa	Unitary	Unicameral	American
San Marino	Unitary	Unicameral	?
Sao Tomé et Principe	Unitary	Unicameral	Other
Saudi Arabia	Unitary	Unicameral	?
Senegal	Unitary	Bicameral	European

Country	Unitary/federal	Unicameral/bicameral	System of constitutional justice
Serbia	Federal	Unicameral	European
Seychelles	Unitary	Unicameral	American
Sierra Leone	Unitary	Unicameral	American
Singapore	Unitary	Unicameral	American
Slovakia	Unitary	Unicameral	European
Slovenia	Unitary	Bicameral	European
Solomon Islands	Unitary	Unicameral	European
Somalia	Unitary	Unicameral	?
South Africa	Federal	Bicameral	European?
Spain	Unitary	Bicameral	European
Sri Lanka	Unitary	Unicameral	European
Sudan	Unitary	Bicameral	European
Suriname	Unitary	Unicameral	European
Swaziland	Unitary	Bicameral	American
Sweden	Unitary	Unicameral	American
Switzerland	Federal	Bicameral	Mixed
Syria	Unitary	Unicameral	European
Taiwan	Unitary	Unicameral	Mixed
Tajikistan	Unitary	Bicameral	European
Tanzania	Unitary	Unicameral	American
Thailand	Unitary	Bicameral	European
Timor-Leste	Unitary	Unicameral	?
Togo	Unitary	Unicameral	European
Tonga	Unitary	Unicameral	American
Trinidad & Tobago	Unitary	Bicameral	American
Tunisia	Unitary	Bicameral	Other
Turkey	Unitary	Unicameral	European
Turkmenistan	Unitary	Unicameral	Other
Uganda	Unitary	Unicameral	European
Ukraine	Unitary	Unicameral	European
United Arab Emirates	Federal	Unicameral	?

Box 14.6

CHECKS AND BALANCES IN 191 INDEPENDENT COUNTRIES (continued)

Country	Unitary/federal	Unicameral/bicameral	System of constitutional justice
United Kingdom	Unitary	Bicameral	None
United States of America	Federal	Bicameral	American
Uruguay	Unitary	Bicameral	European
Uzbekistan	Unitary	Bicameral	European
Vanuatu	Unitary	Unicameral	American
Venezuela	Federal	Unicameral	Mixed
Vietnam	Unitary	Unicameral	Other
Yemen	Unitary	Bicameral	European
Zambia	Unitary	Unicameral	European
Zimbabwe	Unitary	Bicameral	Other

Source: Data on whether a country is unitary or federal are from Bednar (forthcoming). Data on whether a country employs a unicameral or bicameral legislature are from the Inter-Parliamentary Union (2008) at http://www.ipu.org/english/home.htm. Data on the type of constitutional justice system employed by a country are from Dr. Arne Mavčič (http://www.concourts.net/).

Note: Unitary/federal data are for 2000; unicameral/bicameral legislature data are for 2007; constitutional justice system data are for 2004. The two main types of constitutional justice system are European and American; "Mixed" means some combination of the American and European models; "Other" means that the system of constitutional justice is unique or unclassifiable; "None" means that there are no mechanisms for constitutional review; and "?" means that the system is unknown according to the source.

15 Consequences of Democratic Institutions

Proportional representation will thus create a situation where everyone has his will represented exactly but where no one's will is carried out.

Dankwart A. Rustow, "Some Observations on Proportional Representation," 1950

OVERVIEW

- Democratic institutions reflect the interests of voters in different ways. Two fundamentally different perspectives on how democracy should work are known as the majoritarian and consensus visions of democracy. These two visions of democracy have important implications for things like accountability, government mandates, and representation.

- Political institutions influence economic policy and outcomes in different ways too. Research suggests that the choice of electoral institutions in a country has an important influence on who gets to govern and what types of economic policies they are likely to implement when given the chance.

- Electoral laws and federalism affect the likelihood of ethnic conflict. Comparative politics may have advice to offer constitutional designers in ethnically or religiously diverse societies.

- Particular institutional choices might influence the survival of democracy. In particular, we look at whether the prospects for democratic consolidation are greater in countries that adopt parliamentarism or in countries that adopt presidentialism.

As we have seen over the last four chapters, there is what sometimes appears to be a dizzying array of different democratic institutions around the world. For example, democracies can be presidential, parliamentary, or mixed. Democracies can employ majoritarian, proportional, or mixed electoral rules. Democracies can have many parties or just a few, they can be federal or unitary, they can be bicameral or unicameral, and they can allow constitutional review or not. Democracies can also have very different types of government: single-party majority, minimal winning coalition, surplus majority, minority coalition, or single party minority. Indeed, the list of democratic features presented here barely scratches the surface of the set of institutional choices that are available to designers of new constitutions. For instance, the decision to establish a parliamentary democracy with proportional electoral rules simply opens up a whole new round of institutional choices that need to be made: whether to require an investiture vote, whether to employ a constructive vote of no confidence, what district magnitude to use, whether to employ an electoral threshold, whether to use the single transferable vote or some party list system, and so on.

The immense variety of democratic institutions observed in the world should come as no surprise. As our discussion of Arrow's Theorem in Chapter 10 illustrates, there is no ideal decision-making mechanism; institutional choice is ultimately an exercise in the choice of "second bests" and likely depends on the particular context in which a country finds itself. This does not mean, however, that constitutional designers mix and match institutions with reckless abandon. As seen in the next section of this chapter, for example, particular sets of institutions repeatedly recur around the world. On the whole, constitutional designers choose particular sets of institutions to bring about the political, social, and economic outcomes that they desire. This presumes, of course, that they have a good idea about how different democratic institutions affect these outcomes. It is to the effects of particular democratic institutions that we now turn.

In this chapter, we introduce you to four different literatures, each of which examines the effect of particular democratic institutions on important political, social, and economic outcomes. In the first section of this chapter, we examine the way in which various democratic institutions reflect the interests of voters. Democracy gets much of its moral authority from being a form of government "of the people, for the people, and by the people." In Chapter 10, we examined the theoretical reasons why such a notion of democracy is complicated. In this chapter, we evaluate the extent to which different institutions facilitate this notion *in practice*. We then examine some of the ways in which the institutions that vary across democracies influence economic policy and economic outcomes. We report findings from this literature suggesting that the choice of electoral institutions has an important influence on who gets to govern and what types of economic policies they are likely to implement when given the chance. Later, we consider the effects of electoral laws and federalism on the likelihood of ethnic conflict in an attempt to discover whether comparative politics has any advice to offer constitutional designers in ethnically or religiously diverse societies. In the final section of this chapter, we use the knowledge we have learned in the second half of this book about institutions to supplement some of the answers provided in the first half of the book about the economic and cultural determinants of the emergence and survival of democracy. We then ask if there are particular institutional choices, such as parliamentarism or presidentialism that might influence the survival of democracy.

COMBINING INSTITUTIONS: MAJORITARIAN OR CONSENSUS DEMOCRACY?

As Arrow's Theorem makes clear, in the designing of institutions there is a fundamental tension between the desire to guarantee that a group of individuals will be able to make coherent and stable choices (group transitivity) on the one hand and the ability to guarantee the freedom of these individuals to form their own preferences (universal admissibility) and have those preferences influence group decisions (non-dictatorship) on the other. In effect, constitutional designers face an institutional "trilemma" (see Figure 10.10) in that they are only able to design institutions that satisfy at most two of these three desirable attributes—group transitivity, universal admissibility, and non-dictatorship. There is no way around it—constitutional designers have to make trade-offs.

Although constitutional designers could theoretically make different trade-offs for each individual institution that they create, a look at the real world suggests that they frequently make a particular trade-off for the system of government as a whole. In practice, constitutional designers have (implicitly) responded to Arrow's institutional "trilemma" in one of two ways—by creating institutions that disperse power or by creating institutions that concentrate it. Democracies in which power is concentrated are referred to as majoritarian democracies, whereas democracies in which power is dispersed are referred to as consensus democracies (Lijphart 1984).[1] Thus, although there are theoretically many possible combinations of democratic institutions that could occur in the world, political scientists often think in terms of two basic types of democracy: majoritarian or consensus (Steiner 1971; Powell 1982, 2000; Huber and Powell 1994; Lijphart 1999). We now describe these two types of democracy, compare their objectives in regard to producing citizen representation, and evaluate how well each performs in light of its objectives.

Majoritarian and Consensus Visions of Democracy

As we have noted elsewhere, policy decisions in contemporary democracies are not made by citizens themselves but rather by their elected representatives. If democracy is understood as a system in which citizens should be able to influence policy decisions, then it follows that elections must play an important role in any well-functioning democracy. Indeed, to the

---

1. Majoritarian democracies are sometimes referred to as "Westminster democracies," and consensus democracies are sometimes referred to as "proportional democracies." We believe that the terms *majoritarian* and *consensus* are more indicative of how these models of democracy are supposed to work in practice.

extent that elections allow citizens to participate in the policymaking process, they can be considered the primary "instruments of democracy" (Pitkin 1967; Cohen 1971; Powell 2000). It turns out that the influence that the citizenry should be able to exert over the policy decisions made by their elected representatives can be thought of from two entirely different perspectives, each of which has a long historical tradition in democratic theory. These two perspectives can be thought of as two different visions of how democracy should work (Powell 2000). These two visions of democracy see the role that elections play in giving citizens influence over the policymaking process in very different ways.

According to the majoritarian vision, elections are supposed to be events in which citizens get to choose between two alternative teams of politicians that are competing to form the government. Whichever team wins an electoral majority gets to form the government and is supposed to implement the policies that it ran on during the election campaign. In this majoritarian vision, citizens know that whichever team forms the government is responsible for the policies that do (or do not) get implemented during its tenure. As a result, citizens can use their evaluations of the policy record when deciding whether to reward or punish the incumbents in the following election. If citizens wish to reward the government for their performance in office, then they vote for the incumbent at election time. And if citizens wish to punish the government, then they vote for the opposition team. As this description of the majoritarian vision of democracy illustrates, citizens get to exert influence over policy decisions only at election time. In effect, citizens choose a team of politicians at election time to implement the set of policies outlined in the team's campaign manifesto. Only when the next election rolls around do citizens get another opportunity to assert their influence over the policymaking process—they get to assert their influence by deciding whether the policies of the incumbent government should continue or whether they should be replaced by the policy proposals of the opposition. Thus, citizens are expected to exert no influence over policy decisions between elections in the majoritarian vision of democracy.

One of the central ideas behind the majoritarian vision of democracy is, as its name suggests, that policy should be determined by what the majority of citizens want; in effect, citizens who hold minority preferences should have no influence in the policymaking process. As Tocqueville ([1835] 1945, 264), an early proponent of this view, puts it, "The very essence of democratic government consists in the absolute sovereignty of the majority." To make sure that only the majority rule, the majoritarian vision of democracy essentially requires that all policymaking power be concentrated in the hands of a majority government. Power is not to be dispersed among different political actors or institutions because this will almost certainly require the involvement of minority opposition members in the policymaking process; this is something that is seen as illegitimate. In fact, the ability of citizens to control their elected representatives and, hence, policy decisions through the electoral process requires that there be a clear concentration of power in the hands of a single majority team of politicians in the majoritarian vision of democracy.

According to the consensus vision of democracy, elections are supposed to be events in which citizens choose representative agents from as wide a range of social groups as possible, and these agents then go on to bargain over policy in the legislature. In this vision of democracy, elections are not designed to serve as some sort of referendum on the set of policies implemented by the government as they are in the majoritarian vision of democracy. Instead, elections simply provide citizens with the opportunity to choose representatives who they believe will be effective advocates for their interests when bargaining over policy finally begins after the election. With this in mind, one of the central goals of elections in the consensus vision of democracy is to produce a legislature that is, in some sense, a miniature reflection of society as a whole. Such an emphasis on having a legislature whose preferences accurately correspond to those of the nation as a whole has a long history in democratic theory, dating back at least as far as the seventeenth century (Pitkin 1967; Skinner 2005). For example, Burke ([1770] 1949, 28) writes that the "virtue, spirit, and essence" of a legislature lies "in its being the express image of the feelings of the nation," whereas Mill ([1859] 1991, 116) claims that a legislature should be "an arena in which not only the general opinion of the nation, but that of every section of it . . . can produce itself in full light."

It is important to note that the elected representatives in the consensus vision of democracy are *not* elected to enact a precise set of policies; rather, they are elected to bargain with each other in the legislature over what policies should be implemented. This frequently means the existence of shifting majorities in the legislature as political actors build different legislative coalitions, depending on the particular policy that is under consideration. It should be easy to see from this that the consensus vision of democracy has a view very different from that of the majoritarian vision of when citizens should be able to influence the policymaking process. Whereas we have seen that the ability of citizens to influence policy decisions essentially begins and ends at election time in the majoritarian vision of democracy, in the consensus vision of democracy citizens are able, through the ongoing bargaining of their elected representatives, to continue to exert influence over the policymaking process between elections. In effect, the consensus vision of democracy demands that policy decisions continuously respond to changes in the preferences of the citizens rather than just at election time.

One of the central ideas behind the consensus vision of democracy is that policy should be determined by as many citizens (and their representatives) as possible. Unlike the majoritarian vision of democracy, citizens with majority preferences are not to be given any privileged status in the policymaking process; instead, all groups of citizens, including minorities, should have the power to influence policy decisions in direct proportion to their electoral size. In line with this view, Dahl (1989, 104) writes, "If we accept the idea of Intrinsic Equality, then no process of lawmaking can be morally justified if it does not take equally into account the interests of every person subject to the laws." One obvious objective of the consensus vision of democracy, then, is to prevent the majority from riding roughshod over the preferences of the minority. As proponents of this vision of democracy note, the best way to guarantee that the majority take account of minority preferences is to disperse power in such a way that the minority has some valuable policymaking influence with which to defend its interests. If power becomes too concentrated, then there is always the risk that the majority will capture it and use it against the minority; this is something that is seen as illegitimate.

Mueller (1991, 334) summarizes the differences between the majoritarian and consensus visions of democracy in the following way: "Basically there are two alternatives: (1) the citizens can elect 'a government,' i.e. select that party whose policies they most prefer, that party they wish to see run the executive branch, or (2) the citizens can elect a truly representative body, i.e. a group of representatives that will vote as the citizens themselves would have voted had they taken part in a grand 'town meeting' of the entire electorate." Lijphart (1999, 1–2) provides an even more succinct summary of the differences when he argues that the two visions of democracy can essentially be defined in terms of the answer they give to the following question: "Who will govern and to whose interests should the government be responsive?" For the majoritarian vision, the answer is a majority of the people. And for the consensus vision, the answer is as many people as possible. In effect, the **majoritarian vision of democracy** demands that political power be concentrated in the hands of the majority, whereas the **consensus vision of democracy** demands that it be dispersed among as many actors as possible.

> The **majoritarian vision of democracy** is based on the idea that power should be concentrated in the hands of the majority. The **consensus vision of democracy** is based on the idea that power should be dispersed among as many political actors as possible.

Why might political actors wish to privilege one vision of democracy over another? Theoretically, one could argue that the majoritarian vision of democracy would be better in some circumstances and the consensus vision of democracy in others. Powell (2000, 8–9) notes:

> Where the issues are clear-cut and a unified citizenry has an overwhelmingly clear set of preferences, voters might well prefer to take most of the choices out of the hands of the negotiators and be sure that the election results are in themselves decisive. But where the issues are complex, the citizens divided, and problems that the citizens cannot anticipate arise, each group of citizens may well prefer to be represented by trustworthy agents who can be relied upon to negotiate for their constituents. Citizens who fear being in the minority on the issues that dominate a single election outcome, but anticipate being part of a majority on other issues, may especially prefer to have representative agents bargaining for them anew on each separate issue.

Practically speaking, for a democracy to function efficiently it needs relatively stable rules, and so key institutions cannot be continuously restructured depending on whether the most important issues of the day are "clear-cut" or "complex." Thus, a choice about whether to set up a majoritarian- or consensus-style democracy must be made and this choice is likely to endure. But how does one go about making this choice? Which institutions, or sets of institutions, create systems of government that most closely approximate one or the other of the two different visions of democracy? We now reexamine the institutions discussed in Chapters 11–14 in light of whether they concentrate or disperse power; that is, in light of whether they pull systems of government toward the majoritarian or consensus vision of democracy.

Majoritarian and Consensus Institutions

Every democracy has a set of rules that specify how policy gets made and who gets to make it. As we saw in Chapter 14, many of these rules are explicitly written down in a country's constitution. If a constitution encourages the election of single-party legislative majorities that can control the executive and concentrates power in the hands of a single-party government, then it can be considered majoritarian in nature. If the constitution encourages the equitable representation of multiple parties and the dispersal of policymaking power among these parties, however, then it can be considered consensual in nature (Powell 2000, 21). It is possible to think of the two visions of democracy as representing opposing end points of a majoritarian-consensus dimension that captures how widely power is dispersed. To a large extent, the institutions that we examined in Chapters 11–14 can be thought of in terms of whether they disperse or concentrate power. Depending on their characteristics, therefore, they influence the extent to which constitutions are majoritarian or consensual.

In Table 15.1, we illustrate when a particular "institution" can be considered more majoritarian or more consensual.[2] As we will demonstrate, the decisions to adopt majoritarian or consensus institutions are not entirely independent of one another. In other words, choosing to adopt certain majoritarian institutions can virtually guarantee having to live with other majoritarian institutions. Similarly, choosing to adopt certain consensus institutions virtually guarantees having to live with other consensus institutions. This is because many of these institutions are causally related. Indeed, it is this causal interdependence among institutions that helps to explain why constitutional designers are not mixing and matching institutions with reckless abandon and why democracies, despite their great institutional variety, tend to come in just two main types—majoritarian or consensus (Lijphart 1999; Powell 2000).

It is relatively easy to see how electoral systems fit onto a majoritarian-consensus dimension. As our discussion of electoral systems in Chapter 12 points out, majoritarian electoral systems tend to concentrate power in that only those candidates or political parties with the

---

2. The information in Table 15.1 gives the impression that institutions are either majoritarian or consensus. This, however, is somewhat misleading because the extent to which institutions disperse or concentrate power is best thought of as a continuum rather than a dichotomy. For example, some forms of bicameralism disperse power more than others. Similarly, some electoral systems are more proportional than others. The point here is that the extent to which particular institutions, such as the electoral system, bicameralism, federalism, and so on, disperse power depends crucially on exactly what form they take.

TABLE 15.1	**Institutions and the Majoritarian-Consensus Dimension**	
Institution	Majoritarian	Consensus
Electoral system	Majoritarian	Proportional
Party system	Two parties	Many parties
Government type	Single-party majority	Coalition/minority
Federalism	Unitary	Federal
Bicameralism	Unicameral	Bicameral
Constitutionalism	Legislative supremacy constitution	Higher law constitution
Regime type	Parliamentary	Presidential
Interest-group relations	Pluralism	Corporatism
Prototypical examples	Barbados, New Zealand (prior to 1996), United Kingdom	Belgium, Netherlands, Switzerland

most votes win; indeed, in most majoritarian systems only one candidate wins. In contrast, proportional electoral systems tend to disperse power among candidates or parties in proportion to the share of electoral support that they win. As a result, even candidates winning minority support obtain some policymaking power. The more proportional the electoral system, the more it disperses power and the more it approximates the consensus vision of democracy. The size of the party system can also be conceptualized along a majoritarian-consensus dimension in a fairly straightforward manner. For example, power is concentrated in two-party systems in that there are two dominant political parties in the legislature and only these parties have a realistic chance of holding power. In contrast, power is dispersed in multiparty systems in that there are multiple parties in the legislature and more than two parties have a realistic chance of holding power. The more parties there are in the party system, the more that power is dispersed. The type of government in a country also fits neatly into our notion of a majoritarian-consensus continuum. For instance, power is concentrated in the hands of a single party in single-party majority governments but dispersed more widely among multiple parties in coalition or minority governments.[3]

---

3. That power is dispersed in coalition governments is largely self-evident in that there are multiple parties in the cabinet. It is important to recognize, however, that power is also dispersed in minority governments. This is even true of single-party minority governments, at least in parliamentary democracies. Although there is only one cabinet party in single-party minority governments, we know from our discussion of minority governments in parliamentary democracies that some other party or parties in the legislature must be supporting the government for it to remain in power. The ability of these "support" parties to bring the government down means that the government will have to share policymaking power with them if it wants to stay in office.

These three institutions—the electoral system, the party system, and the type of government—are all causally related. As our discussion of Duverger's theory in Chapter 13 illustrates, majoritarian electoral systems tend to be associated with small party systems, whereas proportional electoral systems tend to be associated with large party systems (at least in countries with sufficiently high levels of social heterogeneity). And as our discussion of the government formation process in Chapter 11 illustrates, the size of the party system, in turn, influences the type of government that forms. Specifically, single-party majority governments are much more likely to form when there are few political parties, because small party systems increase the likelihood that a single party will win a legislative majority. In contrast, coalition and minority governments are much more likely to form when there are many political parties, because large party systems reduce the likelihood that a single party will win a legislative majority. As this indicates, the choice of a constitutional designer to adopt a particular type of electoral system—majoritarian or proportional—tends also to be a choice to have a particular type of party system and government. This is why we tend to see either (a) countries with a majoritarian electoral system, a small party system, and a high frequency of single-party majority governments, or (b) countries with a proportional electoral system, a large party system, and a high frequency of coalition or minority governments.

Federalism, bicameralism, and constitutionalism are three other institutions that can easily be conceptualized in terms of a majoritarian-consensus dimension. For example, federal states disperse power between at least two territorial levels of government; in contrast, unitary states concentrate power in the national government. Bicameral states disperse power between two legislative chambers; in contrast, unicameral states concentrate power in a single legislative chamber. Higher law constitutions disperse power by giving certain institutions, like constitutional courts, the authority to invalidate acts of government; in contrast, legislative supremacy constitutions concentrate power in the legislature and do not allow constitutional review.

To a large extent, federalism, bicameralism, and constitutionalism are also closely related. Why? Imagine that you are a constitutional designer for a country and that you see significant advantages to setting up a decentralized form of government to better take account of regional disparities in preferences. A problem, though, is that for decentralized forms of government to be stable and credible, it must be the case that regional governments do not try to take advantage of each other and, more important, that the central government does not try to usurp power from the regions. If these conditions do not hold, then some constituent regional units might decide that it is preferable to withdraw from the system of government altogether. But how can these conditions be achieved? One way you might think to do this is to explicitly write into the constitution that sovereignty is to be divided between governments from different territorial levels. In other words, you might think to write a federal constitution, thereby constitutionally protecting the decentralized system of government. Although this could help, you should ask yourself why actors would necessarily act in accordance with the federal system merely because it is written down somewhere in the constitution. Why, for example, would a central government interested in centralizing power comply with federal provisions in a constitution?

Concerns about compliance might lead you to create an institution like a constitutional court with the authority to punish attempts by political actors to violate constitutional federal provisions. But would the creation of something like a constitutional court be sufficient to make the federal system stable and credible? Not necessarily. For example, a legislative majority at the national level may emerge that wishes to amend the constitution so as to create a more centralized and unitary form of government.[4] To prevent this from happening, you might decide to create a system of checks and balances that makes it harder for national majorities to form that wish to centralize power. One way to do this is to establish a bicameral legislature in which the upper legislative chamber is specifically designed to represent the interests of the different regions.[5] This upper chamber would obviously have a stake in maintaining the federal system. By combining these institutions—federalism, bicameralism, and constitutionalism—it is possible to enhance the stability and credibility of decentralized systems of government (Bednar, Eskridge, and Ferejohn 2001; Bednar, forthcoming). The line of reasoning that we have just outlined helps to explain why constitutional designers who wish to disperse power in the form of a decentralized system of government frequently choose to adopt all three of these institutions.

As the information in Table 15.1 illustrates, the choice of whether to adopt a parliamentary or presidential form of democracy can also be thought of in terms of a majoritarian-consensus continuum. Presidential systems fall at the consensus end of the spectrum because power is dispersed between the executive and the legislature. Indeed, presidential systems are often referred to as "separation of powers" systems for precisely this reason. In contrast, parliamentary systems fall at the majoritarian end of the spectrum because power is concentrated in the hands of an executive that is supported by a legislative majority. Where, you might wonder, do mixed regimes fall on the majoritarian-consensus dimension? To a large extent it depends on whether there is cohabitation or not. Recall from Chapter 11 that cohabitation occurs when the president is from one political bloc and the prime minister is from another. Mixed regimes fall at the consensus end of the spectrum when there is cohab-

---

4. You might also wonder whether a constitutional court would be sufficiently independent of the national government to check its attempts at centralizing power. As we saw in Chapter 14, this concern arises because a constitutional court has to rely on other institutions to enforce its decisions (see Box 14.4, "Judicial Power and the Judicialization of Politics"). To the extent that a constitutional court is institutionally dependent on other national institutions to enforce its decisions, it may act like a creature of the national government and be reluctant to check its powers (Bednar, Eskridge, and Ferejohn 2001).

5. There are obviously other ways to help fragment political power at the national level so as to prevent the emergence of national majorities that might wish to centralize power. For example, electoral systems that inhibit the formation of unified and disciplined political parties could be adopted. As we saw in our discussion of electoral rules in Chapter 12, there are many ways, such as choosing open instead of closed party lists, that this might be done. Another is to adopt institutions that encourage the formation of regionally based, as opposed to nationally based, political parties (see Box 13.4, "Nationalizing Party Systems"). Indeed, several scholars have argued that having a decentralized party system is crucial for having a healthy federal system (Riker 1964).

itation, because power is dispersed and divided between the president and the prime minister. Mixed regimes fall at the majoritarian end of the spectrum, though, when there is no cohabitation, because power is concentrated in the hands of the president, who effectively runs the entire show.

Finally, how interest group relations are organized can also be conceptualized in terms of a majoritarian-consensus dimension. Recall from Chapter 11 that corporatist interest group relations occur when key social and economic actors, such as labor, business, and agriculture groups, are integrated into the formal policymaking process. In contrast, pluralist interest group relations occur when interest groups compete in the political marketplace outside of the formal policymaking process. By bringing interest groups into the formal policymaking process, corporatism disperses power. And by excluding interest groups from the formal policymaking process, pluralism concentrates it. As our discussion of the government formation process in Chapter 11 also indicates, the structure of interest group relations in a country is causally related to the type of government that is likely to form. As we learned there, corporatism tends to encourage the formation of minority governments—another institution at the consensus end of the spectrum.

In Figure 15.1, using data from Lijphart (1999, 311–314), we provide additional information showing how majoritarian institutions tend to go together and how consensus institutions tend to go together. Lijphart examines thirty-six democracies around the world from 1945 to 1996 and codes their institutions in regard to how majoritarian or consensus-oriented they are. In Figure 15.1, we use star-plots (one for each country) to graphically portray this information for the eight institutions shown earlier in Table 15.1.[6] Following Lijphart, we divide the eight institutions into two dimensions: executive-parties dimension and federal-unitary dimension. The executive-parties dimension, shown in the left half of Figure 15.1, includes information on the electoral system, party system, regime type, government type, and interest group relations. And the federal-unitary dimension, shown in the right half of Figure 15.1, includes information on federalism, bicameralism, and constitutionalism. The lines radiating from the center of each star-plot represent the various institutions in each dimension. The lengths of these lines indicate how majoritarian these institutions are—the longer the lines, the more majoritarian the institution. This means that the area encapsulated by each star-plot provides a good visual representation of how majoritarian each country's institutions are as a whole. Countries with large star-plots are very majoritarian, and countries with small star-plots are very consensus oriented. On the executive-parties dimension, Jamaica, the Bahamas, and Trinidad are the most majoritarian, whereas

---

6. Lijphart uses different scales to measure how majoritarian each institution is. For example, he measures how majoritarian the party system is by the effective number of legislative parties and he measures how majoritarian the government type is by the percentage of time that there is a single-party majority government. To make sure all of the institutions are measured on comparable scales, we standardize each of Lijphart's measures. It is these standardized measures that are plotted in Figure 15.1.

FIGURE 15.1 How Majoritarian Is Your Democracy?

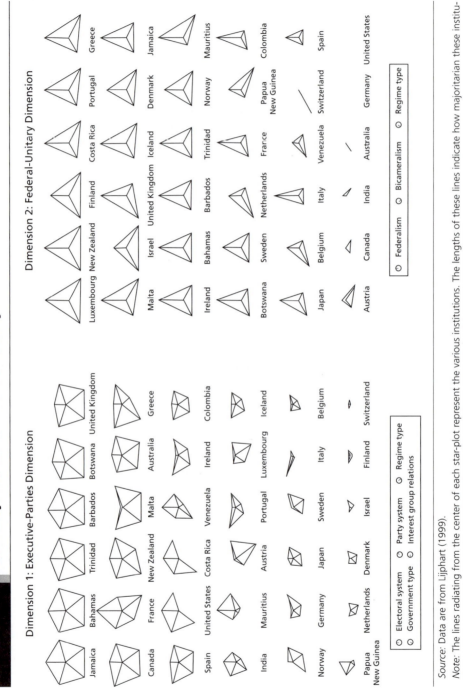

Source: Data are from Lijphart (1999).

Note: The lines radiating from the center of each star-plot represent the various institutions. The lengths of these lines indicate how majoritarian these institutions are: the longer the lines, the more majoritarian the institution. Data are for the period 1945 to 1996.

Switzerland, Finland, and Israel are the least majoritarian. On the federal-unitary dimension, Luxembourg, New Zealand, and Finland are the most majoritarian, whereas the United States, Germany, and Australia are the least majoritarian. As Figure 15.1 illustrates, most countries tend to have either a relatively large star-plot (majoritarian) or a relatively small star-plot (consensus).

Historically, the prototype for majoritarian democracies has been the United Kingdom. Indeed, majoritarian democracies are sometimes referred to as Westminster-style democracies because the British House of Commons meets in the Palace of Westminster in the heart of London. According to Lijphart, though, the country that comes closest to the ideal type of majoritarian democracy during his period of study (1945–1996) is New Zealand. New Zealand fits the "Westminster" model even better than the United Kingdom does because two large parties dominated the parliament and one of the two always had a legislative majority. Unlike the United Kingdom, third parties barely managed to get representation in the New Zealand Parliament.[7] In addition to having pluralist interest group relations, New Zealand is also unitary and unicameral. All in all, New Zealand's institutions from 1945 to 1996 were extremely majoritarian. As we mentioned at the end of Chapter 12, though, New Zealand has recently adopted more consensus-oriented institutions and is no longer the prime example of a majoritarian democracy. Specifically, New Zealand replaced its single-member district plurality electoral system with a more proportional mixed electoral system in 1996. This has led to an increase in the size of the party system and an increase in the frequency of coalition, as opposed to single-party majority, governments. Even the United Kingdom is not the model of a Westminster system that it once was if you take into account recent policies toward devolution and the increasing strength of third parties. Today, the most majoritarian democracies in the world exist in the Caribbean in places like Barbados, the Bahamas, Jamaica, and Trinidad and Tobago.

The prototype for consensus democracies is Belgium. Belgium is federal (since 1993), bicameral (since 1995), and employs constitutional review (since 1984). Its PR electoral system encourages a large party system, which in turn generates broad coalition governments. Belgian cabinets are required to have an equal number of French- and Flemish-speaking ministers (not including the prime minister). Because the parties are split along linguistic lines, the language-parity requirement has the effect of increasing the number of parties in a typical Belgian cabinet. In order to implement any new policies in Belgium, many different actors must agree to the change. The positive spin on this state of affairs would be that politicians must build broad coalitions. This typically involves compromising with many different political actors and taking minority views into account. The negative spin would be to

---

7. Although the New Zealand case is close to being the ideal type of a majoritarian democracy, it is not perfect. One area in which it deviates from majoritarianism is in the special, larger districts that are reserved for the Maori, an indigenous group that make up about 12 percent of the population in New Zealand. The goal of the larger districts is to ensure minority representation (Lijphart 1999, 22).

Supporters for unity in Belgium demonstrate in Brussels on November 18, 2007. Thousands marched through Brussels in support of Belgium's survival, demanding an end to a deadlock that kept a government from taking office and stoking fears that this nation of 10.5 million Dutch and French speakers would break up after 177 years of at times uneasy unity.

simply point out the difficulties that political actors in Belgium sometimes face in reaching agreements on any policy changes. After the June 2007 legislative elections for the lower house, for example, eleven different parties won seats. A new government did not enter office until December of that year, fully eight months after the election (Golder 2008).[8] In the meantime, Belgian citizens had descended onto the streets to protest the absence of an effective government, and some European Union reports on the government formation crisis estimated that the bargaining delay was having deleterious effects on the Belgian economy. According to widespread media reports at the time, the government formation crisis even prompted some Belgians to think seriously about whether their country should simply cease to exist, splitting along linguistic lines into Wallonia and Flanders.

Given our discussion of the government formation process in Chapter 11, it should come as no surprise that a country with a large number of parties would experience delays in the length of time that it takes to form a government. Nor should it come as a surprise that the coalition governments that do form in such a country tend to be unstable and short lived. All institutional choices present trade-offs. We can have a broad representation of social groups, but this may lead to instability in the government. Or we can have a stable and efficient government, but at the cost of dramatically limiting citizens' choices at the ballot box. Whether you prefer the majoritarian vision or the consensus vision of democracy depends on how you value representation and meaningful choices versus efficiency and accountability. We now examine in more detail what the two visions of democracy mean for things like representation and accountability.

Evaluating Majoritarian and Consensus Visions of Democracy

As we have just seen, the institutional choices confronting a country tend to push it toward either a majoritarian or consensus vision of democracy. But how should we evaluate these different views of democracy? Our analysis of democratic decision-making procedures in

---

8. The deadlock was finally broken after King Albert II, the head of state, intervened to urge an interim government to take office for three months so that some pressing reforms could be addressed by the legislature.

Chapter 10 revealed that there is no perfect set of institutions. Rather, different types of institutions reflect trade-offs that are made along different dimensions. Here, we examine several attributes that seem particularly important for democratic governance and evaluate how well different institutional arrangements perform in producing these attributes. In particular, we focus on accountability, mandates, and representation. As you will see, majoritarian democracies value accountability and mandates over representation, whereas consensus democracies embody the opposite trade-off.

Accountability and Mandates

Accountability refers to the extent to which it is possible for voters to reward or punish parties for the policies that they introduce while in office. Put slightly differently, accountability is about how easy it is for citizens "to throw the rascals out." Many view accountability as important because it provides incentives for politicians to pursue policies that will keep the voters—or, at least, a winning coalition of the voters—satisfied. Accountability basically requires that citizens look at how an

> **Accountability** is the extent to which voters are able to reward or punish parties for their behavior in office.
>
> **Retrospective voting** occurs when voters look at the past performance of incumbent parties to decide how to vote in the current election.

incumbent party has behaved in the past in order to decide whether to reward or punish it at the next election. Such behavior on the part of voters is referred to as **retrospective voting** (Fiorina 1981; Erikson, MacKuen, and Stimson 2002). If citizens decide that an incumbent party has performed sufficiently well in office, they will reward it by voting for it. In contrast, if citizens decide that an incumbent party has not performed sufficiently well, they will punish it by voting for another party. If accountability works well, incumbent parties that perform well are reelected into office and incumbent parties that perform poorly are removed from office.

The extent to which citizens can hold their governments accountable through elections varies from country to country. Consensus democracies tend to have relatively low levels of accountability. The reason for this is that voters in these countries typically do not get to directly choose the government. As you will recall from our discussion of the government formation process in Chapter 11, it is relatively rare for a single party to win a legislative majority when there are many parties. As a result, elections in consensus-style democracies almost never determine the identity of the government; instead, they usher in periods of negotiations in which party leaders bargain over the identity of the future government. The choices of these party leaders may or may not accurately reflect the preferences of the citizens. As we have noted elsewhere, it is also common for governments in these types of countries to be removed from office in interelection periods without the voters' being directly consulted. This clearly diminishes the ability of voters to reward or sanction their elected officials (Hellwig and Samuels 2007). Another reason why consensus democracies tend to have low levels of accountability is that citizens may vote against a particular incumbent party at election time and yet find that this party is still a member of the next coalition government because the other parties could not form a cabinet without it. There are numerous examples of parties losing votes and seats in consensus democracies but nonetheless finding themselves in the next government. Perhaps the most egregious case of this is Switzerland, where the four main parties have agreed since 1959 to form governments together irrespective of how the citizens vote; this arrangement is commonly known as the "magic formula" (Kerr 1987; Caramani 1996).[9] In contrast to consensus democracies, it is much easier to throw the rascals out in majoritarian democracies that are characterized by single-party majority governments and two-party systems. If the citizens in a majoritarian democracy are dissatisfied with the performance of the party in power, they simply vote for the opposition party to replace it.

> **Clarity of responsibility** is the extent to which voters can identify exactly who it is that is responsible for the policies that are implemented.

A concept that is closely related to accountability is **clarity of responsibility.** Clarity of responsibility refers to the ability of citizens to identify exactly who it is that is responsible for the policies that are implemented (or not implemented). Clarity of responsibility is obviously a necessary condition for voters to be able to hold their government accountable. If citizens cannot identify who is responsible for the policies that get implemented, they will not be able to appropriately reward or punish those parties for their behavior in office.

As with accountability, clarity of responsibility varies from country to country. The more that power is concentrated, the greater the clarity of responsibility. One factor that affects clarity of responsibility is the type of government in a country. For example, clarity of responsibility is very high in those countries in which power is concentrated in the hands of a single-party majority government. In such countries, citizens know exactly whom to blame—the party in power—at election time. Clarity of responsibility is less high in countries in which power is dispersed among multiple parties in a coalition government, because it is not always obvious which coalition party is responsible for the policies that get implemented. Are all of the parties in the coalition government equally responsible for the government's performance? Or are some parties more responsible than others? Does a party's responsibility vary by policy area? Clarity of responsibility is even lower in minority governments, in which citizens may not know who is keeping the government in power and, hence, who is responsible for the policies that get implemented. Indeed, different parties in the legislature may be keeping the minority government in office at different points in time. The reason for this is that minority governments frequently build shifting legislative majorities on different issues to stay in power.

Other institutions that disperse power, such as bicameralism and federalism, also reduce clarity of responsibility. As we noted in Chapter 14, federalism can make it difficult for citi-

---

9. The original "magic formula" was replaced in December 2003 by a new formula in which the Swiss People's Party gained an additional guaranteed cabinet seat and the Christian Democratic People's Party lost one.

zens to know which level of government is responsible for policy successes and which is to blame for policy failures (Arceneaux 2005; Gomez and Wilson 2008; Maestas et al. 2008; Malhotra and Kuo 2008). For example, is the poor performance of the regional economy the result of policies adopted by the subnational government or of those implemented by the national government? In this type of situation, neither the subnational nor the national government will want to take responsibility for the poor economic performance and will likely try to blame the other. In this way, federalism facilitates blame shifting (and credit claiming), thereby making it difficult for citizens to know exactly who is responsible for what. Bicameral systems can have a similar effect, particularly if the two legislative chambers are equally powerful and controlled by opposing political sides.

Other factors also influence clarity of responsibility. One such factor is the length of time that a government remains in office.[10] As we noted in Chapter 11, governments in nonpresidential democracies can fall in the middle of an interelection period. This means that voters can find themselves going to the polls to pass judgment on a government that has not been in power for a particularly long period of time. If several different governments have been in office since the previous election, who is responsible for the policies in place and the outcomes being experienced on the day the election is held? As we have shown elsewhere, such governmental instability is more likely to occur when there are many parties in the legislature and when these parties reflect a wide variety of policy positions. This is more likely to occur in consensus democracies than majoritarian ones. Similarly, in consensus systems, in which the opposition has a greater role within the legislature itself, the lines between the government and opposition can be blurred somewhat, thereby making the attribution of blame for policy even more difficult.

In Figure 15.2, we plot different political systems in a two-dimensional space capturing accountability and clarity of responsibility. In dictatorships, clarity of responsibility is very high because everyone knows that the dictator is responsible for whatever policies get implemented. Although clarity of responsibility is high in dictatorships, accountability is essentially nonexistent because citizens have almost no chance of throwing the dictator out through electoral means.[11] By concentrating power, majoritarian democracies tend to produce both high levels of accountability and clarity of responsibility. Not only do majoritarian institutions make it easy for voters to identify which political actors are responsible for the policies that get implemented, they also make it easy for voters to reward or punish these

---

10. The level of party discipline also affects clarity of responsibility. If the leaders of a party in government enjoy strong party discipline, they are the ones to be held accountable for the policies championed by the party. If the party is split into factions, or if the rank-and-file members are fairly independent of their party leadership, however, it is less clear who to blame within the party. It might be the case that a voter agrees with the policies pursued by the party leader but that party in-fighting prevented their enactment. In such a case, who is to be rewarded and who is to be blamed? If a voter does not have a chance, at the ballot box, to make such a distinction, how is she to vote?

11. The Selectorate Theory that we examined in Chapter 9 points out that dictators *are* accountable to their winning coalition. This process of accountability, however, almost never works through electoral means, which is the focus here.

actors for their performance in office. By dispersing power, consensus democracies tend to produce relatively low levels of accountability and clarity of responsibility. Consensus-style institutions make it hard for voters to know exactly which political actors are responsible for the policies that a government enacts. And even if voters can figure this out, consensus-style institutions make it hard for voters to reward or punish these actors for their performance in office. Given that, as we have argued, clarity of responsibility is a necessary condition for accountability, there are no political systems with low clarity of responsibility and high accountability (bottom right in Figure 15.2).

If you think that accountability is an important attribute of a democratic system, then the evidence that we have just presented would suggest that you should prefer majoritarian institutions to consensus ones. But does this mean that consensus-style democracies are doing a bad job because they make it difficult for their citizens to hold governments accountable? We do not think so. Accountability is critically important in the majoritarian vision of democracy, and it would be a significant failing if majoritarian democracies could not provide it. As we noted earlier, however, accountability is not particularly important in the consensus vision of democracy. As a result, it is not clear that consensus-style democracies are failing if they do

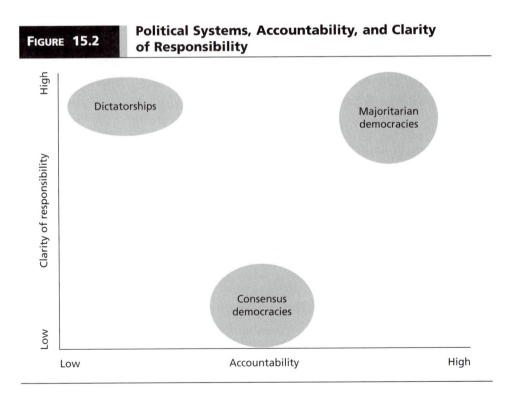

FIGURE 15.2 **Political Systems, Accountability, and Clarity of Responsibility**

not do a great job of allowing their citizens to hold governments accountable. Implicit in this reasoning is that we should probably use different criteria to evaluate majoritarian and consensus democracies, because their democratic visions and goals are not the same.

Like accountability, mandates are extremely important in the majoritarian vision of democracy but not in the consensus vision. A **mandate** is a policy, or set of policies, that the government is both authorized and obligated to carry out once in office. In the majoritarian vision of democracy, parties that make policy commitments during an electoral campaign are authorized, and obligated, to carry out those policies once in office. In

> A **mandate** is a policy that the government is both authorized and obligated to carry out once in office.
>
> **Prospective voting** occurs when voters base how they will vote in the current election on the expected performance of incumbents and challengers.

effect, elections in majoritarian democracies are not just about throwing the rascals out based on their past performance; they are also about giving the next government a mandate to implement the policies that they ran on during the electoral campaign. This means that voters in majoritarian democracies are expected to engage in prospective, as well as retrospective, voting. **Prospective voting** occurs when voters look at what parties say they will do while in office in order to form the expectations about future performance that help them decide how to vote. In contrast to the majoritarian vision of democracy, mandates are not that important for the consensus vision. Indeed, the consensus vision of democracy actually views mandates as being bad because they mean ignoring the preferences of the minority not in power.

Governments around the world frequently claim to have won a mandate at election time. But what exactly is required for a government to have a mandate? Presumably, a government should be able to claim that it has a mandate only if voters can meaningfully be said to have voted for it. This requires that voters be able to identify the different government alternatives when they go to vote. Political scientists refer to the extent to which voters can identify what government alternatives they are voting for at election time as **government identifiability.**

One factor that affects the degree of government identifiability in a country is the expected

> **Government identifiability** refers to the extent to which voters can identify what government alternatives they are voting for at election time.

government formation scenario. As we illustrate in Table 15.2, government identifiability is highest in countries where a single-party majority government is expected to form. For example, a single party nearly always gets to form the government in countries like Greece, Spain, and the United Kingdom. As a result, when voters in these countries go to the polls to vote for a particular party, they know exactly what government and, hence, what set of policies they are voting for. Government identifiability is lower in countries in which a coalition government is expected to form. It is especially low in those countries, like Belgium and Finland, where the government formation process does not start until after the elections. Government identifiability is somewhat better in countries in which parties regularly form

TABLE 15.2	Government Identifiability and Expected Government Formation Scenario

Expected government formation scenario	Identifiability
Few parties; single-party majority likely.	High
Many parties, preelectoral coalitions.	
No preelectoral coalitions; certain government coalitions likely.	↑
Many parties; government coalitions known only after the election.	Low

preelectoral coalitions or in which voters have a good idea of what the likely coalitions will be. In Australia, France, or Germany, for example, it is common for parties to form preelectoral coalitions, indicating what the government will look like if they win. As a result, the voters in these countries have some sense of how their vote will affect which government ultimately forms. Even without preelectoral coalitions, voters in some countries have a fairly strong expectation about which parties are likely to be in government.

For example, if either the left-wing bloc or the right-wing bloc is expected to win a majority of the seats, then voters will expect the government to form from among the mainstream elements of whichever side wins the majority. This was the expectation prior to the 2006 legislative elections in the Czech Republic.[12] In general, government identifiability is higher in majoritarian democracies than in consensus-oriented ones.

Government identifiability is a necessary condition for mandates, but it isn't a sufficient condition. For a government to claim that it has a mandate for its policies, most people believe that it should also win, at a minimum, a majority of the votes cast. How can a government claim to have a mandate if a majority of the electorate did not vote for its policies? The problem is that although government identifiability is high in majoritarian democracies, it is extremely rare for a single party to actually win more than 50 percent of the vote. Although we regularly observe single-party majority governments in majoritarian democracies, these governments typically enjoy only what are called "manufactured majorities." A manufactured majority refers to a situation in which a party that does not win a majority of the votes manages to obtain a majority of the legislative seats because of the disproportional way that majoritarian electoral systems translate votes into seats. Obviously any incoming government in a majoritarian democracy has an incentive to claim that it has a mandate. But, given that a majority of voters have typically voted for other parties, do you think that it is entirely legitimate for it to do so?

---

12. Of course, the voters' expectations do not always turn into reality. As we discussed in Chapter 11, the left- and right-wing blocs in the Czech Republic won exactly the same number of legislative seats, leaving them deadlocked for months following the election.

Another thing to consider here is whether a government actually has the ability to implement a mandate, even if it can legitimately claim to have won one. If power is dispersed, as it is in consensus democracies, it will likely be difficult for the government to fulfill its mandate. For example, veto institutions, such as bicameralism or federalism, may block the ability of governments to implement their policy platforms. Thus, even if a government with a high level of identifiability were to come to power in a consensus democracy, it is not clear that it would be able to implement its campaign pledges, because other actors have the ability to influence or block legislation. In a majoritarian democracy, such difficulties with implementing the government's preferred policy are minimized.

In majoritarian democracies, then, government identifiability tends to be high and mandates are relatively easy to implement. A problem, though, is that governments in majoritarian democracies rarely win the support of a majority of the voters. This means that if someone wants to argue that governments in majoritarian democracies have mandates, then he must argue that mandates are acceptable even when governments win only a plurality of the vote. In consensus democracies, government identifiability tends to be poor. Moreover, governments that wish to implement any mandate will likely find it difficult to do so because of the presence of veto players. We should recall, though, that assigning mandates to governments is not one of the goals of the consensus vision of democracy.

Representation

Another attribute that is important for democratic governance is representation. We now examine what the goals of the two visions of democracy are with respect to representation and how close majoritarian and consensus democracies come to achieving those goals in practice. **Representation** can usefully be conceptualized in terms of (a) responsiveness and (b) congruence.[13] **Responsiveness, or dynamic representation,** refers to how well elected representatives respond to changes in the preferences of the

> **Representation** can be conceptualized in terms of (a) responsiveness and (b) congruence. **Responsiveness, or dynamic representation,** refers to how well elected representatives respond to changes in the preferences of the electorate. **Congruence, or static representation,** refers to how well elected representatives match the preferences of the electorate.

electorate. Many political scientists look at responsiveness in terms of how well the policies of elected representatives respond to changes in the preferences of citizens (Page and Shapiro 1983; Page 1994; Burstein 2003; Ezrow 2007; Barabas 2008). For example, do policies shift in line with changes in public opinion? In what follows, though, we look at responsiveness slightly differently. Specifically, we look at responsiveness in regard to how accurately the policymaking power of legislative parties tracks changes in their electoral support. In other words, do parties see an increase in their ability to influence policy when their electoral support goes up? In contrast to responsiveness, **congruence, or static representation,** refers to how well elected rep-

---

13. There are many different ways to think about representation. For a useful introduction to the literature on representation, see Pitkin (1967).

resentatives match the (static) preferences of the electorate. For example, does the government's policy position accurately match the preferences of the electorate? Does the legislature accurately reflect the full range of citizen preferences?

Let's begin with responsiveness. Responsiveness is an important goal for both the majoritarian and consensus visions of democracy. The exact way that responsiveness is conceptualized, however, differs quite markedly between the two visions of democracy. Recall that in the majoritarian vision, power is to be concentrated in the hands of the majority. This implies that a party should not gain control over policymaking power until it obtains 50 percent of the vote. In effect, a party with less than 50 percent of the vote should have no policymaking power, whereas a party with more than 50 percent of the vote should have all the policymaking power (at least until the next election). In contrast to the majoritarian vision, power is to be dispersed among as many political actors as possible in the consensus vision. Indeed, power is supposed to be distributed among political actors in direct proportion to their electoral size. As a result, in the consensus vision of democracy there should be a close connection between the percentage of votes that a party wins and the percentage of policymaking power that it enjoys. In Figure 15.3, we graphically illustrate the two ideals of responsiveness outlined by the majoritarian and consensus visions of democracy (adapted from Powell 2000, 126). As you can see, they are very different.

| FIGURE 15.3 | **Two Ideals of Democratic Responsiveness (percent)** |

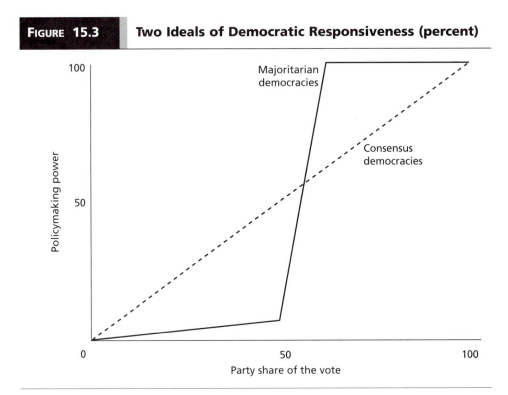

How well do majoritarian and proportional democracies approximate their respective ideals of democratic responsiveness? In line with the majoritarian vision of democratic responsiveness, most governments in majoritarian democracies are single-party majority governments that dominate the policymaking process. The problem, as we saw earlier, is that many of these single-party majority governments do not actually obtain a majority of the votes. Thus, all we can really say is that the party that wins the most votes almost always gets to form the government and control the levers of power in majoritarian democracies. As Powell (2000, 129) notes, "Analysts and defenders of the majoritarian vision . . . are seldom inhibited from replacing expectations about majorities with expectations about pluralities." It is not clear whether this "inhibition" is appropriate, and we leave this judgment call up to the reader. Perhaps we should simply say that majoritarian democracies are fully responsive when the party with a majority of the votes controls the government, and they are only partially responsive when the party with a mere plurality of the votes controls the government.[14]

Consensus democracies come close to approximating their ideals on responsiveness in some respects but not others. On the one hand, the fact that consensus democracies employ proportional electoral rules means that there tends to be a close connection between the percentage of votes that a party wins at election time and the percentage of legislative seats that it obtains. On the other hand, the complicated nature of the government formation process means that there is only a weak connection between the percentage of seats (and votes) that a party wins and its share of government power. For example, it is not always the case that the largest party in the legislature is in the government. It is important to remember, though, that consensus democracies do not concentrate power entirely in the hands of the government; instead, they disperse it (to differing degrees) among both governmental and nongovernmental parties. One way in which they do this is by having legislative committees on which opposition parties receive representation play a significant role in the policymaking process or by having corporatist interest group relations. Powell (2000) ultimately finds that consensus democracies come close to satisfying their ideals of responsiveness if one focuses on the actual policymaking power of political parties as opposed to simply looking at whether these parties are in the government or not. The bottom line is that both majoritarian and consensus democracies come close to, but fall short of, realizing their ideals of democratic responsiveness.

Whereas responsiveness is a *dynamic* measure of representation, congruence is a *static* measure of representation. For democratic theorists of most persuasions, congruence is an important characteristic to be encouraged—democratic governments and legislatures are

---

14. Of course, it does sometimes happen that the translation of votes into seats in a majoritarian democracy results in a situation in which the party with the most votes is not the party with the most legislative seats. This is a more troubling phenomenon from the perspective of the majoritarian vision of democracy. If this situation arises too frequently, it can undermine the voters' faith in the responsiveness generated by the electoral system. Powell (2000, 130) estimates that this type of scenario occurred in about 20 percent of the forty-five elections in the six majoritarian democracies that he examines in his book.

supposed to reflect the preferences of their citizens (Mill [1861] 1991; Dahl 1956; Pitkin 1967).[15] The simplest way to think about congruence is to think of a single citizen and a single representative. In this situation, congruence is just the proximity or absolute distance between the ideological positions of the citizen and the representative. The closer the representative is to the ideological position of the citizen, the higher the level of congruence. Most comparative scholars, though, focus on how congruent governments are with the preferences of their citizens. In most cases, scholars simply conceptualize congruence in regard to the ideological distance between the government and the median citizen. Theoretically, high levels of congruence could be achieved in both majoritarian and consensus democracies. For example, we should observe the two parties in the ideal majoritarian democracy converge to the position of the median voter (see Box 10.1, "The Median Voter Theorem and Party Competition"). Thus, congruence should be high. In a consensus democracy, the party closest to the median voter is likely to play an important role in the government formation process and, therefore, pull government policy toward the policy position of the median voter. Again, this should result in relatively high levels of congruence. Empirically, however, most studies suggest that governments are more congruent with the ideological preferences of the people in consensus democracies than in majoritarian democracies (Huber and Powell 1994; Powell 2000, 2006; Powell and Vanberg 2000; McDonald, Mendes, and Budge 2004; McDonald and Budge 2005).[16]

A slightly different way to approach the question of congruence is to shift the focus from the government to the legislature and ask how accurately the legislature as a collectivity reflects the ideological positions of the citizens. For example, if 10 percent of the population holds Communist policy preferences, is there a Communist Party that holds 10 percent of the legislative seats, and so on. As we saw earlier, having a legislature that is a miniature reflection of the society as a whole is an important objective of consensus democracies but not majoritarian ones. One simple way to conceptualize this type of ideological congruence is by the similarity between the distributions of citizen and representative preferences—the greater the similarity across the two distributions of preferences, the higher the level of congruence. In line with the consensus vision of democracy, a study by Golder and Stramski (2007) finds that legislatures in countries that employ proportional electoral rules (consen-

---

15. Although congruence is desired by most democratic theorists, they frequently disagree as to the exact form that congruence should take. Some emphasize the importance of "descriptive representation"; that is, how accurately legislatures and governments mirror the gender or racial makeup of the citizenry (Mansbridge 1999; Gay 2001; Pantoja and Segura 2003; Atkeson and Carillo 2007; Karp and Banducci 2007). Others emphasize "substantive representation"; that is, how accurately legislatures and governments mirror the ideological makeup of the citizenry (Huber and Powell 1994; Powell 2000, 2006; Powell and Vanberg 2000; McDonald, Mendes, and Budge 2004; McDonald and Budge 2005; Blais and Bodet 2006; Budge and McDonald 2007; Golder and Stramski 2007). In what follows, we focus on congruence in regard to substantive representation.

16. Two new studies (Blais and Bodet 2006; Golder and Stramski 2007) have challenged what appeared to be a growing empirical consensus that consensus democracies produce more ideological congruence between governments and their citizens.

sus democracies) do tend to more accurately reflect the diversity of ideological opinions in society than legislatures in countries that employ majoritarian electoral rules (majoritarian democracies).

A consensus has emerged in recent years that democracies employing majoritarian institutions are better at promoting mandates, accountability, government identifiability, clarity of responsibility, and the like, whereas democracies employing consensus institutions are superior at dispersing power, providing choice, and generating ideological congruence between citizens and their representatives. In effect, this consensus states that there is an explicit trade-off to be made by constitution writers when they are choosing between majoritarian and consensus institutions. For example, they can obtain high levels of government identifiability and accountability by adopting majoritarian institutions, but this may well mean sacrificing congruence between citizens and their representatives.

Throughout this section, we have focused solely on the ideal types of majoritarian and consensus democracies. A few countries, however, employ a mixture of majoritarian and consensus institutions. The most common institutional departure from the pure majoritarian and consensus models of democracy involves the choice of whether to adopt parliamentarism or presidentialism. For example, some democracies that have primarily majoritarian institutions happen to be presidential. As shown by the Belgian case discussed earlier, the converse is also true. It is not unusual, for example, for countries that have primarily consensus institutions to be parliamentary rather than presidential, even though parliamentarism is the more majoritarian of the two regime types.

The United States is probably the best example of a hybrid between the two ideal types of democracy. On the one hand, the United States is an extremely majoritarian democracy in its electoral system, its party system, its government type, and its interest group relations. On the other hand, the United States is an extremely consensus-oriented democracy in that it has constitutional review and it is presidential, federal, and bicameral. We leave it to you to evaluate the quality of democracy in the United States. One could imagine an argument that holds that the trade-off between accountability and representation implied by the choice between majoritarian and consensus institutions is optimized by systems that combine some majoritarian institutions with some consensus ones. There is, however, no consensus on this among scholars. Some see such combinations as "the best of both worlds," whereas others are frustrated by polities that are "neither fish, nor fowl."

From a normative standpoint, you probably have your own preferences by now for whether a country should adopt majoritarian or consensus institutions. If you are having trouble deciding which type of democracy you would recommend to the framers of a new constitution (should you find yourself in a position to be making such recommendations), however, perhaps you need some information about the substantive consequences that are likely to follow from the institutional choices that you would make. In the following three sections, we examine the effects of different institutional choices on economic policy, ethnic conflict, and democratic stability.

THE EFFECT OF POLITICAL INSTITUTIONS ON FISCAL POLICY

There is an extremely large and expanding literature on the effect of institutions on economic policies and economic outcomes. Anything like an adequate review of this important topic would cover at least a whole book. Thus, we focus our attention in this section on the effects of democratic institutions on fiscal policy. **Fiscal policy** refers to the set of government policies related to the raising of revenues through taxation and to the set of policies accomplished through government spending.

Fiscal policy involves the manipulation of tax and spending decisions to accomplish governmental goals.

Historically, policymakers during the Great Depression of the 1930s began to view fiscal policy through what is known as a Keynesian perspective.[17] **Keynesianism,** named after the British economist John Maynard Keynes (1883–1946), is a particular view of how governments can use fiscal policy (taxing and spending) and monetary policy (interest rates and the supply of money) to control the trajectory of their economies. The essence of Keynesian economic policymaking is the idea that economies naturally experience cycles of booms and busts because of fluctuations in the demand for the goods and services an economy produces. When overall, or "aggregate," demand for the goods and services an economy produces goes down, the economy sinks into a recession, national income goes down, and unemployment increases. In contrast, when aggregate demand increases rapidly, the result is inflation—a rise in the general level of prices—because, according to Keynesians, increased demand "bids up" prices. Inflation is considered to be an economic problem because all prices are not likely to change in lock step and, as a result, uncertainty about relative prices increases. This increase in uncertainty can discourage saving and investing, which are key sources of economic growth.[18] Keynesian economics essentially promised to help governments smooth out these "boom and bust" cycles through the use of "counter-cyclical demand management."

Keynesianism is a particular view of how to use fiscal policy (taxing and spending) and monetary policy (interest rates and the supply of money) to smooth out boom and bust cycles in the economy through countercyclical demand management.

Prior to Keynesianism, the so-called "classical school" of economics held that these economic fluctuations would sort themselves out and that the economy would reach equilibrium on its own in the long run. In response to this argument, John Maynard Keynes ([1923] 2000, chap. 3) quipped that "in the long run, we are all dead"—meaning that while the economy was sorting itself out, a good deal of human suffering was likely to occur. Keynes argued that much of this suffering could be alleviated if governments "leaned against" the economy. During recessions, the government ought to use fiscal and monetary policy to stimulate aggregate demand, and during boom periods the government could avoid inflation by restricting aggregate demand. Fiscal policy could be used toward this end if the government cut taxes or increased government spending (or both) during economic downturns and took

---

17. See Hall (1989) for an excellent introduction to the way Keynesianism came to influence government policy.

18. Inflation also has important distributional consequences. The value of people's savings erodes; but so does the value of people's debts. Consequently, net creditors are hurt more by inflation than net debtors (who may actually be helped).

the opposite actions when the economy was thought to be heating up. Similarly, monetary policy could influence aggregate demand in a countercyclical fashion if interest rates were lowered and the money supply expanded during economic downturns, and if interest rates were raised and the money supply contracted as the economy neared the top end of the business cycle. Keynesianism held that if the manipulation of monetary and fiscal policy instruments was timed just right, governments could smooth out the business cycle and provide a foundation for high levels of growth and low levels of unemployment and inflation.

Keynesianism has been criticized on both theoretical and empirical grounds, but its influence over economic policy for more than half of the twentieth century cannot be debated. Indeed, its influence continues to this day. The utility of Keynesianism as a way of explaining macroeconomic behavior is, though, not our direct concern here. Instead, we are interested in understanding if and how the political institutions that we examined in Chapters 11–14 influence the way that governments manipulate the economic policy tools at their disposal. To examine these questions, we adopt what is known as a *political economy* approach. A political economy approach to understanding the political sources of economic policy is based on the recognition of two fundamental assumptions: (a) economic policy is typically made by elected officials (or technocrats appointed by elected officials) who may have goals other than the provision of "stable growth," and (b) economic policies tend to have distributional consequences—that is, they do not affect all citizens in the same way. These two assumptions are central to almost all attempts to understand economic policy and outcomes from a political economy perspective.

In contrast to the political economy perspective, traditional, or "welfare," economics typically assumes that economic policy is made by a "benevolent social planner"—a hypothetical policymaker who weighs the interests of all members of society and chooses the policies that best meet the needs of society as a whole. Because the benevolent social planner is a single individual, the problems that arise from group decision making, such as those we examined in Chapter 10, are assumed away. According to the political economy perspective adopted here, though, economic policy is fraught with conflicts of interests—between the government and citizens, between citizens themselves, and between members of the government representing different groups of citizens—that should not be assumed away. Although these conflicts of interest arise in all areas of macroeconomic policymaking, we restrict our attention in this section of the chapter to fiscal policy. We do this partly because of space limitations but also because fiscal policy is often explicitly used for the purpose of redistribution, because the raising of revenues is central to what it means to be a state, as we saw in Chapter 4, and because fiscal policy is frequently used as a measure of the overall size of government.

According to the traditional view of Keynesianism, governments everywhere should act essentially in the same way—during bad times they should cut taxes and increase spending in an attempt to put resources in the hands of consumers and, therefore, stimulate demand. And during economic booms they should take the opposite position—restrict demand by raising taxes and decreasing spending. A look at the real world, however, suggests that there is a tremendous amount of cross-national variation in fiscal policy. In Figure 15.4, we present a "box and whisker plot" showing how total public fiscal activity—central government revenue and expenditures as a percentage of GDP—varies both within and between twenty-one advanced industrialized countries from 1947 to 1997 (Franzese 2002, 16). The black dots indicate the average level of total public fiscal activity for each country; the "boxes" and "whiskers" display how the level of total public fiscal activity varied within each country during the postwar period. When the boxes stay close to the country average, as in the United States and Switzerland, it means that total fiscal policy varied little during the postwar period. In contrast, when the boxes are large, as in Belgium, the Netherlands, and Sweden, it means that total fiscal activity varied quite a bit in that country. The "whiskers," or vertical black lines, indicate the maximum and minimum levels of total public fiscal activity in each country during the postwar period. The main thing to note from Figure 15.4 is that there is considerable cross-national variation in the level of fiscal activity. For example, in many countries, such as the United States, Japan, Canada, Spain, and Switzerland, the total fiscal

FIGURE 15.4 — **Total Public Fiscal Activity in Twenty-one OECD Countries, 1947–1997**

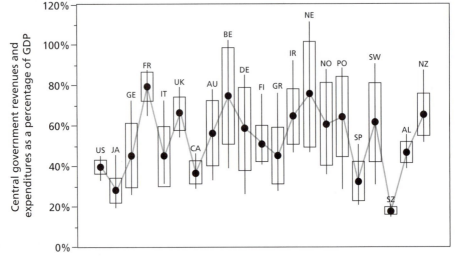

Source: Franzese (2002, 16).

Note: AL = Australia; AU = Austria; BE = Belgium; CA = Canada; DE = Denmark; FI = Finland; FR = France; GE = Germany; GR = Greece; IR = Ireland; IT = Italy; JA = Japan; NE = Netherlands; NO = Norway; NZ = New Zealand; PO = Portugal; SP = Spain; SW = Sweden; SZ = Switzerland; UK = United Kingdom; US = United States. The black dots indicate the mean level of total public fiscal activity for each country; the vertical black lines indicate the maximum and minimum levels of total public fiscal activity in each country; the vertical size of each box indicates one standard deviation above and below the mean in each country.

policy activity is relatively low, near or below 50 percent of GDP. And in many other countries, such as France, Belgium, and the Netherlands, the total fiscal policy activity is relatively high, above 75 percent of GDP. What explains this cross-national variation in fiscal policy? It is this question that we address in the remainder of this section. We begin by briefly examining economic and cultural determinants of fiscal policy. We then turn to our primary task, which is to examine the ways in which political institutions influence fiscal policy.

Economic and Cultural Determinants of Fiscal Policy

Total public fiscal activity is interpreted by many economists as the "size of government" because it gives an indication of the ratio of total government economic activity to overall economic activity within a country. The traditional explanation for the size of the government is "Wagner's Law," named after the German economist Adolph Wagner (1835–1917), who predicted that the size of government would grow as countries became more industrialized. Wagner's Law is often interpreted to mean that the size of government increases as countries become wealthier. In the broadest sense, Wagner's Law seems consistent with the facts—as European countries became richer and more industrialized, the role of the government in the economy did increase as predicted. For example, we illustrate in Figure 15.5 that there was, indeed, an upward trend in total public fiscal activity among Organization for Economic Cooperation and Development (OECD) countries during the postwar period, a period generally considered a time of economic growth and increased industrialization. This can be seen by looking at how the black dots, which represent the OECD average level of total public fiscal activity in each year, rise over time. Note, though, that not only do the black dots rise over time, but so do the lengths of the "boxes" and "whiskers." This indicates that not only did the mean level of government fiscal activity among OECD countries increase during the postwar period, but so did the cross-national variance in the level of government fiscal activity.[19] Wagner's Law does not provide a straightforward explanation for this continued and increasing variation in the level of fiscal activity across countries that, in regard to wealth and industrialization, were probably becoming increasingly similar over time (Li and Papell 1999; Le Pen 2005).

What might explain this cross-national variation in the level of fiscal activity? One explanation that has been offered as an improvement over Wagner's Law emphasizes the conflicts that exist between citizens over fiscal policy. Recall from our discussion of the Meltzer-Richard model in Chapter 9 that there are good reasons to believe that citizens will differ systematically in their views about fiscal policy (Meltzer and Richard 1981). One way to think about this is to consider what would happen in a hypothetical world in which the government taxed every citizen at the same rate ($0 < t < 1$) and then turned around and trans-

---

19. Franzese (2002) suggests that this increased variation in the level of total public fiscal activity is the result of governments' choosing very different ways to respond to the oil crises of the 1970s.

FIGURE 15.5	**Total Public Fiscal Activity by Year in Twenty-one OECD Countries, 1947–1997**

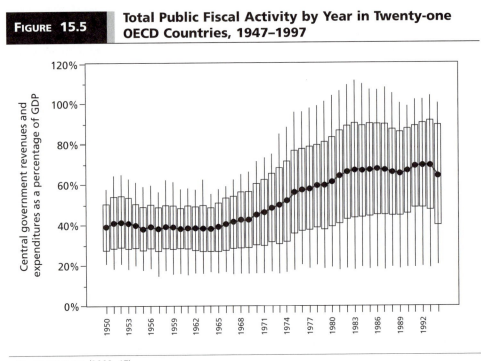

Source: Franzese (2002, 17).

Note: The black dots indicate the mean level of total public fiscal activity for each country; the vertical black lines indicate the maximum and minimum levels of total public fiscal activity in each country; the vertical size of each box indicates one standard deviation above and below the mean in each country.

ferred all tax revenues in the form of an equal subsidy (*s*) to every citizen. You can think of the subsidy that each citizen (*i*) receives as the dollar value that the citizen places on the public goods provided by the state. Because taxes are taken from citizens as a rate, the tax bill of each citizen (*T*) will be an increasing function of her gross income (y_i):

$$T = y_i t.$$

That is, although all citizens pay the same share of their income in taxes, those with large incomes will have larger tax bills than those with low incomes. This means that the overall benefit (*B*) of living under a particular tax and transfer system for citizen *i* will be:

$$B_i = y_i + s - y_i t.$$

If an individual's income is unrelated to the tax rate, by which we mean that taxes are *non-distortionary* in that they do not change an individual's level of income by affecting the trade-offs they make between work and leisure, then the citizen will be concerned only with the net effect of the government's tax and transfer regime ($s - y_i t$).

If we assume, for the purposes of illustration, that the government budget must be balanced over the medium run (that is, that the total subsidies paid out to the citizens must equal the total taxes collected from the citizens), then some citizens will be net recipients and some citizens will be net contributors to the government's tax and transfer system. In Figure 15.6, we plot the tax bill paid and the subsidy received by citizens at different levels of income for a given tax rate and subsidy size.[20] In this economy, the citizen earning slightly more than $20,000, which is the average income in our hypothetical example, is indifferent with respect to the tax and transfer regime—her tax bill is exactly equal to the subsidy she receives from the government.[21] All citizens with below-average incomes are net recipients—they receive more in subsidies than they pay in taxes. All citizens with above-average incomes are net contributors to the tax and transfer scheme—they pay more in taxes than they receive in subsidies.

The distributional implications of this particular tax and transfer system are clear. Low-income citizens (to the left of the vertical dotted line in Figure 15.6) are net recipients of the tax and transfer system and high-income citizens (to the right of the vertical dotted line) are net contributors. Consequently, citizens with high incomes would prefer a system with a tax rate of zero and no subsidies. In contrast, citizens with low incomes are quite happy with this tax and transfer system; in fact, low-income citizens can be expected to support even higher tax rates because they would get the full benefit (B) of a more aggressive tax and transfer system but pay only a fraction of the cost ($y_i t$). Put differently, the tax rate in our economy determines the slope of the line in Figure 15.6. If the tax rate goes up, then the slope of the "Tax bill" line increases (gets steeper). This results in an increase in the size of the net *benefits* going to citizens who have an income below the national average but an increase in the size of the net *contributions* paid by citizens who have an income above the national average.

The analysis so far helps to show that fiscal policy preferences are likely to be related to one's income. High-income voters are likely to be less enthusiastic about increased taxation and spending than low-income voters. Some readers may be concerned that this result is derived from a model that differs in substantial ways from most observed tax and transfer systems in the real world. For example, real-world taxation systems do not apply a single tax rate to all earners. Similarly, governments do not spend equally on all members of society— some individuals receive more government services, subsidies, and so on, than others. These observations, however, do not challenge the usefulness of the analysis presented here unless it can be shown that changing our assumptions to reflect these realities changes our conclusions in a fundamental fashion. Although it is true that governments tend to choose differ-

---

20. In our specific hypothetical example, the tax rate is 20 percent and the subsidy is $4,100 dollars. We should note, however, that any numbers would produce similar figures as long as subsidies weren't so high compared with revenues that everyone was a net recipient, which would produce unsustainable deficits, or tax rates weren't so high that everyone was a net contributor, which might lead to either a tax revolt or costly repression (Levi 1988).

21. The fact that the average earner breaks even in our example is a result of the assumption that the budget must balance.

FIGURE 15.6	The Relationship between Income, Taxes, and Government Subsidies in a Hypothetical Tax and Transfer System (thousands of dollars)

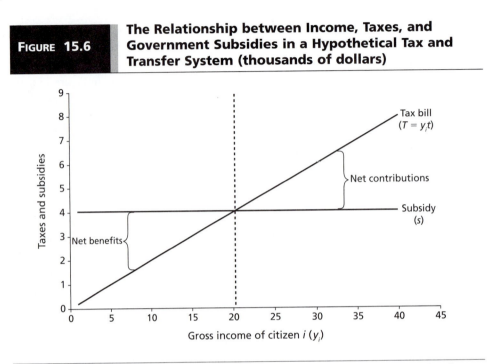

Note: Subsidy (*s*) = the total subsidy awarded to citizen *i*; tax bill ($T = y_i t$) = the total tax paid by citizen *i*.

ent tax rates and subsidies for voters at different levels of income, the standard pattern is for tax rates to be progressive—that is, high-income earners typically face higher tax rates than low-income earners. Similarly, many government-spending programs are aimed at citizens with below-average income. The first of these insights would have the consequence of causing the line plotting individual tax bills in Figure 15.6 to curve upward as income increases. The second insight—that spending tends to be targeted at low-income voters—would have the consequence of causing the line plotting subsidies awarded to citizens to slope downward as income increases. Neither of these changes would alter the central result of our analysis that tax and spend systems necessarily divide the population into net contributors and net recipients, and that rich voters tend to fall in the former category and poor voters tend to fall in the latter category. The only tax and transfer systems that would not have this characteristic would be ones in which the tax system was regressive (the rich taxed at a lower rate than the poor), subsidies went disproportionately to the rich, or there was no budget constraint so that subsidies could be so large that all citizens were "net recipients." Nothing like these systems is observed in modern polities.[22]

22. One might think of a possible exception with respect to the last of these scenarios. For example, some oil-rich countries give out large subsidies to all citizens, thereby making large portions of the citizenry net recipients. But even here the subsidy given to all citizens is likely to be smaller than the tax bill of the richest citizens, and so the point of intersection of the lines in Figure 15.6 would move upward and to the right, but the general pattern of the lines would probably remain the same.

The Meltzer-Richard model predicts that the greater the income inequality in society, the greater the demand from citizens for a large tax and transfer system.[23] In the context of the current setup, we can better understand the Meltzer-Richard model by asking what would happen if actors at different income levels could dictate fiscal policy. The voter with the average income would be indifferent between the existing tax and transfer system and one in which the tax rate and subsidies are both zero. Voters with more income than the average-income earner would be increasingly anxious to *lower* taxes and subsidies. And voters with less income than the average-income earner would be increasingly anxious to *raise* taxes and subsidies. The Meltzer-Richard model shows why preferences over tax rates will be a function of a voter's income, and it assumes that the median voter, who is the citizen with the *median* income, will get to dictate fiscal policy. Because every country in the world has some degree of income inequality—there is a relatively small number of citizens at the top end of the income scale and a relatively large number of individuals at the bottom end of the income scale—the *median* voter always has less income than the *average*-income earner (he is always to the left of the vertical dashed line in Figure 15.6). As a result, the median voter is always a net recipient of redistributive taxation and is, therefore, enthusiastic about increased spending and the taxes that make such spending possible. The more income inequality there is in society (the greater the income gap between the median voter and the average income earner), the more enthusiastic the median voter will be for a large tax and transfer system.

As you can see, the Meltzer-Richard model helps us move toward an explanation of the cross-national variation in total fiscal policy activity—total fiscal policy activity increases with the level of income inequality in a country. Like Wagner's Law, however, the explanation provided by the Meltzer-Richard model is incomplete. Although there is a growing consensus that voter preferences over fiscal policy are likely to be tied to the voters' income levels, it is important to recognize that these preferences affect policy only after they are filtered through political institutions. Consider the implicit assumption in the Meltzer-Richard model that all earners vote. This assumption is contradicted by numerous empirical studies showing that high-income earners are much more likely to vote than low-income earners (Wolfinger and Rosenstone 1980; Leighley and Nagler 1992). Some studies have found little evidence for the positive association between income inequality and larger tax and transfer systems predicted by the Meltzer-Richard model (Iversen and Soskice 2006), but this may be because high-income earners are much more likely to turn out to vote than low-income earners and because voter turnout varies across countries. The fact that high-income earners are more likely to turn out than low-income earners means that the income gap between the average income *earner* and the median *voter* is likely to be smaller than the income gap between the average-income earner and the median-income earner. As a result, the demand for redistribution in the real world is likely to be smaller than that predicted in the Meltzer-

---

23. See also Romer (1975).

Richard model. In addition, since voter turnout is known to vary systematically across countries, the Meltzer-Richard model can be expected to fit the data better in high-turnout countries than in low-turnout countries. In fact, Franzese (2002, 62–125) finds support for exactly this when he examines the interaction between voter participation and income inequality in predicting total fiscal policy activity in OECD countries. Specifically, he finds that the effect of income inequality on the size of the tax and transfer system is largest when voter participation is high. This suggests that institutional factors that influence voter turnout, such as compulsory voting, voter registration rules, and the proportionality of the electoral system, should also have an influence on fiscal policy.

The connection between the proportionality of the electoral system and voter turnout might require a word of explanation. As we saw in Chapters 12 and 13, single-member district plurality electoral systems tend to reward candidates from large parties and punish candidates from small parties. As a result, voters who support a party that is unpopular in their district are likely to either vote strategically for a second-choice party or abstain from voting altogether. Consequently, voter participation rates tend to be higher in PR systems than in SMDP systems (Powell 1982). It is for this reason that we might expect total fiscal policy activity to be larger in countries with PR systems than in countries with plurality electoral laws. Although there is a growing consensus that PR electoral rules are linked with higher fiscal activity, as we will see, there is little agreement among scholars about exactly why this is the case.

So far, we have examined an argument that says that voters will differ in their evaluation of fiscal policy based on their incomes. High-income voters will seek to reduce the size of government, and low-income voters will seek to expand it. The Meltzer-Richard model, in essence, predicts that the size of the state will vary across countries and time as the size of these groups varies. Where income inequality is high, there are many more poor voters than rich voters and the state will, therefore, be large; conversely, where income inequality is low, there are relatively few poor voters compared with rich voters and the state will, therefore, be small. One problem with this approach is that it implicitly assumes that voter preferences are frictionlessly translated into fiscal policy. If, however, voter preferences are refracted through political institutions in complex ways, fiscal policy may have as much to do with cross-national differences in political institutions as it has to do with the distribution of voter preferences. As we learned in Chapter 13, voter preferences are typically aggregated through political parties. So one way to put a little bit of institutional structure on the Meltzer-Richard model is to ask what would happen if there were competing teams of candidates (political parties) that claimed to represent different segments of the income spectrum. This is exactly the approach taken by what is known as the **partisan model of macroeconomic policy.**

According to the partisan model of macroeconomic policy, left-wing parties represent the interests of low-income voters and right-wing parties represent the interests of high-income voters. The main prediction of the partisan model is that changes in the partisan control of the government will lead to changes in fiscal policy. Specifically, left-wing governments are expected to be associated with a higher level of total fiscal policy activity and they are also likely to be associated with "expansionary" fiscal policies in general because such policies are thought to be favored by left-wing voters (Hibbs 1977).[24] Because space constraints prevent a review of the extensive literature aimed at testing various versions of the partisan model, we will simply state that the empirical evidence is somewhat mixed. Some scholars find evidence that left-wing parties do, indeed, adopt more expansionary fiscal policies than right-wing governments; some scholars find no rela-

> The **partisan model of macroeconomic policy** argues that left-wing parties represent the interests of low-income voters and that right-wing parties represent the interests of high-income voters. The main prediction of the partisan model is that changes in the partisan control of the government will lead to predictable changes in fiscal policy.

tionship between the partisan orientation of the government and fiscal policy; and some find evidence that, if anything, right-wing governments are more expansionary than left-wing governments. Of course, difficulty in establishing a difference in fiscal policy behavior between left- and right-wing governments is not evidence in and of itself that these parties—and the voters they represent—do not wish to implement different policies. It may very well be the case that they would like to implement different fiscal policies but that the vagaries of political competition or the "structural dependence of the state on capital" (as discussed in Chapter 9) prevent them from effectively acting on these desires. In the former case, perhaps competition between the parties in a country leads parties of all stripes to reluctantly choose policies to win the support of the median voter. If this is true, then parties representing different constituencies may act very much the same.

Of course, there is the possibility that the relative policy preferences (income position) of the median voter might differ from one country to the next. If the median voter is farther to the left in some countries and this results in left-wing parties being in government more frequently in these countries, then we might expect to see evidence for a *cross-national* version of the partisan model. In other words, one version of the partisan model is about the differences in macroeconomic policy between parties *within* nations and another version is about the differences in macroeconomic policy between parties *across* nations. In a seminal article in the study of the politics of macroeconomic policy, David Cameron (1978) presents evidence to support the cross-national version of the partisan model. In Figure 15.7, we reproduce a scatter plot from Cameron's article showing a positive association between the percentage of the government's electoral base composed of left-wing parties between 1960 and 1975 and the growth of government revenues as a share of GDP during the same period. As you can see, Sweden and the United States represent polar extremes. Sweden was ruled by a left-wing party during the whole period (the Swedish Social Democratic Party) and it experienced a 20 percentage point increase in government revenues as a share of GDP. In contrast, the United States was ruled by a right-wing party during the whole period and it expe-

---

24. For a critical review of the partisan model of fiscal policy, see Clark (2003, 41–84).

| FIGURE 15.7 | The Partisan Composition of Government and the Expansion of the Public Economy, 1960–1975 (percent) |

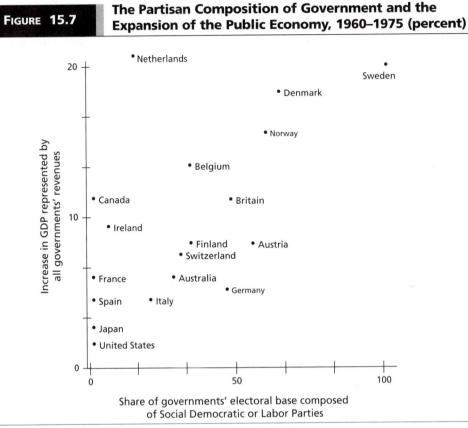

Source: Cameron (1978, 1255, fig. 1).

rienced almost no growth in government revenues as a share of GDP.[25] Between these two extremes in fiscal policy, there is a fairly close relationship between the percentage of time that a country experiences left-wing rule and increases in the size of government.[26]

The cross-national version of the partisan model suggests that cross-national differences in the partisan composition of governments reflect cross-national differences in voter preferences. So far we have presented very little evidence that voters' preferences vary across countries and, if it exists, we have little theory to explain this variance. Some scholars have suggested, however, that the absence of a "European style" welfare state in the United States can be explained by differing attitudes toward the poor in Europe and the United States. Alesina,

---

25. Like many comparativists, Cameron (1978, 1248 n. 12) considers both the Republican and Democratic Parties in the United States to be "center-right" parties compared with the parties in other developed democracies.

26. Canada, Ireland, and the Netherlands don't quite fit the pattern—they experienced a larger growth in the size of the government than the partisan composition of their governments would predict.

Glaeser, and Sacerdote (2001), for example, use data from the World Values Survey to show that Europeans are twice as likely as Americans to say they believe the poor are trapped in poverty, and almost twice as likely to say that luck determines income. Americans are twice as likely as Europeans to say that the poor are lazy. And Europeans are twice as likely as Americans to self-identify as leftists. To some extent, these data, which are shown in Table 15.3, suggest that differences in attitudes toward the poor might be what is driving broad differences in the left-right placement of citizens between the United States and Europe. Although there is some truth to this, Alesina, Glaeser, and Sacerdote note that things are more complicated when we look at the individual level rather than the national level. It appears that many Europeans who are not leftists hold what might be thought of as charitable views toward the poor; indeed, the number of people holding these views is about twice as large as the number identifying as leftists.

There are at least two possible explanations for the lack of a close link at the individual level between attitudes toward the poor and self-identification as a leftist. One is that the presence of a large number of leftists in a country may shift the terms of debate about welfare in such a way that the attitudes they hold about the poor come to be accepted by some non-leftists as well. The second is that leftists may not have a monopoly on these attitudes about the poor. In most European countries, for example, there are parties and substantial numbers of voters that ascribe to what are sometimes called "Christian democratic" attitudes. Christian democrats often espouse a form of conservatism, not often articulated in the United States, which combines interventionist social welfare attitudes with morally conservative views on social issues. Thus, it may be that the large number of non-leftist Europeans expressing "charitable" views to the poor are Christian democrats.[27] For this reason, many careful studies of the partisan sources of fiscal policy divide parties into three categories—right-wing, left-wing, and Christian democratic—and typically expect parties of the last two varieties to act alike (for example, Huber, Ragin, and Stephens 1993).

TABLE 15.3 — European and American Attitudes toward the Poor (percent)		
Item	**European Union**	**United States**
Believe poor are trapped in poverty	60	29
Believe luck determines income	54	30
Believe the poor are lazy	26	60
Identify themselves as on the left of the political spectrum	30	17

Source: World Values Survey data from 1981–1997 as reported in Alesina, Glaeser, and Sacerdote (2001, table 13).

---

27. See Kalyvas (1996) for an explanation of the rise of Christian Democratic parties in Europe and their relationship to traditional conservative parties.

There is also some empirical evidence that attitudes toward the poor are associated with fiscal policy that goes beyond the United States–European comparison that we have just presented. In Figure 15.8, we reproduce a scatter plot from Alesina, Glaeser, and Sacerdote (2001) showing the relationship between the national average response concerning the belief that luck determines income and the national average share of GDP devoted to social spending. Although there is considerable variation in social spending for any given set of beliefs, countries in which relatively few people believe that income is determined by luck have substantially lower levels of social spending and, with the exception of Portugal and Brazil, countries in which most people believe income is determined by luck have substantially higher levels of social spending. Overall, the data presented by Alesina, Glaeser, and Sacerdote (2001) suggest that fiscal policy is influenced not only by economic factors, such as income inequality, but also by cultural factors, such as attitudes toward the poor and beliefs about the extent to which luck determines income.

| FIGURE 15.8 | **Relationship between Social Spending and the Belief that Luck Determines Income** |

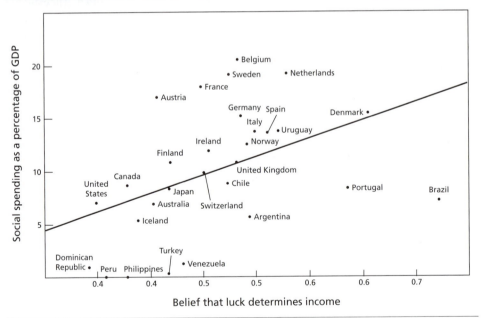

Source: Alesina, Glaeser, and Sacerdote (2001, 244).

Note: Social spending as a percentage of GDP is the average for the 1960–1998 period; the belief that luck determines income is the mean value for a country, measured as an index from 0 to 1, for the 1981–1997 period.

We now turn to an examination of how political institutions influence fiscal policy. In particular, we focus on the relationship between electoral laws and fiscal policy.

How Electoral Laws Influence Fiscal Policy

Over the last decade or so, a steady stream of research has sought to explain that fiscal policy in countries that employ PR electoral systems differs from that in countries that employ majoritarian electoral systems. In particular, this scholarship has sought to explain why PR systems appear to be associated with more public goods, larger and more redistributive social welfare programs, and a larger overall size of government than majoritarian systems (Iversen and Soskice 2006; Persson and Tabellini 2004). Although there is a growing consensus that fiscal policy activity is higher in countries that employ PR electoral systems, there is little agreement as to exactly why this is the case. In what follows, we present three sets of arguments linking fiscal policy to the electoral laws employed in a country. The first set of arguments states that proportional representation election laws influence the amount of redistribution that governments engage in because it facilitates the election of left-wing governments. The second set of arguments states that fiscal policy is different under different electoral systems because some electoral systems encourage targeted spending in small districts, whereas others encourage spending on broader public goods. The third set of arguments states that proportional representation encourages government spending through its effect on the number of parties in government.

Proportional Representation Leads to More Redistribution by Facilitating the Election of Left-wing Governments

Although it is important to look at the way cross-national differences in attitudes affect the propensity to elect left-wing governments, as we saw earlier, many scholars have suggested that electoral laws may play an important role in determining the partisan composition of governments. Specifically, several studies have argued that proportional representation electoral systems encourage the election of left-wing governments and that majoritarian electoral systems encourage the election of right-wing governments (Iversen and Soskice 2006; Rodden 2006).

Rodden (2006) argues that electoral institutions influence "who rules" because of the geographic distribution of support for left-wing parties and the way electoral laws overlay this geographic distribution. He points out that left-wing parties have traditionally drawn their electoral support from concentrated pockets of voters in urban industrial areas and mining centers. This geographic concentration of support for left-wing parties is the product of industrialization in an era when transportation costs were sufficiently high that workers needed to live close to where they worked. This pattern of left-wing support has persisted, even after such large-scale social changes in recent decades as de-industrialization and gentrification. As Rodden (2006, 2) puts it, "Densely populated manufacturing and mining regions vote overwhelmingly for parties of the left and less industrial and rural areas for parties of the right throughout Europe, even in many settings where cities are affluent and rural areas are mired in poverty." Right-wing parties, in contrast, tend to draw their voters from a much broader geographic base. The higher geographic concentration of left-wing support, Rodden argues, is a much greater liability in single-member district plurality electoral systems than in PR systems. This is because of the distortionary effects of SMDP that we examined in Chapter 13. In Chapter 13, we emphasized that votes for a losing party in a district were, in a sense, wasted because they contributed nothing to the party's representation in the legislature. Rodden's argument emphasizes that votes can also be wasted in districts where parties succeed. In SMDP systems, the best a party can do in a particular district is to elect a single representative and to do so it merely needs to win more votes than any other party. Any additional votes are "surplus" and they contribute nothing to enhancing the party's control of the legislature. Consequently, if support for left-wing parties is more geographically concentrated than support for right-wing parties, then left-wing parties will be electorally competitive in a smaller number of districts than right-wing parties, and a larger number of left-wing votes will be wasted than right-wing votes. In contrast, in PR systems, seats in legislatures are distributed in a manner that reflects underlying electoral support, and thus fewer votes are wasted and the bias for right-wing parties caused by left-wing geographic concentration is reduced (or even disappears).

There is, in fact, a strong association between the type of electoral system in a country and the propensity for left-wing parties to win enough seats in the legislature to control the government. In Table 15.4, we present data from seventeen advanced industrialized democracies between 1945 and 1998 showing that a left-wing government was in power about three-quarters of the observed time in countries with PR systems, but only one-quarter of the observed time in countries with majoritarian electoral systems (Iverson and Soskice 2006). Note that we are not necessarily claiming that the electoral system *causes* left-wing electoral success but merely that the two go together. This is important because several scholars have pointed out that ruling elites in European countries in which left-wing parties were strong replaced their majoritarian electoral systems at the beginning of the twentieth century with proportional ones (Boix 1999). This suggests that the causal relationship between PR and left-wing electoral success may run in both directions—countries in which left-wing parties are strong have tended to adopt PR and PR, in turn, is likely to reinforce the representation of left-wing parties in government.

| TABLE 15.4 | Electoral Systems and the Number of Years with Left and Right Governments, 1945–1998 |

Electoral system	Government partisanship		Proportion of left governments
	Left	Right	
Proportional	342	120	0.74
Majoritarian	86	256	0.25

Source: Iversen and Soskice (2006, fig. 1).
Note: Data are from seventeen advanced industrialized democracies; centrist governments have not been included.

Rodden argues that the electoral system affects not only the probability of left-wing parties gaining power but also the way that left-wing parties behave once in power. Specifically, he claims that left-wing parties in SMDP systems are less aggressive in pressing for redistributive fiscal policies than they are in PR systems. The reason is that, to the extent that parties have incentives to court the median voter, parties have incentives to court the *national* median voter in PR systems but the *marginal constituency* median voter in SMDP systems. Marginal constituencies are basically constituencies in which the electoral support for the two biggest parties is evenly split. In SMDP systems, national parties have incentives to ignore voters in "safe districts"—ones where they are likely to win and ones that are "safe" for their competitors where they are likely to lose. Elections in SMDP systems are won and lost in marginal constituencies because that is where the "swing voters" are. Because of the geographic concentration of support for left parties mentioned earlier, the median voter in marginal constituencies is likely to be far to the right of the average voter of the left-wing party. As a result, left-wing parties in SMDP systems have an incentive to not be as redistributive in regard to fiscal policy as they would be in PR systems.

Iversen and Soskice (2006) make claims that are very much like those made by Rodden, but they provide a different causal logic. Iversen and Soskice agree that left-wing parties are likely to participate in government more frequently in PR systems than in SMDP systems. They argue, however, that this is because of the difference in coalitional bargaining across the two systems and not because of the geographic distribution of support for left-wing parties. Iversen and Soskice present a game-theoretic model in which there are three equal-size groups in society based on income level (*Low, Middle,* and *High*). According to their model, the preferred tax and transfer scheme of low-income voters is to tax the high- and middle-income groups at the highest possible rate and redistribute this wealth to themselves. The preferred tax and transfer scheme of middle-income voters is to tax the high-income group and divide this wealth between themselves and low-income voters. Finally, as in the Meltzer-Richard model, high-income voters prefer zero taxes and no redistribution.[28]

Iversen and Soskice assume that because of the reductive effect of SMDP electoral laws on the number of parties gaining representation that we outlined in Chapter 13, there will be only two parties in the legislature of SMDP systems, with the middle-income group splitting its vote between the two other income groups: some middle-income voters will form a party with low-income voters, whereas others will form a party with high-income voters. We will call the two parties in SMDP systems the *Center-Left* and *Center-Right* Parties. Median voter dynamics lead both the *Center-Left* and *Center-Right* Parties to campaign on the poli-

---

28. We should note that these policy preferences are not assumed; instead, they are derived directly from their model. Two particular assumptions of their model lead directly to the policy preferences that we outline in the text. The first assumption is that the lump sum tax on the high-income group is larger than the tax on the middle-income group, which, in turn, is larger than the tax on the low-income group. The second assumption is that the entire system is nonregressive; that is, the difference between the benefits received and the tax paid ($s - y_i t$) in our analysis at the start of this section is smallest for the high-income group and biggest for the low-income group.

cies preferred by middle-income voters. The problem is that neither the *Center-Left* nor the *Center-Right* Parties can credibly commit to implement these policies once the election is over. The problem basically arises from the fact that if middle-income voters split their support between the *Center-Left* and *Center-Right* Parties, then they will be a minority faction in each party.[29] The middle-income voters must, therefore, worry that after the election each party will implement the preferences of its majority faction.

Middle-income voters in SMDP systems are, therefore, confronted with a decision about how to vote under uncertainty. With probability p, each party will keep its campaign promise to implement policies preferred by the middle-income group: tax high-income voters and share the proceeds with low-income voters. Think of the probability p as being equal to the credibility of each party's campaign promise to implement centrist policies. With probability $1 - p$, each party will defect from its campaign promise to implement policies preferred by the middle-income group. If a party defects from its campaign promise, the *Center-Right* Party will implement policies preferred by the high-income group and the *Center-Left* Party will implement policies preferred by the low-income group. Thus, if we let L, M, and H stand for the value that middle-income voters place on the policies preferred by low-, middle-, and high-income voters, then the expected payoff to middle-income voters of *Center-Left* rule is $pM + (1 - p)L$ and the expected payoff to middle-income voters of *Center-Right* rule is $pM + (1 - p)H$. Given these equations, middle-income voters will prefer the *Center-Left* Party if:

$$pM + (1 - p)L > pM + (1 - p)H.$$

Because pM appears on both sides of the above inequality, we can ignore it. This means that the problem facing middle-income voters of whether to support the Center-Left Party or not essentially comes down to whether:

$$(1 - p)L > (1 - p)H.$$

Remember that $1 - p$ is the probability that either party defects from its promise to implement centrist policies. If both parties' campaign promises are perfectly credible ($1 - p = 0$), then middle-income voters will be unconcerned about what each party's "true preferences" are and they will be indifferent between the two parties because both parties will implement the preferences of the middle-income group. If the parties' campaign promises are not fully credible (but are equally credible), however, the middle-income voters' decision is driven by which bad outcome is least unpleasant; that is, whether L is greater or less than H. According to the setup of the model, it is easy to see that if middle-income voters cannot get their most preferred policies implemented, then they prefer the policies of high-income voters (zero tax, zero subsidy) to the policies of low-income voters (tax high- and middle-income voters,

---

29. This is true because of the assumption that the three groups of voters are of equal size.

and distribute to low-income voters). In other words, *H* is greater than *L* for middle-income voters. As a consequence, the expected payoff of *Center-Right* rule is greater than the expected payoff of *Center-Left* rule. This suggests that middle-income voters will have a greater tendency to vote for center-right parties in SDMP systems than center-left parties.[30]

What about PR electoral systems? In PR electoral systems there is no barrier to representation of any of the three income groups in society and so the legislature is composed of three parties, each representing one of the three groups. We will call the three parties in PR systems the *Left, Center,* and *Right* Parties. All of the income groups are assumed to be of equal size, so no single party will control a majority and the three parties will likely have to negotiate the formation of a coalition government. Once again, the middle-income voters will be pivotal. The middle-income voters do not have to worry, however, that the *Center* Party will deviate to the left or right. They can be confident that the *Center* Party will represent the interests of middle-income voters during coalition negotiations with the parties of the left or right. Iversen and Soskice predict that, more often than not, the *Center* Party will form a coalition with the *Left* Party in these circumstances. Why? It is assumed that parties will bargain over policy when forming the government, and so the policy implemented by any coalition government will be a compromise between the most-preferred policy of each party in the coalition weighted by the bargaining strength of the parties.[31] Because, by assumption, the tax and transfer system is nonregressive (that is, low-income voters cannot do worse than middle-income voters, who cannot do worse than high-income voters), it is possible for the *Center* Party to form a coalition with the *Left* Party that redistributes income away from the rich, but it is not politically feasible for the *Center* Party to form a coalition with the *Right* Party that redistributes income away from the poor. Roughly speaking, then, the *Center* Party's choice is between (a) a coalition with the *Left* Party that places some tax burden on high- and middle-income voters and distributes resources to low- and middle-income voters and (b) a coalition with the *Right* Party that distributes the same pot of resources among all three income groups. Because the *Center* Party gets, roughly, half of the government spending pie if it forms a coalition with the *Left* Party but only about one-third of the pie if it forms a coalition with the *Right* Party, the *Center* Party, and the middle-income voters that it represents, will do better by forming a coalition with the *Left* Party. As a result, there is a greater tendency to have center-left government coalitions in PR systems than center-right government coalitions. Iversen and Soskice (2006, 171) nicely summarize the implications of their model in the following way:

---

30. The model that Iversen and Soskice (2006) present is more subtle and elegant than the one we present here. Our goal, though, is to state the main thrust of their argument as clearly as possible.

31. The bargaining model used by Iversen and Soskice (2006) is called the Rubinstein bargaining model, a model that is named after economist Ariel Rubinstein. Simple versions of this model can be found in Dixit and Skeath (2004) and Morrow (1994).

Note that in a PR system the incentive of [the *Center Party*] to pick [the *Left Party*] as a coalition partner follows from the fact that [the *Left Party*] can never be entirely shut out from sharing in redistributive spending, even when [the *Left Party*] is not in the coalition. This implies that [the *Center Party*] has to share with both [the *Left Party*] and [the *Right Party*] in a [*Center-Right*] coalition, whereas [the *Center Party*] only has to share with [the *Left Party*] in a [*Left-Center*] coalition. [The *Center Party*] therefore has a common interest with [the *Left Party*] in soaking the rich. In a majoritarian system, by contrast, the main concern of [middle-income voters] will be to avoid being soaked by the poor.

Iversen and Soskice's model implies, therefore, that the electoral system will influence both the partisan orientation of the government and the level of redistribution in society. Using data from the Luxembourg Income Study that are based on national surveys of households in fourteen industrialized democracies, they present empirical evidence suggesting that this is, indeed, the case. These data provide measures of income inequality before and after the government's tax and transfer system that can be used as an indicator of the redistributive effect of fiscal policy. In short, the first measure of income inequality is based on people's "gross incomes" and then it is recalculated based on their "net incomes" (net of taxes taken out and benefits received). If these two measures of inequality are essentially the same, then we say that the tax and transfer system has little redistributive impact. But if the measure of inequality using "net" incomes is much lower than the measure of inequality using "gross" incomes, then we say that the tax and transfer system has a large redistributive impact. Consistent with their theoretical expectations, Iversen and Soskice find that right-wing governments are associated with less redistribution; that is, a smaller gap between income inequality before and after the government's tax and transfer system. Importantly, this is true even when the partisan orientation of the government is measured relative to the ideological orientation of the median voter. Thus, it is not simply the case that countries with right-wing voters elect governments that redistribute less. Whichever party gets into power, thanks in part to the electoral system, matters too. Iversen and Soskice also show that fiscal policy is more redistributive in countries with PR systems and that this is true even when taking account of the partisan orientation of the government. Thus, proportional representation does not lead to more redistribution just because it leads to more left-wing governments (although they show that it does have this effect). But, for the reasons outlined above, should a left-wing government come to power in an SMDP system, it is likely to engage in less redistribution than left-wing parties that are elected in PR systems.

Proportional Representation Leads to More Redistribution through Its Effect on the Size of Electoral Districts

Persson and Tabellini (1999, 2000, 2004) provide an alternative explanation for why countries with PR systems experience more redistribution than countries with SMDP electoral systems. They argue that political competition is fiercer in SMDP systems and that party leaders have to focus on winning the votes of ideologically flexible swing voters through the use of targeted transfers. As a result, fewer government resources will be available for the provision of broader public goods, which, they assume, tend to be more redistributive. The notion that government spending will be focused on public goods in PR systems but on "pork-barrel projects" that favor local interests at the expense of broader national interests in majoritarian systems is expressed in many different ways in the political economy literature. Since Weingast, Shepsle, and Johnsen's article (1981), this argument has been known as the "law of *1/n*." In other words, if individual legislators care only about spending projects in their district but taxes are not directly linked to those spending projects (because, for example, taxes are proportional to income, as we have been assuming in this section), then taxing and spending decisions take on aspects of what is known as a **common pool resource problem**.[32] A common pool resource problem exists if each legislator has an incentive to maximize government spending in his own district in order to please voters but the costs of that

> A **common pool resource problem** exists when actors can consume some commonly held resource and pay only a share of its cost. As a result, they consume more of the resource than is socially optimal; that is, they consume more than they would if they had to pay the full social cost of the resource.

spending are spread across society as a whole. If there are *n* districts in a country, the people in each district get the full benefit of a spending project but pay only *1/n* of the cost.[33]

Because there tends to be a large number of small districts in SMDP systems and a small number of large districts in PR ones, this argument has important implications for the effect of electoral laws on fiscal policy. Specifically, legislators in SMDP systems can be expected to vote for lavish spending projects in their own districts and shift the cost of paying for such projects onto the legislature as a whole. If legislators adopt a norm called "universalism" in which each legislator is expected to support the spending proposed for her colleagues' districts in exchange for her colleagues' support for spending in her own district, then the result is a level of national spending that is higher than each of the legislators desires (Weingast 1979). The legislators are, in effect, trapped in a prisoner's dilemma that is played out among hundreds of legislators. In contrast, if fiscal policy were controlled by a single actor that answered to a national constituency (such as a president), then that actor would pay the total cost of spending projects and only projects that yielded a national benefit greater than their total cost would be approved. Because legislators in PR systems are elected from a smaller number of larger districts, they bear a larger share of the total cost of spending projects and,

---

32. Common pool resource problems have the same strategic dynamic as a prisoner's dilemma (Chapter 4) played among *N* actors. See Hardin (1968) and Ostrom (1990) for treatments of the general problem. A similar problem has been described as a "collective action dilemma" (Olson 1968; Hardin 1982).

33. E. E. Schattschneider (1935) made a similar argument with respect to trade protectionism. McGillivray (2004) argues that whether spending is concentrated in marginal or safe districts, and whether redistribution would be greater in SMDP than PR systems, depends on the degree of party discipline.

therefore, refuse to pay for at least some projects that have little national benefit. As a result, we might expect legislators in SMDP systems to push for a large number of costly projects with concentrated benefits and legislators in PR systems to limit the overall level of government spending and to have a tendency to adopt only spending projects that produce broader benefits. To the extent that projects producing broader benefits are more redistributive than projects producing concentrated benefits, PR systems will, therefore, be associated with higher levels of redistribution.

It should be noted that the selectorate model of politics discussed at length in Chapter 9 is related to this line of research (Bueno de Mesquita et al. 2003). In a parliamentary democracy with SMDP electoral rules, such as the United Kingdom, a government needs to win a little more than half the votes in a little more than half the districts to stay in power. In other words, the winning coalition in an SMDP system like this is roughly 25 percent of the electorate. In contrast, in the archetypical PR system that has one nationwide electoral district, such as the Netherlands, the government needs to win about half the votes in the country to stay in power. In other words, the winning coalition in a PR system like this is roughly 50 percent of the electorate. As this comparison indicates, PR systems generally have larger winning coalitions than SMDP systems. As a result, they should provide more public goods and spend fewer government resources targeted at narrow minority groups than SMDP systems.

Franzese and Nooruddin (2004) argue that legislators making spending decisions might also consider the interests of the nation as a whole or, perhaps more realistically, the interests of a particular ideologically defined constituency, which they call the legislator's "partisan constituency." Franzese and Nooruddin suggest that legislators probably respond to both the constituency in their electoral district and their partisan constituency and that the weight they put on each of these constituencies is determined by the degree of party discipline that exists. Party discipline can be thought of as the degree to which party leaders are able to punish individual legislators who put the concerns of their local constituency over the concerns of the party leadership (which might be thought of as responding to the party's national constituency).[34] Consequently, when party discipline is high, legislators are likely to think about the broad group or class that the party represents, and when party discipline is low, legislators are likely to focus their efforts on meeting the needs of their electoral district. According to this line of reasoning, the law of *1/n*, therefore, describes the special case in which legislators feel little pressure to support partywide goals and instead focus on their geographically defined constituency.

---

34. A more complete understanding of what drives party leadership would, following Michels' iron law of oligarchy, recognize that leaders often develop interests that are distinct from any group they represent, but it would also recognize that party leaders sometimes have an interest in releasing legislators from voting the party line because forcing them to toe the party line might cause them to lose control of their constituency seats to a competing party.

Proportional Representation Affects Government Spending and Debt through Its Effect on the Composition of Governments

The common pool resource problem that we have just described has also been used to explain a related question—the overall size of government spending and, by extension, the size of government debt and deficits. Once again, many different arguments link electoral rules to overall levels of government spending and debt, each of which highlights a slightly different causal process.

One argument emphasizes the incentives that electoral rules create for legislators to cultivate a "personal vote." A personal vote occurs when an individual votes based on the characteristics of a particular candidate rather than the characteristics of the party to which the candidate belongs. As we briefly mentioned in Chapter 12, there are many factors in addition to district size that influence the propensity for candidates to put the concerns of their district over their party and, therefore, cultivate a personal vote (Carey and Shugart 1995). The most important of these factors may be the type of ballot used in PR systems. In a closed list system, voters can express a preference only over parties, leaving party leaders the power to determine which candidates will fill the seats that the party wins. In contrast, in an open list system, voters can indicate the particular candidates they support, and these votes determine which candidates fill the seats won by the party. Clearly, candidates have an incentive to curry favor with the party leadership in closed list systems but to cultivate a personal vote by making direct appeals and distributing resources to voters in their own district in open list systems. Hallerberg and Marier (2004) argue that the common pool resource problem in fiscal policy will be most severe where legislative candidates have strong incentives to cultivate a personal vote. They go on to note, however, that the adoption of "centralizing" fiscal institutions can mitigate this problem. For example, they present evidence from twenty-five Latin American and Caribbean countries during the period 1988–1997 showing that an increase in an index measuring the personal vote is associated with larger government deficits when executive influence over budgets is at its minimum, but that this positive effect disappears as executive influence over the budget grows.

An alternative argument states that the relevant common pool resource problem in relation to fiscal policy occurs not in the legislature, as we have suggested up to this point, but in the cabinet. According to this argument, each minister seeks to maximize the size of her own ministry's budget while shifting the costs of such spending on to the government as a whole (Hallerberg and von Hagen 1999; Bawn and Rosenbluth 2006). As a consequence, any factor that reinforces "fiscal centralization"—that is, spending decisions that encourage policymakers to consider the full cost, rather than a fraction, of spending—is expected to lead to lower levels of government spending, smaller deficits, and less government debt. The literature that makes this argument typically assumes that political parties have mechanisms to discipline only their own ministers, and so the severity of the common pool resource problem is really an increasing function of the number of parties in government. For example, single-party majority governments often delegate power to a strong finance minister who is able to discipline overspending ministers (Hallerberg 2004). In contrast, coalition governments tend to find it much more difficult to reign in cabinet ministers, because some of them belong to different parties. Neither the prime minister nor the finance minister will necessarily control instruments to discipline cabinet ministers from outside his party.[35] As a result, we would expect that countries with a larger number of parties in government would be associated with higher spending levels, larger deficits, and bigger debt levels. Because we expect SMDP systems to have a reductive effect on the number of parties in the legislature (see Chapter 13) and to encourage the formation of single-party governments (see Chapter 11), this amounts to a specific argument about the way electoral laws influence fiscal policy. Many papers have explored the causal connections that we have just outlined, but perhaps the clearest evidence in support of this line of reasoning comes from a paper by Persson, Roland, and Tabellini (2007). This paper finds positive associations between PR systems and party system fragmentation, between party system fragmentation and coalition government, and between coalition government and higher levels of government spending.

George Tsebelis (2002, chap. 8) offers an interesting rejoinder to those studies that find evidence of a link between the number of parties in government and high levels of government spending or debt. He argues that veto player theory predicts that all policies requiring legislative approval will change more slowly when there are a large number of veto players. Because each party in the cabinet can be thought of as a veto player, we should expect fiscal policy to change more slowly when the number of parties in government is large. But can veto player theory explain the *level* of spending in addition to explaining the rate at which spending levels will change? Tsebelis argues that we ought to consider the fact that almost all of the countries included in studies finding a relationship between the number of parties in government and the level of government spending were greatly affected by the oil crises of the 1970s. Because of the oil crises, these countries were saddled with extremely high levels of spending and debt that were, in effect, exogenously determined. Countries with few veto players were able to reduce debt levels relatively quickly after the oil crises eased, whereas countries with a large number of veto players took longer to turn fiscal policy around and reduce debt levels. Consequently, the positive association found in many studies between fiscal policy and the number of parties in government may be the result of a historical accident (oil crises) that produced high levels of debt in many countries and the fact that the number of partisan veto players in a country determines the amount of fiscal policy inertia. This suggests that if analysts were to examine a different time period, one that did not include the effects of the 1970s oil crises, they might not find any association between the number of parties in government and the level of government spending and debt.

---

35. Some countries with frequent coalition governments have adopted fiscal policy institutions, such as "fiscal contracts" and "negotiated targets," to help limit spending (Hallerberg 2004).

Summary

As we have demonstrated, there are good reasons to believe that political institutions in democracies have an important influence on macroeconomic policies.[36] For example, we presented evidence that PR electoral laws are associated with coalition governments and with having left-wing parties more frequently enter into government. Both of these factors were, in turn, shown to be associated with more extensive government redistribution and higher levels of spending, larger deficits, and higher debt levels. Although there remains considerable debate about the particular causal mechanisms at work here, there is little question that constitutional choices have important effects on the way that governments manage their economies. Central to our perspective throughout this section has been the idea that macroeconomic outcomes are distributional in nature—that is, they tend to help some citizens and harm others. It is not, therefore, possible to suggest on the basis of this literature what the best institutions for encouraging good macroeconomic performance would be. Our goal, rather, is to show that there are trade-offs to be made and that a knowledge of comparative politics can be useful in helping citizens and policymakers evaluate some of these trade-offs.

In the next section, we explore the effects of different democratic institutions on the likelihood of ethnic conflict. Because it is hard to find supporters of ethnic conflict, it might seem that comparative politics will be able to offer unqualified recommendations in this area. As you may have come to suspect, however, reality is a bit more complicated than that.

ELECTORAL LAWS, FEDERALISM, AND ETHNIC CONFLICT

In recent decades a debate has raged between political scientists regarding the effect of institutional choice, including the choice of electoral laws and federalism, on ethnic conflict. In the last few years the debate has taken on a great deal of urgency as the United States and various international organizations have become increasingly ambitious about nation building. Are there constitutional choices that might encourage successful democratic consolidation in ethnically divided countries such as Iraq? A firm understanding of the way the insti-

---

36. In this section, we have only had space to focus on the relationship between electoral institutions and fiscal policy. It is important to recognize, however, that this is merely the tip of the iceberg when it comes to the literature examining the effect of institutions on economic policies and outcomes. In an argument closely related to the constituency size hypotheses we discussed earlier, some scholars have argued that presidents in presidential democracies have an incentive to curb spending and, therefore, strengthen the position of the finance minister in budgetary negotiations (Persson and Tabellini 1999, 2004; Persson, Roland, and Tabellini 2000; Hallerberg and Marier 2004; Cheibub 2006). Clark, Golder, and Golder (2002) examine whether electoral laws influence the extent to which there are partisan differences in fiscal policy. Whereas we have focused in this section on the effect of institutions on fiscal policy, there is also a large literature showing that institutions influence the conduct of monetary policy as well. For example, Goodhart (1999) finds that governments are more likely to manipulate monetary policy for electoral purposes when a single party holds power, and Keefer and Stasavage (2002) find that the number of veto players in a country helps to determine the extent to which central bank independence reduces inflation. In addition, scholars have drawn links between electoral laws and trade policy (Rogowski 1987; McGillivray 2004) and the extent to which governments favor producers over consumers (Rogowski and Kayser 2002).

tutions we studied in Chapters 11 through 14 operate will be essential for answering these questions. But before examining whether there is an "institutional fix" for ethnic conflict, it is important to ask a prior question, and that is, are ethnically diverse societies inclined toward conflict in the first place?

Ethnic Diversity and Conflict

Although large-scale ethnic or religious conflict can be devastating, we should recognize that such conflict is the exception and that interethnic peace is the rule. This may be surprising, because when such conflict occurs the memory of its horror tends to stay with us. Indeed, when asked, it may be easy for people to provide a list of tragically violent interactions between ethnic or religious groups. For example, you might think of the conflicts during the 1990s between Hutus and Tutsis in Rwanda or between Serbs, Croats, and Bosnians in the former Yugoslavia. Or you might think of the current conflicts between Africans and Arabs in Sudan; between Shias, Sunnis, and Kurds in Iraq; or between various ethnic groups in post-Communist states, such as Azerbaijan, Georgia, Moldova, and Russia. There are two problems, however, with simply enumerating ethnic conflicts in this way. First, it tends to ignore the even larger list of "non-events"—incidents in which groups of people with ethnic or religious differences live in relatively peaceful co-existence. Second, such enumerations frequently fail to ask the question, "Compared with what"? That is, if we say groups with ethnic differences tend to be conflict prone, we are implicitly arguing that they are *more* conflict prone than relations within an ethnic group or between nonethnic groups. That may be the case, but a list of conflicts between groups is not enough to establish this claim.

James Fearon and David Laitin (1996) argue that once we address these concerns, ethnic conflict can be seen as a relatively rare event. Table 15.5 reproduces their analysis of data from thirty-six countries in sub-Saharan Africa, an area of the world often thought to be particularly prone to ethnic violence. Fearon and Laitin rely on data from a study by Morrison, Mitchell, and Paden (1989) that examines four different forms of what might be considered ethnic violence: ethnic violence, irredentism, rebellion, and civil war. Morrison, Mitchell, and Paden (1989, 129) define "ethnic violence" as "an event of short duration . . . in which two identifiable communal groups are antagonists in violence to secure some short-term goal." The other three forms of violence that they examine are also ethnically based in that they involve a conflict between an identifiable communal group and the state. They define "irredentism" as occurring when a communal group attempts to change its allegiance from the government of its current territorial unit to a government in which the ruling authorities share the communal identification of the irredentist group. They define "rebellion" as the use of violence by a communal group in an effort to gain greater autonomy from state authorities. And they define "civil war" as a communal group's use of violence in an attempt to "form a new political system based on boundaries of ethnic community." Fearon and Laitin summarize the data in an extremely helpful way that allows us to compare the number of actual incidents of ethnic violence with an estimate of the number of potential incidents of ethnic violence, yielding a ratio of actual incidents of violence to all

	Actual and Potential Communal Violence in Thirty-six Sub-Saharan African Countries, 1960–1979				
TABLE 15.5					
Type of communal violence	Number of incidents for all countries and years[a]	Country mean of incidents per year[b]	Number of potential incidents for all countries and years[c]	Country mean of potential incidents per year[d]	Ratio of all actual incidents to all potential incidents[e]
Ethnic violence	20	0.03	38,383	59	0.0005
Irredentism	29	0.04	18,757	26	0.0015
Rebellion	27	0.04	18,757	26	0.0014
Civil war	52	0.10	18,757	26	0.0028

Source: Fearon and Laitin (1996, 717), based on data from Morrison, Mitchell, and Paden (1989).

Note: See Fearon and Laitin (1996) for how the number of ethnic groups is determined.

a. Cases of communal violence that persist for three years are counted three times, once for each year. Two independent conflicts in the same year are coded as two incidents for that year.

b. The mean for all countries is all incidents in a country divided by the number of full years since independence through 1979; countries that became independent before 1960 are treated as if they became independent in 1960.

c. For irredentism, rebellion, and civil war, potential cases per year in each country are estimated as the number of ethnic groups in the country less one ($N - 1$), under the assumption that typically one group holds power and potential challengers come from all other groups. These numbers are then summed across countries and years to get the figures in this column. For potential cases of ethnic violence, a conservative estimate of the number of ethnic groups engaged in interactions, namely, the smaller of $2N$ and $N(N - 1)/2$, is summed across countries and years. If there are N groups, then the total number of dyads is $N(N - 1)/2$.

d. The mean for all countries of potential incidents per year.

e. Computed by dividing the number of incidents for all years and all countries by the number of potential incidents per year for all years and all countries.

potential incidents of violence across different forms of communal violence. Their summary of the data is shown in Table 15.5.

The comparison of actual to potential events is achieved by moving across the rows of Table 15.5. Beginning with the row "Ethnic violence," we see that there were twenty incidents of ethnic violence in these thirty-six countries between 1960 and 1979. Although we would never seek to minimize the human suffering caused by such violence, it is important to keep these incidents in perspective. Because the sample includes thirty-six countries observed over nineteen years, there are approximately 680 country-years in the data set.[37] One way to estimate the frequency of ethnic conflict, therefore, is to take the ratio of the number of conflicts to the number of country-years in the data set. The third column shows that this figure is 0.03. This means that there have been three incidents of ethnic conflict for every one hundred country-years in this group of countries. This is, however, still an overestimate of the frequency of ethnic conflict because it assumes that each country-year represents just

---

37. There are actually somewhat fewer observations because some countries did not become independent until after 1960.

Box 15.1

ETHNIC CONFLICT IN SUDAN

Apart from an eleven-year period between 1972 and 1983, Sudan has been at war continuously since independence in 1956.[1] A civil war broke out in 1983 when the government, dominated by northern Arabs, attempted to impose Islamic Sharia law across all of Sudan, including the south, which is dominated by Christians and animists. This civil war between the north and the south—Africa's longest-running civil war—which resulted in the deaths of more than 1.5 million people, finally came to an end after twenty-one years in late 2004 with the signing of a power-sharing peace agreement known as the Comprehensive Peace Agreement (CPA). Under the CPA, the rebel Sudan People's Liberation Army (SPLA) agreed to enter a national unity government with President Omar al-Bashir's National Congress Party (NCP). Although the SPLA agreed to accept Sharia law in the north of the country (but not in the capital, Khartoum), they did manage to secure important government jobs, a larger share of Sudan's oil revenue, and they took de facto control in the south of the country. National elections are to take place in 2009 and a referendum on whether southern Sudan should form its own independent state is scheduled for 2011. Despite the peace agreement, which came into force in 2005, tensions between the north and the south have remained high, with both sides claiming that the other has reneged on its promises and commitments. In October 2007, the SPLA withdrew from the national unity government. Disputes over who should control the oil-rich Abyei region, which has had a special administrative status since 2005 and which can choose to join a possibly independent south in the planned 2011 referendum, pose the greatest threat to continued peace. Conflict broke out in May 2008 between Sudanese government troops and the SPLA in the town of Abyei. Government forces burned the town to the ground, completely destroying 95 percent of the homes; the United Nations reports that about 50,000 Sudanese have since fled the town. Rival troops from the north and south headed toward central Sudan in a move that threatened to further escalate violence and potentially restart the civil war.

As the civil war between the north and south was being waged, a separate conflict broke out in Darfur in western Sudan in 2003 when different rebel groups began attacking government targets. Tension over land, water, and grazing rights in Darfur had been high for many years. Like the rebel groups in the south, the rebel groups in Darfur claimed that the Arab-dominated government was oppressing the black African population in favor of the Arab population. In other words, like the north-south civil war, the conflict in Darfur is primarily between Arabs and non-Arabs. One difference, though, is that the rebel groups in Darfur are mostly Muslim non-Arabs, whereas the rebel groups in the south are mostly Christian or animist non-Arabs. Originally, there were just two rebel groups in Darfur—the Sudan Liberation Army (SLA) and the Justice and Equality Movement (Jem). These rebel groups have subsequently split to such an extent, however, that there are now over a dozen different rebel groups in conflict with the government.

---

1. For up-to-date information on the conflicts in Sudan, see the extensive coverage on the BBC News Online site at http://news.bbc.co.uk/2/hi/in_depth/africa/2004/sudan/default.stm.

Given that the Sudanese government was already fighting a civil war in the south that threatened the unity of the country, it responded with considerable force in Darfur in an attempt to discourage secessionist tendencies from developing there too. This involved using aerial bombings and Arab militias, known as Janjaweed, to destroy African villages accused of harboring rebels. The term *Janjaweed* is an Arab colloquialism meaning "a man with a gun on a horse." The Janjaweed are comprised of members of nomadic Arab tribes who have been in conflict with Darfur's settled black African farmers for many years. Ever since independence in 1956, successive weak Sudanese governments have used Arab tribal militias around the country to exert their authority whenever problems arise because the country is too large for the national army to fully control on its own. Although Arab militias have been around for some time, the Janjaweed in its present form was reportedly set up by security agencies under the control of Vice-President Ali Osman Mohamed Taha in response to the 2003 attacks by rebel groups in Darfur. The Sudanese government has repeatedly denied that it controls or supports the Janjaweed. A BBC reporter reported in October 2004, however, that "in May, I saw him [President Omar al-Bashir] address a meeting of his supporters in Nyala, south Darfur, and salute the assembled Janjaweed fighters: 'Long live the Mujahideen.'" [2] Numerous other individuals and organizations have also claimed that the Sudanese government is arming the Janjaweed militias.

The government's use of aerial bombing and the Janjaweed to target African villages in Darfur has led to the establishment of dozens of refugee camps housing about 2.4 million internally displaced persons; a further 200,000 refugees have fled eastward into neighboring Chad.[3] Individuals in the refugee camps report that after government air raids, the Janjaweed would ride into their villages on horses and camels killing men, raping women, and burning down homes in a form of scorched earth policy; the Janjaweed are accused of trying to cleanse black Africans from Darfur. The United States and several other national governments (but not the United Nations) have described what is going on in Darfur as genocide.[4] By 2006 the death toll was estimated to be over 200,000. China, which buys about 60 percent of Sudan's oil and sells it weapons, has played a key role in helping the Sudanese government avoid UN sanctions. Despite Chinese resistance, diplomatic pressure has forced Sudan's gov-

---

2. BBC News Online, http://news.bbc.co.uk/1/hi/world/africa/3594520.stm.

3. Relations between Sudan and Chad are extremely tense. Chad's government recently accused Sudan of attempting to overthrow Chad's president Idriss Deby in February 2008 by using rebels based in Darfur. Sudan, in return, has accused Chad of arming Jem, the Darfur rebel movement. It appears that Chad and Sudan are both fighting a proxy war using each other's rebels to achieve their military objectives. The political tensions spilled into the nonpolitical realm when worried officials from FIFA (soccer's world governing body) suspended the World Cup qualifying match between Sudan and Chad that was scheduled to take place on May 31, 2008.

4. In June 2008, the chief prosecutor of the International Criminal Court (ICC) compared aspects of the Sudanese government's behavior with that of Nazi Germany, saying that state officials were covering up and denying crimes against humanity. The Sudanese government is currently refusing to hand over Ali Kushayb, a leader of the Janjaweed, and Ahmad Harun, Sudan's current humanitarian affairs minister, to the ICC; the men are charged with fifty-one counts of war crimes and crimes against humanity. For more information, see http://news.bbc.co.uk/1/hi/world/africa/7436472.stm.

ernment to let increasing numbers of international troops and observers in to monitor the situation in Darfur. Originally, in 2004, just 300 African Union troops were allowed into Darfur, and their role was limited to protecting the 120 unarmed observers that had been working in the region. By 2007 the size of the African Union observer mission in Darfur had risen to 7,000 troops. With only a limited mandate to intervene, though, the African Union observer mission has been unable to protect the civilians in the refugee camps and has itself come under repeated attack from the Janjaweed; civilians continue to be killed or raped whenever they venture out of the refugee camps. In late 2007, the United Nations agreed to replace the African Union observer mission with a 26,000 strong UN-African Union peacekeeping mission with a stronger mandate to protect civilians and aid workers. The full deployment of the new peacekeeping troops is not expected to be completed until late 2008, and many observers believe that their numbers are still too small to keep peace in a region the size of France.

Although numerous attempts have been made to reach a peace agreement between the rebel groups in Darfur and the Sudanese government, all have so far failed. At the time of writing this chapter, there seemed to be very little light at the end of the tunnel.

one potential incident of ethnic group conflict. In reality, because the typical country in this sub-Saharan sample has more than two dozen ethnic groups, the potential is there for far more than one ethnic conflict per country-year. Consequently, Fearon and Laitin estimate the number of potential incidents of ethnic conflict based on the number of ethnic groups in a country and find that the ratio of actual incidents of ethnic violence to potential incidents of ethnic violence is lower still (last column): there were just five incidents of ethnic conflict for every 10,000 potential incidents (roughly, ethnic-group-years).

Similar calculations can be conducted to gauge the frequency of the other three forms of violence. We see from the last column, for example, that although communal violence aimed at the state occurs with a greater frequency than group-on-group violence, it is still quite rare. Actual communal-based irredentism and rebellion occur about 1–5 times for every 1,000 potential incidents. Although communally based civil wars occur about twice as often as this, they are still quite rare—only 2.8 civil wars for every 1,000 potential civil wars. One could, of course, say that Fearon and Laitin (1996) have made these phenomena seem rare by dividing them into separate categories, but even if we combine all types of communal violence against the state they are still a tiny fraction of the number of potential events—just 5.8 actual incidents for every 1,000 potential incidents.[38]

One thing is clear from Fearon and Laitin's analysis—even in very poor countries where the state has little capacity to rule effectively and the society is reeling from decades of colo-

---

38. The sum of irredentist, rebellion, and civil war incidents is 108. This, divided by the number of potential incidents (18,757), is 0.0058, or, for every 1,000 potential cases of communal violence against the state, just 5.8 actual incidents.

nialism that left a legacy of externally imposed borders, such as sub-Saharan Africa, ethnic heterogeneity does not lead inexorably to ethnic conflict—either between ethnic groups or between ethnic groups and the state. Simply looking at these data of violent incidents and thinking about how many incidents could have occurred if different ethnic groups were to engage in conflict should lead you to question popular notions about the nature of the link between ethnic heterogeneity and violence.

The above conclusion can be arrived at even before we begin to answer the question of whether ethnic violence is more common than other forms of violence. One way to judge whether ethnic conflicts are more common than other forms of conflict is to examine whether ethnic heterogeneity—having large numbers of ethnic groups—increases the likelihood of civil war. In a different article Fearon and Laitin (2003) analyze a data set that runs from 1945 to 1999 and includes 161 countries and 127 civil wars.[39] They find that, after taking account of wealth and a battery of other variables, countries that experience civil wars are no more ethnically or religiously diverse than countries that do not. Instead, what Fearon and Laitin find to matter most for civil war onset are factors that favor insurgency, such as poverty, oil-dependent export sectors, political instability, and rough terrain. These factors increase the probability of civil war by creating bureaucratically weak states and by creating environments favorable to rebel recruitment.[40] Although the study by Fearon and Laitin challenges the popular belief that having more ethnic groups in a country increases the likelihood of civil war, it is possible that ethnic heterogeneity does increase the risk of civil war, but through an indirect effect that goes undetected in their study. What might this indirect effect be?

Several economists have argued that ethnic heterogeneity has a deleterious effect on economic growth (Easterly and Levine 1997). If this is true, ethnic heterogeneity might contribute to the risk of civil war by helping to keep countries poor. Indeed, an analysis using Fearon and Laitin's own data shows that (a) ethnic diversity is positively associated with the onset of civil war when wealth (measured by GDP per capita) is dropped from their statistical model, and (b) there is a negative association between ethnic heterogeneity and wealth. Taken together, these results suggest that ethnic heterogeneity may not have a direct effect on civil war onset but that it does have an indirect effect by reducing wealth, which, in turn, increases the likelihood of civil war. This causal story is graphically illustrated in Figure 15.9.

Considerable disagreement remains among economists and political scientists as to the exact causal connection between ethnic heterogeneity and economic growth, which somewhat complicates the above discussion. Some economists maintain that ethnic heterogeneity and economic growth are not causally related. And even those that accept that there is a

---

39. Gary Bass (2005) wrote an accessible summary of this literature for the *New York Times Magazine*.

40. Poverty, which lowers tax revenue, and political instability weaken the state, thereby making it easier for rebel groups to challenge it successfully. Rough terrain, like mountainous regions, gives rebel groups hiding places and strongholds that hinder attempts by the state to crush them. Thus, poverty, political instability, and rough terrain increase the likelihood of civil war by increasing the probability that a challenge to the state will be successful. In contrast, the presence of oil increases the likelihood of civil war by increasing the value of gaining control of the state. All of these factors together increase the expected value of civil war on the part of rebel groups.

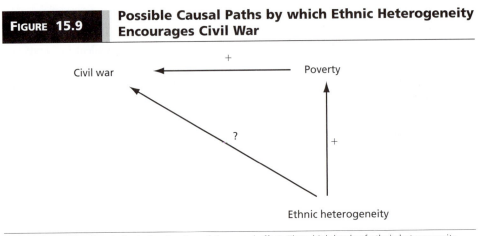

| FIGURE 15.9 | Possible Causal Paths by which Ethnic Heterogeneity Encourages Civil War |

Note: The positive signs indicate the direction of the causal effect. Thus, high levels of ethnic heterogeneity increase poverty, and high levels of poverty increase the likelihood of civil wars. It is unclear whether ethnic heterogeneity had a direct effect on civil war.

causal relationship often disagree about the exact causal process by which ethnic hetero-geneity inhibits economic growth. Easterly and Levine (1997) show that ethnically heteroge-neous African countries experience lower economic growth rates than more ethnically homogeneous African countries. They argue that this is the case because governments in ethnically diverse countries are often politically unstable and tend to choose policies that lead to low levels of schooling, underdeveloped financial systems, distorted financial exchange markets, and insufficient infrastructure. Easterly and Levine suggest that when var-ious ethnic groups in a country have different preferences, they may derive less satisfaction from providing public goods than would be the case in a more homogeneous society. For instance, a public good like a school might lead to lower satisfaction in an ethnically diverse setting if the groups cannot agree on the main language of instruction, location, or general curriculum. The result is that the ethnically diverse society is less likely to end up building the school. Part of the problem is also that members of one ethnic group may not be willing to spend resources on providing public goods that members of other ethnic groups will get to consume. Whatever the reason behind the low level of investment in public goods, eco-nomic growth is likely to be inhibited. Evidence supporting this argument linking ethnic heterogeneity with lower levels of public goods provision can be found in a variety of set-tings, including advanced industrialized democracies. For example, Alesina, Baqir, and Easterly (1999) compare U.S. cities and find that governments in ethnically diverse cities tend to provide fewer public goods than governments in more ethnically homogeneous cities. Significantly, given our upcoming discussion of institutions, Easterly (2001) notes that what economists call "good institutions" (those that reduce bureaucratic delay, enforce con-tracts, reduce risk of nationalization, and provide sound infrastructure) can help to alleviate the negative effects of ethnic heterogeneity on economic growth. In other words, if a country's institutions are of a sufficiently high quality, then ethnic heterogeneity may have no effect on the provision of public goods or on conflict.[41]

The arguments that we have examined so far focus on the claim that it is the number of ethnic groups in a country that increase the risk of conflict and violence. Recently, though, scholars have begun to argue that it is not the number of ethnic groups (ethnic heterogeneity) per se that matters for conflict but, rather, the distribution of ethnic group memberships. For example, some studies have suggested that it is *ethnic polarization* and not ethnic heterogeneity that increases the likelihood of things like civil wars (Estaban and Ray 1999, 2008; Reynal-Querol 2002; Montalvo and Reynal-Querol 2005; Estaban and Schneider 2008). This literature suggests that the risk of civil war is higher when there are a few large ethnic groups with opposing interests than when there are many small ethnic groups. Along similar lines, Chandra and Boulet (2005) argue that democratic stability is put at risk not by ethnic heterogeneity but by the existence of a permanently excluded ethnic minority. The reasoning is that an ethnic minority that sees no democratic means by which it can ever come to power is more likely to break with democracy than one that foresees coming to power from time to time through the electoral process. Chandra and Boulet go on to claim that far from hurting democratic stability, having a large number of evenly sized ethnic groups in a country can help to stabilize democracy by making a variety of shifting ruling coalitions possible, thereby lowering the likelihood that particular ethnic groups will be permanently excluded from power. Empirical evidence for a corollary of this theory comes from Collier and Hoeffler (2004), who show that the risk of civil war is highest when one ethnic group comprises between 45 and 90 percent of the population. That is, they provide evidence that civil war is more likely when a single ethnic group is in a position to act as a permanent *majority*— presumably because for every permanent majority, there is at least one potentially disgruntled permanent minority.

As we will see, arguments about the effect of electoral laws on ethnic conflict are closely tied to arguments about the existence of permanent ethnic minorities. The main dispute is whether these minorities should receive a guarantee of permanent representation or should be encouraged to form coalitions with other groups and, thereby, avoid being placed in the position of permanent opposition. But before we examine the effect of electoral laws on ethnic conflict in detail, it is important to recognize that other factors influence how responsive voters are to ethnic-based appeals from politicians and, hence, how likely it is that there will be group-based conflict. For example, Varshney (2001, 2002) argues that the pattern of social ties between citizens is an important factor influencing the probability of group-based conflict. Specifically, he argues that peace is promoted when citizens form interethnic social ties. Interethnic civic engagement, he finds, promotes peace, and its "absence or weakness opens

---

41. Easterly (2001) uses four measures from the *International Country Risk Guide* in Knack and Keefer (1995) to construct his index of institutional quality. These measures are: (a) freedom from government repudiation of contracts, (b) freedom from expropriation, (c) rule of law, and (d) bureaucratic quality.

up space for ethnic violence" (Varshney 2001, 363). As he notes, though, not all forms of interethnic civic engagement are equally effective at promoting peace. For example, he argues that joining formal associations, such as interethnic business associations, sports teams, reading or film clubs, and labor unions, is more effective in promoting ethnic peace than more everyday forms of interethnic contact, such as regularly eating together or allowing children to play together. Although both forms of interethnic civic engagement promote peace, Varshney finds that the associational form is sturdier than everyday engagement, especially when politicians attempt to polarize people along ethnic lines. This evidence suggests that vigorous associational life, if it has an interethnic aspect, acts as a serious constraint on the ability of politicians to mobilize voters along ethnic lines, even when ethnic polarization is in their political interest. The more the associational networks cut across ethnic boundaries, the harder it is for politicians to achieve such polarization (Varshney 2001, 363).

Most of the studies on ethnic politics that we have examined so far take ethnic identities and how these identities are manifested in associational life as given. As we saw in Chapter 13, however, institutions, such as electoral laws, are likely to influence the type of ethnic identities that become politicized in the first place (Chandra and Boulet 2003; Chandra 2004, 2005; Posner 2004, 2005). Chandra (2005) argues that one reason why so many studies find an inherent tension between ethnic heterogeneity and things like democratic stability is that they treat ethnic identity as given rather than as something that is socially constructed. To demonstrate this point, Chandra presents a model of electoral competition under a single-member district plurality electoral system in which party leaders are free to define ethnic groups strategically. The results of the model show that there are conditions in which party leaders will choose to redefine group identity in order to attract voters across ethnic lines. In other words, it is not always the case that party leaders will choose to mobilize voters along ethnic lines. This is an important result because it suggests that the conflict and extremism predicted by traditional models of **ethnic outbidding,** in which the politicization of ethnic divisions inevitably gives rise to one or more competing ethnic parties (Rabushka and

> **Ethnic outbidding** is a process in which ethnic divisions are politicized and the result is the formation of increasingly polarized ethnic parties.

Shepsle 1972; Horowitz 1985), are the result of assuming that ethnic identities are fixed rather than the mere presence of ethnic differences.

According to models of ethnic outbidding, once a single ethnic party emerges, it "infects" the political system because it results in a new and more extreme ethnic party emerging to oppose the first one. This, in turn, leads the first ethnic party to become more extreme, and so on, producing a downward spiral in which nonethnically based competitive politics is destroyed altogether. Essentially what Chandra (2005) shows is that this ethnic outbidding process need not occur if ethnic identities are not fixed. Interestingly, Chandra's study suggests that far from being a cause of concern, ethnic heterogeneity may actually help ensure democratic stability by increasing the number of dimensions along which interethnic alliances can form. In effect, majorities that are constructed along one dimension are unlikely to be permanent and, hence, dangerous when there is ethnic diversity, because politicians from groups that comprise a minority on that dimension can try to mobilize voters along a different dimension, one in which they will be part of a majority.

We should note at this point, though, that Chandra has analyzed these dynamics under only one type of electoral system—single-member district plurality rule. Further analysis is required to support her conclusion that "some institutional contexts produce benign forms of ethnic politics, while others produce malign forms" (Chandra 2005, 245). Fortunately, there is a rather vigorous debate that we can draw on about the effect of electoral laws on the relationship between ethnic conflict and democratic stability. It is to this debate that we now turn.

The Hypothesized Effect of Electoral Laws on Ethnic Conflict

We learned in Chapter 13 that electoral laws influence whether or not social cleavages are reflected in a country's party system. PR electoral laws with a high district magnitude allow social cleavages to be translated directly into the party system. In contrast, less permissive electoral systems, such as SMDP rule, create incentives for political entrepreneurs and voters to put aside some of their differences in an attempt to capture a difficult-to-obtain electoral prize. Anticipating the effect of electoral rules, members of ethnic groups are likely to engage in what Chandra (2004) refers to as an "ethnic head count"—they will look around to see if there are enough members of their ethnic group, given the electoral rules in place, to make a plausible ethnic-specific bid for a legislative seat. If there are, they will be encouraged to support a party that appeals mainly to their specific ethnic group. But if the perceived electoral threshold exceeds their subjective assessment of the size of their ethnic group, then they will likely support a more broadly based party—either a nonethnic party or an ethnic party that defines the ethnic group in a more inclusive manner. Political entrepreneurs play an important role in all of this. For example, political entrepreneurs may try to influence voters' perceptions about the presence of their co-ethnics by organizing cultural, religious, sporting, and sometimes even explicitly political events that encourage ethnics to reveal their group membership. But political entrepreneurs will also be aware of how electoral thresholds interact with group size to determine the likelihood that such strategies will succeed. Because electoral thresholds are directly affected by electoral laws, the propensity for elites to make ethnic-specific appeals or make interethnic alliances, and the likelihood that voters will respond to such appeals or eschew them and support more broadly based parties, will be a function of the interaction between group size and electoral laws.[42]

---

42. Suggesting that actors condition their behavior on the probability of success in achieving their goals is controversial for some. An alternative view is that actors sometimes choose behaviors because they see such behaviors as the "right thing to do," independently of expected consequences (Varshney 2004). This is, to some extent, true; the difficulty, though, comes in determining *ex ante* when individuals will and will not make such sacrifices. Work on suicide bombings has demonstrated that even these acts of self-sacrifice can be understood from within a standard rational actor framework (Berman and Laitin 2006).

Scholars wishing to influence the design of constitutions in societies characterized by ethnic heterogeneity do not disagree about the role played by electoral institutions. They all recognize that, given high levels of social heterogeneity, the choice of electoral laws will play an important role in determining whether many ethnically homogeneous parties or a smaller number of broadly based parties, each drawing support from multiple ethnic groups, will form. Rather, the debate is whether democratic stability is best ensured by taking ethnic groups as given and ensuring that minorities are guaranteed adequate representation, or by assuming that group identities are malleable and can be successfully channeled into regime-supporting, rather than regime-challenging, behaviors.

Arend Lijphart is the most recognized champion of the view that we should take ethnic groups as given and ensure that minorities receive adequate representation. His approach to dealing with ethnic heterogeneity has come to be known as **consociationalism.** According to Lijphart (2004), ethnic minorities pose an acute danger to democratic stability when they are excluded from participation in formal political institutions. But if ethnic minorities are able to gain access to formal institutions and those institutions are designed to reflect the interests of as broad a set of the population as possible, then these minorities will have a stake in the continued survival of the democratic system. According to Lijphart, it is important that there also be multiple checks on governmental power so as to minimize the likelihood that the state can be used to systematically abuse minority rights. As you can see, consociationalism is closely related to the consensus vision of democracy. As outlined earlier in this chapter, the consensus vision of democracy envisions the adoption of institutional mechanisms that divide power and make it necessary for the government to seek input from as wide a range of citizens as possible. In effect, consociationalism is a particular strategy for implementing the consensus vision of democracy that involves the adoption of institutions guaranteeing the representation of minority groups.

> **Consociationalism** is a form of government that emphasizes power sharing through guaranteed group representation.

Consociationalism has its roots in the religious and social conflicts experienced by the Netherlands in the late nineteenth and early twentieth centuries. These conflicts eventually resulted in the division of Dutch society into four "pillars," representing Calvinist, Catholic, Socialist, and liberal citizens. Each pillar had its own schools, hospitals, university, newspapers, political parties, and institutional guarantees of representation. Another famous application of consociationalism is Lebanon, where Maronite Christians, Sunni Muslims, and Shia Muslims are guaranteed representation by the constitution written in 1943, following Lebanon's independence from France. The 1943 National Pact stipulated that the president was to be a Maronite Christian, the prime minister a Sunni Muslim, and the speaker of parliament a Shia Muslim. In addition, representation in parliament was to reflect a six-to-five ratio between Christians and Muslims; this ratio was based on the 1932 census. The fifty-four Christian seats were further divided, with a fixed number of seats allocated to Maronite (thirty), Orthodox (eleven), Catholic (six), Armenian (five), and other (two) Christian groups. Similarly, the forty-five Muslim seats were divided among Sunni (twenty), Shia (nineteen), and Druze (six) politicians. Ministerial portfolios, as well as many government positions in the executive, legislative, and judicial branches, were also allocated along religious lines. Even positions such as those of judges and teachers were divided up, with some attention paid toward sectarian quotas (Bannerman 2002). Lebanese **confessionalism,** as consociationalism is known when it is applied to religious groups, was initially thought to be highly successful. Demographic changes, the inflow of Palestinian refugees starting in 1948, and conflicts over regional politics, however, led to a protracted and violent civil war in Lebanon that started in 1975 and ended in 1990. The October 1989 Taif Agreement, or Document of National Accord, that helped end the civil war changed the ratio of parliamentary representation to a fifty-fifty Christian-to-Muslim ratio.

> **Confessionalism** is a form of government that emphasizes power sharing by different religious communities through guaranteed group representation.

You will probably have noticed that consociationalism's goal of institutionalizing ethnic (religious) groups is precisely the type of policy that Chandra (2005, 245) argues against on the grounds that it tends to "impose an artificial fixity on ethnic identities." In what follows, we do not engage in a protracted examination of the pros and cons of consociationalism per se. Instead, we focus on the effect of two institutional choices—PR and federalism—that are typically part of consociational arrangements. We begin by examining the effect of electoral laws on ethnic divisions and conflict. We then examine the use of federalism for guaranteeing minority rights and preventing conflict.

Lijphart (2004, 99) states that "the most important choice facing constitution writers is that of a legislative electoral system." He goes on to state that "for divided societies, ensuring the election of a broadly representative legislature should be the crucial consideration" and that PR is "undoubtedly the optimal way of doing so" (100). To demonstrate his point, Lijphart claims that there is a scholarly consensus in the literature against the use of majoritarian electoral laws in deeply divided societies on the grounds that they can lead to the indefinite exclusion of significant societal groups. Not only are PR electoral systems better in divided societies than majoritarian systems according to Lijphart, but they are also better than the mixed electoral systems that are increasingly being adopted around the world. As you will recall from our discussion of electoral rules in Chapter 12, mixed electoral systems combine both majoritarian and proportional components. The extent to which such systems yield minority representation tends to depend on the extent to which the proportional component is compensatory; that is, the extent to which the PR component is specifically designed to counteract the disproportionality produced by the majoritarian component. If the PR component is not compensatory, "the results will necessarily be less than fully proportional—and minority representation less accurate and secure" (Lijphart 2004, 100). If the PR component does override the majoritarian component, though, these mixed systems are, according to Lijphart, essentially proportional with the same benefits as straight PR systems. Some countries, such as Colombia, Croatia, and Pakistan, seek to deal with ethnic diversity by providing guaranteed representation for specified minorities.[43] For Lijphart, however, guaranteed minority representation is inferior to simply using PR electoral rules, because it requires governments to address the difficult and politically incendiary question of which minorities require special representation guarantees and which do not. PR, in contrast, treats all groups the same and, if done correctly, produces the desired minority representation.

The basic assumptions behind Lijphart's argument is that ethnic and other deep-seated conflicts can be mitigated as long as all the relevant parties to a dispute receive adequate legislative representation and that proportional electoral rules are the best way to achieve this representation. As we saw in Chapter 12, though, scholars have pointed to several drawbacks to proportional electoral rules. For example, some point to how PR systems sometimes facilitate the election of small antisystem parties that become locked in cycles of legislative conflict, which can then spill over into violent social conflict. The most dramatic and troubling example of this occurred in Weimar Germany, whose highly proportional electoral system helped Hitler's Nazi Party come to power. Others point to how PR systems frequently wind up giving small parties a disproportionate influence in the government formation process. Because it is rare for parties to obtain a legislative majority in PR systems, large parties often rely on the support of smaller parties to get into government. These smaller parties can frequently use their leverage to wring concessions from the larger party. Some of these concessions can be quite radical and lack the support of an electoral majority. In Israel, for example, ultra-religious parties have won support for many of their policies by threatening to pull out of the government.

More important, some scholars claim that the representation of distinct groups is neither necessary, nor sufficient, to bring about intergroup peace (Barry 1975). For instance, Horowitz (1991, 119) argues that even if highly proportional systems guarantee that small parties win seats in parliament, this is not the same as saying that "minority interests will receive attention in the legislative process." Indeed, if conflicts exist in divided societies, one might wonder why simply using PR systems to replicate the societal divisions that led to these conflicts in the legislature will be of any help if there are no incentives for cross-party cooperation and accommodation. What is needed, according to these critics, is an institutional mechanism that encourages compromise and moderation. Many of these scholars believe that majoritarian electoral laws provide such a mechanism.

Donald Horowitz (1985, 1991) presents the most widely recognized alternative to PR for deeply divided societies: the alternative vote. Recall from Chapter 12 that the alternative vote is, essentially, an "instant-runoff" system in which one legislator is elected from each district and voters have the opportunity to rank order all the candidates. The candidate who wins an absolute majority of the first-preference votes is elected. If no candidate wins an absolute

---

43. Golder (2005) notes that after 1985, for example, Pakistan provided ten guaranteed seats in the legislature for specific religious minorities: Christians (four), Hindus (four), Sikhs (one), and Ahmadis (one).

majority, the candidate with the lowest number of first-preference votes is eliminated and her ballots are reallocated among the remaining candidates according to the indicated second preferences. This process continues until a candidate receives an absolute majority of votes. Unlike with SMDP systems, voters have little incentive to vote strategically because voters know that their vote will not be wasted if their most preferred candidate is unlikely to win; their vote is simply transferred to the next candidate. This means that voters motivated by ethnic identity are likely to indicate a co-ethnic as their first preference and the least unsavory candidate from an alternative ethnic group as their second preference. In highly diverse districts, candidates realize that their electoral success will likely depend on the transfer of second preferences from other ethnic groups. Consequently, successful candidates will typically be those who are effective at making broadly based centrist appeals that cross ethnic lines. It is for this reason that many scholars believe that the alternative vote encourages moderation and compromise across ethic lines (Horowitz 1985, 1991; Reilly 1997, 2001). Empirical evidence to support this belief comes from Australia, where the major parties frequently attempt to negotiate deals with smaller parties for their second preferences prior to an election (Reilly 2001, 55–56). Additional evidence that the alternative vote encourages the building of coalitions across ethnic groups comes from Papua New Guinea and Fiji (Horowitz 2004, 513–514).

To sum up, you can think of the choice between PR and the alternative vote as being a choice between replicating ethnic divisions in the legislature hoping that political leaders will cooperate after the election (PR) and creating institutional incentives that seek to weaken or even transcend the political salience of ethnicity altogether (AV). Given the centrality of the above debate to questions of institutional design, it is surprising that few attempts have been made to use systematic empirical evidence to adjudicate the competing claims put forward by Lijphart and Horowitz. On the whole, the literature is full of evidence from a small number of cases presented by partisans of one view or the other to support their claims; systematic evaluations of the purported benefits of PR or the majoritarian alternative vote for divided societies are relatively rare.

Some studies find support for the claim that PR systems reduce the likelihood of violent conflict (Cohen 1997; Reynal-Querol 2002; Saideman et al. 2002). There are, however, several reasons to be cautious about these results. First, these studies rarely make a direct comparison between PR and majoritarian democracies. For example, many of the studies cited above combine both democratic and undemocratic countries. As a result, PR democracies are being compared with a heterogeneous mixture of majoritarian democracies and dictatorships in the sample. The study by Reynal-Querol (2002, 37) appears to compare parliamentary democracies that use either proportional or majoritarian electoral rules with presidential and mixed democracies as well as dictatorships. Again, this is not the appropriate comparison to evaluate the competing claims put forward by Lijphart and Horowitz. Second, although various scholars have looked at the association between PR and conflict, none has examined whether PR systems *modify* the way that ethnic heterogeneity influences the probability of conflict. In other words, none of them is testing the precise causal story put forward by Lijphart, which is that ethnic heterogeneity leads to conflict in majoritarian democracies but less so or not at all in proportional democracies.[44] Finally, it should be noted that none of these studies distinguishes among the variety of majoritarian electoral systems that exists. As a result, we have little to no systematic evidence as to whether the alternative vote produces the sort of moderating effects that reduce violence in divided societies that Horowitz claims that it does. One reason why so few studies have focused specifically on the impact of the alternative vote is that so few countries around the world actually use this electoral system—this makes conducting statistical analyses problematic. There is no great barrier, however, to evaluating the broader comparison between majoritarian and proportional democracies. It is a little puzzling, therefore, as to why this comparison has been so rarely made in the existing literature.

We expect that future studies on the impact of electoral rules on ethnic conflict and democratic stability—perhaps some that begin as undergraduate research projects—will likely result in clearer policy recommendations for constitutional designers. It is likely that such recommendations will have to take account of how electoral rules might interact with other institutions. It is to one of these institutions—federalism—that we now turn.

The Hypothesized Effect of Federalism

Recent events in Iraq and Afghanistan have led to a renewed debate among political scientists as to the role that federalism can play in stabilizing democracy in divided societies. Historically, comparative political scientists have seen incongruent and asymmetric federalism as a particularly appealing form of government for those countries in which policy preferences differ in significant ways across geographically concentrated ethnic groups.[45] By bringing the government closer to the people, increasing opportunities to participate in government, and giving groups discretion over their political, social, and economic affairs, incongruent and asymmetric federalism is thought to reduce ethnic conflict and dampen secessionist demands, thereby stabilizing democracy. In effect, federalism helps ethnic groups to protect their interests and concerns—such as language, education, culture, security, and economic development—at the regional level. By providing increased autonomy to regional governments in which national minorities might constitute majorities, federalism effectively shifts power to minorities, thereby making them more content to live within a unified state despite being permanent minorities in the national electorate. These purported advantages have led many scholars to view federalism as the most promising means for hold-

---

44. The study by Reynal-Querol (2002) represents a partial exception. Reynal-Querol finds evidence that "inclusive democracy"—by which she appears to mean parliamentary systems that use PR—reduces the likelihood that "religious polarization" will lead to civil war.

45. Recall from Chapter 14 that incongruent and asymmetric federalism occurs when the political boundaries of the subnational units are specifically aligned with the geographic boundaries of social groups and when some territorial units enjoy more extensive powers than others relative to the central government.

ing heterogeneous and conflict-ridden countries together (Riker 1964; Lijphart 1977, 1996, 1999; Tsebelis 1990; Horowitz 1991; Stepan 1999; Lustik, Miodownik, and Eidelson 2004). In support of this line of reasoning, it is commonly accepted that federalism has played an important role in stabilizing democracies in ethnically diverse countries, such as Belgium, Canada, India, Spain, and Switzerland.

Several scholars have recently called for the adoption of federalism in Iraq as an institutional means for dealing with the ethnic conflict between Kurds, Sunnis, and Shias. For example, Brancati (2004, 7–8) states:

> [B]y dividing power between two levels of government—giving groups greater control over their own political, social, and economic affairs while making them feel less exploited as well as more secure—federalism offers the only viable possibility for preventing ethnic conflict and secessionism as well as establishing a stable democracy in Iraq . . . [A federal] system will help the United States not only to build democracy in Iraq but also to prevent the emergence of a Shi'a-dominated government in the country. Without this form of federalism, an Iraq rife with internal conflict and dominated by one ethnic or religious group is more likely to emerge, undermining U.S. efforts towards establishing democracy in Iraq as well as the greater Middle East.

Although federalism has historically been seen as helpful in dampening the flames of ethnic conflict and secessionism, several studies have challenged this view. Some of these studies even go so far as to suggest that federalism might actually intensify, rather than reduce, ethnic conflict. One way in which federalism is thought to do this is by reinforcing regionally based ethnic identities (Hardgrave 1994; Kymlicka 1998). Rather than encouraging the construction of political coalitions across ethnic lines, federalism creates incentives for the politicization of ethnic identities by officially recognizing particular ethnic groups and giving them a sense of legitimacy. In this way, federalism leads to the strengthening, rather than the weakening, of ethnic divisions.

Another way that federalism is thought to intensify ethnic conflict is by providing access to political and economic resources that ethnic leaders can then use to bring pressure against the state. In other words, decentralizing power to the regional level by establishing a federal form of government may have the unfortunate consequence of supplying groups with the necessary resources—regional legislatures, regional police forces, and regional forms of media—to more effectively engage in ethnic conflict and secessionism in the first place (Roeder 1991; Kymlicka 1998; Bunce 1999; Leff 1999; Hechter 2000; Snyder 2000). Indeed, leaders of multiethnic states like Sri Lanka and Indonesia have historically opposed federalism on precisely these grounds, seeing political decentralization as a slippery slope that is only likely to strengthen secessionist groups and generate demands for additional autonomy. A third way in which federalism is thought to encourage ethnic conflict is by making it easier for ethnic groups at the subnational level to produce legislation that discriminates against regional minorities (Nordlinger 1972; Horowitz 1991).

Several recent cross-national studies that support this line of reasoning present suggestive evidence that federalism may not be the panacea for ethnic conflict in divided societies that it is traditionally thought to be. For example, some studies find that although federalism tends to decrease outright rebellion, it increases protest activity among minority groups (Hechter 2000; Lustik, Miodownik, and Eidelson 2004). Another study finds that federalism has no effect on the level of attachment that minority (or majority) groups feel toward the state (Elkins and Sides 2007).

To a large extent, scholars have viewed the impact of federalism on ethnic conflict in black-and-white terms—it either always reduces the likelihood of ethnic conflict or it always increases it. In reality, though, we believe that most political scientists would accept that political decentralization has been helpful in curbing ethnic conflict and secessionism in some countries, such as Belgium and India, but that it has proved to be a failure in other countries, such as Nigeria and the former Yugoslavia. This suggests that the question we really need to ask ourselves is why federalism seems to be helpful in some contexts but not in others.

Brancati (2006) provides one potential answer to this question. She suggests that much has to do with the strength of regional parties in a country. Specifically, she argues that political decentralization reduces ethnic conflict when regional parties are weak but that it can increase ethnic conflict when regional parties are strong. Her causal story is graphically illustrated in Figure 15.10. On the one hand, Brancati believes that political decentralization reduces ethnic conflict by bringing the government closer to the people, increasing opportunities to participate in government, and giving groups discretion over their political, social, and economic affairs. On the other hand, though, she claims that political decentralization increases ethnic conflict by strengthening regional identity-based parties.

As we saw in Chapter 13 (see Box 13.4, "Nationalizing Party Systems"), political decentralization increases the strength of regional parties through the opportunities it provides these parties to win elections and influence policy in regional legislatures (Chhibber and

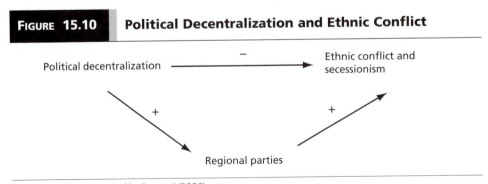

FIGURE 15.10   Political Decentralization and Ethnic Conflict

Note: Causal story posited by Brancati (2006).

Kollman 1998, 2004). According to Brancati, this strengthening of regional parties has a detrimental effect on ethnic conflict because these parties frequently reinforce regionally based ethnic identities, produce legislation that favors certain groups over others, and mobilize groups to engage in ethnic conflict and secessionism or support terrorist organizations that participate in these activities. Regional parties, by their very nature, tend to reinforce regional and ethnic identities by making people who share certain attributes or who live in particular areas think of themselves as a group with shared needs and goals. For example, the Northern League, a regional party in Italy, has gone to great lengths to make the people of northern Italy think of themselves as Northern Italians rather than simply as Italians. The Northern League even produces and distributes special identification cards for residents of the "Free Republic of Padania." Regional parties also frequently attempt to pass laws that discriminate against regional minorities. As an example, regional parties in Moldova exacerbated ethnic tensions with minority Romanians in Transnistria in 2004 when they passed a law closing schools that did not use the Cyrillic alphabet, thereby preventing Romanians in this region from being educated in their language. Regional parties also sometimes help violent insurgent groups in their activities against the state. For instance, regional parties in Northern Ireland and Spain, such as Sinn Féin and Herri Batasuna, have helped such organizations as the Irish Republican Army (IRA) and the Basque Euskadi Ta Azkatasuna (ETA) in their secessionist campaigns against the state. As Brancati notes, Batasuna has supported ETA financially by collecting the proceeds of ETA's "revolutionary tax" on local businesses, has used Basque media to support ETA and its goals, and has even used its offices to store ETA's guns and ammunition.

In sum, Brancati argues that whether federalism is helpful in reducing ethnic conflict or not depends on the extent to which decentralization leads to the strengthening of regional parties. If she is correct, then the key for policymakers interested in reducing ethnic conflict and stabilizing democracy is to combine incongruent and asymmetric federalism with other institutional features that lower the likelihood that regional parties will form and do well. As we saw in Chapter 13 (again see Box 13.4), one factor influencing the success of regional parties is the presence and timing of presidential elections (Golder 2006). As we noted then, the presidency is nearly always the most important electoral prize in a presidential democracy. Typically, however, there are only a small number of viable presidential candidates because only one person can become the president. Given the importance of the presidency, parties that do not have a viable presidential candidate, even if they are electorally strong in particular regions, are likely to find themselves abandoned by both voters and political entrepreneurs at election time. Parties that have a national base and, hence, a viable presidential candidate, will naturally benefit from this strategic behavior. The end result is a nationalized party system in which regionally based parties are likely to struggle to compete. The extent to which presidential elections exert nationalizing pressures on a country's party system will depend on how important it is to win the presidency and the temporal proximity between presidential and legislative elections. Specifically, party systems in presidential democracies are more likely to be stacked against regional parties if the president's power is large relative to that of other political actors and if presidential elections occur at the same time as regional ones (Hicken, forthcoming).

Electoral laws can also be written to discourage the emergence and success of regional identity-based parties. As we saw in Chapter 12 and as we noted earlier in this section, for example, preferential voting systems such as the alternative vote should encourage political parties to make broadly based centrist appeals beyond their core set of supporters, because their electoral success is likely to depend on the transfer of preference votes from other groups. In effect, preferential voting systems attempt to weaken or even transcend the political salience of regional as well as ethnic identities (Horowitz 1985, 1991; Reilly 1997, 2001). As a result, they are likely to discourage the emergence and success of parties that focus their campaigning on a particular identity (regional or ethnic) group. An alternative strategy to penalize regional parties would be to impose cross-regional vote requirements that force parties to compete in a certain number of regions and to win a certain percentage of the vote in these regions if they wish to be elected to the federal government. Russia, Indonesia, and Nigeria have explicitly adopted such cross-regional voting laws in an attempt to prevent identity-based parties from forming (Brancati 2004). Overall, it appears that incongruent and asymmetric federalism can help reduce ethnic conflict and stabilize democracy in countries with geographically concentrated ethnic groups. But this might be the case only if it is combined with institutional mechanisms designed to prevent regionally based identity parties from dominating the subnational governments.

PRESIDENTIALISM AND DEMOCRATIC SURVIVAL

To finish this chapter, we bring our discussion back to the question that dominated Part II of this book: why are some countries democratic, whereas others are not? In Chapters 6 and 7 we examined economic and cultural explanations for the emergence and survival of democracy. Having studied at some length the different institutions that democracies can adopt, we are now in a position to look at a third set of explanations for the survival of democracy: institutional explanations. Institutionalist approaches to democracy ask the following question: if democracy emerges, are there institutions, or combinations of institutions, that make the survival of democracy more or less likely? Although many institutional choices are thought to affect the prospects of democratic survival, one that has generated an enormous literature in comparative politics is the choice of whether to adopt a presidential or parliamentary form of democracy (Linz 1990a, 1990b, 1994; Shugart and Carey 1992; Mainwaring 1993; Stepan and Skach 1993; Jones 1995; Gasiorowski 1995; Mainwaring and Shugart 1997; Przeworski et al. 2000; Bernhard, Nordstrom, and Reenock 2001; Cheibub 2002, 2007; Valenzuela 2004). It is on this institutional choice that we focus in this section.

Considerable historical evidence suggests that democracy is less stable in presidential regimes than in parliamentary ones. Indeed, Przeworski et al. (2000, 129) present evidence showing that the expected life of democracy under presidentialism (twenty-one years) is about three to five times shorter than it is under parliamentarism (seventy-three years). This type of evidence has led some to talk of the "perils of presidentialism" (Linz 1990a). For many years comparative politics scholars have debated whether the fragility of democracy in presidential regimes is really due to something inherent in the structure of presidentialism itself or not, and, if so, what this might be. Answers to these questions are important because, despite the historical pattern showing that democracy is less likely to survive in presidential regimes, many new democracies have adopted presidential constitutions. Indeed, as Figure 11.2b in Chapter 11 illustrates, the percentage of democracies with presidential constitutions has recently doubled from 16 percent in 1978 to 32 percent in 2002. If the survival of democracy is inherently problematic in presidential regimes, this does not bode well for some of these newly democratic countries. In what follows, we suggest that some presidential democracies, specifically those with multiparty systems, are more unstable than others. As we go on to note, though, ongoing economic development around the world is making all presidential democracies more stable than they were in the past.

The Perils of Presidentialism

What are the consequences of presidentialism and parliamentarism for how the executive and legislative branches make policy? The first thing to note is that presidents are different from prime ministers. Unlike prime ministers, presidents fuse the symbolic attributes of the head of state with the pragmatic powers of the head of government. This creates "an aura, a self-image, and a set of broader expectations which are all quite different from those associated with a prime minister, no matter how popular he might be" (Linz 1990a, 53).[46] Supporters of presidential democracy argue that presidents provide an important check on the legislature that does not exist in parliamentary democracies. They point out that whereas presidents are accountable to the nation as a whole, legislators are typically elected by only a subset of the electorate and thus have particularistic interests that may run contrary to the interests of the nation as a whole. Having a president, it is claimed, can help to ameliorate and discipline the particularistic tendencies of legislators.

Shively (2001) summarizes what are commonly thought to be five of the main consequences of presidentialism. First, presidentialism is thought to lead to a situation in which policymaking power is concentrated in the hands of the president. At first glance, this claim might seem counterintuitive, given that presidentialism is typically thought of as a mechanism for the separation of powers between the executive and legislative branches of the government. But the president, through his ability to appeal directly to voters and fuse the powers associated with the head of state and head of government, is able to wield a degree of

---

46. Linz (1990a) traces this characterization of the presidential role back to the nineteenth-century constitutional scholar Walter Bagehot.

power unavailable to most prime ministers, who, by comparison, are "first among equals" in the legislature. Second, presidentialism is thought to make it difficult for citizens to identify who is responsible for policies; that is, it is thought to produce low clarity of responsibility. In effect, the separation of powers between the executive and legislative branches in presidential democracies allows each to blame the other when outcomes are bad and each to engage in credit claiming when outcomes are good. Third, presidentialism is thought to make it difficult for policy to be made quickly. In presidential democracies, new legislation in response to exogenous changes in a country's environment must work its way through the legislature and be accepted by the president before it can be enacted. Such negotiations are often protracted because, unlike in parliamentary democracies, a presidential government can face a legislature controlled by parties that do not support the president's legislative goals; as we saw in Chapter 11, a parliamentary government cannot survive without the support of a legislative majority.

Fourth, presidentialism is thought to produce a pattern of executive recruitment very different from that found in parliamentarism. In many parliamentary democracies, prime ministers tend to be selected from the leadership of a party's legislative delegation. As we illustrated in Chapter 13, membership in that leadership is typically restricted to parliamentarians who have worked their way up from lowly "backbench" positions by gaining policy expertise, honing their debating skills, and demonstrating their loyalty to the party. In contrast, presidential candidates are often drawn from outsiders who are seen to be free from commitments to the party elite.[47] Significantly, this means that presidential candidates are also frequently free of legislative experience and policymaking expertise. Fifth, presidentialism is thought to make it difficult to produce comprehensive policy. As we have already mentioned, the policymaking process in presidential democracies typically involves complex bargaining between the executive and legislative branches of government. A result is that some policies in presidential systems get adopted simply because they are crucial to gaining acquiescence from another branch of government on an unrelated matter. In contrast, because, by definition, the cabinet in a parliamentary democracy enjoys the confidence of the legislature, it is thought that parliamentary governments have a better chance of putting together comprehensive, rationalized, legislative programs.

As you might imagine, most of these purported consequences of presidentialism are viewed as liabilities. To be fair, though, it is important to recognize that many of these purported consequences are not unique to presidentialism—they occur in some parliamentary systems as well. For example, parliamentary democracies that have coalition governments are also likely to experience difficulty in (a) making policy quickly, (b) locating responsibil-

---

47. In presidential democracies, it is possible for complete political outsiders to win the presidency. This is precisely what happened when the academic and TV presenter Alberto Fujimori surprisingly won the 1990 presidential elections in Peru. The election of such a candidate to the "equivalent" position of prime minister in a parliamentary democracy is almost unthinkable.

ity for policy, and (c) making comprehensive policy. Indeed, we often hear people make the case that presidentialism, far from being a cause for concern, is, in fact, the solution to these problems in parliamentary democracies. Rather than talk about the "perils of presidentialism," some scholars choose to focus on the "problems of parliamentarism."

The problems of parliamentarism are, perhaps, best illustrated by the French Fourth Republic (1946–1958). As many scholars have noted, the French Fourth Republic was characterized by high levels of **immobilism** and government instability (Rioux 1989). In the twelve

> **Immobilism** describes a situation in parliamentary democracies in which government coalitions are so weak and unstable that they are incapable of reaching an agreement on new policy.

years of its existence, the French Fourth Republic witnessed twenty-four different governments under sixteen different prime ministers (Huber and Martinez-Gallardo 2004). A consequence of this instability was that French governments were unable to deal with the main issues of the day, particularly those having to do with its colonies in Indochina and Algeria. Much of the problem lay with the Fourth Republic's proportional electoral system that helped to produce a highly fragmented and polarized legislature. For example, roughly 30 percent of the seats in the National Assembly regularly went to parties on the extreme right (Gaullists and Poujadists) and the extreme left (Communists) that were not viewed as viable government coalition partners. This meant that the five or six small moderate parties that existed in the center of the policy space were forced to try to build legislative majorities from the remaining 70 percent of seats, something that proved extremely difficult. Governments typically had to choose between immobility—doing nothing and remaining in power—and attempting to push forward with their legislative program, which normally resulted in their quick removal from office. In May 1958 a majority of legislators in the National Assembly eventually voted themselves and the constitution out of existence, and delegated power to General Charles de Gaulle to write a new constitution. One of the goals of de Gaulle's new constitution was to concentrate power in the hands of a strong president so that he could override the stalemates that dogged the Fourth Republic and rule in the interest of the nation at large. For de Gaulle, a stronger president was the solution to the problems of parliamentarism as exhibited in the Fourth Republic.

Other parliamentary systems have experienced the same sort of chronic government instability and immobilism that plagued the French Fourth Republic. For example, another well-known case of a country characterized by endemic cabinet instability is postwar Italy. Between 1948 and 1991, the average duration of an Italian cabinet was less than a year (Merlo 1998). As with the French Fourth Republic, many scholars put this cabinet instability down to a proportional electoral system that helped to create highly fragmented and polarized legislatures. These legislatures, in turn, made it difficult for party leaders to form stable government coalitions or get much done. Explanations of immobilism nearly always start with the use of proportional electoral systems. As Rustow (1950, 116) put it, PR, "by facilitating cabinet crises, parliamentary stalemates, and legislative inaction, will tend to prevent any exercise of power whatever."

We should recall at this point, though, that a focus on government instability can often lead us to overstate the actual amount of political instability in a country. As we noted in Chapter 11, for example, government instability need not imply a lack of political or portfolio experience among cabinet ministers (Huber and Martinez-Gallardo 2004, 2008).[48] Consider the case of Italy again. Although postwar Italy has been ruled by shifting and unstable government coalitions, there has always been a great deal of political continuity just below the surface. For example, the Christian Democratic Party, the largest party in parliament for most of the postwar period, participated in every cabinet from 1948 to 1992 in coalition with a rotating set of junior partners comprised of the Liberal, Republican, Social Democratic, and Socialist Parties. As several scholars have noted, each new cabinet was essentially composed of the exact same people from the previous cabinet. According to P. A. Allum (1973, 119), "behind the façade of continuous cabinet crises, there [was] a significant continuity of party, persons, and posts" in postwar Italy. Scholars of French politics make an almost identical argument in regard to the government instability in the French Fourth Republic. In short, it is important to remember that cabinet instability in parliamentary democracies need not imply ministerial instability. More significant, *cabinet* instability, as we will see, does not imply *democratic* instability either.

So where does this leave us? Are the dangers of parliamentarism greater than the dangers of presidentialism, or vice versa? Although the examples of immobilism in the parliamentary democracies of postwar Italy and the French Fourth Republic are somewhat illustrative, ransacking history for supportive cases in favor of one's favorite or most hated institution is not good scientific practice. As a result, we will now turn our attention to a more systematic analysis of how presidentialism and parliamentarism affect democratic survival.

Stepan and Skach (1993) claim that the prospects for the survival of democracy are worse under presidentialism than under parliamentarism. They argue that the reason for this can be traced to the fact that the essence of parliamentarism is *mutual dependence,* whereas the essence of presidentialism is *mutual independence.* In a parliamentary democracy, the legislative and executive branches are mutually dependent. On the one hand, the government needs the support of a legislative majority to stay in power. On the other hand, the government can dissolve the legislature by calling new elections. In other words, the government and the legislature cannot continue to exist without the support of the other in a parliamentary democracy. In a presidential democracy, in contrast, the executive and legislative branches are mutually independent. Both the legislature and the president have their own independent sources of legitimacy and their own fixed electoral mandates. The legislature cannot remove the president from office and the president cannot remove the legislature.

---

48. By "political experience" we mean the amount of experience that ministers have in any cabinet portfolio. And by "portfolio experience" we mean the amount of experience that ministers have in a specific cabinet portfolio.

Stepan and Skach (1993) argue that the mutual dependence of parliamentarism encourages *reconciliation* between the executive and legislative branches, whereas the mutual independence of presidentialism encourages *antagonism* between them. In presidential democracies, this antagonism, which can arise when the president is faced by a legislature dominated by opposition parties, can lead to legislative deadlock. With no constitutional mechanism to resolve the deadlock, politicians and citizens in presidential democracies may look to the military to break the stalemate. In contrast, if deadlock occurs between the executive and legislative branches in a parliamentary democracy, there are constitutional means for resolving the crisis. Either the legislature can pass a vote of no confidence and remove the government, or the prime minister can dissolve the parliament and call for new elections. It is the existence of these constitutional means in parliamentary democracies for resolving deadlock situations that is thought to be at the heart of why democratic stability is greater in parliamentary democracies than in presidential ones.

Stepan and Skach (1993) present an impressive array of facts to support their claim that democratic consolidation is more likely in parliamentary democracies than in presidential ones. They begin by asking how many of the countries that became independent democracies between 1945 and 1979 were able to sustain democracy throughout the 1980s. In Table 15.6a, we list the names of all eighty countries that became independent democracies between 1945 and 1979. We also list whether they adopted a parliamentary, presidential, or mixed form of democracy. As you can see, countries that became independent in the post–World War II period were about as likely to adopt parliamentarism (forty-one) as they were to adopt presidentialism (thirty-six). In Table 15.6b, we list the names of those countries that were continuously democratic from 1979 to 1989 and the form of democracy that they had. Of the eighty countries that became independent democracies in the postwar period, only fifteen were continuously democratic through the 1980s. Incredibly, all fifteen of these countries had adopted parliamentarism; none of the thirty-six countries that adopted presidentialism managed to sustain democracy during the 1980s.

Lest a focus on newly independent countries be a source of bias, Stepan and Skach next present evidence from all countries that experienced democracy between 1973 and 1989 but that were not members of the Organization for Economic Cooperation and Development (OECD).[49] They wanted to know how many non-OECD countries that experienced democracy for at least a year between 1973 and 1989 were able to sustain it for a continuous ten-year period. Their data are shown in Table 15.7. As you can see, countries that experienced democracy for at least a year between 1973 and 1989 were about as likely to adopt parliamentarism

---

49. The Organization for Economic Cooperation and Development is essentially a club of rich democracies set up by the Allied powers after World War II. Stepan and Skach focus on non-OECD countries because it is in poor countries that democracy is most unstable and that institutional choice is arguably most important for the survival of democracy. This last point is one that we return to at the end of this section.

| TABLE 15.6 | Democratic Survival in Newly Independent States after World War II |

a. Form of Democracy Adopted

Parliamentary N = 41		Presidentialism N = 36		Mixed N = 3
Bahamas	Mauritius	Algeria	Madagascar	Lebanon
Bangladesh	Nauru	Angola	Malawi	Senegal
Barbados	Nigeria	Benin	Mali	Zaire
Botswana	Pakistan	Burkina Faso	Mauritania	
Burma	Papua New Guinea	Cameroon	Mozambique	
Chad	St. Lucia	Cape Verde	Niger	
Dominica	St. Vincent	Central African Rep.	Philippines	
Fiji	Sierra Leone	Cyprus	Rwanda	
Gambia	Singapore	Comoros	Sao Tomé	
Ghana	Solomon Islands	Congo	Seychelles	
Grenada	Somalia	Djibouti	Syria	
Guyana	Sri Lanka	Equatorial Guinea	Togo	
India	Sudan	Gabon	Taiwan	
Indonesia	Suriname	Guinea	Tunisia	
Israel	Swaziland	Guinea Bissau	Vietnam (N)	
Jamaica	Tanzania	Ivory Coast	Vietnam (S)	
Kenya	Trinidad and Tobago	Korea (S)	Yemen (S)	
Kiribati	Tuvalu	Korea (N)	Zambia	
Laos	Uganda			
Malaysia	Western Samoa			
Malta				

b. Continuously Democratic Countries, 1979–1989

Parliamentary N = 15/46		Presidentialism N = 0	Mixed N = 0
Bahamas	Nauru		
Barbados	Papua New Guinea		
Botswana	St. Lucia		
Dominica	St. Vincent		
India	Solomon Islands		
Israel	Trinidad and Tobago		
Jamaica	Tuvalu		
Kiribati			

Source: Data are from Stepan and Skach (1993, 8–9).

TABLE 15.7	**Democratic Survival in Fifty-three Non-OECD Countries, 1973–1989**	
	Parliamentary	Presidential
Democratic for at least one year	28	25
Democratic for ten consecutive years	17	5
Democratic survival rate	61%	20%

Source: Data are from Stepan and Skach (1993, 11).

(twenty-eight) as they were to adopt presidentialism (twenty-five). Of those countries that managed to sustain democracy for a continuous ten-year period, though, almost none had a presidential form of democracy. By comparing "democratic experimenters" with "democratic survivors," we can calculate a "democratic survival rate." As Table 15.7 illustrates, the democratic survival rate for parliamentary regimes is three times that for presidential regimes.

Although these simple comparisons suggest that there is something to the notion that presidentialism imperils democratic survival, they say almost nothing about why this might be the case. In other words, they say very little about the causal link between regime type and democratic survival. Recall, though, that Stepan and Skach do provide a potential causal story for the results in Tables 15.6 and 15.7. Specifically, they argue that presidentialism is more likely to lead to the kind of deadlock between the executive and legislative branches that invites extraconstitutional behavior. Thus, an observable implication of their theory is that military coups should be more common in presidential democracies than in parliamentary ones. Is this actually the case in the real world? In Table 15.8 we present data on the frequency of military coups collected by Stepan and Skach in the same fifty-three non-OECD countries as before. As you can see, military coups are more than twice as likely in presidential democracies as they are in parliamentary ones. Whereas 40 percent of the non-OECD countries that adopted presidentialism experienced a military coup between 1973 and 1989, just 18 percent of the countries that adopted parliamentarism did. This higher coup rate in presidential regimes is exactly as Stepan and Skach (1993) predict.

TABLE 15.8	**Military Coups in Fifty-three Non-OECD Countries, 1973–1989**	
	Parliamentary	Presidential
Democratic for at least one year	28	25
Number that experienced a coup	5	10
Coup susceptibility rate	18%	40%

Source: Data are from Stepan and Skach (1993, 12).

Although these simple statistics are quite illustrative, it is probably the case that some factors that cause democracies to fail are also associated with the choice to adopt parliamentarism or presidentialism in the first place. This raises the concern that it may be these other factors, and not presidentialism per se, that lead to the collapse of democracy. In other words, the failure to take account of these other factors might lead us to overestimate the true effect of regime type on democratic survival. Recognizing this concern, Stepan and Skach attempt to deal with it by leaning on the work of a Finnish political scientist named Tatu Vanhanen.

Recall from Chapter 6 that modernization theory predicts a strong association between democracy and societal development. In an attempt to evaluate modernization theory, Vanhanen (1991) constructed an index of democratization—a measure capturing the level of democracy in a country—and what he calls an index of power resources—a measure capturing the level of societal development in a country.[50] If modernization theory is accurate, then countries with a high score on the power resource index should also have a high score on the democratization index. Indeed, this is exactly what Vanhanen finds. Although Vanhanen finds a strong association between the power resource index and the democratization index, the fit is certainly not perfect. Some countries, for example, score significantly higher on the democratization index than their level of modernization, as revealed by the power resource index, would predict. Similarly, some countries score significantly lower on the democratization index than their level of modernization would predict. Stepan and Skach label those countries that score surprisingly high on the democratization index as "democratic overachievers." And they label those countries that score surprisingly low on the democratization index as "democratic underachievers." In Table 15.9, we present data from Stepan and Skach (1993) showing whether the democratic overachievers and underachievers are presidential or parliamentary democracies.

Stepan and Skach interpret the comparison of democratic overachievers and underachievers in Table 15.9 to mean that, after taking account of a set of modernization variables thought to influence democratic survival, parliamentary systems are five times more likely

TABLE 15.9	**Democracy Underachievers and Overachievers by Regime Type**	
	Parliamentary	Presidential
Overachievers	31	10
Underachievers	6	12
Ratio of overachievers to underachievers	5.17	0.83

Source: Data are from Stepan and Skach (1993, 10).

---

50. Vanhanen's (1991) index of power resources combines six factors related to modernization: the percentage of urban population, the percentage of the population in nonagricultural occupations, the percentage of students in the population, the literacy rate, the percentage of land in family-owned farms, and the degree of decentralization of nonagricultural economic resources.

to be democratic overachievers than they are to be democratic underachievers; in contrast, presidential systems are slightly more likely to be democratic underachievers as they are to be democratic overachievers. A different way to look at the data is that democratic over-achievers are about three times more likely to be parliamentary regimes as they are to be presidential ones; in contrast, democratic underachievers are about twice as likely to be presidential regimes as they are to be parliamentary ones. Overall, the evidence in Table 15.9 provides strong support for the claim that the prospects of democratic survival are lower in presidential systems than they are in parliamentary systems even after controlling for other factors that affect the survival of democracy.

We now briefly present some new statistical evidence to further support this conclusion. In Chapter 6 we used data provided by Przeworski et al. (2000) on 135 countries from 1950 to 1990 to examine how economic factors, such as a country's status as an oil producer, its wealth, and its economic growth, affect the probability that it will remain democratic. We can use the same data to examine whether the choice of parliamentarism or presidentialism also affects the probability of democratic survival. The results of our analysis using a dynamic probit model are shown in Table 15.10.

TABLE 15.10	**Effect of Regime Type on Democratic Survival**

Dependent variable: Probability that a country will be a democracy this year if it was a democracy last year.

Independent variables	1946–1990	1946–1990
Presidentialism	−0.58***	−0.32*
	(0.14)	(0.16)
GDP per capita		0.0002***
		(0.00005)
Growth in GDP per capita		0.04***
		(0.01)
Oil producer		−0.12
		(0.28)
Constant	2.22***	1.29***
	(0.10)	(0.18)
Number of observations	1584	1576
Log-likelihood	−170.85	−142.15

Source: Data are from Przeworski et al. (2000).

Note: Robust standard errors are in parentheses.

  * = greater than 90% significant.
 ** = greater than 95% significant.
*** = greater than 99% significant.

Recall that the coefficients indicate the direction in which the explanatory variables affect the probability that a democracy remains democratic. Thus, a positive coefficient indicates that an increase in the explanatory variable in question increases the probability of democratic survival, whereas a negative coefficient indicates than an increase in the variable reduces the probability of democratic survival. Recall also that the standard error beneath the coefficient essentially tells us how confident we are in our results. We tend to be more confident in our results the smaller the standard error is relative to the coefficient. Typically, as a rule of thumb, we claim that we can be 95 percent confident that the coefficient is correctly identified as being either positive or negative if the coefficient is bigger than twice the size of the standard error. If the coefficient is much larger than twice the size of the standard error, then we become even more confident. To save the reader from doing this calculation in their heads, authors often use stars next to the coefficient to indicate their confidence in the results. In Table 15.10, one star indicates that we are over 90 percent confident in our results; two stars that we are over 95 percent confident; and three stars that we are over 99 percent confident in our results. No stars next to a coefficient indicates that we cannot be confident that this variable has any effect on the probability of democratic survival.

So what do the results tell us? In line with the evidence presented by Stepan and Skach (1993), the coefficient on presidentialism is negative and significant. This indicates that democracies with presidential regimes are less likely to remain democratic than democracies with nonpresidential regimes. This is the case even when we take account of the economic factors thought to affect democratic survival that we examined in Chapter 6. At this point you might be wondering exactly how much a country's regime type matters for the survival of democracy? For example, how much less likely would it be for a non-oil-producing democracy with average GDP per capita ($3,494) and an average growth rate (2.24 percent) to remain democratic if it adopted presidentialism rather than parliamentarism? It is possible to answer this question using the results in Table 15.10 (although we do not show exactly how to do this here). The answer is that a democracy with the characteristics outlined above would be 50 percent more likely to collapse into dictatorship if it adopted presidentialism rather than parliamentarism. As this example illustrates, regime type is a very important determinant of democratic survival.

The Difficult Combination: Presidentialism and Multipartism

So far, the empirical evidence suggests that the prospects for democratic survival are greater in parliamentary democracies than in presidential ones. But recall our earlier discussion of immobilism in the French Fourth Republic. As you will remember, de Gaulle argued that concentrating power in the hands of a president was the key to solving the problems of highly fragmented legislatures, government instability, and immobilism in the French Fourth Republic. De Gaulle's belief that we should call upon a "strong man," such as a president, who can bring the country together in moments of crisis is quite widespread. As we now suggest, this has important implications for any causal connection between presidentialism and democratic survival. Specifically, if presidentialism is adopted in moments of crisis, then presidential regimes may fail at a higher rate than parliamentary regimes, not because there is something inherently problematic about presidentialism, but simply because presidentialism tends to be adopted in difficult circumstances.[51] One way to think about this is that presidentialism is like a hospital for ailing polities. We would not want to say that "hospitals kill people" just because large numbers of people die in hospitals. If people who go to the hospital are, on average, in poorer health than those who do not, then the explanation for high mortality rates in hospitals is likely to have more to do with the fact that people in a hospital are very sick than it does with the fact that they are in a hospital. Maybe the same is true for presidentialism. Until we can convince ourselves that countries that adopt presidentialism are the same as countries that adopt parliamentarism, studies such as Stepan and Skach's run the risk of overstating the deleterious effects of presidentialism.

The standard way to address this issue is, to continue our metaphor, to find a measure of "poor health" and include it as a control variable in an analysis of the relationship between mortality and being in a hospital. With one exception, we know of no empirical analysis that has adopted this approach when examining the relationship between presidentialism and democratic survival.[52] This may, in part, be because the analytical problem before us is probably more complicated than the one suggested by our hospital metaphor. For example, the factors that cause death in humans—cardiovascular diseases, parasitic diseases, respiratory diseases, and so on—affect those in a hospital and those not in a hospital the same way. But it may be the case that some factors that are "dangerous" for democracy are dangerous only in parliamentary regimes or only in presidential ones. If this is true, and presidential and parliamentary regimes are different sorts of organisms that process factors such as legislative fragmentation in fundamentally different manners, then it may prove extremely difficult to measure the underlying health of a regime independently of its status as a presidential or parliamentary system.

The work of one political scientist, Scott Mainwaring, suggests that presidential and parliamentary democracies *do* process political factors differently. In particular, it suggests that they process legislative fragmentation differently. Whereas legislative fragmentation always increases the likelihood of instability, the instability that is produced in parliamentary democracies is different from that produced in presidential ones. Specifically, legislative frag-

---

51. We owe this insight to an impromptu remark from a New York University undergraduate student during a class on comparative politics that we were teaching. Shugart (1999) makes a similar argument claiming that presidentialism tends to be adopted in large and complex societies with highly unequal income distributions and great regional disparities. Shugart argues that it is these inhospitable conditions rather than presidentialism itself that makes it difficult to sustain democracy.

52. The exception is Cheibub's (2007) analysis of presidentialism and democracy. He argues that what has made presidential regimes more fragile than parliamentary ones is that presidential regimes are more likely to emerge in countries in which the military has traditionally had a strong political role. As Cheibub demonstrates, any democratic regime, parliamentary or presidential, is more likely to fail in countries with a strong military tradition than in countries without such a tradition. This leads him to conclude that presidential democracies are more likely to fail not because they are presidential but because they are more likely to be adopted in difficult circumstances—when the military has a strong political presence.

mentation increases the likelihood of *cabinet instability* in parliamentary systems, whereas it increases the likelihood of *democratic instability* in presidential systems. The work by Mainwaring (1993) ultimately suggests that if legislative fragmentation is viewed as a political ailment in parliamentary democracies, as, say, critics of the French Fourth Republic like de Gaulle and others claim, then presidentialism could well be a form of medicine that is worse than the disease.

Why is legislative fragmentation likely to lead to such different outcomes in parliamentary and presidential democracies? One reason is that legislative fragmentation is more likely to lead to legislative deadlock in a presidential regime than in a parliamentary one. Legislative deadlock in a presidential democracy occurs when a legislative majority opposed to the president is large enough to pass bills in the legislature but not large enough to override a presidential veto. As we have already seen, legislative fragmentation increases the chances that the president's party will not command a legislative majority and, hence, the chances that legislative deadlock will occur. But why is legislative fragmentation more likely to lead to legislative deadlock in presidential systems than in parliamentary systems? The answer is that in a parliamentary democracy, the head of government, the prime minister, serves at the pleasure of the legislature and is, therefore, obliged to form a cabinet made up of a coalition of parties that *does* command a legislative majority. As we saw in Chapter 11, presidents do sometimes form coalitions (Cheibub, Przeworski, and Saiegh 2004; Amorim Neto 2006; Cheibub 2007).[53] The key difference, though, between parliamentary and presidential democracies is that when legislators vote against a president's legislation in sufficient numbers the legislation is blocked, but when legislators vote against a prime minister's legislation there is a good chance that the government will fall. In other words, a coalition government in a parliamentary democracy implies a legislative coalition, whereas this presumption is not the case in presidential democracies.[54] A consequence of this is that legislative fragmentation is much more likely to produce deadlock in a presidential democracy than it is to produce immobilism in a parliamentary democracy.

The problem of legislative deadlock created by legislative fragmentation in presidential democracies tends to be exacerbated by the way presidents are recruited to office. As we noted earlier, presidential candidates are often political outsiders who have relatively little policymaking expertise or experience dealing with the legislature. One of the main reasons for this is that presidents tend to be directly elected by the people and, therefore, have less need to build links with legislative actors than prime ministers do. A consequence of this, though, is that presidents tend to lack the necessary skills or experience to build legislative

---

53. Although presidents do sometimes form coalitions, coalition governments are less common and minority governments are more common in presidential democracies than in parliamentary ones (Cheibub, Przeworski, and Saiegh 2004; Amorim Neto 2006; Cheibub 2007).

54. As Mainwaring (1993, 221) puts it, "the extension of a cabinet portfolio does not necessarily imply party support for the president, as it does in a parliamentary system."

coalitions to resolve deadlock situations when they arise. Even when they do manage to build a coalition, it has been argued that coalition partners in presidential regimes have acute incentives to distance themselves from the president's policy goals. One reason for this is that they expect to run against the president in a winner-take-all contest in the next election and they want to be able to criticize his policies (Coppedge 1994, 168). In contrast, prime ministers tend to be individuals who have worked in the legislature for many years, who have gained enormous amounts of policy expertise, and who have been schooled in the art of coalition building. A result of this is that prime ministers are often better placed than presidents to build legislative coalitions to resolve deadlock situations when they emerge. Thus, according to Mainwaring (1993), presidential democracies are not only more apt than parliamentary democracies to have executives whose policy programs will be consistently blocked by the legislature, but they are also more apt to have executives who are less capable of dealing with problems when they arise.

When legislative deadlock does occur, it is much more likely to lead to democratic instability in presidential democracies than in parliamentary ones. If legislative deadlock occurs between the executive and legislative branches in a parliamentary regime, then there are constitutional means for resolving the crisis. Either the legislature can pass a vote of no confidence and remove the government, or the prime minister can dissolve the parliament and call new elections. As Mainwaring (1993, 208) notes, though, in presidential democracies, "there are no neat means of replacing a president who is enormously unpopular in the society at large and has lost most of his/her support in the legislature." Thus, the absence of a vote of no confidence may ensure the stability of the head of government in presidential regimes, but it introduces a rigidity that can threaten democratic stability by encouraging frustrated elites or masses to call for the removal of the president, or the dissolution of parliament, as a way to break the deadlock (Linz 1994). Although there are some circumstances under which political actors can accomplish this within the bounds of some presidential constitutions, the solution to deadlock is more likely to be extraconstitutional in presidential regimes than in parliamentary ones. As this argument makes clear, legislative deadlock is more likely to produce *democratic* instability in presidential democracies; if and when immobilism occurs in parliamentary democracies, it is more likely to produce *cabinet* instability.

Earlier, we presented evidence suggesting that democracy was more fragile in presidential regimes than in parliamentary ones. An important implication of Mainwaring's argument, though, is that democracy should be more fragile in some presidential regimes than in others. Specifically, his argument implies that democracy should be more fragile in (perhaps only in) presidential democracies that are characterized by high levels of legislative fragmentation than in those characterized by low levels of legislative fragmentation, because legislative fragmentation increases the likelihood of deadlock, which, in turn, increases the likelihood of democratic instability. When legislative fragmentation is low, the likelihood of deadlock and, hence, democratic instability will also be low.

To evaluate his claim that presidential democracies will be unstable particularly (or only) when legislative fragmentation is high, Mainwaring (1993) examines all countries that experienced uninterrupted democracy for the twenty-five-year period between 1967 and 1992. Although twenty-four parliamentary regimes were able to sustain democracy during this period, just four presidential regimes were able to do so: Colombia, Costa Rica, the United States, and Venezuela. Mainwaring wanted to know what made these presidential regimes different from other presidential regimes. His answer was that they all effectively had two-party systems, as illustrated in Table 15.11; none of them had multiparty systems. At the time of his writing in 1993, Mainwaring argued that only one multiparty presidential regime had historically managed to sustain democracy for a twenty-five-year period. And this exception was Chile, a democracy, begun in 1932, that experienced a dramatic "death" in 1973 when a military coup overthrew the Socialist president Salvador Allende and replaced him with the dictator General Augusto Pinochet. Allende had been elected in 1970 with a slim plurality of the vote (35.3 percent) and was immediately beset with problems from every side in the country's highly fragmented and deeply polarized legislature.[55]

In Table 15.12, we use data from Mainwaring (1993, 205–207) to calculate a democratic success rate for parliamentary regimes, multiparty presidential regimes, and two-party presidential regimes. Democratic success is defined here as a sustaining of democracy for an uninterrupted twenty-five-year period at any time between 1945 and 1992. The information in Table 15.12 suggests that democratic consolidation is possible in two-party presidential regimes but not in multiparty presidential regimes. Interestingly, the democratic success rate for two-party presidential regimes (0.50) is almost as high as the democratic success rate for parliamentary regimes (0.57). These results provide strong evidence that it is the combination of presidentialism and multipartism rather than just presidentialism that is inimical to democracy. Indeed, Mainwaring refers to the combination of presidentialism and multipar-

TABLE 15.11	Presidential Regimes that Sustained Democracy from 1967 to 1992 and Their Party System Size
Country (year)	**Effective number of legislative parties**
Colombia (1986)	2.45
Costa Rica (1986)	2.21
United States (1984)	1.95
Venezuela (1983)	2.42

Source: Amorin Neto and Cox (1997, 169–170).

---

55. We are generally reluctant to invoke the "exception that proves the rule," but if this hackneyed phrase ever applies, this seems to be the case.

TABLE 15.12	Regime Type, Party System Size, and Democratic Consolidation, 1945–1992
Regime type	**Democratic success rate**
Multiparty presidentialism	1/15, or 0.07
Two-party presidentialism	5/10, or 0.5
Parliamentarism	25/44, or 0.57

Source: Data are from Mainwaring (1993, 205–207).

Note: The democratic success rate refers to the percentage of countries that were able to sustain democracy for an uninterrupted twenty-five-year period at any time between 1945 and 1992.

La Moneda, the Chilean presidential residence, under ground and air attack by Chilean armed forces during the September 11, 1973 coup d'état that led to the ruthless dictatorship of General Augusto Pinochet. The democratically elected Socialist president Salvador Allende is thought to have committed suicide during the palace siege.

tism as "the difficult combination" for precisely this reason.

It is worth noting that Stepan and Skach (1993) also provide evidence in support of Mainwaring's conjecture in their own analysis of presidentialism and democratic survival. Although they do not make too much of it, they provide data on the size of party systems in those countries that became independent after 1945 and that managed to sustain democracy during the 1980s. These data are shown in Table 15.13. As you can see, long-lived multiparty parliamentary regimes are not particularly rare but long-lived multiparty presidential regimes are.

The data presented thus far seem to support Mainwaring's claim that it is not presidentialism per se that imperils democracy but rather presidentialism combined with a highly fragmented legislature. There are, however, a couple of reasons to be concerned about our approach up to this point. First, the scholarly work that we have examined so far has imposed some fairly arbitrary cut-offs on the data. Why, for example, should we consider a democracy long lived if it survives at least twenty-five years instead of, say, at least twenty-four years or twenty-six years, as Mainwaring does? Why should we consider continuous democratic rule for ten years (in the 1980s) a natural measure of "democratic consolidation" as Stepan and Skach do? Why should we classify countries as having multiparty systems if they have an effective number of legislative parties greater than 2.9? Second, we have made no attempt to take account of other factors that might be associated with democracy, regime

TABLE 15.13	**Consolidated Democracies by Regime Type and Party System Size**	
	Effective number of legislative parties	
Constitution	**Fewer than three**	**Three or more**
Parliamentary	23	11
Mixed	0	2
Presidential	5	0

Source: Data are from Stepan and Skach (1993, 8–9).

Note: The numbers in the table refer to those countries that became independent after 1945 and that sustained democracy for a continuous ten-year period from 1979 to 1989.

type, and party system size. We now end our discussion of the supposed "difficult combination" with a brief presentation of statistical results meant to address these concerns.

Earlier in this section, we estimated a dynamic probit model to examine the effect of presidentialism on the probability of democratic survival, taking into account such economic factors as wealth, economic growth, and oil production (Table 15.10). We now modify this model in such a way that it also tests to see whether the effect of presidentialism on the probability of democratic survival varies with the size of the party system. Recall that Mainwaring's hypothesis is that presidentialism will have a stronger negative effect on the survival of democracy when the party system is large than when the party system is small. Indeed, presidentialism may have no negative effect on the survival of democracy at all when the party system is sufficiently small. Because our hypothesis is a conditional one—the effect of presidentialism varies with party system size—the interpretation of our empirical results is a bit more complicated than it was earlier in the section (Brambor, Clark, and Golder 2006). Because it is easier to show the relevant information for testing Mainwaring's hypothesis in the form of a figure than in a table of results, we turn to Figure 15.11.

In Figure 15.11, the vertical distance between the gray horizontal line and the solid black downward-sloping line indicates the estimated effect of presidentialism on the probability of democratic survival for any given effective number of legislative parties.[56] The downward slope in the solid black line indicates how the effect of presidentialism on the probability of democratic survival changes with the effective number of legislative parties. The important point to notice is that the line starts off close to, but below, zero, and becomes more and

---

56. Figure 15.11 is based on a dynamic probit model that takes account of GDP per worker, growth in GDP per worker, and a country's status as an oil producer. A qualitatively similar figure is obtained if we use GDP per capita and growth in GDP per capita as our proxies for wealth and economic growth. Party system size is measured by the effective number of legislative parties. Data come from Przeworski et al. (2000) and cover 135 countries from 1950 to 1990. In Figure 15.11, we plot the effect of presidentialism on the probability of democratic survival for the specific case in which a country is not an oil producer, its GDP per worker is $14,468, and its growth in GDP per worker is 2.41 percent; this is the "average democracy" in our sample.

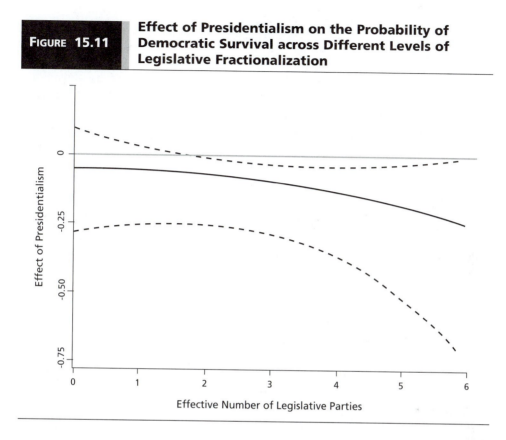

FIGURE 15.11	**Effect of Presidentialism on the Probability of Democratic Survival across Different Levels of Legislative Fractionalization**

more negative as the effective number of legislative parties increases. This tells us that the effect of presidentialism on democratic survival is always negative and that this negative effect becomes stronger—that is, increasingly negative—as the effective number of legislative parties increases.

The solid downward-sloping line shows the direction of the effect of presidentialism on democratic stability (negative) but not whether this effect is statistically significant or not. To know whether the effect is statistically significant, we need to look at the dashed curved lines on either side of the solid downward-sloping line. These dashed lines represent the upper and lower bounds of what political scientists call the "95 percent confidence interval." Together, these dashed lines indicate how certain we are that we have correctly identified the effect of presidentialism on democratic survival as being negative. When the upper and lower bounds of the confidence interval are on either side of the gray horizontal line drawn through the zero point on the y-axis, then we cannot reject the possibility that presidentialism has no effect on democratic survival. This situation is equivalent to a coefficient's having no stars in the table of results presented earlier in the section (and elsewhere in the book). When the upper and lower bounds of the confidence interval are both below the zero line, though, as occurs when the effective number of legislative parties is greater than 2, then we can be 95 percent confident that presidentialism has a negative effect on continued democratic survival. To sum up, Figure 15.11 demonstrates that presidentialism has a significant negative effect on continued democratic survival once the effective number of legislative parties is greater than about 2. This significant negative effect grows larger as the effective number of legislative parties increases.[57] This is exactly as Mainwaring predicts. We should remind the reader at this point that Figure 15.11 is generated by a model that takes account of economic factors such as wealth, oil production, and economic growth.

Summary

In this section we examined, and found considerable support for, an argument that says that presidential constitutions make successful democratic consolidation more difficult than parliamentary constitutions, particularly when the legislature is highly fragmented. The key weakness of presidentialism appears to be its inability to find legal ways out of executive-legislative deadlock, something that is more likely to occur when the legislature is highly fragmented. It is possible to put this finding in a broader perspective by comparing it with the analysis of veto players than we did in the last chapter. In Chapter 14 we discussed various arguments about the effect of multiple veto players on policy stability. All else equal, it was argued, an increase in the number of veto players is expected to make it more difficult to change the status quo policy. This was particularly true if the veto players held diverse policy preferences. What we characterized in the last chapter as policy stability induced by veto players is equivalent in many ways to what we have referred to in this chapter as deadlock or immobilism. The father of modern veto player theory, George Tsebelis, has conjectured that although large numbers of veto players with diverse preferences may encourage policy stability, they may also encourage political instability (Tsebelis 1995, 322). The Mainwaring claim that multipartism and presidentialism form a "difficult combination" for democratic consolidation can be interpreted in light of veto player theory. If Tsebelis is correct that an increased number of veto players leads to policy stability, which in its extreme form manifests itself as "deadlock," then we should expect presidentialism and parliamentarism to affect the type of political instability that ensues.

In other words, multiple veto players leads to policy stability (deadlock), but the form of political instability that results depends on a country's constitution. As we have already argued, if the constitution is presidential, then policy stability or deadlock is likely to encour-

---

57. If we were to extend the upper and lower bounds of the confidence intervals in Figure 15.11 further to the right, they would indicate that presidentialism no longer has a statistically significant negative effect on continued democratic survival when the effective number of legislative parties is slightly greater than 6.1. This is little comfort for presidential democracies in general, however, because only about 3 percent of the presidential observations in our sample have a party system larger than this.

age a coup or some other form of democratic instability. If, however, the constitution is parliamentary, the policy stability of immobilism is likely to lead to a vote of no confidence, a cabinet reshuffle, or elections leading to the formation of a new cabinet; that is, cabinet instability. This causal argument is presented in Figure 15.12.[58]

At this point, we would like to point out one last subtlety that involves our discussion of democratic survival in this section and our discussion of the effects of wealth on democratic survival from Chapter 6. Recall that Przeworski et al. (2000) argue that wealth is, essentially, a sufficient condition for democratic survival. As they indicate, countries above a certain wealth threshold (about $6,055 per capita in 1985 PPP U.S. dollars) are likely to stay democratic forever, should they, for whatever reason, become democratic in the first place (see Chapter 6, Box 6.1 for a discussion of purchasing power parity [PPP]). The claim that wealth is sufficient to ensure democratic consolidation leads to a surprising result—the choice of political institutions, say, the combination of multipartism and presidentialism, is likely to have a bigger effect on the chances that democracy will survive in poor countries than in rich ones. This is because, according to Przeworski et al. (2000), democracy is likely to survive in rich countries whether they have chosen felicitous institutions or not. In other words, institutional choice matters much more in poor countries than in rich ones, at least when it comes to democratic consolidation.[59] This result is somewhat surprising because traditional

| FIGURE 15.12 | **Veto Players, Policy Stability, and Different Types of Political Instability** |

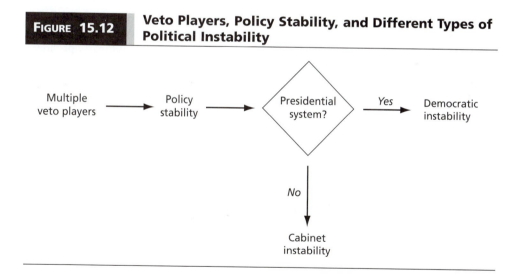

---

58. We should note that we have simplified matters throughout this section by ignoring mixed democracies.

59. Evidence consistent with this line of reasoning comes from Boix (2003, 153–154). In a study of democratic survival from 1850 to 1990, for example, he finds that presidential democracies are more likely than parliamentary democracies to fail only in underdeveloped countries; he finds no difference in the democratic survival rates of parliamentary and presidential regimes in developed countries.

approaches in this area predict that formal institutions are more important in rich countries, where they are more likely to be accompanied by the rule of law, than in poor countries.[60] One of our former students tested this implication in her undergraduate honors thesis at New York University (Ferrer 2003). Her findings, consistent with a veto player interpretation of the Mainwaring argument, show that the probability of democratic regime failure increases as the number of veto players increases *but only in poor countries*.[61] These results are suggestive enough to warrant future work on the interactive effect of institutional and economic variables on the survival of democracy (Bernhard, Nordstrom, and Reenock 2001).

Finally, we would like to point out that whereas the choice between presidentialism and parliamentarism is typically addressed explicitly by constitution writers, the size of the party system is not entirely under their direct control. As we say in Chapter 13, though, comparative politics scholars know quite a bit about why some countries have many parties and some have few. Specifically, we can expect a country with high levels of social heterogeneity to produce a highly fragmented legislature unless specific electoral institutions (majoritarian ones) are adopted with the goal of reducing the number of parties. Consequently, the results in this section suggest that if a presidential constitution is chosen for some reason, then adopting permissive electoral laws such as PR with a high district magnitude is likely to cause problems. In the presence of social heterogeneity, permissive electoral laws can be expected to produce multipartism, which, combined with presidentialism, is likely to inhibit democratic consolidation. Of course, the finding of Przeworski et al. (2000) on the apparent sufficiency of wealth may suggest that relatively rich countries have a greater margin of error in choosing their institutions than poor countries. This may explain why some multiparty presidential regimes in Latin America have managed to stay democratic since the wave of transitions to democracy that began there in the mid-1980s. For some time now many of these countries have exceeded Przeworski et al.'s "magical" threshold of wealth at which democracy is immune to breakdown.

CONCLUSION

We have, perhaps, gone on long enough. We hope, however, that this chapter has convinced you that contemporary comparative politics has a great deal to say that is of vital interest to citizens and policymakers who would like to know how the institutions they choose are likely to affect the political, social, and economic outcomes they will experience. Let us briefly summarize the basic results that we have presented in this chapter. First, we have shown pat-

---

60. Recent studies in this area strongly suggest that the importance of rule of law and other legal institutions for democratic consolidation itself varies across different levels of societal development (Reenock and Staton 2008; Reenock, Staton, and Radean 2008).

61. In this case, "poor" is defined as $6,055 per capita GDP, Przeworski et al.'s (2000) cut-off point.

terned differences in the way that majoritarian and consensus democracies represent the interests of voters. Second, we have demonstrated that electoral laws influence both who is chosen to rule and how they are likely to wield that power—at least with respect to redistributive fiscal policy. Third, we have highlighted the ways in which constitutional elements, such as electoral laws and federalism, are likely to affect the probability of ethnic conflict. And finally, we have reported results suggesting that the choice of electoral laws and the decision about whether to adopt presidentialism or parliamentarism are likely to influence strongly the survival of new democracies—especially if the country's level of wealth is not sufficiently high to, by itself, make democratic survival likely.

Many questions remain about how these results interact with each other. We invite students to speculate about such matters and to develop the tools necessary to evaluate their answers. Comparative politics raises and attempts to answer questions with life and death implications. We hope that as you finish this book, your development as a student of comparative politics is just beginning.

KEY CONCEPTS

accountability, *689*

clarity of responsibility, *690*

common pool resource problem, *719*

confessionalism, *735*

congruence, or static representation, *695*

consensus vision of democracy, *680*

consociationalism, *734*

ethnic outbidding, *732*

fiscal policy, *700*

government identifiability, *693*

immobilism, *745*

Keynesianism, *700*

majoritarian vision of democracy, *680*

mandate, *693*

partisan model of macroeconomic policy, *709*

prospective voting, *693*

representation, *675*

responsiveness, or dynamic representation, *695*

retrospective voting, *689*

PROBLEMS

The following two problems are designed to incorporate material covered in the earlier sections of the book with the material presented in this final chapter, and to encourage you to synthesize what you have learned so that you can make practical policy recommendations.

1. After a long experience with authoritarianism, a new democracy is looking to install a constitution that will maximize its chances of survival. As an expert in comparative institutions, you have been hired as a consultant by the transitional government. They have asked you to develop a proposal in which you are to make recommendations on specific institutions that you believe will enhance their chances of never returning to authoritarianism. To aid in their selection, they have asked you to rank your reform recommendations according to

their likely impact on regime survival. What are your recommendations? Be sure to support your claims with evidence from the literature (both theoretical and empirical). Is there information about the country, such as its wealth and ethnic heterogeneity, which would shape your recommendations?

2. You have received a telephone call from the new interim leadership in Burma (formerly Myanmar), following the collapse of the military junta in the wake of a devastating cyclone. The caller, a policymaker, asks you to explain the pros and cons of parliamentarism versus presidentialism and to advise whether a mixed form of democracy would capture the benefits of both parliamentary and presidential systems while taming the problems commonly associated with each of them. In your reply, you should draw on both theory and empirics. Be sure to discuss what other institutions the caller needs to consider and under what conditions some sets of institutions might be preferable to others. (In answering part of this question, it might be useful to refer back to the section on the making and breaking of governments in mixed democracies in Chapter 11.)

Appendix A

The Failed States Index is produced by the Fund for Peace and the magazine *Foreign Policy*. It is based on the twelve indicators of state vulnerability listed below. Each indicator is scaled from 0 to 10, with 0 being the most stable and 10 being the least stable. A country's overall "vulnerability" or "instability" score, which runs from 0 to 120, is determined by simply adding up its scores on the twelve indicators. Each country is then ranked into four categories: Alert (90–120), Warning (60–89.9), Moderate (30–59.9), and Sustainable (0–29.9). The complete ranking of 177 countries along with their individual scores on the twelve different indicators are shown in Table A.1. For more information, see http://www.foreignpolicy.com/story/cms.php?story_id=3865.

SOCIAL INDICATORS

1. Mounting Demographic Pressures.
2. Massive Movement of Refugees or Internally Displaced Persons Creating Complex Humanitarian Emergencies.
3. Legacy of Vengeance-Seeking Group Grievance or Group Paranoia.
4. Chronic and Sustained Human Flight.

ECONOMIC INDICATORS

5. Uneven Economic Development along Group Lines.
6. Sharp and/or Severe Economic Decline.

POLITICAL INDICATORS

7. Criminalization or Delegitimization, or both, of the State.
8. Progressive Deterioration of Public Services.
9. Suspension or Arbitrary Application of the Rule of Law and Widespread Violation of Human Rights.
10. Security Apparatus Operates as a "State Within a State."
11. Rise of Factionalized Elites.
12. Intervention of Other States or External Political Actors.

TABLE A.1	Ranking of 177 Countries according to the Failed States Index												
Rank	Country	1	2	3	4	5	6	7	8	9	10	11	12	Total
1	Sudan	9.2	9.8	10	9	9.1	7.7	10	9.5	10	9.9	9.7	9.8	113.7
2	Iraq	9	9	10	9.5	8.5	8	9.4	8.5	9.7	10	9.8	10	111.4
3	Somalia	9.2	9	8.5	8	7.5	9.2	10	10	9.7	10	10	10	111.1
4	Zimbabwe	9.7	8.7	8.8	9.1	9.5	10	9.5	9.6	9.7	9.5	9	7	110.1
5	Chad	9.1	8.9	9.5	7.9	9	8.3	9.5	9.1	9.2	9.6	9.7	9	108.8
6	Cote d'Ivoire	8.6	8.3	9.8	8.4	8	8.9	9.5	7.9	9.2	9.6	9.3	9.8	107.3
7	Democratic Republic of Congo	9.4	8.9	8.8	7.6	9.1	8	8.3	8.7	8.9	9.6	8.6	9.6	105.5
8	Afghanistan	8.5	8.9	9.1	7	8	8.3	8.8	8	8.2	9	8.5	10	102.3
9	Guinea	7.8	7.4	8.1	8.3	8.5	8.5	9.6	8.9	8.6	8.1	9	8.5	101.3
10	Central African Republic	8.9	8.4	8.8	5.5	8.6	8.4	9	8	8.2	8.9	9.3	9	101
11	Haiti	8.6	4.2	8	8	8.2	8.4	9.2	9	9.1	9.3	9.3	9.6	100.9
12	Pakistan	8.2	8.5	9	8.1	8.5	5.8	8.7	7.1	8.7	9.5	9.5	8.5	100.1
13	North Korea	8	6	7.2	5	8.8	9.6	9.8	9.5	9.7	8.3	7.9	7.9	97.7
14	Burma/Myanmar	8.5	8.5	9.1	6	8.9	7.6	9.1	8.3	9.8	9	8.2	4	97
15	Uganda	8.1	9.4	8.5	6	8.5	7.5	8.5	8.2	8.2	8.3	7.8	7.4	96.4
16	Bangladesh	8.6	5.8	9.6	8.4	9	6.9	9	7.4	7.8	8	9.5	5.9	95.9
17	Nigeria	8.2	5.6	9.5	8.5	9.1	5.4	9.1	8.7	7.1	9.2	9.5	5.7	95.6
18	Ethiopia	9	7.9	7.8	7.5	8.6	8	7.9	7	8.5	7.5	8.9	6.7	95.3
19	Burundi	9.1	8.9	6.7	6.7	8.8	8.2	7.1	8.9	7.5	6.8	7.5	9	95.2
20	Timor-Leste	8.1	8.5	7.1	5.3	6.5	8.5	9.5	7.9	6.9	9	8.8	8.8	94.9
21	Nepal	8.1	5.2	8.9	6.1	9.2	8.2	8.5	6.6	8.8	8.3	8.5	7.2	93.6
22	Uzbekistan	7.7	5.4	7.1	7.1	8.6	7.5	9.2	6.8	9	8.9	9.2	7	93.5
23	Sierra Leone	8.6	7.4	7.1	8.7	8.7	8.7	8	8	7	6.5	7.7	7	93.4
24	Yemen	8	6.7	7.3	7.2	8.7	8	7.8	8.1	7.2	8	9	7.2	93.2
25	Sri Lanka	7	8.6	9.5	6.9	8.2	6	8.9	6.5	7.5	8.7	9.2	6.1	93.1
26	Republic of the Congo	8.7	7.3	6.8	6.1	8.1	8.3	8.5	8.8	7.9	7.9	7.2	7.4	93
27	Liberia	8.1	8.5	6.5	6.8	8.3	8.4	7	8.6	6.7	6.9	8.1	9	92.9
28	Lebanon	6.9	8.6	9	7	7.1	6.3	7.3	6.4	7	9	8.8	9	92.4
29	Malawi	9	6	6	8	8.8	9.2	7.9	9	8	5.4	7.5	7.4	92.2
30	Solomon Islands	8.5	4.8	8	5.1	8	8	8.5	8.5	7.1	7.7	8.8	9	92
31	Kenya	8.4	8	6.9	8	8.1	7	8	7.4	7	7.1	8.2	7.2	91.3
32	Niger	9.2	5.9	8.9	6	7.2	9.2	8.2	8.8	7.1	6.7	6	8	91.2

Rank	Country	1	2	3	4	5	6	7	8	9	10	11	12	Total
33	Colombia	6.8	9.5	7.4	8.4	8.4	3.8	8.2	6	7.4	8.3	8.5	7	89.7
33	Burkina Faso	8.6	5.6	6.4	6.6	8.9	8.2	7.6	8.9	6.6	7.6	7.7	7	89.7
35	Cameroon	7	6.8	7	7.9	8.7	6.1	8.5	7.5	7.2	7.7	8	7	89.4
36	Rwanda	9.1	7	8.7	7.6	7.1	7.5	8.5	6.9	7.4	4.6	8.2	6.6	89.2
36	Egypt	7.7	6.5	7.8	6.2	7.8	7	9	6.7	8.5	6.1	8.3	7.6	89.2
38	Guinea Bissau	7.6	6.5	5.4	7	8.6	8	7.2	8.5	8	8	6.8	7.2	88.8
39	Tajikistan	7.7	6.1	6.3	6.4	7.3	7.3	9	7.3	8.6	7.8	8.8	6.1	88.7
40	Syria	6.5	8.9	8	6.8	8.1	6.8	8.5	5.3	8.5	7.4	7.5	6.3	88.6
41	Equatorial Guinea	8	2	7	7.4	9	4	9.4	8.6	9.4	8.9	8.5	6	88.2
41	Kyrgyzstan	7.5	6.2	6.8	7.4	8	7.5	8.2	6.3	7.9	7.9	7.5	7	88.2
43	Turkmenistan	7	4.5	6.2	5.6	7.3	7.4	9	7.7	9.6	8.5	8.2	6.5	87.5
44	Laos	8	5.5	6.5	6.6	5.7	7.1	7.9	8	8.5	8.2	8.6	6.6	87.2
45	Mauritania	8.7	6.2	8	5	7	7.8	6.8	8.1	7.1	7.4	7.9	6.7	86.7
46	Togo	7.5	5.4	6	6.5	7.5	8.2	7.7	8	7.8	7.8	7.6	6.6	86.6
47	Bhutan	6.5	7.5	7	6.7	8.7	7.9	8	6.5	8.5	4.6	8	6.5	86.4
48	Moldova	7	4.7	7.3	8.4	7.5	7.5	7.9	7.1	6.8	6.3	7.5	7.7	85.7
48	Cambodia	7.6	5.9	7.3	8	7.2	6.4	8.5	7.6	7.1	6.2	7.5	6.4	85.7
50	Eritrea	8.1	7.1	5.4	6	5.9	8.4	8.3	7.7	7.4	7.5	7.2	6.5	85.5
51	Belarus	8	4.6	6.5	5	7.5	6.8	9.1	6.9	8.5	6.7	8.5	7.1	85.2
52	Papua New Guinea	7.5	3.5	8	7.9	9	7.3	7.8	7.8	6.1	7	6.7	6.5	85.1
53	Angola	8.5	7.5	5.9	5	8.7	4.2	8.6	7.7	7.5	6.2	7.5	7.6	84.9
54	Bosnia	6.1	8	8.3	6	7.2	6	7.6	5.6	5.3	7.3	8.3	8.8	84.5
55	Indonesia	7	7.5	6	7.5	8	6.5	6.5	7	7	7.3	7.2	6.9	84.4
56	Philippines	7	5.7	7.2	6.7	7.6	5.8	8.2	5.9	6.8	7.6	7.8	6.9	83.2
57	Iran	6.2	8.6	7.1	5	7.2	3.3	7.8	5.7	8.7	8.3	8.9	6	82.8
58	Georgia	6.3	6.8	7.6	5.7	7	5.7	7.9	6.1	5.4	7.8	7.8	8.2	82.3
59	Bolivia	7.4	3.7	7	7	8.5	6.4	7.2	7.4	7	6.2	8.3	5.9	82
60	Guatemala	7	6	7.1	6.7	8	7	7.4	6.6	7.1	7.3	5.9	5.3	81.4
61	Swaziland	8.7	4	4	5.3	6	7.7	8.8	8.1	7.5	7.1	7.1	7	81.3
62	Russia	7.5	5.9	7.7	6.5	8.2	3.9	7.6	6.2	8.5	6.8	8.5	3.9	81.2
62	Lesotho	9	4.5	5.5	5.4	5.5	9.1	7.5	8.9	6.7	6.2	6.7	6.2	81.2
62	China	8.7	5.1	8	6.5	9	4	8.5	6.5	9	5.3	7.5	3.1	81.2
62	Azerbaijan	6	7.5	7.3	5.3	7.4	6.3	7.8	6	6.4	7.2	7.5	6.5	81.2
66	Serbia	6	8	7.7	5.5	7.7	6.5	7.5	5	6.1	6.3	8	6.8	81.1
66	Cape Verde	7.9	4.8	4.8	8.2	6.2	8	7	7.4	6.4	6.1	6.4	7.9	81.1
66	Maldives	8	7	4.9	7	4.9	7.3	7.9	7.1	7.7	6.1	7.2	6	81.1
69	Zambia	9.1	6.2	5.2	6.7	7.4	7.9	7.6	7.9	5.8	5.5	5.2	6.1	80.6

Rank	Country	1	2	3	4	5	6	7	8	9	10	11	12	Total
69	Dominican Republic	6.5	6.4	6.1	8.3	8.1	5.8	6	6.9	7	6.5	7.4	5.6	80.6
71	Djibouti	7.9	6.5	5.5	5	6.1	6.9	7.4	7.5	6	7	6.9	7.6	80.3
72	Nicaragua	6.7	5.1	6.4	7.1	8.6	7.8	6.5	7	5.4	6.5	7.2	5.7	80
73	Ecuador	6.2	6	6.7	7.1	8	5.3	7.5	6.8	6.6	6.6	7.6	5.5	79.9
74	Venezuela	6.9	5.2	6.8	6.9	8.2	4	7.5	6.3	7.9	6.9	7.5	5.7	79.8
75	Israel	7	7.9	9	3.5	6.9	3.7	7.3	7	7.4	5.3	7.2	7.4	79.6
76	Tanzania	7.4	7.1	6.2	6	6.9	7.4	6.3	7.8	6	5.7	5.5	7	79.3
77	Sao Tome	7.9	4.8	5.1	7.4	6.1	8.5	7.3	8.1	5.3	5.8	5.9	6.4	78.6
77	Cuba	6.5	4.7	5.5	6	7.2	6.3	7.6	3.8	7.8	7.7	7.8	7.7	78.6
79	Comoros	6.2	3.6	5.3	5.7	6.1	7.6	7.9	8.7	6.6	6.7	6.5	6.9	77.8
79	Vietnam	6.5	5.9	5.3	7	6.2	6.2	7	6.5	6.9	7.4	7	5.9	77.8
81	Mozambique	7.5	2.2	4.7	8	7.2	7.5	7.4	8	7	5.9	5.6	5.9	76.9
82	Jordan	6.2	6.8	6.5	5	7.7	6.6	6.2	5.6	6.2	6.4	6.5	6.9	76.6
83	Madagascar	8.5	3	5.1	5	7	7.5	5.7	8.7	5.7	6.1	6.7	7.5	76.5
83	Saudi Arabia	5.9	7.2	7.7	3.6	6.5	2.3	8.8	4.3	8.8	7.3	7.6	6.5	76.5
85	Peru	6.6	4	6.9	7.5	8.1	5.6	6.6	6.2	5.2	7.7	7	5	76.4
86	Morocco	6.6	7.5	6.8	6.2	7.3	6.6	7.8	6	6.6	5.2	5.4	4	76
86	Gambia	6.4	5.2	4.2	6	7	8	7.9	6.6	6.8	5.8	5.9	6.2	76
86	Thailand	7	5.8	7.8	4.4	7.5	3	8	5.5	6.3	7.2	8	5.5	76
89	Algeria	6.1	6.7	7	5.6	7.3	3.5	7.3	7	7.4	6.4	5.9	5.7	75.9
90	Fiji	5.9	4	7.5	5.4	7.5	5.9	9	4.1	5.9	7	8.2	5.3	75.7
91	Mali	8.5	4.4	6.1	7.9	6.6	8.7	4.7	8.6	4.6	4.8	3.7	6.9	75.5
92	Turkey	6.9	5.8	7.4	5	8.7	4.7	6.1	5.4	5.1	6.7	7.1	6	74.9
92	El Salvador	7.6	5.6	6	7	7.3	5.4	7	6.9	6.9	5.8	3.9	5.5	74.9
94	Honduras	7.8	2	5.3	6	8.7	7.6	7.4	6.6	5.8	5.9	6.3	5.4	74.8
95	Macedonia	5.4	4.7	7.1	7	7.4	5.9	7.3	5.1	5.3	6.1	6.4	6.4	74.1
96	Suriname	7.1	4.2	6.1	6.7	8.3	6.9	6.4	4.9	5.7	6.2	5.1	6.3	73.9
97	Samoa	6.8	3.8	5	7.9	7.2	6.3	6.7	4.7	4.9	6.7	5.4	8.4	73.8
98	Micronesia	7.7	3.2	5	8.1	7.1	6.5	6.9	7.1	2.5	6	5.4	8	73.5
99	Guyana	6.9	4.1	5.4	7.9	8.1	6.8	6.4	5.7	5.6	5.9	4.9	5.6	73.3
99	Gabon	6.6	5.7	3	6	7.8	4.9	7.3	7	6.7	5.3	7.2	5.8	73.3
101	Paraguay	6.5	1.6	6.2	6	7.4	6.7	8.1	6.5	7.9	4.3	7.5	4.2	72.9
102	Mexico	6.9	4	6.1	7	8.4	6.2	6.1	5.7	5.1	6.1	4.8	6.2	72.6
103	Kazakhstan	5.7	3	5.2	4	6.2	6.6	7.5	6.1	7	6.7	7.7	6.6	72.3
104	Benin	6.5	5.2	4	6.9	7.4	7.1	6.4	8.1	4.8	5.2	3.8	6.6	72
105	Grenada	5.9	3.6	5	7.9	7.1	6.5	6.5	4.1	5.1	5.9	5.7	8.3	71.6
106	Ukraine	6.5	3.6	7	7.5	7	5	7.5	4.5	5.9	3	7.9	6	71.4
107	Seychelles	6.9	5	5.5	4.7	6.9	4	7.9	4.1	6.7	6.2	6.7	6.7	71.3

Rank	Country	1	2	3	4	5	6	7	8	9	10	11	12	Total
107	Namibia	6.5	5.1	5.4	7.9	8.2	5.9	4.4	7.5	5.7	5.5	3.2	6	71.3
109	Brunei Darussalam	6.3	5.6	7.4	4.2	7.9	3.2	7.7	3.3	6.6	6.9	7.4	4.7	71.2
110	India	8.3	3.2	7	7.1	8.9	4.6	4.8	6.7	5.4	5	5.6	4.2	70.8
111	Albania	6.5	2.7	5.4	7.5	6.1	6.8	7.4	6.2	5.4	5.5	5.4	5.6	70.5
112	Armenia	5.8	7.6	5	6.9	6	5	6.5	6.2	5.5	4.5	5.8	5.5	70.3
113	Cyprus	5.1	4.2	8.3	5.7	7.5	4.8	5.5	3.8	3.5	4.2	8.4	9.2	70.2
114	Belize	6.6	5.2	5.2	6.9	7.6	6	6.5	5.7	3.8	5.7	5	5.6	69.8
115	Libya	6.2	2.6	5.6	4	7.3	5.3	7.4	4.5	8.1	5.3	8	5	69.3
116	Trinidad and Tobago	5.9	3.8	5.2	6.4	8.1	3.8	6.4	5.8	5.4	5.7	5.7	5.4	67.6
117	Senegal	7	4.5	5.2	5.1	6.9	5.7	5.7	6.7	5.6	5.2	3.8	5.5	66.9
117	Brazil	6.6	3.4	6.1	5	8.8	3.2	6.2	6.3	5.3	6.9	4.5	4.6	66.9
119	Botswana	9.2	5.8	3.4	6	7	5.6	5.4	6.5	4.8	3.9	2.8	6	66.4
120	Malaysia	6.3	4.1	5.5	3.6	6.6	4.6	5.9	5.4	6.5	6.3	5.3	5.8	65.9
121	Antigua and Barbuda	5.2	3.6	5.2	7.9	7.1	4.8	6.3	4.9	5.5	5.2	4.6	5.4	65.7
122	Tunisia	5.6	3.4	5.1	5.1	7.4	4.3	6.4	5.9	7.3	5.9	6.2	3	65.6
123	Jamaica	6.1	2.4	4.3	6.7	6.7	5.4	7	5.8	5.4	5.6	3.7	6	65.1
124	Kuwait	5.9	4.8	4.5	4.1	6.1	3.1	6.9	3.3	6.5	5.3	7.6	4	62.1
125	Ghana	6	4.5	5.1	8	6.8	4	5.5	6.9	4.5	2.4	3.5	4.7	61.9
126	Romania	5.5	3.8	5.2	5.2	6.1	5.7	6.1	5.2	4.8	3.4	4.5	5.4	60.9
127	Croatia	5.3	6.5	6	5	5.7	5.7	4.2	4.1	4.5	3.9	3.9	5.7	60.5
128	Bulgaria	5.4	4.1	4.2	5.9	6.2	4.3	5.7	5	4.7	5.4	3.9	5.5	60.3
129	Bahamas	6	3.6	5.3	5.4	7.2	3.2	6.4	4.1	3	5.4	5.3	5.2	60.1
130	Barbados	4.1	3.6	5.8	6.9	7.6	5	6.1	2.6	3	5.3	4.8	5.1	59.9
131	Panama	6.6	3.1	4.4	5	7.5	5.8	4.8	5.6	4.7	5	2.9	4	59.4
132	Mongolia	6	1	4.1	2.1	5.4	5.2	6	5.3	6.7	4.8	4.9	6.9	58.4
133	South Africa	8.2	6	4.7	4	8.5	2.8	4.3	5.7	4.1	3.2	3.9	2	57.4
134	Bahrain	5.3	3.6	6	3.7	5	3.5	6.8	3.7	4.7	3.4	6	5.3	57
135	Latvia	5.2	5.7	4.6	5	7	5.8	4.7	4	3.8	2.2	4.4	4.3	56.7
136	Montenegro	5.4	4.1	5.8	2.5	4.3	4	4.5	3.6	5.6	4.8	6	5	55.6
137	Qatar	5	3.6	5.6	3.6	4.8	4.9	7	2.6	4.7	2.5	4.7	4.6	53.6
138	United Arab Emirates	5.6	3.6	4	3.7	5.2	2.6	7	4.1	6.1	2.1	3.6	4	51.6
139	Hungary	3.7	3.6	3	5	6.3	4.1	6	3.8	4	2.1	5.5	4.1	51.2
140	Estonia	4.8	4.8	4.5	4	4.9	3.7	5	3.8	3.7	2.1	5.9	3.3	50.5
140	Costa Rica	5.6	4.4	4	5	6.6	4.8	3.9	2.9	3.5	2	3.3	4.5	50.5
142	Slovakia	4.3	1.8	4.4	5.5	6.5	4.5	4.2	4.1	3.9	2	4.2	3.9	49.3
143	Lithuania	5.4	3.4	3.5	5.4	6.2	4.5	4.2	3.7	3.7	2	3	4	49
144	Malta	3.8	6.1	3.9	4.8	4.5	3.5	4.5	3.3	3.5	4.5	1.6	4.5	48.5
145	Poland	4.9	3	3.2	6.5	4.8	4.3	4.2	4.2	3.5	2	3	4	47.6

Rank	Country	1	2	3	4	5	6	7	8	9	10	11	12	Total
146	Oman	3.1	1.1	3	1.1	2	3.7	6.3	4.2	6.6	5.3	7.1	2	45.5
147	Greece	4.7	2	3.5	5.4	5	3.5	4	3.1	3.9	3.1	1.6	3.7	43.5
148	Mauritius	3.6	1.1	3.5	2.1	5.9	3.8	5.1	4.4	3.9	3.5	3	2.8	42.7
149	Czech Republic	4	3.3	3.2	5	3.9	2.8	3.7	3.8	3.5	2	3.5	3.4	42.1
150	Argentina	3.8	1.5	4	4	5.2	4.6	3.4	3.8	3.7	1.9	2.7	2.8	41.4
151	Uruguay	5.1	1.1	2	5.9	5.1	3.5	2.9	4	2.5	3	2.3	3.5	40.9
152	South Korea	4	3.9	3.5	5.5	2.4	1.4	3.9	2	2.7	1	2.9	6.5	39.7
153	Spain	3.7	1.8	5.7	1.6	5	3.4	1.4	1.9	2.8	4.3	5.6	2	39.2
154	Germany	3.9	4.8	4.9	3	5.5	3	2.3	1.7	2.9	2.5	1.8	2.1	38.4
155	Slovenia	4	1.7	3.4	3.5	5.4	3.2	3.2	3.5	3.5	3	1.1	2	37.5
156	Italy	3.6	3.5	3.5	3	4.5	3.8	3.7	2	1.8	2.5	3.2	2	37.1
157	France	4.1	3.6	5.8	2	4.8	2.9	1.5	1.4	3.2	1	1.8	2	34.1
157	United Kingdom	3.4	4	4.2	2	4.7	1.4	2.2	1.8	2.6	3	2.7	2.1	34.1
159	Chile	3.8	1.1	3.5	2.1	4	3.8	1.6	3.7	3.7	2	1.5	3	33.8
160	United States	3.5	5.5	3.2	1	5.8	1.8	2.8	1.4	4.6	1.3	1.7	1	33.6
161	Singapore	2.9	1.1	3	3	2.5	3.4	3.6	1.5	4	1	4	3	33
162	Portugal	4.8	1.1	2.5	2.1	3.9	3.7	1.5	3.7	3.3	1	1.3	3.5	32.4
163	Netherlands	3.2	4	4.8	2.5	4	2	1.3	1.4	1.4	1	1	2	28.6
164	Japan	4.1	1.1	3.8	2	2.5	2.6	1.8	1.2	3.5	1	1.3	3.6	28.5
165	Luxembourg	2.1	1.8	3.7	1.2	2.5	2	3.3	2.6	1.6	2	3	2.3	28.1
166	Austria	2.8	2.2	3.5	1.1	5	1.9	1.3	1.4	1.5	1	2	2.3	26
167	Belgium	3.2	1.6	4	1.1	4	2.1	1.5	1.4	1.5	1.6	1.5	2	25.5
168	Canada	3.3	2.4	2	2.1	5	1.5	1.5	1.2	2	1	1.6	1.5	25.1
169	Australia	2.9	1.6	3	1.1	4.4	1.8	1	1.4	2.5	0.9	1.5	1.1	23.2
170	Denmark	3.2	2.6	2.5	2	1.9	2.1	1	1.4	1.5	1	1	2	22.2
171	Iceland	1	0.9	1	3.2	2.5	3.5	1.3	1.3	2.1	1	0.8	2.5	21.1
172	New Zealand	1.1	1.2	2	2.1	4	3	1.1	1.4	1.5	1	1	1.1	20.5
173	Switzerland	3.3	1.7	2.1	2	2.6	1.5	1	1.4	1.7	1	1	0.9	20.2
174	Ireland	1.6	1.5	1	2.1	2.9	2.1	1.5	1.8	1.5	1	1	1.5	19.5
175	Sweden	3.2	2.8	1	2	2	1.3	1	1.2	1.4	0.9	1	1.5	19.3
176	Finland	2.5	1.6	1	2.1	1.9	2.2	0.9	1.2	1.5	0.9	0.7	2	18.5
177	Norway	2	1.6	1	1.1	2	2.1	1	1.3	1.5	1	1	1.5	17.1

Source: Reproduced with permission from The Fund for Peace.
Note: Shading indicates the country's category: Alert (90–120), Warning (60–89.9), Moderate (30–59.9), or Sustainable (0–29.9).

Appendix B

Three Different Measures of Regime Type in 2002

Country	PACL	Polity IV (−10 to 10)	Freedom House (1 to 7)
Afghanistan	Dictatorship		Dictatorship (6)
Albania	Democracy	Democracy (7)	Mixed (3)
Algeria	Dictatorship	Mixed (−3)	Dictatorship (5.5)
Andorra	Democracy		Democracy (1)
Angola	Democracy	Mixed (−3)	Dictatorship (5.5)
Antigua	Democracy		Mixed (3)
Argentina	Democracy	Democracy (8)	Mixed (3)
Armenia	Democracy	Mixed (5)	Mixed (4)
Australia	Democracy	Democracy (10)	Democracy (1)
Austria	Democracy	Democracy (10)	Democracy (1)
Azerbaijan	Dictatorship	Dictatorship (−7)	Mixed (5.5)
Bahamas	Democracy		Democracy (1)
Bahrain	Dictatorship	Dictatorship (−7)	Mixed (5)
Bangladesh	Democracy	Democracy (6)	Mixed (4)
Barbados	Democracy		Democracy (1)
Belarus	Dictatorship	Dictatorship (−7)	Dictatorship (6)
Belgium	Democracy	Democracy (10)	Democracy (1)
Belize	Democracy		Democracy (1.5)
Benin	Democracy	Democracy (6)	Democracy (2.5)
Bhutan	Dictatorship	Dictatorship (−8)	Dictatorship (5.5)
Bolivia	Democracy	Democracy (9)	Democracy (2.5)
Bosnia-Herzegovina	Dictatorship		Mixed (4)
Botswana	Dictatorship	Democracy (9)	Democracy (2)
Brazil	Democracy	Democracy (8)	Democracy (2.5)
Brunei	Dictatorship		Dictatorship (5.5)
Bulgaria	Democracy	Democracy (9)	Democracy (1.5)
Burkina Faso	Dictatorship	Mixed (0)	Mixed (4)

Country	PACL	Polity IV (–10 to 10)	Freedom House (1 to 7)
Burma	Dictatorship	Dictatorship (–7)	Dictatorship (7)
Burundi	Dictatorship		Dictatorship (5.5)
Cambodia	Dictatorship	Mixed (2)	Dictatorship (5.5)
Cameroon	Dictatorship	Mixed (–4)	Dictatorship (6)
Canada	Democracy	Democracy (10)	Democracy (1)
Cape Verde	Democracy		Democracy (1.5)
Central African Republic	Democracy	Mixed (5)	Mixed (5)
Chad	Dictatorship	Mixed (–2)	Dictatorship (5.5)
Chile	Democracy	Democracy (9)	Democracy (1.5)
China	Dictatorship	Dictatorship (–7)	Dictatorship (6.5)
Colombia	Democracy	Democracy (7)	Mixed (4)
Comoros	Dictatorship	Mixed (4)	Mixed (4.5)
Congo (Brazzaville)	Dictatorship	Democracy (–4)	Mixed (5)
Congo (Kinshasa)	Dictatorship	Mixed (0)	Dictatorship (6)
Costa Rica	Democracy	Democracy (10)	Democracy (1.5)
Ivory Coast	Democracy	Mixed (4)	Dictatorship (6)
Croatia	Democracy	Democracy (7)	Democracy (2)
Cuba	Dictatorship	Dictatorship (–7)	Dictatorship (7)
Cyprus	Democracy	Democracy (10)	Democracy (1)
Czech Republic	Democracy	Democracy (10)	Democracy (1.5)
Denmark	Democracy	Democracy (10)	Democracy (1)
Djibouti	Dictatorship	Mixed (2)	Mixed (4.5)
Dominica	Democracy		Democracy (1)
Dominican Republic	Democracy	Democracy (8)	Democracy (2)
Ecuador	Dictatorship	Democracy (6)	Mixed (3)
Egypt	Dictatorship	Dictatorship (–6)	Dictatorship (6)
El Salvador	Democracy	Democracy (7)	Democracy (2.5)
Equatorial Guinea	Dictatorship	Mixed (–5)	Dictatorship (6.5)
Eritrea	Dictatorship	Dictatorship (–7)	Dictatorship (6.5)
Estonia	Democracy	Democracy (6)	Democracy (1.5)
Ethiopia	Dictatorship	Mixed (1)	Mixed (5)
Fiji	Dictatorship	Mixed (5)	Mixed (3.5)
Finland	Democracy	Democracy (10)	Democracy (1)
France	Democracy	Democracy (9)	Democracy (1)
Gabon	Dictatorship	Mixed (–4)	Mixed (4.5)
Gambia	Dictatorship	Mixed (–5)	Mixed (4)

Country	PACL	Polity IV (−10 to 10)	Freedom House (1 to 7)
Georgia	Dictatorship	Mixed (5)	Mixed (4)
Germany	Democracy	Democracy (10)	Democracy (1)
Ghana	Democracy	Democracy (6)	Democracy (2.5)
Greece	Democracy	Democracy (10)	Democracy (1.5)
Grenada	Democracy		Democracy (1.5)
Guatemala	Democracy	Democracy (8)	Mixed (4)
Guinea	Dictatorship	Mixed (−1)	Dictatorship (5.5)
Guinea-Bissau	Democracy	Mixed (5)	Mixed (4.5)
Guyana	Democracy	Democracy (6)	Democracy (2)
Haiti	Democracy	Mixed (−2)	Dictatorship (6)
Honduras	Democracy	Democracy (7)	Mixed (3)
Hungary	Democracy	Democracy (10)	Democracy (1.5)
Iceland	Democracy	Democracy (10)	Democracy (1)
India	Democracy	Democracy (9)	Democracy (2.5)
Indonesia	Democracy	Democracy (7)	Mixed (3.5)
Iran	Dictatorship	Mixed (3)	Dictatorship (6)
Iraq	Dictatorship	Dictatorship (−9)	Dictatorship (7)
Ireland	Democracy	Democracy (10)	Democracy (1)
Israel	Democracy	Democracy (10)	Democracy (2)
Italy	Democracy	Democracy (10)	Democracy (1)
Jamaica	Democracy	Democracy (9)	Democracy (2.5)
Japan	Democracy	Democracy (10)	Democracy (1.5)
Jordon	Dictatorship	Mixed (−2)	Dictatorship (5.5)
Kazakhstan	Dictatorship	Dictatorship (−6)	Dictatorship (5.5)
Kenya	Democracy	Democracy (8)	Mixed (4)
Kiribati	Democracy		Democracy (1)
Korea, North	Dictatorship	Dictatorship (−9)	Dictatorship (7)
Korea, South	Democracy	Democracy (8)	Democracy (2)
Kuwait	Dictatorship	Dictatorship (−7)	Mixed (4.5)
Kyrgyzstan	Dictatorship	Mixed (−3)	Dictatorship (5.5)
Laos	Dictatorship	Dictatorship (−7)	Dictatorship (6.5)
Latvia	Democracy	Democracy (8)	Democracy (1.5)
Lebanon	Dictatorship		Dictatorship (5.5)
Lesotho	Democracy	Democracy (8)	Democracy (2.5)
Liberia	Dictatorship	Mixed (0)	Dictatorship (6)
Libya	Dictatorship	Dictatorship (−7)	Dictatorship (7)

Country	PACL	Polity IV (–10 to 10)	Freedom House (1 to 7)
Liechtenstein	Democracy		Democracy (1)
Lithuania	Democracy	Democracy (10)	Democracy (1.5)
Luxembourg	Democracy	Democracy (10)	Democracy (1)
Macedonia	Democracy	Democracy (9)	Mixed (3)
Madagascar	Democracy	Democracy (7)	Mixed (3.5)
Malawi	Democracy	Mixed (5)	Mixed (4)
Malaysia	Dictatorship	Mixed (3)	Mixed (5)
Maldives	Dictatorship		Dictatorship (5.5)
Mali	Democracy	Democracy (6)	Democracy (2.5)
Malta	Democracy		Democracy (1)
Marshall Islands	Democracy		Democracy (1)
Mauritania	Dictatorship	Dictatorship (–6)	Mixed (5)
Mauritius	Democracy	Democracy (10)	Democracy (1.5)
Mexico	Democracy	Democracy (8)	Democracy (2)
Micronesia	Democracy		Democracy (1.5)
Moldova	Democracy	Democracy (8)	Mixed (3.5)
Mongolia	Democracy	Democracy (10)	Democracy (2)
Morocco	Dictatorship	Dictatorship (–6)	Mixed (5)
Mozambique	Dictatorship	Democracy (6)	Mixed (3.5)
Namibia	Dictatorship	Dictatorship (–7)	Democracy (2.5)
Nauru	Democracy		Democracy (1.5)
Nepal	Dictatorship	Dictatorship (–6)	Mixed (4)
Netherlands	Democracy	Democracy (10)	Democracy (1)
New Zealand	Democracy	Democracy (10)	Democracy (1)
Nicaragua	Democracy	Democracy (8)	Mixed (3)
Niger	Democracy	Mixed (4)	Mixed (4)
Nigeria	Democracy	Mixed (4)	Mixed (4.5)
Norway	Democracy	Democracy (10)	Democracy (1)
Oman	Dictatorship	Dictatorship (–8)	Dictatorship (5.5)
Pakistan	Dictatorship	Mixed (–5)	Dictatorship (5.5)
Palau	Democracy		Democracy (1.5)
Panama	Democracy	Democracy (9)	Democracy (1.5)
Papua New Guinea	Democracy	Democracy (10)	Democracy (2.5)
Paraguay	Democracy	Democracy (7)	Mixed (3.5)
Peru	Democracy	Democracy (9)	Democracy (2.5)

Country	PACL	Polity IV (−10 to 10)	Freedom House (1 to 7)
Philippines	Democracy	Democracy (8)	Democracy (2.5)
Poland	Democracy	Democracy (10)	Democracy (1.5)
Portugal	Democracy	Democracy (10)	Democracy (1)
Qatar	Dictatorship	Dictatorship (−10)	Dictatorship (6)
Romania	Democracy	Democracy (8)	Democracy (2)
Russia	Democracy	Democracy (7)	Mixed (5)
Rwanda	Dictatorship	Mixed (−4)	Dictatorship (6)
St. Kitts & Nevis	Democracy		Democracy (1.5)
St. Lucia	Democracy		Democracy (1.5)
St. Vincent	Democracy		Democracy (1.5)
Samoa	Dictatorship		Democracy (2)
San Marino	Democracy		Democracy (1)
Sao Tomé et Principe	Democracy		Democracy (1.5)
Saudi Arabia	Dictatorship	Dictatorship (−10)	Dictatorship (7)
Senegal	Democracy	Democracy (8)	Democracy (2.5)
Serbia & Montenegro	Dictatorship	Democracy (7)	Democracy (2.5)
Seychelles	Dictatorship		Mixed (3)
Sierra Leone	Democracy	Mixed (5)	Mixed (4)
Singapore	Dictatorship	Mixed (−2)	Mixed (4.5)
Slovakia	Democracy	Democracy (9)	Democracy (1.5)
Slovenia	Democracy	Democracy (10)	Democracy (1)
Solomon Islands	Democracy		Mixed (3)
Somalia	Dictatorship	Mixed (0)	Dictatorship (6.5)
South Africa	Democracy	Democracy (9)	Democracy (1.5)
Spain	Democracy	Democracy (10)	Democracy (1)
Sri Lanka	Democracy	Democracy (6)	Mixed (3.5)
Sudan	Dictatorship	Dictatorship (−6)	Dictatorship (7)
Suriname	Democracy		Democracy (1.5)
Swaziland	Dictatorship	Dictatorship (−9)	Dictatorship (5.5)
Sweden	Democracy	Democracy (10)	Democracy (1)
Switzerland	Democracy	Democracy (10)	Democracy (1)
Syria	Dictatorship	Dictatorship (−7)	Dictatorship (7)
Taiwan	Democracy	Democracy (9)	Democracy (2)
Tajikistan	Dictatorship	Mixed (−1)	Dictatorship (5.5)
Tanzania	Dictatorship	Mixed (2)	Mixed (3.5)

Country	PACL	Polity IV (−10 to 10)	Freedom House (1 to 7)
Thailand	Democracy	Democracy (9)	Democracy (2.5)
Togo	Dictatorship	Mixed (−2)	Dictatorship (5.5)
Tonga	Dictatorship		Mixed (4)
Trinidad & Tobago	Democracy	Democracy (10)	Mixed (3)
Tunisia	Dictatorship	Mixed (−4)	Dictatorship (5.5)
Turkey	Democracy	Democracy (7)	Mixed (3.5)
Turkmenistan	Dictatorship	Dictatorship (−9)	Dictatorship (7)
Uganda	Dictatorship	Mixed (−4)	Mixed (5)
Ukraine	Democracy	Democracy (7)	Mixed (4)
United Arab Emirates	Dictatorship	Dictatorship (−8)	Dictatorship (5.5)
United Kingdom	Democracy	Democracy (10)	Democracy (1)
United States of America	Democracy	Democracy (10)	Democracy (1)
Uruguay	Democracy	Democracy (10)	Democracy (1)
Uzbekistan	Dictatorship	Dictatorship (−9)	Dictatorship (6.5)
Vanuatu	Democracy		Democracy (1.5)
Venezuela	Democracy	Democracy (6)	Mixed (3.5)
Vietnam	Dictatorship	Dictatorship (−7)	Dictatorship (6.5)
Yemen	Dictatorship	Mixed (−2)	Dictatorship (5.5)
Zambia	Democracy	Mixed (1)	Mixed (4)
Zimbabwe	Dictatorship	Dictatorship (−7)	Dictatorship (6)

Appendix C

188 Independent Countries and Their Electoral Systems in 2004

Country	Electoral system for legislature	Electoral system family	Electoral system for president
Afghanistan	SNTV	Majoritarian	TRS
Albania	Dependent (SMDP & list PR)	Mixed	
Algeria	List PR	Proportional	TRS
Andorra	Independent (PBV & list PR)	Mixed	
Angola	List PR	Proportional	TRS
Antigua	SMDP	Majoritarian	
Argentina	List PR	Proportional	TRS
Armenia	Independent (SMDP & list PR)	Mixed	
Australia	AV	Majoritarian	
Austria	List PR	Proportional	TRS
Azerbaijan	Independent (TRS & list PR)	Mixed	TRS
Bahamas	SMDP	Majoritarian	
Bahrain	TRS	Majoritarian	
Bangladesh	SMDP	Majoritarian	
Barbados	SMDP	Majoritarian	
Belarus	TRS	Majoritarian	TRS
Belgium	List PR	Proportional	
Belize	SMDP	Majoritarian	
Benin	List PR	Majoritarian	TRS
Bhutan	None	None	None
Bolivia	Dependent (SMDP & list PR)	Mixed	TRS
Bosnia-Herzegovina	List PR	Proportional	SMDP
Botswana	SMDP	Majoritarian	
Brazil	List PR	Proportional	TRS
Brunei	None	None	None
Bulgaria	List PR	Proportional	TRS
Burkina Faso	List PR	Proportional	TRS

Country	Electoral system for legislature	Electoral system family	Electoral system for president
Burma	SMDP	Majoritarian	
Burundi	List PR	Proportional	
Cambodia	List PR	Proportional	
Cameroon	PBV/List PR & SMDP	Majoritarian	SMDP
Canada	SMDP	Majoritarian	
Cape Verde	List PR	Proportional	TRS
Central African Republic	TRS	Majoritarian	TRS
Chad	Dependent (PBV/list PR) & TRS	Mixed	TRS
Chile	List PR	Proportional	TRS
China	None	None	None
Colombia	List PR	Proportional	TRS
Comoros	TRS	Majoritarian	SMDP
Congo (Brazzaville)	TRS	Majoritarian	TRS
Congo (Kinshasa)	In transition	In transition	In transition
Costa Rica	List PR	Proportional	TRS
Ivory Coast	SMDP & PBV	Majoritarian	TRS
Croatia	List PR	Proportional	TRS
Cuba	TRS	Majoritarian	
Cyprus	List PR	Proportional	TRS
Czech Republic	List PR	Proportional	
Denmark	List PR	Proportional	
Djibouti	PBV	Majoritarian	TRS
Dominica	SMDP	Majoritarian	
Dominican Republic	List PR	Proportional	TRS
Ecuador	List PR	Proportional	TRS
Egypt	TRS	Majoritarian	
El Salvador	List PR	Proportional	TRS
Equatorial Guinea	List PR	Proportional	SMDP
Eritrea	In transition	In transition	In transition
Estonia	List PR	Proportional	
Ethiopia	SMDP	Majoritarian	
Fiji	AV	Majoritarian	
Finland	List PR	Proportional	TRS
France	TRS	Majoritarian	TRS

Country	Electoral system for legislature	Electoral system family	Electoral system for president
Gabon	TRS	Majoritarian	TRS
Gambia	SMDP	Majoritarian	TRS
Georgia	Independent (TRS & list PR)	Mixed	TRS
Germany	Dependent (SMDP & list PR)	Mixed	
Ghana	SMDP	Majoritarian	TRS
Greece	List PR	Proportional	
Grenada	SMDP	Majoritarian	
Guatemala	List PR	Proportional	TRS
Guinea	Independent (SMDP & list PR)	Mixed	TRS
Guinea-Bissau	List PR	Proportional	TRS
Guyana	List PR	Proportional	SMDP
Haiti	TRS	Majoritarian	TRS
Honduras	List PR	Proportional	SMDP
Hungary	Dependent-Independent	Mixed	
Iceland	List PR	Proportional	SMDP
India	SMDP	Majoritarian	
Indonesia	List PR	Proportional	TRS
Iran	TRS	Majoritarian	TRS
Iraq	List PR	Proportional	
Ireland	STV	Proportional	AV
Israel	List PR	Proportional	
Italy	Dependent (SMDP & list PR)	Mixed	
Jamaica	SMDP	Majoritarian	
Japan	Independent (SMDP & list PR)	Mixed	
Jordon	SNTV	Majoritarian	
Kazakhstan	Independent (TRS & list PR)	Mixed	TRS
Kenya	SMDP	Majoritarian	TRS
Kiribati	TRS	Majoritarian	SMDP
Korea, North	TRS	Majoritarian	
Korea, South	Independent (SMDP & list PR)	Mixed	SMDP
Kuwait	BV	Majoritarian	
Kyrgyzstan	TRS	Majoritarian	TRS
Laos	BV	Majoritarian	
Latvia	List PR	Proportional	
Lebanon	BV	Majoritarian	

Country	Electoral system for legislature	Electoral system family	Electoral system for president
Lesotho	Dependent (SMDP & list PR)	Mixed	
Liberia	In transition	In transition	In transition
Libya	None	None	None
Liechtenstein	List PR	Proportional	
Lithuania	Independent (TRS & list PR)	Mixed	TRS
Luxembourg	List PR	Proportional	
Macedonia	List PR	Proportional	TRS
Madagascar	SMDP & list PR	Mixed	TRS
Malawi	SMDP	Majoritarian	SMDP
Malaysia	SMDP	Majoritarian	
Maldives	BV	Majoritarian	
Mali	TRS	Majoritarian	TRS
Malta	STV	Proportional	
Marshall Islands	SMDP & BV	Majoritarian	
Mauritania	TRS	Majoritarian	TRS
Mauritius	BV	Majoritarian	
Mexico	Dependent (SMDP & list PR)	Mixed	SMDP
Micronesia	SMDP	Majoritarian	
Moldova	List PR	Proportional	
Mongolia	TRS	Majoritarian	TRS
Morocco	List PR	Proportional	
Mozambique	List PR	Proportional	TRS
Namibia	List PR	Proportional	TRS
Nauru	Modified BC	Majoritarian	
Nepal	SMDP	Majoritarian	
Netherlands	List PR	Proportional	
New Zealand	Dependent (SMDP & list PR)	Mixed	
Nicaragua	List PR	Proportional	TRS
Niger	Independent (List PR & SMDP)	Mixed	TRS
Nigeria	SMDP	Majoritarian	TRS
Norway	List PR	Proportional	
Oman	SMDP	Majoritarian	
Pakistan	Independent (SMDP & list PR)	Mixed	
Palau	SMDP	Majoritarian	TRS
Panama	Independent (List PR & SMDP)	Mixed	SMDP

Country	Electoral system for legislature	Electoral system family	Electoral system for president
Papua New Guinea	AV	Majoritarian	
Paraguay	List PR	Proportional	SMDP
Peru	List PR	Proportional	TRS
Philippines	Independent (SMDP & list PR)	Mixed	SMDP
Poland	List PR	Proportional	TRS
Portugal	List PR	Proportional	TRS
Qatar	None	None	None
Romania	List PR	Proportional	TRS
Russia	Independent (SMDP & list PR)	Mixed	TRS
Rwanda	List PR	Proportional	SMDP
St. Kitts & Nevis	SMDP	Majoritarian	
St. Lucia	SMDP	Majoritarian	
St. Vincent	SMDP	Majoritarian	
Samoa	SMDP & BV	Majoritarian	
San Marino	List PR	Proportional	
Sao Tomé & Principe	List PR	Proportional	TRS
Saudi Arabia	None	None	None
Senegal	Independent (PBV & list PR)	Mixed	TRS
Serbia & Montenegro	In transition	In transition	In transition
Seychelles	Independent (SMDP & list PR)	Mixed	TRS
Sierra Leone	List PR	Proportional	TRS
Singapore	PBV & SMPD	Majoritarian	SMDP
Slovakia	List PR	Proportional	TRS
Slovenia	List PR	Proportional	TRS
Solomon Islands	SMDP	Majoritarian	
Somalia	In transition	In transition	In transition
South Africa	List PR	Proportional	
Spain	List PR	Proportional	
Sri Lanka	List PR	Proportional	SV
Sudan	SMDP	Majoritarian	TRS
Suriname	List PR	Proportional	
Swaziland	SMDP	Majoritarian	
Sweden	List PR	Proportional	
Switzerland	List PR	Proportional	
Syria	BV	Majoritarian	

Country	Electoral system for legislature	Electoral system family	Electoral system for president
Taiwan	Independent (SNTV & list PR)	Mixed	SMDP
Tajikistan	Independent (TRS & list PR)	Mixed	TRS
Tanzania	SMDP	Majoritarian	TRS
Thailand	Independent (SMDP & list PR)	Mixed	
Togo	TRS	Majoritarian	TRS
Tonga	BV	Majoritarian	
Trinidad & Tobago	SMDP	Majoritarian	
Tunisia	Independent (PBV & list PR)	Mixed	SMDP
Turkey	List PR	Proportional	
Turkmenistan	TRS	Majoritarian	TRS
Uganda	SMDP	Majoritarian	TRS
Ukraine	Independent (SMDP & list PR)	Mixed	TRS
United Arab Emirates	None	None	None
United Kingdom	SMDP	Majoritarian	
United States of America	SMDP	Majoritarian	TRS
Uruguay	List PR	Proportional	TRS
Uzbekistan	TRS	Majoritarian	TRS
Vanuatu	SNTV	Majoritarian	
Venezuela	Dependent (SMDP & list PR)	Mixed	SMDP
Vietnam	TRS	Majoritarian	
Yemen	SMDP	Majoritarian	TRS
Zambia	SMDP	Majoritarian	SMDP
Zimbabwe	SMDP	Majoritarian	TRS

Source: Data are from a variety of sources including Golder (2005) and Reynolds, Reilly, and Ellis (2005).

References

PREFACE

Brambor, Thomas, William Roberts Clark, and Matt Golder. 2006. "Understanding Interaction Models: Improving Empirical Analysis." *Political Analysis* 14:63–82.

———. 2007. "Are African Party Systems Different?" *Electoral Studies* 26:315–323.

Clark, William Roberts, and Usha Nair Reichert, with Sandy Lomas and Kevin Parker. 1998. "International and Domestic Constraints on Political Business Cycle Behavior in OECD Economies." *International Organization* 52:87–120.

Richards, David M., and Neil J. Mitchell. 2006. "A Makeover for the Introductory Comparative Politics Course: Revising the College Board's Advanced Placement Program (AP) Course in Comparative Government and Politics" *PS: Political Science and Politics* 49:357–362.

CHAPTER 1

Brambor, Thomas, William Roberts Clark, and Matt Golder. 2006. "Understanding Interaction Models: Improving Empirical Analysis." *Political Analysis* 14:63–82.

———. 2007. "Are African Party Systems Different?" *Electoral Studies* 26:315–323.

Clark, William Roberts, and Usha Nair Reichert (with Sandy Lomas and Kevin Parker). 1998. "International and Domestic Constraints on Political Business Cycle Behavior in OECD Economies." *International Organization* 52:87–120.

LaPalombara, Joseph. 1974. *Politics within Nations.* Englewood Cliffs, N.J.: Prentice Hall.

Morgenthau, Hans. 1948. *Politics among Nations.* New York: Knopf.

Ramseyer, J. Mark, and Eric B. Rasmusen. 2003. *Measuring Judicial Independence: The Political Economy of Judging in Japan.* Chicago: University of Chicago Press.

CHAPTER 2

Braumoeller, Bear F., and Gary Goertz. 2000. "The Methodology of Necessary Conditions." *American Journal of Political Science* 44:844–858.

Camerer, Colin. 2003. *Behavioral Game Theory: Experiments on Strategic Interaction.* Princeton: Princeton University Press.

Clark, William Roberts, Michael J. Gilligan, and Matt Golder. 2006. "A Simple Multivariate Test for Asymmetric Hypotheses." *Political Analysis* 14:311–331.

Collier, David. 1993. "The Comparative Method." In *Political Science: The State of the Discipline II*, ed. Ada W. Finifter. Washington, D.C.: American Political Science Association.

Davis, Douglas, and Charles Holt. 1993. *Experimental Economics.* Princeton: Princeton University Press.

Derry, Gregory. 1999. *What Science Is and How It Works.* Princeton: Princeton University Press.

Feynman, Richard. 1967. *The Character of Physical Law: The 1964 Messenger Lectures.* Cambridge: MIT Press.

Gleick, James. 1987. *Chaos: Making a New Science.* New York: Penguin Books.

Gould, Stephen Jay. 1985. *The Flamingo's Smile: Reflections in Natural History.* New York: Norton.

Hildebrand, David K., James D. Laing, and Howard Rosenthal. 1977. *Analysis of Ordinal Data: Quantitative Applications in the Social Sciences.* Beverley Hills: Sage Publications.

Kagel, John, and Alvin Roth, eds. 1995. *The Handbook of Experimental Economics.* Princeton: Princeton University Press.

Kalyvas, Stathis. 1996. *The Rise of Christian Democracy in Europe.* Ithaca, N.Y.: Cornell University Press.

Katznelson, Ira. 1985. "Working-Class Formation and the State: Nineteenth-Century England in American Perspective." In *Bringing the State Back In,* ed. Peter B. Evans, Dietrich Rueschmeyer, and Theda Skocpol, 257–284. New York: Cambridge University Press. Lave, Charles, and James March. 1975. *An Introduction to Models in the Social Sciences.* New York: Harper and Row.

Lieberson, Stanley. 1991. "Small N's and Big Conclusions: An Examination of the Reasoning in Comparative Studies Based on a Small Number of Cases." *Social Forces* 70:307–320.

———. 1994. "More on the Uneasy Case for Using Mill-Type Methods in Small-N Comparative Studies." *Social Forces* 72:1225–1237.

Lijphart, Arend. 1971. Comparative Politics and the Comparative Method. *American Political Science Review* 65:682–693.

———. 1975. "The Comparable-Cases Strategy in Comparative Research." *Comparative Political Studies* 8:158–177.

Mill, John Stuart. [1874] 1986. *A System of Logic, Ratiocinative and Inductive: Being a Connected View of the Principles of Evidence and the Methods of Scientific Investigation.* 8th ed. New York: Harper and Brothers.

Moore, Barrington, Jr. 1966. *Social Origins of Dictatorship and Democracy: Lord and Peasant in the Making of the Modern World.* Boston: Beacon Press.

Popper, Sir Karl. [1959] 2003. *The Logic of Scientific Discovery.* New York: Routledge.

———. 1962. *Conjectures and Refutations: The Growth of Scientific Knowledge.* New York: Basic Books.

Przeworski, Adam. 2005. "Democracy as an Equilibrium." *Public Choice* 123:253–273.

Przeworski, Adam, and Henry Teune. 1970. *The Logic of Comparative and Social Inquiry.* New York: Wiley-Interscience.

Ragin, Charles. 1987. *The Comparative Method: Moving beyond Qualitative and Quantitative Strategies.* Berkeley: University of California Press.

Schelling, Thomas C. 1978. *Micromotives and Macrobehavior.* New York: Norton.

Sekhon, Jasjeet. 2004. "Quality Meets Quantity: Case Studies, Conditional Probability, and Counterfactuals." *Perspectives on Politics* 2:281–293.

Skocpol, Theda. 1979. *States and Social Revolutions: A Comparative Analysis of France, Russia, and China.* New York: Cambridge University Press.

———. 1984. "Emerging Agendas and Recurrent Strategies in Historical Sociology." In *Vision and Method in Historical Sociology.* ed. Theda Skocpol, 365–391. New York: Cambridge University Press.

Theil, Henri. 1971. *Principles of Econometrics.* New York: Wiley.

Weber, Max. [1930] 1992. *The Protestant Ethic and the Spirit of Capitalism.* New York: Routledge.

CHAPTER 3

Althusser, Louis. 1969. *For Marx.* London: Penguin Books.

Block, Fred. 1977. "The Ruling Class Does Not Rule: Notes on the Marxist Theory of the State." *Socialist Revolution* 33:6–27.

Bueno de Mesquita, Bruce. 2006. *Principles of International Politics: People's Power, Preferences, and Perceptions.* Washington, D.C.: CQ Press.

Cameron, Charles M. 2000. *Veto Bargaining: Presidents and the Politics of Negative Power.* New York: Cambridge University Press.

Clark, William Roberts, Matt Golder, and Sona Golder. 2008. "The Balance of Power between Citizens and the State: Democratization and the Resource Curse." Florida State University.

Dixit, Kamalakar Ramachandra, and James Edward Skeath. 1999. *Games of Strategy.* New York: Norton.

Dowding, Keith, Peter John, Thanos Mergoupis, and Mark Van Vugt. 2000. "Exit, Voice, and Loyalty: Analytic and Empirical Developments." *British Journal of Political Science* 37:469–495.

Dutta, Prajit K. 1999. *Strategies and Games: Theory and Practice.* Cambridge: MIT Press.

Epstein, David, and Peter Zemsky. 1995. "Money Talks: Deterring Quality Challengers in Congressional Elections." *American Political Science Review* 89:295–308.

Garton Ash, Timothy. 1999. *The Magic Lantern: The Revolution of '89 Witnessed in Warsaw, Budapest, Berlin, and Prague.* New York: Vintage Books.

Hirschman, Albert. 1970. *Exit, Voice, and Loyalty: Responses to Decline in Firms, Organizations, and States.* Cambridge: Harvard University Press.

Jacobson, Gary C. 2001. *The Politics of Congressional Elections.* New York: Longman.

Kuhn, Harold W., John C. Harsanyi, Reinhard Selten, Jörgen W. Weibull, Eric van Damme, John F. Nash Jr., and Peter Hammerstein. 1996. "The Work of John Nash in Game Theory." *Journal of Economic Theory* 69:153–185.

Kuran, Timur. 1991. "Now Out of Never: The Element of Surprise in the East European Revolution of 1989." *World Politics* 44:7–48.

Lindbloom, Charles. 1977. *Politics and Markets.* New York: Basic Books.

———. 1982. "The Market as Prison." *Journal of Politics* 44:324–336.

Morrow, James D. 1994. *Game Theory for Political Scientists.* Princeton: Princeton University Press.

Nasar, Sylvia. 2001. *A Beautiful Mind: The Life of Mathematical Genius and Nobel Laureate John Nash.* New York: Touchstone.

Osborne, Martin J. 2004. *An Introduction to Game Theory.* New York: Oxford University Press.

Poulantzas, Nicos. 1975. *Political Power and Social Class.* London: Verso.

———. 1980. *State, Power, and Socialism.* London: Verso.

Przeworski, Adam, and Michael Wallerstein. 1988. "Structural Dependence of the State on Capital." *American Political Science Review* 82:11–19.

CHAPTER 4

Anderson, Benedict. 1991. *Imagined Communities: Reflections on the Origin and Spread of Nationalism.* New York: Verso.

Arce, Daniel G., and Todd Sandler. 2005. "Counterterrorism: A Game-Theoretic Analysis." *Journal of Conflict Resolution* 49:183–200.

Axelrod, Robert. 1981. "Emergence of Cooperation among Egoists." *American Political Science Review* 75:306–318.

———. 1984. *The Evolution of Cooperation.* New York: Basic Books.

Baradat, Leon P. 2006. *Political Ideologies: Their Origins and Impact.* Englewood Cliffs, N.J.: Prentice Hall.

Blackbourn, David, and David Eley. 1984. *The Peculiarities of German History: Bourgeois Society and Politics in Nineteenth-Century Germany.* New York: Oxford University Press.

Brubaker, Rogers. 1996. *Citizenship and Nationhood in France and Germany.* Cambridge: Harvard University Press.

Enders, Walter, and Todd Sandler. 1993. "Effectiveness of Anti-Terrorism Policies: Vector-Autoregression-Intervention Analysis." *American Political Science Review* 87:829–844.

Fogel, Robert. 2004. *The Escape from Hunger and Premature Death, 1700–2100: Europe, America, and the Third World.* New York: Cambridge University Press.

Ford, Caroline. 1993. *Creating the Nation in Provincial France: Religion and Political Identity in Brittany.* Princeton: Princeton University Press.

Gellner, Ernest. 1983. *Nations and Nationalism.* Ithaca, N.Y.: Cornell University Press.

Golder, Matt. 2005. "Democratic Electoral Systems around the World, 1946–2000." *Electoral Studies* 24:103–121.

Gourevitch, Philip. 1998. *We Wish to Inform You That Tomorrow We Will Be Killed with Our Families: Stories from Rwanda.* New York: Picador.

Hardin, Garrett. 1968. "The Tragedy of the Commons." *Science* 162:1243–1248.

Hobbes, Thomas. [1651] 1994. *Leviathan.* Edited by Edwin Curley. Indianapolis: Hackett Publishing.

Hobsbawm, Eric. 1997. *Nations and Nationalism since 1780.* New York: Cambridge University Press.

Hobsbawm, Eric, and Terence Ranger, eds. 1997. *The Invention of Tradition.* New York: Cambridge University Press.

Huntington, Samuel P. 1968. *Political Order in Changing Societies.* New Haven: Yale University Press.

King, Gary, and Langche Zeng. 2001. "Improving Forecasts of State Failure." *World Politics* 53:623–658.

Lane, Frederick C. 1958. "Economic Consequences of Organized Violence." *Journal of Economic History* 18:401–410.

Leesom, Peter T. 2006. "Better Off Stateless: Somalia before and after Government Collapse." George Mason University.

Levi, Margaret. 1989. *Of Rule and Revenue.* Berkeley: University of California Press.

Lewis, I. M. 2002. *A Modern History of the Somali: Nation and State in the Horn of Africa.* 4th ed. Athens: Ohio University Press.

Locke, John. [1690] 1980. *Second Treatise of Government.* Edited by C. B. Macpherson. Indianapolis: Hackett Publishing.

Mendelsohn, Ezra. 1983. *The Jews of East Central Europe: Between the World Wars.* Bloomington: Indiana University Press.

Milliken, Jennifer, ed. 2003. *State Failure, Collapse, and Reconstruction.* Oxford: Blackwell.

Mukhtar, Mohamed Haji. 2003. *Historical Dictionary of Somalia.* Lanham, Md.: Scarecrow Press.

Nest, Michael W. 2002. "The Evolution of a Fragmented State: The Case of the Democratic Republic of Congo." PhD diss., New York University.

Nohlen, Dieter, Michael Krennerich, and Bernhard Thibaut. 1999. *Elections in Africa: A Data Handbook.* Oxford: Oxford University Press.

North, Douglas C. 1981. *Structure and Change in Economic History.* New York: Norton.

Powell, Robert. *In the Shadow of Power: States and Strategies in International Politics.* Princeton: Princeton University Press.

Prendergast, John. 1997. *Crisis Response: Humanitarian Band-Aids in Sudan and Somalia.* London: Pluto Press.

Rotberg, Robert I. 2002. "Failed States in a World of Terror." *Foreign Affairs* 81:127–140.

———, ed. 2005. *Battling Terrorism in the Horn of Africa.* Washington, D.C.: Brookings Institution Press and the World Peace Foundation.

Rousseau, Jean Jacques. 1762. *The Social Contract, or Principles of Political Right.* http://www.constitution.org/jjr/socon.htm.

———. 1988. "Discourse on the Origin and Foundations of Inequality among Men." In *Rousseau's Political Writings,* ed. Alan Ritter and Julia Conaway Bondanella. New York: Norton.

Sahlins, Peter. 1991. *Boundaries: The Making of France and Spain in the Pyrenees.* Berkeley: University of California Press.

Sandler, Todd, and Walter Enders. 2004. "An Economic Perspective on Transnational Terrorism." *European Journal of Political Economy* 20:301–316.

Spruyt, Henrik. 1994. *The Sovereign State and Its Competitors.* Princeton: Princeton University Press.

Taylor, Michael. 1976. *Anarchy and Cooperation.* New York: Wiley.

Tilly, Charles. 1985. "War Making and State Making as Organized Crime." In *Bringing the State Back In,* ed. Peter B, Evans, Dietrich Rueschmeyer, and Theda Skocpol. New York: Cambridge University Press.

U.S. Congress. 2006. House of Representatives. Committee on International Relations, Subcommittee on Africa, Global Human Rights, and International Operations and the Subcommittee on International Terrorism and Nonproliferation. *Somalia: Expanding Crisis in the Horn of Africa.* Joint hearing, 109th Cong., 2nd sess., June 29, 2006. http://www.foreignaffairs.house/gov/archives/109/ 28429.pdf.

Waltz, Kenneth N. 1979. *Theory of International Politics.* New York: McGraw-Hill.

Weber, Eugen. 1976. *Peasants into Frenchmen: The Modernization of Rural France, 1870–1914.* Stanford: Stanford University Press.

Weber, Max. [1918] 1958. "Politics as a Vocation." In *From Max Weber: Essays in Sociology,* ed. H. H. Gerth and C. Wright Mills, 77–128. New York: Oxford University Press.

Whaples, Robert. 2006. "Do Economists Agree on Anything? Yes!" *Economists' Voice* 3, art. 1.

CHAPTER 5

Adcock, Robert, and David Collier. 2001. "Measurement Validity: A Shared Standard for Qualitative and Quantitative Research." *American Political Science Review* 95:529–546.

Ahmad, Zakaria Haji. 1988. "Malaysia: Quasi Democracy in a Divided Society." In *Democracy in Developing Countries: Asia,* ed. Larry Diamond, Juan J. Linz, and Seymour Martin Lipset. Boulder, Colo.: Lynne Rienner.

Alvarez, Michael E., José Cheibub, Fernando Limongi, and Adam Przeworski. 1996. "Classifying Political Regimes." *Studies in Comparative International Development* 31:1–37.

Aristotle. 1996. *The Politics and the Constitution of Athens.* Edited by Stephen Everson. New York: Cambridge University Press.

Baradat, Leon P. 2006. *Political Ideologies: Their Origins and Impact.* Englewood Cliffs, N.J.: Prentice Hall.

Bollen, Kenneth A., and Robert Jackman. 1989. "Democracy, Stability, and Dichotomies." *American Sociological Review* 54:612–621.

Cheibub, José Antonio, and Jennifer Gandhi. 2004. "Classifying Political Regimes: A Six-Fold Measure of Democracy and Dictatorship." Paper presented at the annual meeting of the American Political Science Association, Chicago, September 2–5.

Collier, David, and Robert Adcock. 1999. "Democracy and Dichotomies: A Pragmatic Approach to Choices about Concepts." *Annual Review of Political Science* 2:537–565.

Collier, David, and Steven Levitsky. 1997. "Democracy with Adjectives: Conceptual Innovation in Comparative Research." *World Politics* 49:430–451.

Coppedge, Michael. 1997. "Modernization and Thresholds of Democracy: Evidence for a Common Path and Process." In *Inequality, Democracy, and Economic Development*, ed. M. Midlarsky. New York: Cambridge University Press.

Dahl, Robert A. 1971. *Polyarchy: Participation and Opposition.* New Haven: Yale University Press.

Elkins, Zachary. 2000. "Gradations of Democracy? Empirical Tests of Alternative Conceptualizations." *American Journal of Political Science* 44:287–294.

Freedom House. 2005. "Annual Survey of Political Rights and Civil Liberties, 1973–2005." http://www.freedomhouse.org/.

Golder, Matt. 2005. "Democratic Electoral Systems around the World, 1946–2000." *Electoral Studies* 24:103–121.

Hanson, Russell L. 1989. "Democracy." In *Political Innovation and Conceptual Change*, ed. Terence Ball, James Farr, and Russell L. Hanson. New York: Cambridge University Press.

Herodotus. 2005. *The Histories.* Translated by G. C. Macaulay. New York: Barnes and Noble Classics. King, Gary. 1995. "Replication, Replication." *PS: Political Science and Politics* 28: 443–499.

———. 2003. "The Future of Replication." *International Studies Perspectives* 4:72–107.

Machiavelli, Niccolò. 1998. *The Discourses.* Translated by Leslie J. Walker. New York: Penguin Books.

Macpherson, C. B. 1966. *The Real World of Democracy.* Oxford: Clarendon Press.

Marshall, Monty G., and Keith Jaggers. 2003. "Polity IV Project: Political Regime Characteristics and Transitions, 1800–2003." http://www.cidcm.umd.edu/inscr/polity/index.htm.

Marx, Karl. [1850] 1952. *The Class Struggle in France, 1848 to 1850.* Moscow: Progress Publishers.

Montesquieu. [1752] 1914. *The Spirit of the Laws.* London: G. Bell and Sons. http://www.constitution.org/cm/sol.htm.

Muhlberger, Steve, and Phil Paine. 1993. "Democracy's Place in World History." *Journal of World History* 4:23–45.

Munck, Gerardo L., and Jay Verkuilen. 2002. "Conceptualizing and Measuring Democracy: Evaluating Alternative Indices." *Comparative Political Studies* 35:5–34.

Offe, Claus. 1983. "Competitive Party Democracy and the Keynesian Welfare State: Factors of Stability and Disorganization." *Policy Sciences* 15:225–246.

Piven, Frances Fox, and Richard A. Cloward. 1988. *Why Americans Don't Vote.* New York: Pantheon Books.

———. 2000. *Why Americans Still Don't Vote: And Why Politicans Want It That Way.* Boston: Beacon Press.

Plato. 1991. *The Republic of Plato.* Translated by Allan Bloom. New York: Basic Books.

Przeworski, Adam, Michael E. Alvarez, José Cheibub, and Fernando Limongi. 2000. *Democracy and Development: Political Institutions and Well-Being in the World, 1950–1990.* New York: Cambridge University Press.

Rhodes, P. J. 2003. *Ancient Democracy and Modern Ideology.* London: Duckworth.

Roemer, John E. 1998. "Why the Poor Do Not Expropriate the Rich: An Old Argument in New Garb." *Journal of Public Economics* 70:399–424.

Rosanvallon, Pierre. 1995. "The History of the Word 'Democracy' in France." *Journal of Democracy* 6:140–154.

Rousseau, Jean Jacques. 1987. *The Social Contract.* Translated by Maurice Cranston. New York: Penguin Books.

Schumpeter, Joseph A. 1947. *Capitalism, Socialism, and Democracy.* New York: Harper Brothers.

Shively, W. Phillips. 1990. *The Craft of Political Research.* Englewood Cliffs, N.J.: Prentice Hall.

Treier, Shawn, and Simon Jackman. 2008. "Democracy as a Latent Variable." *American Journal of Political Science* 52:201–217.

CHAPTER 6

Acemoglu, Daron, and James A. Robinson. 2000. "Why Did the West Extend the Franchise? Democracy, Inequality, and Growth in Historical Perspective." *Quarterly Journal of Economics* 115: 1167–1199.

———. 2001. "A Theory of Political Transitions." *American Economic Review* 91:938–963.

———. 2006. *Economic Origins of Dictatorship and Democracy.* New York: Cambridge University Press.

Barro, Robert J. 1997. *Determinants of Economic Growth.* Cambridge: MIT Press.

———. 1999. "Determinants of Democracy." *Journal of Political Economy* 107 (6, pt 2): S158–S183.

Bates, Robert H., and Da–Hsiang Donald Lien. 1985. "A Note on Taxation, Development, and Representative Government. *Politics and Society* 14: 53–70.

———. "The Economics of Transitions to Democracy" *PS: Political Science and Politics* 24:24–27.

Beblawi, Hazem. 1987. "The Rentier State in the Arab World." In *The Rentier State: Nation, State, and the Integration of the Arab World,* ed. Hazem Beblawi and Giacomo Luciani. London: Croom Helm.

Boix, Carles. 2003. *Democracy and Redistribution.* New York: Cambridge University Press.

Boix, Carles, and Susan Carol Stokes. 2003. "Endogenous Democratization." *World Politics* 55:517–549.

Bollen, Kenneth A., and Robert W. Jackman. 1985. "Political Democracy and the Size Distribution of Income." *American Sociological Review* 50:438–457.

———. 1995. "Income Inequality and Democratization Revisited: A Comment on Muller." *American Sociological Review* 60:983–989.

Bueno de Mesquita, Bruce, and Alastair Smith. 2004. "Foreign Aid and Policy Concessions." New York University.

Bueno de Mesquita, Bruce, and George Downs. 2005. "The Rise of Sustainable Autocracy." *Foreign Affairs* 84:77–86.

Bueno de Mesquita, Bruce, Alastair Smith, Randolph M. Siverson, and James D. Morrow. 2001. "Political Competition and Economic Growth." *Journal of Democracy* 12:58–72.

———. 2003. *The Logic of Political Survival.* Cambridge: MIT Press.

Burnside, Craig, and David Dollar. 2000. "Aid, Policies, and Growth." *American Economic Review* 90:847–868.

Clark, William Roberts, John Doces, and Robert Woodbery. 2006. "Aid, Protestants, and Growth." Paper presented at the annual meeting of the American Political Science Association, Philadelphia, August 31–September 3.

Collier, Paul, and Anke Hoeffler. 2002. "On the Incidence of Civil War in Africa." *Journal of Conflict Resolution* 46:13–28.

———. 2005. "Resource Rents, Governance, and Conflict." *Journal of Conflict Resolution* 49:625–633.

Drake, Paul W. 1996. *Labor Movements and Dictatorships: The Southern Cone in Comparative Perspective.* Baltimore: Johns Hopkins University Press.

Dunning, Thad. 2005. "Resource Dependence, Economic Performance, and Political Stability." *Journal of Conflict Resolution* 49:451–482.

———. 2006. "Authoritarianism and Democracy in Rentier States." PhD diss. University of California, Berkeley.

Easterly, William. 2002. *The Elusive Quest for Growth: Economists' Adventures and Misadventures in the Tropics.* Cambridge: MIT Press.

Epstein, David L., Robert Bates, Jack Goldstone, Ida Kristensen, and Sharyn O'Halloran. 2006. "Democratic Transitions." *American Journal of Political Science* 50:551–569.

Fearon, James. 2005. "Primary Commodities Exports and Civil War." *Journal of Conflict Resolution* 49:483–507.

Gerschenkron, Alexander. 1962. *Economic Backwardness in Historical Perspective: A Book of Essays.* Cambridge: Harvard University Press.

Haber, Stephen, Armando Razo, and Noel Maurer. 2003. *The Politics of Property Rights: Political Instability, Credible Commitments, and Economic Growth in Mexico, 1876–1929.* New York: Cambridge University Press.

Herbst, Jeffrey I. 2000. *States and Power in Africa: Comparative Lessons in Authority and Control.* Princeton: Princeton University Press.

Humphreys, Macartan. 2005. "Natural Resources, Conflict, and Conflict Resolution: Uncovering the Mechanisms." *Journal of Conflict Resolution* 49:508–537.

Huntington, Samuel P. 1991. *The Third Wave: Democratization in the Late Twentieth Century.* Norman: University of Oklahoma Press.

Inglehart, Ronald, and Christian Welzel. 2005. *Modernization, Cultural Change, and Democracy: The Human Development Sequence.* New York: Cambridge University Press.

Jensen, Nathan, and Leonard Wantchekon. 2004. "Resource Wealth and Political Regimes in Africa," *Comparative Political Studies* 37 (7): 816–841.

Karl, Terry Lynn. 1997. *The Paradox of Plenty: Oil Booms and Petro-States.* Berkeley: University of California Press.

Lipset, Seymour Martin. 1959. "Some Social Requisites of Democracy: Economic Development and Political Legitimacy." *American Political Science Review* 53: 69–105.

———. 1960. *Political Man: The Social Bases of Politics.* New York: Doubleday.

Londregan, John B., and Keith T. Poole. 1996. "Does High Income Promote Democracy?" *World Politics* 49:1–30.

Mahdavy, Hussein. 1970. "The Patterns and Problems of Economic Development in Rentier States: The Case of Iran." In *Studies in the Economic History of the Middle East,* ed. M. A. Cook. London: Oxford University Press.

Moore, Barrington, Jr. 1966. *Social Origins of Dictatorship and Democracy: Lord and Peasant in the Making of the Modern World.* Boston: Beacon Press.

Morgenthau, Hans. 1962. "A Political Theory of Foreign Aid." *American Political Science Review* 56:301–309.

North, Douglass C., and Barry R. Weingast. 1989. "Constitutions and Commitment: The Evolution of Institutions Governing Public Choice in Seventeenth Century England." *Journal of Economic History* 49:803–832.

O'Donnell, Guillermo. 1973. *Modernization and Bureaucratic Authoritarianism: Studies in South American Politics.* Berkeley: Institute for International Studies, University of California.

Powner, Leanne C., and D. Scott Bennett. 2006. *Applying the Strategic Perspective: Problems and Models.* Washington D.C.: CQ Press.

Przeworski, Adam. 2005. "Democracy as an Equilibrium," *Public Choice* 123:253–273.

Przeworski, Adam. 2006. "Self-enforcing Democracy." In Donald Wittman and Barry Weingast, eds., *Oxford Handbook of Political Economy.* New York: Oxford University Press.

Przeworski, Adam, Michael E. Alvarez, José Cheibub, and Fernando Limongi. 1996. "What Makes Democracies Endure?" *Journal of Democracy* 7:39–55.

———. 2000. *Democracy and Development: Political Institutions and Well-Being in the World, 1950–1990.* New York: Cambridge University Press.

Przeworski, Adam, and Fernando Limongi. 1993. "Political Regimes and Economic Growth." *Journal of Economic Perspectives* 7:51–69.

———. 1997. "Modernization: Theories and Facts." *World Politics* 49:155–183.

Przeworski, Adam, and John Sprague. 1988. *Paper Stones: A History of Electoral Socialism.* Chicago: University of Chicago Press.

Reenock, Christopher, Michael Bernhard, and David Sobek. 2007. "Regressive Socioeconomic Distribution and Democratic Survival." *International Studies Quarterly.* 51:677–699.

Roemer, John E. 1998. "Why the Poor Do Not Expropriate the Rich: An Old Argument in New Garb." *Journal of Public Economics* 70:399–424.

Rogowski, Ronald. 1998. "Democracy, Capital, Skill, and Country Size: Effects of Asset Mobility and Regime Monopoly on the Odds of Democratic Rule." In *The Origins of Liberty: Political and Economic Liberalization in the Modern World,* ed. Paul W. Drake and Mathew D. McCubbins, 48–69. Princeton: Princeton University Press.

Rosendorff, B. Peter. 2001. "Choosing Democracy." *Economics and Politics* 13:1–29.

Ross, Michael Lewin. 1999. "The Political Economy of the Resource Curse." *World Politics* 51:297–322.

———. 2001. "Does Oil Hinder Democracy?" *World Politics* 53:325–361.

Rostow, W. W. 1960. *The Stages of Economic Growth: A Non-Communist Manifesto.* Cambridge: Cambridge University Press.

Rueschemeyer, Dietrich, Evelyne Huber Stephens, and John D. Stephens. 1992. *Capitalist Development and Democracy.* Chicago: University of Chicago Press.

Shafer, D. Michael. 1994. *Winners and Losers: How Sectors Shape the Developmental Prospects of States.* Ithaca, N.Y.: Cornell University Press.

Sirowy, Larry, and Alex Inkeles. 1991. "The Effects of Democracy on Economic Growth and Inequality: A Review." In *On Measuring Democracy,* ed. Alex Inkeles. New Brunswick, N.J.: Transaction.

Smith, Benjamin. 2004. "Oil Wealth and Regime Survival in the Developing World, 1960–1999." *American Journal of Political Science* 48:232–246.

Stasavage, David. 2002. "Credible Commitment in Early Modern Europe: North and Weingast Revisited." *Journal of Law, Economics, and Organization* 18:155–186.

Stepan, Alfred. 1985. "State Power and the Strength of Civil Society in the Southern Cone of Latin America." In *Bringing the State Back In,* ed. Peter B. Evans, Dietrich Rueschemeyer, and Theda Skocpol. New York: Cambridge University Press.

Tocqueville, Alexis de. [1835] 1988. *Democracy in America.* New York: Harper Collins.

Van de Walle, Nicolas. 2001. *African Economies and the Politics of Permanent Crisis, 1979–1999.* New York: Cambridge University Press.

Wood, Elisabeth J. 2000. *Forging Democracy from Below: Contested Transitions in Oligarchic Societies.* New York: Cambridge University Press.

CHAPTER 7

Abootalebi, Ali. 1999. "Islam, Islamists, and Democracy." *Middle East Review of International Affairs* 3:14–24.

Achen, Christopher H. 1987. *The Statistical Analysis of Quasi-Experiments.* Berkeley: University of California Press.

Almond, Gabriel A., and Sydney Verba. [1965] 1989. *The Civic Culture: Political Attitudes and Democracy in Five Nations.* London: Sage Publications.

Balmer, Randall. 2006. *Thy Kingdom Come: An Evangelical's Lament.* New York: Basic Books.

Barro, Robert J. 1999. "Determinants of Democracy." *Journal of Political Economy* 107:158–183.

Barry, Brian. 1970. *Sociology, Economists, and Democracy.* Chicago: University of Chicago Press.

Bednar, Jenna, and Scott Page. 2007. "Can Game(s) Theory Explain Culture? The Emergence of Cultural Behavior within Multiple Games." *Rationality and Society* 19:65–97.

Bhatt, M., and C. F. Camerer. 2005. "Self-referential Thinking and Equilibrium as States of Mind in Games: fMRI Evidence." *Games and Economic Behavior* 52:424–459.

Boix, Carles, and Daniel N. Posner. 1996. "Making Social Capital Work: A Review of Robert Putnam's *Making Democracy Work: Civic Traditions in Modern Italy.*" Working Paper 96-4, Harvard University.

Brady, Henry E. 1985. "The Perils of Survey Research: Inter-Personally Incomparable Responses." *Political Methdology* 11:260–290.

Camerer, Colin. 2003. "Strategizing in the Brain." *Science* 300:1673–1675.

Dahl, Robert A. 1971. *Polyarchy.* New Haven: Yale University Press.

Dalton, Russell J., and Nhu-Ngoc T. Ong. 2004. "Authority Orientations and Democratic Attitudes: A Test of the 'Asian Values' Hypothesis." Manuscript.

Davis, Douglas D., and Charles A. Holt. 1993. *Experimental Economics.* Princeton: Princeton University Press.

Eickelman, Dale F., and James P. Piscatori. 1996. *Muslim Politics.* Princeton: Princeton University Press.

Emmerson, Donald K. 1995. "Singapore and the 'Asian Values' Debate." *Journal of Democracy* 6:95–105.

Esposito, John L. 2003. "Practice and Theory: A Response to "Islam and the Challenge of Democracy." *Boston Review,* April–May.

Esposito, John L., and John O. Voll. 1996. *Islam and Democracy.* New York: Oxford University Press.

Fearon, James D. 2003. "Ethnic and Cultural Diversity by Country." *Journal of Economic Growth* 8:195–222.

Fearon, James D., and David Laitin. 1996. "Explaining Interethnic Cooperation." *American Political Science Review* 90:715–735.

———. 2003. "Ethnicity, Insurgency, and Civil War." *American Political Science Review* 97:75–90.

Filali-Ansary, Abdou. 1999. "Muslims and Democracy." *Journal of Democracy* 10:18–32.

Fish, M. Steven. 2002. "Islam and Authoritarianism." *World Politics* 55:4–37.

Frechette, Guillaume R., John H. Kagel, and Massimo Morelli. 2005. "Gamson's Law versus Non-Cooperative Bargaining Theory." *Games and Economic Behavior* 51:365–390.

Friedman, Edward. 2002. "On Alien Western Democracy." In *Globalization and Democratization in Asia,* ed. Catarina Kinnvall and Kristina Jonsson. New York: Routledge.

Fukuyama, Francis. 1992. *The End of History and the Last Man.* New York: Penguin.

———. 1995a. "Confucianism and Democracy." *Journal of Democracy* 6:20–33.

———. 1995b. "The Primacy of Culture." *Journal of Democracy* 6:7–14.

Geertz, Clifford. 1973. *The Interpretation of Cultures.* New York: Basic Books.

Gerber, Alan S., and Donald P. Green. 2000. "The Effects of Canvassing, Direct Mail, and Telephone Contact on Voter Turnout: A Field Experiment." *American Political Science Review* 94:653–663.

Gintis, Herbert. 2003. "Towards a Unity of the Human Behavioral Sciences." Working Paper 03-02-015, Santa Fe Institute.

Greene, Joshua D., R. Brian Sommerville, Leigh E. Nystrom, John M. Darley, and Jonathan D. Cohen. 2001. "An fMRI Investigation of Emotional Engagement in Moral Judgment." *Science* 293: 2105–2108.

Grosser, Jens, and Arthur Schram. 2006. "Neighborhood Information Exchange and Voter Participation: An Experimental Study." *American Political Science Review* 100:235–248.

Gschwend, Thomas, and Marc Hooghe. 2008. "Should I Stay or Should I Go? An Experimental Study on Voter Responses to Pre-Electoral Coalitions." *European Journal of Political Research* 47:537–555.

Habyarimana James, Macartan Humphreys, Daniel Posner, and Jeremy Weinstein. 2005. "Ethnic Identity: An Experimental Approach." University of California, Los Angeles.

———. 2007. "Why Does Ethnic Diversity Undermine Public Goods Provision?" *American Political Science Review* 101:709–725.

Hefner, Robert W. 2000. *Civil Islam: Muslims and Democratization in India.* Princeton: Princeton University Press.

Henrich, Joseph, Robert Boyd, Samuel Bowles, Colin Camerer, Ernst Fehr, Herbert Gintis, and Richard McElreath. 2001. "In Search of Homo Economicus: Behavioral Experiments in 15 Small-Scale Societies." *American Economic Review* 91:73–78.

Henrich, Joseph, Robert Boyd, Samuel Bowles, Colin Camerer, Ernst Fehr, Herbert Gintis, Richard McElreath, Michael Alvard, Abigail Barr, Jean Ensminger, Natalie Smith Henrich, Kim Hill, Francisco Gil–White, Michael Gurven, Frank Marlowe, John Q. Patton, and David Tracer. 2004. "Economic Man in Cross-Cultural Perspective: Behavioral Experiments in 15 Small-Scale Societies." *Behavior and Brain Sciences* 28:795–815.

Horowitz, Donald L. 1993. "Democracy in Divided Societies." *Journal of Democracy* 4:18–38.

Huntington, Samuel P. 1991. "Democracy's Third Wave." *Journal of Democracy* 2:12–34.

———. 1993a. "The Clash of Civilizations?" *Foreign Affairs* 72:22–49.

———. 1993b. *The Third Wave: Democratization in the Late Twentieth Century.* Norman: University of Oklahoma Press.

———. 1996. *The Clash of Civilizations and the Remaking of World Order.* New York: Simon and Schuster.

Im, H. B. 1997. *The Compatability of Confucianism and Democratic Civil Society in Korea.* Paper presented at the International Political Science Association Seventeenth World Congress, Seoul, Republic of Korea, August 17–21.

Inglehart, Ronald. 1990. *Culture Shift in Advanced Industrial Society.* Princeton: Princeton University Press.

Inglehart, Ronald, and Christian Welzen. 2005. *Modernization, Cultural Change, and Democracy.* New York: Cambridge University Press.

Jackman, Robert W., and Ross A. Miller. 1996. "A Renaissance of Political Culture?" *American Journal of Political Science* 40:632–659.

Kagel, John H., and Alvin E. Roth, eds. 1995. *The Handbook of Experimental Economics.* Princeton: Princeton University Press.

Kalyvas, Stathis. 1996. *The Rise of Christian Democracy in Europe.* Ithaca, N.Y.: Cornell University Press.

———. 1998. "Democracy and Religious Politics: Evidence from Belgium." *Comparative Political Studies* 31:291–319.

———. 2000. "Commitment Problems in Emerging Democracies: The Case of Religious Parties." *Comparative Politics* 32:379–399.

Karatnycky, Adrian. 2002. "Muslim Countries and the Democracy Gap." *Journal of Democracy* 13:99–112.

Khan, M. A. Muqtedar. 2003. "The Priority of Politics. A Response to 'Islam and the Challenge of Democracy.'" *Boston Review: A Political and Literary Forum,* April.

Kim, Yung-Myung. 1997. "Asian-Style Democracy: A Critique from East Asia." *Asian Survey* 37:1119–1134.

Kinder, Donald, and Thomas R. Palfrey. 1992. "On Behalf of an Experimental Political Science." In *Experimental Foundations of Political Science,* ed. Donald Kinder and Thomas R. Palfrey. Ann Arbor: University of Michigan Press.

King, Gary, Christopher J. L. Murray, Joshua A. Salomon, and Ajay Tandon. 2004. "Enhancing the Validity and Cross-Cultural Comparability of Measurement in Survey Research." *American Political Science Review* 98:191–207.

King, Gary, and Jonathan Wand. 2007. "Comparing Incomparable Survey Responses: Evaluating and Selecting Anchoring Vignettes." *Political Analysis* 15:46–66.

Laitin, David D. 1983. "Rational Choice and Culture: A Thick Description of Abner Cohen's Hausa Migrants." In *Constitutional Democracy: Essays in Comparative Politics: A Festschrift for Henry W. Ehrmann,* ed. Fred Eidlin. Boulder, Colo.: Westview Press.

———. 1986. *Hegemony and Culture: Politics and Religious Change among the Yoruba.* Chicago: University of Chicago Press.

———. 1992. *Language Repertoires and State Construction in Africa.* New York: Cambridge University Press.

Lewis, Bernard. 1993. "Islam and Liberal Democracy." *Atlantic Monthly.*

———. 1996. "Islam and Liberal Democracy: A Historical Overview." *Journal of Democracy* 7:52–63.

Leys, Simon. 1997. *The Analects of Confucius.* New York: Norton.

Lieberman, M. D., D. Schreiber, and K. N. Ochsner. 2003. "Is Political Cognition Like Riding a Bike? How Cognitive Neuroscience Can Inform Research on Political Thinking." *Political Psychology* 24:681–704.

Lijphart, Arend. 1977. *Democracy in Plural Societies.* New Haven: Yale University Press.

Lipset, Seymour Martin. 1994a. "The Social Requisites of Democracy Revisited: 1993 Presidential Address." *American Sociological Review* 59:1–22.

———. [1959] 1994b. *Political Man: The Social Bases of Politics.* Baltimore: Johns Hopkins University Press.

Mazower, Mark. 1998. *Dark Continent: Europe's Twentieth Century.* New York, Vintage Books.

Mill, John Stuart. [1861] 2001. *Representative Government.* Ontario: Bartoche Books. http://socserv2. socsci.mcmaster.ca/~econ/ugcm/3ll3/mill/repgovt.pdf.

Montesquieu. [1721] 1899. *The Persian Letters.* London: Gibbings. http://fsweb.wm.edu/plp/.

———. [1752] 1914. *The Spirit of the Laws.* London: G. Bell and Sons. http://www.constitution.org/ cm/sol.htm.

Moore, Barrington, Jr. [1966] 1999. *Social Origins of Dictatorship and Democracy: Lord and Peasant in the Making of the Modern World.* Boston: Beacon Press.

Morton, Rebecca, and Kenneth C. Williams. 2006. "From Nature to the Lab: Experimental Political Science and the Study of Causality." Manuscript.

Muller, Edward N., and Mitchell A. Seligson. 1994. "Civic Culture and Democracy: The Question of Causal Relationships." *American Political Science Review* 88:635–652.

Newton, Kenneth, and Pippa Norris. 2000. "Confidence in Political Institutions: Faith, Culture, or Performance?" In *Disaffected Democracies: What's Troubling the Trilateral Countries?* ed. Susan Pharr and Robert Putnam, 52–73. Princeton: Princeton University Press. Norris, Pippa, and Ronald Inglehart. 2004. *Sacred and Secular: Religion and Politics Worldwide.* New York: Cambridge University Press.

Ochsner, K. N., and M. D. Lieberman. 2001. "The Emergence of Social Cognitive Neuroscience." *American Psychologist* 56:717–734.

Phelps, E. A., and L. A. Thomas. 2003. "Race, Behavior, and the Brain: The Role of Neuroimaging in Understanding Complex Human Behavior." *Political Psychology* 24:747–758.

Posner, Daniel N. 2004. "The Political Salience of Cultural Difference: Why Chewas and Tumbukus Are Allies in Zambia and Adversaries in Malawi." *American Political Science Review* 98:529–545.

———. 2005. *Institutions and Ethnic Politics in Africa.* New York: Cambridge University Press.

Price, Daniel E. 1999. *Islamic Political Culture, Democracy, and Human Rights: A Comparative Study.* New York: Praeger.

Przeworksi, Adam, José Antonio Cheibub, and Fernando Limongi. 1998. "Culture and Democracy." In *Culture and Development.* Paris: UNESCO.

Przeworski, Adam, Michael E. Alvarez, José Antonio Cheibub, and Fernando Limongi. 2000. *Democracy and Development: Political Institutions and Material Well-Being in the World, 1950–1990.* New York: Cambridge University Press.

Putnam, Robert D. 1993. *Making Democracy Work: Civic Traditions in Modern Italy.* Princeton: Princeton University Press.

———. 2000. *Bowling Alone: The Collapse and Revival of American Community.* New York: Simon and Schuster.

Pye, Lucian W. 1985. *Asian Power and Politics.* Cambridge: Harvard University Press.

Rabushka, Alvin, and Kenneth A. Shepsle. 1972. *Politics in Plural Societies.* Columbus, Ohio: Merrill.

Rahman, Fazlur. 1979. *Islam.* Chicago: University of Chicago Press.

Sachedina, Abdulaziz. 2000. *The Islamic Roots of Democratic Pluralism.* New York: Oxford University Press.

Scalapino, Robert. 1989. *The Politics of Development: Perspectives on Twentieth Century Asia.* Cambridge: Harvard University Press.

Seligson, Mitchell A. 2002. "The Renaissance of Political Culture or the Renaissance of the Ecological Fallacy?" *Comparative Politics* 34:273–292.

Sen, Amartya. 1999. "Democracy as a Universal Value." *Journal of Democracy* 10:3–17.

———. 2002. "Health: Perception versus Observation." *British Medical Journal* 324:860–861.

Stark, Rodney. 2004a. "SSRC Presidential Address: Putting an End to Ancestor Worship." *Journal for the Scientific Study of Religion* 43:465–475.

———. 2004b. *The Victory of Reason: How Christianity Led to Freedom, Capitalism, and Western Success.* New York: Random House.

Stepan, Alfred. 2000. "Religion, Democracy, and the 'Twin Tolerations.'" *Journal of Democracy* 11: 37–57.

Thompson, Mark R. 2001. "Whatever Happened to 'Asian Values'?" *Journal of Democracy* 12: 154–165.

Tingley, Dustin. 2006. "Neurological Imaging as Evidence in Political Science: A Review, Critique, and Guiding Assessment." *Social Science Information* 45:5–33.

UNDP (United Nations Development Programme). 2000. *Human Development Report.* New York: Oxford University Press.

Wantchekon, Leonard. 2003. "Clientelism and Voting Behavior: Evidence from a Field Experiment in Benin." *World Politics* 55:399–422.

Weber, Max. [1930] 1992. *The Protestant Ethic and the Spirit of Capitalism.* New York: Routledge.

Weingast, Barry R. 1997. "The Political Foundations of Democracy and the Rule of Law." *American Political Science Review* 91:245–263.

Woodberry, Robert D. 2004. "The Shadow of Empire: Christian Missions, Colonial Policy, and Democracy in Postcolonial Societies." PhD diss., Department of Sociology, University of North Carolina.

Woodberry, Robert D., and Timothy S. Shah. 2004. "The Pioneering Protestants." *Journal of Democracy* 15:47–60.

Yazdi, Ibrahim. 1995. "A Seminar with Ibrahim Yazdi." *Middle East Policy* 3:15–28.

Yew, Lee Kuan. 1994. "Culture Is Destiny." An interview with Fareed Zakaria. *Foreign Affairs* 73:109–126.

CHAPTER 8

Brinks, Daniel, and Michael Coppedge. 2006. "Diffusion Is No Illusion: Neighbor Emulation in the Third Wave of Democracy." *Comparative Political Studies* 39:463–489.

Brown, Nathan. 2002. *Constitutions in a Nonconstitutional World: Arab Basic Laws and the Prospects for Accountable Government.* New York: State University of New York Press.

Bueno de Mesquita, Bruce, and George W. Downs. 2006. "Intervention and Democracy." *International Organization* 60:1–23.

Bueno de Mesquita, Bruce, Alastair Smith, Randolph M. Siverson, and James D. Morrow. 2003. *The Logic of Political Survival.* Cambridge: MIT Press.

Carothers, Thomas. 2002. "The End of the Transition Paradigm." *Journal of Democracy* 13:5–21.

Cohen, D. 1983. "Elections and Election Studies in Africa." In *Political Science in Africa: A Critical Review,* ed. Y. Baronga. London: Zed Books.

Colomer, Josep M. 1991. "Transitions by Agreement: Modeling the Spanish Way." *American Political Science Review* 85:1283–1302.

DeNardo, James. 1985. *Power in Numbers.* Princeton: Princeton University Press.

Diamond, Larry. 2002. "Thinking about Hybrid Regimes." *Journal of Democracy* 13:21–35.

Ekiert, Grzegorz. 1996. *The State against Society: Political Crises and Their Aftermath in East Central Europe.* Princeton: Princeton University Press.

Forsythe, David P. 1992. "Democracy, War, and Covert Action." *Journal of Peace Research* 29:385–395.

Gandhi, Jennifer, and Adam Przeworski. 2006. "Cooperation, Cooptation, and Rebellion under Dictatorships." *Economics and Politics* 18:1–26.

Garton Ash, Timothy. 1999. *The Magic Lantern: The Revolution of '89 Witnessed in Warsaw, Budapest, Berlin, and Prague.* New York: Vintage Books.

Geddes, Barbara. 2005. "Why Parties and Elections in Authoritarian Regimes?" Paper presented at the annual meeting of the American Political Science Association, Washington, D.C., September 1–4.

Gershenson, Dmitriy, and Herschel I. Grossman. 2001. "Cooption and Repression in the Soviet Union." *Economics and Politics* 13:31–47.

Gilligan, Michael, and Stephen John Stedman. 2003. "Where Do the Peacekeepers Go?" *International Studies Review* 5:37–54.

Ginkel, John, and Alastair Smith. 1999. "So You Say You Want a Revolution? A Game Theoretic Explanation of Revolution in Repressive Regimes." *Journal of Conflict Resolution* 43:291–316.

Gleditsch, Nils Petter, Lene Siljeholm Christiansen, and Håvard Hegre. 2004. "Democratic Jihad? Military Intervention and Democracy." Paper presented at the annual meeting of the International Studies Association, Montreal, March 17–20.

Granovetter, Mark. 1978. "Threshold Models of Collective Behavior." *American Journal of Sociology* 83:1420–1443.

Gunther, Richard, Hans-Jürgen Puhle, and P. Nikiforos Diamandouros, eds. 1995. *The Politics of Democratic Consolidation: Southern Europe in Comparative Perspective.* Baltimore: Johns Hopkins University Press.

Gurr, Ted Robert. 1970. *Why Men Rebel.* Princeton: Princeton University Press.

Herbst, Jeffrey. 2001. "Political Liberalization in Africa after Ten Years." *Comparative Politics* 33:357–375.

Hitchcock, William I. 2004. *The Struggle for Europe: The Turbulent History of a Divided Continent, 1945 to the Present.* New York: Anchor Books.

Huntington, Samuel P. 1991. *The Third Wave: Democratization in the Late Twentieth Century.* Norman: University of Oklahoma Press.

Kalyvas, Stathis. 2000. "Commitment Problems in Emerging Democracies: The Case of Religious Parties." *Comparative Politics* 32:379–399.

Kaminski, Marek M. 1999. "How Communism Could Have Been Saved: Formal Analysis of Electoral Bargaining in Poland in 1989." *Public Choice* 98:83–109.

———. 2004. *Games Prisoners Play: The Tragicomic Worlds of Polish Prison.* Princeton: Princeton University Press.

Kant, Immanuel. [1785] 1993. *Grounding for the Metaphysics of Morals, with On a Supposed Right to Lie Because of Philanthropic Concerns.* Indianapolis, Ind.: Hackett.

Karl, Terry Lynn. 1995. "The Hybrid Regimes of Central America." *Journal of Democracy* 6:72–87.

Kegley, Charles W., Jr., and Margaret G. Hermann. 1997. "Putting Military Intervention into the Democratic Peace: A Research Note." *Comparative Political Studies* 30:78–107.

Kuran, Timur. 1989. "Sparks and Prairie Fires: A Theory of Unanticipated Political Revolution." *Public Choice* 61:41–74.

———. 1991. "Now out of Never: The Element of Surprise in the East European Revolution of 1989." *World Politics* 44:7–48.

Levitsky, Steven, and Lucan A. Way. 2002. "The Rise of Competitive Authoritarianism." *Journal of Democracy* 13:51–65.

———. 2003. "Autocracy by Democratic Rules: The Dynamics of Competitive Authoritarianism in the Post–Cold War Era." Harvard University.

Lohmann, Susanne. 1994. "The Dynamics of Informational Cascades: The Monday Demonstrations in Leipzig, East Germany, 1989–91." *World Politics* 47:42–101.

Lowenthal, Abraham F. 1991. *Exporting Democracy: The United States and Latin America—Themes and Issues.* Baltimore: Johns Hopkins University Press.

Lucas, Russell E. 2005. *Institutions and the Politics of Survival in Jordan: Domestic Responses to External Challenges, 1988–2001.* Albany: State University of New York Press.

Lust-Okar, Ellen. 2005a. "Elections under Authoritarianism: Preliminary Lessons from Jordan." *Middle East Election Guide.* http://www.kas.org.jo/home/.

———. 2005b. *Structuring Conflict in the Arab World: Incumbents, Opponents, and Institutions.* New York: Cambridge University Press.

Mazower, Mark. 2000. *Dark Continent: Europe's Twentieth Century.* New York: Vintage Books.

Meernik, James. 1996. "United States Military Intervention and the Promotion of Democracy." *Journal of Peace Research* 33:391–402.

O'Loughlin, John, Michael D. Ward, Corey L. Lofdahl, Jordin S. Cohen, David S. Brown, David Reilly, Kristian S. Gleditsch, and Michael Shin. 1998. "The Diffusion of Democracy, 1946–1994." *Annals of the Association of American Geographers* 88:545–574.

Olson, Mancur. [1965] 1971. *The Logic of Collective Action: Public Goods and the Theory of Groups.* Cambridge: Harvard University Press.

Perzkowski, S., ed. 1994. *Secret Documents of the Politburo and the Secretariat of the Central Committee: The Last Year, 1988–89.* London: Aneks.

Powner, Leanne C., and D. Scott Bennett. 2006. *Applying the Strategic Perspective: Problems and Models.* Washington, D.C.: CQ Press.

Przeworski, Adam. 1991. *Democracy and the Market: Political and Economic Reforms in Eastern Europe and Latin America.* New York: Cambridge University Press.

Przeworski, Adam, Michael E. Alvarez, José Cheibub, and Fernando Limongi. 2000. *Democracy and Development: Political Institutions and Well-Being in the World, 1950–1990.* New York: Cambridge University Press.

Rosenberg, Tina. 1996. *The Haunted Land: Facing Europe's Ghosts after Communism.* New York: Vintage Books.

Schedler, Andreas. 2002. "The Menu of Manipulation." *Journal of Democracy* 13:36–50.

Schwedler, Jillian. 2000. "Framing Political Islam in Jordan and Yemen." PhD diss., New York University.

Shepsle, Kenneth A., and Mark S. Bonchek. 1997. *Analyzing Politics: Rationality, Behavior, and Institutions.* New York: Norton.

Solzhenitsyn, Aleksandr Isaevich. 1975. "The Smatterers." In *From under the Rubble*, by Aleksandr Isaevich Solzhenitsyn, Mikhail Agursky, and Evgeny Barabanov. Boston: Little, Brown.

Starr, Harvey, and Christina Lindborg. 2003. "Democratic Dominoes Revisited: The Hazards of Governmental Transitions, 1974–1996." *Journal of Conflict Resolution* 47:490–519.

Svolik, Milan. 2007. "Authoritarian Reversals and Democratic Consolidation." Paper presented at the annual meeting of the Midwest Political Science Association, Chicago, April.

Wantchekon, Leonard, and Zvika Neeman. 2002. "A Theory of Post–Civil War Democratization." *Journal of Theoretical Politics* 14:439–464.

Zakaria, Fareed. 1997. "The Rise of Illiberal Democracy." *Foreign Affairs* 76:22–41.

CHAPTER 9

Acemoglu, Daron, and James A. Robinson. 2000. "Why Did the West Extend the Franchise? Democracy, Inequality, and Growth in Historical Perspective." *Quarterly Journal of Economics* 115: 1167–1199.

———. 2001. "A Theory of Political Transitions." *American Economic Review* 91:938–963.

———. 2006. *Economic Origins of Dictatorship and Democracy.* New York: Cambridge University Press.

Banfield, Edward C., and Laura Fasano Banfield. 1958. *The Moral Basis of a Backward Society.* Glencoe, Ill.: Free Press.

Barro, Robert J. 1989. "A Cross-Country Study of Growth, Saving, and Government." NBER Working Paper 2855, National Bureau of Economic Research, Cambridge, Mass.

———. 1990. "Government Spending in a Simple Model of Endogenous Growth." *Journal of Political Economy* 98:S103–S125.

———. 2000. "Rule of Law, Democracy, and Economic Performance." In *Index of Economic Freedom.* Washington, D.C.: Heritage Foundation.

Blais, André. 2000. *To Vote or Not to Vote: The Merits and Limits of Rational Choice Theory.* Pittsburgh: University of Pittsburgh Press.

Block, Fred. 1977. "The Ruling Class Does Not Rule: Notes on the Marxist Theory of the State." *Socialist Revolution* 33:6–28.

Boix, Carles. 2003. *Democracy and Redistribution.* New York: Cambridge University Press.

Bueno de Mesquita, Bruce. 2006. *Principles of International Politics: People's Power, Preferences, and Perceptions.* Washington D.C.: CQ Press.

Bueno de Mesquita, Bruce, Alastair Smith, Randolph Siverson, and James D. Morrow (BDM^{2}S^2). 2003. *The Logic of Political Survival.* Cambridge: MIT Press.

De Schweinitz, Karl, Jr. 1959. "Industrialization, Labor Controls, and Democracy." *Economic Development and Cultural Change* 7:385–404.

Drake, Paul W. 1996. *Labor Movements and Dictatorships: The Southern Cone in Comparative Perspective.* Baltimore: Johns Hopkins University Press.

Dunning, Thad. 2006. "Authoritarianism and Democracy in Rentier States." PhD diss., University of California, Berkeley.

Fogel, Robert William. 2004. *The Escape from Hunger and Premature Death, 1700–2100.* New York: Cambridge University Press.

Galenson, Walter. 1959. *Labor and Economic Development.* New York: Wiley.

Geddes, Barbara. 2003. *Paradigms and Sand Castles: Theory Building and Research Design in Comparative Politics.* Ann Arbor: University of Michigan Press.

Ghobarah, H. A., P. Huth, and B. Russett. 2004. "Comparative Public Health: The Political Economy of Human Misery and Well-Being." *International Studies Quarterly* 48:73–94.

Haber, Stephen, Armando Razo, and Noel Maurer. 2003. *The Politics of Property Rights: Political Instability, Credible Commitments, and Economic Growth in Mexico, 1876–1929.* New York: Cambridge University Press.

Hibbs, Douglas A. 1987. *The Political Economy of Industrial Democracies.* Cambridge: Harvard University Press.

Huntington, Samuel P. 1968. *Political Order in Changing Societies.* New Haven: Yale University Press.

———. 1993. *The Third Wave: Democratization in the Late Twentieth Century.* Norman: University of Oklahoma Press.

Huntington, Samuel P., and Jorge I. Dominguez. 1975. "Political Development." In *Macropolitical Theory,* ed. F. I. Greenstein and N. W. Polsby, 1–114. Reading, Mass.: Addison-Wesley.

Lake, David A., and Matthew Baum. 2001. "The Invisible Hand of Democracy: Political Control and the Provision of Public Services." *Comparative Political Studies* 34:587–621.

Leblang, David A. 1996. "Property Rights, Democracy, and Economic Growth." *Political Research Quarterly* 49: 5–26.

———. 1997. "Political Democracy and Economic Growth: Pooled Cross-Sectional and Time-Series Evidence." *British Journal of Political Science* 27:453–466.

Leighley, Jan E., and Jonathan Nagler. 1992a. "Individual and Systemic Influences on Turnout—Who Votes? 1984." *Journal of Politics* 54:718–740.

———. 1992b. "Socioeconomic Class Bias in Turnout, 1964–1988—The Voters Remain the Same." *American Political Science Review* 86:725–736.

Lindblom, Charles. 1977. *Politics and Markets.* New York: Basic Books.

Marshall, Monty G., and Keith Jaggers. 2003. "Polity IV Project: Political Regime Characteristics and Transitions, 1800–2003." http://www.cidcm.umd.edu/inscr/polity/index.htm.

McGuire, James. 2002. "Democracy, Social Provisioning, and Child Mortality in Developing Countries." Wesleyan University.

McGuire, M. C., and Mancur Olson. 1996. "The Economics of Autocracy and Majority Rule: The Invisible Hand and the Use of Force." *Journal of Economic Literature* 34:72–96.

Meltzer, Allan H., and Scott F. Richard. 1981. "A Rational Theory of the Size of Government." *Journal of Political Economy* 89: 914–927.

North, Douglass C. 1990. *Institutions, Institutional Change, and Economic Performance.* New York: Cambridge University Press.

North, Douglass C., and Robert Paul Thomas. 1973. *The Rise of the Western World: A New Economic History.* New York: Cambridge University Press.

O'Donnell, Guillermo. 1973. *Modernization and Bureaucratic Authoritarianism: Studies in South American Politics.* Berkeley: University of California, Institute for International Studies.

Olson, Mancur C. 1991. "Autocracy, Democracy, and Prosperity." In *Strategy and Choice,* ed. R. J. Zeckhauser. Cambridge: MIT Press.

Przeworski, Adam. 1991. "Could We Feed Everyone? The Irrationality of Capitalism and the Infeasibility of Socialism." *Politics and Society* 19:1–38.

Przeworski, Adam, Michael E. Alvarez, José Antonio Cheibub, and Fernando Limongi. 2000. *Democracy and Development: Political Institutions and Well-Being in the World, 1950–1990.* New York: Cambridge University Press.

Przeworski, Adam, and Fernando Limongi. 1993. "Political Regimes and Economic Growth." *Journal of Economic Perspectives* 7:51–69.

Przeworski, Adam, and Michael Wallerstein. 1988. "The Structural Dependence of the State on Capital." *American Political Science Review* 82: 11–29.

Rao, Vaman. 1984. "Democracy and Economic Development." *Studies in Comparative International Development* 19:67–81.

Rigobon, Roberto, and Dani Rodrik. 2004. "Rule of Law, Democracy, Openness, and Income: Estimating the Interrelationships." NBER Working Paper 10750, National Bureau of Economic Research, Cambridge, Mass.

Roemer, John E. 1998. "Why the Poor Do Not Expropriate the Rich: An Old Argument in New Garb." *Journal of Public Economics* 70:399–424.

Rose-Ackerman, Susan. 1999. *Corruption and Government: Causes, Consequences, and Reform.* New York: Cambridge University Press.

Rosendorff, B. Peter. 2001. "Choosing Democracy." *Economics and Politics* 13:1–29.

Ross, Michael. 2006. "Is Democracy Good for the Poor?" *American Journal of Political Science* 50: 860–874.

Sen, Amartya. 1981. *Poverty and Famines: An Essay on Entitlement and Deprivation.* New York: Oxford University Press.

———. 1999. *Development as Freedom.* New York: Knopf.

Sirowy, Larry, and Alex Inkeles. 1991. "The Effects of Democracy on Economic Growth and Inequality." In *On Measuring Democracy,* ed. Alex Inkeles, 125–156. New Brunswick, N.J.: Transaction.

Smith, Alastair. 2005. "Why International Organizations Will Continue to Fail Their Development Goals." *Perspectives on Politics* 3:565–567.

———. 2007. "Pernicious Foreign Aid? A Political Economy of Political Institutions and the Effect of Foreign Aid." New York University.

Stepan, Alfred. 1985. "State Power and the Strength of Civil Society in the Southern Cone of Latin America." In *Bringing the State Back In,* ed. Peter B. Evans, Dietrich Rueschemeyer, and Theda Skocpol. New York: Cambridge University Press.

Throup, David W., and Charles Hornsby. 1998. *Multi-Party Politics in Kenya.* Athens: Ohio State University Press.

Verba, Sidney, Kay Schlozman, and Henry Brady. 1995. *Voice and Equality: Civic Voluntarism in American Politics.* Cambridge: Harvard University Press.

Wolfinger, Raymond E., and Steven J. Rosenstone. 1980. *Who Votes?* New Haven: Yale University Press.

CHAPTER 10

Arrow, Kenneth. 1963. *Social Choices and Individual Values.* New Haven: Yale University Press.

Black, Duncan. 1948. "On the Rationale of Group Decision-Making." *Journal of Political Economy* 56:23–34

Borda, Jean-Charles de. 1781. "Mémoire sur les élections au scrutin." *Mémoires de l'Académie Royale des Sciences,* 657–665.

Condorcet, Marie Jean Antoine Nicolas de Caritat (Marquis de). 1785. *Essai sur l'application de l'analyse à la probabilité des decisions rendues à la pluralité des voix.* Paris: L'Imprimerie Royale.

Dixit, Avinash K., and Susan Skeath. 2004. *Games of Strategy.* 2nd ed. New York: Norton.

Downs, Anthony. 1957. *An Economic Theory of Democracy.* New York: Harper and Row.

Geanakoplos, John. 2005. "Three Brief Proofs of Arrow's Impossibility Theorem." *Economic Theory* 26:211–215.

Goodin, Robert E., and Philip Pettit, eds. 1993. *A Companion to Contemporary Political Philosophy.* Oxford: Blackwell.

Hinich, Melvin J., and Michael C. Munger. 1997. *Analytical Politics.* New York: Cambridge University Press.

Hotelling, Harold. 1929. "Stability in Competition." *Economic Journal* 39:41–57.

McCarty, Nolan, and Adam Meirowitz. 2007. *Political Game Theory: An Introduction.* New York: Cambridge University Press.

McKelvey, Richard D. 1976. "Intransitivities in Multidimensional Voting Models and Some Implications for Agenda Control." *Journal of Economic Theory* 12:472.

Monroe, Alan. 1983. "American Party Platforms and Public Opinion." *American Journal of Political Science* 27:27–42.

Morrow, James D. 1994. *Game Theory for Political Scientists.* Princeton: Princeton University Press.

Page, Benjamin. 1978. *Choices and Echoes in Presidential Elections: Rational Man and Electoral Democracy.* Chicago: University of Chicago Press.

Plott, Charles. 1967. "A Notion of Equilibrium and Its Possibility under Majoritarian Rule." *American Economic Review* 57:787–806.

Riker, William. 1982. *Liberalism against Populism: A Confrontation between the Theory of Democracy and the Theory of Social Choice.* San Francisco: Freeman.

Schofield, Norman J. 1978. "Instability of Simple Dynamic Games." *Review of Economic Studies* 45: 575–594.

Sen, Amartya K. 1970. *Collective Choice and Social Welfare.* San Francisco: Holden-Day.

Shepsle, Kenneth A. 1992. "Congress Is a 'They' Not an 'It': Legislative Intent as Oxymoron." *International Review of Law and Economics* 12:239–257.

Varian, Hal R. 1993. *Intermediate Economics: A Modern Approach.* New York: Norton.

CHAPTER 11

Allum, P. A. 1973. *Italy—Republic without Government?* New York: Norton.

Amorim Neto, Octavio. 2006. "The Presidential Calculus: Executive Policy Making and Cabinet Formation in the Americas." *Comparative Political Studies* 39: 415–440.

Amorim Neto, Octavio, and David Samuels. 2006. "Democratic Regimes and Cabinet Politics: A Global Perspective." Paper presented at the annual meeting of the Midwest Political Science Association, Chicago, April 20–23.

Amorim Neto, Octavio, and Kaare Strøm. 2006. "Breaking the Parliamentary Chain of Delegation: Presidents and Non-Partisan Cabinet Members in European Democracies." *British Journal of Political Science.* 36:619–643.

Andersen, Walter K. 1990. "Election 1989 in India: The Dawn of Coalition Politics?" *Asian Survey* 30:527–540.

Bergman, Torbjörn. 1993. "Formation Rules and Minority Governments." *European Journal of Political Research* 23:55–66.

Bernhard, William, and David Leblang. 2006. *Pricing Politics: Democratic Processes and Financial Markets.* New York: Cambridge University Press.

Blais, André, and Indriði Indriðason. 2007. "Making Candidates Count: The Logic of Electoral Alliances in Two-Round Legislative Elections." *Journal of Politics* 69:193–205.

Budge, Ian, Hans-Dieter Klingemann, Andrea Volkens, Judith Bara, and Eric Tanenbaum. 2001. *Mapping Policy Preferences: Estimates for Parties, Electors, and Governments, 1945–1998.* New York: Oxford University Press.

Carroll, Royce A., and Gary W. Cox. 2007. "The Logic of Gamson's Law: Pre-Electoral Coalitions and Portfolio Allocations." *American Journal of Political Science* 51:300–313.

Carruba, Clifford J., and Craig Volden. 2000. "Coalitional Politics and Logrolling in Legislative Institutions." *American Journal of Political Science* 44:521–537.

Cheibub, José Antonio. 2007. *Presidentialism, Parliamentarism, and Democracy.* New York: Cambridge University Press.

Cheibub, José Antonio, and Jennifer Gandhi. 2004. "Classifying Political Regimes: A Six-Fold Measure of Democracies and Dictatorships." Paper presented at the annual meeting of the American Political Science Association, Chicago, September 2–5.

Cheibub, José Antonio, and Fernando Limongi. 2002. "Modes of Government Formation and the Survival of Democratic Regimes: Presidentialism and Parliamentarism Reconsidered." *Annual Review of Political Science* 5:151–179.

Cheibub, José Antonio, Adam Przeworski, and Sebastian Saiegh. 2004. "Government Coalitions and Legislative Success under Presidentialism and Parliamentarism." *British Journal of Political Science* 34:565–587.

Clark, William Roberts. 2003. *Capitalism, Not Globalism: Capital Mobility, Central Bank Independence, and the Political Control of the Economy.* Ann Arbor: University of Michigan Press.

Diermeier, Daniel, and Peter van Roozendaal. 1998. "The Duration of Cabinet Formation Processes in Western Multi-Party Democracies." *British Journal of Political Science* 28:609–626.

Diermeier, Daniel, and Randolph T. Stevenson. 1999. "Cabinet Survival and Competing Risks." *American Journal of Political Science* 43:1051–1098.

Döring, Herbert, ed. 1995. *Parliaments and Majority Rule in Western Europe.* New York: St. Martin's Press.

Downs, William. 1998. *Coalition Government, Subnational Style: Multiparty Politics in Europe's Regional Parliaments.* Columbus: Ohio State University Press.

Druckman, Jamie, and Paul V. Warwick. 2001. "Portfolio Salience and the Proportionality of Payoffs in Coalition Governments." *British Journal of Political Science* 31:627–649.

———. 2006. "The Paradox of Portfolio Allocation: An Investigation into the Nature of a Very Strong but Puzzling Relationship." *European Journal of Political Research* 45:635–665.

Duverger, Maurice. 1980. "A New Political System Model: Semi-Presidential Government." *European Journal of Political Research* 8:165–187.

Elgie, Robert. 1998. "The Classification of Democratic Regime Types: Conceptual Ambiguity and Contestable Assumptions." *European Journal of Political Research* 33:219–238.

———, ed. 1999. *Semi-Presidentialism in Europe.* Oxford: Oxford University Press.

Ferrara, Frederico, and Erik S. Herron. 2005. "Going It Alone? Strategic Entry under Mixed Electoral Rules." *American Journal of Political Science* 49:16–31.

Frechette, Guillaume R., John H. Kagel, and Massimo Morelli. 2005. "Gamson's Law versus Non-Cooperative Bargaining Theory." *Games and Economic Behavior* 51:365–390.

Gallagher, Michael, Michael Laver, and Peter Mair. 2006. *Representative Government in Modern Europe: Institutions, Parties, and Governments.* New York: McGraw-Hill.

Gamson, W. A. 1961. "A Theory of Coalition Formation." *American Sociological Review* 26:373–382.

Garrett, Geoffrey. 1998. *Partisan Politics in the Global Economy.* New York: Cambridge University Press.

Giesbert, Franz-Olivier. 1996. *François Mitterrand, Une Vie.* Paris: Editions du Seuil.

Golder, Sona N. 2006. *The Logic of Pre-Electoral Coalition Formation.* Columbus: Ohio State University Press.

———. 2007. "Bargaining Delays in the Government Formation Process." Paper presented at the annual meeting of the Midwest Political Science Association, Chicago, April 12–15.

Golder, Sona N., and Courtenay Ryals. 2008. "Conceptualizing Government Duration and Stability." Paper presented at the annual meeting of the Midwest Political Science Association, Chicago, April 3–6.

Herman, Valentine, and John Pope. 1973. "Minority Governments in Western Democracies." *British Journal of Political Science* 3:191–212.

Huber, John. 1996. *Rationalizing Parliament.* New York: Cambridge University Press.

Huber, John, and Cecilia Martinez-Gallardo. 2004. "Cabinet Instability and the Accumulation of Experience in the Cabinet: The French Fourth and Fifth Republics in Comparative Perspective." *British Journal of Political Science* 34:27–48.

Indriðason, Indriði, and Christopher Kam. 2005. "The Timing of Cabinet Reshuffles in Five Westminster Parliamentary Systems." *Legislative Studies Quarterly.* 30:327–363.

Kaminski, Marek. 2001. "Coalitional Stability of Multi-Party Systems: Evidence from Poland." *American Journal of Political Science* 45:294–312.

———. 2002. "Do Parties Benefit from Electoral Manipulation? Electoral Laws and Heresthetics in Poland, 1989–1993." *Journal of Theoretical Politics* 14:325–358.

Kayser, Mark Andreas. 2005. "Who Surfs, Who Manipulates? The Determinants of Opportunistic Election Timing and Electorally Motivated Economic Intervention." *American Political Science Review* 99:17–28.

Kim, Dong-Hun, and Gerhard Loewenberg. 2005. "The Role of Parliamentary Committees in Coalition Governments: Keeping Tabs on Coalition Partners in the German Bundestag." *Comparative Political Studies* 38:1104–1129.

King, Gary, James E. Alt, Elizabeth Burns, and Michael Laver. 1990. "A Unified Model of Cabinet Dissolution in Parliamentary Democracies." *American Journal of Political Science* 34:846–871.

Kristinsson, Gunnar Helgi. 1999. "Iceland." In *Semi-Presidentialism in Europe,* ed. Robert Elgie, 86–103. New York: Oxford University Press.

Laver, Michael, Scott de Marchi, and Hande Mutlu. 2007. "Bargaining in N-Party Legislatures." New York University.

Laver, Michael, and W. Ben Hunt. 1992. *Policy and Party Competition.* London: Routledge.

Laver, Michael, and Norman Schofield. 1998. *Multiparty Government: The Politics of Coalition in Europe.* Ann Arbor: University of Michigan Press.

Laver, Michael, and Kenneth A. Shepsle. 1994. "Cabinet Government in Theoretical Perspective." In *Cabinet Ministers and Parliamentary Government,* ed. Michael Laver and Kenneth Shepsle. New York: Cambridge University Press.

———. 1996. *Making and Breaking Governments: Cabinets and Legislatures in Parliamentary Democracies.* New York: Cambridge University Press.

Leblang, David. 2002. "Political Uncertainty and Speculative Attacks." In *Coping with Globalization: Cross-National Patterns in Domestic Governance and Policy Performance,* ed. Steve Chan and James Scarritt. London: Frank Cass.

Leblang, David, and Bumba Mukherjee. 2006. "Elections, Partisanship, and Stock Market Performance: Theory and Evidence from a Century of American and British Returns." *American Journal of Political Science* 49:780–802.

Lijphart, Arend. 1984. *Democracies: Patterns of Majoritarian and Consensus Government in Twenty-One Countries.* New Haven: Yale University Press.

———. 1999. *Patterns of Democracy: Government Forms and Performance in Thirty-Six Countries.* New Haven: Yale University Press.

Linz, Juan J. 1994. "Presidential or Parliamentary Democracy." In *The Failure of Presidential Democracy: The Case of Latin America,* ed. Juan J. Linz and Arturo Valenzuela. Baltimore: Johns Hopkins University Press.

Luebbert, Gregory M. 1984. "A Theory of Government Formation." *Comparative Political Studies* 17:229–264.

Lupia, Arthur. 2003. "Delegation and Its Perils." In *Delegation and Accountability in Parliamentary Democracies,* ed. Kaare Strøom, Wolfgang C. Müller, and Torbjörn Bergman, 33–54. Oxford: Oxford University Press.

Lupia, Arthur, and Kaare Strøm. 1995. "Coalition Termination and the Strategic Timing of Legislative Elections." *American Political Science Review* 89:648–665.

Martin, Lanny W., and Georg Vanberg. 2003. "Wasting Time? The Impact of Ideology and Size on Delay in Coalition Formation." *British Journal of Political Science* 33:323–344.

———. 2004. "Policing the Bargain: Coalition Government and Parliamentary Scrutiny." *American Journal of Political Science* 48:13–27.

Martin, Lanny W., and Randolph T. Stevenson. 2001. "Government Formation in Parliamentary Democracies." *American Journal of Political Science* 45:33–50.

Müller, Wolfgang C., Torbjörn Bergman, and Kaare Strøm. 2003. "Parliamentary Democracy: Promise and Problems." In *Delegation and Accountability in Parliamentary Democracies,* ed. Wolfgang C. Müller, Torbjörn Bergman, and Kaare Strøm. New York: Oxford University Press.

Müller, Wolfgang C., and Kaare Strøm, eds. 2000. *Coalition Governments in Western Europe.* Oxford: Oxford University Press.

Powell, G. Bingham, Jr. 2000. *Elections as Instruments of Democracy: Majoritarian and Proportional Visions.* New Haven: Yale University Press.

Przeworski, Adam, Michael E. Alvarez, José Antonio Cheibub, and Fernando Limongi. 2000. *Democracy and Development: Political Institutions and Well-Being in the World, 1950–1990.* New York: Cambridge University Press.

Rasmussen, Jorgen. 1991. "They Also Serve: Small Parties in the British Political System." In *Small Parties in Western Europe: Comparative and National Perspective,* ed. Ferdinand Müller-Rommel and Geoffrey Pridham. London: Sage.

Samuels, David. 2007. "Separation of Powers." In *The Oxford Handbook of Comparative Politics,* ed. Carles Boix and Susan C. Stokes. New York: Oxford University Press.

Sartori, Giovanni. 1997. *Comparative Constitutional Engineering: An Inquiry into Structures, Incentives, and Outcomes.* London: Macmillan.

Shugart, Matthew Soberg, and John M. Carey. 1992. *Presidents and Assemblies: Constitutional Design and Electoral Dynamics.* New York: Cambridge University Press.

Shugart, Matthew Soberg, and Scott Mainwaring. 1997. "Presidentialism and Democracy in Latin America: Rethinking the Terms of the Debate." In *Presidentialism and Democracy in Latin*

America, ed. Scott Mainwaring and Matthew Soberg Shugart. Cambridge: Cambridge University Press.

Smith, Alistair 2003. "Election Timing in Majoritarian Parliamentary Systems." *British Journal of Political Science* 33:397–418.

———. 2004. *Election Timing.* New York: Cambridge University Press.

Stepan, Alfred, and Cindy Skach. 1993. "Constitutional Frameworks and Democratic Consolidation: Parliamentarism versus Presidentialism." *World Politics* 46:1–22.

Strøm, Kaare. 1984. "Minority Governments in Parliamentary Democracies." *Comparative Political Studies* 17:199–227.

———. 1990. *Minority Government and Majority Rule.* Cambridge: Cambridge University Press.

———. 1995. "Parliamentary Government and Legislative Organization." In *Parliaments and Majority Rule in Western Europe,* ed. Herbert Döring. New York: St. Martin's Press.

Strøm, Kaare, Ian Budge, and Michael J. Laver. 1994. "Constraints on Cabinet Formation in Parliamentary Democracies." *American Journal of Political Science* 38:303–335.

Strøm, Kaare, Wolfgang C. Müller, and Torbjörn Bergman, eds. 2003. *Delegation and Accountability in Parliamentary Democracies.* Oxford: Oxford University Press.

Thatcher, Margaret. 1993. *Margaret Thatcher: The Downing Street Years.* London: HarperCollins.

Thies, Michael F. 2001. "Keeping Tabs on Partners: The Logic of Delegation in Coalition Governments." *American Journal of Political Science* 45:580–598.

Verney, Douglas. 1959. *The Analysis of Political Systems.* London: Routledge and Kegan Paul.

Warwick, Paul V. 1994. *Government Survival in Parliamentary Democracies.* New York: Cambridge University Press.

Woldendorp, Jaap, Hans Keman, and Ian Budge. 1998. "Party Government in 20 Democracies." *European Journal of Political Research* 33:125–164.

Young, Hugo. 1990. *One of Us: Life of Margaret Thatcher.* London: Pan.

CHAPTER 12

Andrews, Josephine T., and Robert W. Jackman. 2005. "Strategic Fools: Electoral Rule Choice under Extreme Uncertainty." *Electoral Studies* 24:65–84.

Barkan, Joel D. 1995. "Elections in Agrarian Societies." *Journal of Democracy* 6:106–116.

Bawn, Kathleen. 1993. "The Logic of Institutional Preferences: German Electoral Law as a Social Choice Outcome." *American Journal of Political Science* 37:965–989.

Benoit, Kenneth. 1996. "Hungary's Two-Ballot Electoral System." *Representation* 33:162–170.

———. 2000. "Which Electoral Formula Is the Most Proportional? A New Look with New Evidence." *Political Analysis* 8:381–388.

———. 2004. "Models of Electoral System Change." *Electoral Studies* 23:363–389.

———. 2005. "Hungary: Holding Back the Tiers." In *The Politics of Electoral Systems,* ed. Michael Gallagher and Paul Mitchell. Oxford: Oxford University Press.

———. 2007. "Electoral Laws as Political Consequences: Explaining the Origins and Change of Electoral Institutions." *Annual Review of Political Science* 10:363–390.

Benoit, Kenneth, and Jacqueline Hayden. 2004. "Institutional Change and Persistence: The Evolution of Poland's Electoral System, 1989–2001." *Journal of Politics* 66:396–427.

Benoit, Kenneth, and John W. Schiemann. 2001. "Institutional Choice in New Democracies: Bargaining over Hungary's 1989 Electoral Law." *Journal of Theoretical Politics* 13:159–188.

Birch, Sarah. 2003. *Electoral Systems and Political Transformation in Post-Communist Europe.* Basingstoke: Palgrave-Macmillan.

———. 2007. "Electoral Systems and Electoral Misconduct." *Comparative Political Studies* 40: 1533–1556.

Birch, Sarah, Frances Millard, Kieran Williams, and Marina Popescu, eds. 2002. *Embodying Democracy: Electoral System Design in Post-Communist Europe.* Basingstoke: Palgrave-Macmillan.

Blais, André, and R. K. Carty. 1987. "The Impact of Electoral Formulae on the Creation of Majority Governments." *Electoral Studies* 6:99–110.

———. 1990. "Does Proportional Representation Foster Voter Turnout?" *European Journal of Political Research* 18:167–181.

Blais, André, and Agnieszka Dobrzynska. 1998. "Turnout in Electoral Democracies." *European Journal of Political Research* 33:239–261.

Blais, André, and Louis Massicotte. 1997. "Electoral Formulas: A Macroscopic Perspective." *European Journal of Political Research* 32:107–129.

Blais, André, Louis Massicotte, and Antoine Yoshinaka. 2001. "Deciding Who Has the Right to Vote: A Comparative Analysis of Election Laws." *Electoral Studies* 20:41–62.

Blaydes, Lisa. 2006a. "Electoral Budget Cycles under Authoritarianism: Economic Opportunism in Mubarak's Egypt." Paper presented at the annual meeting of the Midwest Political Science Association, Chicago, April 20–23.

———. 2006b. "Who Votes in Authoritarian Elections and Why? Vote Buying, Turnout, and Spoiled Ballots in Contemporary Egypt." Paper presented at the annual meeting of the American Political Science Association, Philadelphia, August 31–September 3.

Boix, Carles. 1999. "Setting the Rules of the Game: The Choice of Electoral Systems in Advanced Democracies." *American Political Science Review* 93:609–624.

Bowler, Shaun, and Bernard Grofman, eds. 2000. *Elections in Australia, Ireland, and Malta under the Single Transferable Vote: Reflections on an Embedded Institution.* Ann Arbor: University of Michigan Press.

Brady, D., and J. Mo. 1992. "Electoral Systems and Institutional Choice: A Case Study of the 1988 Korean Elections." *Comparative Political Studies* 24:405–430.

Brams, Steven J., and Peter C. Fishburn. 1978. "Approval Voting." *American Political Science Review* 72:831–847.

Brechtenfeld, N. 1993. "The Electoral System." In *Atoll Politics: The Republic of Kiribati,* ed. H. Van Trease. Canterbury, New Zealand: Macmillan Brown Centre / Suva, Fiji: Institute of Pacific Studies, University of the South Pacific.

Carey, John M., and Matthew Soberg Shugart. 1995. "Incentives to Cultivate a Personal Vote: A Rank Ordering of Electoral Formulas." *Electoral Studies* 14:417–439.

Cohen, Denis. 1983. "Elections and Election Studies in Africa." In *Political Science in Africa: A Critical Review,* ed. Yolamu Barongo. London: Zed Books.

Cox, Gary W. 1987. "Electoral Equilibria under Alternative Voting Institutions." *American Journal of Political Science* 31:82–108.

———. 1997. *Making Votes Count: Strategic Coordination in the World's Electoral Systems.* New York: Cambridge University Press.

Dahl, Robert A. 1971. *Polyarchy: Participation and Opposition.* New Haven: Yale University Press.

———. 1989. *Democracy and Its Critiques.* New Haven: Yale University Press.

Dummett, M. 1997. *Principles of Electoral Reform.* Oxford: Oxford University Press.

Emerson, P. 1998. *Beyond the Tyranny of the Majority.* Belfast: De Borda Institute.

Farrell, David M., and Ian McAllister. 2000. "Through a Glass Darkly: Understanding the World of STV." In *Elections in Australia, Ireland, and Malta under the Single Transferable Vote: Reflections on an Embedded Institution,* ed. Shaun Bowler and Bernard Grofman. Ann Arbor: University of Michigan Press.

Gallagher, Michael. 1991. "Proportionality, Disproportionality, and Electoral Systems." *Electoral Studies* 10:33–51.

———. 1992. "Comparing Proportional Representation Electoral Systems: Quotas, Thresholds, Paradoxes, and Majorities." *British Journal of Political Science* 22:469–496.

Gallagher, Michael, Michael Laver, and Peter Mair. 2005. *Representative Government in Modern Europe: Institutions, Parties, and Government.* New York: McGraw-Hill.

Gandhi, Jennifer. 2003. "Political Institutions under Dictatorship." PhD diss., New York University.

Gandhi, Jennifer, and Adam Przeworski. 2006. "Cooperation, Cooptation, and Rebellion under Dictatorships." *Economics and Politics.* 18:1–26.

Geddes, Barbara. 2005. "Why Parties and Elections in Authoritarian Regimes." Paper presented at the annual meeting of the American Political Science Association, Washington, D.C., September 1–4.

Gibbard, Allan. 1973. "Manipulation of Voting Schemes: A General Result." *Econometrica* 41:587–601.

Golder, Matt. 2005. "Democratic Electoral Systems around the World, 1946–2000." *Electoral Studies* 24:103–121.

Golder, Matt, and Jacek Stramski. 2007. "Ideological Congruence and Two Visions of Democracy." Florida State University.

Golder, Matt, and Leonard Wantchekon. 2004. "Africa: Dictatorial and Democratic Electoral Systems since 1946." In *Handbook of Electoral System Design,* ed. Josep Colomer. London: Palgrave.

Guinier, Lani. 1994. *The Tyranny of the Majority.* New York: Free Press.

Horowitz, D. L. 1985. *Ethnic Groups in Conflict.* Berkeley: University of California Press.

———. 1991. *A Democratic South Africa? Constitutional Engineering in a Divided Society.* Berkeley: University of California Press.

Kaminski, Marek. 1999. "How Communism Could Have Been Saved: Formal Analysis of Electoral Bargaining in Poland in 1989." *Public Choice* 98:83–109.

Kaminski, Marek, Grzegorz Lissowski, and Piotr Swistak. 1998. "The 'Revival of Communism' or the Effect of Institutions? The 1993 Polish Parliamentary Elections." *Public Choice* 3:429–449.

Karklins, Rasma. 1986. "Soviet Elections Revisited: Voter Abstention in Noncompetitive Voting." *American Political Science Review* 80:449–470.

Katz, Richard S. 1980. *A Theory of Parties and Electoral Systems.* Baltimore: Johns Hopkins University Press.

———. 1997. *Democracy and Elections.* New York: Oxford University Press.

Kolk, Henk van der, Colin Rallings, and Michael Thrasher. 2006. "The Effective Use of the Supplementary Vote in Mayoral Elections: London 2000 and 2004." *Representation* 42:91–102.

Lijphart, Arend. 1986. "Degrees of Proportionality of Proportional Representation Formulas." In *Electoral Laws and Their Political Consequences,* ed. Bernard Grofman and Arend Lijphart. New York: Agathon Press.

———. 1990. "Electoral Systems, Party Systems, and Conflict Management in Segmented Societies." In *Critical Choices for South Africa: An Agenda for the 1990s,* ed. R. A. Schreirer. Cape Town: Oxford University Press.

———. 1991. "The Power-Sharing Approach." In *Conflict and Peacemaking in Multi-Ethnic Societies,* ed. J. V. Montville. New York: Lexington Books.

———. 1994. *Electoral Systems and Party Systems: A Study of Twenty-Seven Democracies, 1945–1990.* Oxford: Oxford University Press.

———. 1997. "Disproportionality under Alternative Voting: The Crucial—and Puzzling—Case of the Australian Senate Elections, 1919–1946." *Acta Politica* 32:9–24.

———. 1999. *Patterns of Democracy: Government Forms and Performance in Thirty-Six Countries.* New Haven: Yale University Press.

———. 2004. "Constitutional Design for Divided Societies." *Journal of Democracy* 15:96–109.

Lust-Okar, Ellen. 2005. *Structuring Conflict in the Arab World: Incumbents, Opponents, and Institutions.* New York: Cambridge University Press.

———. 2006. "Elections under Authoritarianism: Preliminary Lessons from Jordan." *Democratization* 13:456–471.

Lust-Okar, Ellen, and Amaney Ahmad Jamal. 2002. "Rulers and Rules: Reassessing the Influence of Regime Type on Electoral Law Formation." *Comparative Political Studies* 35:337–366.

Magaloni, Beatriz. 2006. *Voting for Autocracy: The Politics of Party Hegemony and Its Demise.* New York: Cambridge University Press.

Massicotte, Louis, and André Blais. 1999. "Mixed Electoral Systems: A Conceptual and Empirical Survey." *Electoral Studies* 18:341–366.

Mickey, Robert W. 2009. *Paths Out of Dixie: The Democratization of Authoritarian Enclaves in America's Deep South, 1944–1972.* Princeton: Princeton University Press.

Morton, Rebecca B., and Thomas A. Rietz. Forthcoming. "Majority Requirements and Minority Representation." *New York University Annual Survey of American Law.*

Nagel, Jack H. 2004. "New Zealand: Reform by (Nearly) Immaculate Design." In *Handbook of Electoral System Design,* ed. Josep Colomer. London: Palgrave.

Nohlen, Dieter, Florian Grotz, and Christof Hartmann. 2001. *Elections in Asia and the Pacific: A Data Handbook.* Vol. 1. New York: Oxford University Press.

Nohlen, Dieter, Michael Krennerich, and Bernhard Thibaut. 1999. *Elections in Africa: A Data Handbook.* New York: Oxford University Press.

Posner, Daniel N. 2005. *Institutions and Ethnic Politics in Africa.* New York: Cambridge University Press.

Powell, G. Bingham. 1982. *Contemporary Democracies: Participation, Stability, and Violence.* Cambridge: Harvard University Press.

———. 2000. *Elections as Instruments of Democracy: Majoritarian and Proportional Visions.* New Haven: Yale University Press.

Powers, Timothy, and J. Timmons Roberts. 1995. "Compulsory Voting, Invalid Ballot, and Abstention in Brazil." *Political Research Quarterly* 48:795–826.

Przeworski, Adam. 1991. *Democracy and the Market: Political and Economic Reforms in Eastern Europe and Latin America.* New York: Cambridge University Press.

Rae, Douglas. 1967. *The Political Consequences of Electoral Laws.* New Haven: Yale University Press.

Reilly, Ben. 1997. "Preferential Voting and Political Engineering: A Comparative Study." *Journal of Commonwealth and Comparative Politics* 35:1–19.

———. 2001. *Democracy in Divided Societies: Electoral Engineering for Conflict Management.* New York: Cambridge University Press.

————. 2002a. "Social Choice in the South Seas: Electoral Innovation and the Borda Count in the Pacific Island Countries." *International Political Science Review* 23:355–372.

————. 2002b. "Sri Lanka: Changes to Accommodate Diversity." In *The International IDEA Handbook of Electoral System Design,* ed. Andrew Reynolds and Ben Reilly. Stockholm: International Institute for Democracy and Electoral Assistance.

Remington, Thomas F., and S. S. Smith. 1996. "Political Goals, Institutional Context, and the Choice of an Electoral System: The Russian Parliamentary Election Law." *American Journal of Political Science* 40:1253–1279.

Reynolds, Andrew, and Ben Reilly. 2002. *The International IDEA Handbook of Electoral System Design.* Stockholm: International Institute for Democracy and Electoral Assistance.

Reynolds, Andrew, Ben Reilly, and Andrew Ellis. 2005. *Electoral System Design: The New International IDEA Handbook.* Stockholm: International Institute for Democracy and Electoral Assistance.

Roberts, N. S. 1997. "A Period of Enhanced Surprise, Disappointment, and Frustration? The Introduction of a New Electoral System in New Zealand." In *Electoral Systems for Emerging Democracies: Experiences and Suggestions,* ed. Jorgen Elklit. Copenhagen: Danida.

Roeder, Philip. 1989. "Electoral Avoidance in the Soviet Union." *Soviet Studies* 41:462–483.

Rudd, C., and I. Taichi. 1994. *Electoral Reform in New Zealand and Japan: A Shared Experience?* Palmerston North, New Zealand: Massey University Press.

Satterthwaite, Mark A. 1975. "Strategy-Proofness and Arrow's Conditions: Existence and Correspondence Theorems for Voting Procedures and Social Welfare Functions." *Journal of Economic Theory* 10:187–217.

Schaffer, H. B. 1995. "The Sri Lankan Elections of 1994: The Chandrika Factor." *Asian Survey* 35: 409–425,

Shugart, M., and M. Wattenberg, eds. 2001. *Mixed-Member Electoral Systems: The Best of Both Worlds?* New York: Oxford University Press.

Shvetsova, Olga. 1999. "A Survey of Post-Communist Electoral Institutions: 1990–1998." *Electoral Studies* 18:397–409.

Sinnott, Richard. 1992. "The Electoral System." In *Politics in the Republic of Ireland,* ed. John Coakley and Michael Gallagher. Dublin: Folens and PSAI.

Taagepera, Rein, and Matthew Soberg Shugart. 1989. *Seats and Votes: The Effects of Determinants of Electoral Systems.* New Haven: Yale University Press.

Tideman, Nicolaus, and Daniel Richardson. 2000. "A Comparison of Improved STV Methods." In *Elections in Australia, Ireland, and Malta under the Single Transferable Vote: Reflections on an Embedded Institution,* ed. Shaun Bowler and Bernard Grofman. Ann Arbor: University of Michigan Press.

Young, H. Peyton. 1994. *Equity in Theory and Practice.* Princeton: Princeton University Press.

CHAPTER 13

Afonso Da Silva. 2006. "Duverger's Laws: Between Social and Institutional Determinism." *European Journal of Political Research* 45:31–41.

Aldrich, John H. 1993. "Rational Choice and Turnout." *American Journal of Political Science* 37: 246–278.

————. 1995. *Why Parties? The Origin and Transformation of Political Parties in America.* Chicago: University of Chicago Press.

Amorim Neto, Octavio, and Gary Cox. 1997. "Electoral Institutions, Cleavage Structures, and the Number of Parties." *American Journal of Political Science* 41:149–174.

Anckar, Dag, and Carsten Anckar. 2000. "Democracies without Parties." *Comparative Political Studies* 33:225–247.

Argersinger, Peter H. 1980. " 'A Place on the Ballot': Fusion Politics and Antifusion Laws." *American Historical Review* 85:287–306.

Arrow, Kenneth J. 1963. *Social Choice and Individual Values.* New Haven: Yale University Press.

Bartolini, Stefano, and Peter Mair. 1990. *Identity, Competition, and Electoral Availability: The Stabilization of European Electorates, 1885–1985.* New York: Cambridge University Press.

Betz, Hans-Georg. 1994. *Radical Right-Wing Populism in Western Europe.* New York: St. Martin's Press.

Blais, André, and Indriði Indriðason. 2007. "Making Candidates Count: The Logic of Electoral Alliances in Two Round Legislative Elections." *Journal of Politics* 69:193–205.

Brambor, Thomas, William Roberts Clark, and Matt Golder. 2007. "Are African Party Systems Different?" *Electoral Studies* 26:315–323.

Bredin, Jean-Denis. 1986. *The Affair: The Case of Alfred Dreyfus.* New York: George Braziller.

Bulmer-Thomas, Ivor. 1965. *The Growth of the British Party System I, 1640–1923.* London: John Bake.

Campbell, Angus, Philip E. Converse, Warren Miller, and Donald Stokes. 1960. *The American Voter.* New York: Wiley.

Campbell, James E., Mary Munro, John R. Alford, and Bruce A. Campbell. 1986. "Partisanship and Voting." In *Research in Micropolitics,* ed. Samuel Long. Greenwich, Conn.: JAI Press.

Carey, John M., and John Polga-Hecimovich. 2006. "Primary Elections and Candidate Strength in Latin America." *Journal of Politics* 68:530–543.

———. 2007. "The Primary Elections 'Bonus' in Latin America." Dartmouth College.

Chandra, Kanchan. 2004. *Why Ethnic Parties Succeed.* London: Cambridge University Press.

———. 2005. "Ethnic Parties and Democratic Stability." *Perspectives on Politics* 3:235–252.

———. 2006. "What Is Ethnic Identity and Does It Matter?" *Annual Review of Political Science* 9: 397–424.

Chandra, Kanchan, and Cilianne Boulet. 2003. "A Model of Change in an Ethnic Demography." Department of Political Science, MIT.

Chhibber, Pradeep, and Ken Kollman. 1998. "Party Aggregation and the Number of Parties in India and the United States." *American Political Science Review* 92:329–342.

———. 2004. *The Formation of National Party Systems: Federalism and Party Competition in Canada, Great Britain, India, and the United States.* Princeton: Princeton University Press.

Clark, William Roberts, Michael Gilligan, and Matt Golder. 2006. "A Simple Multivariate Test for Asymmetric Hypotheses." *Political Analysis* 14:311–331.

Clark, William Roberts, and Matt Golder. 2006. "Rehabilitating Duverger's Theory: Testing the Mechanical and Strategic Modifying Effects of Electoral Laws." *Comparative Political Studies* 39:679–708.

Cox, Gary. 1997. *Making Votes Count: Strategic Coordination in the World's Electoral Systems.* New York: Cambridge University Press.

Cox, Gary, and Emerson Niou. 1994. "Seat Bonus under the Single Nontransferable Vote System: Evidence from Japan and Taiwan." *Comparative Politics* 26:221–236.

Dahl, Robert A. 1956. *A Preface to Democratic Theory.* Chicago: University of Chicago Press.

Dixon, Patrick. 1996. *The Truth about Westminster.* London: Hodder.Dolan, Ronald E., and Robert L. Worden, eds. 1994. *Japan: A Country Study.* Washington, D.C.: GPO for the Library of Congress.

Downs, Anthony. 1957. *An Economic Theory of Democracy.* New York: Harper and Row.

Duverger, Maurice. 1954. *Political Parties.* London: Methuen.

Engels, Friedrich. [1893] 1968. "Letter to Mehring." In *Marx-Engels Correspondence.* Geneva, Switzerland: International Publishers.

Fiorina, Morris. 1980. "The Decline of Collective Responsibility in American Politics." *Daedalus* 109:25–45.

———. 1981. *Retrospective Voting in American National Elections.* New Haven: Yale University Press.

Flanagan, Scott. 1987. "Value Change in Industrial Societies." *American Political Science Review* 81: 1303–1319.

Friedrich, C., and Z. Brzezinski. 1961. *Totalitarian Dictatorship and Autocracy.* New York: Praeger.

Gallagher, Michael, Michael Laver, and Peter Mair. 2006. *Representative Government in Modern Europe: Institutions, Parties, and Governments.* New York: McGraw-Hill.

Gershenson, Dmitriy, and Hershel I. Grossman. 2001. "Cooption and Repression in the Soviet Union." *Economics and Politics* 13:31–47.

Gill, Anthony. 1998. *Rendering unto Caesar: The Catholic Church and the State in Latin America.* Chicago: University of Chicago Press.

Golder, Matt. 2002. "An Evolutionary Approach to Party System Stability." Paper presented at the annual meeting of the American Political Science Association, Boston, August 29–September 1.

———. 2003. "Explaining Variation in the Electoral Success of Extreme Right Parties in Western Europe." *Comparative Political Studies* 36:432–466.

———. 2006. "Presidential Coattails and Legislative Fragmentation." *American Journal of Political Science* 50:34–48.

Golder, Sona N. 2005. "Pre-Electoral Coalitions in Comparative Perspective: A Test of Existing Hypotheses." *Electoral Studies* 24:643–663.

———. 2006. *The Logic of Pre-Electoral Coalition Formation.* Columbus: Ohio State University Press.

Gomez, Brad T., Thomas G. Hansford, and George A. Krause. 2007. "The Republicans Should Pray for Rain: Weather, Turnout, and Voting in U.S. Presidential Elections." *Journal of Politics* 69:649–663.

Habyarimana, James, Macartan Humphreys, Daniel Posner, and Jeremy Weinstein. 2005. "Ethnic Identity: An Experimental Approach." University of California, Los Angeles.

Hicken, Allen. Forthcoming. *Building Party Systems in Developing Countries.* New York: Cambridge University Press.

Hirano, Shigeo. 2005. "Electoral Institutions, Hometowns, and Favored Minorities: Evidence from Japanese Electoral Reforms." Columbia University.

Hitchcock, William I. 2003. *The Struggle for Europe: The Turbulent History of a Divided Continent, 1945 to the Present.* New York: Anchor Books.

Hough, Jerry F. 1980. *Soviet Leadership in Transition.* Washington D.C.: Brookings Institution.

Ignazi, Piero. 1992. "The Silent Counter-Revolution: Hypotheses on the Emergence of Extreme Right-Wing Parties in Europe." *European Journal of Political Research* 22:3–34.

Inglehart, Ronald. 1977. *The Silent Revolution: Changing Values and Political Styles among Western Publics.* Princeton: Princeton University Press.

———. 1990. *Culture Shift in Advanced Industrial Society.* Princeton: Princeton University Press.

———. 1997. *Modernization and Postmodernization.* Princeton: Princeton University Press.

Katz, Richard S. 1980. *A Theory of Parties and Electoral Systems.* Baltimore: Johns Hopkins University Press.

Kitschelt, Herbert P. 1988. "Left-Libertarian Parties: Explaining Innovation in Competitive Party Systems." *World Politics* 40:194–234.

———. 1996. *The Radical Right in Western Europe: A Comparative Analysis.* Ann Arbor: University of Michigan Press.

Laakso, M., and Rein Taagepera. 1979. " 'Effective' Number of Parties: A Measure with Application to West Europe." *Comparative Political Studies* 12:3–27.

Lacouture, Jean. 1986. *De Gaulle: Le Souverain, 1959–1970.* Paris: Seuil.

Laitin, David D. 1986. *Hegemony and Culture: Politics and Religious Change among the Yoruba.* Chicago: University of Chicago Press.

———. 1992. *Language Repertoires and State Construction in Africa.* New York: Cambridge University Press.

———. 1998. *Identity in Formation: The Russian-Speaking Populations in the Near Abroad.* Ithaca, N.Y.: Cornell University Press.

Lipset, Seymour Martin. 1996. "What Are Parties For?" *Journal of Democracy* 7:169–175.

———. 2001. "Cleavages, Parties, and Democracy." In *Party Systems and Voter Alignments Revisited,* ed. Lauri Karvonen and Stein Kuhnle, 3–10. London: Routledge.

Lipset, Seymour Martin, and Stein Rokkan. 1967. "Cleavage Structures, Party Systems, and Voter Alignments: An Introduction." In *Party Systems and Voter Alignments: Cross-National Perspectives,* ed. Seymour M. Lipset and Stein Rokkan. New York: Free Press.

Lust-Okar, Ellen. 2005. *Structuring Conflict in the Arab World: Incumbents, Opponents, and Institutions.* New York: Cambridge University Press.

Mair, Peter. 1997. *Party System Change: Approaches and Interpretations.* Oxford: Clarendon Press.

Marx, Karl. [1847] 1995. *The Poverty of Philosophy.* Amherst, N.Y.: Prometheus Books.

Michels, Robert. [1911] 2001. *Political Parties: A Sociological Study of the Oligarchical Tendencies of Modern Democracy.* Kitchener, Ontario: Batoche Books.

Mill, John Stuart. [1861] 1991. *Considerations on Representative Government.* Buffalo, N.Y.: Prometheus Books.

Minkenberg, M. 1992. "The New Right in Germany: The Transformation of Conservatism and the Extreme Right." *European Journal of Political Research* 22:55–81.

Mitra, S. 1988. "The National Front in France—A Single-Issue Movement?" *West European Politics* 11:47–64.

Morton, Rebecca. 1991. "Groups in Rational Turnout Models." *American Journal of Political Science* 35:758–776.

Ordeshook, Peter, and Olga Shvetsova. 1994. "Ethnic Heterogeneity, District Magnitude, and the Number of Parties." *American Journal of Political Science* 38:100–123.

Orwell, George. [1949] 1977. *1984: A Novel.* New York: Harcourt, Brace and World.

Pitkin, Hanna Fenichel. 1967. *The Concept of Representation.* Berkeley: University of California Press.

Posner, Daniel N. 2004. "The Political Salience of Cultural Difference: Why Chewas and Tumbukas Are Allies in Zambia and Adversaries in Malawi." *American Political Science Review* 98:529–545.

———. 2005. *Institutions and Ethnic Politics in Africa.* New York: Cambridge University Press.

Przeworski, Adam, and John Sprague. 1986. *Paper Stones: A History of Electoral Socialism.* Chicago: University of Chicago Press.

Reed, Steven, and Michael F. Thies. 2000. *The Causes of Electoral Reform in Japan.* Oxford: Oxford University Press.

Richardson, Bradley. 1997. *Japanese Democracy: Power, Coordination, and Performance.* New Haven: Yale University Press.

Schattschneider, E. E. 1942. *Party Government.* New York: Rinehart.

Schlesinger, Jacob M. 1997. *Shadow Shoguns: The Rise and Fall of Japan's Postwar Political Machine.* New York: Simon and Schuster.

Shively, W. Phillips. 2001. *Power and Choice: An Introduction to Political Science.* New York: McGraw-Hill.

Stokes, S. C. 1999. "Political Parties and Democracy." *Annual Review of Political Science* 2:243–267.

Strøm, Kaare, Ian Budge, and Michael J. Laver. 1994. "Constraints on Cabinet Formation in Parliamentary Democracies." *American Journal of Political Science* 38:303–335.

Uhlaner, Carole. 1989. "Rational Turnout: The Neglected Role of Groups." *American Journal of Political Science* 33:390–422.

Van Cott, Donna Lee. 2005. *From Movements to Parties in Latin America: The Evolution of Ethnic Politics.* New York: Cambridge University Press.

Voslensky, Michael. 1984. *Nomenklatura: The Soviet Ruling Class.* Garden City, N.Y.: Doubleday.

CHAPTER 14

Alesina, Alberto, and Enrico Spolaore. 1997. "On the Number and Size of Nations." *Quarterly Journal of Economics* 112:1027–1056.

Arzaghi, Mohammad, and J. Vernon Henderson. 2005. "Why Countries Are Fiscally Decentralizing." *Journal of Public Economics* 89:1157–1189.

Barber, Sotirios A. 1993. *The Constitution of Judicial Power.* Baltimore: Johns Hopkins University Press.

Bednar, Jenna. Forthcoming. *The Robust Federation.* New York: Cambridge University Press.

Billikopf, David Marshall. 1973. *The Exercise of Judicial Power: 1789–1864.* New York: Vantage Press.

Binder, Sarah. 1999. "The Dynamics of Legislative Gridlock, 1947–1996." *American Political Science Review* 93:519–533.

———. 2003. *Stalemate: Causes and Consequences of Legislative Gridlock.* Washington, D.C.: Brookings Institution Press.

Buchanan, James. 1995. "Federalism as an Ideal Political Order and an Objective for Constitutional Reform." *Publius: The Journal of Federalism* 25:19–28.

Buchanan, James, and Gordon Tullock. 1962. *The Calculus of Consent: Logical Foundations of Constitutional Democracy.* Ann Arbor: University of Michigan Press.

Caldeira, Gregory, and James Gibson. 1995. "The Legitimacy of Transnational Legal Institutions: Compliance, Support, and the European Court of Justice." *American Journal of Political Science* 39:459–489.

Cameron, Charles M. 2002. "Judicial Independence: How Can You Tell It When You See It?" In *Judicial Independence at the Crossroads: An Interdisciplinary Approach,* ed. Stephen B. Burbank and Barry Friedman. Thousand Oaks, Calif.: Sage Publications.

Cao, Yuanzheng, Yingyi Qian, and Barry R. Weingast. 1999. "From Federalism, Chinese Style, to Privatization, Chinese Style." *Economics of Transition* 7:103–131.

Carrubba, Clifford J. 2005. "Courts and Compliance in International Regulatory Regimes." *Journal of Politics* 67:669–689.

Clinton, Robert Lowry. 1994. "Game Theory, Legal History, and the Origins of Judicial Review: A Revisionist Analysis of *Marbury v. Madison.*" *American Journal of Political Science* 38:285–302.

Congleton, Roger D. 2006. "Asymmetric Federalism and the Political Economy of Decentralization." In *Handbook of Fiscal Federalism*, ed. Ehtisham Ahmad and Giorgio Brosio. Northampton, Mass.: Edward Elgar.

Diaz-Cayeros, Alberto. 2006. *Federalism, Fiscal Authority, and Centralization in Latin America*. New York: Cambridge University Press.

Elazar, Daniel J. 1987. *Exploring Federalism*. Tuscaloosa: University of Alabama Press.

———. 1997. "Contrasting Unitary and Federal Systems." *International Political Science Review* 18:237–251.

Epstein, Lee, and Jack Knight. 1998a. *The Choices Justices Make*. Washington, D.C.: CQ Press.

———. 1998b. "On the Struggle for Judicial Supremacy." *Law and Society Review* 30:87–120.

Epstein, Lee, Jack Knight, and Olga Shvetsova. 2001. "The Role of Constitutional Courts in the Establishment of Democratic Systems of Government." *Law and Society Review* 35:117–167.

Erikson, Robert S., Michael B. Mackuen, and James A. Stimson. 2002. *The Macro Polity*. New York: Cambridge University Press.

Ferejohn, John, and Charles Shipan. 1990. "Congressional Influence on Bureaucracy." *Journal of Law, Economics, and Organization* 6:1–20.

Gibson, James, and Gregory Caldeira. 1992. "The Etiology of Public Support for the Supreme Court." *American Journal of Political Science.* 36:459–489.

Gibson, James, Gregory Caldeira, and Vanessa Baird. 1998. "On the Legitimacy of National High Courts." *American Political Science Review* 92:343–358.

Ginsburg, Tom. 2003. *Judicial Review in New Democracies: Constitutional Courts in Asian Cases*. New York: Cambridge University Press.

Gunther, Gerald. 1991. *Constitutional Law*. 12th ed. Westbury, N.Y.: Foundation Press.

Hallerberg, Mark. 1996. "Tax Competition in Wilhelmine Germany and Its Implications for the European Union." *World Politics* 48:324–357.

Hayek, Friedrich von. [1939] 1948. "The Economic Conditions of Interstate Federalism." Repr. in *Individualism and the Economic Order*. Chicago: University of Chicago Press.

Hechter, Michael. 2000. *Containing Nationalism*. New York: Oxford University Press.

Helmke, Gretchen. 2002. "The Logic of Strategic Defection: Court-Executive Relations in Argentina under Dictatorship and Democracy." *American Political Science Review* 96:305–320.

———. 2005. *Courts under Constraints: Judges, Generals, and Presidents in Argentina*. New York: Cambridge University Press.

Hinich, Melvin J., and Michael C. Munger. 1997. *Analytical Politics*. New York: Cambridge University Press.

Horowitz, Donald L. 1985. *Ethnic Groups in Conflict*. Berkeley: University of California Press.

———. 1991. *A Democratic South Africa? Constitutional Engineering in a Divided Society*. Berkeley: University of California Press.

Lambert, Edouard. 1921. *Le gouvernement des juges et la lutte contre la législation sociale aux Etats-Unis*. Paris: Marcel Giard.

Lasser, William. 1988. *The Limits of Judicial Power: The Supreme Court in American Politics*. Chapel Hill: University of North Carolina Press.

Lijphart, Arend. 1996. "Puzzle of Indian Democracy." *American Political Science Review* 90:258–268.

———. 1999. *Patterns of Democracy: Government Forms and Performance in Thirty-Six Countries*. New Haven: Yale University Press.

Ludwikowski, Rett R. 1996. *Constitution-Making in the Region of Former Soviet Dominance.* Durham, N.C.: Duke University Press.

Marshall, Monty G., and Keith Jaggers. 2003. "Polity IV Project: Political Regime Characteristics and Transitions, 1800–2003." http://www.cidcm.umd.edu/inscr/polity/index.htm.

Mastias, Jean, and Jean Grangé. 1987. *Les secondes chambres du parlement en europe occidentale.* Paris: Economica.

Mayhew, David R. 1991. *Divided We Govern: Party Control, Lawmaking, and Investigations, 1946–1990.* New Haven: Yale University Press.

McRae, Kenneth D. 1983. *Conflict and Compromise in Multilingual Societies: Switzerland.* Waterloo, Ontario: Wilfrid Laurier University Press.

Monroe, Burt L. 1994. "Disproportionality and Malapportionment: Measuring Electoral Inequity." *Electoral Studies* 13:132–149.

Montesquieu [1752] 1914. *The Spirit of the Laws.* London: G. Bell and Sons, http://www.constitution.org/cm/sol.htm.

Montinola, Garbriella, Yingyi Qian, and Barry Weingast. 1994. "Federalism, Chinese Style: The Political Basis for Economic Success in China." *World Politics* 48:50–81.

Murphy, Walter F., C. Hermann Pritchett, and Lee Epstein. 2001. *Courts, Judges, and Politics: An Introduction to the Judicial Process.* New York: McGraw-Hill.

Navia, Patricio, and Julio Ríos-Figueroa. 2005. "The Constitutional Adjudication Mosaic of Latin America." *Comparative Political Studies* 38:189–217.

Oates, Wallace. 1972. *Fiscal Federalism.* New York: Harcourt Brace Jovanovich.

Ostrom, Vincent. 1991. *The Meaning of American Federalism: Constituting a Self-Governing Society.* San Francisco: Institute for Contemporary Studies.

O'Toole, Laurence J. 1993. *American Intergovernmental Relations: Foundations, Perspectives, and Issues.* Washington, D.C.: CQ Press.

Peck, Malcolm C. 2001. "Formation and Evolution of the Federation and Its Institutions." In *United Arab Emirates: A New Perspective,* ed. Ibrahim al Abed and Peter Hellyer. London: Trident Press.

Peterson, J. E. 1988. "The Future of Federalism in the United Arab Emirates." In *Crosscurrents in the Gulf: Arab Regional and Global Interests,* ed. H. Richard Sindelar III and J. E. Peterson, 198–230. London: Routledge.

Peterson, Paul. 1995. *The Price of Federalism.* Washington, D.C.: Brookings Institution.

Ramseyer, J. Mark, and Eric B. Rasmusen. 2003. *Measuring Judicial Independence: The Political Economy of Judging in Japan.* Chicago: University of Chicago Press.

Riker, William H. 1964. *Federalism: Origin, Operation, Significance.* Boston: Little, Brown.

———. 1975. "Federalism." In *Handbook of Political Science 5: Governmental Institutions and Processes,* ed. Fred I. Greenstein and Nelson W. Polsby, 93–172. Reading, Mass.: Addison-Wesley.

Rodden, Jonathan. 2002. "The Dilemma of Fiscal Federalism: Grants and Fiscal Performance around the World." *American Journal of Political Science* 46:670–687.

———. 2004. "Comparative Federalism and Decentralization: On Meaning and Measurement." *Comparative Politics* 36:481–500.

Rodden, Jonathan, and Erik Wibbels. 2002. "Beyond the Fiction of Federalism: Macroeconomic Management in Multitiered Systems." *World Politics* 54:494–531.

Rogers, James R. 2001. "Information and Judicial Review: A Signaling Game of Legislative-Judicial Interaction." *American Journal of Political Science* 45:84–99.

Rose-Ackerman, Susan. 1978. *Corruption: A Study in Political Economy.* New York: Academic Press.

———. 2000. "The Economics and Politics of Federalism: Tensions and Complementarities." *APSA-CP Newsletter* 11:17–19.

Rosenberg, Gerald. 1991. *The Hollow Hope: Can Courts Bring About Social Change?* Chicago: University of Chicago Press.

Samuels, David, and Richard Snyder. 2001. "The Value of a Vote: Malapportionment in Comparative Perspective." *British Journal of Political Science* 31:651–671.

Schleifer, Andrei, and Robert Vishny. 1993. "Corruption." *Quarterly Journal of Economics* 108:599–617.

Schwartz, Hermann. 1999. "Surprising Success: The New Eastern European Constitutional Courts." In *The Self-Restraining State,* ed. Andreas Schedler, Larry Diamand, and Marc Plattner, 195–214. Boulder, Colo.: Lynne Rienner.

Shapiro, Martin, and Alec Stone Sweet. 1994. "Introduction: The New Constitutional Politics." *Comparative Political Studies* 26:397–420.

Staton, Jeffrey K. 2004. "Judicial Policy Implementation in Mexico City and Mérida." *Comparative Politics* 37:41–60.

———. 2006. "Constitutional Review and the Selective Promotion of Case Results." *American Journal of Political Science* 50:98–112.

———. 2008. "Why Do Judges Go Public? Strategic Communication, Judicial Power, and State Consent." Book manuscript, Emory University.

Stepan, Alfred C. 1999. "Federalism and Democracy: Beyond the U.S. Model." *Journal of Democracy* 10:19–34.

Stone Sweet, Alec. 1992. *The Birth of Judicial Politics in France: The Constitutional Council in Comparative Perspective.* Oxford: Oxford University Press.

———. 2000. *Governing with Judges: Constitutional Politics in Europe.* New York: Oxford University Press.

———. 2008. "Constitutions and Judicial Power." In *Comparative Politics,* ed. Daniele Caramani. New York: Oxford University Press.

Tate, C. Neal, and Torbjörn Vallinder, eds. 1995. *The Global Expansion of Judicial Power.* New York: New York University Press.

Tiebout, C. M. 1956. "A Pure Theory of Local Expenditures." *Journal of Political Economy* 64:416–424.

Treisman, Daniel. 2000. "Decentralization and Inflation: Commitment, Collective Action, or Continuity?" *American Political Science Review* 94:837–857.

———. 2002. "Decentralization and the Quality of Government." University of California, Los Angeles.

Tsebelis, George. 1995. "Decision Making in Political Systems: Veto Players in Presidentialism, Multicameralism, and Multipartyism." *British Journal of Political Science* 25:289–326.

———. 1999. "Veto Players and Law Production in Parliamentary Democracies: An Empirical Analysis." *American Political Science Review* 93:591–608.

———. 2002. *Veto Players: How Political Institutions Work.* Princeton: Princeton University Press.

Tsebelis, George, and Jeannette Money. 1997. *Bicameralism.* New York: Cambridge University Press.

Tullock, Gordon. 1969. Federalism: Problems of Scale." *Public Choice* 6:19–29.

Vanberg, Georg. 1998. "Abstract Judicial Review, Legislative Bargaining, and Policy Compromise." *Journal of Theoretical Politics* 10:299–326.

———. 2000. "Establishing Judicial Independence in Germany: The Impact of Opinion Leadership and the Separation of Powers." *Comparative Politics* 32:333–353.

———. 2001. "Legislative-Judicial Relations: A Game-Theoretic Approach to Constitutional Review." *American Journal of Political Science* 45:346–361.

———. 2005. *The Politics of Constitutional Review in Germany.* New York: Cambridge University Press.

Volcansek, Mary L. 1991. "Judicial Activism in Italy." In *Judicial Activism in Comparative Perspective*, ed. Kenneth Holland. New York: St. Martin's Press.

Walsh, Correa Moylan. 1915. *The Political Science of John Adams: A Study in the Theory of Mixed Government and the Bicameral System.* New York: Putnam's.

Weingast, Barry. 1995. "The Economic Role of Political Institutions: Market-Preserving Federalism and Economic Development." *Journal of Law, Economics, and Organization* 11:1–31.

Wibbels, Erik. 2000. "Federalism and the Politics of Macroeconomic Policy and Performance." *American Journal of Political Science* 44:687–702.

World Bank. 2000. "Decentralization: Rethinking Government." In *World Development Report 1999/2000.* New York: Oxford University Press.

Wright, Deil S. 1988. *Understanding Intergovernmental Relations.* Pacific Grove, Calif.: Brooks/Cole.

CHAPTER 15

Alesina, Alberto, Reza Baqir, and William Easterly. 1999. "Public Goods and Ethnic Divisions." *Quarterly Journal of Economics*, 114:1243–1284.

Alesina, Alberto, Edward Glaeser, and Bruce Sacerdote. 2001. "Why Doesn't the United States Have a European-Style Welfare State?" *Brookings Papers on Economic Activity* 2:187–277.

Allum, P. A. 1973. *Italy—Republic without Government?* New York: Norton.

Amorin Neto, Octavio. 2006. "The Presidential Calculus: Executive Policy Making and Cabinet Formation in the Americas." *Comparative Political Studies* 39:415–440.

Amorin Neto, Octavio, and Gary Cox. 1997. "Electoral Institutions, Cleavage Structures, and the Number of Parties." *American Journal of Political Science* 41:149–174.

Areceneaux, Kevin. 2005. "Does Federalism Weaken Democratic Representation in the United States?" *Publius: The Journal of Federalism*, 35:297–311.

Atkeson, Lonna Rae, and Nancy Carillo. 2007. "More Is Better: The Influence of Collective Female Descriptive Representation on External Efficacy." *Politics and Gender* 3:79–101.

Bannerman, M. Graeme. 2002. "Republic of Lebanon." In *Government and Politics in the Middle East and North Africa*, 4th ed., ed. David E. Long and Bernard Reich. Boulder, Colo.: Westview Press.

Barabas, Jason. 2008. "Measuring Democratic Responsiveness." Florida State University.

Barry, Brian. 1975. "Political Accommodation and Consociational Democracy." *British Journal of Political Science* 5:477–505.

Bass, Gary J. 2005. "What Really Causes Civil War?" *New York Times Magazine*, August 13.

Bawn, Kathleen, and Frances Rosenbluth. 2006. "Short versus Long Coalitions: Electoral Accountability and the Size of the Public Sector." *American Journal of Political Science* 50:251–265.

Bednar, Jenna. 2009. *The Robust Federation.* New York: Cambridge University Press.

Bednar, Jenna, William N. Eskridge Jr., and John Ferejohn. 2001. "A Political Theory of Federalism." In *Constitutional Culture and Democratic Rule*, ed. John Ferejohn, John Riley, and Jack N. Rakove, 223–267. New York: Cambridge University Press.

Berman, Eli, and David Laitin. 2006. "Hard Targets: Theory and Evidence on Suicide Attacks." University of California, San Diego. http://econ.ucsd.edu/~elib/.

Bernhard, Michael, Timothy Nordstrom, and Christopher Reenock. 2001. "Economic Performance, Institutional Intermediation, and Democratic Survival." *Journal of Politics* 63:775–803.

Blais, André, and Marc André Bodet. 2006. "Does Proportional Representation Foster Closer Congruence between Citizens and Policymakers?" *Comparative Political Studies* 39:1243–1262.

Boix, Carles. 1999. "Setting the Rules of the Game: The Choice of Electoral Systems in Advanced Democracies." *American Political Science Review* 93:609–624.

———. 2003. *Democracy and Redistribution.* New York: Cambridge University Press.

Brambor, Thomas, William Roberts Clark, and Matt Golder. 2006. "Understanding Interaction Models: Improving Empirical Analyses." *Political Analysis* 14:63–82.

Brancati, Dawn. 2004. "Can Federalism Stabilize Iraq?" *Washington Quarterly* 27:7–21.

———. 2006. "Decentralization: Fueling the Fire or Dampening the Flames of Ethnic Conflict and Secessionism?" *International Organization* 60:651–685.

Budge, Ian, and Michael D. McDonald. 2007. "Election and Party System Effects on Policy Representation: Bringing Time into Comparative Perspective." *Electoral Studies* 26:168–179.

Bueno de Mesquita, Bruce, Alastair Smith, Randolph Siverson, and James D. Morrow. 2003. *The Logic of Political Survival.* Cambridge: MIT Press.

Bunce, Valerie. 1999. *Subversive Institutions: The Design and the Destruction of Socialism and the State.* New York: Cambridge University Press.

Burke, Edmund. [1770] 1949. "Thoughts on the Cause of the Present Discontents." In *Burke's Politics: Selected Writings and Speeches of Edmund Burke on Reform, Revolution, and War,* ed. Ross J. S. Hoffman and Paul Levack. New York: Knopf.

Burstein, Paul. 2003. "The Impact of Public Opinion on Public Policy: A Review and an Agenda." *Political Research Quarterly* 56:29–40.

Cameron, David R. 1978. "The Expansion of the Public Economy: A Comparative Analysis." *American Political Science Review* 72:1243–1261.

Caramani, Daniele. 1996. "The Swiss Parliamentary Election of 1995." *Electoral Studies* 15:128–137.

Carey, John M., and Matthew Soberg Shugart. 1995. "Incentives to Cultivate a Personal Vote: A Rank Ordering of Electoral Formulas." *Electoral Studies* 14:417–439.

Chandra, Kanchan. 2004. *Why Ethnic Parties Succeed: Patronage and Ethnic Head Counts in India.* New York: Cambridge University Press.

——— 2005. "Ethnic Parties and Democratic Stability." *Perspectives on Politics* 3:235–252.

Chandra, Kanchan, and Cilanne Boulet. 2003. "A Model of Change in an Ethnic Demography." Department of Political Science, MIT.

———. 2005. "Ethnic Cleavages, Permanent Exclusions, and Democratic Stability." Paper presented at the Conference on Alien Rule and Its Discontents, University of Washington, Seattle. June.

Cheibub, José Antonio. 2002. "Minority Governments, Deadlock Situations, and the Survival of Presidential Democracies." *Comparative Political Studies* 35:284–312.

———. 2006. "Presidentialism, Electoral Identifiability, and Budget Balances in Democratic Systems." *American Political Science Review* 100:353–367.

———. 2007. *Presidentialism, Parliamentarism, and Democracy.* New York: Cambridge University Press.

Cheibub, José Antonio, Adam Przeworski, and Sebastian Saiegh. 2004. "Government Coalitions and Legislative Success under Presidentialism and Parliamentarism." *British Journal of Political Science* 34:565–587.

Chhibber, Pradeep, and Ken Kollman. 1998. "Party Aggregation and the Number of Parties in India and the United States." *American Political Science Review* 92:329–342.

———. 2004. *The Formation of National Party Systems: Federalism and Party Competition in Canada, Great Britain, India, and the United States.* Princeton: Princeton University Press.

Clark, William Roberts. 2003. *Capitalism, Not Globalism: Capital Mobility, Central Bank Independence, and the Political Control of the Economy.* Ann Arbor: University of Michigan Press.

Clark, William Roberts, Matt Golder, and Sona Nadenichek Golder. 2002. "Fiscal Policy and the Democratic Process in the European Union." *European Union* 3:205–230.

Cohen, Carl. 1971. *Democracy.* New York: Free Press.

Cohen, Frank. 1997. "Proportional versus Majoritarian Ethnic Conflict Management in Democracies." *Comparative Political Studies* 30:607–630.

Collier, David, and Anke Hoeffler. 2004. "Greed and Grievance in Civil War." *Oxford Economic Papers* 56:563–595.

Coppedge, Michael. 1994. *Strong Parties and Lame Ducks: Presidential Partyarchy and Factionalism in Venezuela.* Stanford, Calif.: Stanford University Press.

Dahl, Robert. 1956. *A Preface to Democratic Theory.* Chicago: University of Chicago Press.

———. 1989. *Democracy and Its Critics.* New Haven: Yale University Press.

Dixit, Avinash K., and Susan Skeath. 2004. *Games of Strategy.* New York: Norton.

Easterly, William. 2001. "Can Institutions Resolve Ethnic Conflict?" *Economic Development and Cultural Change* 49:687–706.

Easterly, William, and Ross Levine. 1997. "Africa's Growth Tragedy: Policies and Ethnic Divisions." *Quarterly Journal of Economics* 112:1201–1250.

Elkins, Zachary, and John Sides. 2007. "Can Institutions Build Unity in Multiethnic States?" *American Political Science Review* 101:693–708.

Erikson, Robert S., Michael B. MacKuen, and James S. Stimson. 2002. *The Macro Polity.* New York: Cambridge University Press.

Estaban, Joan, and Debraj Ray. 1999. "Conflict and Distribution." *Journal of Economic Theory* 87:379–415.

———. 2008. "Polarization, Fractionalization, and Conflict." *Journal of Peace Research* 45:163–182.

Estaban, Joan and Gerald Schneider. 2008. "Polarization and Conflict: Theoretical and Empirical Issues." *Journal of Peace Research* 45:131–141.

Ezrow, Lawrence. 2007. "The Variance Matters: How Party Systems Represent the Preferences of Voters." *Journal of Politics* 69:182–192.

Fearon, James D., and David D. Laitin. 1996. "Explaining Interethnic Cooperation." *American Political Science Review* 90:715–735.

———. 2003. "Ethnicity, Insurgency, and Civil War." *American Political Science Review* 97:74–90.

Ferrer, Meghan. 2003. "The Impact of Institutions: Do Veto Players Influence Regime Duration." Honors thesis, Department of Politics, College of Arts and Sciences, New York University. (http://politics.as.nyu.edu/object/politics.undergrad.honorstheses.html).

Fiorina, Morris P. 1981. *Retrospective Voting in American National Elections.* New Haven: Yale University Press.

Franzese, Robert J. 2002. *Macroeconomic Policies of Developed Democracies.* New York: Cambridge University Press.

Franzese, Robert J., and Irfan Nooruddin. 2004. "The Effective Constituency in (Re) Distributive Politics: Alternative Bases of Democratic Representation, Geographic *versus* Partisan." Paper presented at the Midwest Political Science Association Annual Meeting, Chicago, April 15.

Gay, Claudine. 2001. "The Effect of Black Congressional Representation on Political Participation." *American Political Science Review* 95:589–602.

Gasiorowski, Mark J. 1995. "Economic Crisis and Political Regime Change: An Event History Analysis." *American History Analysis* 89:882–897.

Golder, Matt. 2005. "Democratic Electoral Systems around the World, 1946–2000." *Electoral Studies* 24:103–121.

———. 2006. "Presidential Coattails and Legislative Fragmentation." *American Journal of Political Science* 50:34–48.

Golder, Matt, and Jacek Stramski. 2007. "Ideological Congruence and Electoral Institutions: Conceptualization and Measurement." Paper presented at the annual meeting of the American Political Science Association, Chicago, August 30–September 2.

Golder, Sona. 2008. "Bargaining Delays in the Government Formation Process." Florida State University.

Gomez, Brad T., and J. Matthew Wilson. 2008. "Political Sophistication and Attributions of Blame in the Wake of Hurricane Katrina." *Publius: The Journal of Federalism* 38.

Goodhart, Lucy. 1999. "Political Institutions and Monetary Policy." Harvard University Program in Political Economy. http://citeseer.ist.psu.edu/337482.html.

Hall, Peter, ed. 1989. *The Political Power of Economic Ideas: Keynesianism across Nations.* Princeton: Princeton University Press.

Hallerberg, Mark. 2004. *Domestic Budgets in a United Europe: Fiscal Governance from the End of Bretton Woods to EMU.* Ithaca, N.Y.: Cornell University Press.

Hallerberg, Mark, and Patrik Marier. 2004. "Executive Authority, the Personal Vote, and Budget Discipline in Latin American and Caribbean Countries." *American Journal of Political Science* 48:571–587.

Hallerberg, Mark, and Jurgen von Hagen. 1999. "Electoral Institutions, Cabinet Negotiations, and Budget Deficits in the European Union." In *Fiscal Institutions and Fiscal Performance,* ed. James Poterba and Jurgen von Hagen, 209–232. Chicago: University of Chicago Press.

Hardgrave, Robert, Jr. 1994. "India: The Dilemma of Diversity." In *Nationalism, Ethnic Conflict, and Democracy,* ed. Larry Diamond and Marc F. Plattner. Baltimore: Johns Hopkins University Press.

Hardin, Garrett. 1968. "The Tragedy of the Commons." *Science* 162:1243–1248.

Hardin, Russell. 1982. *Collective Action.* Baltimore: Johns Hopkins University Press.

Hechter, Michael. 2000. *Containing Nationalism.* New York: Oxford University Press.

Hellwig, Timothy, and David Samuels. 2007. "Electoral Accountability and the Variety of Democratic Regimes." *British Journal of Political Science* 38:65–90.

Hibbs, Douglas A., Jr. 1977. "Political Parties and Macroeconomic Policy." *American Political Science Review* 71:1467–1487.

Hicken, Allen. Forthcoming. *Building Party Systems in Developing Democracies.* New York: Cambridge University Press.

Horowitz, Donald L. 1985. *Ethnic Groups in Conflict.* Berkeley: University of California Press.

———. 1991. *A Democratic South Africa? Constitutional Engineering in a Divided Society.* Berkeley: University of California Press.

———. 2004. "The Alternative Vote and Interethnic Moderation: A Reply to Fraenkel and Grofman." *Public Choice* 121:507–516.

Huber, Evelyne, Charles Ragin, and John D. Stephens. 1993. "Social Democracy, Christian Democracy, Constitutional Structure, and the Welfare State." *American Journal of Sociology* 99:711–749.

Huber, John D., and Cecilia Martinez-Gallardo. 2004. "Cabinet Instability and the Accumulation of Experience in the Cabinet: The French Fourth and Fifth Republics in Comparative Perspective." *British Journal of Political Science* 34:27–48.

———. 2008. "Replacing Cabinet Ministers: Patterns of Ministerial Stability in Parliamentary Democracies." *American Political Science Review* 102:169–180.

Huber, John D., and G. Bingham Powell. 1994. "Congruence between Citizens and Policymakers in Two Visions of Liberal Democracy." *World Politics* 46:291–326.

Iversen, Torben, and David Soskice, 2006. "Electoral Institutions and the Politics of Coalitions: Why Some Democracies Redistribute More than Others." *American Political Science Review* 100:165–181.

Jones, Mark P. 1995. "Presidential Election Laws and Multipartism in Latin America." *Political Research Quarterly* 47:41–57.

Kalyvas, Stathis. 1996. *The Rise of Christian Democracy in Europe.* Ithaca, N.Y.: Cornell University Press.

Karp, Jeffrey A., and Susan A. Banducci. 2007. "When Politics Is Not Just a Man's Game: Women's Representation and Political Engagement." *Electoral Studies* 27:105–115.

Keefer, Philip, and David Stasavage. 2002. "Checks and Balances, Private Information, and the Credibility of Monetary Commitments." *International Organization* 56:751–774.

Kerr, Henry H. 1987. "The Swiss Party System: Steadfast and Changing." In *Party Systems in Denmark, Austria, Switzerland, the Netherlands, and Belgium,* ed. Hans Daalder. New York: St. Martin's Press.

Keynes, John Maynard. [1923] 2000. *A Tract on Monetary Reform.* Amherst, N.Y.: Prometheus Books.

Knack, Stephen, and Philip Keefer. 1995. "Institutions and Economic Performance: Cross-Country Tests Using Alternative Institutional Measures." *Economics and Politics* 7:207–227.

Kymlicka, Will. 1998. "Is Federalism a Viable Alternative to Secessionism?" In *Theories of Secessionism,* ed. Percy B. Lehning. New York: Routledge Press.

Leff, Carol Skalnick. 1999. "Democratization and Disintegration in Multi-National States: The Breakup of the Communist Federations." *World Politics* 51:205–235.

Leighley, Jan E., and Jonathan Nagler. 1992. "Socioeconomic Class Bias in Turnout, 1964–1988—The Voters Remain the Same." *American Political Science Review* 86:725–736.

Le Pen, Yannick. 2005. "Convergence among Five Industrial Countries (1870–1994): Results from a Time Varying Cointegration Approach." *Empirical Economics* 30:23–35.

Levi, Margaret. 1988. *Of Rule and Revenue.* Berkeley: University of California Press.

Li, Qing, and David Papell. 1999. "Convergence of International Output: Time Series Evidence for 16 OECD Countries." *International Review of Economics and Finance* 8:267–280.

Lijphart, Arend. 1977. *Democracy in Plural Societies: A Comparative Exploration.* New Haven: Yale University Press.

———. 1984. *Democracies: Patterns of Majoritarian and Consensus Government.* New Haven: Yale University Press.

———. 1996. "Puzzle of Indian Democracy." *American Political Science Review* 90:258–268.

———. 1999. *Government Forms and Performance in Thirty-Six Countries.* New Haven: Yale University Press.

———. 2004. "Constitutional Design for Divided Societies." *Journal of Democracy* 15:96–109.

Linz, Juan J. 1990a. "The Perils of Presidentialism." *Journal of Democracy* 1: 51–69.

———. 1990b. "The Virtues of Parliamentarism." *Journal of Democracy* 4:84–91.

———. 1994. "Democracy: Presidential or Parliamentary: Does It Make a Difference?" In *The Failure of Presidential Democracy?* ed. J. J. Linz and A. Valenzuela. Baltimore: Johns Hopkins University Press.

Lustik, Ian S., Dan Miodownik, and Roy J. Eidelson. 2004. "Secessionism in Multicultural States: Does Sharing Power Prevent or Encourage It?" *American Political Science Review* 98:209–229.

Maestas, Cherie, Lonna Rae Atkeson, Thomas Croom, and Lisa Bryant. 2008. "Shifting the Blame: Federalism, Media, and Public Assignment of Blame Following Hurricane Katrina." *Publius: The Journal of Federalism* 38.

Mainwaring, Scott. 1993. "Presidentialism, Multipartism, and Democracy: The Difficult Combination." *Comparative Political Studies* 26:198–228.

Mainwaring, Scott, and Matthew Sobert Shugart, eds. 1997. *Presidentialism and Democracy in Latin America.* New York: Cambridge University Press.

Malhotra, Neil, and Alexander G. Kuo. 2008. "Assigning Blame: The Public's Response to Hurricane Katrina." *Journal of Politics* 70:120–135.

Mansbridge, Jane. 1999. "Should Blacks Represent Blacks and Women Represent Women? A Contingent 'Yes.' " *Journal of Politics* 61:628–657.

McDonald, Michael D., and Ian Budge. 2005. *Elections, Parties, Democracy: Conferring the Median Mandate.* New York: Oxford University Press.

McDonald, Michael D., Silvia M. Mendes, and Ian Budge. 2004. "What Are Elections For? Conferring the Median Mandate." *British Journal of Political Science* 34:1–26.

McGillivray, Fiona. 2004. *Privileging Industry: The Comparative Politics of Trade and Industrial Policy.* Princeton: Princeton University Press.

Meltzer, Allan H., and Scott F. Richard. 1981. "A Rational Theory of the Size of Government." *Journal of Political Economy* 89:914–927.

Merlo, Antonio. 1998 "Economic Dynamic and Government Stability in Postwar Italy." *Review of Economics and Statistics* 80:629–637.

Mill, John Stuart. [1859] 1991. "On Liberty." In *J. S. Mill: On Liberty,* ed. John Gray and G. W. Smith, 23–130. London: Routledge.———. [1861] 1991. *Considerations on Representative Government.* Buffalo, N.Y.: Prometheus Books.

Montalvo, José G., and Marta Reynal-Querol. 2005. "Ethnic Polarization, Potential Conflict, and Civil Wars." *American Economic Review* 95:796–816.

Morrison, Donald, Robert Mitchell, and John Paden. 1989. *Black Africa: A Comparative Handbook.* New York: Paragon Press.

Morrow, James D. 1994. *Game Theory for Political Scientists.* Princeton: Princeton University Press.

Mueller, Dennis. 1991. "Choosing a Constitution in Eastern Europe: Lessons from Public Choice." *Journal of Comparative Economics* 15:325–348.

Nordlinger, Eric. 1972. *Conflict Regulation in Divided Societies.* Cambridge: Harvard University Center for International Affairs.

Olson, Mancur. 1968. *The Logic of Collective Action.* Cambridge: Harvard University Press.

Ostrom, Elinor. 1990. *Governing the Commons: The Evolution of Institutions for Collective Action.* New York: Cambridge University Press.

Page, Benjamin I. 1994. "Democratic Responsiveness? Untangling the Links between Public Opinion and Policy." *PS: Political Science and Politics* 27:25–29.

Page, Benjamin I., and Robert Y. Shapiro. 1983. "Effects of Public Opinion on Policy." *American Political Science Review* 77:175–190.

Pantoja, Adian D., and Gary M. Segura. 2003. "Does Ethnicity Matter? Descriptive Representation in Legislatures and Political Alienation among Latinos. *Social Science Quarterly* 84:441–460.

Persson, Torsten, and Guido Tabellini. 1999. "The Size and Scope of Government: Comparative Politics with Rational Politicians." *European Economy Review* 43:699–735.

———. 2000. *Political Economics: Explaining Economic Policy.* Cambridge: MIT Press.

———. 2004. "Constitutional Rules and Fiscal Policy Outcomes." *American Economic Review* 94:24–45.

Persson, Torsten, Gerard Roland, and Guido Tabellini. 2000. "Comparative Politics and Public Finance." *Journal of Political Economy* 108:1121–1161.

———. 2007. "Electoral Rules and Government Spending in Parliamentary Democracies." *Quarterly Journal of Political Science* 2:155–188.

Pitkin, Hanna Fenichel. 1967. *The Concept of Representation.* Berkeley: University of California Press.

Posner, Daniel N. 2004. "The Political Salience of Cultural Difference: Why Chewas and Tumbukas Are Allies in Zambia and Adversaries in Malawi." *American Political Science Review* 98:529–545.

———. 2005. *Institutions and Ethnic Politics in Africa.* New York: Cambridge University Press.

Powell, G. Bingham. 1982. *Contemporary Democracies: Participation, Stability, and Violence.* Cambridge: Harvard University Press.

———. 2000. *Elections as Instruments of Democracy: Majoritarian and Proportional Visions.* New Haven: Yale University Press.

———. 2006. "Election Laws and Representative Governments: Beyond Votes and Seats." *British Journal of Political Science* 36:291–315.

Powell, G. Bingham, and Georg Vanberg. 2000. "Election Laws, Disproportionality and the Left-Right Dimension." *British Journal of Political Science* 30:383–411.

Przeworski, Adam, Michael E. Alvarez, José Cheibub, and Fernando Limongi. 2000. *Democracy and Development: Political Institutions and Well-Being in the World, 1950–1990.* New York: Cambridge University Press.

Rabushka, Alvin, and Kenneth Shepsle. 1972. *Politics in Plural Societies: A Theory in Democratic Instability.* Columbus, Ohio: Charles E. Merrill.

Reenock, Christopher, and Jeffrey K. Staton. 2008. "Substitutable Protections: Socioeconomic Insulation and Credible Commitment Devices." Florida State University.

Reenock, Christopher, Jeffrey K. Staton, and Marius Radean. 2008. "The Uneven Effects of Legal System Quality on Democratic Survival." Florida State University.

Reilly, Ben. 1997. "Preferential Voting and Political Engineering: A Comparative Study." *Journal of Commonwealth and Comparative Politics* 35:1–19.

———. 2001. *Democracy in Divided Societies: Electoral Engineering for Conflict Management.* New York: Cambridge University Press.

Reynal-Querol, Marta. 2002. "Ethnicity, Political Systems, and Civil Wars." *Journal of Conflict Resolution* 46:29–54.

Riker, William H. 1964. *Federalism: Origin, Operation, Significance.* Boston: Little, Brown.

Rioux, Jean-Pierre. 1989. *The Fourth Republic, 1944–1958.* New York: Cambridge University Press.

Rodden, Jonathan. 2006. "Red States, Blues States, and the Welfare State: Political Geography, Representation, and Government Policy around the World." Work in Progress Series, Massachusetts Institute of Technology.

Roeder, Phillip G. 1991. "Soviet Federalism and Ethnic Mobilization." *World Politics* 43:196–232.

Rogowski, Ronald. 1987. "Trade and the Variety of Democratic Institutions" *International Organization* 41:203–223.

Rogowski, Ronald, and Mark Andreas Kayser. 2002. "Majoritarian Electoral Systems and Consumer Power: Price-Level Evidence from the OECD Countries." 46:526–539.

Romer, Thomas. 1975. "Individual Welfare, Majority Voting, and the Properties of a Linear Income Tax." *Journal of Public Economics* 4:163–185.

Rustow, Dankwart A. 1950. "Some Observations on Proportional Representation." *Journal of Politics* 12:107–127.

Saideman, Stephen M., David J. Lanoue, Michael Campenni, and Samuel Stanon. 2002. "Democratization, Political Institutions, and Ethnic Conflict: A Pooled Time-Series Analysis, 1985–1998." *Comparative Political Studies* 35:103–129.

Schattschneider, E. E. 1935. *Politics, Pressure, and the Tariff.* Englewood Cliffs, N.J.: Prentice Hall.

Shively, W. Phillips. 2001. *Power and Choice: An Introduction to Political Science.* New York: McGraw-Hill.

Shugart, Matthew Soberg. 1999. "Presidentialism, Parliamentarism, and the Provision of Collective Goods in Less-Developed Countries." *Constitutional Political Economy* 10:53–88.

Shugart, Matthew Soberg, and John M. Carey. 1992. *Presidents and Assembles: Constitutional Design and Electoral Dynamics.* New York: Cambridge University Press.

Skinner, Quentin. 2005. "Hobbes on Representation." *European Journal of Philosophy* 13:155–184.

Snyder, Jack. 2000. *From Voting to Violence: Democratization and Nationalist Conflict.* New York: Norton.

Steiner, Jürg. 1971. "The Principles of Majority and Proportionality." *British Journal of Political Science* 1:63–70.

Stepan, Alfred. 1999. "Federalism and Democracy: Beyond the U.S. Model." *Journal of Democracy* 10:19–34.

Stepan, Alfred, and Cindy Skach. 1993. "Constitutional Frameworks and Democratic Consolidation: Parliamentarism versus Presidentialism." *World Politics* 46:1–22.

Tocqueville, Alexis de. [1835] 1945. *Democracy in America.* Translated by Henry Reeve, Francis Bowen, and Phillips Bradley. New York: Random House.

Tsebelis, George. 1990. "Elite Interaction and Constitution Building in Consociational Societies." *Journal of Theoretical Politics* 2:5–29.

———. 1995. "Decision Making in Political Systems: Veto Players in Presidentialism, Parliamentarism, Multicameralism, and Multipartisin." *British Journal of Political Science* 25:289–325.

———. 2002. *Veto Players: How Political Institutions Work.* Princeton: Princeton University Press.

Valenzuela, Arturo. 2004. "Latin America Presidencies Interrupted." *Journal of Democracy* 15:5–19.

Vanhanen, Tatu. 1991. *The Process of Democratization: A Comparative Study of 147 States, 1980–1988.* New York: Crane Russak.

Varshney, Ashutosh. 2001. "Ethnic Conflict and Civil Society: India and Beyond." *World Politics* 53:362–398.

————. 2002. *Ethnic Conflict and Civic Life: Hindus and Muslims in India.* New Haven: Yale University Press.

————. 2004. "Nationalism, Ethnic Conflict, and Rationality." *Perspectives on Politics* 1:85–99.

Weingast, Barry R. 1979. "A Rational Choice Perspective on Congressional Norms." *American Journal of Political Science.* 23:245–262.

Weingast, Barry R., Kenneth A. Shepsle, and Christopher Johnsen. 1981. "The Political Economy of Benefits and Costs: A Neoclassical Approach to Distributive Politics." *Journal of Political Economy* 89:642–664.

Wolfinger, Raymond E., and Steven J. Rosenstone. 1980. *Who Votes?* New Haven: Yale University Press.

Photo Credits

Page	Credit
2	AP Photo/Jerome Delay
23	Library of Congress
60	The Granger Collection, New York
61	AP Photo/Charles Rex Arbogast
93	AP Photo
197	AP Photo/Denis Farrell
228	AP Photo/David Longstreath
261	AP Photo/Jeff Widener
266	AP Photo/STF
279	AP Photo/Reportagebild
315	AP Photo/Naashon Zalk
330	Peer Grimm/dpa /Landov
345	The Granger Collection, New York
412	AP Photo/Jockel Finck
434	REUTERS/Regis Duvignau
453	AP Photo/RTR Russian Channel
465	REUTERS/Fadi Al-Assaad
489	AP Photo/Government Information Service
516	AP Photo/Sandor A. Szabo
539	AP Photo/Rob Cooper
544	REUTERS/Eriko Sugita
558	AP Photo/Francois Mori
688	AP Photo/Yves Logghe
757	COLECCION MUSEO HISTORICO NACION/AFP/Getty Images

Index

Note: Boxes, figures, notes, tables, and maps are indicated by b, f, n, t, and m following the page number.

A

Abu Dhabi. *See* United Arab Emirates
Acheson, Dean, 454
Acuerdo del Club Naval (Naval Club Accord; 1984), 276
Adam, Lyn Terangi, 479
Adams, John, 632
Adenauer, Konrad, 265
Aeschylus, 208–209
Afghanistan. *See also* al-Qaida; Taliban
  electoral rules in, 525
  as a failed state, 7
  Loya Jirga (Grand Assembly) in, 229
  September 11, 2001, and, 7
  Soviet invasion of, 260
  Taliban in, 114, 228
  terrorist groups in, 102
  U.S. invasion of, 7
Africa. *See also* individual countries
  decolonization in, 195
  democratization in, 257, 468, 476, 520, 525
  economic growth in, 730
  ethnic conflict in, 724–725
  ethnic heterogeneity in, 730
  ethnic parties in, 564
  modernization theory and, 170
  selectorate in, 333
African National Congress (ANC), 188b, 544
Age of revolution, 150
Agendas and agenda setting. *See* Decision making
Aggregation and disaggregation, 162, 163, 165, 166
Agriculture, 182–183, 190
Aideed, Mohamed Farah, 98
Albania, 513
Alesina, Alberto, 711, 712, 730
Algeria, 154, 227, 539

Allende, Salvador, 756
Allum, P.A., 442, 746
Almond, Gabriel, 212, 214, 215, 218
Alvarez, Michael E., 154–156, 161
America. *See* United States
Amorim Neto, Octavio, 445, 446, 448, 453
Analyses. *See* Methods—specific
Anarchists and anarchism, 145
ANC. *See* African National Congress
Andorra, 512
Angola, 256
Anne (Queen of England), 623
Antecedents. *See* Arguments
Argentina, 319, 487, 498, 609, 614
Arguments
  antecedents and consequents in, 33, 34–36, 38, 39t, 40
  conclusions, 33
  valid and invalid arguments, 33–36, 38, 39t
Aristotle, 149–151, 152, 630
Aristocracies, 150, 630, 631, 632
Armenia, 449
Arms races, 127–128
Arrow, Kenneth, 380. *See also* Theorems
Ashton, Joe, 541
Asia, 257, 520, 639
Asian Values Debate, 209, 224
Attributes. *See* Social issues
Australia
  constitution of, 636
  democratic institutions of, 685, 687
  elections and electoral system in, 430–431, 470, 471, 472b, 477, 480–481, 483, 488, 507, 511, 737
  federalism in, 616
  legislature in, 625, 626, 627, 633

preelection coalitions in, 694
Austria, 261, 265b, 423, 427, 430, 625, 626
Austro-Hungarian empire, 564
Authoritarian regimes, 255. *See also* Dictatorships
Autocracies, 151
AV (alternative vote) systems. *See* Elections and electoral systems—specific

B

Bacquet, J. Paul, 485
Bahamas, 626, 685, 687
Bahrain, 606
Baillie, Gavin, 477, 481
Balladur, Edouard, 451
Balmer, Randall, 227
Bangkok Declaration (1993), 224
Baqir, Reza, 730
Barbados, 471–472, 626, 687
Barre, Mohamed Siad, 96, 97
Barro, Robert J., 314–315, 317
Barry, Brian, 214
Bates, Robert H., 183, 184, 190, 194
Bawn, Kathleen, 522
BC (Borda Count) systems. *See* Decision making; Elections and electoral systems—specific; Votes, voters, and voting
Belgium
  analysis of democracy in, 21–25, 26–27
  Catholicism in, 227
  cleavages in, 568, 687–688
  consensus democracy of, 687–688
  constitution of, 427–428
  Eighty Years' War and, 555
  electoral system and rules in, 472b, 687

Belgium—*continued*
  federalism in, 611, 612, 615,
    617, 687
  government in, 427–428, 436,
    439, 443, 688
  legislature in, 625, 629b, 687
  Leopold II and, 344, 345
Belize, 471, 474
Benin, 497, 500
Benoit, Kenneth, 525
Bergman, Torbjörn, 423
Berlin Blockade and Airlift
    (1948), 263–264
Berlin Uprising (1953), 264, 271
Berlin Wall, 76, 258, 262, 264–265.
    See also Germany, East
Bhutan, 465
Bicameralism. *See* Legislatures
    and legislators
Birch, Sarah, 525
Black Hawk Down (Bowden), 99
Blair, Tony, 624
Blais, André, 470, 471
Blaydes, Lisa, 467
Blix, Hans, 2
Block, Fred, 322–323
Blunt, Charles, 477, 481
Bodin, Jean, 150
Boix, Carles, 175, 196, 522
Bolivia, 315, 470, 565
Bollen, Kenneth A., 161
Borda, Jean-Charles de, 363, 478
Borda Count (BC). *See* Decision
    making; Elections and elec-
    toral systems—specific;
    Votes, voters, and voting
Bosnia-Herzegovina, 484
Botswana, 155, 544, 615
Boulet, Cilianne, 565, 731
Bowden, Mark, 99
Bowling Alone (Putnam), 213
Brancati, Dawn, 739, 740–741
Brandeis, Louis D., 618
Brandt, Willy, 265b
Brazil
  cabinets in, 448
  democratization in, 257b, 258b,
    276
  elections and electoral system in,
    467, 470, 472b, 497, 500, 506
  federalism in, 608–609, 611, 615
  political parties and party
    system in, 551

Brezhnev, Leonid, 280b
Brown, Nathan, 278–279
Brunei, 465, 466
Brzezinski, Zbigniew, 542
Buddhism, 226. *See also* Democ-
    racy and democratization—
    cultural determinants;
    Religion and religious issues
Bueno de Mesquita, Bruce, 259,
    331, 332, 334b, 335, 337, 346b
Bulgaria, 470, 498
Bulmer-Thomas, Ivor, 552
Burke, Edmund, 679
Burkina Faso, 199–200, 201, 466
Bush, George W.
  arguments for invading Iraq,
    2, 6
  elections of 2000 and, 582
  views of democracy, 2, 6, 7,
    8–10, 259
BV (block vote) system. *See*
    Elections and electoral
    systems—specific

C

Cabinets
  common pool resource problem
    and, 721–722
  instability of, 746
  in mixed democracies, 453
  political parties and, 536, 722
  veto players in, 722
Cabinets—parliamentary
  appointment and formation of,
    409–410, 435–436, 437–438,
    445, 448
  coalition cabinets, 410, 411, 416,
    428, 435–436
  collective cabinet responsibility,
    403
  in corporatist countries, 423
  Gamson's Law and, 415, 448
  government duration and, 438
  instability of, 442–443, 753–754,
    761
  ministers in, 402–403, 411–412,
    415
  policymaking powers of, 412,
    744
  politicians and, 414, 437
  portfolio allocation in, 415
  preelectoral coalitions and, 434
  single-party cabinets, 411

surplus majority government
    and, 426
Cabinets—presidential
  coalitions and, 445–447
  composition of, 447–449
  ministers in, 447
  political parties and, 444, 448
  portfolio allocation in, 447–448
  responsibilities of, 403
  size of, 445–447
Callaghan, James, 541
Calvin, John, 554
Cameron, David, 709
Cameroon, 492
Canada
  cabinet in, 443
  elections and electoral systems
    in, 458, 471, 472b, 474
  ethnic parties in, 565
  federalism in, 612, 615
  legislature in, 543, 626
  Muslims in, 228
  preelection coalitions in, 430,
Candidates. *See also* Electoral
    systems; Political parties;
    Politicians and political
    elites
  alternative vote and, 736–737
  incumbents, 80–83
  incumbents versus challengers,
    341–342
  party lists and, 502–507, 721
  personal votes of, 721
  political parties and, 536
  presidential candidates, 744,
    754
Cape Verde, 500, 525
Capitalism and capitalists. *See*
    Economic issues
*Capitalism, Socialism, and
    Democracy* (Schumpeter), 5
Caribbean region, 517, 520
Catholicism, 9, 222–224, 227,
    230–239, 554–555, 556. *See
    also* Cleavages; Democracy
    and democratization—
    cultural determinants;
    Religion and religious issues
Causes and causation
  definitions and concepts of, 28
  deterministic causes, 28–29
  interaction effects, 29–30
  minimalist views and, 161

Mill's methods and, 19–32
principle of uniformity of
    nature and, 43
probabilistic causes, 28–29
CBOS. *See* Center for Public
    Opinion Research
CPDP. *See* Comparative
    Parliamentary Democracy
    Project
Ceauçsescu, Nicolae, 266
Center for Public Opinion
    Research (CBOS; Poland),
    290, 291, 523
Central African Republic, 485, 525
Chad, 492
Chandra, Kanchan, 563–564, 565,
    593, 731, 732–733, 735
Charles II (King of England), 552
Checks and balances. *See*
    Constitutional issues;
    Political issues
Cheibub, José Antonio, 154–156,
    225, 277, 445, 447
Chernobyl disaster (1986), 260
Chhibber, Pradeep, 586
Chiang Kai-shek, 344
Chile
    democratization of, 276–277
    dictatorial constitution in, 279
    elections in, 500
    military coups and dictators in,
        315, 319, 333
    stability of, 756
    voting in, 470, 471
China, 228, 344. *See also* People's
    Republic of China
Chirac, Jacques, 259, 433, 434,
    451, 455, 487, 582
Christian democrats and
    Christian Democratic
    parties, 558, 711
Christianity, 222, 224, 226–227,
    734–735. *See also* Democ-
    racy and democratization—
    cultural determinants;
    Religion and religious issues
Churchill, Winston, 385
Citizens. *See also* Exit, Voice, and
    Loyalty game; Votes, voters,
    and voting
    accountability and, 689–690, 744
    clarity of responsibility and,
        690, 744

in East Germany, 262
electoral rights of, 471–472
ethnic and minority issues and,
    731–732
exit options of, 197, 202
majoritarian and consensus
    views of democracy and, 680
policy making and, 677–678
political parties and, 535–536,
    538–540, 542
right and left political divide of,
    710–711
states and, 74–79, 193, 195
Civic Culture, The (Almond and
    Verba), 212, 215
Civil Constitution of the Clergy
    (1790; France), 556
Civilizations, 230–231. *See also*
    Cultural issues
Civil libertarianism, 119
Civil society, 113–119, 170–171,
    225, 289
Civil War of 1642 (England), 555
Civil wars, 724, 728, 729, 730*f*,
    731
Clark, William Roberts, 589, 596
*Clash of Civilizations and the
    Remaking of World Order,
    The* (Huntington), 221
Cleavages. *See also* Cultural issues;
    Social issues
    attributes and, 567
    class cleavage, 558–561
    confessional (religious)
        cleavage, 554–556
    cross-cutting cleavages, 573,
        574, 583
    electoral institutions and,
        583–585
    ethnic and linguistic cleavages,
        563–565, 592–593
    politicized cleavages, 565–572,
        588*b*, 590, 733
    post-materialist cleavage,
        561–563
    reinforcing cleavages, 573, 574
    secular-clerical cleavage,
        556–558, 561
    urban-rural cleavage, 554, 559,
        561
Coalitions. *See* Government;
    Political issues
Coding. *See* Methods—specific

Cohabitation. *See* Mixed
    democracies
Cold war, 5, 6
Collective action and collective
    action problem (free rider),
    267–271
Collier, David, 731
Colombia, 105, 315, 496, 565, 627,
    628, 756
Communism
    collapse of, 260–261, 275–276,
        639
    stability of, 258
    winning coalitions and, 335
Communist Party, 335, 535
Communist Party—specific
    countries
    China, 535
    Cuba, 535
    Czechoslovakia, 280*b*
    Poland, 279, 288, 289, 290, 291,
        523–524, 542, 544
    Soviet Union, 537–538, 542
Comoros, 485, 525
Compact or Constitution of
    Medina (622 A.D.), 229
Comparative Parliamentary
    Democracy Project (CPDP),
    404–405
Comparative political science, 19,
    27–28, 604
Comparative politics, 1, 2, 3–6.
    See also Politics
Concordat of 1801 (France), 556
Conditions, 19–21
Condorcet, Marie Jean Antoine
    Nicolas de Caritat, Marquis
    de, 359, 361
Condorcet's Paradox. *See*
    Paradoxes
Confucianism, 221, 223, 224,
    225–226, 227, 228. *See also*
    Democracy and democrati-
    zation—cultural determi-
    nants; Religion and religious
    issues
Congo Free State, 344, 345
Consequents. *See* Arguments
Constitutional courts, 635
Constitutions and constitutional-
    ism. *See also* Legal issues
    amendments to, 636
    bill of rights and, 637, 638, 639

Constitutions and
    constitutionalism—
      continued
cabinet formation and, 445
caretaker governments and, 410
checks and balances, 12, 226,
    453, 604, 631, 632, 667–673
constitutional challenges, 644
constitutional courts and jus-
    tice, 635, 637, 639, 644,
    646–648
constitutional judges, 645
constitutional review, 637,
    642–643, 644, 646, 649
criteria for federal states in, 605
deadlock situations and, 747,
    760–761
decision making and, 384–385
definitions and concepts of,
    604, 634–635, 636, 637, 638
design of, 11, 676, 677, 683–684,
    699, 723, 734, 735, 738, 741,
    761
in dictatorships, 278–279
differences between, 11
economic issues of, 723,
    761–762
federalism and, 612–613
human rights and, 635
judicial independence and, 12
judicial power and, 635
judicial review and, 646
legislative supremacy and,
    634–635
majoritarian and consensual
    constitutions, 681
new constitutionalism, 634–639
in parliamentary democracies,
    405*b*, 407
policy making and, 613, 681
political issues of, 534
presidential constitutions, 401*f*,
    743, 755, 760, 762
power and, 683–684
surplus majority governments
    and, 427
systems of constitutional jus-
    tice, 634, 642–648, 667–673
types of, 635–639, 683
veto players and, 12, 648–649
Constitutions and constitutional-
    ism—specific

Australia, 636
Austria, 638
Baltic states, 639
Belgium, 427–428, 568
Brazil, 608–609
Bulgaria, 470
Chile, 276, 279, 457–458, 470
Czech Republic, 639
France, 450, 451, 637, 745
Germany, West, 638, 639
Greece, 407
Hungary, 639
India, 610, 611*b*
Iraq, 638
Ireland, 410, 457
Israel, 635
Italy, 638, 639
Japan, 12, 458, 636
Laos, 638
Netherlands, 470
New Zealand, 635, 637
North Korea, 638
Poland, 639
Portugal, 639
Qatar, 465
Romania, 639
Russia, 639
Saudi Arabia, 638
Slovakia, 639
Spain, 639
Sri Lanka, 489
Switzerland, 636
United Arab Emirates, 607
United Kingdom, 635, 636, 637
United States, 12, 196, 319–320,
    612, 632, 634, 649
Vietnam, 638
Weimar (Germany), 456–457
Yugoslavia, 639
Constructivism and construc-
    tivists, 564, 565
Contracts, 185
Cook, Robin, 403
Costa Rica, 448, 487, 756
"Counterterrorism: A Game-
    Theoretic Analysis" (Arce
    and Sandler), 136
Countries. *See* States; individual
    countries
Courts. *See* Legal issues
Credible commitment, 184,
    185–188

Croatia, 449
Cuba, 97, 544
Cultural issues. *See also* Cleavages;
    Democracy and democratiz-
    ation—cultural determi-
    nants; Social issues
attitudes toward the poor,
    710–712
causal arguments, 210–211,
    214–215
civic culture, 212–221, 249
classical cultural arguments,
    208–211
constructivist arguments for, 208
cultural clashes, 224, 227–228
cultural entrepreneurs, 227–228
cultural and ethnic diversity,
    232, 233, 236, 239, 246–247
democratic culture, 233
elements of civic culture, 212,
    214–215, 218, 221
fiscal policy, 703–713
political behavior, 208, 212
politicization of cultural differ-
    ences, 570–571
primordial arguments for, 208
types of political culture, 212
Ultimatum and Dictator games,
    239–243, 248–249
Culture Shift (Inglehart), 215
Cyclical majorities. *See* Decision
    making
Cyprus, 257
Czechoslovakia, 258, 266, 275,
    280, 525
Czech Republic, 409, 437,
    471–472, 694

D

Dahl, Robert, 152–153, 155–156,
    157, 159, 162, 163, 469*b*, 679
Darfur, 726–728
Data, 165–166, 244
Decision making. *See also*
    Electoral systems; Votes,
    voters, and voting
agenda setters and, 366–368,
    379, 380, 384, 385
Arrow's Theorem, 355, 380–385
bargaining, 363
Borda Count, 363–366,
    379–380, 382

Chaos Theorem, 379, 392
Condorcet's Paradox, 355, 357–363, 374–375
cyclical majorities, 360–361, 374–375, 378, 379, 380, 392
decision-making rules, 357–366, 374
democracy and, 355, 356, 379, 380, 385, 386
design of decision-making institutions, 383–384
fairness of, 380–384, 385, 386
instability and, 379, 380, 386, 392–394
institutional trilemma, 383–384, 386
irrelevant alternatives, 365–366, 382, 383–384
majority rule, 355, 357–363, 366–379, 380, 382, 384
Median Voter Theorem, 355, 370–379, 380
non-dictatorship condition, 381
preference ordering, 359, 360, 361–363, 364, 365, 366–367, 368–369, 370–371, 374, 380, 384
problems with group decision making, 357, 361, 362
Reversal Paradox, 363–366
round-robin tournaments, 358–371, 379, 380
sincere and strategic voting and, 366, 367
single- and multi-issue dimensionality, 374, 380
single-elimination tournaments, 380
trade-offs in, 357
transitivity and intransitivity, 359, 360, 361–363, 365, 368, 382, 383, 384–385
unanimity, 382, 383–384
universal admissibility condition, 381
Decolonization, 5, 170, 195, 256
Definitions and concepts—A–B
accountability, 689
alternative vote system, 477
antecedent, 33
anti-clericalism, 556
apparentement, 501

arguments, valid and invalid, 33–35
Arrow's Theorem, 383
assets, fixed and liquid, 194
attributes, 565, 567
backward induction, 65
ballot structure, 464
best reply, 109
bicameralism, 620, 622, 627
block vote system, 492
Borda Count, 363, 478
bottom-up process, 255, 257
branches, 59, 62
burying vote, 479
Definitions and concepts—C
cabinets, 402
capital flight, 322
cardinal payoffs, 115
caretaker governments, 410
categorical syllogism, 33
cause, 22, 28–29
Chaos Theorem, 379
choice nodes, 59, 62
civic culture, 212, 249
civil rights, 114
civil society, 114–115
civil war, 724
clarity of responsibility, 690
coalitions, 416, 417
coefficients, 198
cohabitation, 450
collective action, 266–267
collective action problem, 267
collective cabinet responsibility, 403
common pool resource problem, 719
comparative method, 19
comparative politics, 1, 17, 19, 92
complete information game, 287
complete preference ordering, 359
compromising vote, 479
conceptualization, 160
conclusion, 33
conditional statement, 33
Condorcet's Paradox, 359
Condorcet winner, 360
confessionalism, 735
congruence, 695, 697–698

connected coalitions, 417
consensus view of democracy, 677, 680, 734
consequent, 33
consequentialist ethics, 356
consociationalism, 734
constitutionalism, 634, 638
constitutional justice, 634
constitutional review, 637, 642
constitutions, 635, 636, 637
constructive vote of no confidence, 397
constructivist arguments, 208
contestation, 152
continuous measure, 156
contractarian view of the state, 91, 92, 105
corporatist interest group relations, 423
credible commitment problem, 184
critical probability, 309
critical tests, 45
cultural modernization theory, 210
cumulation, 506
Definitions and concepts—D
data, experimental and observational, 244
data-generating process, 244
decentralization, 612
decrees, presidential, 446
delegation problems, 411
democracy, 12, 154, 357, 400, 677
demokratia, 149
deontological ethics, 356
deterrence, 136
devolution, 609
dichotomous measure, 156
dictators and dictatorships, 151b
discount rate, 142
disenfranchised, 332
district magnitude, 464, 499
divisor or highest average systems, 498
dominant strategy, 112, 125
Duverger's theory, 583
Definitions and concepts—E–G
electoral formula, 464
electoral systems, 464

Definitions and concepts—
    E–G—*continued*
electoral thresholds, 501
electoral tiers, 500
ethnic groups, 563
ethnic outbidding, 732
ethnic party, 564
ethnic violence, 724
exit, voice, loyalty, 57
expected payoff, 309
experiments, field, Internet, lab-
    oratory and natural, 244–245
explanations, ex post or ad hoc,
    231
face validity, 218
failed states, 91
falsificationism, 40
federalism, 605, 611, 612, 613,
    616, 617
fiscal centralization, 721
fiscal policy, 700
foreign aid, 195
formateur, 407
free-rider problem, 267
games, 58, 59
game theory, 58
game tree, 59, 62
Gamson's Law, 415
GDP per capita, 172, 173*b*
glasnost (openness), 260
government identifiability, 693
governments, 420, 426, 444, 449
group transitivity, 677
Definitions and concepts—H–L
homo economicus, 240
ideal point, 369
identity category, 565
immobilism, 745
inclusion, 152
incomplete information game,
    307
independency from irrelevant
    alternatives condition, 382
indifference curve, 375–376
individualism, 381
informateur, 409
information set, 307
interaction effects, 29
interest group relations, 423
interest groups, 534
international politics, 1
interval measures, 164
investiture vote, 405

irredentism, 724
judicial review, 637
Keynesianism, 700
laïcité, 556, 557
legislative coalition, 444
legislative responsibility, 397
legislatures, 620
list proportional representation
    systems, 495
Definitions and concepts—M–N
majoritarian view of democ-
    racy, 677, 680
majoritarian electoral systems,
    473
malapportionment, 626
mandates, 693
manufactured majorities, 694
measures or indicators, 151
mechanical effect of electoral
    laws, 575
median voter, 370
Median Voter Theorem, 370
Michels' iron law of oligarchy,
    561
Mill's methods of agreement
    and difference, 25
minimal and least minimal
    winning coalition, 416
minimalist view of democracy,
    152
ministerial responsibility, 403
minister's portfolio, 402–403
minority government, 420
mixed democracy, 400, 449
mixed electoral systems, 511,
    513
modified Borda Count, 479
Nash equilibria, 59, 65,
    108–109, 111, 112
nations and nation states,
    92–93
natural resources, 194
natural rights, 114
necessary and sufficient condi-
    tions, 21
necessary conditions, 19, 21
nominal measures, 163, 164
non-dictatorship condition, 381
non-excludability, 267
non-rivalry, 267
Definitions and concepts—O–P
ordinal measures, 164
ordinal payoffs, 82, 108

overhang seats, 514
panachage, 506
pareto optimality condition,
    382
parliamentary democracy, 400
partisan model of macroeco-
    nomic policy, 708–709
party block vote system, 492
party identification, 535–536
party lists, 502
party systems, 543
payoff matrix, 107
payoffs, 59, 82
perestroika (restructuring), 260
personal votes, 506, 721
pluralist interest group
    relations, 423
policy of liberalization, 277
political economy approach,
    701
political parties, 533, 534
political science, 1, 6, 19, 55, 56
politicians, 414
politics, 55, 56, 92
polyarchy, 153
portfolio coalition, 444
power, 55, 56
predatory view of the state, 91,
    92, 119, 148, 182, 183, 184
preelectoral coalitions, 428, 429
preemption, 136
preference falsification, 272
preference ordering, 108, 359,
    368, 369
preference or preferential
    voting, 477
premise, 33
present value, 142
presidential democracy, 400,
    444
presidents, 444
prime ministers, 402
primordialist arguments, 208
principal-agent problems, 411
procedural view of democracy,
    152
prospective voting, 693
public goods, 267
purchasing power parity (PPP),
    173
Definitions and concepts—Q–S
quasi-rents, 193
quotas, 495

rational decision makers, 59, 359
rebellion, 724
reliability, 164
rentier states, 194
replicability, 165
representation, 695, 697–698
research, experimental and non-experimental, 244
resource course, 194
responsiveness, 695
retrospective voting, 689
reversion point, 444
revolutionary bandwagon, 276
revolutionary cascade, 274
revolutionary threshold, 272
round-robin tournament, 358
science, 17, 18, 42
scientific method, 42
scientific statements, 41
selectorate, 313, 332, 333
Selectorate Theory, 332
sincere vote, 366
single-member district plurality systems, 474
single nontransferable vote system, 490
single-party majority government, 404
single-peaked preference ordering, 369
single transferable vote system, 507
social contracts, 114
sovereign debt, 184
standard error, 198
state of nature, 105
states, 91, 92–95, 604–605
strategic effect of electoral laws, 579
strategic entry, 580
strategic or sophisticated vote, 367
strategic situation, 58
strategies, 59, 112
structural dependence of the state on capital, 323
subgame, 65
subgame perfect Nash Equilibrium, 65
substantive view of democracy, 152
sufficient conditions, 20, 21
suffrage, 468

supplementary vote, 488
surplus majority government, 426
syllogism, 33
Definitions and concepts—T–W
tautology, 42
technological possibility frontier, 320
terminal nodes, 62
theory, 32, 43
third wave of democratization, 256
time inconsistency problem, 184
top-down process, 255, 257
two-round electoral systems, 484
unanimity, 382
unanimity core, 664
uniformity of nature, 43
universal admissibility, 381, 677
universalism, 719
universal suffrage, 468
utility function, 368–369
validity, 162, 218
variables, 198
veto players, 648
vote of confidence, 398
vote of no confidence, 397
waves of democracy, 257b–258b
welfare economics, 701
whips (party), 540–541
winning coalitions, 332
winsets, 376, 650, 664
de Gaulle, Charles, 538–539, 745, 752
Democracy and democratization.
    See also Decision making;
    Constitutions and constitutionalism; Democratic transitions; Electoral systems;
    Federalism; Mixed democracy; Parliaments and parliamentary democracies;
    Presidencies and presidential democracies; Votes,
    voters, and voting
accountability and clarity of responsibility in, 689–693
Bush, George W. and, 2, 6, 7, 8–10
cabinets in, 448
causes and determinants of, 8–9, 21–27, 313–314

classification of, 151–153, 154, 395–400, 453–454, 469b, 520, 534, 549, 597, 648–649
class issues and, 19
comparison with dictatorships, 10, 311–312
contestation and inclusion and, 152–153, 154, 469b
corruption, 339
democratic cascade, 275
democratic over- and under-achievers, 750–751
effects of, 9–10, 223, 723
elections and electoral systems in, 154, 335, 434, 464, 467–472, 520, 521, 522–525, 526, 677–678
ethnic minorities and, 731, 734
federalism and, 738–742
free rider problem and, 271, 291–292
government performance in, 328–331, 342–344
historical perspective of, 147–151
interstate comparisons of, 11
institutional differences of, 12, 681–688
judicial systems of, 12
loyalty norms in, 339, 341
measures of, 154–166
modernization and, 750–751
number and percentage of democratic countries, 256, 401, 402t
perceptions of, 217
political participation, 157–158
political parties and party systems and, 534, 535, 537, 539–540, 543, 547, 551–552
power in, 154–155, 695, 696
as a public good, 267
representation and responsiveness in, 319, 695–699
rule of law and, 314–317
selectorate in, 333–334
special interests and, 327
stability of, 213, 214, 216, 734, 742–743
survival of, 200–202, 236–239, 742–760, 761–762
Transition Game and, 281–291
transitive preference ordering, 359

Democracy and democratization—
continued
treatment of women and,
231–232
U.S. role in growth of, 10–11
veto players and, 762
waves of, 256, 257
Democracy and democratization—
cultural determinants. *See
also* Cultural issues
causal arguments for, 210–211,
214–215, 221–222, 232,
249–250
civic culture, 212–221, 249–250
cultural modernization theory,
207, 210, 214
democratic performance and
stability, 213, 214
political culture, 212, 214
religion, 207, 221–239, 250
test for compatibility between
religion and democracy,
232–239
Democracy and democratization—
economic determinants. *See
also* Economic issues
assets and asset holders, 194,
199, 313–314, 324
causal arguments for, 210–211,
313–317, 323, 328
classic modernization theory
and, 169–181, 182, 198–199,
239
consumption versus investment
and, 325–327
cultural factors and, 210, 214
distribution of private and
public goods, 342
economic distribution and
redistribution and, 324, 330
economic growth and performance, 197–199, 200, 201–202,
236, 239, 313–328
Exit, Voice, and Loyalty game
and, 184, 188–192, 194–195,
197
foreign aid, 195
GDP per capita and, 200
government performance and,
328–331, 349–350, 356
human capital, 194–195
inequality, 196–197

material well-being, 328–331,
349–350, 356
natural resources, 194
oil, 194, 200
political participation, 320
property rights, 314, 319, 325
rule of law and, 314–317, 325
taxes and, 319–320
variant of modernization theory
and, 182–201
Democracy and democratization—
types of
consensus democracies,
679–680, 681–688, 689–691,
692, 693, 695–699, 734
externally-imposed democracy,
259
majoritarian democracies,
677–678, 680, 681–688,
691–692, 693, 694, 695–699
nonpartisan democracy, 543
unitary democracy, 12
Democracy and democratization—
views of
classification and views of,
151–153, 154
continuous views of, 161–162
dichotomous views of, 161–162
minimalist views of, 152,
160–161, 217
substantive views of, 152,
160–161, 217
Democratic Party, 75
Democratic Republic of the
Congo, 148
Democratic People's Republic of
North Korea, 148
Democratic transitions. *See also*
Revolutions
bottom-up processes of, 255,
257, 258–276, 291
top-down processes of, 255,
257, 276–291, 292
problems and games for,
293–310
taxes and redistribution and,
319, 322, 323
Transition Game, 281–291
Demokratia, 149
Denmark, 505, 634
Derry, Gregory, 418
Deterrence, 136

Development and developing
countries, 170–181,
182–183, 210, 326. *See also*
Economic issues
Devolution, 609*b*–611*b*
Dictatorships. *See also*
Authoritarian regimes
accountability in, 691
bottom-up democratic transitions in, 255, 257, 258–276
clarity of responsibility in, 691
classifications of, 151–152, 154,
520
collective action theory and, 271
corruption in, 340, 343
decision-making processes in,
356, 382
distribution of private and
public goods, 342
economic factors of, 194,
197–199, 199–200, 319, 320,
326, 327, 330
elections and electoral systems
in, 278, 290, 463, 520, 526
externally-imposed democracy
and, 259
federal dictatorships, 606
foreign aid to, 195
free-rider problem in, 267, 292
government performance in,
343, 344, 349–350
institutional dictatorships, 288
liberalization and broadened
dictatorships, 277–291, 292
loyalty norms of, 340–341
material well-being in, 328,
330–331, 356
military coups and, 319
modernization theory and, 169,
170–171, 174, 175–181,
182–201
natural resources and, 169, 182,
194, 195, 199, 343
number of, 256
political dissidents and,
272–273
political parties in, 535, 537,
542, 543, 544
preference falsification in, 216,
255, 272, 275, 287, 291, 292,
523
representation in, 319

rule of law in, 315–317
selectorate in, 333
special interests and, 327
stability of, 9
top-down democratic transitions in, 255, 257, 276–291, 292
Transition Game and, 281–291, 292
winning coalitions in, 335, 340
Diermeier, Daniel, 437
Disaggregation. *See* Aggregation and disaggregation
Discourse on the Origin and Foundations of Inequality among Men (Rousseau), 130
Discourses (Machiavelli), 151*b*
Districts, 464, 499–500, 511. *See also* Elections and electoral systems—specific
Djibouti, 492
Dominican Republic, 498, 500, 615
Downs, Anthony, 371*b*
Downs, George W., 259
Dreyfus Affair (France), 557
Dreyfus, Alfred, 557
Druckman, Jamie, 415*b*
Dubai. *See* United Arab Emirates
Dubček, Alexander, 280*b*
Dummet, M., 478
Duverger, Maurice, 572–575, 585, 588. *See also* Hypotheses—specific; Theories—specific

E

Easterly, William, 730–731
Economic issues. *See also* Democracy and democratization—economic determinants; Taxes and taxation
assets, 193–195, 199, 202, 322
capital flight, 322, 324
capitalists and capitalism, 5–6, 77, 221, 222, 321–324, 559, 560
class conflict, 559
classical school of economics, 700
classic modernization theory, 170–181
common pool resource problem, 719, 721
consumption, 325–327

culture, 210, 214
in dictatorships, 174–175, 177
distribution and redistribution, 319–325
in Eastern Europe, 275
economic development, 183–184, 188–192, 326
economic growth and performance, 197–198, 200, 348–349
economic sectors, 182–183
elections, 441, 442*b*
electoral laws, 713–723
equality and inequality, 196–197, 322, 323–324, 707, 708, 718
ethnic heterogeneity, 729–731
exchange rates, 173*b*
"exit option," 183
federalism, 616, 618, 619
fiscal and macroeconomic policies, 700–723
foreign aid, 195
GDP per capita, 172, 173*b*, 177, 181, 198–199, 200
globalization, 195
government formation, 437
government spending and debt, 721–722
human capital, 194–195
income and luck, 712
investment, 315, 323, 324, 325–327
Keynesianism, 700–702
market economies, 318
material and natural well-being, 328–331, 346–349
partisan model of macroeconomic policy, 708–711
productivity, 318–319, 320–321, 323–325
property rights, 313–325
purchasing power parity (PPP), 173
quasi-rents, 193–194, 199, 202
redistribution, 188*b*, 196–197, 318–325, 330, 701, 707, 713, 715, 718, 720, 723
resource curse, 194
revenue sharing, 614
right and left political divide, 562, 708–709, 713–718
rule of law, 314–315, 325

selectorate, 346–349
socialists and socialism, 560
socioeconomic factors, 182, 210
survival story, 173–181
technological possibility frontier, 320–321
variant of modernization theory, 182–201
winning coalitions, 346–349
workers, 559, 560
Economic Theory of Democracy, An (Downs), 371*b*
Economist magazine, 173*b*
Ecuador, 551, 565
EDSA Revolution (1986), 266
Egypt, 277–278, 544, 607
Eighty Years' War (Dutch Revolt), 555
Eickelman, Dale F., 227
Einstein, Albert, 50, 60
Electoral laws. *See* Electoral systems
Electoral systems. *See also* Democracy and democratization; Elections; Votes, voters, and voting
accountability and, 689
ballot nullification, 467
choice of, 520–526
classification and categorization of, 463, 464, 472, 526
costs of, 488, 490
in democracies, 154, 464, 467–472, 520, 526, 678–679, 693
in dictatorships, 278, 290, 463, 464–465, 466–467, 520, 526
district magnitude and, 464, 499–500, 718–720
dual ballot instructions, 429–430
economic factors of, 713–723, 718–723
electoral formulas, 469, 472–473, 495–500, 526
electoral institutions, 5, 522, 565, 568–570, 572*f*, 574–575, 583, 584*f*, 597, 675, 676, 713, 734
electoral laws, 11, 575–583, 588, 593, 594–595, 713–723, 732, 733–738, 741, 742
electoral thresholds, 501–502

Electoral systems—*continued*
electoral tiers, 429–430, 500, 511
endogenous election timing, 440, 441–442
Freedom House study of, 520, 521
geographic distribution of, 517, 510–520
independently elected presidents, 398–399
indirect elections, 625
judicial power and, 641
legislative authority and, 636
mandates and, 693
multimember districts, 490–492, 595–596
nomination agreements, 429
overviews of, 464–473, 517–527, 678
preelectoral coalitions, 428–434
primaries, 537
proportionality of, 472–473, 499, 510, 511, 513–514, 515, 574, 575, 579–580, 581, 583–585, 588, 590–591
quotas, 495
right and left political divide and, 713–718
rules and rights of, 434, 468–472, 501, 574, 721
single-member districts, 474–490, 595–596
summary statistics of, 468, 469*t*, 517
types of, 11, 463, 472
universal suffrage and, 156
voting and, 476
Electoral systems—specific
alternative vote (AV) systems, 474, 477–484, 488, 736–737, 738, 742
block vote (BV) systems, 474, 492
Borda Count (BC) systems, 474, 478–479
disproportional representation systems, 406
divisor or highest average systems, 498–499

list proportional representation (list PR) systems, 493, 495, 501–502, 517, 520, 721
majoritarian systems, 472, 473–492, 493–494, 511, 520, 522, 681–682, 683, 714, 735, 736, 738
mixed electoral systems, 511–517, 735
party block vote (PBV) systems, 474, 492
party list systems, 502–507
proportional representation (PR) systems, 405, 472, 493–511, 522, 576–577, 580, 583–584, 585, 682, 683, 708, 713–723, 735–736, 737–738, 745
single-member district plurality (SMDP) systems, 474–476, 484, 487, 490, 491, 517, 520, 575, 577, 578, 580, 581, 585, 588, 593, 708, 714–720, 722
single nontransferable vote (SNTV) systems, 474, 490–491, 511, 545
single transferable vote (STV) systems, 493, 507–511, 524
supplementary vote (SV) system, 488–489
two-round systems (TRS), 474, 484–490
England. *See also* United Kingdom
democratization in, 314
economic issues in, 183–184, 186
elections in, 332–333, 492
Exit, Voice, and Loyalty game for, 188–192, 193
first bicameral legislature in, 631
life expectancy in, 113
political parties in, 547, 552–554
religious conflict in, 555
voting in, 559
Environment, 56–58. *See also* Exit, Voice, and Loyalty game
Epstein, David, 83
Eritrea, 97, 102, 465, 544

Ethics and morality issues
consequentialist ethics, 356
decision-making procedures, 374, 380
deontological ethics, 356
lawmaking, 679
majority rule, 380
Ethnic and minority issues
civil war, 729, 730*f*, 731
constitutional design and, 734
definition of ethnic group, 563–564
definition of nation and, 92
democracy and, 233, 236–239, 731
economic factors, 729–731
effective number of ethnic groups, 549*t*, 593
electoral laws, 731, 732, 733–738
electoral systems, 476, 484, 491, 492, 494, 731, 735–737
ethnic conflict, 723–742, 737–742
ethnic group hypothesis, 233
ethnic head counts, 733
ethnic identities and identifiability, 246–247, 564, 732, 734
ethnic and linguistic cleavages, 563–565, 592–593
ethnic outbidding, 732–733
ethnic polarization, 731
federalism, 612, 617, 738–742
government stability, 730, 731, 732, 734
interethnic civic engagement, 731–732
political parties, 75, 503, 593–597, 733, 734
Ethiopia, 95–97, 100–101
Europe. *See also* individual countries
attitudes toward the poor in, 710–711
cleavages in, 556, 557–558, 559, 561, 562–563, 574
constitutional justice in, 646–648
democracy in, 230–231, 257, 314
early rulers in, 120, 121
economic issues of, 703
election systems in, 502

fascism in, 639
freezing hypothesis of, 561–562
left-right political divide in, 562–563
maturation in, 183, 201
parliamentary democracies in, 405
party systems in, 561
political divide in, 559
political geography of, 121
political parties in, 558, 561–563
religious conflicts in, 554–555
Europe, Eastern. *See also* individual countries
collapse of Communism in, 258, 260–261, 266, 275–276, 290, 524
constitutional courts in, 639
democratization in, 257, 449
electoral systems in, 501, 515, 522, 525
free-rider problem in, 267
Gorbachev, Mikhail and, 260
government types in, 427
political culture in, 212
preference falsification in, 272, 275, 276
Europe, Western. *See also* individual countries
electoral systems in, 520
end of governments in, 440
government duration in, 438
government formation in, 434–436
government types in, 419, 420*t*, 421, 424, 425*t*, 427
political parties in, 563
EVL. *See* Exit, Voice, and Loyalty game
Exclusion Bill and Crisis (1681; England), 552
Exit, Voice, and Loyalty game (EVL). *See also* Definitions and concepts; Games; Game theory
credible exit threats, 66–77, 189–192, 197, 324
diagrams of, 62, 65, 67, 68, 69, 71, 72, 73, 189, 190, 191
economic development and, 184, 188–192, 194, 195, 197

evaluation and conclusions of, 74–79
fundamentals of, 55, 57–58
illustration of, 62–65
solving of, 65–74, 189–192
subgame perfect Nash equilibrium in, 65, 68–70, 74
Exit, Voice, and Loyalty: Responses to Decline in Firms, Organizations, and States (Hirschman), 56

F

Failed States Index, 103
Falsificationism. *See* Scientific issues
Farrell, David M., 510–511
Fascism, 639
Fearon, James, 724–725, 728–729
Federalism. *See also* Democracy and democratization; States—federal
advantages of, 617–619, 738
asymmetric federalism, 612, 738, 742
choice of, 616–620
clarity of responsibility and, 690–691
congruent federalism, 611, 612
criticisms of, 619–620, 690–691
decentralization and, 612–615, 620, 739, 740
definitions and concepts of, 12, 603, 604, 605, 611, 612, 616, 617
de facto federalism, 604–605
de jure federalism, 604–605
devolution versus federalism, 609*b*–611*b*
economic effects of, 616, 618, 619, 620
electoral laws and, 738–742
ethnic conflict and, 738–742
incongruent federalism, 611–612, 738, 742
policy making and, 613, 618
stabilizing effects of, 738
symmetric federalism, 612
Federalist Papers, 413*b*, 640
Feynman, Richard, 44
Figueiredo, João, 276

Fiji, 481–483, 484, 565, 737
Finland, 427, 506, 564–565, 685, 687
Fiorina, Morris, 540
Fish, M. Steven, 230
Fogel, Robert, 112, 325
Foreign aid, 182, 195
Formateurs. *See* Political issues
France. *See also* French Revolution; individual presidents and prime ministers
cohabitation in, 450–452
constitution of, 450, 451, 637, 745
constitutional challenges in, 644
Constitutional Council in, 645, 649
constitutional review in, 647
democracy in, 399
economic factors in, 190, 314
elections of 2002, 433–434, 485, 486*t*, 487, 582
elections of 2007, 486
electoral system in, 153, 334, 471, 485–486, 525, 745
government in, 427, 430–431
immobilism and instability in, 745
legislature in, 625, 633, 745
as a mixed democracy, 450–452, 455
political divide in, 559
political parties and party system in, 421, 429, 538–539, 547, 745
preelection coalitions in, 694
presidents in, 451
prime ministers in, 451
secular–clerical cleavage in, 556–557
Franco, Francisco, 224, 257, 296
Franzese, Robert J., 708, 720
Freedom House, 520, 521
Freedom House measure, 158–160, 161, 162, 163, 164, 165, 166, 230, 231
Free-rider problem. *See* Collective action and collective action problem
French Revolution (1789), 150–151, 556

Friedman, Edward, 226
Friedrich, C., 542
Frota, Sylvio, 276
Fukuyama, Francis, 223, 228
Fujimori, Alberto, 537
Fund for Peace, 103

G

Gallagher, Michael, 510
Games *See also* Game theory;
    Nash equilibria
  backward induction in, 65,
    66–71, 80–83
  branches of, 59, 62
  choice nodes of, 59, 62, 66–74
  complete and incomplete infor-
    mation games, 287, 296–298,
    307–310
  cooperative and non-cooperative
    games, 60–61
  costs of, 63
  definition of, 58
  dependency in, 67, 70, 76
  diagrams of, 62, 65, 67, 68, 69,
    71, 72, 73, 84, 85, 86, 87, 89,
    282, 284, 298, 299, 302, 304,
    308
  exit payoffs in, 63
  extensive form games, 59, 80–90
  game trees, 59, 62, 64, 65f, 66,
    70, 71–72 73–74, 80–83, 107
  illustration of, 62–64
  mixed motive games, 582
  Nash equilibria for, 65, 68–70,
    72, 74, 80–83, 111–112, 115,
    116, 124, 126–127
  normal or strategic form games,
    59, 65, 107, 109, 123–125, 128
  outcomes and solving of, 62–74,
    80–83, 107–112, 115–118, 124
  payoff matrix in, 107, 124
  payoffs in, 59, 63–74, 78, 80–83
  players in, 59, 63, 66
  prehistory of, 62, 64, 77
  rules of, 59
  strategies of, 59, 69, 112, 116,
    124–125, 140–141, 143
  subgames, 65
  terminal nodes of, 62, 66,
    69–70, 71, 73
  writing of, 80–83, 296–297

Games—specific. *See also* Exit,
    Voice, and Loyalty game
  American Football Game, 134
  Asymmetric Coordination
    Game (Battle of the Sexes),
    132
  Civil Society Game, 114–118, 141
  Coordination and Democracy
    Game, 252–254
  counterterrorism games,
    136–139
  Democratic Consolidation
    Game, 293–296
  Dictator Game, 239–243,
    248–249
  Dictatorship Party Game,
    301–303
  Entry Deterrence Game, 81–83
  Free Trade Game, 139–141
  Game of Chicken, 128–129
  Legislative Pay Raise Game,
    88–90
  Mafia Game, 135
  Nuclear Arms Race Game,
    127–128
  Prisoner's Dilemma Game,
    108n18, 125–128
  Pure Coordination Game, 131
  Religious Party Game, 303–306
  Rock, Paper, Scissors Game, 133
  Senate Race Game, 84–85, 86f
  Stag Hunt Game, 130
  State of Nature Game, 107–112,
    113, 117, 127, 141, 143, 145
  Strategic Entry Game, 581–582
  Terrorism Game, 86–88,
    297–301
  Transition Game, 277, 281–291,
    292, 296, 307–310
  Ultimatum Game, 239–243,
    248–249
Game theory. *See also* Exit, Voice,
    and Loyalty game; Games
  benefits of, 70
  definition of, 58
  game-theoretic model of top-
    down transitions, 277–291
  origins of, 60–61
  state of nature and, 106
  use of, 58, 61, 70, 78, 80–83,
    106–107, 281

Gandhi, Jennifer, 467, 542
Geddes, Barbara, 278
Gedi, Mohamed, 100
Geertz, Clifford, 208
Geisel, Ernesto, 276
George, Andrew, 577
George I (King of England), 553
George III (King of England), 623
German Democratic Republic
    (East Germany), 76, 258,
    260–266, 271, 272, 275
Germany
  Constitutional Court in, 645
  democratic institutions of, 685,
    687
  division of, 263, 265b
  electoral rules in, 471, 472b, 501
  electoral systems in, 513, 515, 522
  federalism in, 615
  government in, 427
  government duration in, 443
  legislature in, 625, 626, 627, 633
  political parties in, 580–581
  post–World War II, 2, 10, 398,
    427
  preelection coalitions in,
    429–430, 431, 434, 694
  pre–World War II, 154, 397–398
  reunification of, 258, 265
Germany, East. *See* German
    Democratic Republic
Germany, Federal Republic of
    (West Germany), 11, 12,
    265b, 404, 406–407,
    413–418
Germany, West. *See* Germany,
    Federal Republic of
Gershenkron, Alexander, 170
Gershenson, Dmitriy, 278, 542
Ghana, 466
Gierek, Edward, 289
Gilligan, Michael, 589
Glaeser, Edward, 711, 712
Glorious Revolution (England,
    1688), 184, 192
Golder, Matt, 589, 596, 698
Golder, Sona N., 426, 428–429,
    431–432, 433, 437
Gonzales, Alberto, 454
Good Friday Agreement (1998;
    Northern Ireland), 609

Gorbachev, Mikhail, 260, 262, 275, 280*b*
Gore, Al, 582
Government. *See also* Cabinets; Democracies and democratization; Dictatorships; Federalism; Legislatures and legislators; Parliaments and parliamentary democracies; Presidencies and presidential democracies; States
accountability and clarity of responsibility of, 617–618, 620, 690
classification of regimes, 149–150
coalitions and, 406–407, 410, 411–413, 416, 418, 428–434, 445, 447, 494, 569, 654–655, 688, 690, 694, 722
collapse, fall or end of, 396, 397, 410, 413, 439–440, 691
confessionalism, 735
consociationalism, 734, 735
in corporatist countries, 423
corruption of, 150
decision making in, 384–385
delegation or principal-agent problems in, 411–413
duration of, 438–443, 691
economic factors of, 700–723
effect of democracy on government performance, 328–331, 342–344
electoral systems and, 494, 721
formation of, 395–396, 404–418, 423, 427, 428, 432, 434–438, 444, 539–540, 683, 688, 693
government identifiability, 693–694, 695
ideological spread of, 433, 437
instability of, 746
legislatures in, 278, 396, 397–398, 418, 444, 454
mandates of, 693, 694–695
office- and policy-seeking and, 414–418, 432
political parties and, 422, 539–540, 587, 722
reforms in, 619

responsibility to presidents, 399–400
support and toleration of, 423
taxes and spending by, 317–318
veto players and, 695
votes of confidence and no confidence, 397–398, 404, 407
Government—types of, 395–396, 418–428, 442
caretaker governments, 410, 413, 436–437, 444
crisis governments, 427
divided government, 450, 654
effect of regime type on economic growth, 313–328
minority governments, 420–426, 690
mixed and simple government, 630–631
national unity governments, 427
oligarchy, 150, 190, 560, 561, 630–631
single-party government, 404–405, 411, 472, 475, 690, 693, 697, 721–722
support and toleration of, 423
Great Britain. *See* England; United Kingdom
Great Compromise (1787; U.S.), 632
Great Reform Act of 1832 (England), 559
Greece, 257, 429, 430, 630, 632
Grossman, Herschel I., 278, 542
Guatemala, 319
Gueffroy, Chris, 265
Guinier, Lani, 490

H

Habyarimana, James, 246–247
Haiti, 485
Hallerberg, Mark, 721
Hallstein Doctrine (Germany), 265
Hamilton, Alexander, 618, 640
Hardin, Garrett, 113
Hare, Thomas, 507
Harris, David, 577
Harsanyi, John C., 61
Hassan II (King of Morocco), 279

Hassan, Abdikassim Salad (transitional president of Somalia), 99
Heads of state, 407, 409, 444. *See also* Monarchs and monarchies; Presidents; Prime ministers
Heath, Edward, 407
Hegel, Georg Wilhelm Friedrich, 150
Henry VII (King of England), 623
Heseltine, Michael, 455
Hicken, Allen, 587
Hirano, Shigeo, 545
Hirschman, Albert, 56
Hitchcock, William I., 260, 538–539
Hobbes, Thomas, 105–106, 112, 113–114, 118, 141, 150, 192–193
Hoeffler, Anke, 731
Hollobone, Philip, 474
Holy Roman Empire, 554–555
Honduras, 315, 496
Honecker, Eric, 261, 262
Horowitz, Donald L., 736, 737, 738
Hotelling, Harold, 371*b*
Hough, Jerry F., 542
House of Lords Act (1999; England), 622, 624
"How Communism Could Have Been Saved" (Kaminski), 523
Howe, Sir Geoffrey, 454–455
Huber, John, 442–443
Human Rights Act (1998, U.K.), 635
Hungary, 258, 260, 261, 275, 515*b*–517*b*, 522
Huntington, Samuel P., 105, 195, 221, 223, 224, 225, 228, 230, 238, 256, 257*b*
Husák, Gustáv, 280*b*
Hussein (King of Jordan), 278, 279–280
Hussein, Saddam, 2, 294, 333, 341, 466, 556
Hypotheses, 42, 44–46. *See also* Theories
Hypotheses—specific
corporatist hypothesis, 423, 424
cultural group hypothesis, 234

Hypotheses—specific—*continued*
  Duverger's Hypothesis, 585
  ethnic group hypothesis, 233
  freezing hypothesis, 561–563
  hypothesized effect of electoral
    laws on ethnic conflict,
    733–738
  hypothesized effects of federal-
    ism, 738–742
  investiture hypothesis,
    423–424
  office and policy seeking and
    coalitions hypothesis, 416, 417
  opposition strength hypothesis,
    422–423, 424
  religious group hypothesis, 234
  strong party hypothesis, 424

I

Iceland, 409
Identity categories. *See* Social
    issues
Implications. *See* Hypotheses
Incumbents. *See* Candidates
India
  cleavages in, 555–556
  devolution in, 610–611
  economic factors of, 35
  elections and electoral system
    in, 472*b*, 474
  ethnic parties in, 565, 593
  federalism in, 615, 617
  health in, 217
  legislature in, 625
  political parties in, 539, 544
Indonesia, 333, 500, 742
Industrial Revolution and indus-
    trialization, 559, 713
Information, 78–79, 617–618
Inglehart, Ronald, 210, 212, 214,
    215, 218, 222, 562
Instrumentalists, 564
Interest groups
  corporatist interest group
    relations, 423
  definition and concepts of, 534,
    685
  economic effects of, 327
  majoritarian-consensus dimen-
    sion of, 685
  pluralist interest group relations,
    423

International politics, 1, 3, 4. *See
    also* Politics
Inter-Parliamentary Union, 620
IRA. *See* Irish Republican Army
Iran, 228, 315
Iraq. *See also* Hussein, Saddam
  constitution of, 638
  democracy in, 8, 9, 13, 259, 294
  economy of, 8
  elections and electoral laws in,
    12, 154, 466, 525
  ethnic and sectarian groups in,
    12, 13, 187
  government and government
    formation in, 427, 436, 739
  Iraq War, 403
  political parties in, 12
  religious cleavages in, 556
  selectorate in, 333
  weapons of mass destruction in,
    24
Ireland. *See also* Northern Ireland
  constitution of, 457
  democratization in, 257*b*, 399
  ethnic parties in, 565
  government in, 402, 405*b*, 410
  legislature in, 625, 626
  political parties in, 430, 434
  religious conflict in, 555
Irish Republican Army (IRA), 187
Iron Curtain, 261. *See also*
    Europe, Eastern; Soviet
    Union; individual countries
Islam. *See also* Democracy and
    democratization—cultural
    determinants; Muslims;
    Religion and religious issues
  democracy and, 9, 207, 221,
    223, 224–225, 226, 227,
    229–230, 231, 232–239, 250
  in Eritrea, 102
  government and political sys-
    tems in, 226, 227, 228
  orthopraxy in, 222
  in Somalia, 99–100
  treatment of women in, 225,
    230, 231–232
Islamic Salvation Army, 154
Israel
  constitution of, 635
  democratic institutions of, 685,
    687

democratization of, 257*b*
  ethnic and minority parties in,
    565, 736
  government in, 397
  political parties in, 429, 495,
    501, 502, 547
  rule of law index and, 315
Italy
  cabinet instability in, 745, 746
  Catholic Church in, 224
  Constitutional Court in, 645
  democratization in, 257*b*
  electoral system in, 399,
    471–472
  government in, 213, 405*b*, 427,
    436, 438, 439, 442, 746
  legislature in, 626, 627, 628, 745
  Northern League in, 741
  political parties in, 411, 424
  prime minister in, 402
Iversen, Torben, 715–718

J

Jackman, Robert, 161
Jackman, Simon, 163
Jamaica, 546, 547, 626, 685, 687
Jamal, Amaney Ahmad, 520
James II (Duke of York, King of
    England), 552, 555
Japan
  constitution of, 636
  democracy in, 12, 155
  electoral coalitions in, 430
  electoral system in, 11, 490, 512,
    545
  judicial system of, 12
  legislature in, 12, 626, 627
  political parties and party
    systems in, 544, 545–546
  post-World War II, 2, 10
Jaruzelski, Wojciech, 289, 290, 523
Jefferson, Thomas, 118–119
Jews and Judaism, 92, 222. *See
    also* Israel
John (King of England),
    332–333
Johnsen, Christopher, 719
Jordan, 277–278, 279
Jospin, Lionel, 433, 434, 451, 582
Juan Carlos (King of Spain), 296
Judiciary and judges. *See* Legal
    issues

June Resistance (South Korea; 1987), 266
Juppé, Alain, 451

K

Kaminski, Marek, 291, 523, 524
Kant, Immanuel, 150
Karatnycky, Adrian, 230
Kashmir, 556
Kekulé, August, 41
Kalyvas, Stathis, 227
Kenya, 100, 334b, 342, 466, 476, 615
Kenyatta, Jomo, 342
Keynes, John Maynard, 700
Keynesianism, 700
Kim, Dong-Hun, 411–412
King, Gary, 165
King, Martin Luther, Jr., 93
Kinnock, Neil, 454
Kiribati, 486, 543
Kiszczak, Maria Terese, 524
Kitschelt, Herbert P., 562, 574
Klaus, Vaclav, 409
Kohl, Helmut, 265b, 413
Kollman, Ken, 586
Krenz, Egon, 262
Kubiak, Hieronim, 524
Kumaratunga, Chandrika, 452, 489
Kun, Roland, 479
Kuran, Timur, 276
Kuwait, 492
Kyrgyzstan, 485

L

Lackland, John, 332–333
Laitin, David, 724–725, 728–729
Lane, Frederick, 94
Laos, 492, 544, 638
LaPalombara, Joseph, 3
Latin America. *See also* individual countries
    democratization in, 257
    constitutional courts in, 639
    coups in, 196, 319
    elections and electoral systems in, 485, 502, 520, 537
    ethnic parties in, 565
    federal states in, 609
    government in, 445
    secular-clerical cleavage in, 558

Laver, Michael, 424, 426, 510
LDP. *See* Liberal Democratic Party
Leaders and leadership. *See also* Politicians and political elites
    accountability of, 540
    corruption of, 340, 341–342, 343, 346
    declaration of state religions, 555
    in democracies, 341
    in dictatorships, 340–341
    distribution of public and private goods by, 340–342, 349
    electoral systems and, 522
    incumbents versus challengers, 341–342
    loyalty norm and, 338–341, 343–344, 349
    Michels' iron law of oligarchy, 561
    political parties and, 537, 540, 560–561
    public policy and, 340–341, 344
    winning coalitions and, 337–346, 349
Lebanon, 492, 556, 734–735
Lee Kuan Yew, 224, 227, 315
Lee Teng Hui, 225, 227
Legal issues. *See also* Constitutions and constitutionalism
    constitutional challenges, 644
    constitutional courts and justice, 635, 637, 639, 644, 646–648
    constitutional judges, 645
    constitutional laws, 637–638
    constitutional review, 637, 642–643, 644, 646–647, 649
    electoral laws, 575–583, 589–592
    judicial power, 639b–640b
    models of constitutional justice, 646–648
    rule of law, 314–315
Leggett, Dudley, 481
Legislatures and legislators. *See also* Government; Parliaments and parliamentary democracies

appointment to, 625
clarity of responsibility and, 690–691
coalitions and, 416
common pool resource problem, 719, 721
congruence and, 698–699
consensus democracies and, 679, 689, 695
constitutions and, 636–638, 735
fiscal policies and, 719–720
government and, 413, 442
history of, 630–634
malapportionment in, 625–626, 627t
majoritarian democracies and, 695
manufactured majorities in, 694
minority governments and, 420–426, 690
mixed electoral systems and, 515
partisan veto players and, 649
personal votes and, 721
policy making by, 722
political parties and, 437, 535, 717, 722
pork-barrel spending by, 719
presidents and, 398–399
quotas and, 495–496
translating votes into seats, 495–500, 502–507, 508–509, 512–515
universalism in, 719
votes of no confidence and, 398
Legislatures and legislators—internal issues
    legislative committees, 411–412, 422
    legislative conflict and deadlock, 628b–629b, 736, 747, 754
    legislative form in 191 independent countries, 667–673
    legislative fragmentation, 753–760
    legislative majorities, 421
    legislative parties, 549
    legislative responsibility, 397, 444, 621
    legislative supremacy, 634–635, 636–637

Legislatures and legislators—
    types of
    bicameral legislatures, 604,
        620–622, 625–634, 683, 690,
        691
    elected legislatures, 397, 625
    unicameral legislatures, 620,
        621, 622, 683
Leopold II (King of Belgium),
    344, 345–346
Le Pen, Jean-Marie, 433, 487, 563,
    582
Levine, Ross, 730
Liberal Democratic Party (LDP;
    Japan), 545–546
Liberal parties, 558
Liberation Tigers of Tamil Eelam
    (LTTE; Tamil Tigers), 452
Liberia, 543–544
Liechtenstein, 153, 470
Lien, Da–Hsiang, Donald, 183,
    184, 190
Life Peerages Act (1958; England),
    623
Lijphart, Arend, 626, 685, 734,
    735–736, 737, 738
Limongi, Fernando, 154–156, 225,
    227, 328
Linz, Juan J., 445
Lipset, Seymour Martin, 170, 171,
    221, 222, 224, 558, 561, 562
List PR (list proportional repre-
    sentation) systems. See
    Electoral systems—specific
Lithuania, 449, 512
Locke, John, 105, 106, 114, 150,
    192
Loewenberg, Gerhard, 411–412
Logic, 33–36
London Agreements (1948),
    263–264
Louis XIV (King of France), 556
LTTE. See Liberation Tigers of
    Tamil Eelam
Luebbert, Gregory M., 422–423,
    425
Lust-Okar, Ellen, 277, 278, 520
Luther, Martin, 554
Luxembourg, 427, 430, 439, 506,
    685, 687
Luxembourg Income Study, 718

M

Macedonia, 565
Machiavelli, Niccolò, 151*b*
Macpherson, C.B., 148
Madagascar, 512, 625
Madison, James, 413*b*, 618
Mainwaring, Scott, 753–754, 755,
    756–758
Mair, Peter, 510
Majorities. See Decision making
Major, John, 455, 541
Making Democracy Work
    (Putnam), 213
Malawi, 476, 570*b*–571*b*
Malaysia, 155, 470, 612, 613,
    615
Maldives, 470
Mali, 247, 471, 485, 525
Malta, 430, 471–472, 507
Manhattan Project, 60
Manifesto Research Group, 433
Marcos, Ferdinand, 266, 333,
    340
Marier, Patrik, 721
Marshall Islands, 543
Martinez-Gallardo, Cecilia,
    442–443
Martin, Lanny W., 411, 437
Marxism and Marxists, 77, 322,
    323, 325. See also
    Theories—specific
Marx, Karl, 150, 560
Massicotte, Louis, 470, 471
Mauritania, 625
Mauritius, 492
Mauroy, Pierre, 455
Mazower, Mark, 230–231
Mazowiecki, Tadeusz, 524
McAllister, Ian, 510–511
McGuire, James, 328
Measurement, 166–167
Measures
    aggregation issues of, 162, 163,
        165, 166
    attributes of, 162–163
    continuous measure, 156
    dichotomous measure, 156
    evaluation of measures of
        democracy, 160–166
    inter-observer reliability, 165
    interval measures, 164

measurement levels, 163–164
    minimalist measures, 152, 162,
        166
    nominal measures, 163–164
    ordinal measures, 164
    procedural measures, 152, 162
    purchasing power parity (PPP),
        173*b*
    reliability of, 164–165, 166
    replicability, 165–166
    validity of, 162–164, 165*f*, 166
Measures—specific
    Big Mac index, 173*b*
    Freedom House measure of
        democracy, 158–160, 161, 162,
        163, 164, 165, 166
    PACL measure of democracy,
        154–156, 159–160, 161–162,
        163–166
    Polity IV measure of democ-
        racy, 157–158, 159–160, 161,
        162, 163, 164, 165–166
Median Voter Theorem (MVT).
    See Decision making;
    Theorems
Method of Agreement, 21–25,
    27–32, 39–40
Method of Difference, 25–32,
    39–40
Methods. See also Method of
    Agreement; Method of
    Difference
    of comparative politics, 4–6
    empirical methods, 32
    experiments in political science,
        244–247
    measurement error, 29
    science as a method, 18
    surveys, 215–221
    testing, 37–40, 44, 45–46, 48
    triangular data and, 330
Methods—calculations and
    equations
    effective number of ethnic
        groups, 593
    effective number of parties,
        548–549, 598
    electoral thresholds, 501
    expected payoff, 309
    probability of regime transition,
        176, 179

probability of transitioning to democracy, 180

probability of transitioning to dictatorship, 180

quotas, 495, 508

value of defecting, 339, 340

Methods—specific

allocation of seats, 496–497, 512, 513

analysis of collective action problem, 268–271

analysis of revolutionary threshold, 273–274

analysis of winning coalitions and selectorates, 346–349

box and whisker plot of fiscal activity, 702

coding, 158, 164–166, 223

comparative methods, 4, 19, 28, 31, 39–40

doughnut graphs, 575, 576f

estimation of frequency of ethnic conflict, 725, 728

example of STV with a Droop quota, 507–509

falsificationism, 40

hypothesis testing, 45–46

mapping W and S onto regime typologies, 335–337

measurement of government duration, 439

Mill's methods, 21–32

plotting majoritarian-consensus dimensions of democracy, 685–687

systems research designs, 27

test for compatibility between religion and democracy, 232–239

test for cultural diversity, 239–243, 248–249

World Values Survey, 215–216, 217–221

Mexico, 25–27, 155, 448, 513, 609

Michels' iron law of oligarchy, 561

Michels, Robert, 560–561

Micronesia, 543

Middle East, 5, 278, 294, 333, 520, 556. See also individual countries

Military coups, 96, 319, 543–544, 655, 749, 760–761

Military juntas, 312, 333, 335, 343, 344, 346, 349–350

Mill, John Stuart, 19, 22, 23b, 25, 32, 209–210, 211, 214, 679

Mill's Method of Agreement. See Method of Agreement

Mill's Method of Difference. See Method of Difference

Mill's methods, 19–21

Minority and ethnic issues. See Ethnic and minority issues

Mitchell, Robert, 724

Mitterrand, François, 450–451, 455

Mixed democracies

cabinets in, 453

classification of, 400

cohabitation in, 450–453, 654, 684–685

government in, 449–453, 455

legislative majorities in, 450, 621

overview of, 400, 401, 402t

power in, 684–685

presidents in, 621

Mixed electoral systems. See Elections and electoral systems—specific

MMP (mixed member proportional) systems. See Elections and electoral systems—specific

Mobutu Sese Seko, 340

Models and modeling. See also Theories

art and process of, 43–45

example of, 47–49

fertile models, 45

game-theoretic model of top-down transitions, 277–291

Meltzer-Richard model of size of government, 317–320, 703, 707–708

model of voter income and right left political divide, 716–717

models of ethnic outbidding, 732

purpose and simplicity of, 44

simple model of government formation, 413–418

spatial models, 389–391, 657–662

structural dependence of the state on capital, 320

technological and capitalism possibility frontiers, 320–323

testing of, 44–46

tipping or threshold models, 255, 271–276

Mogadishu (capital city of Somalia), 98, 99, 100

Mohamed, Ali Mahdi (Somali politician), 98

Moldova, 449, 741

Monarchs and monarchies. See also Heads of State; United Kingdom

corrupted monarchies, 150

democracy and, 150

elections and electoral systems in, 332, 520

in France, 191

government and, 312, 343, 344, 349–350, 400, 407

in Italy, 213

in Jordan and Morocco, 279–280

legislatures and, 622, 625

in the Netherlands, 409

preference for, 346

selectorate in, 333, 335, 337

in the United Kingdom, 191, 622–624

Money, Jeannette, 621–622, 631, 634

Mongolia, 487

Montesquieu, Charles, 150, 209, 210, 211, 214, 224, 618, 631

Moore, Barrington, Jr., 19, 192

Morgenstern, Oskar, 60

Morgenthau, Hans, 3

Morocco, 277–278, 279–280

Morrison, Donald, 724

Morrow, James D., 60, 331, 332, 334b, 335, 337, 366b

Morton, Rebecca B., 490

Movement for Democratic Change in Zimbabwe, 342

Mozambique, 256

Mubarak, Hosni, 544
Mueller, Dennis, 680
Mugabe, Robert, 539, 544
Muller, Edward N., 214, 215
Müller, Wolfgang C., 411
Muhammad (Prophet), 229. *See also* Islam; Muslims
Munck, Gerardo L., 166
Muslim Brotherhood, 278
Muslims. *See also* Islam
  consultation between, 226
  in democratic countries, 228
  divisions between, 556
  in France, 557
  in Lebanon, 734–735
  violence and, 223, 224–225
Mussolini, Benito, 224
MVT (Median Voter Theorem).
    See Decision making;
    Theorems

N

Nader, Ralph, 582
Namibia, 472*b*, 496
Napoleon Bonaparte, 556
Nasar, Sylvia, 61
Nash equilibria. *See also* Games
  definitions, 59, 65
  origins of, 61
  subgame perfect Nash equilib-
    rium, 65, 68–70
  types of, 65
Nash, John, 60–61
National Organization for the
    Reform of Marijuana Laws,
    272–273
Nations and nation states, 92–93,
    723. *See also* States
Natural resources, 8, 182, 194, 199.
    See also Dictatorships; Oil
Nature. *See* State of nature
Nauru, 479, 543
Nepal, 474
Netherlands
  cabinet in, 415*b*, 416*t*
  consociationalism in, 734
  district magnitude of, 500
  Eighty Years' War and, 555
  elections and electoral system
    in, 430, 470, 501, 506
  government in, 427, 436, 438,
    443

informateur and formateur in,
    409
legislature in, 625, 626, 627
political parties and party sys-
    tem in, 411, 429, 430, 543, 547
secular-clerical cleavage in, 558,
    734
Neves, Tancredo, 276
Newell, Neville, 481
New Zealand
  constitution of, 635, 637
  democratic institutions of, 685,
    687
  elections and electoral system
    of, 430, 470, 471, 513, 515,
    515–526, 687
  ethnic parties in, 565
  legislature in, 687
  majoritarian democracy in, 687
  political parties in, 421
Nicaragua, 487
Nigeria, 159*t*, 466, 474, 503*f*, 556,
    742
1984 (Orwell), 537
Nooruddin, Irfan, 720
North Africa, 520
North America, 517, 520
North, Douglass, 93—94, 183,
    184, 185
Northern Ireland, 86, 93, 555, 579,
    609, 741. *See also* Ireland
North Korea, 335, 544, 638
Norway, 423, 430, 626
Novotny, Antonín, 280*b*

O

Obote, Milton, 278, 526
Oceana, 520
Ogaden War (*1977-1978*; Somalia-
    Ethiopia), 96–97, 101*m*
Oil, 199, 200, 202, 324, 722. *See
    also* Natural resources
Olmert, Ehud, 547
Olson, Mancur, 267
Operation Restore Hope (UN;
    Somalia), 99
Orange Revolution (Ukraine),
    452, 539
Organization for Economic
    Cooperation and
    Development (OECD), 693,
    708, 747

Orwell, George, 537
Osborne, Martin J., 61

P

PACL. *See* Przeworski, Adam;
    Alvarez, Michael E.;
    Cheibub, José; Limongi,
    Fernando
PACL measure, 154–156,
    159–160, 161–162, 163–166
Paden, John, 724
Pahlavi, Mohammed Reza (Shah),
    315
Pakistan, 470, 555–556, 629*b*
Palau, 543
Papua New Guinea, 475, 483, 484,
    737
Paradoxes, 355, 357–366, 374, 379
Parliament Acts (1911, 1949),
    621, 633
Parliaments and parliamentary
    democracies. *See also*
    Cabinets—parliamentary;
    Democracy and democrati-
    zation; Prime ministers
  accountability in, 745
  classification of, 400
  coalitions in, 444, 447, 720,
    744–745, 754, 755
  components of government in,
    402
  constitutional theories of, 403
  democratic consolidation and,
    747
  democratic survival and, 743–760
  duration of, 13
  executive recruitment in, 744
  government composition in,
    447–448
  government formation in, 395,
    404–413, 436, 444
  government responsibility to
    the legislature in, 399–400, 746
  immobilism in, 745–746, 754,
    755, 761
  instability in, 755, 757
  investiture votes in, 404
  leadership in, 537
  legislative committees, 411–412
  legislative deadlock in, 754
  legislative responsibility in, 398,
    399, 412, 445

legislature and legislators and, 404, 406, 454, 455, 621, 744, 746–747, 753–760
ministers of, 402–403, 455
minority governments in, 445
mutual dependence in, 746
overview of, 400, 401, 402*t*
policymaking in, 744–745
political careers in, 536–537
power in, 684
preelectoral coalitions and, 434
presidents in, 399, 400
reversion points in, 444
votes needed to stay in power, 720
Paterson, Ian, 481
Paul (Saint), 17, 18
Payoffs. *See* Definitions and concepts; Games
PBV (party block vote) system. *See* Elections and electoral systems
Peace of Westphalia (1648), 555
People Power Revolution (Philippines; 1986), 266
People's Republic of China decentralization in, 614
as a dictatorship, 148
elections in, 465
federalism in, 615
inclusion and contestation in, 152–153
political parties in, 544
Tiananmen Square demonstrations, 261
Persia, 149
Persians, The (Aeschylus), 208–209
Persson, Torsten, 718–719, 722
Peru, 448, 486, 537
Philippines, 266, 333, 340, 471, 626
Pinochet, Augusto, 276–277, 279, 315, 333, 756
Piscatori, James P., 227
Plato, 149, 150, 630
Plott, Charles, 394
PMs. *See* Prime ministers
Poland. *See also* Solidarity communism in, 258
democratization in, 275, 277, 281, 288–291, 339, 449

electoral systems in, 501, 502, 522, 523–524, 542
liberalization in, 260–261
political parties in, 501, 542, 544
prime minister in, 402
Politics (Plato), 149
Policies and policy making. *See also* Political issues; Politicians and political elites
accountability for, 494
by coalition and single-party cabinets, 411, 412
economic policy making, 700
exit, voice, and loyalty and, 57–58
federalism and, 613, 618
government formation and, 421
government policy positions, 433
judges and, 640
legislative committees and, 422
in majoritarian and consensus democracies, 677–680, 697
mandates for, 693, 694
minority government and, 424
multidimensionality of, 374–379
opposition strength and, 422–423
policy space and, 417–418
political parties and, 422, 535, 697
power and, 78
preelectoral coalitions and, 433
presidential powers of, 743
representation and responsiveness and, 695
stability of, 650–656
surplus majority government and, 427
tax revenues and, 614
unanimity core and, 664–665
veto players and, 649–655, 722, 760
winsets, 376, 393, 650–655, 664
Political economy, 3. *See also* Economic issues
Political issues. *See also* Governments; Leaders and leadership; Politicians and

political elite; Political parties; Political party systems
checks and balances, 12, 226, 453, 604, 631, 632, 667–673
coalitions, 332, 333*f*, 334–335, 337, 338–349, 411–413, 435–436, 437–438
credible commitment problems, 185–188
defection, 338–341
delegation or principal-agent problems, 411–413
disenfranchised, 332–333
distribution of private and public goods, 337, 342
economic factors, 718–719
elections, 441
ethnic and minority groups, 732, 733
formateurs and informateurs, 409, 436, 437–438
government formation, 407
interest group relations, 423
judicialization of politics, 639–641
macroeconomic and fiscal policies, 708–709
minority governments, 422–423
partisan veto players, 649
political culture, 212, 214
political dissidents, 273
political identity, 565
political participation, 157–158
right-left political divide, 559
Selectorate Theory and selectorate, 331–349
single- and multi-issue dimensionality, 374, 380
social and cultural cleavages, 565–572
taxes, 338
veto players, 760
votes of confidence, 398
Political parties. *See also* Political issues; Political party systems; Politicians and political elites
accountability and, 689, 690
cabinets and, 448
common poor resource problem and, 721–722
decentralization and, 740–741

Political parties—*continued*
in dictatorships, 148, 278, 288
elections and electoral systems
    and, 270, 427, 432, 574–575,
    597, 736, 742
ethnic conflict and, 740–741
ethnic parties, 564–565,
    593–597, 732, 733
formation of, 572–572,
    574–575, 584–585, 588
government formation and,
    406, 697
liberalization and, 277
manufactured majorities of, 694
majoritarian and consensus
    dimensions of, 682, 689, 697
mechanical effect of electoral
    laws, 575–583
merging of, 583
multiparty systems, 547, 682,
    756–757
number of parties, 548–551,
    574–575, 588, 597, 598, 683,
    722
partisan veto players and, 649
party discipline, 720
party whips, 540–542
policy making and, 422, 535
presidential candidates and,
    587, 741
primary elections and, 537
regional parties, 740–742
representation and responsive-
    ness and, 695–699
right and left divide in,
    561–562, 574, 713–718
in single-party systems, 543–546
size of, 583, 736
small parties, 415*b*, 417, 428,
    432, 575, 578, 579, 580, 581,
    583, 584, 597
social cleavages and political
    identity and, 551–575,
    592–593, 597
strategic entry and, 580–583,
    584, 592
two-party systems, 371*b*,
    546–547, 585, 682, 756
what they are and what they do,
    534–543
where they come from, 551–552

Political party systems. *See also*
    Political issues
apparentement in, 501–502
Arrow's Theorem and, 385
cabinets and cabinet members
    and, 410, 411, 435–436
coalitions and, 428, 429, 432,
    494, 689–690
in consensus democracies,
    689–690
in dictatorships, 278
district magnitude and, 499
electoral laws and, 11, 12,
    589–592, 597
electoral and legislative parties,
    590–591
electoral systems and, 475–476,
    482–483, 485, 491, 492,
    493–495, 501, 509–511, 515,
    522, 525
extremist parties, 495
form, size, and structure of, 534,
    597
formateurs and, 409, 437–438
fragmentation of, 722
government duration and, 442
government formation and,
    407, 409, 437
government spending and, 722
joint lists, 429
legislatures and, 437–438
majoritarian electoral systems
    and, 473–474
Median Voter Theorem and
    party competition, 371*b*
minority governments and,
    421–426
nationalization of, 585, 586–588
nomination agreements in, 429
in parliamentary democracies,
    404–405
party lists, 502–507
policy convergence and, 371
political competition and, 11–12
power and, 682
principal-agent or delegation
    problems and, 411–413
social structures and, 12
surplus majority governments,
    426, 428
types of party systems, 543–551

Politicians and political elites. *See
    also* Political issues; Political
    parties
accountability and, 689–690
cabinet appointments of,
    409–410
constitutional challenges and, 644
ethnic polarization by, 732, 733
federalism and, 619
as formateurs, 407, 409
in national unity governments,
    427
office- and policy-seeking
    politicians, 414–418, 421
policy making and, 678
political parties and, 536–538
representation and responsive-
    ness and, 695–699
strategic entry of, 580–583
Politics. *See also* Comparative pol-
    itics; International politics
American politics, 3–4
political games, 58–59
political mobilization, 76–77
state demands and benefits and,
    118
study of, 3–5, 13–15, 50–51
winners and losers in, 56–57
Politics among Nations
    (Morgenthau), 3
Politics within Nations
    (LaPalombara), 3
Polity IV, 157–158, 161, 162, 163,
    164, 165–166, 328, 605
Polyarchy, 153
Popper, Karl, 17, 18, 39, 41
Portugal, 256–257, 429, 430, 471,
    472*b*, 498
Posner, Daniel N., 570–571
Potsdam Conference (1945), 263
Poverty and the poor
    attitudes toward, 701–711
    consumption by, 326–327
    in democracies and dictator-
        ships, 328
    democratic survival and,
        761–762
    universal suffrage and, 196
Poverty of Philosophy, The (Marx),
    560
Powell, Colin, 24

Powell, G. Bingham, 422, 680, 697
Powers
  definitions of, 55, 56
  delegation and, 412–413
  effectiveness of, 70, 74–75
  relationships between citizens
    and states, 74–79
  separation of powers, 454, 646,
    684, 743–744
  use of voice and, 77–78
PPP (purchasing power parity).
    See Economic issues
PR (proportional electoral)
    systems. *See* Elections and
    electoral systems
Prague Post Online, 437
Prague Spring (Czechoslovakia;
    1968), 280
Preemption, 136, 137–138
Preference falsification. *See*
    Dictatorships
Preference ordering. *See* Decision
    making
Presidencies and presidential
    democracies. *See also*
    Cabinets—presidential;
    Democracy and democrati-
    zation; Presidents
  clarity of responsibility and, 744
  classification of, 400
  coalitions in, 444, 445–447,
    754–755
  deadlock in, 747, 749, 754, 760
  democratic consolidation and,
    747
  democratic survival and,
    742–760
  divided government in, 450
  duration of, 13
  elections in, 587, 741
  executive recruitment in, 744
  government composition in,
    447–448, 449*t*
  government formation in,
    395–396, 443–445
  government types in, 445,
    446–447
  instability in, 753–754, 755,
    756–760
  leadership in, 537
  legislative majorities in, 445, 621

legislative responsibility in, 398,
    399, 444, 454
legislature and, 744, 746–747,
    753–760
mutual independence in, 746
overview of, 400, 401, 402*t*
perils of presidentialism,
    743–752
policymaking in, 744
political careers in, 536–537
political parties in, 587, 741–742
power in, 684, 743–744
separation of powers in, 454,
    684
Presidents. *See also* Heads of state;
    Presidencies and presiden-
    tial democracies
  cabinet appointments of, 450,
    537
  decrees of, 446
  expectations of, 743
  as formateurs, 444
  government responsibility to,
    399–400
  independently and indirectly
    elected presidents, 398–399
  legislatures and, 398–399, 444,
    447, 743, 754–755
  in mixed democracies, 449–453
  in parliamentary democracies,
    399–400, 407
  policymaking power of, 743–744
  political parties and, 448, 537
  power of, 447
  presidential elections, 587, 741,
    754
  role of, 444
Prime ministers (PMs). *See also*
    Heads of state; Parliaments
    and parliamentary
    democracies
  cabinet appointments and,
    409–410, 445, 447, 448, 454,
    537, 754
  as formateurs, 409
  legislature and, 444, 445, 454,
    455, 744, 746, 754, 755
  minister's portfolio, 402–403,
    410
  in mixed democracies, 449,
    450–453

powers of, 744
role of, 402
titles of, 402
Primordialists, 564
Principe, 525
Private goods, 337, 341, 342
Probability, 176
Problems
  classifying democracies,
    456–458
  classifying political regimes, 350
  conceptualizing and measuring
    democracy, 167–168
  constitutional design, 763–764
  credible commitment, 185–188,
    204
  cultural determinants of
    democracy, 251–254
  decision making, 386–394
  democratic institutions, 458–459
  democratic transitions, 293–310
  dependent and independent
    variables, 204–205
  economic development, 353
  electoral systems, 528–531
  Exit, Voice, and Loyalty game,
    203–204
  game theory and games, 80–90,
    123–145, 252–254
  government formation, 459–461
  government types, 461
  Median Voter Theorem, 387–389
  modernization theories, 202–203
  oil and democracy (resource
    curse), 205
  presidentialism versus parlia-
    mentalism, 764
  public and private goods,
    351–352
  scientific method, 51–54
  Selectorate Theory, 351–353
  social cleavages and party
    systems, 598–602
  veto players, 657–667
  winning coalitions, 351–353
Progressive problem shifts, 123
Property rights. *See* Economic
    issues
*Protestant Ethic and the Spirit of
    Capitalism, The* (Weber),
    221

Protestantism, 221–222, 225, 227, 230, 231, 232–239, 554–555. *See also* Cleavages; Democracy and democratization—cultural determinants; Religion and religious issues

Proxy wars, 96–97

Przeworski, Adam, 154–156, 170, 171, 174, 176, 197, 198, 225, 227, 320, 322, 328, 445, 447, 542, 560, 743, 751, 761

Public goods
  definition and concept of, 267
  democracy and, 267, 311–312
  dictatorships and, 311–312
  distribution of, 341, 342
  political distribution of, 337, 344

Purchasing power parity (PPP). *See* Economic issues

Putnam, Robert, 213

Q

al-Qaida, 7

Qatar, 465–466, 606

Quebec (Canada), 612

Quotas and quota systems, 495–499, 507–508

R

Racial and minority issues. *See* Ethnic and minority issues

Raffarin, Jean-Pierre, 451

Rao, Vaman, 326

Ra's al-Khaimah. *See* United Arab Emirates

Rationality, 359–360, 363

Realism, 105n14

Reform Act (1867; England), 559

Reliability. *See* Measures

Religion and religious issues, 233t, 554–556, 565. *See also* Cleavages; Democracy and democratization—cultural determinants; individual sects and religions

Replicability. *See* Measures

Republic, The (Plato), 149

Republic of Hungary. *See* Hungary

Republicanism, 632

Republican Party, 75

Revolutions. *See also* Democratic transitions; individual revolutions

causes of, 274

collection action theory and, 266–271

predictability of, 275

preference falsification and, 255, 275, 276, 292

rarity of popular revolutions, 9, 255

revolutionary bandwagon, 276

revolutionary cascade, 273–274, 275

revolutionary threshold, 272

tipping models and, 271–276, 292

Reykowski, Janusz, 524

Reynal–Querol, Marta, 737

Rietz, Thomas A., 490

Riker, William H., 381

Rodden, Jonathan, 619, 713–714, 715

Rogowski, Ronald, 194

Roh Tae Woo, 266

Rokkan, Stein, 558, 561, 562

Roland, Gerard, 722

Romania, 266, 449, 565

Rose-Ackerman, Susan, 340

Ross, Michael, 202

Rostow, Walt W., 170

Round-robin tournaments, 358–361

Roundtable Talks (Poland; 1988), 260, 289–290

Rousseau, Jean Jacques, 105, 106, 114, 120, 130, 151b

Rural issues. *See* Cleavages

Russia, 105, 449, 512, 522, 564, 565, 612, 742. *See also* Soviet Union

Rustow, Dankwart A., 745

S

Sacerdote, Bruce, 711, 712

Saiegh, Sebastian, 445, 447

St. Lucia, 471

Sakharov, Andrei, 273

São Tomé, 525

Sarkozy, Nicolas, 557

Saudi Arabia, 465, 638

Schumpeter, Joseph, 5

Schwedler, Jillian, 278

Science. *See also* Methods
  as a culture, 18

definitions and concepts of, 17, 18, 42

example of the scientific process, 47–49

as a method, 18, 40–46, 50

myths about, 50–51

Scientific issues. *See also* Hypotheses; Measures; Methods;
  falsificationism, 40–42, 50
  scientific explanations, 17
  scientific statements, 17, 41
  scientific theories, 39
  scientific typologies, 3

Scores
  Autocracy score, 157–158
  Democracy score, 157–158
  Freedom House score, 158–159, 161
  Polity IV score, 157–158, 159

Scotland, 579

Scotland Act (1998), 635

Security dilemma, 119. *See also* States

Selectorate Theory. *See* Theories—specific

Seligson, Mitchell A., 214, 215

Selton, Reinhard, 61

Sen, Amartya, 217

Senegal, 247, 466

September 11, 2001 (9/11), 7

Shapiro, Martin, 635

Sharjah. *See* United Arab Emirates

Shepsle, Kenneth A., 424, 426, 719

Shively, W. Phillips, 536, 743

Sierra Leone, 486–487, 496

Sieyès, Abbé (Emmanuel Joseph), 634

Singapore, 315, 470, 492

Siverson, Randolph, 331, 332, 334b, 335, 337, 346b

Skach, Cindy, 455, 746–751, 757

Skocpol, Theda, 28

Slovakia, 471–472, 500

SMDP (single-member district plurality). *See* Elections and electoral systems—specific

Smith, Alistair, 331, 332, 334b, 335, 337, 346b, 442b

SNTV (single-non-transferable vote). *See* Elections and electoral systems—specific

Social issues. *See also* Cleavages;
    Cultural issues
  attributes and identity categories, 565–571
  civil society, 113–119, 170–171, 225, 289
  social classes, 558–561, 632
  social cleavages and divisions, 554–565, 588, 592–593
  social heterogeneity, 588–589
  social structure, 588
  social welfare attitudes, 711
  value shifts, 562
Social Contract, The (Rousseau), 151*b*
Socialism and socialists, 559–560
Socialist parties, 261, 450, 451, 522, 560
Social Origins of Dictatorship and Democracy (Moore), 19
Society and societal issues, 182
Socrates, 17, 188
Solidarity (Poland), 260, 275, 279, 289–290, 291, 523
Solzhenitsyn, Aleksandr, 272, 273
Somalia
  electoral systems in, 525
  as a failed state, 7, 102–103
  history of, 95–105, 120
  Islamic state in, 99–100, 114
  Soviet Union and, 96–97
  as a state of nature, 112, 118*n*23
  UN and, 98, 99
  U.S. and, 96–97, 98, 99–100
Somali Democratic Republic, 96
Somaliland, 96
Soskice, David, 715–718
South Africa
  apartheid in, 187–188, 197, 333–334
  contestation and inclusion in, 153
  electoral rights and rule of law in, 315, 470
  electoral systems in, 484, 504
  legislature in, 629*b*
  political parties in, 544
  selectorate in, 333–334
South Korea, 281, 512
Sovereigns, 113–114, 116–117, 119, 141. *See also* Monarchs and monarchies

Soviet Union. *See also* Arms races;
    Berlin; Germany, East; Russia
  collapse of, 468
  Communist Party in, 537–538, 542
  contestation and inclusion in, 152
  Eastern Europe and, 258, 260, 262, 275, 280*b*
  elections and voting in, 466, 467
  Ethiopia and, 97
  glasnost and perestroika, 260, 275, 280*b*
  Gorbachev, Mikhail and, 260, 281
  liberalization of, 281
  Poland and, 289, 290
  political elite in, 537
  selectorate in, 333
  Somalia and, 96–97
Spain
  Catholic Church in, 224
  Constitutional Court in, 645
  democratization of, 257, 296
  ethnic parties in, 565
  federalism in, 617
  government duration in, 439
  legislature in, 625
  regional parties in, 741
Spirit of the Laws (Montesquieu), 150, 631
SPNE (subgame perfect Nash equilibrium). *See* Nash equilibrium
Sprague, John, 560
Sri Lanka, 452, 453, 488–489, 506, 522, 565
Stark, Rodney, 222
State of nature, 105–106, 114–118, 192–193
States. *See also* Exit, Voice, and Loyalty game; Federalism; Government; Nations and nation states; Policies and policy making
  asset holders and, 193–194
  centralization of, 613–614
  citizens and, 74–79, 193, 195
  class conflict and, 559
  compliance in, 122
  contractarian view of, 91, 92, 105–119

cooperation in, 113, 114, 122, 141–145
  definitions of, 91, 92–95, 105, 604, 605
  economic issues of, 322–323, 560
  independent, democratic, and authoritarian countries, 256
  institutions of, 332–335
  Marxist view of, 77, 322
  policy making and, 613
  predatory states, 91, 92, 119–122, 193, 194
  rentier states, 194
  rise of the modern state, 121–122
  state religions, 555
  terrorism in, 102
  as a third-party enforcer, 114
  unitary states, 605, 609*b*, 611*b*, 613, 615*f*, 625, 633–634, 667–673, 683
  use of physical force by, 93
States—failed. *See also* Afghanistan; Somalia
  continuum of, 103, 105
  definitions of, 91, 94
  examples of, 94–95, 104
  history of a failed state (Somalia), 95–105
  political and economic instability and, 7
  terrorism in, 102
States—federal. *See also* Brazil; Federalism; United Arab Emirates; United States
  centralization of, 613–614
  characteristics of, 605, 611–612
  constitutional criteria for, 605, 609*b*
  definitions and concepts of, 603, 604, 605, 611, 612, 616
  federal countries, 605, 606*t*, 609*b*, 615, 616*f*, 667–673
  governance of, 605
  policy making by, 613
  power in, 683
  regional units of, 605
  tax revenues of, 614, 615*f*
Staton, Jeffrey K., 640, 641
Status quo proposals, 374–378
Stepan, Alfred, 455, 746–751, 757*f*
Stokes, Susan Carol, 175

Stone, Alec, 635
Stramski, Jacek, 698
Strategies, 145. *See also* Definitions and concepts; Games
Strøm, Kaare, 411, 421–423, 425, 426, 453
STV (single transferable vote) systems. *See* Elections and electoral systems—specific
Suárez, Adolfo, 296
Sudan, 726–728
Suffrage. *See* Votes, voters, and voting
Suharto, 333
Survival story. *See* Economic issues
SV (supplementary vote) electoral system. *See* Elections and electoral systems—specific
Swaziland, 625
Sweden
    economic factors in, 709
    electoral system of, 471, 472*b*, 500, 503, 505
    federalism in, 615
    government in, 103, 421
    interest groups in, 423
    legislature in, 634
    political parties in, 424
    religious issues in, 555
Switzerland
    coalition governments in, 690
    constitution of, 636
    democratic institutions of, 685, 687
    democratization in, 257*b*
    elections and electoral systems in, 153, 334, 506–507
    federalism in, 605, 611, 612, 616
    legislature in, 625, 627, 628, 633
    political parties in, 506–507
Syria, 492, 544, 607
System of Logic, A (Mill), 19
Szczepkowsa, Joanna, 290

T

Tabellini, Guido, 718–719, 722
Taiwan, 344, 490, 522
Taliban, 7. *See also* Afghanistan; al-Qaida

Tamil Tigers. *See* Liberation Tigers of Tamil Eelam
Tanaka Kakuei, 545–546
Tanzania, 100, 466
Taxes and taxation. *See also* Economic issues
    in democracies and dictatorships, 319
    in exchange relationships, 116–118
    fiscal policy preferences and, 703–713, 715
    government spending and, 317–318
    political issues of, 338
    productivity and, 318–319
    tax and transfer systems, 323, 324, 325, 705, 706, 707, 718, 719
Terrorists and terrorism, 7, 99–100, 101, 102, 119, 136–138
Testing. *See* Methods
Thatcher, Margaret, 77, 410, 454–455, 622. *See also* Prime ministers
Theorems
    Arrow's Theorem, 355, 379–384, 655–656, 676, 677
    Chaos Theorem, 379, 392
    Median Voter Theorem, 355, 370–379, 380
Theories. *See also* Game theory; Hypotheses; Models and modeling
    construction of, 231
    evaluation, falsification, and corroboration of, 46, 50
    as steps in the scientific method, 43–44
    testing of, 37–40, 44
Theories—specific
    aims of social and democratic parties, 560
    bicameralism, 631–632
    capitalism possibility frontier, 321–322
    collective action theory, 255, 266–271, 291
    constitutional theory, 403
    contractarian theory of the state, 91, 92, 105–119

democratic theory, 226, 271
    Duverger's Theory of party formation, 572–597, 683
    Gamson's Law, 415
    Marxist theory, 320, 559–560
    Michels' iron law of oligarchy, 560–561
    modernization theory, 750
    modernization theory, classical, 169, 170–181, 194, 201, 210
    modernization theory, cultural, 207, 214, 249
    politicized cleavages, 565–572
    predatory theory of the state, 91, 92, 119–123
    Selectorate Theory, 259, 311–312, 313, 331–350, 720
    social contract theory, 106, 114, 118–119, 122
    structural dependence of the state on capital, 320, 323, 560, 709
    survival story, 173–181
    technological possibility frontier, 320–323
    variant of modernization theory, 182–201
    veto player theory, 604, 648–655, 656, 664, 722, 760
    Wagner's Law, 703
Theory of Games and Economic Behavior (von Neumann), 60
Thies, Michael, 411
Thirty Years' War, 555
TI. *See* Transparency International
Tiananmen Square demonstrations (1989; China), 261
Tilly, Charles, 93–94, 120–121
Tobago, 471, 474, 549–550, 687
Tocqueville, Alexis de, 196, 678
Tongo, 492
Topolanek, Mirek, 409
Tories, 552–554, 558
"To What Extent Forms of Government Are a Matter of Choice" (Mill), 209
Trade issues, 139
Transitions. *See* Democratic transitions; Revolutions

Transitivity and transitive preference ordering. *See* Decision making
Transnistria, 741
Transparency International (TI), 342
Treaty on the Final Settlement with Respect to Germany (1990), 265
Treier, Shawn, 163
Treisman, Daniel, 620
Triangular Table Talks (Hungary; 1988), 260–261
Trinidad, 471, 474, 549–550, 626, 685, 687
TRSs (two-round systems). *See* Elections and electoral systems—specific
Trucial States. *See* United Arab Emirates
Tsebelis, George, 621–622, 631, 634, 722, 760
Tsvangirai, Morgan, 342, 539
Turkey
 as a democracy, 159*t*
 challenges to the state, 105
 electoral system in, 498, 501, 502, 512
 ethnic parties in, 565
 Greece and, 257
Turkmenistan, 544
Tuvalu, 543

U

UAE. *See* United Arab Emirates
Uganda, 466
UK. *See* United Kingdom
Ukraine, 449, 452–453, 485, 512, 539
UN. *See* United Nations
United Arab Emirates (UAE), 466, 606–608
United Arab Republic, 607
United Kingdom (UK). *See also* England; Prime ministers; individual prime ministers
 analysis of democracy in, 21–25, 26–27
 civic culture in, 212
 coalitions in, 430, 475
 constitution of, 635–636, 637

devolution in, 609*b*, 611*b*
disproportional electoral rules in, 405
elections and electoral system in, 441, 442*b*, 474, 475, 492, 577–579
electoral rules in, 471, 472*b*
federalism in, 617
formation of government in, 407, 435–436
government duration and, 439, 443
government in, 403*t*, 421
Iraq War and, 403
legislature and legislative process in, 621–624, 633
majoritarian democracy in, 687
nomination agreements in, 429
party whips in, 540–541
peerages in, 623
political careers in, 536
political parties and party system in, 546, 547, 577, 578–579, 580–581, 583, 585, 624
right to vote in, 470
United Arab Emirates and, 606
United Nations (UN), 98, 99, 100, 265*b*
United Nations Development Fund, 102–103
United States (U.S.). *See also* Arms races
 analysis of democracy in, 24–25, 26–27
 attitudes toward the poor in, 710–711
 cabinets in, 448
 civic culture in, 212, 213
 constitutional justice in, 646–648
 contestation and inclusion in, 153
 democratization and democratic institutions of, 10–11, 259, 685, 687
 divided government in, 450
 economic factors in, 319–320, 709–710
 elections and electoral systems in, 474, 476, 506, 537
 elections of 2000 in, 582
 electoral rules in, 470, 472*b*

executive orders in, 446
Ethiopia and, 97, 100
federalism in, 611, 612, 616
government in, 586
health in, 217
judicial system of, 12
legislature in, 12, 621, 626, 627, 628, 632–633, 649
majoritarian and consensus aspects of, 699
as an occupying force, 10–11
political parties and party system in, 543, 544, 546, 547, 586
Somalia and, 97, 99–100
stability of, 756
veto players in, 648–649
welfare reform in, 618
University of California, 246
University of Michigan, 215
University of Pittsburgh, 241
University of Southern California, 246
Urban issues. *See* Cleavages
Urban, Jerzy, 524
Uruguay, 276
U.S. *See* United States
USSR. *See* Soviet Union
Utility function, 368–370, 371

V

Validity. *See* Measures
Vanberg, Georg, 411, 437
Vanhanen, Tatu, 750
van Roosendahl, Peter, 437
Vanuatu, 490
Varian, Hal R., 382
Varshney, Ashutosh, 731–732
Velvet Revolution (Czechoslovakia; 1989), 266
Venezuela
 cabinets in, 448
 democracy in, 218
 economic factors in, 325
 elections and electoral systems in, 471, 472*b*, 625
 federalism in, 604, 605, 615
 legislature in, 625, 626
 political parties in, 500, 565
 rule of law index and, 315
 stability of, 756
Verba, Sydney, 212, 214, 215, 218

Verkuilen, Jay, 166
Veto players, 12, 162, 604, 648–649, 650–656, 760. *See also* Constitutions and constitutionalism; Democracy and democratization; Government; Policies and policy making; Theories—specific
Vico, Giambattista, 150
Vietnam, 544, 638
Violence, 3, 223, 224–225
Volensky, Michael, 537
Von Neumann, John, 60
Votes, voters, and voting. *See also* Citizens; Decision making; Electoral systems
accountability and clarity of responsibility and, 474–475, 483, 494, 540, 689, 691–692
alternative vote systems, 474, 477–484, 488, 736–737
ballots, 467, 477, 503*f*, 504*f*, 505*f*, 508*t*, 721
chain of delegation and, 412
class cleavage and, 559
in direct and indirect elections, 399
economic effects of, 721
effective number of electoral parties and, 548–549
fiscal policies and, 703–713
franchise and suffrage, 150, 153, 156, 196, 320, 332, 468, 470, 559, 561
government formation and, 434
government identifiability and, 693
inclusion and, 152–153
linkage between voters and representatives, 500
mandates and, 693
Median Voter Theorem, 355, 370–379
minority governments and, 421
one person, one vote principle, 625, 626
party lists and, 502–507, 721
political parties and, 538–539, 708
power of the median voter, 372–373

preelection coalitions and, 693–694
preference swapping, 484
priorities of, 562
proportional electoral rules and, 434
right and left political divide and, 560, 713–718
rights and rules of, 469–472
strategic effect of electoral laws, 579–583
translating votes into seats, 495–500, 512, 513, 515, 575–579, 583–584, 590–591
universal admissibility condition and, 381
universal suffrage, 196, 468, 470, 561
voter abstention, 467
voter turnout, 538, 707, 708
Votes, voters, and voting—types of
alternative vote systems, 474, 477–484, 488, 736–737
block vote and party block vote systems, 492
Borda Count, 363–366, 379–380, 382, 478–479
instant run-off vote, 477
investiture votes, 410, 423, 426, 442
personal votes, 721
preference or preferential voting, 477–484, 487, 494, 507, 509–510, 742
prospective voting, 693
retrospective voting, 689, 693
sincere voting, 366, 476, 487, 494, 579–580
single-elimination tournaments, 380
split and split-ticket voting, 506, 513
strategic voting, 367, 476, 478–479, 483, 487, 494, 579–580, 584, 585, 592, 737
supplementary vote, 488
two-dimensional voting, 374–379, 392–394
votes of no confidence, 397, 404, 420, 755
"voting with one's feet," 618

wasted votes, 502, 509, 584, 714, 737
Voting Rights Act (1964), 153

W

Wagner, Adolph, 703. *See also* Theories—specific
Wakeham Commission, 624
Walesa, Lech, 289, 290
War, 96–97, 108, 121–122
Warsaw University, 291
Wars of religion, 554–555
Warwick, Paul V., 415*b*
Washington, George, 543
Weber, Max, 92, 93, 221
Weimar Republic, 495, 501, 736
Weingast, Barry R., 183, 184, 185, 233, 719
Welzen, Christian, 210
Whaples, Robert, 139
Whigs, 552–554
Wibbels, Erik, 619
Wickremasinghe, Ranil, 452
Woodberry, Robert, 222
World Values Survey (University of Michigan), 215–216, 217–218, 711
World War II, 2, 5, 10

Y

Yanukovych, Viktor, 452, 453, 539
Yemen, 607–608
Yoshinaka, Antoine, 470, 471
Yuschenko, Viktor, 452–453, 539

Z

Zaire, 340
Zambia, 466, 570*b*–571*b*
Zemsky, Peter, 83
Zenawi, Meles (Ethiopian prime minister), 100
Zimbabwe, 342, 539, 544